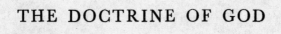

THE DOCTRINE OF GOD

CHURCH DOGMATICS

BY

KARL BARTH

VOLUME II

THE DOCTRINE
OF GOD

FIRST HALF-VOLUME

EDITORS

REV. G. W. BROMILEY, PH.D., D.LITT.
REV. PROF. T. F. TORRANCE, D.D., D.THEOL.

EDINBURGH: T. & T. CLARK, 38 GEORGE STREET

THE
DOCTRINE OF GOD

BY

KARL BARTH, Dr.Theol., D.D., LL.D.

TRANSLATORS

Rev. T. H. L. PARKER, B.D.

Rev. W. B. JOHNSTON, B.D.

Rev. HAROLD KNIGHT, D.Phil.

Rev. Prof. J. L. M. HAIRE, B.D., M.Th.

EDINBURGH: T. & T. CLARK, 38 George Street

Original German Edition
DIE KIRCHLICHE DOGMATIK, II:
Die Lehre von Gott, 1

Published by
EVANGELISCHER VERLAG A.G.
ZOLLIKON—ZÜRICH

Authorised English Translation
© 1957 T. & T. CLARK LTD.
EDINBURGH

PRINTED IN SCOTLAND BY
MORRISON AND GIBB LTD.
FOR
T. & T. CLARK LTD., EDINBURGH

0 567 09021 3

FIRST PRINTED 1957
LATEST IMPRESSION. . . 1976

EDITORS' PREFACE

WITH this volume Barth passes from the introduction to dogmatics to its content, beginning with two massive volumes on the doctrine of God. Here we have the basis upon which the whole of Barth's teaching rests, for, as he says in this half-volume, the whole of revelation is summed up in the statement that " God is." This is particularly worth noting by those who think that Barth merely resolves all doctrine, and not least the doctrine of God, into Christology.

This half-volume is devoted to two chapters on " The Knowledge of God " and " The Reality of God." In the first chapter Barth insists that our knowledge of God is grounded in the action of God, in which He objectifies Himself to us, and meets us on our own plane as a Subject calling for a corresponding action on our part in the obedience of faith. Barth draws a valuable distinction here between God's primary objectivity which is never abstracted from His own self-giving, and God's secondary objectivity in the sign-world used by His self-revelation to man. He speaks of this as " a sacramental objectivity." The real basis and essence of this sacramental reality of His revelation is to be found in the human nature of Jesus Christ. It is here for the first time that we really get anything like an " epistemology " from Barth, and we get it here because the possibility of knowledge of God cannot be discussed apart from the actuality of our knowledge of Him. In other words, we can only understand how God is knowable from the way in which He actually gives Himself to be known. Hence, a true epistemology can be derived only from the actual unfolding of the content of the Word of God, and therefore might best come at the end rather than at the beginning of our dogmatics.

In this part of the work we have a searching and profound examination of the main theses of Natural and Roman Theology, in respect of the distinction between the possibility and the actuality of our knowledge of God, which involves an underlying cleavage between God's being and His action. The repudiation of this cleavage in God is fundamental to the whole of Barth's theology. If this is a critical it is also a sympathetic examination in which Barth takes trouble to understand the persistent vitality of Natural Theology. It is, he holds, the theology of the natural man, and springs out of his attempt to assure his own place in ultimate reality, and is therefore his only trust in life and death. Since only the positive content of our knowledge of God in Christ gives us real ground for calling natural knowledge of God in question, we have no right to deprive the natural man of his only trust in life and death before he attains the true knowledge of God in Jesus Christ.

In the second chapter Barth expands the statement that " God is " into the statement that " God is He who He is in the act of His revelation," or that " God is He who lives and loves in freedom." Here Barth is concerned to correct the scholastic and philosophical separation between the being of God and His actions and attributes, but he is equally careful to avoid the other error which thinks of God's being only in terms of His ways and works, as if it were exhausted in them or passed wholly into them. As in the first chapter he would not allow the possibility of our knowledge to be detached from its actuality, on the ground that this makes the knowability of God a predicate of man rather than of God, so here he seeks to avoid the subtle nominalism that often lurks in traditional doctrines of the attributes of God. He prefers, therefore, to speak of the perfections or properties of God rather than His attributes ; for God's grace and holiness, mercy and righteousness, patience and wisdom are the properties of the divine love, and God's unity and omnipresence, constancy and omnipotence, eternity and glory are the properties of the divine freedom, and are not simply what we attribute to God. They are the perfections of His being and nature manifested and expressed in the active love and freedom in which He seeks and creates fellowship between Himself and us. The richness and beauty of Barth's treatment of these themes gives substance to his own claim in this volume that dogmatics is the most beautiful of all the sciences.

Attention may be drawn to the brief theological autobiography which Barth gives us on pp. 634 ff., since many readers will find this a considerable help to the proper understanding of his theology.

Four scholars have been responsible for the present rendering : the Rev. T. H. L. Parker for pp. 3-254 ; the Rev. W. B. Johnston, for pp. 257-297 ; the Rev. Dr. Harold Knight for pp. 297-439 ; and the Rev. Prof. J. L. M. Haire for pp. 440-677. Mr Parker wishes to express his thanks to Mr Paul Roubiczek for his kind and helpful scrutiny of part of his portion in MS. And to Mr Parker himself we are again indebted for his careful proof reading, and for many enlivening comments which unfortunately cannot be shared with our readers.

CONTENTS

PAGE

EDITORS' PREFACE vii

CHAPTER V

THE KNOWLEDGE OF GOD

§ 25. THE FULFILMENT OF THE KNOWLEDGE OF GOD
    1. Man before God 3
    2. God before Man 31

§ 26. THE KNOWABILITY OF GOD
    1. The Readiness of God 63
    2. The Readiness of Man 128

§ 27. THE LIMITS OF THE KNOWLEDGE OF GOD
    1. The Hiddenness of God 179
    2. The Veracity of Man's Knowledge of God . . 204

CHAPTER VI

THE REALITY OF GOD

§ 28. THE BEING OF GOD AS THE ONE WHO LOVES IN FREEDOM
    1. The Being of God in Act 257
    2. The Being of God as the One who loves . . 272
    3. The Being of God in Freedom . . . 297

§ 29. THE PERFECTIONS OF GOD 322

§ 30. THE PERFECTIONS OF THE DIVINE LOVING
    1. The Grace and Holiness of God . . . 351
    2. The Mercy and Righteousness of God . . 368
    3. The Patience and Wisdom of God . . . 406

ix

x   *Contents*

§ 31. THE PERFECTIONS OF THE DIVINE FREEDOM   PAGE
      1. The Unity and Omnipresence of God   .   .   .   440
      2. The Constancy and Omnipotence of God .   .   .   490
      ·3. The Eternity and Glory of God   608

    INDEXES
        I. Scripture References   679
       II. Names   690
      III. Subjects   693

CHAPTER V

THE KNOWLEDGE OF GOD

CHAPTER V

THE KNOWLEDGE OF GOD

§ 25

THE FULFILMENT OF THE KNOWLEDGE OF GOD

The knowledge of God occurs in the fulfilment of the revelation of His Word by the Holy Spirit, and therefore in the reality and with the necessity of faith and its obedience. Its content is the existence of Him whom we must fear above all things because we may love Him above all things ; who remains a mystery to us because He Himself has made Himself so clear and certain to us.

1. MAN BEFORE GOD

In the Church of Jesus Christ men speak about God and men have to hear about God. About God the Father, the Son and the Holy Spirit ; about God's grace and truth ; about God's thoughts and works ; about God's promises, ordinances and commandments ; about God's kingdom, and about the state and life of man in the sphere of His lordship. But always and in all circumstances about God Himself, who is the presupposition, meaning and power of everything that is to be said and heard in the Church, the Subject who absolutely, originally and finally moves, produces, establishes and realises in this matter. In dogmatics it is the doctrine of God which deals with this Subject as such. In the doctrine of God we have to learn what we are saying when we say " God." In the doctrine of God we have to learn to say " God " in the correct sense. If we do not speak rightly of this Subject, how can we speak rightly of His predicates ?

But in relation to this Subject, we are at once confronted with the problem of knowledge. All speaking and hearing in the Church of Jesus Christ entirely rests upon and is connected with the fact that God is known in the Church of Jesus Christ ; that is to say, that this Subject is objectively present to the speakers and hearers, so that man in the Church really stands before God. If it were not so, if man did not really stand before God, if God were not the object of his perception, viewing and conception, and if he did not know God —whatever we understand by " know "—then he could not speak and hear about Him. Then everything declared and heard in the Church

3

would have no Subject and would be left in the air like an empty sound. Then the Church, if it lives only by what is said and heard in it, would not be alive ; or its life would be merely an apparent life, life in a dream-world with those subjectless images and concepts as the phantasies of its imagination. But if the life of the Church is not just a semblance, the knowledge of God is realised in it. This is the presupposition which we have first of all to explain in the doctrine of God. We have to learn how far we can know God and therefore speak and hear about Him.

It is not a question whether God is actually known in the Church.

I believe I learned the fundamental attitude to the problem of the knowledge and existence of God which is adopted in this section—and indeed in the whole chapter—at the feet of Anselm of Canterbury, and in particular from his proofs of God set out in *Prosl.* 2–4. May I therefore ask the reader to keep that text in mind, and to allow me to refer to my book *Fides quaerens intellectum: Anselms Beweis der Existenz Gottes* (1931), for an understanding of it.

We start out from the fact that through His Word God is actually known and will be known again. On principle we have to reject any anxiety about this occurrence as not only superfluous but forbidden. Knowledge of God within the Christian Church is very well aware that it is established in its reality and to that extent also called in question by God's Word, through which alone it can be and have reality, and on the basis of which alone it can be fulfilled. But precisely because the knowledge of God cannot call itself in question in its effort to understand itself, it cannot ask whether it is real from some position outside itself. This question can be put to it only from God's Word. And from the Word of God this question is in fact put to it. And it is also given the answer there. But it will not want to be set under the Word of God just in order to make its own existence problematical. It is made problematical by the Word of God, but thanks to that same Word it need not fear that it will be made problematical anywhere else. For in the Word of God it is decided that the knowledge of God cannot let itself be called in question, or call itself in question, from any other position outside itself. The Word of God will not let it move from its own place into another. And even if it wanted to, there is no other place from which somebody or something can compete with the Word of God which establishes the knowledge of God : Not because the knowledge of God bestowed upon the Church makes itself absolute ; but because it cannot affront the truth, worth and competence of the Word of God. It must refuse to let its reality be debated from any position, and must start out by establishing its own reality. It is another matter that it can do this only in reflection and response to the Word of God which establishes it. But it cannot retreat from its own reality. Therefore we cannot ask whether God is known.

But this also means that the question cannot be whether God is knowable. .Where God is known He is also in some way or other knowable. Where the actuality exists there is also the corresponding possibility. The question cannot then be posed *in abstracto* but only *in concreto* ; not *a priori* but only *a posteriori*. The *in abstracto* and *a priori* question of the possibility of the knowledge of God obviously presupposes the existence of a place outside the knowledge of God itself from which this knowledge can be judged. It presupposes a place where, no doubt, the possibility of knowledge in general and then of the knowledge of God in particular can be judged and decided in one way or another. It presupposes the existence of a theory of knowledge as a hinterland where consideration of the truth, worth and competence of the Word of God, on which the knowledge of God is grounded, can for a time at least be suspended. But this is the very thing which, from the point of view of its possibility, must not happen. Just as the reality of the Word of God in Jesus Christ bears its possibility within itself, as does also the reality of the Holy Spirit, by whom the Word of God comes to man, so too the possibility of the knowledge of God and therefore the knowability of God cannot be questioned *in vacuo*, or by means of a general criterion of knowledge delimiting the knowledge of God from without, but only from within this real knowledge itself. Therefore it is quite impossible to ask whether God is knowable, because this question is already decided by the only legitimate and meaningful questioning which arises in this connexion.

The only legitimate and meaningful questions in this context are : how far is God known ? and how far is God knowable ? These questions are legitimate and meaningful because they are genuine questions of Church proclamation, and therefore also genuine questions of dogmatics—genuine objects of its formal and material task. How God is known and is knowable has to be a matter of continual reflection and appraisal for the teaching Church, and it has to be continually said to the hearing Church so that it may be called to new witness. And with the questions put in this way, both the teaching and the hearing Church will walk in the path of the Word of God. Put thus, they are not inquisitive and superfluous questions ; much less are they questions that insult the Word of God by suspending its truth, worth and competence. On the contrary, they are both permitted and commanded, as questions about the right understanding and correct elucidation of the Word of God. In this section we will deal first with the former question—that of the how of the knowledge of God in its actual fulfilment.

This fulfilment is taking place. The Church of Jesus Christ lives. It lives, of course, by the grace of the Word. Therefore the Word is not bound to it, or only so far as the Word, in once bestowing itself upon the Church, has bound itself to it as promise for the future. In view of this promise, however, we have to say that the fulfilment of the knowledge of God is taking place, and that we can only ask about its mode. But also, in view of this promise, we can ask about the reality and possibility of the knowledge of God from within the unambiguous, unreserved and unconditional binding of the Church to the Word. This means above all that the question of the object of this knowledge, like the question of its mode, cannot be regarded as open. There can be no reservations about whom or what we have to think when we ask about the knowledge of God. When the knowledge of God is under discussion we are not free perhaps to think of Him who in the Bible is called God and Lord, but perhaps equally well to think of some other entity which can similarly be described and proclaimed as " God," and which has in fact been described and proclaimed as " God " somewhere and at some time. We cannot equally well ask about the knowledge of the World-Ground or the World-Soul, the Supreme Good or Supreme Value, the Thing in itself or the Absolute, Destiny or Being or Idea, or even the First Cause as the Unity of Being and Idea, as we can ask about the knowledge of Him who in the Bible is called God and Lord. The problem of the knowledge of God will have to be posed quite differently from what has been suggested if, in relation to the knowledge of God, we are just as free to look in the various directions to which these concepts point as in the direction to which the biblical concept of God points. There will then be no need, no possibility even, of avoiding the questions whether the knowledge of God is real and whether it is also possible. If what we take to be our knowledge of God is only the knowledge of an entity which we ourselves can find to be the Godhead, choosing it as " God " from among other possibilities and ourselves describing it as God ; if our knowledge of it does not settle the question that this entity and it alone is God, then, of course, we can never be too insistent in our enquiry as to the reality and possibility of such a knowledge of God. Over against the positions occupied by such a knowledge of God there is more than one other position from which the reality and possibility of this knowledge can and must be questioned. If we try to leave open only for a moment the question of who or what is to be understood by " God " ; if we try even for a moment to understand the fulfilment of the knowledge of God (with the mode of which we have here to occupy ourselves) as one particular case in the series of many other similar fulfilments executed in the same freedom ; then, of course, we revert to the question whether this knowledge is real and possible, and we are forced to make sure of the reality and possibility of what is supposed to happen in what we regard as the fulfilment of our knowledge of God. But the fulfilling of the knowledge of God with which we are concerned most certainly does not rest on a free choice of this or that object, of this or that " God." It must be established at once from the knowledge of God with which we are concerned that everything that is described as " God " on the basis of a free choice cannot possibly be God ; and that everything that is declared, on the grounds of this presupposition, to be the knowledge of God cannot have any reality or possibility as a knowledge of God. The knowledge of God with which we are here concerned takes place, not in a free choice, but with a very definite constraint. It stands or falls with its one definite object, which cannot be different, and which cannot be exchanged for or even joined with any other object. Because it is bound to God's Word given to the Church, the knowledge of God with which we are here concerned is bound to the God who in His Word gives Himself to the Church to be known as God. Bound in this way it is the true knowledge of the true God.

If we are not concerned with the God who in God's Word gives Himself to the Church to be known ; or if we think about this God as if He also were an entity freely chosen and called " God " on the basis of a free choice ; if He is known otherwise than with this constraint ; if it is therefore possible to treat of Him openly or secretly like one of those freely chosen and designated entities, and to form Him after their image ; then we must not be surprised if we find ourselves in a position where the reality and possibility of our knowledge of God is at once questioned again from without, a position where we begin to experience anxiety and doubt ; and this will apply most heavily, not at once to the particular and perhaps unconquerable content of knowledge, but to its possibility and reality as such. For if the knowledge of a " God " is or even can be attacked from without, or if there is or even can be anxiety and doubt in the knowledge of him, then that " God " is manifestly not God but a false god, a god who merely pretends to be God.

True knowledge of God is not and cannot be attacked ; it is without anxiety and without doubt. But only that which is fulfilled under the constraint of God's Word is such a true knowledge of God. Any escape out of the constraint of the Word of God means crossing over to the false gods and no-gods. And this will shew itself by leading inevitably to uncertainty in the knowledge of God, and therefore to doubt. A knowledge of God which is the knowledge of false gods can be attacked and, indeed, is attacked. Under the constraint of the Word, however, only the question as to the mode of the knowledge and of the knowability of God can be put—in the freedom and therefore in the certainty which reigns when the choice is not arbitrary. The battle against uncertainty and doubt is not foreign to man even here. But here it will always be a victorious battle. For it goes to the very root of uncertainty and doubt, and it will be simply the one good fight of faith—the fight for a renewal of the confirmation and acknowledgment of our constraint by God's Word as the point of departure from which uncertainty and doubt become impossible possibilities.

Therefore between the constraint of God's Word (or of the God attested by His Word) and the certainty of our knowledge of God there exists the same necessary relationship as between our free choice of this or that " God " and the uncertainty which will then afflict our knowledge of God. We must remember that these two circles do not touch one another but are mutually exclusive ; and that therefore a direct transition from the one into the other is impossible. Uncertainty will never be possible in this constraint of the Word of God and therefore in the knowledge of the God revealed therein. And on the other hand, certainty will never be possible in freedom from the Word of God and therefore in the alleged knowledge of God which rests upon a free choice of this or that " God." Questions as to its reality and possibility which may be addressed to the true knowledge of God from without can never carry any weight. Addressed to a false knowledge of God they are always weighty. Of course, our being bound to God's Word cannot, must not and will not prevent us from subsequently explaining the fact and reason why (since the object of our knowledge of God is the One who is presented to us by God's Word and no other) we do not know God but only false gods, no-gods, in all the other entities which offer themselves to us as gods. But such a demarcation can and will come to pass in the constraint by God's Word and therefore also with the pre-determination which is of necessity given in this constraint. It will have the character of a supplementary, incidental and implicit apologetics, comparable to the subsequent substantiation of a judgment of the supreme court which has already been given and come into force and hence whose validity cannot be questioned. It will presuppose the reality and possibility of the knowledge of God as grounded in itself and as already distinguished from the unreal and impossible knowledge of all false gods. Therefore in its polemic against them it will have to show, not that they are false gods, but only to what extent they are false gods. The fact that they are false gods has already been manifested by God showing Himself in His Word as the true God. An apologetics which is conscious of its tasks and limitations as an account of what happens when God is known will as soon undertake this demonstration outside or above the constraint of the Word of God as it will the demonstration of the truth of God Himself. It will testify both to the truth of the true God and to the falsity of the false gods simply on the ground that these facts are previously and finally testified by God's Word and need from the Church only this repetitive and confirmative witness. It is submission to this order which decides whether the demarcation brings certainty—with a resultant authority and power as a ministry to the Word of God — or whether it re-introduces uncertainty into the knowledge of God — in which case it will definitely not have the authority and power of a witness, the authority and power of the ministry of the Word of God. But we must consider just as closely the converse that even where these entities are freely chosen as gods, the leap into constraint can still be considered and undertaken as a final possibility—perhaps after all other possibilities have been exhausted or have proved doubtful—as the *salto mortale* of free thought, as the last in the series of free choices. All apologetics which are false because they are not really bound to what has already happened, and all arbitrary demarcations between the knowledge of the true God and that of false gods, will, sooner or later, end here. Apparently in sublime, sovereign freedom, open on every side, interested in anything and everything, taking every possible and impossible knowledge of " God " with a tragic seriousness (as if it were or could be serious !), this apologetics will definitely at some point or other suddenly declare the *sacrificium intellectus* to be the one possibility remaining to it. Then, probably assuming a parsonic voice, it will praise this very *sacrificium* as the last and best choice. At this point the false apologetics will start to speak of a necessary constraint of the Word of God ; and it will begin talking about Jesus, or the Bible, or the dogma of the Church. But there is no need to deceive ourselves or let ourselves be deceived, for it will not be possible at this juncture to speak of these things with certainty and thus with power and authority. The possibility of constraint running alongside these many other possibilities, but finally freely chosen instead of them, is certainly not identical with the original constraint by the Word of God, even though it now declares and designates itself to be such.

We can only come from the real and original constraint by the Word ; we cannot come to it. If it is an experiment—even the last and greatest—in a series of other experiments ; if we think that after trying this or that we will and can in the last resort try also a religious philosophy of authority, and then in this framework give Jesus, the Bible or Church dogma a trial too, we simply cannot expect to think and speak with the certainty of the true knowledge of God. The *sacrificium intellectus* as the last despairing, audacious act of self-confidence, in which man thinks he can decide upon his very knowledge of God, has always turned out to be a bit of conjuring, about which no one can be happy in the long run. Even interpreted as a leap into faith, it does not create a position which cannot be attacked and is not attacked. For why should not a religious philosophy of authority be just as open to attack, and just as freely attacked, as any other philosophy ? The doubter cannot free himself from doubt, even by persuading himself to will to doubt no more, even by performing this *sacrificium*. And the doubter cannot free other doubters from their doubt by exacting this *sacrificium* from them—perhaps by making it convincing, perhaps by inducing them to perform it for themselves. He must not be a doubter at all if help is to come to him and through him to others. But that means that he must not think that he can choose and therefore that he can help himself and others. He must be bound already to the Word of God. Any desire to bind himself to the Word of God can only demonstrate to himself and others that in fact he is not yet bound. And any supposed certainty, built on a desire for this self-binding, will only show his actual uncertainty to himself and others. Binding by the Word of God must take place at the beginning. That is, where there is no sort of intention of creating a position for ourselves, but where we find ourselves in a position without self-willing or choosing. At the beginning, where possibilities other than those indicated by the Word of God do not come into consideration at all, and therefore where there can be no question of a particular despair and therefore no *salto mortale* as the last resort of audacity or embarrassment. If this constraint does not take place at the beginning it does not occur at all. There, at the point of departure we are constrained by the Word of God. And so we must fight the good fight of faith in order that the constraint may be acknowledged and that we may let it come upon us. The words of Psalm 127$^{1-2}$ are quite decisive here : " Except the Lord build the house, their labour is but lost that build it. Except the Lord keep the city, the watchman waketh but in vain. It is but lost labour that ye haste to rise up early and so late take rest and eat the bread of carefulness, for so he giveth to his beloved in sleep ". Good apologetics is distinguished from bad by its responsibility to these words.

That the knowledge of God in its fulfilment by the revelation of the Word of God is bound to its one, determined and uniquely distinct object, and that it is knowledge of this object and not of another— knowledge of the God who gives Himself to be known in His Word —means further that, without any prejudice to its certainty, but in this very certainty, it is mediated knowledge. That is to say, God is and remains its object. If God gives Himself to man to be known in the revelation of His Word through the Holy Spirit, it means that He enters into the relationship of object to man the subject. In His revelation He is considered and conceived by men. Man knows God in that he stands before God. But this always means : in that God becomes, is and remains to him Another, One who is distinct from himself, One who meets him. Nor is this objectivity of God neutralised by the fact that God makes man His own through the Holy Spirit, in order to give Himself to be owned by him. For what else does this mean but that He gives Himself to man in His Word as a real object ? He makes man accessible for Himself. He lets Himself be considered and conceived by man. Man cannot and must not know himself apart from God, but together with God as his " opposite." Again, the objectivity of God is not restricted by the fact that we have to understand God Himself as the real and primarily acting Subject of all real knowledge of God, so that the self-knowledge of God is the real and primary essence of all knowledge of God. That God is originally and really object to Himself does not alter the fact that in a very different way He is also object to man. And the fact that God knows Himself immediately is not neutralised by the fact that man knows Him on the basis of His revelation and hence mediately, and only mediately, and therefore as an object. The reality of our knowledge of God stands or falls with the fact that in His revelation God is present to man in a medium. He is therefore objectively present in a double sense. In His Word He comes as an object before man the subject. And by the Holy Spirit He makes the human subject accessible to Himself, capable of considering and conceiving Himself as object. The real knowledge of God is concerned with God in His relationship to man, but also in His distinction from him. We therefore separate ourselves from all those ideas of the knowledge of God which understand it as the union of man with God, and which do not regard it as an objective knowledge but leave out the distinction between the knower and the known. It is not as if we can arrive at the real knowledge of God on this view. On the contrary, this view can help us only by making clear what it means if man is not yet or no longer engaged in fulfilling the knowledge of God.

We are vividly reminded of one of the most beautiful but also most dangerous passages in the *Confessions* (IX, 10) of Augustine—the conversation between Augustine and his mother Monica at the garden window at Ostia. They were talking about the *vita aeterna sanctorum, quam nec oculus vidit, nec auris audivit, nec in cor hominis ascendit* (1 Cor. 2⁹). Augustine tells how his mother and himself, leaving behind them the contemplation of even the highest *delectatio* that could be mediated through the senses, mounted together *in idipsum* (Ps. 4⁹ Vulg.—*In pace in idipsum dormiam et requiescam* . . .). They wandered step by step through all the corporeal world, including the heavens and all their constellations. Climbing yet higher in wondering review of the works of God they arrived at the spirit of man and then passed beyond even this, *ut attingeremus regionem ubertatis indeficientis, ubi pascis Israel in aeternum veritatis pabulo et ubi vita sapientia est, per quam fiunt omnia ista, et quae fuerunt et quae futura sunt; et ipsa non fit sed sic est ut fuit et sic erit semper; quin potius fuisse et futurum esse non est in ea sed esse solum, quoniam aeterna est: nam fuisse et futurum esse non est aeternum. Et dum loquimur et inhiamus illi attigimus eam modice toto ictu cordis, et suspiravimus et reliquimus ibi religatas primitias spiritus, et remeavimus ad strepitum oris nostri ubi verbum et incipitur et finitur.* And then they said : If the *tumultus carnis* could be silenced in man, and all the images (*phantasiae*) of the earth, sea and air, and even the soul itself *et transeat se non se cogitando, sileant somnia et imaginariae revelationes, omnis lingua et omne signum et quidquid transeundo fit, si cui sileat omnino; quoniam si quis audiat, dicunt haec omnia: Non ipsa nos fecimus sed fecit nos qui manet in aeternum*—if everything was silent, listening to God Himself : *et loquatur ipse solus, non per ea sed per se ipsum, ut audiamus verbum eius, non per linguam carnis, neque per vocem angeli, nec per sonitum nubis nec per aenigma similitudinis, sed ipsum quem in his amamus, ipsum sine his audiamus, sicut nunc extendimus nos, et rapida cogitatione attigimus aeternam Sapientiam super omnia manentem*— if all else ceased, if all other sights vanished *et haec una (visio) rapiat et absorbeat et recondat in interiora gaudia spectatorem suum, ut talis sit sempiterna vita, quale fuit hoc momentum intelligentiae cui suspiravimus—nonne hoc est: Intra in gaudium Domini tui ?* (Mt. 25²¹). *Et istud quando ? An cum omnes resurgemus, sed non omnes immutabimur ?* (1 Cor. 15⁵¹). The beginning and end of the passage shew that Augustine wishes to speak of the eternal vision of God at the end of time, and we are not now concerned with the specifically eschatological side of the problem. But Augustine does not speak only of a future, eternal vision, but very definitely of an experience on that day at the garden window at Ostia. Here for a little while everything became silent ; here he aspired to that *idipsum* and here also he found it ; here the timeless Wisdom met him in time ; here he saw and heard God without concepts, without an image, without a word, without a sign—God Himself speaking, not through something else, but through Himself, *ipsum sine his*, so that the One seen is already about to take up into Himself the one who sees : " Enter thou into the joy of thy Lord." However it may be with the reality and contents of this experience, it is certain that the reality of the knowledge of God is not reached by way of the image of such a timeless and non-objective seeing and hearing. In this context reference may be made to the fact that elsewhere (*De civ. Dei* XXII, 29) Augustine himself described the eternal vision of God quite differently : *ut Deum ubique praesentem et universa etiam corporalia gubernantem per corpora quae gestabimus et quae conspiciemus . . clarissima perspicuitate videamus . . . incorporeum Deum etiam per corpora contuebimur . . . ut videatur ab altero in altero, videatur in se ipso, videatur in coelo novo et in terra nova atque in omni quae tunc fuerit creatura, videatur et per corpora in omni corpore.* In the knowledge of God in His Word here and now we are definitely concerned with such a mediate, objective knowledge. What Augustine describes in *Conf.* IX, 10 is, according to his own account, the consequence of an *ascendere* and *transcendere* of all the limitations and restrictions of man's existence and situation. Whether that is a possible beginning we will not pursue further. But it is certain that this *ascendere* and *transcendere* means abandoning, or at any rate wanting to abandon, the place where God encounters man in His revelation and where He gives Himself to be heard and seen by man. But on the other hand Augustine himself has said the right word about this arbitrary procedure : *Optimus minister tuus est, qui non magis intuetur hoc a te audire, quod ipse voluerit, sed potius hoc velle, quod a te audierit.* If we really soar up into these heights, and really reduce all concepts, images, words and signs to silence, and really think we can enter into the *idipsum*, it simply means that we wilfully hurry past God, who descends in His revelation into this world of ours. Instead of finding Him where He Himself has sought us—namely, in His objectivity—we seek Him where He is not to be found, since He on His side seeks us in His Word. It is really not the case, therefore, that if we have a knowledge of God in the form of that experience, we have reached a higher or the highest step on a way which began with an objective perceiving, viewing and conceiving of God, as though that were only an early and sensuous mode of thought. It is not the case that in the non-objective we are dealing with the real and true knowledge of God but in the objective with a deceptive appearance. Just the reverse. If we regard ourselves as bound by God's Word we shall certainly find a deceptive appearance in that *ascendere* and *transcendere* so far as what happens there—whatever else it may be —claims to be knowledge of God. For how can it make this claim except where the fulfilment of the real knowledge of God in God's Word has either not yet begun or has ceased again ? Where it is being fulfilled, the hasty by-passing of God's revelation or the flight into non-objectivity cannot possibly occur. Where it is being fulfilled, knowledge is bound to the objectivity of God just as it is bound to this definite object who is the God who gives Himself to be known in His Word. And it is bound to the fact that His very revelation consists in His making Himself object to us, and so in His making a flight into non-objectivity not only superfluous but impossible. Thus the straight and proper way in this matter can never be from objectivity into non-objectivity, but only from non-objectivity back into objectivity.

The fact that man stands before the God who gives Himself to be known in His Word, and therefore to be known mediately, definitely means that we have to understand man's knowledge of God as the knowledge of faith. In this consists its reality and necessity, which are not and cannot be attacked from without. And from this follow all determinations of the mode of its fulfilment. We must now discuss the assertion that the knowledge of God is the knowledge of faith.

In the first instance, it is simply a confirmation of the fact that the knowledge of God is bound to the object set before it by God's Word —and to this object in its irrevocable objectivity. Faith is the total positive relationship of man to the God who gives Himself to be known in His Word. It is man's act of turning to God, of opening up his life to Him and of surrendering to Him. It is the Yes which he pronounces in his heart when confronted by this God, because he knows himself to be bound and fully bound. It is the obligation in which, before God, and in the light of the clarity that God is God and that He is his God, he knows and explains himself as belonging to God. But when we say that, we must at once also say that faith as the positive relationship of man to God comes from God Himself in that it is utterly and entirely grounded in the fact that God en-counters man in the Word which demands of him this turning, this Yes, this obligation ; becoming an object to him in such a way that in His objectivity He bestows upon him by the Holy Spirit the light of the clarity that He is God and that He is his God, and therefore evoking this turning, this Yes, this obligation on the part of man. It is in this occurrence of faith that there is the knowledge of God ; and not only the knowledge of God, but also love towards Him, trust in Him and obedience to Him. But these various determinations of faith are not to be understood as parts or even certain fruits of faith. Each one is the determination of faith in its entirety. If we speak of the knowledge of faith, we do not speak of something which is faith as well as being all sorts of other things, but we speak—even if from a distinct angle—of faith in its entirety. Everything that is to be said of the nature of faith in general will also have to be said of the know-ledge of God as the knowledge of faith. And we cannot speak of the knowledge of God except by speaking of the nature of faith in general —even if from a distinct angle.

In view of the importance of the standpoint which we have to adopt here, it is a serious question whether the knowledge of God will not have to be the decisive and ruling factor in a definition of faith, and one to which all others will have to be added. That Calvin certainly thought so is to be seen from the well-known opening of his Catechism : *Quelle est la principale fin de la vie humaine ? C'est de cognoistre Dieu;*—and the definition of saving faith : *fidem esse divinae erga nos benevolentiae firmam certamque cognitionem, quae gratuitae in Christo promissionis veritate fundata, per Spiritum sanctum et revelatur mentibus nostris et cordibus obsignatur.* (*Inst.* III, 2, 7 ; cf. Catechism, ed. W. Niesel, Qu. 111.) Since no other concept besides *cognitio* is used in this definition to describe faith as such, at a first glance all the other factors seem to be lacking. But in reality they are, so to speak, posited in the object and from it made visible. It is a procedure that has much to be said for it. And it is an obvious weakening when afterwards in the *Heidelberg Catechism*, Qu. 21—perhaps not without the intention of correcting Calvin slightly—faith is defined not only as a certain knowledge, whereby I hold everything for true . . . but also as a hearty trust. . . . However, we do not have to decide this point now. What is certain is that faith must also be described as knowledge and can also be described thus in its totality.

It is when we understand faith as knowledge that we understand it as man's orientation to God as an object. It was previously our second point that the positive relationship of man to God is created and established by God becoming and being its object. But this takes the first and central place in the faith that is understood as knowledge. The turning, the self-opening, the surrender in faith, the Yes of faith, faith as obligation, love, trust and obedience in faith—all this presupposes and includes within itself the union and the distinction which man fulfils between himself and the God whose existence and nature make it all possible and necessary. This orientation which unites and distinguishes is the knowledge of God in. faith. Without it faith could not be all those other things as well. As knowledge it is the orientation of man to God as an object. And only as it is this can it be those other things as well.

We do not say all that so as to commend some sort of realism or objectivism. Nor are we reporting on any sort of experiences. It is a decisive mark of what the Bible calls faith that everything stated about man as such, and about his bearing and circumstances, appears absolutely as the determination of his orientation to God as an object and therefore as the determination of his knowledge. Biblical faith excludes any faith of man in himself—that is, any desire for religious self-help, any religious self-satisfaction, any religious self-sufficiency. Biblical faith lives upon the objectivity of God. In one way or another, God comes into the picture, the sphere, the field of man's consideration and conception in exactly the same way that objects do, uniting Himself to man, distinguishing Himself from him, evoking by His existence and nature man's love, trust and obedience ; but before and in and above all this, bearing witness to Himself by establishing from His side this orientation of man, this uniting and distinguishing. Biblical faith stands or falls with the fact that it is faith in God. When the Early Church confessed : *Credo in Patrem, in eius Filium Jesum Christum, in Spiritum sanctum,* it thought it had nothing further to confess about its faith as such, because with this *in* it thought it had said everything necessary. God speaks ; He claims ; He promises ; He acts ; He is angry ; He is gracious. Take away the objectivity of this *He*, and faith collapses, even as love, trust and obedience. The objectivity of this *He* must not be taken out of biblical faith—either out

of Abraham's faith in the promise, or out of Paul's πίστις Χριστοῦ (Phil. 3⁹ᶠ·).
That God is worthy of love, trust and obedience, that man is able to render them
to God, that he really does so, and the nature of love, trust and obedience : all
these things spring from the fact that God is *He*, that He is an object on the
human plane just like other objects, that He puts Himself in a relationship to
man and man in a relationship to Himself, and makes orientation to Himself
possible and necessary. In the Bible faith means the opening-up of human
subjectivity by and for the objectivity of the divine He, and in this opening-up
the re-establishment and re-determination of human subjectivity. " But it is
good for me to hold me fast by God, to put my trust in the Lord God, and to speak
of all thy works." (Ps. 73²⁸). Thus, in the Bible, faith decidedly means—the
knowledge of God.

But our first task is not to understand faith as the knowledge of
God, but the knowledge of God as faith. Inasmuch as faith rests upon
God's objectivity it is itself knowledge of God. That must be said in
advance. But if we wish to understand this knowledge of God we
must still go back to faith itself—not now to its special determinations
as love, trust and obedience, but to the special determination of its
object which makes it possible and necessary not only as knowledge
but also as love, trust and obedience. Precisely because we understand faith as the knowledge of God, we must go further and say that
we are concerned with the knowledge of the God who is the object
of faith. Therefore it is not any sort of object ; not an object that
can give itself to be known and will be known just like any other
object ; not an object which awakens love, trust and obedience in
the same way as other objects. Its objectivity is the particular and
utterly unique objectivity of God. And that is tantamount to saying
that this knowledge is the particular and utterly unique knowledge
of faith.

If God becomes the object of man's knowledge, this necessarily
means that He becomes the object of his consideration and conception.
On the strength of this it becomes possible and necessary to speak
and hear about God. If it were not so, there would be no knowledge
of God and no faith in Him. God would simply not be in the picture.
We could not hold to Him. We could not pray to Him. To deny
the objectivity of God is to deny the life of the Church of Jesus Christ
—which lives on the fact that God is spoken of and heard. It is to
deny prayer to God, the knowledge of God, and with knowledge faith
in God as well. But not every object is God ; and so not all our
human consideration and conception is knowledge of God. For
although God has genuine objectivity just like all other objects, His
objectivity is different from theirs, and therefore knowledge of Him
—and this is the chief thing to be said about its character as the
knowledge of faith—is a particular and utterly unique occurrence in
the range of all knowledge. Certainly the same thing happens in
faith that happens always and everywhere when man enters into that
uniting and distinguishing relationship to an object, when his sub-

jectivity is opened up to an objectivity and he is grounded and determined anew. But in faith the same thing happens quite differently.
This difference consists in the difference and uniqueness of God as
its object. Knowledge of faith means fundamentally the union of
man with the God who is distinct from him as well as from all his
other objects. For this very reason this knowledge becomes and is
a special knowledge, distinct from the knowledge of all other objects,
outstanding in the range of all knowledge. What our consideration
and conception mean in this context cannot be determined from a
general understanding of man's consideration and conception, but only
in particular from God as its particular object. On the strength of
the fact that God in His particularity is its object, and as such is also
known, it becomes possible and necessary to speak and hear about
God. It must again be said that if God is not object in this particularity there will be no knowledge of God at all. God is not God if
He is considered and conceived as one in a series of like objects. But
then prayer and the life of the Church will necessarily cease, i.e.,
dissolve into the relationship of man to what he knows or thinks he
knows as one object in a series of other objects. As one in this series
He will not be worshipped, nor will He have a Church. Faith will
have to be denied if we want to take our stand on this presupposition.
God, as the object of knowledge, will not let Himself be placed as one
in a series. If faith can be denied, yet the fact remains unaltered that
the faith which is not denied is the direction of man to the one object
who forbids this procedure, who will not let Himself be placed with
any other object in a series, but who distinguishes Himself from all
other objects, and therefore makes a particular knowledge of Himself
possible and necessary.

We do not teach this distinction between the knowledge of God and its object
on the ground of a preconceived idea about the transcendence and supramun-
danity of God ; nor do we teach it in the form of an affirmation of our experience
of faith. On the contrary, we teach it because of what we find proclaimed and
described as faith in Holy Scripture. There can be no doubt about this point.
Just as He who in the Bible encounters man in the objectivity of the divine
He is not identical with any human subject who knows Him, so also He is
not one object in the series of other objects of man's cognisance. In the Bible,
faith in God occurs by way of separation. That is to say, God separates Himself
as well as the believing man. God sanctifies Himself, i.e., makes Himself known
as distinct from all other objects. And at the same time He also sanctifies man
in his relationship to Himself, i.e., puts him into a separated position. Israel is
taken out from among the peoples. The existence of the Church is nothing but
the comprehensive continuation of this process in the form of the removal
of men (but now men from all nations) into one particular position distinct from
all other positions. This particular position is the position of faith. In the Bible
faith means sanctification. And in the Bible sanctification is the execution of a
choice—of particular places, times, men, events or historical sequences. Where
this sanctification and therefore this choice occurs, there, according to the Bible,
knowledge of God occurs also. The foundation and subject of this sanctification
and choice is, however, the object of scriptural faith, electing and consequently

sanctifying Himself in glory. And this object is God, the one who is certainly an object, but the utterly unique object of a unique human knowledge ; the object who, according to Isaiah 42⁸ and 48¹¹, will not give His glory to another. What happens throughout the Word of God is the history of this choice and sanctification. It is this history that we recount ; and our own faith only comes into play in so far as we keep to this history. In this way, and only in this way, do we come to distinguish God from other objects, and therefore knowledge of Him from all other knowledge. This means, however, that we cannot possibly help distinguishing God from other objects.

If we ascribe objectivity to God (as we inevitably do when we speak of the knowledge of God) a distinction becomes unavoidable. As He certainly knows Himself first of all, God is first and foremost objective to Himself. We shall return to this point in the second part of the present section. In His triune life as such, objectivity, and with it knowledge, is divine reality before creaturely objectivity and knowledge exist. We call this the primary objectivity of God, and distinguish from it the secondary, i.e., the objectivity which He has for us too in His revelation, in which He gives Himself to be known by us as He knows Himself. It is distinguished from the primary objectivity, not by a lesser degree of truth, but by its particular form suitable for us, the creature. God is objectively immediate to Himself, but to us He is objectively mediate. That is to say, He is not objective directly but indirectly, not in the naked sense but clothed under the sign and veil of other objects different from Himself. His secondary objectivity is fully true, for it has its correspondence and basis in His primary objectivity. God does not have to be untrue to Himself and deceive us about His real nature in order to become objective to us. For first to Himself, and then in His revelation to us, He is nothing but what He is in Himself. It is here that the door is shut against any " non-objective " knowledge of God. As such, it would not be knowledge of God, for God is objective to Himself. He is immediately objective to Himself—for the Father is object to the Son, and the Son to the Father, without mediation. He is mediately objective to us in His revelation, in which He meets us under the sign and veil of other objects. It is in, with and under the sign and veil of these other objects that we believe in God, and know Him and pray to Him. We believe in Him in His clothed, not in His naked objectivity. That we know Him in faith has a double significance. We really know Him in His objectivity (even if it is clothed) ; and we really know Him only in His clothed objectivity. We do not ask first of all why this must be so, but are content to establish the fact that it is so. Man therefore stands before God in the knowledge of faith. He really and truly stands before God. God is object to him—the object from whom he sees himself to be distinct, but with whom he sees himself united ; and conversely, the object with whom he sees himself united, but from whom he sees himself to be distinct. But he always stands indirectly before God. He stands directly before another object, one of the series of all other objects. The objectivity of this other object represents the objectivity of God. In the objectivity of this other object he knows God, i.e., between himself and this other object the acts of distinguishing and uniting, uniting and distinguishing, take place. This other object he genuinely perceives, considers and conceives—but in and with this other object, the objectivity of God. This other object is thus the medium by which God gives Himself to be known and in which man knows God.

We must now describe in greater detail the particular, outstanding knowledge of God of which we have already spoken. It is the particular occurrence of an encounter between man and a part of the reality surrounding him which is different from God. In the encounter the reality of this piece of his environment does not cease to be a definite, creaturely reality, and therefore it does not become identical with God, but it represents God. That is to say, it represents God in so far as it is determined, made and used by God as His clothing, temple, or sign ; in so far as it is peculiarly a work of God, which above and beyond its own existence (which is also God's work, of course) may and must serve to attest the objectivity of God and therefore to make the knowledge of God possible and necessary. Thus, to the particularity of this event which, in contrast to all other objects, is grounded in the nature of God, there corresponds the particularity of one such object which, in the sphere of creaturely reality, points to the nature of God, a uniqueness which does not belong to this object in itself and as such, but which falls to its lot in this event in which it is now effective. But it is effective, not on account of its own ability, but in virtue of its institution to the service which this object has to perform at this point. In other words, it is effective in virtue of the special work to which God has at this point determined and engaged it, because it has become the instrument of this work and has been marked off and is used as such. For now it is not only what it is to and in itself. Of course it is always that. But over and above its own self it is now this special work of God, God's sign, the garment of His objectivity, the means by which He gives Himself to be known to man and by which man knows Him —man, who as creature cannot stand directly before God but only before other objects. Here too we have a *conditio sine qua non*. At bottom, knowledge of God in faith is always this indirect knowledge of God, knowledge of God in His works, and in these particular works —in the determining and using of certain creaturely realities to bear witness to the divine objectivity. What distinguishes faith from unbelief, erroneous faith and superstition is that it is content with this indirect knowledge of God. It does not think that the knowledge of God in His works is insufficient. On the contrary, it is grateful really to know the real God in His works. It really lets itself be shown the objectivity of God by their objectivity. But it also holds fast to the particularity of these works. It does not arbitrarily choose objects

to set up as signs, in that way inventing a knowledge of God at its
own good-pleasure. It knows God by means of the objects chosen by
God Himself. It recognises and acknowledges God's choice and sanctification in the operation of this knowledge. And, for its part, it uses
these special works of God as they ought to be used—as means of the
knowledge of God. It lets their objectivity become a witness—yet
only a witness—to the objectivity of God. Where the worship of
God is made possible and necessary by God Himself, it does not
establish an idol worship. Faith, and therefore the knowledge of God,
stands or falls with all these determinations of the clothed objectivity
of God. It is under these determinations that God is spoken about
and heard in the Church of Jesus Christ. Not a single one of them can
be set aside or altered without radically injuring the life of the Church.

Here again we have pointed to a thread running through the Bible. It is well
known what great weight Luther laid upon it. It was for him no less than a
principal rule of all knowledge of God. He continually spoke of it with great
energy in all possible connexions. When we speak and hear about God we are
not concerned with the *nuda essentia* or *natura* of God, but with the *velamen*, the
volucra, the *certa species*, the *larvae* of His works. We must keep to them according to God's wise and unbreakable ordinance. We must be thankful for them.
We must not disregard them, or prefer any direct, non-objective knowledge of
God. If we do, we run the risk, not only of losing God, but of making Him hostile
to us. We must seek Him where He Himself has sought us—in those veils and
under those signs of His Godhead. Elsewhere He is not to be found. There can
be no doubt that these affirmations have no little force in the Bible itself, in view
of what it indicates and declares to be faith.

It is definitely a mistake to point to the visions and auditions of the prophets
and others (in which, apparently, no means or signs enter in), or to the ever-
recurring simple formula : " And God spake," as a proof that the Bible allows
revelation of God and therefore knowledge of God in His naked, primary objectivity as well, and therefore without the veil of His works and signs.

In opposition to that we have to set first Ex. 33$^{11-23}$. We can hardly understand
this except as a confirmation of Luther's general rule, and it forms a background
for the understanding of all the rest. It says there of Moses that the Lord spake
with him face to face, as a man speaks with his friend (v. 11). What does that
mean ? We read in what follows that Moses called upon God in consequence of
God saying to him : " I know thee by name, and thou hast also found grace in
my sight." Thereupon Moses wished to know of God's " ways "—that is, to
" know " Him (v. 13) as the One who would " go up with them " in the move
from Sinai to Canaan which He had commanded. " If thy presence go not with
me, carry us not up hence. For wherein shall it be known here that I and thy
people have found grace in thy sight ? is it not in that thou goest with us ? so
shall we be separated, I and thy people, from all the people that are upon the
face of the earth " (v. 15 f.). God replies that this very thing shall take place.
Moses insists that he would see the glory of the Lord (v. 18). And not even this
request meets with a blank refusal. No ; God will make to pass before him " all
his glory," and he shall hear the name of the Lord : " I will be gracious to whom
I will be gracious, and will shew mercy on whom I will shew mercy " (v. 19).
But it is precisely in the passing before of God that Moses is to hear His name.
" Thou canst not see my face : for there shall no man see me, and live " (v. 20).
This " passing before " obviously means that His prayed and awaited going with
them had begun, that God actually does go before him and the people. And in
this " passing before " God will place him in the cleft of a rock and spread His

hand over him so that he can only see Him from the back (and hence in the process of that passing before and going with and going before). It is in this way and not in any other that he can and shall see the glory of God. It is in this way that God speaks with Moses " face to face, as a man speaketh with his friend." God really speaks with him. Moses hears God's name. He is really encouraged and given directions by God Himself. He knows God, as he has prayed—God in His extremest objectivity. But all this comes to pass in God's passing before and going before, in God's work and action, in which he does not see God's face but in which he can only follow God with his eyes. In this case, more than that would not only be less, but even nothing at all—indeed, something negative. Man cannot see God's face, God's naked objectivity, without exposing himself to the annihilating wrath of God. It would indeed have to be a second God who could see God directly. How could man escape destruction by God ? Hence God shows Moses a two-fold mercy : not only does He actually receive him according to His promise ; but also He does it in a way that is adapted to him as a creature, and speaks to him through the sign of His work. We can hardly presuppose that any of the other scriptural passages and references that should be considered in this context teach anything in opposition to this indirect knowledge of God. Rather we shall have to assume that, even in those passages where means and signs of God's appearance or speaking are not expressly mentioned, they are nevertheless taken for granted by the biblical writers. They always mean the God who is present and revealed to man in His secondary objectivity, in His work.

As far as the prophetic formula : " And God spake " is concerned, we cannot sufficiently keep in mind that the whole of Old Testament prophecy seeks to be, and is, nothing but the proclamation of God in the form of continual explanation of the divine work, of the action of God in the history of Israel, that is to say, in what had happened and what was happening to Israel, beginning with the Exodus as its epitome. It is this God in action, and indeed, this God in His action itself—and hence the God whom they can only follow with their eyes, whom they only know from behind in His secondary objectivity—who speaks to the prophets, and whose words the prophets deliver and whose name they proclaim. How else or whence else could they know Him ? What else could they have to say about Him ? He really stands before them ; He really speaks to them ; they really hear Him. But all this takes place, not in a direct, but in an indirect encounter. What directly confront them are the historical events, forms and relationships which are His work. They see this work, but as followers, as contemporaries of this history, and partly also in expectation of its future continuation. This " Opposite " speaks to them and they hear His voice. Yet not in the same way that we let any sort of event or all events work upon ourselves, and attempt to read out of history in general or out of this or that piece of history what we have first read into it. But they hear Him as prophets of God—and as such, as God's special witnesses and bearers of the divine work—before whose eyes that special event is placed as what it is, the secondary objectivity of God Himself, in which He gives Himself to be known and in which they really know Him.

Moreover, the message of the New Testament is nothing but the proclamation of the name of God on the ground of His gracious " passing before." And it is given in the form of a continual explanation of a definite historical event—of the same historical event that began with the Exodus, even with the call of Abraham, even with the covenant with Noah. But now its concrete aim and its totality become quite clear. The Messiah, the promised Son of Abraham and David, the Servant of Yahweh, the Prophet, Priest and King has appeared ; and not only as sent by God, but Himself God's Son. Yet the Word does not appear in His eternal objectivity as the Son who alone dwells in the bosom of the Father. No ; the Word became flesh. God gives Himself to be known, and is known, in the substance of secondary objectivity, in the sign of all signs, in the work of God which all the other works of God serve to prepare, accompany and continue, in the manhood which He takes to Himself, to which He humbles Himself and which He raises through Himself. " We saw His glory " now means : we saw this One in His humanity, the humanity of the Son of God, on His way to death, which was the way to His resurrection. Hence, it is again an indirect encounter with God in which the apostles, as the witnesses of the New Testament, find them-selves. They, too, stand before a veil, a sign, a work of God. In the crib of Bethlehem and at the cross of Golgotha the event takes place in which God gives Himself to them to be known and in which they know God. The fact that they see this in the light of the resurrection, and that in the forty days they see it as what it really is, God's own presence and action, does not alter the fact that in the forty days they do see this unambiguously secondary objectivity, and in it as such, and attested by it, they know the primary objectivity and hence God Himself. The fact that the God-manhood of the Mediator Jesus Christ is the fulfilment of the revelation and reconciliation proclaimed in the New Testament is equivalent to the fact that the knowledge of faith in the New Testament is indirect (and for that very reason real !) knowledge of God.

And it is precisely this knowledge of faith, attested in the Old and New Testa-ments as the knowledge of God from His works, which is now the content of know-ledge in the message of the Church of Jesus Christ. Since this message is the Gospel of its Lord and therefore of the God-man, the Mediator, it stands in explicit contrast to any message having the pure and naked objectivity of God Himself as its object. It is the Gospel of faith and the summons to faith in that it pro-claims God—really God Himself—in His mediability, in the sign of His work, in His clothed objectivity. And it is this just because it does not leave the realm of indirect knowledge of God, but keeps to the fact that in this very realm God Himself—and therefore all things—is to be sought and found, and that this indirect knowledge is the right and true knowledge of God because it is chosen and ordained by God Himself. Letting this be enough for oneself is not resigna-tion but the humility and boldness of the man who really stands before God in faith, and in faith alone. The Gospel of the Church of God is therefore of necessity a defined, circumscribed and limited message. It does not contain and say any-thing and everything. Its content is not the ἄπειρον, the boundless and ground-less that human presumption would like to make God out to be. It does not destroy perception but integrates it. It does not oppose a definite and concrete view but establishes it. It does not teach thought to lose itself in an unthinkable one and all, but forms it to very definite concepts—affirming this and denying that, including this and excluding that. It contains the veritable Gospel, the Gospel of Jesus Christ, the Messiah of Israel, the true God who became also true man in His own time and place. It explains, not an idea of God, but His name revealed in His deeds. And in correspondence with its content it is itself objective in form—visible Church, audible preaching, operative sacrament. These con-stitute an area of objectivity among and alongside so many other areas of objec-tivity ; but this is grounded on the witness of the apostles and prophets which must be shown and proved objectively. Nor is it ashamed of this witness : on the contrary, it boasts of it as just one book among many others. Christian faith as knowledge of the true God lets itself be included in this area of objectivity, and allows itself to be kept in this area, which in itself and as such is certainly not identical with the objectivity of God. But in it God's work takes place, and hence God's own objectivity gives itself to be known and is to be known, and this on the strength of the choice and sanctification of His free grace. We shall have to destroy the very roots of the Church of Jesus Christ and annihilate faith itself if we want to deny and put an end to the area of secondary objectivity ; if, to reach a supposedly better knowledge of God, we want to disregard and pass over the veil, the sign, the work in which He gives Himself to be known by man

without diminution but rather in manifestation of His glory as the One He is.
Faith either lives in this sphere, or it is not faith at all. And just the same thing
is also true of the knowledge of God through faith.

But we have not yet come to the end. As knowledge of faith
the knowledge of God is just like any other knowledge in that it also
has an object. We have seen that thereby the primary objectivity
of God is to be distinguished—but not separated—from the secondary.
But as knowledge of faith the knowledge of God is unlike all other
knowledge in that its object is the living Lord of the knowing man :
his Creator, from whom he comes even before he knows Him ; his
Reconciler, who through Jesus Christ in the Holy Ghost makes knowledge of Himself real and possible ; his Redeemer, who is Himself
the future truth of all present knowledge of Himself. He and none
other is the object of the knowledge of faith. Its difference from all
other knowledge—a difference based on its object—is that the position of the knowing man in relation to this object is the position of
a fundamentally and irrevocably determined subsequence, of a subsequence which can in no way be changed or reinterpreted into a
precedence of man. It is the position of grace. Knowledge of God as
knowledge of faith either occurs in this position or it does not take
place at all. But this means that knowledge of this object can in
no case and in no sense mean that we have this object at our disposal. Certainly we have God as an object, but not in the same way
as we have other objects. This is true of God both in His primary and
also in His secondary objectivity, and therefore in the whole extent of
the sphere which it marks out. We have all other objects as they
are determined by the pre-arranged disposition and pre-arranged
mode of our own existence. And this is so because we first of all
consciously have ourselves. The problematic of this two-fold having
—of ourselves and of our objects—and the philosophical ambiguity
of this correlation, is a separate question which we have not now to
investigate. Whatever the answer to this question may be, the claim
of our own precedence will always, in some form or other, be awake
and valid and plead for consideration ; it will at least be debatable
whether we may not equally well ascribe to the subject a similar, a
greater, or even the sole right of disposal over the object as *vice versa*.
When it is a case of God being the object, discussion is excluded from the
very outset. The position of grace, which is the position of faith, and
in which God is known, is as such the position of subsequence which
makes any disposal of the object impossible. Knowledge of God is
thus not the relationship of an already existing subject to an object
that enters into his sphere and is therefore obedient to the laws of this
sphere. On the contrary, this knowledge first of all creates the subject
of its knowledge by coming into the picture. There cannot be allowed
here any precedence of man which can entitle his subsequence—in
which God has become the aim of his direction, the object of his

knowledge—to ascribe to itself a right of disposal over the object, to make use of a power of disposal over it—as man does continually and obviously in regard to all other objects, whatever the theory of knowledge that he may hold. The precedence which alone comes into consideration here, and which never ceases as such to come into consideration, is the precedence of this object. Only because God posits Himself as the object is man posited as the knower of God. And so man can only have God as the self-posited object. It is and remains God's free grace when he is object for us in His primary and secondary objectivity. He always gives Himself to be known so as to be known by us in this giving, which is always a bestowal, always a free action. How would it be His objectivity if this were not so ? How could He be our Creator, Reconciler and Redeemer, how could He be the living Lord, if it were not so, and if His being for us were ever to be separated from His activity, so that a direction of man to God's being could exist that was grounded in something other than his being directed by God's activity ? Faith stands or falls with the fact of man being directed by God's action, by the action of His being as the living Lord. Man's being directed is his direction to God and thus of necessity his direction to the living Lord ; not to any other sort of being, but to the actual being of God. The knowledge of God by faith is therefore concerned with Him and with Him alone. It cannot draw conclusions from the fact that its object creates its own precedence. It cannot withdraw before the actuality of its object into any sort of a safe place from which it can contemplate Him *in abstracto* in His being as if it corresponded to a pre-arranged being of the contemplating man himself. For its part it can perform only the act of that being of man which is created and set up by the act of the divine being. It can only perform this act in the way that it has to be carried out on the basis of this creation and setting up : for on the basis of this creation and setting up, man's being is quite incapable of any other act ; but this act is absolutely necessary to his being. Therefore it cannot—as it would if man were directed from anywhere else—be directed to anywhere else than to the living Lord. It will in no way be able to precede this act of God, but will only be able to succeed it. It is therefore of decisive practical importance for the content of the knowledge of God (i.e., for the final question, whether it is false or true knowledge of God) whether a man knows or not that he must of necessity pray for its fulfilment as real knowledge of God, that God may give Himself to be known. The position of grace cannot be taken up and held in any other way than by asking and praying for it. The prayer that has to be made here is that God will set Himself as our object and ourselves as knowers of Him. For this will not take place except as His free gift, in the act of His grace—and this in spite of the fact that He is in fact object in Himself and in secondary objectivity in His revelation, in Jesus Christ, in the witness of the Scriptures, in the visibility of the Church, in the audibility of preaching, in the operation of the sacraments, in the whole world of His work and sign. His primary and His secondary objectivity is objectivity for us, since He Himself makes Himself into object for us and us into knowers of Him. We understand His work and sign very badly if we want to understand it as an object like other objects, and therefore to use it as a sort of atlas of revelation from which we can read the being of God without God Himself speaking to us through it all in His act as the living Lord, according to His free grace. We understand His work and sign very badly if we think that with their help we can survey and master God from some sort of humanly logical, ethical, or religious precedence. The whole world of His work and sign is then at once changed into a world of dead gods or all too living demons. Necessarily, it is all up with the truth of God's work and sign if we cease to adore its grace. For just as certainly as grace is truth, so certainly can truth only be had as grace.

As we turn back again to the Bible we remember that what is there described as the knowledge of God stands in contrast to all other human cognition in that it always in fact coincides with some action of God. God is known, not simply because He is God in Himself, but because He reveals Himself as such ; not simply because His work is there, but because He is active in His work. Biblical knowledge of God is always based on encounters of man with God ; encounters in which God exercises in one way or another His lordship over man, and in which He is acknowledged as sovereign Lord and therefore known as God. They are encounters which are always initiated by God, and which for man always have in them something unforeseen, surprising and new. They may be preceded by a whole history of man's relationship to God. Man may for a long time past have " found grace in his sight." He may for a long time have been chosen, called, enlightened and commissioned. But in these encounters he has as it were continually to begin afresh with God, returning and finding himself. They are encounters which can certainly be continuations of earlier encounters. At the same time, however, all these precedents are reconsidered in them, and the knowledge of God becomes the object of new decisions. For example, it is not the case that Abraham, Moses and David, once chosen, called, enlightened and commissioned, knew once for all how they stood with God. But what was once for all decided concerning them by God had to be worked out and fulfilled in them in a long history of renewals—for as long, indeed, as they lived. And as the renewals take place and become effective these men have what the Bible calls knowledge of God. The Exodus stands before all eyes as the work and sign of God, as the great objectivising of God Himself which is the basis of knowledge. Nevertheless, for it to be seen and understood as such it continually has to receive a new form and voice. The veritable God of the Exodus has to speak and speak again to the prophets and through the prophets, so that in His work and sign He may be known and known again. There is indeed at all times in the history of Israel a faith in Yahweh which, seeing this and other signs, imagines that in them it can have Yahweh in the way that one can have the Baalim but not Yahweh. It is therefore a secret apostasy from faith in Yahweh and it soon comes out into the open as apostasy to strange gods. Without new grace and without the effectiveness of God in His works Israel would have departed from God at every turn and then have been inwardly destroyed. Everything depends on the fact that God does not cease to bear witness to Himself as the one eternal God in new manifestations of His presence, in new revelation of His former ways, leading His people continually from old to new faith. To this extent, the indicating of the people's sin and secession, even of the contradiction and errors of the very greatest men of God, is indispensable to the biblical—or at any rate, to the Old Testament —representation of the knowledge of God. What would become of this knowledge if it were not continually renewed and re-established by its object ? Where would there be truth among these men if it were not continually spoken to them as grace ?

In the New Testament we are concerned with a situation which in this respect is apparently more complicated. It is clear enough that, according to the Synoptics as well as to John, the Old Testament thread continues unaltered in the presence of Jesus Christ—at any rate, up to His death, and properly speaking, even to His ascension. Quite apart from the " people " and the scribes and Pharisees, even the disciples whom Jesus chose and called are not in any sense portrayed as those who finally believe and know, being fully established and possessing a finally assured knowledge of God. On the contrary, like the people of Israel and its men of God in the Old Testament, they are continually revealed to be insecure, doubting, erring and offending, continually needing and receiving instruction, admonition and confirmation. So long as Jesus is among them the picture they present is apparently a continuation and repetition of the picture that we meet with throughout the Old Testament. The positive thing that is to be seen and said about them is the faithfulness of Jesus in which the renewal is continually fulfilled in them. And the figure of Judas the traitor, standing immediately beside Peter who confesses and yet denies, shows the abyss on whose brink they are upheld only by this faithfulness of Jesus and not by what they themselves are or were. This picture becomes strikingly different, at least as far as the apostles and the bearers of the apostolic office are concerned, in the Acts or more precisely from Pentecost onwards. The point at issue is no longer the weakness, doubting and erring of these men. (Gal. 2 is in this respect the exception that proves the rule.) The fact that they can fall and have to be renewed like Abraham, Moses and David, and the whole nation under the old covenant, is at any rate no longer emphasised ; indeed, it is not mentioned again intentionally. In relation to the Jews, the Gentiles, and the mighty in this world but especially in relation to the communities gathered out from Jews and Gentiles, they themselves now seem to have become the fixed pole which only Jesus was in the Gospels. It is the others who are now contrasted with the disciples. To them the name of Jesus Christ has to be proclaimed and has already been proclaimed. They need new grace and new instruction, consolation and admonition. If this involves a riddle, the solution is to be found in their function. In their office as such—and it is in this office that they appear from Acts onwards—the apostles do not need new grace for the confirmation and establishment of their knowledge of God. It is not denied that as men they need it just as much as before. But this fact becomes, so to say, irrelevant, just as now from their point of view the neediness of the Old Testament witnesses also becomes irrelevant. Now, on this side of the resurrection and ascension of Christ, the importance and interest of these men is only in their role as living participators in the work of God that was performed in Jesus Christ. What is important is the fact that it now happens through them, not that it has happened to them. The Gospels have already spoken clearly of the fact that it has happened, and have said how it happened, and that it happened as a subsequence. But so far as it happens through the apostles, and so far as they themselves are instruments of grace, they are obviously not in need of that renewal. The problem of renewal has reference to them only as it arises for the others for whom and to whom they are instruments, and not for themselves. In their existence as apostles the secondary objectivity of the human appearing of Jesus Christ Himself is repeated. And hidden within this is the primary objectivity of God Himself, calling to faith, awakening faith, establishing and renewing faith, and with faith the knowledge of God—not by these men's own strength but by the power of the Holy Spirit communicated to them, in the freedom of grace. (And, looking back, we must affirm that, in respect of their office, just the same thing is true of the witnesses of the old covenant—in fact, in regard to their commission among the nations, of the people of Israel as such.) After the Head of this people had been born, after it had been revealed to whom the prophets bore witness, the fact that in them the fixed pole, the secondary and primary objectivity of God, was already given and operative became more important than the other undeniable fact— that they became what they were through God alone, since He continually made Himself object to them and continually made them knowers of Himself. For all that, we must notice that the apostles pray, just as the man Jesus, in His solidarity with His disciples and with His people, also prayed. This praying of the apostles is a clear reminder that in the bearers of this office, even in the instruments of illuminating grace, we have to do with men who as such were in need of the renewal of their knowledge of God. Hence there can be no question of the emergence of a new type of man standing in a position of grace, in which, as the man who knows God, he now stands in a relation of precedence towards God There can be no question of a fundamental alteration in the situation of the man who knows God in the New Testament as compared with that of the man who knows Him in the Old. We see this at once if we look at the men in Acts and even more so in the Epistles, to whom the apostles turned with their witness as founders and guides of the rising Church. The position of Israel emerges clearly again at this point—in its positive as well as in its critical aspect, in its danger as well as in its promise. Here, among the men to whom God's work comes, there obviously has to be continual instruction, admonition and consolation, a continual beginning at the beginning. And often enough this takes place in such a way that we see the edge of the abyss on which it happens here too. There is a building up indeed —but only on faith. And that means, on Jesus Christ, the foundation and corner-stone ; on the object and not on the subjects of faith ; on the content of the Gospel which was delivered by the apostles and received by the churches, and not on a human precedence which has to be taken into consideration. The precedence is simply Jesus Christ proclaimed, handed down and believed, and He as the living Lord and in His free grace (which remains free), as the One whom even Paul, according to Phil. 3[12f.], did not think he had apprehended, but whom he follows after so that he might apprehend Him in consequence of being apprehended by Him. In this and only in this situation does the knowledge of God come to pass in the New Testament community also. The Reconciler, Jesus Christ, who in the Holy Spirit makes the knowledge of God real and possible, is also the Creator, from whom man can only proceed as one who knows God. But He is also the Redeemer and therefore the future truth of all knowledge of God, the truth which the man who knows God must approach in the humility of hope. God—God Himself, God's Son in the Holy Spirit—is faithful. God never ceases to make continual new beginnings with men. God is continuously effectual in His work. This is the content of the New Testament picture of man standing before God and knowing God.

We come now to the final point. In view of all this, what becomes of the knowing man ? An answer has still to be given to this question. And what other possible answer can be given than this ? The knowing man and his knowing as such ; his faith as his direction to God ; in faith, his self-distinction from God and self-union with Him ; all this is in its totality the subsequence following the divine precedence. We are not returning to the critical aspect of the statement : that it is not in any sense a precedence. It has also and above all a positive meaning. Knowledge of God is obedience to God. Observe that we do not say that knowledge of God may also be obedience, or that of necessity it has obedience attached to it, or that it is followed by obedience. No ; knowledge of God as knowledge of faith is in itself and of essential necessity obedience. It is an act of human decision corresponding to the act of divine decision ; corresponding to the act of the divine being as the living Lord ; corresponding to the act of grace in which faith is grounded and continually grounded again in God. In this act God posits Himself as our object and ourselves as those who know Him. But the fact that He does so means that our knowing God can consist only in our following this act, in ourselves becoming a correspondence of this act, in ourselves and our whole existence and therefore our considering and conceiving becoming the human act corresponding to the divine act. This is obedience, the obedience of faith. Precisely—and only—as this act of obedience, is the knowledge of God knowledge of faith and therefore real knowledge of God. Were it something else, did it not spring from obedience and therefore from faith, it would miss God and would certainly not be knowledge of God. For God will be known as the One He is. But precisely as the One He is, He acts. It is as this One who acts, however, that He will be known. And to know Him as the One who acts means to become obedient to Him. It is only now perhaps that we see the decisive importance of our previous definition of the knowledge of God as the knowledge of His free grace, as the knowledge of the real activity of God in His work. It is only now that we can more closely define prayer, which we have already mentioned as the essentially necessary determination of the knowledge of God. Since it is the prayer that God will posit Himself as our object and ourselves as those who know Him, it must obviously run concretely : " Lead us not into temptation—into the temptation of an objectivistic consideration of God's secondary and primary objectivity ; a disinterested non-obedient consideration which holds back in a place which it thinks secure. Lead us not into the temptation of the false opinion that Thou art an object like other objects which we can undertake to know or not just as we wish, which we are free to know in this way, or even in that. Lead us not into the temptation of wanting to know Thee in Thy objectivity as if we were spectators, as if we could know, speak and hear about Thee in the slightest degree without at once taking part, without at once making that correspondence actual, without at once beginning with obedience." Obviously this temptation does not threaten from the side of God's objectivity, but always from our side. When we can no longer evade the objectivity of God, we can and will still evade God Himself ; we can and will still see the objectivity of God changed into that world of dead gods or all too living demons, into a world whose essence we can contemplate without giving ourselves into the hands of God, but for that reason being all the more enslaved by these gods and demons. This is the characteristic temptation of those who are already called to the people and Church of God. If we give way to it, the knowledge of God is not merely partially but totally lost in the sphere of this people, in the sphere of this Church. What proceeds out of ourselves will always be this temptation—and this is true even of those who are chosen and called, enlightened and commissioned. Therefore we have to pray that we may overcome this temptation. The being of God for us is His being in hearing this prayer and therefore by the act of His grace. The being of God is either known by grace or it is not known at all. If, however, it is known by grace, then we are already displaced from that secure position and put in a position where the consideration of God can consist and be fulfilled only in the act of our own decision of obedience. The object of this consideration is God in His almighty and active will. But if it is consideration of God in His almighty and active will, how can it fail to lead at once to decision ? Either the consideration will become a flight before what is considered, and therefore disobedience, and therefore meaningless, thus ceasing to be the knowledge of God ; or the consideration will become that correspondence, and therefore obedience, and as such real knowledge of the real God. *Tertium non datur.* But where by grace it is really consideration of God in His almighty and active will, it has already passed this Either-Or, and has become obedience and therefore real knowledge of God. Concretely, this means that the distinction and union between God and man in which the knowledge of God comes to pass will be fulfilled in the order laid down by the almighty and active will of God. It will not be any sort of freely chosen union and distinction, but will be concerned under all circumstances with the gracious God on the one hand and sinful man on the other. This qualifying of God and man will be the norm and criterion of all union and distinction, and therefore of the knowledge of God, and therefore of all speaking and hearing about Him. This qualifying is, however, unthinkable as naked thought. It will not be realised, or man will not know what he is doing in realising it, if, when he realises it in thought, it is not fulfilled beforehand in himself ; if he does not know the gracious God as his God and himself as the sinful man distinct from God and yet united with Him ; if he is not the man directed by the act of God the living Lord ; if, therefore, in his direction to God he does not stand in obedience. Just as truth is certainly only to be had as grace, so the securing of grace will certainly have to consist in the decision of obedience.

We have already cited Calvin's definition of faith : *cognitio divinae erga nos benevolentiae.* In accordance with this definition, he described the knowledge of God at the beginning of the *Institutio*: *ad quam nos deduceret genuinus naturae ordo, si integer stetisset Adam: Neque enim Deum, proprie loquendo, cognosci dicemus ubi nulla est religio nec pietas. Pietas,* the presupposition of *religio,*

Calvin describes as *coniuncta cum amore Dei reverentia, quam beneficiorum eius notitia conciliat*. *Religio pura germanaque*, born of *pietas*, means according to Calvin : *fides cum serio Dei timore coniuncta: ut timor et voluntariam reverentiam in se contineat et secum trahat legitimum cultum qualis in Lege praescribitur*. Only in such *pietas* and *religio* is there real knowledge of God. Observe that the *voluntaria reverentia* and the proper reverence of God, corresponding to the Law of God, is based upon the sincere fear of God. This fear, however, is itself a supplement of *fides* which, for its part, is grounded in the *notitia beneficiorum Dei*. Therefore, when we ask about God, everything depends upon the *sensus virtutum Dei*. Everything depends upon His being recognised as the *fons omnium bonorum*. Our question must be, not *quid ?* but *qualis sit Deus ? Quid iuvat Deum cognoscere quocum nihil sit nobis negotii ?* In respect of God known as Lord and Father and just Judge, we must ask ourselves : *quomodo mentem tuam subire queat Dei cogitatio, quin simul extemplo cogites, te, quum figmentum illius sis, eiusdem imperio esse ipso creationis iure addictum et mancipatum ? vitam tuam illi deberi ? quicquid instituis, quicquid agis, ad illum referri oportere ? Id si est, iam profecto sequitur, vitam tuam prave corrumpi nisi ad obsequium eius componitur, quando nobis vivendi lex esse debet eius voluntas* (I, 2, 1–2). According to Calvin, the whole of existence and the whole course of the world is in itself an answer not only to the question *quid ?* but also to *qualis sit Deus ?* and a unique summons *ad Dei notitiam, non quae inani speculatione contenta in cerebro tantum volitet, sed quae solida futura sit et fructuosa, si rite percipiatur a nobis, radicemque agat in corde. A suis enim virtutibus manifestatur Dominus, quarum vim quia sentimus intra nos et beneficiis fruimur, vividius multo hac cognitione nos affici necesse est, quam si Deum imaginaremur cuius nullus ad nos sensus perveniret* (I, 5, 9). Therefore under these objective and subjective aspects Calvin has already described what he understood by the *Dei notitia hominum mentibus naturaliter indita* (I, 3). This is still only an anticipation of what is later described as the knowledge of God mediated through Holy Scripture and realised in Jesus Christ. The objective basis of real knowledge of God, and the *virtutes Dei* revealed in creation, are actually hidden from natural man as a result of the fall, so that according to Calvin also real knowledge of God in the form of natural knowledge of God does not occur : *quum frustra Deus omnes populos ad se invitet caeli terraeque intuitu* (I, 6, 4). This being the case, the revelation of God in Jesus Christ attested in the Scriptures means objectively that for us now *probe et ad vivum a suis operibus describitur Deus, dum opera ipsa non ex iudicii nostri pravitate, sed aeternae veritatis regula aestimantur* (I, 6, 3). The *divina benevolentia* now, so to speak, rends the veil of human non-understanding and misunderstanding, and the rule of all real knowledge of God now comes into force—and this is the subjectively new thing which takes place on the basis of revelation : *Omnis recta Dei cognitio ab obedientia nascitur* (I, 6, 2). *Quodnam vere doctrinae initium est, nisi prompta alacritas ad audiendam vocem Dei ?* (I, 7, 5). *Les hommes ne suyvront point Dieu en dormant: encores qu'ils s'y efforcent beaucoup* (*Serm. on Deut.* 5²⁸⁻³³; C.R. 26, 413). No : *Dei cognitio est efficax . . . nec vero hoc tantum ex Dei natura manat, ut cognitum statim amemus, sed idem Spiritus, qui mentes nostras illuminat, inspirat etiam cordibus conformem scientiae affectum. Quamquam hoc secum fert Dei cognitio, ut eum timamus et amemus. Neque enim dominum et patrem, ut se ostendit, possumus agnoscere, quin praebeamus nos illi vicissim morigeros filios et servos obsequentes* (*Comm. on* 1 Jn. 2³; C.R. 55, 311). For Calvin the fulfilment of the real knowledge of God is a cycle. God gives Himself to be known in His will directed towards us. God is known by us as we are submissive to this His will. It is obvious that this cycle corresponds exactly to what is called knowledge of God in the Old and New Testaments. The encounters between God and man in the sphere of that secondary objectivity of God mean singly and in the aggregate the taking place of a history (Calvin : a *negotium*) between God and man. This history begins with a voluntary decision of God and continues in a corresponding voluntary decision of man. This history develops systematically and completely. The will of God offers itself as good will towards men and is met by faith. Man with his will yields and becomes submissive to the will of God. Faith becomes the determination of his existence and therefore obedience. And in this way the knowledge of God takes place. According to the Bible there is no knowledge of God outside this cycle. Knowledge of God means knowledge of the way or ways of God, which as such are good, true, holy and just. How can they be known except as God gives them to be known, i.e., gives Himself to be known as the One who goes these ways? Everything depends on this divine precedence. But again, how can they be known except as man for his part travels ways which in his sphere correspond to the ways of God—ways of wisdom, of life, of peace, which are indeed no longer his own ways, no longer the ways of the heathen and godless? Thus everything depends too on this human proceeding and going with God. It is therefore of more than external significance that according to the Gospels all the dealings of Jesus with His disciples take place in such a way that He is with them and they are with Him on the way—not any sort of way, but on the way determined by Him. In His going this way and their going with Him, their knowledge of God is fulfilled. That is to say, they reach the faith which as such— as faith in Him whom God has sent—is knowledge of Him as the One sent by God and therefore knowledge of the God who has sent Him. So decisive is this connexion that, according to Jn. 14⁶, Jesus calls Himself absolutely " the Way," and thus the Truth and the Life (i.e., revelation and salvation). Again, after Pentecost the preaching of His name and faith in Him is described just as absolutely as " this way " (Acts 9², 22⁴, 24¹⁴. Cf. 2 Peter 2²). A break in this connexion, and therefore the establishment or presupposition of real knowledge of God apart from this way, without manifestation of the divine will or without the corresponding human decision of will, can hardly be found in the sphere of the biblical witness of God. Where God in His *benevolentia* gives Himself to be known by man, and where man stands before Him as the one who knows this *benevolentia* as such and is therefore determined by it and obedient to it, there and there alone is there a fulfilment of the real knowledge of God.

To summarise, we started out from the fact that we are concerned with the problem of the knowledge of God as bound to the Word of God. The task we set ourselves was to understand how this came to pass. We first of all established that it is as such objective and therefore real knowledge ; it is not identical with God Himself, but it has its object in God. That is to say, it is the knowledge of faith, in which God becomes object to man. It is a particular, separating and sanctifying object distinguishing between itself and the knowing man, so that knowledge of God necessarily has to be understood as an event outstanding in its relationship to other events. We saw, moreover, that this objectivising of God always occurs concretely in the use of a medium, in the putting on of a veil, in the form of a work of God ; and therefore knowledge of God occurs in the fact that men make use of this medium. But, on the other hand, this medium, and therefore this mediate knowledge of God, is not to be thought of apart from the grace in which God the Lord controls and uses this medium and is Himself its power. Thus the knowledge of God can be understood only as the bestowal and reception of this free grace of God. And finally, because in this act of His free grace God makes Himself object to us and makes us knowers of Himself, the knowledge of this object cannot be fulfilled in neutrality, but only in our relationship to this act, and therefore only in an act, the act which is the decision of obedience to Him.

And now we look back to the beginning. All this, regarded first from man's side, is the fulfilment of the knowledge of God as bound to the Word of God. At the outset we said of the knowledge of God as bound in this way that neither its reality nor its possibility can be questioned from without. We said that in regard to both its reality and its possibility we have to keep to its fulfilment, understanding both its reality and its possibility from within. We shall now have to take a second step. We shall have to understand it, not from man's side, but from God's. The first step should have made it clear that when we delimited the bound knowledge of God from other ostensible or real knowledge of God by rejecting any other understanding of its reality and possibility than that which proceeds from within outwards, we were not guilty of an arbitrary absolutising of any human position. Of course, this bound knowledge of God is also formally a human position, and materially a human affirmation. It is a human thesis like any other, to which as such the question coming from without seems to be not only permissible but even necessary. There can be no question of ascribing to this human position as such a special legal title, a particular superiority and certainty over against other human positions. It does not lay claim to any such things. It is even more unassuming than all other human positions in that it quite simply takes its stand beside them without any legal title, without proof of its superiority and certainty, even without proof of its equality of rights. But on the other hand, the unpretentiousness in which we represent the position of the bound knowledge of God as a human position must not be regarded as a cause and ground for misunderstanding the essence and nature of this position ; nor should motives of humility lead us to transform it into the essence and nature of any other human position. It is quite essential to this human position of the knowledge of God bound to the Word of God that it cannot let its reality and possibility be questioned from without, that it can reply to such questions only by a reference to its fulfilment, or rather only by the fulfilment itself, allowing its own actuality to speak for itself. If anything else takes place, this human position has already been transformed, betrayed and finally destroyed. In this way—and this way alone—can it be adopted, defended and maintained. We have to assert this, in a friendly but emphatic manner, when all other human positions complain about the self-sufficiency and pride which reigns here, or the ambiguity which arises when this problem is rejected, or the " dangers " of isolation and illusion which we are supposed to have incurred. Those who want to support and hold this human position cannot impress this fact sufficiently upon themselves. It is possible to leave this position (although seen from within, it has to be said that in point of fact we cannot leave it), but it is quite impossible to defend and maintain it unless we represent its reality and possibility from within outwards, and do not try to establish its reality and possibility from outside. " From outside " means from the point of view of a human position where truth, dignity and competence are so ascribed to human seeing, understanding and judging as to be judge over the reality and possibility of what happens here. But this is the very thing which is excluded by the inner understanding of what happens, as we are taught at least by our first step. Already we have had to understand the knowledge of God bound to the Word of God as an event utterly undetermined by man but utterly determined by God as its object. God distinguishes Himself from man in this event. God also distinguishes this event from all other events. God's work is the medium of this event, and that in such a way that if this event comes to pass God is and remains the operator of His work. And in respect of this event man is himself already immitted into this event. He is already brought on to a way parallel with God's way, and thus placed in the impossibility of ascribing to himself—himself the judged—the office of judge over this event. If the knowledge of God bound to the Word of God is the knowledge of faith, and if we have represented it correctly in our analysis, how can there subsequently be acknowledged a human judgment upon this event ? What else can this mean but that the absolute lordship of God as the One who is known over the man who knows is again denied ? But this is the very thing which must not happen—either from the need humanly to assure the human position of the knowledge of God bound to the Word of God, or even out of humility towards other human positions.

2. GOD BEFORE MAN

We have tried first to understand the knowledge of God bound to the Word of God from its human side. Our aim was to ascertain how men reach the position of speaking and hearing about God. We have therefore tried to clarify how, in the fulfilment of this knowledge, man stands before God. But this very analysis has shown us all along the line that man's standing before God, in which this knowledge becomes real, and therefore the realising itself, can be understood throughout only as a second act which is preceded by a first as its presupposition, determination and restriction, and that the second act can be fulfilled only in confirmation and acknowledgment of this first act. But this first act consists in God standing before man. Knowledge of God comes into force as the knowledge of faith by God awakening man to faith ; in and by His showing Himself to man as his object ; and in and by His opening man's eyes to see God Himself in His objectivity. In and by this way man comes to stand before

God, in a situation in which he can perceive and consider and con- ceive God, distinguishing God from himself and himself from God, and uniting God with himself and himself with God. If God does not have the precedence, if God does not stand before man so that man may stand before God, how can man take even a single step forward ? God is objective and therefore He can be truly known. He encounters man. He encounters him in such a way that man can also know Him. He encounters him in such a way that in this encounter God is and remains God and thus raises up man really to be a knower of Himself. But that this is the case is wholly and utterly God's own being and work, which man can only follow. If we want to be clear what man is and does when he knows God, step by step we have to be clear who the God is and what the God does whom he knows. If we want to see how man stands before God, at every point we have to see how God stands before man. If we want to know about the fulfil- ment of this knowledge, we have to keep wholly and utterly to its content. Therefore we can see already that the doctrine of the know- ledge of God does not form an independent prolegomenon to the actual doctrine of God. It is itself already a part of that doctrine, because it can consist only in a representation of the being and activity of God. But we are dealing with a particular determination of the being and activity of God. For it is not only the basic reality to which all human speaking and hearing about God is related. As the basic reality, it is also a basis of knowledge from which all human speaking and hearing about God originates. We shall now investigate the fulfilment of the knowledge of God as bound to the Word of God along a second line of thought with express reference to this point of view.

In the thesis at the head of this section we stated the content of the knowledge of God in this way : " the existence of Him whom we must fear above all things because we may love Him above all things ; who remains a mystery to us because He Himself has made Himself so clear and certain to us." This is God before man, God as He encounters man and acts towards man according to the knowledge of God as bound to the Word of God. This is the God who in the fulfilment of this knowledge precedes man, whom man, in the fulfilment of this knowledge, can only follow. The fact that He is the One who is to be feared above all and to be loved above all and, indeed, to be feared above all because He is to be loved above all, certainly seems at first sight to have nothing to do with the establishment of His knowledge by man. But in reality, the fact that He is this God is decisive and definitive for everything that is to be said about His knowledge by man. It is with this thought, that He is this God and none other, that we now begin.

God is He whom we may love above all things. God exists, and is the object of our knowledge, as this One who is to be loved above all things. If we are bound to God's Word we cannot contradict this.

To be bound to God's Word means that we may love above all things Him who speaks this Word to us. We emphasise—*may*. Binding to the love of God is first and foremost a permission, a liberation, an authorisation. We do not yet, or no longer believe and trust the Word of God, our obedience to Him is not yet, or no longer the obedience of faith, it is not yet, or no longer real obedience, if our love to God is not an exercise of this permission, if God is not the One whom we may love, and love in such a way as we may love no one and nothing else. If, in regard to some person or thing—whoever or whatever it may be—we stand in some other relationship than that of being allowed and having the freedom to love that person or thing above all things, then that person or thing is not yet in any circumstances God, or is no longer God, and the knowledge of that person or thing has therefore to be distinguished very definitely from the knowledge of God. So, then, the problematic of the knowledge of all objects to which we may stand in another relationship than this, must not be introduced into the investigation of the knowledge of God. This investigation must start out from the fact that God is He with whom we stand in this relationship and not another. The permission with which we are concerned is, however, three-fold. It consists first in the fact that God is in Himself the One who is worthy of our love, and in a way that no one and nothing else is worthy, so that in loving Him disappointment does not await us. Secondly, the permission consists in the fact that God makes Himself known and offers Himself to us, so that we can in fact love Him as the One who exists for us in such a way that it is obvious that He Himself will be loved by us because He offers us reason and cause to love Him. And it consists finally in the fact that God creates in us the possibility—the willingness and readiness—to know Him ; so that, seen from our side also, there is no reason why this should not actually happen. But to love means not to wish any longer to be and have oneself without the beloved object. It is obvious that in the full sense of the concept, because in it our whole existence is at stake, love can come into consideration only in relation to the object which is in itself so constituted that it can invite and demand of us to put our whole existence at stake—only in relation to the object which makes the invitation and demand actually befall us—only in relation to the object which actually moves us to accept the invitation and demand. God is just this object. It is He whom we may love. It is in relation to Him that we may put our existence at stake. In relation to Him the verse is true in this three-fold sense : " Whom have I in heaven but thee ? and there is none upon earth that I desire in comparison of thee " (Ps. 73[25]).

But precisely because this is true, precisely because God is He of whom it may be true, we must now go further, and say that God is the One whom we must fear above all things. We must fear Him above all things because we may love Him above all things. Again, if we

2

are bound to God's Word, we cannot contradict this. The fear which is not in love, the fear which is driven out by perfect love (I John 4[18]), is certainly not the fear with which we must fear God above all things, but is a fear in which we fear persons and things other than Him whom we may love above all things. Of course such a fear is driven out by love ; such a fear cannot be in love. But according to the whole of the Old and New Testaments, to be bound by God's Word undoubtedly means that we must fear above all things Him who speaks this Word to us. This time the emphasis falls on—*must*. The compulsion in the fear of God—we have to say this here—is a command, a seizure, an expropriation which is made upon us. And it derives its seriousness and power from the fact that God is the One whom we may love above all. Again, there is no belief and trust in the Word of God, no obedience of faith, and therefore no obedience in general, if man is not compelled to fear God. If we stand in any other relationship to a person or thing, whoever or whatever it might be ; if we are not forced to fear that person or thing above all things ; but if we sometimes fear and sometimes cannot fear, then that person or thing is not yet or no longer God ; and however real in itself may be our knowledge of that person or thing, it is not in any circumstances the knowledge of God. Again, the caution must be given that the problematic of the knowledge of an object which we are not compelled to fear above all things must not be introduced into our investigation of the knowledge of God. This investigation must not be burdened with questions and difficulties which may be meaningful in their own context, but cannot be meaningful in this context, in relation to the knowledge of Him who is to be feared above all things. The compulsion of which we speak is again three-fold. It consists first in the fact that God is in Himself to be feared, so that escape from Him is unimaginable. Second, it consists in the fearful encounter with God, so that He exists for us in such a way that it is obvious that, since He offers us reason and cause for fear, He Himself wills that we should fear Him. It consists finally in God opening our eyes and ears to His fearfulness, so that our fear before Him is realised. And all this in such a way that between love and fear there is no contradiction but the closest and most necessary—even if a quite determined and irreversible—connexion. Just because we may love Him in that three-fold sense, we must also fear Him in this three-fold sense. Just because we have the permission, the freedom and the authorisation to love Him above all things, we receive also the command, and that seizure and expropriation is made upon us in which we must fear Him : fear Him as the One who does not owe us that permission, freedom and authorisation, but who, by giving them to us, receives a right over us against which we can oppose no counter claim either before or after ; and fear Him as the One whom we may perhaps neglect or omit to love even although everything is ready for it. The man who loves God knows that it is a permission which he has not taken for himself but which is given to him. He knows that God has first loved him so that he may love Him in return in that three-fold sense. And for that very reason he will fear Him as the One without whom he may not love, and as the One whom not to love must mean his own end in terror. For in the full sense of the concept, fear means necessarily to expect the cessation of one's existence at the hands of someone or something. Where the expectation is anything less, or less than necessary, we have not really learned to fear. What we do not fear above all things we do not properly fear at all. And the object of this fear can only be He whom we may love above all. It is He whom we have to fear above all things for this reason. If we are not permitted to love Him and if we do not love Him, we can only expect the cessation of our existence at His hands. Him, therefore, we must fear just because we may love Him. This object is God. How can we stand before Him in the possession of the freedom to love Him without reflecting that this is His unmerited gift and that it is legitimate for us to make use of this gift ? In this very reflection we have to fear God. If this freedom is not bestowed upon us (and it does not have to be bestowed), or if we do not make use of it (and when do we not have to ask ourselves if and how far we do that ?) to stand before God cannot fail to mean our destruction. God stands before man as the One whom he may love and must fear—may really love and must really fear—above all things. He stands before man as the One whom he may and must love in such a way that there is no other love and fear and therefore no other permission and compulsion.

At this point we have adopted the two concepts of fear and love which Luther used in the *Smaller Catechism*, first as a paraphrase of the first commandment, and then as leading concepts for the explication of the other nine. He was evidently of the view that the normal standing of man in relation to God, and therefore also of God Himself in His relationship to man, cannot be better described than by the words : " We should fear and love God." In the first commandment he introduced a third concept, which does not reappear : " fear, love and trust." The addition shows that Luther wanted the content of the first commandment to be understood only as the demand for faith ; which means of course that the God, of whom it speaks already, can be understood only as the God who is revealed to us in Jesus Christ. What other God can be loved and feared in earnest ? The life which is lived in trust towards this God and therefore in obedience to Him is life in fear and love to Him. The keeping of the commandment consists in this twofold attitude, which obviously has to be understood as a movement, and which according to Luther is the movement from fear to love. Now in Luther's sense it may perhaps be justifiable to understand God as Him through whom the man He encounters is put into this double attitude and therefore into this movement. But when we ask about this God, when it is decided that we have to do with the God who is revealed to us in Jesus Christ, and when we look back again from that position to man, the movement of man has actually to be described as the very reverse of what Luther said. Fear has to follow love, and not conversely. Love has to be named and understood as the basis of fear. Fear has to be explained from love—not any sort of fear from any sort of love, but the fear of God from love to God. It is only then that we understand the fact and reason why there has to be fear of God. It is only then that we also understand the fact and reason why in the whole of Scripture (yes, in the New Testament, too!) the fear of God keeps its place alongside love to God, and that it is *this* place. Not an independent place. Not one from which love can again be threatened. Not one from which anxiety can again break into the life of him who trusts God above all things according to the first commandment. But certainly the place from which love is determined and delimited by the remembrance that it is grounded in the love of God to us and is answerable to it. The love which is accompanied by the fear of God and determined and delimited by it will remain in the truth without being the less love for that. It will be genuine and strong love by remaining in the truth—that is, by driving out all false fear and persisting in loving God above all things. This need is met by the fear of God which accompanies, determines and delimits it. How can it be really accompanied, determined and delimited by the fear of God, if this fear does not continually grow out of love as out of a root? How can another fear which springs from a second and certainly muddy source having this saving power, and therefore deserve to be mentioned in the *Catechism*? Of the same God of whom it is true that we may love Him above all things, and true in just the same way that we must fear Him above all things; He is the One whom we must fear above all things because we may love Him above all things. That is why the fear of God has this saving power, and the love which is accompanied, determined and delimited by the fear of God is genuine and strong. That is why we want to see the two concepts placed in the reverse order from that of Luther in the *Catechism*.

The content of the knowledge of God as bound to the Word of God is the existence of Him whom we must fear above all things because we may love Him above all things. When this is understood, then in relation to the fulfilment of this knowledge, the first point which will emerge is the one with which we concluded the first part of our investigation. Knowledge of God is in obedience to God. This obedience is not that of a slave but of a child. It is not blind but seeing. It is not coerced but free. But for this very reason it is a real obedience. It is because this is so that this knowledge is so indisputable and holds such a strong position. This position is strong not only against third parties who from a human position try to contest and combat it like another human position. Above all it is strengthened in opposition to the knowing man himself. Standing over against the object of his knowledge in a relationship of obedience, man acknowledges and confirms that the fulfilment of this knowledge results in binding to God's Word. This is independent of his own choice and will. Therefore he renounces the possibility either of generally withdrawing from the knowledge of this object or of trying to fulfil it otherwise than the object itself demands. Moreover, this obedience itself is not only evoked but also determined by this object. It cannot, therefore, be anything but a childlike, seeing and free obedience; an obedience which results in the fear of God which is rooted in love to God. Because we may love God we must therefore fear Him and we will and shall therefore obey Him. The fact that this takes place means, therefore, that our knowledge of God is strengthened against all third parties and above all against ourselves. We have only to get the relationship between " may " and " must " right to be able to understand how it comes about that in the knowledge of God we are forthwith and finally extracted from any neutrality towards this object, and then contrariwise how our knowledge of God becomes a position of neutrality over against those various human positions which others or even we ourselves might wish to take up in regard to it—and the neutrality one of full superiority and unassailability. In the love to God which is accompanied, determined and delimited by the fear of God it happens that on the one hand our neutrality is taken from us and that on the other hand the position of our knowledge of God acquires the complete neutrality of the superiority and unassailability of God Himself.

It is a question of what Paul calls in Rom. 1⁵ and 16²⁶ ὑπακοὴ πίστεως and in 2 Cor. 10⁵ ὑπακοὴ τοῦ Χριστοῦ, and what Acts 6⁷ calls ὑπήκουον τῇ πίστει. Πίστει καλούμενος Ἀβραὰμ ὑπήκουσεν (Heb. 11⁸). In Rom. 6¹⁷ and 10¹⁶ and 2 Thess. 1⁸ right decisions taken towards the Gospel are called obedience. Phil. 2¹² praises that Church because they were obedient on every occasion. 1 Pet. 1¹⁴ calls Christians τέκνα ὑπακοῆς and the description of the " elect strangers " in 1 Pet. 1¹⁻² runs : " according to the foreknowledge of God the Father, through sanctification of the Spirit, εἰς ὑπακοὴν καὶ ῥαντισμὸν αἵματος Ἰησοῦ Χριστοῦ ". It certainly cannot be the intention of all these New Testament passages to replace or even to complete the concept of faith by that of obedience. And again they are concerned far too centrally with man's basic position in his relationship to what is preached to him for us to understand by " obedience " something incidental happening alongside faith. The only alternative is to understand faith as obedience, to the extent that faith, as " trust of the heart," is now distinguished from any other sort of trust of the heart by being grounded in the must of the fear of God which is inseparable from the " may " of love to God. If faith is really the act in which in regard to the God revealed to him in Jesus Christ man makes use of that " may," how can it occur otherwise than in the " must " which—so necessary for the sake of truth—accompanies, determines and delimits that " may " ? In all the passages cited above it is a question of child-like, seeing and free obedience, and hence of the obedience of faith In face of the object of which they speak, how can it be a question of another obedience ? But again, in regard to this object, how can it fail to be a question of obedience ? How can there be love without fear ? And, as love in fear, how can it fail to be obedience ?

Therefore, when God stands before man as the One who awakens, creates and sustains his faith, and when God presents Himself as the object and content of the knowledge of his faith, He does it in this being and doing. That is, He does it as the One whom we must fear above all things because we may love Him above all things, and in just such a way as the One who awakens, creates and upholds our knowledge of Himself as a work of obedience and for that very reason as a work which is no longer contestable—not even by ourselves. The love in fear, which this object of necessity evokes, will never let us fall out of the knowledge of the object. It holds us to the object, and this in the way that is demanded by the nature and being of the object. The knowledge that springs from this love will continually be real because it is itself from God. In love we are set on the circular course in which there is no break, in which we can and shall only go further—from faith to faith, from knowledge to knowledge—never beginning with ourselves (and that means, with our own ability for faith and knowledge) but therefore also never ending with ourselves (and that means, with our own inability for faith and knowledge).

But we have mentioned a second pair of concepts in our thesis. The same God whom we must fear above all things because we may love Him above all things is also He who remains a mystery to us because He Himself has made Himself so clear and certain to us. We have certainly seen that the fact that God is He whom we may love and whom we must fear has also an independent meaning for the problem of the knowledge of God by men (that is to say, for its establishment and preservation). For in fear, He makes the problem of this knowledge become for the one who loves a problem of obedience, and the knowledge of Himself a decision made necessary by His being and nature. But now the meaning of this fact encroaches upon the shape and form of this knowledge because it is connected with the other order indicated by the second pair of concepts. It is connected with the order in which on the one hand the clarity and certainty in which God stands before us and on the other the mystery in which He stands before us are bound together. The clarity and certainty in which He offers Himself to us correspond to love towards Him, as we are permitted to have it. How can there be reconciliation if there is no revelation ? Faith—making use of that permission—means receiving God's revelation ; and it is by receiving God's revelation that we make use of the fact that we may love Him. But the mystery in which He offers Himself to us corresponds to the fear which we must have before Him. How can there be reconciliation without judgment, and so how can revelation be without mystery ? Faith—treating that " must " seriously—means knowing and acknowledging God's mystery in God's revelation. And it is by knowing and acknowledging God's mystery in God's revelation that we treat seriously the fact that we must fear Him. This is the first thing that we have to consider in detail.

Here again we begin with the positive fact that God is He who has made Himself clear and certain to us. We really must begin with this positive fact. Everything that is to be said about God's mystery in His revelation can only be related to the fact that He is revealed to us as fear is related to love. The mystery accompanies, determines and delimits the clarity and certainty in which God offers Himself to us. But yet it is only a case of it accompanying, determining and delimiting them. Here is no reversible but an irreversible relationship. Clarity and certainty on the one hand and mystery on the other do not stand over against one another in logical convertibility. But the fact that God gives Himself to us to be known, and, indeed, gives Himself to be known clearly and certainly, fully and sufficiently, is the first and most important thing to be considered here. We again step out of our constraint by God's Word if we try to see and say it otherwise. If we are bound to God's Word, we must begin with His existence—namely, with the existence of God in which He has made Himself clear and certain to us. We emphasise : He—Himself. We are bound to His existence on the strength of being bound to His Word. But this does not mean that we have procured for ourselves in some way or other a clarity and certainty about His existence, and that now, thanks to the confidence in which we look back to this event, we regard ourselves as bound to His existence. We do not merely regard ourselves as bound ; we are bound. And it is not because we procured clarity and certainty for ourselves with more or less of success that we are bound, but it is by God Himself making Himself so clear and certain to us. So clear—and this is the criterion—that we may love Him, i.e. that we can no longer be without Him, that we wish neither to be nor to have ourselves any longer without Him. Our own existence stands or falls with the existence of God. In the light of the existence of God it is less—infinitely less—clear and certain to us than His existence. In the light of the existence of God : that is, in consequence of the fact that He Himself has made Himself so clear and certain to us. If our situation in relation to Him is different ; if we have no clarity and certainty about Him and if His existence is a problem to us as the existence of other objects can be a problem, then it is definitely not He who stands before us. But again, He does not stand before us and we are not concerned with God if His existence is perhaps no problem for us because in some way we have procured for ourselves clarity and certainty about it, and we can now look back to this successful undertaking with more or less of confidence. Knowledge of God can always proceed only from the knowledge of His existence in the two-fold sense that we always already have this knowledge and that we must have it from God Himself, in order consequently to know Him. But the fact that He Himself makes Himself so clear and certain to us means that He is, and He shows Himself to us, as object. And He does so in such a way that as such He can be considered and conceived by us as the object whom we may love above all things and for that very reason must fear above all things. Therefore in His own existence God sees to it that He not only does not remain hidden from us, but is known so well that we know our existence only in that relationship of love and fear to His existence, that thus we cannot be ignorant of His existence, but, knowing ourselves, must also know Him. It is He who sees to it. It cannot be any concern of ours to put our existence into this relationship when it is so definitely that relationship of love and fear which can be established only in its object. But again, He does see to it. He is indeed the One who is to be loved and feared above all things and He has actually entered into our ken, and therefore He has actually brought our existence into that relationship. And He sees to it in such a way that we can alter nothing in this relationship ; that we can as little break it off as we can set it up. That is revelation in so far as we mean by the word what is attested in Holy Scripture as the revelation of God to men. The acknowledgment of the fact that revelation has taken place is faith, and the knowledge with which the revelation that has taken place begins is the knowledge of faith. And for the knowledge of faith, the existence of God is the problem already solved in and by the clarity and certainty of the existence of God Himself in His revelation.

But precisely because that is so, precisely because God is He who makes Himself so clear and certain to us, we must now go further and say that He is the One who remains a mystery to us. How can or dare we make that positive statement without at once speaking also of this limitation ? Not so as to deny the positive statement. Not so as to make new obscurity out of clarity, new uncertainty out of certainty. Not so as to make what is in its nature unproblematic problematical again. But in order to consider the necessary determination and limit which is here set us in the fact that the known object is God while we are only the knowing men. If we know Him in consequence of His giving Himself to be known by us in His revelation, then indeed we know Him in His mystery.

" In His mystery." In these words we are saying only that we know Him as He gives Himself to be known by us. But in these words we also make the important declaration : thus and only thus, in this clarity and certainty and in no other. The fact that we know God is His work and not ours. And the clarity and certainty in which we know Him are His and not ours. The possibility on the basis of which this occurrence is realised is His divine power. The actuality in which it happens is the actuality of His will and decision. The order in which it happens is the free disposition of His wisdom. If we ought and want to give an account of how this happens, we can and will certainly understand and know ourselves to be those who are permitted to be the subject here. We can and will understand and know ourselves as those who know God, but in such a way that we go on at once to understand and know that only in our witness to God can it come to pass that we are the subjects of the knowledge of Him. Any assertion which is to be made about us as these subjects can be truly made only in the form of assertions in which the known and therefore God Himself is declared to be the Subject of the knowledge of God. We cannot understand anything at all in this matter except as deriving from God—neither the possibility nor the actuality in which we know God, neither the order in which it happens nor the fact that it happens in that indisputable clarity and certainty. Bound to the Word of God in regard to our knowledge of God we have to give the glory to God Himself and indeed to God alone. Bound to the Word of God, we cannot ascribe to ourselves any other knowledge of God than that of the faith in which we cleave to His Word. But it is the knowledge of God which cannot at any moment or in any respect try to understand itself other than as the knowledge made possible, realised and ordered by God alone. Precisely in the knowledge of faith God is and remains a mystery to us by giving Himself to be known by us. It is not God who stands before us if He does not stand before us in such a way that He is and remains a mystery to us. Mystery means that He is and remains the One whom we know only because He gives Himself to be known. He is and remains the light visible and seen only in His own light. The love to God which is accompanied, determined and delimited by the fear of God makes it absolutely impossible for us to deny this. We cannot dream of any reversal whatsoever of this situation. We cannot think of being able to explain our knowledge of God in any way from itself instead of its object. We cannot imagine any possibility or actuality or ordering of our knowledge of God apart from that which God Himself has established. To love God means in fact that we no longer are and have ourselves without Him, that we wish to be the subject only in our direction towards Him as He Himself has determined and realised it. How can we love Him if we want to take from Him something of what He does to us and for us and in our place, ascribing and appropriating it to ourselves ? He who loves God, loves Him in the mystery in which He gives Himself to be known by us. And to fear God means that we tremble before the possibility that we will not love Him— either that we will not be permitted to love Him or will not make use of that permission. But we have that permission in the very fact that God Himself has made Himself clear and certain to us. And our making use of it consists in the very fact that we love Him as the One who lets Himself be loved by us by making Himself clear and certain to us. How can we fear God if we want to diverge from this permission and then love Him in that divergence ? As if that were still love to Him ! If we know God in love and fear and therefore in obedience, it will necessarily mean that we give Him the glory and therefore confess that He remains a mystery to us and that we know Him with clarity and certainty in His very mystery and not otherwise. For how can these two statements—the mystery that He is and remains to us, and the clarity and certainty in which He gives Himself to be known—constitute a contradiction ? The assertion that God remains a mystery to us for the very reason that He has made Himself so clear and certain to us, is obviously just as evident as the assertion that we must fear God for the very reason that we may love Him. The fact that we admit to ourselves that He remains a mystery to us is the criterion by which we know that we are among those to whom He has made Himself clear and certain. If it is not the case that in knowing God we must praise His grace, then that grace has not come upon us. Because it has come upon us and we have to praise it and, indeed, praise it as grace, we are not in a position to contest a single jot or tittle of the mystery of the possibility, actuality and order of our knowledge of God. To deny, or not to know, or to cease to know the mystery in which God exists for us, is to deny, or not to know, or to cease to know the clarity and certainty of the revelation of His existence for us.

In this connexion we may recall the following passages of the Bible. In Jn. 1⁹ Jesus is called the true light who, coming into the world, enlightens every man. God has made Himself clear and certain in this indisputable way in the fact that this has happened and in the manner in which it has happened. " The life was the light of men " (1⁴), i.e., the reconciliation was the revelation. The same thing is expressly affirmed for us by Jesus Himself : " I am the light of the world. He that followeth me shall not walk in darkness, but shall have the light of life " (8¹²; cf. 9⁵). And again "I am come a light into the world, that whosoever believeth on me should not abide in darkness" (12⁴⁶). Throughout the Fourth Gospel, to believe in Him and so to have life means to receive and therefore to know this light : that is, to know Jesus Christ as the One He is ; to believe and to know that He is the Son of God (6⁶⁹) ; to know in Him the Father and the Father in Him ; and therefore to know God. " This is life eternal, that they might know thee the only true God, namely (καί !) Jesus Christ, whom thou hast sent " (17³). He is the way, since He is the truth and thus the life (14⁶). For : " Have I been so long time with you, and yet hast thou not known me, Philip ? he that hath seen me hath seen the Father ; and how sayest thou then, Shew us the Father ? Believest thou not that I am in the Father, and the Father in me ? " (14⁹ᶠ·). In faith it is obviously impossible to be ignorant of God, for it is He Himself who in Jesus Christ gives Himself to faith to be known. That is why Paul described his apostleship (2 Cor. 4²) as φανέρωσις τῆς ἀληθείας, and explained (v. 6) how he came to this office : " The same God, who commanded the light to shine out of darkness, hath shined in our hearts to give the φωτισμὸς τῆς γνώσεως τῆς δόξης τοῦ θεοῦ in the face of Jesus Christ." But we do well to notice that the verse immediately preceding this declares : " We preach not ourselves, but Christ Jesus the Lord ; and ourselves your servants for Jesus' sake." (v. 5). Obviously Paul, as the subject of knowledge, only wants to come into the picture in order to bear witness to Him who is known on the strength of the knowledge actually bestowed upon him by God. He does not want to declare and emphasise this knowledge of his as an event which is in any sense independent of the work of its object. He " hath called us out of darkness into his marvellous light." (1 Pet. 2⁹). " The light shineth in the darkness." But seen from the side of darkness and therefore of men as such, it must always be said : " the darkness comprehended it not." (Jn. 1⁵). And in this connexion, Heb. 11²⁷ says of Moses : " He clave to the invisible as if he saw him " (for " invisible " Luther has " him whom he saw not "). In this connexion Col. 2²⁻³ says of Christ that in Him the mystery of God is known and yet nevertheless " all the treasures of wisdom and knowledge " are hidden in Him. According to Eph. 3¹⁹, we know " the love of God surpassing knowledge." According to Phil. 4⁷, the peace of God which keeps our hearts is ὑπερέχουσα πάντα νοῦν. Obviously these passages all prepare us for the remarkable inversion in a few Pauline sayings, an inversion which in its whole paradoxicality is quite the clearest expression of the connexion between the clarity and certainty of the knowledge of God on the one hand and its mystery on the other. In 1 Cor. 8¹ᶠ· γνῶσις and ἀγάπη are opposed in such a way that it is said of γνῶσις (of which is assumed : πάντες γνῶσιν ἔχομεν) that it " puffeth up," but love builds up. If knowledge is opposed to love in this way, and if it is obviously not knowledge grounded in love, then this is what we do in fact have to say about it. But Paul at once puts the matter right : " If any man think that he hath known anything, he knoweth nothing yet as he ought to know. But if any man love God, the same is known of him." And this knowledge is not that puffing-up knowledge, because, since the one who knows loves God, it is obviously nothing other than the confirmation of the fact that God knows him, i.e., that he is chosen and called by God. No one can boast of this ; our own knowledge can indeed only bear witness to it. And so in Gal. 4⁸ᶠ· Paul points out to his readers : " When ye knew not God, ye did service unto them which by nature are no gods." But now, γνόντες θεόν, μᾶλλον δὲ γνωσθέντες ὑπὸ θεοῦ, it is quite impossible for them to turn back again to " the weak and beggarly elements." Now obviously the impossibility of the idolatry which Paul finds again in their judaizing legalism is not in any way established by the fact that they are γνόντες θεόν. They are, however, γνωσθέντες ὑπὸ θεοῦ. God knows them as His own, as those who are chosen and called by Him. It is on this fact that the impossibility is unhesitatingly and irrevocably established. It is because of this that they are in truth those who know God. If there is a legitimate sense, and one which avoids the danger of " puffing up " and idolatry, in which I myself not only know but know with the unrestricted autonomy with which I am known (καθὼς καὶ ἐπεγνώσθην, i.e., because here and now as I know God I am known of Him)— then according to 1 Cor. 13¹² this is the knowing God face to face which here and now we can only wait for and in which here and now we certainly do not participate. Here and now I can be certain of the truth of my knowledge of God only by reflecting that God has known me and that I therefore may know Him. Only by the fact that this is so can my knowledge of God be protected from error.

To summarise, where God stands before man as the One who awakens, creates and upholds his faith, and where God offers Himself to man as the object and content of the knowledge of his faith, He does it in this being and action—as the One who remains mystery to us because He Himself has made Himself so clear and certain to us. It is just in this way that He awakens, creates and upholds our knowledge of Himself as a work of obedience, which cannot as such be attacked either by others or by ourselves if only we do not fall out of obedience, out of this relationship between the given clarity and certainty and the guarded mystery. Within obedience the knowledge of God cannot be destroyed, because its object cannot cease to be this object and God cannot cease to be the One who is and acts in this way. If our obedience springs from God, necessarily we are always in the same obedience towards God. In this obedience we are set on the circular course in which we can go only from faith to faith and similarly from knowledge to knowledge. Because we do not in any sense begin with ourselves, with our own capacity for faith and knowledge, we are secured against having to end with ourselves, i.e., with our own incapacity.

We have described God's being and action in regard to the man before whom He stands. This man may love Him and must fear Him. Clarity and certainty is given to him, while at the same time the boundaries of mystery are set up against him. He is placed in obedience. But obviously God is the One from whom all this has to be and is, whose will and wisdom is executed in it all and whose work it all is. This is what justifies our conclusion. It is for this reason that we are not making God in our own image. For we do not under-

stand man in his own light. In all these determinations we understand
him as the man who is set before God by God Himself. Nor do we
understand God and man together in the light of arbitrary presuppositions, but as we are directed by the Word of God itself. Following
this direction we are not merely permitted but commanded to go
the way of this conclusion—in other words, when the question of God
arises in relation to the knowledge of God, to answer it in the light of
the work of God and therefore of the man before whom God stands.
But in the light of this work of God, it can and must be our exclusive
task to understand and portray the fulfilment of the knowledge of
God expressly and exclusively as the being and action of God Himself.
Is it, then, really the case—as we have hitherto assumed—that God
is known through God and through God alone ?   And if so, why ?

Now obviously no critical or agnostic epistemology either can or should force
us to make this assumption. If, on the basis of the Word of God, we had to say
that it is God's pleasure to be known in such a way by man that human knowledge as such receives an independent significance alongside and over against
the work of God, and that therefore the operation of the knowledge of God must
be described as an occurrence in a two-fold and reciprocal relationship—then of
course that would be the case and we should have to accept it, and theologically
at any rate it could not be opposed in the Church on epistemological grounds.
But as it is, our starting point is not in any sense epistemological. However
man's capacity for knowledge may be described, whether more narrowly or more
broadly, yet the conclusion that God is known only through God (we speak of the
God who has revealed Himself in His Word) does not have either its basis or
origin in any understanding of the human capacity for knowledge. And for that
very reason it cannot be assailed from that quarter. Its basis is not in the subject,
but in the object of the knowledge concerned. It is grounded in the God revealed
in His Word. It is because He is who He is and does what He does that we have
made that assumption and reckoned and worked with it all along. But now we
must show how far this basis, which is so clearly distinct from a human theory
of knowledge, does actually compel us to make that assumption. In so doing,
we can gather together all that has to be said about the fulfilment of the knowledge of God in the final statement that God is known through God and through
God alone.

God speaks to man in His Word. Thereby He gives Himself to
him to be known ; therein He is known by him. In this way, as the
One who speaks to him, God stands before man, and it comes to pass
that man stands before Him, and that man for his part—as happens
in the Church of Jesus Christ—can speak and hear about Him.
But God speaks about Himself in His Word. Everything that He
says to man depends upon the fact that when God speaks to man
He does not say this or that, but declares Himself. This is its life
and truth and reality. This is what makes it a Word of enlightenment
and salvation. Because of this man is no more alone and without
God, but is in covenant with God through the Word of God. God's
Word is therefore the covenant-making turning of God Himself towards
the man turned away from Him. In this covenant, and therefore
through God's Word about Himself which sets up this covenant,

there is given to man all the truth and reality, the enlightenment and salvation that God has to say to him, that is bestowed by God upon the man standing before God, and that man for his part can then say and hear about God in the Church of Jesus Christ. Therefore to know God in His Word means primarily and comprehensively to know Him Himself. He Himself stands before man, and He Himself is either known in this way or He is not known at all.

But God speaks in His Word about Himself as the Lord. He is always the Lord of the covenant established in His Word. His Word, and that means His Word about Himself, creates this covenant. The man with whom it is concluded is the man turned away from God. With the conclusion of this covenant he is told that he is this man turned away from God, who as such does not yet stand in this covenant relationship, who cannot and will not conclude it from his side. The fact that this covenant is concluded and exists is God's will and work. In this covenant therefore God, and not man, is always the Lord. As the Lord He stands before the man who for his part is not under any circumstances the Lord. As the Lord He gives Himself to be known by man, and as the Lord He is known by him or He is not known at all.

But He is always the Lord in such a way that He makes Himself known and acts as the One who is in fact man's Lord, and who has therefore the right and the might always to be the Lord in this covenant. That is, He makes Himself known and acts as man's Creator. Man is indebted to Him for everything, and he therefore owes everything. But he cannot discharge this debt. God therefore makes Himself known and acts as the One who all the same and on that very assumption maintains and demonstrates His own faithfulness by Himself being and doing everything for him, by Himself accepting the debt, by being gracious to man, not for what he deserves, but for His own sake. Again, He makes Himself known and He acts as the One from whom man can expect all things ; that is, as the One who promises the man who lives wholly and utterly by His grace, and lets him go the way of the promise, that in the future he will be in himself as righteous and holy and blessed as here and now he is in the unmerited and merciful judgment of His grace. By making Himself known and acting in this way, God proves His right and power always to be the Lord in this covenant concluded in His Word with man. He shows that the One who unites Himself to man in His Word is in fact the Lord of man. Therefore, in this self-demonstration He stands before man as his Lord, and gives Himself to be known by him and is known by him, or else He is not known at all.

But who is the One who, in accordance with this self-demonstration, is the Lord of man ? As we have seen, He is Lord in accordance with His self-demonstration. He forcefully carries through this self-demonstration by His Word and in His covenant with man established by His Word. In this self-demonstration He reveals to man

the truth, to which man has no other truth to oppose, indeed, in
whose light he must recognise all other supposed truths to be lies.
His Word is the truth beside which there is none other, and by which
all other supposed truth is judged. But if this is the case, then the
One who carries through this self-demonstration is not only the Lord
incidentally in this self-demonstration. He is not only one Lord,
equipped with one authority and power—to which He does, of course,
establish a claim by making Himself known and acting in the covenant
with man, although in Himself and absolutely He is perhaps very
different. We might, of course, ask whether He is not perhaps the
Lord in the strictest sense of the concept of lordship and yet only,
say, a subordinate Lord. Is He only the servant and representative
of quite another and a still higher Lord, so that His covenant with
man is a transaction beside which there can ultimately be other and
higher transactions, so that it will be possible—and in the end necessary—to by-pass Him and enter into an immediate relationship to
that higher and real Lord ? Or is He a Lord side by side with other
lords without there being any question of a real and highest Lord ?
Is the last reality, under whose majesty we find ourselves, a multiplicity of lords and powers of which His is only one, so that if necessary others than He may rule over us, so that we can choose for
ourselves another lordship and power than His to rule over us ? Or
is He perhaps the one real Lord, but in such a way that the lordship
which He exercises through His Word, and therefore in the covenant
concluded with man, is simply an appearance of His lordship, a provisional arrangement, an economy, beside which there can perhaps be
other economies which in their provisional character can never have
a decisive or definitive significance ? As He is in truth, is He quite
different from the One who meets us in that self-demonstration ? Is
there again the possibility that we can look past His self-demonstration,
groping perhaps in the darkness, or perhaps penetrating through cracks
and fissures in His concealing veil to His real and ultimate being and
lordship ? Well, if it is true that He forcefully carries through that
self-demonstration in His Word, and in the covenant established with
man by His Word, all these questions are *ipso facto* excluded. But
does He ? This is obviously the decisive question which no man can
answer for another. In face of it we can only point others—and
indeed ourselves—to the answer given by that self-demonstration.
Not even formally can we ask whether the inward compulsion which
we may or may not feel in that self-demonstration is greater or lesser.
We can wait for the rest of our lives and the whole of eternity, and
we will have to do so to our eternal loss, if we want the inner compulsion, the constraint of our personal experience, to become strong
enough to be a reason for yielding to that self-demonstration. And
even if sooner or later we do yield to it because we think we are obliged
to follow this inner compulsion and the constraint of our personal

experience, we are definitely not doing so in the proper way. We are not really convinced by it. We are not led to the indisputable and definitive knowledge of the God who makes Himself known and acts in His Word as one supreme and only Lord. We are building secretly on the sand, i.e., on ourselves. But in face of the question whether the self-demonstration of God in His Word is forcefully carried through we can only ask about the demonstration itself and therefore about what God does in His Word. We can ask whether it is true or not that He who speaks here is the One to whom we are indebted for everything, and still owe everything, and therefore live as such by His grace, but, living by His grace, have the promise of eternal life. The self-demonstration of God in His Word consists in these materials of revelation. Whether the self-demonstration is forceful or not is therefore decided by the material question whether it is true or not. But if it is forceful—and we can only refer one another to the fact that He who demonstrates it does carry it through forcefully—then *ipso facto* all other questions are excluded. There can be no question of the Lord who carries through this self-demonstration being the satrap of another who is the real overlord and God, or a Lord alongside other lords. His lordship as proved in this way cannot be only the provisional appearance of His real and different nature and lordship. The truth of His self-demonstration judges other supposed truths, unmasking them as lies. Or, positively, it is the truth of the one supreme and true lordship of Him who carries through this demonstration. He is in Himself the Lord, the Lord who makes Himself known and acts in this way. He is the Lord of all lords, the unique Lord of heaven and earth, the Lord of all times and places, of all actual or possible worlds, the One who makes Himself known and acts in this way. And He is this Lord not only in time but from eternity to eternity ; not only in a particular, provisional and transient economy, but as the One He was and is and will be ; not only for us, but for us as and because He is in inward truth this One and not another—and for us in such a way that He does not have another being in which He can always be for us something different from His proclamation and action. Therefore He is the Lord in a way which makes flight or evasion quite impossible. For not even conceptually can flight or evasion ever bring us to a sphere in which He is not the Lord, this Lord. As this Lord He stands before us, gives Himself to be known and is known—or else He is not known at all.

But the inner truth of the lordship of God as the one supreme and true lordship revealed and operative in His proclamation and action —the inner truth and therefore also the inner strength of His self-demonstration as the Lord, as this Lord, consists in the fact that He is in Himself from eternity to eternity the triune God, God the Father, the Son and the Holy Spirit. The fact that, according to that self-demonstration, man is indebted to Him for everything and owes Him everything is grounded in God's own eternal Fatherhood, of which any other fatherhood can be only an image and likeness, however much we may owe to it, however much we may be indebted to it. And that self-demonstration constrains us to gratitude and indebtedness and therefore to the knowledge of God the Father as our Lord, because in eternity God is the Father of His own eternal Son and with Him the source of the Holy Spirit. Further, the fact that according to that self-demonstration God Himself is and does everything for the man who still owes Him everything is grounded in the fact that God is in Himself eternally the Son of the Father, eternally equal to the Father and therefore eternally loved by Him, although and because He is the Son. And that self-demonstration constrains us to adoration of His faithfulness and grace and therefore to the knowledge of God the Son as our Lord, because in eternity God is the only Son, begotten of the Father, and with the Father, and along with Him the source of the Holy Spirit. And finally, the fact that according to that self-demonstration God is the One from whom we have to expect everything is grounded in the fact that God is Himself eternally the Holy Spirit, proceeding from the Father and the Son, and of one essence with them both. And that self-demonstration constrains us to hope, and therefore to the knowledge of the Holy Spirit, because in eternity God is also the Holy Spirit proceeding from the Father and the Son, and their unity in love. In this way the self-demonstration, and in this way the proclamation and action of God through His Word in the covenant concluded with man, is grounded in God Himself. In this way and on this ground it has its compelling force. Because God is in Himself the triune God, both in His Word and in the work of creation, reconciliation and redemption, we have to do with Himself. It is therefore impossible for us to postpone the decision —which means the encounter with Him—on the grounds that He is perhaps quite different from the One who proclaims Himself and acts in this way. And because God is in Himself the triune God, in this His Word we have to do with the final revelation of God which can never be rivalled or surpassed. It is, therefore, quite impossible to ask about other lords alongside and above this Lord. In the life of God as the life of the triune God things are so ordered and necessary that the work of God in His Word is the one supreme and true lordship in which He gives Himself to be known and is known. When God speaks about Himself, He speaks about the fact that He is the Father, the Son and the Holy Spirit. And therefore everything else that He has to say to us, all truth and reality, all enlightenment and salvation, depends on the fact that primarily and comprehensively He is speaking about Himself.

But in the light of this the problem of the knowledge of God must be re-stated in a new way. If it is true that God stands before man, that He gives Himself to be known and is known by man, it is true only because and in the fact that God is the triune God, God the

Father, the Son and the Holy Spirit. First of all, and in the heart of the truth in which He stands before us, God stands before Himself ; the Father before the Son, the Son before the Father. And first of all and in the heart of the truth in which we know God, God knows Himself ; the Father knows the Son and the Son the Father in the unity of the Holy Spirit. This occurrence in God Himself is the essence and strength of our knowledge of God. It is not an occurrence unknown to us ; rather it is made known to us through His Word ; but it is certainly a hidden occurrence. That is to say, it is an occurrence in which man as such is not a participant, but in which He becomes a participant through God's revelation and thus in a way inconceivable to himself. It is not self-evident that we become participants in it, that our knowledge of God acquires truth as the external expression of that inner truth. It does, in fact, acquire truth only as the external expression of that inner truth ; that is to say, on the strength of the fact that God is the triune God who knows Himself. If we laud and magnify God on the strength of our own knowledge, bestowed upon us by His revelation, it must always mean that we laud and magnify Him in the hiddenness of His self-knowledge, on the strength of which alone the knowledge of God can ever become real. Our knowledge of God is derived and secondary. It is effected by grace in the creaturely sphere in consequence of the fact that first of all, in itself and without us, it is actual in the divine sphere— in the sphere of God as the sphere of His own truth, of the inner truth even of our knowledge of God, who is always inaccessible to us as such. We stand here before the root of the necessity to fear God because we may love Him, to revere Him in His mystery because He has made Himself so clear and certain to us. The love, clarity and certainty have reference to the fact that God does actually reveal Himself to us as the One who He is. The fear and the mystery have reference to the fact that He reveals Himself to us as the One who He actually is, as the One who first knows Himself in that inner truth of our knowledge of God without which it would be only an empty and evanescent appearance. But again, we stand here before the root of the problem of the objectivity of God. We have already seen that without the objectivity of God there is no knowledge of God. It was proper to seek this objectivity first in God's revelation, in His works and signs, in His veiling and unveiling in the creaturely sphere ; and we shall have to return to this. But even in that connexion we have already seen that without God's objectivity to Himself there is no knowledge of God ; without the truth of a primary objectivity of Him who reveals Himself to us there is no truth of His secondary objectivity in His revelation. But the primary objectivity of God to Himself is reality in His eternal being as the Father, the Son and the Holy Spirit. As the triune God, God is first and foremost objective to Himself. When therefore, in consequence of being objective to

Himself in His own sphere, He also becomes objective to us in the creaturely sphere, it does not mean any renunciation or surrender, but only the confirmation and exemplification of His divine nature. He does become objective. We can and must accept His revelation in this our sphere. We can and must know Him in His works and signs. But in His works and signs we may and must know God Himself—the One who first of all and apart from us is objective to Himself. To say this, however, is to say that His unveiling in His works and signs always means for us His veiling too, that His revelation always means His hiddenness, that love towards Him cannot be without fear before Him, that the clarity and certainty of His existence bestowed upon us cannot be without His remaining a mystery to us. We cannot celebrate and receive the sacrament ordained by Him without looking beyond the sacrament as such and finding Himself in the sacrament. The knowledge bestowed upon us through His revelation cannot be fulfilled without the confession in humility that we not only do not know Him apart from His revelation, but that even in His revelation we know Him only in consequence of the fact that knowledge of God is real as God's own hidden work in His being as the triune God from eternity to eternity.

It is in this connexion that we must understand the texts of Scripture which speak of a complete hiddenness and therefore ignorance of God in apparent (but only apparent) contradiction to God's revealedness in His works and signs. We are thinking of the Old Testament passages—Jer. 23[18] ; Is. 40[13-14] ; Job 15[8]— which Paul took up in Rom. 11[33f.] : " How unsearchable are his judgments, and his ways past finding out. For who hath known the mind of the Lord ? or who hath been his counsellor ? " We are thinking of the designation of God as the φῶς οἰκῶν ἀπρόσιτον, ὃν εἶδεν οὐδεὶς ἀνθρώπων οὐδὲ ἰδεῖν δύναται (1 Tim. 6[16]). We are thinking of the categorical declaration of Jn. 1[18]: θεὸν οὐδεὶς ἑώρακεν πώποτε, and of the almost consonant 1 Jn. 4[12] : θεὸν οὐδεὶς πώποτε τεθέαται. We are thinking of Jn. 5[37] : " Ye have neither heard his voice at any time, nor seen his shape," and of Jn. 6[46] : " Not that any man hath seen the Father, save he which is of God, he hath seen the Father." But the last saying is the one which sets the matter in the right light : He which is of God, the Son, has most certainly seen the Father. This is what we read in the introduction in Jn. 1[18] : " The only begotten Son, which is in the bosom of the Father, he hath declared him ; " and, in agreement with this, Jn. 8[19] : " Ye neither know me, nor my Father : if ye had known me, ye should have known my Father also ; " and Mt. 11[27] : " No man knoweth the Son, but the Father ; neither knoweth any man the Father, save the Son, and he to whomsoever the Son will reveal him ; " and Jn. 10[14f.] : " Mine own know me, even as the Father knoweth me, and I know the Father." For as the Father is revealed only through the Son, so also the Son is revealed only through the Father (Mt. 16[17f.]). We must also include 1 Cor. 2[9-12] : " Eye hath not seen, nor ear heard, neither have entered into the heart of man, the things which God hath prepared for them that love him. But God hath revealed them unto us by his Spirit : for the Spirit searcheth all things, yea, the deep things of God. For what man knoweth the things of a man (τὰ τοῦ ἀνθρώπου) save the spirit of man which is in him ? even so the things of God (τὰ τοῦ θεοῦ) hath only the Spirit known. Now we have received, not the spirit of the world, but the Spirit of God ; that we might know the things that are freely given to us of God." We can see that everything here rests upon revelation, on the sending of the Son and the communication of the Holy Spirit. But at the same time an occurrence takes place in God Himself which is, so to say, copied in the revelation in which man participates. Without this occurrence it cannot therefore take place in revelation. But that means that in revelation itself we again see God's self-knowledge, God's own and original objectivity in the modes of being of the Father and of the Son through the mode of being of the Holy Spirit. But if that is the case, when we make use of " the things that are freely given to us of God," and therefore when we avail ourselves of God's permission to love and know Him in the clarity and certainty of His own unreserved truth, we cannot cease to be grateful that from eternity to eternity He precedes our knowing. He is the One who gives it this truth by knowing Himself in original truth. And it is in consequence of this that in our creaturely sphere, because in His revelation He gives us a share in this occurrence, we can follow Him, perceiving, considering and conceiving His truth as He thinks right.

Only by proceeding downwards from the triune existence of God can we understand how God stands before us, how in His revelation He gives Himself to be known and is known by us. The revelation of God, in which man's fulfilment of the true knowledge of God takes place, is the disposition of God in which He acts towards us as the same triune God that He is in Himself, and in such a way that, although we are men and not God, we receive a share in the truth of His knowledge of Himself. Certainly it is the share which He thinks proper and which is therefore suitable for us. But in this share we have the reality of the true knowledge of Himself. This share is given as God unveils Himself to us in that other, second objectivity, that is to say, in the objectivity of His works and signs in our creaturely sphere, before the eyes and ears and in the hearts which as such and of themselves alone are quite incapable of knowing Him. But the heart of it all is that it is He Himself, the one, supreme and true Lord, who thus unveils Himself to us ; that in revelation we have to do with His action as the triune God, and therefore with Himself in every creaturely work and sign that He uses. On this basis and only on this basis can there be real knowledge of God.

But if it is He Himself who unveils Himself to us, the revelation is characterised as revelation of the truth beside which there is no other and above which there is none higher. Therefore the idea of impartation must not be taken to mean that in His revelation God gives Himself to be known by us only in part, so that we still have to await the revelation of another God in another and higher order, or the revelation of the same God in a different form. The fact that we receive only a share in the truth of His knowledge of Himself does not mean that we have to do only with a limited quantity of His being and not, or not yet, with some other quantity. God is who He is, the Father, Son and Holy Spirit, Creator, Reconciler and Redeemer, supreme, the one true Lord ; and He is known in this entirety or He is not known at all. There is no existence of God behind or beyond this entirety of His being. Whatever we can know and say about the being of God can be only a continual explanation of this entirety. But that means that there can be no knowledge of God in time or even in eternity which will lead us beyond this entirety of His being. On the contrary, a further knowledge of God will only lead us deeper into just this entirety of His being. Again, God exists in this entirety of His being and therefore not in any kind of parts. He exists in the unity of His existence as Father, Son and Holy Spirit, as Creator, Reconciler and Redeemer, as the one supreme and true Lord. At no time or place does He exist in only one of His modes of existence, or in only one sphere of His proclamation and action, or in only one particle of His lordship. A separable being of this kind or one part of such a separable being would have nothing whatever to do with the being of God. But again, that means that no knowledge of God can have as its object one such part of His being, not even if that part is called the uniqueness of God, or the irresistibility of His lordship, not even if it has the name of Jesus Christ. When this name is rightly given, it is not given to a part but to the being of God in His unity and entirety. We either know God Himself and therefore entirely, or we do not know Him at all. If our knowledge of God is under a quantitative limitation it is obviously under a limitation of its truth. But this is excluded by the self-demonstration of God in His Word. Therefore, although there is of course a limitation—in revelation—we cannot think of it as quantitative. The fact that God gives to us only a share in the truth of His knowledge of Himself cannot mean that He does not give Himself to be known by us as the One He is.

But God gives Himself to be known—and this is the limitation that we have to bring out in the idea of impartation—in an objectivity different from His own, in a creaturely objectivity. He unveils Himself as the One He is by veiling Himself in a form which He Himself is not. He uses this form distinct from Himself, He uses its work and sign, in order to be objective in, with and under this form, and therefore to give Himself to us to be known. Revelation means the giving of signs. We can say quite simply that revelation means sacrament, i.e., the self-witness of God, the representation of His truth, and therefore of the truth in which He knows Himself, in the form of creaturely objectivity and therefore in a form which is adapted to our creaturely knowledge. In what, then, does the limitation of this our knowledge consist, if it cannot consist in a quantitative limitation?

We have to reckon with such a limitation even on the presupposition that there is this impartation, that the Son reveals to us the Father and the Father the Son through the Holy Spirit. We can see this at once from 1 Cor. 13⁸ᶠ·, which says quite unequivocally of knowledge: καταργηθήσεται. And it obviously means the knowledge of God which is bestowed upon us here and now. But if one day it is to be dissolved, obviously it takes place here and now under a definite limitation, which there and then will be removed. Paul confirms this in what follows, when he describes it as a γιγνώσκειν ἐκ μέρους and again as a γιγνώσκειν δι' ἐσόπτρου ἐν αἰνίγματι, and when he compares it with the being, speaking and thinking of a child. This knowledge is then (v. 10) contrasted with τὸ ἐκ μέρους καταργηθήσεται. The childish is put away (v. 11). I shall know face to face, even as God knows me (v. 12). Neither in Paul nor in the rest of Scripture is there any doubt that I know God in consequence and on the strength of the fact that He knows me, and that I certainly know Him in truth as the One He is. But while that is true, I do not yet know Him here and now as He already, here and now, knows me. That is to say, we know here and now in such a way that the object of knowledge directly perceived and considered and conceived by us is something different which God has instituted and used as the medium, sign and witness of His own objectivity. Because God has instituted and used it for this purpose, this thing becomes, and is adapted as, the organ of the divine self-witness. Here and now we know by way of faith. It is the way of faith to cleave to God by cleaving to the work of God taking place in the creaturely sphere. But this work as such stands before us always as a fragment. That is, it is a provisional part or moment of the history of the covenant between God and us. It is a reference which always needs to be confirmed and completed by other references. It needs the continuation of that history and therefore new forms of the revealing work of God. Not as it comes from God, but as it presents itself to be perceived and considered and conceived by us, it is a " mirror " in which, while we certainly know in truth the One who is reflected in it, we do so only indirectly, only with the peculiar inversion of left and right, which means that even the best mirror shows a thing quite differently from what it is in itself. We know, then, in an " enigma," and therefore in a form which declares by concealing and conceals by declaring. We know like " children." In intention, and to that extent in truth, the being and play and pursuits of a child comprehend and indeed are themselves the whole life of man with all its heights and depths and joys and sorrows. The transition is almost imperceptible from the prelude of life to life itself, and for the moment life can be actualised only to this degree, as a prelude to itself. When Paul described the limitations of our knowledge in this way, he subtracted nothing from the truth of our knowledge of God and from the fact that when we know God we know God Himself and God in His entirety. But by describing it in this way he characterised it as the indirect knowledge of faith. Its mode is to be distinguished from that of sight (2 Cor. 5⁷), from that of seeing face to face, from the manner of the knowledge with which God knows us. What distinguishes it is that it is bound to that secondary objectivity of God, to the fact that God has instituted and used those means and instruments, and therefore to the creaturely limitations of these means and instruments.

We must now try to reach a basic clarity about the nature of this limitation—but we can also say positively, of this divinely willed and ordained determination—of our knowledge of God on the basis of His revelation and therefore in the mode of faith.

1. When God gives Himself to us to be known in the truth of His self-knowledge as the triune God, He permits some one of His creatures or a happening in the sphere and time of the world created by Him to speak for Him. The basic reality and substance of the creatureliness which He has commissioned and empowered to speak of Him, the basic reality and substance of the sacramental reality of His revelation, is the existence of the human nature of Jesus Christ. *Gratia unionis*, i.e., on the ground of and through its union with the eternal Word of God, this creature is the supreme and outstanding work and sign of God. Because the eternal Word Himself became flesh, because the revelation of God took place once and for all in

Jesus Christ, we know the same revelation of God wherever it is attested in expectation and recollection. For, in the light of the attestation which occurred through the man Jesus, we find the attestation of God wherever it is the attestation of that occurrence. That the eternal Word as such became flesh is a unique occurrence. It happened only once. It is not therefore the starting-point for a general concept of incarnation. But its attestation through the existence of the man Jesus is a beginning of which there are continuations ; a sacramental continuity stretches backwards into the existence of the people of Israel, whose Messiah He is, and forwards into the existence of the apostolate and the Church founded on the apostolate. The humanity of Jesus Christ as such is the first sacrament, the foundation of everything that God instituted and used in His revelation as a secondary objectivity both before and after the epiphany of Jesus Christ. And, as this first sacrament, the humanity of Jesus Christ is at the same time the basic reality and substance of the highest possibility of the creature as such. Not of and by itself, but of and by God's appointment and grace, the creature can be the temple, instrument and sign of God Himself. The man Jesus is the first to rise out of the series of creatures which are not this. But the fact that He does so is a promise for the rest of God's creation. He and no other creature is taken up into unity with God. Here we have something which cannot be repeated. But the existence of this creature in his unity with God does mean the promise that other creatures may attest in their objectivity what is real only in this creature, that is to say, God's own objectivity—so that to that extent they are the temple, instrument and sign of God as He is. Here we have the function which can be repeated in the confirmation and proclamation of that unique happening of the unity of Creator and creature ; and in the Church of Jesus Christ, the Church of the old and the new covenants, it actually is repeated.

It is plainly in this sense that in Rev. 3¹⁴ Jesus is called the " true and faithful witness " and as such ἡ ἀρχὴ τῆς κτίσεως. What is meant is that here in Him, in His existence and in His office as witness, the creation received the beginning of its new being in the commission and authorisation to speak about God in the place of God. It is obviously in the same sense that in Col. 1¹⁵ Jesus Christ is called εἰκὼν τοῦ θεοῦ τοῦ ἀοράτου, and as such, πρωτότοκος πάσης κτίσεως, and directly after, ἡ κεφαλὴ τοῦ σώματος τῆς ἐκκλησίας. What from the first point of view is simply the fulfilling and consequence of the incarnation, is, from the second, the accomplished selection of a creature by God's disposition and grace, and from the third, the promise given to the creature in general. The creature cannot become one with God like the human nature of Christ. But because the human nature of Christ was also creature, and did not cease to be so, it can be a witness to God in its creatureliness, when and where the disposition and grace of God permit it. And where it is this, there is the Church—the self-witness of God in the sphere and time of the world created by Him.

But it is now obvious that what is for the creature a selection or distinction is for God Himself a renunciation of the visibility of His distinction over against the creature. When the creature in its objectivity becomes the representative of the objectivity of God Himself, it hides it. When God makes Himself visible for us through it, He accepts the fact that He will remain invisible as the One He is in Himself and as He knows Himself. He makes Himself known to us, but in the means and sign which He uses to be known by us, He makes Himself foreign and improper to Himself. When He raises us to Himself through the speech of this creature, He lowers Himself to us. All that is already true of the humanity of Jesus Christ. And when we remember that the goal and climax of the epiphany of the Son of God in the man Jesus consisted in His death on the cross, and that as the risen Lord He is still the man who died on the cross, we are even forced to say that it is precisely and supremely the humanity of Jesus Christ which means God's self-humiliation and self-alienation, the remaining invisible of the distinction from all creatures which is proper to Him as God, the concealment of His objectivity by the quite different objectivity of the creature. It is certainly true that He reveals His glory in this way. But we must not overlook the fact that in revealing Himself in this way, He also conceals Himself. He reveals His glory to faith, which sees it in this hiddenness. He reveals it in that it makes itself knowable to faith in spite of and in this hiddenness. This is true, however, of the whole sacramental reality instituted and used as the attestation to His revelation and to that extent as the means of the knowledge of Himself. It is the case everywhere that when there is unveiling there is also veiling, when God sets up His lordship it means the self-humiliation and self-alienation of God, when He reveals Himself His hiddenness is confirmed. Revelation occurs for faith, not for unbelief. God exposes Himself, so to speak, to the danger that man will know the work and sign but not Himself through the medium of the work and sign. A complete non-recognition of the Lord who has instituted and used this medium is possible. The misunderstanding is also possible which thinks it ought to see and honour the Creator in the creature as such. The call to worship God can mean the temptation to idolatry. Revelation occurs in the form of this sacramental reality, i.e., in such a way that God elevates and selects a definite creaturely subject-object relationship to be the instrument of the covenant between Himself the Creator and man as His creature. The knowledge of God is fulfilled in the sphere of this sacramental reality and not otherwise or elsewhere. Yet the sacramental reality, the selected subject-object relationship, is not in itself and as such identical either with revelation or with the real knowledge of God. It serves it, because God reveals Himself and is known. But it can also not serve it ; it can even hinder and prevent it. The very thing can fail to happen which, because this form is given, ought to happen. The direct opposite can even happen. The blindness of man can continue in face of the work and sign of God. Even in face of the work and sign of God offence can be taken. The demand that the objectivity of God must be known in the objectivity of the creature can be rejected because of the too great humiliation and alienation in which the glory of God has to be believed and known. God Himself can be rejected in the grace of His condescension to the creature. Therefore the reality of the fulfilment of the true knowledge of God, as the act in which God gives Himself to be known and is known, must always be distinguished from the necessary limitation in which it happens. And the limitation has to be understood as both the means and limit of the fulfilment of the true knowledge of God. The limitation as such means both the openness and closedness of God towards man and therefore both the way and the frontier of our knowledge of God. We have to recognise and acknowledge the closed-ness of God, too, and the frontier of our knowledge. We have to recognise and acknowledge them even in the light of the fulfilment of real knowledge of God. It is essential to this fulfilment that in it (by the grace of God and in faith, but only by the grace of God and only in faith) veiling becomes unveiling in virtue of the lordship of God even in and above His work and sign.

It is not as if the objectivity of God is, so to speak, naturally inherent in the objectivity of the creature instituted as a sacrament and used as such. It is not even present in the man Jesus merely by reason of the fact that this man exists, so that we can assure ourselves of it by assuring ourselves of the existence of this man. The fact that in Jesus we are concerned, in Luther's well-known phrase, with the " mirror of the fatherly heart of God," is not true apart from God Himself and therefore apart from faith. At this point, too, we have to consider that, according to 1 Cor. 13, knowledge in the mirror always means knowledge in enigma. Even the man Jesus as such is always enigma as well. If He is not only enigma, if as enigma He is also illumination, disclosure and com-munication, then it is thanks to His unity with the Son of God and therefore in the act of the revelation of the Son of God and of the faith in Him effected by the Holy Spirit. The cross of Christ is to those who are perishing foolishness (1 Cor. 1[18]). It is by the foolishness of the preaching of the cross that it pleased God to save them who believe (1 Cor. 1[21]). Between this foolishness of Christ known after the flesh (2 Cor. 5[16]) and the salvation, which He has effected, of those who believe, and therefore the fulfilled knowledge of God in His face (2 Cor. 4[6]), there stands, objectively, His resurrection, and subjectively, the outpouring of the Holy Spirit, through which believers are what they are—a new creature (2 Cor. 5[17]). But if their knowing of God coincides with the knowledge of the man Jesus, the crucified Son of God (1 Cor. 2[2]), if those who are chosen and called as fools (1 Cor. 1[26f.]) by what is to the Greeks foolishness and to the Jews a stumbling-block, come to know the power of God and the wisdom of God (1 Cor. 1[23f.]), this simply means that for them, and particularly for them, the hiddenness of God continues in His revelation. The change from foolishness to wisdom, from the flesh to the Spirit, is not their work, but the work of Him who has availed Himself of foolishness in His dealings with the foolish : ἐξ αὐτοῦ δὲ ὑμεῖς ἐστε ἐν Χριστῷ Ἰησοῦ, ὃς ἐγενήθη σοφία ἡμῖν ἀπὸ θεοῦ, δικαιοσύνη τε καὶ ἁγιασμὸς καὶ ἀπολύτρωσις. (1 Cor. 1[30]). Their participation in the self-knowledge of God in His Son—because and in so far as it is mediated by the man Jesus, the crucified Son of God—is always a gift of participation. It is certainly effected by this means, but under the institution and use of this means by God Himself. And the mystery which limits the knowledge of God must not be denied on the subjective side either. The concept of faith which we find in the Bible and the Early Church must not be reinterpreted in the direction of mysticism. In faith it is not at all the case that on an irrational and supra-empirical interior level of human consciousness man arrives at a unity with God in the form of the suspension of the subject-object relationship of the limitation in which God is revealed to us. Nor is our faith, and with it our knowledge of God, fulfilled in such a way that deep down God's own knowing of Himself is naturally inherent in our being and activity in faith. According to Heb. 11¹, our being and activity in faith are, as relationship to God, an ὑπόστασις ἐλπιζομένων, an ἔλεγχος πραγμάτων οὐ βλεπομένων. Even as our own action they are not an "experience of God." If they are an experience at all, they are an experience of His work and sign, an experience in the limits and in the ambiguity and danger of the subject-object relationship. Even our faith as such belongs to the medium, mirror and enigma instituted and used by God. Even our faith as such belongs to the veiling and limitation of revelation. Our knowledge of faith itself is knowledge of God in His hiddenness. It is indirect and mediate, not immediate knowledge. It is knowledge which in itself and as such could equally well be the knowledge of unbelief, or error, or superstition, and therefore not knowledge of God. In itself it is not in any way protected from remaining or becoming a knowledge which is not knowledge. Even between faith as such and the fulfilment of the real knowledge of God there stands, objectively, the resurrection of Christ, subjectively, the gift of the Holy Spirit, the turning which does not stand in our power but in which man, by the power of God, becomes a new creature. It is in this way, as this new creature and not on any mysterious interior level of his consciousness, that man receives a share in the self-knowledge of God. Faith as such grasps only the promise given to it in God's work and sign. To that extent it remains a blind faith in which man is a sojourner and stranger upon earth (Heb. 11¹³).

2. The limitation of our knowledge of God, which is also its determination, can be more properly understood if we are clear about the following point. When God gives Himself to us to be known in the truth of His self-knowledge as the triune God, what happens is this. In one of His creatures, i.e., in a happening in the sphere and time of the world created by Him, He is not only pleased to be what He is in Himself and for Himself. In and for Himself He is I, the eternal, original and incomparable I. As such He is the Lord above whom is no other lord, the Subject who precedes all other subjects, to whom all other subjects are objects and from whom they can derive and lease their subjectivity and I-ness. God is object in Himself and for Himself : in the indivisible unity of the knowledge of the Father by the Son and the Son by the Father, and therefore in His eternal and irrevocable subjectivity. But in His revelation God is not only I. He is known—from outside, for in an incomprehensible way there is an outside in relation to God—as Thou and He. He is known as many thous and hes and innumerably more its are known : existences which are characterised as creatures and therefore as objects of our knowledge, to which and about which we can speak and hear, by the fact that we give them a name, and that by this name we can distinguish them from the other things which we perceive and apprehend in the world, and also give them their place in this world. Revelation of

God means that although as Father, Son and Holy Spirit God is self-sufficient in His own inward encounter—for otherwise He would not be God—He now encounters us. It is only perhaps from this point that we can see the real significance of the self-humiliation and self-alienation of God in His revelation. It begins with the possibility of an *opus ad extra*, with the will and deed of God the Creator. God does not need a creature. He is an object to Himself. No other object can be an object to Him in the way that He is to Himself. And still less can God Himself be an object for any other object in the way that He is to Himself without any precedence and subsequence of the knower and the known : the Father to the Son and the Son to the Father, in the eternally irrevocable subjectivity of His own divine objectivity. But the actuality of revelation and of the knowledge of God based on revelation is just this : that God has not only created a world different from Himself ; that He not only has therefore objects of His knowledge which are different from Himself ; but that He also becomes an object Himself for these objects created by Himself. There is, therefore, a reciprocity of relationship between Him and these objects. Man is determined, called and enabled by God's revelation to put this reciprocity into practice. He can therefore perceive and consider and conceive God, and therefore Him who in Himself is pure I, just as if He were Himself man. And the means by which this reciprocity is represented, the sphere in which God makes it actual so that it can be actualised by man too, is just the sacramental reality, the work and sign of His self-attestation in the creaturely world, which begins with the existence of the man Jesus. Bearing witness to Himself, but also veiling Himself by means of this sacramental reality, God comes before man as the One who addresses him and who is to be addressed in return, a He who says " thou " to us and to whom we may say " Thou " in return. Yes, God Himself, for it is He who has instituted and used this means, and it is He who demonstrates His divine lordship by this means, so that, since He makes use of this means, we can no longer question whether God, and whether the One who does this, is the one supreme and true God. God Himself, for He attests Himself to us and therefore *ad extra* : otherwise than as He knows Himself, and yet not as another. Knowing Him in His revelation we know Him in this His attestation for us and therefore *ad extra* and therefore in this otherness : that is, in such a way that, by His being revealed to us as He and as Thou, He remains hidden from us as I and therefore in the being and essence of His Godhead. This limitation of our knowledge of God has to be seen and noted. The One whom we know as He and Thou is the I who, as such, is known only to Himself. Certainly we know God Himself on the basis and in the form of the reciprocity created by Himself. But in His I-ness God remains withdrawn from this reciprocity and therefore from our knowledge, even though in revealing Himself to us, in His even becoming man in His Son, He certainly does not cease to be God ; even though it is He, the Lord over all, who gives Himself to us to be known in the manhood of Jesus Christ. We do not know Him as He knows us. And we do not know Him as we men know one another. He knows us as the original and creative I, from whom the created I has received and as it were leases its I-ness, by whom the created I is fathomed and understood before it fathoms and understands itself, and with a perfect clarity in relation to which the self-inspection and self-understanding of the creature can only be a provisional and therefore an impotent approximation. There can be no question of a real knowledge of the real God which presupposes a reversal of this relationship. We may perhaps know one another so far as the approximation in which we attempt to know ourselves provides us with an analogy by means of which we can undertake the same attempt in regard to others. But an application of this analogy to the knowledge of God obviously leads back to the reversal of this relationship between creating and created I, and it cannot therefore be considered. We know God as He gives Himself to us to be known as Thou and He. But we neither know Him as He knows us nor as we know one another. Our participation in His self-knowledge is true and real, but it is this indirect participation. We cannot give God a name as we do to creatures. When we do call God by a name, we must keep to the name which He gives Himself. But God gives Himself a name in His revelation, in what He does in covenant with man, and therefore in the setting up of that sacramental reality. When we hear this name, revealed in His deeds, when we accept it and use it to call upon Him and to proclaim Him, we know God. As Thou and He God is not unknown to us but known. But we must not be surprised if He is known to us even as Thou and He only in such a way that at the same time He remains unknown to us as I. We can put questions about His I only in the form of new questions about His Thou and He. And such answers to these questions as we may expect from Him can consist only in a new making known of His Thou and He. It is in this way that He makes known His name and in His name Himself. We can know indeed that it really is His name, the name of God, and not the name of a creature, which is here made known to us : the eternal, the holy, the glorious name ; the name which is above every name. We can know indeed that in this name we are dealing with God Himself. But we must not be surprised if the name is such that we cannot either hear or express it without remembering that it is a question of Him whom we can only name in consequence of the fact that He has named Himself and as we see and hear this His self-naming. We must not be surprised if this name of His—which we accept, with which we praise and laud Him and call upon Him, in which we can know Him, in which He unveils Himself to us—does at the same time accomplish His veiling, so that, looking forward, we are continually referred to Himself, to His own self-unveiling. If it were otherwise, it would not be the name of God. But just because it is a fact that His name reveals and therefore veils God's I only as Thou and He, it is the name of the Lord. In this determination but also in this limitation we know God.

We are reminded of the clear presentation of this matter in Exodus 3—the meeting of Moses with Yahweh at Horeb. Moses sees the angel of God and therefore Yahweh Himself under this form. But the form is that of a thorn bush which burns without burning away : a devouring fire, which is not consumed ; a creature living and sustained ; and at the heart of it the presence of Him who is its boundary and dissolution ; sacramental reality (v. 2). This incomprehensible event is the revelation of Yahweh. The text emphasises that Moses is at first inclined to regard and understand this event in the way that man will always attempt to regard and understand even the most incomprehensible event in his world of created things (v. 3). In fact, revelation takes place in his place and sphere. But now, from out of the burning bush he is addressed by his human name of Moses by Him who reveals Himself. And the summons is a warning. He cannot and must not approach here in the way that we approach any conceivable or inconceivable being in the creaturely sphere : " Put off thy shoes from off thy feet, for the place whereon thou standest is holy ground " (v. 5). Who is He who is present and speaks here in the form of a burning yet not consuming fire ? What is the significance of this creature which Moses sees, supremely threatened and yet sustained ? Why and to what degree is this holy ground ? Behind the first form there now appears a second. Yahweh speaks. He is the God of his fathers, the God of Abraham, the God of Isaac and the God of Jacob. And now it says of Moses that he hid his face, " for he was afraid to look upon God." The One who acts towards and with the patriarchs, who called and led and delivered them—He is the One who consumes and sustains, who sustains and consumes. Moses now knows that the One whom he would consider and understand comes to him in the way that He came to his fathers. For this reason he knows that he cannot look upon Him. For this reason, he is afraid (v. 6). And the One who comes to him as the God of his fathers does so by now calling and commissioning him also. His action of consuming and sustaining, sustaining and consuming, will continue by his ministry in the future history of Israel. Yahweh is " come down to deliver them out of the hand of the Egyptians, and to bring them up out of the land, unto a land flowing with milk and honey " (v. 8). But Moses still seems not to have fully understood, and asks : "Who am I, that I should go unto Pharaoh, and that I should bring forth the children of Israel out of Egypt ? " (v. 11). And in strict correspondence with this self-defensive question, he asks another : " What is thy name ? " (v. 13)—as if the name " the God of your fathers " were not sufficient. His first question is answered : " I will be with thee," and the second is answered, obviously again in strict correspondence with the former answer : " I am that I am " (v. 14). The translation, " I am He who truly is " has been attempted in the light of the LXX ('Εγώ εἰμι ὁ ὤν) but it is quite impossible in this context. For if the annunciation of this name by God Himself represents, so to speak, a third form of the revelation in which He gives Himself to be known to Moses, the third form definitely has to be understood in the same direction and as an interpretation of the other two. " I am that I am " is none other than the God of the fathers. This is borne out by what follows. If the Israelites ask " who has sent him," then, according to v. 14, he is to say : " I am " has sent me to you. Or, according to v. 15, again expressly: " Yahweh the God of your fathers, the God of Abraham, the God of Isaac, and the God of Jacob, hath sent me unto you : this is my name for ever and this is my memorial unto all generations." Whether we take the verb as present or as future " I am that I am" means: "I am who *I* am (or, who *I* will be)." But that means the One of whom there is no other objective definition but what He gives of Himself by being who He is and by acting as He does. There is therefore no objective definition that we can discover for ourselves. We might say of this revelation of His name that it consists in the refusal of a name, but even in the form of this substantial refusal it is still really revelation, communication and illumination. For Yahweh means the Lord, the I who gives Himself to be known in that He exists as the I of the Lord and therefore acts only as a He and can be called upon only as a Thou in His action, without making Himself known in His I-ness as if He were a creature. We must now glance at Exodus 33[19], where the same name is expressly paraphrased by the words: " I am gracious to whom I am gracious and shew mercy on whom I shew mercy." God is the One who is called in this way and not another : as He posits and gives Himself in His action. God is the One whose being can be investigated only in the form of a continuous question as to His action. Any other name is not the name of God. Any knowledge of any other name is not the knowledge of God. It is in this way and not another that God stands before man.

3. We shall now try to see and understand the same order along a third line of approach. When God gives Himself to us to be known in the truth of His self-knowledge as the triune God, He lowers Himself to be known in time. When God knows Himself, the Father the Son and the Son the Father through the Holy Spirit, then that happens at a stroke and once and for all in the same perfection from eternity to eternity. But our knowing of God is obviously not like this. We can and must ascribe it to Him, for He stands before us as the God and Lord, whose cognition—and primarily and supremely His cognition of Himself—is the origin and the reality and the measure of all creaturely cognition. But, though we ascribe it to Him, we cannot realise even the concept of His cognition, because the concept of cognition with which we make the attempt can only be the concept of our own creaturely cognition, which as such is neither perfect nor eternal cognition and therefore not the cognition of a perfect and eternal cognition. Yet in His revelation God lowers Himself to be known by us according to the measure of our own human cognition. He lowers Himself and He lets Himself be known in truth as the One He is, yet not at all as He knows Himself, but rather in a temporal way. And this brings us to the third limitation which we have to bear in mind. For temporally means in repetition, in a cognition which progresses from one present to another, which constantly begins afresh in every present, in a series of single acts of knowledge. If we want it all to be different, if we want to know God as He knows Himself and as He knows us, and therefore at a stroke and once and for all, we shall certainly not know Him. The fact that God stands before man and is known by man does not happen at a stroke and once and for all, in the way that it did of course happen at a stroke and once and for all in the unity of the eternal Word with the man Jesus at the heart of time. It happens in the whole circumference of this centre, in the whole circumference of sacramental reality, in a succession

of attestations and cognitions, which all expect and indicate each other, which all determine and are determined by each other. Not as if each one does not always exist in complete truth. But it does so in such a way that the whole truth is always truth for us temporally. It is truth which always needs to be repeated. It has to become truth afresh in a new attestation and cognition. Again, it does so in such a way that our standing before God in truth is a walking before Him in consequence of His walking before us in ever new forms of His one revelation with us. Again, it does so in such a way that while God's revelation is always ready for us, we on our side are never ready. For God has not finished with us but given us time. In our creaturely time, although it is our time, and therefore the time of our sin, He has given us His divine time. He allows us our time in order that we may always have time for Him—no, in order that in it He may always have His time for us, revelation time. The participation which we are given in God's self-knowledge consists in this, in the continual concession of revelation time by means of the sacramental reality at the heart of our time.

26

THE KNOWABILITY OF GOD

The possibility of the knowledge of God springs from God, in that He is Himself the truth and He gives Himself to man in His Word by the Holy Spirit to be known as the truth. It springs from man, in that, in the Son of God by the Holy Spirit, he becomes an object of the divine good-pleasure and therefore participates in the truth of God.

1. THE READINESS OF GOD

To ask about the " knowability " of God is to ask about the possibility on the basis of which God is known. It is to look back from the knowledge of God and to ask about the presuppositions and conditions on the basis of which it comes about that God is known. Only in this way, only with this backward look, is it possible to ask about the knowability of God in the Church's doctrine of God. We come to it from " the knowledge of God in its fulfilment." It is from there that we go on to ask about the knowability of God. The type of thinking which wants to begin with the question of the knowability of God and then to pass on from that point to the question of the fulfilment of the knowledge of God is not grateful but grasping, not obedient but self-autonomous. It is not theological thinking. It does not arise from the Church, or rather, from the Church's basis, and it does not serve the Church. What it affirms to be knowable and then to be actually known—whatever else it may be—is certainly not God the Father, the Son and the Holy Spirit whose revelation and work is attested by the Holy Scriptures and proclaimed by the Church. If this God is God—and there is no other God—there is no way from the question of the knowability of God to that of the actual knowledge of Him. There is only the descending way in the opposite direction.

Now in relation to the question of the knowledge of God in its actual fulfilment we have already established the fact that it cannot be: " Is God really known ? " as though we had first to establish this from some other source than the real knowledge of God. In view of the fact that the knowledge of God is actually fulfilled we can only ask about its mode. On the presupposition that God is known, how and how far does this happen ? But self-evidently we can ask about the knowability of God, too, only in this way and not otherwise. We

cannot ask : " Is God knowable ? " For God is actually known
and therefore God is obviously knowable. We cannot ask about an
abstract possibility of the knowledge of God. We can ask only about
its concrete possibility as definitely present already in its actual
fulfilment. Our questioning can relate only to that foundation of the
knowledge of God which is already laid and laid in a quite definite
manner. It cannot relate to one which has still to be laid and determined in one way or another. Otherwise our question will again
betray an untheological type of thinking, i.e., a thinking which derives
from some other source than gratitude and obedience. When we think
gratefully and obediently, we can start only with the fact that the
possibility is also given on the basis of which God is known. And
it is given in a quite definite way. Therefore the presuppositions and
conditions of that fulfilment are firmly established in themselves, so
that their reality is reality. In relation to their reality and kind they
do not first have to be discovered by enquiry, far less do they have
to be established or even created in their reality and kind by the
various answers which we may discover. In this matter, too, we are
asking about the mode, about the how and the how far.

Put in this way, the question of the knowability of God is also
meaningful and necessary. It constitutes the second step on the way
of the indispensable investigation of the knowledge of God, which
forms the presupposition for the understanding of what is said and
heard about God in the Church. This investigation as a whole is
indispensable because the presupposition has to be kept in the consciousness of both the teaching and hearing Church, and therefore it
has to be continually recalled to mind. There can be no right understanding and no right explanation of the revealed Word of God,
attested in the Bible and proclaimed in the Church, without an understanding and explanation of the knowledge of Him whose Word is
to be spoken and heard in the Church. But the investigation which
this involves cannot be content merely to establish and describe the
fact of this knowledge. If the knowledge of God which establishes
the Church's language and hearing about God is to be understood and
explained aright and therefore to be recalled critically and positively
to the Church's consciousness, it is essential that, after the question
as to its actuality, the question of its possibility must also be explicitly
raised and answered. And this is the question of the genesis of its
actuality. We are not dealing with a question which arises from an
idle or even an anxious, but either way a dangerous, curiosity which
has an inquisitive desire to probe back behind the only healthy and
self-sufficient fact of the knowledge of God in its fulfilment in order
to reassure itself from some superior position. If our present enquiry
is on the right lines, this kind of curiosity will definitely not have its
reward. But as we can conjecture at the outset from these preliminary
remarks on the putting of the question, the result or at any rate one

result of our enquiry will be that there is no such superior position in respect of this fact and therefore no reassurance to be gained from it. There is only the certainty inherent in the fact itself and as such. But we must conduct this further enquiry in such a way that it eliminates the conjecture that behind or above the fact of the real knowledge of God there is a kind of empty space which can be filled up by the assertions of an overlapping doctrine of being and knowledge in general. The temptation which necessitates this idea of an empty space must be attacked at its roots. It must be made explicit that the possibility of the knowledge of God is the possibility—and only the possibility—which is contained in the reality as we have described it in the foregoing section. Or conversely, the knowledge of God described there has its possibility, its presuppositions and its determinations in itself. Therefore the fact itself bears direct witness to its genesis. The knowability of God can be known only in the real knowledge of God. But it can really be known. It can never be superfluous to make all this explicit. As it is done, the glory of the knowledge of God becomes visible in a new dimension and therefore so much the clearer and the more to be adored. If it is not done the door will stand wide open for error in this dimension. But again, it can never be dangerous to make all this explicit. If only it is done in the right way there is no risk that we will be led away from the only healthy and self-sufficient fact of the knowledge of God in its fulfilment —indeed, we will be led all the more into the depth of its nature.

We must begin with the fact that there is a readiness of God to be known as He actually is known in the fulfilment in which the knowledge of God is a fact. In the first instance and decisively the knowability of God is this readiness of God Himself. " God is knowable " means : " God can be known "—He can be known of and by Himself. In His essence, as it is turned to us in His activity, He is so constituted that He can be known by us.

But obviously we are not going far enough if we try to be satisfied with saying that the knowability of God is " in the first instance " and " decisively " His own readiness to be known by us, i.e., the readiness grounded in His own being and activity. Later on we shall have to speak of a corresponding readiness of man for this knowledge—for it is certainly a question of our human knowledge of God. If there is not a corresponding readiness of man, there can be no knowability of God—at any rate, not a knowability which will ever be a problem for us. There can be only the knowability of God for Himself, and even this not in a way that it can be the theme of our enquiry. We will have to understand and explain the knowability of God with reference to both God and man, if we are going to understand and explain it properly. But if from the very outset we fix and keep our eyes on this, it must at once become clear to us that the readiness of man cannot be independent. It is a readiness which cannot finally be grounded

3

in itself, i.e. in the nature and activity of man, so that between it and the readiness of God there is a relationship of mutual conditioning, the readiness of man meeting the readiness of God halfway, so to speak, God and His readiness having to wait, as it were, for the readiness of man in order that together they may constitute the knowability of God which establishes the knowledge of God. If we speak about the readiness on His side and ours in this way, it is evident that we are not speaking about the knowability of God, but about the knowability of another object different from God, about a relationship within the creation, within the world that is in need of reconciliation and redemption. But if we speak about the knowledge and knowability of God, we are not speaking—or at any rate, we are not speaking only—of a relationship of this kind. Even when He becomes visible to us within the world and therefore an object, God is the Lord, the Creator, Reconciler and Redeemer. In knowing Him, there can be no readiness of man that is finally grounded in itself, as generally there can be no being and activity of another that is finally grounded in itself. If there is this readiness on the side of man, it can have only a borrowed, mediated and subsequent independence. It can be communicated to man only as a capacity and willingness for gratitude and obedience. It can be opened and apportioned to man only from the source of all readiness—the readiness of God Himself, beside which there cannot ultimately be a second. With good reason, therefore, we have to speak first of the readiness of God. And it is not merely the first and decisive readiness. It is the readiness which in principle comprehends, establishes, delimits and determines the readiness of man in the sovereignty of his Lord, Creator, Reconciler and Redeemer. In the last resort therefore, and properly, it is the only readiness of which we have to think when we ask about the knowability of God. If we are going to speak later of the readiness of real man and therefore of the real knowability of God, this is where we must begin. The knowledge of God is wholly and utterly His own readiness to be known by us, grounded in His being and activity. Real man is the man who stands before God because God stands before him. The question of the readiness of this real man will arise later. Yet no final independence can be ascribed to the readiness of this real man, but only the character of a capacity and willingness for gratitude and obedience communicated by God to man and returning to its source. It will have to be traced back to and grounded wholly and utterly in the readiness of God which fundamentally precedes it and which is finally alone independent. The knowability of God is not the knowability of God if finally—even considered from man's side—it is something other than a work of God Himself (and therefore an object of praise).

The superordinate, and therefore in the last resort not only the superordinate but the only readiness which we have to understand

and explain as the knowability of God, is the readiness that is grounded in the nature and activity, the being and existence of God. He is the Lord of the event which we call the knowledge of God. He is also the substance of the possibility, presuppositions and conditions of this event.

If this is to become quite clear, we must first go back to the decision which is prior to all our questions about the knowledge and knowability of God (and is therefore their origin and at the same time their answer). This decision was made from eternity and in eternity by the fact that God is who He is. We therefore have to go back to a sphere which, since we are men and not God, might be entirely closed to us. But in the fulfilment of the true knowledge of God, it is not actually closed. This is the sphere of what God is in Himself, then to be the same among us and for us. The power of all that He is among us and for us lies in the fact that it is originally and properly His power, i.e., the eternal power of what He is in Himself from eternity and in eternity. In this way and for this reason the power of what He is among us and for us is distinguished from all other powers by the fact that it is the divine power. Therefore even the knowability of God among us and for us, which lies at the foundation of the fulfilment of our real knowledge of God, is first and properly God's own possibility. From eternity and in eternity God is knowable to Himself. For this reason and in this way He is also knowable among us and for us. It is because this is so that the foundation of our knowledge of God is so sure, and the knowledge of God such a powerful and irresistible event. How can there be opposition, how can there be doubt and difficulty, when we have to do with the actualisation of an eternal possibility, God's own possibility? When God is really known, the decision which is made contains within itself the cognizance that God is knowable, and that He is knowable on the strength of His own being and activity. Although this decision is taken only in faith, in time, and in the dialectic of our thinking, which is a human and not the divine thinking, it has all the weight which is proper to it, because God is knowable to Himself. We are guilty of no encroachment when we go back to this sphere. In all its invisibility and incomprehensibility this sphere, which might of course be closed to us, is not actually closed to us. If there is any encroachment here, it is the encroachment which God Himself has made in His revelation in Jesus Christ by the Holy Spirit. Of course, we accept the fact of this encroachment. We think of it when we look back to the fulfilment of the knowledge of God. There is real knowledge of God in the power of His self-demonstration. But this self-demonstration is His revelation as the triune God. We know God in consequence of God knowing Himself—the Father knowing the Son and the Son the Father by the Holy Spirit of the Father and the Son. Because He is first and foremost knowable to Himself as the triune God, He is knowable to us as well. We cannot speak of the knowability of God as an abstract possibility. For it is concretely realised by God Himself, in the Father and in the Son by the Holy Spirit. And by God's revelation we, too, receive and have a part both in His self-knowledge and also in His self-knowability. Though mediated and not immediate, it is nevertheless a real part.

We are rightly describing this possibility as concretely realised by God Himself, and the nature of God Himself as understood in the light of this possibility, when we say quite simply: " God is the truth," characterising the readiness of God, in which alone in the first instance and decisively and finally we can know his knowability, by the fact that God is Himself the truth. The truth—not simply a truth. For the origin and substance of all truth lies in the fact that God is not hidden from Himself but is open to Himself. Truth means unhiddenness, openness. Because God is open to Himself—the Father to the Son and the Son to the Father, by the Holy Spirit, He, the Lord of all things—all things are open to Him, all openness which exists elsewhere is originally and properly His openness. There is, therefore, no openness that we can investigate under the impression that it may be greater than His, and therefore necessary to elucidate it. But in revelation we have to do with the openness which we are given for the openness of God Himself, with the truth of the truth itself. Again, we have to remember that it is not immediate but mediated. Yet within the limits and in the manner appropriate to us, we do have to do with the truth of the truth itself. If this is so—and we have only to keep to God's revelation as the revelation of the Father in Jesus Christ by the Holy Spirit to assure ourselves that it is so—then we can dismiss any nervous fear that we are becoming guilty of an encroachment by going back to that sphere. The only encroachment is the divine encroachment, in the power of which the real knowledge of God is effected. And this not only allows but commands us and even constrains us to see that the foundation and possibility of our knowledge of God has been laid in God Himself, and therefore to regard it as a safe foundation and a given possibility. Our first, decisive and comprehensive answer to the question about the knowability of God must be this—that even as we raise it, the question is superfluous. It has already been raised and answered by the One whose knowability we are investigating. Therefore, in all that follows, we can only proceed from the decision which has already been taken in God Himself. The illegitimate encroachment on our part is to resist the divine encroachment when we have to do with the truth of the truth itself, and to ask after a truth which is superior to the openness between the Father and the Son by the Holy Spirit, as if this openness were not the original and real openness, the source and norm of all others, and as if there were a higher criterion than the fact that God is God and that in His revelation is also God among us and for us. If we do not become guilty of this encroachment, our whole enquiry as to the knowability of God can consist only in a conscious and therefore finally a confident return to the decision which has been taken in the being of God Himself—the decision that God is knowable.

But now we cannot be too definite when we go on to say that we are thinking of the grace of God when we say that God is knowable. We are thinking of the grace of God when we designate and understand our whole enquiry as to God's knowability only as a return to this decision which has already been taken. For it is by the grace of God and only by the grace of God that it comes about that God is knowable to us. How do we come to refer ourselves to God Himself and to the fact that He is Himself the truth ? It is simply that we have referred ourselves to His revelation, to the fact that He gives Himself to us to be known, thus establishing our knowledge. But we cannot arbitrarily refer ourselves to God's revelation. Not, at any rate, in the way that we do to any other datum of our experience, or to any other real or supposed axiom of our thinking. God's revelation is not in our power, and therefore not at our command. God's revelation takes place among us and for us, in the sphere of our experience and of our thinking. But it has to be seriously accepted that it happens as a movement " from God." It is by the truth itself that in revelation we have to do with the truth itself. And it is only in the truth itself that, summoned and authorised and directed by it, we can effectively refer and appeal to the truth itself.

A test may easily be made in this connexion. We have just referred *in concreto* to the fact that, according to the revelation attested by the Holy Scriptures, the Father is knowable to the Son and the Son to the Father by the Holy Spirit. We have described this self-knowability of God as the truth. We have therefore thought of God as knowable among us and for us as well. And there is no doubt at all that this is theologically correct. But it is also theologically correct if we do not just leave it at that, but maintain further that the strength of this reference and the indication it gives cannot possibly lie in what we have done, or in the view which we have more or less adopted, in the act of thought which we have more or less efficiently accomplished, or even in the correct adherence we have shewn to the Church's doctrine of the Trinity, or even in the tacit recollection of specific biblical and especially Johannine texts, in which it has all naturally taken place. The truth is not to be had so simply, nor is the knowability of God into which we are enquiring to be known so easily— not at any rate effectively and with power. Humanly speaking, we have no assurance at all in face of the possibility that the effected reference and demonstration will fail to enlighten us ; that they will not in fact say to us what they might say and what considered in themselves they can say. The alternative possibility, the possibility of the power and effectiveness of this reference and demonstration, is one which we ourselves do not possess. If they are to be powerful and effective, we ourselves must stand in the truth. Only as we stand in the truth, only as we are summoned, authorised and directed by it, can we refer and appeal powerfully and effectively to the truth, and therefore in a way that will genuinely enlighten both ourselves and others. If not, we may carry out a theological movement which is correct in itself. But seen from outside, it will have the appearance perhaps of a theological trick leading out of nothing into nothing. Yet it is not in our power to attain the one thing and avoid the other. It is not in our power to place ourselves in the truth and therefore to become those who are summoned and authorised and directed by it. If we are these things, it is by the truth itself. If we are not, then we can become them only by the truth itself.

But it is not at all the case that in face of this uncertainty we can and should break off the theological investigation of the question of the knowability of God. It is still far too soon to call in Christian life and experience, or to accede to the demand that we abandon what is obviously captious theory for more promising practice. The appeal to " real life " ought not to be despised. But to break off the investigation at this point in favour of that appeal may easily mean the breaking in of error. For it will perhaps imply the advice that in face of the uncertainty we should go forward confidently with our thinking, as if we stood in the truth and were therefore master of the truth and could therefore refer and appeal to revelation without more ado, in other words as if the truth were to be had fairly easily. Now it is a fact—even this honour is not lacking to it—that in its own way (but only in its own way) the truth can be had very simply. But this way wants to be very carefully considered and to be distinguished from other ways, in which it cannot be had on any account. It is in a consideration of the way in which the truth can in fact be had simply, and therefore the knowability of God can be known simply, that we now continue our investigation by turning to the very important recollection that it is by the grace of God that God is knowable to us. We may, therefore, venture to assert that God is in fact knowable, knowable because He is Himself the truth.

What the expression " the grace of God " means in this (and not only in this) connexion we shall best make clear by returning to the pictorial way of speaking that we used before. In the revelation of God, in the power and effectiveness of which there is knowledge of God, we have to do with a divine " encroachment." We did, of course, hesitate when it was a question of going back to the sphere of what God is in Himself, to God's own possibility of knowing Himself. The question arose whether in this we ourselves were not guilty of an encroachment. We had to overcome a mistrust against ourselves in this respect. Our first task was to make clear to ourselves that the real encroachment on our part consists in resisting the divine encroachment that takes place in the revelation of the truth, in thinking past it instead of our adapting our thinking to it. Now we surely did well and we do well to hesitate at this point. The hesitation had to be overcome. It still has to be. But that did not and does not mean that we are mistaken. For it is something peculiar and exceptional if it is a fact that what is open to God—Himself—is also open to us ; if we can therefore regard our knowledge of God as possible and established and therefore certain. This sphere might still be quite closed to us. It is peculiar and exceptional that it is not closed to us ; that the truth is revealed to us ; and that the use that we make of the fact that the truth is open to us has power and effectiveness and is not an empty movement of thought. It could so easily be an empty movement of thought—that is to say, if, in the movement which he regards as the knowledge of God, man is really alone and not occupied with God at all but only with himself, absolutising his own nature and being, projecting it into the infinite, setting up a reflection of his own glory. Carried through in this way the movement of thought is empty because it is without object. It is a mere game. As far as concerns the knowledge of God, it is pure self-deception. This betrays itself in the equivocal certainty of its conclusion. It is a certainty bounded always and everywhere by uncertainty. To-day it is certainty, to-morrow it degenerates into uncertainty. But we must not conceal from ourselves, and we all know well enough, that this is, so to speak, the natural, general and normal aspect of everything which we call our knowledge of God. On this aspect, we are not dealing with God but at bottom with ourselves. We may also add that on this aspect there is no genuine theological knowledge of God, but only an apparent knowledge. On this aspect, we continually perform an empty movement of thought when we think that we attain the sphere of God Himself, and therefore that we can make ourselves masters of His truth and know God in His openness for Himself. On this aspect, it is never more than our own openness for ourselves that we know in this way. And, in the last resort, we even deceive ourselves if we think that we are really open for ourselves, and that we really have to do even with the truth of man in consequence of this movement of thought. We certainly do not have to do with God. But we do not even have to do with ourselves in a way which enables us to escape that dialectic of certainty and uncertainty in relation to ourselves. We will not wholly escape it even in regard to ourselves. And now let us note carefully that, formally considered, even our theological knowledge of God, even our movement of thought as it is properly concerned with the triune God and directed and determined by the Bible and dogma, still has this natural, general and normal aspect, viewed from which it is empty and therefore objectless, viewed from which we are still concerned with nothing but ourselves and not even with ourselves in truth. And it is not in any sense a matter of course that our knowledge of God does not have only this side. It is really something peculiar and exceptional if it has another aspect, seen from which we are concerned not only with ourselves but genuinely with God, and—because genuinely with God—genuinely with ourselves also. It is something peculiar and exceptional if the limitation of that natural, general and normal aspect of our knowledge of God enlightens us in such a way that we are not only driven into a certain scepticism but are really disturbed, and see ourselves really and definitely compelled to look above and beyond it. How do we come even to reckon with the fact that this aspect is not the whole ? Why is not this self-deception in relation to God and ourselves (including the necessary scepticism which cannot itself free us from it) the final term, the boundary by which we are surrounded and above and beyond which we cannot look ? How are we going to be really disturbed, really compelled and enabled to look at another aspect ? If we are, it is certainly more than a lengthening or deepening of the natural, general and normal aspect of our knowledge of God. It is not as if in the fulfilment of our being and nature we are ultimately pressed forward so far that at last we find that we are no longer alone but before God and therefore in the midst of the fulfilment of a real knowledge of God. It is actually the case that in and with the peculiar and exceptional thing that has taken place an entirely new aspect is opened up. For this very reason the right time for us to stop short, to hesitate and to consider what we are doing is the moment when we dare to go back to the sphere of what God is in Himself. It is the case, then, that we have come to a knowledge of the truth by the truth ? Then we are not somehow engaged in trying to persuade ourselves that we are capable of arriving finally at our goal, of pressing forward to the truth and to God Himself by absolutising our own being and nature, which is a way of self-deception, because even though we refer to the Bible and dogma, it is all of ourselves and therefore otherwise than by the truth ? The peculiar and exceptional thing that we think we have discovered is not that of a most audacious *Sic volo sic iubeo!* at the conclusion of our movement of thought, which is just as empty, i.e. objectless, at the end as it was at the beginning ? We have not deceived ourselves, thinking that we are inside—inside with God—at the very moment when all the time we are supremely and most terribly outside ? supremely and most terribly because with this defiant assertion we deny even the human honesty of our being outside. If this were the case, a return to the dialectic of certainty and uncertainty would very soon make us see that the gateway of the sphere of the inner divine being cannot in fact be stormed and forced from without. But the very attempt, or the failure of the attempt, to fulfil the revelation of God for ourselves can blind our eyes in a most destructive manner to the fact that it actually has been and is fulfilled—not by us, not from without, not as the last step on our own way, but by God, and therefore from within, as the first step on His way. The first encroachment that we allow ourselves by trying to obtain the presence of God titanically will thus involve the second, that, disillusioned by the failure of this undertaking, we resist and withdraw from the presence of God as it is actualised on God's initiative and by the work of His self-revelation in His own divine encroachment, perhaps even resisting and withdrawing from it in a way which is almost completely irreparable.

At this point we may recall an historical precedent. How did it come about that at the end of the 19th century Protestant theology allowed itself to be gripped and almost completely dominated by that astonishing *ennui* with revelation ? It alleged that it was in conflict with a false metaphysics, but in actual fact it was in conflict with the knowledge of the real presence of the genuinely speaking and acting God. And the danger was that in the long run it would become only a historical representation and psychological analysis of the religious life of man. Now we can understand this phenomenon only by recalling that this theology, and the age to which it belonged, originated in a very radical disillusionment. Perhaps it was not really tired of revelation, although it did in fact oppose it. But it was certainly tired of the heaven-storming Idealism of the first half of the century, in which the best and profoundest spirits in philosophy and theology had gone to great pains to understand God's revelation and presence as the last and highest result of man's concern with himself and finally to introduce it as an affirmation. Even at that time—as regards theology, we are thinking of the schools of Schelling, Schleiermacher and Hegel—express reference was still made to the Bible and dogma. In biblical and dogmatic statements they believed they saw the last and supremely useful keys to unlock the mysteries of being recognised in the natural, general and normal way. In this context we can only lay it down as a historical fact that in the eras before and after the middle of the 19th century philosophy and theology had everywhere tired in the most disruptive manner of this last and deepest result of the Idealist movement, its faith in God. Did the reality of man's being outside assert itself all the more strongly in proportion as it was denied in this Idealistic faith ? Is it with impunity that we can train real man to titanism, as the Idealists with their faith in God finally did ? However that may be, the wave of doubt and negation, provisionally checked at the end of the 18th century, now swept more strongly and heavily than ever before over supposedly Christian Europe. And it was not opposed only to faith in the most cleverly conceived God of the theologico-philosophical metaphysics of the Idealists. At the same time—although blindness was now so general that the difference could not be appreciated—it was opposed to faith even in the God of the biblical revelation. The first encroachment carried the second automatically in its train. To philosophy and theology, the collapse of the speculative system seemed to leave nothing but a positivistic historicism and psychologism. Of course, dissatisfaction with this positivism could not be suppressed for long. But the situation round about 1910 (at the time of the hey-day of Troeltsch) was not too promising. The only alternative to oppose to its staunch adherents seemed to be the desperate possibility of a revival of the Idealistic metaphysics which had so mysteriously collapsed between 1830 and 1870. But for good reasons (namely because there was no second Hegel or Schleiermacher, but only feeble epigones and eulogists) this possibility was never realised. It is fortunate that this was the case, for thought had already gone right round the *circulus vitiosus* twice (in the 18th and again in the 19th century). To take the same way again could only involve harmful and dangerous deceptions, no matter what precautions might be taken.

If we really dare to go back to the sphere of what God is in Himself, it must have nothing whatever to do with an absolutising of human nature and being. Indeed, it must not be that we try arbitrarily to withdraw from our own sphere—and therefore from the sphere in which we have to do only with ourselves—as if it lay in our discernment and power to set up or even to choose another. If the sphere of God is not closed to us, the singularity is not only by reason of the singularity of God in the distinction of His nature and being from ours, but it is to be found in the fact that this singularity of God as such is evident to us, and that we come to ask about it and to reckon with it. The self-deception in which we stand in relation to God and even in regard to ourselves might so easily be final. It might be quite impossible for us to look to another side, to the true side, of what we call the knowledge of God. If it is not impossible, and if we understand the significance of the fact that it is not in fact impossible, then —by abstaining from the encroachment on our side—we recognise and acknowledge the encroachment which has occurred and still occurs from the side of God. The fact that God is revealed to us is then grace. Grace is the majesty, the freedom, the undeservedness, the unexpectedness, the newness, the arbitrariness, in which the relationship to God and therefore the possibility of knowing Him is opened up to man by God Himself. Grace is really the orientation in which God sets up an order which did not previously exist, to the power and benefit of which man has no claim, which he has no power to set up, which he has no competence even subsequently to justify, which in its singularity—which corresponds exactly to the singularity of the nature and being of God—he can only recognise and acknowledge as it is actually set up, as it is powerful and effective as a benefit that comes to him. Grace is God's good-pleasure. And it is precisely in God's good-pleasure that the reality of our being with God and of His being with us consists. For it is Jesus Christ who is God's revelation, and the reality of this relationship in Jesus Christ is the work of the divine good-pleasure. God's revelation breaks through the emptiness of the movement of thought which we call our knowledge of God. It gives to this knowledge another side, seen from which it is not self-deception but an event in truth, because it happens by the truth. It makes us those who do not have to do only with themselves but also with God. It provides our knowledge of God with its object. And all this because it is God's good-pleasure. For we, real men, have to do with the real God because the mercy of His good-pleasure comes upon us in all the majesty, freedom, undeservedness, unexpectedness, newness and arbitrariness of grace.

In His good-pleasure God is among us and for us—in the encroachment, proceeding from Him alone and effected by Him alone, in which He makes Himself ours. In His good-pleasure He is open to us in the openness in which He is open to Himself. His good-pleasure is the truth by which we know the truth. Hence, God's good-pleasure is His knowability. In it rests the undialectical certainty of the realisation of the true knowledge of God. When we are really unsettled by the dialectic of certainty and uncertainty which is our part in this event, we are really summoned and compelled to look out to its other side. And then we always stand before the good-pleasure which is its divine side. In this good-pleasure the decision as to God's knowability has already been taken before and beyond the decision of our faith and cognition. It has not been taken only in a being and nature of

God which would perhaps be closed to us. In virtue of that encroachment it has been taken among us and for us. The result is that the truth of the being and nature of God stands actually and perceptibly before us in all its divine certainty, and it can genuinely be apprehended by us. The dialectic still remains on our part : yet not in such a way that we are still in the grip of that dialectic ; rather in such a way that the dialectic is directed and controlled from the side of the event which is God's part. For us the event of our knowledge of God shews itself to be a continual winning and losing, winning again and losing again. But through it all the will of God is there as the preponderant force, so that we are not lost in that ascending and descending movement, but held—held as by the mercy of God, but for that reason really held.

" Yea, though I walk through the valley of the shadow of death, I will fear no evil : for thou art with me ; thy rod and thy staff they comfort me " (Ps. 23⁴). " For the Son of God, Jesus Christ, who was preached among you by us . . . was not yea and nay, but in him was yea. For all the promises of God in him are yea, and in him Amen, unto the glory of God by us " (2 Cor. 1¹⁹⁻²²).

God's being and nature are not exhausted in the encroachment in which He is God among us and for us, nor His truth in the truth of His grace and mercy. But whatever else He may be, God is wholly and utterly the good-pleasure of His grace and mercy. At any rate, He is wholly and utterly in His revelation, in Jesus Christ. And therefore it is not only justifiable but necessary for us to understand His whole being and nature as comprehended and ordered in His good-pleasure. In this way and not otherwise He has turned towards us. If we want to assure ourselves of the knowability of God and therefore of the certainty of our knowledge of God, we have no way which by-passes the grace and mercy of the divine good-pleasure. We have no authority to accept anything other than the encroachment which God has effected and is effecting. If the divine readiness which underlies our knowledge of God is not understood as the mystery of the divine good-pleasure, if even for a moment we cease to give God the thanks which are His due because He acts so majestically towards us when His truth is revealed to us, then the divine readiness is not understood at all. Let us try to clarify this in detail.

We possess no analogy on the basis of which the nature and being of God as the Lord can be accessible to us. We certainly think we are acquainted with other lords and lordships. But it is not the case that we have only to extend our idea of lord and lordship into the infinite and absolute and we will finally arrive at God the Lord and His lordship. The decisive distinguishing mark of the lordship of God is this fact that He is really the Lord over all things and therefore supremely over ourselves, the Lord over our bodies and souls, the Lord over life and death. No idea that we can have of " lord " or " lordship " will ever lead us to this idea, even though we extend it infinitely. Outside the ideas that we can have, there is a lordship over our soul, a lordship even over our being in death, a genuinely effective lordship. Only as we know God's lordship will our own ideas of lordship have content, and, within their limits, existence. But if an analogy of God fails at this decisive point, if God Himself has to be added to give content and substance to what is supposed to be analogous to Him, it is obviously useless as an analogy of God. Can the ideas of lords and lordships even help us to know God ? Of themselves they can only hinder. For in the last resort they do not point us to God, but to ourselves, to our God-alienated souls, to our threatened life on this side of death, to a merely possible lordship set in the sphere of our choosing. If they do not hinder us from knowing God, it is not that they have helped us to know Him, but that there has come to them, and to us too, a fundamental conversion and renewal. If we know about God as the Lord, it is not because we also know about other lords and lordships. It is not even partly because of this previous knowledge and partly because of God's revelation. It is in consequence of God's revelation alone. But in consequence of God's revelation—as the " alone " tells us—means by the good-pleasure of the divine grace and mercy, i.e., on the basis of God's free initiative and in His mystery, so that in face of our knowledge of God nothing is left for us but gratitude for the fact that He is and that as such He is not hidden from us but open to us.

Moreover, we have no analogy on the basis of which the nature and being of God as Creator can be accessible to us. We know originators and causes. We can again extend their series into the infinite. When we reach the point where we grow tired of extending it, we can call that point " god " or " creator." Within the series we can talk presumptuously of creators and creations. But we can as little attain to the idea of the real Creator and the real creation as to that of the real Lord and the real lordship. What we can represent to ourselves lies in the sphere of our own existence and of existence generally as distinct from God. But creation means that our existence and existence generally as distinct from God are opposed to nothing, to non-existence. Creator means one who alone exists, and everything else only as the work of His will and Word. Creator means : *creator ex nihilo*. But within the sphere of the ideas possible to us, *creatio ex nihilo* can appear only as an absurdity. And so it is again the case that in the long run the ideas of originators and causes that we may have can have content and, within their limits, substance, only if there stands behind and above them this absurd conception of *creatio ex nihilo* and therefore the concept of the real and divine Creator. Either way, they obviously have no value, and they cannot therefore be used as analogies of God. In themselves—the misuse of the concept of creation shews this clearly enough—they will point us away from the real Creator rather than to Him. The last and profoundest word that they can give us is that of the original relatedness and unity of man and the world, spirit and nature, knowing and being. It is therefore a quantity which is definitely not identical with God, but which is calculated only to make God appear to be superfluous as the Creator, to exclude His truth in favour of the truth of a cosmos resting and moved in itself. If we do know about God as the Creator, it is neither wholly nor partially because we have a prior knowledge of something which resembles creation. It is only because it has been given to us by God's revelation to know Him, and what we previously thought we knew about originators and causes is contested and converted and transformed. Again, it is given by grace and mercy, on the basis of His free initiative and in His mystery. Again, it is given in such a way that in face of our knowledge of God we can only give thanks for the fact that He is God and that as God He is not hidden from us.

Moreover, we have no analogy on the basis of which the nature and being of God as the Reconciler can be accessible to us. Why can analogies not be introduced in this sphere too? We know many disagreements, but we do not know any which cannot finally be overcome. We know many wounds, but we do not know any which cannot finally be cured. Is it not possible to think of the whole course of things as a succession of separations and reunions, disruptions and resumptions? To that extent is it not a unique analogy of the divine reconciliation? But when God makes peace with the world in His Son, He does something very different from completing what we with unbroken optimism find prepared in all nature and history, and in all the maturing experience of our life. For God the Reconciler is not in any sense the principle of synthesis that we apparently find it so easy to think or feel in relation to this world and life of ours. God the Reconciler is the One before whom even a world which was perfectly reconciled in itself would be utterly lost and abandoned to righteous judgment if He Himself had not so loved it that for it He delivered up His only Son. God the Reconciler is the One before whom even the most successful theoretical and practical synthesists are still sinners condemned to death, and no peace which is made elsewhere can ever help them, but only a readiness to be taken up in faith into the peace which passeth all understanding. God the Reconciler is the One who overcomes the disagreement which cannot be overcome, the One who heals and saves from the wound which cannot be cured. If there are genuine syntheses and reconciliations apart from that which God Himself has effected and does effect, they do not have their content and substance in themselves, but only from His work. In themselves and as such they have no force and value as analogies of God. Indeed, they are calculated to hinder the knowledge of God. For in themselves and as such they are only too well adapted to obscure the divine reconciliation. They can so easily veil its necessity and actuality. This can so easily cover over the abyss which separates from God the man who is supposed to be reconciled in himself, and the mystery of the condescension in which God removed this separation by Himself in the mystery of Jesus Christ and His Holy Spirit. They can so easily point man to quite different and apparently more obvious and promising possibilities. If we know about God the Reconciler it is not even partly because we know about other reconciliations. It is simply and solely because God Himself has revealed Himself as the Reconciler. And in so doing He has radically compromised all other reconciliations. He has judged the peace which the world thinks it has and cannot have. He has shown Himself to be the end and the beginning of real reconciliations. Hence it can come about only through God's good-pleasure, and again, only on the basis of His own free initiative and in His mystery, if we know about Him as the Reconciler. All that we can do is to be grateful that He is this God, and therefore God among us and for us. We certainly cannot boast that we have contributed to this knowledge with the help of what we know elsewhere about reconciliation.

And finally we have no analogy on the basis of which the nature and being of God as the Redeemer can be accessible to us. We do know something about goals and attempts to attain them. We do know the future as an empty form of the time which is still perhaps before us. Again, we do know as an empty form the idea of a perfection which is basic and prior to becoming. But what has all this to do with redemption and with God as the Redeemer? Just as God the Creator is not the X at the beginning of our world picture, so, as Redeemer, He is not the X at its end. We can put our question mark at both, but for that reason we cannot know God at either. Redemption does not mean that the world and we ourselves within it evolve in this or that direction. It means that Jesus Christ is coming again. Redemption means the resurrection of the flesh. It means eternal life as deliverance from eternal death. The expectations of redemption that we can know and have do not point in this direction. They presuppose the very thing that is disavowed by the reality of God our Redeemer, and in so doing they disavow just what it promises to us. The analogy of the hopes that we can have fail at the decisive point in exactly the same way as the analogies of our ideas of lordship, creation and reconciliation. It cannot be carried through as an analogy of God. If there is real hope, hope which has content and substance, a confident, joyful, active looking to the future, then this future is the future of God the Redeemer. Here, too, the relationship must not be reversed. In themselves and as such the expectations of redemption that we can cherish will always obscure and cover up the expectation of Jesus Christ, of resurrection and eternal life, just as definitely as in themselves and as such the supposed analogies of God the Creator and the Reconciler will always obscure and cover up the truth of these concepts. Again, therefore, if this does not happen, if we know about

God the Redeemer, neither wholly nor partially is it from what we knew elsewhere about redemption. It is only through the revelation of His future. Therefore, it is through God's good-pleasure, on the basis of His free initiative and in His mystery. And the only possibility that we for our part can visualise is that of being grateful.

In this discussion, the opponent whom we have not so far named is the doctrine of the knowability of God which has found its classical and sharpest expression in the basic theology of the Roman Catholic Church. Our identification of the truth by which the truth is revealed to us with the good-pleasure of God is in flat contradiction to what is said in the *Constitutio dogmatica de fide catholica* of the Vatican Council, *cap. 2 De revelatione* (April 24th, 1870, Denz. No. 1785) : *Eadem sancta mater Ecclesia tenet et docet, Deum, rerum omnium principium et finem, naturali humanae rationis lumine e rebus creatis certo cognosci posse.* And we have done what is condemned in a canon of the same Council (*De rev. 1*, Denz. No. 1806): *Si quis dixerit, Deum unum et verum, creatorem et Dominum nostrum, per ea quae facta sunt, naturali rationis humanae lumine certo cognosci non posse, anathema sit.* In contrast to this doctrine we have affirmed that God can be known only through God, namely in the event of the divine encroachment of His self-revelation. There can be no question of any other *posse*, i.e., a *posse* which is not included in and with this divine encroachment. Let us now try to clarify in what sense and on what grounds we oppose this doctrine.

What we have said is that the accessibility of the nature and being of God as Lord, Creator, Reconciler and Redeemer is not constituted by any analogy which we contribute but only by God Himself. Now when we compare this with what the *Vaticanum* says, the first thing to strike us is that right from the very outset in our outline of the problem of the knowability of God we have been dealing quite unequivocally with the Christian concept of God. Right from the very outset we have been speaking of the one, triune and true God in His work and action as they are knowable in His revelation. Of this God and of His truth we have said that He is knowable only by the truth, i.e., only by His own grace and mercy. Now the *Vaticanum* does not wish to speak about another God, or about only a part of this one God. But its procedure in the noetic question is different from in the ontological. To that extent it certainly intends to make a provisional division or partition in regard to the knowability of God, and this will inevitably lead to a partitioning of the one God as well. For it cannot be overlooked or denied that in the second passage to which we referred, although God is once called *Dominus noster*, everywhere else and decisively He is no more or not yet more than *rerum omnium principium et finis*, or *creator*. And in regard to this one side of God a knowability of God is affirmed other than that which is grounded in the revelation of God. The primary reference of our contradiction is to this partition. Of course, we too understand by " God " *principium et finis omnium rerum* and also *creator*. But God is not only this. He is also God the Reconciler and Redeemer. We have taken the unity of God seriously, not only in theory but in practice. We have answered the question of the knowability of God in the light of His unity, and for that very reason we have had to answer it in the way we have. Every single thing that we have said has been conditioned by this total view. For instance, in our discussion of the lordship of God we kept in mind the fact that it is the lordship of the Holy One in the world of sinners, and for that reason we affirmed that the lordship of God evades all the analogies that we can bring. In our discussion of God the Creator we kept in mind that He is the same One who, as God the Redeemer, awakens the dead, and for that reason we affirmed that the creation of God also evades all the analogies that we can bring. On the other hand, in our discussion of God the Reconciler and Redeemer we certainly did not forget to emphasise that He is also Lord and Creator. But there can be no question of a special theology of the first article, grounded and established in itself, and with special noetic presuppositions. The unity of God has led us necessarily to the answer that we have given in regard to the knowability of God. Therefore, whatever may be the content of his answer, we have to put to our Roman Catholic opponent the following question : In defining what we have to understand by " God," in this question of His knowability, how can we possibly take any other view ? How can we carry through the division—even if it is only meant to be provisional—which enables us in the first instance to investigate the knowability of God the Creator *in abstracto* ? Are we really speaking of the one true God if even provisionally we think of only one side of God—in this instance of God the Lord and Creator ? Are we really speaking of the real Lord and Creator ? Are we speaking of the One who even in the *Vaticanum* is called *Dominum nostrum* ? On what ground do we think we can speak about His knowability in this abstraction, in the light of only one side of God ? The Word of God testified in Holy Scripture gives us no reason to think this, unless it is heard and read very differently from how it is meant to be heard and read. If it is heard and read in its context, even when it speaks of God the Lord and of God the Creator, it also speaks of the one God of Abraham, Isaac and Jacob, of the Yahweh of the history of Israel, of the God who forgives sins and is His people's salvation. In other words, it speaks of God the Reconciler and Redeemer no less than of God the Lord and Creator. It speaks of the one God who in Jesus Christ has revealed His one triune nature and His one triune name. What word of Scripture can be legitimately understood if it is not understood as witness to the one God ? How can that partition of God be effected from the Scriptures ? If, according to Roman Catholic doctrine, it has to take place, will it not be on some other ground than that of Scripture and therefore of the Word of God ? Is not the *Deus Dominus et creator* of this doctrine the construct of human thinking—a thinking which in the last resort is not bound by the basis and essence of the Church, by Jesus Christ, by the prophets and apostles, but which relies upon itself ? And although the knowability of this construct can rightly be affirmed without revelation, do we not have to ask what authority we have from the basis and essence of the Church to call it " God " ? Obviously, in the doctrine of the Roman Catholic Church this partition is already presupposed when the doctrine is put. It therefore assumes the very thing which it wants to affirm in regard to the knowability of God, i.e., the fact that man can and actually does know about God without revelation. It is definitely not summoned and authorised to make this partition by God's revelation. It makes use of a different sort of knowing about Him. Indeed, properly speaking, it explains only this other sort of knowing. It thinks of God as the origin and goal of all things, the Creator. And then quite logically it goes on to say of Him that He is as such knowable without the grace and mercy effectual in His revelation. But if Jesus Christ as attested by the prophets and apostles is the basis and essence of the Church, then this different sort of knowing is alien to Christian doctrine and it is impossible for the Church to make the partition. In the Church and its scholarship the unity of God must be taken seriously, not only in theory but in practice, and therefore in relation to the knowability of God.

This first contradiction now leads us on to a second and more important one. In our answer to the question of God's knowability, the unity of God which we had in mind was the unity of His work and action. We were thinking of Him as the Lord, the Creator, the Reconciler and Redeemer, the Subject of the history of Law and grace in which God really is among us and acts towards us ; really as the One who was, is and will be, really as the supremely real being, but as this being for us in this work and action. We asked about the knowability of this being, about the truth of the real being of the Subject of this history. And to this question we gave the answer that God's knowability is good-pleasure. It is what takes place in the act of the divine encroachment and nothing else. But the

Roman Catholic doctrine does not even put this question, and therefore its answer, the statement about the knowability of God, is not an answer to this question. If we again except the formula *Dominum nostrum*, there is not a single word in the *Vaticanum* to suggest that the God referred to is engaged in a work and activity with man, which is for man a matter of life and death, of blessedness and damnation, nay more, which is for God a matter of His honour and therefore of the miracle of His love, and from which we cannot abstract for a single moment when it is a matter of the relationship of God and man and in particular of the knowability of God. Apparently Roman Catholic doctrine can and must make this abstraction. It does, of course, know about this work and activity, and the necessity and reality of the divine action. But it is able to postpone its treatment of it, deferring it for later consideration. In the first instance, therefore, it can handle the question of God in a very different and more convenient situation ; in a situation in which we do not have to consider the being of God in His work and activity, but only as such and *in abstracto*. It is in this other situation that the question of His knowability is answered. It looks, as it were, away and above what God is among us and for us. It thinks it necessary for assurance about the truth of God to look away and above in this way. It first establishes the fact of the existence of God, i.e., of the beginning and end of all things, God the Creator. In the light of this affirmation it then decides that God is knowable— knowable even without His revelation. The situation in which all this takes place can be called " convenient " for the following reason. The knowability of God without His revelation is affirmed in the light of the being of God abstractly understood. But over against this being of God a certain being is also ascribed to man, although on another plane and in another manner. In the first instance God and man are seen together on a ground common to both and therefore neutral. It is on this ground that the question of truth is decided in Roman Catholic theology. From this starting-point, but only from this starting-point, it will then go on, as it must go on, to consider the activity of God as well. It need not surprise us that this theology believed it could affirm a knowability of God even without His revelation. Such a knowability can easily be asserted of a being *in abstracto*. It was with this kind of being that Roman Catholic theology was dealing (under the impression that it was dealing with God). This being the case, at the present stage in our discussion it can easily make the following reply to all that we for our part—who are dealing with God in His work and activity—have adduced in favour of His knowability in His revelation alone. You ascribe being to God in His work and activity. But you also ascribe it to man, even if in infinite and qualitative disparity. Therefore, whatever may be said about the inadequacy of all other analogies, and as the meaning and justification of all other intrinsically ambiguous analogies, you acknowledge an analogy between God and man, and therefore one point at which God can be known even apart from His revelation. That is to say, you acknowledge the analogy of being, the *analogia entis*, the idea of being in which God and man are always comprehended together, even if their relationship to being is quite different, and even if they have a quite different part in being. As himself a being, man is able to know a being as such. But if this is so, then in principle he is able to know all being, even God as the incomparably real being. Therefore if God is, and if we cannot deny His being, or on the other hand, our own being and that of creation, necessarily we must affirm His knowability apart from His revelation. For it consists precisely in this analogy of being which comprehends both Him and us. (Cf. P. Daniel Feuling, " Das Gotteswort der Offenbarung," *Benedikt. Monatsschrift*, 1934, *Heft* 3/4, pp. 123 ff. ; J. Fehr, " Offenbarung und Analogie," *Divus Thomas*, 1937, *Heft* 3, pp. 291 ff.) Of course, we cannot take it for granted that when we maintain the knowability of God only from His revelation, the Roman Catholic answer will ultimately reduce itself to this line of thought, i.e., to this interpretation of the *analogia entis*. It ought to be mentioned that Gottlieb Söhngen has written two essays (" *Analogia fidei," Catholica*, 1934, *Heft* 3 and 4) in which he advances a doctrine of this subject which is an important deviation from this line. As he sees it, the knowledge of the being of God is not to be superordinated, but subordinated to the knowledge of the activity of God. In theology, therefore, the *analogia entis* is to be subordinated to the *analogia fidei*. *Pulchra et altissimae theologiae utilis est philosophia Aristotelis, si non secundum mentem humani auctoris, sed secundum mentem Verbi divini applicatur, i.e., secundum mensuram seu analogiam fidei. Ergo: gratia non est ens ut qualitas, quomodo metaphysicus ens et qualitatem intelligit et de hac re loquitur, sed secundum veram analogiam entis ut qualitatis concipitur et haec analogia entis est sub mensura fidei* (*loc. cit.*, p. 136). " *Operari sequitur esse*—action follows being. This is valid in the order of being. And therefore the metaphysician strives to trace activities back to their entitative foundations. But this very procedure shews that our knowledge moves in the reverse direction. *Esse sequitur operari*—the knowledge of being follows the knowledge of activity " (p. 198). " An *analogia et participatio divinae naturae* is able neither to evolve nor to become accessible to us out of the *analogia et participatio entis*. And not even in the slightest degree can we men sense the existence and mode of being of a self-disclosure of God. The self-disclosure of God can itself be known only in this divine self-disclosure " (p. 204). To bring out *analogia entis* there has to be an *assumptio* of the *analogia entis* by the *analogia fidei*,—" the *analogia fidei* is *sanans et elevans analogia entis*." But that means, by Jesus Christ : "*Verbum divinum assumens humanam naturam est nostra analogia fidei assumens analogiam entis* " (p. 208). According to this view the contradiction of our thesis follows the warning implied in 1 Cor. 15¹²ᶠ·: " If it is now preached that the Word really participates in our manhood, how then can some among you say that we do not have a real participation of being in Him and by Him (but only the bare participation of Word and hearing) ? If we men do not really participate in Christ, then Christ has not really participated in our manhood " The call of God itself makes us the children of God. Therefore the *participatio fidei* cannot be opposed to the *participatio entis*. On the contrary, it is participation in being—" not a gracious participation in God by reason of a purely human ability for participation, but a truly human participation in God by reason only of the divine power of grace " (pp. 134 f.). A concern for the *actualitas verbi et fidei* must be linked " with a concern for the *substantia verbi et fidei*. Otherwise the substance of the Word and of faith will be swallowed up by a movement of actuality and of events in which the substance will degenerate into movement or even into spiritual and historical ' movements,' and it will therefore become a mere object of movement. For the Word of God must always be the sovereign Subject in every living movement of faith, which is always its own movement because it is carried by its substance and in that substance it has the inward constructive power consistent with its essence " (p. 185). If this is the Roman Catholic doctrine of *analogia entis*, then naturally I must withdraw my earlier statement that I regard the *analogia entis* as " the invention of anti-Christ." And if this is what that doctrine has to say to our thesis, then we can only observe that there is every justification for the warning that participation in being is grounded in the grace of God and therefore in faith, and that substance and actuality must be brought into this right relationship. If we are going to present our thesis correctly we certainly must not neglect to take heed to this warning and comply with it. But I am not aware that this particular doctrine of the *analogia entis* is to be found anywhere else in the Roman Catholic Church or that it has ever been adopted in this sense. Indeed, we may well ask : Can this conception possibly be approved by wider circles in Roman Catholic theology, let alone by the teaching office of the Church ? Will it not have to be repudiated at once by the latter ? To me at any rate—seeing I can only assent to its main features—it is quite incomprehensible how, if we look at it from the historical and practical standpoint, this conception can be accepted as authentically Roman Catholic. For the time being, therefore, we must keep to the more usual interpretation of the *analogia entis* as represented by writers like Feuling and Fehr in opposition to our thesis. But then the following questions arise : How is it that the formula *Dominus noster* was not taken seriously in the *Vaticanum* ? How is it that Roman Catholic theology does not seriously and unambiguously investigate the being of the God who acts among us and towards us as His one true being, besides which there is no other ? How is it that it abstracts from the fact that He is this God, i.e., the God who does these things, the God who condemns to death and leads from death to life, the God who loves us in incomprehensible mercy ? Can we set all this aside in order first to consider the being of this God in itself and as such ? Can we interpret the being of this God as one that has its own if supreme part in being in general, in an idea of being ? Can we compare with that being, and therefore set against it, the certainly very modest part of all other being, and therefore our own part in being in particular ? Can we say, therefore, that they belong together, that they are on the same plane ? Only if we accept this can theology take its stand on the ground where the God who is to be known and the man who knows can be considered and compared and therefore apprehended together, prior to and quite irrespective of any particular act of God to restore this fellowship Only if we accept this can the analogy of being be identified with the knowability of God apart from His revelation. But how can we accept this ? By the mere fact that we are in being, how can we possibly stand on the same plane as God in His being ? Certainly not in virtue of what God is in Himself apart from His revelation. For as God in Himself He is what He is as God in His revelation—the Lord and Creator and Judge and Redeemer from all eternity and in His essence as the triune God. How can this being, which is the origin and boundary of all being, have only a part as we do in some being in general ? How can this being, therefore, come to stand on the same plane as our own being ? Certainly God in His being does not come to stand on the same plane as we do in our being merely in virtue of what we are apart from His revelation. For what will become of what we are without His revelation if we really encounter God in His being ? Will not this being of ours be given over to death ? Will it not be so questioned that we can be sure only of its not being ? And where then is the comparability between His Creator-being and our creature-being, between His holy being and our sinful being, between His eternal being and our temporal being ? Where then is the analogy on the basis of which the knowledge of God is possible to us ? If there is a real analogy between God and man—an analogy which is a true analogy of being on both sides, an analogy in and with which the knowledge of God will in fact be given—what other analogy can it be than the analogy of being which is posited and created by the work and action of God Himself, the analogy which has its actuality from God and from God alone, and therefore in faith and in faith alone ? How can we assert any other analogy, any general *posse* ? Only if we enlist the aid of that abstraction. Only if we change the *Esse sequitur operari* into a " metaphysical " *Operari sequitur esse*. This reversal alone can legitimise the abstraction. But this reversal is just as foreign to the Church as the partitioning of the Christian concept of God in which, indeed, it has its roots. The Word of God will never lead Roman Catholic theology to this reversal. For where do we ever find in the Bible any other being of God than that of the Subject of His work and action towards man, of the God of Israel, who is also the Father of Jesus Christ, who is also the Word made flesh, who is also the Holy Spirit and who is not, in and for Himself, another God. When it makes this abstraction, which is so necessary to its thesis, Roman Catholic theology makes use at this point too of a very different knowledge of God, i.e., a knowledge which is not grounded in God's revelation. It develops this knowledge in its discussion of the being of God for Himself, and the logical deduction is that God can be knowable apart from the good-pleasure operative in His revelation. *Operari sequitur esse* : that is either the self-evident order of being, which as such is always reserved to God Himself and cannot be our order of knowledge ; or if it is understood as the order of knowledge, it is that of Aristotle—an Aristotle understood *non secundum mentem Verbi divini sed secundum mentem humani auctoris*. It is certainly not the order of knowledge which is prescribed by the basis and essence of the Church, by the Jesus Christ attested to us by the prophets and apostles. From the standpoint of this basis and essence of the Church, that other knowledge of God is a foreign body. In the Church and its scholarship the being of God in His activity must be taken seriously, not only in theory but in practice, and therefore in relation to the knowability of God.

It is in this sense and for these reasons that we oppose the Roman Catholic doctrine of the knowability of God, and therefore that *certo cognosci posse*. Our opposition does not begin with the different answer that we have to give. It only emerges at that point. It begins with our different putting of the question. And we are compelled to say that it is at this point and this point alone that we regard it as decisive and critical. If Roman Catholic doctrine affirms that reason can know God from the world, in the last resort that is only the necessary answer to the question as put by it. And ultimately—particularly when we have regard to the careful formulation of the *Vaticanum*, which never speaks of more than a *posse*—it is not in itself absolutely intolerable as an interpretation *in meliorem partem*. The intolerable and unpardonable thing in Roman Catholic theology is that the question is put in this way, that there is this splitting up of the concept of God, and hand in hand with it the abstraction from the real work and activity of God in favour of a general being of God which He has in common with us and all being. To put the question in this way is to commit a twofold act of violence which means the introduction of a foreign god into the sphere of the Church. The fact that knowability is ascribed to this god, apart from his revelation, is in no way surprising. In itself it is even quite proper. This god really is knowable *naturali humanae rationis lumine e rebus creatis* apart from God, i.e., apart from God's special help. But to affirm that the true, whole God, active and effective, the Head and Shepherd of the Church, can be knowable in this way is only possible if He has already been identified with that false god. What thanks do we owe to that god for the benefit and the grace and mercy of his revelation ? Between him and man the relationship is obviously very different. It is not that a door can be opened only from within. On the contrary, man has free ingress and egress of his own authority and power. Quite apart from grace and miracle, has not man always had what is in relation to the being of the world the very " natural " capacity to persuade himself and others of a higher and divine being ? All idols spring from this capacity. And the really wicked and damnable thing in the Roman Catholic doctrine is that it equates the Lord of the Church with that idol and says of Him therefore the very thing that would naturally be said of it. This is the decisive difference between them and us. There is therefore no sense in contrasting their theses and ours in detail and discussing them in this contrast. Our primary contradiction is not of the " natural theology " of the *Vaticanum* as such. This is only a self-evident consequence of our initial contradiction of its concept of God. We reject this because it is a construct which obviously derives from an attempt to unite Yahweh with Baal, the triune God of Holy Scripture with the concept of being of Aristotelian and Stoic philosophy. The assertion that reason can know God from created things applies to the second and heathenish component of this concept of God, so that when we view the construct on this side we do not recognise God in it at all, nor can we accept it as a Christian concept of God. But that means that for us the assertion has no solid foundation. We cannot, therefore, attack it in detail. For how can we attack it ? We can only say Yes and Amen to it as far as it applies to the god, the false god, to whom it refers. It is in itself incorrigible. But we cannot allow that it says anything about God at all, or that it is one of the assertions which have to be made in the Christian doctrine of God.

One would think there was nothing simpler and more obvious than this. God—the God in whom we believe as the Head and Shepherd of the Church—is the Lord, the Creator, the Reconciler and Redeemer. Therefore we can find His knowability only in the readiness of God Himself, which is to be understood as His free good-pleasure. Therefore, in order to assure ourselves of it, and thus of the certainty of our knowledge of God, we must restrict ourselves to the reality of the encroachment carried out by God. Therefore, we can only give thanks for His knowability. Therefore, we can find it, not in a place where to some degree we already have and take it for ourselves, not in an already existent analogy, but only in an analogy to be created by God's grace, the analogy of grace and faith to which we say Yes as to the inaccessible which is made accessible to us in incomprehensible reality. One would think that nothing could be simpler or more obvious than the insight that a theology which makes a great show of guaranteeing the knowability of God apart from grace and therefore from faith, or which thinks and promises that it is able to give such a guarantee—in other words, a " natural " theology—is quite impossible within the Church, and indeed, in such a way that it cannot even be discussed in principle.

It cannot even be discussed because, as we have seen from our debate with the Roman Catholic doctrine, it is possible only on the basis of a mortal attack on the Christian doctrine of God, and it certainly cannot be the case that this attack is the starting-point for the Christian doctrine of God, and with it, dogmatics, and therefore the question of pure doctrine. What good can come of it if at this point we immediately orientate ourselves in another direction than to the basis and essence of the Church ? If we allow ourselves this liberty, how will it be with everything else ? How are we going to treat the nature of God, and then creation, the Law, the covenant of God with sinful man ? Can we ever speak properly of grace and faith if at the very outset we have provided ourselves with a guarantee of our knowledge of God which has nothing to do with grace and faith ? Does it not necessarily change and even falsify everything if at this point we are guilty of enmity and conflict against grace ?

Why is it, then, that our statement on the knowability of God is not so simple and self-evident that the question of a basis of our knowledge of God in ourselves and our relationship to the world cannot be settled once and for all, but seems as though it must continually arise again in different forms and phases ?

1. It may perhaps be pointed out that the establishment of our knowledge of God in this way is in fact possible and practicable, and that it vouches for its own legitimacy and necessity by its actual fulfilment. But what does it mean to be possible and practicable ? And what does it mean that it vouches for itself ? We have to do here with the attempt of man to answer the riddle of his own existence and of that of the world, and in that way to master himself and the world ; with his attempt to strike a balance between himself and the world ; even with his attempt to put these questions in the belief that he can regard

the supposed goal of his answers or even the supposed origin of his questions as a first and final thing and therefore as God. This attempt is, of course, possible and practicable. This attempt does really exist, of course, in an infinite variety of forms. We can say at once that prior to any theology this attempt is the meaning and content of the natural life of man. The natural man is permanently occupied with it, even if with degrees of energy and in very different forms. For the natural man, i.e., man as he thinks he can understand and rule himself without God, it is the meaning and content of life to master himself and the world, and regard the goal and origin of this endeavour as a first and last thing and therefore as his god. Does this attempt succeed ? Certainly it succeeds. How can it fail to succeed, although not always so obviously and happily ? With all the failures, the history of mankind and the history of the individual will always be in part and even in very large part a history of the success of this attempt. Our whole existence bears witness to the fact that we can know " God." But for what does this witness vouch ? For the knowability of God ? In other words, is that which we can know (as, of course, our whole existence bears witness) really God ? that final goal of our answers, that origin of our questions ? Do we really know a first and last thing which can even be measured or compared with what Holy Scripture calls " God," let alone identified with Him in such a way that, from the starting-point of Holy Scripture and hence of the basis and essence of the Church, we can and must say that God is known here and therefore that God is knowable ? What is " God " to the natural man, and what he also certainly calls his " God," is a false god. This false god is known by him and is therefore knowable to him. But as a false god it will not lead him in any sense to a knowledge of the real God. It will not in any way prepare him for it. On the contrary, it will keep him from it. Its knowledge and knowability will make him an enemy of the real God. Therefore, there can be no question of either a knowledge or a knowability of God. It is simply that the contradiction is ignored which Holy Scripture sets up against the identification of God with idols. Holy Scripture and therefore the basis and essence of the Church are abandoned. A general—and from the scriptural standpoint limited—concept of " God " is arbitrarily adopted as a criterion, and—measuring by this criterion—there is ascribed to the natural man, or to the witness of his life's endeavour, a competence and trustworthiness which Holy Scripture at any rate does not ascribe to him.

But again, this witness in itself and as such has never yet appeared with such competence and trustworthiness ; it has never yet asserted itself so permanently, so unanimously, so obviously and convincingly that, compelled by this fact, we are perhaps obliged to overlook the contradiction of Holy Scripture and to confess that here—in another, special way, different from the picture of God in Holy Scripture—God is really known and therefore known in His knowability ; that the natural man can therefore know God without revelation, simply on the strength and in the success of his attempt to master himself and the world. There is no such compulsive fact in the whole known circle of human history. Certainly we have the various attempts of man. We have his answers and questions along these lines. We have his images of God and knowledges of God. But nowhere do they have such force, and even in the aggregate they are not so impressive, as to compel us to admit, in opposition to the contradiction of Holy Scripture, that man's ability (which is, of course, incontestable) stands in a relationship to the real God, and can therefore be claimed as a natural knowledge of God. Even when a man thinks he is obliged to set aside the judgment of Scripture, after all the discoveries he thinks he has made in this respect, sooner or later he will be persuaded that caution is still necessary, and that for the sake of prudence it is better to make only a poetic use of these discoveries. At many times and in many ways the natural man has certainly succeeded in being his own prophet, regarding this or that first and last thing as his god and proclaiming it as such. But where and when has this happened in such a way that, even if we will not and cannot hear the judgment of Scripture, we stand before a fact which compels us to admit that the natural man can know God ? which presents this capacity of the natural man with such force that Christian theology has no option but to recognise it, giving it the necessary consideration at its own basis ? Such a fact would have to be itself a second revelation of God. And although it may be argued that the most forceful attempts of the natural man in this direction have at best the force of supposed and alleged revelations, they have never yet demonstrated the force of a second revelation. In none of its forms are the achievements of " natural " theology so imposing that they compel us to state that God, the real God, is " naturally " knowable.

We must be clear, of course, that even when we claim that this imposing fact is not present, our starting-point is the judgment of Holy Scripture, without which we can hardly escape in the long run the impostures and self-deceptions which are possible in this connexion. It certainly is the case that all the supposed and alleged knowability of God in the sphere of the natural man has not the force effectively to attest that even in this sphere God is knowable to the natural man. But the fact that it is so is the judgment of Holy Scripture. And we can never perceive that it is so except as we hear this judgment. And however that may be, the actuality of natural theology as it is constantly affirmed in the theology of the Church cannot be explained merely by the superior strength of the incontestable fact of natural theology. The strength of this fact is not so great that we are obliged to disavow what seems at a first glance to be necessarily the true situation : that the force of the true knowledge of God on the basis of His revelation, of that killing and making alive again, and the fire of the eternal love which we encounter in it, are incomparably greater and that they therefore render the hypothesis of a "natural" knowability of God quite impossible in Christian theology. The tenacity with which this hypothesis obtrudes itself cannot be explained by its superiority.

2. If this is so, the further question can be asked : Is the practical desirability or necessity of this hypothesis so evident and urgent that we must try to find a readiness of God other than that which is present in the grace of His Word and Spirit ? There are pedagogic and pastoral standpoints from which it is customary to recommend and defend at least a supplementary introduction into Christian theology of the presupposition of a " natural " knowability of God in Christian theology.

We are told that what is in mind is nothing more or less than a common basis of conversation between the Church and the world, between faith and unbelief. This basis is, of course, presumed to be necessary to the existence and activity of the Church. What is in mind is the possibility that the proclamation of the Bible and the Church, which as such is at once alien to man, will " contact " something which is already familiar. What is in mind is the possibility that man can be reminded of his responsibility—and especially of his responsibility for the unbelief which he will perhaps oppose to the Gospel. In this way the presupposition will be created on which he can be addressed to his guilt before God, and told meaningfully and intelligently of the grace of God. In this connexion—in the rather doubtful company of Dostöevski's " Grand Inquisitor "—it can even be represented as the duty of love consciously to take this step towards the natural man. What is the nature of this pedagogy ? Clearly its art will have to consist decisively in this. Theology will have to have its own part in that life-endeavour of the natural man, in his attempt to master himself and the world. Of course, in a very remarkable way, if it really has and keeps before it this pedagogic aim ! For if this is the case, it will take part only in appearance, or at any rate not with the seriousness with which the natural man engages in this pursuit, but with the tolerant superiority of one who understands him but has already seen through the final vanity of his labour. In a sense, it will have to play with him in order to convince him in a wise and friendly manner of the fact that after all it is only a game, and in order to prepare him for that which it does take seriously, and to which it wants to lead him. The idea will be this. The real decision on faith or unbelief, on knowledge or ignorance of God, can and will occur only in and with man's encounter with God's revelation. But the sphere of the life-endeavour of the natural man, which involves a certain " natural " knowability of God, can be considered as a preliminary stage, a game which is played with natural man with a view to leading him beyond this preliminary stage and placing before him the actual decision itself. It always has to be recognised, of course, that this childish game is not without a certain childish seriousness which does at least point very definitely to the actual seriousness. So then a preliminary decision can be taken even here, and it will be meaningful in relation to the true goal. It is to precipitate this decision that theology has first to take part in this game in a kind of anticipation of its real task.

We have to ask ourselves whether this pedagogic experiment is so promising that it forces us to reckon with the " natural " knowability of God presupposed in it. Is it not, perhaps, so full of promise that we necessarily have to reckon with it in spite of the contradictions raised by Scripture, and even when the actual performances of " natural " theology do not impress us so forcibly as all that ?

We must first consider this experiment in the light of the facts. And we have to confess at once that in the sphere of man's life-endeavour, and therefore in respect of the knowability of God now under consideration, decisions are without doubt taken which are important and interesting, and that it can be very rewarding in itself to appraise and discuss the different possibilities now in question. In itself, it is not a thing indifferent whether man is conscious or unconscious of the fact that his life will be, in one way or another, an answer to the question about his development from animality to humanity. It is not a thing indifferent on which step of this development he actually finds himself at any given time. It is not a thing indifferent whether it is clear or less clear to him that in this development an act of his own freedom and therefore responsibility is at any rate also involved ; whether his conscience, his critical faculty is weak or asleep ; whether his way stands under the sign of a naturalistic or idealistic, an optimistic or pessimistic, a naively utilitarian or ethico-critical, an individualistic or collectivistic view of life ; whether his knowing and acting form a unity or not ; whether, by deciding in this or that way, he knows or does not know what he is doing ; and finally, corresponding to all this, of what sort the first and last and therefore the " god " is, who in this sphere is undoubtedly knowable to him in his own way. Now all this is in its own way very important and interesting. But it all boils down to the question whether in this sphere there exists as a possibility somehow attainable within the life-endeavour of natural man the knowability of a god whose disclosure will bear the character of an outstanding decision, of a decision which is previous to the decision of faith or unbelief, and for the sake of which theology must betake itself to this preliminary field of operation with at least a preliminary seriousness simply because this god is identical with the real God whom the Christian Church must proclaim, so that the establishing of his knowability in the natural sphere, in the sphere of the human life-endeavour, will in fact mean a preparation for the establishing of His knowability in His revelation. If this question has to be affirmed, the pedagogic necessity of a " natural " theology as a prelude to real theology will obviously force itself upon us. Man will have to be incited and instructed to make the right use of this position of his, i.e., to make a general survey of his different possibilities and perhaps their gradation, in order finally to discover the possibility from which he can be told that it is not only his, but that as his it is the divine possibility attested in God's revelation. He will have to be led into that previous decision which he certainly cannot make without learning to know, if not the content of revelation, at least the form, the meaning, the theoretical and practical significance which it can have for him. When and because that god—as, so to speak, the legitimate representative of the real God of revelation—becomes knowable to him, the real God must and will also become knowable to him. If, then, the question has to be answered affirmatively, why should it not be a task of theology— " another," preliminary, but necessary task—to participate in the life-endeavour of natural man ? Not for its own sake. Not in the belief that it can as such lead to the goal. Not, then, with the intention of persisting in " natural " theology. Not with real seriousness. But certainly with a childish seriousness, or with the seriousness of teachers coming down to the child's level. For the sake of the pre-decision which points away beyond this sphere, but still takes place in this sphere. All this is quite in order if the question has to be answered affirmatively, and if within this sphere there does exist the knowability of a god who is to be identified with the real God of revelation. But this is not the case. It cannot be denied that there are gods who in fact are knowable to us there. But it is very much to be denied that we have the right to identify any of them with the real God. The decisions taken there may be very important and interesting. The distinctions of our vision of the first and last, and therefore of God, may be very important and interesting. But no distinction which emerges is so great that it can be equated with the distinction there is between the Lord, the Creator, Reconciler and Redeemer of the divine revelation, and therefore the real God on the one hand, and images of the enthusiasm and phantasy of the natural man on the other. The knowledge of the one distinction is not so great that it can prepare the way for a knowledge of the other. The knowledge of these gods in their diversity from one another cannot prepare the way for the knowledge of the real God in His difference from all gods. On any other view, we simply slip back into the Roman Catholic method of a dissolution of the unity of God and an abstract consideration of His being. We do not make any use of the knowledge that the real God, where He is known, kills the natural man with all his possibilities, in order to make him alive again. We put another concept of God into the place of the Christian concept. If we do not do this, if we are prevented by the contradiction raised by

Holy Scripture from allowing some other than the Lord and Shepherd of the Church to be called God and to be accepted as such, then we cannot take into account a knowability of God in the sphere of the life-endeavour of the natural man. He cannot be told that in his childish earnestness he is on the point of transition to real earnestness. The establishment of the knowability of the one god or all the gods in question cannot, therefore, be advertised as a preliminary step towards the establishment of the knowability of the real God. It will then be borne in mind that if we start from the knowledge of the gods in question we can only be blind to the real God and enemies of the real God. It will then be borne in mind that even the highest account to which man can be called here, and therefore even the highest responsibility which he can know, means fundamentally no more than that he is confronted in extreme seriousness with himself, and that he is instructed to take himself seriously in the highest degree. But the possible—and indeed necessary—result will be that now he does not take the real God seriously at all ; that now he withdraws from this encounter ; and that now his responsibility before his God remains completely hidden. And if it comes about that the life-endeavour of man must sooner or later end with his more or less radical self-despair, if the image of the first and last which can emerge in his life-endeavour is finally that of a critically or sceptically intended question mark, what right has he to regard this image as an image of the real God ? Why should he not see that this question mark is the most idolatrous idol ? And why should he not see that the self-despair of man in which he now sets up this idol is the most audacious form of his strife against the real God ? In the knowledge of the real God, why should not the despair of the natural man, and the image of god born of his despair, be given up to death together with the natural man himself ? It is therefore quite impossible to see in the decision for the great question mark a pre-decision which will prepare for the decision of faith or unbelief. But if this is the case, then the trustworthiness of this pedagogy is at once denied in respect of the goal it sets itself. It is established that no matter how loving and friendly towards man the intention may be, it cannot alter in the very least the fact that what this pedagogy wants is factually quite impossible. When a man stands in the decision of faith or unbelief, he has not arrived at this position from any of the pre-decisions which are possible to him apart from God's revelation. But—and this is a very different thing—the real God Himself has come to him.

It will perhaps be worth our while to think through this problem of the pedagogic establishment of natural theology from its other side as well, i.e., in its significance for the man who is to be educated or prepared for the knowledge of God in His revelation. Again, we must concede at the outset the legitimacy of the question concerning a common basis of communication between the Church and the world, between faith and unbelief—the task of pointing the way which leads from the ignorance to the knowledge of God. How can it fail to be the highest and most comprehensive work of love to point this way which is for every man the one way of salvation ? It is also very precipitate to say that this task is impossible, that nothing can be done about it, that we can only leave others to the work of divine revelation, and that in the meanwhile we must wholly renounce our own efforts to effect this task. How can the Church be the Church if it is not actively engaged in this work ; in the work of inviting and guiding from the one point to the other, from the ignorance to the knowledge of God, and therefore from ungodliness to salvation ; in the work of pointing the way that leads from the one to the other, and to that extent certainly also in the work of striving for a common basis of communication ? But the moment this is conceded, the question has to be put in all its sharpness : What is this work to be ? How can and shall this conversation be pursued if it is really going to be the work of love to which the Church is in fact committed ? And it is very much to the point if on this question of the " How " we begin by stating that this conversation must in all circumstances be pursued by the Church in full candour towards the other partner and therefore with faith as the starting-point. He must not be met by a mask. He must not first be deceived by being addressed from his own stand-point, which is the standpoint of unbelief. If we are really going to address this other person from faith with any prospect of being heard by him, then we must say to him what we have to say to him out of faith. He can then come to grips with it, and it will be able to bring him to the point of decision, and therefore to the decision of faith itself.

It rests on a false interpretation when appeal on behalf of the opposite procedure is made to the precedent of Anselm of Canterbury. Anselm pledged himself (especially in the *Cur Deus homo*) to give satisfaction to Jews and heathen with his theological proofs *sola ratione* (I, 20, II, 11, 22 ; cf. also *Monol.* I). *Remoto Christo, quasi nunquam aliquid fuerit de illo . . . quasi nihil sciatur de Christo* (*C.D.h. praef.*, cf. I, 10, 20, II, 10, 11) he especially wants to explain the *necessitas* of the reconciling work of Christ. But the *ratio* as well as the *necessitas* of which Anselm speaks is that of the *veritas* of God, which is for him identical with the divine Word and with the content of the Christian creed. Since he believes it, he wants to know it and prove it ; he wants *ratione* (by means of his human reason) to make clear its *rationem* (its divine reasonableness) ; or *necessitate* (thinking fundamentally) to make clear its *necessitatem* (its divine basis)—*in concreto* the reasonableness and the basis of this or that article of faith (e.g., that of the reconciling work of Christ). Under the presupposition that this article of faith is true, Anselm examines and shows how far it is true. In so doing, he does not make use for the time being of the validity and authority of this article (to that extent, e.g., in the case of the *C.D.h.: Remoto Christo . . .*), but demonstrates its basis and to that extent its rationality in the context of all the other articles of faith which are presupposed as valid and authoritative. There can be no question of his occupying a position where faith and unbelief have equal rights, as the whole contents of the *C.D.h.* shew. None of the writings of Anselm is " apologetic " in the modern sense of the concept. For speaking to the Jews and heathen, he attempts—in the form of sound theology—to make the faith as such intelligible to them, as grounded in itself and rational. He speaks with artless simplicity. He is not the right man to appeal to as the patron saint of natural theology.

Now, suppose the partner in the conversation discovers that faith is trying to use the well-known artifice of dialectic in relation to him. We are not taking him seriously because we withhold from him what we really want to say and represent. It is only in appearance that we devote ourselves to him, and therefore what we say to him is only an apparent and unreal statement. What will happen then ? Well, not without justice—although misconstruing the friendly intention which perhaps motivates us—he will see himself despised and deceived, and indeed doubly despised and deceived. He will shut himself up and harden himself against the faith which does not speak out frankly, which deserts its own standpoint and merely pretends to take up the contrary standpoint of unbelief. What use to unbelief is a faith which obviously knows different ? And how shocking for unbelief is a faith which only pretends to take up with unbelief a common position. But supposing he does not discover that we are not treating him seriously because we do not feel any compulsion to treat even ourselves seriously ? If this insincerity of procedure as such remains hidden to him, then the following dilemma is posed. On the one hand, the conversation may succeed between unbelief and the faith which does not speak properly and sincerely. That is, it may lead to a positive result. On the ground of unbelief, which it pretends to occupy, there may be instructions, conversions and decisions corresponding to the intention of faith masked as unbelief. Within its own sphere unbelief may be led to the possibilities, and persuaded by the quality of the possibilities, of which it is hoped that the decision for them will form the preparation for the decision of faith. But then who or what is going to guarantee that this expectation will be fulfilled ; that unbelief will not limit itself to the possibility which is attainable in its own sphere and indicated by a masked faith ; that it will not take up its abode in it—which is certainly the most likely possibility—and fortify itself all the more against faith (which so far, of course, has not addressed it at all as such) ? And what right has a masked faith really to expect anything else ? Can it hope to gather grapes from thistles ? Or, on the other hand, the conversation may fail. That is, it may lead to a negative result, to a result that is unwelcome to the masked faith. Unbelief may not let itself be led by the nose in its own sphere. Perhaps the masked faith is not quite so versed and competent in the sphere of unbelief as it imagines. Perhaps it does not find it quite so easy to steer unbelief in the direction it wants it to go, that is, to the hopeful borders of its own possibilities. Or perhaps unbelief is not unskilful in defending itself from within against the projected unsettlement. And if this is so—and it may be so more often than the great apologists know—then unbelief will be of the opinion that it has successfully defended itself against faith, when it has grappled only with the inner unsettlement vainly attempted against it and has not come up against faith at all. It will only be the more heartened and assured of its own case over against faith, which has encountered it only in this not unconquerable form of one of its own possibilities. We cannot see how the pedagogy of natural theology is able to escape this double dilemma. For if the subject of this educative process sees how preliminary and unreal is the action by which natural theology thinks it can point unbelief beyond itself, the effect will necessarily be a hardening, because a faith which obviously treats neither itself nor even unbelief seriously is not trustworthy and can only effect a hardening. But even if the insincerity is not perceived, it will still bring about a hardening, for either it will offer a new home and stronghold to unbelief because its intention succeeds too well, or contrary to its intention it will offer unbelief the possibility of renouncing faith at the same time as it renounces this home and stronghold offered to it. This dilemma betrays the inner contradiction in every form of a " Christian " natural theology. As a " Christian " natural theology, it must really represent and affirm the standpoint of faith. Its true objective to which it really wants to lead unbelief is the knowability of the real God through Himself in His revelation. But as a " natural " theology, its initial aim is to disguise this and therefore to pretend to share in the life-endeavour of natural man. It therefore thinks that it should appear to engage in the dialectic of unbelief in the expectation that here at least a preliminary decision in regard to faith can and must be reached. Therefore, as a natural theology it speaks and acts improperly. And at this point—this betrays the contradiction—it is guilty of definite error, not only in regard to the subject, but now also in regard to man, in regard to the world, in regard to unbelief. And it is an error which not only injures truth but also and directly love. It is a theological error which reveals itself to be such by the fact that it is obviously a pedagogic error as well. The unbelieving man who is the partner in this conversation is not a child playing games, to whom we are in the habit of speaking down in order the more surely to raise him up. If we think we can play with him, we will get our fingers bitten. And how will that help his education ? Unbelief, and therefore ignorance of God (including a knowledge of the false gods who are the indices of the human life-endeavour undertaken in unbelief), is an active enmity against God. It is not in any sense a hopeful and lovable inexperience which can be educated above itself with soft words and in that way led at least to the threshold of faith. Unbelief—just because it is unbelief towards God—is far too strongly and far too inwardly orientated to the truth, and (even if only negatively) interested in it, for us to be able to convince it of its wrongness and confront it with the truth by a skilful handling of what is after all, however preliminary and pedagogic in intention, further untruth. Unbelief is hatred against the truth and therefore deprivation of the truth. If we do not meet it sincerely and with the truth, we cannot make clear to the man the truth which he hates, nor approach him with the truth of which he is deprived. If we proclaim the truth, which is indeed the task of the Church, but without telling it to him, we can only plunge him into new hatred against truth and increase the smart of his deprivation of the truth. We cannot experiment with unbelief, even if we think we know and possess all sorts of interesting and very promising possibilities and recipes for it. We must treat unbelief seriously. Only one thing can be treated more seriously than unbelief; and that is faith itself—or rather, the real God in whom faith believes. But faith itself—or rather, the real God in whom faith believes—must be taken so seriously that there is no place at all for even an apparent transposition to the standpoint of unbelief, for the pedagogic and playful self-lowering into the sphere of its possibilities. When faith takes itself seriously, who has place or freedom for this apparent assimilation, for this game with unbelief? Who is it who really has to stoop down at this point? Not one man to another, a believer to an unbeliever, as all natural theology fatally but inevitably supposes. He who stoops down to the level of us all, both believers and unbelievers, is the real God alone, in His grace and mercy. And it is only by the fact that he knows this that the believing man is distinguished from the unbeliever. Faith consists precisely in this— in the life which is lived in consequence of God's coming down to our level. But if this is faith, and the knowledge of faith is the knowledge of this, the believing man is the one who will find unbelief first and foremost in himself. First and foremost he will find only unbelief in himself; enmity against the truth and deprivation of the truth. How, then, can he have place and freedom to descend to the level of other men, to play that game with unbelief? How, then, can he oppose to his own unbelief, and that of others, anything other than, in the deepest humility and yet at the same time in supreme certainty, faith itself, or rather the real God in whom faith believes? How, then, can he still expect something from the possibilities in the sphere of unbelief? How can he fail to know from his own experience the double dilemma which exists where faith does not venture to stand utterly and entirely on its own feet, to live and to speak out of itself, where by way of experiment it dresses up as unbelief, where it thinks it can play with unbelief? How can he fail to know that he has to guard himself with all diligence against this game—and against the hardening which inevitably threatens in this game—for his own sake and also for the sake of others? How can he fail to know that there is only one remedy against unbelief, and that is faith taking itself seriously, or rather taking the real God seriously, since everything else can only confirm and strengthen it as unbelief, can only increase

its hatred against the truth and its deprivation of the truth ? To be
sure, we have to do with a work that must take place between faith
and unbelief, between the Church and the world, and therefore between
believing and unbelieving men. But this work must be the work of
faith itself and alone, and therefore of a faith acting sincerely towards
unbelief. This is the work which must be done in any such conversation.

Unbelief will, in this case, be immediately occupied with faith itself and as
such. And that certainly means with the faith of men who, because they are
believers, are in no way less sinful men than their unbelieving partners in the
conversation, and therefore men who have no power over their faith, and who as
such also lack the power to conquer with their faith, and to overcome the unbelief
of others. What they can, in great insignificance and unpretentiousness, contribute to the conversation, is simply the fact of their faith. The hope in which
they enter upon this conversation is founded only on the fact that the divine
counter-witness will not be lacking in the human witness of faith which they
can make and which they will want to make seriously in all openness. But just
in this way they can and will meet unbelievers sincerely, in the humility of
a full and honest solidarity with them ; but also confidently, having regard
to the, in the long run, irresistible power of the matter they represent. They
do not first need to condescend to them. They do not need any particular art to
draw near to them. They are, indeed, already with them. For they stand with
their witness of faith as poor sinners alongside other poor sinners. They are not
superior to them. They have nothing to hide from them, not even preliminarily.
They can stand and converse with them at once before the secret of the last
decision itself and not merely on the preliminary ground of provisional decisions.
In these circumstances, it will be quite impossible for the first dilemma to arise.
Unbelief will at least not be able to complain that faith does not take it seriously—
because it does not take itself seriously either. From the outset the situation will
be clear. Faith and unbelief are as close together as possible. But they also
confront one another as openly as possible. Unbelief is acknowledged by faith
to be a position only too well known to faith. From it the unbeliever can as little
come to faith by his own strength as the believer has come to faith by his own
strength. But faith, too, stands over against unbelief as a position over which
the believer has no power. He has no authority to abandon it again even by way
of experiment. For the sake of the unbeliever himself, he can only possess it
unambiguously and hold it unambiguously, in the insecurity but also in the
divine certainty which are both involved in the fact that it is the position of faith.
The situation is then ripe for serious and clear-cut decision. But in these circumstances, again, it will be quite impossible for the second dilemma to arise. For
even objectively unbelief is no longer concerned with the possibilities of its own
sphere. Faith will not now offer it any prospect of satisfaction with a supposed
best possibility within this sphere on appeal to the direction given it by faith.
There can be no hope of utilising the instruction provided by faith simply to
entrench itself within this sphere. But again, faith will not offer it any chance of
defending itself against this instruction. It cannot be the conqueror and master
in its own sphere in relation to the instruction provided. It cannot reject faith
itself along with the best possibility offered and rejected within this sphere.
Faith will not assist the hardening which is possible in a twofold manner. It
will merely enter the conversation in the simple form of a witness. It will at
once speak properly. It will thus engage the partner at once in conversation with
itself. It will occupy him only with the possibility of faith. How can the believer
have all ready to hand a recipe which promises results ? His position will not,
indeed, be that of faith if he has not renounced all such recipes at the outset, if
he deals with faith as something which is in his own power. When he confesses

in his human witness he will pray that there will not be denied him the divine counter-witness, without which, as he well knows, he can do nothing at all. But precisely by praying for it, he will work by bearing his human witness. He will do so in obedience, and therefore in the prospect of the power of the promise which alone promises a result. But this means that he will do so in the love toward the other which alone deserves to be called love. There is no guarantee that the other will not be able to harden himself. But at least he will not have helped in that hardening. If it does not lie in his power to put him on the way of faith, at least he has not led him into the way of error. Though he can only do something human, at least he does not do anything abitrary. He simply does the one thing which is necessary—because commanded—if he is to be a believer and not an unbeliever. If he has no prospect of a triumph, and if the triumph of faith which can occur in this conversation is definitely not the triumph of the believer, at least he does something which, whether it has any result or not, offends neither his own conscience nor that of the other, and therefore something which alone, in view of the real result, can at any rate be full of promise.

Even in regard to man as the object of the practice here under consideration, a careful answering of the pedagogic question will lead to the conclusion that he is better served if no use is made of natural theology at all. But for the moment we ask only whether the introduction of natural theology into the foundation of the doctrine of God is for some reason unavoidable in our understanding of the knowability of God; whether out of respect for some hitherto unconsidered facts and necessities we are perhaps forced to accord it a place. To that, at any rate, our answer must be that even in the light of the possibility of its pedagogic-pastoral application it does not so obtrude that we cannot escape it. That it *will* obtrude in the light of this possibility is plain enough. But it is far more plain that a pedagogic-pastoral practice which is conditioned by it is most unreliable, not only in regard to its actual goal, but also in respect to its way of dealing with men. In face of the picture which this practice yields after closer consideration, we cannot see that we are compelled to decide otherwise in regard to natural theology. The acknowledged vitality of natural theology must be explained in some other way—if it can be explained at all.

It is also not true that, from the point of view of missionary practice, i.e., under the pressure of the real necessities of missionary work, we are impelled to a different decision. In accordance with the development in the European and American home Churches, there has, of course, been a long period in which modern missions to the heathen have thought it necessary to allow the use of all sorts of natural theologies for the purpose of linking the Christian Gospel to the heathen situation. But their experience along these lines has not been happy—as attested by the complete chaos which was the result of the missionary conference at Jerusalem (March-April 1928)—and there are signs that they will relinquish this way within a perceptible time, or even that they have already begun to leave it. For the homiletic and linguistic side of this matter, see the essays of Heinrich Wyder, " Die Rechtfertigung in der Missionspredigt " and " Die Übertragung biblischer Grundbegriffe ins Chinesische ". (*Ev. Theol.*, 1936, pp. 87 ff. and 472 ff.)

3. But we have not yet named a third and most important authority in explanation of the vitality of natural theology. Our thesis, that the

knowability of God is to be equated with His grace and mercy in the revelation of His Word and Spirit, is based on the witness of Holy Scripture. We have asked about the knowability of Him whom the Church calls God because He is designated God by Holy Scripture. We have asked about the knowability of the God of the prophets and apostles. We have said of this God that He is knowable to us only through the grace and mercy of His revelation. But supposing Holy Scripture itself authorises or even constrains us to reckon with a different knowability of this God of the prophets and apostles, a knowability which is not given in and with His revelation, nor bound to it? Supposing Holy Scripture itself does to that extent allow and necessitate a genuine Christian natural theology? Supposing Holy Scripture itself lays upon us " another " task of theology alongside the task of expounding God's revelation—the task of expounding a knowledge about God which has its foundations elsewhere than in Scripture? Do we perhaps stand here before a satisfactory explanation of the question at issue? If so, we obviously cannot withdraw from attempting that " other " task of theology even according to our own presuppositions. The concept of " the Word of God," from which we must create the Christian doctrine of God as well as all the other doctrines of Church dogmatics, will have to be extended beyond what God says to us about Himself in His revelation. On the very basis of a divine direction in that same revelation, it will now have to include what we have to say to ourselves about Him on the basis of knowledge from elsewhere.

It is immediately apparent that this will be of the greatest significance not only for the establishing of the doctrine of God, and therefore not only for the question of the knowledge of God, but also for the whole doctrine of God, and therefore (for God is the Subject of all the divine speech and activity presented in dogmatics) for the doctrine of creation, reconciliation and redemption as well. Everywhere, then, the Word of God which formally and materially underlies the presentation, everywhere the norm and source of this presentation, will be not merely the revelation of God attested in Holy Scripture, but at least side by side with it, the voice of the knowledge of God which we can have from elsewhere. Even by Holy Scripture itself we shall then be urged forward at every point to this extended understanding of the presupposed norm and source of our presentation. Even by the authority of Holy Scripture itself we shall then be partly released from its authority (and therefore from the authority of Jesus Christ and the Holy Spirit) ; and we shall be put under another authority, namely, that of the cognition possible to us without the grace and mercy of revelation, without Jesus Christ and the Holy Spirit. Even in the exposition of Holy Scripture we shall then have to learn that theology has—also at any rate—to concern itself with the task of that completely other exposition (which will then necessarily, of course, be in one way or another a self-exposition of man). It is unnecessary to point out what doors, hitherto closed to us, will at once be opened again on every side— and this time on the basis of a judgment given by the highest court. If this explanation of the vitality of natural theology is correct (the explanation that it has a biblical foundation), may it not be that we will have to take up again our discussion of its actual performance and practical usability, and let ourselves be taught something better in both respects? What is certain is that in spite of the considerations which we have advanced we shall have to find a place for it, and find a place at every point : the place which at every point (sometimes explicitly and sometimes implicitly) it does actually have in Roman Catholic theology; the place which it has procured for itself at every point even in Protestant theology wherever its solid claim is thought to be discerned. But how can its solid claim fail to be discerned in Protestant theology if appeal can justly be made to its attestation by Holy Scripture ? Here, therefore, we stand without doubt before a decision of extraordinary importance. But then, of course, it has to be asserted on the other side that the attestation of the claim of natural theology by Holy Scripture is not really proved, and therefore if the vitality of natural theology is not adequately explained from the fact that it is grounded in the Bible, then we are definitely not demanded to give way to its intrusion—either here in the doctrine of God, or in the rest of dogmatics. And if its establishment is not to be explained from Scripture, our objections in relation to its actual perform-ance and practical usability retain all their weight, and we can regard these objections as at any rate confirmed in principle. Indeed, we have here a final warning against embarking upon natural theology.

At this point, too, it is best for us to begin with an open concession. There are not only individual passages, but a whole strand running through Scripture, in face of which we can certainly raise the question whether we are not invited and summoned to natural theology by Holy Scripture itself. Indeed, we must raise it in order that we may give it a correct answer. This strand runs through the whole Bible in so far as the witness of the prophets and apostles to God's revelation not only appeals, as it does primarily, to the confirming witness of God Himself, but also appeals to the confirming witness of the man who hears their word. Not only God, but man too—according to the invariably evident presupposition of the Bible itself—can confirm that what the Bible says about God is the truth : man at the heart of the created spacial and temporal, natural and historical cosmos, the voice of which he can hear—a voice which, so far as it is actually heard, incidentally acquires the character of an independent and third witness. Therefore, God is a witness for the truth of the prophetic-apostolic Gospel, but so, too, is man, and along with man, and summoning him for his part to witness, the whole created cosmos.

We have to ask ourselves : Does all this argue the right and neces-sity of a natural theology because it argues a knowability of God independent of His revelation but affirmed by the Bible itself ? This will obviously be the case if what the Bible says on these lines can be separated in such a way from what it says about God's revelation itself that what is said on these lines receives the character of an independent series of statements. In this case, we shall certainly be dealing in Scripture with at least three independent and sharply dis-tinguished series of assertions. In the middle, so to speak, there stands the real prophetic-apostolic witness to God's speaking and acting in the history of Israel and in the history of Jesus Christ. But on its right there stands independently the reference to the direct confirma-tion by God Himself, which is in some sense the result of the direct

speaking of the Holy Spirit. To appeal directly to this and to learn
it directly is obviously a possibility, quite apart from His revelation.
Then on the left of the prophetic-apostolic witness there stands independently the reference to man in the cosmos : man provided with
the ability to receive the voice of the cosmos ; or, if we prefer it, the
reference to man himself on the one hand and the reference to the
cosmos on the other ; but to both on account of their ability to confirm
the truth of the prophetic-apostolic witness to revelation independently
of it and therefore independently of God's revelation itself. If the
Bible draws these three independent lines, there is actually affirmed
in it a knowability of God independent of His revelation, a knowability
of God which cannot be equated with the grace and mercy of the
divine good-pleasure. The right and necessity of a " natural theology "
is, therefore, biblically demonstrated.

We will even be compelled to look around for a twofold " natural theology " :
first, for an immediate and direct in which we have to do with the confirmation of His revelation which is to be expected from God Himself independently
of His revelation ; and then for a mediate and indirect in which we have to do
with the confirmation of the witness of revelation of which man is now capable
in the cosmos independently of God's revelation.

But does the Bible really say what it will have to say if all this is
true ? It can at least be demonstrated that there is no such thing in
the Bible as an independence of the witness on the right. If the Bible
witnesses appeal to God Himself as a witness for the truth of what
they assert about Him in His name, not even incidentally do they in
any sense look past the One who has spoken to them, and therefore
past His revelation, on the basis of which they themselves speak of
Him : as if His revelation either has to or can receive its divine confirmation from any other source or in any other way than from His
revelation and by itself ; as if God is accessible to them and their hearers
in any other place or as any other than at the point where He has,
according to His good-pleasure, placed Himself and made Himself
accessible to them. The appeal to the witness of God Himself adds
nothing new to their witness of His revelation. It only accentuates
the fact that they and their witness are not the light, but bear witness
to it. It only accentuates the fact that the hearers of their witness
too ought not to hear them, but the One of whom they bear witness—
the One who would not be God if in all human witness and beyond all
human witness He and He alone were not His own witness.

When the witnesses in the Old Testament call upon God to bear witness, they
do not appeal to a court which stands somewhere behind or above the God of
Israel's history. They do not appeal to a God whom they expect to speak to
men in some other way than in the history of Israel itself and as such. What they
do is to comfort and exhort themselves and their hearers by pointing them
above their own word as such to its object, i.e. to the witness of Israel, to the
miraculous and divine ways which speak for themselves in this history. It is to the

fact that He who speaks and acts and hence reveals Himself in these ways is His own witness, and not really to some court to be distinguished from His revelation, that those on the right hand point when they place this other witness alongside their own. And the case is exactly the same when in the New Testament an appeal is made to God—and here particularly and expressly to the Holy Spirit —as the confirming witness of the apostolic word. As He is in the essence of God Himself the Spirit of the Father and of the Son, the Holy Spirit does not come independently, or for Himself, as immediate truth to man, but through the Son and as the Spirit of the Son, as the power in which the truth of God lays hold of man in this very mediacy, in the incarnate Son of God. Where in the New Testament can the Holy Spirit of Pentecost be anything other than the light of Christmas, the light of Good Friday and of Easter Morning ? Where can man be enlightened by the gift of the Spirit in such a way that he is placed as judge over Jesus Christ ? Where not, rather, in such a way that precisely through the Spirit the judgment of Jesus Christ is pronounced upon him ? Again, the witness of God to Himself certainly means that confirmation is added to the human witness of the revelation. But this confirmation happens through revelation itself. It does not come to it as something different and new. It does not delimit it—as it certainly does the human witness about it—but it is fulfilled by it. To this fulfilment Scripture refers us when it refers us to the witness of God Himself.

If this is so in respect of the witness of God Himself encountered in the Bible, will it be otherwise in respect of the witness of man in the cosmos, at any rate as encountered in the Bible ? If, according to the Bible, there is no immediate or direct natural theology, can there be one that is mediate and indirect ? If, when they speak of God, the biblical witnesses refuse even in passing to look and point beyond the God who speaks and acts in His revelation to an entity who is " God Himself " behind or above His revelation, are they really going to do on the left hand what they omitted to do on the right, and therefore, even incidentally, to look and point to man in the cosmos as a court from which, independently of God's revelation, its confirmation can be expected ?

In one respect we certainly agree with the representatives of a " Christian " natural theology, that is, one which is regarded simply as a preparation. Even on this side, there can be no question of anything more than a looking and pointing away which is quite incidental. When it comes to their word as such and as a whole, in its real central contents and aim, the biblical witnesses do not base it on the voice of man in the cosmos, but on God's revelation. Any other view is quite impossible exegetically.

The representatives of a " Christian " natural theology may, for example, lay great stress on the 19th Psalm, interpreted in their sense. But even so they cannot deny that if we take the Gospel of the Psalter as such and as a whole (as indeed the second half of the 19th Psalm shews, though this is usually forgotten or dismissed on literary critical grounds), its starting-point is the declaration of the glory of God by the Exodus, by the election of the patriarchs, by the sending of Moses, Joshua and the Judges, by the founding and upholding of the royal house of David, and not directly, at any rate, by " the heavens " ; even allowing that it does undoubtedly say here : " The heavens declare the glory of God." Or again, they may emphasise strongly, for example, Rom. 1$^{19f.}$ and 2$^{12f.}$ (likewise interpreted in their sense). But even so they cannot deny that no matter what Paul says in these places and no matter what their meaning may be, he certainly did not intend the Gospel of his Roman Epistle to be gathered from what the heathen too can know about God. On the contrary, he grounded it exclusively on what the first chapter of this Epistle calls God's ἀποκάλυψις. Therefore, the fact that the leading and decisive strand in the biblical Gospel goes back to the knowability of God in His revelation, and not to a knowability of God existing for man in the cosmos as such, does not need to be argued here. The rationalistic interpretation of the Bible at the end of the 18th century transposed even those statements about a special revelation which belong to the main biblical strand into statements about a general revelation of God in nature, history and human reason. But (at least for the time being) this has long since been abandoned even in those quarters where the full implications of this distinction are not understood. Among thoughtful exegetes there can be no question that at its heart and decisively the Bible intends to speak from no other source than a particular revelation of God as distinct from a general revealedness—or from revelation itself as distinct from the knowledge of man in the cosmos as such.

The only possible argument, therefore, is whether this other strand —particularly in its form on the left hand—does have the character of a true and proper parallel line, i.e., a line which is really distinct from the recognised " main line " of the biblical Gospel and which accompanies it as an independent parallel. It is not to be disputed that the biblical witnesses do appeal to the witness of man in the cosmos. The question arises, therefore, whether when they do so, even if only in passing and *sotto voce* and less authoritatively, they are saying something new and different from what they say about God's revelation. If this is the case, it may well be only a secondary doctrine according to its content, but it is obviously a biblical doctrine that, alongside the knowability of God in His revelation which is attested as central and decisive, there is somewhere and somehow for man in the cosmos as such, and therefore apart from God's revelation, a knowability of God which has to be taken into consideration and with which we have to reckon. " Natural theology " may then be only a preliminary or even a supplementary accessory. It may speak only *sotto voce* and less authoritatively. But as the kind of natural theology which a Christian natural theology claims to be, it is justified and demanded by Holy Scripture. But this is just the question : Does this line really have this independent significance in the Bible ?

On this point the following observation may be made. It is *a priori* extremely improbable in itself that where, as we have seen, God Himself is not seen and understood as independent of His revelation, but only as attesting Himself in His revelation, this independent witness will of all things be ascribed to the partner on the left, namely, to man in the cosmos. Ought we not to presume at the outset that in this question no other position can fall to man on the one side than falls to God on the other ?

The appeal to Yahweh Himself can refer only to the self-witness of the One who reveals Himself in His speaking and acting towards Israel. The appeal to the Holy Spirit can refer only to the work of the incarnate Word. Is it likely, then, that the appeal to man in the cosmos will refer elsewhere, to a divine self-witness which is at his beck and call quite independently of the history of Israel and of Jesus Christ ? When God confirms and verifies His Word by His Word alone, is it likely that man in the cosmos will be in a position to confirm and verify it from elsewhere, namely, from his being as man and his being in the cosmos ? What a singular relationship ! And is it in this singular relationship that the prophets see God on the one side and on the other man in the cosmos ? Do we find in their statements no true side line in respect of God Himself, but one in regard to man in the cosmos ?

The improbability of this assumption is strengthened, however, if we ask a further question. In the light of the recognised main line of the biblical statements, and of the biblical witness to revelation as such, how is it possible for man in the cosmos, and his witness, to arrive at this independent position? On this main line the whole relationship of God and man is effected on the presupposition that God is holy but man a sinner fallen from Him and therefore lost ; that God is eternally living in Himself, but man lies in death ; that God is in light unapproachable, but man in darkness. According to the statements which follow on the main biblical line, what takes place between God and man takes place in the free election, calling and illumination, in the undeserved justification and sanctification of man by God. What unites man with God on this main line is, from God's side, His grace, in which, before all, there is disclosed to man the judgment under which he stands—and from man's side, the faith in which he bows beneath this judgment, and in so doing grasps the grace of God. If we look at the matter from the point of view of this main line, how can there possibly be this side line on which man in the cosmos can have another relationship with God, i.e., a relationship not founded by God's election and therefore not determined by the grace of God in judgment ? From this point of view, how can he be in a position where we can appeal to him as an independent witness—independent of the order of revelation ?

At the beginning of the Bible we twice find (Gen. 6⁵ and 8²¹) the emphatic expression that God looked upon the evil of the thoughts of man's heart. In the first passage it says that in face of this fact it repented God that He had made man and that He resolved to destroy man from the face of the earth. And, conversely, in the second passage the same fact is given as the reason why God will no more curse the ground for man's sake, and will no more smite all things living. Therefore the judgment upon man as such is not annulled. On the contrary, the truth of it is the reason why the covenant of grace is established with Noah—the covenant which is announced already in the context of the first passage (6⁸). How is it possible that on the basis of creation an independent relationship to God can be declared for the man who in all circumstances stands under this judgment, and is given grace only in this way, and only in this way exists before God ? It is in fact compromised as an independent relationship by this judgment. If, nevertheless, the relationship exists—and according to the covenant with Noah it does exist—it certainly does not exist independently. It is determined by the grace which God exercises towards man on the basis of the judgment which compromises it. But this being the case, how can the creation narrative in Gen. 1–2 possibly be understood as a statement which is independent of God's revelation of grace ?

In Ps. 14² ³ we read : " The Lord looked down from heaven upon the children of men, to see if there were any that did understand, and seek God. They are all gone aside, they are all together become filthy : there is none that doeth good, no, not one." Now certainly, this same Psalm ends with the words : " When the Lord bringeth back the captivity of His people, Jacob shall rejoice, and Israel shall be glad " (v. 7). And in Ps. 51⁴ ⁵ we read : " Against thee, thee only, have I sinned, and done this evil in thy sight. . . . Behold, I was shapen in iniquity ; and in sin did my mother conceive me." And then later, of course, in the same Psalm : " Then will I teach transgressors thy ways ; and sinners shall be converted unto thee. Deliver me from bloodguiltiness, O God, thou God of my salvation ; and my tongue shall sing aloud of thy righteousness. O Lord, open thou my lips ; and my mouth shall shew forth thy praise " (vv. 13–15). We ask : Is it really possible that in the Psalter—whatever else we may find in it—there is ascribed to the man who obviously has so full a knowledge of the judgment of God, and therefore of His grace, an independent relationship to God, and, on the basis of this, the capacity for an independent witness apart from grace and judgment, and therefore apart from God's revelation ? Do these passages not decide at once the way in which certain other passages in the Psalms most definitely cannot be understood ?

In Rom. 3²²ᶠ· we read : " For there is no difference : for all have sinned and come short of the glory of God ; being justified freely by his grace through the redemption that is in Christ Jesus." This verse sums up what has already been unfolded on the one hand (all have sinned), and what is afterwards to be unfolded on the other hand (being justified freely). In Rom. 1¹⁸–3²⁰ Paul had spoken of the revelation of the wrath of God upon all ungodliness and unrighteousness of men, the heathen as well as the Jew, the Jew as well as the heathen. In Rom. 3²¹ᶠ· he will speak in exactly the same way of the revelation of the righteousness of God which by means of the πίστις Ἰησοῦ Χριστοῦ comes for all who believe. We ask : Is there a place between this twofold (but in the wisdom and will of God obviously undivided) determination of man by the wrath and righteousness of God, where it is possible for man in the cosmos as such, and grounded in himself, to stand in an independent relationship to God, i.e., in a relationship untouched by the wrath and righteousness of God, and therefore—in contradiction to 1 Cor. 2, where the very opposite is written—to become the bearer of an independent witness to God ? In face of this context of Rom. 1–3, is there even a remote possibility that the passages 1¹⁹ᶠ· and 2¹²ᶠ· can still point in this direction?

In Ac. 17²²–³¹ we read how on the Areopagus Paul preached the resurrection of Jesus Christ. The " times of ignorance " which God has " winked at " is what he places before his hearers as their past, but as their future, repentance in face of the world judgment imminent in the risen Christ. In v. 32 f. we read that this Gospel was received by the Athenians (when they heard of the resurrection of the dead), partly with mockery, partly with boredom. Paul leaves them. A few individuals join him and become believers. This is the main biblical line in this famous passage. Is it, therefore, probable that in the same story there is also a genuine side line, in which it can be said that, in view of their great religiousness (δεισιδαιμονεστέρους, v. 22), and in view of their altar to the " unknown God " (v. 23), and in view of their knowing about the kinship of man with God and about the unity of the human race (vv. 26–28), the Athenians stood in an independently assured relationship to God apart from Jesus Christ, and were to be addressed on this relationship as such ? Can the appeal to the witness of man in the cosmos (which does obviously have a place in this passage) really bear this meaning ?

The affirmation of the existence of a side line, in which the Bible says this, is obviously only possible if the assertions of the main line are understood in a weakened, hyperbolical or poetical sense. What the Bible calls death is only sickness. What it calls darkness is simply twilight. What it calls incapability is merely weakness. What it calls ignorance is only confusion. The grace of God which comes to man according to the assertions of the main line does not really come to lost sinners. From the word perversion it may be gathered that even if it is perverted a certain uprightness still persists even in corruption ; and from this it may be deduced that even in this perversion which is full of concealed uprightness (and which is hastily equated with the biblical concept of sin), man stands in a relationship to God, an independent and self-grounded relationship. But if this weakening of what are recognised to be the main assertions of the Bible is illegitimate and therefore impossible, it ought to be clear that, at any rate starting from within, we cannot give to these side assertions an interpretation on the basis of which there is ascribed to man that which in the primary statements is plainly denied him. From the primary assertions everything that the Bible says about the witness of man in the cosmos can be understood only as this man is made and summoned to be a witness by revelation itself : made to be something that as man in the cosmos he is not in himself ; summoned to do something which as man in the cosmos he undoubtedly cannot do in himself ; yet nevertheless made and summoned by revelation itself to do this. From the main biblical assertions man in the cosmos is to be understood only as a dependent witness ; not as a primary, but only as a secondary witness.

There is another alternative. We want to establish a series of biblical statements on man in the cosmos as an independent witness, but we cannot co-ordinate them with the main biblical statements. Is it the case, then, that here in the Bible itself we are up against a contradiction ? Are there elements which cannot be brought under the common denominator of the main biblical statements, which are, on the contrary, opposed to them, but the significance of which, seeing they too are obviously elements of the biblical statement, we can as little " avoid " as the others ? The question sounds right enough, but it is as wrong as it possibly could be. If we ask it, we surely cannot realise what we are saying of the biblical witnesses. For as their witness is to be seen in their acknowledged main statements, it is not a kind of logically developed human doctrine and theory which, like every human doctrine and theory, for all its logic can and necessarily will reveal at some point an hiatus and contain and tolerate its own contradiction within itself. The biblical witness is not at all a doctrine and theory of this kind. It is the witness of God's revelation. In other words, it does not spin out a human idea, alongside which other and contradictory ideas can and must have a place, as is the case with all human systems of thought ; but even in the form of human thoughts it points above all human thoughts to the event of the encounter of God with man in Jesus Christ, and therefore to the occurrence of the truth in which there is no Yes and No, and to which therefore we cannot refer in terms of Yes and No. If the biblical witnesses can say Yes and No alongside each other, and if they are free to teach an independent union with God of man in the cosmos alongside the sovereign grace of God in His revelation, they deny to themselves the claim to be witnesses of revelation. As has happened a thousand times in the theology of the Christian Church, they deal with revelation as with a systematic principle which can be worked out logically and consistently only to become inconsistent at some point and necessarily to involve contradiction. They then betray themselves as finally un-bound and therefore finally un-free thinkers : as un-bound, because, like all human systematicians, they can obviously do something else ; as un-free, because, like all human systematicians, they obviously must be able to do something else—as moved and delimited by the contradiction in which man exists with himself, and which means at once his greatness and his misery. The main biblical passages in themselves and as such become false in the company of such a contradiction. Even if the biblical witness is made in the realm of human systematics and therefore in the realm of human self-contradiction, it is still the witness of God's revelation, so that the possibility of saying Yes and No simultaneously, of simultaneously teaching the gracious God and man in the ,cosmos united with God, cannot be attributed to it as such. Even if, as men, the prophets and apostles were as little delivered from that greatness and misery of man as any other men, yet their witness is valid, not as witness to an object sharing with them and all men in this greatness and misery, but as witness to Him who does not contradict Himself, and who cannot allow them— else they would not be His witnesses—to contradict themselves in what they must say about Him. And we too, for our part, so far as we hear them as His witnesses, have to keep ourselves to the fact that they have not said and could and would not say all kinds of things or many things, but only one thing : viz. that which forms the content of the acknowledged main statements of the Bible. We for our part have not to receive this in the way that we receive human thoughts which as such have their hiatuses and limits and also contain their contradiction within themselves and openly or secretly have it already alongside themselves. We for our part have not to make a systematic principle out of what is intended and said as witness of God's revelation ; a principle which can justly and fairly be bracketed and called in question from without. If we see to this, there can be no question on our side of a side statement contradicting the main biblical statement. We can then lay down that the biblical witness does not say the one thing in one way only, but in many ways, not on one line only, but on several converging lines, and therefore not without difference and contrast, but yet without contradiction. It is on the " without contradiction " that we have to insist. There is always the one thing ; not something else alongside it—something which will limit and call in question the one thing, something which will be a real second or third rather than again and all the more the one thing. It is true that the side statement of the Bible as such, and the problem raised by it, is certainly not to be overlooked and underestimated. Yet if at the very outset we do not want to receive the main biblical statement in quite a different way from the sense in which it presents itself, we can only expect from the very outset that the side statement will not conflict with the main statement but will simply underline it and confirm it. But that means that in the side statement there can be no invitation and summons to natural theology, to a biblical doctrine which underlies, makes possible and justifies natural theology. The correctness of this fundamental consideration is confirmed, as indeed it must be since it is an exegetical consideration, when we let the Bible itself speak about this side line.

If we survey the biblical material of which we can think when a side statement is under consideration, it must first of all be noticed formally that it can be separated only in the rarest instances, even externally, from the material clearly belonging to the main biblical statement.

For example, there is no passage in the Bible to which we can appeal even *a parte potiori* in opposition to others as particularly representative of this side statement. And there is hardly a consistent context within the individual biblical writings in which this side statement is accented so purely and independently that we have exegetical cause to put this question. What amputations (open or secret) have to be undertaken to make the biblical text really say what has to be said to find a biblical basis for natural theology ! Rom. 1-2 must be read without regard for the fact that the relevant sections are so embedded in the development of the main biblical statement of God's revelation of wrath and righteousness that it is, properly speaking, impossible to understand them otherwise than strictly from this point of view. In Paul's speech on Areopagus (Acts 17) there has to be a total or partial disregard for the decisive conclusion and its reference to the resurrection of Christ, which forms the point of departure and the material centre of the whole of Acts, and in the light of which vv. 22-29 must also be understood. In contrast to this procedure we may read the Psalms with the unbiased question : Even on this side line do they speak about man in the cosmos thematically, that is to say, independently, centrally and properly ? Do they speak about him in such a way that the question about the independence of his witness can be put with exegetical justification ? Certainly, the side line is evident in the Psalms. An audible call is made to all things to praise God : to all lands (Ps. 100[1]), to all the earth (Ps. 66[4]), to all people (Ps. 67[5]), even to the congregation of the gods (Ps. 82[1]), to everything that hath breath (Ps. 150[6]), to all things that are (Ps. 148). We hear continually that the earth as such is God's (Ps. 24[1-2], 50[10], 95[4f.]), and therefore that all the blessings of creation come from God (Ps. 36[6-10], 65[7-14]) ; but also that the lordship and the judgment over all and upon the whole world is God's (Ps. 96, 97, 99). Again and again the heavens, the sea, the storm, the mountains, the earthquake, the world of plants and beasts, the nations and their rulers, and in the height the angels, are all appealed to as the creatures, the servants and instruments and therefore the loudly speaking witnesses of God. How can all this be overlooked ? But where is it all spoken about abstractly ? Where is it spoken of otherwise than in such a way that it is quite clear, in the immediate or more distant contexts, that the reference is not to any sort of godhead which is or may be open to a man in the cosmos as such, but that (according to what is almost always to be read immediately before and after these passages) it is only to the God of Israel, i.e., the God who acts towards and in Israel and reveals Himself in this action ? He it is who, after He has made Himself visible in His action, now also (but always as this One who acts) becomes visible in heaven and on earth and in everything which is therein. It is his light, shining in revelation, which falls on the world ; and only in this light that light is seen there too (Ps. 36). It is to be bearers of all the power and wisdom and goodness and righteousness of God that heaven and earth and all that is therein are summoned and named. But where is all this spoken of abstractly and in such a way that we can designate and understand what is said as, so to speak, first-hand information ? Where in such a way that the God who is spoken about really emerges as the God known independently by man in the cosmos ? If we test more carefully the relevant Psalms and passages in them, in the light of their immediate and more distant context we can almost always establish what is perhaps paradigmatically clear in the 147th Psalm : the witness of man in the cosmos does not come about independently, but in utter co-ordination with and subordination to the witness of the speaking and acting of God in the people and among the men of the people of Israel. Ps. 147 does not stand alone. The short Ps. 117 may be cited as no less paradigmatic : " O praise the Lord, all ye nations : praise Him, all ye people. For his merciful kindness is great toward us : and the truth of the Lord endureth for ever. Praise ye the Lord." The passages Ps. 24$^{1-2}$, 33$^{5-8}$, 36$^{6-9}$, 66$^{1-4}$, 74$^{13-17}$ are all put on the same footing by the rest of the contents—Ps. 29$^{1-10}$ by v. 11, Ps. 93$^{1-3}$ by vv. 4–5, Ps. 148$^{1-13}$ by v. 14, and so on. And why not also Ps. 19$^{1-6}$ by vv. 7–14 ? In the case of Ps. 90, we may disregard the fact that it is directly ascribed to " Moses the man of God," but vv. 13–17 safeguard it against the conjecture that in it we are concerned with an abstract consideration of the transitoriness of human life. In the same way, Ps. 139 is safeguarded by the interposed verses 19–22 against an understanding which would find in it a representation of the omniscience and omnipotence of God *in abstracto*. If I see them aright, only Ps. 8 and Ps. 104 remain as pure " nature Psalms" (if Ps. 19$^{1-7}$ is not classed as independent). But in Ps. 8 (Zurich Bible : " Universe and man as witnesses of God's glory ") what are we to make of the enemies and the vengeful who, according to v. 2, are to be brought to sentence by God's work ? And in Ps. 104, what are we to say concerning the destruction of the sinners and godless, for which v. 35 prays ? And it is acknowledged that Ps. 104 stands in the closest literary correspondence and connexion with Ps. 103, which is orientated in apparently quite a different direction. Nor must we forget the material difficulties in which we are inevitably involved if we try to interpret Ps. 8 and 104 really as " pure " testimonies to man in the cosmos. The possibility of restoring the lost purity of the side line by the operations of textual criticism is certainly present, not only with regard to Ps. 19, but in a whole series of other Psalms. But even then we certainly have to reckon with the fact that at any rate in the final redaction of the Psalter no regard was had for this purity of the side line, but it was upset and destroyed by additions. And in any case it is a fact that in the overwhelming majority of the Psalms the problem does not arise at all, because, apart from a few traces, they move, so to speak, unambiguously along the main line. Therefore on the formal grounds of exegesis we cannot say that it is possible to demonstrate in the Psalter an independent witness to man in the cosmos as such.

But this formal finding points to a very definite material order. For just as the statements made about man in the cosmos or put into his mouth cannot in the biblical text be severed from the statements about God's revelation in Israel and in Jesus Christ, so the biblical witness cannot be dismembered in context in such a way that on the one hand the witness of revelation and on the other an independently confirmatory witness of the world or nature or history are brought into confrontation in an order of similarity, however distant and remote. On the contrary, the contents of the Bible constitute a single witness, and this is to be understood strictly and exclusively as the witness of God's revelation of grace in His covenant with Israel and in the fulfilment of the promise of the Messiah of Israel establishing this covenant, and therefore of the incarnation of the divine Word and the outpouring of the Holy Spirit on all flesh. There is no element in the biblical witness which does not testify to this, or which points in another direction. We have already seen that there is nothing which points immediately to God Himself, to the unrevealed God as such, existing in Himself. The fact that God exists as God in Himself is certainly the power of the truth of His revelation. But the biblical witness points to God in His revelation and in this way only, and not otherwise, to the God existing in Himself. It does not point past His revelation. It bears witness to Him, and in this way and only in this way to Himself. Therefore it certainly bears witness to Himself, but always only in such a way that it points back to His revelation. In this way it does not even on the other side point past revelation to man in the cosmos. Certainly it also points to man in the cosmos, and it is for this very reason that we are concerned with this side line. But, to understand to what it points, and what this pointing means, we must be clear from where it points and to what end.

First, from where does it point ? The answer must be given : definitely not from another authority and responsibility than the one which is given to the biblical witnesses in and with their one single commission as witnesses to God's revelation. What is our conception of a prophet or apostle if we believe that in spite of his commission and even without warning he will dare to incorporate into his proclamation, or to place side by side with it, statements which he derives from some other source ? In all cases, what is to be said on the side line in the Bible can be said only from the one and only authority and responsibility of the witness to revelation as such.

We know how Paul, say, continually provided against the possibility that, as a missionary and the spiritual leader of his Churches, he might say and have to say something other than what was entrusted and committed to him as an apostle of Jesus Christ. " For I determined not to know anything among you, save Jesus Christ, and him crucified " (1 Cor. 2²). Can we regard it as probable that the same Paul, writing from the same Corinth to which he had written these words, would still write to Rome in virtue of another knowledge, in virtue of a particular knowledge about the original union with God of man in the cosmos ? What, according to Rom. 1–2, he may also have known about man in the cosmos, he can have known only from the point of view of Jesus Christ the Crucified— if we do not want to reckon with a very curious μετάβασις εἰς ἄλλο γένος. But it must also be heard and understood as said from this point of view. In the same way, the standpoint from which the side line is drawn is also quite unambiguously clear in the Old Testament—for example, in the Psalms again. The God whom the Psalmists know is the God of Israel, the Lord of the Exodus and of the wandering in the wilderness, the Giver of the Law, the Hope of David, His wisdom, His power, His goodness, His righteousness, originally and conclusively this God alone. And what they may also say on the side line, they say from this point of view, in exposition and application of their knowledge of this God and no other. We must hear and understand it under all circumstances as said from this point and not from any other.

To what end, then, do they draw the side line and point also to man in the cosmos ? It is already settled that they cannot do it in order to point their hearers to another and second source of possible knowledge about God, in order to invite them to approach this source as well as the other. They cannot try to direct others to a point from which, because of their authority and responsibility, they themselves cannot come. Therefore, in the passages under consideration, there can be no question whatever of their readers and hearers being offered a discharge, as it were, from the faith demanded of them ; of the assurance of faith exacted of them being grounded or supported by a reference to the possibility of a second assurance coming to faith from without—the certainty which man in the cosmos as such can have. But we must now turn to the positive side. Coming from the only possible starting-point, they do in fact come also to man in the cosmos. It is he whom their Gospel reaches, and on the other side of their Gospel, God's revelation itself. The fact that it reaches him, and the way in which it does so, is of necessity the all-determining and really ruling content of their Gospel ; what we have called the biblical " main line." But how can the revelation and therefore the Gospel of revelation reach him without including the fact that it is *he* whom they reach ? The statement on the side line of the Bible arises to the extent that this fact is included. The voice of the Word of God—this is to be understood first of all quite objectively, and therefore quite apart from the question of man's faith or unbelief—awakens an echo. Where the light of the Word of God falls, it causes—this is also to be understood first of all quite objectively—a light and a brightness. The place in which the revelation takes place becomes (and the biblical witnesses testify to this by testifying to God's revelation) objectively another place by now becoming the place of revelation. Man in the cosmos, who is confronted with God's revelation (long before he is aware of the fact, long before he has to make a decision and whatever this decision may be) becomes, as the man confronted by God's revelation, objectively another man.

By way of illustration, it may here be remembered that according to 1 Cor. 7[14] the heathen husband is "sanctified " by his Christian wife, the heathen wife by her Christian husband, the children by their Christian parents.

But this otherness of man is—always in the first place quite objectively—his truth, his unveiled reality : the truth and reality also of his cosmos. Revelation is indeed the truth : the truth of God, but necessarily, therefore, the truth of man in the cosmos as well. The biblical witnesses cannot bear witness to the one without also bearing witness to the other, which is included in it. How can they proclaim the revelation of God as what it is, namely as God's seizure of power

in relation to man, if at the same time they do not first bear witness
to God as the One to whose power man is already subjected as it is
proclaimed to him; if they do not testify to man that he is not concerned with a foreign Lord but with his own, not with a man but with
his eternal Lord, i.e., his Lord who holds and rules his whole time in
and with His hands. As they proclaim God's revelation to man they
must claim man himself as the man already objectively changed by
the event of revelation. It is because this last takes place that the
side line of the Bible arises. Hence our answer to this question is:
The biblical witnesses point also to man in the cosmos in order to
interpret the revelation of God in its necessary and compulsive direction
and relation to the one to whom it is addressed; in order to characterise
his existence and all that it involves, including the whole place in
which he exists, as one which cannot legitimately be withdrawn from
the claim of revelation, because the most real and original right under
which it stands is the right which the God has over it who claims it
in His revelation, and because this very fact that God is its Lord, that
it belongs to God and lives in His service, is its truth and its unveiled
reality. Because this fact, too, must always be attested, this side
line of the Bible exists. Our contention is that it is not drawn from
any other point than revelation itself. And how can it be drawn to
any other place than back to this main line? Everything that can be
said on this line means the objective otherness of man in the cosmos,
which becomes audible as the echo of the Word of God, and visible
as the reflection of His light. In Holy Scripture man in the cosmos is
addressed upon this echo and reflection, and starting from revelation
he is referred back all the more surely to revelation itself.

Turning again to the Psalms, we must first consider the saying in Ps. 36⁹,
which belongs so completely to the context of this side line: " With thee is the
fountain of life: in thy light shall we see light." Even in the praise of the
Creator which immediately precedes this verse, even in what are supposed to be
the purest "nature Psalms" it cannot be the case that a contemplation and
devotion, oriented directly to heaven and earth in their abstract being and
nature, and nourished by them, are spokesmen to proclaim the mystery of
heaven and earth as it is inferred by their thinking and foresight, and therefore
in the last resort to proclaim themselves. We must not overlook or deny the fact
that in terms of current psychology the form of the relevant Psalms or passages
in the Psalms does belong to the sphere of this contemplation and devotion, and
that this contemplation and devotion is, so to speak, worked into and sublimated
in them (partly even in dependence on the models of Babylonian and Egyptian
myth-piety). Certainly there is no reason why the Psalmists should not have
directly considered the stars of heaven and hearkened to the voice of the storm,
and why, when they tried to speak of them, they should not have made profitable
use of what they heard the cultured neighbours of Israel sing and say about all
sorts of light gods and serpent beings. It is indeed quite obvious that they
have actually done so. But this again does not alter the fact that the decisive
statement which they then make is that the heavens declare the glory of God,
that the earth is His and all that therein is, that He is great and good in all His
works. And in relation neither to its subject nor to its predicate is this statement

read either out of Babylonian or Egyptian precedents or out of the text of the cosmos, but it is rightly and properly read both into the text of these literary precedents and also into the text of the cosmos itself. In itself and as such the text of the cosmos is, indeed, mute, as it says expressly in Ps. 19[3]: " Without speech, without words and with inaudible voice " one day speaks to another and one night declares to another. And we can say the same, *mutatis mutandis*, of the relevant literary precedents. " In thy light shall we see light." It is because and as God speaks and acts in Israel that man in the cosmos becomes objectively another, namely one who in the whole compass of his existence can now know and has to acknowledge the might and glory of this God. *This* God—for we must remember that whatever he there knows as the wisdom and power and goodness and righteousness of God is simply an exact reflection of the wisdom and power and goodness and righteousness which he has known before in God's speaking and acting in Israel. We may say quite confidently that there is no overlapping. We do not see the features of any other god than the God of Sinai and Zion declared in the main line. What emerges is simply an extensive repetition of what is seen and said there intensively. And it is only this extensive repetition which is intended. In order that what is said on the main line may be understood so much the better in the dynamic in which it is revealed from within, namely, from God, the Lord of Israel, it is said again on this side line—not this time from without, but certainly in a movement from within outwards, and therefore with special reference to man in the cosmos, in the form of an appeal to his position as witness, indeed, in the form of a witness to this man himself.

We can now see what is involved in this remarkable biblical reference to man in the cosmos as such. There can be no doubt that the biblical witnesses remain true to themselves on this point. By pointing to man in the cosmos, they point to a certain extent through him to the man of the revelation of God, i.e., to the man who, in the covenant of God with His people, in the unity of the members of the body of Christ with their Head, is a participant in the divine good-pleasure and therefore in the knowledge of God. They do not consider taking man in the cosmos seriously and addressing him in his " nature "— which really means in his self-understanding. Rather they say to him that he no longer really exists as such ; that in his self-understanding he now exists only in one monstrous misunderstanding. For his original and proper truth has now been opened up to him by God's revelation. They point through him to the One with whom God is well pleased, to the man Jesus of Nazareth, to the judgment fulfilled in Him, to the grace which man has found before God in Him. They point to Him as the origin and future of man in the cosmos. And therefore their pointing is here also a prophetic and apostolic pointing in the narrowest and strictest sense. They do not point to a truth which man in the cosmos already possessed somewhere and somehow. According to God's revelation, their source and end, he has already lost his own truth, his own being in the good-pleasure of God. Therefore they point to his truth as in and with this same revelation of God (which is grace as well as judgment) it has already broken in upon him and mastered him as his original and future truth, alien, transcendent and irresistible. It has mastered him so thoroughly that he is no longer to be taken seriously in his self-understanding, in his nature, but is in all seriousness to be addressed in relation to his future. It is for this reason and in this sense that reference is now made to him. Therefore this pointing does not mean that in his self-understanding he becomes interesting to the biblical witnesses and is addressed by them in his self-understanding as the witness of a particular union with God. His truth to which they point is not his truth as he has fetched it out from somewhere within himself, but his lost truth as it has now become new to him and come upon him. Not an analytic but a synthetic statement is made concerning him. His property as a witness—the distinctive expressions of the doctrine of justification cannot be avoided here—is imputed, reckoned, or ascribed to him. He is designated and instituted as one who he certainly is not and cannot be in himself, who he can be only in the realisation of the revelation of God as the proclamation of the truth of God and therefore also of man—but who he has now actually become. For this reason it does not mean a deviation from the one biblical Gospel when in the Bible they actually do speak along this line. And for the same reason they do not do so *sotto voce* and half-grudgingly, but with the same definiteness and joyfulness with which they speak elsewhere in the Bible.

When the Bible points us to man in the cosmos, we have to do with a genuinely prophetic and apostolic pointing, with the future truth of man from God's revelation. That this is the case can be illustrated from the two pure " nature Psalms " —Ps. 8 and Ps. 104. Supposing we try to understand Ps. 8 in the sense that an appeal is made to man in the cosmos in himself and as such as a witness of God. What, then, does it mean when it says : " Out of the mouth of babes and sucklings hast thou ordained strength " (v. 2) ? and afterwards, in contrast to the heavens, the moon and the stars as the works of the finger of God : " What is man, that thou art mindful of him ? and the son of man, that thou visitest him ? For thou hast made him a little lower than the angels, and hast crowned him with glory and honour. Thou madest him to have dominion over the works of thy hands ; thou hast put all things under his feet : all sheep and oxen . . ." (v. 4 f.)? and again, when this statement is made a basis for the recognition : " O Lord our Lord, how excellent is thy name in all the earth " (vv. 1 and 9) ? Is there a way from the one to the other, if the first reference is really to the man whom we think we know in his createdness as a howling suckling and as a ruler of all sheep and oxen, etc. ? What do we really learn of the glory of the name of God either from his wailing or later from his power, which is so limited and above all exercised with such little prudence over his fellow-creatures ? What an unreliable witness ! And what a false presumption we have to put in the Psalmist's mouth to expound the Psalm in this way. Ought we not to be warned against this exposition by the form of the question that is asked in the decisive sentence in v. 4 : " What is man, that thou art mindful of him ? " Yes, indeed ! What is man ? and who is the man referred to ? Everything becomes very clear if we follow the lead given by Hebrews 2[st.], where Ps. 8 is cited, and where it says : " For in that he put all in subjection under him, he left nothing that is not put under him. But now we see not yet all things put under him. But we see Jesus, who was made a little lower than the angels for the suffering of death, crowned with glory and honour " (v. 8 f.). If this Jesus is actually the man in the cosmos of Ps. 8, the estimate is true, which otherwise could only be described honestly as false. Even out of the mouth of other babes and sucklings, according to Mt. 21[16f.], God has actually prepared strength, when they accompanied Jesus on the way to suffering and glory with their childish cries, unconscious of their meaning. It is true—in the mouth of this man who from the revelation of God is future to the natural man it is true : " O Lord our Lord, how excellent is thy name in all the earth." The position is exactly the same in Ps. 104, which is concerned with the order and harmony that is so wonderfully visible in great things and small, and by which man in the cosmos finds himself surrounded and upheld. But can we understand this as a direct seeing ? Is the man whom we know, the natural man in his self-understanding, really in a position to read out of all the things by which he sees himself surrounded and conditioned, and to which he himself does not belong, this praise : " O Lord, how manifold are thy works ! in wisdom hast thou made them all : the earth is full of thy riches " (v. 24) ? Thy works ? In wisdom ? Thy riches ? And therefore the conclusion : " I will sing unto the Lord as long as I live : I will sing praise to my God while I have my being. My meditation of him shall be sweet : I will be glad in the Lord " (v. 33 f.) ? I will be glad ? Who can say this, say it as the Psalm obviously intends, so that no Lisbon earthquake will bring tumbling down, like a house of cards, the optimism in which it might possibly be said ? There is an illuminating and comforting ring about it when we read in v. 27 f. : " These all "—the beasts of the forest, the young lions, man who goeth forth unto his work, the small and great beasts of the sea, " leviathan, whom thou hast made to play therein "—" these wait all upon thee ; that thou mayest give them their meat in due season. That thou givest them, they gather : thou openest thine hand, they are filled with good." But can it be overlooked here that what we see and know of this happening, this happening in the realm of our cosmology, involves the cruel struggle for existence of all against all ? Will joy in the Lord survive even in the face of this aspect of the matter ? And can we overlook the fact that the passage continues immediately : " Thou hidest thy face, they are troubled : thou takest away their breath, they die, and return to their dust " (v. 29) ? Will the joy in the Lord that is nourished on the visible works of God grow even from this dialectic of the divine work to which the Psalm expressly refers ? But, if we are confident that the Psalmist's praise of the Creator is so radical that it can easily bear such further enquiries, is it not blatantly self-evident that when he makes man in the cosmos a witness of God, he does not at all allow the world picture of this man as such to speak for itself, but through this picture, in such a way that it is as it were transparent, he causes the picture of the future world to speak, in which the divinity and wisdom and goodness of creation again come to us, although here and now they are completely concealed from us ? Where and how far will the world picture as such testify to an order and harmony in which we can directly perceive the divinity and wisdom and power of the Creator ? Can we rightly understand Ps. 104 even for a single moment without the commentary of Rev. 21¹⁻⁵ : " And I saw a new heaven and a new earth : for the first heaven and the first earth were passed away ; and there was no more sea. And I John saw the holy city, new Jerusalem, coming down from God out of heaven, prepared as a bride adorned for her husband. And I heard a great voice out of heaven saying, Behold, the tabernacle of God is with men, and he will dwell with them, and they shall be his people, and God himself shall be with them, and be their God. And God shall wipe away all tears from their eyes ; and there shall be no more death, neither sorrow, nor crying, neither shall there be any more pain : for the former things are passed away. And he that sat upon the throne said, Behold, I make all things new." I ask : Can we, in a genuine, linguistic, historical explanation of Ps. 104, disregard even for a single moment the fact that it is only from this point—because in the Psalm itself this is first read *into* the cosmology of natural man with prophetic and apostolic authority, and only then read *out* of it—that there can be and actually is the praise of God in the ordered harmony of His creation which constitutes the content of this Psalm ? Let us notice another important document of this side line of the Bible—God's answer " out of the storm " at the end of the Book of Job (38 f.). To understand this passage we must obviously start from the fact that according to the author's intention this is to be the solution of Job's problem and therefore (according to the author's intention) the sufficient and satisfactory answer to Job's question about the righteousness of God in His direction of the world. Job knows all about it after the answer has been given. Yet not in the form of a theory of the matter, but much better, much more fundamentally : " I have uttered that I understood not ; things too wonderful for me, which I knew not. Hear, I beseech thee, and I will speak : I will demand of thee, and declare thou unto me, I have heard of thee by the hearing of the ear : but now mine eye seeth thee. Wherefore I abhor myself, and repent in dust and ashes " (42³⁻⁶). The righteousness of God is known as we fall down before Him because He is the One who is right —that is what the author obviously wants to say. But how is his Job brought to this point ? The content of Job 38 f. is admittedly extremely remarkable. In two passages, chapters 38–39 and 40–41 (unfortunately it is the custom to excise the second as an addition to the real Book of Job), God Himself gives a simple account of certain works of His creation which are by their very nature necessarily quite enigmatical to man. In both passages everything proceeds in the form of questions : Who hath laid the measures thereof ? (38⁵). Or who shut up the sea with doors ? (38⁸). Have the gates of death been opened unto thee ? (38¹⁷). Canst thou bind the sweet influences of Pleiades ? (38³¹). Who provideth for the raven his food ? (38⁴¹). Knowest thou the time when the wild goats of the rock bring forth ? (39¹). Hast thou given the horse strength ? (39¹⁹). Doth the hawk fly by thy wisdom ? (39²⁶). Similarly, in the second passage, where only the hippopotamus and the crocodile, Behemoth and Leviathan, are summoned by God Himself as His monstrous witnesses, it is repeatedly asked whether man is able even remotely to match these monsters of the divine creation with his understanding, his cleverness and powers ; whether, in face of these works of the Creator, he can even remotely dream that he is himself the lord. But in the description of Leviathan even the question finally dies away into silence. It is swallowed up in the description as obviously superfluous, and God's speech about Leviathan concludes : " Upon earth there is not his like, who is made without fear. He beholdeth all high things : he is a king over all the children of pride " (41³³ᶠ·). How far can all this lead Job to the knowledge that God is He who is right ? It is obviously not a direct understanding of God's works ; for this text most emphatically stresses that the works of God are not understandable to man but incomprehensible, indeed dark and strange, in their being and nature. Is it then, perhaps, just their darkness as such, the hopelessness of all questions about the inward and external possibilities of man in regard to them ? But it is from such questions on the course of the world or on God as its Lord, and from the hopelessness of such questions, that Job starts out, and are they to be answered and will they really be answered by all this ? Obviously, then, it is neither positively nor negatively the being and nature of these works of creation as such that instructs and converts him. The fact that the world is large and strange is not the new thing that brings him to the repentance to which his friends, those learned masters of apologetics, could not bring him. But of course this new thing can consist only in the fact that—and this is not given with the existence and nature of the world as such—God Himself speaks with him about His works ; God Himself makes His works the content of His own Word to him. God Himself, by whose Word these works of His have come into being ! Therefore, obviously, not a God who will be the content of what man himself can, in an emergency, say about a kind of world-mystery in face of Behemoth and Leviathan, but the God who just in His Word is the Lord over all, and as such the Lord also of Behemoth and Leviathan, and as such also the truth of the mystery of Behemoth and Leviathan, and of all His works. Job heard this Word of God in the reference to the mystery of the works of God. It is not too much to say that the mystery of chapters 38 f. which leads Job to repentance is in fact identical with the mystery of revelation, i.e., with the mystery of the election and leading of Israel, of the cross and resurrection of Jesus Christ. If Job did not see through the works of God to *the* work of God by which God speaks His Word, how did he arrive at the place to which he himself and all the speeches of his friends (even Elihu) could not bring him ?

And now we can put and answer our last question independently : To what is the reference properly made when in Holy Scripture reference is made to man in the cosmos ? As we have said already, the reference is through everything that he is in his self-understanding to his being in the good-pleasure of God. It is through his own present to Jesus Christ as his future. We now add comprehensively : It is through the word which man in the cosmos can say to himself to the Word which God as his Lord has already said and will say again. It is therefore to a truth which transcends man in the cosmos in himself and as such, but which in all its transcendence has been made by God immanent in him, so that it is now possible and meaningful actually to point to him, or through him. His knowledge about himself is fundamentally surpassed, but at the same time also included, in a higher knowledge, and, despite its limitation, raised into this higher knowledge. He is put in the wrong with his own will and accomplishment. And for this very reason he is instituted as an unwilling representative and proclaimer of the right which is asserted against him and to him. He is disqualified from being an independent witness, and so qualified to become a real and dependent witness for the testimony which it is the one purpose of the biblical witnesses to effect, and to confirm which is the one thing that they can expect, but do very definitely expect, of man in the cosmos. Their pointing to man in the cosmos is an eschatological pointing ; but as such it is of course intended seriously. Yet the ἔσχατον towards which they move and to which they refer is identical with the πρῶτον from which they come and to which they must necessarily refer back. They always mean God's revelation. They always mean the covenant of grace. They always mean Jesus Christ and Him as Lord, over against whom man in the cosmos has no more actuality of himself to assert ; to whom they see already here and now every knee bowed in heaven and on earth and under the earth ; over against whom they here and now acknowledge no other possibility than that of the willing or unwilling testimony to His glory. The willing testimony is their own function and that of the Church. The unwilling testimony is the function to which they call man in the cosmos. This man is also present—namely in the resurrection of Jesus Christ. He also is to be engaged in the work of its proclamation ; for he also has in his way become objectively another by its happening ; to him also it is now plain that he belongs to Jesus Christ and stands to serve Him. What comes out of it for him, whether his will be faith or unbelief, willing or finally unwilling testimony, deliverance or ruin, is a separate question, and certainly it is for the biblical witnesses the real and chief question. But the preliminary question concerning the presupposition of the decision which is made in Jesus Christ one way or the other about man, the preliminary question concerning the power of Jesus Christ over all creatures, is answered by the fact that the creature is the place of His revelation and is confronted with His revelation. To this answer or preliminary answer the biblical witnesses point when they point to man in the cosmos. " The kingdoms of this world are become the kingdoms of our Lord, and of his Christ ; and he shall reign for ever and ever " (Rev. 11¹⁵).

Let us realise what it means from this point of view that there is in the Bible a creation history, and especially the creation history as we have it in the two accounts of Gen. 1 and 2. There is no doubt that in these narratives emphatic and interested reference is made to man in the cosmos as such ; that a cosmogony and anthropogony are also advanced ; that to this extent we are given something of a total view of things, which as such is only partly Israelitic in origin, but is obviously to a large extent formed by general Near-Eastern, and especially Babylonian, creation myths. But it is to be noted in these accounts how much is obviously read both into the text of man's understanding of the world and of himself and also into the text of the Babylonian patterns ; and how the two texts are transformed by this treatment from independent witnesses of an immediate union between God and man in the cosmos into dependent witnesses of the relationship between God and man in the cosmos into dependent witnesses of the relationship between God and man grounded in God's revelation. Where, according to the statement of the (in this respect very paradigmatic) Babylonian myths, man's self-understanding is still only acquainted with a dialectic within the world in which the distinction between the gods and the world is obviously relative and reversible, in the Bible God stands out from the very first line as sovereign in relation to everything which is not Himself, as the One who acts not only in and with, but first and foremost towards the world. Where in the former instance it is all a question of emanations and evolutions, in the latter only the Word of God comes into consideration as the crisis from non-being into being of what is not Himself. And if we still try to see in this conception as such the product of a deepened and radicalised human self-understanding, it is hardly possible to sustain this view in face of the following considerations. The creation narrative in P (1¹–2⁴) clearly lays all the emphasis on a twofold fact. First, the work of creation takes place in the existing framework of the six-working-day week with the following Sabbath. Thus the covenant of God with Israel consists in the ordering of the life of His people in the succession of day and night as an ordinance obviously pointing towards God's Sabbath even before its historical founding in and with the creation of the world itself. And secondly, the created world is good in God's sight and judgment. It is not only created by God but upheld in its created existence and nature by His grace. For that reason it can and must serve what God does within its sphere. For that reason God cannot seriously and definitively repent of having created it or refrain from continuing to uphold it (Gen. 8²¹ᶠ·, 9⁸ᶠ·). For that reason Jer. 31³⁵ᶠ· can say : " Thus saith the Lord, which giveth the sun for a light by day, and the ordinances of the moon and of the stars for a light by night, which divideth the sea when the waves thereof roar ; The Lord of hosts is his name : If those ordinances depart from before me, saith the Lord, then the seed of Israel also shall cease from being a nation before me for ever. Thus saith the Lord ; If heaven above can be measured, and the foundations of the earth searched out beneath, I will also cast off all the seed of Israel for all that they have done, saith the Lord." On the basis of the divine judgment that it is good, the created world is the minor from which may be concluded the major of the certainty of the divine promises. J in his creation narrative (2⁵⁻²⁵) obviously turns his attention to man. The first narrative had already said of him that God had created him " in his own image " (v. 27), i.e., as the one whose determination is to be the " eye of the whole creation " (W. Vischer, *Das Christuszeugnis im A.T.*, 1934, p. 60, *E.T.*, p. 47), reflecting God Himself. His existence is already clearly understood in the light of an event which is to him as such transcendent. But the decisive statements in the second narrative also are as such only to be understood above and beyond human creatureliness as such. What does it mean when according to 2⁷ man becomes a " living soul " by—and only by—God breathing His own breath of life into his nostrils ? What does it mean when in v. 8 f. not simply—as might be inferred from the former narrative—the whole earth as such or some undefined place on the earth, but the definite, particularised place of the Garden of Eden—obviously represented as a sort of oasis in the midst of the desert of the world—is given to man as a dwelling-place ? And what is the significance of the river that flows from it, first as a single stream and then dividing into four parts ? What does it mean when in v. 17, as the sin forbidden to man, the arbitrary grasping after the possibility of the distinction between good and evil and therefore after the possibility of choice, which means already even in Paradise the strife against grace, is designated as the real sin ? And finally, what is meant by the very strange account of the making of woman in v. 18 f. ? Is the man for whom, according to the divine judgment, it is not good to be alone ; the man who—obviously in practical demonstration of his dominion over all other creatures which is ascribed to him in the first narrative (1²⁸ᶠ·)—gives names to all the beasts and birds, and yet nevertheless is still alone, namely without the " help " who can also be an " opposite " to him ; the man out of whose ribs is formed the woman who now really becomes this " help " to him as one who is not merely similar but is actually taken from man—is this man to be understood exhaustively as the sexual being " male " ? Is he not perhaps also and at the same time to be understood as the man whom God does not leave to stand alone above all creatures, who longs for a help, and for whom a help arises by God's creative power out of the mortal wound given him by the same God, and who now can do nothing other than love and nourish and cherish her as his own flesh, the member of his own body ? " Therefore shall a man leave his father and his mother, and shall cleave unto his wife : and they shall be one flesh " (Gen. 2²⁴). This is quoted in Eph. 5³¹, which then goes on : " This is a great mystery : but I speak concerning Christ and the church " (v. 32). If Paul has read Gen. 2¹⁸ aright—and how could it be properly read in any other sense ?—then at this point too, where there is undoubtedly a concrete reference to man in the cosmos, the creation story also points far and fundamentally beyond and above him, to attain a genuinely concrete understanding from this further point, in the light of his own ἔσχατον. In the Bible the creation story is already—and it is this that finally distinguishes the biblical from similar non-biblical texts—something more than a creation story, a cosmogony and anthropogony. It is this as well. But at the same time it is the promise of revelation and reconciliation, the designation and characterisation of the world as a " good " world, i.e., a world determined and adapted as the theatre of revelation. But this means that it really makes clear in advance in all its characteristics the fact that in this good realm, i.e., this realm determined and adapted for it, God's revelation will again be something particular, that it will be free grace, that it will be called Jesus Christ. And in this very way it is true and genuine creation history and reliable cosmogony and anthropogony, and it says the last and proper thing which is to be said about man in the cosmos as such.

And now in conclusion let us address the same question : To what does it point ? to the well-known New Testament passages to which we have already made several incidental allusions, and to which appeal is commonly made for confirmation of a biblical foundation for natural theology. We will begin with Rom. 1[18ff.] (for the exposition of which cf. also *Church Dogmatics*, I, 2, pp. 304 ff.). The passage is the formulation of an accusation. God's wrath is revealed from heaven upon the men who seize and hold down the truth in unrighteousness. From the continuation (1[22f.]), and the clear companion passage (2[1f.]), we gather that it is the heathen who are thought of in these men (Paul says : the Greeks). There is no doubt that his reference here is to man in the cosmos. And of this man he says straight out that God is knowable to him (literally, God is revealed to him in His knowability) ; God reveals Himself to him. For He, the invisible (literally, His invisibility), i.e., His eternal power and Godhead, is, from the creation of the world, clearly seen in His works, so that men are without excuse, because, having the knowledge of God, they still did not render Him honour and thanks as God. It is unquestionable that knowledge of God is here ascribed to man in the cosmos, and knowability is ascribed to God. If Rom. 1[18-21] existed for us on its own, perhaps in the form of a fragment, as the work of a known or unknown secular author (one of the Stoics, say) of the age— and the possibility of an isolated consideration of this kind has been far too often presupposed in the exposition of this passage—we should hardly have any other choice than to acknowledge that it says that man in the cosmos in himself and as such is an independent witness of the truth of God. But as a matter of plain fact, it stands in a quite definite context in Paul's Epistle to the Romans. In this context it does not say this, and what is more, it cannot say it. From the immediate context of the passage it follows at once that in Romans 1[18ff.] Paul is not speaking of the heathen in themselves and in general, just as later in Rom 2[1ff.] he is not speaking of the Jews in themselves and in general. He is not, then, speaking of man in the cosmos in himself and in general. The Jews and the heathen of whom he speaks are very definitely characterised as Jews and heathen objectively confronted with the divine ἀποκάλυψις in the Gospel (1[15-16]). The theme of the epistle as a whole is the representation of this ἀποκάλυψις as the ἀποκάλυψις τῆς δικαιοσύνης τοῦ θεοῦ (1[17] ; 3[21]). There can be no doubt that Paul meant by this the revelation of the grace of God in Jesus Christ. But this revelation of the righteousness of God has for him first of all a shadow side, on which it is the revelation of the ὀργή, the wrath of God. It is of this shadow side that he speaks in the first part of the epistle (1[18]-3[20]). The nerve of the statements in this first part is evident in the sentence in 3[9] (cf. also 2[9] ; 2[12] ; 3[23]) : Jews and heathen all stand in a collective solidarity under sin. What is the starting-point for this statement ? In the end, the question of the correct exposition of Romans 1[18ff.], along with many other questions, is decided by the answer to this question. Does Paul actually stand in this first chapter within the development of the theme announced in 1[17] ? Or is everything in this chapter to be understood as a great excursus whose content is acquired from elsewhere than the Gospel (1[16]) ? Is God's revelation of wrath, during the exposition of which Paul formulates this general accusation, and therefore in particular the accusation against the heathen, actually only the shadow side of His revelation of righteousness ? Or is he thinking of a very different revelation independent of it ? Does he speak in this chapter too as the apostle of Jesus Christ, or does he, between 1[18] and 3[20], speak anthropologically, as a religious and historical philosopher ? Does his knowledge of the judgment under which the Jews stand alongside the heathen, the heathen alongside the Jews, come from the fact that he sees it in the light of the cross and resurrection of Jesus Christ ? Or does he arrive at it on the basis of religio-ethical observations and principles acquired independently of what happened in Christ ? Our presupposition is that at any rate in respect of the Jews, in respect of the killing work of the Law, he does not come to his knowledge from a particular experience with the Law as such preceding his conversion and vocation, but on the basis of the conversion in which he was called to the obedience of faith in Jesus Christ and to be its apostle, and in which also the fulfilling of the Law in Jesus Christ, and therefore also the impossibility of any fulfilling of the Law by himself, was revealed. If this presupposition is valid ; if the statements of Rom. 7 and 8 form a unity which is not to be severed either biographically or factually ; if the assertion of Rom. 3[20], that the knowledge of sin came by the Law, is the meaningful statement of a Christian apostle ; if the whole Pauline doctrine of the Law and therefore also the application of that doctrine in Rom. 2 and 3 is to be understood as an integrating component of the evangelical *kerygma* of Paul, then, in face of the literary inseparability of Rom. 1 and 2, the same must also be said of the accusation of Rom. 1[18ff.], as directed against the heathen in particular. We may observe how expressly Paul continually names together Jews and heathen and brings them under a common denominator in good and in evil (1[16] ; 2[9ff.] ; 3[9]). We have seen in another connexion how improbable it is in the light of 1 Cor. 1 and 2 that Paul should address the Church in Rome from the point of view of another knowledge than his knowledge as a Christian apostle. But even in the context of Rom. 1 itself it is incomprehensible how, from v. 18 onwards, Paul can commence an excursus dependent on so vastly different a knowledge. And if he does not, then the passage 1[18ff.], which is of course decisive in the context of Rom. 1, must also be understood as an integral component of his evangelical *kerygma*. This *kerygma* has in fact—for its object is Jesus Christ both crucified and risen, and faith in it is both death and life— a shadow side. If this is not known its light side is quite unintelligible. The declaration of this side (which is the theme of Rom. 1–3) is therefore the necessary starting-point for the great exposition intended in the epistle. But the evangelical *kerygma* is, for all who hear it, the proclamation of revelation, the proclamation of something new. This is true not only on its light side, but just as certainly on its shadow side as well. For the Jews, the newness consists in the fact that their possession of the Law does not, as they imagine, justify them, but condemns them, because it demands of them the very thing which, in rejecting Jesus Christ, they have refused. They are lost if they do not—in faith in this Jesus Christ whom they have crucified but whom God has raised from the dead—look upon themselves as the transgressors they have shown themselves to be. The Jew confronted with Jesus Christ is objectively found guilty of the transgression of his own Law ; he has no more excuse (2[1]) ; his alleged keeping of the Law is shown on Golgotha to be its complete violation. Without respect of persons (2[11]), God will judge him also and especially (2[8f.]), and from this judgment he will in no way be able to escape (2[3f.]). The only possibility of salvation remaining to him is the other side of the same *kerygma* that is so threatening to him : the righteousness of faith which is also revealed in Jesus Christ ; the keeping of the Law in the grateful acknowledgment of its fulfilment by the Messiah alone, rejected by them but established by God as the Messiah. But this newness is true for the Greeks in another way. In the light of the death and resurrection of Jesus Christ there are no longer guilty heathen—guilty because they are heathen, because they do not know the Law of Israel. If the Law of Israel cannot justify the Jews, if by the Law itself—namely, by the Law fulfilled in Jesus Christ— they are, on the contrary, unmasked as its transgressors, why should the heathen be guilty because they are heathen and do not know the Law ? " For as many as have sinned without law shall also perish without law : and as many as have sinned in the law shall be judged by the law " (2[12]). For the Greeks as well there is an unmasking (spoken of in 1[18-21]). From this same Golgotha where it is revealed that the Jews have never kept their own Law, it becomes clear that the heathen also have always sinned no less responsibly against God. They have sinned against the truth which they too knew so well. God was revealed to them from the very first. The world which always surrounded them was always His creation and spoke of His great works and therefore of Himself. Judged objectively, even when they also denied and betrayed the truth, they always stood in a positive relationship to it. For this reason they, too, are guilty (1[20]). Against them, too, accusation may be brought with complete justice. Upon them, too, the wrath of God does not come as a blind fate. They, too, must acknowledge that it comes upon them justly. They must acknowledge it as the judgment of God ($\delta\iota\kappa\alpha\acute{\iota}\omega\mu\alpha$ $\tau o\hat{\upsilon}$ $\theta\epsilon o\hat{\upsilon}$) that they who do such things—namely, such things as manifestly and consistently result from their suppression of the truth—are worthy of death (1[32]). Let us observe carefully that all this is not, so to speak, catechised out of the heathen as the content of a knowledge which they apply to the Gospel, as the content of a reflection which they had already advanced or could advance for themselves. It is all just as new for them as the judgment that the Jews never kept the Law but have always broken it is quite new to the Jews. That is, it is the truth of revelation proclaimed by the apostle of Jesus Christ. It is all ascribed, reckoned, and imputed to the heathen as the truth about themselves in consequence of the fact that in and with the truth of God in Jesus Christ the truth of man has been revealed. It is not, therefore, timeless, general, abstract truth. It is not the structure of an anthropology or philosophy of religion or apologetic. It cannot be separated even for a moment from the apostolic *kerygma*. On the contrary, it is all the shadow side, the judgment side, of the Gospel declared to the heathen. It is all the objective judgment upon men which is grounded only in the fact that the Jesus Christ who was rejected and crucified by the Jews and rose again on the third day has, in and with the truth of God, also brought to light the truth of man, namely, that he is directed towards God. In His light, light is seen in the midst of darkness. For light in darkness means no less, but also no more, than what Paul saw and said according to this whole context : the heathen can justify themselves before the judgment of God as little as the Jews ; the righteousness of faith which appeared in Jesus Christ is for them, too, the only salvation. And this light, too, is as such only seen and to be seen in His light, from Golgotha, just as also the lostness and transgression of Israel is only to be seen from there. It is impossible to draw from the text a statement (which can then be advanced as timeless, general and abstract truth) concerning a natural union with God or knowledge of God on the part of man in himself and as such. In the rest of this Epistle and in the other Pauline Epistles we find nothing to suggest that he took such a truth into account. He does not describe man in the cosmos as a willing but as an unwilling witness of revelation. He surpasses and transcends him in the same way as man had already been permanently surpassed and transcended in the creation narrative. Of course, for this reason he takes him really seriously ; he addresses him in the most concrete manner. But here, too, the seriousness and the concreteness lie in the fact that God's revelation is read into man in the cosmos with all the sovereignty of the prophetic-apostolic authority. We can certainly call what Paul does a " making contact." But if we do, we must take into account that the " point of contact " is not regarded as already present on man's side but as newly instituted in and with the proclamation of the Gospel. The speech on Areopagus in Ac. 17 points still more sharply and succinctly in the same direction. We have already referred to the situation at the end of the chapter. When Paul declared the Word of resurrection, everything immediately became clear and mockery and boredom was the answer of the Athenian philosophers. But when he turned his back on them a few others joined him. We must now take note of the introductory situation in v. 16 f. On Paul's part there is " indignation in the spirit " at the abundance of idols to be seen in Athens. From the philosophers comes the question : " What will this babbler say ? ", or : " He seemeth to be a setter forth of strange gods: because he preached unto them Jesus and the resurrection " (v. 18). They would like to hear this $\kappa\alpha\iota\nu\grave{\eta}$ $\delta\iota\delta\alpha\chi\acute{\eta}$: " For thou bringest certain strange things to our ears " (v. 19 f.). And Luke adds in explanation that the Athenians loved nothing so much as to tell, or to hear something new (v. 21). The sermon on Mars Hill lies between this introduction and the epilogue. Is it really possible to maintain that, in distinction to what Paul had to say elsewhere to Jews and heathen, it consisted 'for the greater and decisive part in a declaration that without and before God's revelation in Jesus Christ men already stood in a relationship to God, and that in the proclamation of the Gospel they were to be addressed on this basis as a possession in which they had at least the possibility of becoming, independently and of themselves, witnesses to the truth of the Gospel ? If the author of Acts understood the sermon in this sense, it is obviously very strange that, at the end of the story, the stoic and epicurean philosophers addressed on this possibility are not seen in the kind of light the sermon itself would lead us to expect according to this understanding. Paul has addressed them on a possibility which on this occasion, at any rate, obviously does not become an actuality. The story should not have ended in this way if this was the meaning of the sermon ; for this story, at any rate, does not bear witness to a natural addressibility of man for the Gospel. Surely Luke ought to have seen this ? Surely he ought to have seen it on this second occasion ? For a similar question arises in relation to the short speech at Lystra (Ac. 14¹⁵⁻¹⁷). And there, too, the supposed attempt at contact ends in an open failure. Perhaps we can explain it as a literary blemish which Luke has repeated. But if not, neither speech can have had this superficial meaning as Luke himself saw them. On the contrary, what appears a failure of the Pauline missionary preaching is for him the normal crisis upon man brought about by the Word. At the back of his mind in both these accounts is the saying in 1 Cor. 1²³ : that the crucified Christ is a scandal to the Jews and foolishness to the heathen. And he cannot have understood the Pauline sermons to the heathen as attempts to circumvent this state of affairs. As he sees it, Paul proclaims on the Areopagus the crucified Christ in what is basically the same manner as he proclaimed Him always and everywhere. One thing at least is clear : the sermon on Mars Hill (vv. 22–31) contradicts the opinion that in the apostolic Gospel we are perhaps concerned with a ξενίζοντα, with a καινὴ διδαχή, with one of the many spiritual novelties which capture the world's interest just because they are novelties. This Gospel does not belong to this category. It is the utterly and really strange and new thing because it does not belong to this category. From it we can see, and see through, this category —the category of the spiritual novelties of man mutually concurring and surpassing one another—as something which has been wholly and utterly surpassed, as the category of one long and guilty and as such empty misunderstanding. This is what the sermon says. It is not an attempt to understand the world of the Athenian philosophers from their own viewpoint and to overcome it from within. It is the announcement of the judgment which comes upon this world from without— certainly upon *this* world, but upon this world *from without*. So superstitious is this Athens—thus Paul begins—that among its other shrines (σεβάσματα) one finally comes upon an altar " to the unknown God " ! When Paul in v. 23b says : " Whom therefore ye ignorantly worship, him declare I unto you," he does not describe either the Athenian cultus as a whole nor this cult of the unknown God in particular as a point of contact, as the door to freedom standing, to a certain extent, open to them : he says, indeed, ἀγνοοῦντες εὐσεβεῖτε. The altar itself merely confirms that they have no such door into freedom. If they had really known this unknown God, they would not have erected a special altar to Him in distinction to their relationship to other deities whom they also worship. He is indeed—they do not know this, and Paul tells it to them—the Lord who has formed the heavens and the earth and all that is therein, who as the Lord of the heavens and the earth dwells not in temples made with hands, and who is not served by men's hands as though He needed anything. The very fact that this altar stands beside all their other altars means that even in this their apparently highest and best possibility they are not the willing but the unwilling witnesses to this God. All along the line they can bear witness only to the fact, and they can do so only in objectivity, that they need that the true God should be preached to them. Their addressibility consists very simply in the fact that, obviously walking round in a circle from one supposed novelty to another, in ever new " piety," in continual ignorance, they are those who have turned aside from the truth, to whom it is therefore indispensable that the truth should be preached. God is the One who Himself needs nothing, who as the Lord of the world and history has given and daily gives all things to all men, who is not far from everyone of us—" in him we live, and move, and have our being " (as one of their own poets has said in unconscious piety : " We are his offspring ") ; but they themselves and of themselves bear witness to this truth of God in such a way that they treat of God as if He could be equated with χάραγμα τέχνης καὶ ἐνθυμήσεως ἀνθρώπου, as if He belonged to this cosmos, as if He could therefore be sought and felt after and found like one novelty with others. It is on this ignorance of theirs in regard to God, which betrays itself even in their best possibilities but of which they as such are quite insensible, that Paul addresses these Athenians. From within there was absolutely nothing to understand and overcome. Arguing from within, understanding and confirming their own possibilities, leading them further within their own possibilities to a limit visible from within themselves, the most that Paul could have done would be to get them to put up another altar, to treat God like another χάραγμα. But he does not argue from within. He argues against them strictly from outside. Against their whole desire for seeking, feeling after and finding God—summarised as " the times of ignorance"—he opposes the grace of God, in which God has declared the times of ignorance to be " overlooked," i.e., past. The desire to seek, feel after and find God is past. The stoic and epicurean philosophies and all other philosophies are at an end. The whole inclusion of God in the cosmos, with all the novelties which may arise from this undertaking, is now quite obsolete and has, as such, become impossible. They can witness to it objectively only in its obsoleteness and impossibility. And in this way they are objectively unwilling witnesses to the truth of the Gospel. For the Gospel is that God now—how and from what source can the Athenians know this already or have even a possibility of knowing it from their own world ?—commands all men (we can fill this out to include both Jews and heathen, as in Rom. 1-2) to repent, namely, because He has appointed the day of righteous judgment upon the whole world in the man whom He has ordained and whom He has sealed by raising Him from the dead. Here absolutely everything that Paul has to say to the Athenians is plainly focused upon them and applied to them as the knowledge of a Christian apostle concerning them. If one of them now knows about the God proclaimed to them by Paul, it is definitely not in confirmation of what he knew before, perhaps as a member of the sect that worshipped the unknown God, or as a reader of Aratus. It is in a quite new knowledge of his previous complete ignorance. It is as he is discovered and convicted in the guiltiness of all his strivings after a god who could not be God as the object of these strivings. It is in repentance before the Judge of his whole spiritual world. It is in faith in Jesus Christ, in whom the new world-time of the knowledge of the true God—namely, of the gracious Creator and Lord of the world—has broken in. The fact that there are actually only a few who now know about this God and therefore give another answer to Paul's sermon than mockery or boredom is in fact understandable as the normal course of the crisis caused by the Word of God. The man in the cosmos who emerges in Acts as a witness of the Gospel is, as in Rom. 1, and as in the Old Testament texts previously adduced, the man who is seen at the outset in the light of Jesus Christ, the man who at the outset and fundamentally is surpassed and transcended in his self-understanding.

In all these deliberations and investigations our aim has been to clarify the material order in which in the Bible reference is made to man along this " side line " as the witness of the great acts of God in His revelation. What we have learned is that the statements under

discussion can no more be severed materially than they can formally
from the statements of the " main line." In them we are not referred
to anything other than God's revelation of grace, and the content of
the Bible is not, therefore, a twofold but a unitary witness. On the
side line too, from the starting-point of revelation, we are pointed to
revelation for the sake of revelation and in agreement with revelation.

A final illustration of this material order in regard to man in the cosmos is to
be found in the vision of the four living creatures (*chajat*) with the face of a man,
of a lion, of an ox and of an eagle. The vision occurs first in Ezek. 1^{4-28}, 10^{8-17},
11^{22}, and is distinctively repeated in Rev. 4. As described in their astonishing
central position between angel, man and beast (individually they are certainly
symbols of the four quarters of the heavens, the four seasons of the year or the
four respective groups of the zodiac), both in Ezekiel and Revelation they undoubtedly represent the divine creation as such. In all its movement this is
unequivocally set in only one direction—" they went everyone straight forward "
(Ezek. 1^9). In Ezekiel it is distinguished from the course of the world, which is
no less remarkably depicted in the form of the four wheels. But at the same time
it is co-ordinated with it. For " whithersoever the spirit was to go, they went,
thither was their spirit to go ; and the wheels were lifted up over against them :
for the spirit of the living creature was in the wheels. When those went, these
went ; and when those stood, these stood ; and when those were lifted up from
the earth, the wheels were lifted up over against them : for the spirit of the living
creature was in the wheels " (1^{20-21}, 10^{16-17}). *Ideo quoties nos sollicitant res confusae
ad desperationem, veniat nobis in memoriam haec sententia, nempe spiritum ani-
malium esse in rotis. Et certe quando subinde trepidamus in rebus dubiis: quid
fieret, nisi acquiescamus in hac doctrina?* (Calvin: *Comm. on* Ezek. 1^{21}. C.R.
40. 48.) The fact that the Spirit of these living creatures rules the wheels, and
thus the course of the world, is comforting, however, because these living creatures
themselves and therefore the work of the divine creation as such, whether its
wings are in movement or at rest, stand under a bright firmament (*rakia* : a
cover ?) resembling a sapphire stone, with the likeness of a throne upon it,
" and upon the likeness of the throne was the likeness as the appearance of a man
above upon it . . . and it had brightness round about. As the appearance of the
bow that is in the cloud in the day of rain, so was the appearance of the brightness
round about. This was the appearance of the likeness of the glory of the Lord "
(1^{26-28}). Is it legitimate, indeed is it not obligatory, to emphasise the fact that this
is all given, not as a direct view of the world and its course, but in form and content
as the object of a prophetic vision, which as such is not to be separated from the
other themes of the prophetic message ? Moreover, is it legitimate, indeed is it not
obligatory, to assume that it is from that form in the heavens that the living
creatures have their Spirit who operates again in the wheels ? Moreover, is it
legitimate, indeed is it not obligatory, in respect of the brightness of this form
which resembles the rainbow, to think of Gen. $9^{12f.}$, where the rainbow is described
as the sign of the covenant between God and all living things, of the covenant with
Noah which then becomes the presupposition of the covenant of Sinai and Golgotha ? And finally, is it legitimate, indeed is it not obligatory, to accept the interpretation of Calvin (*ibid.* 40^{56}), that this human form, which undoubtedly occupies
the place of God Himself, is the *tota Deitas manifestata in carne*, i.e., Jesus Christ ?
In the parallel passage in the New Testament (Rev. 4) it is noticeable that no express use is made of this part of the Ezekiel text, nor is there any mention of the
four wheels alongside the four living creatures. For.this reason the vision becomes
more comprehensible in other respects. There is a door in heaven which the seer
sees opened ; he is invited to come " up hither," and a voice explains : " I will
shew thee things which must be hereafter " (v. 1). In this way the eschatological

character of the vision now described is obviously more unequivocally emphasised. And then the four living creatures appear within a definite order arranged round the throne of the glory of God, and within this order they have a quite definite function. They stand as the innermost circle next to the throne, which here, too, is surrounded by a rainbow (v. 3). They are separated from it only by the glassy sea which seems to have replaced the firmament of Ezekiel ; they are then (as by a second circle) surrounded in their turn by the seven Spirits of God which are called lamps of fire (in the Apocalypse the seven Spirits have the same significance as the one Holy Spirit in the rest of the New Testament) ; while around these in their turn (as the third and outermost circle) the four and twenty elders have their place on four and twenty thrones, and adorned with golden crowns—obviously the heavenly representatives of the Church. We may ask whether the arrangement—naturally regarded from the throne of God which constitutes the centre and overshadows everything else—is not thought of in terms of an amphitheatre, so that the four living creatures form the innermost but at the same time the lowest circle, enlightened by the seven Spirits who occupy the middle position between them and the elders. Certainly attention must be paid to this mediating role of the Spirit when in relation to the function of the four living creatures we are told that " they rest not day and night, saying, Holy, holy, holy, Lord God Almighty, which was, and is, and is to come " (v. 8). We must consider the implications of the *Sanctus* in Isaiah 6³, which is trinitarian and at the same time reflects the economy of salvation. The fact that God is God in the three times of expectation, presence and recollection now emerges—and obviously in the mouth of the creation—as the actual predicate of the almighty God. The creation itself knows and proclaims this very God. And as response to this praise of God it then comes about that in the third and outmost circle the four and twenty elders rise from their thrones, throw themselves down, lay their crowns before the throne of God and for their part raise a hymn of praise to the Creator : " Thou art worthy, O Lord, to receive glory and honour and power : for thou hast created all things and for thy pleasure they are and were created " (vv. 9–11). In distinction to the uninterrupted song of praise of creation, this is obviously a single and, as it were, historical event. In the point on which everything depends, Rev. 4 and Ezek. 1 and 10 correspond exactly. As the four living creatures in Ezekiel are the bearers of the throne of man surrounded by the glory of God, so in Revelation they sing the praise of the triune God (for it is obviously He who sits on the throne) and consequently it is this God who is praised (by the Church) as the Creator. Thus the two accounts illustrate the fact that even if the Bible assumes the witness of man in the cosmos into its own witness, it does not allow its own witness to cease, or to be replaced by another, but includes this other in its own witness, so that on this line too, from the starting-point of revelation, we are actually pointed to revelation for the sake of revelation and in agreement with revelation.

We may conclude, therefore, that Holy Scripture neither imposes the necessity nor even offers the possibility of reckoning with a knowability of the God of the prophets and apostles which is not given in and with His revelation, or bound to it ; and therefore to that extent with a " Christian " natural theology. Holy Scripture does not present us with " another " task of theology, nor are we allowed to impose it upon ourselves. Holy Scripture neither urges nor even authorises us to look around for a readiness of God for man which is different from His readiness in the grace of His Word and Spirit. And in the present context this means that even this third explanation of the actual vitality of natural theology is not sufficient. If it were sufficient—and we have acknowledged this already—it would be quite important enough of itself to justify natural theology. We should then have to reconsider what was said on the first two points and form another and better judgment in relation to them ; finding some way of bringing them into line with the fact that Scripture itself had now shed a new light on the whole problem. But it is from Scripture that we now hear the very definite command not to ask about another knowability of God than the one bestowed upon us in the grace of His revelation. This means that the earlier considerations which led us to what is substantially the same result are now shewn to be in conformity with Scripture.

4. It remains only to ask in conclusion whether perhaps another, fourth answer to our question is possible and will prove acceptable. After all that has gone before, we may perhaps be discouraged, and simply tolerate the fact that the vitality of natural theology is obviously an unexplained phenomenon of Church history, and that without examining it from within we must be content simply to know the reason why it must be judged negatively, and why, therefore, it must be left alone. But we cannot take up this attitude because the question is far too serious, and it is always far too demanding in practice, for us to be able to leave it behind unanswered. Even if we can pass this negative judgment and obediently take the corresponding decision, we still have to know what we are doing and not doing. Otherwise obedience is not true obedience, and we run the continual danger of falling unawares into disobedience again. Unless we are able to account for the real possibility of the origin and existence of natural theology in the sphere of the Church, and for the real possibility of the seemingly irrepressible desire and call for it, we are not free from it and we simply do not know what it means to be really free from it. And in spite of the unsatisfactory results of our previous deliberations, it is not really impossible to account for it along a path that we have not so far trodden.

We started out from the proposition that apparently nothing is more simple and self-evident than the knowledge that we find God's knowability only in the readiness of God Himself, that we can accept it gratefully only out of the free grace and mercy of His revelation as the inaccessible made accessible to us, and therefore that a theology which seeks another knowability of God is incontestably impossible in the sphere of the Church ; incontestably, because from the very outset a theology of this kind looks in another direction than where God has placed Himself, and therefore involves, from the very outset, a violation of the Christian concept of God. Why, then, is all this not so simple and self-evident ? Why, then, in spite of all the refutations like those we have just made, can a theology of this kind continually arise, announcing itself anew in ever new forms (as if nothing had been said against it and as if it had not been refuted), creeping into theological ventures which have quite different intentions, and like a rank weed clinging even to what is apparently the soundest stalk, weakening it and finally killing it ? It cannot be disputed—and there is no sense in shutting our eyes to the fact—that it actually can do this. And it can do it to a degree that we cannot rate too highly, and with a weight which, once released, will generally sweep away all opposing considerations and even the most careful and complete refutations.

We have only to recall the historical facts. Even in the early post-apostolic Church, the Church of the martyrs, it was supposed to be an indispensable instrument in the literary warfare against heathendom. In this way it was able to become at once a secondary, self-evident classicising support for Christian theology. The same was true in the case of Augustine. In spite of his truly consistent development of the soteriological principle of grace, it could commend itself to him in the form of the platonic idea of God as the scientific foundation of his ecclesiastical and Christian thinking. The same was true in mediaeval theology. Not without a connexion with the new external order of the relationship between Church and Empire initiated by Constantine, it was able, after the rediscovery of Aristotle, to acquire over this theology the power which is finally revealed in the formulae of the *Vaticanum* (which canonises the supreme achievement of Thomas Aquinas). Perhaps its masterpiece to date is that it was able to keep itself hidden or to represent itself as something harmless under what were usually the very sharp eyes of the Reformers. The Reformers witnessed a new confession, even excelling Augustinianism, to free grace according to the soteriological material side of this concept. And positively, with their re-establishment of the Scripture principle, they witnessed a new confession to the unity of the revelation of God in Jesus Christ. But unhappily on the negative side they did not attain with the same clarity to a fundamental excision of the question concerning another revelation and knowledge of God. For this reason, uncertainties and even, it cannot be denied, inconsistencies became possible even with them. Contemporaneously with the Reformation, in the so-called humanism which consisted in a rediscovery of the Stoicism of the Silver Age of Rome, natural theology was able to attain new forms and find new points of entry which were soon revealed in the teaching of the 16th century enthusiasts both inside and outside the Church. It could again recommend itself to a martyr Church—this time the French—in such a way that, in contradiction to Calvin's proposal, the mischief could be done which may now be read in article 2 of the *Confessio Gallicana*, from which it quickly spread to the *Confessio Belgica* (art. 2–3). And once the Reformers were dead (in a century which in other respects is certainly to be reckoned in the " heroic " age of Protestantism), it could impress itself on their disciples as the indispensable prolegomena of theology, a part of the same development by which the Evangelical Churches allowed themselves, almost without thinking, to be steered into a new position as State Churches far surpassing anything ever seen before. Then in the 18th century it was able publicly to enter on the overlordship which for a long time it had already exercised in secret. In connexion with the revolutions in world outlook it was able to assume for the scientific as well as the popular consciousness of the new age the appearance of being the real basic dogma and central doctrine of Christianity which can be affirmed free of doubt in every storm and stress. And so far there has not been a single attempt at renewal in Evangelical theology to which openly or secretly, from near or from far, it has not clung with its octopus-like arm, compromising any genuine renewal and sooner or later ruining the attempt. All refutations apart, natural theology can do so much that we must seriously ask whether there is not good reason to represent the history of Christian theology and of the Church in general as one long history of the relationship of reason and revelation, of philosophy and theology, and this means as one long history of " Christian " natural theology. Certainly this is a poor, tedious and ultimately fruitless and false conception. But we can understand those who do not see how to evade it and understand the theme of Church history as a theme that is to be posed and treated independently. What natural theology has been able to do is not a little thing. It has been able apparently to control the whole picture of Church history. And we must be very clear about the reason why this is so if we are not to be forced to concede that it actually has controlled it, and to weary of the contest against this Hydra even when we have recognised it as such. In defence of a Christian natural theology there is no reason to treat only as a last resort the appeal to the *consensus ecclesiae*, to the more or less solid occurrence of this phenomenon in every period and place, as compared with which any radical attack upon it may be suspected as an unheard-of innovation. The only question is to what *consensus ecclesiae* we are referring, and this is the question which we shall now consider.

2. THE READINESS OF MAN

Our fourth investigation into the question of the vitality of natural theology belongs to an independent sphere ; namely, to the sphere of the second theme of our section. It is part of the investigation into the question of the knowability of God which we now have to understand as the readiness of man. We are already agreed on the point that there can be no knowability of God if it is not also to be understood as a readiness of man. This cannot be an independent readiness. It cannot have its final basis in itself (i.e., in the nature and activity of man). It cannot in any sense delimit the readiness of God. There does not exist a relationship of mutual conditionedness between it and the readiness of God. But this does not mean that it is to be denied. " God is knowable " means : " God can be known." In the first part of this section we have understood this ability to consist not only first and decisively, but solely, in the readiness of God, i.e., in the knowability of God bestowed upon us in the grace and mercy of His revelation. But in this readiness of God, which alone comes under consideration in this connexion, the readiness of man is enclosed. With and in the fact that God is ready within Himself to be known by man, man is also ready to know Him. There is no presumption in affirming this. It would be rebellion to deny it. Man's readiness to know God is encompassed and established, delimited and determined by the readiness of God ; it is not independent but mediated ; subsequent to the readiness of God ; called by it out of nothingness into being, out of death into life ; utterly dependent of and by itself upon the knowability of God, but in this complete dependence real in the way in which creation generally can only be in its relationship to the Creator. And it is obviously in the sphere of the problem which this poses that our reflections on the phenomenon of " natural theology " must arrive at their goal. In its own way all natural theology circles about the problem of the readiness of man to know God. It does so in its own way, i.e., by elevating the readiness of man into an independent factor, so that the readiness of God is not understood as the only one which comes under consideration, nor is the readiness of man regarded as included within it, and completely dependent upon it. It handles the problem in such a way that alongside the knowability of God in His revelation it affirms a second grounded in another way. It speaks of " another " task of theology besides that of explaining the revelation of God. We have to reject this treatment of the problem. But the problem itself we cannot reject. If God is knowable, then it is necessary also to ask how far He is knowable to man. If this question is to receive the right answer, in and with this right answer the fact must become plain which cannot become plain to us from the achievements and pedagogic usefulness and biblical foundation of natural theology, i.e., the possibility of the origin and existence, and along with it the secret of the vitality, of the wrong answer given by natural theology. And only then will the possibility and importance of our rejection of this wrong answer become plain to us in the depth in which alone it can be meaningful and well founded as a rejection.

It seems at first relatively simple to classify what must always belong to the readiness of man as it is included in the readiness of God. As we have seen, the readiness of God is God's grace. Hence the readiness of man must obviously be his readiness for grace. What does this mean ? Obviously his receptivity, his openness for grace ; but that means his openness for the majestic, the free, the undeserved, the unexpected, the new openness of God for man established entirely in God's own authority. We may also say his openness for the miracle that God is not only in Himself the Lord, the Creator, the Reconciler and Redeemer, and not only open to Himself as the Father, the Son and the Holy Spirit, but that He is all this for men also. Without more ado it is evident that if this openness does not exist, then there is no knowability of the God who is knowable to us in His grace. As a further description of this openness we can now make a threefold distinction. We begin with the need of man for this miracle of grace. He cannot dispense with this miracle. And God will not become knowable to him otherwise than in this miracle. His situation is objectively such that he has need of God's grace, and that he is dependent upon God's grace as grace. He cannot exist just as well without knowing God. And he cannot know Him just as well without His grace. Grace is necessary to him in this twofold sense. Secondly, there belongs to this openness a definite knowledge : first the knowledge of his need in the twofold sense just described ; and then the knowledge that God's grace is objectively real. The one is not to be known without the other. Where the need is not evident the grace of God will not be evident either. And without seeing the grace of God no one can see his own need. And thirdly, there belongs to

5

this openness the subjective willingness of man to accept God's grace for his need ; the willingness to let the divine encroachment overcome him as the answer to his own deprivation of God, to his own inaptitude to know Him ; the willingness, therefore, not to evade the miracle of grace but resolutely to accept it. So far everything is tolerably clear and obvious ; the readiness of man to know God consists—and this in such a way that all three cohere and mutually condition one another—in his need for grace, in his knowledge of grace and in his willingness for it. How can there be a knowability of God for men (if the knowability of God is His grace) without the fulfilment of this one and threefold presupposition ?

All this is correct—only too correct ! For in face of the undeniable actuality and completeness with which we can make such statements it is easy to overlook the fact that in everything that is so properly and necessarily to be said on this level absolutely nothing is said about the real readiness of man to know God. Naturally, it is very true that where God is knowable, and therefore where, included in His own readiness, the corresponding readiness of man also exists, there necessarily exists too, as, so to speak, the *conditio sine qua non*, the openness that we have described. But this openness in itself and as such is still not that readiness. Taken simply as it stands, and therefore as it is described as the openness of man, it may equally well be accompanied by man's complete closedness against the readiness of God. Indeed, we must say straight out that simply as such, simply as the openness of man, it is in fact always accompanied by this complete closedness. The deepest and most real need of man for the miracle of grace does not lie in the fact that he needs it objectively, and that he has objective need that it should come to him as grace, but in the fact that he is in a position to cover up and hide from himself this need of his ; to be to himself, and—even if illusorily— to God also, not this needy man, but a rich man who can live without God's grace and who can even allot it to himself. But he is not in this position only accidentally and transitorily, but permanently, because originally. As a natural man he always and everywhere makes use of this possibility. In his objective misery he plays the rich man always and everywhere. But engaged in this game he is necessarily closed against God. And the knowledge of his need and the knowledge of the grace of God will not in itself and as such lead him further. Certainly, in the light of his need, he can become sensible of the truth of grace, and in the light of the grace of God of his own neediness. But we must not forget that in itself and as such the knowledge of man is a knowledge which is not strong but very weak, not to salvation but to condemnation. It is the knowledge of good and evil, with the possession of which man wished to become like God only in this way to fall into misery and to become alien to the grace of God. Under these circumstances what can and will it mean if man knows

his need and God's grace ? Under these circumstances will he really
know his real need satisfied ? Will not the need which he knows be
an abstract misery which has nothing to do with his true standing
before God, which may perhaps hurt him but which can as such
degenerate quickly enough into its opposite, namely into the ecstasy
of the Pharisee pretending to be a publican, of the beggar feeling he
is a king ? And under these circumstances will he really know God's
grace satisfying his need ? Will not the grace known by him be an
abstract law which casts him down to the ground by its sublimity
and severity, only to leave him to dream again that he can perhaps
fulfil it ? In spite and on account of his knowledge he will in this
way be closed against the readiness of God afterwards as well as before.
And however great his willingness, he will not be able to break through
this closedness. For what can even his greatest willingness mean in
itself and as such but his readiness to surrender himself in the usual
way to the dialectic of need and grace which he himself knows. The
willingness of his own will cannot burst the fatal cycle of this dialectic. He will certainly be willing to live as a needy man. Yet
even in his greatest neediness he will not be able to help feeling
and behaving at some point as the rich man who knows very well
how to come to terms with his need and therefore knows very well
how to live otherwise than as a real pauper. And he will certainly be
willing to live by God's grace ; but in fact he will not do this with
complete willingness, because he can be occupied with God's grace
only in a form in which he either has to want it (when it will become
for him a law and cast him into despair), or can want it (when it will
become what he supposes to be his possession, which will necessarily
make him careless). Either way, in spite and on account of his willingness, he will remain closed to the readiness of God afterwards as well as
before. Therefore our analysis of the presentation of human openness
has brought us no nearer to the real readiness of man to know God.
However we may extend and deepen this analysis, we are driven to the
fact that the openness of man in itself and as such not only can mean,
but in fact and in practice does mean, his closedness for the readiness
of God, his own unreadiness, and therefore not the knowability
but the unknowability of God. In that which meets us on man's side
(even as included in the readiness on God's side) we shall necessarily
see only this closedness " in disobedience " (Rom. 11[32]).

Nor will it help us if we try to advance from the presupposed idea
to the idea of a real openness and therefore of a real need, knowledge
and willingness of man. This attempt can, of course, be made, and
it is rewarding to consider what form it necessarily takes. Namely, it
may be objected that in our deliberations hitherto we have not at all
taken into consideration the reality of the factors coming into consideration both on the side of man and on that of God. On the side
of man first : man lives an existence which is really guilty, which is a

real straining at his limits, and which ends very really with his death. He can really doubt the meaning of his existence. He can really fear. He can really despair. And at some level he is openly or secretly really aware of this position and can really be addressed on this basis. Therefore he is just as really in need of God's grace. The lie against this with which he tries to make light of his lost condition, the lie in which he plays the rich man, is not reality. We have to understand man better than he wants to understand himself : namely, as the man who is really entangled in guilt and really submerged in death ; as the man who in one way or another is really filled with fear and despair. And we cannot deprive this man as such of a real knowledge both of his need and also of God's grace, and finally of a real willingness for this grace. Considered in the reality of his existence—and what sense is there in considering it in any other way ?—he has already broken through his closedness against the readiness of God. He can no longer wish to be like God. He stands before Him as the publican and beggar that he really is in relation to him. In this his own reality, then, God is knowable to him. And, of course, we have to take account of the same reality also and especially on God's side. God has really revealed Himself to man, and in His revelation God's grace has really come to him. In consequence, we have not only the right but the duty to consider Him only in His reality as disclosed by the grace of revelation. In consequence, we have the right and the duty to make the presupposition that man can really believe in the fact that God's grace will come to help him in his wretchedness. Is not this a necessary presupposition of the proclamation of the Church in word and sacrament, and of the Word of God which establishes and upholds the Church ? Can we then deny to man, the man who believes in God's Word, a real knowledge of grace. Is not his closedness over against the readiness of God pierced from this side too, and his false likeness to God destroyed ? Does he not stand now before God in real openness, and therefore in real need, knowledge and willingness, in the way in which we have to stand before God if He is to be knowable to us as the gracious God ? We cannot simply contradict all this. On the contrary, we have to allow that it is good to realise what is involved in a real openness of man for God's knowability bestowed upon us in His grace. A real readiness on the side of man and real grace on the side of God will necessarily mean this. The attempt to advance above and beyond the idea of man open to God's grace to the idea of the reality of his openness points us to a *conditio sine qua non* (which we shall certainly have to consider further) of the readiness of man which is in question. Only in regard to the man who really needs grace and really longs for it because he is real man, and only in view of the real Word of God which therefore really brings and offers grace to him, can the question of this readiness of man arise. Any other readiness is not at all the readiness of man which is included in the readiness of God, and therefore genuine and powerful readiness. If even for a moment we try to think away the reality of need and help, we shall definitely be thinking of another readiness than this genuine and powerful one. Nevertheless, even when we think of the whole reality of this need and help, of the real revelation of the neediness of man's existence in the light of the real Word of the grace of God, we have not arrived at the real readiness of man for God. As such, even the object of this idea can still be man closed to the readiness of God, shut up under disobedience. Indeed, we must go further and say that in itself and as such the object of this idea can be nothing other than man closed to the readiness of God. For what does reality mean if and so long as we merely talk of man as such ? Even if he is man fathomed in his final perdition, even if he is man addressed by the preaching and sacraments of the Church and therefore finally by the Word of God itself, and therefore believing man, in himself and as such he is still man closed to the readiness of God. The reality in which man can be guilty and delimited and finally die and be lost ; the reality in which he can be in need of grace, and know grace and be willing for it ; but the reality, too, in which he can be a recipient of the grace of God in His Word, in which he can be a believer ; this reality in itself and as such is not in any sense the penetration of his closedness against God's readiness. If there is to be any serious question of a penetration of this kind, something quite different must come to this reality of his from without ; or rather, this reality of his must be rooted and grounded in Someone quite other outside himself ; so rooted and grounded that it lives entirely by Him, and derives its whole reality from Him. If we disregard this and understand it as his own inner reality, we have to say of it that in it this closedness is not destroyed by a long way, that, on the contrary, it is confirmed in it. The very existence of man considered in its reality, i.e., its reality as disclosed by the grace of God, shows us man in himself and as such not at peace but at war with grace. If it is otherwise, we are definitely not thinking only of this reality, of this reality in itself and as such. If we keep to it in itself and as such it shows us man all along the line as the one who not only can, but actually does, contradict grace. In the last resort, what difference does it make that he is ever so really entangled in guilt and sunk in death and filled with fear and despair ? And in the last resort, what difference does it make that he knows only too well in principle that this is the case ? Man can bear this, and what is more, he does bear it. Through it all, he can uphold and assert himself. In it all, and perhaps especially in it all, even in all his poverty he can still dream the dream of a rich life, i.e., of being sufficient to himself. And as far as the eye reaches, as far as we know ourselves and others, the only thing we see is that man actually does do this in one way or another. If we keep seriously to the reality, the shattering of man by the reality of his existence,

by his entanglement in guilt and death, is not actually so comprehensive and radical as we might think and as we are accustomed to
make it out to be.   He endures this reality far rather and far more
easily than the grace of God by which he might be expected finally
to let himself be carried instead of trying to bear his own life.   The
reality is that man does not want to be carried.   But this picture is
not altered when we consider him in the light of the Word of God.
On the contrary, in the light of the Word of God it simply emerges
in all its clarity and necessity.   Man can also bear it that God's grace
meets him as really as possible in the word and sacrament, even in
God's own revelation.   Man can also bear it that he really comes to
faith, and therefore to the knowledge of his need and to the knowledge of grace, and, above and beyond this, to willingness for it.   So
far as all this is still no more than his own reality, the light of divine
truth in the prism of his own existence, what this reality has to show
us will, as far as the eye can reach, be, not his peace with grace, but
his war against it, and therefore his wretchedness.   He will believe in
grace ; he will affirm that he feels it and rejoices over it ; he will perhaps appraise it, perhaps teach it, perhaps defend it ; and he will do
all this in sincerity.   But through it all, he will not live by grace ;
perhaps by his faith, perhaps by his zeal for grace, or his knowledge
of grace and his willingness for it ; but not by grace itself—only against
it.   He will know how to uphold and affirm himself even on this side.
He will rebel against any questioning of the richness which he thinks
he can secure in this way.

   The reality of the life of real Christians, of Church Christians, even of good
Protestant Christians, and the reality of the life of the Church as such, nowhere
bears witness to an openness of man for grace.   If it does witness to it, then it
is definitely not this reality as such.   On the contrary, this reality as such bears
witness with particular eloquence to the degree to which man is in fact and in
practice still closed on the side on which he should at all costs be open.

   This openness is, therefore, lacking.   Considered even in its reality,
all the supposed need and knowledge and willingness in which this
openness must consist is obviously the very opposite of this openness.
It follows, then, that even when we put the question in this deeper
form we have still not caught a glimpse of the readiness of man
which we can equate with his readiness for God's grace, and in which
we can also rediscover the knowability of God for man which follows
and is enclosed in God's readiness.   We are indeed pressed forward
from a possibility to a reality : to the last reality attainable by us,
even to the deepest human reality ; for is there deeper human reality
than that of the man addressed by God's Word and therefore awakened
to his real existence ?   But even our deepest reality is still separated
by an abyss from our openness for God's grace and therefore from the
knowability of God for us.
   Already we can take a first look back at the problem of " natural

theology." Whatever decision we may reach concerning it, one thing is certain. In it we are not concerned with a kind of fortuitous phenomenon which can emerge and then vanish. The position in which a man thinks he must and can place beside the knowability of God in His revelation a knowability grounded elsewhere is not just any kind of position. It is a kind of key position from which a perhaps unending number of other positions can be surveyed and occupied, while on the contrary perhaps all these positions can be evacuated and abandoned without the key position being endangered or destroyed. Again, it is certain that the conception of another knowability of God of this kind—beyond every serious objection that may be levelled against it—is grounded mischievously deep and firm even in the sphere of the Church, and therefore particularly in its form as a Christian natural theology. It is grounded so deep and firm that initially it is very hard to see in what way and (i.e., above all) from what point it can be decisively and effectively attacked. In other words, natural theology is no more and no less than the unavoidable theological expression of the fact that in the reality and possibility of man as such an openness for the grace of God and therefore a readiness for the knowability of God in His revelation is not at all evident. Natural theology is very plainly the herald and advocate of this the only evident possibility and reality of man. With this possibility and reality as a starting-point, enquiry will necessarily be made concerning that very different knowability of God. With this as a starting-point it is possible to maintain a knowability of that kind. Indeed, from this starting-point it necessarily will be maintained. It is the man closed to the readiness of God who cannot and will not let himself be deprived of the fact that a readiness for God is at his disposal even apart from the grace of God. As we have seen, the attempt to preserve and affirm himself is not only the possibility but the deepest reality of his existence, even of his existence as placed in the light of the divine revelation, even of his believing existence. And this attempt certainly cannot end in any other way than with the affirmation that even apart from God's grace, already preceding God's grace, already anticipating it, he is ready for God, so that God is knowable to him otherwise than from and through Himself. Nor does it only end with this. In principle it begins with it. For in what does it consist but in the arrogation, preservation and affirmation of the self-sufficiency of man and therefore his likeness with God? Man can, and indeed does, bear himself even in and in spite of his existence in the shadow of guilt and death. He can also bear, and does bear, the offer of the Word, without being thrown off his course. But this means that he has already lived a theology before he has thought and developed it as such. The core of this theology is that for him the truth can be had without the truth itself, because he himself is the truth itself, or at any rate, he is also the truth itself, in independence of the truth of God. This theology of life only needs to be made explicit as such and the whole of natural theology is in force in its basic idea. It is really there in force because behind it and co-inherent in it is the strength of that attempt at self-preservation and self-affirmation which is the reality of man. It involves self-denial to deny the basic idea of all natural theology, no matter whether it has been explicitly evolved and developed or not. It involves self-abnegation. And how is that possible ? How can man jump over his own shadow ? Even in the Church, where he is attacked from both sides, on the one hand by the real offer of grace and on the other by his real existence as finally exposed by this offer, he will never be anything different as considered in himself. He will always be the one who wants to carry everything, even—a very Atlas—the whole world. Under no circumstances will he let himself be carried. Therefore finally and at the deepest level he will always be an enemy of grace and a hater and denier of his real neediness. On that soil and in that atmosphere the growth of natural theology is inevitable. Its affirmation by the natural and original human knowledge of God and union with God is quite plainly its self-interpretation and self-justification. What does this affirmation really mean but simply that man is not really needy, that he is already rich and self-secure and therefore that he is not dependent on God's grace ? What else is the God whom he affirms he knows immediately, and to whom he says he is immediately united, but his own reflection, the hypostasising of his self-consciousness in which he knows that he encounters and defies sin, death and devil, but also the preaching and sacrament of the Church and the Word of God itself ? Perhaps he will not find it immediately necessary to think out and state explicitly the basic idea of natural theology. He may even omit to do it altogether. He will perhaps be content for the most part simply to assert it, to affirm its possibility. But his original and therefore tenacious interest in natural theology will show itself at once if its possibility is fundamentally questioned. He will then see at once that his most sacred possession and he himself with it are questioned along with this possibility. And the defence of natural theology will at once be undertaken with all the powers with which he is originally engaged in self-preservation on the left hand and on the right. This defence will at once be undertaken with a seriousness and energy which are not even remotely comparable with those displayed in an ordinary theological controversy or even a war of religion. Surrender of this possibility is self-surrender.

We have also to consider that as seen from its origin and native soil natural theology does not only acquire this natural force as such, but in its exercise it at once assumes a position of monopoly. It has its origin in the only visible possibility and reality of man. Hence it is not as if man can for long halt between natural theology and any other. Coming from the position he does, it is self-evident (i.e., there are no other possibilities to consider) that man will engage in natural theology and none other. In relationship to any other theology, natural theology has the initial advantage of the utterly known and certain over against the utterly new and uncertain. Even when in the first instance and to all appearance it is only a matter of defending it as also possible, also right, and also valid, the secret vitality of its defence is in the fact that in reality it is for man the only possible, right, and valid theology. The passion in this defence is not directed against the contesting of one possibility amongst others, but against the contesting of what is (as far as one can see) the one and only possibility of theology. All the skill which can be applied in its defence will derive right at the outset, even if it is denied by some, from the power —which finally needs no skill—of the very comprehensible and very illuminating desire not to surrender at any price this one and only possibility. And all the skill which can be summoned to contest it suffers from the outset because it is directed against a desire whose power is so strong that at a pinch it can frustrate all opposing skill even without counter-skill. It is not, then, the phenomenon of natural theology as such which is noteworthy, strange and in need of explanation. It is the phenomenon of the fact that in the sphere of the Christian Church (as also in the sphere of other religions) natural theology can apparently tolerate at least another theology, a theology of revelation. We do not now speak of man in general but of man in the Church ; of the man who is effectually attacked on both sides : by sin, death and devil on the one hand ; and by preaching, sacrament and the Word of God on the other. And so what concerns us at the moment is not any kind of natural theology, but Christian natural theology. It is a theology, then, which at least for a start and in appearance does not contest straight out the knowability of God from His revelation and the corresponding theology, but simply places itself at the side of the theology of revelation by appealing to another knowability of God which is also to be affirmed. It is a theology which at least for a start and in appearance makes a very unassuming and modest entrance. It does not want to speak thetically, but only hypothetically. It does not want to handle theology proper but only the prolegomena to it, the so-called *praeambula fidei*. It does not want to make the statement itself but only to introduce it, to prepare an understanding of it. It is, then, a natural theology which not only acknowledges revelation and grace as well, but even gives them materially and formally the precedence, indeed the unconditionally greater importance and correctness. The astonishing fact, which is in need of explanation, is that natural theology can make an entrance and surrender in this way ; that it can use this disguise ; that, if we can really trust its own declaration, it can make this sacrifice of the power and monopoly which are proper to it in virtue of its origin. What are we to say to the fact that it really can also speak in this extremely restrained tone, and can come forward in this extremely modest form ? At any rate we cannot say that all this is in itself necessarily and unambiguously a sign of the fact that its power is limited ; that a plain halt can be called to it in the Church by the fact of revelation which we cannot entirely overlook but have obviously very much to respect ; that here it is or can be relegated to a sphere within which, as a little subsidiary possibility alongside the other great decisive possibility, it is or can be made actually harmless. To be sure, the disguise of its position of monopoly is a distinctive feature of natural theology in the Church (even in Catholicism), and it can only be seen and understood as a sign of the defeat threatening it at the hands of revelation. But do not let us on any account expect that this juxtaposition of the two possibilities—apparently so clear in its superordination and subordination—is already in itself this sign. Let us not expect that this juxtaposition cannot also be seen and understood as a sign pointing in quite another direction. We may expect that this juxtaposition signifies the limitation and finally the defeat of natural theology, but not from a consideration of the immanent relationship of the two possibilities as such. We may expect it only from the fact that a light out of quite another dimension falls upon this relationship, just as we may expect the limitation and finally the defeat of natural theology in general only from that light falling out of quite another dimension into the sphere of the Church. If we consider the sphere of the Church as such and therefore as a human sphere ; if in this sphere we consider the peculiar relationship of these two possibilities, on the one hand the natural theology which speaks in an extremely restrained manner and enters in an extremely modest way, respectfully and humbly retiring before the revelation which really establishes the Church, merely preparing, merely serving, and on the other hand the proper and second task of theology ; if we consider this whole process in its immanent reality, we can in fact only break out in new astonishment at the vitality—which no life in the Church can break—of man and his resistance against grace, and therefore at the life-force of natural theology as it reveals itself in continually new appearances and applications. For what has really taken place when a natural theology and the theology of revelation are brought into this most harmless, indeed, even most promising relationship of juxtaposition or reciprocity ? Are the power and monopoly of natural theology perhaps surrendered and broken by it ? Or is not the chief proof of its power and monopoly the fact that it knows so well how to come to an arrangement with revelation and the theology of revelation ? What does it really effect by leaving open a special place for it ? What does it effect by first acknowledging the superiority of this place and then also the superiority of revelation and of a theology occupied with revelation ? Well, it means that although man was for a moment slightly disturbed and disquieted by this phenomenon which seemed to place him in question, he has now absorbed and domesticated revelation itself. He has transformed it from a question which is put to him into an answer which is given by him—yes, by him. Without any sacrifice, notice, of his own possibility and even in line with it, he has also chosen revelation as his possibility, with all that it is and means. He now lays hands on this as well. He now has the disposal of this as well. His own possibility (very far from being sacrificed) has at once undergone an immense inner enrichment, an addition, so to speak, to its furniture. God (with all the emphasis which the word has when God Himself speaks about Himself in His revelation, and in the mouth of the witnesses of His revelation) ; God's grace ; God's miracle, in which God testifies to His grace as free grace ; Holy Scripture ; love to God and neighbour as described in Holy Scripture ; the Church with its special commission and life—all this has now become a possibility which man can also choose. Undoubtedly it is a possibility which is far superior to that which formerly stood in his choice and at his disposal, yet even as such it is still a possibility which man himself can choose, and which he has at his disposal, without giving up the competence of his self-consciousness, indeed, in a first real exercise of this competence. For has he not now exercised his mastery ? Has he not won his battle against grace ? If grace is alongside nature, however high above it it may be put, it is obviously no longer the grace of God, but the grace which man himself ascribes to himself. If God's revelation is alongside a knowledge of God proper to man as such, even though it may never be advanced except as a prolegomenon, it is obviously no longer the revelation of God, but a new expression (borrowed or even stolen) for the revelation which encounters man in his own reflection. If the miracle acknowledged by man—perhaps an inspired Scripture or an infallible Church—is included in his own reckoning, if it is placed by him alongside the other phenomena of his world, it is obviously no longer the miracle of God, but an astounding element in man's view of the world and of himself. No supranaturalism which man can choose on this higher rung can hold its own against the fact that in the last resort, as chosen by man, it is only a higher, though masked, naturalism. God's real revelation simply cannot be chosen by man and, as his own possibility, put beside another, and integrated with it into a system. God's real revelation is the possibility which man does not have to choose, but by which he must regard himself as chosen without having space and time to come to an arrangement with it within the sphere and according to the method of other possibilities. By treating it as if it does not do the choosing but is something to be chosen, not the unique but just one possibility, Christian natural theology very respectfully and in all humility re-casts revelation into a new form of its own devising. But for all that its behaviour is so respectful and forbearing, for all that it subordinates itself so consciously and consistently, natural theology has already conquered it

at the very outset, making revelation into non-revelation. This will
certainly show itself in what it does with the revelation that has been
absorbed and domesticated by it. For the naturalism which already
exists in the systematisation of the two possibilities will not leave
permanently unmolested the supranaturalism of this higher stage which
is at first respected and forborne.

The necessary reinterpretations and reductions of this higher possibility will
certainly come about in due course once it has become one opportunity among
others, a possibility to be chosen by man. Man's criticism, which is in itself
very justifiable in regard to his own possibilities, is not to be restricted even in
regard to this possibility. As one of these possibilities, is it not possible and right
and necessary that God's revelation should be understood otherwise, more simply,
more clearly and more practically, than as it first appears in itself ? Is it not the
case that its supranaturalism is a self-misunderstanding of man which is destined
to disappear as it is overcome by explanation ? Yea, hath God said . . .? The
God of natural theology certainly cannot object. His vote will always be given to
the most extreme reinterpretations and reductions of the possibility of revelation.
And in the course of this critique the absorption and domestication of revelation
by natural theology can go so far that in the end natural theology again commands the field in its original state and its monopoly is again externally revealed,
so that even externally it is obvious that revelation has found its master.

But it is quite unnecessary to expand this theme. More than once
in Church history it has been expanded on a grand scale. There is no
doubt at all that even in the sphere of the Church, even in its moderate
Christian form, natural theology does not really sacrifice its original
power and monopoly. On the contrary, it triumphs here as perhaps
nowhere else. It even masters revelation. It is even able to change
the theology of revelation, which it tolerates and acknowledges alongside itself, and even consciously superordinates to itself, into an
image which is only too like itself, and which at bottom is itself nothing
but natural theology. Natural theology is still (or again) bungling
and therefore ineffectual when its aim is to rule not only independently
but alone, when it tries to deny revelation, to have absolutely nothing
to do with it, deriving the knowability of God exclusively from the
capability of man in the cosmos. When it acts in this way it still
(or already again) plays its role badly as an advocate and herald of
the reality and possibility, i.e., the self-affirmation and self-defence,
of man. In these circumstances man can still be surprised and overtaken by the genuine, unabsorbed and undomesticated revelation of
God as by an armed man, and there can be no saying whether he will
prove a match for it. But the natural theology to which we refer is pure
and good. It is faithful and circumspect in the service of its principal.
It is a natural theology which enters into friendship with faith, which
accepts revelation undaunted as another and obviously higher possibility, and which then instructs man to come to an understanding
with revelation, adjusting himself to it in the light of his self-consciousness and under guarantee of its unbroken existence. The man prepared

like this need fear no enemy. He is armed with the enemy's own weapon. He knows and can say himself everything that a theologian of revelation may have to say. He has heard long since whatever may be addressed to him from this source, what is said about God, God's Word, sin, grace, forgiveness, and miracle. He has grown accustomed to it. He has seen that it is moving, and indeed inspiring, but in the last resort harmless. Perhaps he has openly or secretly shaken it off again. Or perhaps he has quite quietly and positively assimilated it, according to the instruction of natural theology, as his own possibility, as a matter for consideration, which he can accept, but of which he is fundamentally the master, which does not cause him any inconvenience, indeed in the possession of which he is doubly secure, justified and rich.

I need not say that in all this there is described, not the evil peculiarity of a particular sect or heretical movement, but what, quite plainly, can happen to the Gospel in the Church at any moment. It is what threatens to happen, and actually does happen, when from an object of faith the Gospel becomes the object of our own experience of faith ; when from the gift of God it becomes an element in our own real existence, and therefore, in a larger content, in the life of the people, the community, the family, or society generally. The triumph of natural theology in the Church, described as the absorbing and domesticating of revelation, is very clearly the process of making the Gospel respectable. When the Gospel is offered to man, and he stretches out his hand to receive it and takes it into his hand, an acute danger arises which is greater than the danger that he may not understand it and angrily reject it. The danger is that he may accept it peacefully and at once make himself its lord and possessor, thus rendering it innocuous, making that which chooses him something which he himself has chosen, which therefore comes to stand as such alongside all the other things that he can also choose, and therefore control. What is all open unbelief, and how hopeful it seems, compared with a " victory of faith " in which man has really conquered faith by being a believer along with all the other things he is, by making even the Gospel into a means of his self-preservation and self-defence ! We can make only a brief reference to the abundance of religious, moral, political, philosophical and scientific forms in which this can take place. The important thing is that wherever the Gospel is proclaimed, both in Church extension on the mission field and in the existing Church, it is exposed at once to the danger of respectability. Indeed, the danger has already been incurred, for as far as can be seen it does always succumb to this process of domestication. And the real hero in the process is always the man who maintains a typical respectability by intending to hold his own against grace, but knowing that the best way to do it is not to contradict its proclamation but to put himself into an orderly relation with it, not to deny but to affirm it—yet circumspectly and in such a way that he reserves his rights over against it, so that it cannot become dangerous to him. The Gospel can be handled in this way and it is actually handled in this way. As far as can be seen—and let none try to make a rash exception of himself—this respectable Gospel is the only one there is. And it is this which forms the key position and the indestructible power and monopoly of natural theology in the Church itself. It is this which constitutes the great importance and influence in which it continually exists and asserts itself in spite of all its inward impossibility and every refutation of it. For what speaks here is not one of the many heresies. It is the one heresy which is necessary by its very nature. And none of us can deny what it says because in the Church it is always in our heart and on our lips. It is the respectable Christian who is speaking. And in himself and as such, what Christian can ever speak as anything else ? For this reason he will always recognise only too clearly his own voice in the voice of natural theology. For this reason he will always welcome it with secret sympathy when natural theology again manifests in a new direction that it is not yet at the end of its wisdom, that it is still that which both generally and in the Church has the last word—which was also the first. It will always remind him of what is in principle his own intention and desire, and of the fact that in the last resort even his choice of faith and attachment to the Church is only a clever concession, and that his real intention and desire, which the concession is meant only to serve, must not on any account be forgotten. Who or what can resist natural theology when it so obviously conducts the case for man himself, who even in the Church is still—or is it not so ?—the first and the last ? In short, we can say nothing more simple and yet more penetrating in praise of natural theology than that which is told us by its so wisely chosen name : that it is simply natural theology, i.e., the theology from which man comes when he starts from nature, from the nature which he has not lost even as a Christian, but which he still puts into effect as a Christian in a way which is particularly triumphant and formally conclusive ; that is to say, by domesticating the Gospel, which is to make it innocuous, indeed, to make use of it in the conflict against grace which is man's own deepest and innermost reality. It is in its naturalness, i.e., its respectability, that it has its indestructible glory. It is as a natural, i.e., a respectable, theology that in spite of every refutation it can successfully boast even in the Church of all its achievements, of its pedagogic usefulness, of the scriptural proofs for it. As we have seen, we look in vain for the secret of this success in these arguments as such. But we do not look for it in vain, but understand even the mysterious charm of these arguments (which are in themselves so unsatisfying), if we keep simply to the fact that even in the midst of the Church it is the theology which is natural to us all.

We now return to our line of thought ; to the question of the knowability of God understood as the readiness of man. Our deliberations so far have ended with a negative result. Making a postulate, we tried to see how the readiness of man must be constituted as included in the readiness of God. We described it as the openness and therefore the neediness, knowledge, and willingness of man in relationship to grace. Making a further postulate, we also gave to it reality ; i.e., we understood this open man expressly as man in the Church, as man placed by the Word of God under judgment, but also under grace. But we saw that even in this man we cannot really discern the man who is opened for the grace of God and therefore the knowability of God. It is not in his reality as such that we find the human readiness enclosed in the readiness of God, about which we ask. His reality as such is the conflict against grace, his attempt to preserve himself and hold his own. Our only positive gain from these considerations is unhappily that they enable us to understand only too well the existence and vitality of natural theology in the Church.

Does this conclusion mean that our main question is to be answered negatively ? Is there simply no readiness of man for the knowledge of God ? Is the enmity of man against grace, and therefore his closedness against God, the last thing to be said of him ? Let us be clear what this would mean. It would mean at once that all that we have described as the readiness of God does not really exist. God is not gracious to man. If He is gracious to him, and therefore if He is of Himself ready for him, this necessarily includes the fact that man is also ready for Him. Otherwise grace is not grace, i.e., God is not ready for him, man. If it is really true that man is not ready for God, if his enmity against grace is really the last word to be said about him, the conclusion is inescapable that God is not gracious to man. But that means at once that God is not knowable to him. Man with his know-ledge is left to himself, alone with himself. In his loneliness he may describe and recognise as God either himself, the world, this or that thing in the world, or his unity with the world. But this has nothing whatever to do with the knowledge of the true God his Lord, Creator, Reconciler and Redeemer, because—since there is no grace—he cannot and in fact he does not know this God who can be knowable to him only in His grace and by His grace. One element in his sphere of loneliness is the Church with its message and the possibility of faith in this message. In the world of man, as the sign of another order, objectively perhaps significant, but impotent in practice because as such unknowable, there is also the fact that man in his natural being and course can be to some extent disturbed, disquieted and arrested, that an attempt can be made to recall the depth of his need, and at the same time another help than his own. But man remains the true lord in his whole sphere and therefore in this part of his sphere. Even in this part there has been no power to master his whole sphere, to invade and open it up from without ; there has been no victory of grace to make man a friend of grace instead of an enemy, to bestow the knowability of God upon him. Here too, and here especially, he can actually speak the last word himself and he will actually do so. Even the Church, and with the Church the reality of his need and of the help proclaimed from elsewhere, are in practice included in his own possibility of maintaining and asserting himself, but they are also included in his own impossibility of knowing God. As concerns natural theology it will follow at once that it is right, and that it alone is right ; right in itself and right also in its particular relationship with the revelation of grace proclaimed in the Church. In this case, too, it is only making a legitimate use of the power and monopoly that really falls to its lot. It has the right and the duty to apprehend and there-fore to treat revelation as a human possibility like any other. It has the right and the duty to submit it to an acute critical reinterpretation. It has the right and the duty conclusively to assert itself as that which here too has the last word. Natural theology—a theology which grounds itself on a knowability of God distinct from the grace of God, i.e., on a knowability of another God than Him knowable only in His grace—a theology of this kind is as such the only and therefore fundamentally the right theology ; and in the sphere of the man who does not know the true God there can be no doubt that it is the right theology. These are the results if our main question as to the readiness of man included in the readiness of God is really to be answered negatively. We can see that the results are so far-reaching that, quite apart from the problem of natural theology, we cannot estimate them too seriously.

If in face of this position we look round for a positive answer to our question, we certainly cannot make any further use of anthropological postulates. Postulates of this kind in relation to the readiness of man may be formulated very precisely and accurately, but they can be of no value in so far as their presupposition and therefore the measure of their material determination is man : man who cannot simply be reinterpreted as though he were a friend of grace instead of an enemy ; man to whom readiness for God and God's grace cannot be ascribed by means of even the most complete postulates, because no postulate can reach him where, beyond all the more detailed determinations that are possible, he himself is, and therefore an enemy of grace, or because the postulate, on the ground of which he has to be something other than this, is meaningless, because as such it no longer has any reference to man himself. Therefore if we are to continue our search for a positive answer to our question, we shall not have to dwell any further on man as such, whether in his possibility or in his reality. Nor will it be of any help for us if we try to underline and intensify the ecclesiological position in which we have seen and understood mar from the beginning. For it is to be feared that the only real result will be pathetic protestations, for example of the revivifying power of proclamation and faith. Of course, these protestations are right in substance. They assert the fact that, born again by the Word and the Spirit of God, man may certainly become what he is not in himself and as such, namely, an obedient child of God and His grace. In fact, he does become this. But as we have seen, statements of this kind are not true in themselves as expressed of man. As expressed of man, they are in themselves highly contestable and actually contested. When they are expressed of man as such, they always have behind and above them man himself in his possibility and in his reality. And he is always contradicted by man, even by man in the Church. Even regenerate man continually has to recognise himself as unregenerate man. It is as well for him when he does at least do this. For even if he does not know it, his regeneration as such, his faith, his renewal, his divine sonship, and his love for God's grace will, in fact, always be contradicted by himself. The Church is always the world as well. As such it is not at all that which has overcome the world. It is really lost with the world if it imagines itself to be something of this kind. Therefore when we ask concerning the readiness of man we must not dwell long on the Church and on man in the Church as such. The decision which we are investigating can as little appear on the basis of ecclesiology as it can on that of anthropology.

There is an aspect of man of which we have so far made no use. Under this aspect the picture is altered and the decision which we are investigating does emerge : the readiness of man included in the readiness of God, man's openness for God's grace and therefore God's real knowability.   But this other aspect will certainly have to be viewed and considered in its distinction from the aspect of the problem previously discussed.   Otherwise in our attempt to make use of it we may unwittingly remain entangled or fall back into that earlier aspect. Our deliberations have not only been fruitless, but fruitless in a very singular and disturbing way.   It is not at all the case that we simply entered a false road when we began with the postulate of a Christian anthropology—that openness of man for God's grace must mean his neediness, his knowledge, and his willingness in regard to it.   As we have already said, this is in itself correct.   What else can this openness mean ?   And we could be even more sure that we were on the right road when we approached man in the light of Christian ecclesiology ; when we understood him expressly as the man reached and encountered by the Word of God, judged and pardoned in the light of the truth of this Word.   But the disturbing thing is that we were blocked even on this right road : not by a theoretical and technical difficulty, which could certainly have been removed ; but simply by the nature of the object, namely, of the man whose readiness we had to ask about. Neither in the one way nor in the other could we ascribe this readiness to man as such with an easy conscience.   Whether we looked at it the one way or the other, man as such always remained, contradicting this definition.   In spite of all the postulates about what his openness could and must mean, and in spite of all the definitions—however right —of his real determination by the judgment and grace of God, the fact is that finally and in the last resort man is always to be understood as the enemy of grace.   And this fact emerges as the annoying indivisible remainder in a division, which does ultimately indicate a certain rule of its divisibility, but for this very reason shews itself not actually to be divided.

It is to be recommended, not only in dogmatics but also for preaching, for teaching and for the pastoral work of the Church, that this state of affairs be kept quite clearly in mind. In this matter we can come to no conclusion even on the most correct of roads. We cannot reinterpret the man who is an enemy of grace into a friend of grace. Therefore we cannot ascribe to man as such any readiness corresponding to the readiness of God. We cannot display the fact and extent of an inclusion of the readiness of man as such in the readiness of God. If we try to presuppose any such thing we are treading on air. Man does not lend himself to the fulfilling of this presupposition. The knowability of God is not, therefore, to be made intelligible as the predicate of man as such. The indivisible remainder in this calculation can, of course, be hidden rhetorically in the form of an edifying protestation. And quite an immense amount of passion in theological reflection and in Church proclamation will year in year out be applied simply to hiding this remainder, to assuring the Church and the world that in the long run, attacked on both sides by the judgment and the grace of God, even man as such can in the form of Christian man become and be another, a man ready for God. This can be assured in such an impressive and powerful way that those who hear it may actually regard themselves as assured by it for a while. But we must not deceive ourselves. In reality they are not assured, nor indeed can they be. For we cannot be sure of what is not true. The victories of theology and Church proclamation to be won in this direction are pyrrhic victories. They will lead sooner or later to new victories of man as such, of the natural man, who has no thought at all of becoming and being a man ready for God, but whom we have only to persuade that this is the case really to arm him against God. And even if he may choose this possibility, and let himself be conquered by this theology and proclamation, thus becoming genuinely victorious over the Gospel, there is the other possibility that for some reason he may be so discerning and honest as to perceive or at any rate suspect the untrustworthiness of such a theology and proclamation, rejecting the strengthening of his position offered him by Christianity, regarding himself as strong enough even without this assurance, and conducting his work of self-preservation and self-affirmation, and therefore his strife against grace, in his own strength and without a Christian foundation. To be sure, he does not conduct his case quite so cleverly if he adopts this line. From his own point of view, he might do better with a Christian foundation than without it. The really clever natural man is not to be sought and found in the so-called world but always in Christian circles. But the less clever natural man among the children of the world has his great strength too ; he has even a certain promise beyond his cleverer brother in the advantage he has of somehow seeming to smell out the true state of affairs, namely, the untrustworthiness of a theology and proclamation which wants to persuade him that at any rate in the Church there exists the man as such who is not closed but open towards God. This will probably lead him to scrutinise men in the Church. He will then find that even these men, of whom it is said to him that they are saved, do not look as saved as all that. Their particular humanity will not seem to him especially attractive or thoroughly convincing. With sharp eyes he will perceive that between his own godlessness and the piety and morality of those within there exist certain not unimportant similarities. He will certainly have no few occasions to cry in triumph : " Behold ! we savages are the better men ! " He will at any rate find that the price he must pay to be within is too high for what is clearly offered to him there. To begin with, and perhaps also at the end, he will be content simply to pay his Church rates and perhaps even that will be too much for him. It is, of course, a well-known fact that this discernment and honesty of the children of the world does not stand on too sure feet. Without knowing how it happens, it may be surprised overnight by a religious " movement " and fall away from this protestation in extraordinary or at any rate what are for itself novel forms. But this is a separate matter, which simply means that the clever natural man has now become even cleverer and seen his true interests more clearly. If we assume that the contradiction of the less clever natural man remains, it is quite inappropriate to see in this contradiction a direct outworking of the scandal of the cross of Christ and to take steps to deal with it from the standpoint of 1 Cor. 1–2. The question is whether Christian theology and proclamation have really proclaimed the cross of Christ to the congregation and the world, or whether the offence taken at them is not the customary and not at all unjustified annoyance at the fact that they declare facts that are not true, namely, affirmations about the Christian man which, looked at in the light, when for some reason the magic of the edifying protestation no longer captivates, cannot be sustained, and which in themselves and as such are finally and ultimately illusions. In face of this contradiction it is surely much better strictly to examine whether theology and proclamation to the congregation and the world have not perhaps set up a sign which must be contradicted in all seriousness from the point of view of their own presuppositions : namely, the sign of the Christian man as such, the sign

of the great reinterpretation or reconstitution of this man into a man ready for
God. When theology and the Church are occupied with the telling of this story,
when the religious movements of revival which arise from time to time are
finally only chapters in this story, when their invitation to Christians and children
of the world is to become characters in this story, then, if they fail, they ought
not to hide behind the cloak of 1 Cor. 1-2 applied in quite a different way, and
if they succeed, they have cause for more alarm than if they fail. For the cross
of Christ is not really proclaimed at all. There is no question of His scandal,
or of the salvation revealed in Him. But a game is played in the foreground
which in itself may be harmless—why should we not tell ourselves stories on
earth if it does us good ?—but which is criminal and hurtful if there is nothing
to follow, if the real task of theology and the Church in regard to man is forgotten
or omitted in this game. It is to be noted carefully that the attraction and therefore the danger at this point is so great because in this construction of the Christian
man as such we do not see a false but an entirely correct road, because theoretically no mistake is made but everything is in order. Openness for God's grace
does really mean neediness, knowledge and willingness. And man in the Church,
attacked on both sides by the judgment and grace of God, is undoubtedly the
man who is ready for God, to whom God is actually knowable. Just one little
thing is forgotten : this man in himself and as such does not actually say Yes
to God's grace, but through all the postulates and realities of his existence as
such says No. It is this which, in view of the tidiness in which the rest of the
calculation can be arranged, is so easily overlooked in dogmatics as well as in
Church proclamation, and is not only suppressed but even transformed into its
opposite. And this is the very thing which must not happen. A sound theology
and proclamation (i.e., one that rests, not on spurious results, but on its responsibility to the matter in hand and to man) will notice this state of affairs and
acknowledge it to the congregation and the world, so that there may be an end
of all false positions. It must learn to renounce all those correct things about the
Christian man which are so dangerous and untrustworthy and in the end rather
tedious. It must learn instead to want to tell the truth.

It is, of course, rather remarkable that the praise of the Christian
man's readiness for God can be sung in this very correct, if finally very
ineffectual, way. Where does this praise derive its immanent correctness ? How does it come about that we can, in fact, give tolerably
exact and positive information about the determination of the life of
a Christian, even if we have subsequently to acknowledge that the
Christian as a man does not thoroughly fulfil this determination of his
life ? By what truth do the illusions live which are customarily propounded about the Christian man ? If what we have just considered
is correct in itself—but *de facto* ineffectual—this means necessarily
that there is the inherent possibility of a man who is ready for God,
but what overturns everything is that man as such is not this man who is
ready for God. And the fact that we can even advance considerations
which are correct in themselves necessarily means further that we
know about such a man who is ready for God, although we err when
we deduce from it conclusions concerning man as such, who is not this
man who is ready for God.

It is certainly true that the man who is ready for God is truth
and life ; but he is not identical with man as such. As truth and life,
he needs to be sought, known and found—for the salvation of man

as such—beyond man as such, and especially beyond the Christian man as such. It is certainly true that the whole (and wholly dubious) realm of the Christian man has as its true meaning and intention this transcendent man who is ready for God in life and truth. If this man were revealed, if he were the Lord in the realm of the Christian man, the latter would also be freed by him from his questionableness; and in his immanence chosen, separated, justified and glorified (Romans 8²⁹ᶠ·). Everything which in relation to him as such can only be said with such painfully ineffectual correctness could then be said at once relevantly, impressively and in living truth. The stirring, unsettling, exciting element in everything that can be said about man on this level is just that it is so trite, but that in its triteness—without becoming in itself other and better, without being able to make itself other and better, as a purely negative indication, it points by its inward lack to the other dimension in which it is confronted by the man who is ready for God in living truth. Seen from this man and with reference to him, it is not necessarily trite; it can be true and living. Christian theology and proclamation does not intend and wish to romance when it speaks of the man who is ready for God. It does not mean to lie when it presupposes and affirms his reality so unconcernedly. It does not mean to lie when it ignores that indivisible remainder in what are often such astonishing ways. It does not mean to lie when it applies such unavailing passion to the suppression of this remainder. Its definite intention is the man ready for God who is not identical with man as such, but who confronts him in infinite promise. How can it be Christian theology and proclamation if in all this—even in its illusions, even when it identifies the man who is ready for God with man as such —it does not mean Jesus Christ? But if Christian theology and proclamation is not to lie against its will, if it is not to be all romance and illusion, this is the very thing which needs to be expressly stated and explained, which needs to be lifted out of all ambiguity into unambiguity, which needs, in contradiction to all Ifs and Buts and Boths and Ands, to be known and confessed. It is the decision before which there really is no decision. It is the conclusion beside which all the conclusions of our deliberations and assertions in that first dimension are in themselves really no conclusions. It is truth and life in the height, beside which there can be truth and life in the depth, in the sphere of man, even of the Christian man, only as truth and life come down out of the height where they are into the depth where they are not, and therefore only as they are continually sought and expected in the height.

The only aspect of man under which the picture we have already drawn is actually altered, and the decision investigated (i.e., the readiness of man included in the readiness of God and therefore God's real knowability) is actually disclosed, is the christological. Anthropological and ecclesiological assertions arise only as they are borrowed from Christology. That is to say, no anthropological or ecclesiological assertion is true in itself and as such. Its truth subsists in the assertions of Christology, or rather in the reality of Jesus Christ alone. We can certainly say to man that he can and should believe. But if we want to understand and say truly what this means, we must understand and say it of the One in whom he believes. We can certainly say to man that he becomes another man by the judgment and grace of God. But if we want to understand and say it in truth, we must understand and say that the judgment and grace of Jesus Christ is meant, outside which there is no judgment and no grace ; we must understand and say that Jesus Christ is this Other and how far He is this Other. We can certainly see and testify that there is a new birth of man to divine sonship. But if this is to be seen and attested in truth, this seeing and attesting must consist, and consist only, in a seeing and attesting of Jesus Christ the only begotten Son of God, who is come in our flesh and as whose brethren alone we can become the children of God. If we look past Jesus Christ, if we speak of anyone else but Him, if our praise of man is not at once praise of Jesus Christ, the romance and the illusions begin again, and we fall back again into the aspect under which it is impossible to see, or with a good conscience to speak about, the man who is ready for God in life and truth. In Christian doctrine, and therefore in the doctrine of the knowledge and knowability of God, we have always to take in blind seriousness the basic Pauline perception of Colossians 3³ which is that of all Scripture—that our life is our life hid with Christ in God. With Christ : never at all apart from Him, never at all independently of Him, never at all in and for itself. Man never at all exists in himself. And the Christian man is the very last to try to cling to existing in himself. Man exists in Jesus Christ and in Him alone ; as he also finds God in Jesus Christ and in Him alone. The being and nature of man in and for themselves as independent bearers of an independent predicate, have, by the revelation of Jesus Christ, become an abstraction which can be destined only to disappear. If we acknowledge His revelation as such, if we are in the Church, how can we make use of it to prevent the vanishing of this abstraction, to try if possible to breathe new life into it ? Only the enormous cunning of the natural man explains the riddle that it can happen. But surely it is possible to see through and strike down this cunning of the natural man, not in virtue of the natural man himself, but in virtue of Jesus Christ ? Christian doctrine at any rate cannot utter a single sound word unless it has seen through and laid low this cunning. Therefore if we want to press forward to a positive answer to our question—and we have no other choice : we do not press forward to it, but it presses forward to us— the christological aspect of the problem must now be permitted at once ruthlessly and totally to replace every other. At once—for every other, especially the anthropological and ecclesiological just considered, receives meaning and form as a real aspect only from this point. It does receive them from this point. But it is quite meaningless in any independent use. We can, therefore, anticipate the positive answer to our question by stating simply that the readiness of man included in the readiness of God is Jesus Christ. And therefore Jesus Christ is the knowability of God on our side, as He is the grace of God itself, and therefore also the knowability of God on God's side.

But who is Jesus Christ that we must say this of Him, and can say it of Him only ; and can say it of man and therefore of ourselves only as we first and properly say it of Him ? If now, in naming Jesus Christ, we are again speaking of a postulate ; if we are speaking of Jesus Christ as the ideal case of a man who is ready for God, or as the idea of human readiness for God, everything is lost once more, and we do not attain the real aspect which opens up a positive answer to our question, even if we try to describe and designate it as Christology. For no ideal case and no idea of man can in any way alter the fact that man in himself and as such is not ready for God, and therefore that God is not knowable to him. But Jesus Christ is attested to us by the Old and New Testaments in such a way that we are in fact deprived of the possibility of speaking of a further postulate instead of Him. Jesus Christ is attested to us in such a way that we can say of Him either nothing at all, or, wholly unequivocally, that He is the Lord. Every word of the biblical witness about Him so binds Him to us that it marks Him off against us in such a way that we are deprived of the possibility of understanding Him from ourselves and therefore as an ideal case or an idea of our possibility and reality. Every word of the biblical witness about Him so binds us to Him that He stands above, while we come to stand beneath. In this irreversible order He is the One He is. Already this irreversibility means assurance against a repetition here of the old fruitless game played wherever we are occupied with man as such. Here, too, we have a man. But he is definitely not man as such. It is only if we erase or " spiritualise " His prediction by what took place in the covenant with the fathers and with Israel, His miracles and above all the miracle of His own existence, the Virgin Birth and the resurrection of Jesus Christ ; only if we strangely reinterpret both His Gospel of the kingdom of God, which is as such His self-attestation, and ultimately every word which is said to us by Him or about Him, that we can create for ourselves the possibility of reading into Him an interpretation of man as such and therefore of understanding Him in the light of man as such. Any exegesis which does not manipulate but respects the subject-matter, and therefore the text itself, will certainly tell us that we are here concerned with a man, but it will also assure us against the error that we are here concerned with man as such, with an ideal case or with an idea of natural man. It will tell us, whatever position we may take up towards it, that we are here concerned with the Lord : with the only begotten, unique and eternal Son of God, and therefore with God Himself ; and therefore always with the One who is ready and open for God and to whom God is knowable. For this reason, when and because we are concerned with Jesus Christ, we stand in the mystery and at the same time in the revelation of God, in His own innermost reality. God is knowable to Himself ; the Son to the Father, but also the Father to the Son. This is the first and last thing which is to be said about the knowability of God even from the point of view of the readiness of man. Of course, at this point man still seems to stand outside. Everything still seems to be invalid for him. For we are not God. Indeed we are not. But God is man. For Jesus Christ, the Lord attested in the Old and New Testaments, is as little God in Himself and as such as He is man in himself and as such. He is God who is man. This is Jesus Christ. In Him we do not stand outside but inside ; we participate in this first and last. In Him the fact that God is knowable is true not only for God Himself, not only between the Father and Son, but for man, for us. For in Him man is ready for God. But what does this mean ? What can it mean in view of the fact that man as such is never actually ready for God but closed to Him, because he is not a friend but an enemy of grace, and so turns his back on God's revelation ? Now, we have already heard what it means concretely that Jesus Christ is man. It means that the only begotten Son of God and therefore God Himself, who is knowable to Himself from eternity to eternity, has come in our flesh, has taken our flesh, has become the bearer of our flesh, and does not exist as God's Son from eternity to eternity except in our flesh. Our flesh is therefore present when He knows God as the Son the Father, when God knows Himself. In our flesh God knows Himself. Therefore in Him it is a fact that our flesh knows God Himself. At this point we are keeping intentionally and emphatically to the word " flesh " as used in Jn. 1^{14}, because in the Bible this word means man as such, man as the enemy of the grace of God. It is this manhood, defined in this way, that the Son of God has taken and made His own. He has not entered the fellowship of the humanity defined in this way without being affected by or participating in its inner impossibility in relation to God. No : He, the pure, holy Son of God, obedient to the Father from eternity to eternity, has Himself become a man like this. As the Son of God, He was certainly in the fellowship of the humanity defined in this way, provoking and enduring the enmity of man against the grace of God as all prophets and apostles must provoke and endure it ; nailed to the cross as the last and decisive proof of the definitive disposition of man as such in relation to God. But however decisive this is as the full revelation of the accusation brought against man as such, however conclusive the word spoken in the fact that man as such could act only in this way to the Son of God who had come to him, the real decision and settlement fulfilled in the cross of Jesus Christ works itself out in a very different direction. As man, He has suffered the being of man at enmity with grace in terms not merely of what came on Him from without, from man's side, in the place of God, but also—and this is more—in terms of what came on Him from within, from God's side, in the place of man. He Himself has entered into this being ; He has really moved over against God in the place of man, not to do again in this place what this man always does, but truly in this place. And in this place He has not only borne man's enmity against God's grace, revealing it in all its depth. He has borne the far greater burden, the righteous wrath of God against those who are enemies of His grace, the wrath which must fall on us. For it is we who are enemies of the grace of God. It is we who do that which by its very nature cannot be forgiven, because it is the despising of forgiveness itself. It is we who are accused and convicted by the crucifying of Jesus Christ. It is we who have deserved death, eternal death. But the Son of God—who is this same Jesus Christ—has entered into our place when He became flesh. He has taken to Himself the very accusation which was directed against us, the very judgment which was passed upon us. He has borne the punishment which was rightly ours. As the Son of God He could enter into our place, into the place of every individual man, of the whole human race. And as the Son of God He has actually done it. But this means that our very enmity against grace ceases at the moment at which it is perfectly revealed, when the accusation against it becomes inevitable and crushing because it has risen to the point of hating and wanting to destroy God Himself. At this very moment it ceases to be the object of God's wrath against us. It no longer exists as the cause of *our* accusation, condemnation and punishment. For our enmity, the enmity in which man as such stands against grace, is expiated and abandoned before God by God Himself, before the Father by His only begotten Son, but by the incarnate Son of God and therefore in our place. It is expiated, because He suffered in our place the accusation, condemnation and punishment which must come upon us from God. It is abandoned, because He accepted God's grace in our place and therefore rendered to God the obedience which we continually refuse. For this very reason, however, the enmity of man against God is annulled, done away, obliterated. And if it is obliterated before God, it is obliterated in truth. What happens in the truth, what is indeed the truth, is what happens before God, by God, in our place. And it has happened before God, by God, in our place, that our enmity against His grace has been expiated and abandoned. This is the victory of grace over human enmity against grace. And this has been finally and unambiguously revealed in the crucifixion of the Son of God, for where man in final consistency fancies he can maintain and assert himself by pushing away from himself the fulfilment of the whole promise of grace, even the grace of God become man, where he loses forgiveness by responding to the fulness of the divine forgiveness with his own religious and moral activity and therefore with the capital sentence which condemns himself—" grace did much more abound " (Rom. 5^{20}). And where man is finally and unambiguously revealed as the transgressor of the law, as the one who does not love in return but hates the One who has loved him from eternity—there (miracle of all miracles) the truth is revealed by which all transgression of the law, all enmity of man against grace, is revealed and destroyed as falsehood. This truth is the man who satisfies the Law by suffering the punishment of its transgression and who at the same time keeps and fulfils it by doing what it commands. That is the victory of grace over man's enmity against grace. And the revelation of the truth and life of the man who is open to grace and therefore ready for God is that God Himself became man. He suffered the enmity of man in its most fearful promise and fulfilment. He revealed the judgment under which this man stands. But He did not reveal it in order to fulfil it upon him, but in order to take it upon Himself and under the Law to do what this man does not do, namely to praise and reveal and glorify His grace. This victory of grace, this revelation of the truth and life of a new man, is called Jesus Christ : the crucified Jesus Christ, very God and very man, in His suffering and in his obedience, in His submission to the Law and in His fulfilling of the Law, in His blood which He permitted to be shed by man that He might shed it for man ; the crucified Christ who is also risen, i.e., who has in Himself brought life and revealed to all the world this new man (out of the death in which He had buried the first and old man in Himself). This other, new man is in Himself the man ready for God, for whom we looked in vain so long as we looked to man as such, even to Christian man. But we no longer look for him in vain, nor for the knowability of God for man, if we see clearly that it is not man as such, and not even Christian man, but Jesus Christ, the incarnate Son of the Father, revealed in His cross and resurrection, who is the truth and life of man—the real man, to whom we have to keep if we do not want to speak meaninglessly and futilely, but with final substance and content, of man and of his relationship to God and of his readiness for Him. We have only to speak His name, the name of Jesus Christ, and in this name we say the one thing, but also the most positive thing, which is to be said about man's readiness for God. In Him the enmity of man against the grace of God is overcome, therefore man is no more outside, where God must be unknowable to him because he does not accept the grace in which God makes Himself knowable to him. He is inside, where God is knowable to Himself, the Father to the Son and the Son to the Father, where in the Son, therefore, God is also knowable to him, man. In Him—it cost Him His humiliation to our station, His blood, His suffering of the wrath of God and the quite incomprehensible fact of His obedience in suffering, but it is so. In Him we have a part in the first and final truth that God is not hidden but revealed to Himself.

We can now see the true desire and intention behind those most astonishing and perverted ways, and the illusions to which Christian theology and proclamation to some extent surrenders. We can now see the truth by which they live and are enabled to declare so many things which for all their ineffectiveness are perfectly correct. The correctness springs just from the fact that the man ready for God, whose existence they presuppose and affirm in so doubtful a way, does actually exist, and that He does in fact—His name is Jesus Christ—form the foundation and being of the Church. The essence of the doubtfulness and pervertedness of their activity, and the source of its ineffectiveness, is the fact that they do not actually confess to their true intention and desire, namely, to Jesus Christ, His cross and resurrection. But they pass Him by, so that His name becomes an empty sound and Christology merely an ideology. They keep to man as such, and in consequence know nothing of the man who is really ready for God, so that they can only falsely presuppose his existence and therefore the knowability of God. The way to the healing of Christian doctrine is quite plain : *Haec sola est ratio tam retinendae quam restituendae purae doctrinae: Christum ponere ob oculos qualis est cum bonis suis omnibus* (Calvin, *Comm. on* Col. 1[12], C.R. 52, 83). Christian theology and proclamation have only to consider why it is that they can say ineffectively so many things that are correct. They have only to track down this correctness to its origin, to the real intention and desire. They have only to look up instead of down. They have only in fact—they do it often enough in words—to keep to the man, " who is even at the right hand of God, who also maketh intercession for us " (Rom. 8[34]). If they do this, they will not speak falsehood but the truth. And we can and must also add that when and so far and in the measure that they actually do this, in the measure that—in all the perversity, and in all their illusions in regard to Christian man himself— they nevertheless proclaim the crucified and risen Christ, they speak the truth, they speak it not merely correctly but rightly and effectively, edifying the community, evangelising the world, putting the children of the world in the wrong and having to proclaim to them the real and eternal salvation. It is good that the power of the truth of the Son of God, His cross and resurrection, has always been and always will be greater than the power of the knowledge and confession of Him in the Church. It is good that this power has never been entirely ineffectual even in the erring Church. But that does not excuse the erring of the Church. On the contrary, it must lead the Church to repentance. But again, there has never been an age in the Church in which it has not been called to the repentance which consists in the fact that it returns to the Lord whom it has so easily and so often—and often for so long—forgotten ; allowing Him again to be the Head in whom alone the members can have their life.

But another question still remains to be answered. It can, of course, be only a counter-question, which we ask for the sake of cross-checking and understanding. For when we name the name of Jesus Christ and remember the new creation of man that has taken place in Him, we have really spoken the last Word—not our last word, but God's (and therefore ours as well). Or rather, we have repeated God's own Word after Him. Beyond this last Word there are no questions. All our questions arise only as we are questioned by this last Word. All our questions can be only stages on the way to a knowledge of this last Word, which as such stands under no question, but is unadulterated answer. Even the question which still remains can be only a question of understanding, a question which presupposes the givenness of its answer. As such it can be put in this way : How far is it the case that in Him, Jesus Christ, we are really inside and not outside, and therefore in a place where God is knowable to Himself, and so to us as well ? How far is it the case that I, this man, who as such is not ready for God and who is also not identical with Jesus Christ, am really ready for God in Jesus Christ ? How far is that which is true of Him in the height true of me in the depth ? Or we may formulate the question in this way : How far, alongside and under Christology, is there also a Christian anthropology and ecclesiology wholly dependent of course on it and with strict reference to it ? How do we come to participate in what Jesus Christ is ? The question is not false ; it is even very necessary and urgent. But there is a danger that we may be enticed by it to return answers in which we again lose sight of the true and necessary subject of the question.

It is easy to reply at once with the fact that at this point we are referred to the possibility, necessity and reality of faith. And we shall again be saying something which in itself is no doubt correct. For, indeed, how can the victory of grace, won in Jesus Christ over human enmity against grace, be relevant, valid and saving for us except as we believe in Jesus Christ ? Yet if we refer at once and directly to faith, how easily the first ineffective aspect submerged in Jesus Christ can emerge again. On the one hand, there is God's grace in the height ; and on the other we ourselves in an only too well-known depth. And of us it is demanded, in a new form of the Law (or is it not still the old ?), that we should believe. But, in ourselves, afterwards as well as before, we are what we are. We can and actually will withdraw from grace even if, and so far as, we believe, so that ultimately our faith as such will still be ineffectual. Now, according to the witness of all Scripture, it is certainly a question of faith, and what is more, only of faith in Jesus Christ. But the question is asked : What actually is faith, namely faith in Jesus Christ, as distinct from other possible forms of ineffectual and unsaving faith or unbelief or heresy or superstition, and how are we actually to arrive at this faith, this faith which is no longer to be compromised by ourselves and our own . enmity against grace ? If the question is intended and put seriously, it asks concerning a faith which cannot be compromised, a victory of grace towards and in ourselves which corresponds to the death and resurrection of Jesus Christ and is like the divine certainty of Jesus Christ. The fact that we are here in the depth cannot mean, then, that our relationship to Him who is in the height, and our participation in Him, can again be thought and spoken of only hypothetically, whilst our own reality, the enemy of grace living in us all, still remains to jeopardise the whole relationship. It is not merely a matter of faith, but of true and certain faith. Therefore if our question is to be answered aright, an answer must be given it which does not start from the believing man but from Jesus Christ as the object and foundation of faith.

Basically, then, the right answer can only be that as the one and only man ready for God, Jesus Christ has not only lived, died and risen for us once in time, so that the abounding grace of God might be an event and at the same time revelation among us, but that as this same One He stands before His Father now in eternity for us, and lives for us in God Himself as the Son of God He was and is and will be. Thus our appropriation of what he has won for us has not first to be executed by us. By the fact that He is for us in eternity in God Himself the man who is ready for God, it is executed in eternity, in God Himself, by Him, in the eternal continuation of His high-priestly office. But this means—and what follows can only be a sequel and explanation of this proper and original truth—that Jesus Christ Himself sees to it that in Him and by Him we are not outside but inside. He Himself sees to it that His readiness is valid for us who are not identical with Him, and who in ourselves are not ready for God. He sees to it that what is true in Him in the height is and remains true in our depth. It is not another work that begins at this point, a work that will have to be ours. We do not here fall into the hands of another God. For what is accomplished on this side also is simply the one work of God's Son ; in the fact, that is, that He exists and represents us at the right hand of the Father in our flesh, but as the conqueror of our enmity. As His work, the work of God's Son, this representing of Jesus Christ is an eternal representing and therefore one which is contemporary to all time. Again, as His work, the work of the Son of God, it is an almighty and therefore a wholly effectual representing. This is what we must first remember if we want to see the answer to our question. We have not merely been once represented by Him. We are so at any time because in eternity. He who represents us is no less a person than the Son of God who is consubstantial with the Father and who therefore has God's own power and God's own will to represent us. We are therefore effectually represented by Him. But if this is true, the question as to our presence is already answered by His eternal divine " for us ". If He is for us, this means—and in the last resort this alone means— that with the eternal certainty proper to the Son of God we too are present, genuinely participating in what He is and has done.

According to Rom. 8$^{31-39}$, none can be against us, none can condemn us, none can separate us from the love of God which is in Christ Jesus our Lord. If death and life, angels, principalities and powers, things present and things to come, height and depth cannot do it, then neither can that indivisible remainder of enmity against grace which is the final and proper thing in us men as such. " O wretched man that I am ! who shall deliver me from the body of this death ? I thank God through Jesus Christ our Lord. So then with the mind I myself serve the law of God ; but with the flesh the law of sin. There is therefore now no condemnation to them which are in Christ Jesus. For the law of the Spirit of life in Christ Jesus hath made me free from the law of sin and death " (Rom. 7^{24}–8^2). " And if any man sin, we have an advocate with the Father, Jesus Christ the righteous " (1 Jn. 2^1). And " if our heart condemn us, God is greater than our heart." Just because this is so, we know that we are in the truth, and therefore can and shall assure our hearts before God (1 Jn. $3^{19\text{-}20}$). How do we " hold fast our profession " ? As " we have a great high priest, that is passed into the heavens, Jesus the Son of God. For we have not an high priest which cannot be touched with the feeling of our infirmities ; but was in all things tempted like as we are, yet without sin. Let us therefore come boldly unto the throne of grace, that we may obtain mercy, and find grace to help εἰς εὔκαιρον βοήθειαν " (Heb. $4^{14f.}$).

It must be understood wholly from this height of the occurrence in God Himself, when Holy Scripture as a rule expressly describes our participation in the person and work of Jesus Christ as a work of the Holy Spirit. The Holy Spirit is holy because He is God's Spirit, and therefore the Spirit, the moving and unity of the Father and of the Son from eternity and in eternity. The fact that by the Holy Spirit we are ready for God in Jesus Christ is in the first instance and in itself only a confirmation of what we have just said. Because and as Jesus Christ, the Son of God, is for us in eternity, and the Father also, it is true—beyond anything that may still be true anywhere else, and especially in ourselves ; so true that in the light of it anything else that may be true, and therefore our own enmity against grace, becomes a lie—that God is for us. In the Holy Spirit as the Spirit of the Father and of the Son there is, in the height of God, no " Against us " but only the " For us " which has been spoken and is true once for all. Just because this is how it is and not otherwise in this height, in the height of God, it cannot be otherwise in our depth. What depth can be so deep that it is withdrawn from what is true and valid in the height of God ; that something else can be true and valid in it ; that everything in it that seeks to be true in and for itself is not unmasked from this height as a lie ? So then between us and God, however it may be with ourselves and our enmity against grace, there can be no strife. So then our enmity is outstripped and overcome. So then the world is reconciled to God (2 Cor. 5^{19}). And this is just as certain as that Father, Son and Holy Spirit are the one eternal and almighty God, and that between the Son and the Father in the height there is no strife, but peace and unity in the Holy Spirit from eternity to eternity. Thus everything that is to be said about our participation in the person and work of Jesus Christ, here in the depth as such, can properly consist only in this : It lies in the nature of what happens there in God, in eternal continuation of the reconciliation and revelation accomplished in time, that in full reality it happens here also to and in us—even in face and in spite of what we are to and in ourselves as long as " there " and " here " still mean two different things. This participation of ours in the person and work of Jesus Christ does not

have to be added as a second thing. As the one thing which has to
be done it is already wholly and utterly accomplished in Him. As
that which has taken place in God—in which we are indeed participators
on the strength of the nature of the person and work of Jesus Christ—
it is in itself and from the very outset something which has taken
place to and in us. It would not be this happening if we still had to
think of ourselves as outside, and for us to be within it had to be
superseded by another special happening. Holy Scripture speaks only
of the temporal presence of the eternally present when it speaks of
the outpouring and gift, of the work of the Holy Spirit to and in us,
or concretely, of the life of the Church quickened by the Holy Spirit,
or, with regard to the individual man, of the life of the children of
God quickened by the Holy Spirit. The life of the Church and the life
of the children of God is, as the work of the Holy Spirit, nothing but
the unity of the Father and the Son in the form of time, among and
in us men whose existence as such is not yet at home with the Lord
but still in the far country, although in Jesus Christ it is no longer in
the far country but already at home with the Lord. In the Holy
Spirit this " already " is valid ; for the Holy Spirit is the temporal
presence of the Jesus Christ who intercedes for us eternally in full
truth. Therefore for us life in the Holy Spirit means " already," even
in the midst of the " not yet," to stand in the full truth of what,
considered from our " not yet," is pure future, but on the strength
of this " already " pure present, in which therefore we can already
live here and now, expecting the annulment of the duality. In the
full truth, namely, in the truth that God is for us. Therefore—as the
truth is beyond the lie—beyond our truth ; on the far side of our
enmity against God.

And for this reason life in the Holy Spirit is the life of faith. Faith
does not consist in an inward and immanent transformation of man,
although there can be no faith without such a transformation. Basically, faith is more than all the transformation which follows it. As
the work of the Holy Spirit it is man's new birth from God, on the
basis of which man can already live here by what he is there in Jesus
Christ and therefore in truth. Faith is the temporal form of his eternal
being in Jesus Christ, his being which is grounded on the fact that
Jesus Christ intercedes for us before the Father ; that in Jesus Christ
we are ready for God in the height of God and therefore also in our
depth. Faith extinguishes our enmity against God by seeing that
this enmity is made a lie, a lie confessed by ourselves as such, expiated
and overcome by Jesus Christ, trodden underfoot and destroyed.
Our truth is not the being which we find in ourselves as our own.
The being which we find in ourselves as our own will always be the
being in enmity against God. But this very being is a lie. It is the
lie which is seen to be a lie in faith. Our truth is our being in the
Son of God, in whom we are not enemies but friends of God, in whom

we do not hate grace but cling to grace alone, in whom therefore God is knowable to us. This is man's truth believed by faith. And it is the work of the Holy Spirit that the eternal presence of the reconciliation in Jesus Christ has in us this temporal form, the form of faith, which believes this truth. The man in whom Jesus Christ has this temporal form does not then in any sense believe in himself. By faith he will still find his own being uncovered, always uncovered as a being in enmity and therefore in the lie which is outstripped and destroyed. He will still be able to live only in such a way that he turns his back upon himself, and away above himself " seeks those things which are above " (Col. 3¹). He still exercises in faith " a confidence of things hoped for, an evidence of things not seen " (Heb. 11¹). To believe means to believe in Jesus Christ. But this means to keep wholly and utterly to the fact that our temporal existence receives and has and again receives its truth, not from itself, but exclusively from its relationship to what Jesus Christ is and does as our Advocate and Mediator in God Himself. Faith is not, therefore, a standing, but a being suspended and hanging without ground under our feet. Or conversely, in faith we abandon whatever we might otherwise regard as our standing, namely, our standing upon ourselves (including all moral and religious, even Christian standing), because in faith we see that it is a false and unreal standing, a hanging without support, a wavering, and falling. We abandon it for the real standing in which we no longer stand on ourselves (on our moral and religious, or even our Christian state), and in which we obviously do not stand on our faith as such, but—now at last firmly and securely—on the ground of the truth of God and therefore on the ground of the reconciliation which has taken place in Jesus Christ and is confirmed by Him to all eternity. It is a standing which seen from ourselves (but what we see from ourselves is a lie) may well appear to be an impossible and intolerable hanging and suspension. We will always be afraid of it as we see things from ourselves. We may well try to flee from it as if our lives were at stake (as indeed they are, though in the very opposite sense). We shall continually surprise ourselves on the flight from faith. But there is no sense in going further into this phenomenon. Indeed it is dangerous to do so. For it is identical with the phenomenon of our enmity against God's grace. This phenomenon will, of course, continually emerge. But this phenomenon no longer applies to us. It is not a subject we can possibly consider. Consider it just a moment too long, and, like Lot's wife, we become a pillar of salt. We have to do something better ; we have to do the one thing that is needful. We have to believe : not to believe in ourselves, but in Jesus Christ. In Him, along with our enmity against God's grace, our flight from faith too is limited, ended and destroyed. In Him faith finds itself again. In Him the believing man, beyond and despite the darkness which is in himself, finds himself in the light, ready for God ; he finds God knowable, and he does so with all the eternal definiteness, certainty and blessedness which is proper to faith, so far as it is faith in Him, as the temporal form of the eternal truth of Jesus Christ, which is our own truth.

But it is the Church which lives by the Holy Spirit and in faith. We have already given three answers to the question : How far are we ourselves, in Jesus Christ, not outside but inside with God ? (1) We are within on the strength of the fact that Jesus Christ is for us in eternity. (2) We are within in the Holy Spirit. (3) We are within in faith. It must be clear to us that we have here three forms of the same answer, or a twofold repetition of the first answer. We are again repeating the first answer when we name the Church. Where the Holy Spirit is and therefore where faith is, there is the Church, there are men gathered and united in a temporal form on the ground of what in Jesus Christ is their common eternal truth, and therefore gathered for service, for hearing and teaching His Word and therefore for their edification, i.e., for the renewal and proclamation of their faith, and therefore to the glory of the Lord in whom they believe. Our participation in the person and work of Jesus Christ takes place by the fact that we are in the Church, that we ourselves are the Church. But like the receiving and possessing of the Holy Spirit, or faith, this does not mean an autonomous way or means of salvation. The Church is not the Church when it tries to be this. The Church with its preaching and sacraments, with its ministry of the Word to those inside and outside, does not live in and from itself. So far as it lives in and from itself it is a religious community like any other, serving the enmity against God's grace. It lives literally and really only in Jesus Christ as its Head to which it is the body ; or in Jesus Christ its heavenly body of which it is the earthly form. This is just as literally and really the case as the Holy Spirit in us is only the temporal presence of Jesus Christ Himself, or faith is only our relationship to Him. The Church is the historical form of the work of the Holy Spirit and therefore the historical form of faith. In the Church it becomes evident that the lordship of God, as the reconciliation that took place and eternally exists in Jesus Christ, comes out of the height into our depth, not only in the form of a line or many lines, but in the form of an entirely new plane. It does not have to acquire historical breadth, e.g., with the gathering of believers as an aggregate of individual points. It has it already originally and in itself. It is a totality in the manhood taken by Jesus Christ, in His heavenly body, crucified and transfigured in His resurrection but now existing in the glory of the Father. The Church is not another body. It is just the earthly form of this His own heavenly body, the manhood reconciled in Him and represented by Him above (and because above also below). The same which is in Him invisibly above, is here below visible in His service, in the renewal and proclamation of faith, in the honour which faith renders to Him. For this very reason this service can only be service and cannot become lordship. For this very reason it can be fulfilled only in the renewal and proclamation of faith, in the rendering of praise to God and in the hope of future vision. For this very reason the Church also lives by the fact that it looks out above itself. As soon as it looks into itself it finds only the religious community. But it must not do this. It, too, must learn from Lot's wife what must not happen. As the earthly body of Jesus Christ it may—as is believed and proclaimed in the Lord's Supper—be nourished by its own eternal truth in its form as the heavenly body of Jesus Christ. It cannot be nourished in any other way. If it nourishes itself in any other way it can only die as the Church. But as it lives by this nourishment, as therefore it realises the unity of its earthly with its heavenly form, the fact that this is already realised in Jesus Christ and (since this realisation is itself His ordinance and gift) actual in the work of the Holy Spirit, means that, as the Church of God, it is already perfected even in its imperfection, that even as a religious community it is already the tabernacle of God among men and therefore the answer to the question how we come to participate in Jesus Christ and His person and work.

This, then, is the positive answer to our question. There is for man, included in the readiness of God, a readiness of man for God and therefore for the knowledge of God. The enmity of man against grace and therefore his closedness against God is not the final and proper thing to be said of man. The final and proper thing to be said of him is rather that we have peace with God (Rom. 5[1]), and in this peace we stand in such a relationship to God that the knowability of God which He has bestowed upon us in His grace is received and accepted as such by us. In this our peace with God the circle is closed. In view of it the assertion that God is knowable to us becomes meaningful to us on the human side as well. Now we know where we have to seek this peace and shall find it, and where not. When we speak of this peace, and therefore of the man ready for God to whom God is knowable, we are speaking of Jesus Christ, of the reconciliation of man with God that took place and is eternal in Him the Son of God. It is in this way, and only in this way, that we speak genuinely and really about ourselves, because in the reality of Jesus Christ everything is also accomplished for us that must and can be accomplished ; because in eternity He intercedes for us ; and because in the Holy Spirit the unity of the Father and the Son becomes effectual among and in us too in the twofold form of faith and the Church. We have only to accept the witness about Jesus Christ, and we have then only to look to Jesus Christ—and it is indeed the work of the Holy Spirit, it is indeed the nature of true faith and of the true Church that this happens—to see the man to whom God is knowable, to see and understand ourselves as those to whom God is knowable. And then

6

we can go on to speak in truth of man in His relationship to God, and there can and will actually be a Christian anthropology and ecclesiology. We must not, of course, look in any other direction than to Jesus Christ. We must not formulate any other assertions than those of which He is always the true subject. About man as such, about autonomous man, existing otherwise than in Jesus Christ, the only thing we need to know is that he has brought Jesus Christ to the cross and that in this same cross his sins are forgiven ; that in his independence he is judged and removed, really removed, i.e., moved and taken up into fellowship with the life of the Son of God. Absolutely everything that is to be said about his relationship to God, and therefore about his whole truth, his sin therefore, and the Law against which he has sinned, and his creaturely existence as such, has now to be said and can only be said from this point, from his being in Jesus Christ. If this rule—which is the basic rule of all sound doctrine—is followed, the statement that God is knowable to man can and must be made with the strictest possible certainty, with an apodictic certainty, with a certainty freed from any dialectic and ambiguity, with all the certainty of the statement " the Word was made flesh." The positive answer to our question depends, then, upon whether we follow this rule, not allowing other aspects of man beside the christological to continue to play an independent role, allowing man as such to speak only as the man reconciled in Jesus Christ. For our question is not answered at all if it is not answered with apodictic certainty. But this certainty depends upon whether it is put and answered under the christological aspect of man, and under the christological aspect alone.

And we must reflect that this rule does not involve any extraordinary demand or impose any extraneous law from without. What else does it express but the Gospel by which Christian faith and the Christian Church always and everywhere affirm that they live and by which both faith and the Church really do live ? At bottom, has it not been acknowledged always and everywhere and by all that Jesus Christ is the first and last word of Christian faith and the Christian Church, and that except in His name there is no salvation ? Our rule does not say anything but this very simple thing. It only wants the Gospel really to be respected as the rule of Christian thinking and speaking. It wants to put an end to all false and partial and unreliable certainties. It wants Christian faith and the Christian Church to live by Jesus Christ and to proclaim and hear the name of Jesus Christ, so that they will not stand on a marsh but on solid rock. If this is to happen, faith and the Church and first of all theology must be brought to recognise the marsh as marsh and the rock as rock, so that it may tread on the rock as its own ground and never leave it. This, and therefore the following of its most proper and natural rule of life, is what is demanded of it by the rule that it shall seek man in Jesus Christ and nowhere else.

Our next task is to take a fresh look from this point at the problem of natural theology in the sphere of the Church.

We have had to admit that at a first glance it is not at all apparent how (i.e., from what point) natural theology is to be decisively attacked, because it is no more and no less than the herald and advocate of the evident, and indeed the only evident, possibility and reality of man as such, in which there is not at all an openness for the grace of God and therefore a readiness for the knowledge of God in His revelation. This possibility and reality inevitably involves the investigation of another sort of knowability of God. The affirmation of a natural and original knowledge of God and union of man with God, that does not need grace and its revelation, is simply the necessary self-exposition and self-justification of man as such. We have seen that its power and monopoly are also not broken but rather strengthened and confirmed by the fact that within the Church it can tolerate a theology of revelation beside and even above itself. In this way it still possesses all the vitality of the natural man. Even in the most modest position—so long as it has a position at all—it possesses openly or secretly life and victory and lordship. Starting from man as such we can arrive only at the domestication of the Gospel that takes place continually in natural theology.

But in the meanwhile we have found the positive answer to our chief question—to the question about the knowability of God which is to be understood as the readiness of man. Our last conclusion in regard to the problem of natural theology cannot remain unaffected by this answer. We now know that there is a man who is ready for God and knows God. We now know who he is, what he is called, and the fact and extent that we can recognise and understand ourselves in him. Knowing this, we can understand natural theology only as the attempt, in opposition to the rule just formulated, to confer again on man as such an independent word and right in the sphere of faith and the Church, and therefore not only to fail to assert the unique sovereignty of Jesus Christ in this sphere but even to contest it. For at this point there is no third possibility, no neutrality between the acknowledgment and the non-acknowledgment of the rule. If it is valid and respected, man as such has no independent word and right in the sphere of faith and the Church, and therefore there is no sense in his summoning himself to be his own herald and advocate in this sphere. On the contrary, if in the sphere of faith and the Church man as such has the offices of herald and advocate, if in this sphere the assertion of his possibility and aspirations can become a particular concern of his own, which can enter into a variously ordered relationship of reciprocity or even concurrence with the concern for the assertion of revelation, the rule has been definitely broken, which means that Jesus Christ is no longer understood as the only sovereign Lord, but must, as the man Jesus Christ ready for God, divide His kingdom with the man ready for God whom natural theology affirms it can know and discuss. He has ceased to be the measure, but is Himself measured by the other. He no longer speaks the first and last word, but only at best an additional word. As one factor in the assimilated and domesticated theology of revelation, He is caught up into the process of making the Gospel respectable. Neither He in particular nor the knowledge of God in general can any longer be spoken about with apodictic certainty. And we must definitely not imagine that we have given a positive answer to our chief question.

In face of this alternative we must now address ourselves for the last time to our side question : What is the secret of the vitality of natural theology ? How does it come about that it can continually arise and exist ? Not a great deal of light is shed by its achievements, its pedagogic value or its biblical foundation. Nor does it seem to be explained exhaustively by referring to the *brutum factum* of incorrigible respectability in the Church. Indeed, in this matter we have no right to dwell on this respectability, i.e., on man as such, as though he were the final factor. Have we not had to agree that he is not to be taken so seriously ? What does he mean, and what does his fatal mouth-piece, natural theology, mean, from the point of view that, no matter how unruly he may pretend to be, to him there is to be proclaimed the peace with God concluded in Jesus Christ, the already accomplished annulment of his separate existence, right and suffrage ?

It is at least clear that if we are going to take our rule seriously we cannot on any account concede to him, and with him to natural theology, the dignity and excellence of a self-established and self-assured counter-position opposed to Jesus Christ. To do this, we should again have to look elsewhere than to the Jesus Christ who intercedes both in the height above and also effectively in the depth here below for the man who is so at enmity with grace. We should again have to evade the work of the Holy Spirit and step out of the sphere of faith and the Church in which there can no longer be that independent entity. We should be forced on our side, even if only for the sake of repudiation, to place natural theology alongside the theology of revelation again, and therefore to concede to it fundamentally the very position which it has every reason to covet.

It is when we adopt to natural theology a position of repudiation that we must be particularly careful not to commit at the last minute these dangerous mistakes. They all amount to the same thing. We are trying to free ourselves from natural theology. We want to attack it. We are still somewhat shaken by the fact of its vitality. We actually take it seriously as a contradiction that is finally indis-soluble and real in this indissolubility. And as such we nail it fast and contest and deny it. But we can do this only by wrestling with it, whereas the best procedure is to start from the fact that it is already destroyed, and therefore to give it only incidental and supplementary attention. A good deal of atten-tion has actually been paid to it in these pages. But we may now point out expressly that it has taken a form which will make it quite clear that there has never been any real question of wrestling with it. The battle was already fought and the positive presentation of the knowability of God already lay behind us when we realised, and tried to explain, that with this presentation we had affirmed the very thing which the *Vaticanum* denies, and denied the very thing which it affirms. And it was only as we asked the astonished question : How is this possible ? that step by step we became involved in a supplementary treatment of the claims and promises of natural theology in general as classically embodied in the *Vaticanum*. And in this second part of our section—at the very point where man comes under consideration—it became perfectly clear that in the last resort we can know man to whom God is knowable only in Jesus Christ, and therefore that the decision in respect of the problem of the knowability of God is taken in a place where the problem of natural theology has not even arisen, and that in any case it is quite independent of the answer to that problem. It is only supplementarily and as to a side issue that we can return to it. It can no longer have any importance of its own. It can no longer lay claim to an independent interest. Even when we repudiate it, there can be no question of dealing with natural theology as with a contestant who has to be taken with full and final seriousness. The repudiation especially can consist only in a final attempt to answer the astonished question : How is this possible ? Any other and tragic treatment of the problem of natural theology will betray the fact that we have already lapsed into it. From the standpoint of the decision taken in our main question, natural theology has no real opposition to offer and therefore no opposition which is to be taken seriously. It is really repudiated and overcome only when this is perceived and the whole procedure in relation to it is determined by this insight. It is not, therefore, repudiated and overcome by the presupposition that there is at least so much in it that it must and can be negated with full and final seriousness. What is already negated in itself—and this is the case with natural theology—we cannot want specifically to negate again. It can only be recognised and indicated as self-negated from the very outset. If we try to treat it in any other way, we are not really free from it.

The vitality of natural theology is the vitality of man as such. In the sphere of man as such his own vitality is the phenomenon controlling the whole field of vision. For this reason natural theology can recommend so impressively, and so powerfully intrude, a consideration which is seriously addressed to the sphere of man. For this reason it can always triumphantly produce in this sphere new arguments for its right to exist. For this reason it can here evade every counter-argument, however illuminating. It always has power so long as this sphere is assured in itself, so long as this ground is solid, or so long as it is regarded as solid, and therefore so long as consideration is seriously given to this sphere as such. But we now know that this consideration rests on an error. For the ground is not solid. The sphere is not assured in itself. On the contrary, the presupposed independent existence of a man as such is an illusion. It is a powerful, illuminating and (if we want to leave out Jesus Christ) unconquerable illusion. As such it is, of course, so powerful that like many others the phenomenon of the power of natural theology is not really inexplicable. Yet, when we do not leave out Jesus Christ, but refer to Him, it is still an illusion. And as such it does not form a counter-position over against the truth visible in Jesus Christ. Nor, if we really refer to Jesus Christ, can we handle it and attack as a counter-position. Everything depends on whether we really refer to Jesus Christ. It is not enough to say that we do, or to act as if we do. We really have to look to Him as the revealed truth about God and therefore about man as well. If we do this, and read the truth about man out of the existence of Jesus Christ, we must now say not only that the ground on which natural theology can thrive so powerfully is not solid, but that standing on this ground was always an illusion, that in fact it was always a falling and crashing. And this very fact has become manifest in Jesus Christ for anyone with eyes to see. For in Jesus Christ there is no independent man as such. Man as such is in Jesus Christ the man taken up and accepted by God in the war of grace against his enmity against grace ; the man whose affairs God has taken out of his hands so as to make them His own ; the man for whom God Himself comes forward to stand security for him in time and in eternity. The event of Good Friday and Easter Day would have to be wiped out, the eternal event between the Father and the Son, the work of the Holy Spirit as the temporal form of this eternal event, would have to be arrested, faith as our relationship to this event, realised by the Holy Spirit, would have to be annulled, and the Church, as the unity of faith realised by the same Holy Spirit, would have to be shattered, if even for a single moment man could and should again exist as such independently, and therefore be interesting in and for himself—interesting in such a way that his possibilities and aspirations as such had to be taken seriously, and his plain enmity against God's grace had again had to be specifically discussed as if it were still there. This is, of course, quite impossible. But beyond that, it is unnecessary and illegitimate. We are not to hold him responsible for his position, establishing and addressing him in it.

It is not the case that he and his recognised contradiction still form, as it were, one element in the situation which we have to take very seriously. He has no claim at all to be solemnly considered and attacked in his corruption. Where this happens the game is already lost even because it has begun. For this is just the treatment he wants. He will submit to it with joy. For in this treatment, by the very fact that it has begun, he will be given the first and in the long run the only thing he needs, his one real concern, the possession which guarantees his victory, that is, the confirmation that he exists, that his enmity against grace is a " fact," that he can stand and hold his ground in and with it even over against Jesus Christ, even under the severest threats which it may entail. For what can rejoice us more (with all the threats it may involve) than to hear that we are so interesting—" interesting sinners " ? And this is the confirmation which we must not be given. Only unbelief, only that which is not the Church, can wish to supply this confirmation to man. Faith and the Church will have to ask themselves carefully whether they have not already become unbelief and not the Church if they stand in a relationship to man as such in which they actually supply him with this confirmation. There is no serious reason for them to do this. On the contrary, every serious reason tells against it. Man in contradiction against God has (to his salvation) no well-grounded claim to this solemn treatment, no claim that we have to take his contradiction seriously and again make it a subject of specific discussion with him. He is not so interesting as he thinks. And the great kindness we owe him is to make it clear to him from the very beginning that he is not so interesting as he thinks. It is not true that he stands and upholds himself. It is not true that he can acquire substance by his resistance. Whatever we may think, it is definitely not true in Jesus Christ. The truth of his existence is simply this—that Jesus Christ has died and risen again for him. It is this and this alone which is to be proclaimed to him as his truth. But if this is proclaimed to him, how can we still hold him responsible for his contradiction and establish and address him in it ? Do we fear perhaps that he does not know the divine Law and experience the divine judgment without which he cannot receive salvation in Jesus Christ ? But there is no other Law and judgment than that in which it is established and settled that in Jesus Christ God has taken man's affairs out of his hands and made them His own affair. Are we afraid that the responsibility into which he must definitely be led by the proclamation of faith and the Church will not go far enough ? But there is no severer responsibility than that into which he is led by the fact that God has taken all responsibility for us upon Himself in Jesus Christ. Is it our concern that man will fall into frivolity or despair when he hears that he is not taken seriously ? But what really makes us frivolous and what really brings us to despair is simply the deadly seriousness which, however strongly it may act against us, serves ultimately only to confirm us in the fact that we stand and can uphold ourselves even over against Jesus Christ, thus confirming us in our splendid misery, in our great illusion. And, in any case, why is there this constant anxiety, anxiety, anxiety in regard to the proclaiming of Jesus Christ ? Is it really necessary or possible or right to help Jesus Christ with our anxiety ? Does Jesus Christ only become a serious person when there is set against Him the serious person man, who is therefore haled and condemned to responsibility by our private law and judgment ? In this kind of proclamation does not Jesus Christ cease to be a serious person, namely, the divine person who is seriously revealed as the fulness of all salvation, and in whom, therefore, we are to believe with corresponding seriousness ? The solemn seriousness in which we anxiously affirm that we are taking man seriously by confirming him in his independence is not serious at all, but an empty masquerade. We do not take him seriously in this way. We make a fool of him. Both for the sake of its object and for the sake of the true and only salvation of man, the proclamation of faith and the Church must start out in all strictness from the fact that there is no independent man as such. There is only the man for whom Jesus Christ has died and risen again, whose affairs He has taken into His own hands. And everything that it has to say to man can only be an explanation of this his true existence. It is only in the form of this explanation and therefore only in a fundamental ignoring of his illusionary existence as an independent entity that— where faith is faith and the Church is the Church—grace and judgment, Gospel and Law, righteousness and the wrath of God will be proclaimed in Jesus Christ.

But for this very reason all the ways of natural theology are automatically and radically cut off for the proclamation of faith and the Church and with it for a theology of the Word of God which has a true understanding of itself. They are cut off so radically that basically any discussion with it can consist only in the supplementary explanation which follows the establishment of the proper theme of theology. Christian theology has no use at all for the offer of natural theology, however it may be expressed. For it is busied in quite another direction. It has good reason to regard as quite uninteresting the man for whom natural theology can always be interesting. It is wholly and utterly the prisoner of its own theme, namely, the Word of God spoken in Jesus Christ. It is claimed so completely by the task of explaining the true existence of man in Jesus Christ that it has absolutely no place or time for natural theology as the self-explanation of man as such. Natural theology is not in any sense the partner of a theology of the Word of God which has a true understanding of itself. From the point of view of this theology, it quietly drops away as superfluous. This is the meaning and in this consists the peculiar radicalness of the repudiation it encounters.

In conclusion, it will be rewarding to set clearly before our eyes the fact that this and this alone can be the meaning of its rejection. From the standpoint of a theology of the Word of God which has a true understanding of itself we do not contest natural theology as such. From the standpoint of this theology we are forced at once quietly to concede to it a certain necessity and justification. Natural theology is the doctrine of a union of man with God existing outside God's revelation in Jesus Christ. It works out the knowledge of God that is possible and real on the basis of this independent union with God, and its consequences for the whole relationship of God, world and man. It is a necessary undertaking in the sphere of man as such —presupposing that there is such a sphere and that it can therefore be the object of serious consideration. Whatever we may think of its character as reality or illusion, this sphere arises and exists in the fact that man depends on himself over against God. But this means that in actual fact God becomes unknowable to him and he makes himself equal to God. For the man who refuses His grace God becomes the substance of the highest that he himself can see, choose, create and be. It is of this that he gives an account in natural theology. He must do it, because this is the self-exposition and self-justification of the being of man in this sphere. To strive against this undertaking

as such is meaningless. In this sphere it is inevitable. Naturally man
will attempt to understand and confirm and defend himself even, and
especially, in the position of his appropriated likeness to God. Even
in this position he has not ceased to be man. He now uses his human
capabilities to assure himself and others (and, if one may say so,
the very God forsaken by him and unknowable to him) that even,
and especially, in this position outside the grace of God he is not in
any sense godless, but that here too he is a very God-fearing and God-
respecting man, that here too he is full of God. And how can we talk
him out of this if we ourselves are in the same position and accept it
as a reality ? The whole basis of this position is that man imagines
that it is a real position. And if we cannot talk him out of this imagination, if we cannot persuade him to abandon this position—as we certainly cannot—we cannot try to forbid the undertaking of natural
theology. He is in no position to let himself be forbidden. For this
prohibition attacks his very existence. He will defend himself against it
with the energy with which he defends his existence. It will only
strengthen him in his undertaking, in its necessity and justification. It
will not only not be helpful to him, but definitely harmful. " The law
worketh wrath." Even the law against natural theology can only work
wrath. We ought not to make it. We ought to be merciful and understand—and what has to be understood is unmerciful enough—that
natural theology is the only comfort of the natural man in life and death.
A captious, untenable, false, pernicious comfort no doubt—but this
is the very thing which cannot be seen by the man who has shunned
the possibility of real comfort. If we cannot make him into an altogether different man or cancel his enmity against God's grace—and
we certainly cannot do this : neither he himself nor others can bring
this about—we ought not to want to take from him his false comfort.
The whole attempt to do this will itself have far too much natural
theology about it to be commendable. For in it we will have to treat
man as a free man : free to renounce this undertaking which is so
necessary to him ; and certainly free to translate himself out of this
position (in which this undertaking is necessary to him) into another.
But if we do this we simply confirm and strengthen him in the very
thing in which he must not be confirmed and strengthened. The only
thing that can help him is that the grace of Jesus Christ Himself in
its revelation comes triumphantly to him, freeing him from the illusion
and therefore from natural theology. It is not that he himself decides
for grace and therefore proceeds in a sort of self-disillusionment to
free himself from natural theology. The grace for which we think
we ourselves can decide is not the grace of God in Jesus Christ.
The illusion that we can disillusion ourselves is the greatest of all
illusions. And a theology which thinks it can persuade man against
natural theology and forbid it to him is still itself definitely natural
theology. We must not lead ourselves and others into the temptation

of wanting to attack and defend natural theology directly and as such.

Only one thing cannot be granted to natural theology, namely, that it has a legitimate function in the sphere of the Church, or that in this sphere it has any other destiny than to disappear. The proclamation of the Christian Church or the theology of the Word of God that has a true understanding of itself can have nothing to do with it. It cannot wish to make use of it, and therefore it cannot in fact have any proper use for it. As the content of proclamation and theology it can have no place at all. It can be treated only as non-existent. In this sense, therefore, it must be excised without mercy. For proclamation and theology are busied with the Word of God and therefore with Jesus Christ. They cannot take both Jesus Christ and man as such seriously, but only Jesus Christ and man only in Him. They cannot testify to the work of the Holy Spirit and then also to the work of man that has its roots and summit in natural theology, but only to the work of the Holy Spirit. They cannot serve two masters, but only the one real Master. There can be no question of taking thought for the affairs of man as such alongside the task of proclaiming the grace of Jesus Christ which adopts and accepts man. Quite apart from them, good care is taken that the affairs of man will not turn out too badly. But if God's revelation to His Church is the truth and is understood by it as the truth, and if Jesus Christ has not died and risen again for us in vain, proclamation and theology must take their own way and course. They cannot and must not look back to extirpate the natural theology which leads its dark existence there behind them. But they also cannot and must not look back to render it their own honour and assistance. Its destruction cannot be our business; far less can its assertion and cultivation. If we must be restrained from polemical undertakings, for which we have no commission, by fear that the preaching of the Law will work wrath, fear of the will of the patient God and fear of His judgment which alone is powerful, far more our real commission must restrain us from undertaking unnecessarily to give man a particular reconfirmation, or even to let ourselves be confirmed by it. Either way natural theology can be for us only that which is behind, of which the only thing to be said is: "I forget those things which are behind" (Phil. 3¹³). For as the commission of Christian proclamation and theology, deriving from God's revelation and the existence of the Church, our commission is to stretch out after that which is before. But we cannot do this if at the same time we stretch out after that which is behind. We cannot, alongside this commission, receive and execute another. It belongs to the realism of proclamation and theology to let natural theology drop as something which has been repudiated already, ignoring and refusing to participate in it. If there is any theme of human activity which demands strict realism, it is that of the proclamation and theology of the Christian Church. And this theme—the grace of God in Jesus Christ—does demand this definite realism. It demands a christological understanding of man on the basis of which his self-understanding must be ignored as triviality. And on this point the fact ought again to be emphasised that where there is this realism, and therefore this ignoring, proclamation and theology will exercise the only possible and actual love and mercy between man and man. They will not exercise love and mercy if they want to take from him that which they cannot take from him at all, in which they can only confirm him with all their polemics, which can be taken from him only by God Himself. But they will practise love and mercy all the less if for their part they confirm him in his illusionary possession; if they join with him in making a false use of the patience of God; if with him they forget that time is left us by the forbearance of God as the time of grace; if they put themselves on his level and pursue with him a natural theology. Over man as such there is indeed suspended somewhere, as yet invisible to him, the sword of the great and frightful assault of the divine judgment in the exposure of the whole perversity of his appropriated likeness to God, of the whole reprehensibility of his enmity against God's patience, of the whole damnation and misery of his illusionary position and sphere. All this may leave him unassailed a little longer, but not for ever, not into eternity. He may perhaps comfort himself in relation to it for a little while—for every " little longer " can really mean only " a little while "—but not always and not in eternity. What still is and is true now will no longer be so one day. To be and to be true will one day be only that which is already the object of the proclamation and theology of the Church. The strength of the comfort with which he now comforts himself in the form of his natural theology may be ever so great, but one thing is certain, that this sphere has its boundary, which may or may not be called to man's remembrance by his death, but which at any rate exists, the existence of which will one day be fearfully revealed. For what is beyond this boundary can only be the judgment. None of the supposed data of natural theology can alter this judgment in the slightest. Even if it were true, which it is not, we shall certainly not stand in this judgment because we were originally united to God in such a way that we knew Him immediately. This will be no comfort to us in the unimaginable assault of the divine judgment. The very fact that we may comfort ourselves with this will mean all the more that we shall stand without comfort before the judgment of God. Christian proclamation and theology know and say now that in this unimaginable assault we shall have Jesus Christ, and therefore God Himself, for us and be saved in Him. But they also know and say that the only thing which will save us is that we shall have Jesus Christ, and in Him the divine Judge, for us. Obviously they do not exercise love and mercy if they say anything else; if, at any rate on the left hand, they strengthen poor man with the comfort with which he comforts himself. And any word of natural theology will indeed strengthen him in this way, causing him to hope where he ought to fear, and giving him a false security by which his real and frightful insecurity will only be increased. How can Christian proclamation and theology wish to work even incidentally and on the left hand in this direction as well ? Do they not need both hands for this one task : not to destroy false gods, but to prepare a free way for the one God, who has taken man's part, as the one, true and perfect salvation. How can they possibly evade the exclusiveness of this their commission ? Perhaps by appealing to God the Creator ? But God the Creator is indeed this one God of the one salvation. Perhaps by appealing to God's forbearance ? But God's forbearance is indeed the forbearance of His grace, and its one and only work is to give us time for His grace. Perhaps by appealing to the fact that the Church, itself within the world, has also a responsibility of solidarity for this world ? Certainly it has this responsibility, but its responsibility is to be a light burning and shining in the world, to tell the world that by which alone, if at all, it will stand in the assault of the divine judgment, namely this, that Jesus Christ has died and risen again for it, that God has so loved it that He has given His only begotten Son for it. If the Church does not say this to the world, and if it does not say it in the express form which the matter itself demands and in which alone it can be heard (if it is going to be heard), then it neglects the responsibility of the solidarity in which it exists with the world. It must not withhold from the world, nor must it confuse and conceal, the fact that God is knowable to us in His grace, and because in His grace, only in His grace. For this reason it can make no use of natural theology with its doctrine of another kind of knowability of God. It rejects it by not saying the thing that natural theology says so untiringly. It rejects it because it is already rejected by the positive thing that it has to say. It rejects it because on the twofold ground of realism and of love it cannot say the two things side by side.

We will conclude with a short historical commentary on the first article of the *Theological Declaration* of the Synod of Barmen on May 31st, 1934. The text is as follows :

" *I am the way, the truth, and the life: no man cometh unto the Father, but by me* " (*Jn.* 14[6]).

" *Verily, verily, I say unto you, He that entereth not by the door into the sheepfold, but climbeth up some other way, the same is a thief and a robber. . . . I am the door: by me if any man enter in, he shall be saved* " (*Jn.* 10[1, 9]).

Jesus Christ, as He is attested to us in Holy Scripture, is the one Word of God, whom we have to hear and whom we have to trust and obey in life and in death.

We condemn the false doctrine that the Church can and must recognise as God's revelation other events and powers, forms and truths, apart from and alongside this one Word of God.

This text is important and apposite because it represents the first confessional document in which the Evangelical Church has tackled the problem of natural theology. The theology as well as the confessional writings of the age of the Reformation left the question open, and it has actually become acute only in recent centuries because natural theology has threatened to turn from a latent into an increasingly manifest standard and content of Church proclamation and theology. The question became a burning one at the moment when the Evangelical Church in Germany was unambiguously and consistently confronted by a definite and new form of natural theology, namely, by the demand to recognise in the political events of the year 1933, and especially in the form of the God-sent Adolf Hitler, a source of specific new revelation of God, which, demanding obedience and trust, took its place beside the revelation attested in Holy Scripture, claiming that it should be acknowledged by Christian proclamation and theology as equally binding and obligatory. When this demand was made, and a certain audience was given to it, there began, as is well known, the so-called German Church conflict. It has since become clear that behind this first demand stood quite another. According to the dynamic of the political movement, what was already intended, although only obscurely outlined, in 1933 was the proclamation of this new revelation as the only revelation, and therefore the transformation of the Christian Church into the temple of the German nature- and history-myth.

The same had already been the case in the developments of the preceding centuries. There can be no doubt that not merely a part but the whole had been intended and claimed when it had been demanded that side by side with its attestation in Jesus Christ and therefore in Holy Scripture the Church should also recognise and proclaim God's revelation in reason, in conscience, in the emotions, in history, in nature, and in culture and its achievements and developments. The history of the proclamation and theology of these centuries is simply a history of the wearisome conflict of the Church with the fact that the " also " demanded and to some extent acknowledged by it really meant an " only." The conflict was bound to be wearisome and even hopeless because, on the inclined plane on which this " also " gravitated into " only," it could not supply any inner check apart from the apprehension, inconsistency and inertia of all interested parties. Actually in these centuries too the Church was—as always miraculously—saved because the Bible remained in face of the " also " of invading natural theology and its secret " only." For it threw its own " only " into the scales, and in this way—not without the co-operation of that human apprehension, inconsistency and inertia—did at least maintain the point that for their part God's revelation in Jesus Christ and faith and obedience to Him are " also " not actually to be reduced to silence and oblivion. Thus things were not carried as far as the logic of the matter really demands. The logic of the matter demands that, even if we only lend our little finger to natural theology, there necessarily follows the denial of the revelation of God in Jesus Christ. A natural theology which does not strive to be the only master is not a natural theology. And to give it place at all is to put oneself, even if unwittingly, on the way which leads to this sole sovereignty. But during the developments of these centuries this whole state of affairs was almost entirely hidden, particularly from the eyes of those who wanted in good faith to defend the validity and value of the biblical revelation. It is noteworthy that it was conservative movements within the Church, like those inspired by Abraham Kuyper and Adolf Stöcker, which acted most naively. But the naivete reigned at every point. The concept of revelation and that of reason, history or humanity were usually linked by the copulative particle " and," and the most superficial provisos were regarded as sufficient protection against all the possible dangers of such combinations. Happy little hyphens were used between, say, the words " modern " and " positive," or " religious " and " social," or " German " and " Evangelical," as if the meaning then became self-evident. The fact was overlooked that all this pointed to the presence of a trojan horse within which the superior enemy was already drawn into the city. For in the long run the fundamentally peaceful acknowledgment of the combination came to be accepted as the true orthodoxy, as the basis of theology (especially of Church governments). The resistance occasionally offered to it necessarily came under suspicion as fanatical one-sidedness and exaggeration.

This was how matters stood when the Church was confronted with the myth of the new totalitarian state of 1933—a myth at first lightly masked, but unmasked soon enough. It need not be said that at first the Church stood entirely defenceless before this matter and simply had to succumb to it for the time being. Once again, as so often for two hundred years—or so it seemed—the representative of a new trend and movement of the human spirit knocked at the door of the Church. Its petition was very understandable in the light of every precedent. It asked simply that its ideas and ideals should be allowed into the Church like those of all earlier times and phases. Its argument was that they constituted a more timely form, a new historical hinterland, a point of contact given by God Himself, *rebus sic stantibus*, for the proclamation of the Gospel, which in itself, of course, would remain unaltered. Exactly the same thing had happened at the beginning of the 18th century with the reviving humanism of the Stoa ; or a century later with Idealism ; or, in its train, with Romanticism ; and then with the positivism of the bourgeois society and scholarship of the 19th century ; and the nationalism of the same period ; and a little later socialism : they had all wanted to have their say in the Church. And in face of these clear precedents there could be no basic reason for silencing this new nationalism of race. Whether it was as worthy as its predecessors to be heard and to have its say in the Church is a matter on which there might be different opinions outside Germany. A negative answer would normally be given where the phenomenon of race nationalism is unknown or known only from a distance, and a different political and philosophical position causes it to be regarded with repugnance. But we must not fail to realise that inside Germany an affirmative answer could be given with what is basically just the same right. If it was admissible and right and perhaps even orthodox to combine the knowability of God in Jesus Christ with His knowability in nature, reason and history, the proclamation of the Gospel with all kinds of other proclamations—and this had been the case, not only in Germany, but in the Church in all lands for a long time—it is hard to see why the German Church should not be allowed to make its own particular use of the procedure. And the fact that it did so with customary German thoroughness is not really a ground of reproach. What the " German Christians " wanted and did was obviously along a line which had for long enough been acknowledged and trodden by the Church of the whole world : the line of the Enlightenment and Pietism, of Schleiermacher, Richard Rothe and Ritschl. And there were so many parallels to it in England and America, in Holland and Switzerland, in Denmark and the Scandinavian countries, that no one outside really had the right to cast a stone at Germany because the new combination of Christian and natural theology effected there involved the combination with a race nationalism which happened to be rather uncongenial to the rest of the world, and because this combination was now carried through with a thoroughness which was so astonishing to other nations. Now that so many other combinations had been allowed to pass uncontradicted, and had even been affectionately nurtured, it was about two hundred years too late to make any well-founded objection, and in Germany there were at first good reasons to make a particularly forceful stand for this new combination. It had the merit of recommending itself especially to German Lutheranism as, so to say, its distinctive and perhaps definitive solution of the question of the relationship of Christian and natural theology and proclamation. It could seem like the powerful river in which the different separate streams of the older and oldest history of the German Church and religion might possibly unite. It seemed to promise the exponents of culture and fellowship the unexpected fulfilment of their deepest wishes. It seemed to raise like a tidal wave the ship of the Church which many people felt had run aground, and at last, at long last to be trying to bear it back again to the high seas of the real life of the nation and therefore into the sphere of reality. Humanly speaking, it was inevitable that in 1933 the German Evangelical Church should accede to the demand made of it, to the new " also," and the " only " which lay behind it, with exactly the same abandon as it had done to so many other demands, and as the Church in other lands—wittingly or unwittingly—had continually done to so many other demands. The only question was whether the Bible, which was not at first to be suppressed, and the usual apprehension, inconsistency and inertia of all concerned, would not this time too act as a counter-weight and prevent matters being carried to extremes.

It was, therefore, an astonishing fact—and this is the significance of the first article of the Barmen *Declaration*—that within Germany there arose an opposition to the new combination which was aimed not only at this particular combination, but basically at the long-accustomed process of combination, at the " and " which had become orthodox in Germany and in the whole world, at the little hyphen as such and therefore at no more and no less than the condominion of natural theology in the Church. For when in Barmen Jesus Christ as attested to us in Holy Scripture was designated as the one Word of God whom we have to trust and to obey in life and in death ; when the doctrine of a source of Church proclamation different from this one Word of God was repudiated as false doctrine ; and when, in the concluding article of the whole *Declaration*, the acknowledgment of this truth and the repudiation of this error were declared to be the indispensable theological foundation of the German Evangelical Church—an assertion was made (far above the heads of the poor " German Christians " and far beyond the whole momentary position of the Church in Germany) which, if it was taken seriously, contained in itself a purifying of the Church not only from the concretely new point at issue, but from all natural theology. The German Christians were contradicted by the contradiction of the whole development at whose end they stood. The protest—this was expressed with blunt words at Barmen by Hans Asmussen, who had to explain the whole proposal—was " against the same phenomenon which for more than two hundred years had slowly prepared the devastation of the Church." The protest was without doubt directed against Schleiermacher and Ritschl. The protest was directed against the basic tendencies of the whole 18th and 19th centuries and therefore against the hallowed traditions of all other Churches as well. And it must be noticed that this protest was formulated in a contemporary application of the confession of the Reformation yet without the possibility of appealing to any express formula in that confession. In the unity of faith with the fathers something was expressed which they had not yet expressed in that way. The venture had to be made, even at the risk of the suspicion and later the actual charge of innovation in the Church. It was under the sign of this protest that the German Church conflict continued from this point. All its individual and practical problems were and still are directly and indirectly connected with the first article of Barmen. The Church was the " confessional " Church precisely in the measure that it took this decision seriously in all its aspects. The conclusions of the Synod of Dahlem in November 1934 clarified its position in relation to Church law. But this clarification was dependent upon the dogmatic clarification of Barmen and could be carried through only in conjunction with it. The accumulated errors and vacillations in the Confessional Church are connected with the fact that the insight expressed at Barmen—Jesus Christ is the one Word of God whom we have to trust and to obey—did not at first correspond to the flesh and blood reality of the Church but contradicted it, and had still to be repeated, attained and practised in a wearisome struggle. Where this did not happen, no other attitude could be reached in practice than that of continual partial retreats and compromises. Where it did happen, it carried with it automatically the will and the power to resist. The German Confessional Church has either the power of the ecumenical gift and task which it received and accepted at Barmen, or it has no power. It either fights for the purification of which the Evangelical Church has long been in need and is everywhere in need, or in reality it does not fight at all. Had it been concerned simply with the German error of 1933, or with certain fatal consequent manifestations of this error, its conflict would have had no less but also no more meaning than the different reactions within the great modern disorder which had never been entirely lacking earlier and are not entirely lacking elsewhere. It would then not have been a real and serious conflict. It is a real and serious conflict so far as it is concerned with the matter as a whole ; and not merely because what is at issue is obviously the opponent natural theology in its newest form, but because it is this time a question of the Church itself in its repudiation of natural theology as a whole, because it is a question of its own fundamental purification. But the very thing which (in what is best described as a cry of need and of joy) is expressed in the first article of the Barmen *Declaration* is that this is at issue. The fact that in 1934 the basic opposition could be made which is laid down in this article, and that, in spite of all uncertainty and reverses, this opposition could since prove and maintain itself as the nerve of the whole attitude of the Confessional Church in a position of the severest tribulation, is something which, however things may develop, we can already describe as one of the most notable events in modern Church history.

It was not the new political totalitarianism, nor was it the methods of beleaguerment which precipitated this event. And it is naive in the extreme to find in " Calvinism " or the activity of this or that professor of theology the effectual power of salvation (or corruption) in this affair. The fact is that, when nothing else was left for the Church, the one Word of God who is called Jesus Christ remained. The fact is that it could not let itself fall into the abyss, as was demanded, but that it could take and had to take a new stand. The fact is that this time the logic of the case worked irresistibly on the other side and therefore this time it was arrested in the Church. And all this has to be appraised spiritually or it cannot be appraised at all. What might have been expected was that, having so often blunted the temptation in its earlier, finer forms, the Church would now be tired and its eyes blurred and it would be inwardly exhausted, so that it would succumb all the more easily and this time for good to the assault of the blatant temptation. But the fact is that this did not happen. The Word of God still remained, in spite of everything, in the same Church in which it had been so often denied and betrayed. Men could still be so terrified by the spectre of the terrible form of the new god and his messiah as not to give way to it. They could still come to the position of knowing that there is another possibility than that of crashing into the abyss. In spite of every weakness they could still reach after this other possibility, reading the Bible again, confessing again its clear assertions, and therefore uttering the cry of need and of joy from Barmen. And they could at once stand and hold their position on this ground after all other grounds had crumbled under their feet. That this could be the case certainly has its spiritual-historical, theological and political presuppositions and determinations. But all the same it was impossible, and in the end a miracle, in the eyes of those who saw it at close quarters. And so the first article of Barmen was not merely a pretty little discovery of the theologians. The position in the spring of 1933 was not one in which a fortune could be made in Germany with little theological discoveries. Basically it was quite simply a public statement of the very miracle that against all expectation had once again happened to the Church. When it had lost all its counsellors and helpers, in the one Word of God, who is called Jesus Christ, it still had God for its comfort. Things being as they were, to whom else could it give its trust and obedience ; to what other source of its proclamation could it and should it cling ? *Rebus sic stantibus*, any other source could only be myth and therefore the end of all things and certainly the end of the Church. But from this very end the Church now saw itself pulled back and guarded by the Word of God in contemporaneous self-attestation. What option had it but to confess this Word of God alone ? If we want really to understand the genesis of Barmen, we shall be obliged to look finally neither to the Confessional Church as such nor to its opponents. For there is not much to be seen here. The Confessional Church was, so to speak, only the witness of a situation in which simultaneously there took place a remarkable revelation, as there had not been for a long time, of the beast out of the abyss, and a fresh confirmation of the one old revelation of God in Jesus Christ. It was only a witness of this event. Indeed, it was often a most inconspicuous and inconvenient witness. But it was a witness. It was obliged to notice what was going to be seen on this occasion—that Satan had fallen from heaven like lightning and that the Lord is mighty over all gods. What it noticed on this occasion was the fact of the unique validity of Jesus Christ as the Word of God spoken to us for life and death. The repudiation of natural theology was only the self-evident reverse side of this notice. It has no independent significance. It affirms only that there is no other help—that is, in temptation—when it is a question of the being or not being of the Church. What helps, when every other helper fails, is only the miracle, power and comfort of the one Word of God. The Confessional Church began to live at the hand of this notice and at its hand it lives to this day. And it is this notice which it has to exhibit to other Churches as the testimony which it has received and which is now laid upon it as a commission. It will be lost if it forgets this testimony, or no longer understands it, or no longer takes it seriously ; the power against which it stands is too great for it to meet it otherwise than with the weapon of this testimony. But it will also be lost if it does not understand and keep to the fact that this testimony is not entrusted to it simply for its own use, but at the same time as a message for the world-wide Church. And it may well be decisive for other Churches in the world, for their existence as the one, ecumenical Church of Jesus Christ, whether they on their side are able to hear and willing to accept the message of the Confessional Church in Germany.

For the understanding of what the first article of Barmen has to say in detail, it is perhaps advisable not to pass over the preceding verses from Jn. 14 and Jn. 10, but to understand everything from them as a starting-point. The emphasis of everything said previously lies in the fact that Jesus Christ has said something, and, what is more, has said it about Himself : I myself am the way, the truth, and the life. I myself am the door. The Church lives by the fact that it hears the voice of this " I " and lays hold of the promise which, according to this voice, is contained in this " I " alone ; that therefore it chooses the way, knows the truth, lives the life, goes through the door, which is Jesus Christ Himself alone. Moreover, it is not on its own authority, or in the execution of its own security programme, but on the basis of the necessity in which Jesus Christ Himself has said that no man comes to the Father but by Him, and that any by-passing of Him means theft and robbery, that the Church makes its exclusive claim, negating every other way or truth or life or door apart from Him. The negation has no independent significance. It depends entirely on the affirmation. It can make itself known only as the affirmation makes itself known. But in and with the affirmation it does and must make itself known. For this reason the positive assertion has precedence even in what follows, and for this reason the resulting critical assertion can be understood only as its converse and unambiguous elucidation. The Church lives by the fact that it hears the Word of God to which it can give entire trust and entire obedience, and that in life and in death—that is, in the certainty that it will be sustained in this trust and obedience for time and eternity. Precisely because it is allowed and invited to entire trust and obedience, it knows that the Word said to it is the one Word of God by which it is bound but in which it is also free, alongside whose Gospel there is no alien law and alongside whose Law there is no alien gospel, alongside or behind or above which we do not have to honour and fear any other power as way, truth, life or door.

And this one Word is not first to be found, but has already given itself to be found : in Him who has the power and the right to call Himself the way, the truth, the life and the door because He is these things.   This one Word means Jesus Christ from eternity to eternity.   In this form it is attested in the Holy Scriptures of the Old and New Testaments.   In this form it has founded the Church ; and upholds and renews and rules, and continually saves the Church.   In this form it is comfort and direction in life and in death.   In this form and not in any other ! It is of the " not in any other " that the concluding critical article speaks.   We may notice that it does not deny the existence of other events and powers, forms and truths alongside the one Word of God, and that therefore throughout it does not deny the possibility of a natural theology as such.   On the contrary, it presupposes that there are such things.   But it does deny and designate as false doctrine the assertion that all these things can be the source of Church proclamation, a second source alongside and apart from the one Word of God.   It excludes natural theology from Church proclamation.   Its intention is not to destroy it in itself and as such, but to affirm that, when it comes to saying whom we have to trust and obey in life and in death, it can have no sense and existence alongside and apart from the Word of God.   Whatever else they may be and mean, the entities to which natural theology is accustomed to relate itself cannot come into consideration as God's revelation, as the norm and content of the message delivered in the name of God.   When the Church proclaims God's revelation, it does not speak on the basis of a view of the reality of the world and of man, however deep and believing ; it does not give an exegesis of these events and powers, forms and truths, but bound to its commission, and made free by the promise received with it, it reads and explains the Word which is called Jesus Christ and therefore the book which bears witness to Him.   It is, and remains, grateful for the knowledge of God in which He has given Himself to us by giving us His Son.

27

THE LIMITS OF THE KNOWLEDGE OF GOD

God is known only by God. We do not know Him, then, in virtue of the views and concepts with which in faith we attempt to respond to His revelation. But we also do not know Him without making use of His permission and obeying His command to undertake this attempt. The success of this undertaking, and therefore the veracity of our human knowledge of God, consists in the fact that our viewing and conceiving is adopted and determined to participation in the truth of God by God Himself in grace.

1. THE HIDDENNESS OF GOD

How far is God known? and how far is God knowable? We have answered these questions in principle in the two previous sections. We may summarise our answer in the statement that God is known by God and by God alone. His revelation is not merely His own readiness to be known, but man's readiness to know Him. God's revelation is, therefore, His knowability. On the ground and in the sphere of this basic answer we now have to give a practical answer—a concrete description of the event between God and man which we call the knowledge of God and which as such is the presupposition, continually to be renewed, of all Christian doctrine, of Church dogmatics and therefore of the preaching of the Church. We have to make this event and the form of the knowledge of God plain and understandable to ourselves. We do so by defining its limits. Since we are dealing with an event, limit is here to be understood in the sense of *terminus*. What happens when God is known becomes clear and understandable to us, and visible to us as a form, when we know the *terminus a quo* and the *terminus ad quem* of this event, the point with which it begins and the point with which it ends. Thus the title of this section might well have been " The way of the knowledge of God." But the nature of this way is determined by the points at which it begins and ends, and is thus determined by the limits of the knowledge of God. The way of the knowledge of God running between these two limits is the Christian doctrine presented so far as it rests on the knowledge of God and produces the knowledge of God. If we again ask how far this doctrine rests on this knowledge and produces this knowledge, and if we ask especially about the form of its knowledge, our question will be more clear and precise if we ask about its limits.

The limit which is our concern in the first part of this section is the *terminus a quo*, the point of beginning and departure in the knowledge of God. We have said that knowledge of God is the presupposition of all Christian doctrine. But this means that it is the basis of the Church and its confession, the basis of the faith of all those who, in the Church and by the Church, are called to fellowship with God and thus to their own salvation and the glorifying of God. Knowledge of God in the sense hitherto defined by us as the knowledge of God which is objectively and subjectively established and led to its goal by God Himself, the knowledge of God whose subject and object is God the Father and the Son through the Holy Spirit, is the basis—and indeed the only basis—of the love of God which comes to us and the praise of God which is expected of us.

It involves, therefore, neither exaggeration nor intellectual restriction when, at the beginning of his *Catechism*, Calvin says that the *praecipuus finis humanae vitae* consists in the fact *ut Deum, a quo conditi sunt homines, ipsi noverint.* Nor is this statement a peculiarity of Calvinist thought. J. Gerhard agrees with it : In creation and by His Word God has stepped forth *ex arcana majestatis suae sede, . . . ut homines Deum recte agnoscerent et veram de Deo doctrinam ab omni errorum fermento puram et illibatam conservarent atque ad posteros suos propagarent* (*Loci theol.*, 1610, *L.* II, 2). It cannot be gainsaid that without the knowledge of God there is no doctrine, i.e., no proclamation of the revelation and reconciliation to which Scripture bears witness. But without doctrine there is no Church, no life of the children of God, no honouring of God by man, no salvation for man. Therefore without the knowledge of God there is no salvation. God's design in His whole action with us, and our determination, beside which we have no other because all others are contained in this one, is in fact that we may know God.

But the more strongly we emphasise this fact, so much the clearer must it become to us that God is known by God. In this knowledge we do not primarily and properly have to do with an undertaking which is to be fulfilled in human strength and will therefore share in a human and relative and assailable result. We have to do with an event which has the capacity that is needed if everything is to be built on it, if the Church and the children of God are to grow and live from this basis. In the foregoing sections we have continually laid down that we are dealing with a cognition which does not have merely a relative certainty, but the absolute, simple and indisputable certainty of God Himself. It cannot be established in this certainty otherwise than by God Himself ; but otherwise than by God Himself it cannot be attacked and annulled. The *terminus a quo* of the knowledge of God is therefore the fact that in it we have to do with God Himself by God Himself, in insurpassable and incontestable certainty, and that therefore it is real knowledge of God. We may equally well say (pending more detailed definition) that this will also be the *terminus ad quem* of which we must speak later.

Again, J. Gerhard expressly describes the *cognitio Dei ex verbo petita* as perfect knowledge, *cognitio perfecta,* and he finds its *perfectio* in the fact that it is *sufficiens ad salutem* (*op. cit.,* II, 90). It is indeed the strength of this knowledge that it is sufficient for our salvation. But what is sufficient for our salvation cannot, as knowledge of God, be other than perfect. It must consist in an event in which we really have to do with God Himself. For what creates our salvation and what establishes the Church and the life of the children of God is nothing less nor other than God Himself : not merely a word about God, but the utterance of the Word of reconciliation as the Word of truth which God Himself speaks and which He alone can speak. Thus the perfection of the knowledge of God consists in the very fact that in it we have to do with God Himself. It is in this that it is real (i.e., true) knowledge of God.

But the fact that in the knowledge of God we have to do in divine certainty with God Himself by God Himself, is one which, as the *terminus a quo* of this event, we must now investigate more closely and define more exactly. We are speaking of the knowledge of God whose subject is God the Father and God the Son through the Holy Spirit. But we men are taken up into this event as secondary, subsequent subjects. Therefore we are not speaking only of an event which takes place on high, in the mystery of the divine Trinity. We are indeed speaking of this event, and the force of anything that is said about the knowledge of God consists in the fact that we speak also and first of this event. But we are now speaking of the revelation of this event on high and therefore of our participation in it. We are speaking of the human knowledge of God on the basis of this revelation and therefore of an event which formally and technically cannot be distinguished from what we call knowledge in other connexions, from human cognition. The fact that it has God not only for its object but also as its origin, and that its primary and proper subject is the Father who knows the Son and the Son who knows the Father in the Holy Spirit, and that it is a sure and perfect and genuine cognition because God is known by God, does not mean either the abrogation, abolition or alteration of human cognition as such, and therefore of its formal and technical characteristics as human cognition. But human cognition is fulfilled in views and concepts. Views are the images in which we perceive objects as such. Concepts are the counter-images with which we make these images of perception our own by thinking them, i.e., arranging them. Precisely for this reason they and their corresponding objects are capable of being expressed by us. If men can speak of God in human words—and this is the presupposition which we have to examine—it is obvious that they can first view and conceive (i.e., perceive and think) God. If this is not so, they do not know Him. Knowledge of God is still only an event enclosed in the mystery of the divine Trinity.

But what are we saying when we affirm that men can view and conceive God and therefore view and conceive Him after a human manner ? When we say this, have we made a statement on human cognitive capacity as such, on a possibility immanent in our viewing and conceiving (i.e., indwelling and proper to it as such)? Does it follow from the fact that we are capable of viewing and conceiving objects in general that in certain circumstances, i.e., presupposing the fact that God reveals Himself to us and therefore makes Himself object to us, we are also capable of viewing and conceiving this object on the basis of the same capacity? Clearly we cannot evade the insight of the whole Early Church and theology that this statement must not be ventured in this sense. If we keep to the fact that God is known only by God, then whatever may be the function of our viewing and conceiving, and however necessary this function may be, it is fixed that we certainly do not know Him by these views and concepts of ours: that is to say, not by their inner power; not in virtue of their own capacity, i.e., of the capacity of human viewing and conceiving as such; not in virtue of a potentiality of our cognition which has perhaps to be actualised by revelation. We definitely cannot deny to this the character and function of an instrument in this event. In the act of the knowledge of God, as in any other cognitive act, we are definitely active as the receivers of images and creators of counter-images. Yet while this is true, it must definitely be contested that our receiving and creating owes its truth to any capacity of our own to be truly recipients and creators in relation to God. It is indeed our own viewing and conceiving. But we ourselves have no capacity for fellowship with God. Between God and us there stands the hiddenness of God, in which He is far from us and foreign to us except as He has of Himself ordained and created fellowship between Himself and us—and this does not happen in the actualising of our capacity, but in the miracle of His good-pleasure. Our viewing as such is certainly capable of receiving images of the divine. And our conceiving as such is certainly capable of creating idolatrous pictures. And both are projections of our own glory. But our viewing and conceiving are not at all capable of grasping God. That is to say, what they grasp as such—as our own viewing and conceiving, as the work of our nature—is as such not God but a reality distinct from God. This is not only so when we are not concerned with God's revelation and our undertaking to view and conceive God is an arbitrary undertaking foreign to faith in God's revelation. We are not simply repeating what had to be said against the undertaking of natural theology. We are now taking a further step in the same direction; or rather, we have now reached the place from which the rejection of natural theology receives its final necessity and strength. For even when we are occupied with God's revelation, when therefore we are concerned with giving an answer in faith to God's revelation, we are still not capable of ourselves of having fellowship with God, and therefore viewing and conceiving Him, and therefore realising our knowledge of God. At this very point it emerges that although the knowledge of God certainly does not come about without our work, it also does not come about through our work, or as the fruit of our work. At this very point the truth breaks imperiously and decisively before us : God is known only by God ; God can be known only by God. At this very point, in faith itself, we know God in utter dependence, in pure discipleship and gratitude. At this very point we are finally dissuaded from trusting and confiding in our own capacity and strength. At this very point we can see that our attempt to answer God's revelation with our views and concepts is an attempt undertaken with insufficient means, the work of unprofitable servants, so that we cannot possibly ascribe the success of this attempt and therefore the truth of our knowledge of God to ourselves, i.e., to the capacity of our views and concepts. In faith itself we are forced to say that our knowledge of God begins in all seriousness with the knowledge of the hiddenness of God.

It is to be noted that the assertion of the hiddenness of God as introduced and represented here has no connexion with a general theory of human knowledge, and therefore must not be measured by either the contradictory or what seem to be the very similar statements of general theories of knowledge. We are certainly in the sphere of human knowledge, but only of the knowledge of God, and of the knowledge of God particularised by its foundation in revelation. This particularisation takes place by the revelation which establishes it, so far as this obliges us not to take account of any other beside the God known in it. Our assertion does not deny what may be called God's revelation in the sphere of a general theory of knowledge which either is unrelated to God's revelation or is not, as this demands, related to it alone. Nor does it maintain and confirm, let alone derive from, what may be called God's hiddenness in a general theory of knowledge. For example, nothing can be more misleading than the opinion that the theological statement of the hiddenness of God says roughly the same thing as the Platonic or Kantian statement, according to which the supreme being is to be understood as a rational idea withdrawn from all perception and understanding. If we have to say that God is in fact withdrawn in this way, this does not mean that the rational idea, surpassing all cognitive experience and all cognitive categories, is identical with God. For on this view God is understood as a rational idea, which, however transcendent, is general, " pure " and non-objective (i.e., objective only in intention). This shows us at once that it has no identity with God, and any such identity must be denied. The God who encounters man in His revelation is never a non-objective entity, or one which is objective only in intention. He is the substance of all objectivity. And when He encounters man as the hidden One, His hiddenness not only concerns human perception and understanding as such, but also the intention which accompanies this perceiving and understanding, i.e., our capacity for it. It concerns the act of human knowledge and its intentions ; it concerns ourselves. And it concerns ourselves even as God's revelation concerns us. God's hiddenness is not the content of a last word of human self-knowledge ; it is not the object of a last performance of human capacity ; it is the first word of the knowledge of God instituted by God Himself, which as such cannot be transposed into self-knowledge, or into the statement of a general theory of knowledge. When we say that God is hidden, we are not speaking of ourselves, but, taught by God's revelation alone, of God.

The hiddenness of God is the content of a statement of faith. We have already said that it is in faith itself that we are forced to dispossess ourselves of any capacity for viewing and conceiving God. It is in faith, and therefore in the fulfilment of the knowledge of God, and therefore in the real viewing and real conceiving of God, that we can understand the fact that we know, view and conceive God, not as a work of our nature, not as a performance on the basis of our own capacity, but only as a miraculous work of the divine good-pleasure, so that, knowing God, we necessarily know His hiddenness. But we must now continue that it is only in faith, only in the fulfilment of the knowledge of God which is real because it is grounded in God's revelation, that we conceive God's hiddenness. The *terminus a quo* of the knowledge of God is not, therefore, identical with the *terminus ad quem* which we can reach when we discern the inability—i.e., the limitation—of our perception and discursive thinking. When we reach this insight, which perhaps forms the end of self-knowledge, we have not even begun to know God. This is just as true when we remain satisfied with the negation as when we think we need to complete it with the corresponding " position," namely, the affirmation of the possibility of an intuitive cognition, of an immediate sight of the reality intended in our perceiving and thinking. God's hiddenness is the hiddenness of God. It is one of His properties. It is indeed that property of God with which His knowledge as such undoubtedly has its formal beginning. It is not reflections about space and time and about the categories of our thought, nor the *aporia* in which we can entangle ourselves with these reflections, thus setting ourselves a more negative or perhaps a very positive limit, but simply the great positions of the biblical attestation and of the Church's confession of the being and activity of God, which move us to assert God's hiddenness. With this assertion we confess that, knowing God, we do not comprehend how we come to know Him, that we do not ascribe to our cognition as such the capacity for this knowledge, but that we can only trace it back to God. It is God alone, and God's revelation and faith in it, which will drive and compel us to this avowal. Without faith we will definitely remain satisfied with the delimitation which we allotted to ourselves. And the lack of seriousness in this delimitation will probably be betrayed in two ways. We shall ascribe to ourselves a capacity for the knowledge of God in opposition to the revelation of God. And we shall, therefore, treat God's revelation as something which stands at our own disposal, instead of perceiving that the capacity to know God is taken away from us by revelation and can be ascribed to us again only by revelation.

When in Ps. 139[6] it says of God's action : " It is too wonderful for me ; it is high, I cannot attain unto it " ; or in Job 36[26] : " Behold, God is great, and we know him not " ; and when Paul calls God invisible (Rom. 1[20], Col. 1[15], 1 Tim. 1[17]), we can ascertain from the more immediate and more general contexts of the passages that there is definitely no question here of the *terminus ad quem* set up by man himself, but of the *terminus a quo* set up by God in His revelation. But this enables us to understand the corresponding voices of the Early Church and its theology, although here we are occasionally faced by the linguistic problem how far they were clear about the fact that, when they spoke of the ἀκαταληψία, the *incomprehensibilitas*, the incomprehensibility of God, they were saying anything basically different from what Plato and Plotinus could also say when they spoke about the inaccessibility of the true and supreme being and the transcendence of the knowledge of this being.

The concept ἀκατάληπτος as a designation of the nature of God is first met with in the Christian sphere in the *First Epistle of Clement* (33³), and then in Athenagoras (*Leg. pro christ.* 10). When at his trial during the persecution of the Gallic Christians under Aurelius the martyr Attalus was asked what was the name of his God, he replied : ὁ θεὸς ὄνομα οὐκ ἔχει ὡς ἄνθρωπος. (Euseb *Ch. Hist.* V, 1, 52), and Justin Martyr even called it an incurable madness to want to give a name to the ἄρρητος θεός (*Apol.* I, 61). God is ἐπέκεινα πάσης οὐσίας καὶ ἀνθρωπίνης ἐννοίας (Athanasius, *C. gent.* 2, cf. 35). *De Deo loquimur, quid mirum, si non comprehendis? Si enim comprehendis, non est Deus* (Augustine, *Sermo* 117, 3, 5). *Ergo Domine, non solum es, quo maius cogitari nequit, sed es quiddam maius quam cogitari possit*, writes Anselm of Canterbury. And he proves his statement in this way God is He than whom no greater can be conceived. But an inconceivable is, as such, conceivable. If it were not identical with God, then it would be a greater than God. Therefore, since no greater than He can be conceived, God is Himself the inconceivable (*Prosl.* 15). (We may notice continually in this construction that the inconceivability of God is imputed to His positive greatness and not deduced from a human deficiency.) So far as I know, it was Anselm who first used the formula—paradoxical but very important and suitable for the whole problem—that the task of theology is *rationabiliter comprehendere* (*Deum*) *incomprehensibile esse* (*Monol.* 64). In the Fourth Lateran Council, 1215 (c. 2, *Denzinger* 428), *incomprehensibilitas* is declared for the first time to be a property of God. And then we read in Thomas Aquinas : *Comprehendere Deum impossibile est cuicumque intellectui creato* (*S. theol.* I, qu. 12, *art.* 7). The matter was obviously felt to be important, for the word could pass over into a whole series of 16th and 17th century Reformed Confessions as a designation of God (*Gall., Belg., Scot. and Westm. Conf.*), and with varying degrees of emphasis the *incomprehensibilitas Dei* could be fairly regularly mentioned and discussed as one of the properties of God in the older Protestant dogmatics. If we remember the " invisible " God of the witness of the Bible we can appreciate the necessity of this and the reasons for it.

But the relationship to the God of the biblical witness, and therefore the character of this assertion as an article of faith, was veiled in a certain obscurity in the Early Church and the Middle Ages and even into the modern period. A favourite anecdote was that of the ancient philosopher Simonides who, challenged by King Hieron to answer the question *Quid sit Deus?*, requested first one, then two, then three days, and more, to consider, and finally replied : " The longer I think about it, the less I know the answer." Calvin and J. Gerhard found this story worthy of notice, and later still Schleiermacher too adopted it with approbation. Did they cite it because they tacitly re-interpreted it as a declaration of the self-understanding of the Christian faith ? Or did they cite it because they just as tacitly thought they saw in the *docta ignorantia* of the natural man, which is obviously expressed in this anecdote, a confession of the hiddenness of God ? The twilight which covers the history of dogma in this respect cannot be entirely dispelled. And it is of a piece with it that the full reach and power of the statement *Deus est incomprehensibilis* were never known in the older dogmatics. When it became an essential part of the doctrine of the properties of God something quite decisive was certainly said and won. A very basic indication was given. But it was as if they had not entirely understood the indication itself. Otherwise, the *incomprehensibilitas Dei* could not have emerged and disappeared again in the series of

other divine properties. It would necessarily have occupied a basic and determinate position—which we are now giving it—in relation to the whole doctrine
of the knowledge of God. In the newer dogmatic literature I know of only one,
the Dutch theologian H. Bavinck, who seems to have perceived this (cf. the
beginning of the 2nd vol. of his *Gereformeerde Dogmatiek*, 1918). The fact that
this was not seen in the older theology seems to me to be explicable only on the
grounds that in those times it was not finally clear whether they really wanted to
understand the incomprehensibility of God from Plato and Plotinus, or from
Ps. 139 and from Paul, and therefore as an article of faith confirming the revelation of God as such. But we cannot easily evade the conclusion that it can only
be the latter. And this being the case, the matter gains a practical importance
which it could not have earlier for all the basic nature of the insight.

Let us first try to come to a closer understanding of the content
of the statement of God's hiddenness. And first, we must establish
linguistically that it is not merely a question of His " incomprehensibility," of the fact that God cannot be conceived, i.e., cannot become
the content of a concept formed by us, in so far as we think of the
ability and capacity of our conceiving as such. It is, of course, a
question of this as well. We cannot conceive God because we cannot
even contemplate Him. He cannot be the object of one of those perceptions to which our concepts, our thought-forms and finally our
words and sentences are related.

As the older theology used the word, the " incomprehensibility " of God is
something very far-reaching. Quenstedt gives it a threefold meaning : 'Ακαταληψία
*sive incomprehensibilitas Dei est qua ipse ratione Essentiae suae ac proprietatum
essentialium a nulla mente finita perfecte concipi aut oculis corporeis comprehendi
aut lingua creata enunciari potest. Hinc tribus velut gradibus constat incomprehensibilitas quorum I. est incognoscibilitas, II. invisibilitas, III. ineffabilitas. Illa
oculos mentis, ista oculos corporis, haec vero loquelam oris a Dei* καταλήψει *seu
comprehensione excludit.* (*Theol. did. pol.*, 1685, I, c. 8, sect. 1, th.21.) But even in
the relevant passages in the Church fathers it is already a question of the whole
sphere of *videre, sentire, aestimare, capere, investigare, explicare*, etc., of the whole
sphere of human apperception or capacity for apperception which precedes and
underlies human speech. This capacity as such is disavowed in relation to God
by the concept of the *incomprehensibilitas Dei*.

But we must go further (even though this is partly against tradition
or at any rate not unanimous with it) and not exempt from what we
have to deny as human capacity the intuitive and immediate cognition
which we may allow accompanies our viewing and conceiving and is
immanent to it. We have already touched on the significance of this.
It means that the non-objective invisible, ineffable, incomprehensible
and inexpressible object of such a cognition is expressly to be distinguished from Him whom we here, on the basis of His revelation, call
the hidden God. We shall have cause to come back to this point.
But to begin with, this differentiation is only of secondary interest.
The subject of our present enquiry is the knowledge which establishes
Christian language and doctrine. What comes under consideration as
such is not immediate knowledge but the mediate knowledge which
passes into viewing and conceiving. The statement of the hiddenness

of God says of it as such that it cannot, on the ground of man's own capacity, be the knowledge of God.

But this very negation now needs detailed material explanation. The assertion of God's hiddenness (which includes God's invisibility, incomprehensibility and ineffability) tells us that God does not belong to the objects which we can always subjugate to the process of our viewing, conceiving and expressing and therefore our spiritual oversight and control. In contrast to that of all other objects, His nature is not one which in this sense lies in the sphere of our power. God is inapprehensible.

We have already seen how God's ἀκαταληψία was understood in the second century : we can give God no *nomen* ; we cannot exercise towards Him the activity which, according to Gen. 2¹⁹f·, is characteristic of man in his relationship to other living creatures. *Nulla definitione poterit proprie determinari* (Augustine, *De cogn. verae vitae* 7). For : *Deus non est in aliquo genere* (Thomas Aquinas, *S. theol.*, I qu. 3, art. 5).

In other words, the lines which we can draw to describe formally and conceptually what we mean when we say " God " cannot be extended so that what is meant is really described and defined ; but they continually break apart so that it is not actually described and therefore not defined. In relation to God the means of definition at our disposal are not sufficient to reassure us, when we have applied them to Him, that we have thought what must be thought and said here. The being apprehended by us in thoughts and words is always either not yet or else no longer the being of God. How, then, did we come even to " mean " what is " meant," to " intend " what has to be " intended " ?· How did we come even to affirm the existence of the being which is here to be perceived and conceived and named ?

Augustine maintained that there can never be a *proprie definiri*, and Quenstedt that there can never be a *perfecte concipi*, of God. This *proprie* or *perfecte*, as Chrysostom noted in his exposition of the Pauline term ἐκ μέρους (1 Cor. 13⁹), has not to be understood quantitatively, as if we apprehend a part of the being of God, but cannot apprehend an even greater part, but disjunctively : we know indeed that God is, but not what He is. " We do not comprehend Him " means " we do not comprehend His being." Οὐχ ὅτι τὸ μὲν αὐτοῦ τῆς οὐσίας γινώσκει, τὸ δὲ ἀγνοεῖ, ἁπλοῦς γὰρ ὁ θεός, ἀλλ' ἐπειδὴ ὅτι μὲν ἔστι θεὸς οἶδε, τὸ δέ τι τὴν οὐσίαν ἐστὶν ἀγνοεῖ (*De incomprehensibili* 1, 5). But this distinction is impracticable. That God is, lies as little in the field of our spiritual oversight and control as what He is. We lack the capacity both to establish His existence and to define His being.

If we now ask why this is so, we must be careful not to be tempted by the older theology on to the paths of general considerations, which will help us to understand the incomprehensibility of the supreme being in the sense of Plato and Plotinus or even Kant, but not the incomprehensibility of God. Or rather, we shall have to divest of their original character the perhaps inevitable elements of a generally " metaphysical " language structure, giving them a clear theological sense by placing them in the theological context. We must not, therefore, base the hiddenness of God on the inapprehensibility of the infinite, the absolute, that which exists in and of itself, etc. For all this in itself and as such (whether it is or not, and whatever it may be) is the product of human reason in spite of and in its supposed inapprehensibility. It is not, therefore, identical with God and is in no way a constituent part of the divine hiddenness. What we shall have to say is that God is not a being whom we can spiritually appropriate. The pictures in which we view God, the thoughts in which we think Him, the words with which we can define Him, are in themselves unfitted to this object and thus inappropriate to express and affirm the knowledge of Him. For God—the living God who encounters us in Jesus Christ—is not such a one as can be appropriated by us in our own capacity. He is the One who will appropriate us, and in so doing permit and command and therefore adapt us to appropriate Him as well. It is because the fellowship between God and us is established and continues by God's grace that God is hidden from us. All our efforts to apprehend Him by ourselves shipwreck on this. He is always the One who will first and foremost apprehend and possess us. It is only on the basis of this, and in the area marked out by it, that there can and should be our own apprehension of God.

It is the case that we resemble what we can apprehend. Thus we certainly resemble the world and everything in it. For with the world we are created by God. And for this reason we can form views and concepts of the world and what is in it. But we do not resemble God. The fact that we are created in the likeness of God means that God has determined us to bear witness to His existence in our existence. But it does not mean that we possess and discover an attribute within ourselves on the basis of which we are on a level with God. When the serpent insinuated this to the first man, Adam missed his true determination and fell into sin. Because, therefore, we do not find in ourselves anything which resembles God, we cannot apprehend Him by ourselves.

Let us put it in another way. We are masters of what we can apprehend. Viewing and conceiving certainly mean encompassing, and we are superior to, and spiritually masters of, what we can encompass. In this sense we are masters of the world and everything in it, in spite of the enigmatic quality and superior power which we apparently encounter in them. For the apparent infinite of the world is in fact limited by the finite just as the apparent finite is limited by the infinite. Absolute and relative, being for itself and being in itself, are dialectical and changeable concepts. Their contradiction is always already overcome and mastered in ourselves, so that theoretically and practically it can always be overcome and mastered. But God is not one whom we can dialectically encompass. If we equate Him with world elements which we will encompass and secretly have already encompassed, we shall encompass and apprehend a world element—but not God. If we incorporate Him into any of our world-views, it may help us to complete this world-view; but at the same time it will reveal its godlessness, and involuntarily we shall have confirmed the hiddenness of God. We are not master of God, and for this reason we cannot apprehend Him of ourselves.

Let us put it in yet another way. We are originally and properly one with what we can apprehend. To apprehend certainly means to possess. But there is no possession without original and proper unity between the possessor and the possessed. Upon this unity rests the secret of our capacity to apprehend in this or that way the world and what is in it. Heaven and earth, invisible and visible, spirit and nature, being and knowing, the world as object and man as subject— all these, however great may be their immanent contrast, are originally and properly one as the creation of God. This is recollected in the act of the knowledge of the world by man, and conversely, as the bolder philosophers have always seen and said, the world achieves self-awareness in man and his knowledge. And this is what makes human apprehending possible and effectual on this plane. But between God and man there is no such unity. Creation by God—even the creation of man—means the institution of an existence really distinct from the existence of God. Between God and man, as between God and the creature in general, there consists an irrevocable otherness. Because this is so, because the mystery of unity underlying all our other apprehension does not exist here, we cannot conceive God of ourselves.

Even within the fellowship between God and us ordained by God's grace, this negation exists and is valid. Made like God by His grace in Jesus Christ, we shall never say that we resemble Him of ourselves. Become master of Him by His grace in Jesus Christ, we shall never say that we are master of Him of ourselves. Become one with God by His grace in Jesus Christ, we shall never say that we are one with Him of ourselves. By the grace of God we are like Him, master of Him, one with Him. This has to be said of His children in the name of His only-begotten Son. But as such we shall honour and acknowledge the revelation of the judgment of truth, according to which we of ourselves are not these things. We shall, therefore, renounce the capacity to conceive God—or rather, we shall be forced to know that this renunciation is imposed upon us. When we think the being of this God, God in Jesus Christ, as we can and must, the possibilities of our apprehending do in fact break apart, and we do not really know what we are saying when we say " God," no matter whether we try to express it by this word or by any other word. And this is the point at which we ourselves must and will avow that this is so, necessarily recognising and confessing the incapacity of our apprehending, and therefore God's hiddenness.

The beginning of our knowledge of God—of this God—is not a beginning which we can make with Him. It can be only the beginning which He has made with us. The sufficiency of our thought-form, and of the perception presupposed in it, and of the word-form based on it, collapses altogether in relation to this God. Of ourselves we do not resemble God. We are not master of God. We are not one with God. We are not capable of conceiving Him. But this means, with a backward reference so to speak, in respect of the views to which our concepts must be related, that no man has ever seen God. What " any man " has seen of himself has always been something other than God. God is invisible. He is invisible to the physical eye of man; He is also invisible to the so-called spiritual. He is not identical with any of the objects which can become the content of the images of our external or inner perception. But it also has a forward reference, in respect of the words which express our concepts, enabling us to impart knowledge to others. No one has ever said, or can say, of himself, in virtue of the dynamic of his words, what God is ; God is inexpressible, *ineffabilis*. But He is not *invisibilis* and *ineffabilis* in the same way as the infinite, the absolute, the indeterminate, the spirit in the world, can also be described as invisible and inexpressible. For then indeed, as all philosophies and outlooks shew, there is no lack of images of concept, perception or expression as there would have to be if man really knew he had no power to apprehend these quantities. But God is invisible and inexpressible because He is not present as the physical and spiritual world created by Him is present, but is present in this world created by Him in His revelation, in Jesus Christ, in the proclamation of His name, in His witnesses and sacraments. He is, therefore, visible only to faith and can be attested only by faith. But this means that He is to be seen only as the invisible and expressed only as the inexpressible, not as the substance of the goal or origin of our seeing and speaking, but because He Himself has given us permission and command to see and speak, and therefore by His Word, and in His free and gracious decision, has given us the capacity to see and speak.

What we have learned from the Early Church and its theology about the incomprehensibility of God or about His invisibility and ineffability is to be estimated critically and expressly augmented and corrected in the light of this truth : *Non videri potest, visu clarior est, nec comprehendi, tactu purior est, nec aestimari, sensibus maior est, infinitus, immensus et soli sibi tantus, quantus est, notus; nobis vero ad intellectum pectus angustum est* (Minucius Felix, *Octavius* 18). When we undertake to conceive God, He is ἐξαναχωροῦν ἀεὶ καὶ πόρρω ἀφιστάμενον τοῦ διώκοντος (Clement of Alex., *Strom.* II, 2, 5, 2). *Sensus capax omnium bene et recte dicetur, sed non similis hominum sensui, et lumen rectissime dicitur, sed nihil simile ei, quod est secundum nos, lumini. Sic autem et in reliquis omnibus nulli similis erit omnium pater hominum pusillitati et dicitur quidem secundum haec propter dilectionem, sentitur autem super haec secundum magnitudinem* (Irenaeus, *Adv. o. h.* II, 13, 4). *Quidquid de Deo dixeris, quidquid tacitae mentis cogitatione conceperis, in humanum transilit et corrumpitur sensum, nec habet propriae significationis notam, quod nostris dicitur verbis et ad negotia humana compositis* (Arnobius, *Adv. nat.* III, 19). *Ipsum quod in semetipso et a semetipso sit et ipse per se sit, quod invisibilis et incomprehensibilis (!) et immortalis—in his quidem honoris confessio est et sensus significatio et quaedam circumscriptio opinandi, sed naturae sermo succumbit et rem ut est verba non explicant. . . . Deficit ergo in nuncupatione confessio et quidquid illud sermonum aptabitur, Deum ut est, quantusque est, non eloquetur* (Hilarius, *De trin.*, II, 7). *In omni nomine a nobis dicto quantum ad modum significandi, imperfectio invenitur, quae Deo non competit* (Thomas Aquinas, *S. c. gent.* I, *c.* 30). We may notice that Hilary too related this expressly to the concept of the incomprehensibility of God. Similarly Augustine : *Ne ineffabilis quidem dicendus est Deus, quia et hoc, cum dicitur, aliquid dicitur* (*De doctr. chr.* I, 6). The hiddenness of God is not, then, in any way denied or circumvented in the transition from an apophatic to a cataphatic theology. In the same way the older Protestant orthodoxy knew that any definition of God *est duntaxat descriptio quaedam Dei, quatenus nobis est patefactus; nam Deus non potest definiri et ad perfecte definiendum Deum Dei ipsius Logica opus fuerit* (Polanus, *Synt. Theol. chr.*, 1609, II, 3, *col.* 857). *Deum quidem cognoscimus, sed non comprehendimus* (J. Gerhard, *Loci theol.*, 1610 f., L. II., 90). If only we could take it that all this is said of the transcendence of the knowledge of God in the grace of His revelation ! The contexts point mostly in another direction. Anselm of Canterbury comes near to the point, describing the hiddenness of God more exactly than almost all the rest of the older orthodox, on the one hand as a predicate of the glory of the Lord present to man, and on the other in its relationship to the sinful closedness of man against this God present to him : *Ideo hanc (lucem) non video, quia nimia mihi est. . . . Non potest intellectus meus ad illam. Nimis fulget, non capit illam, nec suffert oculus animae meae diu intendere in illam. Reverberatur fulgore, vincitur amplitudine, obruitur immensitate, confunditur capacitate. O summa et inaccessibilis lux, o tota et beata veritas, quam longe es a me, qui tam prope tibi sum ! Quam remota es a conspectu meo, qui sic praesens sum conspectui tuo ! Ubique es tota praesens et non te video. In te moveor et in te sum et ad te non possum accedere. Intra me et circa me es, et non te sentio.—Adhuc lates, Domine, animam meam in luce et beatitudine tua et idcirco versatur illa adhuc in tenebris et miseria sua. Circumspicit enim et non videt pulchritudinem tuam. Auscultat et non audit harmoniam tuam. Olfacit et non percipit odorem tuum. Gustat et non cognoscit saporem tuum. Palpat et non sentit lenitatem tuam. Habes enim haec, Domine Deus, in te tuo ineffabili modo, qui ea dedisti rebus a te creatis suo sensibili modo; sed obriguerunt, sed obstupuerunt, sed obstructi sunt sensus animae meae vetusto languore peccati* (*Prosl.* 16–17). We must admit that here at any rate we are close to the insight that we do not have to do with any kind of hiddenness, but with that of the merciful and holy God. Our final point, returning to the beginning of dogmatic history, is that Justin Martyr (*Apol.* II, 6) described the name Christ as the ὄνομα περιέχον ἄγνωστον σημασίαν. We can appropriate what tradition has to say on this matter, if we understand it to be rightly said under this sign.

We thus understand the assertion of the hiddenness of God as the confession of the truth and effectiveness of the sentence of judgment which in the revelation of God in Jesus Christ is pronounced upon man and therefore also upon his viewing and conceiving, dispossessing him of his own possibility of realising the knowledge of the God who encounters him, and leaving him only the knowledge of faith granted to him and demanded of him by the grace of God and therefore only the viewing and conceiving of faith.

But by this same fact we are already impelled to the positive meaning of the statement. Where we really confess God's judgment, we also confess God's grace. The assertion of the hiddenness of God is not, therefore, to be understood as one of despairing resignation, but actually as the *terminus a quo* of our real knowledge of God, as the fundamental and decisive determination, not of our ignorance, but of our cognisance of God. It affirms that our cognisance of God does not begin in ourselves, since it has already begun in God ; namely, in God's revelation and in faith to Him. The confession of God's hiddenness is the confession of God's revelation as the beginning of our cognisance of God. Only in a secondary and derived sense is it also a confession of our own incapacity. The emphasis in the confession of God's hiddenness is not primarily that of humility but first and decisively that of gratitude. Because God forgives us our sins we know that we need forgiveness, and that we are sinners. And because God views and conceives Himself in His Word we know that He is not viewable and conceivable in any other way, and that therefore we are incapable of viewing and conceiving Him of ourselves. The negation is only to be understood from this " position." The moment the confession of the negation becomes indispensable to us, we are separated by an abyss from all resignation and scepticism. The moment we have unreservedly to confess God's hiddenness, we have begun really and certainly to know God. As an assertion of revelation and therefore of faith, as a confession of our grateful responsibility to the God present to us, the insight that God is hidden from us is the infallible indication of the fact that it is by God Himself—namely, by His revelation—that we are led to the knowledge of Him, that we and our knowledge do not stand outside and afar off but in the very presence of God Himself. It is in the real knowledge of God that it is a question of apprehending God in His hiddenness, of *comprehendere incomprehensibile*. Only in the real knowledge of God can this be the case. If we apprehend, view and conceive God in His hiddenness, we stand already in the real knowledge of God.

" The fear of the Lord is the beginning of knowledge " (Prov. 1⁷). If we hear and understand all four terms in this proverb as of equal importance, we shall see at once that in it everything has been said which has to be said at this point. For at this point, in regard to this necessary turning from the negation to the " position "—and from the " position " to what is at first the prominent negation —we now have more solid ground under our feet even in the theological tradition of the Church (whatever the basis of its assertion of God's incomprehensibility). For there was at least agreement in the Early Church that to know God means " to conceive Him in His incomprehensibility." *Sic eum digne aestimamus, dum inaestimabilem dicimus* (Minucius Felix, *Octavius* 18). This is the one and only possible way to know God : *si cogitaverimus id illum esse, quod, quale et quantum sit, non possit intelligi nec in ipsam quidem cogitationem possit venire* (Novatian, *De trin.* 2). *Unus est hominis intellectus de Dei natura certissimus, si scias et sentias nihil de illo posse mortali oratione depromi* (Arnobius, *Adv. nat.* 3, 19). Ἐν τοῖς·γὰρ περὶ θεοῦ μεγάλη γνῶσις τὸ τὴν ἀγνωσίαν ὁμολογεῖν (Cyril of Jerusalem, *Cat.* 6, 2). *Perfecta scientia est, sic Deum scire, ut, licet non ignorabilem, tamen inenarrabilem scias* (Hilary, *De trin.* II, 7). Εἴδησις τῆς θείας οὐσίας ἡ αἴσθησις αὐτοῦ τῆς ἀκαταληψίας (Basilius, *Ep.* 234, 2, *ad Amphilochium*). Καλῶμεν τοίνυν αὐτὸν τὸν ἀνέκφραστον, τὸν ἀπερινόητον θεόν, τὸν ἀόρατον, τὸν ἀκατάληπτον, τὸν νικῶντα γλώττης δύναμιν ἀνθρωπίνης, τὸν ὑπερβαίνοντα θνητῆς διανοίας κατάληψιν, τὸν ἀνεξιχνίαστον ἀγγέλοις, τὸν ἀθέατον τοῖς σεραφίμ, τὸν ἀκατανόητον τοῖς χερουβίμ, τὸν ἀόρατον ἀρχαῖς, ἐξουσίαις, δυνάμεσι, καὶ ἁπλῶς πάσῃ τῇ κτίσει, ὑπὸ δὲ υἱοῦ μόνου καὶ πνεύματος ἁγίου γνωριζόμενον (Chrysostom, *De incompr.* 3, 1). *Sic enim sunt incomprehensibilia requirenda, ne se existimet nihil invenisse qui, quam sit incomprehensibile quod quaerebat, potuerit invenire* (Augustine, *De trin.* XV, 2). *Hoc ergo non est, si comprehendisti, si autem hoc est, non comprehendisti* (*Sermo* 52, 16).

It is not an imperfection but the perfection, not a compromising but the certainty, not a limit but the reality of the knowledge of God, which, in regard to its *terminus a quo*, is indicated by the assertion of the hiddenness of God.

Since this is so, we must not on any account draw from this statement the conclusion that there is no true knowledge of God, and that we are forced to renounce the undertaking to view and conceive God and therefore to speak of Him.

It would be a serious misunderstanding of the *Deus definiri nequit* if we were to conclude from it that theology and proclamation must be completely silenced. The positive origin and meaning of the matter would then not be understood. *Deus definiri nequit* is, rightly understood, the confession of God's revelation by which we certainly affirm that the incapacity of our own viewing and conceiving of God is disclosed, but by which the mouth is not stopped but opened for the delivery of the divine mandate. And again, it would be a misunderstanding if the conclusion were to be drawn from the *Deus definiri nequit* that all theology and proclamation has to take the form only of negative statements, and that in this form, as " cataphatic " theology, in the form of a revocation or relativising of all the definiteness of the divine nature, it is in a position to express and to establish true knowledge of God. Taken in this way, as in Pseudo-Dionysius the Areopagite and all his disciples, the *Deus definiri nequit* is not understood radically enough. Again, we cannot flee from the hiddenness of God into the possibility of a negative comprehensibility, as if this were less our own human comprehensibility than a positive, and not just as incapable. And again, it would be a misunderstanding of the *Deus definiri nequit* if theology and proclamation tried to renounce the viewing and conceiving of God Himself in order to become instead a theology and proclamation of the subjective feelings and experiences of the pious man or a theology and proclamation of the underlying feeling of " absolute dependence." For this time, as in Schleiermacher, it is not understood that the assertion of the incomprehensibility of God does not point us away from God to man, but simply tries to cleave to God, yet to the grace of God in His revelation. The *Deus definiri nequit* means that the Church receives permission and command to keep to the true knowledge of God bestowed upon it and not to escape into the supposed knowledge of God of a self-explanation of the pious man. Taking the latter course, it will know only a god who will certainly be apprehensible, but who will not be the true God. The true God is the hidden God. The Church must not flee from the task of knowing and proclaiming just this God. The misunderstandings of the *Deus definiri nequit* which we have mentioned—they are the misunderstandings of different varieties of mystical theology—are all of them attempts to evade this task, which means, to evade the true God in His hiddenness. It is advisable not to take part in these attempts.

7

Knowing the true God in His revelation, we apprehend Him in His hiddenness. And just because we do this, we know the true God in His revelation. If He is not always the One whom we of ourselves are unable to view and to conceive, the One whom we know is not the true God in His revelation. Again, He is not this true God if His knowledge does not involve a real human viewing and conceiving, founded and ordered of course by Him alone, and not therefore cancelling His hiddenness. If we deny either the one or the other, we deny His revelation and therefore Himself. We still deny it, or we deny it again. Both can occur only in an equally unhappy pre- or post-faith condition. In faith itself, and therefore confronted with the true God in His revelation, we cannot deny either the power of God, our impotence, or our power as the gracious gift of God.

It must be accepted always that the assertion of the hiddenness of God denotes our impotence. In the knowledge of God which takes place in faith in God's revelation, this impotence of ours cannot possibly be denied. If we are allowed to make use of God's permission—if we must obey His command—to undertake the attempt to know Him in our human viewings and conceivings and to speak of Him in our human words, this in no sense means that our human viewing, conceiving and speaking possess their own capacity for God —even a capacity awakened and actualised by revelation and faith. On the contrary, our viewing, conceiving and speaking are placed in a service and put to a use for which they have, of and in themselves, no fitness either after or before this takes place. It is the truth of God that imparts itself to our viewing, conceiving and speaking, which as such are not capable of the truth of God. It is settled that as such our images of perception, thought and words neither are nor can be images of God. They become this. They become truth. But they do not do so of themselves ; they do it wholly and utterly from their object, not by their own capacity but by that of their object. Therefore the hiddenness of God remains. We do not encroach upon Him by knowing Him : we do not of ourselves become like Him ; we do not of ourselves become master of Him ; we do not of ourselves become one with Him. And all this means—we cannot of ourselves apprehend Him.

Augustine expressed this once as follows : *Vide quemadmodum tu contingendo efficeris quod non eras, non illud, quod contingis, facis esse quod non erat.* *Hoc dico: Deus non crescit ex cognitore, sed cognitor ex cognitione Dei.* Our speaking about God must therefore be a *pia confessio ignorantiae magis quam temeraria professio scientiae* (*Sermo* 117, 5). As we have already seen from Polanus there can never be more than a *descriptio quaedam Dei quatenus nobis est patefactus.* We respond as we are permitted and commanded to the revelation of the ineffable *nomen Dei, quod vult cognosci, narrari, celebrari et invocari* (M. Chemnitz, *Loci theol., ed.* 1590, *De Deo, c.* 3) when we speak rightly of God. But the limits of this speaking are also indicated by this source and norm. Its external limit is : *Quid Deus sit, nemo explicare potest praeterquam Deus in verbo suo. Quicumque vero alias opiniones fingunt et diversa ratione Dei cognitionem assequi conantur, hi se ipsos fallunt et idola cordis sui venerantur* (Bullinger, *Comp. chr. rel.*, 1556, II, 2). And its internal limit is : *Definitio ὀνοματώδης dari potest, οὐσιώδης vero minime* (J, Gerhard, *Loci theol.*, 1610 f., *L.* II, 90). Λέγωμεν γὰρ οὐχ ὅσα δεῖ περὶ θεοῦ . . . ἀλλ' ὅσα κεχώρηκεν ἡ ἀνθρωπίνη φύσις καὶ ὅσα ἡ ἡμετέρα ἀσθένεια βαστάσαι δύναται (Cyril of Jerusalem, *Kat.* 6, 2).

It is well to establish explicitly that all this is true of any word which man can express on the ground of his viewing and perceiving. It is not true only of the attempt of scientific theology to speak of God in strict concepts. But it is certainly true of this as well.

There is not, then, as A. E. Biedermann and the Hegelian school in general supposed, a pure conceptual language which leaves the inadequate language of images behind, and which, accessible to the initiates of this high art, is, as such, the language of truth. In fact, the language of the strictest conceptuality participates in the inadequacy of all human language. *Nec nomen sapientiae mihi sufficit ostendere illud, per quod omnia facta sunt de nihilo . . ., nec nomen essentiae mihi valet exprimere illud, quod per singularem altitudinem longe est supra omnia et per naturalem proprietatem valde est extra omnia* (Anselm of Canterbury, *Monol.* 65).

But it is also not true that there is a " simple " thinking and speaking, which, in its " child-likeness," does not stand under the crisis of the hiddenness of God. Even the language of ecclesiastical dogma and that of the Bible is not exempt from this crisis. It is not the case, then, that we have only, say, to rediscover the world of the biblical view and concept or to adopt the biblical language, in order to make the viewing and conceiving and language of truth our own.

This has been the frequent error of biblical orthodoxy. But the Church fathers were already clear that there are no words, not even the simplest of basic Christian words, in the use of which we do not have to take into account this inner limitation of all human language. On the contrary, it was clear to them that even the words Father, Creator, Lord, Sovereign—and even the word God itself—are not in themselves and as such identical with the ineffable name by which God calls Himself and which therefore expresses His truth ; and therefore they cannot in themselves express His truth (cf. Justin, *Apol.* II, 6, Clement of Alex., *Strom.* V, 12, 81, 6). *Quem si patrem dixero, carnalem opineris: si regem, terrenum suspiceris; si dominum, intelliges utique mortalem* (Minucius Felix, *Oct.* 18). Indeed, it belongs already to the concept of the biblical witness that he is a man who in human words witnesses to God's Word and to that extent speaks God's Word ; but his human words as such are confounded by the hiddenness of God like those of any other man, and therefore in their repetition in another man's mouth they are not exempt from the crisis of the hiddenness of God.

It is most important to establish all this expressly, because it follows inevitably that if the inner limitation which divides and separates our viewing, thinking and speaking as such from the being of God is overlooked or forgotten or denied, and if this happens in responsibility towards God's revelation, the external limitation is also lost, as is the character of the revelation of God as the source and norm of our knowledge and speech about God, and the unconditioned subordination of the latter to this source and norm.

The way is then opened up to this or that *diversa ratio Dei cognitionem assequi*, to the kingdom of the pretended *aliae opiniones*. Then *crescit Deus ex cognitore* ; i.e., our cognition ceases to be the mirror of God's revelation and the revelation of God begins to be the mirror of our cognition. Any native and original capacity which is ascribed to our viewing and conceiving of God or to our human language must mean that on the strength of this capacity we have a second source and norm of the revelation of God within ourselves. We will always apply this to the revelation which encounters us in Jesus Christ. We will use it to measure and judge this revelation at least by way of comparison. And because it lies so much closer to us, there is no doubt that secretly, and very soon openly, we will subordinate the revelation to it, so that in what seems to be an irresistible development it finally turns out to be the real and unique source of what we regard as revelation. What God is, is something which primarily, and in the long run exclusively, or at any rate decisively, will be learned from the immanent meaning of the words with which we define Him. But these derive from the views and concepts which are the basis of these words, and of which the words are the expression. In practice, a philosophy or outlook or myth is the determining factor in the content of our knowledge of God even if in its formation we do not entirely neglect at least respectfully and attentively to consult the revelation of God in Jesus Christ. It is difficult to see how this inversion is to be avoided if the assertion of the hiddenness of God is not valid and does not prevent us from understanding our capacity for knowledge in this way.

Only if this assertion is valid are we held fast to the revelation of God as the unique source and norm of our knowledge of God. Indicating its inner limit, it also indicates its external limit. For if we have no capacity of our own to view, conceive and speak in regard to God we are thrown back on the fact that our viewing, conceiving and speaking—whose capacity we must ascribe to God Himself—is necessarily instituted by God's revelation. We are therefore thrown back upon God's revelation, not merely in the sense that all cognition is referred back to its object, but in the sense that the knowledge of God is referred back to God as its object and free origin.

If this is established, and if, therefore, it may be regarded as certain that the capacity to know and therefore to view and conceive God cannot be reinterpreted as a capacity of man but only understood as a divine gift, then we can take a second step and say that the God who quickens us to faith in Him by His revelation can and may and must be spoken about, so that He can and may and must be viewed and conceived by us. The limit within which this takes place must be remembered. But we are not now concerned only with the limit, but also with the matter itself. It is no *sophisma*, but clear and true, if we say of the revelation of God that the statement *Deus definiri nequit* is itself annulled if in spite of its predicate (yet also as the possibility of its predicate) its subject cannot be regarded as knowable, i.e., as viewable and conceivable. Even with the *definiri nequit* we define, conceive and indeed apprehend, and therefore we apprehend something which is apprehensible. God is actually apprehensible in His revelation. He is so in such a way that He makes Himself apprehensible to those who cannot apprehend Him of them-

selves. But He is still apprehensible. Man is not left alone in himself,
as the final presupposition of all mystical theology would make out.
In the miracle of revelation and faith he stands before God, God stands
before him, and he knows God and conceives Him therefore in His
inconceivability.

For an initial understanding of the facts in relation to this conceiving of God
in His inconceivability, we may turn to the fine presentation given by the 13th
century pseudo-Augustinian writing called the *Soliloquia animae ad Deum* (*cap*.
31). In this work too we read of the *Deus definiri nequit: Soli quidem tibi soli,
Trinitas, integre nota es, Trinitas sancta, Trinitas supermirabilis et superinenarra-
bilis et superinscrutabilis et superinaccessibilis et superincomprehensibilis et _tper-
intelligibilis et superessentialis, superessentialiter exsuperans omnem sensum,
omnem rationem, omnem intellectum, omnem intelligentiam, omnem essentiam
supercoelestium animorum: quam neque dicere, neque cogitare, neque intelligere,
neque cognoscere possibile est etiam oculis angelorum.* Does this mean that we
can and should be silent about God ? No, certainly not. (*Domine*) *vae tacentibus
de te, quoniam loquaces muti sunt* (from Augustine, *Conf.* I, 4, 4). *Et ego non
tacébo, quoniam fecisti me et illuminasti me; et inveni me et cognovi me et inveni te
et cognovi te quoniam illuminasti me. Sed qualiter cognovi te ? Cognovi te in te.
Cognovi te non sicut tibi es, sed cognovi te sicut mihi es; et hoc non sine te sed in te,
quia tu es lux quae illuminasti me. Sicut tibi es, soli tibi cognitus es. Sicut mihi es,
secundum gratiam tuam et mihi cognitus es.* By grace. But this means : *Intonasti
desuper voce grandi in interiorem aurem cordis mei et rupisti surditatem meam et
audivi vocem tuam et illuminasti caecitatem meam et vidi lucem tuam et cognovi
quoniam Deus meus es. Propterea dixi quod cognovi te; cognovi te quoniam Deus
meus es; cognovi te solum verum Deum et quem misisti Jesum Christum.*

The hiddenness of God is the inconceivability of the Father, the
Son and the Holy Spirit ; of the one true God, our Creator, Reconciler
and Redeemer, who as such is known only to Himself, and is therefore
viewable and conceivable only to Himself, and alone capable of speaking of Himself aright, i.e., in truth. But He has not omitted to do
this—to speak of Himself aright, i.e., in truth. He has seen to it
that He is to be found by those who seek Him where He Himself has
given Himself to be found. And He has seen to it also that they
might seek Him in this place. If it is not possible for any man, indeed
for any creature, to make God manifest to himself of himself as we
can make other objects manifest to us—because God is the *prius* of
all cognition and of everything known—yet it is possible for God to
make Himself manifest to His creation. And it is this possibility
which is reality. God has in fact revealed Himself and is manifest
by Himself—in His Son, the fact that He became man, and by the
Holy Spirit, His outpouring on all flesh. The first work of the worship
with which we thank Him for the grace of His revelation is to know
and confess Him as the hidden One. The nature of His revelation
(as distinct from other revelations, which may also exist but which
are not revelation in this strict sense) is that it is grace. That is, it is
a bestowal which utterly transcends all our capacity, being and
existence as such, but does not destroy us, does not consume and

break our being and our existence. On the contrary—and from our point of view this is a miracle, an inexhaustible reality that cannot be established, deduced or explained—it is present to us to our salvation, and it can be affirmed and grasped by us in faith, to become a determination of our being and existence. It therefore lies in the nature of this revelation that we can meet it only with the praise of thanksgiving. To thank means to accept with the confession that we have not won or deserved what we have received, that we have not foreseen this accepting, and that we have had no claim to it. To thank means to acknowledge that it is a question of accepting a pure gift, whose reality has no basis elsewhere than in the goodness of the Giver, in view of which, therefore, we can only glorify this kindness of the Giver. By thanking God for His revelation we shall glorify Him in His hiddenness. But in so doing, we acknowledge—and how else can we come to do it ?—that we have already known, that that miracle is already an event, that the pure gift is already made to us, and that we have already accepted it. Having known His hiddenness we have known Himself by the grace of His revelation. We have not known Him in virtue of the capacity of a concept of the inconceivable brought by us, or in virtue of our capacity to set up enigmas as such, or to acknowledge mysteries as such, or to allow the validity of paradoxes as such. How can this capacity as such lead us to God and open us for Him ? In virtue of this capacity every imaginable marvel may be manifest to us, but God always hidden—if, that is to say, God's own capacity is not added to ours by the grace of His revelation, if, in the event of this miracle, in the incarnation of the Son of God, and by the Holy Spirit poured out upon us, our concept of the inconceivable does not become a vessel to contain the inconceivable God. By God Himself in the grace of His revelation it must happen that our confession of God's hiddenness and therefore the worship of our thanksgiving becomes a worship of God and therefore the beginning of our knowledge of God. But it is this very thing which actually does happen by God Himself in the grace of His revelation. And because it happens, in spite of our incapacity, our viewing of the unviewable God and conceiving of the inconceivable God are made by God's own capacity a genuine viewing and conceiving, the whole truth of which is the truth of God, and that in such a way that by the capacity of its object it is a true viewing and conceiving.

As we have seen : *Cognovi te in te*—Thee, the incomprehensible Triunity—namely, *sicut mihi es, et hoc non sine te sed in te, quia tu es lux, quae illuminasti me. Sicut tibi es, soli tibi cognitus es. Sicut mihi es, secundum gratiam et mihi cognitus es.* Thou didst speak from above with Thy powerful voice to my inward ear, and didst pierce my deafness and I heard Thy voice ; and Thou didst enlighten my blindness, and I saw the light and knew Thee that Thou art my God. *Cognovi te solum verum Deum et quem misisti, Jesum Christum !* According to Irenaeus, God is *invisibilis propter eminentiam, ignotus autem nequaquam propter providentiam (Adv o. haer.* II, 6, 1 ; cf. IV, 6, 4). Beyond all negation of our incapacity by the incomprehensibility of God and accepting this negation, according to Clement of Alexandria there is the new possibility—of dipping εἰς τὸ μέγεθος τοῦ Χριστοῦ. That is why Moses said to God: Shew me Thyself, explaining μὴ εἶναι διδακτὸν πρὸς ἀνθρώπων μηδὲ ῥητὸν τὸν θεόν, ἀλλ᾽ ἢ μόνῃ τῇ παρ᾽ αὐτοῦ δυνάμει γνωστόν. ἡ μὲν γὰρ ζήτησις ἀειδὴς καὶ ἀόρατος, ἡ χάρις δὲ τῆς γνώσεως παρ᾽ αὐτοῦ διὰ τοῦ υἱοῦ (Strom. v, XI, 71).

In His revelation, in Jesus Christ, the hidden God has indeed made Himself apprehensible. Not directly, but indirectly. Not to sight, but to faith. Not in His being, but in sign. Not, then, by the dissolution of His hiddenness—but apprehensibly. The revelation of God is that God has given to the creature whom He has chosen and determined for this end the commission and the power to take his place and represent Him, to bear witness to Him. The Word was made flesh : this is the first, original and controlling sign of all signs. In relation to this sign, as the sign of this sign, there is also creaturely testimony to His eternal Word, not everywhere, but where His eternal Word has chosen, called and created for Himself witnesses : a testimony by the word of the prophets and apostles of this Word ; by the visible existence of His people, His Church ; by the Gospel which is delivered and to be heard in it ; by the sacraments in which this Gospel has also a physically visible and apprehensible form ; and finally, by the existence of us who believe this testimony. Jesus Christ and His visible kingdom on earth : this is the great possibility, created by God Himself, of viewing and conceiving Him, and therefore of speaking about Him. For as we men view and conceive Him, so we can speak of Him. We cannot do so without the veil, and therefore without the reservation of His hiddenness, or apart from the miracle of His grace. It is not true that the grace of His revelation ever or in any relationship ceases to be grace and miracle. Nor is it true that God Himself and His free action ever become superfluous because, instead of Him, we have the creature chosen and determined by him. But it is also not true that we men are now left to ourselves, to our ignorance or to the inventions of our own hearts. On the contrary, what is true is that as men, and in the sphere of our human views and concepts, we have a direction which derives from God Himself and corresponds to His will and is furnished with His promise. On the basis of this direction and in accordance with its guidance, we can and ought to view and conceive Him, and therefore to speak of the hidden God in human words. It is not the case, then, that God enters again the sphere of our own survey and control. This can happen only as His revelation is misused or sacrificed. But in the revelation of God, without and against our capacity, in the form of a taking into service of our incapable capacity, we are permitted and commanded to do something which if it came from our own free choice would be madness, but which in the freedom and obedience of revelation is the good sense of God Himself. That is to say, we are to view, conceive and follow the creaturely witnesses willed and ordered by Himself, to receive them as His witnesses, to repeat and render them again as His witnesses. God's revelation is God's condescension to the creature. This condescension is actualised in His Word by His Holy Spirit. When this takes place we are authorised and commanded continually to undertake in faith—not looking back to our own incapacity but trusting only in God's own capacity—the attempt to respond to His revelation with human views and concepts and therefore with human words.

The traditional statements on this matter might have been clearer than they are. They point in this direction ; but they cannot be accepted without caution and criticism. Though there is no creaturely name under which He whom we call the Father, the Creator, the Lord is to be conceived, yet nevertheless there is ἐκ τῶν εὐποιῶν καὶ τῶν ἔργων προσρήσεις (Justin Martyr, *Apol. II.* 6). *De Deo quidem Patre quamvis digne proloqui nemo valeat, tamen possibile est, intellectum aliquem capi ex occasione visibilium creaturarum* (Origen, Περὶ ἀρχῶν I, 3, 1). *Admirare creaturas et glorifica creatorem !* (Ephraem, *Adv. scrut.* 47.) Though there is no single name which is sufficient to express comprehensively the whole essence of God, yet there are many and various names, each one of a particular content of meaning (σημασία), which can mediate to us a viewability and comprehensibility of God which is certainly dark and scanty in relation to the whole, but yet sufficient for us (Basil, *Adv. Eunom.* 10). If we do not know God's *essentia*, yet we know *habitudinem ipsius ad creaturas* (Thomas Aquinas, *S. theol.* I, *qu.* 12, *art.* 12). And perhaps most judiciously Gregorius Eliberitanus in the 4th century : *Quidquid de eo dixeris, efficientiam operum suorum et dispensationes sacramentorum ipsius nominabis* (*Tract. Orig.* 1).

The doubtful nature of all these statements—with the exception of the last—lies in the remarkable generalness with which they refer to a relationship of God to the creature as such in which He makes Himself viewable and conceivable to us. Are they really thinking, then, simply of the creation as such, and therefore of a relative knowability of God in it ? We probably have to take most of these statements in this way, or at least also and primarily in this way. To a large extent, therefore. it is from natural theology or a natural revelation that the fathers derived the relative viewability and conceivability of God bestowed upon us. But obviously we cannot accept their statements so far as they bear this meaning. God's revelation, by which we are authorised and commanded to view and conceive Him according to the measure of our incapable capacity, can only be— if we may take Clement of Alexandria at his word—" the grace of His knowledge by the Son," i.e., the "greatness of Jesus Christ." This revelation occurs in the sphere of the creation of God, but not in the power of the creation as such. Therefore, as we have it in the last of the passages adduced, it is in *dispensationes sacramentorum ipsius* in connexion with the appearing of Jesus Christ Himself, that God—*sicut mihi es*—becomes knowable and therefore viewable and conceivable to us. If, in view of these creaturely *dispensationes*, we for our part venture and are permitted to venture to speak of God in our human viewings and concepts, and therefore to make use of the possibilities given to us in our relationship to the creation in general, the legitimacy and strength of this use does not originate from a revelation proceeding from the creation, but from a revelation entering into the creation and illuminating it. The fact that the one revelation of God in Jesus Christ actually does illuminate the creation and our relationship to it, and therefore also our human possibilities of viewing and conceiving, means that we are given the authorisation and command to make this use of them.

But the authorisation given us by God's revelation demands our trust and its command our obedience. In its consequences it is nothing more nor less than a denial of Jesus Christ and blasphemy against the Holy Spirit, resembling the act of the servant who took and hid the one talent entrusted to him, if we try to value our incapacity more highly than the capacity which God Himself in His revelation confers upon our incapacity; using the appeal to it, and the resigned complaint that God is a hard Master, to justify our failure to attempt to view and conceive Him, and our resort to the way of mystical theology. As God encounters us visibly and conceivably in the witness of His revelation, in the creaturely form of a historical occurrence or a succession of such occurrences, and in the relationships of our own life to these occurrences, we are invited and summoned to know Him as the One who acts and rules in these occurrences and relationships. But this means that our human viewing and conceiving are claimed within their natural limits. They are, of course, claimed by God's revelation of Himself in these visible occurrences and relationships—of God Himself, who as such neither is nor becomes visible. And of course, before and above all viewing and conceiving, it is our faith which is claimed : our faith, which as such is not a viewing and conceiving but consists in our being apprehended by the invisible God. So, then, even if and as they are directed to the occurrences and relationships of revelation, our viewing· and conceiving remain absolutely behind God as their object and behind faith, which is, from our side, the power of their movement. Therefore our knowing reaches its goal only in God Himself and in faith. But this does not at all alter the fact that as our limited viewing and conceiving, it is on the way to this goal, and that on the way to this goal as this limited viewing and conceiving it participates in its truth. Only in God and only in faith is it knowledge of God. But only as the attempt of perceptible conceptual cognition is it our knowing. And, on the basis of the revelation of God, it ought to be and can be, not merely the knowing of God, but also our knowing. As the knowing of God it is powerful ; as our knowing it is powerless. But on the basis of God's revelation the two aspects cannot and must not fall apart but are always held together : God and man, His power and our powerlessness, He as the goal and we on the road to it, and therefore faith, which is already at its goal, and our viewing and conceiving, which can always be only a stage on our journey to this goal. It must not be a cause of regret or too little a thing for us in faith always to be only on the way. It must not be too little to undertake, and undertake continually, the attempt of viewing and conceiving. If we do not want to do it ; if we grow tired of it ; if we think we can or should dispense with it, we are no longer standing in faith and therefore we are no longer at the goal. On the basis of revelation, man can and must, within the limits which are his lot, participate in the knowledge of God, which in its truth is indeed wholly and utterly God's self-knowledge. He can and must, therefore, participate in the truth. On the basis of revelation, even man and his views and concepts, which in themselves and as such are impotent, can and will participate in the truth of the goal to which the way here entered leads.

The fact that no one knows the Father save the Son does not in any way mean, according to J. Chrysostom : πάντες ἐν ἀγνοίᾳ ἐσμέν, but merely that we do not know Him in the same way, namely, immediately, or in His essence, as God knows Himself, and therefore the Son knows the Father (*In Joann.* 15, 1). Even if this final knowledge is debarred to us, our viewing and conceiving on the basis of revelation is not altogether prevented from an approximation (προσέγγισις), i.e., a movement in the direction of the being and essence of God, and it does not therefore lack the ability—the capability added to it by revelation—τοῦ ζητουμένου λαβεῖν εἰκασίαν, to attain a reflection of what it intends and seeks (Gregory of Nyssa, *C. Eunom.* 12).

There would, therefore, be no sense in accompanying the human viewing, conceiving and speaking practised on the basis of revelation, with a fundamental scepticism, perhaps surrounding it at the outset and as such with a mistrust of its ability and therefore of its standard of truth. If the *Deus definiri nequit* is once acknowledged and confessed as an article of faith, if it is and always will be out of the question to reinterpret the ability added to us by revelation as an ability proper to man as such, if therefore we and our viewing, conceiving and speaking do not give the glory to ourselves but to God, namely, to His grace in Jesus Christ, then, even if within the limits of our human cognition, we know Him in truth, and this knowing may and must be a confident knowing. We have always to be self-critical. It belongs to the nature of this knowing that it consists only in " approximations." It cannot, therefore, be perfected. It stands in need of correction at every point. Its preservation and promotion in the Church has to be a continual matter for discussion. But all the same, it is ingratitude and rebellion if, on account of its inadequacy, we try basically to negate or even to doubt its truth. Once the hiddenness of God is rightly understood and acknowledged as it should be, a fundamental resignation is no longer possible or legitimate.

Κἂν γὰρ ἀδυνάτως ἔχωμεν καταλαβεῖν, ὅ τι ποτε ἔστιν, ἀλλ' ἀκούοντες τὸ Πατὴρ καὶ τὸ Θεὸς καὶ τὸ Παντοκράτωρ, οὐχ ἕτερόν τι, ἀλλ' αὐτὴν τὴν τοῦ ὄντος οὐσίαν σημαινομένην νοοῦμεν (Athanasius, *Ep. de synodis* 35). The fact that we understand God otherwise than He understands Himself, must not mean that we understand Him falsely (ψευδῶς) and distortedly (διεστραμμένως). Why should it not be the case that God alone knows Himself perfectly according to His nature, ἡμᾶς δὲ ἀνθρώπους ὄντας ἔλαττόν τε νοοῦντας αὐτοῦ, μὴ πάντως καὶ διεψευσμένας ἔχειν τὰς δόξας (*inferiore modo eum intellegamus, minine tamen falso conceptu* (Cyril of Alex., *Thesaurus* 31) ?

There is, therefore, no reason to suspect or depreciate the human image and human word about God as such. As we have said, they will be liable to criticism, and in only too great a need of it. Nor can we ever forget that with man generally they stand as such under the judgment of God, that they as such have no ability—even by way of sign—to pass on the reality of God, and that the sword of the hiddenness of God hangs over them all. All the same—and we have to say this in opposition to all arrogant and faint-hearted scepticism—it does not lie in the power of any man to set this sword in motion against them. This sword certainly strikes them when and so far as, resting on the free-will and arbitrariness of man, they are formed and expressed with the claim of an independent authority, which can only be a usurped and powerless claim. But who will attack and repudiate them in principle, if and so far as their formation and expression derives from God's revelation ? Man cannot arrogate it to himself that this is truly to be said of his views, concepts and words. It is God's grace which makes it real. But if God's grace makes it real, it cannot be taken from man by an objection in principle that can be raised against it by other men. He need not let himself be assailed by any such objections.

Audio vulgus, cum ad coelum manus tendunt, nihil aliud quam " Deum " dicunt et " Deus magnus est" et " Deus verus est " et " si Deus dederit." Vulgi *iste naturalis sermo est an christiani confitentis oratio ?* (Minuc. Felix., *Octav.* 18). To be sure, this question can always be raised. But as between men, more than a question cannot be raised, nor can a fundamentally destructive verdict be passed. In principle, there is nothing to prevent us confidently associating ourselves with this *vulgus.* Indeed, we will have to do so when the command and authorisation to do so and therefore the command and authorisation for *christiani confitentis oratio* is given us by God's revelation.

But along the same line it is finally to be said that labour for the truth in the sphere of human views and concepts and words about God need not be an impossibility, and therefore superfluous, because it is performed in this sphere. Theology can, of course, be sheer vanity. It is this when it is not pertinent, and that simply means—not humble. The pertinence of theology consists in making the exposition of revelation its exclusive task. How can it fail to be humble in the execution of this programme, when it has no control over revelation, but has constantly to find it, or rather be found by it? If we presuppose this happening—and we can, of course, presuppose it only as we pray and work—theology is as little vanity as the " old wife's " stammering. If she may stammer, surely theology may also try to speak. The attempt may and must be made, within the limits of human cognition, to ask about the truth, to distinguish the true from the false, and continually to carry the " approximation " further—although always knowing that the goal as such is attainable only to faith and not to our viewing and conceiving as such. This means, to seek after better human views and concepts in closer correspondence with their object, and therefore, so far as we are able, to make the witness to the reality of God more complete and clear. If this presupposition is valid—as it can and will be valid—theology can be pursued in the confidence which is not forbidden but commanded us against the background of the hiddenness of God, without any pretensions, but also without any false shame, so much the more so because it is not an arbitrary undertaking, but one which is necessary to the task of the Church's proclamation. If this presupposition is valid, theology is on firm ground for its undertaking—indeed, on disproportionately firmer ground than all other sciences.

We conclude our considerations on the *terminus a quo* of the knowledge of God with Augustine : *Deus, cum de illo nihil digne dici possit, admisit humanae vocis obsequium et verbis nostris in laude sua nos gaudere voluit* (*De doctr. chr.* I, 6). And we remember again the other saying of the same father : *Vae tacentibus de te, quoniam loquaces muti sunt* (*Conf.* I, 4, 4). We are allowed to view and conceive the inconceivable God in obedience, to proclaim the Ineffable in obedience. God rejoices at the praise we render Him in this obedience, even though we know that we are unworthy to speak of Him. And woe betide us if we rely upon our impotence and omit to praise Him !

2. THE VERACITY OF MAN'S KNOWLEDGE OF GOD

Our next concern is with the *terminus ad quem* of the knowledge of God. We do not understand by this the object as such which is attained by it, although we shall certainly have to speak of its object too—this is inevitable. We understand by the *terminus ad quem* of the knowledge of God, the goal and end, determined by its object, of the event, the movement, the human action which we call the knowledge of God ; the limit by which as such it is separated from its object as such, but by which it is also united with it.

Knowledge of God is not only the presupposition but also, as we have already affirmed at the beginning of our first part, the goal of all Christian doctrine. If the Church lives, if its faith and its confession are real and do not evaporate, it not only comes *from* the knowledge of God, but again and again comes *to* the knowledge of God. We have hitherto tried to make clear the fact and extent that the Church comes from the knowledge of God. We have now to understand the fact and extent that at the same time—a circular course is involved—it always goes to meet it. A circular course is involved because God is known by God, and only by God ; because even as an action undertaken and performed by man, knowledge of God is objectively and subjectively both instituted by God Himself and led to its end by Him ; because God the Father and the Son by the Holy Spirit is its primary and proper subject and object. If it is also a human undertaking and action, if as such it also arrives at its goal, this is in consequence of the fact that God does not wish to know Himself without Himself giving us a part in this event in the grace of His revelation. For this reason the undertaking is to be ventured in assurance and confidence. Only for this reason, as we have seen, and therefore with critical prudence, for God is hidden. But for this reason in the assurance and confidence which correspond to the divine faithfulness, and therefore leave behind all mistrust and scepticism. It is only by God Himself that this undertaking and action can be basically assailed. But from the same point of view we have now to ask about its success. And with this second question, too, we cannot place ourselves outside that circular course. The first and the last thing to be said here too must consist in the fact that in the knowledge of God by God Himself we have to do with God Himself, and we have to do with Him in a matchless and incontestable certainty grounded on the faithfulness of God Himself. The beginning of all knowledge of God has now to be understood as its end and goal—God the Father and God the Son by the Holy Spirit as the object of the knowledge of God.

If we are going to explain this in greater detail, in accordance with what was said at the beginning of the first part, we must first establish the fact that subsequently and therefore secondarily and improperly man is included in this event in the height, in the being and essence of God, so that God is now the object not only of His own cognition, but also of that of man. He is really object, in the same way as this may be said of other objects of man's cognition : as the opposite of another, which man can distinguish from himself and from which man can distinguish himself, which he can therefore perceive and contemplate and of which he can speak. For if this is not the case he does not know God. Knowledge of God is then an event enclosed in the bosom of the divine Trinity. A genuine speaking about God, and therefore Christian doctrine, cannot then exist, or at any rate, cannot exist with the promise and claim of being true speech. What is then supposedly and allegedly spoken about God, is not really about Him but about another. Mistrust and scepticism are then far too weak an attitude towards this human undertaking and action, in face of its inner impossibility. It can only be perceived and therefore set aside in its inner impossibility.

But what are we saying when we describe God as the object of human cognition, and an object of human cognition as God ? It is quite clear that such a description is necessary if there is to be speaking about God and therefore Christian doctrine as true language about God. But is God really an object of human cognition ? Is an object of human cognition God ? No postulate, however necessary, can compel this to be true. If it is not true in itself that God wishes to be and will be object, not only to Himself, but, by the grace of His revelation, and therefore by Himself, to us also, we shall certainly have to accept the inner impossibility of this human undertaking and action and therefore the fact that all speaking about God and even Christian doctrine is not true language. For without the grace of His revelation, God is definitely not an object of human cognition, and definitely no object of human cognition is God. It is by God's revelation that we know God as the One who is absolutely perfect and self-sufficient, as the One whose being is absolutely self-determined and self-fulfilled and therefore self-enclosed, because in His being and for the felicity of His being He does not need another in the knowledge of whom He must first be confirmed and verified as the One He is. It is by God's revelation that we therefore know God as the One who only by His revelation, as the free good-pleasure and free activity of His overflowing love, can be the object of our cognition, the object of our substantiation and acceptance. There is not another necessity, that it must be so, or even another possibility, that it can be so. God reveals Himself to us in Jesus Christ as the One who does not owe us Himself, but has bestowed Himself upon us. If we have to do with Him, the possibility and necessity on the basis of which this is so are grounded only on the fact that He wills to have these dealings with us. We can therefore describe God as an object of human cognition, and an object of human cognition as God, only on the assumption that it has pleased and does please God—in an earlier connexion we spoke of a divine "encroachment"—to make Himself the object of our cognition. Just as we ourselves have no capacity for fellowship with God and therefore no capacity to view and conceive God, and, in relation to Him, to be true receivers and creators and therefore subjects of this knowledge, so there is in itself neither a necessity nor even a possibility that God must or can be present as the object of our viewing and conceiving. God is the One who is to and by and in Himself. On the basis of His revelation we shall have to say this with quite another emphasis and weight than we could say it on the basis of a philosophical definition of the absolute. As such, God does not have to be the object of our cognition. As such, He cannot be it at all. If, in spite of this, He is, what is revealed in this fact is only the exuberant freedom of the love in which He is who He is; not a necessity, on the basis of which He has to be this, or even the possibility, on the basis of which He can be. In His self-revelation as Father, Son and Holy Spirit we can see the fact that He is the object of our cognition ; we can find Him as the One who in the depths of His being is in fact none other than the One who loves us, and therefore bestows Himself upon us, positing Himself as the object of our cognition. But because we find Him as this One, it does not mean that we can see why and how, on the basis of what necessity and possibility, He is this One. We know Him very badly in His revelation, in His emergence from His self-sufficient glory, if we do not accept this emergence and His love as free love, or if we try to regard His objectivity for us as necessary or even possible. His objectivity is always grace even in His revelation. Indeed, in His revelation it reveals itself no less as grace than in relation to our capacity to view and conceive Him. The fact that He is the object of our knowledge is just as miraculous, just as much the necessary basis of our praying, praising and thanksgiving, as the fact that we may be the subject of this knowledge. God, who is an object of our cognition, and an object of our cognition which is God—this is certainly a reality within our world. For our knowledge must be knowledge of world-reality if it is really going to be our knowledge. And it is because He makes world-reality into His witness that God becomes objective to us in His revelation, and an objective thing can become a witness of God. But then, this world-reality will always be one which is distinguished from all others by the gracious presence of God. This means, that always by the free grace of the Word and Spirit of God, always in His free choice and call, it comes to pass and is a fact that God is really attested by this object, that this object really attests God, that it is not, therefore, something quite different standing in the place of God, and that therefore our knowledge of God is true. In what other way than in the gracious presence of God can we really have to do with God Himself in a world-reality of this kind ? It would not be God if His presence, objectively bestowed, did not become the necessary basis of our prayer and praise and thanksgiving. Only false gods can be present to us in other ways.

It is as well to remind ourselves again at this point of the meaning and function of the concept of truth as the word is used in the Bible. The Hebrew equivalent *'emeth* indicates first (and to some extent rightly) the propriety of a process or state, and therefore its solidity, force and permanence, and therefore its authenticity, validity, necessity and impregnability. But this very reality, which makes possible and establishes not only human knowing and speaking, but in the long run human life as a whole, does not have its original place and therefore its source in man, so that to know and declare the truth, to establish the truth as such, to live by the truth and in the truth, does not lie in man's capacity and existence. But properly and decisively, and therefore in truth, the truth is seen throughout as a predicate of the prerogative of God as the Lord who speaks and acts in Israel. As numerous places in the Psalms have it, it is " Thy " truth. Again and again it appears in connexion with the great predicates of the revelation and saving activity of God among His people : with God's mercy, goodness, righteousness and light, and in particular, His grace (so Ps. 89^{14} ; 98^3 ; 115^1 ; 117^2 —which is then taken up in, e.g., Jn. 1$^{14f.}$). As the very truth of God it is " shield and hiding place " (Ps. 91^4). It further appears as directly synonymous with the faithfulness with which God issues His promises and stands by them. How He speaks and acts, and at the same time what He wills and seeks and creates with His speaking and acting : this is true as such. And for this reason the truth of man's being, thinking, speaking and acting can consist in nothing other than in man's response with a corresponding faithfulness to the way and work of God, to God's faithfulness. In the truth and therefore the faithfulness of God, that of man has its origin as well as its object and criterion. The New Testament usage does not involve any change in basic meaning. Ἀλήθεια too means in itself and as such that which in itself is permanent, valid and trustworthy, thus giving the character of what is right to human speaking and acting. Nor does it make any material difference if that which is right as understood in this way is now described as ἀλήθεια and therefore related to the concept of God's revelation and indeed identified with it ; if the knowledge of the truth—the LXX had already translated '*emeth* by πίστις—is now expressly understood as the knowledge of faith ; if together with grace and in consequence of grace the truth is described as the fulness of the only-begotten Son of God (Jn. 1¹⁸) ; if it is mentioned along with the πνεῦμα (Jn. 4²⁴ ; 1 Jn. 5⁶) ; if it is equated with " thy word " by which the disciples are sanctified (Jn. 17¹⁷) ; if Jesus Christ Himself is called the truth (Jn. 14⁶) and His Gospel " the word of truth " (2 Cor. 6⁷ ; Col. 1⁵ ; Eph. 1¹³ ; Jas. 1¹⁸) ; if ἀληθεύειν (Gal. 4¹⁶ ; Eph. 4¹⁵) is to be understood simply as the right teaching of the Gospel or as the attitude corresponding to this teaching. We may say that in respect of the concept of truth, whether we consider its basic meaning or its practical application, there is complete unanimity between the Old and the New Testament. There is a truth, in itself proper, and permanent, valid and right as such, which can become the content and order of man's language and action. But this possibility is not an independent possibility which man himself can control. It is a possibility which is imparted to him by the speaking and acting of God. With Him is the truth : it is His truth ; He Himself is the truth. Γινέσθω δὲ ὁ θεὸς ἀληθής, πᾶς δὲ ἄνθρωπος ψεύστης (Rom. 3⁴). If we know the truth, it can happen only by the liberation which comes from the truth itself (Jn. 8³²).

With this as a starting-point, we must now consider the success of the human undertaking to view and conceive God, and therefore the truth or veracity of our human knowledge of God. The success of this undertaking, if success is attained, obviously consists in the veracity of the human knowledge of God, namely, in the fact that, knowing God, we do not have to do with something else or someone else, but validly, compulsorily, unassailably and trustworthily with God Himself. And beyond that, it consists in the fact that we do not have to do with Him only in a loose way, or at random, or with the threat of mistakes from unknown sources, or with the reservation that in reality everything might be quite different, but in a way which is right, which formally as well as materially cannot be separated from the matter itself, and therefore in this respect, too, validly, compulsorily, unassailably and trustworthily. If this undertaking to view and conceive God as an object of our knowledge is authentic in this twofold sense—and if our attempt to speak of God on the ground of this undertaking is also authentic, then the undertaking is one which succeeds. Our undertaking to view and conceive God will not, then, involve self-deception, and our attempt to speak of God will not involve the deception of others. We shall not want to speak of more than an undertaking and attempt, and therefore not of an undertaking that has " succeeded." Our viewing and conceiving of God and our speaking of Him will never be a completed work showing definitive results : and therefore we can never view what we do as something which has already " succeeded." In this respect the hiddenness of God as the point of departure of this activity of ours defines at the outset the limit which will not be infringed even at its finishing point. The perfect work of truth will always be God's own work and not ours. But our work as such—and this is the subject of our present enquiry—can be work which succeeds within its own natural and impassable limits ; that is to say, a work which strives towards its perfection as fulfilled in God alone. When this is the case, when in our knowing we are on the way to the goal hidden in God Himself and in faith in God—and what a distance it always is !—our undertaking to conceive and view Him is not self-deception, and the attempt to speak of Him under the presupposition of our views and concepts is not a deception of others. The undertaking and the attempt are on the way to success—with the success appropriate to us men. And our knowledge of God is then true—as true as it can be as our knowledge, which cannot coincide with the self-knowledge of God.

We are on the way. This certainly indicates the limit, but it also indicates the positive possibility of our cognition. At best, our theology is *theologia viatorum*. But it also stands under the promise of this best : that it really can be *theologia viatorum*. It is as such that it can and will be true. This concept was used in the older theology to designate the distinction of our present temporal from our future eternal knowledge of God, the distinction between faith and sight. In distinction to the former, the latter was described as *theologia comprehensorum* or *theologia patriae*; the knowledge of those who are at home, who, no longer wandering on from one hour to another, from one decision to another, stand once for all at the goal of faith and know God face to face. God will then be no more hidden from us in faith. But God as God, in Himself, will still be hidden from us even then. Even this knowing of God face to face will still be a miraculous bestowal of His grace, an incomprehensible descent of God into the sphere of objectivity of our cognition, and an incomprehensible admission of ourselves into this knowledge—for this is how the older theologians understood this *theologia comprehensorum*. Even as eternal grace, freed from the whole enshrouding veil of our temporality and corruption, grace will still be the grace of God and not our nature. To that extent, even in the eternal redemption, we shall not be at the goal, and the blessedness of our perfect knowing of God will consist in a being on the way, so that it too will have to be described as *theologia viatorum*. It will no longer be the knowing of a Church militant, which is always threatened and encompassed by error, but the knowing of a Church triumphant, which is free from dispute and complete in itself. But through all eternity it will still be the knowledge of the Church of Jesus Christ and not the knowledge of the triune God Himself. The point is that the authenticity of our knowledge will be delivered from every assault and disorder, but to all eternity it will still be an authenticity which is adapted for us as men and creatures, corresponding to the authenticity of God Himself, yet also distinct from it. But for this very reason it must now be said on the other hand that we have to do with a knowledge which is true, not only there and then, but also here and now. We may know and ought to know. The truth of God can and should be known by us in the darkness of faith no less than in the light of sight. If it is known by the blessed and by the angels in heaven otherwise than by us, it is not other for us than for them. We stand together with them before the mystery, but also before the revelation, of God. We are afar off from God, but we are also near Him. And in both cases this nearness is the nearness of His revelation and therefore of His grace.

The veracity of our knowledge of God is the veracity of His revelation. This is the statement which we now have to expound. The truth of the revelation of God consists first and decisively in the fact that it is His, God's revelation. It is not someone or something else which reveals God, but God reveals Himself. At any rate this is how God's revelation is attested in Holy Scripture, and it was in adoption of this witness that the Church of the fourth century defended the Godhead of the Son and the Holy Spirit against those who wanted to see in them simply two principles of revelation distinct from God Himself. The fact that the revelation of God is His own revelation means that it is correct and trustworthy ; that we are not put off by someone or something else, obtruding itself in the place of God ; that we are not totally or partially deceived by false or half-correct information about God. God's revelation is authentic information about God because it is first-hand information, because in it God is His own witness and teacher. The fact that we have to do with Him—no, that He in His revelation has to do with us—makes our knowledge of God true. Whatever we may always have to say about its natural limitations, and whatever critical prudence and frankness we may have to bring to its attainment, priority must be given to the fact that it is correct knowledge of God because the revelation from which it springs and to which it is related is God's own revelation and there-fore correct. Any closer definition, any reservation, any *caveat* can only follow the affirmation that with our knowledge of God we do not draw from our own source or an alien source, but directly from the well of God Himself ; that it is pure praise and thanksgiving to the Father who Himself has represented Himself to us in the Son by the Holy Spirit. For this reason it is true knowledge ; for this reason our undertaking to view and conceive Him is an undertaking that succeeds ; for this reason we speak, as we believe, in the certainty that we do not speak in vain, but, with a good conscience before our-selves and everyman, declare the truth and nothing but the truth.

But, again, because it is God's revelation, it is correct and trust-worthy revelation. It is the will, but also the power of this object, to make Himself known to us. The will—for at any rate in the revela-tion attested to us in the Bible as God's revelation there is no trifling with man on the part of God. It is the revelation of the hidden God. It shows itself as revelation of the true God in the fact that, in it, God is always the Lord, over whom man has no power, nor can have, except the power to be His child, trusting and obedient to Him. But it is genuinely the revelation of this incomprehensible God. The very hiddenness in which He is here revealed is only the mark of the grace of His revelation, with the knowledge of which our knowledge of God must begin and from which it must never depart. But in the revela-tion of God there is no hidden God, no *Deus absconditus*, at the back of His revelation, with whose existence and activity we have also occasionally to reckon beyond His Word and His Spirit, and whom we have also to fear and honour behind His revelation. It may often look like this in certain contexts in Luther. But in the witness of Holy Scripture it does not appear like this. Here also God is God and therefore mystery. But in this very mystery He encounters and gives Himself to man without reservation, without our having to wait for another. And where this will is, there is also the power to make Himself known to us. The world-reality distinct from Him, which He uses to reveal Himself, and which in His revelation necessarily becomes His witness, is certainly never identical with Himself, but, as the world-reality created by Him, it is in no position to set up a real opposition to His will to reveal Himself to us. It cannot separate us from Him, seeing He wills to be for us in the omnipotence of His Godhead. And if our views and concepts are impotent to apprehend Him because they are ours, because in themselves and as such they are capable only of apprehending world-reality and not His reality, even in this their impotence they cannot imply any real hindrance to His power to reveal Himself to us and therefore to give Himself to be known. Where we are impotent He can be all the more powerful ; and willing it He also does it. And the veracity of His revelation— i.e., His will and His power to reveal Himself—means that, however seldom it may appear to us, there is a veracious knowledge of God by man.

We must go further. The veracity of the revelation of God verifies itself by verily laying claim to the thinking and speaking of man. Our thinking, which is executed in views and concepts, is our responsibility to ourselves. Our speech is our responsibility to others. In this twofold responsibility—and this is how the veracity of the revelation of God verifies itself—we are verily claimed by it. That is to say, we cannot be responsible to ourselves and others without at the same time being responsible to God's revelation, as those whom this revelation concerns. By the Word and Spirit of God we are told that God is and who He is, what He wills and does and will do, and what this means for us. We have now to tell ourselves what is told us, and we have also to tell it to others. This claim cannot stand, or it cannot stand unconditionally, if in God's revelation we are not really dealing with God Himself, or with His true revelation. In that case we can be responsible to ourselves and others without thinking of God or speaking of God. But the veracity of God in His revelation, and the veracity of His revelation, establishes the veracity of the claim laid upon us to think of Him and speak of Him. This claim does not annul our human situation. Nor does it ignore and eliminate the fact that apart from God many other things, conditioned by ourselves and by the world-reality around us, are the content of our twofold responsibility and therefore of our thinking and speaking. But it does not constitute any protection against the fact that God too becomes the content of this twofold responsibility. It confirms our human situation as well to the extent that afterwards as well as before we are still powerless to make God the content of our twofold responsibility and therefore of our speaking and thinking about Him. On the contrary, it is the veracity of the revelation of God which brings our impotence home to us, and which therefore puts this judgment on ourselves into our mouth. But the claim is issued—and in this it shews itself to be a true claim—in spite of our powerlessness. It is disclosed to us that we do not view and think of God, that we cannot speak of Him ; and because this is disclosed to us, it is brought home to us that the very thing which has to happen, no matter what the circumstances, is that we must not fail to do it. It is the one characteristic of the revelation of God attested in the Bible that when it is issued it is impossible for man not to proceed to think of God, or to be silent about God. When it is issued, man is convicted of his inability to think of God and to speak of God. And when it is issued, it is required of man that in spite of inability, and even in his inability, he should still do both. On the ground of this requirement, thanks to the truth of God in it, there is a true knowledge of God on the part of man. The human knowledge of God is true in so far as it does not evade this requirement, but fulfils it in obedience.

But we must go still further. We have seen that to the will of God to reveal Himself corresponds His power to do so, and as there is no contradiction against His will, so also there is no real hindrance against His power. And when we say this, we are saying that the claim made upon us by His revelation does not demand anything impossible, and therefore that it is not an impotent and ineffectual claim. If God commands, it is so. And in the present context this means that, if He will have it so, we shall think of Him with what are certainly (from our standpoint) impotent views and concepts, and that we shall speak of Him what (again from our standpoint) are certainly impotent words. It means that God Himself, with His will to reveal Himself and therefore His claim upon us, takes our place, and therefore that, with His power to reveal Himself, He does not ignore or eliminate but fills up the void of our impotence to view and conceive Him. Our inability to perform by our action what is demanded of us is not at all His inability to cause what is demanded to happen by our action. What we of ourselves cannot do, He can do through us. If our views and concepts and words are of themselves too narrow to apprehend God, it does not follow that this sets a limit to God Himself, that it is impossible for God to take up His dwelling in this narrowness. If no heaven or earth or even eternity is too great to allow them to be His sphere of sovereignty and action, why should our views and concepts and words be too small for God to be in them in all His glory ? It is not a question of a power to receive this guest being secretly inherent in these works of ours. They have no power to do this, just as all the heavens are not able to contain Him. But there is a power of the divine indwelling in both the broad and the narrow which our works cannot withstand for all their impotence. This indwelling does not involve a magical transformation of man, or a supernatural enlargement of his capacity, so that now he can do what before he could not do. He cannot do it afterwards any more than he could do before. But he is taken up by the grace of God and determined to participation in the veracity of the revelation of God. In all his impotence he becomes a place where his honour dwells—not his own, but God's. As a sinner he is justified. But because it comes to pass in the truth of the revelation of God, this justification is not an illusion or a game. It is a real and effective justification of the views and concepts in which man is responsible to himself, and of the words in which he is responsible to others, on the ground of the divine claim issued to him. In the sanctification which comes to him through this claim his sin is neither ignored nor excused. Nor is it simply set aside. But it is forgiven, and this means that in his sinful position and behaviour he is the object, and also the instrument, of the divine good-pleasure. In relationship to this divine good-pleasure, both his sin, which is of course disclosed and taken very seriously, and also the sinfulness of his thinking and speaking, no longer have any power of their own, any definitive power. At the same time, however, they cannot and must not be asserted against the divine claim as an argument of the unprofitable servant and therefore of disobedience. The veracity of the revelation of God, which justifies the sinner in His Word by His Spirit, makes his knowledge of God true without him, against him—and yet as his own knowledge, and to that extent through him. By the grace of God we may view and conceive God and speak of God in our incapacity. And we ought to do so. We must not neglect to make use of this permission. We must not neglect it, even though our incapacity cries to heaven for such neglect. When we are obedient, according to our capacity and even our incapacity, we have the promise that God Himself will acknowledge our obedience in spite of our capacity or even incapacity, and this means that He will confer upon our viewing, conceiving and speaking His own veracity. The obedience to the grace of God in which man acknowledges that he is entirely wrong, thus acknowledging that God alone is entirely right, is the obedience which has this promise.

Again, for the sake of the veracity of our knowledge of God, the veracity of the revelation of God will necessarily make us humble. By the grace of God we shall truly know God with our views and concepts, and truly speak of God with our words. But we shall not be able to boast about it, as if it is our own success, and we have performed and done it. It is we who have known and spoken, but it will always be God and God alone who will have credit for the veracity of our thinking and speaking. In the true knowledge of God, it will necessarily be true and known again and again that God is true and all men are liars. But this cannot mean that we are again plunged into nothingness and resignation. Resignation is not humility but the pride which as such does not want to accept the grace of God and the justification of the sinner. And humility is not at all resignation. Humility accepts grace in judgment. Humility, therefore, does not let itself be driven by judgment into a despair which as despair of God can only be the rebellion of a supreme human self-consciousness. On the contrary, humility allows itself to be driven by judgment into the saving unrest (grounded in a final rest) of a continual enquiry concerning God, namely, God in His revelation. And this means concretely that as we, who are claimed by God's true revelation, form our views, concepts and words according to our ability (or inability), we cannot confine ourselves to any one of these works, as if we have already thought of God and spoken of God, and we have only to repeat our concepts and words to attain and express again the knowledge of God. The veracity of our knowledge of God can easily die of this kind of repetition ; for it does not possess in itself the knowledge of God ; it comes to it from the veracity of the revelation of God. The success of our undertaking stands or falls with the fact that we are on the way ; that therefore any goal that is attained becomes the point of departure for a new journey on this way, on which the revelation of God and its veracity are always future to us. A repetition of our work can mean that we no longer tread this way and therefore that we no longer stand under the promise of its goal and therefore of success. That God in His grace will take up His dwelling in the confines of our thinking and speaking cannot mean that He has surrendered Himself to us as our prisoner. He dwells where our thinking and speaking about Him take place in obedience : in obedience to His grace, which is *His* grace, which as such, whether we repeat ourselves or not, needs continually to be bestowed upon us, and therefore continually to be sought by us. A repetition of our work can mean that we want to master God, that we are therefore no longer obedient to His grace. The humility which is not only demanded but induced by the veracity of His revelation can certainly allow us to repeat our way, but it will accompany any such repetition with the warning and summons that, whether in repetition or in a new form of our work, we must reach out and explore for its object, i.e., for the grace of His revelation, from which alone it can ever become and be true.

The decisive thing about the veracity of human knowledge of God is undoubtedly said when we remember the veracity of the revelation of God. The human knowledge of God becomes and is true because God is truly God in His revelation ; because His revelation is true as such ; because in it he truly claims human thinking and speaking ; because in it He truly justifies human thinking and speaking ; because by it He upholds us as those who think of Him and speak of Him in humility before Him. Because this happens our human undertaking to view and conceive God and to speak of Him is an undertaking that succeeds. The grace of the revelation of God, which we came to know as the *terminus a quo* of our knowledge of God, is therefore also its *terminus ad quem*. Just as the hidden God, and therefore faith in Him, forms its beginning, so also the true God, and again faith in Him, forms its goal. Its own veracity consists, however, in the fact that it is on the way from this beginning to this goal and therefore participates in the veracity of this goal within the limitations imposed upon it by its beginning.

There still remains for us the task of defining more precisely the character and bearing of this participation of our knowledge in the veracity of its goal. What we have said is that our knowing has its veracity from its goal, but its determination and limit from its beginning. These statements can, of course, be reversed. The very fact that it proceeds from the hidden God guarantees its veracity, and the very fact that it goes towards the true God gives it its determination and limit. In both cases the reference is to God's revelation. As God veils Himself in His revelation, He also unveils Himself. And as He unveils Himself, He also veils Himself. Not the veiling, however, but the unveiling is the purpose of His revelation, the direction of His will. In our knowledge of Him we certainly cannot affirm His unveiling without at the same time acknowledging His veiling. And, on the other hand, in our knowledge of Him we certainly cannot affirm His veiling without at the same time thanking Him for His unveiling. Yet these two moments in His revelation and in faith are not equally balanced. There is not a mere uniformity between them. Nor is there the relationship of a monotonous and in a sense not obviously necessary alternation and reversal. If it is understood in this way, we are still under the spell of a formal logic raised to metaphysics, which is actually exploded and given the lie by the fact of the revelation of God, and therefore also of faith in Him. God indeed acts towards us and with us in His revelation, and therefore faith in Him also consists in an action, namely, in our following His action. But in the preceding divine and the subsequent human action we do not have either a uniformity of veiling and unveiling, or a continual alternation between the two, but, while the two always go together, they are also distinguished as the starting-point and the goal of the way on which God precedes us and we may follow Him, as the mode and meaning of His revelation. God reveals Himself in the mode of hiddenness ; but the meaning of His revelation is His veracity. He unveils Himself to us in and through His veiling and to that extent beginning with His veiling. But He does unveil Himself : it is for this reason and to this end that He veils Himself and to this extent that His unveiling is the goal of His way and ours. To this extent, in our definition of the *terminus ad quem* of our knowledge of God, while we do not forget or deny its *terminus a quo*, and are therefore determined and delimited by the recollection of God's hiddenness, we have good grounds to ask particularly about the veracity which is proper to it by reason of its goal, in virtue of its participation in the truth of the revelation of God, in virtue of the divine unveiling as the goal of God's way and ours. What sort of a participation is it ?

1. We can understand it only as participation in God's revelation. It is, therefore, right and proper that among our more detailed definitions we should give priority to the fact that basically it can consist only in the offering of our thanks. In this respect our knowledge of God stands under the same ordinance as our human work in general, which may be a response to the work of the Word and Spirit of God. If it really does respond ; if it really is response to this work ; if it really is the work of our following of God on the way on which He precedes us, from His veiling to His unveiling, then it has for its title : " On the Gratitude of Man."

But this means, first of all, that it does not have its necessity in itself ; it does not happen on its own account ; but it is evoked by an object. Nor does it have its necessity in us who do this work ; we do it, not because we are forced by an inner compulsion or enabled by an inner desire, but because the demand for us to do it is imposed upon us from without, because God is God in His revelation, because it is His true revelation and because we are truly claimed by it. There is no other basis for the knowledge of God, for the undertaking of human viewing, conceiving and speaking in regard to Him. This undertaking has only this basis outside itself and outside ourselves. But this basis is sufficient. It is sufficient to incite us to take this work in hand, to expel from us the fear of our insufficiency, to prevent us from wearying in its performance, to maintain our courage in all humility. If God in His revelation is this basis outside ourselves, the permission posited with this basis—the " permission to have Him as the basis of our actions "—is as such so great and strong that it becomes in us an imperative which breaks through all indolence and dilatoriness.

Our knowledge of God as participation in the veracity of His revelation consists in an offering of our thanks. But this means further that from the very first our work can claim only one recommendation and dignity, namely, that it is simply a response to God's revelation. If, then, it takes its place with other—and in their way good—works of man, it cannot try to commend itself as compared with them. If, and so far as, these other human works are also a response to God's revelation, then it is indeed commended as compared with them, and its goodness shines out among them, although there is no question of mutual competition. For how can works of gratitude be at strife with one another ? The work of the knowledge of God as man's participation in the veracity of the revelation of God certainly involves a witness, a question and a summons to all other works. But it takes place as such, as human work, with the same unpretentiousness with which they must all take place, and alone can take place as good works. If they try to be anything else but response to God's revelation, and therefore anything else but works of gratitude, in a very strange and exposed and defenceless way this work, the work of the knowledge of God, will make of itself an exception. It will obviously lack the inner-worldly recommendation and dignity which these works claim for themselves and which they apparently possess. It will have only the goodness which, where God's revelation is not known and acknowledged as the goal and object of the human action, cannot be seen and understood as goodness at all. It will have only its hidden excellence in its character as response to the Word which in this instance has not been heard. In this case—which continually recurs—the knowledge of God will have to be content to be revealed before God in its excellence as a good work. It will take place as such. It will be a witness, question and summons to all other works. But it will not enter into competition and strife with them. Gratitude cannot desire strife : either against other gratitude or even against ingratitude. Gratitude can only take place. It has its goodness only in the goodness which it reflects. It is only a receipt, not a security either to the giver or to any third party. Its necessary strife as a witness, question and summons takes place merely because it is gratitude and exists as such. Of course, a struggle takes place where the undertaking to view and conceive God and to speak of God is in progress. In this struggle, however, it is not we who are the strivers, either for or against anyone, but God Himself strives in this struggle—against all and for all. In this struggle there cannot be a commendation of some and a discrediting of others. For it is God who in this struggle commends Himself and maintains His dignity.

Our participation in the veracity of God consists in the offering of our thanks. But this means further that it can consist only in an acknowledgment of the revelation of God. It cannot consist, then, in a requital, in a work which is comparable in nature with the work of God, in an adequate reply to what has been said to us by God about God. True knowledge of God does not need to be called to order by any critical theory of knowledge to remember the inadequacy of all human views, concepts and words in relationship to this object, because as the work of gratitude it cannot try to be requital and therefore a reply in equal terms to what had been said to man by God. Where man repays like with like, there is no question of thanksgiving but only of a transaction : we are at the market which is ruled by the mutual adjustment of supply and demand, value and price. The giving of thanks for anything can only be acknowledgment, and the one who acknowledges places himself and his action consciously and expressly under the giver and his gift. Even the richest gift given in return as a mark of thanks will then—if it does not spring from the wrong intention of discharging the thanks—be designed only to emphasise the acknowledgment of the giver and the gift and the subordination of the recipient to the giver in accordance with the very nature of thanks. Basically, then, the undertaking to know God in human views, concepts and words belongs to the category of sacrifice, and what is more, to sacrifice in the biblical sense of the term. For in the Bible sacrifice does not mean that the Godhead is enlisted and reconciled and placated by an action equivalent to His own goodness and to that extent satisfying. On the contrary, it is a question of attesting the Godhead as Godhead by an action which does not conform in the very least to His goodness or claim to satisfy Him, by a gift which does not even remotely correspond to the Giver, and of which He does not stand in the slightest need ; of attesting Him as the Lord, to whom man owes everything, to whom he owes himself with everything that he is and has, to whom he owes it to give the glory which belongs to Him in the sphere of our humanity, the glory which He can receive if we do the best we can in His service. As sacrifice in this sense, our undertaking to know God is a sacrifice which is well-pleasing to Him. It participates in the veracity of His revelation, the veracity of the fact that He Himself has bestowed Himself upon us with all His riches.

Our participation in the veracity of the revelation of God is the offering of our thanks. But this means further that as the acknowledgment of His revelation our knowledge of God is put under the measure, order and rule of His revelation. It takes place in the sphere of our humanity and claims our very best—and therefore our best thinking and speaking to this end. But this does not mean that it is abandoned to our arbitrary selection of this best according to our own choice and pleasure. Purposeless or arbitrary thanksgiving, the thanksgiving in which the giver is guided either by chance or by his own humour, fancy or obstinacy, is not thanksgiving at all. For basically it will either not be occupied with the acknowledgment at all, or if it is, it will be more occupied with the acknowledgment than with what it is trying to acknowledge. True acknowledgment cannot come about in this way. True gratitude enquires—and it does not enquire in a soliloquy, but it enquires after Him to whom it wants to show gratitude. Certainly it does not claim to be sufficient for this task. Certainly it does not think that it should even try to requite Him. But it enquires after Him, and enquiring after Him, it acts : not arbitrarily, not according to its own discovery of gratitude, but in such a way that the One to whom it would be grateful is the law of its action. This means that in the true knowledge of God we are not left to ourselves, whether in the form of chance or of the wilfulness of our own general or individual nature, thinking and speaking. It is always a question of acknowledging God's revelation. This definite object rules our thinking and speaking. It claims an affirmation here, a negation there. It establishes connexions here, distinctions there. It reveals relationships here, and does not reveal them there. It brings into relief specific distinctive possibilities of view and concept, and the specific words which correspond to them, suppressing other words and possibilities. It brings before us the possibility and necessity of various perceptions and conceptions, at the same time reminding us of their mutual delimitation, and their common delimitation by their object. All this takes place in the sphere of our humanity. In it all we are not passive, but active. It has all been put in our hands. But this does not mean that it is given over to us. Because it is put in our hands it is expected of us that the work of our hands will be accomplished as responsibility towards this object and therefore towards this object of our gratitude.

There is one final point. The knowledge of God as participation in the veracity of the revelation of God is a work of gratitude. But this means that it cannot take place except in joyfulness. There can be no acknowledgment of the revelation of God unless we ourselves are involved. But, involved in this way, we are placed strictly under the rule of the object and become obedient. This obedience, however, can only mean that we are ourselves requisitioned to be doers of this work. If the revelation reaches us, if it becomes for us the necessary basis of our knowledge, this does, of course, mean that it approaches us from without, but it also means—how else can it reach us?—that it does actually come to us and therefore into us. It does not cease to transcend us, but we become immanent to it, so that obedience to it is our free will. But because God remains transcendent to us even in His revelation, the subjectivity of our acknowledgment of His revelation means our elevation above ourselves. It is this that of necessity makes our knowledge of God a joyful action. A gratitude that consists in an involuntary, mutinous and therefore forced and unjoyful action is not thanksgiving. A tribute to tyranny, however paid, is not thanks. A sacrifice offered in dread and constraint is not, in the biblical sense at least, a real sacrifice. Sacrifice and thanks are only what is offered gladly. And the basis which makes the true knowledge of God necessary is in itself the basis of knowing God gladly. But "gladly" means in the joy of the elevating of man above himself, in the exuberance of the movement in which he certainly remains with himself and yet at least as a sign reaches out above himself, in which he certainly remains a man and within the sphere of his human capacity and yet, in this very sphere of his human capacity, witnesses to what transcends all his possibilities, because he can witness to it on the basis of his present. In this sober exuberance there takes place the true human knowledge of God and the undertaking to view and conceive God humanly and to speak of Him in human words. It is not the undertaking of a slave but of a child. It is childlike even in the restrictive sense of the term, but in such a way that the very limitation of that which is childlike is also the earmark of the peculiar freedom here bestowed upon man. In this exuberance, which has nothing to do with conceit and presumption, in the exuberance of the worship of God in the heart and mouth of the sinful creature, human knowledge of God is an act of gratitude and therefore partakes of the veracity of the revelation of God.

2. Now if the participation of our knowledge of God in the veracity of His revelation consists in the offering of our thanks, we shall have to go rather further back and say that it will always be also an act of wondering awe. We have not been able to speak of gratitude without already touching in many ways on what is meant here : the necessary consciousness of the inadequacy of man as the recipient in relation to the knowledge of God as the gift and God Himself as the Giver in the relationship established by revelation. The knowledge of God will obviously not be an act of gratitude if it does not happen in this consciousness and in the attitude characterised by this consciousness. In our knowledge of God, whether in thought or speech, we always use some kind of views, concepts and words. They may be taken over from others or fresh minted by ourselves. But as human productions they do not stand in any real relationship to this object, nor have they any power to comprehend it. As there is a general incongruence between God and man, there is here a particular incongruence between God as the known and man as the knower. If there is a real knowledge, from our side, it is in this incongruence, and, therefore, in the overcoming of this incongruence. But it cannot be overcome from man's side. The overcoming is therefore from the side of God as the known. It takes place in the grace of His revelation, and it is known by us only in the grace of His revelation. As it is performed by God and known by us in faith, this event of the overcoming of the incongruence between Him as the known and us as the knowers is the object of the awe which to some extent forms the test of the genuineness of our knowing, and to that extent of the genuineness of our participation in the veracity of His revelation. How do we come to think, by means of our thinking, that which we cannot think at all by this means ? How do we come to say, by means of our language, that which we cannot say at all by this means ? The fact that we do actually think it and say it is the sure promise in which we are placed by God's revelation, which we may and shall apprehend in faith ; the event, which is continually before us, of real knowledge of God. But how do we come actually to think and say it ? How do we come to our participation in the veracity of His revelation and therefore in His own veracity ? In face of this *terminus ad quem* of our knowing of God we can only be amazed and, indeed, amazed only in awe. It can never be a question of amazement at ourselves, at the force of our thinking and language. However great this force may actually be, we shall not seize the kingdom of heaven with it. But if our thinking and language in this matter are not without object, if our undertaking to know God succeeds by these means of knowledge, it is because the kingdom of heaven has come to us. Therefore the amazement, without which we cannot put this act into effect as an act of gratitude, will necessarily be amazement at the kingdom of heaven which comes to us, and therefore the amazement of awe.

If the mouth and the tongue and lips of man become the instruments by which God and His truth and righteousness and glory are praised, and His Word is proclaimed, then, according to Holy Scripture, this is never a self-evident occurrence, or a success which man may attribute to himself. For first of all there has taken place at God's hand the overcoming in relation to which the man who uses these instruments, and is himself the instrument, always stands as an awed spectator conscious of his own failure. Prototypical in this respect is the form and attitude of Moses, as it is described in, *inter alia*, Ex. 4[10f.] : " O my Lord, I am not eloquent, neither heretofore, nor since thou hast spoken unto thy servant : but I am slow of speech, and of a slow tongue. And the Lord said unto him, Who hath made man's mouth ? or who maketh the dumb, or deaf, or the seeing, or the blind ? have not I the Lord ? Now therefore go, and I will be with thy mouth, and teach thee what thou shalt say." This is repeated in the confession of Isaiah : " Woe is me ! for I am undone ; because I am a man of unclean lips, and I dwell in the midst of a people of unclean lips : for mine eyes have seen the King, the Lord of hosts," and in what happens to him when in the vision the seraph takes a live coal with the tongs from off the altar : " And he laid it upon my mouth, and said, Lo, this hath touched thy lips ; and thine iniquity is taken away, and thy sin purged " (Is. 6[5ff.]). It is repeated in the call of Jeremiah: " Ah, Lord God ! behold, I cannot speak : for I am a child." " Then the Lord put forth his hand, and touched my mouth. And the Lord said unto me, Behold, I have put my words in thy mouth " (Jer. 1[6ff.]). It is repeated in Ezekiel : " But when I speak with thee, I will open thy mouth, and thou shalt say unto them, Thus saith the Lord God " (Ezek. 3[27]). It is drastically repeated in Daniel : " And when he had spoken such words unto me, I set my face toward the ground, and I became dumb. And, behold, one like the similitude of the sons of men touched my lips : then I opened my mouth, and spake " (Dan. 10[15f.]). " I create the fruit of the lips . . . saith the Lord " (Is. 57[19] ; cf. Heb. 13[15]). " I will put my words in his mouth ; and he shall speak unto them all that I shall command him," says Deut. 18[18] of the prophet of the last days. " The Lord God hath given me the tongue of the learned, that I should know how to speak a word in season to him that is weary " (Is. 50[4]). And therefore we must pray : " O Lord, open thou my lips ; and my mouth shall shew forth thy praise " (Ps. 51[15]). And we must not forget Num. 22[28], where even the mouth of Balaam's ass is opened (as if incidentally to show that the divine possibility involved does not have a limit, let alone a condition, in humanity). And if in the New Testament men have tongues to confess Jesus Christ as Lord, the power is again to be found in the miracle of Easter (Ac. 2[3f.]) behind them and the miracle of the future parousia before them (Phil. 2[11]). " It shall be given you in that same hour what ye shall speak. For it is not ye that speak, but the Spirit of your Father which speaketh in you " (Mt. 10[19f.]). Are we not forced to the express conclusion that the repression of human speech, to which there is universal reference, and its divine overcoming, are not simply a question of technical imperfections and their removal, nor of the ordinary difficulty of human communication, as if the biblical witnesses did not know how to express themselves properly ? No, the difficulty, and indeed the impossibility, to which reference is made, is a basic one. It is that of the object of which they have to speak, and on which, as sinful and weak men, they can only make shipwreck with their words. It is that of the object which obviously can find force and expression only in the shipwreck of their words, conferring suitability upon their words, which are impotent as such.

In this respect we must scrutinise carefully the statements of the fathers when they refer to the inadequacy of all human words to express this object. For what is the factor which really motivates them ? Is it the magic of the ineffable One and All of the Greeks, i.e., the *ineffabile* of man ? Or is it really reverence for the God of Israel who will be known only in His grace and therefore only in acknowledgment of the impotence of our own works and therefore also of our own words ? They knew almost too well and said almost too eagerly that we speak of God humanly and therefore inadequately when we do so in sensible expressions, when therefore, e.g., we speak of His mouth, His arms and hands, His remembering and forgetting, His pity, wrath and repentance. The danger is pressing, and has even become acute, that we may over-emphasise the impropriety of what are in the narrowest sense to be called " anthropomorphisms," ascribing in contrast a kind of moderate impropriety to abstract concepts like the being, wisdom, goodness and righteousness of God, and a genuine propriety only to negative concepts like incomprehensibility, immutability, infinity, etc., and therefore thinking that we can speak only uncertainly of the acts of God in His revelation, as if they were merely images and accommodations, and that we must say rather less in order to find safety on what is supposed to be the surer ground of these generalities and especially these negations. It is evident that this very prejudice against what are in the narrower sense to be called anthropomorphisms can also provide a basis and occasion for the pitiful transition from theology to philosophy, or from the theology of revelation to natural theology. The further we move away from the witness of the Holy Scriptures to the sphere of general conjectures about God, so much the purer, we think, is the air of thought, i.e., so much the less do we need the anthropomorphisms which are found to be particularly suspect. But, if it lets itself be guided by its object, theology ought to try to evade these anthropomorphisms least of all. And there is an obvious error when it is said that they are particularly suspect. " Anthropomorphism " is not merely " the application of expressions which are borrowed from the human, material and corporeal to define the divine and the spiritual " (thus J. Braun, *Handlex. der kath. Dogm.*, 1926, p. 18). For spiritual—i.e., abstract—concepts are just as anthropomorphic as those which indicate concrete perception. As a characterisation of human language about God " anthropomorphic " necessarily has the comprehensive meaning of that which corresponds to the form of man, and does not, therefore, correspond to God. When the fathers dig deeper, they too know this well enough. The difficulty, explains Athanasius, lies in the fact that we can say of man that he creates, he is, and that we can only say the same of God, although God's being and creating is not like that of man but very different (ἄλλως, ἑτέρως) (*Ep. de decr. Nic. syn.* 11). The same is also true, however, of concepts like the *vita, intelligentia, substantia, existentia* of God : *Non proprie nominamus nec appellamus*, but *a nostris actionibus nominamus actiones Dei* (Marius Victorinus, *De gen. div. Verbi* 28). On the wisdom, life and power of God there comes at once a συνταπείνωσις when we speak of His wisdom, His life and His power in accordance with what we know as such. For our nature is transient, our life short, our power weak, our word fickle. And conversely, by the actuality of the divine nature, when it encounters us, everything that we can say of Him is raised συνεπαίρεται (Gregory of Nyssa, *Or. cat.* 1). *Aliter bonum Deum appellamus, aliter hominem. Aliter iustum Deum appellamus, aliter hominem* (Augustine, *De off. minist.* III, 2, 11). When we speak of God, we speak in relation to the world created by Him, its beauty and goodness and being. But : *Nec ita pulchra sunt, nec ita bona sunt, nec ita sunt, sicut tu conditor eorum, cui comparata nec pulchra sunt, nec bona sunt, nec sunt* (*Conf.* XI, 4, 6). If we could only be sure that this *nec ita* or *aliter*, this ἄλλως or ἑτέρως, does not refer only to a superlative of unlikeness, but to a basic difference between God and the creature, and therefore between the divine being and creaturely views, concepts and words ! If only the above-mentioned specific critique of anthropomorphisms in the narrower sense did not shew in what direction they think they have to seek the incongruence of the divine being and human language, namely, in the distinction between the spirituality of this being and the sensuousness of our speech ; and in what direction they seek the congruence of both as reconstituted in the knowledge of God, namely, in a process of spiritualisation, to which creaturely views, concepts and words can be not altogether unsuccessfully subjected ! For what is involved in this case is an incongruence which exists within the world and can therefore be overcome within the world. And in contradistinction to the amazement expressed in the biblical passages the amazement at the fact of this overcoming which was certainly not foreign to the fathers necessarily has in it more of amazement at the *ineffabile* of man, or at the final power of human thinking and speech to overcome all obstacles, than the amazement of awe at the omnipotent miracle of the divine condescension. We must, however, give the fathers due credit for their attention to the biblical passages about the inadequacy of all human language about God and its divine overcoming, and also for their emphasis on the fact to which these passages refer. And there is no doubt that they did aim to interpret this truth of revelation as attested in the Bible. But while we acknowledge this fact, we shall have to underline at any rate more clearly than they did the basic character of the incongruence and the revelational character of the congruence reconstituted when it is overcome.

We say awe, having previously said thanksgiving, and having referred finally to the necessary joyfulness of the knowledge that participates in the veracity of the revelation of God. But as in the case of thanksgiving, and therefore joyfulness, we have to say awe of necessity. Awe refers to the distance between our work and its object. This distance is certainly overcome. But it is still a distance which is overcome only by God's grace, the distance between here and there, below and above. In awe we gratefully let grace be grace, and always receive it as such. We never let reception become a taking. Our knowledge of God is always compelled to be a prayer of thanksgiving, penitence and intercession. It is only in this way that there is knowledge of God in participation in the veracity of the revelation of God.

If it does not come to pass in this amazement of awe, if we do not see the distance between our work and its object, if we ascribe to ourselves the capacity to overcome it in our own strength, if we claim this overcoming as, so to speak, our own act, and try to perform and master it as such, if we evade the school to which the prophets and apostles submitted when they spoke about God on the basis of His revelation, then, on the basis of the revelation of God, we can, of course, arrive at a more or less wonderful theological systematisation of divine truth, but we shall have our reward, for from the very first the worm of a human rapacity and encroachment will be at work in the timber of such a structure. And sooner or later we shall have to observe that the veracity of the revelation is to be had only as the veracity of His grace, and that we, by rejecting and denying it as the veracity of grace, must also lose it as the veracity of His revelation, and that God cannot really be known otherwise than by God.

To the question how we come to know God by means of our thinking and language, we must give the answer that of ourselves we do not come to know Him, that, on the contrary, this happens only as the grace of the revelation of God comes to us and therefore to the means of our thinking and language, adopting us and them, pardoning, saving, protecting and making good. We are permitted to make use, and a successful use at that, of the means given to us. We do not create this success. Nor do our means create it. But the grace of God's revelation creates it. To know this is the awe in which our knowledge of God becomes true.

3. But just what this permission means for the act of our cognition we must now submit to even more detailed investigation. If we presuppose that everything said so far is agreed and acknowledged, what is to be said about the relationship between the views, concepts and words used by us on the basis of the means we are given and God as their object ? There is no doubt that, on the basis and according to the measure of the presuppositions now clarified, this relationship is to be regarded as a positive relationship, i.e., one in which there exists a real fellowship between the knower and his knowing on the one hand and the known on the other. If it is regarded as negative, and this fellowship is denied, God is not revealed to man. His grace is not grace. Man's faith is not faith. Or else God's revelation is not true. That is, either He is not truly God in it, or He is not truly revealed as God. Or again, man's knowledge of God does not take place in participation in the veracity of the revelation of God. The way of human cognition of God has no goal at all, no *terminus ad quem*, which means that it probably has no beginning, no *terminus a quo*. It is simply a fiction, resting on an illusion, that we are on this way at all. But if this fellowship is not to be denied, in what does it consist ? Where do we find the veracity in which we apply to God human words which as such are inadequate to describe Him, as we all do at every point when we speak directly or indirectly about God ?

Does there exist a simple parity of content and meaning when we apply the same word to the creature on the one hand and to God's revelation and God on the other ? We are aware, or we think we are aware, of what being, spirit, sovereignty, creation, redemption, righteousness, wisdom, goodness, etc. mean when we use these terms to describe creatures. We are also aware, or think we are aware, what we are saying when in the sphere of the creature we say eye, ear, mouth, arm or hand, or love, wrath, mercy, patience and such-like. Does all this mean the same thing when we also say it about God ? Is, has and does God all these things as we see creatures are, have and do ? Obviously we cannot affirm this, nor can the veracity of our knowledge be found in a likeness of this kind between our knowledge and Him as the known. For this would mean a denial of God's hiddenness, and His revelation would no longer be understood as an unveiling in veiling. A parity of this type would mean either that God had ceased to be God and become merely a creature, or that man with his capacity had become a God. Therefore this parity means necessarily that the knower and the known are related either as two creatures or as two gods. If we are dealing with the creature on the one hand and God on the other, and if the grace of the revelation of God is the alpha and omega of the positivity of that relationship, this positivity cannot be understood in this way, and there can be no question of a likeness between our word, which as such refers to a creaturely being, and the being of God which it is used to describe.

Ought we, then, to speak of a disparity of content and meaning when we apply a description to the creature on the one hand and to God's revelation and God on the other ?   When we speak of God as being, spirit, sovereign, creator, redeemer, righteousness, wisdom and goodness, but also apply to Him such words as eye, ear and mouth, arm, hand, love, wrath, mercy, patience, do they mean something different from when we use them to describe the creature ?   We must be careful what we are affirming if we wish to affirm this.   There can be an all too human exaggeration of that awe in the knowledge of God, by which we do not praise God but deny Him.   This kind of disparity necessarily means that in fact we do not know God.   For if we know Him, we know Him by the means given us ; otherwise we do not know Him at all.   The fact that we know Him must mean that, with our views, concepts and words, we do not describe and express something quite different from Himself, but that in and by these means of ours —the only ones we have—we describe and express God Himself. Otherwise, without this relationship, under the presupposition of a simple disparity, there cannot possibly be any question of the veracity of our knowledge of God.   The whole relationship will have to be regarded as simply negative, as a relationship of mutual exclusion. There will not then be in fact any fellowship between the knower and the known.   God's revelation will simply be a veiling, and it cannot therefore be understood as revelation.   The impossibility of the thesis of a parity between our word and the being of God must not press us into the counter-thesis of a disparity between them.   On the basis of the same presupposition the latter is just as impossible as the former.

In this perplexity the older theology accepted the concept of analogy to describe the fellowship in question.   By this term both the false thesis of parity and the equally false thesis of disparity were attacked and destroyed, but the elements of truth in both were revealed.   It could therefore be claimed as the correct definition of the matter.   In distinction to both likeness and unlikeness " analogy " means similarity, i.e., a partial correspondence and agreement (and, therefore, one which limits both parity and disparity between two or more different entities).   The term is (cf. above, pp. 75 ff.) burdened by its use in natural theology, and it needs specific clarification in this respect.   But at this point it is as such unavoidable.   If in this fellowship there can be no question of either parity or disparity, there remains only what is generally meant by analogy : similarity, partial correspondence and agreement.   We shall have to reserve for the moment what is to be said about the origin and constitution of this correspondence and agreement as such, and also about the meaning of " partial."   But the object itself—God's truth in His revelation as the basis of the veracity of our knowledge of God—does not leave us any option but to resort to this concept.

8

It is to be noted that this procedure is itself an illustration of the matter of which we are speaking ; or, rather, that this procedure as such brings us at once to the very heart of the matter. We are enquiring into the relationship between what we may say about God with our words which in themselves describe only the creaturely, and what God is and therefore what must be said of Him in words which are not at our disposal. We can also say what is to be said about this relationship only with our words which have reference to the creaturely. Parity, disparity and analogy are all equally such creaturely words, and therefore quite insufficient in themselves to say what is to be said at this point where we have to do with God and the creature. Nevertheless, a selection has to be made. The words parity and disparity have to be rejected and the word analogy preferred. With what right ? Merely regarding the words as such, the one is actually as insufficient as the others to be used in this way. In all three words the co-existence of comparable objects is obviously presupposed. Only under this presupposition can they be described as alike, unlike or analogous. But God is not an object comparable to other objects. Supposing, however, that the relationship between God's being and human words really consists in God's true revelation, because this revelation mediates true knowledge of God to us ? Supposing the knowledge of this relationship also belongs to this true knowledge and there is therefore a word to describe this relationship ? Whatever may have to be said about the insufficiency of the words parity, disparity and analogy to be used in this way, are we not driven into the sphere of these three words (not on account of a secret capacity of the words, but on the strength of the Nevertheless of the true revelation of God, in which God posits Himself as a comparable object) ? It is still the case that we are not concerned with the words as such. In a sense we simply turn our back on them. We look to the true revelation of God. And by it we are pushed away from the words parity and disparity. For the relationship posited in God's true revelation does not bear either description, although in themselves both terms, like the word analogy, can be, and in other contexts (as, for example, the doctrine of the Trinity) actually are, instruments to be used in this way. In this case, however, to answer the concrete question posed by revelation, they obviously cannot be used. They are, therefore, incorrect. And, pressed again by the true revelation of God, we are pushed on to the word " analogy." In itself and as such it is no better than the words parity and disparity. Indeed, in other contexts (as, for example, to describe the relationship between God and Christ) it would be quite out of place. It is not, therefore, correct in itself, even in this context. It becomes correct in this context because the relationship (posited in God's true revelation) which we have here to express in some sense attracts this word to itself, giving it in the sphere of our words, which are insufficient to be used in this way, the character of a designation for the divine reality of this relationship. It is not a relationship either of parity or of disparity, but of similarity. This is what we think and this is what we express as the true knowledge of God, although in faith we still know and remember that everything that we know as " similarity " is not identical with the similarity meant here. Yet we also know and remember, and again in faith, that the similarity meant here is pleased to reflect itself in what we know as similarity and call by this name, so that in our thinking and speaking similarity becomes similar to the similarity posited in the true revelation of God (to which it is, in itself, not similar), and we do not think and speak falsely but rightly when we describe the relationship as one of similarity. It is not a deification of man and of a human word if we ascribe this correctness to it and consequently take it upon our lips. We are not trusting in a power of apprehension and therefore of correctness immanent in us or in this word. We know that it cannot have this in and of itself. But we trust in the true revelation of God coming to us and therefore to these words as well. For the sake of God's revelation man and his human word cannot be abandoned to a nothingness of fundamental godlessness. But the truth is that man with his human word " similarity " participates in the (as such) incomprehensible similarity which is posited in God's true revelation, so that in it God participates in man and his human word. If we are not disobedient but obedient to the truth of this revelation in taking up this particular word ; if our decision for the concept of analogy is not arbitrary ; if it is not self-grounded upon a secret prejudice in favour of an immanent capacity of this concept, but occurs under the compulsion of the object ; if it is not, then, a systematic but an exegetical decision, for this reason and to this extent it was and is a right decision.

We have been analysing the procedure by which the term analogy is selected to describe the relationship between what we say of God and what God is. But at bottom we have to do with the same procedure in the relationship itself. If we can presuppose that the term analogy or similarity is " correct " in the sense explained, the correctness of what we say about God, in its relationship to what God is, is everywhere based on the fact that God's true revelation comes from out of itself to meet what we can say with our human words and makes a selection from among them to which we have then to attach ourselves in obedience. What we say in this attachment we say rightly, and in it—as the *terminus ad quem* of our knowledge of God—we participate in the truth of His revelation. Its *terminus a quo*, God's hiddenness, will not be annulled by it, or denied by us. But we will also not deny that it has pleased and does please God in His true revelation to make Himself comprehensible to us, without prejudice to His hiddenness and therefore within the limits of our comprehension.

Between our views, concepts and words, and God as their object, there exists, on the basis of the revelation of God, the relationship of analogy, of similarity, of partial correspondence and agreement. On the basis of this similarity there is a true human knowledge of God and therefore the human knowledge of God reaches its goal. But how does this partial correspondence and agreement arise ? If it does so only partially, then, as a presupposition of this event, we must affirm that, as and before it occurs, as and before our word comes to participate in it, it obviously subsists in God Himself as the Subject and Lord who in His revelation reveals Himself to us, and as the Creator who in His revelation controls His own work. In Himself He is quite different from what He is in our work. Therefore the relationship between what He is in Himself and what He is in our work is only a relationship of similarity. Yet while this is true, it is also true that both in Himself and in our work He is not Another. And because in our work He is this One on the basis of His revelation, because His revelation in its relationship to us is grace, we shall have to say that He is this One first of all in Himself, and on this basis He is it secondly (not as Another, but in another way) for us, in our work grounded in His revelation. Our work consists in applying to God human views, concepts and words which as such can be applied only to the creaturely. This work of ours, grounded on God's revelation, can become a successful work. Our views, concepts and words, grounded on God's revelation, can be legitimately applied to God, and genuinely describe Him even in this sphere of ours and within its limits. For all their unsuitability, they can still be correct and true. But if this is the case, the capacity does not rest on a lie in which black is called white. In other words, we do not attribute to our views, concepts and words a purely fictional capacity, so that the use we make of them is always hedged in by the reservation of an " as if." But because God, who is always God in this relationship, takes the part of man, there is genuine correspondence and agreement. Indeed, it is not the case that when He authorises and commands us in His revelation to make use of our views, concepts and words God is doing something, so to speak, inappropriate, because, if they are to be applied to Him, our views, concepts and words have to be alienated from their proper and original sense and usage. No, He takes to Himself something that already belongs originally and properly to Him. Although His action is pure grace, He does not perform a μετάβασις εἰς ἄλλο γένος. He is righteous in all His works and therefore in this work too : He " comes unto His own." Creatures who are the suitable object of our human views, concepts and words are actually His creation. But our thought and our language in their appropriateness to this object are also His creation. Therefore the truth in which we know this appropriate object in the way appropriate to us is His creation, His truth. It is His truth in a very different way from what it is ours—with all the distinction of the Creator from the creature. It is obviously His truth originally, primarily, independently and properly, because creatively. It is our truth only subsequently, secondarily, dependently and improperly, because creaturely. Obviously, again, we know our truth only as ours and not as His. A reversal of the relationship, a control of God by man, is, therefore, excluded and impossible. That which follows cannot possibly precede.

For this reason it is not at all the case that with our thinking and speaking in its creaturely reference, while we do not, of course, grasp the thought and truth of the Creator, we still think and intend to conceive at least the idea of God beyond our thinking and speaking and perhaps even to realise it at least in terms of feeling. Our supposed idea of God, the object of our most intimate feeling, will always be the idea of the world and in the last resort of man. It will always be our own reflection, the hypostatisation of our thought and speech. It will be this the more fully if we follow the teaching of A. Ritschl, which was Augustine's before him, and unite it with the idea of a supreme value or good   We cannot even mean God of ourselves. But He not only means us but knows about us. " Thou understandest my thought afar off " (Ps. 139¹). His truth is not our truth. But our truth is His truth. This is the unity of truth in Him who is the truth.

The activity involved in our knowledge of His creation, to be realised in views, concepts and words, has its truth, hidden from us, in God as its and our Creator. In the first instance, whatever is said by us was, is and will be said truly in Him. It will be said in Him in a truth which is original, primary, independent and proper truth ; by us in a truth which is subsequent, secondary, dependent and improper. It will be said in Him infallibly, by us (for we are not only creatures but sinful creatures who have fallen from Him) always in error, and yet in such a way that even in error, doubly hidden from ourselves (by our creatureliness and our sin), and therefore in a double sense without any possibility of reclamation, we live by His infallible truth. With our views, concepts and words we have no claim on Him, that He should be their object. He Himself, however, has every—the best founded and most valid—claim on us and on all our views, concepts and words, that He should be their first and last and proper subject. Therefore, He does not annul His truth or deny it, nor does He establish a double truth, nor does He place us in the doubtful position of an " as if " cognition, when He allows and commands us in His revelation to make use of our views, concepts and thoughts to describe Himself, His Word and His deeds. On the contrary, He establishes the one truth, His own, as the truth of our views, concepts and words. But again, this is not because they are appropriate for it or because they originally mean Him apart from this one truth. As our own they simply do not do this. When He claims them, He does not confirm Himself but us. But in them He does in fact confirm Himself. For the truth is that, as they have His creation for object, and as they are themselves His creation, in them all God the Creator has knowledge of Himself, so that by them all, as by the existence of creation generally, God describes and proclaims Himself. For this reason He, the Creator, claims us and therefore them in His revelation. Thus He does not perform a violent miracle, but exercises a lawful claim and makes a restitution, when, in His omnipotence, He causes the miracle to happen by which we come to participate in the veracity of His revelation, and by which our words become true descriptions of Himself. Our words are not our property, but His. And disposing of them as His property, He places them at our disposal—at the disposal of our grateful obedience—when He allows and commands us to make use of them in this relationship too. The use to which they are put is not, then, an improper and merely pictorial one, but their proper use. We use our words improperly and pictorially—as we can now say, looking back from God's revelation—when we apply them within the confines of what is appropriate to us as creatures. When we apply them to God they are not alienated from their original object and therefore from their truth, but, on the contrary, restored to it.

For example, the words " father " and " son " do not first and properly have their truth at the point of reference to the underlying views and concepts in our thought and language, i.e., in their application to the two nearest male members in the succession of physical generation of man or of animal creation generally. They have it first and properly at a point to which, as our words, they cannot refer at all, but to which, on the basis of the grace of the revelation of God, they may refer, and on the basis of the lawful claim of God the Creator they even must refer, and therefore, on the basis of this permission and compulsion, they can actually refer—in their application to God, in the doctrine of the Trinity. In a way which is incomprehensible and concealed from us, but in the incontestable priority of the Creator over the creature, God Himself is *the* Father and *the* Son.

If we apply these words to God, we do not withdraw from them their original meaning, nor do we speak " as if." On the contrary, we speak in the original truth of these words. And, in the same way, " lordship " is not first and properly what we know as the exercise of power by man over man, but the κυριότης of God exercised and revealed in Jesus Christ. In the same way, " patience " is not primarily the crumb of virtue which we do, or do not, practise under this name, but the incomprehensible being and attitude of God which is shown in the fact that He gives us time to believe in Him. In the same way, the truth of what " love " means may be read from what we know as the desire, surpassing natural self-seeking, of the one for the other, only in the light of what happens between God the Father and the Son by the Holy Spirit, or in the light of the fact that God has loved the world in His Son. In the same way also, words of such simple content as " arm " and " mouth "—which to us are as such incomprehensible—declare their truth only in the place (and therefore in the very place where the spiritualisers think they must find excuses for themselves or the Bible) where the reference is to the arm and mouth of God, His deeds and words. " He that planted the ear, shall he not hear ? he that formed the eye, shall he not see ? " (Ps. 94⁹). " Can a woman forget her sucking child, that she should not have compassion on the son of her womb ? yea, they may forget, yet will I not forget thee " (Is. 49¹⁵). " If ye, then, being evil, know how to give good gifts unto your children, how much more shall your Father which is in heaven give good things to them that ask him ? " (Mt. 7¹¹). In sayings such as these where is the proper and where the improper use of our views and concepts ? Their proper use obviously consists in the fact that they point away and beyond themselves, taking on a new pregnancy, referring to that to which they cannot refer at all as our views and concepts.

Now, it certainly does not lie in our power to return our words to their proper use. There is a deep error here in the misused application which the concept of analogy is ordinarily and continually given in natural theology. In His revelation God controls His property, elevating our words to their proper use, giving Himself to be their proper object, and therefore giving them truth. Analogy of truth between Him and us is present in His knowing, which comprehends ours, but not in ours, which does not comprehend His. But in our knowing, this analogy of truth comes into being in virtue of the decision of His grace, which is to this extent the grace of His revelation. It is not the case that we can anticipate or handle this divine control, elevating and giving ; that even prior to God's decision, or without it, we can understand our truth as secondary to His and therefore His truth in the reflection of ours, our words as inexhaustible, as words that properly mean God. It is not, then, the case that by means of a clarification of the meaning and understanding of our words as such we can press forward to a provisional meaning and understanding of their use in relation to God. The provisional meaning and understanding to which we can, of course, press forward by this kind of clarification is the provisional meaning and understanding of our understanding of the world, and finally of our self-understanding as it may actually come to pass in our encounter or supposed encounter with one of the gods of this world. Our encounter with the God who is the Creator and forgives sins cannot be preceded by this type of provisional understanding. As the encounter precipitated entirely by God, it can only be the first, which our knowing must follow and cannot precede. The reflection of His truth in our truth follows it. The proper use of our words in the employ of this knowing follows it. It follows it because truth and propriety are placed by Him at the disposal of our words. God has to make Himself object to us in the grace of His revelation. He has, therefore, to bestow truth upon our knowing that is directed to creaturely objects—the truth of similarity with Him. Without this bestowal our words have truth in Him but not for us. In our mouths they are words which denote the creature but not God. Indeed they cannot denote Him. This possibility of theirs stands or falls with the reality of the fact that they are enlisted by God's revelation to participate in His truth, that they are in a certain sense raised from the dead. The fact that this does happen to them at the hands of God's revelation, that He gives to them the thing which by nature they cannot have—in their creatureliness the character of an analogy to Himself as the Creator—is, of course, something which is not to be denied.

This giving is originally intended by the doctrine of analogy in natural theology, at any rate so far as it thinks it can call itself Christian natural theology and the cognition of the Church. Its error is that it makes out of the " He " an " it," out of the becoming a being, out of the coming to us by God's revelation something existing and capable of proof even without revelation and otherwise than in faith. This static instead of dynamic understanding of the analogy between our word and God must, therefore, be expressly repudiated if we are to adopt the term. When we make this repudiation, when we understand that the analogy has its basis in the being of God as He may be comprehended by creation and is therefore a mode—the mode which particularly concerns our knowledge of God—of His revelation, and the work of His grace, the peculiar overweighting of the concept, and the danger which its use incontestably involves, is eliminated. We have no grounds for saying No where God has said Yes in His revelation. But it all depends upon our saying Yes where—and only where—God has first said Yes in His revelation.

We cannot open our mouths to speak about God without appropriating the promise that we shall speak the truth in the analogy of His truth itself. But everything depends on our doing it with a good conscience ; and, indeed, everything depends on our actually appropriating His promise and therefore not using our human words without the permission and command of His revelation, on the basis of a provisional understanding, but on the basis of the decision made in His revelation. In this use our words then possess the entire veracity which they have in God Himself, in which God the Creator, who places them at our disposal, knows about Himself, and with which He describes Himself. In this use God Himself lives and speaks in them. In this use the human word becomes God's own word, the human word receives the momentum, the *parresia*, the certainty and authority, which distinguishes genuine preaching from a mere speaking about God and past God, from a mere religious " as if " speech, however earnest and moving it might be. Man has not arrogated anything to himself when he speaks of God. He just speaks what is given to him.

It is to be noted that the human word receives concrete content and concrete form from God, and becomes capable of saying something, by the fact, and only by the fact, that it is spoken on the strength of God's permission and command, and therefore has the definite similarity with its object which is promised and bestowed by God's revelation, and is not arbitrarily discovered and affirmed. Where the latter is to be said of it, necessarily it is or will be unrestrained and therefore sooner or later futile. All kinds of things might be analogous of God, if God had not made and did not make a very definite and delimited use of His omnipotence in His revelation ; that is to say, if the analogy of the creation and the creaturely word effected by His revelation did not mean a selection, determined and carried out by Himself, from among the infinitely many possibilities, and therefore if we were not always referred to quite definite possibilities and definitely referred away from others. And all kinds of things might become analogous of God if it were left to our wisdom or will (appealing to the fact that with God nothing is impossible and that we must not assign limits to Him) to claim this thing or that as an analogy of God, discovering and proclaiming one analogy here to-day and another there to-morrow. In these circumstances human language about God would be a stream of formless inundation, which now in this place and now in that breaks through a bank, flooding streets and villages, and finally creating everywhere the uniformity of death. For although we can attempt arbitrary decisions between real and unreal analogies, they can only be affirmed and executed arbitrarily and in the long run ineffectually. It will only be the perseverance or the stubbornness of one or the other of the philosophical schools which will here affirm the analogy of God in the one case and deny it in the other, thus drawing a boundary, but not knowing at all how long it will be a boundary, or whether it will not soon be drawn very differently.

We must not overlook the fact that the moderate doctrine of analogy in natural theology, as it has been and is represented in particular in the Catholic Church, stands in the closest material and historical connexion with the Liberalism which, under appeal to God's omnipotence, affirms all analogies. Even if it is sanctified by the teaching office of the Church, it is still an arbitrariness, grounded only in philosophy, that Catholicism will not allow Christian thinking and Christian language to draw from the *analogia entis* affirmed by it the consequence of a general analogy of the world to God. On the other hand, Liberalism shows a basic readiness in almost every connexion to discover new analogies in the world, and, whether it knows it or not, it stands in only too great need of the corrective of a philosophical arbitrariness (and a teaching office to sanctify it ?), and necessarily evokes at least a desire for it. Genuine proclamation is not possible on the basis of the opinion that we have to reckon with an analogy of human views, concepts and words, which may be established apart from God's revelation, and therefore on the basis of the doctrine of analogy in natural theology. It is only possible where the analogy is understood as the work and proposition of revelation itself. Genuine proclamation must speak particularly and therefore restrictedly. It must be aware why it says this and does not say that ; why it says this in one way and that in another. But its particularity must not be abandoned to an arbitrary philosophy, to the chances and changes of philosophies, and finally to the dictates of a teaching office. If it is going to be proclamation of God, it must rest on the choice made by God Himself. For this very reason it must always be bound to God's revelation, and must always be the exposition of the revelation of God. Even indirectly it must not become the self-exposition of man, or the exposition of the revelation of God under the presupposition and according to the measure of a preceding self-exposition of man. It is exposition of the revelation of God when it keeps to the human words which are placed at our disposal as we are confronted by God's revelation, and which are therefore designated as serviceable for this employment; when it follows the freedom in which God bestows His grace upon man generally and therefore upon his human views, concepts and words. It will then have something definite to say, and that with a good conscience, with the promise of relevance, i.e., of standing in a real relationship to the reality proclaimed by it, and with the justified claim and well grounded prospect of obtaining a hearing.

But we must take a final step. We saw first that our words about God can stand in analogy to God's being because, as the Creator of all things, God is the first and last truth of all our words as well. We then saw that this ability becomes reality—i.e., our words about God receive analogy to God's being—as God disposes concerning them in His revelation, giving Himself to them as object and thus giving them veracity. This is the goal of our knowledge of God, its *terminus ad quem*. Because this is so, the relationship between the knower and the known on the basis of revelation is to be understood as a positive one. But we must now be clear that this positivity is definitely restricted; that this goal of our knowledge of God (i.e., its veracity) also means in fact its limit to forward progress (corresponding to and in fact coinciding with the incomprehensibility of God). If our knowledge of God is true, our words stand in a correspondence and agreement with the being of God. But we have already seen that this cannot be a correspondence and agreement which mean parity, because that would mean the annulment either of the deity of God or of the manhood of man. If it is also not a question of disparity—for in that case where is the correspondence and agreement, the positivity of the whole relationship, the truth of our cognition and finally also the truth of the revelation of God?—it can only be a question of similarity, of analogy, and therefore of partial correspondence and agreement between our words and God's being. But we still have to explain the " partial " which denotes that the goal is also the limit of our knowledge of God.

We can see at a glance that in itself and as such the word is quite impotent and inadequate to designate the matter in question.

It was fitting, therefore, that when we came up against this concept of analogy, and accepted its validity and adopted it, we stated at once that the concept as such—with which apparently we cannot designate God directly but only our knowledge of God—is undoubtedly in itself an unsatisfactory concept. This is only a confirmation of the fact that, in the doctrine of the knowledge of God, we are already within the doctrine of God itself and not in the sphere of mere prolegomena, where other considerations rule. This is inevitable. The main proposition of all this first chapter of the doctrine of God, both latently and patently, is that God is known by God, and what is more, by God alone. But if this is the case, we are already concerned with God Himself when we want to speak directly of the nature of God. It is not surprising, then, that our concepts and words to describe this fact come under the same particularisation and limitation as the concepts and words used to describe God Himself.

The insufficiency of the concept of analogy emerges in the fact that we have to introduce this word " partial " when we define it more exactly. If we think that, in the relationship between two creaturely entities, we have not to establish disparity or parity, but similarity, we are left with a partial correspondence and agreement. This means that the relationship between the two entities is to be understood and represented algebraically as a plus and minus on both sides : the correspondence and agreement partially exist and partially do not exist. But this kind of algebraic division—and any division that we know and can make is an algebraic division of this kind—is quite out of the question as between God and ourselves.

Much obscurity would be avoided in dogmatic *Loci* if this were clearly perceived. Instead, there is a constant resort to questions and solutions whose presupposition is an algebraic " partial." But as such this can never be sufficient to designate the relationship between God and man. It must not, then, be used without careful examination, i.e., without correction from this object.

God is one. He is the One. He Himself does not consist of quantities. He is not to be understood as resolved into quantities. The same is true of His relationship to us and therefore of our knowledge of Him. In this knowledge, because it is true knowledge, there is similarity between our words and His being. But this cannot mean (as the necessary word " partial " seems at first to suggest) that whereas a quantity in the sense and content of our words corresponds to one quantity in God's being, to another quantity in God's being there is only a corresponding vacuum in the sense and content of our words, so that in the latter respect, or part, our words do not correspond to the being of God. For the parts under consideration here are on the one hand the one, entire and indivisible being of God, who has unreservedly made Himself accessible and imparted Himself to us in His revelation without reservation, and on the other hand our words—i.e., we ourselves—again entire and indivisible in our creatureliness and sinfulness, in the works which correspond to this determination. To designate the positivity and truth of the relationship between these two entities we use the concept of similarity and therefore of a partial correspondence and agreement. But neither the one nor the other of these two entities is calculable. For in this relationship man is confronted by God. He is drawn into the light that is given with the fact that God has entered into relationship with him. Therefore man and his capacity and achievement can no longer be regarded and understood as calculable. In this relationship man arises either entirely or not at all. Therefore in this connexion the " partial " which we have to use in explanation of the concept of analogy means that it is a question of these two " parts " which, in themselves and in their relation to each other, are quite incalculable. God is always God and man is always man in this relationship. It is, then, in this way, in the determination of the particular relationship which exists and can only exist between God and man, in the fulness of this relationship but also in the limitation which is given with the fact that it is this particular relationship, that there is correspondence and agreement between our words and God's being. Because God is always God in this relationship, He is (in His entirety, in the quantitatively as well as qualitatively quite unlimited truth of His being) the object of the views, concepts and words which He places at man's disposal in His revelation, which in His revelation He allows and commands him to use to designate Him. He is this in so far as He is gracious to man and actually accepts him in grace. But because God is always God, He is also in His revelation (again in His entirety and therefore without deduction of a part of His being, of which something else might be said) the hidden God, who is definitely not the object of the views, concepts and words which we may apply to Him, and who has certainly not given Himself by this His permission and command even into the sphere of our apprehension and disposal, much less into our hands. He is hidden in so far as His grace is grace, i.e., in so far as He does not owe it to us but causes it to come to us in His freedom. And because man is always man in this relationship, his views, concepts and words as such, as his own, are not only partly insufficient but wholly and utterly insufficient to designate God, and he cannot take these instruments in hand without realising that they are quite impotent for this employment and in this very impotence are his—man's —part in this matter. They are this so far as they are not awakened and taken into service by God's grace. Again, because man is always man, in virtue of this awakening and being taken into service, his views, concepts and words in their human entirety—without deduction of any of the all too human marks of humanity, and therefore without the omission of certain supposed very crass anthropomorphisms —are sufficient to apprehend God's being (the one, entire, indivisible being of God), and therefore to be true, to express and establish a true knowledge of God. They are this so far as they are formed and expressed in faith in God's revelation, in obedience to the direction given to man in it. The " partial," the limit, in the concept of similarity, and therefore the forward limit of our knowledge of God is this : that when we know God, we must not and will not leave the grace of His revelation. We must not dispense with it. Nor will it become superfluous to us. Each step that we take as we come from the hiddenness of God must, and will, consist in a new reception of the grace of revelation.

But at this point we must take up again and complete a statement that we have made already. We have stumbled again on the co-existence and co-inherence of veiling and unveiling in God's revelation. That God also veils Himself in His revelation certainly excludes the concept of parity as a designation of the relationship between our word and God's being. And that God also unveils Himself in His revelation excludes the concept of disparity. We are therefore forced to avail ourselves of the concept of analogy by the fact that in God's revelation both His veiling and His unveiling are true. But it is now clear that in the veiling and unveiling of God it is not a question of quantity, either on God's side or on man's. In both cases it is a question of the one whole God, and in both cases of the one whole man. Now that this is clear, however, we recall that the relationship between veiling and unveiling is not symmetrical equivocal, vacillating or obscure, nor is it a reversal and alternation dependent on the arbitrariness of God or man. If we want to describe the relationship between the two concepts, and therefore the explanation of the concept of analogy, as dialectical, we must always note that what is involved is an ordered dialectic, and indeed one which is teleologically ordered. With both concepts we speak of the grace of the revelation of God. For God is gracious not only in His unveiling, but also in His veiling ; not only in His pardoning and sanctifying Yes but also in His No of judgment upon our work. And only for the sake of His unveiling does He veil Himself, only for the sake of His Yes will and must He also say No. Unveiling and veiling thus designate the way which God goes with us, not a contradiction which He pronounces against us, into which He impels us, and which we have to suffer and bear as such. From first to last on this way it is a question of the one saving fulfilment of fellowship between Him and us. In the fulfilment of this fellowship He has to be hidden from us to be revealed to us, to become revealed and yet to remain hidden, so that the becoming revealed, the Yes which He says to us, is the goal and end of His way, no matter how hidden it may be under the No. The same cannot be said of His veiling, of His No. If we try to understand the two differently, if we will not understand them (and therefore the rightly understood concept of analogy) in this teleological order, we shall see and understand neither the unveiling as *His* unveiling, nor the veiling as *His* veiling. As His revelation, and therefore as His unveiling and veiling we shall always know it in this teleological order. Outside this order both the Gospel and also the Law as such, as the Gospel and Law of God, are necessarily alien to us. The Gospel rightly seen and understood is always the victorious Gospel. It always has the last word. As such, it has the Law as a taskmaster, not outside— either before or behind itself—but inside itself. The revelation of the Law has to serve the revelation of the Gospel. Therefore the " partial," with its reminder of the hiddenness of God, is certainly in itself and as such a designation of the limit of our knowledge of God, but in its connexion with revelation—it is indeed a question of the partial agreement and correspondence of our words with God's being—it is at the same time the promise which is the travelling portion given to our undertaking to know God if it is an obedient undertaking.

It may be instructive at this point to cast a comparative glance back at the way in which the older theology treated the problem of the veracity of the human knowledge of God in the crucial form of the problem of analogy. For this purpose we will select as a good summary of the results of all earlier studies the presentation of A. Quenstedt (*Theol. did. pol.*, 1685, I., *c.* 8, *sect.* 2, *qu.* 1).

Quenstedt puts the question in this way. In what sense are certain attributes like *essentia, substantia, spiritus, bonitas, sapientia, iustitia* to be predicated simultaneously of God and the rational creature ? With what right is this twofold application made ? Quenstedt gives a threefold answer : *Essentia, substantia, spiritus et consequenter reliqua attributa, quae Deo et creaturis simul tribuuntur, de Deo et creaturis rationalibus non συνωνύμως, univoce, nec ὁμονύμως, aequivoce, sed ἀναλόγως, analogice praedicantur*. We speak *univoce* when the same term, applied to two different objects in the same way, designates the same thing in both of them. *Univoce* there come under one concept : *quae et nomen et rem nomine illo denotatam communem habent aequaliter*. It is asked whether God and the creature come under one concept in this sense. What Quenstedt has in mind at this point is obviously the thesis of parity between human word and divine being (he found it in Duns Scotus and his school). His reply is that what the creatures have in common with God they have in dependence on Him, so that it exists first in Him, then only and through Him in them. Hence it cannot be expressed *univoce* of Him and of the creatures. We speak *aequivoce* when the same term, applied to two different objects, designates a different thing in the one and the other. *Aequivoce* there come under one concept : *quae nomen habent commune, sed non rem nomine significatam*. It is asked whether God and the creature come under one concept in this sense. What is meant is plainly what we called the thesis of the disparity between our words and God's being. Quenstedt found this thesis among others in certain Reformed theologians of the beginning of the 17th century. And in fact we read in Polanus : *Spiritus non dicitur de Deo et angelis ac animis hominum συνωνύμως, univoce, sed ὁμωνύμως, aequivoce* (*Synt. theol. chr.*, 1609, *col.* 859). Quenstedt replies : As God is *essentia et substantia singularissima*, so, too, the creatures are *proprie entia, essentiae et substantiae*, and as God is Spirit in a unique way, the angels and human souls are also spirit in their own way. God has not created *non-entia*, and when Christ took human nature He did not take *non-ens*. But Quenstedt also thought it right to appropriate an argument from Thomas Aquinas, who rejected *aequivoce* because, if we affirm it, it means that God cannot be known from the creature. *Et hoc est tam contra philosophos, qui multa de Deo demonstratione probant quam etiam contra apostolum dicentem Rom.* 1 : *Invisibilia Dei per ea quae facta sunt, intellecta conspiciuntur* (*S. theol.* I, *qu.* 13, *art.* 5c). Hence : *Entia creata non sunt plane nihil, sed posita extra nihil. . . . Deus distat a creaturis toto genere, verum non in esse entis, sed in esse talis entis h. e. infiniti*. We have thus to interpret any passages in Scripture which seem to deprive the creature of true being only as extenuative statements and not as destructive, and therefore not as absolute denials of what is in its own way the true being of creation. *Licet solus Deus sit ens per essentiam, propterea tamen res caeterae non negantur vere esse aliquid, vel rationem entis habere*. And now Quenstedt turns to the third possibility. We speak *analogice* when the same term, applied to two different objects, designates the same thing in both but in different ways. *Analogice* there come under one concept : *quae et nomen et rem nomine designatam communem habent, sed inaequaliter*. It is asked whether God and the creature come under one concept in this sense. Quenstedt agrees with Thomas and the majority of theologians and philosophers, particularly of the Lutheran school, in giving a positive answer. His more precise explanation is this. We do not have here an *analogia inaequalitatis*, the kind of similarity which exists, e.g., between the different *species* of one *genus* (their greater or lesser perfection, etc.). Nor do we have an *analogia proportionalitatis*, i.e., the similarity which exists in the agreement when some determinations of two objects agree but at the same time others disagree. What we have is an *analogia attributionis*, a similarity of two objects which consists in the fact that what is common to them exists first and properly in the one, and then, because a second is dependent upon it, in the second. The *analogia* is *analogans* in the first and *analogata* in the second. This is the similarity between God and the creature—on the basis of which they can come under common concepts. But Quenstedt aims to be even more precise : Between God and the creature we do not have only an *analogia attributionis extrinsecae*, so that the analogy of the *analogatum* and therefore of the creature is proper to the creature only externally in the existence and form of its relationship to the *analogans*, that is, to God, but internally it is proper only to this *analogans* as such. What we have is an *analogia attributionis intrinsecae*. The analogy *proprie* belongs both to the *analogans* and to the *analogatum*. It is inward both to God and to the creature, although to the last only δευτέρως *et per dependentiam*. *Sic de utroque* (*scil. Deo et creatura rationali*) *vere dicitur, quod substantia sit, quod immaterialis sit etc., non tamen eodem modo et sensu*. . . . *Deus substantia est absoluta et independenter, creatura vero dependenter et per participationem.*

Thus far Quenstedt. Now, have we said the same thing as he ? How far and how far not ? A direct answer to this question is historically rewarding. For although Quenstedt is a Lutheran, here as elsewhere he may be regarded as the summariser of the older Protestant theology at any rate in relation to the common questions put by the different confessional schools. By defining our attitude to him we can, therefore, clarify the attitude which we have to take up in this matter in regard to the older theology in general. And the question is materially rewarding. For the comparison can be an occasion to test and explain again the position we ourselves have reached in the light and by the criterion of the classical counterposition. We will first establish what we have in common. In the question of the meaning of the fellowship between the human word and the divine being we have been forced to agree with Quenstedt in deciding against the concept of parity and against that of disparity in favour of that of analogy. And we can also consent to what he says when he tries to understand this analogy as an *analogia attributionis*. In our discussion on the concept of the " partial correspondence and agreement " we too have seen that a calculable *analogia inaequalitatis* or *proportionalitatis* between God and the creature cannot be considered. We, too, have sought and found the analogy in an *attributio*, in the relationship of an *analogans* with an *analogatum*. But when two people say the same thing, it is not always quite the same thing. If we look more closely, the question will at once have to be put again to Quenstedt whether it must not be expressly said that when the term analogy is used in this way, as *analogia attributionis*, it does not admit of any other application than to God and the creature. In other words, as used in this way it becomes wholly and utterly filled out with meaning. With the rejection of the idea of a calculability of the correspondence and agreement at issue, it says something more and other than what it can say in the usage possible to us. Taken up, then, into this usage, it is translated into a new and absolutely unique usage, founded only on the possibility of a fellowship between God and ourselves. If, with Quenstedt, we say *analogia attributionis*, we are not merely naming, as he appears to do (he took over the distinction from Cajetan), a third thing alongside *analogia inaequalitatis* and *proportionalitatis* as the first and second, but it is to be perceived and conceded that the concept is no longer a general, but a specifically and expressly theological concept. Is it an accident that this consideration plays no part in Quenstedt ? The next question we have to put to him is connected with his more detailed explanation of this *analogia attributionis*. We have seen that he tries to understand this *attributio* as *attributio intrinseca*. The analogy will belong, not only to God, but also to the creature, " inwardly," *proprie*. To be sure, it will do so *dependenter et per participationem*. But it will still do so inwardly. This will be *per habitudinem*, on the basis of its relationship to God, but not only as *habitudo*, not in such a way that it consists exclusively in this relationship. What, then, is the meaning of *attributio*? Does it signify the qualification that comes upon the creature by the grace of revelation? We, too, referred to this qualification and therefore to this *dependentia* and *participatio* of the creature. This, then, is how we should have to understand this *attributio*. But if we do, we obviously separate ourselves from what Quenstedt meant by this concept. For there is not a single reference to God's revelation in the whole *quaestio* in which he speaks of this matter. And that *attributio* means for him something different from the grace of the divine revelation, is obvious from the fact that he defines it more closely as *attributio intrinseca*. If he had thought of the grace of revelation, if in this place, too, this Lutheran had remembered the Lutheran doctrine of the forgiveness of sins by grace alone, he would undoubtedly have decided terminologically for the concept of an *attributio extrinseca*. He would have had to say, not merely that the analogy comes to the *analogatum per habitudinem*, but that it is only *in habitudine*, in its relationship to God as the *analogans*, that it has its existence and its truth. It stands or falls with this relationship. It does not belong to the creature as such " inwardly," *proprie*. But at this point Quenstedt did not remember the doctrine of justification. In other places in his works, where he speaks of the meaning of faith for justification (III, *c*. 8, *sect*. 1, *th*. 11), he defines it very precisely : *Ratio causandi, vis iustifica est competens fidei non in se et in sua natura, sive ex liberali Dei aestimatione seu acceptatione dignitatem aliquam sive parvam, sive magnam habens, sed unice ex obiecto iustifico apprehenso, Rom.* 3, 25. Applied to the problem of the knowledge of God, we gather from this statement that what converts the creature into an analogue of God does not lie in itself and its nature, not even in the sense that God will acknowledge and accept as an analogue (in itself) something of that which lies in the nature of the creature. What converts the creature into an analogue of God lies only in the veracity of the object known analogously in the knowledge of God, and therefore in the veracity of God Himself. It therefore possesses it *extrinsece* in the form of *apprehensio* and not at all *intrinsece*. This is what Quenstedt would have had to write in the first part of his work if he had written it " in analogy " to its third part, if he had understood and expounded the first article of the creed " in analogy " to its second article, and therefore in the analogy of faith. But this is just what he flagrantly and very consciously did not do. And not only Quenstedt, but all the orthodox with him, with a few happy exceptions and inconsistencies. When they came to this question of the knowledge of God, although they did not wish to answer it without mentioning and involving in some way the concept of faith, they did not genuinely and consistently treat it as a question of the knowledge of faith and therefore in analogy to the doctrine of justification. And therefore in this context Quenstedt does not recall that this *attributio* has perhaps something to do with the grace of God. In this connexion he can agree unhesitatingly and unreservedly with Thomas Aquinas, ascribing to the creature as well as to the Creator a *proprium* of analogy. Later, of course, he has a passably reformed doctrine of grace. But is he not exposed to the danger that Catholicism will ask why the relationship of God and man is represented so very differently in this case from what it is in the other. How is it that the *proprie* of creaturely similarity with God suddenly has no part to play at this point—in the question of the *liberum arbitrium*? Quenstedt can still evade the *intrinsece* here, but sooner or later will it not necessarily emerge as such in this case too, i.e., in the doctrine of a human readiness for faith preparatory to justification or even following it ? It is already clear that while we used much the same words as Quenstedt we really said something very different. Our attempt was to grasp the problem of the knowledge of God, and in particular that of analogy, in the strictest understanding of the first article in the light of the second. Quenstedt, on the contrary, when he speaks of *dependentia*, obviously has in mind a relationship between the Creator and the creature which as such can be known even apart from the knowledge of God in Jesus Christ. For this reason, although we agree with his attack on the theses of parity and disparity between human word and divine being, in his case it has another sense than with us. With us the rejection of parity is a defence against the denial of the veiling of God in His revelation. But with him it is a defence against the denial of the distinction between absolute and relative being as such. With us the rejection of the thesis of disparity is a defence against the denial of unveiling in God's revelation. With him it is a defence against the denial of the unity of relative and absolute being in truth. This is not only not saying the same thing : it does not even lead to the same thing. If in the question of the veracity of the fellowship between human word and divine being our aim is to confess the veiling and unveiling of God in His revelation, and we have to refuse both the *univoce* and the *aequivoce* for this reason, we are obviously seeking this fellowship in God's revelation and its truth in the grace of this revelation which is denied both by the *univoce* and the *aequivoce*. On the other hand, if our aim is to affirm the distinctions between absolute and relative being on the one side, and the unity of the truth of both on the other, and we refuse the *univoce* and the *aequivoce* because both contradict this affirmation, we are seeking this fellowship in a being which is common to both God and the creature, and its truth in the dialectic of this being—in its distinction and unity, unity and distinction. In both cases the truth of the same relationship is investigated. But it is clearly sought in different places. In both cases we have to do with God and man. But the veracity of their relationship is very different. Quenstedt is thinking of the veracity of being in general. Even before he enters on the problem at all, this is for him a criterion the excellence of which obviously cannot be surpassed. Armed with it, he then decides against the *univoce*. True being is in itself distinguished as absolute and relative being. He also decides against the *aequivoce*. Absolute and relative being is a being true in itself in both forms. This is how he seeks the veracity of this relationship ; or this is how he criticises first the two misinterpretations of this relationship. Now there can be no doubt that as we, too, enter on the question of the same veracity we have our presuppositions and a definite criterion, the excellence of which we, too, presuppose to be unsurpassable. From the very outset we have in mind the veracity of the being which is in itself the particular being of grace. Therefore we can seek it only in God's revelation. We are forced to decide against the *univoce* because it conflicts with the confession of God's veiling in His revelation, and against the *aequivoce* because it contradicts the confession of His unveiling ; against the one as against the other because it cannot be united with the confession of God's grace in His revelation. This is how we seek the veracity of this relationship ; this is how we criticise the two misinterpretations of this relationship. The two presuppositions are clearly distinguished polemically, and they give two very different positive definitions of the concept of analogy. It might seem that we can at least stand with Quenstedt on the first and topmost step of our deliberation—in our affirmation that the truth of our words is originally and properly the truth of God as the Creator, so that He only exercises a lawful claim when in His revelation He places them at our disposal to describe Him. But starting with this statement—that our truth is God's truth—we understood it to be irreversible. We added at once that God's truth is not our truth, and we had to do so, because from the outset we understood God's truth as the truth of His grace. But in this context at any rate Quenstedt understands by God's truth God's being, and by God's being the absolute being to which ours can be related only as relative being. On the basis of this material definition the statement in Quenstedt is clearly to be understood as reversible. Our truth, i.e., our being, which as ours can certainly be only relative, is God's truth so far as God is absolutely what we are relatively. But relatively we are the same as God is absolutely. Thus God's truth is also our truth. If being and not grace is the criterion of truth, this reversal is inevitable.

In Quenstedt revelation is not necessary to make us participants in the truth of God. We are so already, to the extent that we are, if only relatively, what God is absolutely. Thus the second and materially the most important step in our deliberations—the assertion of the divine disposal and bestowal, on the basis of which our words become true—is omitted in Quenstedt. As he sees it, to establish the veracity of our words, it is quite enough to consider (and we can obviously do so without objection) our own being or creaturely being in general. For this brings us face to face with the being which, in the one case relatively, in the other absolutely, is also the being of God. Analogy is discovered by way of this free recollection. For this discovery neither revelation nor faith is needed. It is not quite evident, perhaps, at a first glance. But it is not absolutely concealed. It is not something which must be opened up to us by God in a decision over and above the fact that we are His creation. But this means that on the third and lowest step of our deliberation we cannot possibly stand with Quenstedt. He, too, does, of course, speak of an *attributio*. But in this *attributio* where is the freedom of the gracious God which Quenstedt knows so well when he speaks of *justificatio*? Describing this *attributio* as *attributio intrinseca*, he betrays the fact that he is resisting the idea of a similarity of the creature with God which is simply controlled and bestowed by God Himself, and that he wants this similarity to be understood as one that is given and constant in and with the co-existence of the Creator and the creature. Therefore the *inaequaliter*, by which the similarity is to be distinguished in his definition of parity and disparity, does not denote the distinction between the veracity of the divine being and our words which consists in the fact that the former *is* true, but the latter become true by the special decision of God in His revelation and therefore on the way from His unveiling to His veiling. In Quenstedt, *inaequaliter* designates only the difference of absoluteness and relativity in the being which is without question identical in God and in us.

The significance of this difference between the two lines of thought must not be overlooked. If Quenstedt is right, the knowledge of God happens through man. For between God and man, even apart from God's revelation, even without Jesus Christ, there exists not only a real but also, as real, a perceptible fellowship. We can, therefore, claim this fellowship. It goes back to the fact that the relationship between Him and us is indeed the relationship between the Creator and the creature. This is a relationship of community because both the Creator and the creature are. They are, of course, in different ways, the former absolutely, the latter relatively. But they both are. And the being common to both is a fact not only known to God but also known, or knowable, to man. We need only indicate where this necessarily leads if the presupposed view of the relationship between God and man is taken seriously at every point. The consequence is surely inescapable that the criterion of all truth in this relationship is not God at all, but the being in which God and man—the former absolutely, the latter relatively—participate. And everything that is to be said in this relationship and in consequence of it will necessarily lead up to an explication of this participation, not of man in God, but of God and of man in this final truth of being which is ultimately superior to God. God's grace and man's sin, God's revelation and man's faith, can all be understood only as a modification of this participation in being which God has absolutely, but man also has, if relatively, *intrinsece*, *proprie* and therefore in common with God. Indeed, all specifically Christian truth will be only a modification of the general truth of being (presupposed on the basis of this recollection)—of a being the closer interpretation of which will be abandoned to our own tender mercies, to the change and development of the different views of what deserves to be called true being. It may perhaps be moralistic being, or spiritual, or transcendental, or empirical, or humanistic, or individual. One day it may even be " German " being. And what will this involve for the relationship between God and man that stands and is to be understood in the sphere of this being ? Now, in his theology Quenstedt has not deduced this consequence, much less the consequences of this consequence. Nor have the other older Protestant orthodox. Once they leave the dangerous ground of the general doctrine of God, in the doctrine of the Trinity they return—as if involuntarily—to their normal procedure, not learning about God from what they think they know about being, but about being from what God has revealed of Himself. It is here and not in the introduction—although occasionally there may be suspicious traces of the first statement—that they say what really is to be said about God and man. Christology suddenly appears and breaks through as the proper centre of their theological life. And starting from Christology, as Protestant theologians they come to very different conclusions in relation to original sin and the sin of man, to the *liberum* and *servum arbitrium*, to the justification and sanctification of the sinner, from those which we should naturally expect from their doctrine of the knowledge of God. Here too, then, we are confronted by the phenomenon of the happy inconsistency of Protestant orthodoxy in its general handling of natural theology. If we do not want to become guilty on our side of drawing wrong conclusions, we have, therefore, no cause to belabour them because of this statement of their doctrine of knowledge. But we certainly have cause to remember that in the last two hundred years the fatal consequence has actually been deduced from this (again Catholic or already Neo-Protestant) statement of orthodox Protestant theology. It was hailed triumphantly as a victory over the " older orthodoxy." The consequence *could* be deduced. This statement did not make it clear that that Christology has to be carried through as the life-centre of theology in these other spheres of dogmatic deliberation. Indeed, it could cause it to lose this position. It even lay in the logic of the matter that it would necessarily lose it. It did in fact lose it, and accordingly, i.e., under a consistent application of the sovereignty of this or that interpretation of being, the dogmatic conclusions in these spheres soon became very different from those reached by the older orthodoxy on the basis of this lucky inconsistency.

But this is perhaps the point at which we may suggest a remedy for the wrong emphasis of the 17th century, which did not perhaps do great harm at first, but had a very detrimental influence on all later development. We cannot adopt and repeat the orthodox doctrine of analogy. If we did, we might perhaps succeed in acting later, at any rate from our Christology onwards, as if nothing had happened here, or something very different. But although this can perhaps be understood and excused in the men of the 17th century, it would be an irresponsible and impossible action in the light of what has happened since. Humanly speaking, the same causes would very quickly have the same effects. Warned by this precedent, we have therefore attempted to understand and form the doctrine of analogy otherwise than the older orthodoxy did, and as in truth it must be understood and formed, if we are already aware that Christology really is and must remain the life-centre of theology, of all theology, and if we are also aware that the correct interpretation of Christology, as presented even by the older orthodoxy, is to be found in the doctrine of the justification of the sinner by faith alone. For the point at issue is that it is not a good thing to operate in theology with a twofold truth. The point at issue is that in the doctrine of the knowledge of God, in the doctrine of the knowledge of God by Jesus Christ, we must think and speak and argue from the Word of God and not from elsewhere.

But this means that the necessity and legitimacy of the way we have followed can only be illuminated, not proved, by the warnings of theological history. Why is it that at the decisive place (on the question of the truth of the fellowship between God's being and our words) we were right to enter on the problem with a specific concept of veracity, understanding it from the very first, in distinction to Quenstedt, as the veracity of the grace of God ? We could, of course, answer that we were right to do so because the presuppositions of Quenstedt's doctrine of analogy, or that of the older orthodoxy, undoubtedly prove that its doctrine is in fact identical with the cardinal dogma of Roman Catholicism, namely, with the doctrine of the *analogia entis*, so that if we make this our starting point our further thinking will have to be Catholic or Liberal, and for this reason we must reject the presupposition. Of course, we could answer in this way, and it is all true, but we have still not given the real reason for this rejection and still less the reason for our own choice. The presupposition of Quenstedt's doctrine of analogy is unhealthy—so far as this is the case—for the simple reason that in the last resort it is an arbitrary presupposition. For it is hard to find any genuine reason why 17th century Protestant theology came to agree with mediaeval scholasticism in this distinctive appreciation of the concept of being, exalting it, as least supplementarily, into the criterion of all things. But if we ourselves take a different path, we must not be guilty of a similar act of wilfulness. We can see to-day that, on the basis of its presupposition, this doctrine of analogy means a return to the flesh-pots of Egypt. We can see the fatal results which it has had in theological history. But negatively, and above all positively, we can regard our own decision as solidly grounded only when, for its part, it is that which the other obviously is not, namely, a decision corresponding to what is found in the Bible, and to that extent demanded by the Word of God. Even our theologico-historical assessment of the fateful character of this doctrine, or of the cardinal dogma of Roman Catholicism, needs the foundation of this criterion. Therefore in the last resort we shall not contend with the exponents of this doctrine for the precedence of an *analogia gratiae* over an *analogia entis* or *vice versa*. We shall ask them whether their doctrine of the *analogia entis* has any claim at all to justification as a decision demanded by Holy Scripture and how far it can be justified from this source. Our contention is that so far as we can see this is quite impossible. Conversely, we shall point to the fact that our alternative solution of the problem makes the claim to be sought and found, not arbitrarily, but in orientation to the relationship between God and the creature, God and man, which we have normatively in the Holy Scriptures of the Old and New Testaments. In the Bible, however, it is not a being common to God and man which finally and properly establishes and upholds the fellowship between them, but God's grace. The presupposition and criterion with which we entered on this problem of analogy must therefore be considered in the light of this fact. Were we right or wrong when we took this course, believing that the excellence and purity of this criterion cannot be surpassed ? Appealing to the Scriptures, we are prevented from giving any further answer to this question. Scripture stands as judge between us and the representatives of that other solution, and it can speak for itself. Face to face with this judge, however, we cannot let this historical excursus be our last word. Our last word will have to consist in an express repetition of our appeal to this judge.

We must return to our main theme and its elucidation. As set out in the thesis of our section, our concern is with the success of the undertaking to answer God's revelation in faith on the basis of human views and concepts, and therefore with the veracity of human knowledge of God. We have tried to explain this along three lines of thought. First, we have tried to define the veracity under consideration as the veracity of God in His revelation, which claims us, which therefore leads us into humility and sustains us in it, but which also puts us in the position of a definite and positive participation. Secondly, we have explained that this participation of ours in God's veracity is the relationship of thanks, in which our knowing receives the character of a very definite permission, in which there is bestowed upon our viewing, conceiving and speaking a similarity with its object and therefore the divine veracity as it is adapted to us. And thirdly, we have discussed this similarity in relation to its origin, its emergence and its actuality, all of which have again confronted us with the reality of revelation itself, i.e., with its way from the veiling to the unveiling of God ; with the hiddenness in which God is who He is, and therefore does not regard it as too small a thing to be who He is even in the sphere of our apprehension. These three lines of thought in their mutual relationship still need to be finally consolidated and secured. We might also say that they still need to be finally shaken, destroyed and explained in respect of the fact that we can have taken these paths only under the belief that what we have to describe is the success of the undertaking of *faith*. We might say that this is patent in the fact that with these three lines of thought we have manifestly and admittedly described a circle. We have undoubtedly returned from the hiddenness of God, in which we found the *terminus a quo* of the knowledge of Him, to the hiddenness of God in the assertion of the *terminus ad quem* of the knowledge of Him. But this circular course of our presentation is not in itself a proof that we have really established and understood the truth of the knowledge of God that takes place in faith. The very fact that we have taken a circular course may in itself be evidence that we have not understood our knowledge of God as veracious. There are many kinds of *circuli*. There are, at any rate, *circuli vitiosi*. And if we try to argue in opposition that there may also be *circuli veritatis*, the reply must be made that the very fact that there are also *circuli veritatis*, that is to say, other *circuli veritatis*, raises the suspicion whether—assuming that our *circulus* is a *circulus veritatis*—we have really established the truth of our knowledge of God in our circular course as such. There are in fact other circular courses, which are in their own way legitimate and impressive and full of solutions and fruitful, but in which there is never any question of the knowledge of God, but more or less clearly of one of the different forms of a human self-knowledge metaphysically constructed. At every point we have taken pains to mark ourselves off from these other circular courses, and therefore to take precautions against the confusion of our way with one of these other ways. But who and what protects us finally against the possibility that this delimiting and guarding is perhaps only a suspiciously eager assertion instead of a genuine assurance ? It was indeed inevitable that on this whole way we should continually make use of the possibility which it was the whole point of this way to test and discuss : the possibility of applying general human concepts (as e.g., the main concepts of truth, participation, or similarity) to this matter, to the event of the knowledge of God. We continually found ourselves in the proximity, even in the closest proximity, to expressions that in themselves and as such could refer to objects quite different from this event. Who or what protected us, perhaps in spite of all our attempted safeguards, from thinking ambiguously and speaking without understanding ? The fact that we have continually spoken of the grace of revelation, that we have continually tried to clarify by these concepts all the other concepts applied, is obviously not a final protection at this point. For the concept of revelation, too, is obviously a general human concept, as also is that of grace. It is quite possible that, even with a most central and carefully systematic application of these concepts, we may still represent the immanent truth of a metaphysico-anthropological relation, but not at all the veracity of our knowledge of God. Is this possibility not so threatening that we must now affirm that we are still very far from an understanding of the true knowledge of God ? And even if we are successful in marking off, to some extent, the veracity intended from other thinkable veracities, the first question still lurks menacingly in the background, whether the circular course in which we have openly and avowedly moved is perhaps not a *circulus veritatis* at all, and not even a *circulus vitiosus*, i.e., whether in this question of the relation intended and its veracity we are not chasing a shadow, whether the pains we have taken to mark off ourselves from imminent, generally human lines of thought is not an indication of the fact that we would do better to devote ourselves to the basis of these general lines of thought, which are also *circuli*, but can be more easily shown to be *circuli veritatis* than that in which we are trying to move. We must not be deceived. It is just because of the fact that we have appealed to God's revelation and grace as the necessity and basis of the right to move in this particular circle that the question cannot be suppressed. The point is whether, by letting ourselves be guided by these two concepts, we are not being led into a *circulus vitiosus*, into an undertaking which by its very nature cannot possibly succeed. Are we not asking about a veracity which does not exist at all, or which cannot possibly be established and confirmed, and certainly not with the definiteness which we have attempted ? A theology of revelation and grace is obviously not protected as such (i.e., by the fact that it has made these concepts its leading concepts) from the possibility that it may have set itself an impossible theme. May it not be that this possibility is so threatening that we must now affirm that we have not attained an understanding of the veracity of the knowledge of God ? In short, we set out to understand the undertaking to know God in human views and concepts as a *successful* undertaking. But this was obviously itself an undertaking the success of which involved a problem. Have we succeeded in establishing and understanding this success ? Do there not exist possibilities on the right hand and on the left that, in spite of everything, we may not have been successful, that we may certainly have represented and understood the veracity of a cognition, but not the veracity of a cognition of *God*, or perhaps a cognition of God, but not the *veracity* of it ?

It is clear that the whole problem of our section: "The Limits of the Knowledge of God," is again involved. And this is perhaps to say that we will have to return to the first two sections of the chapter, on the knowledge of God in its fulfilment, and on the knowability of God. The determination of the limits, the question of the veracity of the knowledge of God, presupposes the very thing which we there tried to elucidate : that knowledge of God is real and possible. But was this elucidated there in such a way, and can it be elucidated in such a way, that we can suppress as pointless the question which now arises as we look back at our presentation of the limits of the knowledge of God ? Is not the problem of these earlier investigations, and therefore the whole problem of the knowledge of God, again contained in this question ? Ought it not to be said that in this entire chapter on the knowledge of God we have moved on a circular course, to the whole of which we may now put the question that we now ask in a narrower context : Were we really moving on the *circulus veritatis Dei*, the *circulus veritatis Dei* ? And in face of this question in the narrower and wider context, it is not sufficient simply to maintain that we have thought and said all this in faith and for this very reason in veracious knowledge of God. This may well be just an empty phrase, which does not protect us at all against the menace of the question. For this question asks whether and how far we really have thought and said all this in faith. Nor can we protect ourselves against the menace of the question by entering the narrower and wider circle a second and a third and an *x*th time. The indefatigable repetition of this way as such does not protect us, nor do the insights and outlooks, however important and significant individually, which we may continually recall. It is not by this at all that we can protect ourselves against this question. If our continual appeal to God's grace and revelation—whatever else may be thought of it—was not at any rate for us subjectively a mere playing with words or operating with a systematic *Deus ex machina*, if we at least thought we knew what we were saying with these words, we cannot wish to have it otherwise than that we cannot in fact protect ourselves against this question. If we can, what are we doing to put our whole deliberation under the leading concepts of revelation and grace ? In the same way we only need to take ourselves at our word—that we pursued this way in faith—to see at once that we cannot really wish to protect ourselves against this question. If there is a final consolidation and security here, it must definitely consist in a simultaneous insecurity and destruction. If in faith we have moved on the *circulus veritatis Dei*, on the *circulus veritatis Dei* we must openly and honestly let ourselves be asked whether and how far this really took place in faith. The faith on which everything depends here will never treat itself as a presupposition given without question. We must be clear, of course, that the achievement of a final security and insecurity of our whole line of thought is not an act that we can perform. The question whether we really believe, and as believers truly know God, and know God truly, is far too radical and shattering for us to be able to direct it seriously to ourselves.

We must not be under any illusions as to the seriousness with which we ourselves can direct this question to ourselves. It is not so great as, caught up in our own seriousness, we may well imagine. This is shown by the relative lightness with which we are able to answer it, whether we ascribe to ourselves a faith which is hardly called in question, and with faith the veracity of our knowledge of God, or whether we cease to have confidence in our faith and dare not reckon so rightly with the veracity of our knowledge of God. In this fluctuation of our self-questioning and self-criticism no serious decisions are taken. At best there is only a continuing existence either in an unreflecting confidence or an equally unreflecting lack of confidence. Both of them have, of course, their corresponding images of thought and ways of speech. These are apparently very definite, but in fact absolutely vacillating, and the true knowledge of God has, of course, nothing whatever to do with them. If this question of our faith is directed from ourselves to ourselves it is not only a waste of time (because we should do far better to believe instead of asking whether we believe), but it is a dangerous playing with faith, because it means that we have to cut ourselves loose from faith and consider and handle as it were from without. A man can and may do this with his feeling, personal experiences and practical knowledge, but it is quite impossible in relation to faith. In this way we can only lose faith. In faith we can only again believe, beginning at the beginning and continuing to believe. Everything else is not serious. It can lead only to religious or irreligious pomposity, or to all kinds of pietistic or rationalistic sharp-practice.

If it is radical, the question of our faith, and therefore the necessary unsettlement of our systematic deliberation and establishment of the limits of our knowledge of God and its reality and possibility, already has its derivation in God, who is the source and fulness of its whole answer. It therefore comes to us from without, and not from ourselves on the basis of all kinds of not so important doubts. Therefore, because it comes from God, it comes to our faith. It simply does not comes to us at all if we have dispensed with faith, considering it from without and playing with it, and then arbitrarily deciding either for belief or unbelief. What can God do with us, or the question which He directed to us mean for us, if when He comes He happens to find us not at home, i.e., outside of faith? He can only abandon us to what is in the last resort frivolous and ineffective self-questioning and self-criticism. It needs faith if we are going to let ourselves be asked seriously about our faith, and therefore, in respect of our knowledge, about our standing and going in the *circulus veritatis Dei*. It needs faith if this question is to strike us radically and shatteringly; to strike us in such a way that there can be no question of a happy-go-lucky reply either one way or the other; to strike us in such a way that we cannot actually answer it, that in fact it remains stuck in us like a deadly arrow. It needs faith to participate in temptation.* Temptation is a divine work, like the comfort from which it is not to be separated. If we do not believe, then we may indeed doubt,

---

* *Temptation* is used here with the sense of *testing, tentatio,* or *Anfechtung.*

and doubting fall on the right hand and on the left, seeking our refuge now in this and now in that unreal contention. But the faith which distinguishes John the Baptist and Peter from Judas Iscariot does not doubt ; it cannot doubt, because the divine work of temptation comes upon it by which it is deprived of the time and desire for doubting. Faith falls into temptation and " counts it all joy " when this happens (Jas. 1²f·). "Blessed is the man that endureth temptation" (Jas. 1¹²). For temptation is God's question as to its existence. Nothing can be dearer to faith than to accept this question. By temptation faith is completely destroyed, and in that way completely established. In temptation faith is taken from man that it may be restored to him by its object. In temptation faith is killed that it may be quickened again by Him in whom it believes. This is the blessedness of temptation. We still do not know anything about faith, and therefore about God, and therefore about the knowledge of God in this *circulus veritatis Dei*, if we do not know about the blessedness of temptation, which is as distinct from doubt as heaven is from earth. But in the insecurity which, at the end of a course of thought like that just concluded, is needful for us, what is involved is the blessed temptation which is God's own work directed to our faith. For this very reason the unsettling question under consideration cannot be a work that we can perform as the critical seal to a human system.

Therefore it can only rest on an appalling misunderstanding of what is a necessary critique for us at this point if, looking back to our investigation of the knowledge of God, we still regard it as answered in principle by a critical philosophy, or try to borrow points of view and arguments from such a philosophy, so that, by a final critical bracketing of our investigations and conclusions (in which in a sense we have a place alongside the judging God), we relieve ourselves of the weight of the question directed to us, procuring for ourselves a quiet mind and light shoulders in relation to it. If we can make it our own question, and thus conclude our systematic treatment with an act of self-criticism, what a tremendous relief this will be ! If we can end our heroic career with a hara-kiri, what a supreme triumph of heroism we shall achieve ! But if we can do so, the mere fact that we can will show that everything which precedes this conclusion is *de facto* futile—even our critical conclusion, our supposed unsettlement, being only a final futile attempt at reassurance. A critical conclusion can be important and right at this point only when it does not consist in a theoretical questioning, by which we are again self-justified but also self-accused, but in the wholly factual questioning which takes place only from God, in the blessedness of temptation. Therefore, if we are to denote our actual and true unsettlement we can only point absolutely above ourselves and our possibilities.

But this is even more true of any answer to be given to this question. If it is a real answer to this question, it is so radical, so originally and finally basic, that there can be no question of our being able to provide it ourselves.

We have even less reason to surrender to illusions concerning the seriousness which usually leads us to positive conclusions in relation to the *circulus veritatis*

Dei. There was a time when theology could quieten itself on the question of true faith and its true knowledge of God by assuring itself that the circle in which this knowledge moved was identical with the life circle of the absolute spirit. There was a time also when it found its treasure in the fact that faith is faith, and therefore true knowledge of God, because, as the original act of human self-consciousness, it is, as it were, its own guarantee before the judgment seat of ultimate spiritual reality. Again there was a time when comfort was found in the fact that faith and its knowledge were substantial and justified by their correspondence to the highest value or good of all human being, indeed of all being whatsoever. But positive answers sounding the biblical and Church note could also be worked out, and they were given often enough in the same connexion. Thus the Holy Spirit can be given the last word instead of the absolute, all enquiries being evaded on the plea that they can be answered by the presence and work of the Holy Spirit, that through Him our faith is true faith and our knowledge true knowledge of God. Or again, appeal can be made to the Church, whose doctrine of God and of divine things is founded and corroborated by revelation, by whose existence therefore the question of our faith and of the *circulus veritatis Dei* is decided and settled. But recourse may also be had to practical experience, or to the Holy Trinity, or to Jesus Christ. . . . It is worth noting that in this matter every kind of recourse is, as such, frivolous and of evil derivation. If we have recourse, if we give our own answer, no matter how serious the answer may be in content, we think that we can secure ourselves. But this is just what we cannot do. And it is faith which knows that we cannot do this. We again secretly dispense with faith, and are not at the point where God can find us with His answer, if we think that we are in a position to confirm and guarantee faith, and with faith the veracity of our knowledge of God. When we are caught by the radical and shattering question whether we really believe, when we are caught by temptation and therefore made ready for the divine deliverance, we know that we cannot deliver ourselves.

The substantiation of our faith and therefore the necessary confirmation of our systematic deliberations and affirmations in respect of the knowledge of God must also come to us from without. If they are genuine they cannot come from ourselves as a grasping with which we try to save ourselves. They must be the grasping by which they are grasped. Otherwise they will not be genuine confirmations and substantiation. We cannot grasp at the Holy Spirit, or the Church, or Christian experience, or the Trinity, or Christ—not to speak of other supports—in order to try to create certainty for ourselves. The confirmation which our systematic needs cannot itself be systematic under any name, and least of all under the name which tells us that we are helped in our helplessness, which is itself the answer coming to us from without. Most definitely not, then, under the name of Jesus Christ. And therefore not under the name of the Holy Spirit or the Church or whatever else we may name with perhaps a right intention in the light of God's revelation. To adopt this answer and confirmation we are utterly in need of faith. We need faith to become partakers of the comfort, the substantiation, that we have faith and in faith true knowledge of God. And faith does not have recourse to anything. Faith does not assert and boast. Faith refuses to grasp after any axioms and guarantees. Faith knows that man cannot comfort himself; that comfort, like temptation, is the work of God. It is only when we do not believe, only when we consent to this intermitting of faith, that we can come to think of trying in some way to comfort ourselves. Faith has as little time and desire for this as for doubt. He who believes is saved. Faith lives by this comfort. Its comfort, therefore, stands in direct connexion with temptation. It begins at the very point where temptation is at its height, where faith is taken from us, where it is annulled and killed, so that it may really be given to us, so that in this very way it may be surely grounded and alive. This comfort upholds and substantiates faith from its goal and end. It comforts it by directing it to look beyond itself, by instructing it to point above itself. It comforts it with the truth which is outside and above it in the height as God's truth and therefore as its own, faith's truth. It comforts it with hope. In this way it is the real and divine comfort which is as different from all self-comfort as heaven from earth, as temptation from doubt. Therefore the positive conclusion of our doctrine of the knowledge of God and our answer to the open question of the *circulus veritatis Dei* must have nothing whatever to do with an act of synthesis executed by ourselves. It is an answer only when it is not our answer, or when, as our answer, it is only the witness to God's answer. Only then is it indeed the answer in which faith gives the legitimate answer to the question of its being by acting as faith and thus giving factual proof of the truth of our knowledge of God.

In this sense, it is Jesus Christ to whom we must again refer in conclusion. This does not mean that we are speaking our last word. In respect of the *circulus veritatis Dei* we have no last word to speak. We can only repeat ourselves. We can, therefore, only describe Him again, and often, and in the last resort infinitely often. If we try to speak conclusively of the limits of our knowledge of God and of the knowledge of God generally, we can come to no conclusion. We can only speak of it again and again in different variations as God in His true revelation gives us part in the truth of His knowing, and therefore gives our knowing similarity with His own, and therefore truth. And the question always remains whether we stand in faith so that this can be said of us, and therefore whether we are actually partakers of true knowledge of God. In this matter we have definitely no last word to speak. If we think we have, we have already pronounced our own judgment, because we have denied faith. For this very reason, the reference to Jesus Christ cannot and must not on any account try to have on our side the character of a conclusive word. Jesus Christ is really too good to let Himself be introduced and used as the last word of our self-substantiation. For this very reason we have expressly affirmed that, with regard to this question, it cannot possibly be a matter of self-questioning and, with regard to its answering one way or another, it cannot possibly be a matter of self-judgment. With regard to both the question and the answer it is a matter of Jesus Christ and therefore not of ourselves ; of ourselves only on the basis of the fact that it is a matter disinterestedly of Jesus Christ. We certainly cannot refer to Jesus Christ without making use of various articles of Christology. The mention of the name of Jesus Christ is already a christological statement. But we are not referring to the articles of Christology. If we have these in mind, we are again caught up in the attempt (the attempt of unbelief) to anchor in a safe harbour, whereas in faith it is a question of putting out to sea at Christ's command. We are not referring to Christology. We are referring, christologically speaking, to Jesus Christ Himself. We have already referred to Him by speaking of God's temptation and of God's comfort as the divine reality by which the *circulus veritatis Dei* in which we move is encompassed. This divine reality is Jesus Christ Himself.

Where is it true that in His true revelation God gives us a part in the veracity of His knowledge, and therefore the similarity of our knowing with His own, and in that way veracity ? In our whole line of thought we have presupposed that this may become and be true in *us*. We have also tried to realise, as we must, the limits and therefore the veracity of *our* knowing of God. The restraint with which we have made this presupposition lies in the matter itself, because the central concept of our line of thought has to be that of revelation and therefore of the grace of God, which we cannot take of ourselves. Yet even with this restraint, which as such could also act as a last powerful assurance, we have actually presupposed that the content of our line of thought could become and be true in ourselves. That we do this is quite in order. But the very appeal to God's grace under which we do it—whether it means restraint or assurance—means in any case that we put ourselves in the sphere in which we do not withdraw from the temptation of faith, in which we can be comforted only with the comfort of faith. But this sphere is the sphere of Jesus Christ. Grace is not a general possibility, to which as such we can systematically recur and from which we can withdraw, no matter whether we have in mind restraint or assurance in regard to our action. Grace is the " grace of our Lord Jesus Christ " (2 Cor. 13^{14}). If we appeal to it, we not only acknowledge that we are in need of restraint or of assurance in regard to our own action, but we have confessed that our action (in our case, a line of thought) reveals a vacuum within us which is decisive for the whole, shewing it to be either correct or utterly futile. We have confessed that we cannot fill up this vacuum, not even with a central concept, either by restraint or by assurance. We have confessed that there, in this vacuum of our action and line of thought, stands Jesus Christ : not a christological article which we can now utilise as a key to turn this last lock, and therefore not as a last word in our mouth ; but Jesus Christ Himself as the pre-eminent Judge and Saviour of our action. We have confessed that our action and line of thought can only be originally and properly true in Jesus Christ and can only become and be true in Him in consequence of the fact that Jesus Christ is also really our Judge and Saviour. We have given ourselves into His hand so that according to His own good-pleasure He may be this Judge and Saviour and as such may act towards us from the place where He must establish His own vacuum. This means the appeal to the grace which has accompanied us on our whole line of thought. It means—if it is not the bad information of an all too crafty philosophy—the renunciation both of placing ourselves under the restraint, and also of creating the assurance for ourselves. If it is genuine, it definitely does not mean anchoring but putting out to sea. It means that in regard to our knowledge of God and its veracity we let the temptation of faith befall us, and that we look for nothing but the comfort of faith. It means that we let the place of our knowledge of God be that in which God's temptation and God's comfort have come to pass for us and from which the temptation and comfort of faith come to us. And this is simply Jesus Christ. For it is because He is this place, but only because He is, that we too become and are this place. If we are this place it is only by faith in Him. But this means by our letting Him be this place. " In Him are hid all the treasures of wisdom and knowledge " (Col. 2³). This does not have only the general meaning that we must know Him in order to know God. It has the particular meaning that we must know Him as the first and proper Subject of the knowledge of God. If we have spoken of man aright when we presupposed in our line of thought that it contains and expresses man's truth, then originally and properly we have not spoken about ourselves but about this man Jesus Christ. In Him who is true God and true man it is true that in His true revelation God gives to man a part in the truth of His knowing, and therefore gives to man's knowing similarity with His own and therefore truth. On the basis of the grace of the incarnation, on the basis of the acceptance and assumption of man into unity of being with God as it has taken place in Jesus Christ, all this has become truth in this man, in the humanity of Jesus Christ. The eternal Father knows the eternal Son, and the eternal Son knows the eternal Father. But the eternal Son is not only the eternal God. In the unity fulfilled by the grace of the incarnation, He is also this man Jesus of Nazareth. It is not our knowledge of God, but the knowledge which is and will be present in this man Jesus, that we have described in our description of its reality, its possibility, and now finally its limits. Otherwise we have not described it in faith, or as the knowledge of faith, and therefore not in any sense as the true knowledge of God. When we appeal to God's grace, we appeal to the grace of the incarnation and to this man as the One in whom, because He is the eternal Son of God, knowledge of God was, is and will be present originally and properly ; but again through whom, because He is the eternal Son of God, there is promised to us our own divine sonship, and therefore our fellowship in His knowledge of God. We grasp this promise by ascribing to ourselves true knowledge of God, by venturing to move confidently in this *circulus veritatis Dei*. And as we do this, we enter the sphere of the temptation and comfort of faith, because the temptation and comfort are the form of the grace of the incarnation applied to this man, because all the treasures of wisdom and knowledge are hidden in Him in this form, in the form of temptation and comfort.

What does temptation originally and properly mean ? Not something that we can know and experience in ourselves, and can therefore fashion for ourselves, but what, according to the Scriptures, came from God upon the Son of God in the humiliation of His humanity in His death on the cross ; the judgment of God, under which He placed Himself, taking our place and representing us in this place. It is in this way, as the One who Himself suffers judgment, that He becomes our Judge. It is in this way that He places our faith in question, taking it away, and killing it as our own work. For what remains of our faith when we hear Him cry : " My God, my God, why hast thou forsaken me ? " If the Son of God can confirm faith only by letting it be taken from Him, what can this mean for us but the revelation that our faith as our own work is a lost work ? Yet it is not we but Jesus Christ who has first and properly borne the temptation of God, and our own concern in it can only be to acknowledge it as borne by Him and to accept its validity against all the claims of our own work. Therefore our faith, although our own work, is not a lost work when it consists in the appeal to the fact that the necessary temptation of our faith has already taken place in Jesus Christ and that it is removed in Him. For this very reason it cannot, then, be exchanged for the doubts of our self-questioning and self-judging. And what does comfort mean originally and properly ? Again, nothing that we can know and experience and fashion for ourselves as confirmation and strengthening, but what, according to the Scriptures, has come upon the Son of God in the exaltation of His manhood, in His resurrection from the dead ; the confirmation of the good-pleasure that God has found in Him, and again, in Him in our place. As the One to whom salvation and eternal glory were allotted, this man is our Saviour. It is in this way that He gives us faith again, awakening it from the dead, and making it living faith. It is in this way that He procures for our faith the acknowledgment which we are not able to procure for it, the acknowledgment that He is our righteousness before God. We must not only believe *in* the risen Christ. We must believe *with* the risen Christ, i.e., on the basis of the divine comfort which has come upon Him. The power of our faith is that God has accepted His Son in the flesh, that He has comforted this man Jesus in eternity. And in Him He has already comforted us all in advance. What can we do but let this comfort, like the temptation, have its course, and therefore let it be our own comfort ? And so both the temptation and the comfort can only be the confirmation that, moving in our *circulus veritatis Dei*, we are in the sphere of Jesus Christ, where that which in an earlier context we called the veiling and unveiling of God, the way from the one to the other, forms the household rule from which we cannot except ourselves.　Faith is nothing but the acknowledgment of this rule.　And faith consists absolutely in the fact that we want to know only about the temptation and comfort that have come upon Jesus Christ, only about His cross and resurrection as the question, really directed to us but in this way really answered for us, of our action : of the correctness of our line of thought ; of the limits and the veracity of our knowledge of God.

CHAPTER VI

THE REALITY OF GOD

CHAPTER VI

THE REALITY OF GOD

§ 28

THE BEING OF GOD AS THE ONE WHO LOVES IN FREEDOM

God is who He is in the act of His revelation. God seeks and creates fellowship between Himself and us, and therefore He loves us. But He is this loving God without us as Father, Son and Holy Spirit, in the freedom of the Lord, who has His life from Himself.

1. THE BEING OF GOD IN ACT

God is. This is the simple statement which we have to develop and explain in this chapter on the basis and in the application of what we have learnt in the previous chapter about the fulfilment, the possibility and the limits of our knowledge of God. In so doing we confront the hardest and at the same time the most extensive task of Church dogmatics, behind which also there lies concealed the hardest and at the same time the most extensive task of the whole of Christian preaching. The task consists in defining the subject of all the statements that are here necessary and possible. The problem of definition as such lies behind us (at least, as far as scientific development and statement is concerned). That was our concern in the doctrine of the knowledge of God. It is self-evident that this problem can never leave us, that it will again accompany us at every step on the next stage of our journey (and on what further stages will we be free from it ?). But the result of the considerations that we took up there will have to be authenticated, as we now try to complete the definition of the subject of which we have already given an account as such ; as in the framework and in accordance with the doctrine of the knowledge of God we now try actually to say that God is. This statement and the object of the task confronting us is not just one particular " theologoumenon " among others. Strictly speaking this cannot be said of any single article of faith and therefore of dogmatics. Strictly speaking, in dogmatics and in Church preaching every single statement is at once the basis and the content of all the rest. But inevitably this

9   257

is true in a very particular way of this statement, in which we define completely the subject of all other statements.

Dogmatics, in each and all of its divisions and subdivisions, with every one of its questions and answers, with all its biblical and historical assertions, with the whole range of its formal and material considerations, examinations and condensations, can first and last, as a whole and in part, say nothing else but that God is. According to the measure that it does this, it serves the Church as criticism of its conduct and as counsel and suggestion for its conduct. Inasmuch as it says, or does not say, that God is, it decides not only on its own usefulness or uselessness, but also on its scientific value or lack of value. In every train of thought, in every sentence which directly or indirectly serves the purpose of saying this, dogmatics does what it ought to do, what its very existence demands and justifies. And conversely, in every train of thought or statement which does not serve this purpose, in which it does not say this either directly or indirectly, in which directly or indirectly it says something other than that God is—in every such form, however enlightening or fruitful it may be in other respects, it will most certainly be guilty of aberration, leading the Church into error instead of to the truth, and compromising itself and its right to exist.

This is the case because the Church too, whose commission the science of dogmatics has to serve in its own sphere and manner, lives by the fact and only by the fact that it can hear the word that God is, and because first and last it has this and only this to say to itself and the world in the execution of its commission—the fact that God is. What God according to His Word wills with men and from men is that they should and must hear, believe, know and reckon with this ; in great things and small, in whole and in part, in the totality of their existence as men, they should and must live with the fact that not only sheds new light on, but materially changes, all things and everything in all things—the fact that God is. That this is so—that God wills to let men live with this fact of His own being, and that what God wills happens—is not, of course, the concern of the Church. Indeed, it is not the concern of any man or of any other creature. God Himself sees to it in His Word. But the Church has to serve the Word in which He Himself does see to it. For the Church lives by the Word of God and for the Word of God. It is, therefore, the Church's commission, which the science of dogmatics has also to serve in its own way, that taught and bound by the Word of God and for the sake of it (for it has no other *raison d'être* than to serve the Word of God), it has to say that God is. It is, therefore, to be said of it (and above all of it) that it does what it ought to do, what exclusively but also unconditionally is required of it, what exclusively but also unconditionally justifies its existence, when it says that God is. Because it lives itself by the Word of God and for the Word of God, it knows that what must be said in all circumstances, what it is necessary in all circumstances for men to hear, so that they live with this fact in the totality of their existence, but what it can never in any circumstances say of itself (for the Church has never said it of itself), is the fact that God is. It is true to its commission when taught and bound by the Word of God and for the sake of it, it says this directly or indirectly but unequivocally to itself and to the world. For whatever else it can say, if it is to be said properly, directly or indirectly, it must be this. It would also be true to say that it too (and especially) makes itself impossible if it does not say this, or if directly or indirectly it says something else.

So hard and so extensive is the statement that God is, that we may well ask whether a particular development and explanation of this statement, as if it were an individual statement and not the statement of all statements, is not wholly superfluous and impossible.

Should we not be content with the definition of the subject which we make when we adopt the statements which according to the Word of God are necessary for the description of the action and working of this subject ? To this we make the following answer. If the Word of God forbids the question of God's being as a particular question, or leaves us in doubt about this particular question, it means that it gives us no real revelation of God. It does, of course, reveal to us perhaps a very significant and effective action and working, but it keeps from us, and therefore does not reveal, the fact that it is, and how far it is, the action and the working of God. This action and working becomes and is significant and effective with a significance and effectiveness qualitatively different from any other action and working in virtue of the fact that it is God's action and working. It is not because it is proclaimed and believed in itself, nor because there is proclaimed and believed a creation, reconciliation, and redemption, but because the whole is proclaimed and believed as God's action and working, that there is proclaimed in Jesus Christ, in Holy Scripture, and in the Church, the Word of God as true revelation. Moreover, the true revelation does not remain silent on the particular question of God's being—quite apart from the fact that it is in its entirety one single answer to the question. It is the whole truth. It authorises us and commands us quietly and candidly to halt at this point and to consider specifically what we are saying when we make this hardest and most comprehensive statement that God is. And because this is the case, we shall be guilty of an omission which will recoil on us if we hurry over the statement that God is, as if it were only the common truth in all other statements, as if it were not worth our while to give particular account of its particular truth.

It was, therefore, an act of rashness, of which he rightly repented, when in his *Loci* of 1521 Melanchthon, the first dogmatician of the Evangelical Church, thought he should so suppress the special doctrine of God in order to turn at once to the statement of the *beneficia Christi*. He did this on the ground that : *mysteria divinitatis rectius adoraverimus, quam vestigaverimus. Immo sine magno periculo tentari non possunt.* To this we must say that surely the *beneficia Christi* also belong to the revealed *mysteria divinitatis* which are only to be investigated at some risk ; that the *beneficia Christi* cannot be properly investigated if some consideration of the *mysteria divinitatis* as such has not been undertaken in its proper place ; that the danger of every human *vestigare* of divine truth, here as well as elsewhere, is not to be avoided as such ; that here as well as elsewhere it can be met in the fact that *vestigare* is not separated from *adorare*, i.e., that here as well as elsewhere attention is paid (only) to God's revelation. The second mistake that Melanchthon committed later was if anything worse than the first. It consisted in this. When he later decided to take up again in his *Loci* the doctrine of God, he began to create it from another source than from the revelation of God, namely, from an independently formed and general idea of God. He therefore began to consider the *mysteria divinitatis* apart from their connexion with the *beneficia Christi*. In this he fell right into the *magnum periculum* of which he had been afraid in 1521, and was all the more guilty of the very error which in his first act of rashness he had had a right instinct to avoid as opposed to late medieval scholasticism, thus affording a disastrous example to the whole of Protestant orthodoxy. We must be at pains to avoid both these errors of Melanchthon.

Although we cannot allow as such the objection to the possibility of a special doctrine of God, there is something to be learned from it. When we ask questions about God's being, we cannot in fact leave the sphere of His action and working as it is revealed to us in His Word. God is who He is in His works. He is the same even in Himself, even before and after and over His works, and without them. They are bound to Him, but He is not bound to them. They are nothing without Him. But He is who He is without them. He is not, therefore, who He is only in His works. Yet in Himself He is not another than He is in His works. In the light of what He is in His works it is no longer an open question what He is in Himself. In Himself He cannot, perhaps, be someone or something quite other, or perhaps nothing at all. But in His works He is Himself revealed as the One He is. It is, therefore, right that in the development and explanation of the statement that God is we have always to keep exclusively to His works (as they come to pass, or become visible as such in the act of revelation)—not only because we cannot elsewhere understand God and who God is, but also because, even if we could understand Him elsewhere, we should understand Him only as the One He is in His works, because He is this One and no other. We can and must ask about the being of God because as the Subject of His works God is so decisively characteristic for their nature and understanding that without this Subject they would be something quite different from what they are in accordance with God's Word, and on the basis of the Word of God we can necessarily recognise and understand them only together with this their Subject.

In the preceding chapter we have already had to resist the threatened absorption of the doctrine of God into a doctrine of being : and we shall have to do this again. Yet we must not yield to a revulsion against the idea of being as such, which for some time had a part in modern Protestant theology (occasionally with an appeal to Melanchthon), even as late as the extraordinarily informative book of H. Cremer, *Die christliche Lehre von den Eigenschaften Gottes*, 1897 ; 2nd ed. 1917. God is not swallowed up in the relation and attitude of Himself to the world and us as actualised in His revelation. The dignity and power of His works, of His relation and attitude, depends much more on the fact that as distinct from them, without being any other than the One who manifests Himself in them, He is Himself; that, while He reveals Himself in them, He remains at the same time superior to them. We keep this constantly in mind as we take up the concept of being at this point with complete impartiality.

At the same time we must be quite clear on the other side, that our subject is God and not being, or being only as the being of God. In connexion with the being of God that is here in question, we are not concerned with a concept of being that is common, neutral and free to choose, but with one which is from the first filled out in a quite definite way. And this concretion cannot take place arbitrarily, but only from the Word of God, as it has already occurred and has been given to us in the Word of God. This means that we cannot discern the being of God in any other way than by looking where God Himself gives us Himself to see, and therefore by looking at His works, at this relation and attitude—in the confidence that in these His works we do not have to do with any others, but with His works and therefore with God Himself, with His being as God.

What does it mean to say that " God is " ? What or who " is " God ? If we want to answer this question legitimately and thoughtfully, we cannot for a moment turn our thoughts anywhere else than to God's act in His revelation. We cannot for a moment start from anywhere else than from there.

We stand here before the fundamental error which dominated the doctrine of God of the older theology and which influenced Protestant orthodoxy at almost every point. For the greater part this doctrine of God tended elsewhere than to God's act in His revelation, and for the greater part it also started elsewhere than from there. It is of a piece with this fact that with a surprisingly common thoughtlessness it was usual to begin by deducing the doctrine of the Trinity—theoretically maintained to be the basis of all theology—from the premises of formal logic. In the vacuum which this created, there was no place for anything but general reflections on what God at any rate could be—reflections arising from specific human standpoints and ideas as incontestable data, and then interwoven rather feebly with all kinds of biblical reminiscences. In this way there was created a doctrine of God which could have either no meaning or only a disastrous one for the remaining contents of dogmatics. And also in this way there was created, involuntarily, the basis on which an anti-Christian philosophy (and at the same time and later a heretical theology) could only too easily attack the dogma of the Trinity, and with it all the decisive articles of faith and its knowledge of the Word of God. It was certainly right to define the essence of God : *Essentia Dei est ipsa Deitas, qua Deus a se et per se absolute est et existit* (Polanus, *Synt. Theol. chr.*, 1609, *col.* 865). But even in the definition of this *a se et per se* there ought never to have been an abstraction from the Trinity, and that means from the act of divine revelation. In all the considerations that are brought before us in this chapter we must keep vigorously aloof from this tradition, remembering that a Church dogmatics derives from a doctrine of the Trinity, and therefore that there is no possibility of reckoning with the being of any other God, or with any other being of God, than that of the Father, the Son and the Holy Spirit as it is in God's revelation and in eternity. So then, as dogmatics describes and explains God as the One who is, it cannot make any free speculations about the nature of His being. Whatever may be the standpoints and ideas that are adduced, in this context it has always to win and explain their particular sense in the light of this revelation—the revelation of the being of the triune God.

What God is as God, the divine individuality and characteristics, the *essentia* or " essence " of God, is something which we shall encounter either at the place where God deals with us as Lord and Saviour, or not at all. The act of revelation as such carries with it the fact that God has not withheld Himself from men as true being, but that He has given no less than Himself to men as the overcoming of their need, and light in their darkness—Himself as the Father in His own Son by the Holy Spirit. The act of God's revelation also carries with it the fact that man, as a sinner who of himself can only take wrong roads, is called back from all his own attempts to answer the question of true being, and is bound to the answer to the question given by God Himself. And finally the act of God's revelation carries with it the fact that by the Word of God in the Holy Spirit, with no other confidence but this unconquerable confidence, man allows being to the One in whom true being itself seeks and finds, and who meets him here as the source of his life, as comfort and command, as the power over him and over all things.

Therefore our first and decisive transcription of the statement that God is, must be that God is who He is in the act of His revelation. Hence we have already repeated this sentence in our chapter heading with the concept of " The Reality of God," which holds together being and act, instead of tearing them apart like the idea of " essence." It will be noticed that even in this transcription and comprehension the statement speaks of the being of God and therefore answers the particular question of the subject of all the other articles of the creed. We are in fact interpreting the being of God when we describe it as God's reality, as " God's being in act," namely, in the act of His revelation, in which the being of God declares His reality : not only His reality for us—certainly that—but at the same time His own, inner, proper reality, behind which and above which there is no other.

If we follow the path indicated, our first declaration must be the affirmation that in God's revelation, which is the content of His Word, we have in fact to do with His act. And first, this means generally— with an event, with a happening. But as such this is an event which is in no sense to be transcended. It is not, therefore, an event which has merely happened and is now a past fact of history. God's revelation is, of course, this as well. But it is also an event happening in the present, here and now. Again, it is not this in such a way that it exhausts itself in the momentary movement from the past to the present, that is, in our to-day. But it is also an event that took place once for all, and an accomplished fact. And it is also future— the event which lies completely and wholly in front of us, which has not yet happened, but which simply comes upon us. Again, this happens without detriment to its historical completeness and its full contemporaneity. On the contrary, it is in its historical completeness and its full contemporaneity that it is truly future. " Jesus Christ the same yesterday and to-day and for ever " (Heb. 13⁸). This is something which cannot be transcended or surpassed or dispensed with. What is concerned is always the birth, death and resurrection of Jesus Christ, always His justification of faith, always His lordship in the Church, always His coming again, and therefore Himself as our hope. We can only abandon revelation, and with it God's Word, if we are to dispense with it. With it we stand, no, we move necessarily in the circle of its event or, in biblical terms, in the circle of the life of the people of Israel. And in this very event God is who He is. God is He who in this event is subject, predicate and object ; the revealer, the act of revelation, the revealed ; Father, Son and Holy Spirit. God is the Lord active in this event. We say " active " in this event, and therefore for our salvation and for His glory, but in any case active. Seeking and finding God in His revelation, we cannot escape the action of God for a God who is not active. This is not only because we ourselves cannot, but because there is no surpassing or bypassing at all of the divine action, because a transcendence of His action is nonsense. We are dealing with the being of God : but with regard to the being of God, the word " event " or " act " is *final*, and cannot be surpassed or compromised. To its very deepest depths God's Godhead consists in the fact that it is an event—not any event, not events in general, but the event of His action, in which we have a share in God's revelation.

The definition that we must use as a starting-point is that God's being is *life*. Only the Living is God. Only the voice of the Living is God's voice. Only the work of the Living is God's work ; only the worship and fellowship of the Living is God's worship and fellowship. So, too, only the knowledge of the Living is knowledge of God.

We recall in this connexion the emphatic Old and New Testament description of God as " the living God." This is no metaphor. Nor is it a mere description of God's relation to the world and to ourselves. But while it is that, it also describes God Himself as the One He is. " As I live " or " As the Lord (or God, or the God of Israel) liveth " is not for nothing the significant formula for an oath in the Old Testament. God is " the living fountain " (Jer. 2¹³, 17¹³), " the fountain of life " (Ps. 36⁹). The Father has life in Himself (Jn. 5²⁶). Christ is " the author of life " (Ac. 3¹⁵), even " the life " (Jn. 14⁶, Phil. 1²¹, Col. 3⁴, 1 Jn. 1²), and " eternal life " (1 Jn. 5²⁰), " alive for evermore " (Rev. 1¹⁸). The Holy Spirit is life (Jn. 6⁶³, Rom. 8¹⁰). All this is clearly in contradistinction to the gods and idols who " have no life " (Jer. 10¹⁴, Ac. 14¹⁵). Thus it was quite right when the older theology described the essence of God as *vita*, and again as *actuositas*, or more simply as *actus*. What was meant was : as *actus purus*, indeed *purissimus*. *Domine, cui esse et vivere non aliud atque aliud est, quia summe esse atque summe vivere idipsum es* . . . (Augustine, *Conf.* I, 6, 10). In speaking of the essence of God we are concerned with an act which utterly surpasses the whole of the actuality that we have come to know as act, and compared with which all that we have come to know as act is no act at all, because as act it can be transcended. This is not the case with the act of God that happens in revelation. Of course, when we have said this, we have still not said everything that we must say about God when we describe Him as act, or as living. But we must always say this of Him too (and if we are concerned to understand who God is, we must say it first of all) that He is act or He is living. *Vita Dei est tale attributum, quo Deus semetipsum perfectissime actuat per actus intrinsecos et immanentes cognoscendi et volendi seque semper actuosum demonstrat* (Quenstedt, *Theol. did. pol.*, 1685, I *c.* 8, *sec.* 1, *th.* 22). Polanus is surely right : *Propriissime solus Deus vivere dici potest* (*op. cit., col.* 986). Thomas Aquinas had said the same (*Summa theol.* I, *qu.* 18, *art.* 3 c) : *vita maxime proprie in Deo est*. God really lives. And the definition of Polanus is also instructive (*op. cit., col.* 985) : *Vita Dei est essentialis Dei proprietas seu ipsa divina essentia vivens, per quam Deus actuose vivere et se ipso omnia agere et vi agitandi movendique praeditus esse ac proinde aliis quoque vitam indere significatur.*

But we must be more precise. When on the basis of His revelation we always understand God as event, as act and as life, we have not in any way identified Him with a sum or content of event, act, or life generally. We can never expect to know generally what event or act or life is, in order from that point to conclude and assert that God is He to whom this is all proper in an unimaginable and incomprehensible fulness and completeness. When we know God as event, act and life, we have to admit that generally and apart from Him we do not know what this is. So then, when we know God as event, act and life, He is definitely something different—to be distinguished from what we are accustomed to understand by these views and concepts. God's revelation is a particular event, not identical with the sum, nor identical with any of the content of other existing happenings either in nature or in human history. It is a definite happening within general happening : so definite that, while it takes part in this happening, it also contradicts it, and can only be seen and comprehended together with it in its contradiction, without the possibility of a synthesis, apart from the synthesis proclaimed and already fulfilled in itself. So, too, the action of God that takes place in revelation is a particular action, different from any other happening, even in contradiction to it. *Actus purus* is not sufficient as a description of God. To it there must be added at least " *et singularis.*" The fact that in God the source, reconciliation and goal of all other happenings are together real and discernible, is another matter, which as such is only true in the separation of this action from every other happening. God is also the One who is event, act and life in His own way, as distinct from everything that He is not Himself, even though at the same time He is its source, reconciliation and goal. God is not merely differentiated from all other actuality as actuality generally and as such, or as its essence and principle, so that, while He is differentiated from all other actuality, He is still connected to it—and the idea is both immanent in the phenomenon and transcendent to it. He is, of course, differentiated from it in this way too. His work in the creation and preservation of the world can also up to a point—but only up to a point—be described in this way. But the particularity of His working and therefore His being as God is not exhausted by this dialectical transcendence which, however strictly it may be understood, must always be understood with equal strictness as immanence. On the contrary, without prejudice to and yet without dependence upon His relationship to what is event, act and life outside Him, God is in Himself free event, free act and free life.

We were careful not to understand the biblical description of God as " the living God " as a simile. But again, it is not a mere simile in Holy Scripture when God is described as wrath, mercy, patience, repentance, pleasure, pain, or the like, or as remembrance and forgetting, speech and silence, coming and going, presence and absence ; and when God's action as attested in deeds is of such a kind as to make it necessary in describing it to apply such categories. As we remember from the doctrine of the knowledge of God, not only some but all human standpoints and concepts, even those used by Scripture, are " anthropomorphisms." It is, then, quite arbitrary to describe these in a special way as *attributa metaphorica* (Polanus, *op. cit.*, col. 1231 f.), so that they have first to be divested of their full meaning to make the truth of God visible. In their fulness they are especially adapted to describe the special life and being of God, although quite useless to describe the highest ideal in Plato's teaching, or the πρῶτον κινοῦν of Aristotle. What is described in these views and concepts is the saving contradiction of God found in His revelation, which is more than a mere difference that can be removed dialectically. It is the particularity of revelation amid all other happenings, the particularity of the divine reality as against all other. It is the undialectical transcendence, the free achievement, the free act, the free life of the divine being. And it is not something that can be juggled away by a new idealistic interpretation if at this point we are really to speak of the being of the triune God in His revelation. and not of any other being.

But we must take a further step forward. What is the particularity, what is therefore the specific freedom, of the event, act and life of God in His revelation ? We are obviously speaking with a double meaning when in describing God we speak of event, act and life. Event, act and life could refer to an event in nature, or a transcendent happening, to be investigated after the fashion of what we know as natural events. Now it is true that we cannot simply neglect to seek the being of God along this line if we consider ourselves bound to speak of the God of revelation. Therefore, in the attempt to speak here more unequivocally, we must exercise some care. The differentiation of the divine happening from the non-divine does not coincide in Holy Scripture with the distinction between nature and grace, soul and body, inner and outer, visible and invisible. On the contrary, the event of revelation as described for us in Scripture has everywhere a natural, bodily, outward and visible component—from the creation (not only of heaven but also of earth), by way of the concrete existence of the people of Israel in Palestine, the birth of Jesus Christ, His physical miracles, His suffering and death under Pontius Pilate, His physical resurrection, right down to His coming again and the resurrection of the body. We cannot give a new meaning to this component without explaining away the specific sense of this revelation, and therefore the revelation itself, without giving over the field to another reflection foreign to the basis and message of the Church. And this state of affairs cannot be a matter of indifference for the description of the being of God. Whoever describes this as absolute " spirit," and by this absoluteness understands an as it were chemical purity as against " nature," must ask himself whether at the very source of his consideration of the matter he has not fallen into a misunderstanding of the most fundamental character and with the gravest consequences, confusing the reality of God with the reality of the spiritual world—a reality to be distinguished no less from the reality of God than from that of the world of nature.

Si Deus est Spiritus, nihil ergo de eo terrenum aut carnale cogitandum. Deinde ex analogia spiritualium essentiarum simpliciumque de natura eius iudicium aliquomodo fieri potest. (Polanus, *op. cit., col.* 860). Here the confusion has already taken place, or is irresistibly about to do so.

According to Holy Scripture heaven—or supernatural, imperceptible, spiritual reality—is not in any way to be identified with God, even in its highest sublimations and pinnacles. It is fundamentally God's creation, as earth is. It is creative only in the quite narrow, relative and figurative sense in which we can speak of creation within a created world. If we are not tied by the superstitions of a spirit-nature system which confuses theology with metaphysics, and if we understand that what we know as spirit is in itself and as such no less a creation than what we call nature, then we are free to discern that the nature of God, when we describe it as spirit, cannot for that reason be described (like that of the angels) to the exclusion and denial of nature.

We must keep well in mind that Holy Scripture not only speaks of God's wrath, mercy, etc., but also—to the even greater confusion of all spiritualisers—very obviously and emphatically of His face, His eyes, His mouth, His ears, even His nose, His back, His arm, His hand, His right hand, His finger, His feet. Can it really be maintained that all that is meant *non theologice, sed oeconomice: secundum captum nostrum et ex imbecillae cognitionis nostrae sensu* (Polanus, *op. cit., col.* 1231 f.) ? Are the decisive and in truth very meaningful trinitarian descriptions of God as " Father " and " Son " also not to be understood *theologice?* Is it not to be understood *theologice* that we are to be called God's children ? How can anyone think to explain Holy Scripture when he treats these concepts figuratively, setting over against them something " purely spiritual " as what is really intended ? Does the understanding of all the connexions marked by these concepts not depend to some extent on this—that the reality of the natural component of the divine being indicated in them should in its place and in proper proportion be taken just as seriously as the undeniable spiritual reality ? It is at this point that we can appreciate how the orthodox doctrine of God, as determined by that of the philosophy of pagan antiquity, paved the way for the later Enlightenment with all that that involved.

It is not, of course, that we have to confuse and confound Creator and creature on this side, ascribing to God our created nature. As God's thoughts are not our thoughts, as His Spirit is not our spirit, so obviously His eyes are not human eyes, nor His hands human hands. But it does mean that what is said naturally about God is not to be arbitrarily translated into something spiritual. The divine being must be allowed to transcend both spirit and nature, yet also to overlap and comprehend both, as attested in His revelation according to the testimony of Holy Scripture. We have to enquire into the event and act and life of God—in His transcendence as against the whole created world, in the order appropriate to the matter—but also in the direction of what we think we know as " natural event." Quite apart from the witness given to Him by Scripture, God could not be understood as the Lord of heaven and earth, as the Saviour of soul and body, as the God of all men, if we could only really understand Him by having recourse to these spiritualising abstractions. It is to be noted that it depends on this demarcation from a spiritualising which makes itself systematically absolute, which so to speak obtrudes itself on the God-head, whether we can seriously and properly speak of God's being as deriving from God's act. If God has no nature, if He is that chemically distilled absolute spirit, He does nothing, and in fact He can do nothing.

The statement of Polanus: *quo quid spiritualius est, eo magis activum est* (*op. cit.*, *col.* 860) can only be right in the sense that the " spirit " is the principle of every act, that an act is all the more an act if it is the act of a spirit. But it cannot possibly be right if the reference is to a spirit without nature.

Acts happen only in the unity of spirit and nature. If such a unity is to be denied in regard to God, then—and sooner or later this conclusion has to be drawn one way or another by all who deny it—there is no true, real history of His doings in any genuine sense of the term. There are no decisions and working of God. There is no revelation and reconciliation. There is also no creation and redemption as happening and decision. And, of course, there is no eternal witness of the Son through the Father, no eternal procession of the Holy Spirit from the Father and the Son, no inner life of God. These things are all images and likenesses. They are not strictly and properly true. Their true reality, the truth presumably meant by them, confronts them as the formless, motionless being of a spirit which is open to the serious suspicion that it is nothing but a hypostatisation of our own created spirit. We stand, therefore, at an important and crucial parting of the ways when we assert that we cannot adopt the so-called " purely spiritual " interpretation of the divine being.

Now that we are clear about this, we are free to state the opposite truth that the specific freedom of the event, act and life of God in His revelation and in eternity is, of course, the freedom of the spirit. It is not, therefore, accident or necessity. It does not have the orderliness or fatality of a natural event, although nature is not excluded. It is the freedom of a knowing and willing I, an I which itself distinguishes itself from what it is not, and what it is not from itself, an I which controls nature. The particularity of the divine event, act and life is the particularity of the being of a person. We speak of an action, of a deed, when we speak of the being of God as a happening. Indeed the peak of all happening in revelation, according to Holy Scripture, consists in the fact that God speaks as an I, and is heard by the thou who is addressed. The whole content of the happening consists in the fact that the Word of God became flesh and that His Spirit is poured out upon all flesh. In this happen-ing the world of nature and sense is undoubtedly subordinate. It is the servant. It is the component which is not important and necessary for its own sake, but only in its relationship and function.

Therefore, we must be very careful how we state the so-called spirit-corpo-reality of revelation, however justified it may be against spiritualising. It is a false realism to balance against one another spirit and nature, inner and outer, soul and body, in such a way that their relationship is treated as symmetrical and reversible. In revelation as such the subject treated is undoubtedly spirit. It is for the sake of spirit and only for the sake of it that there is any mention of nature. The well-known phrase of F. C. Oetinger that the end of the way of God is corporeality reveals a historically understandable but essentially doubtful over-simplification, which is only acceptable if we make it read " also corporeality."

In accordance with the happening of revelation we reject a false spiritualising on the one hand and a false realism on the other, and have to understand God's being as " being in person." What is meant is certainly not personified being, but the being that in the reality of its person realises and unites in itself the fulness of all being. In its person means in its unity of spirit and nature. For in this unity, in the due superiority of its spirituality, in the due inferiority of its natural-ness, it is not an " It," nor is it a " He " like a created person. It is genuinely (and therefore also for a genuine understanding) always an " I." It is the I who knows about Himself, who Himself wills, Himself disposes and distinguishes, and in this very act of His omnipotence is wholly self-sufficient.

In this formula we are simply interpreting the triune being of God as Father and Son in the unity of the Holy Spirit proceeding from both. This being as such and in its entirety is the being, the *essentia*, of the Godhead, and whatever else we may have to say about it will have to be understood as a definition of this being. It is in reference to this being that the famous definition of Jn. 4²⁴ : " God is Spirit," is to be understood ; and if we can understand the usual defini-tions of orthodox dogmatics : *Deus est spiritus independens*, or *spiritus existens a se ipso* or the like (cf. J. Wolleb, *Chr. Theol. comp.*, 1626, I, 1, 1), as formed in relation to this being, we have no option but to agree with them.

However, before we explain more precisely the spiritual being of God in our second sub-section, we must make the further point that God's being is being which knows, wills and decides of itself, and is moved by itself. Inasmuch as God's being consists in God's act, it reveals itself as being which is self-moved. It is self-moved in that it differentiates itself both from the abstractly observed being of nature and from the abstractly comprehended being of spirit. Natural being, as far as it can be observable to us as such in this or that material aggregate, is in itself unmoved. We understand it as motivated being only in a series of such aggregates. But in this series, as living nature, it is not observable by us. Comprehensible spiritual being as such is in itself unmoved. We comprehend it as the being of contents, laws and ideas. It has motion only in its relation from individual to individual. But in this relationship it is for us incom-prehensible. As such, then, natural and spiritual being means un-moved being. The being of God as we know it from revelation is moved in itself and therefore motivating.

Hence the impossibility of the assertions of a naturalistic or spiritualistic Deism, to which those of a mystical Pantheism have often enough approximated, and in which God is described as the objectivity or the non-objectivity of a being at rest in itself. No matter how strong the emphasis on its other-worldliness the description of this being as supreme or true being does not of itself mean that God is actually described. It means rather that an abstract view of nature or an equally abstract concept of spirit is the measure of all things. The fact that anyone identifies the measure of all things with God does not in this case imply that he is really speaking of God.

Now, of course, there does exist a concrete view of nature and a concrete concept of spirit, i.e., a knowledge of the moved being of nature and spirit as activated by a movement which comes upon both in their mutual relationship from outside, from a third quarter. We have, therefore, to emphasise the further point that God's being is not only moved being, but self-moved being. Nature and spirit, when they are moved, are not moved by themselves, nor is the one by the other, but both from outside. The only point of origin and beginning that is really known to us in this movement of theirs, the third quarter from which they are both moved, is the knowing, willing, appraising, working, and suffering human being. It is because we live that there is a living nature and a living spirit. The concrete view of nature, the concrete concept of the spirit, is our work. In this work of ours there is achieved a characteristic harmony of both, in which spirit precedes and nature follows, in which spirit is the subject and nature the object, in which nature provides the material, spirit the form. Nevertheless, by the revelation of God, in which God meets us as the Lord of men, we are forbidden and restrained from confusing and comparing the being of God with this working of men. God is not the being moved in and by us which we know or think we know as our movement of nature and spirit. Whatever may be the truth about this movement of ours, if we do not want to be guilty of comparing ourselves with God (and this is precisely what is forbidden and prohibited in God's revelation) we cannot understand this motivated and motivating being of ours as a self-motivated and self-motivating being. It is not only to unmoved nature and unmoved spirit, but to our motivated and motivating being that God's being stands in contradistinction, as the one and only being that is self-motivated.

Hence the impossibility of all those assertions about the nature of God, behind which there is seen to a greater or less extent the moved and moving being of men ; his moving of nature and spirit, his special classifying of both together as the measure of all things : " as Pheidias fashioned a Jupiter . . . when he gave to his own likeness supreme grandeur, dominance, size and beauty " (J. Wichelhaus, *Die Lehre der h. Schrift*[3], 1892, p. 332). Again there is no help to be found even in the strongest and most emphatic underlining of this motivation. We can say " man " in the loudest tones. We can ground our statements about man on the most profound metaphysical premisses. But this does not mean that we say " God." By this very act we perhaps again and more emphatically say " man " in distinction and opposition to God. In fact with this exaggeration we really say " sinful man." Sinful man—according to God's revelation—is man exalting himself, and thinking that by his own efforts he can realise and assert the being of God. Kant speaks forcefully of God. But when he defines God as the necessary postulate of the limit and goal of pure reason, and the equally necessary presupposition of the law-giver and guarantor of practical reason, what else does he do (without adding substantially to his anthropology) but powerfully to speak again and strictly about man (about the depth of the nature of his rational capacity) ? Again, Hegel speaks forcefully of God. But when he describes Him as the process of absolute spirit, which exists eternally in itself, eternally proceeds from itself, and existing in itself and outside itself is eternally the same, this is indeed a forceful and profound description of the movement of nature and spirit which proceeds from ourselves and returns to ourselves. But it is not a description of God, whose movement is infinitely more than our self-movement even when the latter is hypostatised, i.e., projected into eternity, and by whose movement this hypostatisation and projection is necessarily forbidden and prevented. Schleiermacher speaks forcefully of God when he describes Him as the source of the absolute dependence of our consciousness, and therefore not only the ground of all religion, but at the same time and as such the ulterior ground of our whole self-consciousness, the mysterious centre of our intelligent and active existence. Schleiermacher more plainly perhaps than any of his spiritual confreres knows how superfluous is a particular concept of God to describe the moving power of spirit and nature, and above all of man as such. In fact, Schleiermacher takes such little account of a force moving us from outside, and above all self-moved, that he purposed to give his system a final form in which it would be a clear presentation of the self-motivated Christian-religious self-consciousness as such : an undertaking which—in view of the instruction it would have given us we can only say—unfortunately his death prevented from further prosecution. A. Ritschl, too, spoke forcefully of God (as his contemporaries saw it). For in impressive distinction from all ancient and modern theoretical metaphysics, he aimed exclusively at the practical, ethico-religious significance of the idea of God. Nevertheless, it can be truly said that we come out of the frying-pan into the fire when we have to be told by him that God is the power " in and over the world " " which man reverences, because it maintains his spiritual self-feeling against the restraints that arise from nature " (*Theol. und Metaphysik*, 1881, p. 11). Religion is concerned with the solution of the paradox " in which man finds himself as a part of the world of nature and yet as a spiritual personality, which demands of him that he should be lord of the world " (*Rechtf. und Vers.* 4, Vol. 3, 1895, p. 189). Christianity as the highest religion mediates to man a sure appraisal both of himself as a definite spiritual personality, made for the attainment of the supreme good, and also of the world as a contained " whole," and in this way the Christian idea of God is " the ideal link " between our self-consciousness on the one hand and our world-view on the other (*loc. cit.*, p. 190 f.). It will be clear that the attainment of this self-consciousness, the formation of this world-view, and the constitution of the " ideal link " between both, is not so very different from what man ordinarily achieves in his relation to nature and spirit that it is seriously worth while to speak seriously of God at this final point. If God " in and over the world " is only a higher degree of the movement which we know well enough as our own, it is hard to see to what extent beyond this He is necessarily self-motivated, and therefore to what extent there necessarily has to be a particular idea of God.

Just think what is implied if God's being is understood as self-moved being. It implies that the movement of nature and spirit, which occurs in His revelation and is effected by it, does not lead back to any self-movement of man. It cannot be enervated by the consideration whether the man to whom it is related may finally and in the last resort be alone in it with himself. God's revelation draws its authority and evidence from the fact that it is founded on itself apart from all human foundations. God's commandment, God's grace and God's promise have a unique force because they are without reference to human strength or weakness. God's work is triumphant because it is not bound to our work, but precedes and follows it in its own way, which may also be the way of our work. God's righteous demand on man, and His faithfulness in covenant with him, are irresistible and irrevocable because for their confirmation they need only God Himself and no corresponding relation of man. All this is compromised and even belied, not only if we think of God's being as unmoved, but even if we think of it as anything other than self-moved. The fact that God's being is event, the event of God's act, necessarily (if, when we speak of it, we turn our eyes solely on His revelation) means that it is His own conscious, willed and executed decision. It is His own decision, and therefore independent of the decisions by which we validate our existence. It is His conscious decision, and therefore not the mechanical outcome of a process the rationality of which, in so far as we can speak of such a thing, will have to be sought outside itself. It is His willed decision, and therefore not an event occurring through external causes or only in an external relationship. It is His executed decision—executed once for all in eternity, and anew in every second of our time, and therefore in such a way that it confronts what is not divine being, not as a mere possibility, but always as a self-contained, self-containing reality. Certainly God's being in this its self-motivation is spirit. But it is divine Spirit. Certainly it is nature. But it is divine nature. Certainly it is both in the unity and togetherness of a person. But this person is the divine person, whom we must see at once to be distinguished from other persons by the fact that He is self-motivated person. No other being exists absolutely in its act. No other being is absolutely its own, conscious, willed and executed decision. Only in the illusion of sin can man ascribe this being to himself or to the content of the world as a projection of himself. Whenever God confronts him in His revelation, this illusion is destroyed, and this being is denied to him and to the whole world. In the light of the judgment and grace which come to him in God's revelation, man must ascribe this being to God and to God alone. Now, if the being of a person is a being in act, and if, in the strict and proper sense, being in act can be ascribed only to God, then it follows that by the concept of the being of a person, in the strict and proper sense, we can understand only the being of God. Being in its own, conscious, willed and executed decision, and therefore personal being, is the being of God in the nature of the Father and the Son and the Holy Spirit. Originally and properly there is no other beside or outside Him. Everything beside and outside Him is only secondary. It exists only on the basis of His gracious creation and providence, conditioned by His gracious reconciliation of the sinner, and with a view to His future redemption. And it can be known only by God's Word and revelation. We cannot speak of " personalising " in reference to God's being, but only in reference to ours. The real person is not man but God. It is not God who is a person by extension, but we. God exists in His act. God is His own decision. God lives from and by Himself.

God is. The first and basic general definition of this statement has now been given. Whatever else we may have to say must always correspond to this first definition. Anything contradictory will necessarily be false. Every statement of what God is, and explanation how God is, must always state and explain what and how He is in His act and decision. There is no moment in the ways of God which is over and above this act and decision. There is no evasion of this act and decision of the living quality of God. There is only the apprehension of this quality in virtue of the fact that we are apprehended by Him in His revelation. But this means that it is not merely this quality in its supreme form, *par excellence*, but basically and properly it is so in a unique sense : *propriissime solus Deus vivere dici potest*. If we have life on the basis of His creation and in hope on the ground of the resurrection of Jesus Christ, our quality of life can never be confused with His, or compared or contrasted with it as commensurate. The validity of every further statement about God, as a statement about the living God, depends on the avoidance of this confusion, or this comparison and contrast, between His life and ours. But this will happen automatically if the positive content of the rule which has emerged is clear to us, if every further statement what and how God is is always linked with the fact that God is He who is not only to be found alone in His act, but is to be found alone in His act because alone in His act He is who He is. If we keep this clearly in mind, if all our thoughts are always grasped by God's action, because in it we have to do with God's being, we may be sure that they cannot err, and become either openly or secretly thoughts about ourselves.

2. THE BEING OF GOD AS THE ONE WHO LOVES

It would be dangerous and ambiguous if we tried to prolong the definition of the divine essence as His being in act generally, and therefore, the establishment of the form of this essence—His actuality or His life. Once said, the fact that God's being is absolutely His act will not be restated, but taken seriously in the insight that this act of His, which is His being, is not actuality in general and as such, but that in His revelation and in eternity it is a specific act with a definite content. It is personal being in the originality and uniqueness that is applicable only to Him. It is the being of a person, distinguished not by its formal completeness, but by its peculiar, distinctive act as such. We must now enquire further what is this act of His, the divine act which is the divine being, so that we have to conclude from it what is divine, i.e., what it is to be God, what makes God God, what God's "essence" is. Following the considerations of the first section this much is established, that God is what He is absolutely by Himself, and not by anything else that would confer divinity upon Him. Therefore the act that becomes visible to us in God's revelation, in which He is who He is, and from which we must conclude what and how He is, can only make manifest in fact that He is who He is. If it does not make this manifest, it has definitely not made manifest what is divine, what is the essence of God. But the act that is visible in God's revelation is not so constituted that we can conclude from it no more than the tautology "God is God." This very tautology as such we find clarified and explained in God's revelation. For it is nothing less than God's self-revelation. It is the revelation of the name by which He wills to be known and addressed by us, the name which does not add a second and extrinsic truth to the first intrinsic truth of His intimate, hidden essence, but which is the name and the criterion and the truth (i.e., the disclosure and description of the particularity) of His innermost hidden essence. This essence of God which is seen in His revealed name is His being and therefore His act as Father, Son and Holy Spirit. The fact that He makes Himself visible in this name is the solution of the tautology. From this name of His we have to conclude what and how He is in His act and therefore in His being : what is divine, what is the character of Him who is God, what makes God God, what therefore His "essence" is. The fact that we cannot go behind His livingness for a definition of His being means in fact that we cannot go behind this name of His, because in the very revelation of His name there occurs the act which is His being to all eternity. However (in order to define this revealed and eternal being) we can, we may and we must ask what this name has to say to us about the particular being of God in His act.

As it is revealed to us as the definition of that which confronts us in His revelation, this name definitely has this primary and decisive thing to say to us in all its constituents—that God is He who, without having to do so, seeks and creates fellowship between Himself and us. He does not have to do it, because in Himself without us, and therefore without this, He has that which He seeks and creates between Himself and us. It implies so to speak an overflow of His essence that He turns to us. We must certainly regard this overflow as itself matching His essence, belonging to His essence. But it is an overflow which is not demanded or presupposed by any necessity, constraint, or obligation, least of all from outside, from our side, or by any law by which God Himself is bound and obliged. On the contrary, in itself and as such it is again rooted in Himself alone. Yet important

as it is, we will postpone this explanation and keep to the positive statement that God is He who in His revelation seeks and creates fellowship
with us, and who (because His revelation is also His self-revelation) does
this in Himself and in His eternal essence. Creation itself, i.e., the
establishment and maintenance of a reality really distinct from Himself, of which man confronted by God may find himself the spiritual-
natural unity, is already a seeking and creating of fellowship. This seeking and creating is heightened in the work of revelation itself, which is
not so much a continuation of creation as its supersession, and is identical with the reconciliation of sinful man in the incarnation, death and
resurrection of the Son of God. This seeking and creating finds its
crown and final confirmation in the future destiny of mankind as
redeemed in Jesus Christ, in his destiny for eternal salvation and life.
What God does in all this, He is : and He is no other than He who does
all this. But what is it that He does in virtue of His triune name, and
therefore in this whole act of God seen in His revelation ? If it is right
and necessary to bring together the purpose and meaning of this act
in order to understand it, and therefore to understand God, we must
now say that He wills to be ours, and He wills that we should be His.
He wills to belong to us and He wills that we should belong to Him. He
does not will to be without us, and He does not will that we should
be without Him. He wills certainly to be God and He does not will
that we should be God. But He does not will to be God for Himself
nor as God to be alone with Himself. He wills as God to be for us
and with us who are not God. Inasmuch as He is Himself and affirms
Himself, in distinction and opposition to everything that He is not,
He places Himself in this relation to us. He does not will to be Himself
in any other way than He is in this relationship. His life, that is, His
life in Himself, which is originally and properly the one and only life,
leans towards this unity with our life. The blessings of His Godhead
are so great that they overflow as blessings to us, who are not God.
This is God's conduct towards us in virtue of His revelation. There
is no lack of contrariety in this conduct. It establishes and embraces
the antithesis between the Creator and His creatures. It establishes
and embraces necessarily, too, God's anger and struggle against sin,
God's separation from sinners, God's judgment hanging over them
and consummated on them. There is death and hell and eternal
damnation in the scope of this relationship of His. But His attitude
and action is always that He seeks and creates fellowship between
Himself and us. For large stretches it may be for us doubtful, dark
and incomprehensible. For large stretches it will seem to us like the
very opposite of this relationship. It will reveal itself as such through
judgment and grace, through dying and making alive, through veiling
and unveiling. It will always be the light that shines out of darkness
when it is revealed to us as such. We shall have to learn ever and
again what it really means to say that God seeks and creates fellow-

ship between Himself and us. In itself, first and last, it will always be this and no other relationship. God wills and does nothing different, but only one thing—this one thing. And this one thing that He wills and does is the blessing of God, that which distinguishes His act as divine, and therefore also His person as divine. This one thing is therefore the divine, the θεῖον, the essence of God in the revelation of His name, which is the subject of our enquiry. That is to say, we shall find in God Himself, in His eternal being, nothing other than this one thing. As and before God seeks and creates fellowship with us, He wills and completes this fellowship in Himself. In Himself He does not will to exist for Himself, to exist alone. On the contrary, He is Father, Son and Holy Spirit and therefore alive in His unique being with and for and in another. The unbroken unity of His being, knowledge and will is at the same time an act of deliberation, decision and intercourse. He does not exist in solitude but in fellowship. Therefore what He seeks and creates between Himself and us is in fact nothing else but what He wills and completes and therefore is in Himself. It therefore follows that as He receives us through His Son into His fellowship with Himself, this is the one necessity, salvation, and blessing for us, than which there is no greater blessing—no greater, because God has nothing higher than this to give, namely Himself; because in giving us Himself, He has given us every blessing. We recognise and appreciate this blessing when we describe God's being more specifically in the statement that He is the One who loves. That He is God—the Godhead of God—consists in the fact that He loves, and it is the expression of His loving that He seeks and creates fellowship with us. It is correct and important in this connexion to say emphatically His *loving*, i.e., His act as that of the One who loves.

The tempting definition that " God is love " seems to have some possible support in 1 Jn. 4[8, 16]: ὁ θεὸς ἀγάπη ἐστίν. But it is a forced exegesis to cite this sentence apart from its context and without the interpretation that is placed on it by its context, and to use it as the basis of a definition. We read in v. 9 : " In this was manifested the love of God towards us, because that God sent his only-begotten Son into the world, that we might live through him." Again we are told in v. 10 (with a remarkable similarity of predication) : " Herein is love, not that we loved God, but that he loved us, and sent his Son to be the propitiation for our sins." And finally in v. 15 : In this we have knowledge and faith in the love that God has for us, that we confess " that Jesus is the Son of God." The love of God, or God as love, is therefore interpreted in 1 Jn. 4 as the completed act of divine loving in sending Jesus Christ. If we want to follow M. Dibelius in describing v. 8 and v. 16 as an " equation of God," we must at least go on to say that as such (as the equating of God with an abstract content of His action) it is at once resolved again, being replaced by a declaration of God's act as such. This finding is confirmed by a right understanding of Jn. 3[16] : " God so (Vulg. : *sic*) loved the world, that he gave his only-begotten Son, that whosoever believeth in him should not perish, but have everlasting life."

If, then, we now take the decisive turn, directing our attention to the definition and content of the divine being as it confronts us in

God's revelation, and if as our first step we take up the concept of love, it is not because we think that somehow we already know generally what love is as the content of an action which is genuinely good, and that on the basis of this knowledge we can equate God with this content. The proper procedure is very different. By the reality of the divine act we are summoned to give an account of the essence of this act, and thereby of the essence of God Himself. And led by Holy Scripture itself, we may and must venture to bring the concept of love (the peculiar and final meaning of which we admit we do not know in what is otherwise a tempting application) into the service of our present task, the declaration of the act and therefore of the being of God. We must recognise quite frankly the possibility that in this use " love " may take on a meaning which is fulfilled in a way which breaks up and reforms its meaning in the tempting application. Intentionally we have not begun with a definition of love, but with the resolve to let the act of God visible in His revelation speak for itself —God is in His act the One who seeks and creates fellowship with us. If we define this action of His as the love of God, and therefore God as the One who loves, and (in the proper sense) as love, our gaze must always be directed strictly on the fact, i.e., on God's act, and must not be allowed to wander under the influence of a concomitant and supposititious general idea of love. If we say with 1 Jn. 4 that God is love, the converse that love is God is forbidden until it is mediated and clarified from God's being and therefore from God's act what the love is which can and must be legitimately identified with God. The elucidation of this love is our present task.

1. God's loving is concerned with a seeking and creation of fellowship for its own sake. It is the fellowship of the One who loves with the loved himself, and therefore that which the One who loves has to impart to the loved and the loved has to receive from the One who loves. God is not, therefore, the *Good* first, and then the One who loves, because He does not keep this *Good* to Himself but communicates it to others. God is the One who loves, and as such the *Good* and the sum of all good things. God is good in the fact that He is Father, Son and Holy Spirit, that as such He is our Creator, Mediator and Redeemer, and that as such He takes us up into His fellowship, i.e., the fellowship which He has and is in Himself, and beyond which as such there is no greater *Good* which has still to be communicated to us through His fellowship with us. Loving us, God does not give us something, but Himself; and giving us Himself, giving us His only Son, He gives us everything. The love of God has only to be His love to be everything for us.

" He that spared not his own Son, but delivered him up for us all, how shall he not with him also freely give us all things " (Rom. 8³²). Even the knowledge and confession on which so much weight is laid, especially in the Johannine writings, are not concerned with the light and the life, or the way and the truth, which are given us through the Son of God. Nor are they concerned with the gifts, although these are named specifically enough and sufficiently highly praised. But they are concerned with the Giver of these gifts, and therefore with the Son of God as such. For this reason, in the Synoptics the kingdom of God is not an independent reality, but is absolutely bound up with the revealed Messiah, with His Word and His deeds, with faith in Him. This kingdom cannot in any sense be separated from its King. Therefore the answer of the man beloved of God, according to Psalm 73[23f.], is as follows : " Nevertheless I am continually with thee : thou hast holden me by my right hand. Thou shalt guide me with thy counsel and afterward receive me to glory. Whom have I in heaven but thee ? And there is none upon earth that I desire beside thee. My flesh and my heart faileth : but God is the strength of my heart, and my portion for men. For lo, they that are far from thee shall perish : thou hast destroyed all them that go a-whoring from thee. But it is good for me to draw near to God : I have put my trust in the Lord God, that I may declare all thy works." Paul speaks similarly : " For I am persuaded, that neither death, nor life, nor angels, nor principalities, nor powers, nor things present, nor things to come, nor height, nor depth, nor any other creature shall be able to separate us from the love of God, which is in Christ Jesus our Lord " (Rom. 8[38f.]). Shed abroad in our hearts by the Holy Spirit, the love of God as such is the only ground of the hope that maketh not ashamed, and so worketh tribulation and patience (Rom. 5[4f.]). We overlook this if, like Thomas Aquinas, we tie the love of God to the definition : *Amare nihil aliud est, quam velle bonum alicui* (*S. theol.*, I *qu.* 20, *art.* 2 *c*), and then have to continue : *Amans sic fit extra se in amatum translatus, inquantum vult amato bonum et operatur per suam providentiam sicut et sibi* (*ib. ad.* 1). Correctly, i.e., biblically, this sentence as a description of the love of God must read : *Amans sic vult amato bonum et operatur per suam providentiam sicut et sibi, inquantum, fit extra se in amatum translatus.* For it is in this *translatio,* or rather *communicatio,* as such that the *Good* is bestowed on the other when the matter concerns the ways of God, and not *vice versa*. Because and as God loves, His will is a *velle bonum alicui,* for it is only because God loves that there is any *aliquid* or *aliquis* at all, towards whom His will can be or is directed. As there is such another, and as God's will is in fact directed on it, as, therefore, He holds fellowship with it, as He loves it, He wills its good. Because and as He is who He is, because and as it is His will which is directed towards this other, and therefore because and as He loves, His will is good will. If we look for God's good behind His love in a *summum bonum* that is separate from His love, in the act of determining this *summum bonum* we can hardly avoid a relapse into the concept of a pure unmoved being, and will have to defend it in face of the divine witness of revelation. The polemic with which G. Thomasius defended this patristic and scholastic definition of the essence of God : that the definition " God is love " supposes " a positively good content of the self-communicating " and personal life and that otherwise it would be " a bad volatilisation of the self " (*Christi Person und Werk*,[3] 1886, Vol. I, p. 31), is fallacious in both its arguments. The " positively good content " of God's personal life does not exist behind or apart from His communication, but consists in the fact that it is the self-communicating life as such. And the fact that there is no volatilisation of the divine self is due to the fact that God is in Himself as Father, Son and Holy Spirit the self-communicating life. Along the same lines the definition of H. Lüdemann must also be corrected : " The love of God is His self-communication : but He is His innermost self as *summum bonum*. Because He loves the world, He wills that it should have a share in His completeness " (*Dogm.,* 1926, Vol. II, p. 261). No, but His innermost self is His self-communication, and loving the world, He gives it a share in His completeness. And when R. Seeberg (*Chr. Dogm.,* Vol. I, 1924, p. 254) demurs that we cannot possibly characterise the whole activity of God towards the world as love, but that this description applies only to the " specifically Christian experience of God," it must be remembered that according to Jn. 3¹⁶, in virtue of the " specifically Christian experience of God " (which is surely not merely one with others, and cannot be restricted in its reference), God has in a very definite way loved the world, so that we cannot really approve Seeberg's substitution of the omnipotence of God for His love in this connexion.

2. God's loving is concerned with a seeking and creation of fellowship without any reference to an existing aptitude or worthiness on the part of the loved. God's love is not merely not conditioned by any reciprocity of love. It is also not conditioned by any worthiness to be loved on the part of the loved, by any existing capacity for union or fellowship on his side. If he has such a thing, it is itself the prior creation of the love of God. It is not and does not become the condition of that love. It is the object of the divine pleasure which follows the preceding love. The object of the love of God as such is another which in itself is not, or is not yet, worthy of this His pleasure. The love of God always throws a bridge over a crevasse. It is always the light shining out of darkness. In His revelation it seeks and creates fellowship where there is no fellowship and no capacity for it, where the situation concerns a being which is quite different from God, a creature and therefore alien, a sinful creature and therefore hostile. It is this alien and hostile other that God loves. Fellowship with him as such is the fellowship which He seeks and creates. This does not mean that we can call the love of God a blind love. But what He sees when He loves is that which is altogether distinct from Himself, and as such lost in itself, and without Him abandoned to death. That He throws a bridge out from Himself to this abandoned one, that He is light in the darkness, is the miracle of the almighty love of God.

For this reason the Son of Man is " sent to the lost sheep of the house of Israel " (Mt. 15²⁴), and " come to seek and to save that which was lost " (Lk. 19¹⁰). " They that are whole need not the physician, but they that are sick. I came not to call the righteous but sinners to repentance " (Lk. 5³¹). According to Lk. 15 it is the lost sheep, the lost coin and the lost son that are the object of the Messiah's work ; while to the Pharisees Jn. 9⁴¹ must be quoted : " If ye were blind ye should have no sin : but now ye say, we see : therefore your sin remaineth." This is how it is with the love of God that is shed abroad in our hearts—God commends it towards us " in that, while we were yet sinners, Christ died for us " (Rom. 5⁸). Little justice is done to this aspect by the definition of Polanus : *Amor Dei est essentialis proprietas seu essentia Dei, qua oblectans sese in eo quod approbat, ei bonum vult. Hoc enim est amare: oblectare se eo quod placet, eique bonum velle et praestare* (*Synt. Theol. chr.*, 1609, *col.* 1094). We have already discussed the inadequacy of the formula *bonum velle*, which is openly borrowed from Thomas Aquinas. Equally in need of correction is the other assertion that the particular constituent and motivating element of the divine love is a preceding pleasure in the loved. How can God love us if it really depends on an *approbatio* that is our due ? The same holds of the definition of Quenstedt : *Amor Dei est, quo ipse cum obiecto amabili se suaviter unit* (*Theol. did. pol.*, 1685, I, *c.* 8, *sect.* 1, *thes.* 30). It is as *amatus* that the loved of God becomes *amabilis*. He does not become *amatus* because he is *amabilis*. Those who make definitions like this are not thinking of the cross of Christ, of the sin of the chosen and elect people of Israel, of the justification of the ungodly

(Rom. 4⁵), and of faith in Him who quickens the dead and calls those things that are not as though they were (Rom. 4¹⁷), but of a general concept of love, which in itself is highly controversial. In reality the basis of the love of God lies outside the man loved by Him and in God Himself. " I love them that love *me* " (Prov. 8¹⁷). " He that loveth *me* shall be loved of my Father (Jn. 14²¹, cf. 23). " For the Father himself loveth you because ye have loved *me*, and have believed that I came forth from God " (Jn. 16²⁷). And Jesus says of Himself : " Therefore doth my Father love me, because I lay down my life, that I might take it again " (Jn. 10¹⁷). Therefore the idea of an *objectum amabile* cannot be normative when we are concerned with the relationship of the love of the Father for the Son, with which " thou hast loved me before the foundation of the world " (Jn. 17²³⁻²⁶), and above all of the love which is the event in the triune God Himself to all eternity. Certainly God is *objectum amabile* to Himself. But He is not eternal love because He finds Himself worthy of love. He is worthy of love, and blessed in Himself, because in His life as Father, Son and Holy Spirit, He is eternal love.

3. God's loving is an end in itself. All the purposes that are willed and achieved in Him are contained and explained in this end, and therefore in this loving in itself and as such. For this loving is itself the blessing that it communicates to the loved, and it is its own ground as against the loved. Certainly in loving us God wills His own glory and our salvation. But He does not love us because He wills this. He wills it for the sake of His love. God loves in realising these purposes. But God loves because He loves ; because this act is His being, His essence and His nature. He loves without and before realising these purposes. He loves to eternity. Even in realising them, He loves because He loves. And the point of this realisation is not grounded in itself, but in His love as such, in the love of the Father, the Son and the Holy Spirit. And as we believe in God, and return His love, it is not to be understood from itself, but only from His loving as such.

" Because the Lord loved you, and because he would keep the oath which he had sworn unto your fathers, hath the Lord brought you out with a mighty hand and redeemed you out of the house of bondmen, from the hand of Pharaoh, king of Egypt " (Deut. 7⁸). " From afar" the Lord appeared to His people in the wilderness and said : " I have loved thee with an everlasting love : therefore with loving kindness have I drawn thee " (Jer. 31³). " Not a messenger nor an angel, but he himself saved them : in his love and pity he redeemed them " (Is. 63⁹). In this light it is difficult or impossible to agree with the doctrine of the love of God as developed by A. Ritschl. Ritschl's general definition of the love of God is to the effect that it is " the constant will which summons another spiritual, and therefore similar, person to the achievement of its own supreme destiny, and in such a way that the one who loves follows his own final purpose " (*Unterricht*, § 12 : *Rechtf. u. Vers.*⁴, Vol. 3, 1895, p. 263 f.). In accordance with this view the kingdom of God, i.e., the "moral association of the human race through the motive of universal love," " as the final purpose of the world and the *summum bonum* for created souls," is the necessary correlative of the divine self-purpose. According to Ritschl, it is as God wills both—this final purpose of the world, and in and with it His own peculiar purpose—that He is love : and as He wills both constantly, that He is eternal love. " If therefore God loves eternally the community of His kingdom (Eph. 1⁴, ⁶), He also loves the individuals that are bound up in it in so far as He purposes to take them up into the kingdom of God.

If these are presumed to be sinners, God loves even sinners in the light of their ideal destiny, for the realisation of which He chooses them " (*op. cit.*, p. 303). Ritschl was of the opinion that the way of thinking thus described is " not at all difficult." It has " its analogy in the self-reliance and the self-judgment which is ours in the exacted moments of our moral volition, in which we experience the power of our self-determination for good with the disregard of all the hindrances that are present in and outside us " (*op. cit.*, p. 269). We might say that this way of thinking is in fact only too easy, because its object is too similar to the well-known working of our human self-consciousness in its elevated moments. Riveted in this way to his own purpose and that of the loved, man himself may love (although he, too, may often love in other ways than this). But we are not to describe in this way the love which not only realises a purpose of its own and that of another, but also has its purpose in itself, the divine love. If God is riveted in this way, as though He were not God before and without His realising this double purpose, even this event cannot be understood as the divine realisation of divine purposes. He rather stands in a half-light which makes it possible to understand it without any previous mention of the name of God, as the action of human self-consciousness, so that what according to Ritschl is meant to be the analogy is the true reality intended. If we dissolve what God does in love into inflexibility of purpose, we shall find it hard to rediscover the ·divine essence of this action, that which distinguishes it as a holy and gracious, a laudable and sanctifying action. We shall find it hard to differentiate it from the pragmatism of all other possible events, and declare it as the sovereign action of this subject. If we keep this task in view we will postulate of the divine loving that in a reality which is unsearchable it has in itself not only its blessing and its ground, but also its purpose.

4. God's loving is necessary, for it is the being, the essence and the nature of God. But for this very reason it is also free from every necessity in respect of its object. God loves us, and loves the world, in accordance with His revelation. But He loves us and the world as He who would still be One who loves without us and without the world ; as He, therefore, who needs no other to form the prior ground of His existence as the One who loves and as God. Certainly He is who He is wholly in His revelation, in His loving-kindness, and therefore in His love for us. He has not withheld Himself from us, but given us Himself. Therefore His love for us is His *eternal* love, and our being loved by Him is our being taken up into the fellowship of His eternal love, in which He is Himself for ever and ever. All the same it is a " being taken up." It is not part of God's being and action that as love it must have an object in another who is different from Him. God is sufficient in Himself as object and therefore as object of His love. He is no less the One who loves if He loves no object different from Himself. In the fact that He determines to love such another, His love overflows. But it is not exhausted in it nor confined or conditioned by it. On the contrary, this overflowing is conditioned by the fact that although it could satisfy itself, it has no satisfaction in this self-satisfaction, but as love for another it can and will be more than that which could satisfy itself. While God is everything for Himself, He wills again not to be everything merely for Himself, but for this other. While He could be everything only for Himself (and His life

would not on that account be pointless, motionless and unmotivated, nor would it be any less majestic or any less the life of love), He wills— and this is for us the ever-wonderful twofold dynamic of His love—to have it not only for Himself, but also for us. It does not belong to us to have being, and when we have it it does not belong to us in this being of ours to be the objects of the love of God. We might not be at all, and we might be without being the objects of His love. God does not owe us either our being, or in our being His love. If we are, and if we are objects of the love of God, that means that we on our side are debtors to God, without God owing anything to us. If He loves us, if He has preferred our being to our not-being, our lovableness to our unlovableness, that is for us the ever-wonderful dynamic of His love. It is grace and not nature. For it takes place in the whole intervention of the divine action and being. We cannot go back behind this event. We should not seek and think of God anywhere else than in this act, or as any other than as the One who is at this point and in this way. Just because we must hold fast to this, it must be clear that the fact that we can actually hold on to this rests on the overflowing of the divine love. The eternal correlation between God and us, as shown in God's revelation, is grounded in God alone, and not partly in God and partly in us. It means that we are tied to God, but not God to us. So in the highest and last degree (and this is true of what has been said about the goodness, the basis and the purpose of the divine love) the concept of God's love surpasses and oversteps the common concept of love that we ourselves can produce and presuppose. Here especially the common concept must be interpreted according to the particularity of this object. In this connexion especially, we must beware of an unreflecting inversion and therefore of a definition of the divine love on the basis of a common concept of love. If we are not careful at this point we shall inevitably rob God of His deity.

What we have to avoid can be grasped in a crude form from some of the famous aphorisms of Angelus Silesius :

> I know that without me God cannot an instant be.
> He needs must perish at once were death to come to me.

> God owes as much to me as the debt that I must pay,
> I give my help to Him, He keeps me in my way.

> The blessedness of God, His life without desire,
> He doth as much from me, as I from Him acquire.

> What God eternally doth ever wish or long,
> He looketh on in me, as in His likeness strong.

> God truly nothing is, therefore something to be,
> Choosing myself for Him, He hath to be in me.

God loveth me alone, He holdeth me so dear,
That if I love Him not, He dieth of anxious fear.

Nought is but I and thou, and if we two are not,
Then God is no more God, and Heaven itself is nought.

The *Cherubinischer Wandersmann* in which these pious blasphemies are to be read (Rainer Maria Rilke has the same sort of thing on his conscience) is published with the imprimatur of a Roman Catholic bishop, and we may well ask whether this bishop was an imbecile or whether he had a secret understanding with the modern rogue. What is beyond question is that this is the impossible way of talking about the relations of God and man, and yet it is incontestably possible, and even necessary, in a train of logic in which—in view of the indispensable requirement of all human love, a beloved object different from the one who loves— we try to tie the love of God to the existence of an object of this kind, and to exhaust it in the relationship to this other. For example, we find in A. E. Biedermann the definition that the love of God is " the self-determination for the self-positing of the absolute world-process, and the immanence of the absolute God as its basis " (*Chr. Dog.*, 1896, p. 636). But in this sentence, if it is to be acceptable at all, we have to stress the word " self-determination " so strongly that there can be no simultaneous mention of an absolute God and an absolute world-process. The equation of both under an " absolute " necessarily involves an understanding either of God as the world-process or of the world-process as God. And either way the actuality of God's love as seen in His revelation is forsaken and forgotten in favour of a general concept of love (which is not incontestable in itself, like Hegel's). For the same reason the definition of E. Böhl (*Dogmatik*, 1887, p. 61) is perhaps suspect when it is applied to God. It is to the effect that love is " the inclination, the aspiration, the desire of one essence for another, the procession of a personality from itself, with the desire to go over to another or to take up the other into itself. . . . It cannot be alone, but it desires its like." Yet when, loving us, God does not withhold Himself, but gives Himself, this is love, His love, and therefore beyond all our concepts true love, just because it does not involve a transfer of God's person to us or of ours to God's. For when God loves us He is true to Himself. Indeed He is supremely true to Himself when He loves us. In this respect E. Böhl has very rightly seen and said : " Only relatively can the All-highest make creatures the objects of his love. . . . Otherwise we are forced to the position that because God is love, He must always have around Him the creatures to whom He has shown this love. We are thus forced to accept an eternal existence of the world side by side with God—which is a negation of the creaturely, of that which is only willed and created by God. It does not belong to the completeness of this divine love that it communicates itself to a mortal, created essence. It is quite another question if of His own free will God chooses to make the world the object of His love " (*op. cit.*, p. 62). On the other hand we have to ask whether certain passages in the work of H. Cremer already mentioned (e.g., pp. 19 f., 25) do not go beyond what is legitimate in the emphasis on the being of God in its relation to us. When Cremer writes (p. 25) " that we are eternally the object of God's love, or, more specifically, that it is the essence of God's manifestation to us eternally to will and be Himself, not for anyone, not in *abstracto* for any possible object, but wholly and utterly for us, and for us alone," we have to observe that we certainly will never see clearly enough and can never say strongly enough that in loving us God has given and gives Himself to us, and gives Himself fully, since this loving is His own being and essence. How can we ever say too much here, when God has loved and loves and will love us in His own Son ? On the other hand, we must not allow the completeness of His being in love for us to blind us to the fact that we do not speak of His, the divine love, if we try to deny it the movement that is proper to it in itself, even though it is not an attitude to us. The fact remains that God is He who gives everything life and breath and all things, and who therefore does not need the service of men's hands to be who He is (Ac. 17²⁵), the Father of lights, from whom every good and perfect gift ἄνωθέν ἐστιν καταβαῖνον (Jas. 1¹⁷), the μακάριος καὶ μόνος δυνάστης (1 Tim. 6¹⁵), whose word is therefore to be understood as " the gospel of the glory of the blessed God " (1 Tim. 1¹¹). It is in the light of these texts that the older theology spoke with emphasis not only of the love but also (and to some extent much more so) of the blessedness (*beatitudo*) of God : *qua nullius indigus et omnium bonorum complementum se ipso fruitur et in se acquiescit* (*Syn. pur. Theol.* Leiden, 1642, *Disp.* 6, 43). *Nam ipse per se et sua natura semper ab omnibus malis liber, semper omnibus bonis affluens est, semper hanc suam felicitatem perfecte cognoscit, semper sibi αὐτάρκης et sufficiens, semper se ipso contentus est, nullo nostro bono eget* (Ps. 50 ⁷ᶠ· was often quoted at this point) *eoque nihil extra se appetit* (Polanus, *Synt. Theol. chr.*, 1609, *col.* 996). And Augustine had already adduced the differentiation that in so far as it has as its object something other than God, the divine loving is not to be described passively like ours as *frui*, but actively as *uti*, by which *ille usus, qui dicitur Dei, quo nobis utitur, non ad eius sed ad nostram utilitatem refertur, ad eius autem tantummodo bonitatem* (*De doctr. chr.*, 1, 31-32). We have to add only that this very blessedness of God itself is to be understood as the blessedness of His love. *Beatitudo in actu consistit* (Polanus, *op. cit.*). But God's act is His loving. It is His blessedness in so far as it is His essence even apart from us. But He wills to have this same essence, not merely for Himself alone, but also, having it for Himself, in fellowship with us. He does not need us and yet He finds no enjoyment in His self-enjoyment. He does not suffer any want and yet He turns to us in the overflow of the perfection of His essence and therefore of His loving, and shares with us, in and with His love, its blessedness. This blessedness of the love of God is founded on the fact that He is Father, Son and Holy Spirit and as such loves us : as our Creator, Mediator and Redeemer, as love itself, the One who loves eternally. It is as well to make all this clear because it reminds us of the mystery of the divine love which transcends all thought, of its divinity which is different from all other love and eternally surpasses all other love, and of the fact that as we have to do with God's being in God's revelation, we have to do with the one true love to which all other love can only bear witness, not of itself, not by an indwelling power of witness, but only because our creaturely loving is confronted in God's revelation with this one true love, and that we, who love as creatures, are claimed in God's revelation as the objects of this divine, this one, true loving.

This, then, is the particular actuality of the being of God, the content of that which we have previously described in its form as God's acting and living. This is the nature of God disclosed in the revelation of His name. God loves. He loves as only He can love. His loving is itself the blessing which as the One who loves He communicates to the loved. His loving is itself the ground of His loving. His loving has its aim and its purpose in itself. His loving in the turning of the One who loves to a loved different from Himself is an overflowing of the loving with which God is blessed in Himself. This is how God loves. And genuinely and properly this is how only God loves. And this loving is God's being in time and eternity. " God is " means " God loves." Whatever else we may have to understand and acknowledge in relation to the divine being, it will always have to be a definition of this being of His as the One who loves. All our further insights about who and what God is must revolve round this mystery—the mystery of His loving. In a certain sense they can only be repetitions and amplifications of the one statement that "God loves." Even in the question of the mystery of God to be raised in the third sub-section, we cannot for a moment lose sight of the fact that we have to speak of God's loving, of the mystery of that loving, and of its difference and particularity as God's loving. The consideration of the mystery of His freedom cannot lead us in any other direction. It cannot lead us to another god who is not the One who loves. We must also focus on this same centre when we come to discuss the doctrine of the attributes of God, and we try to find a common explanation of the divine loving as such and the divine freedom as such. Everything will depend on our not losing the basic definition that we have now found, that God is the One who loves. What follows must all be in fact a development of this basic definition.

Before we proceed, however, alongside this basic definition of the divine being, we have to repeat and underline a definition on which we touched in a general way, as then required, in the first sub-section but which must now be made more express and exact than it was there. In the light of the definition of His being as a being in act we described God as a person. We must now show, from the closer definition of the divine act, that this was not an arbitrary postulate (from the concept of an act as distinct from that of a mere happening). The One who (in His own way) loves us, who (in His own way) seeks and creates fellowship between Himself and us, also informs us what a person is, in that (in His own way! not as if we knew of ourselves what it is, but in such a way that we now come to recognise it for the first time) He acts as a person. The definition of a person—that is, a knowing, willing, acting I—can have the meaning only of a confession of the person of God declared in His revelation, of the One who loves and who as such (loving in His own way) is *the* person. God is what man in himself never is, what man himself can only understand as he looks to Him, admitting that of himself he does not know what he means when he says it. Man is not a person, but he becomes one on the basis that he is loved by God and can love God in return. Man finds what a person is when he finds it in the person of God and his own being as a person in the gift of fellowship afforded him by God in person. He is then (in his own way as creature) a person wholly and exclusively in the fellowship of Him who (in His way as Creator) is it in Himself. Therefore to be a person means really and fundamentally to be what God is, to be, that is, the One who loves in God's way. Not we but God is I. For He alone is the One who loves without any other good, without any other ground, without any other aim, without any other blessedness than what He has in Himself, and who as He does so is Himself and as such can confront another, a Thou. Without being limited or bound by this other, He can be this other's

limit and bound, the very ground of his being, and in such a way
that He can meet this other on his side as a Thou, and can be understood and addressed by this other as Thou. He is therefore capable
of fellowship—capable of fellowship on the basis of His own power
and act, capable of fellowship and capable of achieving fellowship in
Himself and without the need of this other, but at the same time
capable of fellowship and capable of achieving fellowship with reference to this other. This means really and fundamentally to be I.
The being and therefore the loving of God has alone this character of
being I.

For "such self-determination . . . is the completest self-affirmation; such
activity complete self-activity, complete life in which the subject, its own being
and life, coincides with the determination and activity of others, so that life
proceeds from life, life produces and creates life" (Cremer, *op. cit.*, p. 21).

For this reason the original and proper knowing and willing and
doing that distinguishes an I from an It, and an act from a mere
happening, is the property and the prerogative, not of the human,
but of the divine being as the One who loves. It is only the divine
loving that truly knows, truly wills and truly acts, because in it the
knowing and willing subject, its object, and the seeking and creating
of fellowship with it, are one, quite irrespective of the existence of
another different from itself, and as such they are the ground of
existence of this other and the definition of its relationship to this
other. Thus to know, to will, and to act like God as the One who
loves in Himself and in His relationship to His creation means (in
confirmation of His I-ness) to be a person. God is a person in this
way, and He alone is a person in this way. He is the real person and
not merely the ideal. He is not the personified but the personifying
person—the person on the basis of whose prior existence alone we
can speak (hypothetically) of other persons different from Him. When
He meets us in His revelation as the One who loves, He meets us as
the One who is unique.

What do we know of our own selfhood before God has given us His name, and
named us by our name ? What do we know of what it means to say Thou
before God has named us in this way, and in thanks and praise and prayer we
for our part have called Him Thou ? What do we know of what speaking
means before God has spoken with us ? or what hearing means, before we have
heard God ? or what acting means, before God in Jesus Christ has been manifested
as the One who acts for us ? or what suffering means, before God, and He again
in Jesus Christ, is known as the One Who suffers for us ? or what might and lordship are, without the recognition of His might and His lordship in His Word ?
We are thinking and speaking only in feeble images and echoes of the person of
God when we describe man as a person, as an individual. Consciously or unconsciously it is thanks to the love of God in His revelation that we can describe man
in this way, and consciously or unconsciously it is not the being of man, but the
being of God as the One who loves, i.e., the reflection of God in men unfolded by
His Word, which there confronts us as reality.

The One, the person, whom we really know as a human person, is the person of Jesus Christ, and even this is in fact the person of God the Son, in which humanity, without being or having itself a person, is caught up into fellowship with the personality of God. This one man is therefore the being of God making itself known to us as the One who loves.

It is not the case then—and this is the decisive result of the whole consideration—that we have to blush when we adopt the language of Scripture and talk of God, not in abstract terms as the "highest good" or the "absolute" or "omnipotence" or "omniscience" and the like, but personally as One who is all these things as the knowing, willing and acting I; when in fact we take the metaphor "God is love" and as in 1 John 4 we understand it personally: He is the One who loves. This personal way in which Scripture speaks is not in any way childish or naive or anthropomorphic (or at least it is no more so than all the terms and concepts we use in the service of faith and proclamation on the basis of and in obedience to God's revelation). The personal way in which Holy Scripture speaks corresponds absolutely and exclusively to the fact that God is not something, but someone, the One from whom man merely holds in fee the possibility of being one himself. We have to blush (because then we are talking with false childlikeness, immaturity and impropriety) only if words again slip out in which we do not reckon with the personality of God or do not take it seriously.

But again, it is not the case that this manner of speech stands under the proviso that it is allowed or even commanded us as an element of our anthropomorphic manner of expression, but that we have to remember that beyond this manner of expression of ours God is not really one person but one thing, e.g., the impersonal absolute, the highest good, the world-spirit or world-cause or the like. The fact that in knowing God we cannot comprehend Him because we know Him only as men and not as He knows Himself, has nothing whatever to do with a proviso of this kind (according to which the esoteric claims finally to know Him as He knows Himself). If we know God only in a human way, even in this limit we know Him on the basis of His revelation as the One He is. He is the One who loves, surpassing all our concepts and ideas of love, but still the One who truly loves, and therefore One—person. As One, as person, He surpasses all our concepts and ideas of person, but still He reveals what one, a person, really and truly is. We are therefore allowed and commanded within the limits of what is human to speak the truth when we speak of Him as the One, as personal; the truth, beyond which there is no greater, because in the mystery of His ways which we cannot unravel, God is none other than the One as whom He has made Himself manifest and comprehensible to us in His revelation.

Finally it is not the case that this application of the personal manner of speech to God means the recognition of a paradox in the nature of God that we cannot unravel, because on the one hand we must necessarily understand God as the impersonal absolute, but at the same time (and in unavoidable logical contradiction to this) we must also understand Him as person. In this connexion we must notice that the paradox of the nature of God that we cannot unravel is not in any sense that of a logical tension between two concepts which we can perceive and control as such, as if we knew what " absolute " is on the one hand and " personality " on the other, as if the difficulty consisted only in bringing both together, and as if God's reality were just the overcoming of this difficulty. No: the (to us) inexplicable paradox of the nature of God is the fact that He is primarily and properly all that our terms seeks to mean, and yet of themselves cannot mean, that He has revealed Himself to us in His original and proper being, thus remaining incomprehensible to us even in His revelation, yet allowing and commanding us to put our concepts into the service of knowledge of Him, blessing our obedience, being truly known by us within our limits. It is the paradox of the combination of His grace and our lost condition, not the paradox of the combination of two for us logically irreconcilable concepts. Recognising the true, divine paradox, we shall not see together or put together God's personal-ness and God's absolute-ness in the way that we are often forced to do, with and without logical contradictions, when we describe created realities, but we shall hold to the fact that God has revealed Himself to us as He who He is, that is, as the One who loves and therefore as One—person. There is, then, nothing that we can say to this (whether logically compatible or incompatible). Fixing all our attention on its unique particularity we can say only the one thing with all that it involves—that He is the One. We can say it only in such a way that it corresponds to what He has said to us already in His Word, which will do justice, of course, to what may be truly signified by the " absolute." But we cannot say it as if the truth that He is the One seems to be dialectically delimited and completed by the fact that He is " absolute," as if in order to describe God we must dilate on His personality and His absoluteness in a kind of vacuum, as if God is truly and properly God only in the dialectical conquest of this antithesis. He is God (within the limitations of our human knowledge) as the One who (in His own way) loves, and therefore as the One, and He is all that He is inasmuch as He is this One : not subsequently in His being as the one thing, not in a simultaneity as the one person and the one thing, nor yet in a synthesis beyond this antithesis, but simply inasmuch as (in His own way) He is the One.

From this standpoint we can survey the discussion of the personality of God which has played such a prominent part in the theology of the 19th century and to some extent of the 20th as well.

Its origin is to be found deep down in the doctrine of God of the time of orthodoxy, and even of the Middle Ages. We have already mentioned the common practice in this doctrine of placing the doctrine of the Trinity after the development of a concept of the nature and attributes of God in general. This arrangement led to the temptation of speaking of God apart from His revelation and therefore apart from His being as the One who loves, on the basis of a free appraisal of what can be called divine. The result was an involuntary movement away from the school of Scripture into that of heathen antiquity. The nature of God was defined as a neuter furnished with every conceivable superlative, as the *ens perfectissimum* and the *summum bonum*, which as such, as the *actus purus* of the spirit, is also the *primum movens*. And it was no easy matter to bring together the concept of the existence of this *Deus unus* and that of the biblical *Deus triunus*. The presupposition that this God was one person, not one thing, but all things as the One, was clear and effective in the Reformers and tacitly self-evident in their successors, but it had no real basis and no prominent place in all this older doctrine of God, either from the concept of nature and attributes already mentioned, or even from the doctrine of the Trinity. Indeed, the doctrine of the Trinity only gave rise to further obscurity. For the more the term *persona* (*modus subsistentiae*, manner of being) came to be equated with a " person " (in our meaning of the word) and therefore (in complete contradiction to the intentions of the trinitarian doctrine of the Early Church) the more the idea gained currency of three personalities in God, the less could the being of God be understood as the One who loves, and therefore as the One, in terms of the one life of the threefold God in His revelation and in Himself. In this situation theology was assailed by the inrush of the so-called Enlightenment, the product of the rising anthropology of the new age, with its reduction of the idea of God to the eternal truth of the theoretical and practical aesthetic ideas of human reason, or in the last resort to this parental reason as such (thought of as hypostatised). It was fairly easy to re-recognise this image supposedly identical with the Godhead in the orthodox doctrine of the nature and attributes of God, or to interpret this older doctrine of God according to the measure of this image. For essentially constructed according to the directions of heathen antiquity, what else was it but a hypostatisation of the world of ideas, or of the idea of all ideas, which may just as well and perhaps better be named reason rather than God.

This equation or inversion is, of course, the work of the Idealism of the turn of the 18th and 19th centuries, which appeared to supersede but in reality crowned and completed the Enlightenment. It is from the theological school which made this stimulus most consistently its own, viz., that centred on Hegel, that there came the first conscious and express attack against the idea of the personality of God, which the older theology of the Enlightenment, not yet conscious of the extent of its method of reduction, or not yet intellectually and morally mature, had on the whole failed to do, in spite of the constant accompaniment of Spinozism. If God is in reality only the highest idea, or the origin of all theoretical and practical aesthetic ideas, or " the spirit," if we know Him as we know this spirit, and in it the source of all rationality, and in this the absolute or the highest good of men, it is very hard to see why and how He can and may be One, why and how He can and may be person. What a person is, was now thought to be known from the knowledge of self as person. Person is the individual manifestation of the spirit, its individualisation, which as such is limited, but contingently necessary. How, then, could God be a person ? The esoteric or explicit meaning of this question was : How could God be limited ? How does the infinity of the spirit tally with the finiteness that is prescribed for it with the concept of personality ? *Omnis determinatio est negatio* was echoed in every kind of tone from Spinoza. Personality means a *determinatio*, and therefore a *negatio* incompatible with the absolute. Thus the absolute or God cannot be personality. " As persons we know and feel ourselves only in our difference from other similar persons outside ourselves, from whom we differentiate ourselves, that is, as finite ; in this realm of finitude, and fashioned for it, the concept of personality logically seems to lose every meaning apart from this, and a nature which has no other like itself outside itself seems unable to be a person. To speak of a personal God or a divine personality seems from this point of view to be a combination of ideas, one of which in the last resort excludes and supplants the other. Personality is a self-contained self-hood over against another which it differentiates from itself ; absoluteness is the uncontained and unlimited which excludes from itself nothing but the exclusiveness inherent in the concept of personality. Absolute personality is a *non ens* which we cannot even conceive." (D. F. Strauss, *Die christliche Glaubenslehre*, Vol. 1, 1840, pp. 504 f.) "The concept of personality cannot be taken up by a finite spirit in such a way as to be abstracted thereby from the moment of finitude. Personality is rather the specific form of subsistence of the human spirit as finite, on which the sensuous basis of subsistence constructs both for the form and for the content of personality a constitutive moment . . . The assertion of the personality of God is thus only the shibboleth of a still imaginative Theism. This notion is, however, to be lifted by strict thought into the pure concept of the absolute spirit that is alone adequate for God, which presupposes no finite existence in God Himself, but which is in His being in Himself the absolute pre-supposition for the totality of all finite existence" (A. E. Biedermann, *Chr. Dog.*, 1869, p. 639). That reflection on the nature of " personality," and the conditions which are indispensable for its rise and continuance, make it impossible to speak of a " personality of God," is still asserted with great force by H. Lüdemann (*Chr. Dog.*, Vol. 2, 1926, p. 168).

It is to be observed that this critique was able to invest itself with the form of an almost Calvinistic and puritanical concern for the purity and pre-eminence of the thought of God over against its confusion with a (or rather with *the*) fundamental self-determination of man. Nor is it possible to doubt the subjective sincerity in this respect of the battle waged by the Hegelians. Not without the collusion of the older orthodoxy, there had been an emergence and penetration of confusion between the idea of God and the idea of spirit generally. And this had become so incontestably self-evident through the classical Idealism of the philosophico-theological thinkers of the 19th century that even the acutest exponents of Christian doctrine—even a theologian like Biedermann, who undoubtedly in his day strove honestly and with great and penetrating scholarship to evolve a Church tradition that would without doubt build up and not destroy the Church in the modern situation—were not capable of the insight that by the glorification of an absolute spirit they served a God who, measured by the biblical revelation, was alien, and who indeed, measured by the same standard, was not divine but created. Since they did not know any other god than this (at least as theologians), it necessarily remained hidden from them that it was extremely logical to deny this god personality, and that this logical consistency merely proved they had completely lost sight of the object of an Evangelical theology. The absolute spirit which had become the object of their theology was in fact not person and could not be thought of as such. In this they were quite right in their defence against all their less consistent opponents. As a result of the prejudice arising from this confusion and therefore arising from the true nature of their whole approach, they could not, of course, see the esoteric or implicit meaning of the question—How could God be person ? Thus they were unable to assert the decisive reason why their God could not be a person. For indeed, why does the absoluteness and infinity which is predicated of this God necessarily cause the very idea of personality to appear as the essence of finitude and therefore exclude it ? The explanation—and surely there is a powerful positive pathos hidden behind what seem to be the purely negative assertions of these theologians—is that in their thinking the place where they should speak earnestly, genuinely and realistically of personality was already occupied, and in fact solemnly and conclusively occupied, so that the claim could not be allowed a second time. If personality was self-evidently denied to what was conceived and described as " God," it was no less self-evidently attributed to the subject of this conception and description, namely, to the conceiving, describing man. What did it matter that in distinction to its " God " this subject was referred to the sphere and manner of finitude, if at the same time it was decked with this predicate, if it was understood as the subject which is always capable of itself of conceiving and describing the absolute spirit, the supreme good, infinite being ? The subject which has the merit and the power of being subject of this predicate—does it not fulfil the concept of personal being, the nature of the true I ? Is it not the true knowing and willing I ? What difference does finitude make to it, if it stands in this relation to the infinite, with such creativeness, direction and control, if the infinite as such is obviously the predicate of the finite subject ? The infinite, the God who is subject to his control in this way, obviously cannot be in any way unsettling, menacing or critical, in spite of the subject's finitude. Behind and above His whole infinity there towers all the time the comforting certainty that the finite being itself, as subject of this infinite predicate, is undoubtedly the person at work, supreme in thought and definition over this infinite. This work must obviously abide by only one rule if the finite subject is to remain secure. Under no circumstances may the predicate be conceived or described as the subject (in the same, or perhaps in a basically superior sense, as compared with the human subject), and therefore under no circumstances may God be conceived or described as person. This would be an admission that God's infinity is His own and not that of man. It would involve a denial and abandonment of the presupposition that God is the content of the human concept of reason. It would mean a serious calling in question of that which is based solely on human self-consciousness, and therefore of the final reality of human personality. Man would be finally stripped of his own creative role in relation to the visible and the invisible, and therefore to all things. This was what must never under any circumstances be allowed to happen according to the most sacred convictions of the generations cradled in the Enlightenment, Romanticism and classical Idealism. The predication of God as personality was necessarily for them the absurdity of which no philosopher or theologian must under any circumstances be guilty. For this predication meant an end of the predicating subject. This predication could not meaningfully be understood as a predication at all, but only as the recognition of something which precedes all human predication, as the end of the control under which the neutral infinite so comfortably contemplates and governs itself as man's own infinite, realising itself in the act of his finite personal being. This was the end of all things, which was not allowed to come to pass. The whole advance of the new age, embraced in the equation of God and the idea of reason, was a defence against the destroying of human self-consciousness through the reality or even the mere possibility of a divine self-consciousness materially different. In this destruction there could be discerned only an inrush of primitive barbarity into the preserve of the newly discovered and already self-evident " religion within the limits of pure reason." On these grounds, therefore, the Hegelian theologians necessarily had to deny firmly and strenuously the personality of God. In this position they were very experienced and from their own standpoint rightly vigilant apologists of the neo-Christian Church which since 1700 had begun more consciously and decisively to come together and consolidate. They knew the true enemy and the danger involved. Only from this point of view is their opposition to the personality of God really intelligible. It was irresistibly powerful because it moved in purely analytical statements, because it merely repeated the so-to-speak commonly held presupposition that man is the person who, thinking the idea of his reason, has the power to think God, and that for this reason, and in confirmation of it, God is to be thought of as absolute and infinite, but cannot under any circumstances be thought of as person and therefore as the superior rival of man. On the premises of the Enlightenment, Romanticism and Idealism this opposition to the personality of God cannot be avoided, because it is absolutely vital. If we begin with this equation, willingly and wittingly or not we have already contested the fact that God is a person, and we cannot later recant. For with this equation we have attributed true and proper personality to man as the subject of the idea of reason, thus taking the step which necessarily brings us into insoluble contradiction with belief in the personal God.

The weakness in all the modern vindications of this belief is that they have taken up their position on the same premises as their opponents, namely, on the equation which their opponents must necessarily hold. Naturally, there has been no lack of answers to the suggestions of the Hegelian theologians. Ought not personality to be ascribed to God for the very reason that man describes the truest and the best of his own existence with this concept, and therefore has to complete with it his final, supreme and indeed decisive predications of the absolute spirit ? H. Siebeck has argued it in this way. The inner development of man comes up against a climax which consists in his knowing himself as a unit over against the world—on the one side as part, on the other side as the centre of the world. Understanding himself in this latter sense, he can regard the world as the means of his self-preservation and self-participation. Indeed, personality sees its moral uniqueness as founded on the basis of the world-whole ; the world must be planned for the emergence of personality. And therefore the idea of God must be constructed on the analogy of personality (*Lehrb. der Rel. Phil.*, 1893, pp. 168 f.). " The essence of the personal is projected from experience into the transcendent " (*op. cit.*, p. 363). Siebeck indeed conceded that all the marks of empirical personality, when directed to an absolute essence, incur the loss of their discursive conceivability. But he thought he could set his mind at rest about this by the consideration that without the true personality of God all religious history would have to be explained away as an illusion, and by the specially attractive assertion that all powerful spiritual movements of history have always been born out of the rich depths of the life of particular, spiritually strong personalities (*op. cit.*, pp. 364 f.). H. Lotze argued similarly : " No other form of being than that of personality can satisfy (or even be considered for the purpose) the longing of the soul to grasp as reality the highest which it is given to sense." So firmly is it convinced that living, self-possessing and self-enjoying individuality is the imperative precondition and the only possible source of every good and all good things, so much is it filled by secret disdain of all apparently lifeless existence, that we always find embryo religion in its myth-forming beginnings busy transfiguring natural reality into spiritual : it has never on the other hand felt any need to bring spiritual life back to blind reality as a more solid base " (*Mikrokosmos* [3], Vol. 3, 1880, p. 563 f.). In the same way R. Rothe has explained that it is " a narrow-minded delusion to think that we must regard the blessed God as so superior that He must be denied everything that constitutes the peculiar excellences of human nature " (*Ethik*, Vol. 1, 1867, p. 122). Again, A. Ritschl could say that the recognition of the personality of God discloses " the value which religion asserts for the human spiritual life " (*Rechtf. u. Vers.* [1] Vol. 3, 1874, p. 173). It is clear from all these considerations that they have a common hypothesis with those who deny the personality of God, namely, that God is to be understood as the content of the highest human values. But on this common ground they cannot hold their own against the criticism levelled from the other side.

For one thing, they are *technically* impossible. If it is not to be denied or superseded, infinity of spirit or good or being, so far as these are thought of as the content of a human idea, does not tolerate any other finitude than that which is proper to the subject of this idea as such, but which must therefore be thought of as necessarily superseded in the predicate of this subject and therefore denied. If the absolute is the absolute of human idea, the concept of an

" absolute personality " has to be described with Strauss (*op. cit.*, p. 505) as nonsense, or with Biedermann (*op. cit.*, p. 643) as a *contradictio in adiecto*. For it constantly gives to the predicate the creative finitude which as such can only belong to the subject. The subject will then be defended only too self-evidently against the threatened competition with an eagerness for the purity of its predicate, and it will be all too easily demonstrated that it ill becomes the mark of the subject to be elevated to the predicate. We cannot very well proceed, as Lotze wanted, by first reducing the antithesis of Ego and non-Ego, which constitutes human personality, to the antithesis of the spirit to its manifestations (even though these arise at the instigation of an external world of reality), and then turning round and postulating an unlimited spirit which, being " itself everything that is," does not need any such external cause to be in perpetual activity and therefore to be personality. " When we describe the inner life of the personal God, the current of His thoughts, His feelings, His will, as one which is eternal and without beginning, never at rest, and never excited to movement from any stationary position, we demand of our power of imagination no greater task than is sought of it by any materialistic or pantheistic viewpoint " (Lotze, *op. cit.*, pp. 569-80 : *Grundzüge der Rel. Phil.*[3], 1894, pp. 39-43). That materialistic and pantheistic views claim the power of the imagination in all sorts of ways is cold comfort in view of the dilemma in which we find ourselves in regard to this vindication of the personal God. For it is not clear whether the absolute is absorbed by personality, or personality by the absolute, or perhaps each by the other. The reader is left in a complete fog with regard to the really vital question whether, in spite of assurances to the contrary, he is not confronted here by a materialistic or pantheistic viewpoint. It was a bad omen for the prospects of modern Protestant theology that (from Rothe to Ritschl and in part even to the present day) it found this Lotzian vindication of the personality of God particularly masterly and helpful.

Secondly, this vindication, and the similar attempts of his associates, had the fatal peculiarity that they exposed the distinctively postulatory character of the whole modern doctrine of God in what is undoubtedly a very compromising way. As L. Feuerbach wrote, long before Lotze and Siebeck : " Theology is anthropology, i.e., in the object of religion which we call in Greek *Theos*, in English God, there expresses itself nothing other than the nature of man ; or, the God of mankind is nothing other than the deified nature of man " (*Das Wesen der Religion*, 1848, Lecture 3). " Christianity reproached heathenism for idolatry, Protestantism reproached Catholicism, or early Christianity, for idolatry, and Rationalism now reproaches Protestantism, at least the older orthodox Protestantism, for idolatry, because it worships a man as God, and therefore an image of God—for that is what man is—in place of the original, in place of real being. But I go further and say : Rationalism itself, indeed, every religion and every cult which sets up a God, i.e., an unreal being, a being different and separated from real nature, the real being of man, and which makes it an object of worship, is the worship of images and consequently idolatry . . . For God did not create man in His image, as the Bible has it, but, as I have shown in *Das Wesen des Christentums*, man created God after his image. And even the rationalist, the so-called believer in thought and reason, creates the god whom he worships in his image ; the living archetype, the original of the rationalist god is the rationalist man. Every god is a being of the imagination, an image and in fact an image of man, but an image which man places over against himself, and imagines as an independent being " (*op. cit.*, Lect. 20). " Because for the Christian the spirit, the feeling, thinking, willing being, is his highest being and his ideal, he makes it also his first being, i.e., he changes his spirit into an objective, existing outside him, and different from him. . . . Is the eternal spirit not just the spirit of man desiring to be eternal, complete ? . . . Does not man wish to be free from the confines of the flesh ? does he not wish to be omniscient, omnipotent, omnipresent ? Therefore is not this god, is not this spirit, the realised desire of man to be eternal spirit ? Have we not, therefore, objectivised even in this god the nature of man ? . . . Is, therefore, their god, their eternal spirit, anything other than the image and pattern of what they themselves want to become, the original and copy of their own nature as it is to be unfolded in the future ? . . . The eternal spirit is nothing but the generic concept of the spirit which is symbolised as an independent being by the power of imagination at the command of human wishes and human impulses towards happiness " (*op. cit.*, Lect. 28). We can see how here the mystery of the modern doctrine of God— that the being of God is the predicate of the human subject—was long ago care-lessly exploded by a philosopher who derived from the school of Idealism, but was no longer interested in the Church. We may well wonder that his objection did not make more impression on those who denied the personality of God in so far as he also and particularly attacked their positive assertions. But we must wonder even more how its defenders, with their references to the longing of the human heart, the infinite value of human personality, the import of the history of religion, the meaning of personality in spiritual and world history, with their quite open and express projection of human self-consciousness into the transcendent, could expose themselves so openly to this objection of Feuerbach without apparently taking any account of its existence. It was of little value to the cause advanced that the character of the newer theology as a higher anthropology could be silenced and suppressed, as was thought possible by an ecclesiastically-minded modern like Biedermann. But it was unparalleled naivete that it should be shouted abroad as was done, not by the decriers, but by the protagonists of the personality of God. The only possible result was to make more suspect the statement which they wanted to advocate, and indeed, to compromise with this addition the whole common doctrine of God as eternal spirit.

But let us suppose that their attempt had not been vitiated by its technical impracticability. Let us suppose the real possibility of distinguishing it from a self-admission of the illusion of the modern doctrine of God. Let us suppose that it had genuinely proved what it set out to prove, namely, that the eternal spirit, rightly equated with God, is as such also person, therefore itself subject, the knowing and willing I in real difference from the human I. Let us suppose that we are really prepared to venture this predication of the supreme being (the consistency with which even Lotze was prepared to do it is not beyond question). Granted these things, how very disloyal we are to the whole intention of the modern doctrine of God ! What perspectives we open up in relation to the human subject as the ostensible measure of all things when we do not oppose to it the neutral absolute which can be leisurely surveyed and mastered, but a divine I endowed with this absoluteness ! If we concede the personality of God, we are flagrantly guilty of the absurdity which means the invasion of the sanctity of the unity of life which binds God and the world together in man, thus involving the end of the modern self-consciousness with which it was hoped to unite the Christian faith, and indeed to represent and commend the Christian faith as its deepest wisdom. Only the dullness and the stupidity of the thought-processes of these protagonists of the personality of God could hinder the onset of this end of all things. If anyone had suddenly taken seriously the matter with which at bottom Lotze and Siebeck only played, if anyone had once begun to think of God and speak of God to the effect that God as such was the true, speaking, acting person, if anyone had done this (and it could not happen other-wise), not on the basis of speculative considerations, but on the basis that God is actually present in His revelation, there would have been achieved in the eighties and nineties of the 19th century the fundamental disturbance at any rate of theological, and in that way indirectly of philosophical and, again indir-ectly, of general thinking, which would have taken from the development self-evidently adopted and continued from the 18th century its self-evident character. This did not happen. The reaction represented by Lotze and others could not be effectively dangerous to the modern self-consciousness because it shared its hypotheses. It could actually have been a danger, but the time was not ripe, and therefore it could not have any historical success. But we cannot, of course, deny that in its total weakness it was objectively a symptom of the fact that, although contrary to the prevailing doctrine and irreconcilable with its basic hypotheses, the recollection of the biblical concept of God had not disappeared altogether. Its influence was still felt even within the (to it) strange surroundings of modern anthropological thought, and by this curious detour *via* the concept of human personality.

The fact that the problem remained in spite of their own intentions and systematisation had to be admitted in a most extraordinary way even by the two classical antagonists of the personality of God, Strauss and Biedermann, to the detriment of the clarity and logic of their position. The result was that at the apex of their critique they both showed leanings to a certain compromise. The exposition of Strauss (*op. cit.*, pp. 523 f.) concludes with the statement that God is not just " general substance " to whose being the self-insertion of person-ality does not belong. He is certainly not a person beside and above others. But He is "the eternal movement of the general, continually making itself subject, achieving objectivity and true reality only in the subject, and in so doing abolishing the subject in its abstract self-hood." As eternal personality, He allows that which is other than Himself, nature, to proceed from Himself, so that it can return to Himself as self-conscious spirit. His personality must not be thought of as individual personality but as comprehensive personality. Instead of personifying the absolute, we must learn to understand it as that which eternally personifies itself. When Strauss says this, is he really saying anything different from what Lotze later thought he was saying *against* him ? It is true that with this perversion of the Hegelian doctrine of the Trinity he did not even remotely attain the biblical concept of the personal God, but directly denied it. It is also true that with this " comprehensive personality " he destroyed his own technical concept (he had already defined the absolute so as to exclude irrevocably the concept of personality). But these facts cannot allow us to overlook how strongly and openly in his thought another conception of the nature of God was at work, one which rested on different presuppositions and asserted itself contrary to his intentions. This actual and involuntary com-pulsion of the problem can be seen even more clearly in the case of Biedermann (*op. cit.*, p. 645 f.). After an exemplary proof that the concept of an " absolute personality " must necessarily disintegrate into its several parts, the one necessarily excluding the other, he goes on in this astonishing way. It is still legitimate to postulate an absolute personality. Indeed : " If we think of God rightly and fully as absolute spirit, then, if we can conceive of Him at all, we can do so only as absolute personality." The pantheistic images of a life-force or world-soul poured out through the universe are inadmissible according to Biedermann. God is absolute spirit and therefore impersonal in concept ; but He is absolute personality in our conception, in the " intercommunication of religion " which " goes on between the infinite and the finite spirit within the finite human spiritual life, and which therefore must reach its final conclusion in the form of the latter." Obviously, this proviso is no compensation for the damaging, or indeed the removal, of the biblical concept of God by the previous denial of the personality of God. No compensation is possible on the basis of the modern anthropological presupposition, because the presupposition itself is ultimately responsible. The God who speaks and acts and therefore exists in His revelation is as little to be recognised in the " representation " of Biedermann (whatever its content, and however biblically filled out) as in the gnosticising picture which Strauss finally thought he could sketch positively as the nature of God. The reason for this is that ultimately and irrevocably the " representation " of Biedermann can be only a representation. It can have only subjective truth. This " only " makes Biedermann's doctrine of God ecclesiastically untenable, in spite of the concession with which it finishes. Whatever else He may be, the God who, though He may be person in subjective truth, is in objective truth not person but an impersonal absolute is not to be compared with the God of the biblical revelation. Moreover, in the case of Biedermann we must seriously ask whether by this concession he has not destroyed his own technical concept to the point of unrecognisability. For can the distinction between concept and representation be substantiated in such a way that under the term concept there is described the comprehension of objective truth, under the term representation that of a merely subjective truth, the two being mutually related as higher and lower steps of the same perception ? How is this distinction to be made ? And supposing it is, how is the relationship to be achieved ? Can even the purest concept be more than a representation purified as far as possible from all intuitive evidence, a representation made as mathematical as can be ? To what extent in the concept are we really on a higher step of the knowledge of truth ? And does not the naive representation have necessarily in itself something of the value and pretension of the concept ? To what extent in the representation are we really on a lower step of truth ? The difference between concept and representation can at best be only a difference of clarity ; and how often must the question be asked whether the representation does not enjoy a higher degree of clarity than the concept ? On the other hand, if the difference is maintained on the basis of a particular theory of knowledge, like the difference between objective and subjective knowledge of truth, how can we relate the two as stages in the same knowledge and therefore, e.g., say of the same object that here it cannot possibly have a certain predicate, and there it must of necessity have it ? How do we come to speak of stages in the knowledge of truth instead of a contradiction of true knowledge against false and false against true ? If, however, either the distinction or the relationship cannot be properly sustained, if there is either only a knowledge directed one way or another at the one truth, or only the contradiction between true and false perception, Biedermann has to reply to the whole might of his own critique if he wants to explain the concept of " absolute personality " as impossible on the level of concept, and yet cling to it on the level of representation. Either there must be conflict on the level of representation, or there must be a solution of the conflict on the level of concept. A third course is possible only if there is a double truth—which Biedermann did not want to maintain. It is remarkable enough that with their concession Strauss and Biedermann were untrue to their own systematisation. It is even more remarkable that in working it out they did exactly the same thing—and against the background of their preceding critique they did it even more impressively—as philosophers who attempted directly to recover the personality of God. Contrary to the intention of the whole of the modern doctrine of God, according to their own understanding and admission the problem of the personality of God as such obviously could not actually be denied—the very problem that they wished to deny by raising the question. With all the energy of the idealistic reduction and cleansing of the concept of God, with all the power of the desire that lay behind it to defend the human subject against the superior competition that threatened it from the side of the personality of God, they were not actually in a position completely to ignore the fact that, whether they liked it or not, the concept of God had once meant more, and in the Bible which they still read still meant more, than this sum of human ideas and the eternity which belongs to it as such. If with these conscious concessions they attained as little the concept of God as the contemporary defenders of the personality of God, the fact that even as opponents of the personality of God they ultimately made these conscious concessions bore witness to the fact that the biblical concept of God had not actually disappeared, but that it was always present as a question and a threat, as an error to which justice must somehow be done.

There was, then, a constant vacillation between the intention of this concept of God and the modern doctrine of God, or that of pagan antiquity. The one was affirmed, but there was obviously no ability or desire to sustain it. The other was rejected as untrue, yet its presence had still to be taken into account. There was error, but continual hesitation in error. The error was begun, but the aberration could not be completed. And all this goes to show, as so often in Neo-Protestantism, that it is easy enough to raise trouble and disturbance in the Church by introducing new teaching, but not so easy to break up the Church by raising a consistent counter-doctrine and therefore a counter-Church. Neo-Protestantism in the 18th and 19th centuries certainly tried to lead the Church back to a renewed paganism. But it is self-evident that it did not have the power even to set about this attempt with ultimate seriousness, let alone to see it through. To-day, perhaps, it is to be regarded as an interlude—comparable with Marcionism in the Early Church. There is, therefore, no more point now in being as angry with its champions as we sometimes are when we lose sight of the inner weakness of the whole affair. If we know that we cannot accept what is even in the orthodox doctrine of God the customary transposition of the divine being into a neutral absolute, to an anthropocentricity which is secretly at work in response to the revelation of God, we are not forced into this unhappy state of vacillation. If we can abandon the dialectic to which it necessarily gives rise with all its inconsistencies and illogicalities, if we need not feel coerced by it, then we cannot show too much anger against those who are imprisoned in this dialectic. The dispute about the personality of God then becomes a historical matter. As such it is no doubt very interesting, exciting and informative. But it is still merely historical.

We conclude with two terminological elucidations. The first is that in this context everything depends on the statement that God is the One who loves. But nothing at all depends on the statement that He is or He has personality. The second statement is unknown both to the Bible and to primitive and Reformation dogma. It emerged only when the right and important thing that is meant by it began to be problematical on the grounds that we have discussed. It became a battle-cry attacked by the one side and championed by the other. Taken by itself, however, it does not say the right and important thing that it is meant to say. It can say this only in the context of the statement that God is the One who loves, as the express avowal and affirmation of the fact that God is not something, not a thing, but a person, the One, the speaking and acting Subject, the original and real I. But it is as who He is and therefore as the One who loves that He is this. The concept of personality as such is too colourless to form a necessary basis for our description of this absolutely indispensable moment in the nature of God. We can use it, and shall do so, when the need arises. But we can have no essential interest in the modern debate centred on this concept. We can and must, therefore, concede that we can do without it so long as what is intended in it is assured and accepted. In preaching nothing is to be gained by this concept, and nothing lost. The only thing which matters is that God's Word should be proclaimed as the Word of the One, the One who loves; as the Word of which He Himself as such is the Subject and content; and not as an expression of our own eternity and therefore not as the word of a general, neutral truth or goodness. What will then be proclaimed is not that God is person, but the particular person He is. If this happens, this is all that is needed. And it can and must happen even though the concepts of " personality " and " person " are not employed as such. Secondly, if we accept the concept of the personality of God, we must be conscious of a certain lack of clarity arising from the fact that right up to modern times most people have spoken of divine " persons " in relation to the doctrine of the divine Trinity.

What is meant here is the being of God in the three modes : Father, Son and Holy Spirit. In our treatment of the doctrine of the Trinity we took the view that the concept " person " should be dropped in the description of this matter, because in all classical theology it has never in fact been understood and interpreted in the sense in which we are accustomed to think of the term to-day. The Christian Church has never taught that there are in God three persons and therefore three personalities in the sense of a threefold Ego, a threefold subject. This would be tritheism, which the concept *persona*, understood as *modus subsistentiae*, is in fact meant to avoid. The important and true thing intended by the concept of personality in the modern sense as a description of God is, of course, connected not merely closely, but indissolubly, with the doctrine of the Trinity. Being in Himself Father, Son and Holy Spirit, God is in Himself the One who lives and loves, and therefore One, and therefore the One ; and as we know Him as Father, Son and Holy Spirit, we know Him always as the One who loves, and therefore as the One who meets us, and addresses us and deals with us as Thou. What we can describe as personality is indeed the whole divine Trinity as such, in the unity of the Father, Son and Holy Spirit in God Himself and in His work—not the individual aspects by themselves in which God is and which He has. Not threefold, but thrice—and thrice not in any self-sufficiency of one of the aspects, but in their being with each other and for each other and in each other, in their succession one to another—the one triune God is the One who lives and loves, and therefore One, the One, and therefore, if we want to call it so, personality. There are not three faces of God, but one face ; not three wills, but one will ; not three rights, but one right ; not three Words and works, but one Word and work. The one God is revealed to us absolutely in Jesus Christ. He is absolutely the same God in Himself. This one God as the Triune is—let us say it then—the personal God.

3. THE BEING OF GOD IN FREEDOM

The being of God is His own. His act is His own. His love is His own. In this His being and act God is who He is. After all our previous considerations, we cannot lay too strong an emphasis on this fact in characterising the divine being. But what do we imply by this emphasis ? There are, of course, other beings, other forms of activity ; there are also others who love and other persons. Obviously, when we emphasise that it is of God that we are speaking, we are not distinguishing Him only as when, by the use of the personal demonstrative or possessive pronoun, we distinguish one subject from others of the same class. If we say of God " He," " this," or " His," if in each sentence we give the word God explicitly or implicitly the tone and the weight of meaning that befits it, when we allude to Him distinctively in this way we are also affirming something essential, indeed in some sense the one essential thing that is to be affirmed of Him. His act is in a unique way His act. His love is uniquely His love. He is uniquely who He is. The essential fact that must be affirmed of God consists in the characterisation of the uniqueness of the form and content of His being, and when we distinguish Him from everything else that exists we are necessarily expressing at the same time this essential fact. Already we have found that we could

not properly speak of God's life and love without constantly referring
to the unique mode of His life and love. We speak irrelevantly of
God's life and love if we do not constantly make this distinction and
reference, if we do not constantly look into the depths of the divine
being and keep in view the fact that we have indeed to do with a life
and love, yet not with any life and love, but with the life and love of
God Himself. This object permits and indeed commands us to speak
of a life and love, of a living and loving I, defining, attesting and
proclaiming it. But permitting and commanding us to do so, He
also requires us to understand and name Him beyond all our insights
and ideas as the I who lives and loves in His unique way, to give
Him the honour which cannot even remotely accrue to any but the
living and loving being known to us, but which we must specifically
deny to all other living and loving beings known to us, because it is
properly and originally His honour alone, because we can truly understand all other life, love and being only in virtue of His creation and
therefore as the reflection and echo of His life and love. Only when
we glimpse the depth in which He lives and loves and has His being,
have we truly recognised and understood His being as love and therefore as divine.

We now turn to the question of this depth in the divine being. So
far we have asked and answered it provisionally, but for good or ill
it must now engage our attention directly if our reflection upon the
life of God is not to be incomplete. We must know what we are
thinking and doing when we do not speak of the life and love of God
without reference to their uniqueness, without drawing this vital distinction. We must know what is meant by the special divine character
which is to engage our attention when we make this reference and
this distinction. We must enquire about the determination of the
divine being which makes it necessary for us to study this divine
essence. The difficulty and the doubtfulness of this question are
obvious. As regards its difficulty, how are we even to frame a question concerning the special and distinctive essence of the divine being,
let alone know how to answer it? As regards its doubtfulness, are
we not here necessarily disregarding the revealed being of God and
asking about something else supposedly lying behind it? Must we
not therefore base our answer upon another presupposition, perhaps
that of a presumed universal knowledge of God? We take up at
once the challenge of this second question. This is, of course, the very
thing which must not happen under any circumstances. Even when
we enquire about the special and distinctive element in the life and
love of God, we are not enquiring about the content of a universal
idea of the divine, as though we could glean from this instruction
concerning the special and distinguishing essence of God. We make
our enquiry on the assumption that the object of this universal idea
of God, i.e., of any idea of God formed otherwise than in view of God's

revelation in Jesus Christ, is necessarily other than He who is Lord and salvation, and therefore the object of the faith of the Church and the only true God. We are not trying to discover a characteristic mark of divinity which this God will have in common with other gods. We are not concerned with any idea of the divine under which we will subsume the only true God with other gods. We are well aware that, if we do this, we shall be enquiring in fact not about the idea of God, but, in common with the worshippers of those other gods, about the idea of man, about the sum of his wishes and longings, about the highest embodiment, in absolute form, of our own being. Therefore now as before we do not enquire in disregard of God's revelation, but with our attention concentrated upon it and only upon it.

It is the fundamental weakness of the work of H. Cremer, which we have mentioned more than once and which is so bravely progressive in its basic direction, that formally at least it remains the slave of tradition in that it reckons ultimately with the existence and authoritativeness of an idea of God known also to the heathen, of a universally current predicate of divinity, although this does of course receive its content only through the subject Jesus Christ, the sole true revelation of God, and must therefore be understood and interpreted in the light of this revelation (*op. cit.*, pp. 32 f.). The energy with which Cremer tried to argue this point of view ought not to pass without due appreciation. But is not the biblical message concerning God—even in regard to the predicate of divinity, in regard to what distinguishes God's life and love as His, as divine—much more than a special interpretation of a universal idea of God which the prophets of Yahweh shared with the prophets of Baal, the apostles with the exponents of the mystery religions ? Does not the predicate " divine " as well as the subject " God " belong to that other text which the prophets and apostles and they alone have read ? Has not the predicate become new in the sense that it can be received only in this its newness, and no longer—or only polemically—with reference to its old, universalised significance ?

No change of theme was involved when we spoke first of God's life and then of God's love, first of His being in act and then of His being as the One who loves. It was not as if we knew first and in general of God's life as such and only then provided this generalised subject with its specialised predicate, that it is the life and ruling of love. But God's life itself and as such is in all its depths the loving of God, and only in preparation for this insight, only in development of the prior logical assertion that God is an acting Subject, did we linger for a moment (but in fact only for a moment) to reflect upon God's being in act, which is in no sense act in general but the concrete, specific action of His love. And so, too, when we enquire into the unique and distinctive divinity of God, the characteristic depth of His being, it does not imply the introduction of a new theme, as though we were looking behind the wings of the theatre, as though having answered the question : Who is God ? we could now ask *in abstracto* : What is God ? For as God is not an it but a He, so He is not a He who has first to partake in an it in order to be this He. In God there is no it that is not Himself. There is nothing general that is not His particular being in the uniqueness of its act and therefore its living and loving. Now that we are asking : What is God ? what is His divinity, His distinctive essence as God ? we can only ask again : Who is God ? For He has what He is, not only in Himself and as a concomitant and attribute of His being, but because He is, and is everything that He is. Strictly speaking, there is no divine predicate, no idea of God, which can have as its special content what God is. There is strictly speaking only the divine Subject as such and in Him the fulness of His divine predicates. Properly speaking the idea of God can have only this divine Subject as its content and the divine predicate must be sought only in this Subject as such, outside of which it can have no existence and cannot therefore become the content of an idea. If we now seek to discover what God is, our enquiry will not be presumptuous, foolish and blasphemous only if we at once allow it to be taken out of our hands and rightly framed ; only if we are aware that with the greatest childlikeness, which in this connexion is also the greatest, the only possible profundity, we are again asking : Who is He ? We need only stand on the ground which we took up from the beginning—the question of the reality of God in the actuality of His revelation where He is faithful to Himself and where we are therefore confronted by His being as it is in itself—and the question of the depths of His being, of His unique and distinctive divinity, loses the dubiousness which seems at first to cling to it. Nor in this case need its apparent difficulty cause us any further trouble. It is as difficult (but not more so) as any other question which God's self-revelation raises for us and which we have to answer in the light of it. We can indeed know what we are thinking and doing when we are speaking of God's living and loving as of something distinctive. It is necessary and right and also not impossible for us to be clear about it. We have only to remember that we have to enquire about the distinctiveness of this particular living and loving, not from the point of view of universal criteria and standards, but in view of the reality revealed to us by God Himself.

And we must also recollect that in formulating our question directly we do not approach it empty handed. For we could not complete our consideration of the life and love of God as such without realising at every step the peculiar and distinctive characteristics of this divine living and loving. We understood the being of God as moved, although self-moved, as life living from its own centre. We understood. His loving to be loving for its own sake, an unconditioned, utterly sovereign love, positing its own basis and purpose. Without this more concrete determination, without this characterisation of the uniqueness of His living and loving, we are obviously not speaking of God's living and loving, but of life and love generally, and therefore definitely not of God. We must now take this particular determination as our present point of departure. It was indicated in the title of the section and this third sub-section by the idea of freedom. This does not mean that with this idea we can grasp and exhaust by a long way all that is to be said in answer to our question. It can only suggest the direction in which we are to look. But it can do that. God's being as He who lives and loves is being in freedom. In this way, freely, He lives and loves. And in this way, and in the fact that He lives and loves in freedom, He is God, and distinguishes Himself from everything else that lives and loves. In this way, as the free person, He is distinguished from other persons. He is the one, original and authentic person through whose creative power and will alone all other persons are and are sustained. With the idea of freedom we simply affirm what we would be affirming if we were to characterise God as the Lord. But His lordship is in all circumstances the lordship of His living and loving. Our present question is that of the mode of His lordship and therefore of His living and loving—of the divine characteristics by which, as He who lives and loves, He manifests His sovereignty. This mode is characterised by the fact that it is absolutely God's own, in no sense dictated to Him from outside and conditioned by no higher necessity than that of His own choosing and deciding, willing and doing. If we enquire how, according to His revelation in Jesus Christ, God's lordship differs in its divinity from other types of rule, then we must answer that it is lordship in freedom. It would be senseless to ascribe this characteristic to other kinds of sovereignty, or to any other living and loving but that of God. There are other sovereignties, but freedom is the prerogative of divine sovereignty. Freedom is, of course, more than the absence of limits, restrictions, or conditions. This is only its negative and to that extent improper aspect—improper to the extent that from this point of view it requires another, at least in so far as its freedom lies in its independence of this other. But freedom in its positive and proper qualities means to be grounded in one's own being, to be determined and moved by oneself. This is the freedom of the divine life and love. In this positive freedom of His, God is also unlimited, unrestricted and unconditioned from without. He is the free Creator, the free Reconciler, the free Redeemer. But His divinity is not exhausted in the fact that in His revelation it consists throughout in this freedom from external compulsion : in free utterance and action, free beginning and ending, free judgment and blessing, free power and spirit. On the contrary, it is only manifest in all this. For He has it in Himself quite apart from His relation to another from whom He is free. He in Himself is power, truth and right. Within the sphere of His own being He can live and love in absolute plenitude and power, as we see Him live and love in His revelation.

There is no plainer description of the divinity of God than the phrase which occurs so frequently in the Pentateuch and again in the Book of Ezekiel : " I am the Lord." It is followed hard by that other, analytical phrase : " I am the

Lord your (or thy) God," and it has its exact New Testament parallel in the
"I am" of the Johannine Jesus. It is, of course, obvious that in this biblical
"I am" the Subject posits itself and in that way posits itself as the living and
loving Lord. In doing so, this Subject is God. He who does this is the God of
the Bible. Because He is the One who does so, everything outside Him depends
on His good-pleasure or its opposite. Because of it, His throne is high and lifted
up (Is. 6[1]), being prepared in the heavens by Himself (Ps. 103[19]) above the
cherubim (2 Kg. 19[15]). Because of it His eyes look down upon the earth (Ps. 11[4],
33[13f.], 102[19]). Because of it there is none like Him (Ex. 8[10], 15[11]; Ps. 86[8], 89[8].)
He alone is God and there is no other (Deut. 4[35]; 2 Kg. 19[15]; 1 Chron. 17[20]).
He is the Lord of Lords, the King of Kings (1 Tim. 6[15]; Rev. 17[14], 19[16]). He
is the alpha and the omega, the beginning and the end, the first and the last
(Is. 44[6]; Rev. 1[8, 17], 21[6], 22[13]). Thus we read in Rom. 11[35f.]: "Who hath first given
to him, and it shall be recompensed unto him again?" ὅτι ἐξ αὐτοῦ καὶ δι' αὐτοῦ
καὶ εἰς αὐτὸν τὰ πάντα. αὐτῷ ἡ δόξα εἰς τοὺς αἰῶνας.

The loftiness, the sovereignty, the majesty, the holiness, the glory
—even what is termed the transcendence of God—what is it but this
self-determination, this freedom, of the divine living and loving, the
divine person ? If later on we shall not be able to portray fully the
attributes of divine love except with close attention to their divinity,
i.e., their divine excellence, conversely we shall have to understand
this divinity of God in all its aspects as the sum of His freedom.

By freedom we denote what was called in the theology of the Early Church
the *aseitas Dei*. In content, the idea is already to be seen in the fondness of
the Greek fathers for compounds with the word αὐτός to express the attributes
of God : To God belongs αὐτουσία, αὐτοζωή, αὐτοαγαθία; He is αὐτάρκης,
αὐτοκράτωρ, αὐτόθεος, etc. It was formulated for the first time by Anselm of Canterbury : *summa natura . . . per se ipsam et ex se ipsa est, quidquid est* (*Monol.* 6) *;
summa veritas . . . nulli quidquam debet nec ulla ratione est, quod est, nisi quia est*
(*De verit.* 10) *. . . te tibi omnino sufficiens et nullo indigens quo omnia indigent,
ut sint et ut bene sint* (*Proslog.* 22). And specifically : *Ille igitur solus a se habet,
quidquid habet* (*De casu diab.* 1) Similarly, the older Protestant dogmaticians
frequently included in their definition of God a characterisation such as : *a se
ipso ab aeterno existens*, or something of the sort. This feature was usually
defined as the divine *independentia*, about which W. Baier (*Comp. Theol. pos.*,
1686, I, *c.* 1, 6) made the (in itself correct) statement : *Per hoc enim sicut Deus
ab aliis rebus omnibus adaequate distinguitur, ita nihil est, quod a Deo, tanquam
proprium et determinatum conceptum prius concipere possis, quam quod non sit
ab aliis adeoque a se et necessario exsistat.* But the replacement of the term *aseitas*
by *independentia*, and the content of the explanation, reveal that the tendency was
for that which must always be our primary concern when it is a question of the
being of God, the positive aspect of God's freedom to exist in Himself, to be less
clearly grasped and considered less important than the negative aspect of God's
freedom from all external conditions. The inevitable result was to miss the
biblical idea of God, to which there was a close approximation in the favourite
citation of Exodus 3[14].

Our emphasis in defining the concept must not in any circumstances
fall upon this negative aspect. To be sure, this negative side is
extremely significant not only for God's relation to the world, but
also for His being in itself. We cannot possibly grasp and expound
the idea of divine creation and providence, nor even the ideas of

divine omnipotence, omnipresence and eternity, without constantly referring to this negative aspect of His freedom. But we shall be able to do so properly only when we do so against the background of our realisation that God's freedom constitutes the essential positive quality, not only of His action towards what is outside Himself, but also of His own inner being. The biblical witness to God sees His transcendence of all that is distinct from Himself, not only in the distinction as such, which is supremely and decisively characterised as His freedom from all conditioning by that which is distinct from Himself, but furthermore and supremely in the fact that without sacrificing His distinction and freedom, but in the exercise of them, He enters into and faithfully maintains communion with this reality other than Himself in His activity as Creator, Reconciler and Redeemer. According to the biblical testimony, God has the prerogative to be free without being limited by His freedom from external conditioning, free also with regard to His freedom, free not to surrender Himself to it, but to use it to give Himself to this communion and to practise this faithfulness in it, in this way being really free, free in Himself. God must not only be unconditioned but, in the absoluteness in which He sets up this fellowship, He can and will also be conditioned. He who can and does do this is the God of Holy Scripture, the triune God known to us in His revelation. This ability, proved and manifested to us in His action, constitutes His freedom.

Just for these reasons it was a retrogression when the idea of God's *aseitas* was interpreted, or rather supplanted, by that of *independentia* or *infinitas*, and later by that of the unconditioned or absolute. It is not that these ideas were not serviceable, admissible and even necessary in their place. But in their place means against the background of a positive conception of God's being, which as such (but only as such) includes also a very definite non-being, but which is not exhausted in this non-being, which must be constantly presupposed if this non-being is to be real, if it is to be a divine and not a different kind of non-being. Similarly, the thought of the divine transcendence, if intruded as a substitute, can denote the being of God only when it is remembered that it cannot be exhaustively defined as God's opposition to the reality distinct from Himself, that it can also signify God's positive fellowship with this reality and therefore His immanence within it, that in this connexion, because it has in fact pleased God to establish and maintain this fellowship, it can have " immanence " as its primary connotation, and only within this framework and as an explanation of its method denote what the idea immediately and intrinsically suggests, so that it truly describes the being of God only when it describes Him in His own characteristic freedom which He enjoys beyond and above His opposition to the reality distinct from Himself.

If we fail to bear all this in mind, if we view the being of God in its abstractly understood transcendence in accordance with the disastrous suggestions of Neo-Platonism, i.e., as negative from the point of view of the being of the reality distinct from Himself, then we have substituted for the biblical idea of God an idea which is easily recognisable as the highest idea conceivable to man. For what is the idea of the infinite, the unconditioned or the absolute but the idea of our own limits, which suggest to us both our transcendent goal and origin, but which in themselves can be understood only as our limits and therefore as the negation, the non-being of all that we are ? If we interpret this our non-being as pointing to true being, if we make our limits the object of an apotheosis, we are in no sense testifying to God. On the contrary, by this abuse of the name of God, we are affirming our awareness that these limits suggest our transcendent goal and origin. We are expressing the deep appreciation and esteem we feel for this our goal and origin, and for our own ideal image, carefully purged of all imperfection, but still only postulated as far as its being (even its divine being) is concerned.

God's freedom is the freedom proper to and characteristic of Him. It is His freedom not merely to be like the reality different from Himself, but to be as the Creator, Reconciler and Redeemer acting towards it and in it, and therefore as its sovereign Lord. Again, it is His freedom not merely to be in the differentiation of His being from its being, but to be in Himself the One who can have and hold communion with this reality (as in fact He does) in spite of His utter distinction from it.

According to the self-attestation of His revelation, God is free to reveal His existence within the sphere of the reality that is distinct from Himself. Notice that it is *His* existence, therefore the existence of Him whose being is clearly differentiated from the whole realm of this reality. But it is His *existence*, that is to say His being, independent of our thought about it, preceding and providing the basis for our thought, absolutely objective. And it is this His existence within the reality that is distinct from it, so that in this reality to which man belongs, and in all its differentiation from it, it can be recognised by man ; so that the divine self-revelation can be apprehended by him and grasped according to the possibilities of his knowledge. Now all this obviously does take place as God's self-revelation takes place, creating and finding faith. Therefore it can all take place—it lies within the scope of God's freedom. He shows and proves in His revelation His freedom to begin with Himself : with Himself, without subtraction from His being, without reserving the secret possibilities of a being beyond that which He is at the point where He begins ; to begin with Himself, i.e., not to ground His existence anywhere else but with, or rather in, the life which He here reveals ; to begin with Himself in such a way that no thinking can evade the inescapable, incontestable and unforgettable event of this beginning— and to do it here, in the midst of a reality which is as distinct from Him as He is from it, here, then, where, viewed from either angle, His existence necessarily seems impossible. The freedom to manifest it notwithstanding, is shown and proved by God in His revelation. But this is the freedom of His incarnation in Jesus Christ foreshadowed in His election and rule of Israel, the freedom of His Word, the freedom of His Spirit, the freedom of His grace. It is from first to last the freedom with which He proves His own existence, the proof which every human proof of His existence can only repeat if it is really to prove God's existence and not something very different, that is, if, in the last resort, it is not to prove the existence of man from the awareness of his own limitation.

That it fulfils this condition is the peculiar excellence of the—falsely so-called and as a result permanently misunderstood—ontological proof of God's existence by Anselm of Canterbury (*Prosl.* 2-4). Anselm halted on the very frontier of the great Neo-Platonic error of a God whose being consists only in a hypostatised summary of His non-being in relation to all other kinds of being, a God who is certainly conceivable as an idealisation of man, but whose objective existence can only be demonstrated by sophisms. On the very brink of this error he proved the existence of God by the fact that God has demonstrated and does and will demonstrate Himself. For (deserving our gratitude and answering prayer) He constitutes Himself the point of departure which no thought can by-pass or elude, and with which all thought must begin. In this event of His self-demonstration God is He *quo maius cogitari nequit*. By His holy name, not only His non-existence but even the thought of His non-existence is excluded. Such an error is forbidden man by the fact that God has given Himself to be the object of man's awareness and at the same time has illuminated man's mind to grasp this object.

The freedom in which He proves His existence is the freedom of God in His revelation. And the freedom to exist which He exercises in His revelation is the same which He has in the depths of His eternal being, and which is proper to Him quite apart from His exercise of it *ad extra*. He who begins in this way with Himself in His revelation is He who begins with Himself from eternity, and therefore the One who properly and necessarily exists. And the fact that He is this is what we mean by God's being in freedom.

At this point Catholic dogma (Bartmann, *Lehr. d. Dogm.*[7], Vol. I, 1928, p. 106 f. ; Diekamp, *Kath. Dogm.*[6], Vol. I, 1930, p. 151 f.) joins issue with a theory of the modernist Hermann Schell. According to Schell, the self-existence of God is to be understood as the divine " self-realisation," " self-constitution " and " self-causation." What he has in mind is the phrase of Jerome : *Deus est causa sui.* Objections in formal logic can of course be raised to this statement, that *causa* must be something other than the *causatum*, that it must logically precede it, etc. But these are less decisive than the material point that God as *causa prima* cannot be both *causa* and *causatum*, but only *causa*. Therefore " aseity " cannot in any sense be interpreted as God's act of self-realisation, His self-initiation, as though in a certain sense God arose out of Himself. Obviously in relation to God we can speak only of the ground and actuality of His being which is not in need of any special origin and constitution. The God who takes His origin from Himself or is constituted by Himself is in a certain sense limited by the possibility of His non-being and therefore He is not the free God. Yet the special concern of Schell must be recognised. His intention is suspected by Catholic scholastic dogmatics, and on Catholic ground it can, of course, be fulfilled only with difficulty. For it arose out of his opposition to the scholastic equation of God with the unmoved Mover of Aristotle. What he had in mind was a development of the doctrine of the eternal generation of the Son by the Father, and procession of the Holy Ghost from the Father and the Son. If the inner life of God is the life of Father, Son and Spirit, and if therefore His life resides in this process of generation, then it is hardly possible to raise any decisive objection to the description of God by the idea of self-realisation—later Schell spoke with more reserve about self-actualisation and self-expression. But this is true only if we remember two things : (1) that of the three modes of being of God, that of the Father is not even the object of any self-realisation, which limits

the idea in its application to the life of God ; and (2) that an eternal self-realisation, which alone is possible in the case of God, can have nothing whatever to do
with any idea of God taking His origin from Himself, so that it is at least very
inadequately denoted by the expression *causa sui*. Thus the expression " self-
realisation," in its legitimate use, can mean only the freedom of the divine being
which is in need of no origination (not even an origination from itself).

The freedom in which God exists means that He does not need
His own being in order to be who He is : because He already has His
own being and is Himself ; because nothing can accrue to Him from
Himself which He had not or was not already ; because, therefore,
His being in its self-realisation or the actuality of His being answers
to no external pressure but is only the affirmation of His own plenitude
and a self-realisation in freedom. If, therefore, we say that God is
a se, we do not say that God creates, produces or originates Himself.
On the contrary, we say that (as manifest and eternally actual in the
relationship of Father, Son and Holy Ghost) He is the One who already
has and is in Himself everything which would have to be the object
of His creation and causation if He were not He, God. Because He
is God, as such He already has and is His own being. Therefore this
being does not need any origination and constitution. He cannot
" need " His own being because He affirms it in being who He is. It
is not, of course, that His being needs this affirmation. But He does
actually affirm it in this way. And what He creates, produces and
causes, what needs origination and constitution in order to be, what can
need existence, is not God Himself, or His reality, but the reality which
is distinct from Himself. When we say that God is free to exist, we do
not say that God lifts Himself, as it were, out of non-existence into
existence, that He makes Himself free to exist. What we say is that
the mode of existence is proper to Him which is exempt from any
limitation by the possibility of its non-existence. He is the One
who is in Himself the Existent. By existing in this way He is not
subject to any necessity, as though He must first exist in order to be
who He is. But by His existence He simply reaffirms Himself. It is
not that He needs to reaffirm Himself, but that, being who He is, He
does in fact reaffirm Himself and His existence. When we say that
God begins with Himself, we do not say that He needs a basis in which
He must define and delimit Himself in differentiation from what He
is not, or from His own non-existence, in order to have His being
within this limit. We say rather that He Himself, in being, is His
own basis, and that as such He differentiates His being from what He
is not, His existence from His non-existence, and even from the very
thought of His non-existence, the basis and the differentiation being
confirmed in the very act of His being. Again, it is not that His
being needs this confirmation, but that the very fact of His being,
free from all need, is in fact this confirmation. This is the first primary
meaning of God's being in freedom, in aseity.

The insight expressed in this way is endangered when it is thought essential to complete and deepen the idea of the aseity of God by the Catholic dogma that God's being is necessary, that He is to be defined as the *ens necessarium* : " It is an intrinsic impossibility that He should not be or should be other than He is." This is said to result from the idea of the pure essence or the primary being of God. But because the deduction is only too easily drawn from this idea, we must treat it with great reserve. At any rate the German word *notwendig* is more than doubtful. For in God and for God there can be no " difficulty " (*Not*) which He has to " turn " (*wenden*), or turn from Himself, by His being. But even in the Latin *necesse, necessarium, necessitas* we have a combination of *ne* and *cedere* and therefore the implication of something which it is impossible to evade, not to speak of the Greek ἀνάγκη which really means " straitness." The case is a good illustration of the fact that our words require a complete change of meaning, even to the extent of becoming the very opposite in sense, if in their application to God they are not to lead us astray. We may perhaps be able to say of pure actuality or primary being that if we are to give the true meaning we must speak of " turning difficulties," or the " inescapable," or being " driven into straits." But we certainly cannot say this of God. We cannot apply the terms to God if defined in this way. Of God we can say only that in the actuality of His being He is its affirmation, that in the actuality of His being His non-being or His being other than He is is ontologically and noetically excluded, that it becomes an absolute impossibility, i.e., an impossibility which has no possibility as its background. As distinct from what is meant by these terms, there is no need as a result of which God has to be. But if God is, it is the effect of His freedom, which knows no necessity, no inevitability, no straitness. The fact that He is (and this is the truth of the statement under discussion) does, of course, settle the fact that He exists eternally. His non-existence or the possibility of His non-existence is negated and becomes inconceivable. But this decision results from His actual being as He who is, and it is in obedience to this empirical decision as He is sought and worshipped in it that we have to say that He cannot be non-existent or other than He is. If we seek to establish the intrinsic impossibility that God could not be, or could be other than He is, i.e., if we seek the necessity of His being, or of His being in this particular way, on any other basis than that of this empirical decision, we have to consider whether we are not concerned with a God who in His need to be is not God but the postulated apotheosis of our creaturely existence. We have also to ask ourselves whether the confidence with which we think we can speak of the necessity of the existence of this God can resist the challenge of the question which inevitably arises—whether God might not also not be, or be other than He is ? The genuine necessity to answer this question negatively can spring only from the God who knows no necessity, who, not needing His own being, simply has being as a matter of empirical fact, thus affirming Himself in fact, although He does not need to, as the One who is. The difference between the false and the true negation of our question consists in the fact that the former proceeds automatically from the development of an idea, but the latter can be won only from the hearing of the divine Word in prayer and supplication, from the experience of the struggle between the flesh and the spirit, from the real overcoming of real temptation. In this respect the way of Catholic dogmatics is obviously an easier and smoother way. But it is not apparent to us how we can follow it in obedience or with what promise of reward. For there can be no hope of reward in wishing to cling to something supposedly higher and better than the God who in freedom lives as He who He is.

When we have established this first proposition that God is He who is free in Himself, we can express His aseity in a second proposition, that He is the One who is free from all origination, conditioning or determination from without, by that which is not Himself. The fact that in every way He is independent of all other reality does not in itself constitute God's freedom but its exercise. It does not constitute His divinity, but He is divine in it. If He does not need His own being or any basis or limitation in Himself, if He has and is in Himself being, ground and limit in the actuality of His existence and in the freedom proper to Him, how can He possibly need any other being, or need to be grounded or limited by it ? God is absolute, i.e., utterly independent of everything that is not He. God is, whether everything else is or is not, whether it is in this way or some other. If there is something other, it cannot precede God, it cannot place God in dependence upon itself, and it cannot limit God or change God. If there is something other, it can exist in its own manner of being only by God and from God. It can exist only in subordination to, and in the service of, God. But God was, is and will be who He is without the being and nature of this other existence having any other possible significance than what God is pleased to assign to it. We can and must say all this too, although we refused to say it first, but were first taught ourselves that God is free in Himself.

For we have to be taught first, by the decision made in His actual existence, that God is free in Himself. This statement has to come first as the content of a knowledge whose object cannot be an idea, but only God Himself in His self-evidencing existence. Otherwise how can the second proposition, that God is free from all external conditioning, be distinguished from a product of our own wishful thinking ? Absolute being purged from all subservience to outward conditions may easily signify, as we have seen, the kind of being that we would gladly ascribe to ourselves, and can actually do so with some uncertainty and indefiniteness, in the form of " pure actuality." To what extent is God defined by it and not ourselves ? Obviously, to the exact extent that we have first recognised and acknowledged the freedom of God quite apart from this His independence of all external conditions ; that we have learnt to respect the empirical affirmation of the divine life as such, and therefore to reckon with Him as with the One who is absolute above and beyond the absoluteness in which He confronts that which is not Himself, and in respect of which we are irresistibly drawn to wish ourselves like Him—we can therefore say at once, to reckon with Him as with the One who is alone absolute in sovereign splendour, whom we therefore cannot equal or try to equal, because we are forbidden and prevented from doing so by His demonstration of His own existence, by the factual affirmation of His being. If this is clear to us, we shall be able to guard against the temptation to self-apotheosis which can so easily arise from the elucidation of this secondary freedom of God. This fundamental presupposition will naturally always have to be very clear to us if we are not to succumb tacitly or openly to this temptation.

And a second point is immediately clear if we allow due validity to this fundamental presupposition, viz., that the existence of a reality distinct from God and confronting Him in its difference cannot imply any difficulty in relation to the absolute God. It will necessarily imply such a difficulty in relation to the " absolute " which, as man's own reflection, gains its absoluteness only in virtue of this opposition, only through the denial of its conditioning by this distinct reality. The definition of this absolute will always hover between two extremes. On the one hand, it may be consistently affirmed, with the result that the existence of the other is rendered problematical and finally destroyed and the real world recedes into the ghostly light of ultimate unreality. On the other hand, this other may be inconsistently endowed with a degree of independent reality, so that the so-called absolute is subjected to a certain conditioning by this other and its supposed Godhead to a thoroughgoing determination by the subordinate world. This dilemma is removed if the freedom of God is primarily and fundamentally defined as God's freedom in Himself, and only from that point of view understood as His independence of the world, and therefore His absoluteness in the usual sense of the term. In this case the absoluteness of God—that which makes it a genuine absoluteness—does not derive primarily from the mode of His relationship to the world. For this very reason, He can enter into a real relationship with the latter. There can be a real world confronting Him, not threatened with destruction by the divine absoluteness, but, on the contrary, existing as a world precisely because of it. There can be a world which is not to be understood, on the basis of our idea of God, as a *pudendum*, a contradiction to God, but as something which authenticates His reality and accrues to His glory. In this case, when the world has to be viewed *sub specie aseitatis*, i.e., in the light of the primary creative freedom of God, there can no longer be any question of aloofness or hostility to the world on the part of the absolute God (or rather of a mysticism which worships an idol under the name of God). God has His absoluteness decisively in Himself. For the same reason, also, there cannot be a being and existence of the other which imperils the divine absoluteness or limits the divine freedom or produces even a partial disturbance of the relation of dependence. The relativity of the other is made necessary (here the term is in place) by God's absoluteness. It is made irrevocably necessary. There cannot, then, be any divinisation of the world or demonisations of this other. If, then, the freedom of God is understood primarily as His own positive freedom, it can and must be understood secondarily in His relationship to that which is other than Himself, which exists through Him and in subordination to Him, as His true immanence as well as His true transcendence.

We must notice in this connexion, too, the danger of a different and purely speculative foundation of this secondary absoluteness of God. " Being itself or pure reality depends on no one and needs no other in order to be and work, and it can receive no sort of completion of its being through any other " (Diekamp, *op. cit.*, 152 f.). This may well be true, but it must not be said of God. For again " pure reality " in itself is not to be equated with God, but only in so far as God is reality is He (as the One He is) anything in the nature of pure reality. Pure reality can also be the reflection of our own existence, and will inevitably land us in the dilemma either of being consistent and having to assert the actuality of the " impure " reality distinct from it, or of being inconsistent and limiting the " pure " by the " impure " reality. This dilemma discloses to us the difference between what is connoted by this idea and God.

Against the background of these presuppositions we will now attempt a general explanation of the divine freedom in this secondary connotation of the idea—as the " absoluteness " of God. The fact that God is free in His relationship to all that is not God means noetic-ally that God cannot be classified or included in the same category with anything that He is not. There exists no synthesis in which the same attribute, whether being, spirit, life or love, can be predi-cated in the same sense both of God and of something else ; in which, therefore, God is to be an element embraced with other elements in the one synthesis. Whenever God is placed side by side with another factor (with the explicit or implicit copula "and" or in some other way), we must clearly realise that there can be no question of a synthesis ; that any conceivable synthesis is precluded in advance by the inclusion of the element God along with others ; that the element God stands in such a relation to all other elements that the latter, in spite of indi-vidual variations, are all characterised as one group ; that by their intrinsic difference they are all separated from the divine in such a way that no higher unity is possible between them and God which can be expressed by a higher comprehensive term. If there is here a unity, it is not in any sense a unity which can be expressed by a higher term embracing God and these other elements. If we think and speak of God as an element juxtaposed with others in a series, the very idea or view of the series as such must be fundamentally dis-turbed (which in this case means reinterpreted) by the fact that the element God is in such a way independent of all the other elements and of the series as such, that, whatever may be the common de-nominator, God will not be embraced by it, but will remain detached and independent in regard both to these associated elements and to the common factor which binds them together. *Deus non est in genere*, as we have seen already.

The theological consequences of this first proposition are so far-reaching, logically, that we can only give one or two examples by way of indication. Be-cause *Deus non est in genere*, we must take exception to Roman Catholic theology when—in what seems an incomprehensible contradiction to this statement of Thomas Aquinas—it thinks it possible at every opportunity to fall back upon a concept of being which comprehends God and what is not God, and therefore at bottom to explain all the relations between God and what is not God in the form of an exposition of this general concept. Because *Deus non est in genere*, the doctrine of God in Kant is quite intolerable, for in it the idea of God is put alongside other supreme ideas like freedom and immortality, and with them is subordinated to the crowning idea of reason.   Because *Deus non est in genere*, every theological method is to be rejected as untheological in which God's self-revelation is apparently recognised, but in fact is subsumed beneath a higher term, whether that of truth, or that of divine revelation in general, or that of religion, or that of history, so that it now has to be interpreted in the light of this higher comprehensive idea.   We have already seen that the Bible repudiates such comparisons of God with other values, such attempts to transcend God, as though He were not supreme, the alpha and the omega.   If we refuse to learn this lesson, if we audaciously attempt such equations and subsumptions, if we dare to bracket God along with other things, then, whatever may happen inside the framework of the system, God Himself cannot be spoken of, at any rate not honestly and seriously.   With whatever earnestness and sincerity we may attempt to speak of the God who is embraced by such a system, in the last analysis we are not speaking of God but of the higher synthesis furnished by our controlling idea. The absoluteness of God permits of no such systematisations.

But behind this noetic absoluteness of God there stands decisively His ontic.   This is decisive because in God's revelation it is really a question of His ontic absoluteness, from which His noetic absoluteness inevitably follows.   God's freedom in relation to all that is not God signifies that He is distinct from everything, that He is self-sufficient and independent in relation to it, and that He is so in a peculiar and pre-eminent fashion—as no created being confronts any other.   No created beings are in fact so independent of each other that in spite of this relative mutual independence they have not also to some extent a certain mutual interdependence, in the sense that ultimately none of them would have its being and nature apart from its interlocking with the being and nature of all the others.   But God confronts all that is in supreme and utter independence, i.e., He would be no less and no different even if they all did not exist or existed differently.   God stands at an infinite distance from everything else, not in the finite degree of difference with which created things stand towards each other.   If they all have their being and a specific nature, God in His freedom has conferred it upon them : not because He was obliged to do so, or because His purpose was influenced by their being and nature, but because their being and nature is conditioned by His being and nature.   If they belong to Him and He to them, this dual relationship does not spring from any need of His eternal being.   This would remain the same even if there were no such relationship.   If there is a connexion and relatedness between them and Him, God is who He is in independence of them even in this relatedness. He does not share His being with theirs.   He does not enter with them into a higher synthesis.   He does not mingle and blend Himself with them.   He does not transform Himself into them.   Even in His relationship and connexion with them, He remains who He is.   He creates and sustains this relationship.   Through it He holds sway in an absolute supremacy which is unbroken and uninterrupted in the greatest aspects and also in the smallest.   He would be who He is even without this connexion. Every relationship into which God enters with that which is not Himself must be interpreted—however much this may disturb or correct our preconceived ideas of connexion and relationship—as eventuating between two utterly unequal partners, the sheer inequality consisting in the fact that no self-determination of the second partner can influence the first, whereas the self-determination of the first, while not cancelling the self-determination of the second, is the sovereign predetermination which precedes it absolutely.

From this point of view all the conceptions of God must be excluded *a limine* and definitively which take the form of what is called pantheism or panentheism. God does not form a whole with any other being either in identity with it or as compounding or merging with it to constitute a synthesis—the object of that master-concept, so often sought and found, which comprehends both God and what is not God. God enters into the closest relationship with the other, but He does not form such a synthesis with it. Therefore neither the conception of an identity of God with the universe in its totality is acceptable, nor that of God's identity with the elementary constituent substance of the universe—a view with which the history of Western philosophy began in Ionia—nor again the conception of God's identity with a world-soul or reason penetrating and informing the universe as an *élan vital*, or with the essential spiritual reality behind it, whether conceived statically as the inherently changeless principle behind all human mental and spiritual activity, or dynamically as the propelling force behind human intellectual and religious development. The mythology of a merely partial and to some extent selected identity of God with the world, which under the name of panentheism has been regarded as a better possibility than undiluted pantheism, is really in a worse case than is that of the latter. And again, it would be shortsighted, within the framework of panentheism itself, to give too decided a preference to Idealism, as though its two forms of expression, or one of them, were well adapted to compensate for the fundamental error on which they rest, and lead on to the Christian idea of God. Within the framework of these erroneous presuppositions, the Ionian possibility was not bad of its kind. And so it could not fail to come about that in the second half of the 19th century there was an inversion, and a type of panentheism arose which selected as its mythologumen, not the spirit or soul or reason as in an earlier period, but matter, or the atom, or some other symbol for the universe in its naturalistic aspect, identifying this with supreme being or divinity. We may abuse this procedure as crass materialism. We may also point out with satisfaction that it is not quite so easy to maintain a materialism purged of all spiritual elements as the more careless materialists supposed. But we must not forget that at least the same applies to the affirmation of a " spiritualism " purged of all material elements; that this crass materialism is in fine only a reaction against the equally crass " spiritualism " previously in the ascendant; and that ultimately both of them had little cause to criticise a simple, undifferentiated and therefore crass pantheism, because after all they only represent action and reaction in the same view according to which God can be identified with another. If, as distinct from pantheism, it is desired to hazard only a partial identification, beyond the chosen sphere of the identification God must still be mingled with something else : in the case of Idealists with the (unavoidable) nature of the universe ; in the case of materialists, with the likewise not wholly avoidable spirit. To that extent panentheism in its two forms is more crass than crass pantheism. It is easy to see, however, that there is no place for mutual recrimination, since in every identification of God with another the fundamental error has been committed which in itself and as such can very well develop in a twofold and threefold dialectic, but on the basis of which there can never be a return to honest and serious thinking and speaking about God. In this connexion the essential insight is that God cannot in any way be or constitute a synthesis with that which is other than Himself. The Bible speaks of the God who cannot be or do this. It speaks of the absolute God. It is for this reason that it speaks sincerely and seriously of God. And this is what must happen, at any rate in the Christian Church, as a witness against all false gods.

Now the absoluteness of God strictly understood in this sense means that God has the freedom to be present with that which is not God, to communicate Himself and unite Himself with the other and the other with Himself, in a way which utterly surpasses all that can be effected in regard to reciprocal presence, communion and fellowship between other beings. It is just the absoluteness of God properly understood which can signify not only His freedom to transcend all that is other than Himself, but also His freedom to be immanent within it, and at such a depth of immanence as simply does not exist in the fellowship between other beings. No created being can be inwardly present to another, entering and remaining in communion with him in the depths of its inner life. No such being can create and sustain the life of another, seriously leading and governing, binding itself to the other and the other to itself in eternal faithfulness and whole-hearted devotion. The essence of every other being is to be finite, and therefore to have frontiers against the personality of others and to have to guard these frontiers jealously. It lies in the nature of the created being to have to be true to itself in such a way that with the best will in the world it simply cannot be true to another. It is its very nature that it cannot affirm itself except by affirming itself against others. For this reason it is only by simplification and tentatively, i.e., not with basic seriousness, that created beings can be present with each other, communicating and binding themselves to each other, listening to each other. Therefore between all such beings, as there is no genuine transcendence so there is no genuine immanence. A pantheistic or panentheistic alternation between God and another is required to affirm a true immanence even between created beings, instead of between God alone and all created beings. This affirmation needs a good deal of poetic fancy. But God is free. He is also free to be immanent, free to achieve a uniquely inward and genuine immanence of His being in and with the being which is distinct from Himself.

Therefore God can indeed (and this is His transcendence) be sufficiently beyond the creature to be his Creator out of nothing and at the same time be free enough partially or completely to transform its being or to take it from it again as first He gave it. But, if the expression may be allowed, God can do even more than this. He can (and this is His immanence) so indwell the other that, while He is its Creator and the Giver of its life, and while He does not take away this life, He does not withdraw His presence from this creaturely existence which is so different from His own divine life. Now that it has originated in His will and subsists by His will, He does not detach Himself from it in an alien aloofness, but is present as the being of its being with the eternal faithfulness of which no creature is capable towards another. God can allow this other which is so utterly distinct from Himself to live and move and have its being within Himself. He can grant and leave it its own special being distinct from His own, and yet even in this way, and therefore in this its creaturely freedom, sustain, uphold and govern it by His own divine being, thus being its beginning, centre and end. God can in fact be nearer to it than it is to itself. He can understand it better than it understands itself. He can inspire and guide it at a deeper level than it knows how to do itself—infinitely nearer, better, more deeply, yet not in dissolution but in confirmation of His own divine singularity, and again not in dissolution but in confirmation of the singularity of the creature. The fact that God can do this is His freedom in immanence.

But we must go further. God is sufficiently free to indwell the creature in the most varied ways according to its varying characteristics. The fulness of the movement in which, according to the witness of the Bible, we find God relating Himself to the creature must not therefore be interpreted as inessential and analogical, but as in the strictest sense a reality, because it is in this movement that He shows Himself to be God and not an idol, and therefore free—in contradistinction to the limitedness of a being which, even though it bears the highest attributes, betrays its creatureliness in the fact that its mode of approach and relation to the creature is, from the latter's point of view, inflexible. Of course, God too in His relationship to the world can react only in a certain way and not otherwise—that is, only according to His own standpoint, in correspondence with His divine being, as He determines and wills in His freedom. But in this His freedom, in which He spontaneously binds Himself in a certain way to the world, He remains unbound from the point of view of the world and its specific determinations. His changelessness does not coincide with any one of our constancies. His faithfulness is His own, and not the metaphysical equivalent of any one of the normal features of creaturely existence. His presence in the life and being of the world is His personal and therefore actual presence expressed in continually new forms according to His sovereign decisions.

It is not, then, the rigid presence of a being whose nature we can, so to speak, formulate in this or that principle. God is free to be present with the creature by giving Himself and revealing Himself to it or by concealing Himself and withdrawing Himself from it. God is free to be and operate in the created world either as unconditioned or as conditioned. God is free to perform His work either within the framework of what we call the laws of nature or outside it in the shape of miracle. God is free either to grant His immanence to nature by working at its heart or by exerting His sway at an infinite height above it. God is free to conceal His divinity from the creature, even to become a creature Himself, and free to assume again His Godhead. He is free to maintain as God His distance from the creature and equally free to enter into partnership with it, indeed, to lift the creature itself, in the most vigorous sense, into unity with His own divine being, with Himself. God is free to rule over the world in supreme majesty and likewise to serve in the world as the humblest and meanest of servants, free even to be despised in the world, and rejected by the world. God is free to clothe Himself with the life of the world in all its glory as with a garment ; but free likewise Himself to die the death which symbolises the end of all things earthly, in utter abandonment and darkness. God is free to be entirely unlimited over against the world : not bound by its finitude, nor by its infinitude ; not confined to its time and space as a whole, nor to any one area of space or period of time. He is equally free to limit Himself : to be eternal in the tiny endlessness of our starry heavens, or of our human conceptuality, but eternal also in our finitude ; to be shut up in the totality of our time-space universe, but also in all humility to be confined to this or that time and place as contrasted with other times and places. God is free to ally Himself, within creation, to the spirit as against rebellious nature, but also free to ally Himself with nature in opposition to the undoubtedly more rebellious spirit. God is free to be provoked and to be merciful, to bless and to punish, to kill and to make alive, to exalt us to heaven and to cast us down into hell. God is free to be wholly inward to the creature and at the same time as Himself wholly outward : *totus intra et totus extra* and both, of course, as forms of His immanence, of His presence, of the relationship and communion chosen, willed and created by Himself between Himself and His creation. This is how He meets us in Jesus Christ. His revelation in Jesus Christ embraces all these apparently so diverse and contradictory possibilities. They are all His possibilities. If we deny Him any one of them, we are denying Jesus Christ and God Himself. Instead of recognising and adoring God, we are setting up an idol. For we are imposing upon Him—in defiance of the freedom which He has actually proved to us—a bondage which can be only that of our own self-will that would like to deny God and put itself in the place of God. If only the Word of God breaks through the walls of our self-will, our worship of the freedom of God exercised in His immanence can have no bounds. And then the full inadequacy of all pantheism and panentheism will be exposed to us. For what a poor limited God it is, and what a poor and limited world, whose confines wholly or partially overlap in these systems, so that they have to be wholly or partially interpreted as a unity ! Once the boundless exaltation of God's freedom in immanence is recognised to be necessary and rendered, there can be no further lapse into these systems.

We must go further still. God is sufficiently free to differentiate His presence infinitely, and decisively, not merely with respect to the variations of the creature, but also in Himself, that is, according to the demands of His own intention with regard to the creature. The relationship and fellowship of God with the world is not bound to a definite scheme, to the *quantum* and *quale* of a certain mode of action uniformly proceeding from Him.

Although in His eternal being and action towards the world God is undivided and indivisibly One and the Same, although He is always wholly the One He is, the mode of His action varies. It is one thing in the incarnation of the Word, in the once-for-all and unique assumption of human nature into unity with His eternal Son, into communion with His divine being. It is another thing in the wider kingdom of His grace—in the life of the Church and the children of God, in the power of preaching and the sacraments, in the power of the new conception and birth of man to faith by the Holy Spirit. It is another thing again in the creation, preservation and government of the existence and nature of the world and man, in virtue of which they are always neutral reality. It is another thing again in the future consummation, in the return of Christ, in the resurrection of the dead, in the last judgment and the end when He will be all in all. He acts and speaks variously in the prophets and apostles, in preaching and sacrament, in Holy Scripture, in the writings of the fathers and the creeds of the Church, differently yesterday, and differently to-day, and differently to-morrow. His communion with the angels is certainly different from His communion with the rest of the world. His communion with men is different from His communion with other spiritual creatures. His dealings with the faithful differ from His dealings with men in general. His manifestations in Church history differ from His manifestations in world history as such. And finally He is always infinitely diverse in His communion with each individual angel, thing, man, or believer, as compared with all the rest.

There is not only the infinite individual variation of the divine action *ad extra*, to which we first referred, but as its ground in the being and will of God, in His decrees, there is a whole hierarchy of His decisions and acts, the variation of which does not destroy but confirms the oneness of God as a divine unity in contradistinction to the unity of a natural force or spiritual principle. When we say this, we are not speculating. On the contrary, it would be speculation, an illegitimate simplification, a dishonouring of God, not to say this, seeing it is stated so unambiguously in God's revelation. It is fatal for the Church and a threat to the faith of each individual and his eternal felicity to overlook even a single one of the revealed variations of God's immanence, to deny it, to efface it, or to level it out into something generalised which as such certainly cannot be the divine.

We may say that dogmatics especially, which is always concerned to distinguish and discriminate (and necessarily so for the sake of the purity and fulness of Church doctrine), has its authorisation and justification at this point in the concept of God. If we do not like dogmatics because of its inevitable refinements and distinctions, we must consider whether we are not tilting against God Himself. For He has the freedom in all His *opus ad extra* to remain the One who He is in an apparently inexhaustible abundance of distinctions which have to be noted. And He can be a valid object of our knowledge only if we do not deny Him this freedom and the apparently overwhelming richness of distinctions within His being, but conscientiously reckon with it at every point, being concerned only to realise and accept Him as He is.

The triumph of God's freedom in immanence is seen precisely in this hierarchy of His being and action as it operates in relation to the being which is distinct from Himself. Yet it is not the case—for how otherwise would it be a hierarchy?—that we stand confronted by this richness of the divine being as by an unfathomable ocean of possibilities of any and every kind. According to the testimony of the same revelation which in the first instance simply discloses this richness as such to our gaze, inviting us to take God seriously as God now in this and now in that of His multiple manifestations, the fact emerges that all these possibilities of divine presence and action have a very definite centre, that is, they have their basis and their consummation, their meaning, their norm and their law in Jesus Christ. In the first place, the fulfilled union of the divine and the human in Jesus Christ is, to be sure, one among others of these various possibilities of divine immanence, but over and beyond that, it must be defined, in its once-for-all and unique aspect, as the possibility of all other possibilities. For the Son of God who became flesh in Jesus Christ is, as an eternal mode of the divine being, nothing more nor less than the principle and basis of all divine immanence, and therefore the principle of what we have called the secondary absoluteness of God.

We have seen that the freedom of God, as His freedom in Himself, His primary absoluteness, has its truth and reality in the inner Trinitarian life of the Father with the Son by the Holy Spirit. It is here, and especially in the divine mode as the Son who is the " image of the invisible God " (Col. 1¹⁵), in God Himself, that the divine freedom in its aspect of communion with the other, i.e., the secondary absoluteness of God, has its original truth. Here it is not yet relationship and fellowship with the other that is outside God, with the created world. We should be repeating the error of Philo and Gnosticism, which was unhesitatingly repudiated by the Early Church, if we tried to identify the Son of God with the world, and therefore to introduce the world in some sense as a necessary element, a divine mode, into the life of the Godhead. There could not then be any question of God's freedom in regard to it. But God Himself is the Son who is the basic truth of that which is other than God. As the Son of God this Other is God Himself. But God Himself becomes Another in the person of His Son. The existence of the world is not needed in order that there should be otherness for Him. Before all worlds, in His Son He has otherness in Himself from eternity to eternity. But because this is so, the creation and preservation of the world, and relationship and fellowship with it, realised as they are in perfect freedom, without compulsion or necessity, do not signify an alien or contradictory expression of God's being, but a natural, *the* natural expression of it *ad extra*. The world is, because and as the Son of God is. πάντα δι' αὐτοῦ ἐγένετο καὶ χωρὶς αὐτοῦ ἐγένετο οὐδὲ ἕν ὃ γέγονεν (Jn. 1³). ὁ κόσμος δι' αὐτοῦ ἐγένετο (Jn. 1¹⁰). When we now learn that, over and beyond all this, it is said of the same Son of God : σὰρξ ἐγένετο (Jn. 1¹⁴), that therefore, besides being Creator, He became creature, it is clear that in this singular and supreme relationship and fellowship between God and the world realised in the incarnation we have the quintessence of all possible relationship and fellowship generally and as such, and that in the transcendent freedom of God thus expressed we see the archetype and the norm of all the possible ways in which He expresses His freedom in this relationship and fellowship. As the Son of God takes His place among other creatures, His place is inevitably at their head, controlling them all. He is necessarily the πρωτότοκος πάσης κτίσεως (Col. 1¹⁵), and whatever else is created, is created δι' αὐτοῦ, as well as ἐν αὐτῷ and εἰς αὐτόν. And with whatever freedom God expresses Himself in other ways in the sphere of creation, we shall have to recognise in the way in which He exercises His freedom here, and only here, the meaning, the norm and the goal of all the other ways in which He also does it, and quite differently.

Thus in spite of the almost confusing richness of the forms of divine immanence we are led to recognise a hierarchy, a sacred order, in which God is present to the world. We have only to grasp the fact that Jesus Christ is the focus and crown, and not merely the focus and the crown of all relationship and fellowship between God and the world, but also their basic principle, their possibility and presupposition in the life of the Godhead, and we shall see God's freedom disclose and develop itself. It does not do so as chaos. It does not do so as an ocean of particularities and contradictions. It does not do so as a picture composed arbitrarily and fortuitously, so that one thing is missing here and another might be different there. It does not do so as a pyramid whose apex is the apex and nothing more, based upon elements of a very different nature and origin, with which it unites to form a whole. But it does so as the one work of one unvarying wisdom, which excludes the fortuitous and the contradictory, which does not will at random or juxtapose incompatible elements, but which in the abundance of its effects wills only one thing, namely itself, and which orders all things to its own glory but also to the life and healing of the other which has its being by it and in it. Thus, everything for which God is free and in which God is free will be understood by us as the unity of the freedom of His being if we approach it in this way. It will not confuse us by its manifoldness, but will comfort, warn and rejoice us if we see that it derives from Jesus Christ the Son of God, attesting Him, serving Him and leading to Him, as is in fact disclosed to our sight and hearing in God's revelation. There is no caprice about the freedom of God. The faithfulness which He evinces and proves in His freedom with regard to His creation is His own faithfulness. It cannot, therefore, be reduced to the level of the regularity of a cosmic process. But it is not on this account concealed from us so that as a matter of fact and in practice we do not know to whom and to what we are clinging when we embrace and apprehend by faith this divine loyalty, when we are summoned by it, and consoled by it, and in turn invoke it. But what it purposes and wills is sure, as is the fact that in all its forms it is true steadfastness, responsible dealing and no irresponsible game. The fact is sure that God constantly turns to us, whether He seems near or far, whether He speaks to us in silence and in secret or whether He addresses us openly, whether He blesses us or punishes us, kills or makes alive. The fact is sure that He is none other than the Creator, the Lord of the Church, the Ruler of our hearts and consciences, the Judge at the last day, the same Lord to me and thee and to His angels and archangels, the same yesterday, to-day and for ever, here and now and in the remotest lands and times, ever diversely manifested in His freedom, yet ever the same, never and nowhere a different God. But we are sure of this fact only because God is Jesus Christ and Jesus Christ is God ; only because the divine immanence in all its varied possibilities has its origin in Jesus Christ and therefore its unity in Him, but only in Him, in the diversity of its actions and stages. Therefore we cannot be sufficiently eager to insist, nor can it be sufficiently emphasised in the Church and through the Church in the world, that we know God in Jesus Christ alone, and that in Jesus Christ we know the one God. For this reason we are constantly called to make a decision in this matter, and every decision to which we are summoned will always be in the last resort a decision on this point. Any deviation, any attempt to evade Jesus Christ in favour of another supposed revelation of God, or any denial of the fulness of God's presence in Him, will precipitate us into darkness and confusion when we realise the abundant variety of the divine presence grounded in the divine freedom, because, without the key to the whole, even though He is undoubtedly present and we objectively meet Him, we will not find Him as God, nor be able to recognise and praise Him as God, for we will meet Him only in the diversity, in the curious details and puzzling contradictions of His presence. We will then have to fall back, according to the best of our knowledge and belief and our judgment from some other point of view, upon another basis of unity for His presence. We will then have to seek God here and there, and objectively we will not be mistaken in our search : for where is He not to be sought, He who has first sought and found us in Jesus Christ ? But with what meaning and success can He be sought anywhere when He remains unknown to us in this form, when He is not acknowledged by us here as the one God ; here, where He discloses the unity which embraces the manifold richness of His immanent presence, where He has permitted Himself to be found ? All other unities of immanence which we seek and think we find cannot constitute the unity of His immanence, because we seek them elsewhere than at the point where God Himself has revealed it, where He has first sought and found us. We are simply making an idol of the ruins of His immanence, which seen and accepted as such does not attest but denies Him, and in the service and worship of this idol we can only more and more blind ourselves to the true God present to His creation.

In this way arise the various heathen religions and the various heresies within Christianity. The religions of heathendom come about because man simply does not know or refuses to know the ground of divine immanence in Jesus Christ. The Christian heresies spring from the fact that man does not take seriously the known ground of divine immanence in Jesus Christ, so that from its revelation, instead of apprehending Jesus Christ and the totality in Him, he arbitrarily selects this or that feature and sets it up as a subordinate centre : perhaps the idea of creation, or the sacraments, or the life of the soul, or even the kingdom of God, or the regeneration of man, or the creeds or doctrine. There is also a possibility of idolatry by wresting a part or stage of the hierarchy of divine immanence from its connexion with its divine Head and accepting it in itself and as such as the truth and reality of Christ—oblivious of the fact that this immanence both as a whole and in its parts has Christian truth and reality only in so far as it is founded in Jesus Christ and summed up in Him, so that if, as a whole and in its parts, it is affirmed, preached and believed as a centre in itself and alongside of Christ, the Church will inevitably be led back into heathendom and its worship of the elements.

If the freedom of divine immanence is sought and supposedly found apart from Jesus Christ, it can signify in practice only our enslavement to a false god. For this reason Jesus Christ alone must be preached to the heathen as the immanent God, and the Church must be severely vigilant to see that it expects everything from *Jesus Christ*, and from Jesus Christ *everything* ; that He is unceasingly recognised as the way, the truth, and the life (Jn. 14⁶). This attitude does not imply Christian absolutism or ecclesiastical narrowmindedness, because it is precisely in Jesus Christ, but also exclusively in Him, that the abundance and plenitude of divine immanence is included and revealed. If we do not have Christ, we do not have at all, but utterly lack, the fulness of God's presence. If we separate ourselves from Him, we are not even on the way to this richness, but are slipping back into an impoverishment in which the omnipresent God is not known. The freedom of God must be recognised as His own freedom and this means—as it consists in God and as God has exercised it. But in God it consists in His Son Jesus Christ, and it is in Him that God has exercised it. In all its possibilities and shapes it remains the freedom which consists and is exercised in Jesus Christ. If we recognise and magnify it, we cannot come from any other starting-point but Him or move to any other goal.

Christology, therefore, must always constitute the basis and criterion for the apprehension and interpretation of the freedom of God in His immanence. The legitimacy of every theory concerning the relationship of God and man or God and the world can be tested by considering whether it can be understood also as an interpretation of the relationship and fellowship created and sustained in Jesus Christ. Is it capable of adaptation to the fundamental insights of the Church concerning the person and work of Jesus Christ—the *analogia fidei* ? Or does it stand in isolation from Christ's person and work, so that it can be brought into connexion with these insights only as an introduction or an appendix, neither deriving from them nor leading back to them. There are strictly speaking no Christian themes independent of Christology, and the Church must insist on this in its message to the world. It is at all events impossible to assert the contrary with reference to God and His freedom. If we appeal to God and His freedom, in the last resort, directly or indirectly, we can expound and elucidate only this one theme.

With this we have said conclusively what is to be said at the close of this sub-section and of this whole section. We gave it the title : " The Being of God in Freedom " ; and in it we have spoken of God's aseity and of His primary and secondary absoluteness. We again remind ourselves that in this whole discussion we have not been looking past the revelation of God to a dimension of His being somewhere beyond ; we have not been concerned to define a divine predicate, a general idea of God, but the profundity of the revealed God Himself in His aseity, His primary and secondary absoluteness. Woe to us if we had spoken of freedom generally and ascribed this to God as an attribute the meaning of which we could fathom quite apart from the fact that it is a divine attribute ! We would then have been engaged in erecting at this very spot the worst of all idolatries. When we say that God is free, the accent does not fall on " free " but on " God." What we mean by freedom in this context, in what legitimate sense God can be known and understood as He who dwells in freedom, is something which can be disclosed only as we put the question to God Himself and listen to the answer which He gives us. For this reason we started from the living and loving of God, and now again we must point expressly to the fact that we have not strayed from the living and loving of God, but that it is the aseity, the freedom of the divine living and loving, and only to that extent the divinity of this living and loving, the divinity of God, which has occupied this final section. We cannot get behind God—behind God in His revelation—to try to ask and determine from outside what He is. We can only learn and then attempt to repeat what He Himself alone can tell us and has told us—who He is. But He is who He is as the One who loves, not in a substance in which He can be more or less or something other than the living God. We have seen indeed that the life and act of God is the life and act of His love. The only reason we have to distinguish between the living and loving of God is because He is not merely the idea of love but the One who loves in the very act of His existence. It is not that God first lives and then also loves. But God loves, and in this act lives. If we have interpreted the divinity of His act, or the divinity of God, as freedom, we could not and cannot mean by this notion of freedom anything different from Himself as the One who loves. We cannot mean a " universal " in which He merely participates as the One who loves. We can mean and characterise only the manner, the utterly unique manner, of His love. His loving is, as we have seen, utterly free, grounded in itself, needing no other, and yet also not lacking in another, but in sovereign transcendence giving, communicating itself to the other. In this freedom it is the divine loving. But we must also say, conversely, that only in this divine loving is the freedom described by us divine freedom. If we abstract the love of God and therefore the purpose of God, however circumspect we may be, we describe only a world-principle. Therefore we must not think away the love or the person of God for a single moment if we wish to think rightly and truly of God's divinity. God is free. Because this is the case, we must say expressly in conclusion that the freedom of God is the freedom which consists and fulfils itself in His Son Jesus Christ. In Him God has loved Himself from all eternity. In Him He has loved the world. He has done so in Him, in the freedom which renders His life divine, and therefore glorious, triumphant, and strong to save.

THE PERFECTIONS OF GOD

God lives His perfect life in the abundance of many individual and distinct perfections. Each of these is perfect in itself and in combination with all the others. For whether it is a form of love in which God is free, or a form of freedom in which God loves, it is nothing else but God Himself, His one, simple, distinctive being.

God's being consists in the fact that He is the One who loves in freedom. In this He is the perfect being : the being which is itself perfection and so the standard of all perfection ; the being, that is, which is self-sufficient and thus adequate to meet every real need ; the being which suffers no lack in itself and by its very essence fills every real lack. Such a being is God. He is this being because He lives as such. It is as we return to life as the fundamental element in the divine being that we also move forward to God's perfections. The one perfection of God, His loving in freedom, is lived out by Him, and therefore identical with a multitude of various and distinct types of perfection. There is no possibility of knowing the perfect God without knowing His perfections. The converse is also true : knowledge of the divine perfections is possible only in knowledge of the perfect God, of His loving in freedom. But because God lives His perfect being the knowledge of His perfections is also a way— the way which in the presence of the living God we must tread. In other words, even in the knowledge of the one perfect God we are confronted by His richness. The real God is the one God who loves in freedom, and as such is eternally rich. To know Him means to know Him again and again, in ever new ways—to know only Him, but to know Him as the perfect God, in the abundance, distinctness and variety of His perfections.

As we understand the one being of God from this angle, we enter the region of that complex of teaching which the older dogmatics treated under the heading " The Doctrine of the Attributes of God," His *appellationes, virtutes, attributa, proprietates* or even *perfectiones*. From these suggested terms—while reserving to ourselves the right to make occasional use of the others—we choose the last because it points at once to the thing itself instead of merely to its formal aspect, and because instead of something general it expresses at once that which is clearly distinctive. The fact that God's being has attributes is something which it has in common with the being of others. But that it is identical with a multitude of perfections—if the term is taken strictly—is something which is the " attribute " of God and of God alone.

The old problem of the doctrine of the attributes of God is so far-reaching that in this section we must first devote to it a general treatment, and then develop it concretely in the two following sections.

Let us first attempt to define the problem as such. In this connexion our primary affirmation must be that here too it is a question of nothing else but of God Himself. But because we are thinking of God Himself, we are thinking of the One who at the same time, in confirmation and glorification of His oneness, is also many. We are careful not to say : all. There is much which God is not. God is not creature. God is not sin. God is not death. But He is many, not merely something, not merely one. He is who He is and what He is in both unity and multiplicity. He is the One who is this many, and the many who are this One. The One is He who loves in freedom. The many are His perfections—the perfections of His life. Only perfections come under consideration here, for what He is is perfect because He is it. And every sort of perfection which there can possibly be can be only His perfection. How can He be anything except in perfection, and what can be perfect except in Him ? But everything which can be described as perfect is so because He is this thing. He not only has it as others might have it. He has it as His own exclusively. And not only so, but He *is* it, so that it has its essential being in Him.

> Sed certe quidquid es, non per aliud es quam per te ipsum. *Tu es igitur ipsa vita, qua vivis et sapientia qua sapis et bonitas ipsa qua bonis et malis bonus es* (Anselm of Canterbury, *Prosl.* 12).

Since God is Father, Son and Holy Ghost, i.e., loves in freedom, every perfection exists essentially in Him.

> Deo autem hoc est esse, quod est fortem esse, aut iustum esse, aut sapientem esse et si quid de illa simplici multiplicitate vel multiplici simplicitate dixeris, quo substantia eius significetur (Augustine, *De Trin.* 4, 6, cf. VI, 7, 8). *Hoc enim est Deo esse quod velle, et hoc velle, quod sapere (Conc. Tolet.* XV, 688, Denz. VI, *No.* 294). *Sicut nefas est putare, quod substantia supremae naturae sit aliquid, quod melius sit aliquo modo non ipsum, sic necesse est ut sit, quidquid omnino melius est quam non ipsum. . . . Quare necesse est eam esse viventem, sapientem, potentem et omnipotentem, veram, iustam, beatam, aeternam et quidquid similiter absolute melius est quam non ipsum* (Anselm of Canterbury, *Monol.* 15). And so Calvin wanted all the attributes of God to be understood as *virtutes* of His *aeternitas* καὶ αὐτουσία (*Instit.* I, 10, 2).

To speak of God's attributes as we must and may do, since we are speaking of Him on the ground of His revelation, means therefore to speak again and this time properly, in concrete definition, of His being. It is impossible to have knowledge of God Himself without having knowledge of a divine perfection, and it is impossible to have knowledge of a divine perfection without having knowledge of God Himself —knowledge of the triune God who loves in freedom. For as the triune God, both in regard to His revelation and to His being in itself,

He exists in these perfections, and these perfections again exist in Him and only in Him as the One who, both in His revelation and in eternity, is the same. To grasp and understand this connexion is the special task of the doctrine of God's attributes. In this doctrine we have to attain the insight that God—and here the German language offers a possibility of expression which other languages do not have —is not only the Lord (*Herr*), but the Lord of glory (*Herrlichkeit*), and conversely, that all glory is the glory of God the Lord (*die Herrlichkeit Gottes des Herrn*).

In taking as our point of departure the glory of God we touch on a concept the explanation and exposition of which will form the conclusion to our whole survey of this doctrine and therefore to the doctrine of the reality of God. We cannot well do other than begin at this point with the same concept.

It does not go without saying that with equal emphasis God (or, according to 1 Cor. 2[8] and Jas. 2[1], Jesus Christ) is both the *Lord* and the Lord of *glory* and is recognised and confessed as such. There is always the danger of a cleavage here. The danger is equally great on both sides, and on both sides it jeopardises no less than everything. God as the Lord can be viewed and understood so to speak in a punctual or linear manner. He is the fully existent One, and perhaps also, according to our definition, the One who is utterly loving and free. But as such He is perhaps a very intensive, yet to some extent also a very slender, not to say impoverished and spectral being. He becomes living for us, He acquires for us abundance of life, vividness and palpable reality, only as He enters into relation with us, as there stands over against Him a world and especially man in his manifold movement, in relation to which He Himself acquires movement. But He cannot be taken with true and final seriousness in this movement and therefore in His glory, His glory cannot be accepted strictly, because all that His revelation appears to affirm in this regard has to be understood only as a divine economy which is grounded more in the nature of the world, and in our own nature, than in the nature of God Himself. This nature itself, as the proper being of God, has to be regarded as standing inscrutably beyond and above this economy. That God is mighty, holy, just, merciful, omnipresent, is affirmed more in relation to an analogical world in which He exists for us than in relation to His being in itself as it is in reality. In this case faith in Him can never completely free itself from ultimate suspicion in face of a Lord whom it pleases to yield Himself to us in this or that form in a kind of sport, without disclosing Himself in reality, without giving us any pledge that in Himself He is not perhaps quite other, and so radically different from the forms of glory in the game played with us that it is not worth while perhaps to take part in this game or this economy. In regard to the glory of God understood in this way, we may well prefer the dark secret of our own existence (as a secret with which we are in any case more intimately concerned) to the whole range of this purely economical glory of God, i.e., to the unknown quantity, the inscrutable being who is concealed by it. In this case, we will be strongly tempted, in spite of the ambiguity of our own life, in spite of the frailty of our own glory, finally to accept these tatters, to try to be our own neighbour, instead of committing ourselves to an enigma in regard to which we cannot conclusively know —if we do so commit ourselves—in whose hands we will rest. It is dangerous and ultimately fatal to faith in God if God is not the Lord of glory, if it is not guaranteed to us that in spite of the analogical nature of the language in which it all has to be expressed God is actually and unreservedly as we encounter Him in His revelation : the Almighty, the Holy, the Just, the Merciful, the Omnipresent, the Eternal, not less but infinitely more so than it is in our power to grasp, and not for us only, but in actuality therefore in Himself. Holy Scripture speaks to us of God in such a way as to give us this assurance. It does not point beyond the whole glory of God to this punctual or linear being, as though the latter is the real and true God, while His glory is only a mode of revelation, a phenomenon. But attesting to us the glory of God, it certifies to us that this Lord of glory is as such the real and true God. In this manner Scripture invites us to serious and true faith in God Himself and not merely to committal to the economy or sport of a great Unknown, even though he may be called the One who loves in freedom. To attest and expound this biblical unity of the Lord with His glory is the business of the doctrine of the divine perfections.

But the task must also be viewed from the other angle. The glory of God can be seen and understood in a way which dissipates and dissolves it because it has no Lord. It then consists in a collection of mighty potencies by which man sees himself surrounded and about which, on the basis of revelation, he must believe that in them all he is confronted by the divine. He must believe in an omnipresent One who penetrates all things. He must believe in His infinite and irresistible power. But he must also believe in a holiness and justice governing both himself and the world—a norm by which he is measured and to which he is responsible without ever being able to satisfy it. Besides all this he must believe further in a goodness and mercy, in a patience reigning over all, in a wisdom which orders all things for the best, holding them together and leading them to a goal, and finally in an eternity from which man springs and towards which he moves. What a strange, obviously inscrutable, incoherent and self-contradictory world of ultimates this is in which he thus finds himself !—and so much the more so the more seriously he takes now the one, now the other of these divine potencies, the more sincerely he wishes to lay it to heart that in all of them he has to do with the Deity. Really with the Deity ? Really with God Himself ? That is just the question—whether the whole so-called glory of God is not really a world of conceptual forces, of principalities and powers, which in the last resort, as the objectified projection of human wishes and fears, is no less but much more of the world, in a certain sense, than the rest of the world and man himself. Where and who is God in this His supposed glory ? Is He more than a collective name for all sorts of ultimate values which as such will still be divine without Him ? How mistaken is our understanding of this glory when the recognition that it is God's glory is only a meaningless appendix to the real view, according to which it is only the cosmos, or rather the chaos, of certain hypostatised principles ! What servitude, in this case, is the alleged worship of God and so-called piety ! What rebellion is concealed behind our submission ! What a desire to break free from our bondage to masters whose claim to rule is obviously compromised by their plurality, and who can in any case be so easily handled that man tries to make himself independent of them all, attributing to himself the power to decide what is holy, righteous, good and eternal, and what in all this is really the One ! Again it is inevitably dangerous and ultimately fatal to faith if God is not the Lord of glory, if we have no guarantee that everything which in heaven and on earth is truly glorious, and therefore all power, goodness, justice and wisdom, are not distinct from Him but are in fact Himself. Here again, everything is made plain to us in Holy Scripture. In testifying to us of God's glory, Holy Scripture does not refer us to this and that, to all sorts of potencies about which we must subsequently allow ourselves to be persuaded that they are God's representatives and servants. But according to Scripture, all the glory of God is concentrated, gathered up and unified in God Himself as the Lord of glory. While in Holy Scripture God has quite definite attributes and an abundance of perfections, we are never concerned merely with these attributes or perfections as such, but with them as His, and therefore always directly with Himself. Therefore Holy Scripture can summon us to a faith which does not consist in the affirmation of all sorts of ultimate values, but in the affirmation of a single genuine sovereignty established over us—an affirmation which has nothing in common with slavish submission, which contains no fear and therefore no seed of revolt in itself. There is revolt against this Lord only in the form of a return to slavery, to the unreal worship and piety which we think ourselves called upon to render to a diffused glory which is not that of God. To show the biblical unity of all glory with its Lord is the task of the doctrine of God's perfections viewed from its second angle.

It should be noted that in this matter we have an exact parallel to the concern of the doctrine of the Holy Trinity. In this doctrine the one God in His three modes of being corresponds to the Lord of glory. As it is of decisive importance to recognise the three modes of being, not only economically as modalism does, but, according to the seriousness of the divine presence and power in the economy of His works, as modes of being of the one eternal God Himself, so it is equally important to understand that God in Himself is not divested of His glory and perfections, that He does not assume them merely in connexion with His self-revelation to the world, but that they constitute His own eternal glory. Again, as it is of decisive importance not to dissolve the unity of the Godhead tritheistically into three gods, but to understand the three modes of being strictly as the modes of being of the one God with whom we have to do in all His works, so it is of equal importance to interpret God's glory and perfections, not in and for themselves, but as the glory of the Lord who alone is able to establish, disclose and confirm them as real glory. The attributes or perfection of God are as it were the letters of the divine Word. It becomes a Word only through the sequence and unity of these letters. But again, it is only in this sequence and unity that the letters can constitute the Word. In the same way the doctrine of God's perfections consists at every point only in the development and confirmation of the doctrine of His being. We can in fact only continue to say that He is the One who loves in freedom. Yet in the doctrine of God's perfections there must be this development and confirmation of the doctrine of His being. It must therefore tread this path.

We next turn our attention to the question of the possibility, legitimacy and necessity of speaking here of perfections (in the plural), of the glory of God as a multiplicity of perfections, and therefore of the latter in their individuality and diversity. This possibility, legitimacy and necessity are not at all self-evident.

That there exists objectively in God Himself a multiplicity of this kind, and therefore individuality and diversity, contradicts what we have indicated as the characteristic relation of simplicity and plenitude in the being of Him who is the Lord of glory. And in the history of Christian doctrine it has been disputed more or less consistently and expressly, but very definitely in substance. The multiplicity of attributes as contrasted with the simplicity of the being of God has always been affirmed to be improper. The simplicity of the divine being has always been held to be the only true description of that being. We must discriminate between an' extreme and a more moderate or mediate form of the opposition which confronts us, but it cannot be ignored that we have to meet it equally decisively in both its forms.

The extreme expression of it is seen in the strict nominalistic thesis as represented by Eunomius in antiquity and William of Occam and Gabriel Biel in the Middle Ages. According to this all individual and distinct statements about the being of God have no other value than that of purely subjective ideas and descriptions (*conceptus, nomina*) to which there is no corresponding reality in God, who is pure simplicity. According to Eunomius God is in fact to be characterised only as *nuda essentia*. Schleiermacher too is probably to be understood in the sense of this extreme opposition—which in the form of a thesis of Meister Eckhart (*nulla distinctio in ipso Deo esse potest aut intelligi*) was condemned as heretical by Pope John XXII in 1329. For as he sees it, all attributes which we distinguish in God (whose being is exhaustively defined in the concept of causality) do not denote something distinctive in God but something distinctive in the way we relate our pure feeling of dependence to Him at various stages of our religious self-consciousness (*The Chr. Faith*, § 50). Corresponding to the absolute unity of God we can see in His attributes only an expression, which our thinking cannot avoid, of the Godhead which in itself is absolutely one (R. Seeberg, *Chr. Dogmatik*, I, 1925, p. 399).

According to the main stream of theological tradition which holds the balance in this matter, the emphasis—in distinction to this strict nominalism—falls less upon the negation, upon the "only," than upon the positive point that the statements concerning a multiplicity of perfections in God are statements expressing our vision of God. They may be made quite decidedly in regard to the characteristic limitations of the human understanding face to face with this object. Thus Irenaeus defined the attributes of God as *earum virtutum quae semper sunt cum Deo appellationes, quemadmodum possibile est et dignum hominibus audire et dicere de Deo* (*Adv. o. h.* II, 13, 9). Thomas Aquinas wrote as follows : *De Deo loquentes, utimur nominibus concretis, ut significemus eius subsistentiam, quia apud nos non subsistunt nisi composita : et utimur nominibus abstractis, ut significemus eius simplicitatem. Quod ergo dicitur Deitas vel vita vel aliquid huiusmodi, esse in Deo, referendum est ad diversitatem, quae est in acceptione intellectus nostri et non ad aliquam diversitatem rei* (*S. theol.* I. qu. 3, *art.* 3, *ad.* 1). *Deus in se consideratus est omnino unus et simplex : sed tamen intellectus noster secundum diversas conceptiones ipsum cognoscit, eo quod non potest ipsum ut in se ipso est, videre. Sed quamvis intelligat ipsum sub diversis conceptionibus, cognoscit tamen quod omnibus suis conceptionibus respondet una et eadem res simplex* (*ibid., qu.* 13, *art.* 12 c). And even more positively : *Sicut diversae res uni simplici rei, quae Deus est, similantur per formas diversas, ita intellectus noster per diversas conceptiones ei aliqualiter similatur. . . . Et ideo de uno intellectus noster multa concipiens non est falsus neque vanus, quia illud simplex esse divinum hujusmodi est, ut ei secundum formas multiplices aliqualiter assimilari possint* (*S. c. gent.*, I, 35). Polanus put it this way : *Proprietates Dei essentiales ut non realiter, ita nec ex natura rei sed ratione distinguntur, aut modo potius, id est nostra conceptione et comprehensione seu nostro intelligendi modo* (*Synt. theol. chr.*, 1609, *col.* 902). Quenstedt wrote : *Quia intellectus noster finitus infinitam et simplicissimam Dei essentiam uno conceptu adaequato adaequate concipere nequit, ideo distinctis et inadaequatis conceptibus essentiam divinam inadaequate repraesentantibus eandem apprehendit, qui conceptus inadaequati dicuntur affectiones et attributa Dei* (*Theol. did. pol.*, 1685, I, *c.* 8, *sect.* 1, *th.* 3). And it could be bluntly formulated by Wegscheider as follows : *Cognitio attributorum Dei . . . ob mentis nostrae imbecillitatem ita comparata est, ut . . . anthropopathiam plus minusve redoleat, nec nisi analogice, symbolice atque imperfecte esse possit* (*Inst. Theol.*, 1815, § 60). The emphasis could also be laid on the fact that, in becoming known to us in this multiplicity of attributes, God Himself has condescended to adjust Himself to our capacities of understanding. This was the opinion of John of Damascus : " God is nameless, but in His mercy allows Himself to be named, as befits our need " (*Ekd.* I, 12). Calvin took the same view : " The attributes of God express *non quis sit apud se, sed qualis erga nos: ut ista eius agnitio vivo magis sensu quam vacua et meteorica speculatione constet* (*Inst.* I, 10, 2). So, too, did Wolleb : *Proprietates divinae sunt attributa Dei, quibus se nobis infirmis cognoscendum praebet et a creaturis distinguit* (*Chr. Theol. comp.*, 1626, I, 1, 2). And so the attributes of God according to C. I. Nitzsch are conceptual expressions of the real relation of God to the world : " The idea of God discloses its quality only as the movements and changes of self- and world-consciousness give occasion " (*Syst. d. chr. Lehre*[6], 1851, p. 149). The nominalistic background and tendency of all these opinions is unmistakable. It is clear that on this basis there is no desire simply to abandon and deny the attributes of God, but actually to assert them, as is in fact done. Even Schleiermacher does this, and more so Thomas Aquinas, and especially Protestant orthodoxy which stood foursquare on this ground. The thesis could even be advanced as in Quenstedt : *Attributa divina ante omnem intellectus nostri operationem revera et proprie sunt in Deo* (*Theol. did. pol.*, 1685, I, *c.* 8, *sect.* 2, *qu.* 2), in which the basic nominalism was apparently —but only apparently.—transcended. Even Polanus realised : *Proprietates essentiales Dei sunt in Deo ab aeterno in aeternum . . . non sunt posteriores essentia Dei quia reipsa sunt idem. . . . Sine proprietatibus divinis essentialibus Deus esse non potest, ne sine seipso sit* (*ibid., col.* 903 f.). And also Petrus van Mastricht : *Omnia attributa vere Deo competere. Est enim, non per cogitationem tantum nostram, sed ex naturae suae conditione bonus, sapiens, justus, etc.* (*Theor.- pract. Theol.*, 1698, II, *cap.* 5, 7). But immediately afterwards Polanus continues: *Non sunt proprie loquendo multae proprietates in Deo sed una tantum, quae nihil aliud est quam ipsa divina essentia . . . sed respectu nostri quasi multae proprietates dicuntur, quia in nobis sunt multae.* And Quenstedt, too, qualifies what he had said: *Si enim proprie et accurate loqui velimus, Deus nullas habet proprietates sed mera et simplicissima est essentia quae nec realem differentiam, nec ullam vel rerum vel modorum admittit compositionem. . . . Quia vero simplicissimam Dei essentiam uno adaequato conceptu adaequate concipere non possumus, ideo inadaequatis et distinctis conceptibus inadaequate essentiam divinam repraesentantibus eum apprehendimus, quos . . . attributa vocamus. Et sic intellectus noster distinguit, quae ex parte rei distincta non sunt* (*ibid., ekth.* 3). So, too, does Petrus van Mastricht: *Attributa Deo competere quasi in esse quodam secundo, quatenus prius essentiam Dei concipimus velut radicem a qua attributa oriuntur. Concipimus enim, Deum esse, antequam concipere possumus, eum misericordem, sapientem, justum esse* (*loc. cit.*). It was gladly conceded that this *modus concipiendi* was *non destitutus omni fundamento in re* (Quenstedt, *ibid., font. sol.*, 5), and on this was based the justification and necessity of speaking *vere et proprie*, not merely anthropopathically, of God's attributes. Even in Catholic dogmatics, which follow St. Thomas, there is much talk of this *fundamentum in re*. But an explanation of what is to be understood by this *fundamentum* has never been vouchsafed. Nor could it properly be investigated. For the presupposition stood firm that by the being of God must be meant His *essentia* as such, i.e., at bottom His *nuda essentia*, whose simplicity must be conceptually the first and last and real thing, the *proprium*, with which we are here concerned, and in comparison with which every other statement can have no further value than that of a concession, a purely secondary truth. It is very plain in Polanus, Quenstedt and van Mastricht that they are making efforts to do justice to the emphasis with which the Bible speaks of the being of God as having specific attributes. The statement that the *proprietates Dei* are not *qualitates aut accidentia* of His being but this being itself, may be defined as the kernel of the older doctrine of the divine attributes. But it was invariably interpreted unfavourably to the *proprietates*, so that in the last resort the latter necessarily lose their reality in favour of the *essentia*. For they were conceived as rooted, not in the *essentia* as such, but—in spite of occasional reservations and occasional happy assertions to the contrary—only in its relation to us and our relations to it. The fact that the life of God was identified with the notion of pure being, the fact that the idea of God was not determined by the doctrine of the Trinity, but that the latter was shaped by a general conception of God (that of ancient Stoicism and Neo-Platonism), was now avenged at the most sensitive spot. Starting from the generalised notion of God, the idea of the divine simplicity was necessarily exalted to the all-controlling principle, the idol, which, devouring everything concrete, stands behind all these formulae. As a result it was impossible to make proper use of what Augustine had so happily indicated with his phrase *multiplex simplicitas* or *simplex multiplicitas*: the triumphant unity in God of the Lord with glory and of glory with the Lord. From this starting-point we can speak only hesitantly about the reality of the divine perfections. On this basis, when we speak of God, we must mean essentially only the simplicity and not the richness, at best the simplicity of the richness, but at bottom only the simplicity. We may try to specify, but in the last resort we can intend and demonstrate only the barrenness of *nuda essentia*. This was done only in the last resort. There was at least a hesitation. The themes suggested by the Bible were not simply abandoned. In spite of the alien presupposition, and within the conditions which it imposed, they were adopted and an attempt was made to exploit them. This was the best feature of all these systems. But there was in fact a hesitation between the reality and unreality, between an objective and a purely subjective discrimination of the divine attributes. As D. F. Strauss (*Die chr. Glaubenslehre*) ridiculed, they were placed in an " unhappy midway position." This is indisputable. It was indeed an unhappy position because the attributes of God had to be affirmed *proprie* and yet they could not be ; because the *proprie* uttered by the lips could be interpreted only as an *improprie* ; because in this position what had to be affirmed had already been denied by the whole approach.

It is to the credit of certain German theologians of the 19th century that in this matter they broke utterly, not only with the total, but also with the partial nominalism of the Thomistic and orthodox Protestant tradition. " Christian faith lives in the countenance of the eternal and omnipresent, the holy and gracious God, and for it these specific attributes belong so little to the purely subjective sphere of a mere perception of God which does not correspond to anything really existing in God that for it God would cease to be the living and true God without such attributes and would become a lifeless shadowy abstraction. That the many, the manifold, the diverse, is thus attributed to God in His self-existence does not embarrass faith or lead it astray as regards God's absoluteness and unity. On the contrary, it would not recognise God as the real, the absolute, the One, if it were not permitted to ascribe to Him also the attributes of eternity, omnipotence and.holiness as objectively belonging to Him." " The dogmatic formulation of these attributes can correspond to faith-consciousness only when both aspects—the objective reality of the attributes as manifold and distinct (in accordance with their meaning), and also the unbroken unity of God on which these attributes ultimately rest, and which alone in fact confers on them their reality—stand out clearly and complete each other without contradiction " (F. H. R. Frank, *Syst. d. chr. Wahrh.*[2], 1885, Vol. I, pp. 222 f.). The statement that the attributes of God are nothing other than His being is correct, as is also the further statement that in them the relationship of God to the other, to the created world, is made known. But it is not right to oppose these statements " as though, because God's relation to the other is expressed in them, these attributes are so much the less or not at all the being of God, or as though, because the attributes actually are and express the being of God, this somehow precludes them from expressing it in its relationship to the other. For they must belong to the divine being, they must constitute and characterise the divine being, if they are at all divine attributes, and if that which is divine cannot come to God from that which He is not " (*op. cit.*, p. 226). " If God exists only in a relationship to the world, then all His attributes are only relations, revelations and effects in the world—and such a view imperils God's independence of the world ; for in that case He becomes what He is only through His relationship to the world. . . . But there is a relationship of God to Himself . . . and in this is grounded the justification for affirming immanent or essential attributes in God " (G. Thomasius, *Christi Person und Werk*[3], 1886, Vol. I, p. 38). J. A. Dorner argued on the same correct lines : " If God refuses to allow us any knowledge of His being in itself, but only of His being in its relation to the world, then He reveals to the world, because not Himself, necessarily some other than Himself" (*System der chr. Glaubenslehre*[3], Vol. I, 1886, p. 191). "Since God cannot wish to appear other than He is, and since no dualistic power checks His will to reveal Himself, then it must be that in God's self-revelations we see revelations of what and how He is (not simply what and how He is not), and therefore the revelation of objective attributes " (*op. cit.*, p. 186). This is the line of thought which we must develop.

We shall develop the truth of the multiplicity, individuality and diversity of God's perfections—in view of the nominalistic contesting and the semi-nominalistic weakening of them and in answer to both— in three explanatory propositions.

1. The multiplicity, individuality and diversity of the divine perfections are those of the one divine being and therefore not those of another divine nature allied to it. In regard to the realistic understanding of the divine perfections, the question has been asked whether it does not imply the existence of a second, alien divinity in God. To such a question our answer must be a flat negative. In so far as God is almighty, eternal, wise and merciful, it does not add anything new or strange or half-divine to His being as the One who loves in freedom. On the contrary, the divine being as the One who loves in freedom is the divine being in the multiplicity, individuality and diversity of these perfections. He does not possess this wealth. He Himself is this wealth. He is not what He is in a height or depth beyond these His perfections in their multiplicity, individuality and diversity. But He is Himself the perfect One in the abundance and variety of these His perfections. Every question : Of what nature is God ? can be understood only as a repetition of the question : Who is God ? and any attempt to answer the former question can be only a repetition of the answer which is given us by God Himself to the latter question—an answer which makes possible and necessary both the question : Who is God ? and the question : Of what nature is God ? In describing God as almighty, eternal, wise, or merciful, we are only repeating this answer ; we are only naming Him again and yet again as the One who loves in freedom. But by reason of the fact that it comes from the living One who loves in freedom this answer is so framed that we must continually repeat it, not speaking of any other but God's one being, but in continual recognition and confirmation of the plenitude and richness of this one being of God. God is in essence all that He is. But He is in essence not only one, but multiple, individual and diverse. And these are His perfections.

The maxim opposed to the realistic understanding of these perfections : *In Deum non cadit accidens*, is therefore correct in itself. But just because it is so true it must be applied from both points of view. When Gilbert de la Porrée (d. 1154) taught that the Godhead as the fulness of the divine attributes was really distinct from God, that God was God through His Godhead, just as man is man through his humanity, Bernard of Clairvaux and the Synod of Reims (1148) in the presence of Pope Eugenius III rightly brought against him the proposition : *non aliquo sensu catholico posse negari, quin divinitas sit Deus et Deus divinitas. Si vero dicitur: Deum sapientia sapientem, magnitudine magnum, aeternitate aeternum, unitate unum, divinitate deum esse et alia huiusmodi—credimus nonnisi ea sapientia, quae est ipse Deus, sapientem esse, nonnisi ea magnitudine, quae est ipse Deus, magnum esse, nonnisi ea aeternitate, quae est ipse Deus, aeternum esse, nonnisi ea unitate, quae est ipse Deus, unum esse, nonnisi ea divinitate, Deum, quae est ipse, id est se ipso sapientem, magnum, aeternum, unum Deum* (Denz. No. 389). Two centuries later the same problem occupied the Greek Church, unfortunately with just the opposite result. It was the monks of the mountain of Athos who under the leadership of Gregorius Palamas expounded the doctrine of an eternal and uncreated light which could yet be communicated to the creature, and had shone among other places on the mount of transfiguration, and had also appeared to them. In the discussion arising from the opposition by the monk Barlaam, these so-called "Hesychasts" (so-called because their real aim was a theological foundation for mysticism) worked out the view that although this light is ἄκτιστον, unearthly, and divine, as comprehending all the divine effects, influences and exercises of power in its relation to the world, it must be distinguished from the true being of God, and represents as it were a halfway stage of the divine, on which it becomes capable of a link with the creature and can communicate to it a higher nature. "It is a question of divine influences (θεότητες) proceeding from God and indissolubly bound up with Him, of emanations from the Trinity which is complete in itself" (*P.R.E.*[3], Vol. 8, art. "Hesychasten"). To this the unfortunately ineffective answer was given, especially by Nicephorus Gregoras, that such a distinction between the being and the effective reality of God must lead either to the affirmation of a further divine hypostasis and therefore to a quaternity in God, or else to the supposition of a divine power in the world without subject, to a doctrine of two gods, an ὑπερκείμενος and an ὑφείμενος. God's being in itself is not without effect, and God's effects are those of His being : God not only has but is αὐτοενέργεια, and it is in Him that there is to be sought and found whatever twofoldness and manifoldness He evinces in His relation to the world. But the abstract conception of the simplicity of the divine being on the one hand, and on the other hand the imperious desire to have a direct mystical experience of the power of God, have always been too strong in the Greek Church and theology for it to be possible to make a halt here. A synod of Constantinople in 1351—without attaining conceptual clarity—ranged itself on the side of the Hesychasts, and Eastern Orthodoxy is committed to their doctrine up to the present day. The Western Church rightly took the part of Barlaam and his defeated supporters : for the Hesychastic doctrine separates what must not be separated if the being and attributes of God are not to become in fact two distinct divine spheres ; if the being of God is not to become completely formless and the form of God completely lacking in being. At the same time it must be asked whether Western orthodoxy, in so far as it transferred itself to the semi-nominalistic line and therefore sought to limit the attributes of God to His relation to the world, is not itself on the path which leads to the errors of Gilbert de la Porrée and Gregorius Palamas (note for instance the above-quoted sentence of Petrus van Mastricht about the *esse quodam secundo* in which the attributes of God have their reality). If it is desired to avoid these errors, we have not only to challenge the separation of the attributes from the being of God, but also to note and emphasise the positive aspect of our proposition—that the perfections of God in their multiplicity and variety do not arise simply from His relation to the world, but are those of His own being as He who loves in freedom.

2. The multiplicity, individuality and diversity of the perfections of God are those of His simple being, which is not therefore divided and then put together again. In God multiplicity, individuality and diversity do not stand in any contradiction to unity. Rather the very unity of His being consists in the multiplicity, individuality and diversity of His perfections, which since they are His are not capable of any dissolution or separation or non-identity, and which again since they are His are capable of genuine multiplicity, individuality and diversity. The plurality which is to be predicated of God can therefore, even in its multiplicity, because it is the multiplicity of God, signify only the unity. The unity which is to be predicated of God must with equal necessity, because it is in reference to God, signify the plurality. Every individual trait which is to be affirmed

of God can signify only the one, but the one which is to be affirmed of Him must of necessity signify also every individual trait and the totality of all individual traits. Every distinction in God can be affirmed only in such a way as implies at the same time His unity and therefore the lack of essential discrepancy in what is distinguished. But again, it would not really be the unity of God if no distinctions were recognised and confessed. Our doctrine therefore means that every individual perfection in God is nothing but God Himself and therefore nothing but every other divine perfection. It means equally strictly on the other hand that God Himself is nothing other than each one of His perfections in its individuality, and that each individual perfection is identical with every other and with the fulness of them all.

Totus ipse sibimet ipsi similis et aequalis est ; totus quum sit sensus et totus spiritus et totus sensualitas et totus ennoia et totus ratio et totus auditus et totus oculus et totus lumen et totus fons omnium bonorum (Irenaeus, *Adv. o.h.* II, 13, 3). Καθ᾽ ὅλον γὰρ οὐδὲν ἐφ᾽ ἑαυτοῦ τῶν ὑψηλῶν τούτων ὀνομάτων διεζευγμένων τῶν ἄλλων ἀρετὴ κατὰ μόνας ἐστίν. Apart from its unity with all the others, no one of the divine perfections will be good and hence divine (Gregory of Nyssa, *Or. cat.* 20). *Proprietates in Deo non sunt . . . res ab essentia aut a se invicem diversae* (Wolleb, *Comp. theol. chr.*, 1626, I, 1, 2, c. 1). *Proprietates Dei non sunt partes essentiae divinae, sed quaelibet proprietas essentialis est ipsamet Dei essentia tota et integra, ita ut essentia Dei et essentialis Dei proprietas non sunt aliud et aliud, sed unum et idem. . . . Quicquid Deus est aut in sese agit, uno et eodem actu, qui est ipsius essentia, id est in sese agit ; ideo uno et eodem actu simplex, infinitus, immutabilis est, uno et eodem actu vivit, intelligit, vult, amat,* etc. (Polanus, *op. cit., col.* 902 f.). But as against this we must also emphasise another statement of Polanus : *Proprietates essentiales Dei sunt in Deo ab aeterno in aeternum . . . non sunt posteriores essentia Dei, qua reipsa sunt idem . . . Sine proprietatibus divinis essentialibus Deus esse non potest, ne sine seipso sit : ipse enim ipsissima sapientia, bonitas, potentia est.* We must reject out of hand the semi-nominalistic reservation that in the last resort we can speak of the *proprietates Dei* only *improprie*, that the most characteristic inner being of God is a *simplicitas* which is to be understood undialectically. If we refuse to do this and to recognise that God's being transcends the contrast of *simplicitas* and *multiplicitas*, including and reconciling both, it is hard to see how we can escape the view of a God who is extremely lofty in His pure simplicity but also quite empty and unreal. It is also hard to see with what justification and emphasis, in consideration of God's relation to the world, we can still speak of His various perfections as those of the one true God. If God is the God who is rich in Himself, and if He is the one true God even in His works *ad extra*, we cannot emphasise either His *simplicitas* or His *multiplicitas* as though the one or the other *in abstracto* were the very being of God, as though the one inevitably precluded the other. We can only accept and interpret God's *simplicitas* and *multiplicitas* in such a way as to imply that they are not mutually exclusive but inclusive, or rather that they are both included in God Himself.

3. The multiplicity, individuality and diversity of God's perfections are rooted in His own being and not in His participation in the character of other beings. The recognition of divine attributes cannot be taken to mean that for us God is subsumed under general notions, under the loftiest ideas of our knowledge of creaturely reality, and that He participates in its perfections. It is not that we recognise

and acknowledge the infinity, justice, wisdom, etc. of God because we already know from other sources what all this means and we apply it to God in an eminent sense, thus fashioning for ourselves an image of God after the pattern of our image of the world, i.e., in the last analysis after our own image. Even less in the ontic sphere is it that God shares in truths and realities distinct from Himself, that He is subordinated to certain general laws of being, so that He can be defined in accordance with this participation and subordination and therefore to have such and such qualities. God is subordinate to no idea in which He can be conceived as rooted or by which He can be properly measured. There are not first of all power, goodness, knowledge, will, etc. in general, and then in particular God also as one of the subjects to whom all these things accrue as a predicate. But everything that God is, and that is in God, is—as the origin of all that is distinct from God and that can be the predicate of other subjects too—first and properly in Him. Indeed, it is first and properly God Himself as the One who loves in freedom, He Himself in His own being. Therefore God does not borrow what He is from outside, from some other. On the contrary, it is the problem of everything that exists outside of Him that it can be what it is only in virtue of the truth and reality imparted to it by God. God is the being of all beings, the law of all laws, and therefore the nature of every nature. In Himself, then, He is rich, multiple, individual and diverse. He does not need to become this by entering into relation with the " golden outpouring of the world."

The older dogmatics expressed this logically by the declaration that God's attributes are not *formae accidentales seu accidentia*, and are not to be understood in the sense that God is subject to the categories of being or of our thought : *Nihil est in Deo non per se subsistens*, i.e. nothing which presupposes as general possibilities quantity, quality, movement, suffering, space, time and so on. But apart from all such presuppositions God is in Himself—as pure act without potentiality—the basis of all such presuppositions, and therefore is in His own being infinite, good, wise and merciful. *Proprietates Dei essentiales sunt actus, prout Deus actus purissimus est et simplicissimus* (Polanus, *op. cit., col.* 904). All this would be excellent, so far as it goes, if it were not for the cloven hoof of semi-nominalism which at once appears and obviously compromises everything again with the explanation : *Proprie loquendo* there is only one *proprietas Dei*, namely His *essentia*—*sed respectu nostri quasi multae proprietates dicuntur, quia in nobis sunt multae : in Deo autem sunt una reipsa ; ratione tantum differunt, rationeque multae sunt, et quidem non ipsius Dei sed nostri ratione, nimirum magis ut intelligentiae nostrae accommodantur, quam ut revera sunt (quae enim creatura eas ut sunt, intelligeret ?) inter se distinguuntur, quoniam tam ὑπερούσιον καὶ ὑπερ-ουράνιον φύσιν explicare aut intelligere non nisi nostris verbis et pro nostri captus ratione possumus. Intellectus noster non potest uno simplici actu, sed necesse habet multis distinctisque actibus, ut alia omnia, ita et Deum cognoscere (op. cit., col.* 904). The fiction which is concealed behind this consideration consists in the fact that, owing to the dazzling effect of the platonic-aristotelian idea of being, in which men thought they had attained knowledge of God, it was felt necessary to ascribe a much higher dignity to the idea of the one as against that of the many—so much higher, in fact, that in the application of this idea of the one it was thought possible to speak of God *proprie*, as though even in this case God is not spoken of *respectu nostri*, *pro nostri captus ratione* ; as though in view of God's (own) hiddenness in His revelation it does not have to be totally conceded that our ideas—including that of the one also—are in themselves unsuitable and inadequate for the comprehension of God ; and as though on the fundamental assumption that God in His hiddenness has revealed Himself to us and has authorised us to apply our conceptual systems to Him, while realising their limitations, the multiplicity of His being is not to be taken just as seriously as its unity. Yielding to this fiction and on the basis of a philosophical prejudice introducing the distinction between *proprie* and *improprie* where everything is in itself to be understood and spoken *improprie*, but *proprie* on the ground and after the pattern of the divine revelation, these thinkers did the very thing which they were trying to avoid. On the one hand, they falsely defined the being of God, which they were supposed to be defining *proprie*, in such a way that it did not transcend but was subject to this notion of unity. On the other hand, they made the multiplicity of the divine attributes, which they wanted to ascribe to God only *improprie*, dependent on the discursiveness of the human intellect and the manifoldness of the created world. In both cases—contrary enough to the original intention—they worked under the presupposition of an intrinsically fixed order of ideas within the framework of which they thought to do God the honour of including His being in the notion of the one but of excluding it from the supposedly less exalted notion of the many. But the whole point was that they should not have subsumed the idea of God at all in either case, but that they should have done justice conceptually to His revealed being as such. That is, they should have given the glory to God in His multiplicity just as seriously and truly as in His unity and confessed Him unreservedly in His multiplicity as such—God Himself as the One, but as the One who is also the Many.

The further fundamental question to which we must now turn, is this : To what extent do these many individual and various perfections of God exist ? How do we come to recognise them as such, and to speak of them *proprie*, i.e., on the basis of God's revelation, and in responsibility to this revelation, without reservation in respect of their truth ?

In traditional theology this question is known as the problem of the derivation and distribution of the divine attributes. The apparent unsuitability of these ideas is obvious at once. We can see how close and tempting at this point is a total or partial nominalism. For what is there to derive and distribute when it is a question of the being of God and His perfections ? Were we not compelled at the outset to declare that each of the divine perfections is materially identical with each of the others and with the fulness of them all, indeed with God Himself ? that every statement about the divine attributes can only be a repetition of the statement about the divine being ? How, then, can there be a derivation and a distribution ? Well, we can and must put the question. One of the useful results of our previous considerations is that we can realise that this is not a meaningless but a necessary question. That God in all His multiplicity is the One and that all multiplicity in Him is He Himself, the One, is only one aspect of the matter, which we must certainly keep in view. But again, it is also written that God not only appears but is almighty, eternal, just, wise, merciful—not merely for us but in Himself. And although in all this He is concealed from us in so far as these words are our words and not His own Word about Himself, yet it remains true that we are invited and authorised by His revelation to name Him with these words of ours in the confidence that in this way we are moving in the sphere of truth and not of falsehood so long as we are always willing to allow Him to be Himself the interpreter of these human words which He has placed upon our lips. If this is the case, the question of understanding His being in detail, the question of the derivation and distribution of His attributes—however inappropriate such ideas may seem to be at first sight—cannot really be meaningless and void. If we are not to renounce altogether the task of saying who and in what mode God is—and in the Christian Church, at any rate in theology, particularly dogmatics, there can be no question of such a renunciation—we will not try to evade this very task, however strange it may appear. The knowledge of God is true knowledge and not vague surmise and sentiment. As knowledge it has to be expressed in words. It cannot spare itself the trouble of formulation. The objectivity of God in His revelation has to be taken seriously, so that in regard to God we cannot be content merely with a devout silence and a rapturous whisper. The humility of our knowledge of God does not consist in the laziness of the servant who took his pound and buried it (Mt. 25[18]), but in the fact that, invited and authorised by revelation to do so, we give God the honour which belongs to Him, to the very best—no less—of our ability, i.e., of the ability which He Himself gives us. But this being the case, we not merely may but must ask in human words and concepts what God is and is not, and in what way He is what He is, and therefore in some sense what are the upper and lower aspects, the right and the left, the contours of His being. And that is the question of the derivation and distribution of His attributes. If we refuse to ask these questions, we must consider whether we are not secretly of the opinion that it is preferable to renounce the attempt to know God, or to abandon ourselves in this matter to our own arbitrary opinion or to chance. We must consider how we can accept responsibility for either the one or the other in view of the fact of divine revelation, which takes from us the pretext of our incapacity, and in face of which we have therefore no excuse if—especially in view of the many attempts in this sphere already undertaken in the history of theology—we should wish to prefer laziness to industry or confusion to order.

No serious attempt to expound the Christian doctrine of God has in fact been able completely to evade the problem which confronts us, although obviously all or the majority of those who have occupied themselves with the subject have had to overcome at this point a certain difficulty. It is rather laughable to notice how again and again earlier attempts to say something appropriate in this connexion, and especially what is supposed to be the chaotic diversity of these attempts, have at once evoked the astonishment, the pity and the rather sceptical amusement of those who came later. But although the latter would obviously have preferred to ignore the whole matter, they found it quite impossible to avoid coming to grips with the question on their own account, taking up some attitude to its problems and finally enriching the wealth of previous material with further possibilities.

If we look closely, the task will be found to be not so impossibly difficult as may at first sight appear. It is going too far to speak of chaos in face of the undeniable abundance of previous attempts to solve the problem. If we talk in this way we shall inevitably lose courage and drop the question as meaningless. Nor is it the case that every newcomer to this question has found a new solution, so that we ourselves will have to find a new answer on the assumption that everything so far accomplished is confused and unserviceable. The case is rather that there are a number of errors which we have to avoid and reject, but that they are relatively easy to discover, summarise and unmask. And on the other hand there is also a classical, and to some extent ecumenical line of theological reflection into which the previous course of our argument readily leads. We shall have to move along it in our own distinctive manner (if we can convince ourselves of its rightness). But from the presence of many companions to the right and left, we may conclude that it does not need any special depth of intelligence to find our bearings correctly in the whole matter.

In this connexion we may consider as obvious errors all those types of a doctrine of attributes which attempt to define and order the perfections of God as though they were the various predicates of a kind of general being presupposed as known already, whereas in reality each of them is the characteristic being of God Himself as He discloses Himself in His revelation. The right way, on the contrary, will consist in understanding the attributes of God as those of this His special being itself and therefore of His life, of His love in freedom.

It is noteworthy that although these errors are ultimately rooted in the mistakes which constantly beset the doctrine of the Early Church, they have become palpably manifest only in more recent types of theology. Orthodoxy, on the other hand, in spite of the doubtful nature of its approach, displayed sure instinct in moving into the right way, at least as regards fundamentals, and in remaining in it. We will now indicate the various principal attempts from which we must dissociate ourselves in view of our previous considerations. They fall into three categories.

1. The attempt has been made to bring the attributes of God as it were within a psychological framework. This has its occasion and its relative justification in the fact that Holy Scripture undoubtedly characterises God as a person and therefore as a thinking or knowing and a willing subject. Rightly, therefore, the dogmatics of the Early Church did not omit to speak of the *intellectus* and *voluntas Dei*, nor can we omit to do so in so far as we interpret God as the One who loves in freedom. In the theology of the 18th and 19th centuries it was thought necessary to broaden this very simple psychology by speaking of a feeling in God (as, for example, A. E. Biedermann, *Dogmatik*, 1869, p. 635,

and R. Seeberg, *Chr. Dogm.*, I, 1925, pp. 334, 428 f.). The ontological aspect of the Godhead in its freedom or absoluteness or aseity, which appears to recede into the background in such an attempt, is understood by its exponents as a framework which fashions and embraces all these psychological categories. In Biedermann's essay, as we have seen, this framework is in fact understood in such a way that it absorbs these categories. The psychological expression of the idea of God is, therefore, a mere form of the inherently impersonal and absolute process of spirit. It is not true in itself, but it has conceptual value. When put in this logical way, the doubtfulness of the whole approach becomes apparent. Orthodoxy did not press it to this logical conclusion. It was willing to allow truth to the psychological attributes of God, although with regrettable nominalistic reservations. And it spoke with equal definiteness of the other attributes of God which cannot be brought under any psychological category because they are the attributes of divine freedom, absoluteness or aseity, and yet as such they are no less (though no more) but with equal truth the attributes of the one divine being. The psychological category must be duly taken into account as a principle of derivation and distribution, seeing that God is the One who does actually love in freedom. But it must not be given the position of a supreme governing principle in the whole doctrine of attributes, because there can be no such overriding principle where God Himself is all. Nor must it subsequently be assigned a position of inferiority as is apparent in Biedermann. The freedom of God is not merely the form of His love nor is His love only the form of His freedom. It is only the arbitrariness of an attempt to make the being of God correspond definitely with the being of man, to find in God the absolute expression of man, which can give rise to this psychological approach. And this arbitrariness betrays itself in its empty formalism, for in the definition of knowing, willing and feeling generally, what after all is said about God ? What happens here to the presupposition that in regard to the attributes of God it cannot be a question of neutral descriptions, but only of divine perfections ? For instance, is the wisdom of God only a specific mode of His knowledge, or the justice, holiness or mercy of God only a specific mode of His will ? Where is the beneficence and the absolute authority of a God who is defined in so human and at bottom so neutral a way ?

2. A further principle of derivation and distribution that has been proposed is the religio-genetic. This second and, in its way, very interesting type is represented by Schleiermacher and his most authentic pupil Alexander Schweizer. We have seen how Schleiermacher tried to interpret the attributes of God as an objectification of the individual aspects of the religious self-consciousness. According to him there results from this consciousness itself (apart from the antithesis of sin and grace) God's eternity, omnipresence, omnipotence and omniscience. From the religious consciousness in antithesis (i.e., the consciousness of sin) there results God's holiness and justice. And from the religious consciousness of a resolution of this disharmony (the consciousness of grace) there results God's love and wisdom. In A. Schweizer (*Chr. Glaubenslehre* [2], Vol. I, 1877) pious feeling finds God in the world of nature as omnipotence, omniscience, eternity and omnipresence, in the world of ethics as goodness, holiness, wisdom and justice, and in the specifically Christian life of sanctification as love and grace, fatherly wisdom and mercy. We must at once concede to this attempt that in its way—here too within the limits of the nominalistic presupposition—it has aimed with obvious sincerity at getting beyond a purely formal idea of God and at bringing out the beneficence and authority of God. But what justification is there for attributing to the actual successive stages in the religious consciousness something specially corresponding in the being of God ? With what right can it be said of the consciousness of sin, for example, that in it is implied the realisation of the holiness and justice of God, or of pious feeling towards the world of nature that it necessarily leads to the knowledge

of God's omnipotence and omniscience ? What place does this leave for the insight so carefully and rightly preserved in orthodoxy that the divine being cannot be torn asunder into a series of attributes each real and true in itself ? Is there at Schweizer's first stage a real knowledge of God's eternity without the knowledge of God's holiness and mercy, which is presumably not reached until the second and third stages ? And is the recognition of God's justice, which is possible at the second stage, really the justice of God without the grace of God, which is presumably not recognisable until the third stage ? Is not the criterion that we are really confronted by an attribute of God the fact that it must be an attribute of the one God Himself and therefore must include in itself every other and the totality of all others ? Do we recognise the being of God otherwise than by recognising God Himself in His absoluteness, and therefore in each distinct attribute every other attribute and the totality of them all ? The creative role which in this approach is assigned to the subject of religious experience, and in particular the naturalistic theology which lies at the basis of it, works itself out in the shape of an utterly catastrophic dissolution and destruction of the whole conception of God. Schleiermacher and Schweizer certainly did not desire such a dissolution. But if it is insisted that the various stages—and this was Schleiermacher's express meaning—are simultaneous strata or aspects of one and the same religious consciousness, why is there this concern for their independence, their value as special sources of knowledge ? If, on the other hand, we take seriously the genetic character of these various stages—as Schweizer did in contradistinction to Schleiermacher—this derivation and distribution leads not so much to the attributes of the one being of God as to a hierarchy of general and particular, superior and subordinate, divine or rather religious ideas and hypostases hanging lifelessly in the air. The whole wrongheadedness of the nominalistic treatment of the doctrine of attributes becomes apparent in this attempt of Schleiermacher and Schweizer. What is found is just what is sought, but only what is sought, viz., the gigantic reflections or projections of the human religious consciousness. What is found is man himself and as such on his supposed way to God which in reality is only the way to his own inner self. And it is only with difficulty that he can be persuaded that in this way he has found God. " This dissolution, according to which God the Creator does not really possess for the disciples of Schleiermacher the attributes of justice, wisdom, mercy, etc., follows quite naturally from the fact that man insists on constructing the idea of God from the human understanding and consciousness, and so utters things about God which have no solidity and reality in themselves, but only formal validity " (J. Wichelhaus, *Die Lehre der hl. Schrift* [3], 1892, p. 333).

3. The third type is perhaps best defined as the historico-intuitive, and it is the one which calls forth the strongest disapproval. For, although it has for some time been very pressingly recommended on account of its supposed great simplification and religious deepening of the problem (F. Nitzsch, *Lehrb. d. ev. Dogm.*, 3rd ed. by H. Stephan, 1912, p. 452), it treats the whole matter in a truncated and innocuous way which completely fails to do justice to its full seriousness, in spite of the many true and important things which are noted. An illustration of the argument used may be taken from the dogmatics of Julius Kaftan (3-4 ed., 1901, §§ 13-18). First it is explained that what has usually been characterised as the freedom of the divine being (" the absolute ") really entered Christian theology only as a result of the world-renouncing nature of early piety and the philosophical tradition of antiquity. It was unfortunately retained by Protestant orthodoxy, which was dependent on scholasticism, and, most regrettably, by Luther himself in *De servo arbitrio*. In face of this tradition we must get back to the divine self-revelation attested in Scripture and to be received in faith, especially as it is rooted and breaks forth in the innermost consciousness of the personal life of Jesus. While the absolute is only a theological framework in every religion of the spirit, we must infer from revelation that God is an

other-worldly personal Spirit. In this connexion other-worldly means only that the divine being and life are distinct from those of the world (i.e., the material world) and that the attributes of this spirit are love, holiness and omnipotence. Holiness is to be understood as the predicate of love, and again omnipotence as the predicate of holy love. What does this involve ? The Neo-Platonism of orthodox tradition has been completely jettisoned and with it the arbitrary speculations of its liberally minded heirs. And God's revelation attested in Scripture seems now to have gained expression. But is this really the case ? Only to the extent that the spirit which is now described as love, distinguished as holy love and finally equipped with almighty power (it differs from the spirit of the Hegelians by reason of its strongly moralistic character), the spirit which constitutes the secret of the personal life of Jesus, is proclaimed as the divine being, and God is subjected to these metaphysical categories, and to this conceptual schema. But this spirit is not really, or in any sense, the divine Spirit. It is a particular interpretation of the human spirit. This is shown by the directness with which, by dint of historical intuitions, its reality is read off from the personal life of Jesus as from a blackboard. There is read out of revelation that which has previously been read into it as an already known universal. In this way there can be constructed the being of a God who is only too familiar apart from all revelation. If the serious defect of the orthodox tradition had really been overcome in this scheme, if the revelation of God had really been allowed to speak, it would have been impossible simply to ignore the problem of the aseity (the freedom) of God to which the orthodox tradition and even the speculative Liberals rightly draw attention even though they handle it with unfortunate results. But this is what inevitably happens when it is thought to avoid the Scylla of speculation by taking refuge in the Charybdis of historical intuition. To what extent are the love, holiness and omnipotence in question really *divine* love, holiness and omnipotence ? This is the question to which the Ritschlians return as unsatisfactory an answer as do the orthodox and their liberal heirs to the question to what extent the infinite simple being (which for them is God) really deserves to be called *divine* being ? If love is lacking to the freedom which the latter rightly stress, freedom is lacking to the love which the Ritschlians again rightly stress. What happens in both cases may be called " a strong simplification " and even, if we like, " a religious deepening ". Obviously, however, it is not a Christian simplification and deepening in either case, but from the Christian aspect the procedure adopted on both sides involves what we can only describe as an over-simplification.

Besides these, there is, however, another and better way. It has all kinds of variations, but the theme remains unmistakable. It was followed by the older theology, and in its track many of the more recent theologians. Briefly this way was and is characterised by the fact that serious attention is paid to the twofold question answered in the preceding section : Who and what is God ? in respect of the diversity as well as the unity of its two parts, with the result that a doctrine of attributes is strictly to be understood and expounded as that which alone it can be—a repetition and development of the doctrine of the being of God. On this path—which for us will mean that we shall have to enquire into the perfections of the divine loving and those of the divine freedom —the orthodox Lutheran theologians of the 17th century distinguished more or less happily and exactly—not without a dangerous admixture of their dangerous basic ideas, but in substance with obvious consistency and accuracy—between *attributa negativa* and *positiva*, or *quiescentia* and *operativa*, or *interna* and *externa*, or *absoluta* and *relativa*, or *immanentia* and *transeuntia*, or *primitiva* and *derivata*, or *metaphysica* and *moralia*. In the older Reformed schools the distinction was almost invariably between *attributa incommunicabilia* and *communicabilia*. Among the later theologians Wegscheider (*Instit. Theol.*, 1815, §§ 62 and 64) distinguished between attributes of the *substantia perfectissima infinita per se spectata* and attributes of the *substantia perfectissima spiritualis*. Martensen (*Chr. Dogm.*, 1856, p. 85) enquired about the relationship between the unity of God and the opposition in which He finds Himself towards the world. Frank (*Syst. d. chr. Wahrheit* [2], 1885, Vol. I, pp. 232 f.) tried to interpret the attributes first as attributes of the absolute God and then as such of the personal triune God, but with not the slightest suggestion " that the attributes which first referred to the absolute God are not at the same time those of the personal being and those connected primarily with the personal God are not also proper to His absolute Godhead." R. A. Lipsius (*Lehr. d. ev. prot. Dogm.*[2], 1879, p. 224) distinguished between the metaphysical and psychological attributes of God, while Wichelhaus (*Die Lehre der hl. Schrift* [3], 1892, p. 333 and E. Böhl, *Dogmatik*, 1887, pp. 45 f.) tried to follow out the same distinction in the light of the distinction between the biblical names for God, Elohim and Yahweh, θεός and κύριος. Even among the Ritschlians, in spite of their quite different point of view, traces of this classical distinction can be detected. O. Kirn (*Grundriss d. ev. Dogm.*, 1930, p. 55) distinguishes between " formal (metaphysical) attributes which express God's transcendence over the world," and " material (ethical) attributes which express the content and direction of the divine will and action." T. Haering (*Der chr. Glaube*, 1906, p. 320) distinguishes attributes of God's holy love and attributes of His absolute being. And finally even for E. Troeltsch (*Glaubensl.*, 1925, pp. 183 f. and 212 f.) and H. Stephan (*Glaubensl.*[2], 1928, §§ 12 and 13) the divine attributes have been grouped under the categories of the holiness and the love or the "nearness" of God. It is worth noting that even H. Cremer (*Die chr. Lehre v. den Eigenschaften Gottes*[2], 1917), who in this matter goes his own way, has in fact reached no other method of classification. The same twofold division—attributes of the divine being and attributes of the divine activity—also governs the exposition of Roman Catholic doctrine (J. M. Scheeben, *Handb. der kath. Dogmatik*, Vol. I, 1925, pp. 513 and 616 ; H. Hurter, *Theol. dogm. comp.*[12], 1907, Vol. II, pp. 23 and 52 ; B. Bartmann, *Lehrb. d. Dogm.*[7], 1928, Vol. I, pp. 116 and 132 ; F. Diekamp, *Kath. Dogm.*[4], 1930, pp. 150 and 184). In spite of all the differences of nomenclature, basis and arrangement in this classification, and in spite of all the doubts which we can and must feel almost everywhere in matters of detail, it is impossible to overlook or deny the fact that in the last resort it is the same thing which is here perceived and meant with greater or lesser acuteness, so that we have a certain broad consensus of Christian theological opinion at this not unimportant point. On the one hand it is a question of the moment of God's aseity, absoluteness or freedom ; of God in the exaltation proper to Him in Himself, as against all that is not Himself. And on the other hand it is a question of the moment of the love of God, of the activity of His personal being. In this matter the chaos of opinion is not as great as perhaps at first sight appears, and it should be clear that in accordance with the presuppositions previously discussed we have no real need to look around for a radically new solution. Indeed, we have absolutely no other choice but to adopt basically—reserving the right of more detailed elucidation and purification—this fourth and, as we may call it, classical line of approach.

A fully restrained and fully alive doctrine of God's attributes will take as its fundamental point of departure the truth that God is for us fully revealed and fully concealed in His self-disclosure. We cannot say partly revealed and partly concealed, but we must actually say wholly revealed and wholly concealed at one and the same time. We must say wholly revealed because by the grace of revelation our human views and concepts are invited and exalted to share in the truth of God and therefore in a marvellous way made instruments of a real knowledge of God (in His being for us and as He is in Himself).

We must say wholly concealed because our human views and concepts (the only ones at our disposal for the knowledge of God, and claimed by God Himself as a means to this end) have not in themselves the smallest capacity to apprehend God. A true doctrine of the divine attributes must in all circumstances attest and take into account both factors—God's self-disclosure and His self-concealment. The knowledge of God must not be swallowed up in the ignorance. Nor, again, must the ignorance be swallowed up by the knowledge. Both demands are laid upon us by God Himself in His revelation : the obedience of knowledge and the humility of ignorance. And in laying down both requirements God is equally the one true God. The one grace of His self-revelation is at the root of both, and, because His self-revelation is His truth, we must add : He Himself, His own most proper reality. And in both ways, through His self-disclosure and His concealment, He is at one and the same time knowable and unknowable to us. In other words, in His self-revelation and concealment He has become for us an object of our human knowledge while remaining completely unknowable to us in both aspects (even in that of revelation). The relation between the two is not such that in His self-unveiling we have grounds for knowing Him, and in His self-concealment for not knowing Him ; in the former case for speaking, in the latter for being silent. We have to know Him integrally and therefore in both these aspects. At every point, therefore, we have to be silent, but we have also to speak. The honour which we give Him is in both cases alike problematical. But we are summoned to both alike. We can evade neither. We have thus to recognise Him both in His hiddenness and in His self-disclosure. It will certainly be true that in both cases He remains completely unknowable to us even as we may and must know Him. In all our thinking and speaking about Him we never become His masters. We are always and must always be His servants, and indeed quite unprofitable servants. But it is also true—and this must be stated just as vigorously—that in both cases He becomes completely recognisable by us, not because of our capacity, thinking and speaking, but because of the grace of His revelation, which we cannot refuse to receive, however little we may be able to control it. In order to do justice to this whole state of affairs it is obviously incumbent upon a doctrine of divine attributes to say two things. We cannot confess simultaneously both our knowing and our not knowing. Nor should we try to do so. For it is in such a way that the two things do not exist simultaneously, but only alongside of each other and in succession, that God has revealed Himself in Jesus Christ. Nor does a temporal simultaneity, if we are to trust His revelation, correspond to God's own reality. But, again, we may not and should not wish to confess the one to the exclusion of the other, thus allowing our knowledge to be swallowed up in a presumed absolute and final ignorance, or on the other hand our ignorance to be dissolved in a presumed absolute and final knowledge. For in God's self-revelation and therefore in God's reality there is no such merging of the one in the other. God's reality is of such a character that the one exists with the other, in the other, alongside of and after the other, an eternal simultaneity and successiveness. So, then, we are not compelled to retire within the limitations of our capacity for knowledge, but speak directly in view of the reality of the object itself, when we say that in any doctrine of divine attributes both factors must be particularly emphasised, alongside each other and therefore successively—God's self-disclosure and also His concealment.

This unity and this distinction corresponds to the unity and distinction in God's own being between His love and His freedom. God loves us. And because we can trust His revelation as the revelation of His own being He is in Himself the One who loves. As such He is completely knowable to us. But He loves us in His freedom. And because here too we can trust His revelation as a self-revelation, He is in Himself sovereignly free. He is therefore completely unknowable to us. That He loves us and that He does so in His freedom are both true in the grace of His revelation. If His revelation is His truth, He is truly both in unity and difference : the One who loves in freedom. It is His very being to be both, not in separation but in unity, yet not in the dissolution but in the distinctiveness of this duality. And this duality as the being of the one God necessarily forms the content of the doctrine of His perfection. The doctrine must consequently treat of the perfections of His love and also of the perfections of His freedom. According to all that we have said, this cannot mean that we shall now begin to speak of two different subjects. The unity of self-disclosure and concealment, of the knowability and unknowability of God, constitutes the biblical idea of the revelation of God, just as the unity of love and freedom constitutes the biblical idea of the being of God. In both cases therefore—and in respect of each individual characterisation—we shall have to speak of the one God integrally. Therefore, explicitly or implicitly, when we speak of the love of God we shall have to speak also of His freedom, when we speak of His freedom we shall have to speak also of His love, and when we speak of one individual aspect we shall have to speak also of all the others. But if we do not wish to deviate from Scripture, the unity of God must be understood as this unity of His love and freedom which is dynamic and, to that extent, diverse. What we have here is, then, a complete reciprocity in the characterisation of the one Subject. Always in this reciprocity each of the opposing ideas not only augments but absolutely fulfils the other, yet it does not render it superfluous or supplant it. On the contrary, it is only in conjunction with the other—and together with it affirming the same thing—that each can describe the Subject, God.

Apart from Frank, T. Haering is the modern theologian who has shown a particularly felicitous touch in these matters, and he evinces a fine understanding of this reciprocity. He expresses it by speaking of " the absolute personality " of God on the one hand and His " holy love " on the other. The emphasis in the former case is on the adjective and in the latter on the substantive. In this way, we are continually reminded of the counterbalancing second concept which is so indispensable for a true understanding : in the one case, that the attributes of the personal God are those of the Self-existent ; and in the other, that whichever name we may give we can speak only of one and the same God. But we cannot speak rightly of this one God except in the mutual characterisation and limitation of these two names—of His love by His freedom, and of His freedom by His love.

For us too, then, there arises the necessity of speaking of God's attributes in a twofold series. The unity and distinction of the complete trust and the complete humility in which the Christian knowledge of God is attained (in view of the complete disclosure and the complete concealment of the one God in His revelation), and the unity and difference in which God loves as the One who is free, and is free as the One who loves, make any other way but this impossible to us. Therefore the two fundamental features of the being of God—His love and His freedom in their unity and diversity—necessarily indicate the two directions in which we shall have to think, now that it can no longer be a question of analysing our knowledge of God as such, but of presenting the One already known. In the following sections, then, we shall have to treat of the perfections of divine love and the perfections of divine freedom.

But before we adopt this line of approach which we know to be basically and generally that of a whole theological tradition, we must come to an understanding with regard to the question how far we may or may not associate ourselves with this tradition. What has previously been attempted on this generally and basically acceptable path is not so consistent, unambiguous and secure that even in regard to the question as a whole, quite apart from any details, we do not have to avoid certain misunderstandings and make certain corrections. Three decisive points are at stake.

1. It is in the nature of the case that when we speak of God's love we have occasion to think chiefly of God in His fellowship with the other, or, to be more specific, with the world which He has created. And on the other hand, when we speak of God in His freedom, it would appear to be chiefly a question of His transcendence over against all that is not Himself and therefore over against the created world. But this cannot be a true and basic distinction. For it is also a question of God's transcendence over everything that is not Himself even in His fellowship with the world which He has created. And again, this transcendence is itself no other than that which He discloses and exercises in His fellowship with the world. God is not first the One who loves, and then somewhere and somehow, in contra-

distinction to that, the One who is also free. And when He loves He does not surrender His freedom, but exercises it in a supreme degree. The principle of division which we recognise at this point cannot mean that out of the distinction suggested but also overcome in revelation we have to establish a separation between a God in Himself and a God for us, in which the essential being of God will probably be decisively sought in His sovereign freedom and the perfections proper to it, eternity, omnipotence and so on, while the love of God and its perfections, holiness, justice, mercy and so on, are treated nominalistically or semi-nominalistically as a question of mere economy, as non-essential, as perhaps purely noetic determinations, so that the final and decisive word in our doctrine of God is the affirmation of God as the impersonal absolute.

It is not to be denied (it would be surprising if it were otherwise) that the various bases of distinction suggested by the Lutheran Orthodox theologians point more or less plainly in this direction. Therefore, if we do not repudiate the principles as such, we must add by way of elucidation that there are no *attributa absoluta* which are not also *relativa*, no *quiescentia* which are not also *operativa*, no *metaphysica* which are not also *moralia*, and on the other hand, no *externa* which are not also *interna*, no *transeuntia* which are not also *immanentia*, no *derivata* which are not also *primitiva*. Even the distinction favoured by the Reformed between *attributa incommunicabilia* and *communicabilia* can be admitted only as a distinction, but in no sense as a separation. For which of the attributes of God, in which as Creator, Reconciler and Redeemer He allows His creatures to share, is not, as His own, utterly incommunicable from the creaturely point of view, i.e., communicable only by the miracle of grace? And again, which of these incommunicable attributes has not God nevertheless communicated to the creature in that His Word was made flesh? Is not God's mercy completely unfathomable and inaccessible to us? And has He not implanted His eternity utterly in our hearts? In His Son God has opened up to us and given us all, His own inmost self. How then can His sovereign freedom be understood as a limitation of His love? How can it be sought elsewhere than in this love itself? Again, the very fact that we know Him and possess Him only because He has revealed Himself and given Himself to us in the miracle of His grace means inevitably that He stands over against us in all the austerity of His majesty and difference from us, and that we ill recognise His love if we do not see in it His freedom. The knowledge of the majesty of God must not be misused to set up that idol of the one and absolute which is " properly " without motion, utterance, or action. Nor must the knowledge of God's condescension be so misused that finally we seek Him only in certain relations in which we must stand and which have to be interpreted as such. But as in the former aspect God must be recognised as eternal love, so in the latter He must be understood as the freedom personally entering our world of time. What He is there in the height for us and for our sakes, here in the depths He is also in Himself. And we are speaking of God only when we know that He is both—and both in this reciprocal relation, and differentiated unity.

We cannot, then, attribute to this whole distinction between God in Himself and God in His relation to the world an essential, but only a heuristic, significance. It does, of course, have this significance. That God is both knowable and unknowable to us, the One who loves and the One who is free, becomes actually clear to us in this distinction.

Neither of the two aspects is self-explanatory. Neither can be simply assumed. Both must become clear to us. The truth of both becomes manifest in the event of revelation in which God makes the transition from there to here, from His being in Himself to His being in fellowship with us, thus disclosing the truth of both these aspects, not in the form of a separation but of a distinction, as the same thing in distinguishable forms. By this distinction in God of His being in Himself and for us, as it is brought out in the event of revelation, the distinction between His love and His freedom can and must become clear to us; His love in that God as He is in Himself wills also to be God for us His freedom in that He will and can be for us no other than as He is in Himself. We recognise the latter distinction through the former, and with it the division of the divine attributes. But we cannot allow it an essential significance if we wish to avoid the well-known traps into which the orthodox doctrine of God has fallen.

2. The division of the divine perfections according to this twofold principle can involve the temptation of attempted epistemological deduction. If, for example, the distinction between God in Himself and God for us is interpreted at this point as primary, it is only a step to the consideration that if the freedom of God is identical with God's being in Himself in its transcendence over all that is distinct from it, its perfections obviously cannot be described by the aid of concepts whose proper objects can be sought only in the realm of realities distinct from God. This being the case, it is necessary in describing them to transcend these realities. But how is this possible since our ideas are indissolubly bound up with these realities of quite a different order? Obviously there is only one answer—which is thought to be the true one—that we have to employ negative concepts, i.e., those which express the negation of the realities which are properly denoted by human ideas, but which through this negation point beyond these realities and therefore—so it is supposed—to God as the One who in sovereign freedom stands over against this realm of earthly reality. And if, on the other hand, the love of God is identical with His being for us, in His fellowship with the world which He has created, the perfections of this divine love cannot be characterised by concepts which have as their content the being and nature of the created world as such, but we can attempt to render these ideas transcendental by expanding, elevating and enriching them, by using them in the superlative, so that they receive a form in which they can no longer denote the world but—so it is supposed—only the love of God turned to the world and manifested in the world. The two possibilities may then be completed, or rather grounded and comprehended, in a third possibility, according to which God in Himself and God for us is seen to confront the world as its basis, and the world is therefore a negative and positive witness to the perfection of its divine basis. Thus human concepts properly denoting the realities

of this world may be employed to denote the being of God and its perfections.

This is the doctrine of the *via triplex* which is well known in dogmatic history in association with the name of Pseudo-Dionysius Areopagita (*De div. nom.* VII, 3)—the *via negationis* (ἐφαιρέσεως), *eminentiae* (ὑπεροχῆς) and *causalitatis* (αἰτίας). The establishment of this doctrine need not necessarily be regarded as the establishment of a rationalistic proof of God's existence and therefore as a substitute for the knowledge of God by revelation. At a pinch it can be interpreted as a proposed method for the formation of theological concepts in complete independence of the question of our knowledge of God. Now obviously it must have been very tempting (and many of the orthodox succumbed to the temptation) to divide the attributes of God summarily into negative and positive, i.e., those falling under the heads of *via negationis* and *via eminentiae*, whilst the third, the *via causalitatis* was (probably rightly) interpreted by Schleiermacher and A. Schweizer as the common presupposition and crown of both, and was not actually used as a third method co-ordinated with the first two.

Even at best, and supposing that we have here to do, not with an attempt at natural theology, but only with a method for the formation of concepts, it must still be pointed out that the division into these two categories ought certainly not to be dependent on an epistemological distinction. As far as the *via negationis* is concerned, it is not the case that if our concepts negate earthly realities, by this their antithesis to that which is not God they automatically imply an approximation to God's being in Himself. How can our negation be a trustworthy transcending of the created world and as such a trustworthy description of God ? And even if it is the case that by reason of their negativity negative conceptions are fitted to express God's being in Himself, this method is suspicious by the fact that, as we have seen, God's freedom is not in any way identical with God's being over against the world, but is just as operative in His relation to the world as in His being in Himself, and therefore is by no means to be exhaustively described in negative concepts—not even if we can rightly attribute to the latter a special appropriateness to describe the transcendent God. God is the One who is free even in His being for us, in which He is certainly not to be apprehended only by means of negative concepts. Again, so far as the *via eminentiae* is concerned, it is not true that as our concepts try to surpass earthly realities in the form of superlatives they necessarily move towards the love of God turned to the world and manifested in the world. This kind of transcending of the created world can be extremely unreliable in itself, and in any event it is an extremely unreliable description of God. But even supposing a reliable transcendence is attainable by this means, even supposing our concepts in this form are in some sense adapted to describe God's being for us—and on the basis of divine grace it may well be that as regards both the *via eminentiae* and the *via negationis* they are so adapted—we have still to remember that God's love is in no way coincident with His being for us. He is the One who loves in Himself quite apart from His relation to the existence of another. Therefore the concepts by which, superlatively, we attempt to transcend this other, make shipwreck on the rock of this eternal self-existence of God. The *via negationis* and the *via eminentiae* may, indeed, perform their specific though limited services in the formation of concepts to describe the divine perfections. But, however that may be, the distinction between the two categories of divine attributes certainly cannot be made coincident with these two methods in the formation of theological concepts, which in any case are not the only ones.

What remains as a secure body of truth in the doctrine of the *via triplex* does not belong to our present argument. It is that which—neutral as regards this fundamental distinction—may be legitimately meant by the *via causalitatis* (assuming that the method of natural theology is not implied). We have already said earlier that our views and concepts, necessarily referring as such to earthly realities, can and may and must—not in virtue of any immanent capacity, which they inevitably lack in this respect, but in virtue of the divine command and blessing—become descriptions of God as the Lord of the world, and therefore theological views and concepts. Why should not the *via negationis* and the *via eminentiae* be considered in this connexion ? At the proper place there is a necessity and freedom to use even these logical possibilities. But these two possibilities cannot possibly form the framework of the Christian knowledge of God and the division of the divine perfections.

3. The order in which these two series of divine attributes are formulated is not a matter of indifference. It is, of course, true that in both cases, whether we are speaking of the love or of the freedom of God, we are concerned with the one God, with the glory of the Lord in its fulness, in which there can be no more or less and therefore no before and after. At a first glance, then, it may well appear that we can begin and end at either point without deriving any particular advantage and without incurring any particular danger. But this conclusion is overhasty. The logical rigour of the dialectic which occupies us must not conceal from us the fact that we are not concerned with any sort of dialectic but with the very special dialectic of the revelation and being of God, in the apprehension of which we are not left to chance or caprice but must adjust ourselves to the order intrinsic to the theme, or realised in it. It is important not to miss this order if we are not to miss the thing itself. But it is undeniable that this order, and to a great extent also the thing itself, has been fairly generally missed in the tradition to which in essentials we have adhered. For instance, theologians have nearly always treated first of the *attributa absoluta, quiescentia, incommunicabilia*, etc., i.e., of the perfections of the divine majesty, or, as we would term it, the divine freedom, and only then have they been willing to discuss the *attributa relativa, operativa, communicabilia*, etc., i.e., the perfections of the divine love. The fundamental error of the whole earlier doctrine of God is reflected in this arrangement : first God's being in general, then His triune nature—with all the ambiguities and sources of error which must

result from this sequence. Its nominalism or semi-nominalism is also reflected in it, for the order undoubtedly implies that it is a question first of what the being of God is properly in itself, and only then of what it is improperly in its relationship *ad extra*. And finally there is reflected what is actually the most doubtful feature of its conception of God : that God is first and properly the impersonal absolute, and only secondarily, inessentially and in His relationship *ad extra* the personal God of love with the attributes of wisdom, justice, mercy, etc. But this sequence corresponds neither to the order of revelation nor to the nature of the being of God as known in His revelation. In God's revelation the disclosure of God is in fact the first and the last, the origin and the end, of the ways of God. God's revelation is first and last a Gospel, glad tidings, the word and deed of divine grace. Not without concealment, for in His revelation God shews Himself to be the secret of all secrets ; not without the revelation of His omnipotence and eternity, of His hidden majesty ; not without the Gospel becoming for us Law and judgment ; not without exposing our sin and helplessness, our distance from God and therefore the transcendence of God over all that He Himself is not. Nor is all this involved only provisionally or apparently or incidentally, in such a way that this aspect of the divine speaking and action can be ignored. It is involved in such a way that this second aspect is seen as complementary to the first, as included in it, and manifesting itself truly only in the light of it. Only now that the mystery of God is disclosed is it seen to be a mystery : for what do we know of the mystery of God without revelation ? Only as God reveals Himself does He also conceal Himself. Only as God speaks and acts do His omnipotence and eternity become real to us. Only as He gives Himself to us as the One who loves does He withdraw from us also in His holy freedom. Only through the power of the Gospel does there arise for us a divinely binding and authoritative Law, and a knowledge of our sin, and therefore of our creatureliness, our distance from God, and therefore the recognition of God's transcendence in Himself and over against all that He is not. It is not that God in His revelation is the second of these aspects to a lesser degree than He is the first. The truth is that He is it differently. He is it Himself in this relationship of the second with the first. He is it in this sequence. And a knowledge of His being and attributes which is to be faithful to the intrinsic character of His revelation must adhere to this sequence. The same point results from a consideration of the being of God as knowable in His revelation. We have seen that the essence of the divine being is to be the One who loves us and who loves in Himself, the One who is active in founding and maintaining fellowship. But He is this as the One who is free, in His freedom, and therefore as the self-existent One, unconditioned by anything else, Himself conditioning everything else. He is it, therefore, in His majesty, omnipotence and eternity. He is it in

His aseity. Nor again is He all this provisionally, apparently or incidentally, in such a way that this aspect of His being can be ignored. Even in His freedom He is the One who loves. Therefore His Godhead, in so far as it is to be understood as His freedom, is the Godhead of His love. It is as the personal triune God that He is self-existent. And although the converse is certainly true, it is only because we must first say that it is as the personal triune God that He is self-existent ; as the One who loves that He is the One who is free. If there is full reciprocity, as we have seen, this order obtains even in the full reciprocity, not signifying a difference of value between the two aspects of divinity, but the movement of life in which God is God, corresponding exactly to His revelation of Himself as God. And in our apprehension and exposition of the perfections of God we must adhere to this order and sequence.

It is clear that the older scholastic doctrine, to whose basic thoughts we formally adhere, will be given a greatly changed appearance by these three modifications and especially by the third—the reversal in the order of the two categories. But it is surely the appearance corresponding to the compulsion of the subject.

30

THE PERFECTIONS OF THE DIVINE LOVING

The divinity of the love of God consists and confirms itself in the fact that in Himself and in all His works God is gracious, merciful and patient, and at the same time holy, righteous and wise.

1. THE GRACE AND HOLINESS OF GOD

God is He who in His Son Jesus Christ loves all His children, in His children all men, and in men His whole creation. God's being is His loving. He is all that He is as the One who loves. All His perfections are the perfections of His love. Since our knowledge of God is grounded in His revelation in Jesus Christ and remains bound up with it, we cannot begin elsewhere—if we are now to consider and state in detail and in order who and what God is—than with the consideration of His love. In the Gospel of Israel's Messiah and His fulfilment of the Law, of the Word that was made flesh and dwelt among us, of Him who died for our sins and rose again for our justification—in this Gospel the love of God is the first word. If then, as is proper, we are to be told by the Gospel who and what God is, we must allow this primary word to be spoken to us—that God is love. We must recognise and understand all His perfections as the perfections of His love. This is in spite of the fact that at a first glance we might suppose that we ought to seek the divinity of the divine being much rather in the freedom of God, i.e., in His unity, constancy and eternity, in His omnipresence, omnipotence and glory. This freedom of God will be - our theme in the next section. God's freedom is in fact no less divine than His love. And God's love is in fact divine only in so far as it is exercised in His freedom. But again, God's love, too, is no less divine than His freedom. And again, God's freedom is divine only in so far as it is the freedom in which He loves. And not according to value and dignity, not in the sense of any hierarchy, but in the sense of the intrinsic manner in which God is God (as was shown at the end of the preceding section), according to the intrinsic order of the divine life, He is first of all the One who loves and then and as such the One who is free. The recognition of this does not mean that first of all, provisionally setting aside God's freedom, we can and will turn exclusively to the love of God as such, and afterwards equally exclusively to His freedom. In a static systematisation of that type we do not do justice to the intrinsic mode of God's being. There is no love of God in itself and as such, just as there is no freedom of God in itself and as such. God's being consists in His being as the One who loves in freedom. Thus in thinking of His love we have constantly to bear in mind His freedom (and later, in thinking of His freedom, we must not forget His love). It can involve only a change of emphasis or key if we now tread a way demanded by the peculiar characteristic of God's being itself. This way can consist only in our thinking first of the love of God as it really exists in His freedom and then of His freedom as it really exists in His loving. But the " first " and " then," the sequence, can be reversed only arbitrarily and at the cost of great artificiality and misapprehension. We cannot allow ourselves such caprice. Therefore we begin with the perfections of the divine love : with the intention and in the confidence that in this way, even if indirectly, we are beginning also with the divine freedom. God is gracious, merciful and patient both in Himself and in all His works. This is His loving. But He is gracious, merciful and patient in such a way—because He loves in His freedom—that He is also holy, righteous and wise—again both in Himself and in all His works. For this is the freedom in which He loves. Thus the divinity of His love consists and confirms itself in the fact that it is grace, mercy and patience and in that way and for that reason it is also holiness, righteousness and wisdom. These are the perfections of His love. In this its divinity consists and is confirmed.

Why precisely in these attributes ? Every doctrine of God's perfections has to come down, in detail, to a certain choice and grouping of concepts—a choice and summary which as such will not be able to appeal to any direct intimation of Holy Scripture nor to the voice of any sort of relative authority. Both Church creeds and the older and more recent dogmatic systems have shewn in regard to the enumeration of individual attributes, as also in regard to their grouping, great differences as well as certain agreements, and in this matter Holy Scripture itself does not anywhere give us authoritative directions. We have here the specific form of a problem which has already arisen in regard to the order of dogmatics as a whole. *Methodus est arbitraria* was our conclusion then, and we repeat it now. The kind of choice and grouping which we must now attempt can always have the basic character only of a trial and proposal. But it must not on that account be arbitrary, i.e., unreasonable or perverse. Our own attempt and proposal rests first upon a consideration of the question by what specific determinations does the love of God—not love according to a general conception, but the love of God in Jesus Christ, as attested in Holy Scripture—become for us an event and reality so that we may and must infer in consequence that these are determinations of the divine being. The first series, grace, mercy and patience, furnishes an answer to this question. Secondly, it rests upon a consideration of the question in what determinations does the freedom of God stand—again not a universal idea of freedom but the freedom of God in Jesus Christ as attested in Holy Scripture—when His love is actualised for us. The second series provides the answer to this question—holiness, righteousness and wisdom. Whether these two answers are correct, satisfying and compelling, and whether consequently our proposal is serviceable, can be seen only from our exposition itself, or from the relationship to the biblical witness to revelation. It is to be noted that what appears to be an unavoidable systematisation is only a means to an end. The end is the most fully concrete answer to the question: Who and what is God?, i.e., the answer which most faithfully follows and corresponds to the self-manifestation of the living God. The means is an exposition of ideas ordered and controlled as far as possible by this object in its self-manifestation. Our proposal relates to this means. A confused essay committing itself impetuously to concepts of any sort, a meaningless or self-willed choice and arrangement, will obviously be a bad means unworthy of the honour of God, who is not a God of confusion but of order (1 Cor. 14³³). A certain degree of systematisation need not then mean a usurpation if it is an unpretentious attempt to think and speak worthily, or at any rate not unworthily, of this object.

We begin our consideration of divine love with a study of the concept of divine grace as it stands directly confronted with and controlled and purified by the concept of divine holiness.

When God loves, revealing His inmost being in the fact that He loves and therefore seeks and creates fellowship, this being and doing is divine and distinct from all other loving to the extent that the love of God is grace. Grace is the distinctive mode of God's being in so far as it seeks and creates fellowship by its own free inclination and favour, unconditioned by any merit or claim in the beloved, but also unhindered by any unworthiness or opposition in the latter—able, on the contrary, to overcome all unworthiness and opposition. It is in this distinctive characteristic that we recognise the divinity of God's love.

Gratia in Deo residens est essentialis proprietas eius nimirum benignissima voluntas Dei et favor, per quem vere et proprie est gratiosus, quo favet et gratis benefacit creaturae suae (Polanus, *Synt. Theol. chr.*, 1609, *col.* 1040). *Gratia Dei est favor eius gratuitus, quo creaturae rationali ac inprimis hominibus credentibus benefacit, vel est benignissima Dei voluntas qua sine merito omni favet et benefacere gaudet* (Quenstedt, *Theol. did. pol.*, 1685, I, *c.* 8, *sect* I, *th.* 31). The formula of Polanus is to be preferred to that of Quenstedt as the more comprehensive.

Above all, we maintain that according to the dominant meaning of the terms *chen, chesed, χάρις* in the linguistic usage of the Bible, grace is an inner mode of being in God Himself.

" I will have mercy on whom I will have mercy " (Ex. 33¹⁹). To promise to show, to give grace, to make grace prevail, to fill or crown with grace, is all God's work, taking place in consequence of the fact that He is gracious in Himself and therefore gives Himself to be known as gracious and acts graciously. Whosoever finds grace, finds it in His eyes, and therefore in His presence. It is the grace of Him who dwells in the burning bush (Deut. 33¹⁶), and therefore of the author of the covenant with Israel, and as such it is everlasting mercy (Is. 54⁸; Ps. 89³), reaching unto the heavens (Ps. 108⁵; cf. Ps. 103¹¹). According to the recurrent formula of Paul, it is the grace of our Lord Jesus Christ, i.e., the grace which dwells and is manifest, knowable, effectual and imparted in the person of Jesus Christ. We must not follow Roman Catholic dogma (cf., e.g., Bartmann, *Lehr. d. Dogm.*⁷, Vol. II, 1929, p. 3 f.), in making an *a priori* and decisive definition of grace as a supernatural gift, and then proceeding to characterise it as a third element mediatorial between God and His creatures. Grace is certainly a gift—and indeed a very supernatural gift. In fact it epitomises all the gifts of God—not merely revelation, reconciliation and redemption, but also creation. But it is a gift—and this must be our *a priori* definitive description—in so far as the Giver, i.e., God Himself, makes Himself the gift, offering Himself to fellowship with the other, and thus showing Himself in relation to the other to be the One who loves. And the supernatural element arising from the fact that God is gracious does not constitute a third factor. On the contrary, divine grace consists in the fact that God as the First founds and maintains direct fellowship between Himself and the second, His creature. The archetypal form of God's gift of grace lies in the incarnation of His Word, the unity of God and man in Jesus Christ. And in this there was no third mediating element between God and man. The secret essence of grace manifested in the fact that out of two beings—entirely by the will and power of the primal being—there has now been made one ; that between God and man there has been instituted the direct peace which Paul is accustomed to mention in connexion with the word grace and clearly as its determining content. Between the gracious God and him to whom He is gracious there must not be intruded the gnosticising conception of grace as a mediatorial sphere. Everything depends here on the immediacy of the relation and on the fact that the being and action of God, of which we are thinking, is really God's *essentialis proprietas* and is understood as God Himself who, as He is Himself and acting according to His nature, is gracious. That is why the Old and New Testaments speak so emphatically with reference to God of " My " or " Thy " or " His " grace. That is why biblical man not only prays : " Help me according to thy grace " (Ps. 109[26]), " Think upon me in thy grace " (Ps. 106[4]), " Quicken me by thy grace " (Ps. 119[88]), " Cause me to hear thy grace " (Ps. 143[8]), and so on, but in most places directly and simply : " Be gracious unto me." On the other hand it is never said : " Give me, lend me grace ! " or anything of that sort. For this reason, too, all that the apostles wish to their congregations can be summed up in the familiar formula of greeting : " Grace be with you." For the same reason the word of God—Ac. 14[3], 20[32]—can quite simply be called the word of grace. And with Paul, grace, his own conversion, his apostolic office and its exercise, and the preaching of the Gospel constitute a single integral whole : " But by the grace of God I am what I am : and His grace which was bestowed upon me was not in vain ; but I laboured more abundantly than they all : yet not I, but the grace of God which was with me " (1 Cor. 15[10] ; cf. Rom. 1[5]). Grace denotes, comprehensively, the manner in which God, in His essential being, turns towards us. This turning, which is that of a superior to an inferior, and takes place in the form of a condescension, is contained even in the meaning of the word χάρις, the Latin *gratia*, our English grace, and most strongly of all the German *Gnade*. Especially the Old Testament contexts in which the word appears make it clear that in His turning everything which God confers on man as a benefit is implied : His truth, His faithfulness, His law, His mercy, His covenant (Dan. 9[4]), or, according to the apostolic formula of greeting, His peace. All this is primarily and fundamentally His grace also.

But grace means a turning, not in equality, but in condescension. The fact that God is gracious means that He condescends, He, the only One who is really in a position to condescend, because He alone is truly transcendent, and stands on an equality with nothing outside Himself. His inmost being in grace is that He wills not to remain in this position. His transcendence stands out as the presupposition of His condescension fulfilled in the saving turning—which includes every conceivable benefit—to that which is not on an equality with Himself. Not on an equality ! Now this means that grace is a being and action of God upon which no one and nothing has any claim. What this implies positively we shall have to show when we come to speak of God's mercy.   In the idea of grace as such, to which we are confining ourselves here, there is included from our present point of view only the negative aspect that God's turning is not the answer and correspondence to something meritoriously performed by the partner to whom He turns.   If there is such a partner deserving of such a response and possessing a claim to God's notice, able to condition His grace, we shall obviously have to speak of an equality, even if only partial, between this partner and God.   But such an equality does not come into consideration with regard to God.   In the grace of God, His transcendence over against every counterpart is thrown into sharp relief.   The mere fact that God is gracious implies that He Himself owes nothing to any counterpart.   His condescension is free, i.e., unconditioned, i.e., conditioned only by His own will.   His inclination, good will and favour which He turns towards His partner in this act of condescension is a sheer gift which something necessarily called forth by it can neither precede nor follow, for, whatever follows it has its ground in this prevenient cause.   It is thus a gift in this strictest sense of the term.

Δωρεὰν ἐλάβετε (Mt. 10⁸).   It is from a gracious election (κατ᾽ ἐκλογὴν χάριτος) that the remnant of Israel and the Church of Jesus Christ derives : εἰ δὲ χάριτι, οὐκέτι ἐξ ἔργων, ἐπεὶ ἡ χάρις οὐκέτι γίνεται χάρις (Rom. 11⁵ᶠ·).   Grace means redemption : καὶ τοῦτο οὐκ ἐξ ὑμῶν, θεοῦ τὸ δῶρον· οὐκ ἐξ ἔργων, ἵνα μή τις καυχήσηται. αὐτοῦ γάρ ἐσμεν ποίημα, κτισθέντες ἐν Χριστῷ Ἰησοῦ ἐπὶ ἔργοις ἀγαθοῖς (Eph. 2⁵, ⁷⁻¹⁰, cf. 2 Tim. 1⁹).   " According to the good pleasure of his will, to the praise of the glory of his grace, God hath made us accepted in the beloved " (Eph. 1⁵ᶠ·).

The biblical conception of grace involves further that the counterpart which receives it from God is not only not worthy of it but utterly unworthy, that God is gracious to sinners, that His being gracious is an inclination, goodwill and favour which remains unimpeded even by sin, by the resistance with which the creature faces Him.   Again, the positive element to be discussed here will fall for special consideration under the heading of God's mercy.   Grace in itself means primarily that the sin of the creature, the resistance which it opposes to God, cannot check, weaken or render impossible the operation of divine grace.   On the contrary, grace shows its power over and against sin.   Grace, in fact, presupposes the existence of this opposition.   It reckons with it, but does not fear it.   It is not limited by it.   It overcomes it, triumphing in this opposition and the overcoming of it.

The grace of Jesus Christ is related to the sin of Adam in such pure superiority and preponderance that more often than not Paul can express it simply by a πολλῷ μᾶλλον which he does not need to argue further (Rom. 5¹⁵, ¹⁷), but which appears to him so decisive and thoroughgoing that he can finally say : οὗ δὲ ἐπλεόνασεν ἡ ἁμαρτία ὑπερεπερίσσευσεν ἡ χάρις (Rom. 5²⁰).   The fact that God is gracious—this is how the superiority is shown—implies that He forgives the sinner his sin (Ex. 34⁹, Num. 14¹⁹).   That is, He Himself with His inclination, good will and favour intervenes on behalf of the one who has sinned against Him.   His own good free will is to Him truer and more significant—infinitely more so—than the evil will of the sinner. He does not regard and treat the latter as he would have to be regarded and treated on the basis of his evil human will, but as he must be regarded and treated on the basis of the good will of God now turned towards him : because He is God, because this covering and wiping out of sin, because this unmerited, kind, and utterly different view and treatment of His creature is not merely in His power but is His right and there-fore His majestic will. " The Lord is merciful and gracious, slow to anger, and plenteous in mercy. . . . He hath not dealt with us after our sins ; nor rewarded us according to our iniquities. For as the heaven is high above the earth, so great is his mercy toward them that fear him. As far as the east is from the west, so far hath he removed our transgressions from us " (Ps. 103⁸ᶠ·). That this should happen and be true for us is the prayer of biblical man when he cries out : " Be gracious unto me." This is what God's inclination, good will and favour means for God Himself and for us. It is always God's turning to those who not only do not deserve this favour, but have deserved its opposite.

It is to be noted how important it is for this supreme meaning of the concept that in understanding its root we maintain against the Roman Catholic conception of divine grace the thesis that grace is not merely a gift of God which He might give or not give, or an attri-bute which might be imputed to Him or not be imputed. No, grace is the very essence of the being of God. Grace is itself properly and essentially divine. This is, of course, the secret of the forgiveness of sins. For this reason the latter does not imply merely a noteworthy episode the scope of which is open to doubt. Forgiveness cannot be an object of uncertainty. It cannot be accepted and treated lightly. It meets us, not in spite of, but in and with all the holiness, righteous-ness and wisdom of God. It claims us, cleansing, judging and re-deeming us. It is also our true and final consolation. For God Him-self is in it. He reveals His very essence in this streaming forth of grace. There is no higher divine being than that of the gracious God, there is no higher divine holiness than that which He shows in being merciful and forgiving sins. For in this action He interposes no less and no other than Himself for us. With His good will He takes up our cause and responsibility for us in spite of our bad will. In this action He is manifested in the whole majesty of His being. As we sin against God Himself, God Himself takes action to reconcile us by being gracious to us. If we find and recognise and receive His grace, we find and recognise and receive no less and no other than Himself. Thus there takes place by grace the only thing that is effective against sin. By grace sin is attacked and wiped out at its root. Therefore there is no more fear and no more self will where grace is found and recognised and received. Where grace is revealed and operative, God Himself is always revealed and operative. It is not necessary for us to strive after a higher, better, more helpful revelation. God's promise and also His command, God's truth and also His power, God's judgment and also His restoration cannot fail where God is gracious. Again, where God is revealed and operative, He is always the gracious God. God is *vere et proprie gratiosus*. He is so even when He is for us the unknown and hidden God. He is so even when He is the God who is denied and hated by us and therefore provoked against us. He is so even as the God against whom we sin and who therefore judges and punishes us. We know and rightly understand our sin only when we have realised it to be enmity against the grace of God. And we turn from our sin only when we return to the grace of God. Any other idea of God, in which He is not yet gracious, or not yet essentially decisively and comprehensively known as gracious, is really, whether it is affirmed or denied, a theology of the gods and idols of this world, not of the living and true God. And to it will correspond the faith that we bring to its object, the confession of sin by which we stand over against it, the conversion to it which we suppose we must experience or have already experienced. All this religious experience will lack real seriousness and power because the true God, in face of whom alone there is real seriousness and from whom alone flows real power, is the gracious God : He alone, for He alone is the living and true God. Fundamentally and decisively God distinguishes Himself from the creature by His grace. Fundamentally and decisively His divinity consists and confirms itself in His grace. Therefore it is not simply that we may, but we must establish as a criterion whether we have found and are worshipping a God or an idol, the following : whether we have found grace—not grace in general or in any arbitrary sense—but grace before Him and in His very presence ; whether it is grace which we have learnt to venerate and worship as God.

This is how God loves. This is how He seeks and creates fellowship between Himself and us. By this distinctive mark we recognise the divinity of His love. For it is in this way, graciously, that God not only acts outwardly towards His creature, but is in Himself from eternity to eternity.

One might object that in His own being there cannot be a creature standing over against Him, still less any opposition from this other, and therefore that there cannot take place any special turning, or condescension, or overcoming of the resistance of the other, and consequently that there cannot be any scope for grace. Our reply is that there is not in fact any scope for the form which grace takes in its manifestations to us. The form in which grace exists in God Himself and is actual as God is in point of fact hidden from us and incomprehensible to us. For this very reason even in its manifestation and effectiveness for our sakes and towards us it is for us always the mystery which can thus be appropriated only as such and in faith. For this very reason grace can be revealed and imparted to us only by grace. But in this mystery it is actually revealed and operative as God's being and action in our midst. How then can it be denied that primarily it is real in God Himself in a form which is concealed from us and incomprehensible to us—in Him who as Father, Son and

Holy Spirit is One, who is utterly at one in Himself, in whom therefore there is neither the need nor the capacity for any turning and condescension, in whom there is no strife and therefore no reconciliation ? Must we not say, then, that just because this is so, just because He who is Father, Son and Holy Spirit is from eternity to eternity the centre and source of all unity and all peace, therefore He must be the origin and essence of that which we know as grace in such a very different form ? How can it have divine reality in the form known to us if it does not have reality in the unfathomable life of God Himself ? From the sphere and source alone where it is not yet a special turning, not yet condescension, not yet an overcoming of opposition, where it is manifest in the pure love and grace which binds the Father with the Son and the Son with the Father by the Holy Spirit—from this sphere and source alone can it become what in our experience we know it to be : a turning towards the creature, a condescension, an overcoming of resistance. And from this divine source it will be this in so far as it has divine reality in the form known to us.

We now place this concept of the grace of God alongside that of His holiness. This cannot mean that we imply a need either to qualify or to expand what is denoted by the concept of grace. In grace we have characterised God Himself, the one God in all His fulness. We are not wrong, we do not overlook or neglect anything, if we affirm that His love and therefore His whole being, in all the heights and depths of the Godhead, is simply grace. But in our heart and on our lips, in our mode of knowledge, this thing grace is in no sense so fully and unambiguously clear, or above all so rich and deep, as it is in the truth of God which by this concept we apprehend—yet apprehend as we men apprehend God by faith, i.e., in such a way that our knowledge must needs expand and grow and increase. For this reason the idea of grace, not in itself, not in God, but in our mode of knowledge, requires qualification and expansion. Our notion of grace is not able to grasp in its clarity and richness all that grace is in God Himself. If we are concerned about the truth of the God who is wholly grace, we cannot and must not cling to our idea of grace as though our understanding of God had no need to grow, as though this idea of ours enabled us to acquire control over God. In our understanding of the being of God it can be a question only of our continually making clear to ourselves how God gains control over us. For this reason we must not cling to any of our ideas. For this reason we must constantly be prepared to allow our ideas to be qualified and expanded. We have already recognised this in presupposing the great reciprocal qualification and expansion of the two leading ideas of the love and freedom of God. In doing this we did not postulate a cleavage and dualism in God, but were obliged and wished to respect the unity of God in the clearness and fulness

of His revelation and being. We must adopt the same procedure at
every point in the details as well. We will therefore make the kind of
distinction which does not imply a second factor alongside a first, but
simply wishes to recognise the one according to the clearness and fulness
with which it is a unity in God. We are not, then, making any crucial
change of theme when we go on to speak of God's holiness. We
are merely continuing to speak of God's grace. In the case of all the
other concepts which will engage our attention in this and the following sections, we shall still continue to speak only of the grace of God.
But if we are to go on to speak of the one rich grace of God, we must
in fact develop further concepts. We shall do so always from the
point of view that God is utterly and wholly grace, yet not by clinging
stubbornly to our idea of grace as the focal point, but by realising
that that one focal point may bear other names and thus by allowing
the one focus to express other ideas and in that way to control what
we think and say.

God's loving is a divine being and action distinct from every other
loving in the fact that it is holy. As holy, it is characterised by the
fact that God, as He seeks and creates fellowship, is always the Lord.
He therefore distinguishes and maintains His own will as against
every other will. He condemns, excludes and annihilates all contradiction and resistance to it. He gives it validity and actuality in this
fellowship as His own and therefore as good. In this distinctiveness
alone is the love of God truly His own divine love.

*Sanctitas Dei est proprietas eius essentialis, per quam intelligitur naturam eius
esse universe et perfectissime iustam, in qua prorsus nihil iniqui, nihil mali, nihil
labis inest ac perinde esse etiam summe puram et castam amantemque et causam
puritatis et castitatis in creaturis rationalibus, contra autem summe abhorrentem
ab omni impuritate et immunditie sive interna sive externa eamque severissime
detestantem et punientem* (Polanus, *Synt. Theol. chr.*, 1609, *col.* 1185). *Sanctitas
Dei est summa omnino labis aut vicii expers in Deo puritas, munditiem et puritatem
debitam exigens a creaturis—sive qua Deus summe purus mundus et sanctus est
omnisque puritatis et sanctitatis in creaturis autor* (Quenstedt, *Theol. did. pol.*, 1685,
I, *c.* 8 sect. 1, *th.* 34). If we can cite the definitions of grace given by these two
authors without essential objection, we must observe concerning their formulation of the idea of divine holiness that in spite of its correctness in detail it makes
the fatal mistake, precisely in regard to the grace of God, of not realising clearly
the unity of the divine being, and of allowing holiness to appear as a second
or third factor in God alongside the primary one. This is also true of the penetrating exposition of Petrus van Mastricht (*Theor. Pract. Theol.*, 1698, II, 19,
5f.), who in the concept of the *sanctitas Dei* wishes to distinguish between:
1. the *segregatio* (in which God is marked off from everything general and as
such " profane "); 2. the *dedicatio* (in which God does what He does for His
own sake, *sibi addictus, seipsum quaerens*); 3. the *repraesentatio* (in which He is
the author and also the fulfiller of His law); 4. the *detestatio* (His utter aloofness
from the evil repudiated and characterised by Him as such). This analysis is
noteworthy in that it makes holiness an aspect of divine freedom. So much
the more deplorable is its failure to note the connexion on the other side. From
the outset, however, the problem is to show the fact and extent that God as
gracious is also holy, and again that as holy He is also gracious. If we allow

ourselves to be guided by Scripture in this matter, we shall not make a distinction here, and therefore we shall not differentiate a second from a first without revealing the connexions and thus remaining within a unified knowledge of the one God.

The common factor linking the biblical concepts of the grace and the holiness of God is seen in the fact that they both in characteristic though differing fashion point to the transcendence of God over all that is not Himself. When we speak of grace, we think of the freedom in which God turns His inclination, good will and favour towards another. When we speak of holiness, we think of this same freedom which God proves by the fact that in this turning towards the other He remains true to Himself and makes His own will prevail. How can we properly separate these two aspects? The freedom with which God remains true to Himself cannot shine more gloriously than in the freedom with which He turns towards the creature without regard to the latter's merit and worthiness. And again, this freedom cannot be manifested and understood except as the freedom with which He remains true to Himself. The bond between the concepts of grace and holiness consists further in the fact that both point to God's transcendence over the resistance which His being and action encounters from the opposite side. When we speak of grace, we think of the fact that His favourable inclination towards the creature does not allow itself to be soured and frustrated by the resistance of the latter. When we speak of holiness, we think, on the other hand, of the fact that His favourable inclination overcomes and destroys this resistance. To say grace is to say the forgiveness of sins; to say holiness, judgment upon sins. But since both reflect the love of God, how can there be the one without the other, forgiveness without judgment or judgment without forgiveness? Only where God's love is not yet revealed, not yet or no longer believed, can there be here a separation instead of a distinction. In this case forgiveness would be inferred *in abstracto* from sin, and judgment from condemnation. It would not be God's judgment in the one case or God's forgiveness in the other. If we speak in faith, and therefore in the light of God and His love, and therefore of God's forgiveness and judgment, as our insight grows we shall distinguish, but we shall certainly not separate, between God's grace and God's holiness. The link between the two is decisively summed up in the fact that both characterise and distinguish His love and therefore Himself in His action in the covenant, as the Lord of the covenant between Himself and His creature.

The holy God of Scripture is certainly not " the holy " of R. Otto, that numinous element which, in its aspect as *tremendum*, is in itself and as such the divine. But the holy God of Scripture is the Holy One of Israel. That is the primary and fundamental thing to be said about Him. But this does not mean first of all and decisively the God who is exalted over Israel, separated from it and confronting it, to be feared by it as the One to whom it has obligations. The holiness of God does mean all this too, but only because it means primarily and decisively this—that God has adopted and chosen Israel as His child, has given it His promise, and has already conferred upon it His gracious help. Note that the saying in Exod. 15¹¹ : " Who is like Thee, O Lord, among the gods ? who is like thee, glorious in holiness, fearful in praises, doing wonders ? " belongs to the hymn of praise uttered because of the deliverance at the Red Sea ; that the saying in 1 Sam. 2² : " There is none holy as the Lord, for there is none beside thee ; neither is there any rock like our God " belongs to the song of Hannah after the hearing of her prayer; and that the saying in Ps. 77¹³ : " Thy way, O God, is holy ! " comes from a song summarising the acts of God performed for His people. According to Is. 41¹⁴, 43³, ¹⁴, 47⁴, 48¹⁷, 49⁷ and 54⁵ the Holy One of Israel is the Redeemer (*goel*). The Israelites will hold His name holy because they will see what His hands have done for them (Is. 29²³). In all these and similar passages holiness could obviously stand for grace, since it characterises God as Him who is and acts for Israel. And the same applies precisely to the most important use of the notion in the New Testament, viz., to the description of the application of the grace of Jesus Christ to the Church and its members by the presence and gift of the Holy Spirit. To be sure, in this case too, and especially, " holy " means separate, that which confronts, arousing awe and the sense of obligation. But it clearly means primarily and fundamentally that which singles out, blesses, helps and restores, and only in this positive connexion does it have that other significance.

It is, then, only as God affirms His victorious good will, as the concept of grace implies, that what holiness specially denotes is true and actual—the aloofness with which God stands over against the resistance He encounters, His judgment upon sin. He exercises this judgment, His judgment, in such a way that it can be manifest and truly appreciated and experienced as divine judgment only in this way, the way of grace. But of course it must also be said that this way leads necessarily and unavoidably to the truth and reality of judgment, and therefore to the holiness of divine grace.

We are thinking here of the solemn warnings of Paul in Rom. 6¹, ¹⁵ : Is it possible to continue in sin that grace may abound ? Can we sin because we do not stand under the law but under grace ? The answer is : μὴ γένοιτο. We are dead to sin, and therefore cannot live to it any longer (v. 2) ; μὴ γένοιτο. Freed from sin, we have become the servants of righteousness (v. 18). This is the holiness of the grace of God.

That God is gracious does not mean that He surrenders Himself to the one to whom He is gracious. He neither compromises with his resistance, nor ignores it, still less calls it good. But as the gracious God He affirms Himself over against the one to whom He is gracious by opposing and breaking down his resistance, and in some way causing His own good will to exert its effect upon him. Therefore the one to whom He is gracious comes to experience God's opposition to him.

" For whom the Lord loveth He correcteth ; even as a father the son in whom he delighteth (Prov. 3¹²). This text is cited emphatically in two places in the New Testament : Heb. 12⁶ and Rev. 3¹⁹. And in Titus 2¹¹ᶠ· we read : " The grace of God that bringeth salvation to all men hath appeared, teaching (or correcting) us." This is the holiness of God's grace. Just because God is gracious we must fear Him. For : " If we sin wilfully after that we have received the knowledge of the truth, there remaineth no more sacrifice for sins, but a certain fearful looking for of judgment and fiery indignation, which shall devour the adversaries. He that despised Moses' law died without mercy under two or three witnesses : of how much sorer punishment, suppose ye, shall he be thought worthy, who hath trodden under foot the Son of God, and hath counted the blood of the covenant, wherewith he was sanctified, an unholy thing, and hath done despite unto the Spirit of grace ? For we know him that hath said, Vengeance belongeth unto me, I will recompense, saith the Lord. And again, The Lord shall judge his people. It is a fearful thing to fall into the hands of the living God " (Heb. 10[26-31]). Note the context of this text (which is perhaps the most emphatic in the whole Bible on the theme of God's holiness). It is a fearful thing to fall into the hands of the God who has sent us His Son, who is the Lord of the covenant sanctified by the blood of Jesus Christ, who is the Spirit of grace. In the last resort this is the only thing to be feared. But it really is fearful. For here there is a conflict between God and the creature, a conflict in which the creature can be only the threatened party. The revelation of God, just because it is a revelation of His love and grace, means the revelation of His opposition to man, i.e., of His opposition to the opposition in which man exists over against Him.

Only in this opposition is God known in His being as love and grace. For only in this relationship of opposition does He actually create and maintain fellowship between Himself and us, and turn towards us. Only in this tension, as we experience and recognise it as such, and subject ourselves to it, do we truly believe in Him and yield to Him the right which He has against us and over us : the right in which we can then place our confidence. If He is not present to us in this tension, He is not present to us at all. If we refuse to recognise and, as is right, to suffer this His opposition to us, we are also repudiating His grace. To believe in God means that we bow to this His opposition to us, accepting, and—despairing of ourselves but not of Him—allowing His good will towards us to be our ground of confidence and hope.

We cannot do this if that which we encounter in God is sheer abstract opposition, and not the opposition of His good but also gracious, beneficent and saving will towards us ; if His opposition is not, so to speak, implicated in the marvellous work of His election and favour : just as the tables of the Law with their annihilating commands and threats were hidden in the ark of the covenant and so placed under the throne of grace besprinkled with the blood of atoning sacrifices. But again this covenant cannot stand without the revelation of the Law of God in all its holiness, and therefore not without the revelation of the divine opposition and judgment, of the wrath of God from heaven against all the ungodliness and unrighteousness of men (Rom. 1[18]). There can, therefore, be no real faith in God which in the presence of the marvellous work of divine election and favour does not feel compelled to utter the cry of Peter in Luke 5[8] : " Depart from me ; for I am a sinful man, O Lord." Rightly understood, it is the believer and the believer alone who speaks in this way. For from grace and only from grace does the judgment proceed which compels a man to speak in this way. The man without grace and faith will not speak in this way. Rather he will attempt to evade the judgment and hide it from himself. In fact, he will not be able to appreciate it. He will merely be judged in fact, and fall an eternal victim to judgment, without realising it. He will suffer without surrendering himself to that which encounters him, without repentance and without knowledge, and therefore without help and without hope. It is a well-known fact that Luther usually referred the consciousness of sin, the fear of God's wrath and penitence, to a special revelation of divine Law, holiness and wrath, separate from the revelation of divine grace ; to a special aspect of God's being, its majesty and hiddenness. In this respect we do not follow Luther because this scheme cannot honestly be maintained in face of the apparently more complicated but in truth far simpler testimony of Scripture. In Scripture we do not find the Law alongside the Gospel but in the Gospel, and therefore the holiness of God is not side by side with but in His grace, and His wrath is not separate from but in His love. But Luther seems fortunately to have contradicted Himself many times. That the Holy Spirit, the One who convicts the world in respect of righteousness (i.e., in the resurrection of Jesus Christ) and of judgment (upon the prince of this world), also convicts the world in respect of sin (Jn. 16⁸ᶠ·), was after all written effectively in his Bible too. And so Luther could express himself in the following terms in a sermon about Peter's draught of fishes (Lk. 5⁴⁻¹¹) : " Yea, what more serious and terrible indication of God's anger over sin could there be than the suffering and death of Christ His Son ? The consequence of it is that when the passion of Christ really moves a man's heart, he must spontaneously see and feel therein the unendurable anger of God over sin, and be terrified that the world is too narrow for him, as St. Bernard also witnesses was his experience ; when he rightly considers the passion of Christ he exclaims : Ah ! I thought I was safe, and I did not know about the judgment and wrath which had gone forth upon me, until I realised that the only Son of God had to die for my sake. For this spectacle is so terrible that even the damned in hell will have no greater pain and consciousness of God's reprobation than what springs from the sight of the death of the Son of God, the effect of which they have allowed to be lost upon them ; just as Judas the traitor, since he refused to heed the friendly warning of the Master or to consider what he was doing to Him, was finally driven to such terror by this realisation that He pronounced his own condemnation when he said : ' I have betrayed the innocent blood,' (Mt. 27⁴). Therefore St. Peter also preaches to him here the law of his sin and of God's wrath from this great benefit of Christ " (1538, E.A., Vol. 13, p. 116 f.). And on another occasion Luther referred to the " sad, piteous, tragic, moving, blood-stained spectacle which is put before us on Good Friday, that Christ hangs there between murderers and dies in great agony. We ought to consider such a spectacle, as we have already said, in such wise that we conclude therefrom that all this has happened because of our sin, that He, the righteous and eternal high priest, has been willing to give Himself as a sacrifice for our sin, and to pay for it with His death. For every man should realise that his sins have wounded Christ and done Him to death in this terrible way, and that the sufferings of Christ are nothing but the bearing of your sins and mine. Therefore as often as we think of such a sad blood-stained spectacle we must think only that we see there our sins and their provocation of God's terrible wrath, into which we fall with our sins, which is so great that no creature can carry it nor effect atonement except the Son of God alone through His own sacrifice and death (*Pred. über Matth.* 28¹⁻¹⁰, 1531, acc. to Dietrich, E.A., Vol. 3, p. 299).

The holiness of God consists in the unity of His judgment with His grace. God is holy because His grace judges and His judgment is gracious.

In this sense Jesus Christ Himself is the Holy One of God (Mk. 1²⁴ ; cf. Ac. 3¹⁴, Rev. 3⁷). The unity of the Old and New Testament is at this point unmistakable and indisputable. The Holy One of Israel in Deutero-Isaiah is the most exact description of the name of Yahweh which determines the whole history of Israel. It sums up the promise given to Israel and Israel's hope and expectation. God deals with Israel from the days of the patriarchs, through Moses and David up to the restoration from Exile, in such a way that He reveals and confirms

Himself once and for all as the Holy One of Israel, i.e., the One who in Israel maintains and fulfils His own will. We certainly cannot say that the idea of holiness as contrasted with the thought of revelation signifies the inaccessibility of God over against His people and as such points to an older stratum in Old Testament theology which was later " rejected " in the New Testament community in favour of the idea of the love and mercy of God (thus A. Ritschl, *Rechtf. und Versöhnung*, Vol. 2, 1900, pp. 89-102). The revelation and hiddenness of God are indeed to be distinguished in the Old Testament, but not separated, and the same applies to God's grace and God's holiness. In revealing Himself, God reveals Himself as the hidden God, but the hidden God reveals Himself. And just because He is gracious God shows His holiness, and as the Holy God He manifests His grace. It is in this unity that God speaks and acts according to the witness of the New Testament. According to 1 Pet. 1[1st.] the God is holy who has called the Christian community as those who are redeemed by the blood of the Lamb without blemish and without spot, and who as such must place their hope entirely in grace. Jesus invokes as holy Father (Jn. 17[11]) the One who will keep the disciples in the name in which He has given them to Him, that they may be one even as the Father and the Son are one. The holy God according to 1 Jn. 2[20] is He from whom Christians receive their anointing and have their being in Christ. As we have already indicated, He is the Holy Spirit, who epitomises all perfected fellowship between God and man, and who according to 1 Cor. 2[10] is also the epitome of the " deep things " of God. And the very fact that specific allusions to the holiness of God in the New Testament are often brought into connexion with Old Testament passages only goes to show that the New Testament witnesses in this matter desired to speak and did in fact speak in conscious unity with the Old Testament. But quite apart from the linguistic aspect, it is puzzling how the heart of the New Testament message, viz., the passion narrative and the indissoluble connexion between Christ's death and resurrection as directly or indirectly attested in so many apostolic texts, can be so disregarded that even momentarily we can lose sight of the necessity of seeing the grace of God in His judgment and therefore His judgment in His grace.

Because, in virtue of what God does to Israel, God and Israel belong together, and because God continues to have dealings with Israel in this partnership and as its Creator, God is holy. That the idea is to be understood in this sense is shown by the fact that the holiness required of Israel—Ye shall be holy; for I am holy (Lev. 11[44]; 1 Pet. 1[16])—has essentially the character of cultic holiness. The holiness of man and of human actions, of things and places, is constituted, so to speak, by their serviceableness in the fellowship founded and initiated by God between Himself and man. Unholiness is therefore unserviceableness to this end. The holiness of God describes the form of His attitude in this fellowship. Sin is whatever disturbs and makes this fellowship impossible. For this reason God's attitude in this fellowship is characterised by holiness, exclusiveness, the condemnation and annihilation of sin. The holiness of God thus involves peril to the man with whom He has fellowship. Since his sin disturbs this fellowship and makes it impossible, man himself becomes impossible. As a sinful man he cannot stand before God. He must perish. That he should himself be holy is not, therefore, a command by which God urges him to secure for himself a status or merit in His presence. But as God's command it is quite simply the command to cleave to His grace. And again, this command to be holy is not a command which man might or might not fulfil. But as a divine command it is simply the command of self-preservation. In the presence of God man stands or falls as he becomes holy. But he becomes holy in virtue of the holiness of the God who graciously takes action on his behalf. The whole concrete content of the Holiness Code simply illustrates—as is necessary in the economy of revelation in expectation of Jesus Christ—this complete, all-embracing divine action for man. It reminds man—and therefore all these commands must be kept—that all along the line God's own holy will is dealing with him, and that he, intrinsically unholy man, is saved by it, not because he sanctifies himself, but because in obedience to these commands he submits himself to the holiness of God. Because the good will of God is His own free will, therefore the content of the Holiness Code cannot be assimilated to a general system of the ethico-teleological type. We are continually astonished that this or that command is grounded in the affirmation : " For I am the Lord." In unending variations—and the multiplicity is not superfluous because it makes clear the point at issue—it is always a question of the same thing, that in the realm of contingent reality, acting personally, inscribing His name' as it were with His own independent curves and lines in personal, everyday, popular life, and again with the same independence cutting out of this life what He destines for His service or has declared to be contrary to it, God binds Himself to this people, giving it His presence and self, being the One who makes it holy and its holiness. And so the keeping of the Holiness Code cannot even remotely signify anything which might be construed as a meritorious righteousness of works. The keeping of it can mean only that Israel accepts this contingent reality of its God, that He may dwell with it in His glory, that He may be its holiness, so that Israel itself may not be consumed by the divine holiness. In so far as it consists inwardly and essentially in adoration of divine grace, in gratitude for the gift of the covenant, obedience simply means dread of the destruction which must at once and at every point overtake Israel if it " transgresses," i.e., oversteps the line marking out the contingent reality of God's self-manifestation in its midst, thus falling a victim to the mortal opposition of God to human sin. There is sin only where man transgresses the commandments of God, i.e., enters the sphere of this opposition. It is just because God is so gracious to Israel that it must so basically and totally fear Him. It is only as God sanctifies Himself in its midst, and therefore requires holiness from it, i.e., the respecting of His own holiness, that He makes it possible for Israel to have fellowship with Him—a fellowship in which as the chosen people it is the redeemed people. We are not exaggerating, but simply noting the plain unmistakable meaning of the text itself viewed in its context, if we declare that the divinity of the love of God is in few other passages of the Bible so distinctly manifest as in that Book which is so often misunderstood and regarded as obscure, useless and imprisoned within the limitations of its period, the Book of Leviticus, and in those parts of the Pentateuch which are related to it—in this connexion we may also think of the Book of the prophet Ezekiel which is viewed with similar disapproval. What is the meaning of Messianic expectation and promise if they are not present here ? here where nature and grace, reason and revelation are so irreconcilably juxtaposed because the Law which slays and the Gospel of God which makes alive are interwoven in the most astonishing way. J. Wichelhaus was certainly right when (long before R. Otto) he wrote on this point : " Man cannot and will not understand that it is just because God is good that He is holy and just because He loves that He is angry and chides and hurts and casts into the flames. The holiness of God is terrible to man. In His holiness God has for man the appearance of a Moloch, a Saturn, a consuming fire. God is in His holiness a consuming fire, and therefore, if man is to be brought back again to God, He must be supremely praised and loved by man in His holiness " (*Die Lehre der hl. Schrift* [3], 1892, p. 343). It was A. Ritschl who in contradistinction to this insight tried to reduce everything that the Old Testament says about the wrath of God to the idea of occasional outbursts of God's passion and destructiveness against the enemies of Israel and those who broke the covenant in Israel itself, by which the righteous in Israel were not affected, but to which they subjected themselves out of sympathy " with the people." As he saw it, this idea, like that of divine holiness generally, recedes more and more in the New Testament behind the thought of divine love and grace. That is to say, it becomes an expression, to be understood " only eschatologically," of the ultimate victory of God against His adversaries. " From what religious point of view can we Christians be interested in applying the concept of the wrath of God to our present-day experiences ? . . . Whoever invokes God as His God is not far from God, nor is God far from him: such a one, therefore, is not exposed at that moment to the divine wrath " (*Rechtf. und Versöhnung* [4], Vol. 2, 1900, pp. 119-156). Quite apart from the exegetical violence done by his thesis, Ritschl failed to see that with the present experience of the divine wrath he was also eliminating its eschatological reality, and that with the elimination of the idea of divine wrath in general he was eliminating that of divine grace and love, converting it into an idea which has scarcely anything in common with the contingent reality in which, according to the witness of the Old and New Testament, God in His own person encounters man. If God does not meet us in His jealous zeal and wrath—exactly as He meets Israel according to the witness of the Old Testament, exactly as He meets it later in the crucifixion of His own Son—then He does not meet us at all, and in spite of all our asseverations about divine love, man is in actual fact left to himself. That man is not abandoned in this way, that God is really gracious to him, is shown in the fact that God confronts him in holiness. It is in this way that God is present with him, taking over and conducting the cause which sinful man is impotent to conduct himself. It is in this way that God reconciles man to Himself. The fact that God does not permit Israel, the righteous, or the Church to perish means that he cannot allow them to go their own way, unaccused, uncondemned and unpunished, when they are and behave as if they were people who do not participate in this salvation and protection. The burning bush of Exod. 3^2 cannot be consumed. But the unconsumed bush must burn. This bush is Israel. And the flame which burns it but does not consume it is the God of Israel, the holy God. When God spake : Let there be light, and there was light, and God saw that it was good, God separated the light from the darkness and the light He called day and the darkness night (Gen. $1^{3f.}$). This separation could only have been avoided if God had not spoken : Let there be light, and there had not been light, and God had not seen that the light was good. Because this is true and actual, it must also be true and actual : " And the light of Israel shall be for a fire, and his Holy One for a flame : and it shall burn and devour his thorns and his briers in one day ; and shall consume the glory of his forest, and of his fruitful field, both soul and body : and they shall be as when a standard-bearer fainteth. And the rest of the trees of his forest shall be few, that a child may write them " (Is. $10^{17f.}$). And at this point how can we help thinking of Is. $6^{1f.}$ where the prophet sees the Lord sitting on a throne high and lifted up, and his train filled the temple? Above it stood the seraphims, and one cried to another : " Holy, holy, holy, is the Lord of hosts : the whole earth is full of his glory. And the posts of the door moved at the voice of him that cried, and the house was filled with smoke." Then the prophet exclaims (exactly like Peter in Lk. 5) : " Woe is me ! for I am undone ; because I am a man of unclean lips, and I dwell in the midst of a people of unclean lips : for mine eyes have seen the King, the Lord of Hosts." And accordingly there follows the terrible touching of his lips with a live coal from the altar, but also the explanation: " Lo, this hath touched thy lips; and thine iniquity is taken away, and thy sin purged." Consider this point. It is not after but in the manifestation of wrath and judgment that there comes the pardon, reconciliation, calling and commissioning of the prophet, in short, the grace, which was obviously from the very outset the secret meaning of this whole revelation of God's holiness. In this sense we clearly have to understand the preaching of judgment to the people with which Isaiah is at once entrusted, and in fact the prophetic preaching of judgment generally, even when it is not completed and qualified by any specific prophecy of salvation. How can it be ignored as the immediate inevitable consequence of the revelation of holiness and the Law of holiness ? It is where the name, the people, the city, the house of God is, that judgment must begin (Jer. 25[29]; 1 Pet. 4[17]). Binding Himself to Israel, God binds Israel to Himself, and binding Israel to Himself, He becomes to it the inextinguishable fire whose flame is nothing else but the flame of His love. Making Himself its God, He subjects it to His Law, His threats and His punishments in order to confer on it His blessings by this subjection. Separating it from among the peoples, in all the things in which its native way of life is the same as that of the heathen, He must deal with it just as He does with the latter, and indeed incomparably more strictly. To this day He must heap misfortunes upon Israel as compared with other peoples in order to accomplish supremely its separation and therefore its promise, and therefore His own gracious election and turning to this people. The *freedom* of grace is revealed in the fact that it is always manifest in judgment. But it is the freedom of *grace* which is revealed in this way. If it is God who enters into fellowship with man, and if this happening spells grace and election, is it not inevitable that the opposition, indeed the consuming opposition, between God and sinful man should be made manifest? And conversely, if God did not make known His consuming opposition to sin and therefore to sinful man, how could He really hold fellowship with man, seeing He can do so only on the basis of grace and election? To accept God's grace necessarily means, therefore, to respect God's holiness, and therefore to accept, heed and keep His laws, to fear His threats, to experience His wrath and to suffer His punishment. Otherwise acceptance of grace is indistinguishable from heathen quietism. But again, respect for God's holiness, if it is not a vain heathen religion of fear, can only mean directly to accept God's grace in thankfulness, to be contentedly replenished by it. "Wherefore we receiving a kingdom which cannot be moved, let us hold fast thankfulness, whereby we may serve God acceptably with reverence and godly fear. For our God is a consuming fire" (Heb. 12[28f.]). Again, if anywhere the unity of Old and New Testaments is visible, if anywhere we not only can but must speak of the Old Testament witness to Christ and of Christ as the fulfilment of the Old Testament, it is precisely in this connexion where the too fashionable exegesis of both Testaments has always tried to divorce Moses and Christ, the Law and the Gospel. For it is the witness of the Old Testament and its fulfilment that God made to be sin (2 Cor. 5[21]) His own beloved Son in whom He was well pleased (Mk. 1[11]), that He condemned sin in Him (Rom. 8[3]), and that because He thus humbled Himself unto the death of the cross, He gave Him the name which is above every name (Phil. 2[9]), and that in all this, in confirmation of what had always been His revelation of holiness, He made His own business the sanctification of His people, the expiation of its sin, the embodiment of His will in the life of His people, thus giving this people the opportunity of receiving and accepting by faith the divine judgment, but also of finding in it the forgiveness of sins and the promise of eternal life and therefore of fleeing sin as surely as it cannot wish to flee from divine grace. "And for their sakes I sanctify myself, that they also might be sanctified through the truth" (Jn. 17[19]) When we look at Jesus Christ we cannot fail to see how the apparently varied threads in the Old Testament witness of God all intertwine, His election and His wrath, His forgiveness of sins and His commandments, His graciousness and His holiness; and that according to the Old Testament witness the Lord who deals with Israel is the one God in all this diversity. Again, the Old Testament attests and affirms that Jesus Christ, in whom God turns to man while remaining completely true to Himself, discloses a life which in the Old Testament sense can be adequately described only by the appellation God. If God's love is what is revealed to us in Jesus Christ, if Jesus Christ Himself is the revealed love of God, there is an end of the divorce between God's grace and holiness, and there remains to us only the recognition and adoration of Him who is both gracious and holy: gracious as He is holy and holy as He is gracious.

We may now say again, with richer insight, that in this way God *loves*. By this mark, that it is holy love, we recognise the divinity of His action and being. For again we must add that God not only acts as the Holy One, but that as He acts He is, from everlasting to everlasting. In Him, of course, there is no sin which He has first to resist. But in Him there is more. There is the purity, indeed He is Himself the purity, which as such contradicts and will resist everything which is unlike itself, yet which does not evade this opposing factor, but, because it is the purity of the life of the Father, Son and Holy Spirit, eternally reacts against it, resisting and judging it in its encounter with it, but in so doing receiving and adopting it, and thus entering into the fellowship with it which redeems it.

2. THE MERCY AND RIGHTEOUSNESS OF GOD

The fact that among the biblical attributes of God we select two further divine perfections, both individually and in their interconnexion, does not mean that we are leaving behind what we have already said of the divine being, i.e., the perfections of His grace and holiness, in order to turn our attention as it were to another aspect of deity. In this whole enquiry and exposition we must never forget that there exists " another " in God only in so far as it is still one and the same thing. But in God Himself, and therefore also for us, there is a fulness of the divine perfections, not in poverty, but in richness, and therefore continually different, and to be viewed and conceived in its development. We continue our consideration and discussion of the love of God and therefore of God Himself as the One who loves in freedom. But continuing to study this one object we come necessarily, if we follow the testimony of Holy Scripture, from the first to the second proposition, that God is merciful and righteous. Continuing! The first assertion, that God is gracious and holy, is not therefore exhausted and abandoned. On the contrary, we can regard the task which now faces us, and indeed all possible tasks in this sphere, simply as a further analysis and elucidation of this first affirmation. In fact we shall have to repeat and understand again that God is gracious and holy. We shall have to repeat it with ever-growing insight. Our second affirmation and all further affirmations can thus be regarded simply as variations of this first theme. But as the being of God in itself is really one in real plenitude and not in poverty, our knowledge of God can be coherently developed yet still be more than the mere logical unfolding of a single principle and proposition. We not only can but must place alongside our first affirmation a second and a third : not with the idea of adding something new, but with the idea of continually saying the one thing, on the presupposition of what has already been said, in ever new forms.

In this sense, we now learn and repeat that the one thing which God is, is also mercy and righteousness.

———————

We begin with the perfection of the divine mercy. The word itself in its Latin and German, but especially its biblical usage, teaches us that in this notion we are not merely in the proximity but in fact at the very centre of the concept of divine love and its specific determination as grace. In a general idea of love, the thought of mercy is not necessarily included—any more than that of grace. Love in itself and in general can also fall under quite other descriptions. But the love of God as the Creator's will for fellowship with His creature bears necessarily the character of grace, i.e., the free inclination of an unconditionally superior towards one who is unconditionally subordinate. If this is true, with the absoluteness with which it must be true of the two partners we are now considering, we must consider these two partners more precisely, the One who loves and the object of His love, and go on at once to say that divine love bears necessarily the character of mercy. The word " necessarily " can and must be understood literally in this connexion. In the relationship between this love and its object, and therefore in the grace of God, we have to do with the " turning " of a " need " (*Not-Wende*). The free inclination of God to His creature, denoted in the biblical witness by grace, takes place under the presupposition that the creature is in distress and that God's intention is to espouse his cause and to grant him assistance in his extremity. Because grace, the gracious love of God, consists in this inclination, it is, and therefore God Himself is, merciful ; God's very being is mercy. The mercy of God lies in His readiness to share in sympathy the distress of another, a readiness which springs from His inmost nature and stamps all His being and doing. It lies, therefore, in His will, springing from the depths of His nature and characterising it, to take the initiative Himself for the removal of this distress. For the fact that God participates in it by sympathy implies that He is really present in its midst, and this means again that He wills that it should not be, that He wills therefore to remove it. We can see at once that the idea of the mercy of God is not evolved logically from a merely general notion of grace. Understood in quite general terms, as the free condescension of a superior to an inferior, it does not necessarily include the superior's participation in, and determination speedily to relieve, the distress of the inferior. Grace in itself and in general might equally well mean an unsympathetic and ineffectual inclination on the part of the superior. But we are speaking of the grace of God and therefore of the concrete relationship in which it becomes actual, of His grace towards the one to whom He is gracious. In this relation mercy is included in grace ; grace itself is mercy. And by this mark and this alone we recognise the divinity of the love and grace of God : by the fact that it is merciful.

Misericordia Dei est gratiosissima voluntatis divinae propensio, qua Deo cordi est miseria hominis, eandemque benevole sublevatam cupit (Quenstedt, *Theol. did. pol.*, 1685, I, *c.* 8, *sect.* 1, *th.* 32). It is a peculiarity of the LXX that the normal translation for the Old Testament *chesed* (where we would expect χάρις)) is ἔλεος, of which the Old Testament equivalents are properly *chanan* and *racham*. But in this way there is correctly suggested the affective aspect of love, peculiar, in fact, to the biblical conception of grace. The concept is, therefore, presented immediately and unmistakably in the concrete content which the biblical background implies. It is well known how often grace and mercy appear side by side in the Old Testament, the one clearly determining and elucidating the other. The New Testament terms ἔλεος and οἰκτιρμοί do not suggest, of course, only a feeling but an action, yet the kind of action which is determined by a feeling. Quenstedt was right exegetically and substantially not to fear the anthropomorphic character of the expression : *qua Deo cordi est miseria*. The main point is, as the Latin and German words make very clear, that God's love and grace are not just mathematical or mechanical relations, but have their true seat and origin in the movement of the heart of God. It is here that we can appreciate the meaning of the idea of personality in God, and what has to be defended by its maintenance against the conception of God as an impersonal absolute. In any other relation between God and creature except that attested in the Bible, in any relation which, if need be, can be described in mathematical or mechanical terms, the idea of personality in God is perhaps dispensable. But in the relation between the merciful God and the " miserable " creature (i.e., in need of mercy) it emerges—and here at last it must emerge—that it is indispensable, and expresses the truth. It was quite natural that Schleiermacher should consider it impossible to ascribe to God a state of feeling specially awakened by the suffering of others and going out to assist them, and therefore that he should try to eject the idea of the mercy of God from the language of dogmatics to that of homiletics and poetry (*Der chr. Glaube*, § 85). The source of the feeling of sheer dependence has no heart. But the personal God has a heart. He can feel, and be affected. He is not impassible. He cannot be moved from outside by an extraneous power. But this does not mean that He is not capable of moving Himself. No, God is moved and stirred, yet not like ourselves in powerlessness, but in His own free power, in His innermost being : moved and touched by Himself, i.e., open, ready, inclined (*propensus*) to compassion with another's suffering and therefore to assistance, impelled to take the initiative to relieve this distress. It can be only a question of compassion, free sympathy, with another's suffering. God finds no suffering in Himself. And no cause outside God can cause Him suffering if He does not will it so. But it is, in fact, a question of sympathy with the suffering of another in the full scope of God's own personal freedom. This is the essential point if we are really thinking of the God attested by Scripture, and speaking only of Him. Everything that God is and does is determined and characterised by the fact that there is rooted in Him, that He Himself is, this original free powerful compassion, that from the outset He is open and ready and inclined to the need·and distress and torment of another, that His compassionate words and deeds are not grounded in a subsequent change, in a mere approximation to certain conditions in the creature which is distinct from Himself, but are rooted in His heart, in His very life and being as God. When, therefore, Polanus says : *Deus est misericors sua aeterna et simplici essentia, non autem qualitate aliqua, non affectu, non passione* (*Synt. Theol. chr.*, 1609, *col.* 1119), he is right to the extent that by this negation he wishes to avoid the conception of a God who can be moved and stirred from without. The " affection " of God is different from all creaturely affections in that it originates in Himself. But in this sense it cannot be denied. In this sense it is God's mercy as it can also be God's wrath. We recall that in Lk. 1⁷⁸ it is expressly a question of the σπλάγχνα —the bowels of God's mercy. Phil. 1⁸ speaks in the same sense of the σπλάγχνα Χριστοῦ Ἰησοῦ. In Phil. 2¹ and Col. 3¹² these σπλάγχνα are linked with οἰκτιρμοί, and in a whole series of Synoptic passages the verb σπλαγχνίζεσθαι is used for " have mercy," and always denotes the compassion of Jesus. In view of all this we shall have to take the positive part of Polanus' sentence as seriously as the negative. The mercy of God really means His σπλάγχνα, and no less than all His other attributes denotes His *aeterna et simplex essentia.* The God whom Jesus Christ calls Father is merciful (Lk. 6³⁶), rich in mercy (Eph. 2⁴), the Father of mercies and therefore the " God of all comfort " (2 Cor. 1³). All that He does gains both its power and its character from this source. Grace is rightly received and understood as such, free and unmerited grace, but in the effectual reality of the turning of God denoted by it, if we note the actual context : " I will be gracious to whom I will be gracious, and will shew mercy on whom I will shew mercy " (Ex. 33¹⁹). The impassibility of God cannot in any case mean that it is impossible for Him really to feel compassion. Where grace is manifest and effectual, it is always a question of the misery of man. In this fact its freedom is implied. It is really a gift made to one who is poor and in misery. But, on the other hand, it is always a question, no more and no less, of the heart, the innermost being of God. This is not closed but open to feel the distress of man. God cannot be moved from outside, but from inside His own being He shares it in sympathetic communion. It is here that we see the power of grace. This means, of course, that in fact it is not merely a gift of God, but God Himself the Giver who gives Himself as the gift. In this connexion we may also think of the passages where the mercy of God at first sight seems to be related " only " to the physical need of man (e.g., Phil. 2²⁷). " His tender mercies are over all his works " (Ps. 145⁹). Measured by the Lord's holiness the whole creation as such lies in need and misery and is dependent on the fact that God's mercy is new every morning (Lam. 3²³). And God does not refuse to give Himself to it. He maintains it as He has created it. He takes into account its frailty and need, giving Himself anew to it every morning. That all this is true becomes especially clear when the work of God assumes the form of His self-revelation, reconciliation and sanctification, the form of His covenant with Israel, the form of Jesus Christ.

We have seen how grace in Jesus Christ stands in victorious opposition to the resistance set up by the creature to God. The mercy of God, too, expresses this opposition. The point is, however, that not merely in regard to its consequences and punishment, not merely in view of the judgment which it brings down upon itself, but ·in itself this resistance has in the light of the merciful grace of God the appearance of man's distress and suffering and misery. Arrogance is seen as pitiable folly, the usurpation of freedom as rigorous bondage, evil lust as bitter torment. It is again true that man by his own fault has plunged himself and is continually plunging himself into these ills, and in view of this we shall have to speak later of the righteousness of God. But it is also true that this resistance of the creature, this sinfulness of man, has in itself and as such the simple meaning of folly, bondage and torment. And as such it is the object of God's compassion. In concrete the mercy of God means therefore His compassion at the sight of the suffering which man brings upon himself, His concern to remove it, His will to console man in this pain and to help

him to overcome it.   The freedom of God is such that His grace and
condescension to man can, may and must have the meaning and effect
of making man's sin and guilt an object of divine compassion, so that
He can hate sin and for this very reason love the sinner, pitying sinful
and guilty man even as He opposes him, and in this pity entering into
dealings with him.   And this pity is no mere sentiment, but power
and deed.   We are assured of this by the fact that it is not too light
a thing for God to turn favourably to man in this way, and indeed to
be open to man in this way, to be for Him the One who is merciful,
even prior to his creation and any turning to him, from all eternity.

> God grieveth in eternity
> My misery beyond measure,
> He called to mind His mercy mild,
> To help me was His pleasure.
> He turned to me His Father's heart,
> 'Twas not for Him the trifler's part,
> He gave His costliest treasure.
>
> For mercy now the time has come,
> To His own Son confiding,
> Away, heart's crown, from heaven's throne,
> Salvation now providing.
> To help poor man from sinful loss,
> Endure for him the bitter cross,
> And be his life abiding.

(Luther: " Nun frewt euch lieben Christen gmeyn . . ." 1523 ? W.A. 35, 424,
4.) Note that God is merciful, i.e., the time can come for Him to be merciful, because He pities in eternity, because He has only to call to mind His mercy.   The
sovereign freedom and power of His mercy are not, then, merely (as H. Cremer
still asserts in his *Lexikon*, Art. ἔλεος) those of an attitude in the economy of salvation, but genuinely and truly the freedom and power of His Godhead.   God the
Father, Son and Holy Spirit is merciful in Himself.   In this essential freedom and
power He speaks and acts mercifully in His revelation, reconciliation and sanctification, in His covenant with Israel, in the epiphany and parousia of Jesus Christ.
We read in Rom. 9[16], in direct connexion with the quotation from Ex. 33[19] :
" So then it is not of him that willeth, nor of him that runneth, but of God that
sheweth mercy " ; and immediately after, in Rom. 9[18]: " Therefore hath he
mercy on whom he will have mercy."   Rom. 11[32] is also to be understood
in this sense: " For God hath concluded them all in disobedience, that he
might have mercy upon all."   God's mercy is God's freedom.   Hence it is
impossible to understand this " all " mathematically and mechanically, as
the sum of all mankind, to whom God owes His grace as such.   On the
contrary, according to the passages in Rom. 9 they are undoubtedly the
elect people which once was no people, but has now become His people,
the people of those who were once without grace but have now found grace
(1 Pet. 2[10]).   As God's mercy it is necessarily a grace which chooses, and it
is manifest and effectual as such to those who love Him (Ex. 20[6]) and fear
Him (Ps. 103[13] ; Lk. 1[50]).   But in this way and to them it is powerfully, incontestably and irresistibly manifest and effectual, that no human sin or guilt can
suspend its working, but it is just human sin and guilt which are the occasion
of the powerful divine compassion.   Again it is of the freedom and the power of
" the tender mercy of our God " that it is said in Lk. 1[78f.] that by it " the

dayspring from on high hath visited us, to give light to them that sit in darkness, and in the shadow of death, to guide our steps into the way of peace." Again it is of the freedom and power of the divine mercy that it is said in 1 Pet. 1³ that by it God " hath begotten us again unto a lively hope by the resurrection of Jesus Christ from the dead," or in Tit. 3⁵ that by it—not on account of any righteous works which we have done—God has " saved us, by the washing of regeneration, and renewing of the Holy Ghost." And, again, when it is a question of the God who is rich in mercy in Eph. 2⁴ᶠ·, it is through mercy that we who were dead in our trespasses—have been made alive with Christ. Again it is mercy in Ps. 78³⁷ᶠ· : " Their heart was not right with him, neither were they steadfast in his covenant. But he, being full of compassion, forgave their iniquity, and destroyed them not." And again in Is. 54⁷⁻¹⁰ : " For a small moment have I forsaken thee, but with great mercies will I gather thee. In a little wrath I hid my face from thee for a moment ; but with everlasting kindness will I have mercy on thee, saith the Lord thy Redeemer . . . for the mountains shall depart, and the hills be removed, but my kindness shall not depart from thee, neither shall the covenant of my peace be removed, saith the Lord that hath mercy on thee." In all these and similar statements we must understand the predicates in the light of the subject and then interpret the subject in its predicates. That God who is provoked to anger is not only angry, but for the sake of that which provokes Him sets bounds to His anger and is compassionate, and that this compassion is His and is therefore active, where His wrath slays, to make alive and renew and enlighten—that is the secret and at the same time the simple and manifest reality of His mercy.

It is to be noted that when we confess God to be merciful it is not even remotely possible to demonstrate this as a logically deducible truth. All that we can do is to acknowledge the actual reality of God. What else can we produce as a proof of this confession except the fact that God has given Himself to be known by us as merciful in the name of Jesus Christ ? How can we try to recognise the reality of the mercy of God except in this name ?

The revelation of this name as the epitome of the expectation of Israel and the recollection of the Church is also in Holy Scripture the epitome of the reality of God's mercy. We cannot get behind this name to learn why God is merciful. But we can infer from this name with unshakable certainty that He is. In this recognition and confession everything depends on the fact that by the Word and Spirit of God we are linked to this name, that in and with this revelation, attested to us by the Word and Spirit, the revelation of the mercy of God stands immediately before us, that by this name we are divinely and therefore incontestably and irresistibly comforted. We are comforted by an acceptance that not merely our creatureliness, not merely the need and the misery of our existence in its sheer dependence, but the very heart of this misery, our revolt against Him on whom we are utterly dependent, is in fact the object of His own participation, His care, His suffering, and therefore also His assistance and intervention. Before we are touched or can be touched by any pain which we have brought on ourselves by our sin and guilt, before we are sorry for or can be sorry for our sin, before death and hell can frighten us, and before we feel the greater terror that we are such sinners as have deserved death and hell, already in the One against whom we sin and are guilty and whose punishment threatens us we have to do with the God who Himself suffers pain because of our sin and guilt, for whom it is not an alien thing but His own intimate concern. And as God is far greater than we His creatures, so much greater is His sorrow on our behalf than any sorrow which we can feel for ourselves. If we recognise God's mercy in

Jesus Christ, this means necessarily that we can no longer try to experience and bear in the sorrow which we have to experience and bear for ourselves an, as it were, divine, eternal, irremovable weight of sorrow. Because God is merciful, a divine pain of this kind is not only taken away from us, but forbidden to us as something presumptuous—a tragic consciousness to which we may not pretend. The height and depth, the inwardness and outwardness of our sorrow is really God's concern—and ours only as it is seen and borne by God. What is our suffering when we recollect that God has Himself felt it so keenly as to give His only begotten Son in order to remove it ? Our suffering for sin has not touched us, and cannot touch us, as it touches Him. So we can never take it to our hearts in this way. When we realise the full depth of our sorrow as it is seen and borne and suffered by God Himself, any complaint of ours as to the form in which it confronts and affects us is silenced. Our lamenting comes too late and is always relatively too weak. Indeed, it is always ineffective and in the end untrue. For what is the use of our lamenting when the heart of our misery is that we are sinners and debtors to God, in face of whom we cannot do anything to make good ? Who can complain when God has to complain, when the right to complain is His right alone ? It is His heart, not ours, which is suffering when we think that we are the sufferers and that we have a right or obligation to lament. His heart is wounded, and wounded through our heart. How can we reverse the relationship and behave as though we have to suffer, as it were, in the void, divinely, eternally, or on our own account ? In the recognition and confession of the mercy of God, what we are accustomed to take so seriously as the tragedy of human existence is dissolved. There is something far more serious and tragic, viz., the fact that our distress—the anguish of our sin and guilt—is freely accepted by God, and that in Him, and only in Him, it becomes real agony. That this is the case is due to the mercy of God. In the face of this mercy we must be silent. In the bearing of our pain, we must be modest and unassuming, as also in our lamentation and protests against it. We not only must, but may. For it is the third and crucial factor in our misery that we think that we ourselves must bear our agony, the agony of our sin and guilt, that we must accuse and judge and cleanse ourselves, and then take pity on ourselves for the consequences of our sin. Sin attains its true form as opposition to the grace of God. It becomes hopeless as such, and its consequences are hopelessly painful. But at this point the grace of God intervenes as the mercy of God. Jesus Christ enters human existence as the great joy which shall be to all people. He breaks down this resistance to grace by Himself appearing as grace triumphant, as the royal removal of our sin and guilt by the action of God Himself. Because our sin and guilt are now in the heart of God, they are no longer exclusively ours. Because He bears them, the suffering and punishment for them are lifted from us, and our own suffering can be only a reminiscence of His. As He takes to Himself our sin and guilt in His Son, we are freed from the necessity of seeing and suffering and lamenting except as His and by faith in Him, i.e., except as a burden of sin and guilt which is lifted from us by Him. It remains for us only to be the sinners whose place He has taken and who must therefore really have their life in Him.

The merciful God has taken action on our behalf both in freedom and in power. In freedom : for our sin and guilt were not His and did not have to become so. Because this is so, faith believes in God's grace and election in virtue of which we receive what we have not deserved. But also in power : for He has really taken to Himself and removed from us our sin and guilt. Therefore faith is joy and gratitude, an assurance which can no longer look back, only forwards. In freedom and power, awakening a humble but assured and unshakable faith,

He took our place because He was God's eternal Son, because it was manifest in Him that God's eternal being is mercy, because there is nothing more real and true behind and beyond this substitution, because this substitution is the very essence of God's own being, of His divinity, for which we must glorify Him in joy and gratitude if we are not to sin wantonly against Him, if we are to let God be God.

That we both must and may is seen again at this point, in the light of God's mercy, to be an inseparable unity. Must or may the heathen praise God for the mercy that has come to them (Rom. 15⁹) ? The question is obviously pointless. The Law of God commands and the Gospel permits us to answer love with love. But is not the converse equally true ?

This, then, is how God loves. His love is merciful love. In the nature of the case, we do not need to emphasise the point that God is as merciful in Himself as He is merciful in His action. For the idea of mercy itself refers back from God's attitude and act to the depths of God's being, to His heart, His mind, Himself. All misunderstanding in regard to the idea of grace, as if it were not eternal in God Himself, becomes quite impossible when we have understood it as merciful grace. For it is then understood, not simply as God's turning towards us, but as His free, effectual compassion. Looking backwards, therefore, it is seen, not simply as an appearance, but as the disposition of the heart and being of God. Viewed as merciful grace the love of God descends to earth more deeply, and climbs higher to heaven, than the idea of grace in itself would permit us to suppose. It is in this sense that we must use it in all our future deliberations.

We now turn to the concept of the righteousness of God, which is specially significant in Scripture and has been so much disputed in the history of the Christian confession. As we do so we must keep well in view a consideration which concerned us when we passed from the idea of the grace to that of the holiness of God, and which subsequently controlled our whole explanation and exposition of the idea of holiness. This is, that we are not concerned with a second thing side by side with a first ; but that in both cases we have to do with one and the same thing. Is it not, then, a question of the second thing ? Of course it is, and absolutely. Indeed, we can even say that it is only a question of the second thing because this second thing is so utterly identical with the first. In this one thing, in God Himself, in the plenitude of His being, there is no division and therefore no mutual qualification and augmentation of His attributes. But this does apply to the concepts by which we are allowed to recognise God on the basis of His revelation and in the truth of His unity and plenitude, i.e., when this process takes place in due humility, and no one of our concepts tries to usurp authority and form a system, and therefore we allow these concepts to qualify and augment each other, and, recognising and attesting the One in His unity and fulness, we pass from one idea to the other. But we cannot do as we like.

We must proceed in order, in the order determined by the object, by the revelation of God in Jesus Christ, and therefore by His being. According to this order, the mercy of God must precede His righteousness, just as His grace had to precede His holiness. It is not that God is less holy and righteous than merciful and gracious. God is altogether everything that He is. In everything that He is, He is Himself. And everything that He Himself is, He is in unsurpassable, unchallengeable perfection. But He is so in His own perfection, not in one which is arbitrarily determined, as, for example, the perfection of a circle or a ball. In the multiplicity of His perfections He is not comparable to the multiplicity of the points on the periphery or surface of an object of this kind, which are all equally near to the centre, and equidistant from it. God cannot be compared to anyone or anything. He is only like Himself. And who and what He is cannot be constructed mathematically or logically or ethically or psychologically. We have simply to listen to Himself on the point. If we do this, if we adhere to His revelation in Jesus Christ, specific relations gradually emerge between His perfections, not in spite of the fact that in each of them He is no less wholly Himself than in all the others, but just because of it. We have seen that there exists a relationship between God's grace and holiness, a relationship of mutual penetration and consummation determined by grace, which necessarily precedes. The relationship between God's mercy and righteousness is similar. We shall have to emphasise the righteousness of God no less than His mercy. If possible, we shall have to emphasise it even more. But we cannot do this, we cannot speak at all of the righteousness of God which is so much emphasised in the Bible, if we do not proceed from a consideration of God's mercy. The relationship between God's mercy and righteousness will also present itself to us as a relationship of mutual penetration and consummation, but here again it will receive its characteristic stamp from the fact that divine mercy necessarily precedes. For only in this way does it correspond to the economy of the revelation and therefore the being of God, which must always be respected and never replaced by any arbitrarily introduced symmetry.

The loving of God is a divine action and being distinct from every other loving in the fact that it is righteous. Our point of departure must be that the righteousness of God is a determination of the love, and therefore of the grace and mercy, of God. And the love and grace and mercy of God have the determination of righteousness necessarily, as they have that of holiness. Necessarily, because if this love were not holy and righteous it would not be the love of God. The characterisation and determination of this love as righteousness and therefore divine springs from the fact that when God wills and creates the possibility of fellowship with man He does that which is worthy of Himself, and therefore in this fellowship He asserts His worth in spite of all contradiction and resistance, and therefore in this fellow-ship He causes only His own worth to prevail and rule. It is only in this characterisation and determination that the love of God is truly His divine love.

The definition must be framed on these lines if there is not to take place here a cleavage in the being of God, if the righteousness of God is to be seen in its unity with His mercy and also with a back-ward reference in its unity with His holiness. In its unity with His mercy : we defined the latter as a determination of the love and grace of God manifested in time as God's effectual participation in the misery of another, a participation prompted by His inmost being. From this it follows, not logically of course, that God is righteous, that, founding and maintaining in this way fellowship with another, He wills and expresses and establishes what corresponds to His own worth. But if it is in fact true that God is righteous in this sense, and on the basis of His revelation we presuppose that it is true, it cannot be asserted of this definition of His righteousness that it is in logical contradiction to the definition of His mercy. God does not have to, but He can, take to Himself the suffering of another in such a way that in doing so, in founding and accomplishing this fellowship, He does what corresponds to His worth. Our definition of the righteous-ness of God can co-exist with that of His mercy and together with it make manifest the unity of God. The same applies in regard to the unity of God's righteousness and holiness. We defined the latter as the self-affirmation of the will of God which takes place in His found-ing and accomplishment of fellowship with another. Again, it does not follow logically that God is righteous, that what He wills and does and realises in this fellowship is what corresponds to His worth. That there is a divine worth which is maintained, defended and realised in this self-assertion of the divine will is something which is not included in it by any necessity of logic. But if in point of fact it is included, because in virtue of God's self-revelation it is clear that God's holiness is His righteousness, there does not exist any contradiction between God's holiness and righteousness according to the definition here given. They can co-exist and equally denote one being of God.

We have seen that the weakness of the definitions of Protestant orthodoxy in respect of the relationship between God's grace and holiness was that they did not make clear the unity of the divine being. The same is true in this connexion.

We read in Quenstedt : *Iustitia Dei est summa et immutabilis voluntatis divinae rectitudo a creatura rationali quod rectum et iustum est exigens. Estque vel remuneratrix, qua bonos praemiis, vel vindicatrix, qua malos suppliciis afficit* (*Theol. did. pol.*, 1685, I, *c.* 8, *sect.* 1, *th.* 35). This definition fits in only too well with the same author's definition of the holiness of God, in which the divine *exigere* plays so decisive a part. Later Schleiermacher defined the righteousness of God on the same lines as " the divine causality in virtue of which, in the condition of universal sinfulness, there is ordained a nexus between evil and real sin " (*Der chr. Glaube*, § 84). But if it is defined in this way, what happens to what even Quenstedt calls the *gratiosissima voluntatis divinae propensio, qua Deo cordi est miseria hominis* ? If God in His righteousness is simply exacting, i.e., rewarding the fulfilment of His demands and punishing their non-fulfilment, how in His mercy can He take to heart the suffering of man ? And if He does the latter, how can He give play to His righteousness, supposing that it is to be understood only as demanding and distributive ? To illustrate its doubtful content we will at once contrast with the thesis of this Lutheran author the words of Luther himself, whose insights were strangely lost during the course of the 16th and 17th centuries. Luther expressed himself as follows in his exposition (1532) of Ps. 51 (on v. 1 : *Miserere mei, Deus, secundum magnam misericordiam tuam*) : *Sancti patres, qui in psalmos scripserunt, fere exposuerunt " iustus Deus " pro eo, quod iuste vindicat ac punit, non pro eo, quod iustificat. Inde mihi accidit iuveni, ut hanc appellationem Dei odissem et ex illa hexei seu habitu adhuc hodie quasi cohorresco, cum audio Deum iustum dici. Tanta est vis impiae doctrinae, si ea animi in prima aetate imbuantur, et tamen veteres doctores fere omnes sic exponunt. Sed si Deus sic iustus est, ut puniat iuste seu pro merito, quis potest subsistere in huius iusti Dei conspectu ? Si quidem omnes sumus peccatores et afferimus ad Deum iustam poenarum infligendarum causam. Procul hinc cum tali iustitia et tali iusto Deo, quia nos omnes sicut " ignis consumens " vorabit. Quia autem Christum salvatorem Deus misit, profecto non hoc modo iustus vult esse, ut puniat pro merito, sed vult iustus esse et dici, ut agnoscentes peccata iustificet et eorum misereatur.* . . . And on v. 14 (*Exultabit lingua mea iustitiam tuam*) : *Hoc vocabulum Iustitiae magno sudore mihi constitit ; sic enim fere exponebant, iustitiam esse veritatem, qua Deus pro merito damnat seu iudicat male meritos. Et opponebant iustitiae misericordiam, qua salvantur credentes. Haec expositio periculosissima est, praeterquam quod vana est, concitat enim occultum odium contra Deum et eius iustitiam. Quis enim eum potest amare, qui secundum iustitiam cum peccatoribus vult agere ? Quare memineritis, iustitiam Dei esse, qua iustificamur seu donum remissionis peccatorum. Haec iustitia in Deo grata est, facit enim ex Deo non iustum iudicem, sed ignoscentem patrem, qui iustitia sua vult uti non ad iudicandos, sed iustificandos et absolvendos peccatores. Hanc tuam iustitiam, inquit, non iustitiam hominum aut Mosi, ego cum gaudio et laetitia praedicabo, etiam si mihi hostes capiendi sint omnes homines, modo tu hoc facias ut etiam coram ecclesia me absolvas* (W.A. 40[II], 331, 25 and 444, 36). And in the preface to his Latin writings of 1545 Luther expressed the same point again in the well-known summary of his theological development : *Miro certe ardore captus fueram cognoscendi Pauli in Epistola ad Rom., sed obstiterat hactenus non frigidus circum praecordia sanguis sed unicum vocabulum, quod est Cap. 1 : iustitia Dei revelatur in illo. Oderam enim vocabulum istud " iustitia Dei," quod usu et consuetudine omnium doctorum doctus eram philosophice intelligere de iustitia (ut vocant) formali seu activa, qua Deus est iustus et peccatores iniustosque punit. Ego autem, qui me, utcumque irreprehensibilis monachus vivebam, sentirem coram Deo esse peccatorem inquietissimae conscientiae nec mea satisfactione placatum confidere possem, non amabam, imo odiebam iustum et punientem peccatores Deum, tacitaque si non blasphemia, certe ingenti murmuratione indignabar Deo, dicens : quasi vero non satis sit, miseros peccatores et aeternaliter perditos peccato originali omni genere calamitatis oppressos esse per legem decalogi, nisi Deus per euangelium dolorem dolori adderet et etiam per euangelium nobis iustitiam et iram suam intentaret. Furebam ita saeva et perturbata conscientia, pulsabam tamen importunus eo loco Paulum, ardentissime sitiens scire, quid S. Paulus vellet. Donec miserente Deo meditabundus dies et noctes connexionem verborum attenderem, nempe : Iustitia Dei revelatur in illo, sicut scriptum est : Iustus ex fide vivit, ibi iustitiam Dei coepi intelligere eam, qua iustus dono Dei vivit, nempe ex fide, et esse hanc sententiam, revelari per euangelium iustitiam Dei, scilicet passivam, qua nos Deus misericors iustificat per fidem, sicut scriptum est : Iustus ex fide vivit. Hic me prorsus renatum esse sensi et apertis portis in ipsam Paradisum intrasse. Ibi continuo alia mihi facies totius scripturae apparuit. Discurrebam deinde per scripturas, ut habebat memoria, et colligebam etiam in aliis vocabulis analogiam, ut opus Dei, id est, quod operatur in nobis Deus, virtus Dei, qua nos potentes facit, sapientia Dei, qua nos sapientes facit, fortitudo Dei, salus Dei, gloria Dei. Iam quanto odio vocabulum " iustitia Dei " oderam ante, tanto amore dulcissimum mihi vocabulum extollebam, ita mihi iste locus Pauli fuit vere porta Paradisi. Postea legebam Augustinum de spiritu et litera, ubi praeter spem offendi, quod et ipse iustitiam Dei similiter interpretatur : qua nos Deus induit, dum nos iustificat. . . . Istis cogitationibus armatior factus coepi Psalterium secundo interpretari* . . . (W.A. 54, 185, 14). If we consider the thesis of Quenstedt in this light, we will certainly be warned against taking up the problem in the way he suggests.

But we must also express at this point a reservation in regard to the Reformed theologian Polanus. He defines the righteousness of God as *voluntas eius per quam ipse iustus est et omnis iustitiae in creaturis autor*, and then continues : *Iustitiae divinae regula summa perfectissima et infallibilis est voluntas eius. Nam Deus sibi ipsi lex est. Quicquid Deus fieri vult, eo ipso quod vult, iustum est : Quicquid Deus facit, scit et vult* (*Synt. Theol. chr.*, 1609, *col.* 1157 f.). We certainly cannot say that this definition of the righteousness of God is in conflict with that of His mercy. We can expand it without fear of contradiction : God's mercy is His righteousness because it is His will, and because the will of God, God being a law to Himself, is necessarily a righteous will. But it is of serious consequence that this expansion has to be made ; that this sequence in which the will of God is revealed as righteous *eo ipso*, and in which it is also righteous *eo ipso* in God Himself, is as little adopted into the definition as it is in the case of Quenstedt. Because this sequence is lacking, the grounding of righteousness in the will of God as such (although it is correct in itself) assumes a certain arbitrary appearance which, contrary to what happens in Quenstedt, threatens to compromise the holiness of God. For if God is in Himself the law and therefore righteous, He is distinguished from a tyrant, who one day caresses and the next day strikes, by the fact that His will, which obeys His own law, shows itself to be a good will, worthy of Himself and therefore really righteous, and that it is such a will in itself. But this cannot be evinced in the abstraction in which Polanus too talks about the righteousness of God. It would have been evinced if he had defined the righteousness of God—on lines which he fortunately picked up again later in his discussion—in close relationship with the concepts of the love and grace and mercy of God as a determination of the manner in which God founds and maintains fellowship. If in Quenstedt it is not clear how the mercy of God can co-exist with His righteousness, it is not evident in Polanus either (at least according to his definition) how God can be both merciful and righteous. And as, in face of the separation of the righteousness of God from His mercy, we can be corrected by Luther, so, in face of the separation of the mercy of God from His righteousness, we can be corrected by Anselm of Canterbury, who usefully impels us to view the problem, as must be done, from this angle too. How can God be good both to the good and the evil ? How then, can He have mercy on the wicked and yet at the same time and in this very way be righteous ? This is how Anselm poses the problem in *Prosl.* 9-11. His answer is as follows. The stream of divine mercy flows from the hidden fundamental goodness of God (the *altissimum et secretissimum bonitatis tuae* as the unfathomable source of His being). Therefore just because God is *totus et summe iustus* He is good even to the wicked too—not simply to all the wicked, but to the wicked too. He is not perfectly good if He is not good both to the good and the bad, but only to the good ; if He does not confront even the wicked as the One who judges and also the One who shows mercy. What flows from His goodness, is also, as such, righteous. *Si misericors es, quia es summe bonus, et summe bonus non es, nisi quia es summe iustus : vere idcirco es misericors quia summe iustus es.* God's mercy—we see how here Anselm proceeds by a method directly opposed to that of Luther, only to arrive at the same result—is known by His righteousness : *misericordia tua nascitur ex iustitia tua.* How is that ? God's righteousness consists in the fact that He is righteous to Himself, i.e., that He is goodness than which no greater can be conceived. But this goodness is a goodness according to which He not only judges but also has mercy, creating good out of evil. *Hoc itaque modo iustum es, ut parcas malis et ut facias bonos de malis.* If He has mercy on the evil, He does not do so in an unjust but in a just manner. He does not do so *quia illorum meritis* (this would be unjust), *sed quia bonitati suae condecens est. . . . Ita iustus es, non quia nobis reddas debitum, sed quia facis, quod decet te summe bonum. . . . Sic ergo nascitur de iustitia tua misericordia tua ; quia iustum est, te sic esse bonum, ut et parcendo sis bonus.* It is just because God wills it. And what God wills is just because He wills what is worthy of Himself. Anselm posed the same problem rather differently, i.e., concretely in relation to the historical action of God in the atonement, in *Cur Deus Homo* I, 12 and 24. Ought not God to be able to forgive sins *sola misericordia* and thus without due reparation of the injury done to His honour ? The answer is that in God's kingdom there is no disorder. If an injustice is left by this *sola misericordia*, if it is, therefore, divinely validated, if it is exposed to no divine punishment, if it needs no divinely just reparation, then this *iniustitia* has, as it were, the character of a second Godhead in the face of God. By the fact that God commands us to forgive our debtors, He reminds us that we must not arrogate to ourselves what is His privilege—to judge. But it is His concern in the freedom of His goodness, in which He stands above all necessity, to preserve His *dignitas* in all circumstances. *Libertas enim non est nisi ad hoc, quod expedit aut quod decet, nec benignitas dicenda est, quae aliquid Deo indecens operatur.* God can will only what is worthy of Himself. But He does will this. Therefore the omission of a due restoration of the order of His kingdom disturbed by sin cannot be rooted in the freedom of His goodness. It is not merciful to mediate forgiveness to man and yet leave him in his unrighteousness. Injustice is not only unrighteousness but also weakness. It therefore means unhappiness. If God's mercy is concerned with man's blessedness, then it must assume the character of this just reparation and therefore of a triumph of God's righteousness.

From Luther on the one side and Anselm on the other we have to learn that there is no righteousness of God which is not also mercy and no mercy of God which is not also righteousness. If this is the case, it is clear that no progress is possible if there is a fluctuation between God's mercy and righteousness, a hesitant and alternating consideration and underlining now of the one and now of the other. Bernard of Clairvaux called righteousness and mercy the two feet of God : *curato, ut neutro frauderis illorum. Si dolore peccati et iudicii timore compungeris, veritatis iudiciique vestigio labia impressisti. Si timorem doloremque divinae intuitu bonitatis et spe consequendae indulgentiae temperas, etiam misericordiae pedem te amplecti noveris. Alioquin alterum sine altero osculari non expedit, quia et recordatio solius iudicii in barathrum desperationis praecipitat et misericordiae fallax assentatio pessimam generat securitatem (In Cant. serm. 6).* But may it not be that this metaphor of the two feet contributes to the fatal idea that we can really " kiss " God's righteousness in abstraction from His mercy and His mercy in abstraction from His righteousness. May it not be that it enhances the dangers of *desperatio* and *securitas* which are rightly indicated ? The unity to which both Luther and Anselm draw our attention seems to have been more acutely realised by Augustine than by Bernard : *intendite ipsam misericordiam et iudicium . . . Ne putetis, quia ista a se possunt in Deo aliquo modo separari. Videntur enim sibi aliquando contraria : ut qui misericors est, non servet iudicium, et qui iudicii tenax est, obliviscatur misericordiam. Omnipotens est Deus, nec in misericordia amittit iudicium, nec in iudicio misericordiam (Enarr. in Ps. 32, on v. 5).*

As regards the biblical basis, we can take as our point of departure the fact that in Holy Scripture the attestation of God's mercy frequently takes the form of an admonition : " Great are thy tender mercies, O Lord ; quicken me according to Thy judgments " (Ps. 119[156]) ; " Rend your hearts and not your garments . . ." (Joel 2[13]) ; " Therefore seeing that we have this ministry . . ." (2 Cor. 4[1]) ; " I beseech you, therefore, brethren, by the mercies of God . . . (Rom. 12[1]). Or with an even more direct application : " Be ye therefore merciful, as your Father also is merciful " (Lk. 6[36]). And in the parable of the wicked servant : " Shouldest not thou also have had compassion on thy fellow servant, even as I had pity on thee " (Mt. 18[33]). On the other hand, there are even in the Old Testament at least as many passages in which, conversely, the thought of God's righteousness and judgment takes the form of expressions of trust, gratitude and joy. We read in Is. 30[18-21] (directly following a warning of judgment) : " And therefore will the Lord wait, that he may be gracious unto you, and therefore will he be exalted, that he may have mercy upon you : for the Lord is a god of judgment : blessed are all they that wait for him. For the people shall dwell in Zion at Jerusalem : thou shalt weep no more : he will be very gracious unto thee at the voice of thy cry ; when he shall hear it, he will answer thee. And though the Lord give you the bread of adversity, and the water of affliction, yet shall not thy teachers be removed into a corner any more, but thine eyes shall see thy teachers : and thine ears shall hear a word behind thee, saying, This is the way, walk ye in it, when ye turn to the right hand, and when ye turn to the left." The Lord in His righteousness guides the footsteps of the man who calls upon him because of his enemies (Ps. 5[8]). He saves him in his righteousness and does not let him be ashamed (Ps. 31[1]), so that God's righteousness and His laws and statutes and judgments, rightly considered, are just as much an object of desire (Ps. 119[16]), joy (Ps. 48[11f.]) and thankfulness (Ps. 7[17]), as they are of awe and fear. Thus when the Old Testament speaks of the Law of God as a revelation of righteousness, even when it is a question of its transgression and of divine threats, we find always (and not merely in Ps. 119) that it is God's great blessing to Israel—His love which remains even though it is misesteemed and despised and repelled, and therefore becomes a curse. This emerges continually even in Paul's polemic against the *nomos* (Rom. 7[7, 12-14, 16]). According to Scripture it is as the merciful God that God is to be feared, and as the righteous that He is to be loved. If we try to separate, or to evade, the alternation of fear and love, we speak of a different God from Him who bears this name in Scripture.

Let us attempt a connected statement. He who in Holy Scripture is called God, is in truth—not only additionally or partially or in one special aspect or appearance of His being, but wholly and utterly— the Judge. His revelation is wholly and utterly the Law, manifesting His will as righteousness, and distinguishing it from all unrighteousness. His activity is wholly and utterly the execution of this Law.

In this respect the New Testament does not differ from the Old. The ministry of the New Testament is also the ministry of righteousness (2 Cor. 3[9]). In the New Testament also there is invoked as Father He who without respect of persons judges every man according to his works (1 Pet. 1[17]). The seat of Jesus Christ proclaimed in the New Testament is a seat of judgment from which every man receives, whether good or ill, according to his conduct in earthly life (2 Cor. 5[10] ; Rom. 14[10]). In the New Testament, too, we are to work out our salvation in fear and trembling " because it is God which worketh in you both to will and to do " (Phil. 2[12-13]), i.e., because we know that in Him who accomplishes this we are dealing with the Judge, and in the work itself with our judgment. In the New Testament, too, in faith in Jesus Christ we live in responsibility towards Him who has revealed Himself to this faith : " For whosoever hath, to him shall be given, and he shall have more abundance : but whosoever hath not, from him shall be taken away even that he hath " (Mt. 13¹²). Neither in the Old Testament nor in the New can the conception of justice ever be interpreted in such a way that there is no longer any true or serious question of the Law, of the Judge and of His judgment. It must sometimes be objected to Luther that the fact that God in His righteousness is in truth the *ignoscens pater* cannot mean that He ceases to be the *iustus iudex*. This point is especially to be made against A. Ritschl. We have to recognise that in his polemic against the *iustitia distributiva* of orthodox dogmatics he has perceived and expressed what is biblically correct and reminded us of the better insight of Luther. But he went too far in the opposite direction—as was only to be expected in view of his attitude to the problem of the holiness and wrath of God—once he dissolved the justice of God into the mere " consistency of the divine guidance of men to salvation which is partly demonstrated in the pious and upright adherents of the old covenant, and partly expected for the community in whose salvation the rule of God will be consummated," trying to interpret it merely as " the criterion of the distinctive operations by which the community of Christ is realised and conducted to its goal " and finally attempting a straightforward identification with grace (*Unter. in d. chr. Rel.*, 1875, § 16). Certainly the righteousness of God is identical with the grace of God, but it is so as righteousness, and we have to see and understand exactly to what extent it is so as righteousness. Thus the concept is weakened when F. Nitzsch tries to give to the righteousness of God the general significance of " clemency " (ἐπιείκεια)—according to Aristotle " the mildness of the judge who, while he does not violate the law or become partial, takes into account individual circumstances." According to Nitzsch God as the King and Saviour of the covenant people handles the norm which governs it, and which springs from His own holiness, in such a way that in consideration of the people's special need of mercy, as a mild Judge and Ruler, He allows grace to rule rather than the principle of a tooth for a tooth (*Lehr. d. ev. Dogm.*³, 1912, p. 467 f.). That God does in fact allow gentleness to prevail will have to be dealt with under the heading of God's patience. But Aristotle is quite irrelevant in this context. In the biblical account of God's exercise of justice there is never any question of a regard for individual circumstances, or a limitation of His justice by His gentleness, or allowing grace to precede strict righteousness, but it is everywhere stated that He unconditionally maintains right as right and wrong as wrong, judging, rewarding and punishing according to this standard without deviating a hair's breadth either to the one side or the other. Only when we admit this unreservedly do we understand what it means that God's justice is also in fact a determination of His love, and His judgment an expression of His grace. To grasp this it must be realised that the communication of His grace is an expression of His judgment. It is as God forgives sins in His mercy that He judges. We have to take it quite literally when Paul declares (Rom. 1¹⁶ᶠ·) that the Gospel is the saving power of God to every believer because in it the righteousness of God is revealed. And it is not a weakened, qualified righteousness, but, as the continuation makes clear in vv. 18 f. (concerning the simultaneous revelation of wrath upon all the ungodliness and unrighteousness of men), the unconditional eternal righteousness of God which it is impossible to evade or warp and which must be understood strictly as *iustitia distributiva*. The mistake of the orthodox dogmaticians was not that they held fast to this concept, but that they did not follow the direction of Scripture and include and explain in their understanding of this concept the mercy of God. When Jesus Christ is set forth to be a ἱλαστήριον ἐν τῷ αὐτοῦ αἵματι as the basis of free justifying grace, it is not, as is twice emphasised in Rom. 3²⁴ᶠ·: πρὸς τὴν ἔνδειξιν τῆς δικαιοσύνης αὐτοῦ, in execution of a divine will discordant with divine righteousness, but in execution of the one righteous will of God : εἰς τὸ εἶναι αὐτὸν δίκαιον καὶ δικαιοῦντα (in justifying) τὸν ἐκ πίστεως 'Ιησοῦ (v. 26). For this reason it is not a later and inconsequent reservation, but the most consistent explanation of the grace which forgives sins, that a few verses later, after an express distinction in v. 28 between righteousness by faith and the righteousness of works, Paul rejects with horror in v. 31 the idea that this might imply the suspension of the Law : μὴ γένοιτο· ἀλλὰ νόμον ἱστάνομεν. And as it is unconditionally the righteous government of God which makes this basis of grace, it is a full and true righteousness which is imputed to the believing sinner (the godless according to Rom. 4⁵), who for his part cannot refer to any justifying works (and does not pretend to be able to perform them). This imputation as such (λογίζεσθαι) is not to be understood as what we usually call an act of grace or an " amnesty." On the contrary, it follows from the fact that righteousness really accrues to the sinner and therefore must be reckoned to him by right. He is in fact in the right against any accusation. He has fulfilled the Law. The godless, as H. Cremer rightly says (*Die Lehre von den Eigenschaften Gottes*, 1917, p. 49), is not saved from the hand of God, but by His hand, and by His righteous hand.

God cannot affirm Himself more strongly as the righteous God, He cannot more effectively attest and implement the Law as the most proper and characteristic revelation of Himself, He cannot bind the impious more closely to Himself as righteous and to His Law, than by His grace which pardons the sinner. For this grace is through and through the proof of the existence of the righteous God. It is so from every point of view : its foundation in the will of God, its execution in the death of Jesus Christ, and its application to believers. God does not need to yield His righteousness a single inch when He is merciful. As He is merciful, He is righteous. He is merciful as He really makes demands and correspondingly punishes and rewards.

That God winks at the times of ignorance (Ac. 17³⁰) does not mean, any more than the ἀνοχή of Rom. 3²⁶, that God accepts ignorance or sins or even that He ignores and condones them. But what is described in Rom. 3 as the demonstration of God's righteousness in which God confronts sin as the Judge is pictured in Ac. 17³⁰f· as the dawning of the day when by the resurrection of Jesus Christ God offers faith (πίστιν παρασχών) to all. Why ? As a back door through which they can escape the demands of His righteousness ? No, but in this way He " commandeth all men everywhere to repent ; because he hath appointed a day (the day of faith) in the which he (according to Ps. 96¹³) will judge the world in righteousness." Here we can and must look back to the Old Testament where, for example in Is. 1²⁴f·, the prophet speaks with the same absoluteness of the gracious action of God towards Jerusalem : " Therefore saith the Lord, the Lord of hosts, the mighty One of Israel, Ah, I will ease me of mine adversaries, and avenge me of mine enemies : and I will turn my hand upon thee, and purely purge away thy dross, and take away all thy tin : and I will restore thy judges as at the first, and thy counsellors as at the beginning : afterward thou shalt be called, The city of righteousness, the faithful city. Zion shall be redeemed with judgment, and her converts with righteousness. And the destruction of the transgressors and of the sinners shall be together, and they that forsake the Lord shall be consumed." This is spoken no less concretely and directly to the contemporary situation because it confronts the latter with the coming day of the Lord. On the contrary, it is because this is the case that the prophet addresses this Word to his contemporaries. And this day of the Lord is no less the day of grace and salvation because it must clearly be described as the day of judgment. On the contrary, it is because God asserts His righteousness as against men and establishes a new righteousness, His righteousness, among them—it is in and through the terror which this implies, that He acts in mercy towards them. He is not merciful if He is even a jot less righteous. It is not the kingdom of heaven, imminent as the kingdom in which sins are forgiven and redemption is offered, if it does not have to be proclaimed with the summons to repent as, according to Mt. 3^2 and 4^{17}, John the Baptist and Jesus did in the selfsame words. And the proclamation of this kingdom has not been heard, and it is not entered, if this proclamation is understood to cancel the Law and the prophets or even the smallest part of their message, if the new kingdom does not introduce a righteousness which is better than that of the scribes and Pharisees (Mt. 5^{17-20}). Israel always misconceived the righteousness of God and of the kingdom of heaven (Rom. 10^3). When the day of the revelation of God's righteousness dawns, when in the epiphany of Jesus Christ, in the proclamation of the Gospel the kingdom of heaven draws near, penitence is the one thing which Israel needs. In the parallel passage in Mark 1^{15} we read : " Repent ye, and believe the Gospel; " but even in this expanded form repentance is interpreted as faith and faith as repentance. As is still very plain in the later New Testament witness (2 Pet. 1^1), in faith it can only be a question of recognising and obeying the revealed righteousness of God.

For according to the Scriptures of the Old and New Testaments what constitutes the demonstration and exercise of God's righteousness, what makes penitence and obedience necessary on man's side, is precisely the fact that God enters into a covenant with him and promises that his sins are to be forgiven and eternal life assured. According to the witness of the Old and New Testaments, the love and grace and mercy of God, Jesus Christ, are the demonstration and exercise of the righteousness of God. And it is only in this way that the divine love and grace and mercy can be truly recognised and felt and appropriated. It is only in this way that Jesus Christ can be believed. He is the righteousness of God. Any other kind of faith, any faith which does not refer consistently to God's righteousness and rest upon it, any kind of piety which is not for its part the righteousness of man, according to what is in this respect the quite unequivocal witness of both Old and New Testaments, necessarily lacks in seriousness, assurance and joy because it obviously has as its object another god than the God whose self-revelation is unfolded to us in Scripture as the being and basis and substance of the Church. For in the very fact that God founds and maintains this covenant with man He distinguishes His action from all caprice and contingency, from all confusion and unrighteousness. He does what is in the highest sense the right : that in which He Himself is righteous ; that which befits Him and is worthy of Him as God. In this covenant He reveals Himself as the One He is, the One who is bound to His own nature, the One who is true to Himself.

It is not the case that in Jesus Christ there has, as it were, been an unforeseen episode in our favour. It is not the case that God in His love and grace and mercy has performed as it were a *tour de force* and brought about an altogether exceptional state of affairs. But it is rather the case that He is wholly Himself and true to Himself in the fact that He is true to us. And the point of faith is to trust wholly in the God who is true to Himself in the fact that He is true to us. For this reason in the first biblical passage in which these two ideas emerge (Gen. 15⁶) faith and righteousness stand in an intrinsically necessary and indissoluble connexion. Therefore biblical faith consists in penitence and obedience, ὑπακοὴ πίστεως (Rom. 1⁵, 16²⁶), ὑπακοὴ τοῦ Χριστοῦ (2 Cor. 10⁵), ὑπακοὴ τῆς ἀληθείας (1 Peter 1²²), a returning and a submission. From this derives its seriousness but also its joyous confidence. It is in the revelation of the righteousness of God (Is. 56¹, Ps. 98²) that faith has its life. To it the heavens declare God's righteousness (Ps. 50⁶, 85¹¹, 97⁶), and allow it to prevail (Hos. 10¹², Is. 45⁸). It sees the justice of God towering like mountains (Ps. 36⁷). It knows it to be eternal (Ps. 111³, 112³, Is. 51⁶). It knows its God only as the One who makes firm His kingdom (Is. 9⁷), who espouses His own in right and righteousness (Hos. 2¹⁹), who clothes them with the mantle of righteousness like the bridegroom who adorns his head and like the bride who decks herself in jewels (Is. 61¹⁰). It calls Yahweh Himself our righteousness (Jer. 23⁶, 33¹⁶, cf. Ps. 4¹). It therefore realises that righteousness and peace kiss each other (Ps. 85¹⁰, cf. Is. 32¹⁷). It prays to be led in God's righteousness (Ps. 5⁸), to be saved by it (Ps. 31¹), to be heard (Ps. 143¹), to be led out of distress (Ps. 143¹¹), to see the face of God (Ps. 17¹⁵), to be allowed to pass through the gate of righteousness (Ps. 118¹⁹). According to the Book of Proverbs, it knows that righteousness makes man's way straight (11⁵), that it is a certain good (11¹⁸), that it preserves the innocent (13⁶), guards a people (14³⁴), saves from death (10²). Not only in the mouth of Job (27⁶, 29¹⁴), it glories in its righteousness. The pious man knows and understands himself to be just. What else can he be if—and in this his piety consists—he holds fast to God ? How can he declare God's righteousness (Ps. 22³¹, 35²⁸, 71¹⁵ etc.) if he does not take seriously and make his own this divine righteousness ? This does not make it any the less God's own righteousness. It is God's righteousness in this way. For God's righteousness is that the man in covenant with Him should be righteous, that he should be such a one as is justified in God's sight because God has addressed him and dealt with him in righteousness, putting him in the right. But again, it is impossible to see how faith in the God who reveals Himself and speaks and acts in righteousness will not necessarily have as such the character of a returning and a submission. For this God calls us to Himself and binds us to Himself, tearing us from ourselves and from all that wills to resist Him and transporting us into an identity of our will with His. This God and only this God is our God in such a way—as we have indicated—that He is our righteousness. *Prodest meditatio haec ad colligendos omnes sensus nostros ad unam Dei iustitiam, ne varie spes nostras partiamur, sed relictis omnibus pravis fiduciis, quibus totus fere mundus circumagitur huc et illud, prorsus defixi in Dei voluntate propensissima ad exhibendam nobis promissam salutem. Neque consilio proprio, neque industriae, neque virtuti inniti, neque ullis opibus, neque hominum auxiliis debemus, ut secure nobis salutem polliceamur, sed hoc unum nobis propositum esse debet, quia iustus est Deus, fieri non posse, ut ab eo deseramur . . . Nihil est tutius quam sicut in clementia et misericordia, ita in iustitia Dei acquiescere ne alio nos quicquam rapiat : nam qui consilio destituti, sibi ipsis prospicere nequeunt, qui obiecti sunt iniuriis, qui cavendis iniuriis minime sunt solertes, qui denique a filiis huius mundi superantur astu et fraudibus, si solummodo in fiducia iustitiae Dei sint firmi, ne utiquam subvertentur. Iustitia Dei exseret se ad ipsos tuendos ; iustitia Dei pericula, quibus salus ipsorum impeditur, depellet* (Polanus, *Synt. Theol. chr.*, 1609, col. 1162 f.).

Faith in God's righteousness is at one and the same time the source of all comfort and the epitome of God's most jealous demand upon man. For in this faith it is a matter of cleaving to God who does what befits Him and what is worthy of Him. That doing this He espouses man's cause, covenanting and keeping faith with him, is the comfort of this faith. But it is also God's strictest claim in that it affirms and apprehends as the covenant-partner of man the God who in this covenant does what befits Him, what is worthy of Himself. We cannot, therefore, appropriate and understand His love and grace and mercy without at the same time hearing and considering the summons with which He lifts us out of all the being and doing in which we try to follow our own ideas of justice, i.e., what befits and is worthy of us. Faith in God's righteousness means necessarily and essentially a choice and decision in favour of His righteousness as opposed to our own; in other words, the choice and decision by which instead of our own righteousness we accept as our own the righteousness of God, or, according to the shorter New Testament definition, of Christ. To this extent the revelation of God's righteousness means in fact judgment upon us, implying our condemnation and the death of the old man. To this extent faith means that we accept this condemnation, the death of the old man, and that as condemned sinners, divested of our own righteousness, we flee from ourselves and take refuge in God who wills alone to be both our righteousness and our life, who, making us righteous by Himself, wills that there should be no division between Himself and us.

In this connexion it is important to notice that the people to whom God in His righteousness turns as helper and Saviour is everywhere in the Old Testament harassed and oppressed people of Israel, which, powerless in itself, has no rights, and is delivered over to the superior force of its enemies; and in Israel it is especially the poor, the widows and orphans, the weak and defenceless. The branch out of the root of Jesse " will have his delight in the fear of the Lord. He shall not judge after the sight of his eyes, neither reprove after the hearing of his ears," which means obviously that he will not vindicate him who in the common opinion is already in the right, " but with righteousness he shall judge the poor, and reprove with equity for the meek of the earth : and he shall smite the earth with the rod of his mouth, and with the breath of his life shall he slay the wicked." And so " righteousness shall be the girdle of his loins and faithfulness the girdle of his reins " (Is. 11$^{3f.}$). For this reason the human righteousness required by God and established in obedience—the righteousness which according to Amos 5^{24} should pour down as a mighty stream—has necessarily the character of a vindication of right in favour of the threatened innocent, the oppressed poor, widows, orphans and aliens. For this reason, in the relations and events in the life of His people, God always takes His stand unconditionally and passionately on this side and on this side alone : against the lofty and on behalf of the lowly ; against those who already enjoy right and privilege and on behalf of those who are denied it and deprived of it. What does all this mean ? It is not really to be explained by talking *in abstracto* of the political tendency and especially the forensic character of the Old Testament and the biblical message generally. It does in fact have this character and we cannot hear it and believe it without feeling a sense of responsibility in the direction indicated.

As a matter of fact, from the belief in God's righteousness there follows logically a very definite political problem and task. But seen and understood *in abstracto*, the latter—i.e., the connexion between justification and law in all its relevance for that between Church and state—cannot really be evident and necessary of itself. It becomes so when we appreciate the fact that God's righteousness, the faithfulness in which He is true to Himself, is disclosed as help and salvation, as a saving divine intervention for man directed only to the poor, the wretched and the helpless as such, while with the rich and the full and the secure as such, according to His very nature He can have nothing to do. God's righteousness triumphs when man has no means of triumphing. It is light when man in himself lies in darkness, and life when man walks in the shadow of death. When we encounter divine righteousness we are all like the people of Israel, menaced and altogether lost according to its own strength. We are all widows and orphans who cannot procure right for themselves. It is obviously in the light of this confrontation that we have all those sayings in the Psalms about God's righteousness and the believer and his righteousness before God. The connexion between God's righteousness and mercy now becomes clear. The righteousness of the believer consists in the fact that God acts for him—utterly, because he cannot plead his own case and no one else can represent him. Faith grasps this full intervention on the part of God and it is therefore *eo ipso* faith in God's mercy, the faith of those who are poor and wretched before God. According to the Gospel of Luke and the Epistle of James, as also according to the message of the prophets, there follows from this character of faith a political attitude, decisively determined by the fact that man is made responsible to all those who are poor and wretched in his eyes, that he is summoned on his part to espouse the cause of those who suffer wrong. Why ? Because in them it is manifested to him what he himself is in the sight of God ; because the living, gracious, merciful action of God towards him consists in the fact that God Himself in His own righteousness procures right for him, the poor and wretched ; because he and all men stand in the presence of God as those for whom right can be procured only by God Himself. The man who lives by the faith that this is true stands under a political responsibility. He knows that the right, that every real claim which one man has against another or others, enjoys the special protection of the God of grace. As surely as he himself lives by the grace of God he cannot evade this claim. He cannot avoid the question of human rights. He can only will and affirm a state which is based on justice. By any other political attitude he rejects the divine justification.

But this is not the point with which we are immediately concerned. Our concern is that at this point the truth emerges that God's righteousness does not really stand alongside His mercy, but that as revealed in its necessary connexion, according to Scripture, with the plight of the poor and wretched, it is itself God's mercy. Just because He is righteous God has mercy, condescending sympathetically to succour those who are utterly in need of His help, who without it would in fact be lost. God is righteous in Himself, doing what befits Him and is worthy of Him, defending and glorying His divine being, in the fact that He is our righteousness, that He procures right for those who in themselves have no righteousness, whose own righteousness is rather disclosed by Him to be unrighteousness, yet whom He does not leave to themselves, to whom rather He gives Himself in His own divine righteousness and therefore becomes the ground on which, against their own merit and worth and solely by His merit and worth, called away from themselves and summoned to surrender themselves to His will, they can truly stand and live. This standing and living of man is not, therefore, threatened but in the true sense established by the righteousness of God when in his confrontation by God man must necessarily confess that—in so far as he stands isolated from God's activity on his behalf—he is a sinner. There is, therefore, only an apparent contradiction between the prayer of Psalm 143[2]: "Enter not into judgment with thy servant : for in thy sight shall no man living be justified " ; and that of Ps. 7[8]: " Judge me, O Lord, according to my righteousness, and according to mine integrity that is in me." If Ps. 7 expresses the confidence of the man whom God has justified and who has in this

way established his case in the teeth of all his accusers and adversaries, Ps. 143 shows how he attains this confidence—namely, by allowing that God is in the right against him, and accepting God as his only righteousness, his own but his real righteousness. It is in this sense that Zion boasts of its hope in Micah 7⁷ᶠ·:
" Therefore I will look unto the Lord ; I will wait for the God of my salvation : my God will hear me. Rejoice not against me, O mine enemy ; when I fall, I shall arise ; when I sit in darkness, the Lord shall be a light unto me. I will bear the indignation of the Lord, because I have sinned against him, until he plead my cause, and execute judgment for me : he will bring me forth to the light, and I shall behold his righteousness. Then she that is mine enemy shall see it, and shame shall cover her which said unto me, Where is the Lord thy God ? " On the other hand, consider how the righteous Job, who is known to be protected by God Himself against all accusations, speaks of his right as such and *in abstracto* : " How should man be just with God ? If he will contend with him, he cannot answer him one of a thousand. He is wise in heart, and mighty in strength: who hath hardened himself against him, and hath prospered ? " (Job 9²⁻⁴). " Behold, he taketh away, who can hinder him ? who will say unto him, What doest thou ? If God will not withdraw his anger, the proud archers do stoop under him. How much less shall I answer him, and choose out my words to reason with him ? Whom, though I were righteous, yet would I not answer, but I would make supplication to my judge. If I had called, and he had answered me ; yet would I not believe that he had hearkened unto my voice " (9¹²⁻¹⁶). " If I speak of strength, lo, he is strong : and if of judgment, who shall set me a time to plead ? If I justify myself, mine own mouth shall condemn me : if I say that I am perfect, it shall prove me perverse " (9¹⁹⁻²⁰). " If I be wicked, why then labour I in vain ? If I wash myself with snow water, and make my hands never so clean, yet shalt thou plunge me in the ditch, and mine own clothes shall abhor me. For he is not a man, as I am, that I should answer him, and we should come together in judgment. Neither is there any daysman betwixt us, that might lay his hand upon us both " (9²⁹⁻³³). " Man that is born of a woman is of a few days, and is full of trouble. He cometh forth like a flower, and is cut down : he fleeth also as a shadow, and continueth not. And dost thou open thine eyes upon such an one, and bringest me into judgment with thee ? Who can bring a clean thing out of an unclean ? Not one " (14¹⁻⁴). The tone of complaint and accusation, the bitterness, the fierce irony with which all this is spoken in the context of Job's speech does not alter the fact that it expresses the truth. And on it is founded the possibility that Job can again say with regard to his right : " Behold now, I have ordered my cause ; I know that I shall be justified. Who is he that will plead with me ? for now, if I hold my tongue, I shall give up the ghost " (13¹⁸⁻¹⁹). " Also now, behold, my witness is in heaven, and my record is on high. My friends scorn me ; but mine eye poureth out tears unto God. O that one might plead for a man with God, as a man pleadeth for his neighbour ! " (16¹⁹⁻²¹). " But I know that my Redeemer liveth, and an Advocate arises for me over my dust. Even when my skin is torn from my body and my flesh has perished, I shall behold God (to salvation), and my eyes shall behold Him, not as an enemy. . . . If you say: How we shall persecute him, and find the root of the matter in him, be afraid of the sword, for wrath falleth on the guilty, that you may know there is a judgment " (19²⁵⁻²⁹). Again, all this is not spoken without defiance and even arrogance. Again, it is true that the consoling and warning counter arguments of Job's friends undoubtedly sound far better theologically, and do in fact serve to put him subjectively even more in the wrong than he himself has already done in his own speeches. But objectively it is still the case that in all this Job speaks the truth, so that according to 42⁷ᶠ· the wrath of God is not kindled against him but against his friends: " For you have not spoken of me the thing that is right, as my servant Job hath." So in spite of his revolt and presumptuousness he

has spoken that which is right about God because in fact, even though sullenly and scornfully, he has confessed himself to be a sinner before God and because again in fact, though not without an element of impudent conceit, he has claimed God's righteousness as his own. In the objectivity of this twofold recognition of truth Job is plainly the prototype of the poor in spirit whose is the kingdom of heaven (Mt. 5³). " If we confess our sins, he is faithful and just to forgive us our sins, and to cleanse us from all unrighteousness " (1 Jn. 1⁹). " Blessed are they which do hunger and thirst after righteousness : for they shall be filled (Mt. 5⁶). It is always and necessarily a subjectively sinful and unrighteous people, confessing its unrighteousness, whose cause before God is just, whose just cause God protects, because He Himself is its just cause. It is the people whose righteousness is as filthy rags (Is. 64⁶). It is the people that must confess (Is. 59⁹ᶠ·) : " We look for light, but behold obscurity ; for brightness, but we walk in darkness. We grope for the wall like the blind, and we grope as if we had no eyes : we stumble at noonday as in the night ; we are in desolate places as dead men. We roar all like bears, and mourn sore like doves : we look for judgment, but there is none ; for salvation, but it is far off from us. For our transgressions are multiplied before thee, and our sins testify against us : for our transgressions are with us, and as for our iniquities we know them ; in transgressing and lying against the Lord, and departing away from our God, speaking oppression and revolt, conceiving and uttering from the heart words of falsehood. And judgment is turned away backward, and justice standeth afar off : for truth is fallen in the street, and equity cannot enter. Yea, truth faileth ; and he that departeth from evil maketh himself a prey." This is the people that can stand and live under the divine answer : " And the Lord saw it, and it displeased him that there was no judgment. And he saw that there was no man, and wondered that there was no intercessor : therefore his arm brought salvation unto him ; and his righteousness, it sustained him. For he put on righteousness as a breastplate, and an helmet of salvation upon his head ; and he put on the garments of vengeance for clothing, and was clad with zeal as a cloke. . . . And the Redeemer shall come to Zion, and unto them that turn from transgression in Jacob, saith the Lord. As for me, this is my covenânt with them, saith the Lord ; my spirit that is upon thee, and my words which I have put in thy mouth, shall not depart out of thy mouth, nor out of the mouth of thy seed, nor out of the mouth of thy seed's seed, saith the Lord, from henceforth and for ever " (Is. 59¹⁵ᶠ·). It is only by the forgiveness of sins that God manifests and exercises His righteousness towards this people, giving it a just cause and Himself espousing its just cause. For " thou hast not called upon me, O Jacob, thou hast been weary of me, O Israel. Thou hast not brought me the small cattle of thy burnt offerings ; neither hast thou honoured me with thy sacrifices . . . but thou hast made me to serve with thy sins, thou hast wearied me with thine iniquities. I, even I, am he that blotteth out thy transgressions for mine own sake, and will not remember thy sins " (Is. 43²²ᶠ·). The message can then continue : " Yet now, hear, O Jacob my servant ; and Israel whom I have chosen. Thus saith the Lord that made thee, and formed thee from the womb, which will help thee; fear not, O Jacob, my servant; and thou Jeshurun, whom I have chosen. For I will pour water upon him that is thirsty, and floods upon the dry ground : I will pour my spirit upon thy seed, and my blessing upon thine offspring : and they shall spring up as among the grass, as willows by the water courses. One shall say, I am the Lord's ; and another shall call himself by the name of Jacob ; and another shall subscribe with his hand unto the Lord, and surname himself by the name of Israel " (Is. 44¹ᶠ·). It is only as they invoke the grace of God which forgives sins that Moses (Ex. 32¹¹ᶠ·, Deut. 9²³), Solomon (1 Kg. 8) and Daniel (9⁴ᶠ·) can intercede with God that He will still graciously accept this people. It is never their own being and doing which constitutes the justice of their cause, and for the sake of which the divine advocacy and action takes place. It takes place only for the reason that Israel's infidelity cannot suspend God's fidelity (Rom. 3³), that God cannot repent of His gracious promises and calling (Rom. 11²⁹), and therefore only for the sake of God's own righteousness. Looking upon Israel's own ways and conduct, God can only judge, reject and punish. In the process of judging, rejecting and punishing, God does not break but keeps His covenant, and therefore comforts, helps and saves. He maintains the right of this judged, rejected and punished people against all other peoples. He does not cease to act towards it as His own people called and chosen by Himself. But this is not the result of any preference which Israel has or has acquired in His sight. It is through and through the *iustitia peccatorum*. It is the triumph only of God's own righteousness. Only in faith in Him, only in that intercession of Moses, Solomon and Daniel for the forgiveness of sins, can Israel be subjectively in the right. But in faith, in that prayer, it is in point of fact subjectively righteous. If it seizes this promise of the divine advocacy and action, in this apprehension it already lives in its fulfilment, and it can and may and will stand before its enemies and in every misfortune. " If ye will not believe, surely ye shall not be established " (Is. 7⁹). And this implies as its complement : " He that believeth shall not be ashamed " (Is. 28¹⁶), or in Luther's translation : " He that believeth shall not flee." With Job the believer can confidently await God's righteous judgment : in spite of and in all the merited and inevitable threat to his own existence as such ; in spite of and in the recognition and confession of his guilt and sin. He can in fact appeal to this first judgment of God as the court before which he is already declared righteous and before which, when it is publicly revealed, he will be justified to all eternity against the accusations of men and of his own heart. For him the day of the Lord will not be, as it is described in Amos 5¹⁸ᶠ·, Joel 2¹¹ and Zeph. 1¹⁴ᶠ·, a day of darkness and terror, but a day of light and joy. On that day—in accordance with the saying in Hab. 2⁴ which is cited in Rom. 1¹⁷ and which assumed such importance for Luther—he will remain alive in virtue of his faith : *iustus ex fide vivet*.

According to the witness of the New Testament the One in whom God's people has its righteous cause, maintained and protected by God, is Jesus Christ. It is in Him that God reveals and does what is worthy of Himself. It is in Him that He reveals and exercises His own righteousness in favour of those whom He has called and chosen, even though their own righteousness is as filthy rags. It is He who had compassion on the people, for they were faint and exhausted like sheep without a shepherd (Mt. 9³⁶). It is His call which is the call to repentance and therefore to faith and therefore to the kingdom of heaven, and at the same time a blessing upon the poor in spirit, upon those who mourn, upon those who hunger and thirst after righteousness, upon those who are persecuted for righteousness' sake, etc. His is the invitation : " Come unto me, all ye that labour and are heavy laden and I will give you rest " (Mt. 11²⁸). It is He who is the righteous Advocate of sinners with the Father (1 Jn. 2¹). It is He who saves " them to the uttermost that come unto God by him, seeing he ever liveth to make intercession for them " (Heb. 7²⁵ ; Rom. 8³⁴). It is He who is made righteousness for us (1 Cor. 1³⁰). And it is faith in Him, the πίστις Ἰησοῦ Χριστοῦ, which is the condition on which the righteous God justifies the ungodly. It is faith in Him which God reckons to the ungodly as righteousness, and in which he becomes and is truly righteous.

But this leads us necessarily to a further consideration. As we envisage and apprehend in Jesus Christ the righteousness of God, and therefore the fidelity which is grounded in and constitutes His very being, the fidelity to Himself in which He is faithful to us, we are warned against the too convenient and facile way of thought which has simply divested the concept of divine righteousness of the notion which is necessarily bound up with the concept of judgment, that of a decision about good and evil, about reward and punishment. As we envisage and apprehend in Jesus Christ the righteousness of God we shall not think that we have exhausted it by viewing it and interpreting it as comfort and help in the misery of human sin, as the promise and fulfilment of pardon for this sin. On the contrary, it is just because—and there can be no surrender or weakening of the righteousness of God, but only its assertion in its true character and rigour—it implies comfort and help in the distress of our sin, the promise and the fulfilment of its pardon, that, if we have really seen it at work in Jesus Christ, a place must be found for a consideration in which (in contradiction to modern interpretations) its character as *iustitia distributiva* is maintained. It is a righteousness which judges and therefore both exculpates and condemns, rewards and also punishes.

Orthodoxy had pushed this aspect of the matter too much into the foreground and thus imperilled the unity of God's righteousness with His mercy. Because, as the righteousness of the God revealed in Jesus Christ, it must be understood essentially as an expression of His love and grace, we have been trying to grasp and interpret it chiefly in its oneness with divine mercy. Its character as *iustitia distributiva* was necessarily obscured in the process. We have seen it so far as a righteousness which decisively exculpates and rewards, that is, in the case of faith. But if it is real righteousness, the essential righteousness of the God revealed in Jesus Christ, we must now see too that it is a righteousness which condemns and punishes. Even as such, of course, it is God's mercy and grace and love. But as mercy and grace and love it is now a righteousness which condemns and punishes. Otherwise its unity with the holiness of God is obscured and we have learned from our introductory references to Anselm that this obscuration is no more legitimate than that of which Ritschl is guilty. We shall have to arrive at a deeper understanding of the mercy of God, and of Luther's insight that God's righteousness is His mercy, as we now address ourselves to the concern which has led orthodoxy into this error (which we have avoided). This concern is rather more than the attempt to complete a purely human idea of righteousness and therefore to apply it in its other aspect. On the contrary, we are plainly compelled by the testimony of Scripture and in particular by the Christian testimony of Scripture, to go a step further than Ritschl did. We have already pointed out more than once the unity of the Gospel with the Law, and the character of faith as penitence. We have understood the distress and poverty of Israel, whom God in His righteousness assists, as the spiritual distress and poverty of the people who must confess their sin and failure before God. We have seen how the understanding in faith of the saving righteousness of God implies that man in himself must perish before God, to live only in Him and with Him. But all this requires special emphasis and explanation if it is to be seriously grasped and affirmed.

We can begin here with the prayer of Solomon uttered on the occasion of the consecration of the temple. Its first petition is (1 Kg. 8³¹ᶠ·) that justice should be proclaimed in the temple and the judgments of God awaited. When this takes place, then, as Solomon prays: "Hear thou in heaven, and do, and judge thy servants, condemning the wicked, to bring his way upon his head ; and justifying the righteous, to give him according to his righteousness." This is obviously an appeal to the *iustitia distributiva* of God. Obviously the righteous God is like this and acts like this even in His mercy. He adjudges guilt to the guilty and causes his deeds to recoil on his own head. Though His fidelity is endless and cannot be suspended by the infidelities of Israel, that is not to deny that it clashes with the offences of Israel. And what then takes place is the condemning and punishing operation of His righteousness. Does this mean that it ceases to be merciful ? Certainly not. His mercy does not cease to be righteousness and His righteousness does not cease to be His holy essence and to show itself as such in conflict with human disobedience. In this clash God is and does what is worthy of Himself. This necessarily means condemnation and punishment where He finds disobedience, and pardon and reward where He finds the obedience of faith.

The witness is unequivocal : " In the day that thou eatest thereof thou shalt surely die " (Gen. 2[17]) ; " Cursed is he that confirmeth not all the words of this law to do them " (Deut. 27[26]) ; " For thou art not a God that hath pleasure in wickedness : neither shall evil dwell with thee. The foolish shall not stand in thy sight : thou hatest all workers of iniquity. Thou shalt destroy them that speak leasing : the Lord will abhor the bloody and deceitful man " (Ps. 5[4f.]) ; and " The face of the Lord is against them that do evil, to cut off the remembrance of them from the earth " (Ps. 34[16]). The threats of the Law and prophets against sinful Israel and against the impiety of the heathen, and the accounts of the actual execution of these threats, also have a place in the Bible, forming in their severity and relentlessness an integral part of its witness to the revelation and therefore the essence of God. Nor do we have here a specific Old Testament concern which was later superseded. That the wages of sin is death is still the message of Rom. 6[23]. Even in the Gospel the man who has no wedding garment at the marriage of the King (Mt. 22[13]), and the unprofitable servant who has buried the talent entrusted to him instead of exploiting it (Mt. 25[30]), are cast out into outer darkness where there is weeping and gnashing of teeth. The fig tree bearing nothing but leaves is cursed by Jesus and withers (Mt. 21[18f.]). The foolish virgins knock at the closed doors of the bridal chamber and are told : " I know you not ! " (Mt. 25[11f.]). To those who have not given food and drink, and lodged and clothed and visited the Son of Man in His lowly brethren, it is said : " Depart from me, ye cursed, into everlasting fire, prepared by my Father for the devil and his angels " (Mt. 25[41f.]). We read expressly in 2 Thess. 1[6f.] : " It is a righteous thing with God to recompense tribulation to them that trouble you . . . when the Lord Jesus Christ shall be revealed from heaven with his mighty angels, in flaming fire taking vengeance on them that know not God, and that obey not the gospel of our Lord Jesus Christ : who shall be punished with everlasting destruction from the presence of the Lord, and from the glory of his power ; when he shall come to be glorified in his saints." Revelation speaks to the same effect ; and on what page of the New Testament is not the same message directly or indirectly proclaimed ? Certainly both the Old and the New Testaments summon Israel and the Church to have faith and in that way to trust in their deliverance from this operation of God's righteousness. But they do not conceal the fact—on the contrary, the whole impressiveness of their summons to faith is that they so powerfully shew that the operation of the righteousness and therefore the mercy of God is the judgment which we certainly will not escape without faith. It is the abyss from which we are held back by faith alone. It is the damnation from which we are preserved only by faith, which in ourselves we have merited and which on our own merits we cannot escape, from which we have refuge only because (and this is the essence of faith) we are no longer expected to live in our own strength, because we see ourselves and act as those who have thankfully found the centre of their being in the faith that God lives for them.

It should be understood that we are not summoned in faith to look past the God who lives for us and stare into this precipice. We have not to fear that it might again threaten us, that we might again be swallowed up by it. We apprehend by faith God's justifying and rewarding righteousness, and it is the unbelief of Lot's wife to try to look back and again reckon or even trifle with the reality or the possibility of damnation and death. For this is not a serious calculation but a wanton trifling. It can only be a false Christian earnestness which causes a man to suspend his faith as it were, to lay aside for a moment the decision about his salvation contained in God's revelation, and to place himself at the critical point where it is seen that the end of one way is eternal glory and of the other way everlasting fire. All heathen eschatology thinks in this symmetrical way, but Scripture never puts these two ways before our eyes. We are not called by its summons to faith to stand at this critical point.

On the contrary, we are clearly invited by this summons to give ourselves to the God who lives for us and saves us by His life for us. But the reference to the condemning and punishing operation of God's righteousness means (and this is why it is essentially a call to faith) that we are to understand God's life for us and therefore our deliverance from judgment as His mercy by which there comes to us that which we have not deserved and of which we are not worthy. It is the negative side of the matter. What we have deserved and what we are worthy to receive in our intrinsic being and conduct is always and will always be the condemning and punishing operation of divine justice. For in our intrinsic being we find ourselves in collision with the faithfulness of God. When we are confronted by the faithfulness of God, our own characteristic reaction to it is always unfaithfulness. We are revealed as foolish virgins, as unprofitable servants, as the murmuring stiff-necked idolatrous people of Israel. " No flesh is just in thy sight " (Rom. 3^{20}). " God saw that the wickedness of man was great in the earth, and that every imagination of the thoughts of his heart was only evil continually " (Gen. 6^5). This is the statement made before the Flood, and it is expressly repeated after the Flood (Gen. 8^{21}) as the presupposition for the suspension of further divine punishment. ". The Lord looked down from heaven upon the children of men, to see if there were any that did understand, and seek God. They are all gone aside, they are all together become filthy : there is none that doeth good, no, not one " (Ps. 14^{2-3}). It is necessary that faith should remember the abyss from which it has been saved and over which it is poised in order that as effective faith it may praise God as the One who has found man in his utterly lost condition, snatching him from the grip of death and translating him into life ; in order that it may give honour to free mercy in the freedom in which it has accomplished the unexpected and incomprehensible ; in order that it may be bound in total obedience to the God who owed it nothing and to whom it owes everything.

But if this worship of the merciful God is to be an unequivocal and worthy worship of the true and living God it must redound also to the glory of His righteousness. His mercy is not truly His, it is not a saving divine mercy, if it is not also righteousness, and we do not praise the mercy of God if in it we do not also praise His righteousness.

The question which we have still to answer, or rather the answer which we have here to ponder as already given in God's revelation and being, the answer to every question about the depth and power and might of His mercy, is as follows. How far is the mercy of God, which is to be apprehended in faith, at the same time the righteousness of His judgment ? And how far is it recognisable in that fact as His, the divine and therefore the eternal and actual, saving and victorious mercy ? God's revelation in Jesus Christ supplies to this question the answer that the condemning and punishing righteousness of God is in itself and as such the depth and power and might of His mercy. Where

{394   § 30. *The Perfections of the Divine Loving*}

Holy Scripture speaks of God's threats and judgments, we do not in point of fact find ourselves on a periphery from which we have finally to look to a very different centre of its message. On the contrary, we find ourselves at the very heart of this message. We can only be overlooking or misunderstanding the biblical message if for one reason or another we try to be spared having to take quite seriously the fact that God is the God who for the sake of His righteousness is wrathful and condemns and punishes. He is not only this, but He is also this. If He were not also this He would not be for us the living God to whom we are summoned to listen when we are invited to have faith. If we are earnestly to cleave to Him, if we are to accept the salvation accomplished in Himself and offered to us through Him, if we are really to look forward in faith rather than backward, we cannot try to overlook or evade by reservations the essential realisation that God also is angry, condemns and punishes. If we truly love Him, we must love Him also in His anger, condemnation and punishments, or rather we must see, feel and appreciate His love to us even in His anger, condemnation and punishment. For we cannot avoid the conclusion that it is where the divine love and therefore the divine grace and mercy are attested with the supreme clarity in which they are necessarily known as the meaning and intention of Scripture as a whole, where that love and grace and mercy are embodied in a unique event, i.e., in Jesus Christ, that according to the unmistakable witness of the New Testament itself they encounter us as a divine act of wrath, judgment and punishment.

Not only as that, for there also takes place there the resurrection of Jesus Christ from the dead, and to that extent what takes place is God's righteousness in an act of divine pleasure, acquittal and reward. But we must not for one moment forget the full implication of the fact that it is the crucified Jesus Christ who rises from the dead. This means that the divine Yes of Easter Day presupposes a divine No from which it is inseparable, without which it is not the divine Yes of God's vindicating and rewarding righteousness. The event of Good Friday embodies the divine No, which contains in itself the divine Yes and is the presupposition of it, but which must not be any the less on that account understood as a definite divine No: as the judgment whose frightfulness causes even the most dreadful judgments threatened and executed by God in the witness of Old Testament Scripture to fade ; or conversely, as the judgment whose continual fire is the light in which is first revealed the true terror of those Old Testament threats and executions of judgment. If we view the latter in themselves, in spite of the terrible contents of almost innumerable Old Testament texts of this kind we may ask whether their terrors cannot be classed with the far too many similar happenings which have been the more or less merited destiny of other ancient and modern and indeed all peoples. Or if on a closer investigation we admit that in spite of its general similarity with that of other peoples the destiny of Israel reveals a consistency and radicalness which makes it of exemplary force even to-day, we may ask whether the Christian Church of every age and people has cause for this reason to see its God in these Old Testament texts, in His wrathful dealings with this people Israel. Why should the terrible fate of this people in this age (or in our own) concern us who do not belong to it ? We will no longer ask this question once we have seen and understood the terror of

Good Friday. The fact is that we cannot regard God's threats and executions of punishment on Israel and Israel's destiny in every time and place as indifferent facts. This is not independent fire shedding an independent light. All that we have mentioned, dreadful as it seems and in fact is in itself, is only a faint reflection compared with the infinitely more terrible happenings that took place on Good Friday. But the light of the fire of this event goes still further. This event is the judgment which reduces to insignificance the seriousness of all the other judgments which from the beginning of the world have been seen to sweep over peoples and individuals—from the great catastrophes of nature and history which have and will come upon thousands and even millions, to that which we all have sooner or later to bear in the deprivation of health, wealth and opportunities in consequence of our own and others' folly or wickedness, and finally in the unique form of our death. It can, again, be more effectively expressed the other way round. The meaning of illness and want, of the mental and physical suffering of each individual, of war, hunger, tyranny and revolution in the life of peoples, of the winding sheet of death spread unceasingly over everything and everyone, is revealed in its true frightfulness only on Good Friday. For we can always relativise and soften and finally forget the pain and suffering, not only of others but also our own. This is true even of the most world-shaking destiny. What is there that has not been forgotten? What will we not all one day have forgotten again? There is nothing so frightful as to be able permanently to affect us : curiously enough, not even the thought that to-morrow we might be dead. But all this inevitably assumes a different complexion as soon as we see it, not in itself as we usually do, but in its inner connexion with the event of Good Friday, with the agony and death endured there. For then we realise that, while it has no profound significance in itself, it acquires it, and in such a way as finally to shake our apathy, from its connexion with the place—the cross of Golgotha—where the infinite weight and meaning of suffering and death has been borne. Our own suffering and death in all their bitterness cannot approach this death and suffering. But as a token of them they assume the character of a witness which we can no longer overlook, though we shall at the same time be thankful that they are only a token of that suffering and death, of the passion of Jesus Christ, His bearing of the eternal wrath of God. For the terrible thing, the divine No of Good Friday, is that there all the sins of Israel and of all men, our sins collectively and individually, have in fact become the object of the divine wrath and retribution. It must be clearly understood : there and there alone ; and therefore not in the great slaughter after the setting up of the golden calf, not in the swallowing up of the sect of Korah, not in the defeat and death of Saul by the Philistines, not in David's sufferings through Absalom, not in the destruction of Samaria and Jerusalem, not in the deportation to Babylon, not in the final overthrow of the temple worship and the state of Judah in A.D. 70. The scale of the Old Testament portrayal of this persistent smiting by Yahweh of His own unfaithful people is far too large, and the accompanying fact that in and through all this divine punishment Israel is not blotted out but continually preserved in a remnant far too singular, for it not to be clear that in spite of the terrible reality in which it is proclaimed and executed, this punishment is not the real divine judgment, but merely points beyond itself to the latter as its adumbration. The Suffering Servant of God in his historical form—whether it be the prophet himself, or the whole people, or the king, or something of them all—is only the representative of Someone very different. The negative and positive predicates heaped upon this Servant are so much more than life-size that the historical embodiment of this figure cannot possibly sustain them. In Israel the really suffering One who bears the wrath and judgment of God is not Israel itself but He to whose advent Israel looks forward and who furnishes the clue to the inner meaning of its existence : Israel's Messiah in the one day of His passion. He and not Israel is also the One who really suffers in all that the Jews of to-day have to endure. He is the One who is intended, aimed at and smitten, hated and pushed aside. And what Israel undergoes up to the present time is undergone as an echo and aftermath of what the heathen long ago did to the Messiah of Israel and had to do as instruments of God, as an echo and aftermath of the one real outbreak, smiting and slaying, of the divine wrath on Golgotha. This is the reason for the ceaseless futility and inevitable ineffectiveness of all that human beings at any time have perpetrated against the Jews or can perpetrate even to-day. They can only set up again the token of the crucifixion of Christ and therefore of the real judgment of God. But the real judgment of God is alone the crucifixion of Christ, and the terror of this event is that it is the reality which all other judgments upon Israel, the world and mankind can only foreshadow or reflect. The awfulness of the crucifixion of Christ is that in it the real essence of all the Old Testament threats and executions of judgment, i.e., the revelation of the wrath of God against all ungodliness and unrighteousness of men (Rom. 1[18])—without which revelation is not divine revelation—was embodied in a unique event. For in the strict sense we can truly say that human sin and sinful man have become the object of divine anger and judgment only as we look at this event. The whole seriousness of man's situation, the effective individual and collective threat to it from both nature and history, the seriousness of the fact that it is man's lot to die, is not at all diminished but only brought out in its full force when it is realised that all that world-history and the life story of each single individual is able to show of slowly advancing or suddenly manifested distress, affliction and catastrophe, every kind of agony and dying (the outpouring of the vials of wrath, Rev. 15 and 16), is not yet or no longer the judgment of God Himself. None of these plagues either was or is the merited end. We have always continued, and do continue, like Israel. Whether we make good or bad use of them is another question, but we always have time and space, and by disregard or interpretation or especially forgetting we can draw away from even the most terrible events which come upon ourselves or others. But could we do this even physically if in what came upon us we had really and ultimately and basically to do with the wrath and judgment of God ? If God's wrath and judgment were really to strike us in all this, and not merely its token (Rev. 15[1]), foreshadowing and reflection—where should we be, where should we have been long since ? Fortunately for us the idea that in the ills we encounter we have to endure the wrath of God Himself is incorrect. The only correct view, i.e., in harmony with the biblical interpretation, is that expressed in the 14th articles of the *Heidelberg Catechism* that " no mere creature can bear the burden of the eternal wrath of God against sin." In face of a real outbreak of God's avenging and smiting wrath, the creature would be annihilated. God's real judgment would mean the end of us. But there is obviously not an end of us, any more than there was or will be of Israel. We obviously still have, and will always have, time and space. Therefore, even though what comes on us from time to time pierces us to the heart, it cannot yet be, or any longer be, the real judgment of God, but only a serious token of it.

The meaning of the death of Jesus Christ is that there God's condemning and punishing righteousness broke out, really smiting and piercing human sin, man as sinner, and sinful Israel. It did really fall on the sin of Israel, our sin and us sinners. It did so in such a way that in what happened there (not to Israel, or to us, but to Jesus Christ) the righteousness of God which we have offended was really revealed and satisfied. Yet it did so in such a way that it did not happen to Israel or to us, but for Israel, for us. What was suffered there on Israel's account and ours, was suffered for Israel and for us.

The wrath of God which we had merited, by which we must have been annihilated and would long since have been annihilated, was now in our place borne and suffered as though it had smitten us and yet in such a way that it did not smite us and can no more smite us. The reason why the No spoken on Good Friday is so terrible, but why there is already concealed in it the Eastertide Yes of God's righteousness, is that He who on the cross took upon Himself and suffered the wrath of God was no other than God's own Son, and therefore the eternal God Himself in the unity with human nature which He freely accepted in His transcendent mercy.

We may rightly say that in fact the whole of the New Testament is concerned with this matter. This is especially true of the Gospels with their unmistakable emphasis on the passion story. It also applies to the Epistles with their many references to the cross or blood or sacrifice of Christ. It is even true of Revelation in which the dominating central figure is the Lamb that was slain. Nor are there lacking specific explanations as to how this happening is to be understood. We may take as our point of departure the well-known text (Jn. 3[16]) which tells us that God so (οὕτως) loved the world that in its revelation and exercise to us His love took this form : " that he gave (ἔδωκεν) his only begotten Son ; " that he " delivered him up for us all : " ὑπὲρ ἡμῶν πάντων παρέδωκεν, as Rom. 8[32] puts it even more plainly and strongly. Or Titus 2[14] : He, our great God and Saviour Christ Jesus, gave Himself for us : ἔδωκεν ἑαυτὸν ὑπὲρ ἡμῶν (cf. Gal. 2[20]). In this giving or self-offering is expressed (Gal. 4[4], Rom. 8[3]) what the Fourth Evangelist especially likes to sum up in the conception of sending, of the divine πέμπειν or ἀποστέλλειν of the Son. This sending means a self-offering grounded in the free will of the Father and the Son in fulfilment of the divine love turned towards the cosmos and the world of man. But it is the case that God in this offering or sending of His Son, and the Son Himself in accepting this mission and allowing Himself to be sacrificed, has exposed Himself to an imposition. In His love God has been hard upon Himself, exacting a supreme and final demand. " He spared not his own Son " (Rom. 8[32]). Christ was rich and for our sake He became poor (2 Cor. 8[9]). He did not snatch at being equal with God but humbled Himself (Phil. 2[6f.]). In what consists this sternness of God against Himself, this self-abasement of God in His only Son ? According to Phil. 2[7] it consisted in the fact that in a self-emptying, in a complete resignation not of the essence but of the form of His Godhead, He took upon Himself our own human form—the form of a servant, in complete likeness to other men : ἐν ὁμοιώματι ἀνθρώπων γενόμενος, allowing Himself to be found in fashion as a man : σχήματι εὑρεθεὶς ὡς ἄνθρωπος. Like all men He was born of a woman (Gal. 4[4]). But what does it mean to take the place of man, to be Himself a man, to be born of a woman ? It means for Him, too, God's Son, God Himself, that He came under the Law (γενόμενος ὑπὸ νόμον), i.e., that He stepped into the heart of the inevitable conflict between the faithfulness of God and the unfaithfulness of man. He took this conflict into His own being. He bore it in Himself to the bitter end. He took part in it from both sides. He endured it from both sides. He was not only the God who is offended by man. He was also the man whom God threatens with death, who falls a victim to death in face of God's judgment. If He really entered into solidarity with us—and that is just what He did do—it meant necessarily that He took upon Himself, in likeness to us (ὁμοίωμα), the " flesh of sin " (Rom. 8[3]). He shared in the status, constitution and situation of man in which man resists God and cannot stand before Him but must die. How could God resist Himself ? How could God sin ? The Son of God knew no sin (2 Cor. 5[21], Jn. 8[46], Heb. 4[15]). But He could enter into man's mode of being, being in the flesh, in which there is absolutely no justification before God (Rom. 3²⁰), but only sin. God could—and not only could but did—allow His Son to be in the body of the flesh (Col. 1²²), and therefore make Him to be sin for our sakes (2 Cor. 5²¹), to become the object which must be the object of His own anger, the victim of His own condemnation and punishment. This is just what has happened. He who was equal with God has become obedient unto death, even the death of the cross (Phil. 2⁸). Where we the unjust should stand, He the Just now stands δίκαιος ὑπὲρ ἀδίκων (1 Pet. 3¹⁸). Where we the weak, the godless, should stand, the Son of God now stands (Rom. 5⁶). Where we the sinners should stand, our Judge now stands (Rom. 5⁸). Where we the enemies of God should stand, God Himself now stands in Jesus Christ (Rom. 5¹⁰). And on Him there now comes what ought to come on us : the condemnation of sin in the flesh (Rom. 8³). In His body—our body of flesh has become His—He bears our sins upon the tree (1 Pet. 2²⁴). He dies for our sin (1 Pet. 3¹⁸, Rom. 6¹⁰). He became a curse for us, as it is written : " Cursed is everyone that hangeth on a tree " (Gal. 3¹³). And all this happened in order that there should be no more condemnation for us (Rom. 8¹), that we who are subject to the Law should be ransomed (Gal. 4⁵), delivered from the curse of the Law (Gal. 3¹³), saved from wrath (Rom. 5⁹), released from sin, healed by His wounds (1 Pet. 2²⁴), redeemed from all lawlessness (Tit. 2¹⁴). For by the event in which God has reconciled us with Himself (ἀποκαταλλάσσειν literally " exchanged ") in which He Himself has therefore become the object of His own severity, His own righteous condemnation and punishment in our stead—in this event it has not only become possible but necessary, and above all actual, that " He does not impute unto us our trespasses " (2 Cor. 5¹⁹). By His blood Jesus Christ has justified us (Rom. 5⁹), procured us the freedom to live in righteousness (Rom. 6¹⁶ᶠ·, 1 Pet. 2²⁴), so that —as He was made sin for us—we have become the righteousness of God in Him (2 Cor. 5²¹). This is the witness of the New Testament concerning the dreadfulness, and in its dreadfulness the liberation and comfort, of the event of Good Friday.

The same truth must again be expressed in the words of Polanus—if only to remind us how fearlessly and unequivocally the older orthodoxy, for all its defects, could speak of this, the heart of the New Testament message : *Nullum exemplum iustitiae, irae et comminationum divinarum est expressius, severius, horribilius quam in Christo. Nam quia omnes homines in Adamo peccaverunt, postulat iustitia Dei, ut, quod adversus summam atque infinitam Dei maiestatem commissum est, id etiam summis atque infinitis, hoc est sempiternis cum animi tum corporis suppliciis luatur, ut sit proportio culpae et poenae. Huic iustitiae satisfaciendum est necessario. At quia nemo hominum satisfacere posset in aeternum ne totum, humanum genus interiret, sponsorem* (a guarantor) *se ultro fecit unigenitus Filius Dei pro illis, quos pater ipsi dederat et ipse sese exinanivit . . . (Phil. 2⁷ᶠ·). Quoniam ergo Filius Dei homo factus constituit se pro electis sponsorem : Deus poenam, quae electis in sempiternum perferenda fuisset, in ipsum transtulit sponsorem et iram suam adversus peccata electorum in eum effudit (Synt. Theol. chr.,* 1609, *col.* 1166).

1. The fact that it was God's Son, that it was God Himself, who took our place on Golgotha and thereby freed us from the divine anger and judgment, reveals first the full implication of the wrath of God, of His condemning and punishing justice. It shows us what a consuming fire burns against sin. It thus discloses too the full implication of sin, what it means to resist God, to be God's enemy, which is the guilty determination of our human existence.

What this means no Old or New Testament command in itself and as such can reveal even in its transcendence of the best that we can will and do. Nor can any divine threat and execution of judgment. Nor can any confession of sin made by us, nor any painful consciousness of sin that we experience. Nor can any of the greater or less judgments which may come upon us. Nor can any repentance and despair, however deep may be our experience of them (but when were we really in despair ?). At the worst, these things in themselves and as such can point only to a great finite act of disobedience and suggest the possibility only of a finite punishment and restitution. None of them has in itself the power to summon us to such penitence before God that we have to recognise and confess ourselves infinitely guilty before Him and infinitely lost sinners abandoned to eternal death. Considered from the standpoint of these things in themselves, our most serious confessions of sin—those corresponding to the insights and language of the Bible—always have an inevitable smack of exaggeration. And—necessarily almost—the question arises in regard to the Old and New Testaments, whether God's reaction of wrath as it is attested to us in the Bible really stands in an intelligible relation to man's opposition to God, to man's sin and guilt ? And how natural it is to propose this question especially when we find or feel ourselves affected by God's token judgments ! " Is God not unjust to exercise His wrath ? " (Rom. 3⁵). Have we really deserved it ? Are we really as guilty as all that, that we should have to suffer it ? This murmuring, this question of Job's, is silenced—but only really silenced—when we remember how it is that God judges the world (Rom. 3⁶), that is, His relentlessness against Himself as we have described it, His allowing Himself so to feel the pain of our sin that He spared not His only Son, but delivered Him up for us all. What do *we* know of God's righteousness, of what is worthy of Him, and therefore of what, when He confronts us as our Creator and Lord, He necessarily and rightfully has against us ? It is here, where He guarantees—but in His love for us and therefore utterly on His own initiative—that He is not against us but for us (Rom. 8³¹), that we have to learn what is His righteousness and our unrighteousness. And it is from this point of view, as a token of the righteousness of God manifested here, that we have to appraise and interpret the righteousness of the Law, of the threats and judgments of the Old Testament, and of those of world history and our own life. It is here that we come to know of what we are accused and guilty, what our trespass is and means. It consists in an alienation from God, a rebellion against Him, which ought to be punished in a way which involves our total destruction, and which apart from our annihilation can be punished only by God Himself taking our place, and in His Son taking to Himself and bearing and suffering the punishment. This is what it costs God to be righteous without annihilating us. The opposition to Him in which we find ourselves is so great that it can be overcome and rendered harmless to ourselves only by God, and indeed only by His entering Himself into this opposition and bearing all the pain of it. Our position is such that we can be rescued from eternal death and translated into life only by total and unceasing substitution, the substitution which God Himself· undertakes on our behalf. When this is clear to us we shall no longer have any objections to raise against the appropriateness of what we may encounter in the Old Testament, in world history and in our own life as a token of God's judgment. What symbol can be plain and strong enough to indicate the enormity of our opposition to God when it has been indicated in this way by God Himself through what He has done in order to overcome it ?

2. Because it was the Son of God, i.e., God Himself, who took our place on Good Friday, what had necessarily to happen—because God is righteous—could happen there. There could happen there—the " could " being understood primarily in a physical sense—that which could not have happened to us without causing our annihilation.

That is to say, the righteousness of God in condemnation and punishment could take its course in relation to human sin.

Jesus Christ, in His solidarity with " human nature which has sinned, could pay the penalty of sin " (*Heid. Catech. Qu.* 16), and at the same time, in the power of His divinity, could " bear the burden of the wrath of God in His humanity " (17). Without any diminution of His divine majesty, in the exercise of the divine majesty of His love He could enter into this " likeness of sinful flesh " to bear, in the same majesty, the judgment of divine wrath without annihilation, to be and to reveal Himself supremely as divine majesty even in His humiliation, to rise from the dead as conqueror of the judgment to which He had subjected Himself, the first fruits of all who were to follow in His steps. He could drink the cup which had to be drunk. Because He was God Himself, He could subject Himself to the severity of God. And because He was God Himself He did not have to succumb to the severity of God. God had to be severe to be true to Himself in His encounter with man, and thus to be true also to man. God's wrath had to be revealed against the ungodliness and unrighteousness of men. But only God could carry through this necessary revelation of His righteousness without involving an end of all things. Only God Himself could bear the wrath of God. Only God's mercy was capable of bearing the pain to which the creature existing in opposition to Him is subject. Only God's mercy could so feel this pain as to take it into the very heart of His being. And only God's mercy was strong enough not to be annihilated by this pain. And this that could happen only by the divine mercy is just what did happen on the cross of Golgotha : that double proof of omnipotence in which God did not abate the demands of His righteousness but showed Himself equal to His own wrath ; on the one hand by submitting to it and on the other by not being consumed by it. In virtue of this omnipotence God's mercy could be at one and the same time the deepest and sincerest pity and inflexible and impassible divine strength. He could yield to His own inexorable righteousness and by this very surrender maintain Himself as God. He could reveal Himself at once as the One who as the servant of all bore the punishment of death which we had deserved, and the One who as the Lord of all took from death its power and for ever vanquished and destroyed it. In this twofold sense God's righteousness triumphed in the death of Jesus Christ.

3. Because it was the Son of God, because it was God Himself who on Good Friday suffered for us, the destruction which took place there of the suffering and death which resulted from human disobedience to God could justly satisfy and indeed fulfil the righteousness of God. As a fulfilment of the righteousness of God it necessarily meant that in the conflict between God's faithfulness and man's unfaithfulness, the faithfulness of God Himself was maintained, and therefore His honour was not violated. It was only in this way that it could also be exercised as His faithfulness to man, for how could man be really helped by a God who actually surrendered His own honour ? On the other hand, the faithfulness of God Himself could not and must not exclude and suspend His faithfulness to man, nor must His honour be safeguarded by the visitation upon man of that which he has properly deserved : eternal death and destruction. In the death of Jesus Christ God remained true both to Himself and to man.

The dilemma seems inescapable. *Either* there is not visited on man what ought to be visited on him in his conflict with God. But in this case permanent injury is done to God's glory. God is no longer God. His faithfulness—a faithfulness in which He is untrue to Himself—can be of no help to man. *Or* there is visited on man just what he deserves. And in this case God's honour is indeed safeguarded and God remains God. But because God is God, in this conflict the precipice yawns in which man can only cast himself headlong and be swallowed up in the abyss. What then becomes of God's faithfulness to man, His mercy ? The solution of this dilemma lies in the interposition for us at Golgotha of the Son of God, and therefore of God Himself. Because God is God, and remaining such can do in this conflict only what is worthy of Himself, therefore this conflict cannot be resolved without the divine condemnation and punishment necessarily proportionate to the trespass which we have committed. The endless consequence of the endless disobedience of which man has made himself guilty towards God and continually makes himself guilty, must be borne by man. " Is God then not merciful ? God is certainly merciful but He is also just. Hence His justice demands that sin which has been committed against the supreme majesty of God should be punished in body and soul with the supreme, i.e., eternal punishment " (*Heid. Catech.* 11). Now consider the following point. Man, who is God's creature and exists wholly by God and is in God's hand, has sinned and sins, and is therefore God's opponent in this conflict. And he has sinned and sins against God alone. Therefore in this conflict the injured and the aggressor have no higher lord and judge. But the injured Himself is also the Lord and Judge. As the wounded and offended party, at the same time He is both the measure and the Subject of the judgment and punishment which are proportionate to the offence. He is not only the measure but also the Subject. That is, He is not only the just norm according to which judgment and punishment takes place, but also the Judge who judges and punishes in righteousness. Because He is the measure, the judgment is necessarily one of condemnation and the punishment eternal death. But because He is also the Subject, because only He can judge and punish in this matter, He cannot be denied the right to execute judgment and punishment according to His good-pleasure. Again God is not God if He does not enjoy this freedom of His good-pleasure in the choice of the fulfilment of His judgment and punishment. Just as God is not God if in condemnation and punishment His righteousness does not take the course which He must take in conflict with the disobedience of His creature, so again He is not God if He is not free to give His righteousness the course which it must take according to the dictates of His mercy. Even if in the execution of His judgment and punishment God is bound, as it were, to an abstract conception of right which is superior to Himself, so that He has to condemn and punish according to this conception, He obviously will not be and do what is worthy of Himself, and He will not therefore be the' righteous God. He is this because He is free to be righteous in His mercy, free to be true to Himself and therefore to remain true to us as well. And this was the character of His righteousness in the judgment executed upon Golgotha. This righteousness clothed in mercy is the meaning of the fact that the Son of God took our place, that He went surety for us, so that our judgment and punishment do not have to be borne by us because they were borne by Him. Let it be clearly understood that it did not have to happen in this way if we mean by that that God was under an obligation to clothe His righteousness in mercy and therefore in fulfilment of His righteousness to give His only Son to die for us. God could have been true to Himself without giving His faithfulness the determination of faithfulness to us. It could easily have been God's good-pleasure to express His righteousness in quite another way, namely in the form of our destruction. God would not have been any the less God if this had happened. We had and have no other claim against Him than that which arises from the fact that in the event His good-pleasure was that of His merciful righteousness. In other words we can say that it had to be so only as we look at what God has in fact done in Jesus Christ, at the way in which His good-pleasure has in fact revealed itself in Him. Looking at Him we must of course say that what did happen had to happen. But doing so we acknowledge and magnify only the decision made in God's good-pleasure and its necessity not that of any recognisable principle existing apart from this decision. We therefore exalt the divine love and grace and mercy. But as we exalt God's mercy, it must not be forgotten that in His mercy God allowed righteousness to have sway ; that He was merciful but He was also just ; that as He was merciful everything had to happen which has happened, which was necessary for the maintenance and preservation of His glory ; that therefore in Him who is so true to us according to His own free good-pleasure we have in fact to do with Him (and this is why His faithfulness is so effectual) who is always true to Himself. God was true to Himself when He gave His Son to die for us. He did not in this way conceal the conflict between man and Himself, let alone ignore or overlook it. He bore it, as it had to be borne, to the bitter end, as it affected Himself as the injured party and man as the violator of His glory. His mercy consists in the fact that He took this conflict to heart, indeed, that He bore it in His heart. But it was nonetheless a conflict between Himself and us that was borne. For in Him who took our place God's own heart beat on our side, in our flesh and blood, in complete solidarity with our nature and con-stitution, at the very point where we ourselves confront Him, guilty before God. Because it was the eternal God who entered in in Jesus Christ, He could be more than the Representative and Guarantor of God to us. He could also be our Repre-sentative and Guarantor towards God. He could be the fully accredited Repre-sentative not only of the divine Judge, but also of the judged : of fallen Adam in his sin ; of the whole of sinful humanity ; of each individual sinner in all his being and sinning. Because He was God's Son, He could take humanity to Himself in such a way that in it He was the Advocate for God to us and to God for us all—this one man for every man. In this fully accredited representation of God to us all and of us all to God, Jesus Christ came into the midst to bear that conflict to the bitter end in righteousness, but in the merciful righteousness of God. In this fully accredited representation He really suffered our distress as the distress in the heart of God Himself. He therefore became the object of divine wrath and judgment and the bearer of our guilt and punishment. Thus we do not have here—as in the travesty in which this supreme insight and truth of the Christian faith is so often distorted—a raging indignation of God, which is ridiculous or irritating in its senselessness, against an innocent man whose patient suffering changes the temper of God, inducing in Him an indulgent sparing of all other men, so that all other men can rather shamefacedly take refuge behind his suffering, happily saved but quite unchanged in themselves. We do not have here an abstract justice of God which is later changed into an equally abstract compassion and indulgence. On the contrary, it is the actual and terrible wrath of God which rules according to God's free good-pleasure in the fulfilment of what is from the first His merciful righteousness, and it does not need any change of mood or weakening, but in its strictest fulfilment it is the self-expression of the eternal unchangeably good will of God. And it is not the fact that a man suffers in patience and innocence which is the motive force of this happening. There is no moving of God by the creature on the basis of which God can then decide on a universal amnesty. But it is God's own heart which moves in creation on the basis of His own good-pleasure. It suffers what the creature ought to suffer and could not suffer without being destroyed. It suffers it with omnipotent vicariousness in virtue of the fact that it is the heart of the almighty Lord and Creator, who, since it is His good-pleasure, cannot be pre-vented from Himself sustaining His creature (even in the face of His own divine wrath), as He has Himself created it. And if the creature accepts this vicarious suffering, accepts its own life on the ground of this divine substitution as a gift of the love and grace and mercy of its Lord and Creator, this cannot mean that before God it hides behind another. As we know, this is what Adam and Eve did in the Garden according to Gen. 3⁸. But it is the very thing which must not happen again. On the contrary, the meaning is that it is dragged out of its hiding place and put fair and square before the face of God as the face of Him before whom it is utterly lost and who alone can now be its Saviour from death and its life. It means, then, that the creature is cast wholly and utterly upon God and bound to God as to Him who alone has conducted its cause and will conduct its cause in eternity.

4. Because it was the Son of God, i.e., God Himself who took our place on Good Friday, the substitution could be effectual and procure our reconciliation with the righteous God, and therefore the victory of God's righteousness, and therefore our own righteousness in His sight. Only God, our Lord and Creator, could stand surety for us, could take our place, could suffer eternal death in our stead as the consequence of our sin in such a way that it was finally suffered and overcome and therefore did not need to be suffered any more by us. No creature, no other man could do that. But God's own Son could do it.

We have seen that He could do it physically and that He could do it lawfully. We must now add specifically that He could also do it effectually, i.e., in such a way that His suffering is in fact reckoned to us, that it need not be suffered any more by us, that we can be free from fear, that in view of the righteousness of God in necessary condemnation and punishment we may cling to Him as to the One in whom satisfaction is done to this necessity. Jesus Christ could take our place with this effectiveness because as the Son of God He became man and had therefore the freedom and power to be in His humanity as that individual the Head and Representative of us all, and therefore not only to speak to us in God's name, but also in our name, as flesh of our flesh, to speak to God. If we hear Him as the Word made flesh, we hear what God also hears as the blood of His own Son cries to heaven to Him. But in His own Word made flesh, God hears that satisfaction has been done to His righteousness, that the consequences of human sin have been borne and expiated, and therefore that they have been taken away from man—the man for whose sake Jesus Christ intervened. In the Word spoken by the blood of His Son God hears that for those whose flesh this His Son has made His own, for those who are in Him, in Jesus Christ, there is now no more condemnation (Rom. 8¹). In this His own Word answering Him out of the depths of humanity, God hears the Word by which we are justified, which as surely as it is His own Word is also our pardon. As we for our part may hear this Word, as there is said to us what God in Jesus Christ His incarnate Word has said to Himself, we hear our pardon. Everything depends on whether we are present at this divine colloquy. Everything depends on whether this Word is also spoken also to us and we also hear it. If it is addressed to us and we hear it, we know that there is no longer an objective judgment passed on us and we need no longer fear such. This is not because God is not just, or not strictly just. It is because He has been strictly just once and for all, but according to the requirements of His mercy and therefore in the sacrifice of His only Son. It is not because we did not deserve His condemnation—we deserved it a thousand times—but because, as the judgment which we have deserved, it has already been executed and suffered. It is not because—as we are in and for ourselves—we did not need to fear it. As we are in and for ourselves we would have to fear it throughout eternity. It is because we now have to fear God only in such a way that we allow His incarnate Word to be addressed to us and hear it—the Word which God has addressed to Himself and by which we are justified in His sight, the Word of our pardon. By faith in this Word we fear God's judgment as it ought to be feared. Everything now depends on whether our primary fear is that we should arbitrarily try to fear God's judgment in a different way. Everything now depends on whether " I live by the faith of the Son of God, who loved me, and gave himself for me " (Gal. 2²⁰). " How art thou just before God ? Only by faith in Jesus Christ, that although my conscience accuses me, telling me that I have grievously sinned against all the commandments of God and have never kept a single one of them, but have always been inclined to evil, yet God, without any merit on my part, of pure grace has granted and imputed to me the complete satisfaction, righteousness and holiness of Christ, as .though I had never committed any sin and had myself performed all the obedience which Christ has rendered for me, if only I will accept these benefits with a believing heart " (*Heid. Catech*. 60). That this faith should be awakened in us and not sleep again, that it should begin and not cease, that it should live and not die, is the victory of God's righteousness and therefore our own real righteousness before God. It is the proper effect of the proper fear of God, which alone is required of us and is possible. Everything depends on whether we attain this fear of God, not letting it go, earnestly and constantly maintaining it. Everything depends on whether we do not remain fixed or again sink into a fear of judgment which in Jesus Christ has become pointless—the fear of a judgment which can still come upon us ourselves even though it has affected God Himself in Jesus Christ, even though God Himself has borne it for us in His own heart, even though God has once for all saved us from it. In view of Jesus Christ this fear of judgment can no longer be called fear of God. We really fear God only in the judgment which in its righteous execution upon the cross of Golgotha has finally procured our pardon. We really fear God only in so far as we allow this pardon to be spoken to us, to be true and valid. From our point of view, the effectiveness of the intervention of God's Son for us lies in the fact that it is the revelation of God by which we are gathered to Jesus Christ as to our Head and Representative, by which we are gathered to His Church, by which, that is, we are awakened and called to the fear of God by faith, and maintained in it. In the revelation of God we are drawn into God's colloquy with Himself. In the revelation of God there is said to us what God has said to Himself in His incarnate Word. This revelation consists, however, in the resurrection of Jesus Christ from the dead as a confirmation that He who suffered eternal death on the cross was the One who by suffering it was destined to overcome it, and also as a confirmation that by placing His own Son, Himself, under the judgment, God would necessarily be the goal and end of judgment. As this conquest of death and this righteous end of judgment, the resurrection of Jesus Christ is both the self-revelation as the Son of God and the revelation of the righteousness of God in its unity with His mercy, and the revelation of faith as our salvation by the righteousness which has been fulfilled in Jesus Christ. It is in this sense that we are to understand Rom. 4²⁴ᶠ· : " We believe in him that raised up Jesus our Lord from the dead ; who was delivered for our offences, and was raised again for our justification," i.e., for the revelation of our righteousness, the revelation of the fact that God's righteousness has prevailed, that according to 2 Cor. 5²¹ we ourselves have become the righteousness of God. We have become this because we are members of the body of which Jesus Christ is the Head : He who is God Himself taking our place. And that we accept this position, that we admit His Godhead and allow Him to be God for us, is faith in Him and therefore the proper fear of God required of us. If by His resurrection He discloses this faith to us, if by the power of His resurrection He awakens and maintains this fear of God in us, His intervention on our behalf, and therefore the righteousness of God, is effective as the love and grace and mercy in which once for all He has turned to us sinners without even the slightest self-betrayal ; as His faithfulness which is powerful for time and eternity because, while evincing it to us, He first and foremost remains true to Himself.

From this standpoint we must look back—really look *back*—to the divine threat and execution of judgment on Israel, but also to the divine judgment continually taking place on the Church and in the world, and again to the divine judgment which always menaces and strikes each individual life—and does so finally in the death towards which each of us is hastening. Only in unbelief, only by overlooking God's revelation in the resurrection of Jesus Christ, only in the selfish fear which has to be overcome by the true fear of God, can it be thought and said that in all this we are already or again and in the same sense dealing with the judgment of God which took place on the cross of Golgotha, which God suffered and consummated in His own heart as both Judge and judged. Of course, even if we could escape by a trick of interpretation what we have in fact to experience, the unitary testimony of Holy Scripture leaves us in no doubt that we do in fact stand under these judgments. The people of God, Israel in the hidden sense of the Old Testament and the open sense of the New Testament, the Church of Jesus Christ, is not in fact immune from divine judgment, but openly or secretly, directly or indirectly, it is subjected to it in every age. Again, according to the unitary testimony of Holy Scripture, there does undoubtedly exist an inner, essential connexion between the one passion of the Son of God and the many sufferings which we see afflicting Israel, the Church, the world and ourselves. The fear of God, in which we must cling to the revealing righteousness of God as the revelation of the conquest of death and the end of judgment, does not preclude that we should constantly be witnesses, and indeed conscious and frank and honest witnesses, of the fact that God is not mocked either in Israel, or in the Church, or in the world, or in our own lives ; that whatsoever a man soweth that shall he also reap (Gal. 6⁷ᶠ·). We can best see the connexion which exists here when we think of the reality of the divine intervention for sinful man which has taken place in Jesus Christ. We saw that the effectiveness of this intervention consists in the salvation of the sinner from judgment and the revelation of the faith in which he may grasp this salvation, knowing and re- joicing in it, giving glory to the Son of God as his Saviour, and placing his whole trust in Him. This effectiveness of the divine intervention, however, stands or falls according as we are taken up into unity and fellowship with the Son of God, and may live in faith as in this unity and fellowship with Him our Head, as members of His body. As the gift and the exercise of this unity and fellowship faith is our reconciliation, our divine righteousness. Is it not inevitable that the effectiveness of God's intervention should involve our seeing and feeling and experiencing and suffering the judgment of God fulfilled and suffered for us in Jesus Christ as He Himself has suffered it for us ? Not in the same way as He has suffered it, for He alone has suffered the eternal death which we have de- served. Our cross is not the cross of Calvary where satisfaction was done to the righteousness of God in condemnation and punishment. But we cannot believe in the righteousness of God triumphing for us on the cross without real- ising that there we have been justified apart from and against our deserts, and therefore without taking our cross upon ourselves and placing ourselves under the signs of the divine judgment. Faith has its life in the submission which this involves. This is the faith which triumphs in Jesus Christ over eternal death. This is the faith which stands in Jesus Christ at the goal and end of all judgment. Faith lives in the self-prostration before God which is necessary and self-evident by reason of the fact that God has intervened on behalf of men, taking up their cause and vindicating it. Man himself could not have done this. As an indica- tion of this the life of the believer must run its course in the shadow of divine judgment. In this respect we cannot speak of more than signs and shadows. The afflictions of Israel, the Church, the world and ourselves are all announcements and echoes of the reality of the divine judgment. The divine judgment itself in its reality is only what happened at Golgotha. But it did really happen there. We therefore find its traces and tokens, its announcements and echoes, in the environs of Golgotha. These environs are Israel, the Church, the world, and our own lives. Therefore alongside the cross of Christ there is our own cross, alongside His suffering our suffering, alongside His death our death. They are not the judgment of God that we have to fear, but the judgment of God that we have to see as vanquished and ended if we are to continue in penitence and obedience. For to see judgment in this way—in the ineluctability in which we ourselves really see it, in the honesty in which we must be prepared to see it, in the readiness to bear the little suffering which seeing involves—this is the necessary exercise of faith. We do not believe if we do not live in the neighbourhood of Golgotha. And we cannot live in the neighbourhood of Golgotha without being affected by the shadow of divine judgment, without allowing this shadow to fall on us. In this shadow Israel suffered. In this shadow the Church suffers. That it suffers in this way is the Church's answer to the world on the question of a "theodicy"—the question of the justice of God in the sufferings inflicted on us in the world. That suffering should be learned in this shadow is in 1 Peter the problem of faith for every Christian community and individual Christian. "Nay, in all these things we are more than conquerors through him that loved us" (Rom. 8[37]). The shadow would not fall if the cross of Christ did not stand in the light of His resurrection. We would not have to suffer if it were not that we are "begotten again unto a lively hope by the resurrection of Jesus Christ from the dead" (1 Pet. 1[3]).

3. THE PATIENCE AND WISDOM OF GOD

We now emphasise two further biblical attributes of God, both individually and in their interconnexion. We must try to understand them as expressions of the perfection of His love. As we do so, we are again reminded of the fact that all further consideration of the divine attributes can but move in a circle around the one but infinitely rich being of God whose simplicity is abundance itself and whose abundance is simplicity itself. We are not speaking of a new object but allowing the one object, God, to speak further of Himself. We are continuing to contemplate the love of God and therefore God Himself as the One who loves in freedom. What end can there be to this development? We are drawing upon the ocean. We are therefore faced by a task to which there is no end. But a third affirmation must now be added to the first two if we are to gain at least the authorised and commanded view of this inexhaustible ocean. We first said that God is gracious and holy. We then continued that God is merciful and righteous. Now that we have developed these two affirmations along the lines indicated by the biblical revelation, a third affirmation necessarily follows which expresses the same truth again, but again differently, that God is patient and wise. The first two points are not left behind when we proceed to this third. They are not exhausted and abandoned. If we proceed to this third point, we acknowledge by this very act that the first and second are not exhausted and abandoned, but that we must reaffirm them in a new way. We have again to pursue the movement demanded by the object and therefore the development of the knowledge of God occasioned by it. We have again to magnify the plenitude of the divine being by not lingering unduly over any one proposition or letting it become the final word or the guiding principle, but by proceeding from one to another, from the second to the third. As we do so, we realise that even if we make a provisional halt at the third, this does not mean that we have spoken the last word. It is simply an indication that we are on a human path where in the very face of God we cannot even try to rival His infinity.

In view of certain specific scriptural passages, there is a clear necessity that after speaking of God's grace and mercy we should consider the perfection of the divine patience as a special perfection of the love and therefore of the being of God.

There is a whole series of Old Testament texts (Ex. 34⁶ ; Joel 2¹³ ; Jonah 4² ; Neh. 9¹⁷, Ps. 86¹⁵, 103⁸, 145⁸) in which, with variations of order, but obviously a certain necessity which has almost become a formula, these three—Yahweh's grace, mercy and patience (or longsuffering), usually completed by the comprehensive thought of His " great faithfulness "—are described as the distinctive marks of the God revealed and active in Israel.

If first and basically we ask what is to be learnt and understood under this concept of the patience of God, it will be helpful if in the first instance we make it clear that in this third stage, too, there can be no question of our inference from a general idea of love. We have already seen that love in general does not necessarily bear the character of grace or of mercy. We must now continue that it does not necessarily bear that of patience. Love can be extremely honest, deep and passionate and at the same time extremely impatient. It may want to possess its object immediately or in a specific qualitative or quantitative way. It may wish to devour it, or, if it is frustrated, vindictively to destroy it. Similarly, grace in general or mercy in general may behave with great impatience. We can mean only the love and grace and mercy of the God revealed in Jesus Christ, and not of an imaginary god, if we confess and affirm that love and grace and mercy must also be patient. We saw that the love of God is necessarily grace because it expresses the condescension of the unconditionally superior to the unconditionally inferior—of the Creator to His creature. It is because this condescension—in the absolute freedom without which it would not be such—is manifest in the God revealed in Jesus Christ that we say that God's love is gracious love. And further, God's grace is essentially merciful because the absolute subordinate in this relation finds himself, the creature as such and as a sinful creature, in a position of needy distress and misery, because God's turning to him, as that of the absolute superior, implies necessarily that God espouses the cause of the creature in all his need and distress, sharing it, making it His own, taking it to His own heart. The fact that He does this, that He is the One whose very being impels Him to do it, means that God's grace—the grace of the God revealed in Jesus Christ—is merciful grace. On the way of knowledge pursued so far we saw that our statements rested on an utterly factual and concrete necessity—that the God revealed in Jesus Christ loves in grace and mercy. The case is exactly the same now that we proceed to affirm that His love bears essentially the character of patience. Patience exists where space and time are given with a definite intention, where freedom is allowed in expectation of a response. God acts in this way. He makes this purposeful concession of space and time. He allows this freedom of expectancy. That He does so lies in His very being. Indeed, it is His being. Everything that God is, is implied and included in the statement that He is patient. But this is no more self-evident than our previous considerations. It cannot in any sense result from a simple development of ideas. God could be gracious and merciful in such a way that His love would consume His creature. He could take to Himself his distress in such wise as to leave him no further opportunities in space and time, but to strip him of both, recalling and annulling his corrupt and twisted existence, destroying the perverse and tortured will of the creature, and again substituting His own good will as the sole effective reality. Does not the condescension of the unconditionally superior to the unconditionally inferior, the activity of the Creator on behalf of the suffering creature, logically and necessarily imply this outcome ? And could it not be the most wonderful, effective and generous proof of divine grace and mercy if God willed it to be all in all in such a way as to be it in Himself to all eternity without creation, the meaning and basis of everything other than Himself without its individual existence, its differentiation from God ? Is not the very existence of all that is other than God identical with its suffering, its suffering with its existence ? Could there be a more radical form of love than that which does not first need the existence of the beloved, that in which the beloved exists wholly and utterly in the lover, that which leads the beloved back to this form of existence ? Could not, then, the possibility of God's annihilating wrath against His creature, which we have already had frequent occasion to consider, be the real fulfilment of divine love. Could not eternal death as the work of this divine wrath be in truth eternal peace, the eternal rest of the creature in God Himself, unviolated and in fact inviolable by all the assaults and torments which are obviously unavoidably bound up with space and time and with our existence as such ?

We have only to listen to what heathen and ostensibly Christian mysticism of all times and countries says about God's love and grace and mercy. We have only to listen to its decisive and culminating utterances. At a pinch mysticism could perhaps have followed us so far—with certain reservations and special explanations. But at the very latest it would have to diverge at the point we have now reached, proclaiming as the culmination of its own teaching concerning God's love and grace and mercy, as the properly and ultimately redemptive word, a doctrine of God's impatience. Here at the very latest the real difficulty of the Christian knowledge of God in relation to every form of mysticism (and even every mystical perversion of the Christian knowledge of God) would be revealed as irreconcilable.

It is a necessary characteristic of Him whom the Christian Church names God not to be impatient but patient. The necessity to which we refer is again a factual, concrete necessity. From the logic of abstract ideas we might equally well infer that God is impatient. If we had to think of God according to the standard of what we think is fine and pleasing and therefore godlike, we might easily suppose Him to be impatient (and we should find ourselves in the best of company). The result would be a fine and complete and satisfying doctrine of God and an equally fine and complete and satisfying doctrine of redemption. Here then we can actually speak of the necessary patience of God only if we take as the pure source and necessary determination of our knowledge the factual and concrete revelation of God in Jesus Christ in its factual and concrete attestation in Holy Scripture. If we adopt this point of view, if we think and speak in the Church and therefore from within the basis and essence of the Church in Jesus Christ, from the very outset our course is so fixed that we cannot journey in the direction desired and initiated by mysticism, i.e., in the direction of a doctrine of God's impatience. This is not because, generally speaking, it is impossible that God should be impatient. And it is not because an impatient God could not be a very fine and profound conception. It is simply because God is in fact patient. When He discloses Himself to our understanding, when alone it is worthwhile to talk of a knowledge of God in the strict and full sense, He gives Himself to be known as the patient and not the impatient God. God reveals Himself in such a way that we have to say that in the concrete context in which God's love and grace and mercy are actualised, they bear unmistakably the mark of patience. They bear it in such a way that we are forced to say that we can know them as divine love and grace and mercy only in so far as they have this characteristic. The divine patience must, then, be for us another differentiating sign between the divine and that which is only apparently so, the demonic.

We define God's patience as His will, deep-rooted in His essence and constituting His divine being and action, to allow to another— for the sake of His own grace and mercy and in the affirmation of His holiness and justice—space and time for the development of its own existence, thus conceding to this existence a reality side by side with His own, and fulfilling His will towards this other in such a way that He does not suspend and destroy it as this other but accompanies and sustains it and allows it to develop in freedom.

Patientia Dei est, qua iram suam erga homines ita moderatur Deus, ut conversionem et resipiscentiam eorum expectet vel poenam differat, vel iram suam totam uno momento non effundat (Quenstedt, *Theol. did. pol.*, 1685, I, c. 8, sect 1, *th.* 33). Polanus defined the concept of divine *patientia* in a very similar way (*Synt. Theol. chr.*, 1609, *col.* 1146), and he linked it with that of the *clementia* of God : *benignissima eius voluntas, per quam etiam in ira misericordiae suae recordans, nobis est propitius parcitque nobis etiam si aliter meriti simus, malens resipiscentiam et conversionem nostram quam mortem* (*ib., col.* 1152). The addition and explanation will have to be accepted : *etiam in ira . . . recordans*, and we can then extract from the orthodox definition at least the following point—that when God is patient, there is no question of a weakness of God in the exercise of His grace and mercy. Nothing can affect or change the fact that God is holy and just. And nothing is to be deducted from what this implies for the creature, for man, in his encounter with God. The fact remains that God's anger burns in this encounter and that it requires on the part of man a complete change of attitude. But the divinity of God's grace and mercy and therefore of His holiness and justice is seen in the fact that in this encounter and therefore in God Himself there occurs a *moderatio* or *recordatio*. The wrath of God is characteristically divine, and therefore a holy and righteous wrath, in the fact that it does not break out like any anger, and (as the anger of Almighty God) take an utterly destructive course, but that it is guided and shaped, that it has its own particular form and limit, not a determination, form and limit imposed upon it from outside but by God Himself who is Lord of His wrath in virtue of what He knows and wills. And that man for his part really has to do with God, with the grace and mercy, the holiness and justice, the wrath of God, and not with a demon to whom also in a certain sense all this could perhaps be ascribed, is revealed by the fact that his allotted part in the encounter with God is not death and destruction, but conversion, *resipiscentia* and *conversio*, and for this purpose he is not deprived of space and time and existence, but as he has been given he is also left them. It is to be noted that God is not more powerful in His action than in His forbearance from action. Indeed there is no antithesis here : God's forbearance is only a specific form of His always powerful doing and being. God is therefore no less effective in His patience than in His grace and mercy, than in His holy and just wrath which includes His grace and mercy. God does not repent when He forbears to act, but it is also—and properly understood, precisely—the unrepentant outbreaking of His whole divine glory that He is patient in His grace and mercy and therefore patient also in His holy and righteous wrath. Polanus is right when he emphasises (*ib., col.* 1145) that the *patientia* of God does not mean a *pati*. We add in elucidation that it does not mean a *pati* to which He is subject as to an external cause, so that it diminishes His majesty. If God restrains Himself, as is implied in the New Testament term ἀνοχή, this self-restraint is also to be understood as the powerful act of God. God could not be more divine, indeed, He would be less divine, He would not be God at all, if He were not patient. " For my Name's sake will I defer mine anger, and for my praise will I refrain from thee that I cut thee not off " (Is. 48⁹). If the other New Testament term for this thought is μακροθυμία, the word " long-suffering " is a bad translation if it suggests hesitation, weakness, indulgence, a stretching of the divine will. On the contrary, the term implies that God's will is great and strong and relentless and victorious. It is this as a gracious, merciful will, and therefore it waits patiently, giving man every freedom and opportunity. But this waiting, by which God grants us liberty, is itself and as such to be understood as a plus, not a minus, of God's freedom, power and activity. It too is to be understood as a specific form of the divine majesty—exactly like His mercy.

The idea of the patience of God expresses an enrichment, a clarification and an intensification of the idea of His mercy, which is itself to be understood in an active and dynamic sense. This enrichment, clarification and intensification by the concept which is for the moment our special concern, consist in the fact that God takes up the cause of the creature, the reality distinct from Himself, in such a way that He accepts it as a reality and intervenes for it in recognition, not in suspension, of its reality. For it as such, He is severe with Himself. He suffers for it. He sacrifices His only Son for it. He does it for the creature as such—which means that God's mercy does not act in such a way as to overpower and blot out its object. God does not take the place of the creature in such a way as to annihilate it. That He takes its plight to His own heart does not mean that He robs it of its independent life, making the latter a mere potentiality or recollection in His own life. The encounter of His eternal love with the creature existing in space and time does not imply the utter dissolution of its space and time and therefore of its existence as such. The fact that God in His mercy intervenes for it must be understood in the full sense of the two words " for " and " it " ; in such a way, therefore, that this divine intervention for the creature does not exclude but includes its independent life—whatever the encounter with God may entail for that life—so that the atoning will of God maintains His will and act as the Creator : " What our God has created He will also uphold, and sooner or later control by His grace." He will control it—but not in such a way that grace means the catastrophic destruction of nature. It means radical judgment upon nature. It means its radical transformation and renewal. But it does not mean its violent end.

In this sense we must admit the truth of that maxim of Thomas Aquinas which is so often put to dangerous use and in the first instance was no doubt dangerously meant : *gratia non tollit (non destruit) sed (praesupponit et) perficit naturam*. God deals with His creature in such a way as to share his wretchedness. This is the meaning of His mercy. In this way it is more powerful than if it had to kill and slay in order to arrive at its goal. It is so powerful that it can wait, allowing us to continue. The abyss in the heart of God is so deep that in it the other, the reality distinct from God, can be contained in all its wretchedness. It does not have to perish. It is allowed to live, i.e., to live as the object of divine mercy, to live under the divine righteousness, to live under the full and strict outworking of what is entailed by its encounter with God, by God's intervention for it. There can be no question of a neutral juxtaposition of God and creature and therefore of a restraint on the part of God which signifies inaction. The relationship between the two is a very definite relationship of action and reaction. It is in this, the God-creature relationship, that there happens to the creature what is in accordance with the will of God. This relationship is part of the full and strict outworking of that encounter. It belongs to it as the will of God that God acts as the One who in His absolute freedom, power and activity maintains what He has created so that it may continue to live. This is the patience of God.

We shall see at once that this patience is the divine being in power and not in weakness if we consider in detail the testimony of Scripture to God's revelation from this particular standpoint.

We begin with the story of Cain (Gen. 4^{1-17} ; cf. W. Vischer, *Jahve der Gott Kains*, 1929). Eve has " gotten a man from the Lord "—the first human birth, Cain in his greatness, but also under the threat which arises from the fall of Adam. It is worth noting that it is not his name but that of his brother Abel which points to this latter fact. That they must both live by God's grace, as they testify with their offerings, leads to the disclosure of human sin in the act and guilt of Cain. Cain, too, has sought grace : yet not as man has to seek the grace of God ; not in upright conduct before God ; not freely looking up to God; but, as the eventual outburst of his jealousy shows, with the object of gaining God for himself. Therefore he finds no grace. Sin lurks before his door and he cannot control it because, seeking grace, he repulses grace. Hatred of grace manifests itself as hatred of his brother, in the murder of his brother, in the lack of a sense of responsibility evinced in his affectation of ignorance : " I know not. Am I my brother's keeper ? " But what he wishes to conceal from God is not concealed : " What hast thou done ? The voice of thy brother's blood cries unto me from the ground." And Cain is cursed. He is driven away with curses from this ground, which shall no more give him fruit. " A fugitive and a vagabond shalt thou be upon the earth." This is the encounter of the creature with its God. This is the intolerable and impossible nature of its existence in this encounter. It cannot be said that in this story God's holiness and righteousness do not receive proper attention. But this is not the end of the story. God's holiness and righteousness seem to require a different interpretation and to be differently determined from what we might have supposed from the story so far. The mood of despair in which alone Cain himself can react to this judgment is not the final thing that is decreed even for him. In his despair he sees and confesses : " My punishment is greater than I can bear." Obviously this cry implies objectively, as does the similar complaint of Job, the truth which Luther has expressed by the translation : " My sin is greater than can be forgiven." But has not Cain now sought God's grace as it must be sought ? Obviously, for now according to the unambiguous statement of the story he has in any event found it. " Everyone that findeth me shall slay me," he thinks in his despair. Yahweh answers him : Not so ! " Whosoever slayeth Cain, vengeance shall be taken on him sevenfold. And the Lord set a mark upon Cain, lest any finding him should kill him. And Cain went out from the presence of the Lord, and dwelt in the land of Nod, on the east of Eden. And Cain knew his wife ; and she conceived, and bear Enoch." We see that the story has as its theme the patience of God which receives pointed expression in the decree that death must not be the punishment of the murderer. Cain the murderer is permitted to live. It is not that he could arrange this himself, but that God wills and allows it to happen. It is not that he did not deserve death, but that God does not will the death he deserves. It is not that he does not stand under the wrath and curse of God. This has come upon Cain and he must bear it. But Cain must not be killed. The sign which God sets upon him is undoubtedly the brand of the sin which necessarily arises from his contempt of grace. It is the mark of the homicide. But this very mark is a protective sign which God has given him. In fact it is a covenantal sign by which Yahweh admits Himself to be the Avenger and Saviour of this murderer ; by which—for the first time in the Bible —God binds Himself to sinful man in a kind of treaty. God is holy and righteous in such a way that He sustains the life of the one who has forfeited his life before God. He sustains it with the intervention of His Word and the gift of a token of Himself as the Lord of man. God is holy and righteous to such effect that whoever is against Cain is not for but against God, the holy and righteous One, and will necessarily be the victim of an even heavier judgment. In God's patience, then, there triumphs the almighty, gracious and merciful, and therefore the holy and righteous, being of God.

The same is true in the story of Noah in Gen. 6-9. This relates an annihilating judgment of God, and yet surely its proper sequence and original meaning are rightly perceived in 1 Pet. 3²⁰, which places it under the heading of the patience of God. For its true content is not that God repented having created man and that He decided and fulfilled His decision to extirpate man and all living creatures. Its true and final Word is that God in His wrath and judgment finds and saves the one man Noah, again not because of Noah's intrinsic excellence, but because he found grace in the eyes of the Lord (Gen. 6⁸) and was seen to be " righteous before him " (Gen. 7¹). The point of this story is that while God destroys the human race and all things living for the sake of His holiness and righteousness, He is at the same time concerned about the further progress and growth of the human race and of all other creatures, and so, after the catastrophic destruction of all flesh upon the earth, He accepts the sacrifice of the rescued Noah and promises him : " I will not again curse the ground for man's sake ; . . . neither will I again smite any more everything living, as I have done " (Gen. 8²¹, cf. 9¹¹) But : " While the earth remaineth, seedtime and harvest, and cold and heat, and summer and winter, and day and night, shall not cease." Again a sign is appointed, the rainbow, as the " token of a covenant between me and the earth " (Gen. 9¹²ᶠ·), which, according to Gen. 9¹⁶, not only man can see, but God Himself " will look upon it," that He may remember His covenant. Again, as in the Cain story, it is a question principally—and in an abstract sense we might almost say, only—of man's life and its conservation, of the place which he is granted on earth, of the existence permitted to him in time and the inevitable revolutions of time, even in spite of the fact that the thoughts of the human heart are evil from youth. But in this very abstraction the story asserts all the more plainly that it also belongs to God's being and action, that it renders His holiness and righteousness divine, that even when He punishes and slays He can still grant place and time. To whom ? To the creature ? Is it a question of the creature and its life in itself and as such ? Obviously it is also a question of the creature, but again obviously—because the creature's life is forfeit—it is primarily and properly a question of God Himself who has not yet finished with this creature ; who wills to continue with it, to have further dealings with it ; who therefore leaves it the gift of life in order that He Himself may have opportunity for what He wills to do and be in His continued future relations with it. Does not the whole story of God's covenant with man, the covenant with Abraham, and the covenant at Sinai, and everything that happens in connexion with them—above all does not the fulfilment of all the promises of all these covenants in Jesus Christ, depend upon the fact that this covenant with Noah was concluded and kept and will always be faithfully kept ? Does not the grace and mercy of God depend upon the fact that there is also a patience of God, that He grants space to the sinful creature, thus giving Himself space further to speak and act with it ? We should certainly have to venerate the omnipotent Godhead of God in the end which He could have willed finally to prepare for all creatures and could have prepared long ago. But since He has willed and wills it otherwise, since He has willed to provide us with the sign of Cain and that of Noah, do we not have to say that the omnipotent Godhead of the living God consists only in the fact that He is not impatient but patient ?

An impatient God would be in fact a petty, human, weak and finally a false god. It is only the patient God who is the great, divine, strong and true God. This truth emerges with particular clarity in the Book of Jonah. Notice the relation between the two parts of the work. First (cc. 1-2) we have Jonah's own disobedience to his prophetic mission, the punishment of this disobedience and his gracious and miraculous deliverance from the belly of the fish as he pleads for it and celebrates it in advance in the Psalm of Jonah 2³ᶠ·. There then follows in cc. 3 and 4, the apparent obedience of the prophet. But the same man who in this mysterious way was the object of God's patience is slow to understand it. Indeed, we might say that he shows crass ignorance in respect of the message read to him. He is called to be the prophet of the fact that in consideration of the penitence of the Ninevites God will repent of His intention to destroy the city. And he, of all people, makes this complaint against God : " For I knew that thou art a gracious God, and merciful, slow to anger, and of great kindness, and repentest thee of the evil." Indeed, he justifies his own original disobedience, thus in a sense repeating the sin that had been so wonderfully forgiven : " O Lord, was not this my saying, when I was yet in my country ? Therefore I fled before unto Tarshish " (4²). This prophet, just rescued from death, wearies of life, and in his final words he, the psalmist of ch. 2, impatiently prays down even upon himself the impatience of God : " Therefore now, O Lord, take, I beseech thee, my life from me ; for it is better for me to die than to live." There then follows in 4⁵ᶠ· the exquisite repetition of the whole in the shape of an unmistakable burlesque. The prophet instals himself in the eastern part of the town to see what will happen. He rejoices in a gourd which gives him the necessary shade as he waits for the outburst of God's anger. " So Jonah was exceeding glad of the gourd." But as a symbolic judgment God sent a worm which smote the gourd that it withered, and Jonah experienced in a most unwelcome way the heat of the sun, and had fresh occasion to desire his own death and therefore God's impatience. The ironical question : " Doest thou well to be angry for the gourd ? " does not help him. Yes, he answers : " I do well to be angry that life has been so spoiled for me." What more can be done ? Who is in the right ? The impatient prophet who raises such a lament for the gourd and thinks " that it is justified," or the patient God whose final word we hear in the question : " And should not I spare that great city, wherein are more than six score thousand persons that cannot discern between their right hand and their left hand ; and also much cattle ? " We are not told that the prophet learned his lesson. But we must obviously learn from his story who and what God is and is not. For again we are not told that Jonah's impatient prayer for the action of an impatient God found any answer. It would seem that with the 120,000 minors and other inhabitants of the town and the mass of cattle he himself did not perish but was left alive—with a life which both he and they had forfeited. The truth of God's patience with Nineveh and with himself for his own salvation is the ultimate message of this Scripture. And in this way does it not express, more powerfully than any picture of judgment and punishment on the city and the prophet could ever do, the omnipotent holy and righteous Godhead of God ?

God does not renounce His government when He exercises patience. If God gives further opportunity to sinful man and grants him life, it is perhaps because, as in the case of the Ninevites, he has already repented and converted. Ezek. 18²¹ᶠ· is obviously to be understood on this presupposition : " But if the wicked will turn from all his sins that he hath committed, and keep all my statutes, and do that which is lawful and right, he shall surely live, he shall not die. All his transgressions that he hath committed, they shall not be mentioned unto him : in his righteousness that he hath done, he shall live. Have I any pleasure at all that the wicked should die ? saith the Lord God : and not that he should return from his ways, and live ? " Or else the patience of God is exercised with the aim and intention of inducing his future repentance and conversion. Paul seems to speak of this in Rom. 2⁴ when he asks the impenitent Jew whether he despises the riches of God's mercy, patience and long-suffering ? " Dost thou not know that the goodness of God leadeth thee to repentance ? " The same point is made in Rom. 9²²ᶠ·, where it is said that although God wills " to show his wrath, and to make his power known," He has " endured with much longsuffering the vessels of wrath fitted to destruction," in order at the same time " to make known the riches of the glory on the vessels of mercy, which he had afore prepared unto glory." Again in 2 Pet. 3⁹ : " The Lord is not slack concerning his promise, as some men count slackness ; but is longsuffering to us-ward, not willing that any should perish, but that all should come to repentance." It was in this sense that in 1 Tim. 1¹⁶ Paul described himself, who later became by God's mercy the type of faith, as an object of the μακροθυμία of Jesus Christ. Under this heading we may also include the remarkable recapitulation of a constantly recurring situation in Israel's history at the beginning of the Book of Judges. According to this survey there is a repeated cycle of Israel's apostasy, God's wrath and Israel's deliverance to its enemies, followed by a new invitation to Israel to return to God, a new manifestation of God's help and deliverance, and then again a fresh apostasy, a fresh outburst of divine wrath and a fresh deliverance to the surrounding nations (Judges 2¹¹⁻²²).

But this raises a problem which has so often involved lax and unworthy conceptions of God's patience. What is the real aim and intention of God when He exercises patience ? What is this human penitence for the sake of which, in prospect or retrospect, God contains His anger, sometimes refusing to execute punishment, but giving men further opportunities of life, sometimes punishing only one, but leaving others the gift of life, sometimes mightily destroying but no less mightily saving ? Indeed, is there anywhere or at any time a real act of human penitence for the sake of which it is worth while to God to spare men and to give them time and life ? Was the human race any better after the Flood than before it ? Did it not immediately think it right to build the Tower of Babel ? Was not all its penitent zeal only too much like Israel's passing cry for help in the time of the Judges ? Where is there in the presentation of the Bible itself a single penitent whose existence really justifies the patience of God and therefore the preservation of the creature ? Abraham, Isaac or Jacob ? Moses or David ? Are there any genuine exceptions to what we read in Is. 65¹ᶠ. " I am sought of them that asked not for me ; I am found of them that sought me not : I said, Behold me, unto a nation that was not called by my name. I have stretched out my hands all the day unto a rebellious people, which walketh in a way that was not good, after their own thoughts ; a people that provoketh me to anger continually to my face ; that sacrificeth in gardens, and burneth incense upon altars of brick ; which remain among the graves, and lodge in the monuments, which eat swine's flesh, and the broth of abominable things in their vessels." What, then, is the meaning of the patience of God ? Is it not the equivalent of weakness ? Does it not mean that God allows Himself to be mocked ? For when and where will not both the actual and the anticipated penitence prove a disappointment ?

But conversely it might equally well be asked : Where is in fact the patience of God ? How often do we not read that God " repented " not only of His anger but also of His kindness and mercy ? How often, to how many people, and how destructively His impatience also seems to take effect ! How radically His wrath, too, seems to take its course ! In spite of everything, how much death and destruction does actually come upon Israel ! And in any case, is not the final thing the catastrophic end of this people behind which, according to the New Testament, we see the final catastrophe which overtakes the whole of humanity and indeed the whole universe, a passing away of heaven and earth ? (Mt. 24³⁵). Where, then, is the patience of God ? What does it really mean when we read in Is. 54⁸ : " In a little wrath I hid my face from thee for a moment ; but with everlasting kindness will I have mercy on thee, saith the Lord thy Redeemer " ? Or in Ps. 30⁵ : " For his anger endureth but a moment ; in his favour is life : weeping may endure for a night, but joy cometh in the morning." Is not this the very opposite of the truth ? Will not a new night of weeping

follow upon this morning and finally a night that is without end ? Ultimately
will it not be found that the kindness and grace of God have been only the affair
of a moment, whereas His wrath is the constant and eternal factor and will
necessarily have the last word ? Has He not always waited and will He not
always wait in vain for real penitence ? When we keep to the biblical testimony
to God's patience, we cannot avoid but we have to ask the question in all seriousness : Is it really possible for God to be patient ? And is He actually so ? And
if we do not at once accept the biblical answer, if we do not frame the question
itself in the light of the biblical answer (i.e., if we do not consider that we have
not yet touched upon the decisive aspect of the biblical testimony), we can
hardly avoid having to give a negative answer to this question. If we look at
the human repentance and conversion which are presumably the aim of divine
patience, we are forced to say that this patience—if we do not regard it as mere
weakness, as a passing failure of God to be God—can in any event be understood
only as a temporary and in the last resort external attitude, that it is not rooted
in His real and intrinsic being, that it is perhaps a determination of His *opus
ad extra*, but that *ad intra* in the proper nature of God there corresponds to it
His impatience, so that finally even *ad extra* there will correspond to it His
wrathful punishment and destruction ; a *dies irae* in which righteous and unrighteous, pious and impious, penitent and impenitent, will equally fail to stand.
This will necessarily be the end, and if God is still to be understood as love, it
will be only as a radically impatient love which consumes its object in fire.
But if this is so, how strange it is that according to the witness of the Bible this
necessary end, and with it the revelation of the inner being of God, is continually
deferred ! How strange it is that according to the biblical presentation there
can be this long interplay of patience and impatience, of mercy and severity, on
the part of God, and of repentance and recurrent apostasy on that of man ! In
the last resort is not this for both partners a needlessly cruel game ? In view
of the Old Testament, may we not ask whether it is not a cat-and-mouse game
which—with an evil, despairing, Promethean defiance, but choosing the lesser
of two evils—man may well prefer to decline and evade ? Is it not a game in
face of which—if it is to be played with us—the best part of wisdom is to close
our eyes ? This chain of thought—and for those who consider themselves strong
enough even its final conclusion—is hardly to be resisted if the decisive moment
of the biblical testimony to God's patience is not expressed. But it can and
must be expressed, and then the real meaning and basis of the aspects so far
touched upon will become clear, and this chain of thought will be arrested.

The decisive moment of the biblical testimony to God's patience
is that according to Heb. 1³ God upholds all things by the Word of
His power. By His Word ! which means in any event that they are
not occasioned by, and dependent on, what becomes manifest and
actual from our side as penitence and conversion. What is manifest
and actual here is in point of fact the alternation of penitence and
impenitence which is sufficiently clear in Israel's example and the
final outcome of which will be Israel's impenitence. To this outcome
in our experience there could correspond on God's part only the
judgment of wrath, and this is actually the case. God cannot sustain
all things or the sinful creature in his wretchedness by means of our
final word. This word is definitely not effective to uphold all things.
But God upholds them by His Word. And this Word as such is
powerful. According to Heb. 1² it is the Word of the Son by whom
He has spoken to us in these last days, i.e., at the end of the days of the

fathers and the prophets, whom He has appointed heir of all things, by whom also He created the worlds, who is the brightness of His glory and the express image of His person. By this His Word in His Son Jesus Christ, He upholds all things and upholds them with power.

" For as the rain cometh down, and the snow from heaven, and returneth not thither, but watereth the earth, and maketh it bring forth and bud, that it may give seed to the sower, and bread to the eater : so shall my word be that goeth forth out of my mouth : it shall not return unto me void, but it shall accomplish that which I please, and it shall prosper in the thing whereto I sent it " (Is. 55[10f.]). We have already pointed out in relation to the story of Noah that God obviously gives His creature space in order that in this way He Himself may have space : time for eternity. This fundamental meaning constitutes the invincible victorious power of the divine patience ; the reason and the effectiveness by which its exercise is distinguished from the unworthy and cruel game which it would otherwise be. The Word of God has not been spoken to man in vain, and God's Son has not Himself become incarnate in vain. But God's Word was spoken for the sake of God Himself, and therefore, included in the will of God, for the sake of man, and therefore meaningfully and effectively. In other words, God's Son became incarnate for the sake of God Himself, and again therefore, included in the will of God, for the sake of man, and again therefore meaningfully and effectively. Because this happened for God's sake and therefore for man's sake, in spite of all its sinfulness human existence is justified before God by God Himself, and therefore the patience of God, which leaves man his existence and space and time for it, is both well grounded and effective. It is because God's Word goes forth out of God's mouth, because God's Word cannot return to Him void out of our impenitent penitence, that God is patient and grants space and time. Strictly speaking, He grants it to His Word and therefore to Himself. He has time. And the fact that He has time for us is what characterises His whole activity towards us as an exercise of patience. Included in this exercise of patience is both God's mercy and punishment, God's salvation and destruction, God's healing and smiting. This all takes place in the course and service of the revelation of His Word. By it all Israel is instructed in the divine Word. It all means that God always, and continually, has time for Israel. That Israel has time to hear God's Word, and therefore time to live for the sake of God's Word and by its power, is shown—only symbolically and provisionally but nevertheless truly—in the very stumbling-block of the alternation of penitence and impenitence in which Israel receives this instruction. And the predominating measure of impenitence reminds us that we have to do primarily and decisively with the will and being of the righteous and holy God and not with the intrinsic merits of man, that man can appropriate this instruction and set up this symbol only in so far as he is justified and sanctified by God, that without the aid of God's Word he cannot and will not provide the token of penitence and repentance, and therefore that in himself he cannot and will not have time, he cannot and will not be the object of God's patience. That in all this, again, Israel receives time from God, time to hear God's Word and therefore time to live for the sake of God's Word and by its power, is shown—again only symbolically and provisionally but nevertheless truly—in the further stumbling-block of the alternation of grace and judgment, mercy and punishment, salvation and ruin, in which God gives this instruction to Israel. And again the apparent prevalence of judgment, punishment and ruin shews that it is God's Word which must be heard in these signs and tokens, and for the sake of which He has time for mankind, so that it must always appear a miracle to man that in this connexion, included in the will of God to speak with him, he too, man himself, continually acquires and has time and acquires it again. It is in this way,

14

however, in the language of God's Word characterised and made unequivocal by this very alternation, that man receives time from God and lives in virtue of God's patience—certainly in order to repent and convert, yet not in virtue of his penitence, but in virtue of God's patience.

But to see and hear and feel and recognise the power of this patience means to believe in Jesus Christ. As regards the question where and when genuine fruits of penitence have been brought forth, in consideration of which it is worth God's while to have patience with man and therefore to grant him space and time, the answer must be that such fruits have never been brought forth at any time or place except in Jesus Christ, but that they have been produced genuinely and finally and in sufficient measure for us all in the perfect obedience which He, the one and only direct and true hearer of God's Word, has rendered in human flesh. For His sake, as it is said in Rom. 3²⁵ᶠ·, the divine ἀνοχή deemed it worth while to overlook sins committed in times past—and in comparison with the time of Christ all other time is past time, an old aeon—in which sins had remained unpunished through the forbearance of God (διὰ τὴν πάρεσιν τῶν προγεγονότων ἁμαρτημάτων ἐν τῇ ἀνοχῇ τοῦ θεοῦ). For the sake of these times and the sins committed in them God has manifested His righteousness in Jesus Christ. But obviously the converse is also true. For the sake of manifesting His righteousness in Jesus Christ, God exercised ἀνοχή in these times. In these times, therefore, there was a πάρεσις τῶν ἁμαρτημάτων. Certainly there was judgment, punishment and destruction. But in and through it all there was a divine patience, a living and letting live in relation to the creature.

The position is now clear that God's patience does not leave man to his own devices. His jealous zeal in and for the creature cannot be more powerfully manifested than in the incarnation of His Word. He has espoused the cause of the creature to the final depths. From this point of view the divine patience certainly cannot consist in an indifferent self-withdrawal of God in relation to its being, action and destiny. If He allows the many to go their own ways, if He leaves them their freedom, if He gives continual time (and food for it), if through it all He constantly waits for them, He does so for the simple reason that He has already overtaken them in the One, His only Son, that in Him He has already walked with them in His own way and at His own time, and to the very end. He does so because, in the One in whom He has given Himself utterly to all, they have already fallen into His hand. He does so because this One stands in place of them all and for them all has accomplished the genuine penitence which was expected from all. For the sake of this One, God has patience with the many.

For the sake of this One, there is space and time for the many. It is not that they have deserved this or ever will or can deserve it by their ambiguous and, in the last resort, insincere penitence. Nor is it, of course, that space and time have been granted to enable them to continue in their impenitence. It is rather that they might have space and time to appropriate the life which has been secured for them by the sincere penitence of that One—space and time to believe in Him in whom as their Head their penitence becomes sincere and acceptable to God. Because there, in the One, the zeal of God is so powerful and attains its goal, therefore the others, the many who are summed up in Him, who in Him are conducted to the goal and have already attained it, can as the many be at their various times on the way—the way of faith on which their footsteps follow His, their freedom is an acknowledgment of His freedom, their time a sharing of His time, and therefore contemporary with Him. To go the way of faith is what God's patience leaves to them and concedes to them. Therefore the meaning of the divine patience is a summons to have faith. We have only to think of the object of faith, of the one Jesus Christ, to believe in whom the many are called by the patience of God, to realise that in the tarrying of the divine patience there can be no question of the indifference of God to His creature, but that this very tarrying of God is His decisive action and work in relation to it.

It is also clear that there can be no question of disappointment or self-deception on the part of God with respect to the sincerity, or insincerity, of the human penitence for which He waits in His patience. God is not short-sighted, nor is He subject to any optimistic illusions, when again and again He saves and preserves Israel only to reap continually wild grapes instead of grapes. God does not, then, experience any disillusionment with regard to His people, the many. He knows very well what is our frame. But because He knows it, He has good ground for being patient with us—the ground which He Himself has created and laid down. His self-restraint in regard to the many is justified by the fact that in the midst of the many, in the person of the One whom He Himself has appointed Head of these many and their Representative before Him, that which He awaits has taken place and is fulfilled, the obedience which He demands from His creature has been rendered.

Because this has happened, because in this happening God Himself has taken action on behalf of the many, something has happened which makes it possible for God in faithfulness to Himself to be faithful to us too ; faithful even in the sense that He can leave us our existence although we ourselves in our own strength, i.e., apart from what has taken place on our behalf in Jesus Christ, cannot produce any justification of our existence. We are reminded of the fact that we cannot do so by the judgment, punishment and destruction to which, tacitly or openly, our existence is continually exposed. These things recall to us our true limits, i.e., refer us to that by which alone we are preserved from the outbreak of the objective anger and judgment of God. They refer us to Jesus Christ and to faith in Him. But in Jesus Christ and by faith in Him we are able in supreme reality to produce a justification, the justification of our existence. In the midst of the judgments and punishments which smite us we can and should find comfort and, indeed, glory in the fact that it is not all up with us. This is not because we have not deserved such an outcome. It is because rightfully—not by denying but by fully asserting His holiness and righteousness—God Himself has seen to it that this cannot be the final outcome for us, that our preservation is meaningful and necessary. It is necessary because God has linked His own life with ours, and has sacrificed Himself for us so that as truly as God Himself lives we cannot perish. As we are summoned by the patience of God to the life of faith, we are invited to seize and affirm this objective divine justification of our existence and with it the justification of the divine patience itself, for our own part giving God the glory which He has assured Himself by creating and establishing this ground for His patience.

Again, it is clear that even the judgments and punishments of God, the whole severity of His conduct towards Israel, do not contradict the truth that He actually wills to maintain and not destroy His creature. They are all temporary and as such symbolic judgments and punishments. They are not the outbreak of the genuine wrath and judgment of God. They are not the eternal death, the abandonment and precipitation into nothingness, which Israel and with Israel all humanity has deserved. They are all to be included in the sway of God's patience. That which we all deserved has been suffered in our place and in Israel's place by the only righteous One, who achieved a perfect penitence—although He had no need of it for Himself—by not refusing to take upon Himself the genuine wrath and judgment of God. Because He has done this in His function as the One who could take our place and suffer for us as our Head, all that which we with Israel have to suffer is shown to be included in the government of God's patience, a reminder of our own incapacity to justify ourselves but also a reminder of the God who justifies us by Himself.

By His own suffering He has characterised our suffering as a token of life and not of death, as a token of His friendship and not of His enmity, as a token which is meant to awaken and maintain and not destroy our faith. It is the shadow of death under which our life stands, the shadow of the eternal death which Jesus Christ has suffered for us. It is this which lends it its seriousness, but takes from this seriousness its absoluteness, thus preventing it from giving rise to fear. It is only the shadow of eternal death. We shall not have to drink this cup. And it is the shadow of the eternal death suffered by Jesus Christ. Thus, although it is a real and a serious shadow—and this cannot be contested or argued away—it is the token of life, eternal life. And it is also the token of the continual maintenance of our life in time by Him and for His sake : that we might have time and space to believe in Him, to believe in His penitence, and in His penitence in the sincerity of our own intrinsically imperfect penitence.

Therefore, as all this becomes clear to us, as we apprehend the Word of God and Jesus Christ to be the power which sustains all things, the power which supported Israel for forty years in the wilderness Ac. 13[18]), the power of the self-restraint in virtue of which God overlooked the times of ignorance (Ac. 17[30]) and was able to forgive the sins committed in these times (Rom. 3[25]), as we hear this Word as God's eternal Word spoken to us, we hear the decisive Word, the central truth of the biblical testimony to God's patience.

We had to ask first : What is the meaning of God's patience in view of our own proven impenitence ? And again : Where is His patience in view of the manifest judgments and punishments of God which come upon us too ? Can God be patient ? And is He really so ? Well, these questions can and necessarily will have to be asked so long as we have not heard the Word of God among the words of the Bible. But the open secret of the whole Bible is precisely the Word of God itself. In His Word God becomes the Protector and Avenger of the murderer Cain. He saves Noah and concludes a covenant with him and his heirs, although they are no better and become no better than the people destroyed in the Flood. He remains patient when Jonah the prophet would call down His impatience over godless Nineveh and his own head. In His Word He is patient even where He strikes and slays, for as He does so He utters His Word and establishes a sign of fellowship between Himself and the creature. Put the two questions side by side. In the light of the central answer and truth of the Bible it is clear that they cancel out each other.

We must accept the fact that God can be patient because He is patient in His Word. While we can still hear it, He keeps time and space for us who have forfeited our existence in His sight and are unable to justify ourselves. We must also learn that God is patient from the fact that He can be patient in His Word which is Himself, that is to say, He can have time and space for us, i.e., for faith. If we believe in His Word, we can no longer doubt either the reality or the possibility of His patience.

From the point of view of faith in His Word there can be no justification for the conception, to which these questions seem to point, of a finally and essentially impatient God, or of the impatient love which consumes its object. For the same reason there can be no question of a game which God plays partly with Himself and partly and even more with us. Nor can there be any place for a possible Promethean defiance in which man tries to evade this game. Ideas like this can arise only outside the sphere of faith in God's Word, i.e., only where the central truth of the biblical testimony to God's patience has not yet been spoken to us or appropriated by us. Belief in God's Word, i.e., in Jesus Christ, will necessarily destroy at its root this whole sequence of thought. The truth which it distorts is, rightly expressed, that we have not deserved God's patience, and that His patience is effectual towards us even in judgment and punishment. But the former does not mean that God cannot be patient, nor does the latter mean that He is not so, or only partially so. On the contrary, His Word is the ground of our confidence, and in His Word He gives us His pledge that He can be patient and is so in fact. In His Word He waits for us to give Him the glory in faith, accepting both the possibility and the reality of His patience. God is the One who lives in His Word and He is no other. In Him is possible and real what is possible and real in His Word. If God reveals His patience to us in His Word, God is the very possibility and reality of patience itself. The way is thus closed both to a God of impatience and also to the Promethean defiance of a man who presumes to lose patience with God. The only way open to us now is the way of gratitude for our life which has been undeservedly left to us ; the way which will become and be of itself the way of the patience that we now have to show in suffering the judgments and punishments which strike us. The fact that, in spite of our infinite guilt, we are permitted to suffer them in the fellowship and shadow of the innocent suffering of Christ, by which we have been spared the suffering of the eternal wrath and judgment of God, is sufficient reason for us to suffer them patiently and to allow them to serve the purpose which they have for us : the conversion from every illusion of our own worthiness; the return to the One who has made us worthy of God, to faith, therefore, in which we can give ourselves to the God who in His Son has taken our cause into His own hands. The relationship with Jesus Christ in which we must suffer is sufficient to overrule our suffering and the gift of our whole life for good (Rom. 8²⁸). In this relationship the worst and the harshest thing that we can encounter, and do encounter, is our inevitable death in time, with which we must finally profess this relationship. But even this, the imminent end of all things, is not only not unbearable—for in its unbearable reality it has all been borne for us by Jesus Christ—but is in fact the outwardly bitter, yet inwardly sweet, promise of the eternal life which has been won for us by Him. To grasp this promise, to be permitted to live with it already in this life as with the certainty in comparison with which everything else pales into uncertainty— this is what is meant by believing in God's Word. From this standpoint we can see the truth of Is. 54⁸ and Ps. 30⁵ : the outburst of God's anger is only the affair of a moment. We do not have to endure and suffer even this moment. It is in truth the moment when Jesus cried with a loud voice : " My God, my God, why hast thou forsaken me ? " (Mk. 15³⁴). But has not this moment in all its darkness all the attributes of that other moment when the trumpet shall sound and the dead shall be raised incorruptible ? In any case, there corresponds to this very moment the eternal loving-kindness, the lifelong enduring grace and favour of God. The sufferings of this present time, which reflect both the light and shadow of this moment, are nothing in comparison with the glory which shall be revealed in us (Rom. 8¹⁷ᶠ·). If we suffer with Him in this hope, and we believe according to God's Word that we have to suffer with Jesus Christ in this hope, we can and may and must suffer in patience : answering His patience with our patience ; giving the right answer to the waiting of His wrath with our waiting for redemption.

If now, coming to a provisional conclusion, we balance or confront the idea of the patience with that of the wisdom of God, the meaning of this juxtaposition is essentially the same as that of the juxtapositions which we have already made. In God wisdom is related to patience as is holiness to grace, and righteousness to mercy. All these ideas express and translate the love of God. But the second set of ideas —holiness, righteousness and wisdom—express with greater distinctness than the first (grace, mercy and patience) the fact that it is His free and therefore distinctively divine love. That God in Himself and in all His works is gracious and therefore holy, merciful and therefore righteous, patient and therefore wise, is the proof and essence of the divinity of His love according to the main theme of the section and the explanations already adduced. We have taken care to speak of the ideas of the grace, mercy and patience of God in such a way that there cannot arise any material antithesis to the ideas of the second category, but that the depth and majesty of all these perfections of the divine love in the divine freedom should, as far as possible, be visible in their proper content. Yet Holy Scripture itself does not allow us to stop here, but leads us at once to survey and think about the same matter from the other side, which is not opposite but in the one hidden being of God distinct. The recognition of the depth and majesty of divine grace called for a special consideration of the divine holiness. The recognition of the depth and majesty of the mercy of God called for a special consideration of His righteousness. Our experience would have been the same if we had begun with the second set of ideas. In our next section we shall in fact begin with the ideas which more definitely characterise and describe the freedom of God as His love. And we shall then find the same thing. The recognition of the attributes of the divine freedom in their depth and majesty will require a special consideration of those attributes which, on the other hand, characterise and describe the divine freedom as the freedom of divine love. The distinctive feature of the knowledge of God and of God Himself is that He is all that He is in particular, apart, newly and differently in the inexhaustible plenitude of His one being, so that in all that He is He wills to be considered and apprehended in particular, apart, newly and differently.

So now, in connexion with the perfections of the divine love, the depth and majesty of God's patience call for a special consideration of His wisdom. The depth and majesty of God's patience, as we have seen, consist in the fact that He upholds all things by His powerful Word. In this it is distinguished from all impatience, but no less from all the weak, non-divine and therefore false patience which derives from indifference or weakness or shortsightedness. In this it is one, not only with the grace and mercy, but also with the holiness and righteousness of God. But, as is evident in the central biblical witness, this secret is a special characteristic in God requiring special consideration. God's Word, revealing the depth and majesty of His patience, is God's will expressed and to be accepted as such from all eternity ; subject to no higher appeal ; thankfully and obediently to be accepted because it is His will. But again, God does not reveal Himself and is not God in such a way that His expressed will is not in itself and as such light and recognisable as light. God's will expressed in His Word is neither in itself nor in its manifestation of such a kind that it can even be comparable, let alone identical, with an abyss of what is ultimately chance or caprice. We are not being led to the edge of this type of abyss when we are invited to recognise the majesty and depth of the patience of God in the power of His Word. There is no magic about what God has performed and completed in His Son. No *sacrificium intellectus* is required of us to know this happening, to know the divine being as the ground of the divine patience which we encounter. In this whole matter of recognising the activity and ruling of His love, it is not a question of our being blinded but of our becoming clear-sighted. If His Word is His declared will, it is of the very nature of its being as His Word that it is not merely truth—as such it could still be the disclosure of an abyss of ultimate chance or caprice—but also wisdom. That is to say, it is meaningful in itself, and it shows itself to be meaningful to us who hear it. The wisdom of God is that God not only wills but knows what He wills. And He knows not only what He wills, but why and wherefore He wills it. And He wills only that of which He knows the why and wherefore, of which the why and wherefore is then His own meaning, plan and intention. To this extent there is in it light and no darkness. Because His Word is His wisdom, because the power of His Word is, therefore, the power of His wisdom, His patience is wise, and the grateful recognition of it is at the same time the recognition and adoration of His wisdom. It is not a closing but an opening of our eyes. It is not suspension of the real knowledge of God, but the basis for it. All other secrets—secrets which are neither directly nor indirectly the secret of God's patience—are fortuitous and capricious.

What the creature in himself, i.e., apart from God and His revelation, considers to be wise, intelligible and purposeful, is fortuitous and capricious. The Word of God, however, as the foundation of His patience is neither fortuitous nor capricious. The Word of God shines as light in the darkness. When we hear it, we hear the reason, meaning, purpose and intention of God. When we hear it, we are instructed, enlightened, knowing and wise. When we hear it, the darkness of chance is lightened. If, then, on the basis of the revealed Word we accept our existence as something conceded to us for the sake of the one Jesus Christ, and if we accept the punishments and judgments which threaten and mark our existence as necessary and redemptive for the sake of our fellowship with Jesus Christ, this very acceptance signifies the acceptance of reason, of the sense and purpose for our life, for which it is not only intended, as surely as we are God's creatures, but which as the sense and purpose of God are the only satisfying sense and purpose, the only reason which our life can accept, because in the last resort they are the only ones there are, and in comparison with them everything else that may be described as such is only senselessness, purposelessness and unreason.

The Word of God which determines us to accept our existence as a gift of God's patience, Jesus Christ Himself, is the one reason, sense and purpose. We repel all reason, sense and purpose and relapse into darkness if we refuse to accept the order of the divine patience. On rational grounds, i.e., the one ground that here and only here we have the possibility of accepting reason, we really cannot not believe. This is the wisdom of God in its general connexion with His patience. This is the special characteristic of God in the power of His Word which makes His patience possible and real.

Before proceeding further it will be useful to extend our lines of reference backwards. The fact that God knows why and wherefore He wills what He wills, that He wills only that of which He knows the why and wherefore, is something which is also to be said of His grace and mercy. These perfections of God and the fact that He turns to His creature and takes its misery to heart, could still stand perhaps in the shadow of a slight suspicion. They are true, no doubt, but it might easily be otherwise. The freedom in which we see God manifest these perfections and give Himself still bears some resemblance to chance or accident. Why is it that God is gracious and merciful? We cannot, of course, try as it were to climb over God Himself with this Why? We cannot try to justify Him from above, measuring Him by this or that standard of value and reasonableness. Nor is it as if there is no answer to this Why? in God Himself, or as if we ourselves cannot understand this answer or know God Himself as the One in whom there is an answer to this question. The answer is that God is wise. He knows why and to what end He is gracious. And this is not something dark in itself, but intrinsically illuminating, intelligible and purposeful. The recognition of it does not mean that we are plunged into darkness but, on the contrary, that we are delivered from the darkness of ignorance and brought into the light of a reason hitherto concealed from us, but now revealing itself as something we have to accept. God is not guilty of impulsiveness or irrationality when He is gracious and merciful, any more than He is of a surrender of His holiness and righteousness. He is not, then, overcome by a whim or a chance inspiration. He is not capricious. But in this as in every other respect He is the God of order. And His order, the order of His wisdom, is that in Himself and in all His works He is gracious and merciful. He would not be gracious, but ungracious ; He would not be merciful, but unmerciful ; or He would be gracious and merciful only weakly and ineffectively, like a creature, if He were not wise. But He is gracious and merciful just because and as He is wise. Again, a connexion must be made with His perfect holiness and righteousness. Here too, perhaps, there remains the shadow of a suspicion. Must we evade the question why God is so zealous to affirm Himself in His holiness or to vindicate Himself in His righteousness ? Could it perhaps be otherwise ? Is the unity between His grace and holiness or His mercy and righteousness only a kind of freak or accident, a *factum brutum* which is simply there and has to be accepted by us as such ? Why is God holy and righteous ? Why as such is He also gracious and merciful ? Here again, of course, there is not as it were a Therefore which we can pronounce about God from without or above. But here too there is the Therefore of wisdom in God Himself. His holiness has nothing to do with defiance nor His justice with tyranny. And the unity of the grace and holiness and the mercy and righteousness of God has nothing to do with a " paradox," as has often been alleged. But the mystery with which these things confront us is that of the reason, meaning and purpose which God has in Himself, which He Himself is. It is the mystery of His wisdom. If He were not wise He would not be holy and righteous, nor gracious and merciful, and still less both in one. He is holy and righteous just because and as He is wise. Strictly speaking, there is no confidence or freedom in our knowledge of God apart from what we have to learn at this final stage. For if God is for us an abyss of chance and caprice, if as far as possible we regard the irrational as the essentially divine, we neither have nor can have any real confidence in relation to God. For confidence is based on the appreciation of reason, meaning and order. So long as we do not have this, the knowledge of God cannot give us any freedom. For freedom comes only from the recognition of reason, meaning and order, and not from the consideration of chaos, chance or caprice. We can only say once again that it all depends absolutely on how far we recognise God as wisdom. God is wise in so far as His whole activity, as willed by Him, is also thought out by Him, and thought out by Him from the very outset with correctness and completeness, so that it is an intelligent and to that extent a reliable and liberating activity. We have to say of His activity in His works and also of His inner activity, of the essential actuality of His divine being, that God is wise, that in Him is wisdom. God Himself is wisdom.

Polanus and Quenstedt, whom we have so far consulted for the orthodox doctrine of God, fail us at this point. For Polanus (*Synt. Theol. chr.*, 1609, *col.* 998 ff.) the wisdom of God seems to be dissolved in the general idea of divine knowledge as omniscience. It is, of course, true that God's all-powerful knowledge is the knowledge of His wisdom. But it must be realised first of all that wisdom constitutes the intelligence and rationality of God's love. It is only in this way that it can be understood as the source of God's all-powerful omniscience. Again, Quenstedt (*Theol. did. pol.*, 1685, I c. 8, *sect.* 1, *th.* 26) can really say about the wisdom of God only that as divine and therefore hidden wisdom it surpasses all human knowledge and understanding. This is also true ; but it does not alter the fact that, like all the divine perfections, it forms the substance of His self-revelation and is therefore an object of faith, and to that extent of human knowledge. It safeguards the truth that God's wisdom surpasses our insight and understanding. But in a Christian doctrine of God the truth must also be safeguarded that God's wisdom is as determinative of His love as are His holiness and righteousness. H. Cremer (*op. cit.*, p. 69f.) defines the wisdom of God at once as the transcendence of His saving counsel in contrast with the law of logical consistency current in the world. This again is true. But just because it is so true, it is advisable to pause and consider further that this God who vindicates the validity of His saving counsel in opposition to the world is Himself as such the source of all true logical consistency. More helpful in this connexion is the view of H. Heidegger. He, too, subordinates the *sapientia Dei* to the idea of divine knowledge. But he gives the fuller definition that it is the quality of the divine being *per quam novit, quibus rationibus res ab eodem producendae gloriam suam illustrare queant, ut eas convenienter suae naturae, perfectioni et gloriae vocare et velle possit*. It is the *moderatrix consiliorum Dei, per quam sic ad decentiam divinam gloriae suae attendit, ne veritati, ordini, pulchritudini in ulla verborum vel operum eius parte desit* (*Corp. Theol.*, 1700, III, 65, quoted from H. Heppe, *Dogm. d. ev. ref. K.*, 1935, p. 49 f.). The allusion to the divine *convenientia* or *decentia* obviously reminds us of the connexion between the wisdom and the holiness and righteousness of God. In God's wisdom, too, it is a question of what is worthy of God as God, what befits Him as He loves. It befits Him to affirm Himself and to carry through His plans. In this reside His holiness and righteousness. But in both these *moderatio* is also proper to Him (and here we are reminded of God's patience). By this they are both conjoined with His divine glory, rooted in it and related to it. In this relationship His holiness and righteousness, His whole being and doing, have truth, order, beauty, meaning, purpose and reason. In this foundation and relationship consists His wisdom.

The wisdom of God is the inner truth and clarity with which the divine life in its self-fulfilment and its works justifies and confirms itself and in which it is the source and sum and criterion of all that is clear and true. It is in this inner truth and clarity that God loves, and this is the source of the dignity with which He is free in His love. In it He also demonstrates the legitimacy, necessity and the sufficiency of His divine existence and action. God is glorious in His wisdom. He attests Himself as God by attesting His wisdom.

The basic meaning of *sapientia* is taste, that of σοφία tact and skill, that of " wisdom " a right orientation. All such words obviously offer correct interpretations of the wisdom of God, for they all emphasise certain qualities which are integral to it. But the root meaning of *chokmah* is that of firmness and steadfastness, and we must think primarily on these lines if we are to speak of the wisdom of God and not another wisdom. The divine taste and skill and right orientation can be known only from the indication given by the Old Testament word. The truth that God is wise must, like His holiness and righteousness, mean primarily that He is steadfast and self-consistent. It is in this that He shows His intelligence, He who needs to apprehend nothing outside His own being, whose apprehension of realities distinct from Himself is already an exercise of His grace, mercy and patience, but who can also and does apprehend what is outside Himself, grace and mercy and patience being His most inward and proper being. The fact that God apprehends Himself and is therefore eternal reason, that He lives and is active in Himself in truth and clarity, attesting Himself, magnifying His own glory and to this extent being firm and steadfast and self-consistent—this is the wisdom of God which in His activity, His works *ad extra*, is revealed as His taste or sense for what will serve its supreme and ultimately its only purpose, His skill in making it contribute to this purpose, His orientation and therefore His guidance, the controlling providence and rule which He exercises in and over this activity. It is to be noted that the wisdom of God characterises His whole activity as reliable and liberating, as something in which we can have confidence, just because His wisdom consists in and finally evinces itself as His firmness and self-consistency, the satisfaction of His *decentia* or *convenientia divina*. When God is apprehended as the One who under all circumstances is intelligence and reason in this way, purposing and deciding and speaking and acting on this basis, the knowledge of God means that we can have confidence in Him, that we can be free, that all the uncertainty and darkness of the capricious and irrational is ended.

That according to biblical insight the wisdom of God is actually bound up with His patience is clear from the fact that just where the idea is to some extent clearly unfolded in the Bible it is defined as a wisdom which creates, maintains and rules the world and therefore as the proper instrument of divine providence. Because God is Himself the truth and clarity which justifies, confirms and attests itself, He can allow time, space and existence to another beside Himself without uncertainty, danger or infidelity, as the Lord of this other, and to the praise of His own glory. And He does all this with the same truth and clarity. In this way His wisdom is the meaning of His patience and forbearance. In this way it is the meaning of the world.

But note—in this way and not in any other! God is not the immanent meaning of the world. The world has meaning as it acquires meaning from Him who alone has and is meaning. The difference between biblical wisdom and the world-idea of the Stoics and Philo and others is quite clear when we realise from the more immediate and wider context of the relevant passages that in the Bible wisdom is related not only to the divine patience but to the divine grace and mercy, and that it is also far too closely related to God's holiness and righteousness to allow the emergence of the idea to be explained by reference to the pressure of the Hellenic need to find a principle of world-interpretation. That the main wisdom passages belong to the third part of the Canon of the Old Testament, and shew more or less clearly the historical contact between Israel and Greece, does not imply an acceptance of foreign interests and ideas, but that there has been here a confrontation of the Israelite conception of God with these alien concerns and ideas. If the God of Israel is the God of grace, mercy and patience, it must be said on the one hand that God creates, maintains and governs all that is in His patience and therefore for His own sake and for the sake of His glory. He has determined everything that is as an arena for His activity. Therefore it exists by Him. This connexion of its determination by Him with its creation, maintenance and ruling by Him is the wisdom of God. And, on the other hand, in the actual being and nature of the creature we do not see the reign of chance and caprice, but of God's patience which has determined it as a theatre for His action and therefore created it out of nothing and still preserves and governs it. Therefore, the connexion between the actual being and its nature, and this its determination, is the wisdom of God.

Because it stands in this unity with the divine patience and therefore with all the other attributes of the God of Israel, because then it is really the wisdom of this God, it can and must appear as it actually does in Prov. $1^{20f.}$, and again $8^{1f.}$, not as a logical-ethical principle but as a person, and obviously indeed as a prophetic person : " Wisdom crieth without ; she uttereth her voice in the streets : she crieth in the chief place of concourse, in the openings of the gates ; in the city she uttereth her words " (Prov. 1^{20-21}). And therefore it comes about that the content of what it cries, preaches and proclaims is clearly nothing other than the well-known preaching of repentance, judgment and salvation, and even the wording might easily be that of a prophet : " How long, ye simple ones, will ye love simplicity ? and the scorners delight in their scorning, and fools hate knowledge ? Turn you at my reproof : behold, I will pour out my spirit unto you, I will make known my words unto you. Because I have called, and ye refused ; I have stretched out my hand, and no man regarded ; but ye have set at nought all my counsel, and would none of my reproof : I also will laugh at your calamity ; I will mock when your fear cometh ; when your fear cometh as desolation, and your destruction cometh as a whirlwind ; when distress and anguish cometh upon you. Then shall they call upon me, but I will not answer ; they shall seek me early, but they shall not find me : for that they hated knowledge, and did not choose the fear of the Lord : they would none of my counsel : they despised all my reproof. Therefore shall they eat of the fruit of their own way, and be filled with their own devices " (Prov. 1^{22-33}). Of the wisdom which acts and expresses itself in this way it is then said in Prov. $3^{19f.}$: " The Lord by wisdom hath founded the earth ; by understanding hath he established the heavens. By his knowledge the depths are broken up, and the clouds drop down the dew." But do we not read the same in Jer. 10^{12} : " It is the Lord who hath made the earth by his power, he hath established the world by his wisdom, and hath stretched out the heavens by his discretion " ? The full meaning of the cosmological determination of divine wisdom in Prov. $3^{19f.}$ may be seen from the rest of the chapter. Very simply it explains and emphasises both the threats and the affirmations made in regard to wisdom—that the merchandise of it is better than the merchandise of silver, and the gain thereof than fine gold (v. 14). " Length of days is in her right hand ; and in her left hand riches and honour " (v. 16). " She is a tree of life to them that lay hold upon her ; and happy is every one that retaineth her " (v. 18). " Then shalt thou walk in thy way safely, and thy foot shall not stumble. When thou liest down, thou shalt not be afraid : yea, thou shalt lie down, and thy sleep shall be sweet. Be not afraid of sudden fear, neither of the desolation of the wicked, when it cometh " (vv. 23-25). How far is all that true ? To the extent that by the same wisdom everything has been created and is maintained (v. 19 f.). To the extent that it does in fact guard man and bring him continued life. And when its preaching of repentance, judgment and salvation is accepted, these its promises become true. Its preaching ? No, God's own preaching ! For how can any other " hypostasis " than that of God's revelation speak and preach and promise ? How can even v. 18 ff. —in what abstraction they would have to be read to be understood in this way !— suddenly have the character of an independent attempt at world interpretation, and wisdom therefore the character of an intermediary between God and the world ? What we learn from this chapter is, in fact, that there is no such independent principle of world interpretation, but only the self-explanation of God, the explanation of His own wisdom which is effective because incidentally it does actually explain the world. And therefore it moves necessarily to the express conclusion : " For the Lord shall be thy confidence, and shall keep thy foot from being taken " (v. 26). It is in just the same context that we must read the even more famous passage (Prov. 8²²⁻³¹) where again wisdom itself speaks in the following terms : " The Lord possessed me in the beginning of his way, before his works of old. I was set up from everlasting, from the beginning, or ever the earth was. When there were no depths, I was brought forth ; when there were no fountains abounding with water. Before the mountains were settled, before the hills was I brought forth ; while as yet he had not made the earth, nor the fields, nor the highest part of the dust of the world. When he prepared the heavens, I was there : when he set a compass upon the face of the depth : when he established the clouds above : when he strengthened the foundations of the deep : when he gave to the sea his decree, that the waters should not pass his commandment : when he appointed the foundations of the earth : then I was with him, as one brought up with him : and I was daily his delight, rejoicing always before him ; rejoicing in the habitable part of the earth ; and my delights were with the sons of men." Even more plainly than in ch. 3 we find here that as God's eternal work produced before all other works as His first attestation and therefore as His witness, intermediary and companion in the creation of all other works, wisdom is equated with God Himself, so that again and more emphatically than before we are told that all the works of God testify to His wisdom as to His first and original work. Here, too, we have only to read the beginning and end of the chapter to be convinced that there is no independent attempt at interpreting the universe even in this exalted cosmological section. Why is it that wisdom has to be described in this way ? Obviously to emphasise, for example : " I love them that love me ; and those that seek me early shall find me " (v. 17). Or v. 35 : " For whoso findeth me findeth life." Obviously to emphasise generally the exhortations of wisdom which precede and follow. The emphasising of these exhortations of this practical revelation of wisdom, i.e., the emphasising of this divine address, consists in the fact that the same wisdom, the same God whose exhortations are summed up in the beginning and end of the chapter, is characterised as the One who has created the world and sustains and rules it in His patience, who therefore has every right to expect that His exhortation will be needed in the sphere of this world, the ground which has been created and is maintained and ruled by Him alone. Those who do not heed it cut the only possible ground from under their feet. Those who do heed it live in accordance with the meaning of every creaturely possibility of life. If we doubt this inference from Prov. 3 and 8 because there it can " only " be drawn from the context and is not made explicit, the desired plainness is to be found at the close of Job 28, which is just as relevant in this connexion. In what is an exact parallel to Prov. 8 we read there : " To make the weight for the winds ; and he weigheth the waters by measure. When he made a decree for the rain, and a way for the lightning of the thunder : then did he see it, and declare it ; he prepared it, yea, and searched it out." And the immediate continuation is as follows : " And unto man he said, Behold, the fear of the Lord, that is wisdom ; and to depart from evil is understanding " (Job 28²⁵ᶠ·). But the very same verse stands at the beginning of Proverbs itself : " The fear of the Lord is the beginning of knowledge ; but fools despise wisdom and instruction " (Prov. 1⁷). It is also repeated in Prov. 9¹⁰ᶠ· : " The fear of the Lord is the beginning of wisdom : and the knowledge of the holy is understanding. For by me thy days shall be multiplied, and the years of thy life shall be increased. If thou be wise, thou shalt be wise for thyself : but if thou scornest, thou alone shalt bear it." Lady Folly, on the other hand, is " clamorous, simple and knoweth nothing " (9¹³). She obviously bases her message on the assumption : " Whoso is simple, let him turn in hither " (9¹⁶), and failure to understand life is what she brings to the man whom she invites into her house : " But he knoweth not that the dead are there ; and that her guests are in the depths of hell " (9¹⁸). The " sum of the matter " at the close of Ecclesiastes is in similar terms : " Fear God, and keep his commandments : for this is the whole duty of man. For God shall bring every work into judgment, with every secret thing, whether it be good, or whether it be evil " (Eccl. 12¹³ᶠ·). What is the meaning of all this ? Divine wisdom is obviously the meaning and ground of creation and therefore of the sphere in which man can live. The whole art of living and understanding life consists in heeding and accepting divine wisdom and in this way becoming wise. But what is this heeding and accepting of the divine wisdom which distinguishes the wise man from the fool and which alone promises the possibility of life in this sphere ? It is here that we have the apparent μετάβασις εἰς ἄλλο γένος which differentiates the Old Testament from all Greek teaching about wisdom. For this heeding and accepting in the fear of God, which alone can save and maintain, consists in an attitude to the divine wisdom active in the creating, ruling and sustaining of the world which is determined by the fact that this wisdom is at the same time holy and just, that it is the meaning and the basis of God's patience with man. The wisdom which man must strive to attain and which is required of him according to the Old Testament is an attitude which corresponds with this divine wisdom. For the further elucidation of this matter, notice that we have the same saying in Ps. 111¹⁰ : " The fear of the Lord is the beginning of wisdom : a good understanding have all they that do his commandments : his praise endureth for ever." But here the exhortation forms the conclusion of a recalling of the works of God which have taken place and still take place in His covenant with His people : " He sent redemption unto his people : he hath commanded his covenant for ever : holy and reverend is his name " (v. 9). If to fear this Lord is the beginning of wisdom, His wisdom is obviously something very different from an abstract world principle and the recognition of it. Similarly the human wisdom corresponding to it is very different from abstract assent to a particular explanation of the universe. On the contrary, it is settled that He and He alone is the world principle who in His revelation to Israel acts as the holy and righteous One. And the only world-explanation lies in the recognition that in the world we are given space and ground to learn how to live in the presence of this holy and righteous One and in covenant with Him a life which is in keeping with His being revealed in the establishment and execution of this covenant, to the end that we might thus live the only possible life. In Job 28 the possibility is unambiguously eliminated which has sometimes been (falsely) detected in the famous passage in Proverbs 8 : the conception of an immanent divine wisdom accessible to and recognisable by man of himself. We are given a concrete picture of man's ability to extract silver and gold and iron and brass from the bowels of the earth : " There is a path which no fowl knoweth, and which the vulture's eye hath not seen : the lion's whelps have not trodden it, nor the fierce lion passed by it. He putteth forth his hand upon the rocks ; he overturneth the mountains by the roots. He cutteth out rivers among the rocks ; and his eye seeth every precious thing. He bindeth the floods from overflowing ; and the thing that is hid bringeth he forth to light " (Job 28⁷⁻¹¹). But it is very different with divine wisdom : " But where shall wisdom be found ? and where is the place of understanding ? Man knoweth not the price thereof ; neither is it found in the land of the living. The depth saith, It is not in me : and the sea saith, It is not with me. It cannot be gotten for gold, neither shall silver be weighed for the price thereof. It cannot be valued with the gold of Ophir, with the precious onyx, or the sapphire " (Job. 28⁷ᶠ·). In short, it cannot be possessed by man as in the last analysis all other treasures can be possessed by him. " Whence then cometh wisdom ? and where is the place of understanding ? Seeing it is hid from the eyes of all living, and kept close from the fowls of the air. Destruction and death say, We have heard the fame thereof with our ears. God understandeth the way thereof, and he knoweth the place thereof. For he looketh to the ends of the earth, and seeth under the whole heaven " (Job 28$^{20f.}$). And this leads to the conclusion already quoted : " And unto man he said, Behold, the fear of the Lord, that is wisdom ; and to depart from evil is understanding " (v. 28).

From this point of view it is necessary, but only from this point of view is it possible, to see why in the Old Testament the reference to the unfathomable wisdom of God is adduced as a proof of the impossibility, and therefore the utter folly, of all idolatry. If the wisdom of God and therefore God Himself could be known by man in the created world, if the flood, the sea, the deep and death disclosed to him what according to Job 28 they do not disclose, if there were not concealed from the eyes of all living creatures that which according to Job 28 is concealed, there would be no real reason why the adoration of God in images of all kinds should not be a justifiable and even necessary result of this natural knowledge of God. But the Old Testament says, quite rightly from its own standpoint, that all idolatry is folly. It is not of course sin, but only sin in the sense of folly. It is the work of those who do not understand life—not the work of the worldly wise, but the work of fools, of those who utterly fail to appreciate the only possible ground on which man can exist, viz., the recognition of God as Creator, Sustainer and Lord of the world. For they foolishly imagine that they can find the place of understanding just as men find the place of gold or brass in the hills. " Who hath measured the waters in the hollow of his hand, and meted out the heaven with the span, and comprehended the dust of the earth in a measure, and weighed the mountains in scales, and the hills in a balance ? Who hath directed the Spirit of the Lord, or being his counsellor hath taught him ? With whom took he counsel, or who instructed him, and taught him in the path of judgment and taught him knowledge, and shewed to him the way of understanding ? Behold, the nations are as a drop of a bucket, and are counted as the small dust of the balance " (Is. 40$^{12f.}$). " To whom then will ye liken God ? or what likeness will ye compare unto him ? " (v. 18). " Have ye not known ? have ye not heard ? hath it not been told you from the beginning ? have ye not understood from the foundations of the earth ? It is he that sitteth upon the circle of the earth, and the inhabitants thereof are as grasshoppers ; that stretcheth out the heavens as a curtain, and spreadeth them out as a tent to dwell in. . . . To whom then will ye liken me, or shall I be equal ? saith the Holy One. Lift up your eyes on high, and behold who hath created these things, that bringeth out their host by number : he calleth them all by names by the greatness of his might, for that he is strong in power ; not one faileth " (v. 21ff.). From this point of view, because God is this unfailing and perfect Creator, Sustainer and Lord of all that is, it is obviously impossible to go back to the work of heathen craftsmen and goldsmiths. For this reason, too, there are no images of God. From this standpoint—that of the true knowledge of God the Creator—there is only the way forward to confidence in Him who discloses Himself and gives Himself to be known as Creator, not in His creation in general, but in His spiritual and merciful dealings with Israel. " Why sayest thou, O Jacob, and speakest, O Israel, My way is hid from the Lord, and my judgment is passed over from my God ? Hast thou not known, hast thou not heard, that the everlasting God, the Lord, the Creator of the ends of the earth, fainteth not, neither is weary ? there is no searching of his understanding. He giveth power to the faint, and to them that have no might he increaseth strength. Even the youths shall faint and be weary, and the young men shall utterly fall : but they that wait upon the Lord shall renew their strength ; they shall mount up with wings as eagles ; they shall run and not be weary ; they shall walk, and not faint " (v. 27 ff.). We started with the confession and worship of God as the real and only source of wisdom in and above all that He has created. We then moved to the knowledge of His unfathomableness and incomparableness and therefore His transcendence of all images. We have now reached the knowledge of Him at the place where He has permitted Himself to be heard by Israel, His recognition as the One who as the Creator and Lord of all things has not forgotten but vindicates, saves and strengthens Israel—and conversely, as the One who, remembering and vindicating and saving and strengthening Israel, is also the Creator and Lord of all things. From the one point to the other it is a direct path in Is. 40. These things are all a unity in the Old Testament knowledge of God, and in order to attain this insight we have only to leave it in its original unity and accept it as expressed in this text, and of course others too (for example, we find the same sequence of thought in Jer. 10$^{1-16}$). The place where we discover the wisdom of God, the place where it really exists and is known in the fear of God, is, if we give due weight to the Old Testament witness in its context and specific utterances, the place where God gives Himself to be recognised as Creator, Sustainer and Lord of the world. And that place is His holy and righteous, gracious and merciful dealings with Israel.

The new truth imparted by the concept of wisdom as compared with those of grace and holiness, mercy and righteousness, or rather its special contribution to the clarifying of these other ideas, is that God is not the slave of His patience when in the dealings of which these other ideas speak He gives Himself time, and also gives us time, and therefore allows space and ground as the Creator, Sustainer and Lord of the world. What moves Him to exercise patience is His holy and righteous, gracious and merciful meaning, His will to unfold to us this meaning, to lead us to penitence, and therefore to make our own lives meaningful. This meaning behind His patience is His wisdom. It is the wisdom of His being and His works. And as the wisdom of His works it is world-wisdom properly understood. It is the philosophy of the created universe and the philosophy of human life. This " philosophy " is certainly not to be derived from reflection upon the universe or upon the being of man. It can be appreciated only by the bearing of God's own Word which as such gives us the right philosophy of the universe and of our own human life. In this connexion it should be clear at once that the testimony to God's wisdom in the Old and New Testaments is not a divided but a united testimony. We shall not, therefore, be surprised to read in Col. 2^3 that in the mystery of God called Christ "are hid all the treasures of wisdom and knowledge," and in 1 Cor. 1^{30} that Jesus Christ is made not only our justification, sanctification and redemption, but with a special emphasis our wisdom : ὅς ἐγενήθη σοφία ἡμῖν ἀπὸ θεοῦ. That Jesus Christ is the meaning of God's patience is the result at which we have really arrived in discussing the perfection of the divine patience.

" The divine wisdom is the principle which orders and determines the world for the divine self-communication active in our redemption " (Schleiermacher, *Der Chr. Glaube*, § 168). This separation between the divine self-communication and a special principle ordering and fashioning the world to that end is untenable. " All things were made by him ; and without him was not anything made that was made " (Jn. 1³). The definition must be corrected to read as follows : " The divine wisdom is the divine self-communication ordering and determining the world for itself."

The Old Testament has already in King Solomon a supremely wise man, endowed by God Himself with wisdom, and therefore made the image and exponent of God's own wisdom upon earth. Tradition has unanimously ascribed to him the wisdom teaching of the third part of the Canon. We are told in I Kings 4²⁹ᶠ· that God gave him " wisdom and understanding exceeding much, and largeness of heart, even as the sand that is on the sea-shore. And Solomon's wisdom excelled the wisdom of all the children of the east country, and all the wisdom of Egypt. For he was wiser than all men." " And he spake of trees, from the cedar tree that is in Lebanon even unto the hyssop that springeth out of the wall : he spake also of beasts, and of fowl, and of creeping things, and of fishes." We read in I Kings 10¹ᶠ· how the queen of Sheba heard of his fame and came to him to prove him with riddles. " And when she was come to Solomon, she communed with him all that was in her heart. And Solomon told her all her questions : there was not any thing hid from the king, which he told her not." And because at God's offer : " What shall I give thee ? " he had asked for wisdom and not for long life, wealth or the life of his enemies, God granted him also what he had not asked for. " Riches and honour : so that there shall not be any among the kings like unto thee all thy days " (I Kings 3⁴ᶠ·). His wisdom thus became manifest in his wealth, in the splendour of his palace and of the temple built by him, in the whole earthly brilliance of his kingdom. We recognise at once the connexion which we have met already in the Book of Proverbs. Human wisdom means the art of living. The wise man as distinct from the fool knows how to make a use of his life and of the whole universe which is in harmony with its creation and preservation by God and therefore meaningful, rich in promise and redemptive. The man who makes this use of his life and of the universe can and will live, and, as the life of Solomon shows, he will do so in unparalleled fulness and dazzling splendour. But there emerges from the Solomon story of the First Book of Kings a second point beyond that of the wisdom teaching of the Ketubim. This is that human wisdom of this kind is not a possibility which man can intrinsically realise. It is a gift of God which has to be sought. It springs from a special divine grace and favour. And as a wonderful divine gift of grace it acquires at once in the human sphere an unparalleled expression and brilliance which casts everything else into the shade. Therefore, and above all, the wisdom of Solomon is not a kind of knowledge or worldly shrewdness which has its meaning and purpose in itself, or in the existence of the individual Solomon. On the contrary, as recorded in I Kings 3⁷ᶠ·, Solomon's prayer for wisdom, which was so richly answered, is as follows : " And now, O Lord my God, thou hast made thy servant king instead of David my father : and I am but a little child : I know not how to go out or come in. And thy servant is in the midst of thy people which thou hast chosen, a great people, that cannot be numbered nor counted for multitude. Give therefore thy servant an understanding heart to judge thy people, that I may discern between good and bad : for who is able to judge this thy so great a people ? " The wisdom of Solomon is not, then, a private wisdom, but a public, official wisdom of kingship and government. In a remarkable inversion of what, according to Gen. 3⁵, was the sinful private desire of Adam at the suggestion of the serpent, it consists (cf. also Is. 7¹⁵) in a gift which marks the competent judge, the power of discrimination between good and evil, the possession of the criterion which the ruler of a people needs to establish justice and peace in his kingdom. What this criterion is, is seen from the singular story of Solomon's judgment (I Kings 3¹⁶ᶠ·) which follows directly upon this prayer and its answer. Which of the two women who appear before Solomon's seat of judgment is the mother of the living child ? The answer is—the one who would rather give up the possession of it than sacrifice its life. Solomon judges that she is in the right and to her the child is now awarded. On the other hand, the woman is in the wrong who would rather sacrifice the child's life than renounce the claim to its possession. What is the meaning of this story ? In fact it is the people of God who are being judged here. Two mothers, that is, two peoples, are secretly hidden and must again and again be distinguished in its midst. The one cherishes a living, the other a dead hope. But which is the one, which the other people ? This question and the divine answer to it is the red thread which runs through the whole of the history of Israel. Does not the people with the dead hope constantly lay claim to have a living hope ? Does it not stealthily creep into the possession of this hope, self-confidently refusing to renounce its claim and passing itself off as the true people of God ? And how does the other stand, which is the true people of the living hope, but cannot prove its possession ? Well, God knows, and King Solomon, endowed by Him with wisdom, will declare, what is good and evil ! Between the two peoples comes the threat that even the living hope will become dead ; there will be an utter end of Israel. The decision might be carried out at once in this terrible way. But the threat of this frightful decision, the sword already drawn against the living child, the threatened destruction of the living hope of Israel, is only Solomon's means of bringing to light right and wrong in his people, and therefore between the two peoples contained in his people. For now it is shown that the people of the dead hope looks on indifferently at the imminent destruction of the living hope to which it had falsely laid claim and still lays claim. In face of this threat the people of the living hope wills only one thing : may the fulfilment of the hope come to whomsoever it will, may the false pretender enjoy it, so long as it only remains and remains alive. The people vindicated in Solomon's judgment is the people which would rather resign its just claim, which would rather renounce the possibility of experiencing salvation, than renounce the life of hope itself ; which would choose hell rather than impiety. It is the people of motherly love which loves not itself in the child but the child for its own sake. And it is revealed in face of the drawn sword as the people which in fact has the true claim to the living hope, as the people to which this hope properly belongs, and which will not have to be deprived for ever of its salvation. This, then, is Solomon's wisdom. This is how it rules in the midst of God's people. This is the criterion which it knows and applies—the living child as a question concerning the true mother, the living hope as a question concerning the true people of God. Solomon's wisdom knows and decides that the true people of God will reveal itself and be known as such in the fact that the living hope in God is dearer to it than its own life. And for that reason it will always retain this hope.

Jesus Christ, who is greater than Solomon (Mt. 12⁴²), stands in the midst of the people of God with all the wisdom of Solomon, and indeed as its embodiment. Again, and this time critically, the question is asked : Which is the true mother ? Again the threat appears—will it again be divisive and decisive ? Again it is possible—and in the strict sense inevitable—that neither is right, i.e., that they are all mothers only of a dead child. Again the wisdom of Solomon, which is divine, pursues a different course. But a greater than Solomon is indeed here. For now the sword is not only drawn. It strikes. The Judge Himself suffers Himself to be both the dead child, the annihilated hope of Israel, and also the true mother bereft of her child, the Israel that has lost all hope. He does so in order that as the sacrificed victim (crucified but risen from the dead on the third day) He may be the living hope which wills to be loved in faith for its own sake, but which rightly belongs to all those who believe, who, like the mother of the child, protest and maintain and desire only that He should live, that He should be always who He is, and who for the sake of this desire are justified. The action of Jesus Christ as King of His people is that as the Judge who pronounces and fulfils this threat, but also as the mother and child who must suffer its fulfilment, He continually looks for faith in Himself, continually distinguishing and separating as justified those who have faith in Him. For them and for all of us there remains the threat, the drawn sword, the sword that has not yet smitten or that smites no longer. The only course open to us all, if we wish to be vindicated and revealed as God's people, is that of faith in Him, the faith in which He Himself will necessarily be dearer and more precious and more significant for us than any claim and expectation we might have in Him for ourselves, the faith which does not find its object in itself but in Him. Again, in faith in Him we retain that which we cannot even try to procure for ourselves as we believe in Him : our justification, our membership of the true people of God, and therefore the promise of life for time and eternity. As we subordinate ourselves to Jesus Christ in faith, or rather as He subordinates Himself to us by giving Himself to us as the object of our faith, He is made unto us wisdom (1 Cor. 1³⁰). Under the patience of God which is shown us for His sake, and in the time which is granted us for His sake, He is the meaning of this patience and this time—He Himself present with us and making us wise as well.

It is from this standpoint that we must read the whole argument of 1 Cor. 1¹⁸⁻²¹⁰. This tells us that the Word of the cross is foolishness to them that are perishing but the power of God to them that are being saved (v. 18). How is this ? Because the foolish are without faith in Him and therefore do not belong to the true people of God, they can obviously see in the news of the death of Jesus Christ (either with or without that of His resurrection, and even more so with it) only the news of a further demonstration of the meaninglessness of human life; and probably indeed the proclamation of the paradox that the meaninglessness revealed here too is as such its true meaning. So then, as is described in Acts 17³², they turn away in impatience or alarm from this foolish Gospel. But they do not realise that by doing this, and by making this judgment, they are already condemned, exposed and revealed as the mother of the dead child. For what happens when they pass this judgment ? " For it is written, I will destroy the wisdom of the wise, and will bring to nothing the understanding of the prudent " (v. 19, Is. 29¹⁴). What happens, then, is simply that in this judgment they and their wisdom are superseded and destroyed and eliminated. This is what is revealed and confirmed when they consider this news to be folly. " Where is the wise ? where is the scribe ? where is the disputer of this world ? (v. 20a). There is none. By the very fact of what God has done through this Gospel He has made *tabula rasa* of all that is published in the world as wisdom but is not. " God has made foolish the wisdom of this world " (v. 20b). Whatever this wisdom may be in itself, confronted with what God has done in this Gospel it is clear that it is assuredly not what it claims to be, the art of living, worldly wisdom, but the exact opposite. For what happened at this point ? Διὰ τῆς σοφίας, applying its own supposed wisdom, the world failed to recognise God ἐν τῇ σοφίᾳ αὐτοῦ, i.e., where His wisdom actually was and acted and revealed itself. But it pleased God by the supposed folly of this preaching to save them that believe (v. 21) : by the preaching of the crucified Christ, unto the Jews a stumbling-block, unto the Greeks foolishness ; but unto them which are called, both Jews and Greeks, not only the power of God, but also the wisdom of God (v. 23 f.). Even this supposed folly of God is in fact wiser than men—so much wiser as Solomon was wiser than all men—and even this supposed weakness of God is in fact stronger than men (v. 25). For this reason, it is not a bad sign for the Church, but an indication of the genuineness of its calling, that not many wise after the flesh, not many mighty, not many noble are in it. In keeping with the presumed folly of this Gospel, God has chosen the so-called foolish ones of this world to confound the wisdom of the wise, the weak to confound the strong, the trivial and contemptible, the things that are not (τὰ μὴ ὄντα) to bring to nothing those that are (ἵνα τὰ ὄντα καταργήσῃ), in order that it may be manifest that no flesh can glory in His presence (vv. 26-29). From this God, in whose presence no flesh can glory, Christians have their life in Jesus Christ : ἐξ αὐτοῦ δὲ ὑμεῖς ἐστε ἐν Χριστῷ Ἰησοῦ. They have it by the power of His resurrection from the dead. Therefore, on the one hand, they clearly participate in the supposed folly, weakness and contemptibility of the divine action which has taken place in Jesus Christ. They must be content, with Jesus Christ, i.e., with God Himself, as His children, to fall under the judgment of that Greek world. But for this very reason, they participate, on the other hand, in the triumph of real divine wisdom over the false human wisdom from which this judgment stems—a judgment which can only reveal the actual folly of this wisdom. For them, Jesus Christ the Crucified, in whom they have their being from God, as God's children, has been made by God Himself by His resurrection, not only justification, sanctification and redemption, but also and above all wisdom (v. 30), in order that in them may be fulfilled the words of Jer. 9²³ff. : " He that glorieth, let him glory in the Lord." The exact wording of the passage runs : " Let not the wise man glory in his wisdom, neither let the mighty man glory in his might, let not the rich man glory in his riches : but let him that glorieth glory in this, that he understandeth and knoweth me, that I am the Lord which exercise loving-kindness, judgment and righteousness, in the earth : for in these things I delight, saith the Lord." If a man boasts in the Lord, there are three reasons why he cannot at the same time boast also in his own wisdom, the human wisdom of this world. 1. Since he boasts in this other, the real wisdom of God, he has no more room for his own, human wisdom. 2. By this wisdom in which he may now glory human wisdom is for him unmasked as unwisdom, as utter and contemptible folly in his eyes. 3. He cannot wish to withdraw from his solidarity with divine wisdom even in regard to its supposed folly and the judgment to which it must be content to submit in this world.

A passing reference may be made to Mt. 11¹⁶⁻¹⁹. It describes this generation as angry with John the Baptist because of his asceticism (" He hath a devil "), and with Jesus because of His freedom from asceticism (" Behold, a man gluttonous, and a wine-bibber, a friend of publicans and sinners "). True wisdom is always different from what this generation has expected and desired, and therefore the latter, like the disappointed children in the market-place, believes itself to have reason to complain : " We have piped unto you, and ye have not danced ; we have mourned unto you, and ye have not lamented." What are the representatives of wisdom to do ? Should they accept these complaints ? Should they determine their conduct accordingly, dancing when there is piping and lamenting when there is mourning. No, but as they continue to do undeviatingly in face of these complaints what as wise men they must do, it happens that wisdom is justified and justifies itself in its works, i.e., in that which the wise as such must faithfully do : καὶ ἐδικαιώθη ἡ σοφία ἀπὸ τῶν ἔργων αὐτῆς. For the true works of wisdom are the works of its representatives so long as the latter—and what else is to be expected when they are John the Baptist and Jesus ?—will only remain faithful and obedient. They, too, do not need to look for any other justification for their works. They are justified as wisdom justifies itself in and by their works.

But this brings us back to the argument of 1 Cor. 1-2. What was Paul trying to prove by his exposition in 1¹⁸⁻³¹ ? According to the first verses of the second chapter it was simply this. He could not come among them καθ᾽ ὑπεροχὴν λόγου ἢ σοφίας (v. 1), or ἐν πειθοῖς σοφίας λόγοις (v. 4), to declare his testimony to God. He could not then, in accordance with their expectation, dance after the pipings of a human wisdom or lament after its mourning. As one whose mission it was to glory in the Lord and only in the Lord he could not please them by glorying at the same time in what was still a human wisdom. He could not declare to them the testimony of God in such form as would have been in keeping with their ambitions as children of this " generation." He could declare it to them only as it actually ran. When he was among them, he could know nothing but Jesus Christ and Him crucified (v. 2). Inevitably, then, he appeared among them in " weakness, and in fear, and in much trembling " (v. 3). His word could have only one foundation, and this of course it had : the ἀπόδειξις πνεύματος καὶ δυνάμεως (v. 4), i.e., obviously the justification of wisdom by its works which takes place whenever the work of man consists solely and supremely in the fact that he yields himself wholly as an instrument at the disposal of God's wisdom, allowing it to say unreservedly, without subtraction or addition, what it wills to say. When this happens we have the demonstration of the Spirit and of power, about the effectiveness of which no one need have any anxiety, but the effectiveness of which again cannot be replaced or completed by that of any other sort of wisdom. And this is just what took place in Corinth, to please no one and to harm no one. Nothing else could take place or could be allowed to take place. For the faith of the Corinthian Christians would not have ripened into genuine faith if Paul had tried to adduce even provisionally any other proof. He could not base his position on the wisdom of men, but only on the power of God with its self-justifying wisdom. And as far as Paul was concerned, such a foundation could be achieved only by one thing, that is, the preaching of the crucified Christ (v. 5). It is with this preaching that Paul speaks wisdom. That is, for the τέλειοι. But again, these are not, as in the mystery religions, the esoterics, the initiates of a human wisdom, who from the point of view of this preaching (1²⁰ᶠ·) could only be the most foolish of all fools. They are simply those who accept the Word of the cross in faith. Those who do this do not deceive themselves or go astray. They are no fools. They are not like the weeping children in the market-place. They do not adopt the judgment of folly, or determine their conduct accordingly. The demonstration of the Spirit and of power has become effective with them because they are wise enough to hear wisdom where fools think to hear folly and, because they are fools, can in fact only hear folly. Certainly what those who are righteous in faith hear when they hear the Word of the cross is not the wisdom of the world, nor the higher wisdom of those angelic powers which are at present the rulers of this world, the ἄρχοντες τοῦ αἰῶνος τούτου (v. 6). But what Paul proclaims only by the Word of the cross, and what they hear, is God's own wisdom : His wisdom which in this mystery (that of the cross of Jesus Christ) is just as concealed (for the world) as it is revealed (for believers) ; the wisdom which before all worlds God has appointed and foreseen for our glorification, as it has already served, and will further serve, to this end in the resurrection of Christ, by which He was made wisdom for us. For this is already our glorification. We already have actually and visibly something of the splendour of Solomon. We live here and now with all joy and gladness in Solomon's temple. For by the resurrection of Christ we have received our life from God as life in Him, the risen Lord. He has been made wisdom for us, God's children, and we ourselves may now be wise in faith. We ! For this wisdom is not only a wisdom apart, alien to all the human wisdom of this world as such, and to that extent, where there is no faith, alien to all who live within it. Not only is all human wisdom unmasked and compromised by its judgment that as so-called wisdom it is folly, and supreme folly in those who justly perhaps can boast that they are perfect in this human wisdom. It is also alien to the higher or supreme wisdom of the angelic powers which rule this world and humanity. Obviously these too have incurred condemnation. For as represented by the governmental authority of the Roman state, they shared in the rejection and murder of Jesus Christ. If they had been alive to the wisdom of God at the point where it lived and spoke, not merely in the form of testimony, but in its original reality ; if they had been receptive of the demonstration of the Spirit and of power as it was given, not in the form of the apostolic word, but by the incarnate Word itself, " they would not have crucified the Lord of glory " (v. 8). They would have been wise enough to perceive His glory, the glory of divine wisdom as such. But they did not do so. It was they who in the last analysis crucified Jesus Christ. There is therefore all the less reason why Paul, in his witness to God, should consult the desires and expectations, the piping and mourning of any kind of human wisdom, and thus give his Gospel any other form than that in which it has clothed itself : the form of the Word of the cross. He must be content with the demonstration of the Spirit and of power, with the self-justification of divine wisdom in face of all the folly of men, as it takes place and will continually take place in the preaching of this Word. It is in this way that the Word of the cross becomes for those who are being saved the power of God—that God has prepared for those who love Him what eye hath not seen, nor ear heard, nor the human heart conceived (v. 9). What is this ? In the wider context it is undoubtedly the revelation of the secret of the cross of Christ and therefore of the wisdom of God predestined and applied to us from all eternity for our future and indeed our present glory. This wisdom of His in its eternally concrete expression is what eye has not seen, nor ear heard, nor the human heart conceived. And God has revealed it to us by the Spirit : ἡμῖν γὰρ ἀπεκάλυψεν ὁ θεὸς διὰ τοῦ πνεύματος (v. 10).

It is evident that even in this New Testament context the wisdom of God is identical with the administrative and judicial wisdom of Solomon which awards to each what is properly appropriate. Folly to fools who do not have so great a love for wisdom that for the sake of it they prefer to be regarded as fools in their own eyes and in the eyes of the world ; and wisdom to the wise whose love of wisdom is such that for the sake of it they are prepared to be able to glory only in the Lord and no longer in their own human wisdom. Folly to fools who in applying and exercising their own presumed wisdom do not hesitate, but are in fact compelled to destroy genuine wisdom, thus revealing their own real folly ; and wisdom to the wise, for whom and in whom, contrary to any ostensible wisdom of their own, the wisdom of God is itself at work—alive, vindicating and justifying itself, as genuine wisdom, the wisdom of God, can and does. But in distinction from the Old Testament picture, or rather supplementing and clarifying it, we find that the three main aspects of the wisdom of God in Solomon's judgment are united in the New Testament presentation of the divine mystery called Jesus Christ. For He is (1) wisdom as the judge, alone knowing, deciding and disposing in sovereign power ; (2) wisdom as the object of accusation and counter-accusation, rejected and destroyed, and yet ever living ; (3) wisdom as the fulfilment of the verdict, imparting itself to the wise and denying itself to fools.

According to the New Testament God is the μόνος σοφός (Rom. 16²⁷, 1 Tim. 1¹⁷) in such a way that His wisdom coincides with His holiness and righteousness, and the recognition of it, i.e., man's attainment of wisdom, with his winning through to faith. That is why Paul can speak as he does (Eph. 3⁸ᶠ·, cf. Col. 1²⁵ᶠ·) about the meaning of his apostolate. It is laid upon him to bring to light the economy (the order or structure) of the mystery eternally concealed in God, the Creator of all things, " to the intent that (ἵνα) now unto the principalities and powers (ἀρχαί and ἐξουσίαι) in heavenly places might be known by the church the manifold wisdom of God (πολυποίκιλος σοφία τοῦ θεοῦ) according to the eternal purpose which he purposed in Christ Jesus our Lord." In accordance with this Paul had already told the Church in Eph. 1⁷ᶠ· : In the riches of His grace exercised in our redemption through the blood of Christ and in the forgiveness of our sins, God has abounded toward us ἐν πάσῃ σοφίᾳ καὶ φρονήσει, for He has made known to us the mystery of His will which is to gather together all things in heaven and on earth in Christ as their Head—their Representative and recapitulation, their core and substance (ἀνακεφαλαιώσασθαι). He had also prayed in Eph. 1¹⁷ᶠ· (cf. Col. 1⁹) that " the God of our Lord Jesus Christ, the Father of glory, may give unto you the spirit of wisdom and revelation in the knowledge of him : the eyes of your understanding being enlightened ; that you may know what is the hope of his calling." He also invites them later in Eph. 5¹⁵ to walk ἀκριβῶς, " not as fools, but as wise " ; or, as we have it in the parallel in Col. 4⁵, " to walk in wisdom toward them that are without." Paul understands his own task to be that of preaching Christ the hope of glory and therefore instructing and warning every man in all wisdom and presenting him perfect (τέλειον) in Christ (Col. 1²⁸). In Colossians and Ephesians wisdom is plainly enough identified with Jesus Christ Himself. But exactly the same wisdom is meant in James 3¹³ᶠ·. The question is asked : " Who is a wise man and endued with knowledge among you ? " and the answer is that he will show it by walking ἐν πραΰτητι σοφίας. Again, in Jas. 3¹⁷ᶠ· the wisdom which is from above is described as " first pure, then peaceable, gentle, and easy to be intreated, full of mercy and good fruits, without partiality, and without hypocrisy." Again, in Jas. 1⁵ᶠ· the man who lacks this wisdom is exhorted to pray to God for it in faith. It is instructive to see that the freedom from doubt, which in 3¹⁷ is a criterion of the wisdom for which we have to pray in faith (1⁵ᶠ·), is defined in this latter passage with great emphasis as the fundamental determination of faith and therefore of a right prayer for wisdom. Wisdom to the wise ! this rule clearly applies here, as it did in the case of Solomon, who had to be already wise in order to pray for wisdom, and in that of Jesus Himself, of whom Lk. 2⁴⁰, ⁵² does not tell us that He received wisdom or became wise, but that He " increased " in wisdom and stature and in favour with God and man. It is clear that in all these New Testament passages wisdom is nothing more nor less than God Himself turning to man in grace and mercy, God in His love but also in His freedom, in the fulness of His love but also in the fulness of His freedom.

The observation with which we opened our discussion of the wisdom teaching of the Old Testament may be repeated in relation to that of the New. It is perhaps a stumbling-block that here too the concept of wisdom is explicitly mentioned only in a relatively small part of the Canon. And there can be no real objection to the historical explanation that—as in the case of Israel's encounter with older Hellenism—this was the necessary consequence of the contact and conflict of the New Testament community with the philosophical and religious movements which gave rise to so-called *Gnosis*. But it should be carefully noted how radically critical this contact was, and how completely the conceptual material perhaps received in the course of this contact was assimilated to the apostolic testimony, not weakening or transforming but underlining and sharpening the Christian message when assumed into the context of other concepts and viewpoints and applied, of course, only in this context—I know of no passage where it could be said to be broken or even disturbed. But whatever may be our attitude to the historical question, there can be no doubt that in the New Testament Canon, as in that of the Old Testament, the wisdom teaching has become an integral part of the apostolic preaching. Paul would not be Paul without 1 Cor. 1-2, and the whole context of Colossians and Ephesians would disintegrate if for some reason it were desired to remove this stone from the edifice. Jesus Christ, our righteousness, sanctification and redemption, is also our wisdom, and faith in Him is our instruction by the wisdom of God. In substance, the witness of John's Gospel is the same, although surprisingly it avoids the use of the term as such. Instead, more penetratingly than any other New Testament document, it brings faith and knowledge into juxtaposition and conjunction.

THE PERFECTIONS OF THE DIVINE FREEDOM

The divinity of the freedom of God consists and confirms itself in the fact that in Himself and in all His works God is One, constant and eternal, and therewith also omnipresent, omnipotent and glorious.

I. THE UNITY AND OMNIPRESENCE OF GOD

We are not turning to any new object, nor are we opening a new volume, if we now turn our attention to the perfections of the divine freedom. We have already spoken about the divine freedom as we spoke about the divine love. We were not able to speak about the latter without continually glancing over to the divine freedom. In speaking of God's holiness, righteousness and wisdom, we have already anticipated in the true sense the content of this second part of the doctrine of the being of God. For it was simply the recollection of the divine freedom which forced us to keep before our eyes particularly God's holiness beside His grace, His righteousness beside His mercy, and His wisdom beside His patience, thus establishing, safeguarding and clarifying the fact that we were not speaking of any kind of grace, mercy and patience but of the divine grace, mercy and patience. The divine nature of God's love consists and confirms itself in the fact that in His very love God is free and therefore in His very grace, mercy and patience He is holy, righteous and wise.

We have now to consider this cohesion, this unity of the being of God from its other side as well. Our thinking now moves in some sense in the opposite direction. We now begin at the point at which we continually ended in the previous section. We now start from the divine freedom. We put this second in correspondence with the order of the divine life. We have seen, however, that this order does not imply a subordination. God's freedom is no less divine than His love. God's freedom is divine as the freedom in which God expresses His love. The opposite is also true. God's love is divine as the love which is free. This entitles and requires us to take His freedom just as seriously, and, as we now consider His being in this second way, to start from His freedom with no less seriousness than we did before from His love. Again, we are already aware that God's freedom does not exist alone by itself. All the time, then, we shall have to remember His love as we now turn to His freedom. Necessarily, therefore, in this second part of the doctrine of the being of God we must recapitulate the first part both implicitly and explicitly. Whatever was perceived and expressed there must always accompany and be present with us. Our recollection of the divine love will require us here as well to consider our subject in two ways. This time they will both be directed to God's freedom, but the second in such a way that it reminds us of the cohesion and unity of God's freedom with His love, thus establishing, safeguarding and clarifying the fact that it is not with any kind of freedom but with the divine freedom that we have to do. The divine nature of God's freedom consists and confirms itself in the fact that even in His freedom, as the One who is free, God is the One who loves. God is One. He is constant and eternal in Himself and in all His works. This is His freedom. This is His majesty and sovereign power. This will be our first concern at each point in this second part of the doctrine of His being. But it is in no accidental or arbitrarily determined way that God is free, majestic and sovereign. It is in a manner wholly determined by Himself. He is, therefore, One in such a way that He is omnipresent, constant in such a way that He is omnipotent, and eternal in such a way that He is glorious. His freedom is the freedom of His love. As we speak of His omnipresence, omnipotence and glory, we glance back again from His freedom to His love, and therefore—in this context—to His divinity. The divinity of His freedom consists and confirms itself in the fact that even in His unity He is omnipresent, in His constancy omnipotent, and in His eternity glorious. This fact is the criterion of the divinity of all the perfections of His freedom.

The question may be raised again at this point how we come to mention these six attributes of the divine freedom in this particular juxtaposition. And again we have to acknowledge that we certainly cannot rely on, or appeal to, any direct (or verbal) precept of Holy Scripture or even to the precedent of any other dogmatics. We have to admit that basically this selection and juxtaposition can possess and claim only the character of an attempt or suggestion. In the light of the biblical witness to revelation—not of some general idea of the being of God—we are asking two questions. First, what are the specific determinations in which the love of God attested in the Bible becomes event and reality in the freedom of God, so that we can and must see them as determinations of His being ? The answer to this first question is given by the series : unity, constancy and eternity. And second—again in the light of the biblical witness to revelation—what are the specific determinations of this love itself in so far as it is the love which becomes event and reality in His freedom, so that we can and must understand these determinations as those of the divine being ? The second series, omnipresence, omnipotence and glory, is the answer to this question. It may now be seen that the questions are the same in substance as those asked at the beginning of the previous section, only now they have been put in the opposite order. We could not ask any others because, keeping to the same source, we have to speak about the same God, the One who loves in His freedom, and therefore the same love and the same freedom, which occupied us earlier as the context of the biblical witness to God. Our selection and juxtaposition of attributes is supported by no previous authority, so that whether it is correct and satisfactory, a significant and serviceable attempt and suggestion, is a question which can be answered, as previously, only by the presentation itself, or its relation to the biblical witness to God. Thus the question must be thrown straight back at the one who raised it. Anyone who wishes to object to the selection and juxtaposition here proposed can do so only by himself making another attempt and suggestion which corrects the inevitable defects and deficiencies. And it must not be forgotten that the unavoidable schematic form here in evidence is only a means to an end. On no account should it attract independent attention, for example on account of the symbolic numbers 2, 3 and 12. Our purpose, now as previously, is to give " the most fully concrete answer to the question : Who and what is God ? i.e., the answer which most faithfully follows and corresponds to the object in its self-manifestation." This is the only purpose to be served by a development of concepts which is as well ordered and clear as possible. Its opposite, a chaotic or riotous presentation, would certainly not be worthy of this purpose, and presumably, therefore, could not serve it.

We begin with the unity of God. All the perfections of God's freedom can be summed up by saying that God is One. And to this extent all the perfections of His love, real and operative in His freedom, and all the perfections of the divine being taken together, can be summed up in this one conception. If we understand it rightly, we can express all that God is by saying that God is One. By this He differentiates Himself from everything that is distinct from Himself. By this He rules and determines it, and by this He is also in Himself what He is. He is One. The word oneness has two meanings. It can mean both uniqueness (*singularitas*) and simplicity (*simplicitas*). As a statement about God it must in fact mean both, and we shall have to deal with both under the one heading.

First we take unity in the sense of uniqueness. What is meant when we say that it belongs to God to be unique ? Naturally not that He alone exists. The world He has created also exists. But God alone is God. He is the only one of His kind. There is not another God, either a second god or many gods. We cannot fail to recognise the fundamental character of the statement that God is One when we use the word in this first sense. From the beginning the Church understood the prophetic and apostolic testimony in such a way that in its confession of faith, in which it responded to that testimony, it had to say first and foremost that He whom this testimony calls God, and whose revelation and work are to be found in this testimony, is One, a unique being, this unique being. A being which was not unique, and not this unique being, would not be God. For this reason any so-called or would-be God which has a second god alongside it is bound to be a false god or no god. The very moment we conceive of a second person or thing of the same kind as God, even if it possesses only one attribute of the divine being, we cease to think of God as God. It is He alone who lives. It is He alone who loves. He alone is gracious, merciful and wise. He alone is holy, righteous and patient. And

He alone is also free, with all that this involves. To be one and unique is true only of Him in the sense proper to Him. For it is only in Him that everything (including uniqueness) is essential, original, proper, and for this reason also creative, so that now it can all belong to other forms of being also in a created, dependent, derived and improper way. In comparison with everything else, God is unique—as who He is and what He is—while everything else is what it is by Him, and therefore only dependently, in a contingent and figurative sense, and therefore not in a way that competes with God. Whatever its nature and mode of existence, it is not God. It cannot stand beside Him as a second of His kind or a multiple of His kind. Thus the knowledge of God, the God attested in His revelation by prophets and apostles, means that all so-called or would-be deities and divinities apart from Him lose their character as gods. The faith and worship offered to them cannot be taken seriously. They fade away as idols and nonentities. And so God's freedom, majesty and sovereignty shine out in His uniqueness. Knowledge of this God brings those who partake of it under a claim that is total and unlimited as regards what is divine. It isolates them unescapably. It confronts them with an exclusive demand that nothing can soften. In respect of God it sets bounds for them which they can break only by giving up the knowledge of this God. In this they experience God's love as grace, mercy and patience. They experience it as God's election in virtue of His freedom, an election in which God not only chooses them for Himself, but in doing so chooses Himself for them, and marks Himself out as the one, true and therefore unique God. They experience His love as an election in which a final decision is reached at every point regarding what is and what is not divine. The decision is reached that this God who chooses them is God alone, and that all other so-called or would-be gods are not what they claim to be. He alone is God, because all that He is and does has its significance and power and stands or falls by the fact that He is it and does it in an incomparable and unique way. There is no other like Him. He does not have to face any competition, either hostile or friendly. His Word does not need to fear any contradiction or His work any opposition, nor of course do they stand in need or are they capable of any assistance, supplementation or authorisation from any other source.

Because the Church from the beginning understood the prophetic and apostolic testimony in this way, it responded from the first with a confession of His uniqueness as a kind of primary assertion. *Quod unus est Deus* is, according to Origen, the first *species eorum quae per praedicationem apostolicam manifeste traduntur* (Περὶ ἀρχῶν I, *Praef.* 4). *Regula fidei una omnino est, sola immobilis et irreformabilis : credendi scilicet in unicum Deum* . . . (Tertullian, *De virg. vel.* 1). *Deus, si non unus est, non est* (*Adv. Marc.* 1, 3). *Neque super eum, neque post eum est aliquid ; neque ab alio motus sed sua sententia et libere fecit omnia quum sit solus Deus et solus Dominus et solus conditor et solus pater et solus continens omnia et omnibus ut sint, praestans* (Irenaeus, *Adv. o. h.* II, 1, 1). *Praeter hanc nullam credimus esse naturam vel angeli, vel spiritus, vel virtutis alicuius, quae Deus est credenda* (*Libellus in modum Symboli* [5th century ?] Denz. No. 19). God is the One *cuius nec magnitudini neque maiestati, neque virtuti quidquam, non dixerim praeferri sed nec comparari potest* (Novatian, *De trin.* 31). Knowledge of God in the sense of the New Testament message, the knowledge of the triune God as contrasted with the whole world of religions in the first centuries, signified, and still signifies, the most radical " twilight of the gods," the very thing which Schiller so movingly deplored as the de-divinisation of the " lovely world." It was no mere fabrication when the Early Church was accused by the world around it of atheism, and it would have been wiser for its apologists not to have defended themselves so keenly against this charge. There is a real basis for the feeling, current to this day, that every genuine proclamation of the Christian faith is a force disturbing to, even destructive of, the advance of religion, its life and richness and peace. It is bound to be so. Olympus and Valhalla decrease in population when the message of the God who is the one and only God is really known and believed. The figures of every religious culture are necessarily secularised and recede. They can keep themselves alive only as ideas, symbols, and ghosts, and finally as comic figures. And in the end even in this form they sink into oblivion. No sentence is more dangerous or revolutionary than that God is One and there is no other like Him. All the permanencies of the world draw their life from ideologies and mythologies, from open or disguised religions, and to this extent from all possible forms of deity and divinity. It was on the truth of the sentence that God is One that the " Third Reich " of Adolf Hitler made shipwreck. Let this sentence be uttered in such a way that it is heard and grasped, and at once 450 prophets of Baal are always in fear of their lives. There is no more room now for what the recent past called toleration. Beside God there are only His creatures or false gods, and beside faith in Him there are religions only as religions of superstition, error and finally irreligion.

There is no doubt that theoretically the ancient and medieval Church worked out the knowledge of the uniqueness of God with great clarity. But except for the significance of this for the original conflict of Christianity with paganism, and especially for the exclusion of Gnosticism, it was really the Reformation of the 16th century, above all the Calvinistic Reformation, which first brought into true focus the character of practical decision, the critical significance which belongs to this knowledge. To be sure, Thomas Aquinas (*S. theol.* I, *qu.* 3, *art.* 5 *s.c.*) had already advocated and established the statement, which is of incalculable importance for the logic of theology, that *Deus non est in aliquo genere*, because *nihil est prius Deo nec secundum rem, nec secundum intellectum*. And Anselm of Canterbury had already declared (*Monol.* 80)—in remarkable anticipation of the tendencies of the Reformation—that God is *non solum Deus sed solus Deus ineffabiliter trinus et unus, de quo solo prospera sunt operanda, ad quem solum ab adversis fugiendum, cui soli pro quavis re supplicandum*. But after the struggles of the Early Church against Gnosticism, it is the Reformation which first seriously and comprehensively makes practical application and especially critical application of this knowledge. It does this internally and not merely externally—in relation to the Church itself and the apostasy which is both possible and real within the Church. Calvin now writes : *Religio* means a binding, and the decisive content of this " binding " is : *ne aliquo transferatur quidquid in divinitatem competit*. If everything divine is not recognised, sought and honoured as the sole possession of the one God, He is robbed of His honour, and the worship apparently offered to Him is profaned (*Instit.* I, 12, 1). By demanding from Jesus (Mt. 4⁹) that He should fall down and worship him Satan showed himself to be Satan, while the angel of God (Rev. 19¹⁰) revealed himself to be an angel of God by refusing for himself the *proskynesis* which belongs only to God. *Si volumus unum Deum habere, meminerimus ne tantulum quidem ex eius gloria delibandum quin retineat, quod sibi proprium est . . . Quaecunque pietatis officia alio transferantur quam ad unicum Deum, sacrilegio non carere (ib.* 12, 3). And for this reason the *Scots Confession* begins with the weighty sentence : " We confesse and acknawledge ane onelie God, to whom only we must cleave, whom onelie we must serve, whom onelie we must worship and in whom onelie we must put our trust." Everything depends on God's not only being recognised as the One who is unique, but on His being treated in the way which is His due, as the One who is unique. Everything depends on the fear, trust, honour and service, which are His due, being given Him as the only One to whom they can possibly apply. It is to be noted that on this knowledge, i.e., the practical and critical application of this knowledge of God as the unique, the one and only God, depends the Scripture principle of the Reformers, their doctrine of justification, and especially their Christology, with all the antitheses and the positive rules for doctrine and life which this involves. Yet this knowledge must be made even more fruitful in its implications than even the Reformers made it. It is not an easy thing to apply it with the required universality.

We now turn to the other side or meaning of the assertion of the unity of God. It means also that God is simple. This signifies that in all that He is and does, He is wholly and undividedly Himself. At no time or place is He composed out of what is distinct from Himself. At no time or place, then, is He divided or divisible. He is One even in the distinctions of the divine persons of the Father, the Son and the Holy Spirit. He is One even in the real wealth of His distinguishable perfections. In specific things that He is and does, He never exists in such a way as to be apart from other things that He also always is and does. But in all other things He also is and does these specific things. And as He is and does these specific things, He also is and does all other things.

In this second sense, too, the assertion of God's unity can be called the basic proposition of the doctrine of God's freedom. Being simple in the sense described, God is incomparably free, sovereign and majestic. In this quality of simplicity are rooted, fixed and included all the other attributes of His majesty : His constancy and eternity, His omnipresence, omnipotence and glory. Nothing can affect Him, or be far from Him, or contradict or withstand Him, because in Himself there is no separation, distance, contradiction or opposition. He is Lord in every relationship, because He is the Lord of Himself, unconditionally One as Father, Son and Holy Spirit, and in the whole real wealth of His being. For every distinction of His being and working is simply a repetition and corroboration of the one being and, in the one being, of all that He was from eternity and therefore from all time, and of all that He will be in eternity and therefore for all time.

Finally, His uniqueness too is based on His simplicity. As the One who is simple, God clearly cannot without self-contradiction—and there is no such contradiction—tolerate a second or third Almighty which is equally simple and eternal. The simplicity of God means that within the Godhead there is no additional or subsequent being.

There is no God beside God. Everything that is Godhead and divine is always God Himself and therefore always the one being.

From the knowledge of the simplicity of God, it follows as a matter of course that His relation to the world cannot on any account be understood and interpreted as a combination, amalgamation or identification of God with the world. From the same standpoint there are also no effluences, emanations, effusions or irruptions of God into the world, in virtue of which, apart from God Himself, there are in a sense islands or even continents of the divine in the midst of the non-divine. We must not understand or interpret creation, or even the incarnation of the Son of God in Jesus Christ, either as a commixture or identification of God with the world, or as a kind of outgoing of God from Himself. God's creation of the world out of nothing means that He does not abandon or give His glory as Creator to anyone else. The fact that Jesus Christ is very God and very man means that in this oneness of His with the creature God does not cease for a moment or in any regard to be the one, true God. And the strength and blessedness and comfort of His work of creation as of reconciliation and revelation consists in the fact that in these works of His too He is never less than wholly Himself.

The early battle for a recognition of the simplicity of God was the same as for the recognition of the Trinity and of the relation between the divine and human natures in Jesus Christ. We can put it equally well both ways. The Church clarified its mind about the simplicity of God by means of the essential unity of the Son and the Holy Spirit with the Father, and the undivided but unconfused unity of the divine with the human nature in Jesus Christ. But it also clarified its mind about the *homoousia* of the Son and the Holy Ghost in the one divine being, and the unity of the two natures in Jesus Christ, by means of the simplicity of God. Properly considered, the two things are one. The unity of the triune God and of the Son of God with man in Jesus Christ is itself the simplicity of God. We shall have to return to the point later, but this background must not be forgotten when we find that the development of the conception in the later theology of the Church appears to be of a purely logical and metaphysical kind. For example, we read in Augustine that this is the *natura simplex: cui non sit aliquid habere, quod vel possit omittere, vel aliud sit habens aliud quod habet* (*De civ. Dei* XI, 10, 2). God is *simplex* for this reason and in this way : *quia non aliud illi est esse, aliud vivere quasi possit esse non vivens; nec aliud illi est vivere, aliud intelligere, quasi possit vivere non intelligens; nec aliud illi est intelligere, aliud beatum esse, quasi possit intelligere et non beatus esse; sed quod est illi vivere, intelligere, beatum esse, hoc est illi esse* (*ib.* VIII, 6). And Anselm of Canterbury tells us that in God is *idem quodlibet unum eorum, quod omnia sive simul sive singula* (*Monol.* 17). *Quomodo ergo, Domine, es omnia haec ? An sunt partes tui, an potius unumquodque horum totum es quod es ? Nam quicquid est partibus iunctum, non est omnino unum, sed quodammodo plura et diversum a se ipso et vel actu vel intellectu dissolvi potest: quae aliena sunt a te, quo nihil melius cogitari potest. Nullae igitur partes in te sunt, Domine, nec es plura sed sic es unum quoddam et idem tibi ipsi, ut in nullo tibi ipsi sis dissimilis; immo tu es ipsa unitas, nullo intellectu divisibilis* (*Prosl.* 18). Or using a mathematical concept : *Punctum in puncto non est nisi punctum: habet enim punctum* (understood in a spatial or temporal sense) *non nullam similitudinem non parum ad eiusdem* (God's) *aeternitatis contemplationem utilem* (*De fide trin.* 9). The older Protestant orthodoxy, too, usually adopted much the same arguments and explanations when it placed and expounded the simplicity of God first among the divine attributes. A typical example is J. Wolleb's definition : *Simplicitas est, qua Deus ens vere unum omnisque compositionis expers intelligitur* (*Chr. Theol.Comp.*, 1626, I, *cap.* 1, 3). There could be no objection to the logic, metaphysics and mathematics of these lines of thought if they had been used only to perform the service of explanation—a service which it is quite possible and even up to a point necessary to render in this way. But we cannot read these things in the older writers with unmixed joy. The trouble is that they are put at the head, and not, as we are trying to do here, in their proper turn. They thus give the impression that what is argued and considered is the general idea of an *ens vere unum* and not the God of the doctrine of the Trinity and of Christology—although this is in flat contradiction to the way in which this recognition originally forced itself on the Church. But again, if the basic concept in the doctrine of God is taken in this way, it leads to an underlying nominalism or semi-nominalism in the doctrine of the attributes, in the light of which the different perfections of God inevitably take on the colourlessness and lack of form which undoubtedly characterise this section of the older Protestant dogmatics and constitute its weakness. On the other hand, this must not be allowed to mislead us in regard to the necessity and scope of the recognition itself. We will have to give it a more distinctly biblical and therefore Christian basis than it had in the Early Church, the Middle Ages and Protestant orthodoxy. We have so far avoided the fatal consequences of a possible non-Christian basis for this recognition and we shall have to continue to do so. But we must still hold fast to the recognition itself. As we have seen, it stands on a firm foundation as a decisive designation of the freedom and therefore of the divinity of God. It is the basis of His uniqueness, the explanation of the diversity and unity of His perfections and finally the criterion for understanding His relation to the creature.

But we must now try to lay even deeper foundations for the statement that God is one, grasping its meaning even more basically, i.e., more specifically than has so far been done. We understand the concept of the unity of God in the first instance as a designation of His freedom, of His being as it is self-grounded and therefore absolutely superior to every other being. When we say that God is one, unique and simple, we mean something different from when we ascribe unity to any other quantity. Anything else to which we can ascribe unity is one side by side with one or many others which are comparable with it and belong with it to a species. It is one instance in a genus. It is, therefore, only relatively unique. But God is an instance outside every genus. God is, therefore, absolutely unique, in a way that is itself unique and cannot be denoted by any concept. Openly or secretly, anything else to which unity can be ascribed is internally divisible and therefore composite, and externally linked with something else and therefore combined or amalgamated. Everything else is only relatively simple. But God is simple without the least possibility of either internal or external composition. God is completely in-dividual. He is absolutely simple. In regard to His uniqueness and equally in regard to His simplicity God is therefore the only being who is really one. His unity is His freedom, His aseity, His deity. It is with His deity alone that our concern must be when we ascribe to Him unity, uniqueness and simplicity. It is His deity alone that we must seek to magnify by these concepts. We have to accept, then, that these concepts are determined and also circumscribed wholly and completely by His deity. We cannot accept the converse that His deity is circumscribed by the concepts of unity, uniqueness and simplicity—concepts which are at our disposal. The relation between subject and predicate is an irreversible one when it is a matter of God's perfections. We shall have to watch this with particular care in this as in all the designations of God's freedom. Otherwise we shall fail to understand them as the designations of God's freedom and therefore of real freedom. We shall violate the mystery of God's majesty in our very desire to glorify it. Necessarily, then, we must say that God is the absolutely One, but we cannot say that the absolutely one is God. This concept of the " absolutely one " is the reflection of creaturely unities. By making them absolute we do not in any sense conceive or proclaim God the Creator, but one of the gods, which as gods (not of themselves, but in virtue of their origin in our imagination, in which alone they can be gods, and also of their plurality) are empty caricatures of God.

A good example of the absolutising of " uniqueness " is provided by the noisy fanaticism of Islam regarding the one God, alongside whom, it is humorous to observe, only the baroque figure of His prophet is entitled to a place of honour. " Monotheism " is obviously the esoteric mystery behind nearly all the religions with which we are familiar, as well as most of the primitive religions. " Monotheism " is an idea which can be directly divined or logically and mathematically constructed without God. It is the reflection of the subjective sub-consciousness, the requirement of freedom and the claim to mastery on the part of the human individual ; or it is the reflection of this as already reflected in the various cosmic forces of nature or spirit, fate or reason, desire or duty ; or more concretely it is perhaps one of the various " incarnations " of these cosmic forces which in his occasional doubts about the divinity of his own individuality man absolutises in an attempt to reach out beyond himself and in this inverted way to advance his own elevation to deity. The artifice adopted by Islam consists in its developing to a supreme degree what is at the heart of all paganism, revealing and setting at the very centre its esoteric essence, i.e., so-called " monotheism." In this way it was able to become a deadly danger to all other forms of paganism and to a Christianity with a pagan conception of the oneness of God. The fact should not be overlooked that this danger, its seductive profundity, consists in what is (compared with other forms of paganism) simply the greater primitiveness with which it proclaims the unique as God instead of God as the One who is unique. Monotheism, the religious glorification of the number " one," the absolutising of the idea of uniqueness, can be impressive and convincing as knowledge of God only so long as we fail to note the many-sided dialectic in which we are thereby inevitably entangled and in which Islam is incurably entangled. For the cosmic forces in whose objectivity it is believed that the unique has been found are varied. It is only by an act of violence that one of them can be given pre-eminence over the others, so that to-day it is nature and to-morrow spirit, or to-day fate and to-morrow reason, or to-day desire and to-morrow duty, which is regarded as the unique thing which constitutes the common denominator of everything else and therefore the theoretical and practical principle for the knowledge and direction of human life. The one objective reality of to-day is quickly enough limited and replaced by another which makes the same claim to divinity. For all his heavenly divinity each Zeus must constantly be very anxious in face of the existence and arrival of very powerful rivals. And even when the conflict in Olympus is settled, will the God who is claimed to be unique and recognised as such be able to master the human " in-dividual," Prometheus ? Who is first and foremost and really the one who is unique—Allah or his prophet, Allah or his devotees ? Monotheism is all very well so long as this conflict does not break out. But it will in-evitably break out again and again. A Hegel will always give rise to a Feuerbach and a Feuerbach to a Max Stirner. The individual will continually and inevitably resist every universal, however unique, with the claim that he is something even more unique. And is there any end to this conflict, even if every conflict in Olympus is settled ? Once we grasp this *aporia* we shall avoid absolutising the idea of uniqueness just as much as any other idea. That which men can divine or construct as well as believe, that which, as an object of human divining or constructing, is as dialectical as the absolutised idea of uniqueness, may be any-thing we like to call it—and we certainly cannot deny that it is something—but it is not God. It is, therefore, unthinking to set Islam and Christianity side by side, as if in monotheism at least they have something in common. In reality, nothing separates them so radically as the different ways in which they appear to say the same thing—that there is only one God.

Similarly, the assertion of the simplicity of God is not reversible in the sense that it could equally well be said that the simple is God. The simple, the concept of a whole which is indivisible or an indivisible which is whole, can certainly be an object and a very natural object of human divining and construction. Indeed, whenever men have begun to worship the unique as a deity, they have always more or less consistently tried to describe it as the simple as well. It is very understandable that, complex as he is and suffering from his own com-plexity as he does, man would like to be different, i.e., simple. He therefore ascribes simplicity to his own reflection, his would-be deity, believing that he sees true deity in the simplicity he longs for and extols. It is further under-standable that, moving from direct to indirect self-deification, man should ascribe this simplicity to the cosmic force which he venerates at any given time, thus believing that he sees the simple and to that extent the divine in one or other of these cosmic forces. But unfortunately it is not true that the simple as such, the simple which can be the object of our divining and constructing, can be unequi-vocally and with certainty contrasted as that which is divine with what is not simple but complex. For, on the one hand, we may try to think out the idea of the simple to its conclusion, attempting to think of it as a being which exists only for itself, in abstraction from all that is complex. But in this case the simple is an utterly unmoved being, remote from this world altogether, incapable of sound or action, influence on or relation to anything else. And over against it we have to understand this whole complex world either as an autonomous world or as a mere appearance, the veil of Maia, so that either way the simple cannot be thought of as having the mastery over it. Or, on the other hand, we may shrink from this conclusion and understand the simple as the unconditioned. In this case we can find room for the existence of a related, conditioned and com-plex world here. But we have to admit that this relationship, and therefore the existence of this world, and therefore its complexity, are all essential to the simple, that it would not be the unconditioned without the correlated totality of the conditioned. Indeed, may we not even have to bring the unconditioned and the conditioned close together until at last they are dialectically identified ? We shall certainly be forced to abandon again the absolute simplicity of the would-be simple, and with it that in which we were seeking the divinity of God. This is the dialectic which enmeshed the orthodox doctrine of God, as it did that of Hegel and Schleiermacher after it, to the extent that its basis was the concept of the *ens simplicissimum*. And if this is the particular difficulty of the concept of simplicity it must not be forgotten that all the time the concrete question necessarily arises : What in fact is the simple ? Where is it to be found ? Which of the cosmic forces can be proclaimed as that which is simple and therefore as God ? With what right and authority is it to be this one and not that one ? And if it is one of them, what about man's own rivalry to it and all of them ? Who will prevent him from regarding perhaps his own vital impulse as the most simple thing of all, and opposing it as truly and properly divine to every would-be simple being in heaven and earth ? In a word, deliverance from the complex to simplicity, the proclamation of the simple as the truly divine, does not prove on examination to be quite so simple as it usually appears to be as a slogan. God is certainly simple and the divine deliverance is certainly deliverance from complexity. But the absolutised idea of simplicity itself belongs to the complexity from which man must be delivered. As such it is no more the divine which saves than is the idea of uniqueness. On the contrary, it is itself enmeshed in complexity and calculated to increase the misery which complexity actually involves.

When the unity of God is turned into the divinity of unity there can only result what are actually caricatures of God. If we are not to end with these caricatures, we cannot think out to its conclusion the unity of God as a determination of His freedom without recalling that, if we are speaking of the one, unique and simple God, we are speaking of the God who is love. Knowledge of the unity of God is not in any sense the result of human divining or construction. It is the result of the encounter between man and God, brought about by God. It is the human result of the event in which *the* " I " meets the human " Thou " and becomes the reality and determination of its existence. It bears all the marks of that which is incomparable (God's uniqueness) and that which is undivided (His simplicity). Recognition of the unity of God is the human response to the summons and the action of this incomparable and undivided being. It is the recognition of His promise under which man is placed. It is obedience to His command, which is given man and accepted by him. Knowledge of the unity of God breaks through the arbitrary assumptions of all monotheism as of all pantheism. This knowledge is necessarily a stumbling block to monotheism and foolishness to pantheism, because its concern is wholly with God and not at all with unity in itself, and because it knows that it is indebted and responsible to the love of God and the love of God alone. For it is in this indebtedness and responsibility that it is knowledge of the One who is both unique and simple.

It is in His love above all that God reveals Himself as the One who is incomparable and therefore unique ; which means that He reveals Himself as the true and essential God. This revelation is of such a nature that He accomplishes at one stroke what the idea of uniqueness is unable to accomplish in any of its various forms and applications. We have referred already to the fact that divine revelation has the character of election, and to the twofold aspect, that as He chooses man in order to reveal Himself to him as God, God also chooses Himself, that He may be revealed to man as God. It is not, however, from the principle or concept of this twofold election that the knowledge of the divine uniqueness comes. It is not unique in this character of election as such. The idea of election itself leads us back only to the idea of uniqueness. Knowledge of this does not give or complete knowledge of the divine uniqueness. This takes place in the actuality of the twofold election as it occurs in God's revelation according to the witness of the Old and New Testament. It is a choice, but it is a choice as an event. It is in this event as such that the love of God reveals itself and acts with the incomparability to which the only appropriate response is the confession of God's uniqueness. It is in this event that the twofold choice is made which excludes even the very idea that God may be subject to the rivalry of other gods.

It is worth while recalling first the whole passage, Deut. 4³²⁻⁴⁰ : " For ask now of the days that are past, which were before thee, since the day that God created man upon the earth, and from the one end of heaven unto the other, whether there has been any such thing as this great thing is, or hath been heard like it ? Did ever people hear the voice of God speaking out of the midst of the fire, as thou hast heard, and live ? Or hath God assayed to go and take him a nation from the midst of another nation, by temptations, by signs, and by wonders, and by war, and by a mighty hand, and by great terrors, according to all that the Lord your God did for you in Egypt before your eyes ? Unto you it was shewed, that thou mightest know that the Lord he is God : there is none else beside him. Out of heaven he made thee to hear his voice, that he might instruct thee : and upon earth he made thee to see his great fire : and thou heardest his words out of the midst of the fire. And because he loved thy fathers, therefore he chose their seed after them, and brought thee out with his presence, with his great power, out of Egypt ; to drive out nations from before thee greater and mightier than thou, to bring thee in, to give thee their land for an inheritance, as at this day. Know therefore this day, and lay it to thine heart, that the Lord he is God in heaven above and upon the earth beneath : there is none else. And thou shalt keep his statutes, and his commandments, which I command thee this day, that it may go well with thee, and with thy children after thee, and that thou mayest prolong thy days upon the land, which the Lord thy God giveth thee, for ever." And then this recalling of the acts of God's love becomes the basis of the repetition of the Ten Commandments (Deut. 5¹ᶠ·). The first of these : " Thou shalt have no other gods before me " is explicitly based on the words : " I am the Lord thy God that brought thee out of the land of Egypt, out of the house of bondage," and the inculcation of the divine law in Deut. 6 has as its basis the *fundamentum classicum* (so P. v. Mastricht, *Theor. Pract. Theol.*, 1698, II, 8) : " Hear, O Israel : the Lord our God is one Lord : and thou shalt love the Lord thy God with all thine heart, and with all thy soul, and with all thy might " (Deut. 6⁴). If we consult Exodus 20 we see that this is not a mere Deuteronomic construction. There the first commandment has the same decisive basis. And in the context in which they appear the whole ten can have the significance only of the proclamation of the truth which is immediately seen to be valid life-truth for Israel by reason of what Yahweh has actually given Israel, a truth which draws its power, and therefore supreme power, wholly from this actuality. It is not at all the case, then, that we have here first a God who says and does all kinds of things, and then an idea of uniqueness, and that these two have to be brought together in some way, so that this God clothes himself or is even clothed with the characteristic of uniqueness. On the contrary, this God is unique from the very first in the things that He is and says and does. The exhibition of His being and action is the proof of His uniqueness. He has only to place Himself beside the would-be gods of the nations, as He really does in the establishing, upholding and guiding of Israel, and He becomes *ipso facto* manifest as the only God among them. " Thus saith the Lord, the king of Israel, and his redeemer the Lord of hosts : I am the first, and I am the last ; and beside me there is no God. And who, as I, shall call, and shall declare it, and set it in order for me, since I appointed the ancient people ? and the things that are coming and that shall come, let them declare. Fear ye not, neither be afraid : have I not declared unto thee of old, and shewed it ? and ye are my witnesses. Is there a God beside me ? yea, there is no rock : I know not any. They that fashion a graven image are all of them vanity : and their delectable things shall not profit : and their own witnesses see not, nor know ; that they may be ashamed " (Is. 44⁶⁻⁹). Hence the prayer of Hezekiah : " Incline thine ear, O Lord, and hear : open thine eyes, O Lord, and see ; and hear the words of Sennacherib, wherewith he hath sent him to reproach the living God. Of a truth, Lord, the kings of Assyria have laid waste the nations and their lands, and have cast their gods into the fire : for they were no gods, but the work of men's hands, wood and stone : therefore they have destroyed them. Now therefore, O Lord our God, save thou us, I beseech thee, out of his hand, that all the kingdoms of the earth may know that thou art the Lord God, even thou only " (2 Kings 19¹⁶⁻¹⁹). Hence, too, the references in Exod. 20⁵, 34¹⁴ and many later passages to the jealousy of God, which is established with painful fulness in the description in Ezek. 23 of the harlotry committed by Judah and Israel, and wonderfully deepened and superseded by the recollection in Hos. 1-3 of the faithfulness of God which forgives and overcomes the unfaithfulness of His people. It is against this background and this background alone that we can understand the commandment : " Thou shalt have no other gods before me," and with it the " monotheism " of the Old Testament in general. It has absolutely nothing to do with the ambiguous charm of the number " one " or the subjective and objective monism of human self-consciousness and world consciousness, On the contrary, it is in conflict with this monotheism, detecting and passing judgment on its hidden dialectic. It attacks man as a fallen creature who is utterly ignorant of the one and only God and therefore of the true God, a creature who is always looking for the one and never finds it. He finds only what is multiple, because the one is the one person from whom man has fallen away and who is hidden from him and can be revealed to him only by that One Himself. Old Testament monotheism consists in God's disclosing and giving Himself to man as the One who is also the one for which man for his part can only ask in vain. He is not, then, an -ism or a system, which is capable of turning into its opposite. On the contrary, He is the divine reality itself in its uniqueness. For this reason and in this way He possesses power as well. This is not the precarious power of an idea that for a while brings conviction and sets up a school, and later fades again and is replaced by another idea. His is the concrete power that preserves the people of Israel through its long history, which from Israel's standpoint is a continual history of opposition and apostasy. It is the power that preserves it in spite of itself (as depicted in Hosea 1-3) in constant selection and separation at the name of Yahweh as the name of the only true God. It is the power of the divine grace, mercy and patience in which His holiness, righteousness, and wisdom do in fact triumph. It is the power to bind this people in the way in which God Himself, as contrasted with an idea, binds men, so that it is not always evident how far men glorify Him, but it is always evident that He does glorify Himself among and in these men, and in such a way that His love in its uniqueness never fails or is renounced or becomes equivocal in relation to these men. The God of the Old Testament is not, then, the God to whom uniqueness accrues or is ascribed as a kind of embellishment drawn from the stores of creaturely glory, which He may now wear as the images of the heathen gods wear their embellishments of gold and silver. On the contrary, He is the God who possesses uniqueness in the love that is actively at work on Israel, a uniqueness that is His own, a divine, a unique uniqueness, unique in comparison with all human uniqueness. He is the God who is unique in Himself, quite apart from any corresponding knowledge or service contributed or offered or provided by Israel. Indeed, Israel's knowledge of God and service of God is to be understood as a divine gift subsequent to God's existence and action and to that extent as obedience to God's command. It is drawn always by " the cords of grace," by the " bands of love " (Hos. 11⁴). There is continual resistance from the human side. There is always breaking out to the left hand or the right. This is how Israel comes to the knowledge and service of God, as God opposes to it His own faithfulness.

" Jewish monotheism ? " It was just when something like this had begun to take shape, when apparently all opposition had been broken and apostasy seemed to belong to the past, when polytheism had apparently become a matter of past history and the idols Israel had worshipped were apparently recognised only as the idols of the despised Gentiles or in recollection of the abomination of their disobedient fathers—it was just then, under the sway of this victorious monotheism, that Israel's Messiah was handed over by Israel to the Gentiles and nailed by them to the cross with Israel's approval. Could there be a better proof that this monotheism is not a final achievement and expression of Israel's obedience to the first commandment ? On the contrary, is it not a proof that, like the monotheism of Islam (its later caricature), it is simply the supreme example, the culmination and completion of the disobedience which from the beginning constituted the human side of the dealings of the one and only God with His chosen people ? The conception of the one and only being now actually reached by Israel has as little as that to do with the uniqueness of God. It is— always—the form taken by the supreme and as it were mature contradiction of the one and only God. This does not occur in the remoter ages when Israel worshipped idols, but at the height of its religious development, when it seemed as if the indictments of Moses and the prophets and the threatenings of the Law no longer applied, and the dogma of God's uniqueness had become something that all the parties of the Jewish Church would of course hold in honour. In these very conditions the fulfilment of the whole history of Israel could be and inevitably was misunderstood. The one and only Son of the one and only God, the very incarnate Word of God to which Moses and the prophets had borne witness, could be and inevitably was rejected by Israel, and its whole history could be and was inevitably proved to be the history of human disobedience to the one and only God in a manner both awesome and final. Could there be any better proof that God's uniqueness is really His, God's uniqueness, not a matter of a human idea of God, but of His revelation, of His speaking and acting, of His inmost being, inseparable from His grace and holiness ? Could there be any better proof that it is as little the discovery of a human mind as His grace and holiness and all His other perfections, and that as a divine reality it is diametrically opposed to creaturely reality, including even the highest human faculty of construction and foresight, and can become an object of human knowledge only in the way in which God in any of His perfections can become such an object ? In face of the cross of Christ it is monstrous to describe the uniqueness of God as an object of " natural " knowledge. In face of the cross of Christ we are bound to say that knowledge of the one and only God is gained only by the begetting of men anew by the Holy Spirit, an act which is always unmerited and incomprehensible, and consists in man's no longer living unto himself, but in the Word of God and in the knowledge of God which comes by faith in that Word. But faith in that Word means faith in the One whom this very Judaism with its monotheism rejected as a sinner against its monotheism, a blasphemer against God. This is the gulf which separates Christian monotheism, if we can use the term, from Jewish monotheism and monotheism of every other kind. It is strange but true that confession of the one and only God and denial of Him are to be found exactly conjoined but radically separated in what appears to be the one identical statement that there is only one God. This one sentence can actually mean what it says, and it can actually not mean this, but its opposite. What distinguishes these two possibilities, raising the one to reality and invalidating the other, is the resurrection of Jesus Christ, the outpouring of the Holy Spirit and faith.

That God is a single unique being is of course stated expressly and in many forms by the New Testament as well (Mt. 19¹⁷, Gal. 3²⁰, 1 Cor. 8⁴ᶠ·, 1 Tim. 2⁵). It says this actually and not merely verbally because, like the Old Testament, it makes the statement in attestation—this time retrospective—of the Word and work of God.

The passages which speak expressly of the uniqueness of God are only in a sense the spokesmen for a far more extensive conception of the uniqueness of the form and content of the event between God and man in which the being of God as the one and only God has been revealed. They are to be read and understood against this background, and not by themselves as abstract statements about God in Himself. The very remarkable fact is to be noted that (in harmony with the predominant " henotheism " of the Old Testament) Paul not only did not deny the existence of many that are called (λεγόμενοι) gods and lords in heaven and on earth (1 Cor. 8⁵), but actually affirmed it : ὥσπερ εἰσὶν θεοὶ πολλοὶ καὶ κύριοι πολλοί. To such an extent is the New Testament doctrine of the singleness or uniqueness of God based on the conception of that event, and so little on a preconceived theory. That God is a single being is clearly reflected, according to the parables of the lost sheep and the lost coin, in the fact that there is more joy in heaven over one sinner that repents than over ninety and nine just persons, who need no repentance (Lk. 15⁷⁻¹⁰). Such is God and such His mercy and righteousness that He is concerned about the individual man in his need and his redemption. Again God as the One who is single and unique is reflected in the fact that Martha is wrong to be worried and anxious about many things. " But one thing is needful : for Mary hath chosen the good part, which shall not be taken away from her " (Lk. 10⁴¹ᶠ·). Such is God and such His grace and holiness that there is simply one thing which He wants from men. Again, in Gal. 5¹⁴ the whole Law is fulfilled in one saying (the saying : " Thou shalt love thy neighbour as thyself "). For Paul there seem to have been two objects of what is in the first instance an indirect view of the singleness and uniqueness of God. First, there is the embracing together of Jew and Gentile both in sin and in the mercy of God or faith—a decisive mark of his Gospel : " Or is God the God of Jews only ? is he not the God of Gentiles also : if so be that God is one, and he shall justify the circumcision by faith and the uncircumcision through faith ? " (Rom. 3²⁹ᶠ·). " For there is no distinction between Jew and Greek : for the same Lord is Lord of all, and is rich unto all that call upon him " (Rom. 10¹²). Or again (and already the connexion with the direct view of God's uniqueness is present here) : " For he is our peace, who made both one, and brake down the middle wall of partition, having abolished in his flesh the enmity, even the law of commandments contained in ordinances ; that he might create in himself of the twain one new man, so making peace ; and might reconcile them both in one body unto God through the cross, having slain the enmity thereby " (Eph. 2¹⁴⁻¹⁶). The saying in Jn. 10¹⁶ belongs to this context : " And other sheep I have which are not of this fold : them also I must bring, and they shall hear my voice ; and there shall be one flock, one shepherd." The second· indirect view of the divine singleness and uniqueness in Paul—and it is of course directly connected with the first—is that of the Church as the one body (Rom. 12⁴ᶠ·, 1 Cor. 10¹⁷, 12¹²ᶠ·). " There is one body, and one Spirit, even as also ye were called in one hope of your calling : one Lord, one faith, one baptism, one God and Father of all, who is over all, and through all, and in all " (Eph. 4⁴ᶠᶠ·). This passage makes it obvious how Paul simply reads off the truth of the singleness and uniqueness of God from the reality of the life of His people created by His Word and work. That this reality represents for him a divine reality is shown by the fact that it is traced back to the reality of the one Holy Spirit both in this very passage (Eph. 4⁴) and in many other places (1 Cor. 12¹ᶠᶠ·, 2 Cor. 12¹⁸, Eph. 2¹⁸). For this reason the gift of revelation and reconciliation, visible in the life of the community in all its unity, may and must be described also as a task, and made the object of apostolic exhortation. It is the singleness and uniqueness of God which is proclaimed when in Gal. 3²⁸ (cf. 1 Cor. 12¹³) not only the distinction between the Jews and Greeks but also that between slave and free and male and female is relativised by the statement that " ye are all one in Christ Jesus." And it is the singleness and uniqueness of God which is proclaimed when in Phil. 1²⁷ Christians are called to stand fast in one spirit, " with one soul striving for the faith of the gospel," or in Phil. 2² " to be of the same mind," having the same love, as σύμ-ψυχοι to be of one mind ; or in Rom. 15⁵ᶠ· to glorify the God and Father of our Lord Jesus Christ " with one accord, with one mouth ; " or when it can in fact be said of the community in Jerusalem in Acts 4³² that the multitude of them that believed were " of one heart and soul."

But all this is, after all, only the indirect conception which serves as a basis for confession of the one God. It cannot be understood except against the background of the proper, direct conception which now calls for consideration. But this direct conception, the one with which knowledge of the singleness and uniqueness of God in the New Testament stands or falls, is that of Jesus the Messiah, rejected by monotheistic Judaism. Already in Ephesians 2 and 4 this view is clearly enough visible as the constitutive centre of what is said about the unity of the congregation. It is dominant, however, in the principal passages 1 Cor. 8⁶ and 1 Tim. 2⁵. The first passage says first : εἷς θεὸς ὁ πατήρ and then : εἷς κύριος Ἰησοῦς Χριστός; the second : εἷς θεός and then : εἷς μεσίτης θεοῦ καὶ ἀνθρώπων, ἄνθρωπος Χριστὸς Ἰησοῦς (" who gave himself a ransom for all "). In neither passage is the connecting καί to be understood as if a second unique being is named alongside a first, but what comes after the καί strengthens, emphasises and interprets what stands in front of it—a common usage. Thus mention of the one Lord or Mediator simply expresses the fact and extent that God the Father is the unique being. He is it in and with the fact that our Lord, the Mediator between God and man, is as such the one unique being. This twofold εἷς does not involve in the least the introduction of a new polytheism, as in the conception of a higher unique being and a lower—analogous to " Allah is great and Mohammed is his prophet." On the contrary, it means the final establishing of the monotheism of Moses and the prophets, the monotheism of the God who is real and revealed, who has His being and makes it known in His Word and work. And it is established by the specific naming of His name. Christian monotheism results from and consists in the fact that Jesus Christ bears witness to Himself and reveals Himself as the Son of His heavenly Father, distinguishing Himself and separating Himself as reigning Lord from the powers and forces of this age, and manifesting Himself as their Conqueror and Master. In the events which not only are caused by God or proceed from Him, but which are identical with His being and action, He reveals Himself and is known in His being as the One who is unique. He is not a unique being in the way in which there are many such. He is *this* unique being. As this unique being He is *the* unique being. Thus everything depends on the revelation and knowledge of this unique being if it is to be a matter of the revelation and knowledge of the uniqueness of God in the New Testament sense.

We must now consider the passages in which the unique God and the unique Christ are not expressly connected, as in 1 Cor. 8 and 1 Tim. 2, but the uniqueness of the divine Word and work as it occurred in Jesus Christ is itself described and emphasised. It is these passages which will be finally decisive for the understanding of New Testament monotheism. For in these passages we go even beyond what has been said above, where the two are set together, and learn the extent to which, in fact, uniqueness—and uniqueness that is divine —is Jesus Christ's by right. According to Mt. 23⁸⁻¹⁰, it is His in the sense that He Himself says to His disciples : " But be not ye called Rabbi : for one is your teacher, and all ye are brethren. And call no man your father upon the earth : for one is your Father, which is in heaven. Neither be ye called masters : for one is your Master, even Christ." The passage frankly sounds intolerable if we fail to realise that this is the claim of the one and only God. Yet it should be noted that the very thing which would be completely intolerable if it were a man's testimony to himself—Jesus' witness to Himself as Messiah—is the basis of New Testament monotheism, just as the basis of Old Testament mono- theism is the witness of Yahweh to Himself as He acts on Israel. We cannot listen to what the New Testament calls " the one God " without listening to His self-testimony. Naturally we may reject this. But in that case we reject not only what is here called " the one God," but this God Himself. This God, the God of the Old and New Testaments, is in His being not only unique, but this unique being. We can react to His self-witness in which He reveals Himself as unique : " I and the Father are one " (Jn. 10³⁰), in the same way as the Jews did according to Jn. 10³¹ : " They took up stones to stone him." But for all that, it still stands as this self-witness and as such it is the one and only approach to what the Old and New Testaments call " God." For a being which is not the unique being attested by this self-testimony may also be unique in its own way, but it is certainly not this God. This and this alone is the admittedly strait way, the admittedly narrow gate, to the one God of the prophets and apostles. And everything that Paul says in his letters about the unity of the Spirit and the Church has as its background this self-witness. " Keep them in thy name which thou hast given me, that they may be one, even as we are " (Jn. 17¹¹). But it is not only through words that this self-witness takes place. For instance, if we read Paul in Rom. 5¹²⁻²¹ (cf. 1 Cor. 15²¹), there does not seem to be a single word about the uniqueness of God. It is all about the alteration that has taken place in the human situation through Jesus Christ, an alteration from the dominion of sin to the dominion of righteousness, from death as man's destiny to the gift of life. It should be noted, however, on the one hand how utterly un- symmetrical is the relationship of these two sides or possibilities. Grace, righteous- ness and life are absolutely superior, as becomes more and more impressively clear as the end is approached. And it should be noted, on the other hand, how in relation to the power that has been overthrown the victorious power is epi- tomised in the form of the εἷς ἄνθρωπος who has redressed the evil done by another and first εἷς ἄνθρωπος. This latter " one man " was Adam. The other " one man " is Jesus Christ and it is He who is the bringer of the grace and righteous- ness of the life that triumphs over death, a grace and righteousness which shows itself divine by its superiority. This happening is now the Messianic witness of Jesus to Himself. At the same time and as such it is witness to the uniqueness of God. Or, to put it the other way round, here too the witness to the uniqueness of God is simply the Messianic witness of Jesus to Himself. This witness outdoes the testimony to sin and death offered by the human race as embraced in the one man Adam. It does so by a victorious decision which ends and excludes all dispute or competition. This one being has gained His right and lordship over the lives of all—or we may also say, this one being has revealed His dignity as Creator and Lord of all—by dying for them all (2 Cor. 5¹⁴). And if human priests proved themselves merely witnesses and types by daily sacrifices, which have always to be repeated and " can never take away sins," He, Jesus Christ, " when he had offered one sacrifice for sins for ever, sat down on the right hand of God ; from henceforth expecting till his enemies be made the footstool of his

feet. For by one offering he hath perfected for ever them that are sanctified"
(Heb. 10[11-14]). This, it must be said, is the unique New Testament proof of the
uniqueness of God.

We conclude by referring to the fact that this was recognised and acknowledged in the Reformation doctrine of justification with the statement that it
is only by faith that man possesses righteousness and holiness. This *sola fide*
is simply the reflection of the *soli Deo gloria* with which the fathers of the Protestant Church were equally accustomed to sum up their profession of faith, just
as conversely this *soli Deo gloria* is simply the reflection of the *sola fide*. Rightly
understood these two *sola* (and the third one, *sola scriptura* too) mean one and
the same thing. *Unicus Deus*, because *unicus summus pontifex, patronus et
pacificator* (*Conf. Scot.* Art. XI), is the archetype, reflected by both, indeed by all
three *sola*. The uniqueness of faith is based on the uniqueness of its object,
and therefore *soli Deo gloria*. But the uniqueness of this object requires faith
to be unique, because it is only God who is feared, loved and glorified by us,
and therefore *sola fide*. But the power of this uniqueness is the power of the
name under which God reveals His being and in which faith may believe. The
Reformation recovered and brought to light the testimony of the whole of Holy
Scripture when it sang : " Ask ye who is this same ? Christ Jesus is His name.
The Lord Sabaoth's Son ; He, and no other one, Shall conquer in the battle."

The simplicity or indivisibility of God too, the deeper essence and
ground of which we have still to investigate, reveals itself to us with
the invincible truth of a determination of the freedom of God only
when we allow ourselves to be reminded, by the witness of Scripture,
that God's freedom and therefore His simplicity are the freedom
and simplicity of His love. Not an idea of simplicity, for, as we have
shown, this could only draw us away from the knowledge of God. In
Scripture the utterly simple is " simply " God Himself in the actuality,
the superior might, the constancy, the obviousness, or even more
simply, the factuality, in which He is present as God and deals as God
with the creature, with man.

If we examine its treatment of the *simplicitas Dei*, we can only be amazed
at the way in which orthodox dogmatics entered on and lost itself in logical
and mathematical reflections. For the results reached it naturally could not
produce a single scriptural proof, and yet this was to form the fundamental
presupposition of its whole doctrine of God and therefore finally of its whole
Christian doctrine. Could it not see the wood for the trees ? Fortunately its
subsequent progress was generally better than its customary beginning. Later
it said everything about God which has to be said if Scripture is guide. And the
rest of Christian doctrine, too, it tried to present and develop in loyalty to the
guidance of Scripture. It is a pity that this happy inconsistency did not survive
in the teaching of a later period. But the question remains why orthodoxy was
not consistent when it worked back to its starting-point, but gave a later period
the possibility of deducing from this unhappy starting point far more unhappy
consequences. Rightly it saw that God must be described as the absolutely
simple. But this absolutely simple can only be God Himself—and not " God
Himself " as interpreted by the idea of the absolutely simple, but God Himself
in His self-interpretation. Theoretically, of course, this was what orthodoxy
sincerely wished to discover in His self-revelation attested in Scripture. But in
practice, for some strange reason, it was not satisfied at this point. It seemed
to imagine that the simplicity of God can be attested and presented—more simply
than by reference to God Himself—by all kinds of speculation on the idea of

the uncomposed and indivisible as such and in general. It did not see that the scientific accuracy necessary to present this object requires us absolutely to accept God Himself in His revelation attested in Scripture as the absolutely simple One, the One who is in fact uncomposed and indivisible, and to allow Him to assert Himself as such. God Himself, this God in His reality, is that which is simple, He who is simple. It is He who is incomparably, uniquely simple—infinitely more simple than all the complexities and even all the would-be simplicities of the rest of our knowledge. God Himself is the nearest to hand, as the absolutely simple must be, and at the same time the most distant, as the absolutely simple must also be. God Himself is the irresolvable and at the same time that which fills and embraces everything else. God Himself in His being for Himself is the one being which stands in need of nothing else and at the same time the one being by which everything else came into being and exists. God Himself is the beginning in which everything begins, with which we must and can always begin with confidence and without need of excuse. And at the same time He is the end in which everything legitimately and necessarily ends, with which we must end with confidence and without need of excuse. God Himself is simple, so simple that in all His glory He can be near to the simplest perception and also laugh at the most profound or acute thinking—so simple that He reduces everyone to silence, and then allows and requires everyone boldly to make Him the object of their thought and speech. He is so simple that to think and speak correctly of Him and to live correctly before Him does not in fact require any special human complexities or for that matter any special human simplicities, so that occasionally and according to our need He may permit and require both human complexity and human simplicity, and occasionally they may both be forbidden us. For the simplicity of God is His own simplicity. His simplicity is God Himself as comfort, exhortation and judgment for all men and over all human endeavour. *Est igitur, ob quod pia αὐταρκείᾳ animum ad simplicitatem assuefaciamus ac rerum varietati unum substituamus Deum omnibus ad omnia sufficientissimum* (P. v. Mastricht., *Theor. Pract. Theol.*, 1698, II, 6, 29).

Who and what is God Himself ? We must not now go back and give an answer which declares what we think the conception of God ought to be, what God must be to be God according to all necessary postulates and ideas in respect of the concept of deity. God Himself is in fact simply the One of whom all prophets and apostles explained that they had heard His voice and had to obey Him, executing the messages and tasks He laid on them, and bearing witness of His will and work to others. In a remarkable way they also recognised His voice in the testimony of each other, at least to the extent that, in a long unbroken chain, admittedly in quite different ways, but in ways which at this point involved no contradiction, they all aimed to be servants and messengers of one and the same God. This One is God Himself, described by the unanimous testimony of prophets and apostles as the Subject of creation, reconciliation and redemption, the Lord. And as they describe and explain these works of His and His dignity, they characterise Him as the One who is gracious and holy, merciful and righteous, patient and wise, but also omnipresent, constant, omnipotent, eternal and glorious. According to this testimony all these perfections are the perfections of this one being. According to this testimony they all have their existence and their essence, not outside of Him, but absolutely in Him. The One who is all this, and in whom all this is, is God Himself. And He is simple, i.e., He is all this indivisibly, indissolubly, inflexibly. The reason for this is that He is in Himself indivisible, indissoluble, and inflexible. According to the testimony of the Bible (which refers us to His revelation as to Him Himself), the simplicity of God consists in the trustworthiness, truthfulness and fidelity which He is Himself, and in which, therefore, He also is what He is, and does what He does. If He were divisible, dissoluble, or flexible, He would not be trustworthy. But the God of the prophets and apostles is trustworthy. And He is not merely casually or accidentally trustworthy, so that He could also be untrustworthy. On the contrary, He is trustworthy in His essence, in the inmost core of His being. And this is His simplicity. It is also, of course, what orthodox dogmatics had in mind when it usually began its doctrine of God with this conception of simplicity. It is to be wished that it had only made clear that this was what it had in mind—the trustworthiness of the God who demonstrates His nature in His Word and work attested in Scripture. In this sense God in His simplicity is what the Bible so often calls Him, the " rock," the unshakable foundation, on which is based not only the doctrine of God but all the doctrines, and not only these but the whole life of the Christian Church, all Christian life, and finally all human life as a whole, and the promise of eternal life. Without this foundation all this necessarily dissolves into nothingness. This divine simplicity, however, is not to be looked for in any other place than that in which the prophets and apostles found it, when it offered itself for them to find and they were found by it—in God's self-demonstration, given by Him in His Word and work, which is in itself the demonstration of His trustworthiness, truthfulness and fidelity. God's simplicity is to be sought in the prayer : " Grant us faithfulness and deliver us from all our distresses," and the flame of this prayer can be kindled only at the fire which Moses saw alight on Horeb, a fire that is always consuming and always preserving, always judging and always saving, always killing and always making alive. The prophets and apostles came to know the One who is active there and in that way as One who is trustworthy in His Word and work, and they attested Him as such. He grants constancy because He Himself is constant. We can trust Him because His essence is trustworthiness. When we know this we know God's simplicity. For revealing Himself in this way He reveals His simplicity. Thus you cannot know it except by knowing Him and we cannot know Him except in the place and way in which He has demonstrated Himself and given Himself to be known as the One He is. In this place and in this way—in His Word and work— He bears witness to Himself as the One who is simple, as He does also to Himself as the One who is unique.

It is, then, what may be called an analytical judgment when in Deut. 7[9] God is called the " faithful God," or in the Song of Moses in Deut. 32[4] the " God of truth." * For this is said of the God " which keepeth covenant and mercy with them that love him and keep his commandments to a thousand generations." And when Paul takes up the phrase : " God is faithful," it is with his eyes on the God " by whom ye were called unto the fellowship of his Son Jesus Christ our Lord " (1 Cor. 1[9]), " who shall stablish you and keep you from evil " (1 Thess. 3[3]). According to 1 Jn. 1[9] God is faithful and just " to forgive us our sins and to cleanse us from all unrighteousness." Because " thou hast redeemed me," He is addressed in Ps. 31[5] as the " God of truth." Note how often this is said in contrast to men's unfaithfulness : Deut. 32[5], Rom. 3[3], 2 Tim. 2[13]. Equally involved in this analytical judgment is the fact that the man to whom this faithful God reveals and binds Himself as faithful has to confess like Jacob : " I am not worthy of the least of all the mercies and of all the truth which thou hast shewed unto thy servant " (Gen. 32[10]). If Ps. 33[4] applies to Him the cognate conception of " truthfulness " and says " the word of the Lord is true (or right) ; and all his works are done in truth," it is matched by Rom. 3[4] : " God is true, but every man a liar." In Jn. 1[9] His Word is called the true Light that comes into the world, but we must also note what follows in verse 10 : " He was in the world, and the world was made by him, and the world knew him not." It is precisely God's faithfulness and truthfulness and therefore His simplicity which characterise His love too, His grace and mercy and patience, as matters of His free and sovereign choice, unmerited by us. It is precisely God's faithful-

* The " truth " of the English A.V. carries, like the Hebrew *'emeth*, the idea of faithfulness, as in the German rendering.—Tr.

ness and truthfulness and therefore His simplicity which in a special way characterise God Himself as the One who gives Himself to be known by Himself, and for His own sake lends and gifts Himself to man to be his God. He who is holy, He who is true according to Rev. 3^7, is "he who hath the key of David, he that openeth and no man shutteth; and shutteth and no man openeth." "True and faithful" is the name of the rider on the white horse in Rev. 19^{11}. The "true witness" of Rev. 1^5 (identical with "the true and faithful witness" of Rev. 3^{14}) is Jesus Christ, "the first begotten of the dead and the prince of the kings of the earth," "the faithful high priest in things pertaining to God" (Heb. 2^{17}). Those who receive His testimony confirm that God is true (Jn. 3^{33}). He has come and "hath given us an understanding that we may know him that is true, and we are in him that is true, even his Son Jesus Christ" (1 Jn. 5^{20}). God is true because Jesus Christ is "in truth arisen" according to Luke 24^{34}. Finally, then, we reach the same point in regard to God's simplicity as we reached in regard to His uniqueness and all the other divine perfections. When we hear Paul call the "true God" to witness that his own word as an apostle was not Yes and No, but a word of truth and therefore a simple word, he finds the one basis for this appeal in the recollection that "the Son of God, Jesus Christ, who was preached among you by us, even by me and Silvanus and Timotheus, was not yea and nay, but in him was yea. For all the promises of God in him are yea and in him Amen, unto the glory of God by us" (2 Cor. 1^{18-20}). God's simplicity reveals itself and consists in His continual self-confirmation in His speech and action; His continual self-confession and self-attestation in His identity. This involves the repetition and also the fulfilment of His promise, which does not mean that it ceases to be a promise, but that for the first time it really becomes one. It involves the unity of His promise and His command, of the Gospel and the Law, and in such a way that the Gospel is the fulfilling of the Law, while the Law is the form of the Gospel. It involves the unity of the election and calling of the sinful people Israel and of the Church of Jews and Gentiles sanctified by grace. It involves the unity of grace and holiness, mercy and righteousness, patience and wisdom, in the total work of His love. It is in this way that God confirms Himself, that He is One and the same. And everywhere that this takes place, even at the points where at first we may think we see difference, opposition, or contradiction, but later find unity, He attests Himself and gives Himself to be known by faith in His simplicity. But the name in which this witness to His unity is made is the name of Jesus Christ, as all the New Testament passages cited above show. All the lines we mentioned, promise and fulfilment, Gospel and Law, Israel and the Church, the love and freedom of God, are not separate, but meet and unite in Christ. The Yea and the Amen of the whole prophetic-apostolic message of all Scripture is, in fact, in Him: for in Him is the Yea and the Amen of the one God Himself. This is the reason why the faithfulness and truthfulness of God are to be regarded and understood as the real meaning and basis of His simplicity. And this is the reason why the meaning and basis of the knowledge of His simplicity is faith, in which man for his part ascribes to God's faithfulness and truth the glory due to it, acknowledging its legitimate right, and to that extent himself ($\pi\iota\sigma\tau\epsilon\acute{\nu}\epsilon\iota\nu$) becoming faithful and true and himself simple. Faith is trust placed in the divine faithfulness. Faith is straightforwardness corresponding to the divine truthfulness. "I believe" means "I put my trust on the fact that I have to do with the God who is trustworthy, and I put my trust on Him in the way in which trust may and must be put on Him." But the God who is trustworthy is the God who, in the incarnation of His Word, has borne witness to both His love and His freedom and in both to Himself. The God who is trustworthy is the Father who is one with the Son and the Son who is one with the Father in the Holy Spirit. It is right to extol the virtue of Christian simplicity as the climax of the attitude required and necessary in the Church. According to Scripture, however, there is no simplicity in the Church except for the simplicity of faith in this God who is trustworthy. There is no simplicity except for that of straightforward trust in the power of the mystery now revealed of the incarnation of the Word and the divine triunity. The simplicity of this straightforward trust will show itself to be the required and necessary simplicity, the true divine simplicity of the Christian, by the fact that it does not deviate a hair's breadth from its committal to the name of Jesus Christ. In this committal it is in fact the *conditio sine qua non* of a knowledge of the simple God, of God Himself, who as such is the unique, the one God.

Because and as God is one, unique and simple, He is for this reason omnipresent. Omnipresence is certainly a determination of the freedom of God. It is the sovereignty in which, as the One He is, existing and acting in the way that corresponds to His essence, He is present to everything else, to everything that is not Himself but is distinct from Himself. It is the sovereignty on the basis of which everything that exists cannot exist without Him, but only with Him, possessing its own presence only on the presupposition of His presence.

God's presence includes His lordship. How can He be present without being Lord? And His lordship includes His glory. How can He be Lord without glorifying Himself, without being glorious in Himself? And if nothing exists without Him, this means that everything is subject to Him. And that it is subject to Him means that it can and must serve His glory. But while we will not forget all this, we can leave it on one side for the moment, since it will have to be weighed and considered in its own place.

The presupposition of all divine sovereignty is that of the divine omnipresence. The whole divine sovereignty is based on the fact that for God nothing exists which is only remote, i.e., which is not near even as it is remote, so that there is no remoteness beside and outside Him which is remoteness without His proximity. There is remoteness as there is proximity. Otherwise there would be no creation. And because creation is God's creation, there is also a divine remoteness and proximity. But in God Himself remoteness and proximity are one. And so in His creation, although there can be remoteness without proximity and proximity without remoteness for His creatures, no remoteness or proximity can exist apart from the divine remoteness and proximity. Remoteness and proximity in created things rest on their multiplicity and differentiation, on the fact that they exist beside one another. But the divine remoteness and proximity rest on the wealth of the divine perfections. And God is One in this wealth of perfections. Therefore God is Lord over these antitheses. He is Himself distant and near in one being. For the same reason He is also, as Creator, both the author of the multiplicity and the differentiation of things which exist side by side in creation, and yet also independent of it. Therefore there is in it no proximity and no remoteness without His proximity and remoteness, and no presence without His presence : a presence with all the wealth and unity of His perfections ; His presence as Himself in the uniqueness and simplicity in which He is Himself.

It is at once apparent that this very freedom of God's being over all and in all, which is the basis of His whole sovereignty, compels us to remember that God is love. The love of God is not contained in the concept of the divine unity as such. We have seen, of course, that, provided we think of it as the unity of the God attested in Scripture, we cannot think through or state clearly the concept of unity without already looking away from the freedom of God (the perfection of which it denotes in the first instance) to the love of God which alone can make the freedom of God clear and understandable as His freedom. It is only if God's freedom is interpreted in this way that we are justified in stating, as we have already proceeded to do, that God is omnipresent because He is One. But the concept of God's omnipresence adds something new to the concept of God's unity as unity, for in the first instance this concept seems to refer only to God's being as such. The concept of omnipresence, on the other hand, contains the reference to a universe, or the possibility of a universe, to which God stands in a very direct and very intimate relationship. He is present to it, yet He is not identical with it, but distinct from it as it is distinct from Him. We are not saying that God is omnipresent only in so far as there is this universe. God's omnipresence, like His other perfections, cannot be resolved into a description of His relationship to His creation. All that God is in His relationship to His creation, and therefore His omnipresence too, is simply an outward manifestation and realisation of what He is previously in Himself apart from this relationship and therefore apart from His creation. Even if creation and this relationship of God to creation did not exist, proximity and remoteness in irresolvable unity (and therefore the basis of what is externally manifested and realised in His omnipresence in relation to His creation) would still be a divine perfection. It is in the fact that there is in God proximity and remoteness in irresolvable unity, no proximity without remoteness and remoteness without proximity ; it is in this fact—we recall anew His triune essence—that God is love. In the outward manifestation and realisation of this eternal love of His, He is also the Creator, and there is also a creation, and in it a creaturely proximity and remoteness, where there is proximity apart from remoteness and remoteness apart from proximity. In relationship to it, not tied but sovereign and controlling, and yet in a real relationship to it, stands God's omnipresence in the meaning of the term in which it does in fact presuppose the existence of a universe distinct from God. We can now say more precisely : The concept of the unity of God as such does not seem to describe God's being in such a way as to explain His being as love.

The concept of the divine omnipresence, however, does this without any ambiguity, and when this term is associated with that of the divine unity, the latter also does. So then we can see why it is that we cannot think through this latter concept without recalling that the God who is unique and simple is the One who loves. The fact that He is this must be our starting-point as we now try to understand His omnipresence as an attribute of His majesty and sovereignty.

Such is God's nature and in such manner is He the One who is unique and single, that He can be the Creator of a world separate from Himself and be its Lord. There does exist in Him the wealth of His attributes. But above all there exists in the very unity of this wealth of His the triunity of His essence. Thus there exists a divine proximity and remoteness, real in Him from all eternity, as the basis and presupposition of the essence and existence of creation, and therefore of created proximity and remoteness. God can be present to another. This is His freedom. For He is present to Himself. This is His love in its internal and external range. God in Himself is not only existent. He is co-existent. And so He can co-exist with another also. To grant co-existence with Himself to another is no contradiction of His essence. On the contrary, it corresponds to it. And this is true also of His own entering into co-existence with this other. This co-existence, of course, can be only one which is posited, limited, conditioned and circumscribed by His own essence. It will be characterised by the unlimited priority of His, the divine existence and therefore by the unlimited subordination of the existence of the other which co-exists with Him. Yet under these presuppositions and in this order this co-existence has both its basis and its possibility in God. God is love in Himself. For this reason and to this extent omnipresence is proper to Him as an attribute of majesty and sovereignty. Without the divine love this would be incomprehensible. For without the divine love there could be no other, no universe beside God and therefore no divine omnipresence in relation to it, and therefore no revelation or knowledge of the omnipresent being of God. But we must note also that there would be no love of God, no incarnation of His Word, and therefore no revelation of His action as Creator, Reconciler and Redeemer, if God were not present to another distinct from Himself on the basis of the fact that He is the One who is omnipresent in Himself. The attributes of God's love about which we have already spoken, His grace and mercy and patience, are in their revelation more precise determinations of His omnipresence, of His sovereign co-existence with another distinct from Himself ; and in their identity with the divine essence they are determinations of the way in which God as the One who is primarily present to Himself can love a world distinct from Himself and can therefore be its Creator, Reconciler and Redeemer. This connexion ensures for us that in considering this divine perfection too we are at the well-known place where we have to hold fast to the Word and work of divine love as the first and last court of appeal for our attempt at interpretation.

In the older theology God's omnipresence was usually coupled with His eternity. The reason is not far to seek. His omnipresence seems to have reference to His relation to space, His eternity to His relation to time. The two, it was thought, could be comprehended under the more general conception of infinity (*infinitas*) and expounded according to the common pattern thus provided. *Infinitatis enim duae quasi species statuuntur, aeternitas et immensitas. Aeternitas est talis Dei proprietas, per quam nullo tempore finiri nec principium nec finem exsistendi habere, sed citra omnem temporis successionem semper totus simul esse significatur. Immensitas est talis Dei proprietas, per quam nullo loco mensurari ac circumscribi, sed omnia et singula loca citra essentiae suae multiplicationem, extensionem, inclusionem ac divisionem penetrare ac replere significatur* (J. Gerhard, *Loci theol.*, 1610 f., II, 171). The parallel between omnipresence and eternity appears obvious. It gives a logical and metaphysical clarity which has perhaps seemed even more satisfactory since the conceptions of space and time began to play their prominent role in Kant's theory of knowledge. For space and time can be understood as the limits within which we ourselves exist and within which the world also exists for us. They are the conditions under which the activity of our human existence, our knowing and willing, take place as such (in time), and in relation to objects (in space). On the other hand, the eternal and omnipresent God is understood as the supreme principle of existence and the universe, which is not itself bound by these limits and conditions, but posits and embraces them.

The first objection we have to bring against this very illuminating scheme is a formal one. It does not represent a true outworking of the Christian knowledge of God if we try to understand and present God's essence (as clearly takes place in this parallel treatment of omnipresence and eternity) from the point of view of the problems of our created existence and our created world, i.e., as the answer and solution to these problems. The Christian doctrine of God has to face and answer questions put to it by the God who confronts man and not by the man who confronts God. If it does this, it will not appear quite so obvious that the divine omnipresence and eternity should be treated as parallel for all the parallels between the problems of space and time. In the last instance we are, of course, saying one and the same thing when we speak of God as omnipresent and when we speak of Him as eternal. But this is true of all the perfections of the divine essence, and not more true of His omnipresence and His eternity than of the others. On the contrary, we are at this point directed along remarkably different lines if we are really dealing with the Christian knowledge of God. As we have seen, God's omnipresence is to be understood primarily as a determination of His love, in so far as God is not only One, unique and simple, but as such is present to Himself and therefore present to everything which by Him is outside Him.

This cannot, however, be said in the same way of His eternity. It is true, of course, that we cannot think through this conception either without understanding God's eternity as qualified by His love, indeed as identical with it, just as we must try to think through the unity of God as the unity of His love if we are really to understand it as His unity. Yet the fact remains that in the first instance, as a distinct perfection in the wealth of God's essence, eternity in itself and as such is to be understood as a determination of the divine freedom. Like the unity and constancy of God, it primarily denotes the absolute sovereignty and majesty of God in itself and as such, as demonstrated in the inward and outward activity of His divine being and operative in His love as His, the eternal love. God's love requires and possesses eternity both inwards and outwards for the sake of its divinity, its freedom. Correspondingly it requires, creates and therefore possesses in its outward relations what we call time. Time is the form of creation in virtue of which it is definitely fitted to be a theatre for the acts of divine freedom. In order that in His outward relationships too God may be the eternal and may act as such, time is required as a determination of creation. If creation were eternal instead of temporal, God, as the Eternal, could not be eternal in the creation, i.e., He could not be free, sovereign and majestic, nor could He act accordingly. In a sense He would be as much bound to creation's eternity as to His own. Thus God's eternity is bound up both with His love and also with time as a determination of creation in the freedom in which both inwards and outwards He is always Himself, one and the same.

All this, again, cannot be said in the same way of the divine omnipresence. It too, of course, is an attribute of God's freedom, like God's omnipotence and glory. But it is not an attribute of God's freedom as such. It is an attribute of God's freedom operative in His love, first in its inward and then in its outward relationship. As this demonstrates and expresses itself as love and in love, it requires and possesses omnipresence both inwards and outwards. Correspondingly, it too requires, creates and therefore possesses in its outward relations what we call space. Space is the form of creation in virtue of which, as a reality distinct from God, it can be the object of His love. That God may be omnipresent outwards (as He is in Himself), space is required as a quality of creation. If creation were itself omnipresent instead of spatial, God, as the Omnipresent, would not be omnipresent in His creation. He would, in a sense, be crowded out by its omnipresence. It could not be the object of His love. God's omnipresence is, then, connected with His freedom, and it is with space as a quality of creation, in the love in which He not only is always and always will be one and the same both inwards and outwards, but is always and always will be the One who encounters and is related and present, first to Himself and then to others also. There is, therefore, an undeniable relationship between God's omnipresence and His eternity, as there is also between these and the problems of space and time. But the relationships are of such a nature that, to understand them, we must not think of them as parallels, as we should have to do if we followed the advice of the older theology. On the contrary, our thinking must first take different directions, and only in this way will it reach the unity which here too, of course, constitutes the object of our whole consideration of the divine essence. It is only by a *tour de force* that the omnipresence and eternity of God can be fitted to the pattern of the anthropological parallelism of the problems of space and time—the demonstration of which is beside our present purpose and may be cheerfully left to the logician, metaphysician or epistemologist.

In addition to this formal objection there is also a material. The more general concept under which the older theology grouped the omnipresence and eternity of God was that of *infinitas*. It was defined as *talis proprietas, quod Deus nec tempore nec loco nec ulla re alia finiri possit, sed sua natura et essentia actu simpliciter per se et absolute sit infinitus* (J. Gerhard, *loc. cit.*, 162). This general concept is purely negative—and obviously so in relation to man and the reality distinct from God. It speaks of the non-finiteness, the non-limitedness or non-limitableness, and therefore the timelessness and non-spatiality of God. According to J. Wolleb (*Chr. Theol. Comp.*, 1626, I, *cap.* 1, 3) God is *omnis mensurae aut termini expers*. In harmony with this another negative term, *immensitas*, was often used for *omnipraesentia* or *ubiquitas*, although in respect of *aeternitas* the usage of the Bible was retained. We can see clearly at this point what is involved when in the definition of the essence of God the starting-point is man rather than God. It is not the essence of God which is defined, but, quite unintentionally, it is again and in the full sense the essence of man. For what can the idea of infinity as such have to do with the essence of God? The concept of infinity is the concept of limit and origin, the consummation of the ideas of space and time as two presuppositions of created existence. It is as such both unavoidable and also possible. We are finite and therefore not infinite, but infinitely limited and defined. But when we have established this limited and defined condition of ours, have we really said anything about God ? Have we not again said something about ourselves, even if only negatively ? Have we not simply heightened or deepened the concept of the reality which is distinct from God, which really tells us nothing about God ? For if the finite is in fact limited by the infinite, the opposite inevitably holds good too. Every finite thing and every sum of finite things may in fact be only a drop in the ocean of the infinite, yet this ocean too, in all its infinity, is only what it is through these drops of the finite. It can consist only in an infinite profusion of these individual drops of finite things. When we set the infinite beside and over against the finite, we are not directing our gaze to the realm of being which is different or separate from the finite. We are offered only a broader characterisation of the reality that is distinct from God when, following the general concept of tradition, Schleiermacher (in *The Christian Faith*, §§52-53) defines the divine eternity and omnipresence as the absolutely timeless (or non-spatial) divine causality, which conditions time (or space) itself along with all that is temporal (or spatial). This is equally true when Biedermann (*Dogmatik*, 1869, p. 627) defines them as " the pure non-temporal and non-spatial internal essence of the absolute ground of the world." Even the fine words of J. Wichelhaus (*Lehre d. hl. Schrift* [3], 1892, p. 339) are no decisive advance on this when he says : " Where God reveals Himself, there space and time draw back, earth's foundations sink, and an essence utterly other makes itself known, an eternal form of being that rests in itself, is complete in itself and in which . . . man too rests perfectly from all his works, from all seeking and craving to be, become or have anything else, because the seen and temporal has passed away and that which is eternal and satisfying in itself and permanent has been found."

Such a withdrawal from space and time, a non-spatial, timeless form of being as the basis of the spatial and temporal does also exist inside creation. In their very limitation space and time are the divinely created qualities of the reality distinct from God. And so, within this reality, temporal and timeless, spatial and non-spatial being touch, supplement and overlap one another. They form the world of earth and heaven, nature and spirit, perception and conception, physics and mathematics. It has been so arranged that even in the world itself we continually meet the distinction and relationship between that which is limited and the unlimited which limits it. All human life exists in this distinction and relationship, this togetherness, encounter and coinherence of time and the timeless, space and the non-spatial. But this mutual relationship must not be confused with the mutual relationship between God and man. God must not be looked for in the unlimited which bounds the limited, or defined as the totality of the timeless and the non-spatial. For we must not overlook the fact that that which limits and that which is limited, within whose difference and whose relatedness our life takes place, never confront one another anywhere with a clarity, unambiguity and irreversibility which entitle us to assert, even with a very moderate certainty, that we are dealing with God on the one hand and the world on the other. Is the material world of nature the sum of finite reality and therefore of the reality distinct from God ? But according to Goethe it is here that we should seek the truly infinite and therefore God, and who can authoritatively assert the opposite ? Or is the life of the spirit infinite in itself, and as such one with the divine life ? Strange as it may seem, what characterises acts of the spirit is to see the finite in the infinite, and to give the infinite form. The infinite which we know as the boundary of the finite never bounds the finite any more than it is itself bounded by it. It is always possible to vacillate in our judgment which is the higher and the lower, the prior and the posterior, the original and the reflection. It is far from certain—as the Idealists would have it—that the non-spatial and timeless alone can be the " basis of the world "

—let alone that they are God, who is surely to be sought elsewhere than in this basis. If we find the essence of God in the non-spatiality and timelessness of the basis of the world, this means neither more nor less than that God is drawn into the dialectic of the world's antithesis. But this leaves the way open for Feuerbach's question whether God might not be in man rather than man in God, and to this question there can be no decisive answer. If the only thing which exists is this antithesis which comprehends God, the relativity of the two spheres cannot prevent us from ascribing now to the one and now the other the dignity and function of deity. And this necessarily is what has always happened and will always happen apart from the knowledge of revelation and faith.

But primarily it is from God's side that we must ask seriously whether the infinite which corresponds and is opposed to the finite is at all adapted to describe God's essence as presupposed in the definition ? Is it the case that God is only infinite, *omnis mensurae aut termini expers*, and therefore that He fully partakes of the properties of only the one sphere, that of non-spatial and timeless spirit ? We certainly do not deny that God is this too, that He is infinite, i.e., that He is not bound to the limits of space and time nor to the forms of space and time generally as the determinations of His creation. But we must add at once that God is infinite in His own divine way, and not in the way in which this can be said of created spirit. On the contrary, He is infinite in a manner in which the antithesis and mutual exclusiveness of the infinite and the finite, non-spatiality and timelessness on the one hand and spatiality and temporality on the other, do not enclose and imprison Him, so that He is confined by His being *omnis mensurae aut termini expers*. How can God suffer this kind of privation ? The infinity which as a concept stands in antithesis to finitude, and therefore to this extent the isolated concept of infinity, is quite insufficient to describe what God is in relation to space and time. God's " infinity," if we want to use this expression, is true infinity because it does not involve any contradiction that it is finitude as well. For there is no reason why God in His essence should not be finite in the same perfect way as He is infinite. But to be finite in this perfect way necessarily means in such a way that His finitude does not prevent His being infinite, and therefore that while finitude is that which limits and is a determination of His creation, it does not involve any limitation or defect in God. It means also that while finitude is made by Him a determination of His creation, it still has its ground and truth antecedently in God Himself, in His essence as God. If we call God infinite, measureless, limitless, spaceless and timeless, this does not mean that we will try to exclude, deny or even question that He is the One who in His whole action posits beginning and end, measure and limit, space and time. If He did not do this but was absolute infinity as the older theology presupposed, how could He be God, love living in freedom, the Lord, the Creator, Reconciler and Redeemer ? God does not do anything which in His own way He does not have and is not in Himself. It is not that in His works God is a God of order, and therefore of measure and limit, and therefore also of space and time, but in Himself, in a hidden, divine realm, which is really that of His essential being, He is the ἄπειρον that He will have to be, if the idea of *omnis mensurae aut termini expers* is to be taken seriously. What pretends to be this ἄπειρον, even if only in pride and revolt against the finite, is the creaturely infinite, created spirit, with all the demonic self-will which is its characteristic in the world of sinful men. But God's revelation is in no sense in harmony with pride and revolt in this world, as it would necessarily have to be to represent and proclaim the content of the real, hidden essence of God. On the contrary, it is against this pride and revolt that God's revelation sets itself with the sharpest and most exclusive opposition as a perversion and destruction of creation. We have therefore no reason to try to see the essence of God in this proud and rebellious ἄπειρον. We have not the slightest cause to allow our knowledge of God to be fitted into the antithesis of the concepts of finitude and infinity, but are definitely warned against it by what we may know of God from His revelation. Otherwise, we have no legitimate complaint against those who in stupified awe before the infinite (which is the divine) usually take refuge in a peaceful finitude, a godless normality. Nor have we any legitimate complaint against those who, in the name of the infinite (which is the divine), see it their duty from time to time to disturb and destroy this peaceful finitude, opening the floodgates in greater or less degree, but certainly no less godlessly to chaos. Reaction and revolution have always drawn their nourishment from the same source, the one in fear, the other in desire, and both in godlessness. This source is certainly not the essence of God as we know it. For this reason the concept of infinity as such is not adapted to serve as a description of God's essence, as a general concept embracing His omnipresence and eternity. And for the same reason we cannot follow the older theory in its imprudent attempt to understand God's omnipresence and eternity as species of His infinity. God is certainly infinite, i.e., He has no basis which is not Himself, no goal which is not Himself and no standard or law which is not Himself. But He is also finite—without destroying, but in His infinity—in the fact that as love He is His own basis, goal, standard and law. It is in this way—and not in that abstract infinity—that God is eternal and omnipresent.

God's omnipresence, to speak in general terms, is the perfection in which He is present, and in which He, the One, who is distinct from and pre-eminent over everything else, possesses a place, His own place, which is distinct from all other places and also pre-eminent over them all. God is the One in such a way that He is present : present to Himself in the triunity of His one essence ; present to everything else as the Lord of everything else. In the one case as in the other, inwards as well as outwards, presence does not mean identity, but togetherness at a distance. In the one case, inwards, it is the togetherness of Father, Son and Holy Spirit at the distance posited by the distinction that exists in the one essence of God. In the other case, outwards, it is the togetherness at a distance of the Creator and the creature. It is in this way, as the One who is present to Himself and to everything else, that God is the One. Presence as togetherness (as distinct from identity) includes distance. But where there is distance, there is necessarily one place and another place. To this extent God's presence necessarily means that He possesses a place, His own place, or, we may say safely, His own space. The absolute non-spatiality of God, deduced from the false presupposition of an abstract infinity, is a more than dangerous idea. If God does not possess space, He can certainly be conceived as that which is one in itself and in all. But He cannot be conceived as the One who is triune, as the One who as such is the Lord of everything else. He cannot be conceived in His togetherness with Himself and everything else, but only in His identity with Himself and therefore with everything else as well. But in this case, is He really conceived as God ? The Christian conception of God at least is shattered and dissolved if God is described as absolute non-spatiality. Non-spatiality means existence without distance, which means identity. God's omnipresence in the Christian sense of the concept has the very opposite meaning that God possesses space, His own space, and that just because of His spatiality, He is able to be the Triune, the Lord of everything else, and therefore the One in and over all things.

This is what we are told by the most explicit of the Bible passages on this subject. They certainly do not deny that God has space. On the contrary, they describe His space in its distinctiveness as also in its pre-eminence over all other spaces. For instance, we read in Solomon's prayer in 1 Kings 8²⁷⁻³⁰ : " Will God indeed dwell on the earth ? " This prayer does not dispute that God actually dwells on earth. Indeed, this is expressly affirmed in the later verses. But it clearly points to the fact that God dwells on earth in His own way, not in the way in which anyone else dwells on earth. " Behold, the heaven and heaven of heavens cannot contain thee." Thus heaven and any place higher than heaven cannot as such be God's place. Again, this does not dispute that God dwells in heaven, and especially in heaven. This, too, is expressly stated lower down. " How much less (may) this house (contain thee) that I have builded ? " The earthly place of Solomon's temple cannot, then, be God's place. But again, Solomon prays later that God will have His earthly place in this temple—from heaven, as is proper to Him as God, but still an earthly place. So the prayer continues : " Yet have thou respect unto the prayer of thy servant, and to his supplication, O Lord, my God, to hearken unto the cry and to the prayer, which thy servant prayeth before thee to-day : that thine eyes may be open toward this house night and day, even toward the place of which thou hast said, My name shall be there : that thou mayest hearken unto the prayer which thy servant shall make toward this place. And hearken thou to the supplication of thy servant, and of thy people Israel, when they shall pray toward this place : and hear thou in heaven thy dwelling place : and when thou hearest, forgive." It is to be noted that although there is a strong emphasis on the particularity with which God possesses space beyond all other spaces, there is also no denial but the assertion that He does actually possess space, His particular space, and that He possesses it also in other spaces, in heaven and on earth. The same presupposition underlies Job. 11⁷⁻⁹. " Canst thou by searching find out God ? canst thou find out the Almighty unto perfection ? It is high as heaven : what canst thou do ? deeper than hell : what canst thou know ? The measure thereof is longer than the earth, and broader than the sea "—the reference being undoubtedly to God's depth and height and width and breadth as distinct from all other depth and height, width and breadth. It also underlies Eph. 3¹⁸, where the knowledge of these very dimensions is not, of course, questioned, but is positively mentioned as the theme of the apostle's prayer for the Church. Yet here, too, we have to do expressly and seriously with real dimensions in God. The same is true of the particularly impressive passage in Ps. 139⁵⁻¹⁰ : " Thou hast beset me behind and before, and laid thy hand upon me. Such knowledge is too wonderful for me ; it is high, I cannot attain unto it. Whither shall I go from thy spirit ? or whither shall I flee from thy presence ? If I ascend up into heaven, thou art there ; if I make my bed in hell, behold, thou art there. If I take the wings of the morning, and dwell in the uttermost parts of the sea ; even there shall thy hand lead me, and thy right hand shall hold me." How can we fail to see in this passage too that God possesses space ? He does so in His own way, of course, differently from all other things, yet not less but more really than anything else. I am not aware of any biblical passage which can be said to teach otherwise : " Am I a God at hand, saith the Lord, and not a God afar off ? Can any hide himself in secret places that I shall not see him ? saith the Lord. Do not I fill heaven and earth ? saith the Lord " (Jer. 23²³⁻²⁴). " He is not far from every one of us ; for in him we live and move and have our being " (Acts 17²⁷⁻²⁸). " The righteousness which is of faith speaketh on this wise, Say not in thine heart, Who shall ascend into heaven ? (that is, to bring Christ down from above), or, Who shall descend into the deep ? (that is, to bring up Christ again from the dead). But what saith it ? The word is nigh thee, even in thy mouth, and in thy heart, that is, the word of faith, which we preach " (Rom. 10⁶⁻⁸). What takes place in all these passages is the relativising of all created space over against the presence of God. This does not mean, however, the denial but the absolutising of the divine space based on the divine presence, and of its special conditions.

We shall now attempt a general definition of the divine spatiality. The spatiality of God is to be distinguished from the spatiality of every other being by the fact that it is the spatiality of the divine being, and that like all other divine perfections it is identical with this being. God is spatial as the One who loves in freedom, and therefore as Himself. Nowhere is He ever spatial as anything other than Himself, or in such a way that His spatiality involves a curtailment or diminution of His deity. He is spatial always and everywhere in such a way that His spatiality means the manifestation and confirmation of His deity. God possesses His space. He is in Himself as in a space. He creates space. He is and does this so that, in virtue of His own spatiality, He can be Himself even in this created space without this limiting Him or causing Him to have something outside Himself, a place apart from Himself, a space which is not His space too in virtue of His spatiality, the space of His divine presence. Or, to express it positively, God possesses space in Himself and in all other spaces. He does this as the being who is completely present in the spatiality that belongs to Him. There is no place where He is not present in His essence, which includes, of course, His knowledge and power. There is no place where He is less present than in all others. On the contrary, He is everywhere completely and undividedly the One He always is, even if in virtue of the freedom of His love He is this in continually differing and special ways. This is the general nature of His omnipresence.

Deus totus ipse intra et extra se omnia continet ut neque infinitus absit a cunctis, neque cuncta ei qui infinitus est, non insint (Hilary, *De trin.* I, 6). The older theology generally quoted at this point a hexameter handed down from the Middle Ages which summed up the general teaching as follows :

Enter, praesenter Deus, hic et ubique potenter.

Augustine's explanations are as follows (*Ep.* 187 *De praesentia Dei*): *Quanquam et in eo ipso quod dicitur Deus ubique diffusus, carnali resistendum est cogitationi et mens a corporis sensibus avocanda, ne quasi spatiosa magnitudine opinemur Deum per cuncta diffundi, sicut humus, aut humor, aut aer, aut lux ista diffunditur (omnis enim huiuscemodi magnitudo minor est in sui parte quam in toto); sed ita potius sicuti est magna sapientia etiam in homine cuius corpus est parvum* (11) . . . *Sic est Deus per cuncta diffusus, ut non sit qualitas mundi, sed substantia creatrix mundi, sine labore regens et sine onere continens mundum. Non tamen per spatia locorum, quasi mole diffusa, ita ut in dimidio mundi corpore sit dimidius et in alio dimidio dimidius, atque ita per totum totus; sed in solo coelo totus, et in sola terra totus et in coelo et in terra totus et nullo contentus loco, sed in seipso ubique totus* (14) . . . *Ideo enim ubique esse dicitur, quia nulli parti rerum absens est; ideo totus, quia non parti rerum partem suam praesentem praebet et alteri parti alteram partem, aequales aequalibus, minori vero minorem, maiorique maiorem; sed non solum universitati creaturae, verum etiam cuilibet parti eius totus pariter adest* (17) . . . *In seipso autem, quia non continetur ab eis quibus est praesens, tanquam sine eis esse non possit.* For : *Deus non, si minus capitur ab illo cui praesens est, ideo ipse minor est* (18). And this is Polanus' summary : *Deus est ubique tota sua individuaque essentia, sed ita, ut essentia divina non sit multiplicata, alibi alia existens; nec sit ubique per magnitudinem molis, nec per rarefactionem et extensionem aut divisionem, hoc est extensa aut divisa, alibi alia sui parte exsistens, nec in dimidio mundi dimidia: sed ut tota et una sit in seipsa tota et una in omnibus et singulis locis et rebus, atque adeo ut sit tota intra omnia et tota extra omnia, nusquam inclusa aut exclusa, omnia continens a nullo contenta —nec propterea immista est rebus aut a rerum sordibus inquinata. Deus est ubique essentia sua, non ut accidens in subiecto, sed ut principium et causa universalis efficiens et conservans adest rei quam efficit.* (*Synt. Theol. chr.*, 1609, *col.* 937). The older theology leaned heavily at this point on the paradox of the " philosopher " Hermes Trismegistus : *Deum esse sphaeram intellectualem, cuius centrum est ubique,* περιφέρεια *vero nusquam.*

But general definitions of this kind are necessarily formal and do not wholly escape ambiguity. For we could say all this of a spaceless principle of space, and therefore of a created reality. Now God as the Creator of all things is certainly the principle of space. But He is not Himself a non-spatial principle. On the contrary, He is the principle of the space in which He Himself is in His own way spatial. This will become clear as we now turn to some of the specific qualities of His omnipresence.

Even the slightest reflection on the being of the God who is to be known in His revelation necessarily leads us to the position that, when we consider the relation of God to space, we cannot play with the concepts *ubique* and *nusquam* as though they were two balls, saying that " God is nowhere " just as easily as we say that " God is everywhere." All the testimony we receive from Scripture concerning God's being and action in this respect asserts that the relation of God to space is an absolutely free and superior relationship, but it definitely does not say that it is a *negative* relationship or, consequently, that God is non-spatial. There is nowhere where God is not, but He is not nowhere. On the contrary, in a way still to be defined more closely, He is always somewhere—from there seeking man and there to be sought by man, there in His remoteness and from there drawing near, present here as the One who is there. If we put our pen through this " somewhere " or change it into a " nowhere," where are we to find the living and the loving God ? And what sort of a divine freedom is it which consists in His being nowhere ? If, as the older theology rightly affirmed, He is not here, there and everywhere under the limitation with which the same can be said of air or light, if He is here, there and everywhere perfectly, undividedly and by Himself, the conclusion to be drawn is certainly not that He is not " really " present here, there and everywhere, or that the " really " must be taken to mean " not really." He is it in His own divine way, but

He is it. He possesses and He is Himself space. And we have no right to limit this statement to God's being in and with creation. God's spatiality cannot, therefore, be related to created space alone, while as He is in Himself He is conceived and described as non-spatial. At this point, as at every other, a distinction of this kind would inevitably mean that in the way in which God exists in and with creation (or to put it concretely, in His revelation), God deceives us as to His true being : He represents Himself and acts as the living and loving God in relation to us, but in Himself He is quite different, non-spatial, and therefore lifeless and loveless. If in and with His creation God is the same as He is in Himself, revealing Himself to us in His revelation as not less or other than Himself, then it is characteristic of Him to be here and there and everywhere, and therefore to be always somewhere and not nowhere, to be spatial in His divine essence.

To play with *ubique* and *nusquam*, as the Fathers often did, may and must be viewed, no matter where we meet it, as a sure indication that those who play in this way are either on the point or have already decided to turn to the lifeless and loveless God of pure human invention (the ultimate secret of all heathen faiths) in place of the God who has Himself given and revealed Himself to us as the One He is. We have good cause, therefore, to regard all their other statements as suspect, or at least to approach them with great care. For we cannot turn to these two Gods at one and the same time. The living and loving God has always been abandoned already when He is in some sense understood as an interpretation of the other lifeless and loveless God, or when *mutatis mutandis* the latter is understood as an interpretation of Him. A choice must be made between the *ubique* and the *nusquam*. Omnipresence cannot mean God's " omni-absence." It is only when we do not speak of God at all, but of the non-spatial principle of all space, that no choice is required and we can play with the two terms, explaining the *ubique* by the *nusquam* and the *nusquam* by the *ubique*. This game and explanation is a characteristic of all mystical teaching about God. It is this which stamps it as an attack on or a flight from the real Christian knowledge of God, even when it takes the form of what is called Christian mysticism. Or, at any rate, it is the factor which brings it into opposition to the true Christian knowledge of God.

But again, if we reflect on the being of the God who is to be known in His revelation, we are forced to adopt a second position alongside the first. The perfection in which God is omnipresent, and therefore not nowhere but somewhere, does mean indeed that He is everywhere undividedly and completely as the One He is and in all the fulness of His being. It does not mean, however, that God is in the least hindered from being present everywhere in a particular way—otherwise it could not be the perfection of His freedom and His love. It does not mean that He cannot be everywhere present in a different way (without this raising any question about His identity with Himself or His simplicity). It does not mean that He cannot be present in an individual way in individual cases, in the individuality which He has Himself and which is determined by Himself. On the contrary, the perfection of God's spatiality triumphs (as does also His identity with Himself, His simplicity) in the fact that He is free in His unity and totality always to be present in one specific way according to His good-pleasure, and in the fact that in His love He is actually always present in a specific way.   In this He is always identical with Himself yet always present in a specific way corresponding to the relation between His unity and His triunity, as also to that between His unity and the wealth of His being.   This means that God can be God and actually is God and present everywhere.   He is not less God or present here or there.   But He is God in a different way here and there, in a relationship between His here and His there, in a movement from the one to the other and *vice versa*, with greater or lesser remoteness or nearness between the two,   He can be and actually is present everywhere in this way in the manifestation of His freedom, the fulfilment of His life and the reality of His love.   If His were, so to speak, an immovable omnipresence, excluding a divine here and there and its relationships and distances, it is inevitable that He would again be lifeless and loveless and therefore fundamentally unfree.   And in that case the distinction of the persons in the unity of His essence, the manifold wealth of this one divine essence, and above all His speaking and acting as the Subject and Lord of His own dealings with His creation, is necessarily shown again to be an impossibility, a mere illusion which will be dispelled at some height or depth. The game of *ubique* and *nusquam* can and inevitably will begin again. For God is now lifeless and loveless in His very spatiality.   He is more or less the prisoner of His own deity, prevented by His perfection from being the One revelation shows Him to be.   " Everywhere " can again be understood, and necessarily will be, as the equivalent to " nowhere."   We will again have to distrust His revelation.   We will again have to assume that He is quite different in Himself from what He is in His revelation and in creation generally.   It is an ill " perfection " of God which means this, and has these consequences.   No, God's true omnipresence, according to the testimony of Scripture, includes the possibility and actuality of His differentiated presence with Himself and with everything else, without any curtailment or weakness or diminution of Himself.   We must not fail to note that this differentiation of the divine presence does not depend on its adaptation to the nature of creation.   To be sure, it is in fact adapted to it, but that is another matter.   It is adapted to it because it is truly grounded on the essence of its Creator, because, prior to all differentiation in creation, God Himself as the One is also differentiated within Himself in this way.   Nothing particular or different exists in creation without God's will and therefore without His essence and therefore without Himself.   Everything, even in its differentiation, is well considered in Himself.   He is present to everything with a presence which is not uniform but distinct and differentiated.

We shall now try to describe some of the most important differences

or differentiations of the divine omnipresence, in which it is first revealed as a divine perfection. And we shall have to begin from the
position that it is not His, God's omnipresence, if it does not include
first and above all the presence in which God is present to Himself
and to Himself exclusively, and therefore the space which is exclusively His own space. If it does not include this space, if it is reduced
to being His presence in and with all kinds of other things, and if
no space exists that belongs only to God and to nothing else, God
Himself is again spaceless, and therefore lifeless and loveless. The
truth is rather this, that God is present to other things, and is able
to create and give them space, because He Himself possesses space
apart from everything else. The space everything else possesses is
the space which is given it out of the fulness of God. The fact is that
first of all God has space for Himself and that subsequently, because
He is God and is able to create, He has it for everything else as well ;
just as He is life and love *ad extra* because He is it first in Himself
with primal power and fulness.

When the prophet Isaiah (6¹) sees the Lord on His throne high and lifted
up (cf. the prophet Micaiah ben Imlah, 1 Kings 22¹⁹), it denotes the sum of God's
holiness and glory, but it also denotes this basic form of His omnipresence, the
space which is God's alone. This throne, erected by God Himself, is to be found
in heaven (Ps. 103¹⁹). It stands fast from the beginning (Ps. 93²). It is the
place from which God looks at all the inhabitants of the earth (Ps. 33¹⁴). From
it " his eyes behold " the earth, " his eyelids try the children of men " (Ps. 11⁴).
This throne is clearly to be found in the same space as the earth. Within this
space, however, it is elevated above earthly space. And it is God's space alone.
Who or what has a right to have a space beside God on this throne ? He who
sits on this throne and dwells there is God Himself and no one else. Note that
in all circumstances it is in this way, as the possessor of this throne, that God
is said to be or dwell " in heaven," to use the general biblical phrase that has
become more or less canonical through the words of the Lord's Prayer (Mt. 6⁹).
According to Scripture heaven, like the earth, belongs to God's creation, which
will one day pass away, be changed and become new. " Heaven " denotes, in
a word, the upper, the invisible, we might say the spiritual side of the reality
created by God and to that extent its higher side. If it is said of God that He
dwells " in heaven," this naturally does not deny that He is the Creator and
Lord of heaven too and of all heavenly beings and all heavenly hosts. Scripture
certainly speaks of " heavens " and therefore of heaven in several senses (2 Cor.
12²), and we know how Jewish speculation, and later that of the Scholastics,
tried to understand and describe it in its varied forms, together with the hierarchy of its inhabitants, forces and orders. In so doing they borrowed to some
extent from Plato and the Platonists. But even the highest of these real or
possible heavens and even the highest of all the heavenly powers are in no sense
identical with God. The fact that God is in heaven cannot on any account mean
this. 1 Kings 8²⁷ is relevant in this respect: " Behold, heaven and the heaven
of heavens cannot contain thee." It makes no difference that in some passages
God's throne is described as heaven itself or heaven as His throne (Is. 66¹, Mt. 5³⁴,
Acts 7⁴⁹). For if in contradiction to the others these passages seem to say that
God's throne is part of His creation and should be distinguished from God Himself, nevertheless it is true in them that, while God shares heaven with the angels
and the heavenly host, He does not share His throne with anyone else. We
must understand these passages, then, as saying that heaven in all its glorious

variety and with all who dwell in it serves as a throne for Him who is its Lord and Creator too in so far as it too is under Him. Of course, God is also " in heaven " or " in the heavens " in the same sense as He is even on earth. That is, as Lord and Creator of the whole world He is fully present to heavenly reality also. He is in the midst of the heavenly hosts and in the lowest of the heavens no less than in the highest. But so far as we have to interpret His being " in heaven " strictly, as a description of God's own particular " dwelling place," we must certainly understand " in heaven " to mean " above heaven." Because heaven is the higher side of the reality created by God, and because God is in all circumstances the highest and is to be sought above, and because for us as His creatures, at least here and now, heaven stands for and denotes what is " above," for this reason and to this extent His holy name can and must be for us here and now that of the " Father in heaven." Note how Col. 3^{1-2}, which tells us to " seek what is above," clearly does not identify " above " with heaven as such, but describes " above " as " where Christ is seated at the right hand of God," thus distinguishing it from heaven as well. The specific contrast intended is between " above " and " on the earth." It is thither that we are to look and think when we think of the " Father in heaven." We are again dealing with a " there," but now it is this " there." We are to think of the throne which God occupies in heaven, and occupying it, is exalted above heaven as He is above the earth. But the space of this throne, while it is also space, is the space which belongs to God alone. It is in this way that God is present there and there only. But as and because He is present there in this way, He can also be present elsewhere in different ways. He who possesses His own space (exclusively His own) is able to be the Creator and Lord of other spaces as well, and in the power of His own spatiality He can be present in these other spaces too. The consequence is—this seems to be the meaning of Scripture—that His space and the other spaces together really form a single space, to the extent that God is present to Himself and in them all, to the extent that He gives space, indeed is space, both to Himself and in different ways in these spaces to everything which is in them. If that were not so, what interpretation could we give to Acts 17^{28}, that " in him we live and move and have our being " ? What truth would correspond to the symbol if everything that Scripture says about our existence and life " in God," " in Christ," " in the Spirit " could bear only a symbolical interpretation, if God were not genuinely and primordially spatial, and indeed in such a way that in the first instance He is it only in and for Himself, but subsequently and in virtue of this for others also, who can obtain space by Him, indeed in different ways can find their own space in Him ? If it is not an incidental or superfluous belief that we can obtain space from God and find space in Him, but a truth which is decisive for the actuality of creation, reconciliation and redemption and the trustworthiness of the Word of God, we cannot evade the recognition that God Himself is spatial. But if this is the case, the biblical picture of the throne of God (at whose right hand His Son sits and is our Representative as the One who wears our humanity) is not merely a picture or symbol. For it denotes the real place of God, and as such the one which is superior to all other places, underlying and controlling them, the place of all places, and therefore the very opposite of Nowhere or Cloudcuckootown, the principle of space itself, real space *par excellence*. This is the true and therefore itself the spatial principle of space of basic divine reality, and not the non-spatial principle of space of our creaturely notions. If a still more definite question is asked about this basic form of the divine omnipresence, and therefore about the throne of God itself, we can refer only to the triunity as such of the one being of God. This settles the fact that although God is certainly the One who alone is God, He is not therefore solitary, but is in Himself both unity and fellowship, the One in three modes of being at one and the same time. This decisively rebuts the view that God is spaceless and therefore lifeless and loveless. As the Triune

He is living and loving, and this is the basis and the ultimately real source of space in God Himself. God's triunity is the space which is exclusively His own space, and as such can become and give itself to be the space of all spaces. As Father, Son and Holy Spirit God uses and has and is space for Himself. But in His being as Father, Son and Holy Spirit He is the Creator and Lord of everything whose being and nature corresponds to His will, decree and act. And as such He uses and has and is also space for all this which is distinct from Himself —space in created space, and therefore space in the space of heaven and earth, space in our spaces, which are as little identical with His space as the world in general can be identical with God. Yet these spaces can be spaces by Him and in Him, enclosed by His space. In them in turn His space must therefore have and actually does have unlimited space by reason of its eternity in the divine triunity. He is present to them all and in them all He is omnipresent.

At all events, in distinction from this basic form of the divine omnipresence it is also His omnipresence *ad extra*, in creation. In the first instance, reserving any further differentiation, we think of it as a whole in relation to all creation as such. The love which God has in Himself as the triune God has also turned and manifested itself in freedom outwards. It did not have to do this. It would not have been any less love if it had not done so. But it has done so. In virtue of the divine existence there is a creaturely existence distinct from it. And in virtue of the divine space there is a creaturely space distinct from it, the space of heaven and earth, our space. And again, in virtue of His own proper spatiality God is present in space and in all the spaces of His creation. Note that He is *present*. This implies both distinction and relationship. There is distinction. For neither as a whole nor in detail is what we have and know as our space God's space, and therefore God Himself. But there is relationship. For what we have and know as our space does not exist apart from God's space. On the contrary, by it and in it God's space is always and altogether in our space as well. As, then, we are in our space, we are in one way or another always in God's space at the same time. Indeed, we are far more in God's space than in our created space. Thus there are certainly different forms, very different forms, of God's presence in His creation, but there is no absence of God in His creation. There are in it many forms of the remoteness and nearness of God, and of His coming and going in the full reality of all that is denoted by these terms. There is a presence of God in wrath and a presence in grace. There is a presence in His hiddenness and a presence in His revelation. And in all these are the most diverse gradations. But there is no non-presence of God in His creation. This is just as true as that everything which exists is in space and therefore in His space too, and therefore also in Himself as well, so that it cannot be withdrawn from Him in the spatiality proper to Him.

At this point we may again recall the words of Ps. 139[5-10] which make it so clear that the God whose being Scripture attests as the being revealed by Himself is the One from whom there is no escape into any spaces which are not primarily and decisively in His space and in which He does not primarily and decisively have His space. His presence in one form in His hiddenness and in another in His revelation does not mean that He can be evaded by any real or imaginary ascent to heaven or descent to hades. He will be present in the one place as the other. He will be present differently in the two, in one way in heaven and in another in hades. But He will be present as the same being that He everywhere is and that He is in Himself. " Neither is there any creature that is not manifest in his sight ; but all things are naked and open unto the eyes of him with whom we have to do " (Heb. 4^{13}). How fearful this is we learn from Amos 9$^{1ff.}$: " He that fleeth of them shall not flee away, and he that escapeth of them shall not be delivered. Though they dig into hell, thence shall mine hand take them ; though they climb up to heaven, thence will I bring them down. And though they hide themselves in the top of Carmel, I will search and take them out thence ; and though they be hid from my sight in the bottom of the sea, thence shall I command the serpent, and he shall bite them." But this is not only fearful. Ultimately and decisively it is not fearful. On the contrary, it is comforting, because God in His love and for His love's sake is present to everything and everywhere. This is the lesson of Isaiah 57^{15} : " For thus saith the high and lofty one that inhabiteth eternity, whose name is holy : I dwell in the high and holy place, with him also that is of a contrite and humble spirit, to revive the spirit of the humble, and to revive the heart of the contrite ones." In different ways God Himself surrounds and encloses His creation. That is why we can speak of His omnipresence in the totality of the things which are distinct from Himself. God's being and dwelling both in His own heavenly or supra-heavenly place and in the particular places in creation which, in distinction from others, He has made in a special way His own, is never attested or emphasised in Scripture for its own sake. These " high places " of God are always spoken of because of their connexions in a different direction, because from His high place God looks and speaks, approaching men and nations, Himself descending into the world that is distinct from His high place. He is always moving out even from those places which are selected and characterised in the world as " holy," to enter into all the rest of the world (or from an earlier or primary sanctuary to a new or secondary one). He is clearly depicted as doing this in Ps. 68$^{17-19}$: " The chariots of God are twenty thousand, even thousands of angels ; the Lord is among them, as in Sinai, in the holy place. Thou hast ascended on high, thou hast led captivity captive ; thou hast received gifts for men, yea, for the rebellious also, that the Lord God might dwell among them. Blessed be the Lord, who daily loadeth us with benefits, even the God of our salvation." In view of passages like this, which form the rule and not the exception in the biblical witness of the relation of God to space, we can only say with reference to God's omnipresence in His creation as a whole that it must be understood strictly as omnipresence. It is not a kind of shroud which is itself unmoved but is spread over the totality that is moved in itself. On the contrary, it is itself that which moves and is moved, which is the real mover and object of movement in this totality. Like God generally it is being and act in one. It could not be otherwise. For it is the omnipresence of the living God.

There is no absence, no non-presence, of God in His creation. But this does not form any obstacle to a whole series of special presences, of concrete cases of God being here or there, which rise like mountain peaks from the plain of God's general presence with His creation. The reason for this is that we are dealing with the presence of the living God. And these special cases take place in the context of what God does as He reveals Himself and reconciles the world with Himself. Indeed, we are forced to say that according to the order of biblical thinking and speech it is this special presence of God which always comes first and is estimated and valued as the real and decisive presence. The general omnipresence of God in His creation is not in any sense a kind of general truth which is seen in a distinctive form in His particular presence. In that case the unexpressed presupposition of the possibility of the latter (and that which safeguards and covers its assertion) would be the fact that God is admittedly omnipresent, and is therefore present primarily, not in a particular place, but everywhere. God is certainly everywhere. But God is not only everywhere. On the contrary, as the matter is presented in the Bible, it is in and along with His particular presence, and not apart from it, that the reality of this general presupposition encounters man. It is as we look back and forwards from God's special presence that His general presence in the world is recognised and attested, and the authenticity and efficacy of the general divine omnipresence consists always and exclusively in the identity of the God who is present generally with the God who is present in particular, and not *vice versa*. The general truth is determined and guaranteed by the special one, and not conversely. The way does not, then, lead directly from the presence with which God, as the Triune, is present to Himself to His presence in the whole world. It does lead, of course, from the one to the other. But it goes, as it were, by way of His special presence, and therefore in the first instance and directly it leads to His special presence. The reason is that it is through God's Word that the world is created, preserved and upheld, and this Word is the essence and mystery of His revelation and so of His special presence in the world. God's presence to the whole world from the beginning and for all time is in His Word, which as the Word of revelation and reconciliation occupies a special space. This being so, God's omnipresence is bound up with the special nature of His presence in His revealing and reconciling work ontologically (in its reality) and not merely noetically (as far as our knowledge of it goes). It is only the One who is present in this special manner and place who is also the God present in the world as a whole.

Note how the very passages which bear witness so emphatically to the general omnipresence of God (Ps. 139[5ff.], Amos 9[1ff.]) do not make this a law which then finds special application also in His presence to man, or the people of Israel, as Lord and Judge. On the contrary, it is in view of this special presence that His general presence is recalled and asserted. Note how Heb. 4[13] too, in accordance with the previous verse, is a statement about the Word of God which is living and active and pierces through everything like a sword. It is to this Word that the omnipresence of God is ascribed, and not, conversely, that to a general presence of God there is ascribed the characteristic, among others, of possessing also the form and efficacy of such a Word of God. We must not think, then, that it is meant or at least has to be understood only symbolically, pictorially and indirectly when in the Old and New Testaments God is constantly characterised and described as the possessor of a place or location, of one or many dwelling places, which in distinction from God's throne in heaven can easily be found on a map and viewed and visited as places, which can and should be approached and left and stayed at, and at which God can and should be sought and worshipped more and better, or at any rate differently from elsewhere without detriment to His omnipresence. If we read in Ps. 103²² : " Bless the Lord, all his works in all places of his dominion," these places of His dominion may be infinitely many. Yet they are in no sense identical with the whole of created space, but are special places within this space. There exists a kind of rivalry between these places and other places. " Why leap ye, ye high hills ? this is the hill which God desireth to dwell in ; yea the Lord will dwell in it for ever " (Ps. 68¹⁶). He that sitteth in the heavens (Ps. 2⁴), who dwelleth on high (Is. 33⁵), in the light which no man can approach unto (1 Tim. 6¹⁶), has the desire, the will and the power to be everywhere, but not only to be everywhere. He has the desire, the will and the power also to be in special places in a special way, and to be everywhere in the special way that He is in special places. We are not to understand Exod. 24¹⁶ figuratively but literally when we read that the glory of the Lord abode upon mount Sinai, and again we are not to understand it as figurative, or in contradiction to this first verse, when it says immediately afterwards (Exod. 25⁸) : " Let them make me a sanctuary, that I may dwell among them." Just as certainly Exod. 29⁴⁵ᶠ· is not to be understood figuratively : " And I will dwell among the children of Israel, and will be their God. And they shall know that I am the Lord their God, that brought them forth out of the land of Egypt, that I may dwell among them : I am the Lord their God." It is not said to every nation that God will be their God. It is not said to Egypt or Assyria, Moab or Midian. No, it is to the particular nation Israel. And as certainly as this is literal, so too is what is said about the particular dwelling of God in the particular places, at Sinai as the temporary goal of the exodus from Egypt, in the tabernacle during the wilderness wanderings and the conquest of the land, and in Jerusalem during the occupation of Palestine. The concreteness of the choice and sanctification of these places corresponds to the concreteness of the choice and calling of this people. And so, when Jacob, waking from his dream (Gen. 28¹⁶ᶠ·), says : " Surely the Lord is in this place : and I knew it not. And he was afraid and said, How dreadful is this place ! this is none other than the house of God, and this is the gate of heaven," this is not simply an expression of pious emotion. On the contrary, it describes the objective condition that lies at the basis of the whole covenant between God and man. Had the Lord not been at this particular place in a particular way, and had it not really been this particular Beth-El, then the dreams of this particular man, Jacob, which he had at this particular place and not at any other, would have been idle fancies. And then the whole covenant between God and man as a definite covenant with definite men would have been invalid both at that time and for all time. In the same way, in Exod. 3⁵ it is God who addresses Moses, and not Moses God, with the words : " Draw not nigh hither : put off thy shoes from off thy feet, for the place whereon thou standest is holy ground." It is a special form of the order without which the existence of Israel in covenant would be quite unthinkable (for it would not have existed at all) when in Deut. 12¹⁻¹⁴, in contrast to the ways of the peoples who " served their gods, upon the high mountains, and upon the hills, and under every green tree," the injunction is given to Israel : " Ye shall not do so unto the Lord your God. But unto the place which the Lord your God shall choose out of all your tribes to put his name there, even unto his habitation shall ye seek, and thither shalt thou come : And thither ye shall bring your burnt offerings and your sacrifices . . . and there ye shall eat before the Lord your God and ye shall rejoice." Note that the gods of the heathen are characterised by the arbitrary and accidental way in which the places of their dwelling and worship are fixed. But the God of Israel dwells in a definite place chosen and designated by Himself. It is objectively and organically necessary that when Ps. 135 depicts the superiority of Yahweh to all gods and idols, as shown in His actions to Israel, it should begin with the words : " Praise ye the name of the Lord, praise him, O ye servants of the Lord, ye that stand in the house of the Lord, in the courts of the house of our God " (v. 1f.), and end with the words : " Blessed be the Lord out of Zion, which dwelleth at Jerusalem. Praise ye the Lord " (v. 21). " For " (necessarily and not arbitrarily) " the Lord (who is so great in his acts) hath chosen Zion : he hath desired it for his habitation " (Ps. 132¹³). And therefore the prayer is really for one and the same thing when it says in Ps. 74² : " Remember thy congregation, which thou hast purchased of old, the rod of thine inheritance which thou hast redeemed : this mount Zion, wherein thou hast dwelt." Thus it is an integral part of the righteousness which the true Israelite knows is promised him, and which he has a right to claim, that he may say also : " Lord, I have loved the habitation of thy house, and the place where thine honour dwelleth " (Ps. 26⁸). It is no poetic exuberance, but for all its warmth the most sober reality, when he confesses in Ps. 84¹ᶠ· : " How amiable are thy tabernacles, O Lord of hosts ! My soul longeth, yea, even fainteth for the courts of the Lord : my heart and my flesh crieth out for the living God. Yea, the sparrow hath found an house, and the swallow a nest for herself, where she may lay her young, even thine altars, O Lord of hosts, my King, and my God. Blessed are they that dwell in thy house : they will be still praising thee " ; and in v. 10 : " A day in thy courts is better than a thousand. I had rather be a doorkeeper in the courts of my God than to dwell in the courts of wickedness." And the images are neither confounded nor confused, but this necessary connexion is again indicated when in Ps. 46⁴ᶠ· that which is defended by the God of Jacob as our sure stronghold, is suddenly itself called the city of God : " the holy place of the tabernacles of the most high. God is in the midst of her ; she shall not be moved : God shall help her, and that right early." Naturally it must be understood that these statements are all made relatively to the dwelling place (the throne of God) which is not to be found on any map. But in this relation they do have to be made. For in the Old Testament testimony and the Old Testament form of the revelation there is always a dwelling-place of God which can be marked on the map. The Old Testament testimony does not, of course, say (as do those who according to Jer. 7³ᶠ· trust in " lying words ") : " The temple of the Lord, the temple of the Lord, the temple of the Lord are these." That is to say, it does not regard the place as holy in itself, trying to have the Lord Himself, possessively, with the holy place. Those who think in this way must be told without any ceremony : " Amend your ways and your doings." They must be reminded by the prophetic preaching of repentance and judgment that it is God who dwells here and who will be recognised and honoured as God. But Jeremiah, too, did not doubt for one moment that God does actually dwell here. God is not imprisoned in this place. What the prayer of Solomon says in this connexion may be regarded as characteristic of the tenor of the whole Old Testament. According to Jeremiah 7¹⁴ᶠ· He can destroy and forsake this house as He forsook that of Shiloh. But He always was and always will be the One who dwells in the midst of Israel and possesses a definite place.

The relativity but also the reality of this dwelling emerges clearly in the New Testament. On the one hand it is a matter of the freedom and therefore the relativity of this divine dwelling. It cannot be said that this is something new in contrast with the Old Testament testimony. There were those who denied God this freedom. Some held Him to be merely a mountain god or a god of the wilderness. Others (confusing Him with the gods of the heathen) regarded Him as the god of the blood and soil of Canaan. Others thought Him tied to the temple buildings in Jerusalem. Others wanted to make Him a distant god in heaven. But those who thought along these lines all failed to know Him in His revelation in Israel. Every divine dwelling-place is placed under the law of the freedom of the divine dwelling as an act in which God controls but is not controlled. We may seek God in special places according to His command, but if we are not willing to seek Him in these special places as the One who possesses His eternal throne, we deceive ourselves. The New Testament gathers up this truth when it says expressly that the " tabernacle " in which the God of Israel dwelt, as " a house made with hands," belonged to the ὑποδείγματα and ἀντίτυπα of the ἐπουράνια and ἀληθινά (Heb. 9²³ᶠ·). The fact is certainly true, and even the New Testament does not deny but confirms it, that it did belong to these things and derived its dignity and power from a heavenly object and original. But it is also confirmed that it had the dignity and power only of an indication or foreshadowing, that it was God's dwelling-place with a relative reality. In contrast to every heathen understanding of the reality of God's dwelling-places—and that means in contrast to every godless understanding— it is now recognised and confessed (in harmony with Solomon and Jeremiah) that " God that made the world and all things therein, seeing that he is Lord of heaven and earth, dwelleth not in temples made with hands ; neither is worshipped with men's hands " (Ac. 17²⁴⁻²⁵). And when the Samaritan woman (Jn. 4²⁰⁻²⁶), also entangled in the heathen idea of God's dwelling-places, sums up the situation in the words : " Our fathers worshipped in this mountain : and ye say, that in Jerusalem is the place where men ought to worship," this is openly repudiated with : " Woman, believe me, the hour cometh, when ye shall neither in this mountain, nor yet in. Jerusalem, worship the Father. Ye worship ye know not what : we know what we worship : for salvation is of the Jews. But the hour cometh, and now is, when the true worshippers shall worship the Father in spirit and in truth : for the Father seeketh such to worship him. God is a spirit : and they that worship him must worship him in spirit and in truth." But at this very point we must pay careful attention to what follows. " The woman saith unto him, I know that Messias cometh, which is called Christ : when he is come, he will tell us all things. Jesus saith unto her, I that speak unto thee am he." This does not mean that the freedom of the divine dwelling had suddenly ceased to be the freedom of an actual dwelling of God, and that its relativity would now rule out its reality. It does not mean that the divine presence in the world had suddenly become that of a mere undifferenti- ated ubiquity, and not of definite and distinct places. The opposite of Jerusalem and Gerizim and all temples made with hands—and we can apply it and say the opposite of Rome, Wittenberg, Geneva and Canterbury—is not the universe at large, which is the superficial interpretation of Liberalism, but Jesus. And the worship of the Father in spirit and in truth is not the undifferentiated worship of a God undifferentiatedly omnipresent. On the contrary, we have only to glance at the way in which the terms " spirit " and " truth " are used elsewhere in St. John's Gospel and we shall see at once that it is worship of God mediated through Jesus as the One who makes everything known to us. According to the testimony of the New Testament, God does not cease to dwell in the world in definite and dis- tinct ways, i.e., even as omnipresent, and without detriment to His omnipresence, He does not cease to be in special places. On the contrary, the reality of the definite, distinct dwelling of God in the world is now made clear in this true but not abstract antithesis, in which it can be said : " The Word (the very Word which was in the beginning, which was with God and which was God, the Word by which all things came into being, this really omnipresent Word) " was made flesh, and dwelt among us, and we beheld his glory " (Jn. 1¹⁴). This was what underlay Beth-El and Sinai, Jerusalem and Shiloh, but not the temples of the heathen gods or Gerizim (" Ye worship ye know not what "). That is why there is in the former real ὑπόδειγμα and ἀντίτυπον. Salvation is really of the Jews. But it is really salvation ; and when it has actually come from the Jews and been rejected by the Jews as such, it is no more simply for the Jews, but from the Jews for all, Jews and Gentiles, who are ready to be worshippers of this kind, in spirit and in truth, as the Father wishes them to be. We are dealing with the fulfilment of the Old Testament predictions of the divine dwelling, and not their annulment. For what is the glory of the incarnate Word of God, which could be beheld ? What does the great voice from the throne cry now in view of the resurrection and return of Jesus Christ ? It now says fully, definitely and distinctively nothing less than this : " Behold, the tabernacle of God is with men, and he will dwell with them and they shall be his people, and God himself shall be with them " (Rev. 21³). Thus a decisive, all embracing and confirming Yes (and not a No) is said here to the testimony of God's definite and distinctive dwelling on earth (with the words of Ex. 29⁴⁵, cf. Lev. 26¹¹f.). It is still true, indeed now for the first time it is really true and manifest, that " out of Zion God hath shined " (Ps. 50²), because He is great there, high above all the peoples (Ps. 99²), and there and there only is He to be seen (Ps. 84⁷), and from there goes forth the Law and the Word of the Lord from Jerusalem (Is. 2³). What the Old Testament had said about the special nature of all these places still obtains—indeed now for the first time it is decisively and finally confirmed. All these places in their special concrete and distinctive character stood for the special nature of God's place, from which His Word, His Law and His salvation always go forth in the special way that corresponds to the special nature of God Himself, that He may now be in His special place for us too in the world, that He may be seen and heard and tasted and believed by men with human faculties and senses. Now that the concealment of the Messiah has passed and His revelation by the people of Israel as such is repudiated, so that this people is no longer the isolated bearer of the covenant, the time has also passed of God's dwelling at those special places whose special nature was bound up with the conditions that have now lapsed. It has passed like the time of the sacrifices and the whole Law of Israel as such. Special places can no longer exist in this sense. If Christianity, for its part, tries to proclaim and accept holy places in this sense, it will mean always a relapse into Judaism, or more correctly, into a pagan self-misunderstanding of Judaism, or even more accurately, a rejection of the true Judaism of Solomon and Jeremiah. Theologically, then, we cannot expect anything for the Jews from a return to Palestine as the holy land ; and recent propaganda for the gathering of all Christian Jews to Palestine as the place of the promise which avails for all who are baptised out of Israel involves a twofold error. Now that Israel's Messiah has appeared, and has been rejected by Israel, and manifested as the Saviour of believers from both Jews and Gentiles, there does not exist any more a holy mountain or holy city or holy land which can be marked on a map. The reason is not that God's holiness in space has suddenly become unworthy of Him or has changed into a heathen ubiquity. The reason is that all prophecy is now fulfilled in Jesus, and God's holiness in space, like all God's holiness, is now called and is Jesus of Nazareth. This holiness is certainly to be encountered in the created space that can be represented on maps. But in this space it is only where Jesus Himself, having entered heaven (in fulfilment of the entering of the high priest into the tabernacle, Heb. 9²⁴), is now present in the world from heaven and therefore from the throne of God in such a way that He calls and quickens men to faith in Him by His Word and His Spirit, and therefore calls and quickens them for that worship in spirit and truth desired by the Father. In Him is Sinai and Zion, Bethel and Jerusalem. And it is all in Him as divine space, as the heavenly Jerusalem (Rev 21²) prepared for His own, who have their country already here and now, but must seek it as strangers and sojourners here and now in this world, having no country in this world which corresponds to it. But again this does not mean that their existence, and with it the secondary existence of Jesus in the world, may be described or understood as non-spatial. It is just as little non-spatial as Jesus' proper and primary existence, as the occupier of the throne of God, is non-spatial. For they cannot evade the fact that their expectation and hope is set, not on a non-spatial form of being, but on a building " from God, a house not made with hands, eternal in the heavens " (2 Cor. 5¹), on their being in the heavenly

Jerusalem and therefore definitely in a space, the divine space itself. For this reason the existence of these strangers and sojourners, founded by the Word and Spirit of Jesus, as the existence of those who believe in Him, is described in spatial terms as their being in Christ or Christ's being in them. And just as the Father (Jn. 14¹⁰), indeed the very " fulness of the godhead " dwells in Christ (Col. 1¹⁹ ; 2⁹), so His Word dwells richly in His own (Col. 3¹⁶), and similarly His power (2 Cor. 12⁹), the Spirit (Rom. 8⁹, 2 Tim. 1¹⁴, Jas. 4⁵), Christ Himself dwells in them, and Christians both in their individual lives on earth and as a whole are seen as a " temple " of God (1 Cor. 3¹⁶ᶠ·, 6¹⁹ ; 2 Cor. 6¹⁶ ; Eph. 2²¹ ; 1 Pet. 2⁴ᶠ·). Although the members of the Church are strangers here and live under this condition, the Church itself is not a mass which is scattered diffusedly about the world, having no boundaries, but intermingled and lost in the form of the world itself. On the contrary, to use what is in this respect too the distinctive expression, it is the body of Christ, and although it is true enough that the body can be recognised only by faith and the Word and Spirit of Christ, yet as a body it has contours like everything else that exists in bodily form, and it fills a particular space in space generally. Consequently the Church and the world, the Church and the state and the Church and the heathen faiths can always meet and separate, attracting and repelling one another even though they may often seem to merge into another. If the eschatological place of the throne of God, the place " where Christ sits at the right hand of God," is the Church's own space and therefore the reason why it stands over against other places, yet as the Church of Him who has His own space there, as the secondary form of His existence, it has also in created space a spatial form of existence and spatial function. It is for this reason that there is an *extra* and an *intra ecclesiam*, in which not the Church but its heavenly Lord decides on acquittal or condemnation, life or death as the future of all men. This spatiality of Jesus Christ in heaven and on earth is what continues even in the New Testament when the earthly Jerusalem was destroyed and could not continue as the dwelling-place of God. It is the constant factor in that which is not constant—its end and also its fulfilment. In this way we find that according to testimony of the New Testament, too, there is maintained, or rather revealed, not only the relativity but also the reality of the special presence of God.

We have spoken about the general and special presence of God in His creation. By the general presence we understood God's presence in His creation in its totality ; by His special presence His presence in His definite and distinct action in His work of revelation and reconciliation within creation. And we maintained the position that according to the order and evaluation of biblical thinking God's special presence is first and decisive. Both noetically and ontologically the general presence is bound to this special presence. For all things are created and preserved by God's Word, by the Word which is nothing other than the Word of His revelation and reconciliation.

But this relationship requires us to make a third distinction within the presence of God in His creation. There is a proper presence of God in His creation which is the basis and constituent centre of His special presence, and therefore the meaning and presupposition of His general presence. This is His presence in His Word, in the Word of His revelation and reconciliation as such, in Jesus Christ. He is therefore the place to which every examination of the Old and New Testament witness to God's special presence must necessarily and unequivocally point in the last instance. If the dwelling of God in Jesus Christ is the fulfilment, the constant factor, to which every other dwelling of God attested in the Old and New Testaments can stand only in the relationship of an impermanent expectation or recollection, this dwelling of God stands out again above every other, and therefore above the totality which we have known as God's special presence. And it does so, not merely quantitatively, but qualitatively. It is not simply a special instance in a series. It is the origin and the goal, the basis and the constituent centre of the whole series of the special self-representations of God. It is the one unique and simple presence, the proper presence of God as the one and simple God in His creation, in which both His special presence in all its diversity and also His general presence with its dynamic identity possess their beginning and their end. If we maintain that the path from the presence with which God as the triune God is present to Himself leads directly and in the first instance to His special presence in creation, we must now take a further step backwards, making a fresh distinction, and upholding the position that strictly speaking it leads directly and in the first instance, within all the special presences, to His proper presence in Jesus Christ. It is as the One who is present here in this way that He is the God who is specially present in Israel and the Church, and as such generally present in the world as a whole and everywhere.

The threefold nature of God's presence *ad extra* was recognised in Scholasticism at least from the time of Peter Lombard. God, he writes (*Sent. I, dist.* 37A), is 1. *praesentialiter, potentialiter, essentialiter in omni natura sive essentia* ; He is 2. *excellentius sc. per gratiam inhabitans in sanctis spiritibus et animis* ; but He is 3. *excellentissime non per gratiam adoptionis, sed per gratiam unionis in homine Christo*. In opposition to the idea contained in this *excellentissime* (or for its correct understanding), J. Gerhard (*Loci theol.*, 1610 II, 187) rightly noted that instead of *excellenter* it is much better to say : *singulariter, . . . quia modus ille praesentiae hypostatica non tantum gradu aut secundum plus et minus, sed toto genere a reliquis praesentiae modis differt*. We are indeed forced to say that this form of divine presence in the world must be radically distinguished from every other form, even the highest, even those forms of special divine presence which according to the testimony of Scripture are to be recognised and acknowledged, in their relativity of course but also in their reality, as forms of God's special presence. It is to be distinguished in just the same way as grace which bestows is to be radically distinguished from grace which is bestowed, or as the coming Messiah from His people, the coming Saviour from His Church, the expectation and recollection of revelation and salvation from its fulfilment and presence. Jacob at Bethel, Moses at the burning bush, and the pilgrims to the temple at Jerusalem are not deluded as to the special presence of God at these earthly places. For the God present in these earthly places attests Himself to them as the One who will occupy and possess a unique place on earth in virtue of His good-pleasure and omnipotence, and who for the sake of this, in view of it and by the proclamation and power of it can and will be present even before it takes place in these other earthly places on earth in a way which is relative but real. Again Paul is not deluded when (presumably accepting and adapting as his own a saying and certainly a sentiment of pagan wisdom) he confesses that in God we live and move and have our being. For God attests Himself to him on the

Areopagus and wherever he may be, as the One who has possessed and occupied this one unique place on earth (Jesus) in virtue of His good-pleasure and omnipotence. There is, therefore, no reason to doubt that for the sake of this one place, in view of it and by the proclamation and power of it, He can and will also be present also here and now in other earthly places relatively to this one place, but really. It is to be noted that the reality of God's special presence in other places rests on this relationship, but so too does the distinction between them and His presence in this one place. They would not have existed as places of His presence without this proper place, just as the circumference of a circle cannot exist without its centre. God is really present in these other places too. Indeed, He is really present everywhere. But He is present in them and everywhere because and as He is present here. He is first present here, and then (either before or after Jesus Christ's epiphany) there and everywhere. He is present here primarily, there and everywhere secondarily. He is really present to Israel and the Church as the body of humanity taken up into His covenant, but He is present in Jesus Christ as the Head which constitutes and controls this body.

In fact, then, the distinction is not merely one of more or less. There is a difference of kind between the Messiah and His people, the Saviour and His Church, the One in whom everything begins and ends and the everything which may begin and end in Him. It is the distinction between *gratia adoptionis* and *gratia unionis*, as Peter Lombard rightly said. God was present to Israel and is present to the Church *gratia adoptionis*. They are children adopted for the sake of Jesus Christ and not for their own sakes. And it is for this reason that they are considered worthy and made partakers of a special divine presence, and in them God's love will glorify itself in His creation, in His reconciling in them of the world to Himself. To adopt means here really to accept, viz., to accept in Jesus Christ, to bring into truth and reality, under the Law and ordinances, into the enjoyment of the fruit of His life, so that everything which can be said of Him, beginning with His divine Sonship and therefore embracing even the real divine presence which is His own, can also be said of these His adopted children in the sense in which it can be theirs. By the proclamation and power of this adoption of Israel and the Church, which has taken place in Jesus Christ, there was and is now as then a real presence of God in places on earth. But this adoption of Israel and the Church which takes place in Jesus Christ has as its distinct presupposition that which took place and is in Jesus Christ Himself. It assumes that He Himself has part in the divine Sonship and therefore in the real presence of God, *gratia unionis*, so that Israel and the Church " received [it] from his fulness." Being accepted into Him they could be the children of God by Him and from Him, and therefore with Him, participating in the real divine presence. Even if it was only as those who are added, they could be this by the proclamation and power of what He is and has. But to be partakers in this way necessarily means to partake differently, as differently as *adoptio* is different from *unio*. *Unio* is the basis of *adoptio*. *Adoptio* is based on *unio*. *Gratia unionis* is the bestowing grace of God, *gratia adoptionis* the divine grace bestowed. That is the difference. On the basis of the *adoptio* there is really a kind of symbolical, sacramental or spiritual presence, the presence bestowed on Israel and the Church. And if we take the matter even further, we shall see that the adoption itself is the basis of something more, because in it the Creator of all things glorifies Himself and therefore makes clear the meaning and purpose of all things. It is the basis of the fact that, again as a gift, God is everywhere, with and in all things. But the *adoptio* is itself based on the *unio*, on the primary, bestowing presence of God in Christ. And this presence, which is the basis of the *adoptio*, and with it every secondary presence of God, whether special or general, is event and reality only in Jesus Christ, and is therefore neither before Him nor after Him. The reason why it is called and is *unio* is this. In the person of His Son, in Jesus Christ, God is not merely present to man as He was and is in Israel and Church, around him and in him in the special form of a blessing or an injunction, an abasement or an elevation, a declaration or an act in connexion with His work of revelation and reconciliation. But God is Himself this man Jesus Christ, very God and very man, both of them unconfused and unmixed, but also unseparated and undivided, in the one person of this Messiah and Saviour. This is what cannot be said about any other creature, even any prophet or apostle. Jesus Christ alone is very God and very man. And it is on the basis of this *unio*, but clearly differentiated from it, that there is an *adoptio*.

Apart from anything else, this means at least one thing, that in Jesus Christ human corporality and therefore creaturely spatiality, is not only, like all other creaturely spatiality, grounded in and created by, and therefore preserved and upheld and surrounded on all sides by the spatiality of God. Jesus Christ is not simply one of the beings—perhaps the highest—which can confess in general or in particular that it lives and moves and has its being in God. On the contrary, in Him dwells the fulness of the Godhead bodily (Col. 2⁹). Σωματικῶς is the adverb to κατοικεῖ and the subject of the sentence is the πλήρωμα τῆς θεότητος. And Col. 1⁹ is even more emphatic : ἐν αὐτῷ εὐδόκησεν πᾶν τὸ πλήρωμα κατοικῆσαι. Both sentences undoubtedly speak of a bodily and proper dwelling of God in His fulness or completeness. They therefore speak unreservedly of a divine position above or behind it which cannot partake in this indwelling. And they say of this bodily and proper dwelling of God Himself, which otherwise takes place only beyond here and the heaven of heavens, that in Jesus Christ as His dwelling it is present not merely, as elsewhere, as the presupposition of His dwelling in creation, but as itself His dwelling even in creation. In Jesus Christ there does exist the distinction between Creator and creature, between God and the created world of heaven and earth, and therefore between divine and created space. Yet there is no diversity or separation, but rather the unity of the two. For here the Creator is at the same time creature, which means in this connexion that the Creator has given the creature not only space but His own most proper space. God has raised man to His throne. God's most proper space is itself the space which this man occupies in the cradle and on the cross, and which He cannot therefore leave or lose again, for, as His resurrection and ascension reveal, it is now His permanent space. How can the dwelling of the fulness of God in Him be cancelled ? Thus the human nature of Christ (and especially in this connexion His corporality and therefore His spatiality), in its unity with the deity of the Son (unconfused with it, but also undivided from it, in real indirect identity), is the revelation, but as the revelation it is also the reality of the divine space, by which all other spaces are created, preserved and surrounded. Viewed and understood in this unity, it is at once the demonstration and the explanation of this divine space. If we take the reality of the human nature of Christ seriously in its unity with the divine nature, if we free ourselves of all gross or refined Docetism, if we give John 1¹⁴ : " and dwelt among us," its full value, there is no room for the old error of God's non-spatiality, and we understand the reality with which Scripture can speak of the spatiality of God in the whole width of His revelation (both before and after the epiphany of Christ), and in His ubiquity in the world. We shall then cease from questioning it or idealising it in different ways. The God who possesses such real space here (in Christ) possesses it also in another form elsewhere (in creation). The God who dwells properly here dwells there symbolically, sacramentally and spiritually. The God who dwells permanently in this place passes through other places. And it is always true that the God who is really present here is really present there as well. What He is here bears witness to what He is there. And in His being here and there together He reveals Himself as the One who is present everywhere ; or, to put it the other way round, the God who is everywhere present is so only if He is identical with the One who is present there and here, and primarily here, in Jesus Christ, in the unity of the Word with what was created and is upheld by the Word.

Rightly understood, it might well be said that with the establishment of this third and proper form of God's presence in His creation, His presence in Jesus Christ, we have in a sense come back to the point from which we began, the affirmation of the presence in which God is present to Himself as the Triune, the occupier of His supraheavenly throne. The God who is present in Jesus Christ is the One who is enthroned over heaven and earth and therefore the God who is present specially in His work of revelation and reconciliation and generally in the world at large. He does not merely give this creature, as He gives all other creatures, his space, created space, from the fulness of His own uncreated and creative space. But He also gives him His own space itself. He is one with this man. He takes him up to sit at His right hand, to occupy His supra-heavenly throne. And it is in doing this that God is, and reveals Himself to be, the One He is, omnipresent in Himself and as such outside Himself, in His special work (whose centre is His action in this creature, the man Jesus Christ), and in His general work which is subservient to this special work, finding its goal and completion and therefore having its meaning and origin in it, and therefore in Jesus Christ Himself.

If we keep this circle and the connexion and distinction of its stages before us, and therefore the differentiations of the reality of God's omnipresence, it should be possible to survey and to some extent settle a dispute that at one time greatly agitated Protestant theology and could easily break out again in some new form. I refer to the unfortunate controversy which arose out of the eucharistic conflict and in the 16th and 17th centuries separated the Lutheran and Reformed Schools in respect of the ubiquity of the human nature of Christ and especially the ubiquity of His body.

It was an unfortunate dispute because the Lutherans did not take seriously enough the distinctions and the Reformed did not take seriously enough the connexion between the stages of the circle in which we cannot cease to think when dealing with this subject. And it was unfortunate because the Lutherans were not willing to note that the Reformed too were aware of the connexion, while the Reformed were not willing to note that the Lutherans too were aware of the distinctions of the stages of the circle. The Lutherans ignored the fact that the Reformed for their part did not altogether disregard or deny the connexion, while the Reformed ignored the fact that the Lutherans did not altogether disregard or deny the distinctions, the trouble on both sides being a failure to take the one aspect or the other seriously enough, or to make it sufficiently clear to what extent they meant to do so. (This is the way in which unhappy and theologically useless controversies arise. Not all controversies are of this nature, but they do exist. On one side there is a foreshortening or one-sidedness which, without amounting to heresy, is a forced contraction of the truth. Opponents who are guilty of a similar foreshortening or one-sidedness are then attacked as if they were the victims of heresy instead of a forced contraction of the truth. This was the course taken by the mutual dealings of the Lutherans and Reformed in the 16th and 17th centuries on this—and indeed other matters.)

When the Lutherans asserted the omnipresence of the humanity and therefore of the body of Jesus Christ (I follow the presentation of the matter by J. Gerhard, *Loci theol.*, 1610, II, 182) they did not wish to deny its creatureliness and therefore the limitation of its spatiality : *Christum ut hominem non dicimus naturaliter et essentialiter . . . esse omnipraesentem.* But they fixed their eyes on the union which the Creator accomplished with the creature in the incarnation. (The one-sidedness and foreshortening consists in the fact that they would understand the union only if stated with this emphasis on the Creator.) And they asserted the omnipresence of the humanity of Jesus Christ : *quatenus ipsius assumpta humana natura in infinitam Λόγου ὑπόστασιν est evecta et in exaltatione ad dextram Patris coelestis collocata.* Generally speaking, this is clearly correct, and when the Lutherans quote as evidence Mt. 18²⁰ (" Where two or three "), Mt. 28²⁰ (" Lo, I am with you "), Eph. 4¹⁰ (" Ascended far above all the heavens, that he might fill all things "), Col. 1¹⁸ (" He is the head of the body "), it must certainly be acknowledged that we cannot easily exclude from these sayings, which establish a presence of Jesus Christ in the world, the presence of His human nature and therefore of His body. Above all, we obviously cannot exclude it from the sayings in the passages on the Lord's Supper which gave rise to the whole dispute. The positive statement of Lutheran doctrine is quite in order : *Logos in et cum natura humana . . . omnes creaturas in coelo ac terra regit non absens sed praesens.* But when it came to the conception of the " right hand of God " as the place where Christ is, a conception which is decisive for the understanding of the presence of the whole Christ, it was a mistake to try to interpret it without proper differentiation, as in the following passage : *quae dextra Dei cum sit ubique praesens nullo loco inclusa, a nullo exclusa, utique etiam Christus ad eam evectus erit omnipraesens.* In this interpretation of the right hand of God, the presence with which God is present to Himself in His supraheavenly place seems to melt or sink into His presence in general, His presence in creation. It has no biblical justification, but is clearly linked up with the fatal and, in this case, violently applied presupposition of all the older theology, that the essence of God is the non-spatial infinite, and that God is omnipresent as this non-spatial infinite. The consequence is that in the Lutheran conception it is not at all clear how far the spatial limitation and even the creatureliness of the body of Christ and His human nature in general can be taken seriously. It is not at all clear whether the true manhood of Christ has not disappeared in His divinity, thus annulling the incarnation and compromising God's revealing and reconciling work in Christ. The Lutherans, of course, did not intend this. But at no stage in the controversy could they make clear how far they could escape ending in Monophysitism and perhaps in Docetism. The correct statement about the omnipresence of Christ even in His human nature should have been interpreted in such a way that the particularity of the divine place, which is also the place of Jesus Christ in His human nature, is safeguarded. It should also have been interpreted in such a way that the creatureliness and therefore the true and limited spatiality of His humanity occupying that divine place is safeguarded, and with it His whole position as very God and very man, Mediator, Revealer and Reconciler.

The Reformed rightly perceived that in the Lutheran position this had not happened in the way that is to be desired. (I follow Polanus, *Synt. Theol. chr.*, 1609, *col.* 942 ff.) For their own part they did not wish to deny the divinity of Christ and with it the omnipresence of the whole Christ. They, too, fixed their eyes on the incarnation as the union of the Creator with the creature. (Their one-sidedness consists in the fact that they tried to understand it with an almost exclusive emphasis on the latter.) They took good care not to apply the *ubique* to the human nature and therefore to the corporality of Christ as such. They understood the " right hand of God " (in this they were biblically correct) as a place that in itself and in the first instance is a distinct place, not only the place of all places, but also the place over all places. On the other hand, they also wanted Bethlehem, Nazareth, Jerusalem and all the other places in which Jesus was present spatially in His humanity to be interpreted as real creaturely places. Above all, they wanted the spatiality of the humanity of Christ to be interpreted as that of His true manhood and therefore as a spatiality limited on any given occasion to a particular place. The gap in the Lutheran argument is in fact pointed out and filled by the Reformed. Both in regard to the biblical record and the exalted Christ they hold firm to His concrete manhood which cannot be compromised. They therefore hold firm to the authenticity of His mediatorship between God and man. In their own argument there is a gap of another kind. They, too, obviously have to do violence both to the texts and to the subject when they boldly assert that in Mt. 18²⁰ and 28²⁰ the reference is not to a bodily presence of Christ. In the latter passage, for example, all that Christ says (as they see it) is : *licet corpore discederet, manere tamen ipsum cum illis deitate, Spiritus virtute, efficacia et maiestate sua ;* in a word, in virtue of His divinity. They do similar violence when they interpret Eph. 4¹⁰ as follows : *ascendit Christus in coelum, ut gratiis et donis Spiritus sancti omnia ecclesiae membra impleret,* or when they will have it that the true body of Christ is only in heaven even in the reception of the Lord's Supper, so that they have to say of believers that, though they can eat both physically and spiritually on earth, they can feed on it in heaven only in virtue of the *spiritualis facultas fidei.* But what about the unity of the humanity with the divinity of Christ ? Is it not annulled now in this opposite sense ? Is not the humanity stripped of His divinity and the divinity active without and apart from the humanity ? But can He really be our Mediator if, in accordance with this teaching, He is more or less hampered and isolated from the rest of the world, as concerns His humanity, first in Bethlehem and Nazareth and later in heaven ? And is it really the " right hand of God " if it is only in heaven and not omnipotently here and everywhere as well ? The Reformed for their part have to face all these questions from the Lutherans, and it is true that they were never at any stage of the controversy able to give exact and satisfying replies to all these objections—although, of course, they had no more desire to draw the dangerous consequences ascribed of them than had the Lutherans those that threatened them. Consider the answers which the *Heidelberg Catechism* gives to questions 47 and 48 : " Is Christ then not with us to the end of the world, as He has promised us ? Christ is very man and very God. He is not now on earth after His human nature, but after His divinity, majesty, grace and Spirit He never withdraws from us. Will not the two natures in Christ be separated from one another if the humanity is not everywhere, as the divinity is ? By no means, for since the divinity is present incomprehensibly and on every side, it must follow that it exists both outside the humanity it has assumed and nevertheless also within the same, and remains personally united therewith." But the question asked by the Lutherans was whether and how far we are dealing here and now with the whole Christ, so that in spite of the true elements in it this reply cannot but appear unsatisfactory or evasive. Reformed Christology could be understood in a Nestorian or even Ebionite sense. Its true statement concerning the indissolubly definite nature of the spatiality of Christ's human nature should have been interpreted in such a way that the divinity of its place is safeguarded, and with it Christ's omnipresence even in His human nature, and therefore the full reality of the unity of His person and work as Mediator. The Reformed had no convincing answer to the Lutheran objection that this had not been done in the way that is to be desired.

This question is, then, one of the matters on which interconfessional discussion in the Protestantism of the time became quite futile. The dispute cannot in fact be settled at the level at which it was started by both sides. On the basis of the hypotheses that we have worked out with regard to God's omnipresence we offer the following suggestion. If God's presence in Jesus Christ is God's proper presence in the world, and we are therefore to understand that in Jesus Christ the space of God Himself (in the strictest original sense of the concept, the throne of God) has become identical with creaturely human space, then it is at once apparent (as the Reformed saw against the Lutherans) that both the

corporality of the historical and exalted Jesus Christ and also the right hand of
God as His place must have a definiteness and distinctness from other spaces,
and this must not be denied for the sake of the truth of Jesus Christ's humanity.
But it is also apparent (as the Lutherans saw against the Reformed) that there
is not only an omnipresence of Jesus Christ in accordance with His divinity.   There
is also a human corporal omnipresence of Jesus Christ.   In virtue of the proper
and original presence of God on His supra-heavenly throne, in which in Jesus
Christ even human nature in its corporality has a part, there does exist also a
relative but real presence in the world (both in particular and in general), not
only of God, but also of man united with God in Jesus Christ.   This cannot
simply be equated with the former (in this we agree with the Reformed against
the Lutherans).   Nor can the former be allowed to merge into it.   The definiteness and distinctness of the space above the world " where Christ sits at the right
hand of God " must be maintained at all costs and with it the truth of the human
nature of Jesus Christ.   But the presence in the world of man united with God
in Jesus Christ must not be denied either (in this we agree with the Lutherans
against the Reformed).   Therefore the presence (in Israel and the Church in
particular, and in the world in general) of the whole Christ as the occupant of
the divine throne must not be restricted to His divinity, His Spirit, His grace,
etc.   Where His Spirit and His grace are, He Himself is wholly present, very
God and very man.   How can they be present, if He is not there as a whole—
the one undivided Mediator between God and man ?   Therefore we say : The
whole Jesus Christ is there at the right hand of God in one way, and the same
whole Jesus Christ is here in Israel and the Church, but also in the world, in
another way.   We make a distinction (with the Reformed) and say : " He is there
properly and originally and here symbolically, sacramentally, spiritually."   But
(with the Lutherans) we draw the two together and say : " He is here no less
than there, but really present both there and here, in both places the whole
Christ after His divine and also after His human nature."   On these lines it is
possible and necessary to take up again the discussion of the individual problems
of exegesis which we cannot pursue in this context.

2. THE CONSTANCY AND OMNIPOTENCE OF GOD

We sum up the results of the previous sub-section in the statement
that God is One in His perfect freedom, and that as such He is present
to Himself and to all that is in His perfect love.   The new statement to
which we now pass is a necessary repetition and endorsement of the
first—that God is constant and God is omnipotent.   Again, by constancy we denote first the perfect freedom of God and by omnipotence
the perfect love in which He is free.   To what extent is this second
statement new or necessary alongside the first ?   Not to the extent
that it seeks or is able to say anything different from the other, but
to the extent that it does say the same thing differently.   This difference is one which is required by the object, so that while the substance
of it is foreseen and intended in the first statement, it could not be
expressed in it as such.   We have spoken about Him who is constantly
One and omnipotently omnipresent.   Otherwise we could not have
spoken about the unity and omnipotence of God.   But we must now
speak about God's constancy and omnipotence expressly and inde-

pendently. We must speak about them expressly. This is demanded by the essence of God, which needs to be seen and understood from the standpoint denoted by the concepts of constancy and omnipotence. We must also speak about them independently. The whole essence of God must be seen and understood from this standpoint too, as if it were the one and only standpoint. For each of God's qualities and perfections declared and knowable in His revelation is at the same time His one, complete essence. This is also true of God's constancy and omnipotence.

All the perfections of God's freedom and therefore of His love, and therefore the one whole divine essence, can and must be recognised and expressed by recognising and saying that God is constant. By this perfection of constancy God differentiates Himself from everything that is distinct from Himself. By it He is what He is in Himself, and by it He also qualifies and directs everything distinct from Himself. Because He is constant, and as the One who is constant, He is also omnipotent. And because He is omnipotent, and as the One who is omnipotent, He is also constant. But because our present task is to view and understand God's freedom, we begin with the fact that He is constant.

What does this mean? God is the one omnipresent God, self-inclosed over against everything else, disclosed to Himself and everything else, enclosing Himself and everything else. His self-inclosure no less than His disclosure and enclosure of all things, His uniqueness and simplicity no less than His spatiality, is grounded in Himself and posited, maintained and executed by Himself. And because by Himself this is all done in such a way that there neither is nor can be, nor is to be expected or even thought possible in Him, the One and omnipresent being, any deviation, diminution or addition, nor any degeneration or rejuvenation, any alteration or non-identity or discontinuity. The one, omnipresent God remains the One He is. This is His constancy. It is not in conflict with His freedom and His love. On the contrary, both His freedom and His love are divine for the very reason that they are the freedom and the love of the One who is constant in Himself, from whose freedom nothing else is ever under any circumstances to be expected but that again and again He will be Himself and demonstrate and confirm Himself as such, and from whose love nothing else is ever in any circumstance to be expected but that it will always manifest itself as love and that He will manifest Himself in it. The constancy of God is not, therefore, in conflict with the life of God either. The one omnipresent God is the living God. But as the living God, He is not Himself subject to or capable of any alteration, and does not cease to be Himself. His life is not only the origin of all created change, but is in itself the fulness of difference, movement, will, decision, action, degeneration and rejuvenation. But He lives it in eternal self-repetition and self-affirmation. As His inner life and His life in all that is, it will never sever itself from Him, turn against Him, or possess a form or operation alien to Him. In all its forms and operations it will be His life. In every alteration and movement it will go out from the peace, return to the peace, and be accompanied, upheld and filled by the peace, which He has in Himself as the only really living One, in so far as His self is neither in need of, capable of, or exposed to any annulment, decrease, increase or perversion into any other self, and His life with its very alteration and movement can, and does gloriously, consist only in His not ceasing to be Himself, to posit and will and perfect Himself in His being Himself. He does not do this of necessity but in freedom and love, or, one may say, with the necessity in virtue of which He cannot cease to be Himself, the One who loves in freedom.

Unfortunately the older Protestant orthodoxy did not display any great felicity in its handling of this matter either. It did, of course, recall the biblical passages which we do have to recall, the " I am that I am " of Ex. 3[14], which we have already discussed in our general consideration of the concept of God's aseity ; Num. 23[19] : " God is not a man that he should lie ; neither the son of man, that he should repent : hath he said, and shall he not do it ? or hath he spoken, and shall he not make it good ? " ; Mal. 3[6] : " For I the Lord change not " ; above all, Ps. 102[25f.] : " Of old hast thou laid the foundation of the earth ; and the heavens are the work of thy hands. They shall perish, but thou shalt endure : yea, all of them shall wax old as a garment : as a vesture shalt thou change them and they shalt be changed : but thou art the same, and thy years shall have no end " ; Jas. 1[17] : " Every good gift and every perfect gift is from above, coming down from the Father of lights, with whom can be no variableness, neither shadow that is cast by turning " ; and Heb. 6[13ff.], which tells us that God confirmed His promise to Abraham by swearing by Himself " since he could swear by none greater," " that by two immutable things (God and His oath), in which it was impossible for God to lie, we might have a strong consolation, who have fled for refuge to lay hold upon the hope set before us, which hope we have as an anchor of the soul, both sure and stedfast, and which entereth into that within the veil, whither the forerunner is for us entered, even Jesus." But in substance as well as terminology we are transported to quite a different world when we read Polanus' exposition and demonstration of God's " immutability " (*Synt. Theol. chr.*, 1609, *col.* 967) : *Deus a nulla re extra ipsum existente moveri mutarive potest: sic enim ipse primus motor et effector omnium bonorum in natura non esset. Ab interno etiam principio moveri aut mutari non potest. Quodcumque enim ab interno principio movetur aut mutatur, in eo aliud sit necesse est, quod moveat, aliud quod moveatur, ac proinde ex diversis rebus compositum. In Deo autem statuere rerum diversarum compositionem non patitur eius simplicitas absoluta, immensitas et summa perfectio. Non igitur aliquid in ipso mobile est, sed totus ipse immobilis existens omnibus aliis rebus motuum causa est. Quapropter etiam totus est immutabilis.* Does this derive from the biblical passages quoted ? Is it therefore true of the God who attests Himself in His revelation ? It is obvious that on the basis of these passages and in face of this God something very different will have to be said about God's " immutability," something which is not in such irreparable conflict with God's freedom, love and life. The source, however, from which Polanus draws is different and is expressly mentioned. It is his development of the idea of the *ipsum ens*, the *actus simplex et perfectissimus*, the *immensitas*, the *primum principium et primum movens*. By definition this is necessarily *immutabile*, and *immutabile* in this sense, which does not correspond in the least with the biblical passages. It must be admitted that Augustine was, relatively, much nearer the facts, when he expressed his opinion about the relation between God's rest and His work (*De civ. Dei* XII, 17, 2) as follows : *Nobis fas non est credere, aliter Deum affici cum vacat, aliter cum operatur: quia nec affici dicendus est, tamquam in eius natura fiat aliquid, quod non ante fuerit. Patitur quippe qui afficitur et mutabile est omne quod aliquid patitur. Non itaque in eius vacatione cogitetur ignavia, desidia, inertia, sicut nec in eius opere labor, conatus, industria. Novit quiescens agere et agens quiescere. Potest ad opus novum non novum, sed sempiternum adhibere consilium, nec poenitendo quia prius cessaverat, coepit facere quod non fecerat. Sed et si prius cessavit et posterius operatus est (quod nescio quemadmodum ab homine possit intelligi), hoc procul dubio quod dicitur 'prius et posterius' in rebus prius non existentibus et posterius existentibus fuit. In illo autem non alteram praecedentem altera subsequens mutavit aut abstulit voluntatem, sed una eademque sempiterna et immutabili voluntate res quas condidit, et ut prius non essent egit, quamdiu non fuerunt, et ut posterius essent, quando esse coeperunt.* Obviously Augustine did perceive at least something of what is at stake here. God's constant divine nature lies beyond the antithesis between rest and movement. Therefore the one cannot be played off as divine against the other as less divine. His rest is not to be denied out of deference to His movement nor His movement out of deference to His rest. But Augustine, too, is suspect because he seems to want to restrict the relation between the two to God's outward activity. To God Himself and in Himself there is ascribed a rest without any *prius* and *posterius*. But the constancy of God attested in these passages of Scripture cannot be an abstract rest. On the contrary, it can be only the rest, the uninterrupted continuity, the unchangeableness, the " immutability," that belongs to the living God, living not merely *ad extra*, but also and primarily in Himself, the Father, the Almighty, the Creator of heaven and earth. I. A. Dorner has made this clear in a way that is illuminating for the whole doctrine of God in his great essay : *Ueber die richtige Fassung des dogmatischen Begriffs der Unveränderlichkeit Gottes*, 1856 (*Ges. Schriften*, 1883, pp. 188-377). Those who know the essay will recognise as they read this sub-section how much I owe to Dorner's inspiration.

It is decisive for a right understanding of this concept to grasp the fact that it is not a matter of recognising God in an immutable more or less consistently conceived as such, but that on the contrary it is a matter of recognising that God is " immutable," the predicate being again determined by the subject, and the subject by His self-revelation, and not an arbitrarily chosen subject by an arbitrarily chosen predicate. To the extent that we are not really able to break away from the first and false way of stating the question in favour of the second, we are in irremediable conflict with the biblical statements, which do not speak of an *immutabile* or *immobile* in itself, but of the " immutable " God in His self-revelation. But if this is the case, whatever we may say about a living God can be said only in uneasy subjection to what is in this connexion a most dangerous presupposition, or in equally uneasy conflict with it. For if the " immutable " as such is in fact to be God, this is undoubtedly the most dangerous assumption conceivable not only for the doctrine of God in particular but for every statement about God.

If it is true, as Polanus says, that God is not moved either by anything else or by Himself, but that, confined as it were, by His simplicity, infinity and absolute perfection, He is the pure *immobile*, it is quite impossible that there should be any relationship between Himself and a reality distinct from Himself —or at any rate a relationship that is more than the relation of pure mutual negativity, and includes God's concern for this other reality. And this being the case, it is only in a most highly figurative way, or in most violent contradiction to our basic assumption, that we can speak of God as the Creator and Lord of the world, of the work of reconciliation and revelation as His real work, of the incarnation, substitution and mediatorship of His Son and, on this basis, of God as the Father and believers as His children, of the gift of the Holy Spirit, of prayer and the promise given us of eternal life. We are then uncommonly near to Schleiermacher's solution—the interpretation of all these things exclusively as the emotions of pious feeling. And beyond Schleiermacher's solution, if the emotions of pious feeling do not appear very significant, we may easily finish up with the solution of atheism. For we must not make any mistake : the pure *immobile* is—death. If, then, the pure *immobile* is God, death is God. That is, death is posited as absolute and explained as the first and last and only real. It is said to have no limit and no end, to be omnipotent, so that there is no conqueror of death and for us no hope triumphant over death. Death itself holds the one place from which victory and hope can come. It is itself Lord of all. And if death is God, then God is dead. In other words it is superfluous to equate them, for it is intrinsically untrue and impossible to deck out the final reality death with all the impotently mutinous utterances of pious feeling about a Creator, Reconciler, Redeemer and Lord, as we impotently deck out graves for whose occupants there is no more sun and springtime. All the consolation and exhortation of religion has simply become an imposture in the face of better knowledge, an empty clerical bogey to which we consent in sentimental moments and moods, but of which we know in our hearts that it has nothing to do with reality, and which we therefore exert ourselves to keep at a safe distance. It is a serious matter to have to note that even the orthodox theology of the Protestant Church, scarcely a hundred years after Luther and Calvin, did not realise that with this *immobile* it was well on the way to receiving and accepting the heathen concept of God, the concept of men who have no hope. And in doing this they not only prepared the way for the Neo-Protestant decay of the Church and theology, or, to state it concretely, for the anthropologising of Schleiermacher and Feuerbach. They also prepared the way for the primitive unbelief of modern times. For when the average man appeals covertly or often openly to " reality " as against all religious declarations, in harmony with ancient and all subsequent heathendom, he means the final reality of death. And according to orthodox teaching, at least under the head *De immutabilitate Dei*, this is supposed to be the reality of God. If death can be and is actually feared there is much to be said for reacting with resolute unbelief when the incredible label " God " is attached to it.

But it is not true that the immutable as such is God. The real truth is—and it is very different—that God is " immutable," and this is the living God in His freedom and love, God Himself. He is what He is in eternal actuality. He never is it only potentially (not even in part). He never is it at any point intermittently. But always at every place He is what He is continually and self-consistently. Hi love cannot cease to be His love nor His freedom His freedom. He alone could assail, alter, abolish or destroy Himself. But it is just at this point that He is the " immutable " God. For at no place or time can

He or will He turn against Himself or contradict Himself, not even in virtue of His freedom or for the sake of His love. What He does in virtue of His freedom for the sake of His love will never be the surrender but always at every point the self-affirmation of His freedom and His love, a fresh demonstration of His life. This self-affirmation is never anywhere an act of holy egotism, but always everywhere an act of the righteousness in which He establishes His glory over all things. And as an act of His righteousness His self-affirmation must be understood as necessary, not subject to any doubt or temptation. The answer, therefore, to the question : " What is the immutable ? " is : " This living God in His self-affirmation is the immutable." The immutable is the fact that this God is as the One He is, gracious and holy, merciful and righteous, patient and wise. The immutable is the fact that He is the Creator, Reconciler, Redeemer and Lord. This immutability includes rather than excludes life. In a word it is life. It does not, therefore, need to acquire life from the impulse of the created world, or above all from the emotions of our pious feeling. It not only has nothing whatever to do with the pagan idea of the *immobile*, which is only a euphemistic description of death, but it is its direct opposite. It does not require, then, any sentimentalisings in sham concealment or embellishment of its terrible reality. For it is not this fearful reality. It is the reality of life and not of death. God's constancy—which is a better word than the suspiciously negative word " immutability "—is the constancy of His knowing, willing and acting and therefore of His person. It is the continuity, undivertability and indefatigableness in which God both is Himself and also performs His work, maintaining it as such and continually making it His work. It is the self-assurance in which God moves in Himself and in all His works and in which He is rich in Himself and in all His works without either losing Himself or (for fear of this loss) having to petrify in Himself and renounce His movement and His riches. The constancy of God is not then the limit and boundary, the death of His life. For this very reason the right understanding of God's constancy must not be limited to His presence with creation, as if God in Himself were after all naked " immutability " and therefore in the last analysis death. On the contrary, it is in and by virtue of His constancy that God is alive in Himself and in all His works. The fact that He possesses selfhood and continuity itself makes Him the living One that He is, and is the basis and meaning of His power and might, the inner divine secret of the movement and wealth itself in which He is glorious on His throne and in all the heights and depths of His creation.

It is not possible, then, to distil a motionless *ipsum ens* out of the " I am that I am " of Ex. 3¹⁴, as if the divine self-affirmation expressly stated in these verses took place and could be understood apart from the fact that it is the self-affirmation of the God who approaches Moses and Israel and deals with both in a very definite manner. There is such a thing as a holy mutability of God. He is above all ages. But above them as their Lord, as the βασιλεὺς τῶν αἰώνων (1 Tim. 1¹⁷), and therefore as the One who—as Master and in His own way—partakes in their alteration, so that there is something corresponding to that alteration in His own essence. His constancy consists in the fact that He is always the same in every change. The opposite of His constancy, that which is ruled out by it, is not His holy mutability, but the unholy mutability of men as described in Isaiah 1²¹ᶠ· : " How is the faithful city become an harlot ! it was full of judgment ; righteousness lodged in it ; but now murderers. Thy silver is become dross, thy wine mixed with water. Thy princes are rebellious, and companions of thieves . . ." ; or in Rom. 1²³ : " They changed the glory of the uncorruptible God into an image made like to corruptible man " ; or in Gal. 3¹ : " O foolish Galatians, who hath bewitched you, before whose eyes Jesus Christ hath been evidently set forth crucified ? ", and 3³ : " having begun in the spirit, are ye now made perfect in the flesh ? ", and 5⁷ : " Ye did run well ; who did hinder you, that ye should not obey the truth ? " It should be noted with what God's immutability is contrasted in Mal. 3⁶ᶠ· : " For I the Lord change not and ye, O sons of Jacob, are always the same (Luther's translation). From the days of your fathers ye have turned aside from mine ordinances. . . ." According to these verses man is constant in his wicked inconstancy. This is just what God is not. God is consistently one and the same. But again His consistency is not as it were mathematical. It is not the consistency of a supreme natural law or mechanism. The fact that He is one and the same does not mean that He is bound to be and say and do only one and the same thing, so that all the distinctions of His being, speaking and acting are only a semblance, only the various refractions of a beam of light which are eternally the same. This was and is the way that every form of Platonism conceives God. It is impossible to overemphasise the fact that here, too, God is described as basically without life, word or act. Biblical thinking about God would rather submit to confusion with the grossest anthropomorphism than to confusion with this the primary denial of God. In biblical thinking God is certainly the immutable, but as the immutable He is the living God and He possesses a mobility and elasticity which is no less divine than His perseverance, and which actually and necessarily confirms the divinity of His perseverance no less than its own divinity naturally requires confirmation by His divine perseverance.

It is not, then, a figurative but a strictly literal statement, and one which does not contradict but bears testimony to the constancy of God, when we are told in Ps. 18²⁵ᶠᶠ· : " With the merciful thou wilt shew thyself merciful ; with the perfect man thou wilt show thyself perfect ; with the pure thou wilt show thyself pure ; and with the froward thou wilt show thyself froward. For thou wilt save the afflicted people ; but wilt bring down high looks." This is the way in which the immutable and as such the living God acted. It is not really the case that Num. 23¹⁹, which says that God is not the son of man that He should repent, is qualified or indeed denied and cancelled by the numerous other passages in which God does in fact repent of having promised, threatened or even done something, and in which He in a sense retracts either once or many times, and sometimes goes on to retract His retraction, returning to what He had originally said or done. According to Gen. 6⁶ᶠ· it repented the Lord that He had made man on the earth and it grieved Him at His heart and He resolved to destroy man whom He had created from the face of the earth. Is this any the less true and in conformity with Him than His decision in Gen. 1²⁶ : " Let us make man in our image, after our likeness," and its execution, or than what God said in Himself after the flood (Gen. 8²¹) : " I will not again curse the ground any more for man's sake," and the execution of this decision in the establishment of the covenant with Noah as described in Gen. 9 ? We read in Gen. 18²⁰ᶠᶠ· how Abraham tried by his intercession to hold back the judgment of God which threatened the cities of Sodom and Gomorrah, and how step by step God made concessions to him. If He finds fifty, if finally He finds only ten righteous men there, God will forgive the entire place. Does this really involve an influencing of God by Abraham ? Is it not rather the confirmation of the fact that according to v. 17 God intended to keep nothing hidden from Abraham of what He proposed to do, and according to v. 19 He had chosen him to command those that came after him to keep the way of the Lord and to do justice and judgment ? The way of the Lord is clearly " kept " in Abraham's intercession and manifest in the divine concessions. Something of the same may well be said of the dialogue between Moses and Yahweh after the setting up of the golden calf in Exod. 32⁹ᶠᶠ·: " And the Lord said unto Moses, I have seen this people, and, behold, it is a stiffnecked people : Now therefore let me alone, that my wrath may wax hot against them, and that I may consume them : and I will make of thee a great nation. And Moses besought the Lord his God, and said, Lord, why doth thy wrath wax hot against thy people, which thou hast brought forth out of the land of Egypt with great power, and with a mighty hand ? Wherefore should the Egyptians speak, and say, For mischief did he bring them out, to slay them in the mountains, and to consume them from the face of the earth ? Turn from thy fierce wrath, and repent of this evil against thy people. . . . And the Lord repented of the evil which he thought to do unto his people." Something of the same may also be said of the eventful 11th chapter of Numbers with its depiction of the kindling, extinguishing and rekindling of the divine wrath against the people as they murmured in the wilderness. The same is true of Amos 7¹⁻⁶ : " Thus hath the Lord God shewed unto me ; and, behold, he formed grasshoppers in the beginning of the shooting up of the latter growth. . . . And it came to pass, that when they had made an end of eating the grass of the land, then I said, O Lord God, forgive, I beseech thee : by whom shall Jacob arise ? for he is small. The Lord repented for this : It shall not be, saith the Lord. Thus hath the Lord God shewed unto me : and, behold, the Lord God called to contend by fire, and it devoured the great deep, and did eat up a part. Then said I, O Lord God, cease, I beseech thee : by whom shall Jacob arise ? for he is small. The Lord repented for this : This also shall not be, saith the Lord God." A decisive passage for the understanding of this subject is Jer. 18¹⁻¹⁰ : " The word which came to Jeremiah from the Lord, saying, Arise, and go down to the potter's house, and there I will cause thee to hear my words. Then I went down to the potter's house, and, behold, he wrought a work on the wheels. And the vessel that he made of clay was marred in the hand of the potter : so he made it again another vessel, as seemed good to the potter to make it. Then the word of the Lord came to me, saying, O house of Israel, cannot I do with you as this potter ? saith the Lord. Behold, as the clay is in the potter's hand, so are ye in mine hand, O house of Israel. At what instant I shall speak concerning a nation, and concerning a kingdom, to pluck up, and to pull down, and to destroy it ; If that nation, against whom I have pronounced, turn from their evil, I will repent of the evil that I thought to do unto them. And at what instant I shall speak concerning a nation, and concerning a kingdom, to build and to plant it ; If it do evil in my sight, that it obey not my voice, then I will repent of the good, wherewith I said I would benefit them." Also in Amos 7⁷⁻⁹ we find the statement : " Thus he shewed me : and, behold, the Lord stood upon a wall made by a plumbline, with a plumbline in his hand. And the Lord said unto me, Amos, what seest thou ? And I said, A plumbline. Then said the Lord, Behold, I will set a plumbline in the midst of my people Israel : I will not again pass by them any more : And the high places of Isaac shall be desolate, and the sanctuaries of Israel shall be laid waste ; and I will rise against the house of Jeroboam with the sword."

It should be noted, however, that it is no accident that both in Amos and Jeremiah the two possibilities of divine repentance are put in a definite order.

God's freedom to chide and His freedom to redeem, to kill and to make alive, are never made parallel or balanced the one against the other. The same is also true when the parable of the potter is taken up again in the New Testament in Rom. $9^{21ff.}$. God is not, as it were, placed in an indeterminate middle point between the two. It is not that He uses them indifferently, causing Himself to repent now of the one and now of the other in a dialectic which is eternally incomprehensible. It is not that at one moment He can choose and perform the one, and at another moment the other. On the contrary, the Book of Jeremiah teaches us that the first divine repentance is His true and proper repentance (although this does not detract from the strict reality of the second repentance as well). This first repentance is the repentance in which He promises to go back and does in fact go back on warnings and even judgments which have already fallen. It is the repentance on account of which He sends His prophets, so that His people too may turn and thus lay hold of this promise and these benefits and confirm and justify God's gracious repentance (Jer. $26^{2-3, 13, 19}$; 36^3; 42^{10}). That God is of such a nature that " He repents of evil " is included with His grace, mercy, forbearance and clemency as one of His divine attributes (Joel 2^{13}; Jonah 4^2). God can certainly repent of having promised or demonstrated His help to Israel in different ways. He can retract in the most terrible manner by showing Himself as the One He is in His wrath. But He cannot and never does repent of being the One He is. He is this One even in His wrath : the God of Israel. It is as the God of Israel that He speaks to Abraham, Moses, Amos and Jeremiah, even when He speaks in wrath. It is as the God of Israel that they come to know Him and cry to Him. It is His Word that they proclaim. Therefore, even when He repents of His help, He is Israel's Helper, just as He is always the Creator of heaven and earth, the Creator and Lord of men, even when He repents of having formed man. It is for this reason that in the strange proclamation of His repentance, the repentance in which He repents of evil has—implicitly or explicitly, but always in fact, and necessarily so—a position of advantage or preponderance over that other repentance. This preponderance may be observed even in Ps. $18^{20f.}$. Therefore as Rom. 11^{29} has it, the first and last word concerning the divine χαρίσματα and the divine κλῆσις must be that " they are ἀμεταμέλητα." This preponderance does not lessen the reality of that other repentance. It does not mean that when God chides He does not do so seriously. But it shows the order in which His chiding occurs. As real chiding it is a function of His love active in freedom.

It would be most unwise, then, to try to understand what the Bible says about God's repentance as if it were merely figurative. For what truth is denoted by the " figure " if we are not to deny that there is an underlying truth? It would be just as foolish to try to see in the alteration which is certainly contained in the idea of repentance only an alteration in man in his relation to God, but not an alteration in God in His relation to man. Of course, in so far as this relationship rests on an attitude of God's, it is immutable in the sense that it is always and everywhere God's relationship to man, the being and essence of the One who loves in freedom. Yet it would not be a glorifying, but a blaspheming and finally a denial of God, to conceive of the being and essence of this self-consistent God as one which is, so to speak, self-limited to an inflexible immobility, thus depriving God of the capacity to alter His attitudes and actions. God is Himself in all His attitudes and actions, as they are manifested in His revelation in concurrence or in sequence. And He Himself does not alter in the alteration of His attitudes and actions (Ps. $102^{26f.}$). In all of them He intends and maintains Himself, His love and His freedom. He neither loses Himself nor becomes untrue to Himself. Yet He is not prevented by this continuity from genuine life and therefore from life in this concurrence or sequence. He is not prevented from advancing and retreating, rejoicing and mourning, laughing and complaining, being well pleased and causing His wrath to kindle, hiding or

revealing Himself. And in all these things He can be always Himself, and therefore He can be them seriously, yet still according to the order of His essence,
and therefore in a definite sequence and gradation. All this is revealed in His
relation to the creation and man, and decisively in His relation to Israel and the
Church. But it is not the case that only in His relation to the creation and man,
in His revelation of grace, does it all become a reality which it is not in God
Himself. On the contrary, the fact that in His relation to creation and man
God relates Himself to them in a way which is conformable to their mutability and alteration is based on the fact that they have this nature of theirs
from Him and even in the perversion of it cannot evade that which they have
from Him. What is conformable or proportionate to them is so because it was
apportioned to them by Him, so that primarily and originally it is based on His
own creative being and essence. If God relates Himself to creation and man in
a way which is conformable to them, this means that He also relates Himself
in a way which, as it is grounded in Himself, is above all conformable to Himself.
But it is in conformity with Himself to be constantly the living God.

This understanding of God's constancy leads at once to the following conclusion in respect of His relation to His creation as such and
in general. That as Creator God posits and maintains by His will
a reality distinct from Himself is something which He does as an
expression and confirmation of His constant vitality. He does it in
the freedom of His love. He does not do it, therefore, because in His
essence He is under the necessity of having the world as well, outside
Himself, perhaps as His fellow-worker or even as His playmate. He
does not do it because He is not great or rich enough in Himself, or because His omnipotence—the omnipotence of the divine knowledge and
will—needs an object distinct from itself, or space for its activity outside
itself. Nor does He do it because of a superabundance which has to
find an outlet, as it were, and if it did not overflow in the creation of
a world would be imperfection, discord or suffering. He does not in
any sense do it because He stands in need of an improvement or
enlargement of Himself and must provide it for Himself. The constancy of the divine essence is repugnant to all conceptions of this
kind. He does it in love. But His love is free. It does not have to
do what it does. This means that when God becomes the Creator
and Lord of the world He does not become anything that He was not
before. As Creator and Lord of the world He is not less or more than
He was before. Creation cannot bring Him any increase, decrease or
alteration of His divine being and essence by reason of its existence
as the reality distinct from Himself, of its essence, its vitality, which
grows and decays and alters. It cannot do this because it is His
creation, the creation of His free love, which has its existence and
essence by Him, while what God has in Himself is the ground of its
existence and essence and not that existence and essence itself. In
God Himself there does exist diversity prior to this, but it is His
own and not that of the world. In God Himself there is also life and
movement, but again it is His own and not that of the world. What
new thing can the world offer, lend or be to Him, when the ground

of the novelty of its existence, and of all the novelties in its essence, is in Himself, and would be so no less even if there were no world. It is by Him that there is the new thing of a reality distinct from Himself, and it is by Him that all the new things in this reality exist. But all these novelties can and do exist by Him because it is in Him Himself that they have their ground, because He is immutable in the fact that He is the One who is eternally new, and because it was in this immutability that He chose to be the Creator and Lord of the world and to manifest His love in freedom. Its freedom consists in the fact that it could choose between the being and not being of the world without being any the less love. But it is love in the fact that it has actually chosen that the world should be without being any the less free. By God the world exists in God. This is how the world exists beside and outside God. This is how it has its existence and essence.

We can see at once that this sets two limits. The first is against all speculation of a monistic kind. According to this the world constitutes an integral part of the essence of God. This part was originally concealed and then manifested. It existed eternally in God. It then became a reality in time in the form of an emanation or division of the divine essence beside and outside Him and yet in secret identity with Him. It will finally return into pure existence in Him. In this speculation the simple fact is overlooked that, while the world certainly exists in God, it does so by Him. The speculation can take two fundamental forms. On the one hand, the existence of the world set in motion beside and outside God can be viewed as a mere passing appearance. It is in a sense a self-misunderstanding or nightmare on the part of God. It is a kind of deviation of God from Himself which will be rectified by the return of the world to God. On the other hand, the existence of the world beside and outside God can be treated seriously by taking it up in all its mutability and change into the essence of God Himself. God's essence is identified with it, or it with God's essence, as if God were God in the fact that the world in its existence and essence is the world. It is clear that according to the first conception the work of creation and the reality of the world in its distinction from God has necessarily to be denied with an audacity which is only really possible where a creature presumes to ascend God's throne over against the rest of the world and to think of himself as a dreaming God. And it is clear that according to the second conception the Creator, indeed the reality of God as such, has necessarily to be denied with an indifference which is only possible when the creature is so satisfied with himself that it means nothing to him to identify his own reality with that of God. It is unnecessary to mention that these two conceptions meet both in their origin and in their consequences, completing one another and finally amounting to one and the same thing. They have in common a failure to see that creation is that which is freely posited by the divine love. They have no knowledge of the distinction between the Creator and the creature. But without this knowledge they cannot give either the Creator or the creature the honour that in different ways belongs to each of them. Without it they cannot honestly or consistently acknowledge or affirm either the existence of God or that of the world. Over against these two speculative conceptions of the existence of the world in God Himself, the affirmation of God's constancy tells us that God is the same both before and after the creation of the world, both without it and with it. Its existence does not mean that He is not destined to be identical with it either in appearance or reality, either dreaming or awake. His relation to the world, binding Him to it yet distinguishing Him from it, is the relation of the Creator and Lord, who, in His free love, has *really* created it in its existence, but has really *created* and upholds it, having and affirming His own existence over against it in this creative and sustaining love.

It is no less a speculation, however, when the distinction between Creator and creature is drawn in a dualistic fashion, so that *in abstracto* immutability is ascribed to the Creator, and mutability to the creature. Thus this involves both the denial of a real participation by the Creator in the existence and essence of the creature moved by Him, and the corresponding denial of a real participation by the creature in the immutability of the Creator. In this speculation, too, the simple fact is overlooked that because the world certainly is by God it is for this very reason in God. Two conceptions are again possible corresponding to the two sides of the problem to which the presupposition gives rise. On the one hand, the emphasis falls on God's immutability and therefore on the fact that the existence and essence of the creature in its mutability is necessarily deprived of God's participation in it, or may enjoy it merely in a form of confrontation that in the last resort is of no significance for either side. The mutable world may be created and preserved by the immutable God—no one knows how or why—but the two live apart as if in semi-detached houses, with no door in the party wall between them. In this case the creature is on the one side with a sad face and a bad conscience, helpless, tortured by the mutability of this world —a world which can certainly be limited by the immutable God, but which in the last resort can receive from Him no comfort and no hope. And the Creator stands on the other side, very high and lofty and superior in His immutability over against the mutability of the creature, but for this reason with a very small portion in us, whose portion is simply this mutability. On this view it will be very hard to avoid the practical conclusion that death is God or that God is dead. This conception can obviously be formed and propagated only where there is for some reason no awareness of the living God. This is always and necessarily the case where His revelation has not been recognised or has been rejected as such. The other form of the conception is the one in which the emphasis falls on the mutability of the creature and therefore on the fact that the Creator has essentially no significance or message for us just because He is excluded from our mutability. Fortunately, then, proximity to the immutable has no effect on the changes in which our life is lived. The metaphor of the party wall is again apposite, except that in this case we do not feel quite so much excluded as protected behind this wall. The separation means that the world acquires a valid autonomy which is affirmed and enjoyed by the creature. Secularism turns to its own advantage the immutability and therefore the absence of God in this mutable world. It is a secularism which is based on itself and confirms and guarantees itself. It is the self-satisfaction of a self-moved world celebrating its triumph on the very basis of what is apparently an essential and very reverent distinction between the Creator and the creature. It is again apparent that this conception can be formed and propagated only where the creature can and does in some sense become intoxicated with its own mutability, not noticing either the fact that at least in the form of death an immutable means the limit of all its possible changes, or the riddle that it necessarily is to itself in so far as its existence this side of death is to exhaust itself in incessant movement. But again it is only when there is knowledge of the living God that there is also knowledge of death and therefore of the riddle of life in movement this side of death. And knowledge of this God requires knowledge of His revelation. Again, we can see the agreement between the two possible conceptions on the basis of this second speculation which separates Creator and creature. The only real difference is that the one possesses a negative note and the other a positive. The aspect disclosed by the one is optimistic, that by the other pessimistic. But they are at one in their presuppositions and significant conclusions. In practice, then, they continually meet and interchange and complement one another, providing for their exponents a wide field of play for various combinations and the opportunity for what is both emotionally and intellectually an immensely rich dialectic. They have in common a failure to see that the divine love is that which has freely posited creation. And so they have no knowledge of the relation between the Creator and the creature. The result of this lack of knowledge is that they too are unable to give either to the Creator or the creature the honour due to each in its own way. They cannot see clearly and accept the essence of God or that of the world. Over against both these forms of speculation on the eternal difference between the immutable God and the mutable world, the affirmation of God's constancy tells us that God is the same both before and after the creation of the world, both without it and along with it. He is not far from the world, but near it even and indeed precisely in its mutability. He is bound to it in His immutable essence because this essence is life in itself before there was a life of the world or life in the world, quite apart from the world's life, and as the basis of this life. This is the reason why the world's life cannot be lived by itself, autonomously and in its own strength, separated from His life by a party wall. On the contrary, because God Himself is constant life, all the world's life lives by Him, and for that very reason it lives in Him. It is, of course, distinct—infinitely distinct—from His life. Yet in its very distinctness it derives from Him and returns to Him. On the one hand, it must not be deprived of a share in His life. And, on the other hand, it cannot raise itself up to independence of His life. There is as little ground for pessimism in its relation to Him as there is for optimism. Pessimism and optimism can arise and be expounded only if men forget the relationship which exists in virtue of the constancy of God and in which creaturely life is lived.

If, then, we are to understand God's constancy in respect of His relationship to His creation as such and in general we must resolutely abstain from both monistic and dualistic speculation. But we will really abstain resolutely, that is, radically, only when we see clearly that monism and dualism are not as distinct from one another as at first sight appears—and this includes the various conceptions under which they can be worked out. Both arise from a failure to see that the world is freely posited by the divine love. Both arise, therefore, from a failure to recognise the being of God as the One who is constant, the One who loves in freedom. It is not really so important whether this false presupposition leads in the one case to the assertion of a false unity or in the other to a false separation between God and the world. Different words may be used (corresponding to the different approaches to the falsely stated problem and different aspects of it), but either way they express one and the same thing, one and the same distortion. In practice at any rate the antithesis shows itself to be what it is—a purely dialectical antithesis. We can vacillate between its terms. Indeed, since it is a false antithesis, we will inevitably do so. But ultimately the error thought and expressed in it is always monotonously the same. But this is changed when we have a right understanding of the assertion of the constancy of God.

We have also to understand it as a proof and a manifestation of God's constant vitality that God has a real history in and with the world created by Him. This is the history of the reconciliation and revelation accomplished by Him, by which He leads the world to a future redemption. In this history God does not become nor is He other than He is in Himself from eternity and in eternity. But again, His constancy does not hinder Him from being the real subject of this real history. On the contrary, it is in virtue of His constancy that He has the capability and capacity and willingness to be this. Even less is He prevented by His being and activity as the Creator. It is this very history which reveals in what sense He is the Creator and Lord of the world and in what way the world is actually posited by His free love, in what way it is really in Him by Him. For the beginning and end and quintessence of this history, at all events on the one hand, is always that the created world is by God, that it never escapes His control by reason of its own reality or autonomy, but that it is wholly and utterly under His dominion and in His hand. And on the other hand, it is also that this world is in God, which means that in its reality, which is distinct from the divine reality, it is always upheld by God, that it never falls out of His hands in this reality and autonomy. This is so because He never ceases to act in His connexion with it, giving Himself wholly in love to this connexion, without detriment to His freedom. So far from contradicting Himself God confirms Himself as the Creator of the world by having a special history with it in His work of reconciliation and revelation. It is, of course, clear that God introduces something really new, distinct from the work of creation as such, in this history, His history with Israel and the Church. It is now a matter of His action and attitude towards the creature which has fallen away from Him and resists Him. It is now a matter of the salvation of that which because of its defection would be lost if it were not for this new divine way of being and acting.

But the fact of resistance to God in the sphere of creation does not involve any conflict in God Himself. It is a mark of the divine nature as distinct from that of the creature that in it a conflict with Himself is not merely ruled out, but is inherently impossible. If this were not so, if there did not exist perfect, original and ultimate peace between the Father and the Son by the Holy Spirit, God would not be God. Any God in conflict with Himself is bound to be a false God. On the other hand, it is a mark of created being as distinct from divine that in it conflict with God and therefore mortal conflict with itself is not ruled out, but is a definite possibility even if it is only the impossible possibility, the possibility of self-annulment and therefore its own destruction. Without this possibility of defection or of evil, creation would not be distinct from God and therefore not really His creation. The fact that the creature can fall away from God and perish does not imply any imperfection on the part of creation or the Creator. What it does mean positively is that it is something created and is therefore dependent on preserving grace, just as it owes its very existence simply to the grace of its Creator. A creature freed from the possibility of falling away would not really be living as a creature. It could only be a second God—and as no second God exists, it could only be God Himself. Sin is when the creature avails itself of this impossible possibility in opposition to God and to the meaning of its own existence. But the fault is that of the creature and not of God. In no sense does it follow necessarily from what God is in Himself.

Nor does it result from the nature of creation. It follows inevitably only from the incomprehensible fact that the creature rejects the preserving grace of God. What belongs to the nature of the creature is that it is not physically hindered from doing this. If it were hindered in this way, it could not exist at all as a creature. In that case, grace would not be grace and the creature would inevitably be God Himself. The fact of evil in the world does not cast any shadow on God, as if evil, i.e., opposition to Him, had any place either in Himself or in His being and activity as the Creator.

Further, no conflict in God is involved in the fact that He for His part opposes the opposition of the creature to Himself. This divine opposition to the defection and destruction of the creature is simply an expression of the fact that God cannot cease to be God and that He cannot cease to act as the Creator and Lord of the world, and therefore of the sinful world. In the whole work of reconciliation and revelation God simply remains the One He is. He is not diverted from His purpose. He is not mocked. He does not allow limitations to be set Him by the opposition of the creature. And He certainly does not allow Himself to be drawn into the conflict. Whatever He decides to do as Judge and Helper of the sinful creature He does as the One He is, undisturbed and intact and true to Himself. However He replies, He does so as the One who is peace in Himself, and who even as Creator and Lord of the world cannot be implicated in its sin. His reply is rather to justify and maintain Himself in relation to the sinful world ; and to bind Himself afresh and as never before, so that He reveals Himself in His constant being, and in it is present to it and active in its midst. The salvation revealed and given by Him to the world in this new work does not in any sense consist in making concessions of any kind or withdrawing in face of it, as if He had to take its defection seriously in the sense that, faced with a *fait accompli*, He could only be different, retracting or qualifying the law of His will, or letting mercy take the place of justice and the like. He neither can nor will be different. Nor would it help the world in any way if He were. The world is helped only by the fact that He remains what He is—and now supremely. It is not by His abandoning His opposition, but by His maintaining and exercising it that the world is saved from the evil of its own opposition. This is what we have to say about God's constancy. It is in His revelation as the Reconciler, as the Lord of Israel and the Church, as the Giver of future redemption, that He is revealed and active in it.

It is at this juncture that we have to recall all the Old Testament sayings in which God the Lord, the Creator of the ends of the earth, fainteth not neither is weary (Is. 40²⁸) ; or Yahweh has loved Israel with an everlasting love and therefore drawn her to Him in loving-kindness (Jer. 31³) ; or, though the mountains depart or the hills be removed, yet His kindness will not depart or the covenant of His peace be removed (Is. 54[10]). And this is also the point to think of New Testament passages like Rom. 9[11], Eph. 1[4f.], 3[11], 2 Tim. 1[9] and 1 Pet. 1[20] in which the salvation proclaimed to the Church in Jesus Christ is traced back to a decision made by God in their favour from all eternity. " I will take my rest, and I will consider in my dwelling place like a clear heat upon herbs, and like a cloud of dew in the heat of harvest " (Is. 18[4]). In fact everything that is said and done in fulfilment of the divine reconciliation and revelation is the execution of the one fixed divine decision, taken once for all. This is so whether in individual cases it means light or shadow, judgment or grace, wrath or patience, Law or Gospel. In virtue of this decision God is always the same in the space occupied by His creation even in face of the defection and rebellion that has taken place in it. This is the best thing and indeed the only thing He can do for the advantage of His creation. Seen and stated from this eminence, God's speech and action has truth and force. It is itself decision and it calls for decisions. It has divine character in the midst of what is otherwise creaturely existence and being. All sin, all enmity against grace in Israel and the Church, has its ultimate root in a failure to recognise this source of the divine speech and action. In his own uncertainty man thinks of God Himself as vacillating. And all obedience, i.e., all faith which is brought to the Word and work of God, has its root in a recognition that it is the Word and work of the One who never can or will be, choose, or do anything other than what in different ways He now reveals as His Word and work with its promise and its claim. If the constancy of God is recognised, there is always trust in His promise and acknowledgment of His claim.

But here, too, the constancy of God must be considered as a perfection of His freedom. It will be appreciated that the opposition with which God confronts the defection in the sphere of His creation is not merely a passive opposition. It is not simply that in Himself, or even as Creator and Lord of the world, God continues to be Himself on His throne on High, and therefore at a distance from the world's error and misery. He certainly does do this. But since He is always the same His work of opposition to sin, as it becomes an event in His revelation and reconciliation, is much more than this. It is a new work, a fresh overflowing of the divine fulness. For God still maintains contact and fellowship with the world even on that assumption of the defection and destruction of the creature which is neither possible in His own being nor chosen by Him in His work of creation. He can be—and in fact is—the God even of sinful man, his Judge and Deliverer, without altering His unalterable being. Indeed, the fact that He is this is simply a confirmation that He is unalterably alive with a life to which sin cannot oppose anything new, strange or superior, but which is—from the very outset—so completely equal to the fact of sin itself that sin is already outstripped and overcome in it. It could not be otherwise. If God is who He is, eternal peace, this does of course settle the fact that in Him there is no sin, but it also settles the fact that He is in opposition to sin, in an active and infinitely superior opposition, so that from the very first sin is contested, confuted and overcome in it (and therefore as our sin by it). And if He is the Creator and Lord of the world, this settles the fact that even in creation sin can only be the impossible possibility, the possibility rejected by His sustaining grace. But it also settles the fact that when sin actually occurs, as the destruction and misery of His creature it goes straight to His heart as the Creator. It is, in fact, quite intolerable to Him as the Creator of His creature, and it is His own most proper concern to resist and overcome it. Newer than the novelty that man has sinned is the new fact that becomes visible and active in the work of His opposition to it in His essential being. This is the divine mercy and the divine wrath in which He does not become different, but confirms Himself anew as the One He has been from all eternity and from the creation of the world. It is to this extent that something new happens when in Abraham God has mercy on Israel and in Israel on all peoples. This is not an emergency measure, an inevitable reaction. God's refusal to leave them in their defection and consequent destruction cannot be regarded as necessitated by creation or the existence of the world, and certainly not by the sin of the creature. He was and is under no obligation to the creature to give this new form to His preserving grace against which it had sinned—a form which confirms and declares it anew as grace. He was just as little under obligation to do this for it as He was either to it or to Himself to create it. If God has befriended man in his sin and continues to befriend him, this was and is again a free act of positing. The New Testament rightly calls it " a new creation." But now that He has done it and does do it, we cannot but recognise the new fulness of His being (new in its overflowing for us), the depth of His grace, in the fact that He wills to be and is the God and Judge and Saviour even of sinful man. And nothing of all that He does or is as such should be regarded by us as less real because it is in fact in this new relationship that He does it, as the Creator and Lord of His fallen creation, and therefore in conformity with its new situation, and not exclusively in His creative function as such. For originally and properly He does this too in conformity with Himself.

In this connexion our attention is necessarily drawn to what are almost all peculiar characteristics of the history of salvation. It is impossible to understand the God of Scripture, and the constancy of this God, if we overlook or blur the fact that at this point we have to do with special characteristics in which God is in some sense to be distinguished from Himself in His being and action as Creator—or better, in which His being and action as Creator and therefore His divine being as such acquires contours which are inconsistent with a general concept of immutability. It is not at all that we have to criticise or idealise these characteristics from the standpoint of a general idea of the immutable. The truth is just the reverse, that in them the God of Holy Scripture wills to be understood in His reality, that in them He wills that we should learn what the really immutable is, and in what sense He, God, is the immutable.

Our first point is simply that although this new work takes place within the sphere of the creation and continuous preservation of the world, it is still a special work, and not directly coincident with the other. Nor can it be understood merely as the continuation and crown of the work of creation (as Schleiermacher would have it) although it certainly is this as well ; for necessarily God the

Creator is alive and active in it, continuing and completing His work. On the contrary, God so surpasses Himself in this new work that it is only here that He can really be known, as it were retrospectively, as God the Creator. Between us and God's being and action as the Creator, there stands our sin and rebellion by which we have forfeited our life as His creatures and our fellowship with Him as our Creator, and perverted our knowledge of Him. The real Creator and Lord of the world is not the principle of the beginning or origin or real essence of all things. If we identify God with this principle, we forget that we have fallen away from God and we repeat and confirm our apostasy by erecting an idol. The real Creator and Lord of the world is the One, and only the One, who befriends us in our very apostasy from Himself, and who in so doing, in confirmation of His creation, has done to us something new and more than by creation itself. It is in and by the knowledge of this second act that we come to know the first. It is in and by the special act that we recognise the general, and not *vice versa*. We have to do with a special act of God to us, corresponding to the special nature of our apostasy, and in this special act we have to do with the really immutable.

This special act of God as the Subject and Lord of the history of salvation appears already in the fact that there are now specific dealings between God and man which according to the Genesis " saga " began directly after the fall. The time of God's general speaking, as recorded in Genesis 1-2, is now past. God walks in the garden in the cool of the day (Gen. 3⁸ᶠ·). He calls the man who has feebly tried to hide from Him. He listens to his excuses and unmasks them as such. He informs him of the new order of his existence on the presupposition of what has occurred ; its curse, and also at once its promise. From now on the being and action of the Creator in His relation to the creation takes the form of these distinct dealings with man. Does this mean that God has altered ? That is impossible. But as the One He is and continues to be, He has and He obviously realises this new possibility too. Does He cease to be the Creator and Preserver of the whole world ? That cannot be. But as such He now reveals Himself and acts in this new reality. Does this mean that His glory, the glory of His love to His creature, is diminished ? The wonder is that it is not. The God of Genesis 3 is more living, because more definite, than the God of Genesis 1-2. And He has turned more intimately to the creature than before. Something other and greater than mere creation has now taken place. It is so much greater that the dangerous saying is forced to our lips : *felix culpa, quae talem et tantum meruit redemptorem* (*Roman Missal*, Liturgy for the Saturday before Easter Day). And in this different and greater thing we see nothing but the glory of the Creator and creation, forfeited by us and now for the first time revealed. But if this is the case, cannot the specific dealings of God with man dissolve into the picture of the general truth of the relation between Creator and creature ? Most certainly not, even for the sake of this general truth itself. For it is in the particular truth of these dealings that the general truth is provided and maintained. If we want to know it and live in it, we must live in the actuality of these dealings, which can be understood only in their actuality.

The special act of God in this new work consists further in the fact that in these dealings God does not disdain to enter into a kind of partnership with man. In Genesis 1-2 it is only God who speaks. But from Genesis 3 on there is a human reply. It now becomes possible and even necessary that there should be scenes like Abraham's intercession for Sodom and Gomorrah (Gen. 18²⁰ᶠᶠ·), or Jacob's struggle with the angel (Gen. 32²²ᶠᶠ·), or the picture of God in the parable of the unjust judge (Lk. 18¹ᶠᶠ·). It is He, as Creator the only and perfect Lord of men, who now enters into a confrontation of this kind. And it is in the freedom which he has snatched on his own authority, in the pseudo-divinity in which he now knows good from evil, that man is now taken seriously. This does not mean only that he is imprisoned in this state of punishment, but also that in this state he receives a new blessing. The divine decisions now aim continually at human ones as well. In the one course of the divine action there is not only the divine predestination, but also a human self-determination; not only the divine faithfulness but also human faith; not only God's command and promise, but also the question of obedience and trust directed to man for man to answer. This cannot possibly mean that God has ceased to be man's Creator and Lord. It cannot possibly mean that He is less in this relationship than previously. On the contrary, is it not the case that God's freedom emerges as all the more majestic now that it obviously includes the freedom of the creature and wills to be known and acknowledged and glorified even in the freedom of the creature? Is it not the case that now for the first time the reality of the creature emerges as a reality distinct from God and the preserving grace of God as grace that as such waits for gratitude and can only really be received in gratitude? Again our thoughts may turn to the *felix culpa*. And again God has certainly not become smaller, but in this new confirmation of Himself really great. Again it would be positively dangerous to deny to the partnership between God and man which has now obviously become possible and necessary its particular reality. For it is in it and it alone that God's sole lordship and activity appear in the way in which God Himself will have them understood.

The special act of God in this new work of God's appears, further, in the fact that from the very outset and in all its stages the history of salvation is based on a choice. The communication and partnership between God and man do not take place in a general way, but between God and specific men who are marked out for it by God Himself. We can see this from Abel through Noah to Abraham, Isaac and Jacob. We can see a continual selection and separation in Israel. We can see the same thing in the calling and gathering of the Church and even within the Church itself. Faith always depends on calling and calling on election and the Spirit always bloweth where He listeth. Of course, God does not cease to be the Creator and Lord of the whole world, and therefore of all men. He does not cease to act as such: " He maketh his sun to rise on the evil and on the good, and sendeth rain on the just and the unjust " (Mt. 5⁴⁵). He does not cease to " will all men to be saved, and to come unto the knowledge of the truth " (1 Tim. 2⁴). On the contrary, it is just in this way that He wills all this. It is for the sake of the preservation of the human race that He makes His covenant with the one man Noah, for the sake of the peoples that He chooses the one elect people of Israel, and for the sake of mankind that He chooses the Church. What is the reason for selection? A selection is made because they have all rejected and forfeited the preserving grace of the Creator as the only condition of their existence, and because it is a matter of its restoration, or rather of its triumph over the opposition raised against it. But this triumph could not take place, and grace would not be grace, if the relation between God and all men were uniform. It belongs to the very essence of the matter that if sinful men are not merely to continue to be God's creatures but are to be called the sons of God, this is something special, an unmerited, freely given differentiation. In this act of selection which constitutes the history of salvation God does not become nor is He different. On the contrary, it is as the Saviour from sin and death in this special form that He is the One He is. Again, His glory and the intensity of His love for creation are not less but greater and more evident in this new form. Again our thoughts turn to the *felix culpa* when we compare the regularity of man's unfallen existence before God in Paradise with the fire of being loved and being able to respond in love that now burns in the hearts of His children on the basis of this selection. Again this second element is simply what is now for the first time revealed as the greatness of the first. Consequently it must never be reduced to the first, just as the truth about God and man must never be sought apart from this divine choice and the human existence based upon it. Rather, the proclamation of God's Word to all men—

in order to be addressed as such to all—must have as its content this selection and therefore this existence, the existence of the special children of God.

The special act of God in this new work appears, further, in the fact that its occurrence, its acceptance by men and its effect on them are always accompanied by the sign of the miraculous, or, to speak in general terms, the extraordinary. When God speaks and acts and is heard and obeyed by men, it is always in the sphere of creation, at some point in the context of the life established and preserved by creation. Yet in this very sphere and context it is on each occasion something completely new. Although it follows some other event and many other events, it does not follow from this other event or the sequence of all others. On the contrary, at the heart of these other events it has the character of a termination of all the rest and at the same time of the beginning of something quite different. God's words and acts, and the faith and obedience with which man meets these (and the unbelief and disobedience with which he withstands them) do take place within the course and development of created things, and have the character of these things. At the same time, however, they have decisively the character of an interruption and annulment of all that precedes in favour of a new order. We do not know of the Spirit whence He comes or whither He goes. Signs, reversals and alterations take place on the same old earth and under the same old heaven as everything else, and in continuity with everything that precedes, and yet at the same time they proclaim a new heaven, a new earth and a new continuity. Neither the work of the Son nor that of the Holy Spirit is understandable if we fail to recognise the miraculous element which accompanies these events, or if we try to conjure away the miracle as such. Again this does not mean that God ceases to be true to Himself, the Creator and Lord of this world. But how can the divine work take place, in which God causes His preserving grace to triumph over man's opposition, without a perception by man of the divine opposition as such ? How can grace meet him as grace if it simply decks itself out as nature, if nature as such is grace ? Grace is the secret behind nature, the hidden meaning of nature. When grace is revealed, nature does not cease to exist. How can it, when God does not cease to be its Creator ? But there is in nature more than nature. Nature itself becomes the theatre of grace, and grace is manifested as lordship over nature, and therefore in its freedom over against it. And again God is not less but more glorious for us in miracle than elsewhere. Again miracle is simply the revelation of the divine glory otherwise hidden from us, on the strength of which we can believe and honour Him elsewhere as Creator and Lord. Miracle must not be reduced to the level of God's other and general being and action in the world. Its miraculous nature must not be denied. It must be maintained—even for the sake of the general truth. For it is miracle alone which opens for us the door to the secret that the Creator's saving opposition to us does not confront us only at individual points and moments, but throughout the whole range of our spatio-temporal existence.

The special act of God in this new work appears, further, in the fact that creation itself gains new depth or perspective in it. This is true of man, but it is also true of the whole sphere and reality of creation. There can be seen in it both the distinction and the connexion between the reconciliation which is to be received here and now in faith and the redemption which is to be revealed one day beyond, and therefore between the provisional and final form of creation, our time and God's time, this life and eternal life, this world and the world to come, or more correctly, this life and this world in the form and manner in which they are known to us here, and in the form and manner of their perfection in which they are known to God alone, but will also be known to us also hereafter ; that is, in the form and manner of the kingdom of God which will then be manifested and seen absolutely, exclusively and without any contradiction. It is this step, this change, this road, the revealing of this perspective as such which is the meaning and the content of the communication between God and His chosen partners. It is this which is also the significance of miracles which are the necessary form of this communication to the extent that as genuine communication it involves man as well as God. Since we have to do with the relation of the creature to God it is also a matter of the creature's own *eschaton*, its final reality as it is already present to God, but still future for itself, still to be revealed to it. Reconciliation is real reconciliation because it makes us men who wait and look and move towards the redemption which has already taken place for us and is ready for us. Revelation is true revelation because, by means of what we are told in it, it forces us to look to the place where our redemption will one day be visible to us, although it is still invisible to us here. Faith is real faith because it is a rebirth to a living hope, as 1 Pet. 1³ says. The work of reconciliation and revelation (which embraces everything else) is a fundamentally new work as compared with the work of creation because it consists in the opening up of this depth or perspective for creation, the vision of the resurrection of the body, eternal life and the new heaven and the new earth. The possession of this perspective does not belong of necessity to the essence and conception of creation as such. But it is to be noted that the fact that it does actually possess this perspective emerges in the work of reconciliation and revelation and therefore—and what unfathomable depths of grace this opens up !—in God's action in relation to the apostasy of the creature. But this being the case, God does not change when He does this second thing after the first. He does not become untrue to that first work or to Himself. But here supremely He is true to both. He does not reply to human rebellion simply with a *restitutio ad integrum*, but with the revelation of a perfection concealed even in the original creation in its integrity. He does not only make the sick whole, but gives him a share in the hope of everlasting life. In retrospect, we may well ask : What would the first work or its restoration be without the second ? Would what God made be good if this depth were missing ? Would its restoration be real, and would there be confidence and a real answer to sin and death, if there were no hope, and God were not the One who in the midst of sin and death renewed us with this hope ? But God was and is under no obligation to be this One to us. We only boast of the fact that He is actually this One. But because He is so in fact, we must boast of it, and we must never in any way smooth over or deny the step, the change and the road which leads from the first to the second and consists in the opening up of this perspective. This special element in God's constant life, the fact that He is our coming Redeemer, must above all be perceived and recognised with gratitude as something special. This will not conflict with the gratitude which we owe Him already as our Creator. It will be the proper gratitude towards the One who has revealed Himself as our Creator and also as our Redeemer because He is in fact both, and not the first without being the second.

We shall conclude this survey by glancing at the special act of God in His new work which in a sense forms a direct question addressed by the God who is active in this new work to the practice of our faith. This consists in the fact that the prayers of those who can and will believe are heard ; that God is and wills to be known as the One who will and does listen to the prayers of faith. His communication with man in the partnership based on His election is so real and so definitely miraculous, and it is the concrete form of the hope given the believer by the opening up of the depth and perspective of creation, that man is not merely permitted to hear God, to answer Him, to worship Him, and in that worship to find comfort, peace and purity, but he may actually call upon God in the most definite way to do for him and give him what he needs, with the expectation that God will do it, and in His wisdom give him what he needs. So real is this communication that where it occurs God positively wills that man should call upon Him in this way, in order that He may be His God and Helper. We need not hesitate to say that " on the basis of the freedom of God

Himself God is conditioned by the prayer of faith ". The basis is His freedom. It is thus a form of His sovereignty, and therefore of His immutable vitality that He is willing not merely to hear but to hearken to the prayer of faith and that He not only permits to faith the prayer which expects an answer but has positively commanded it. The Bible is completely unambiguous about this : " He heareth the prayer of the righteous " (Prov. 15²⁹). " The Lord is nigh unto all them that call upon him, to all that call upon him in truth. He will fulfil the desire of them that fear him : he also will hear their cry, and will save them " (Ps. 145¹⁸⁻¹⁹). " Call upon me in the day of trouble : I will deliver thee, and thou shalt glorify me " (Ps. 50¹⁵). " The effectual fervent prayer of a righteous man availeth much. Elias was a man subject to like passions as we are, and he prayed earnestly that it might not rain ; and it rained not on the earth by the space of three years and six months, and he prayed again and the heaven gave rain, and the earth brought forth her fruit " (Jas. 5¹⁶⁻¹⁸). " Ask and it shall be given you ; seek, and ye shall find ; knock and it shall be opened unto you : For everyone that asketh receiveth ; and he that seeketh, findeth ; and to him that knocketh, it shall be opened. Or what man is there of you, whom if his son ask bread, will he give him a stone ? Or if he ask a fish, will he give him a serpent ? If ye then, being evil, know how to give good gifts unto your children, how much more shall your Father which is in heaven give good things to them that ask him ? " (Mt. 7⁷⁻¹¹). " Hear what the unjust judge saith. And shall not God avenge his own elect, which cry day and night unto him, though he bear long with them ? I tell you he will avenge them speedily " (Lk. 18⁶⁻⁸). The living and genuinely immutable God is not an irresistible fate before which man can only keep silence, passively awaiting and accepting the benefits or blows which it ordains. There is no such thing as a Christian resignation in which we have either to submit to a fate of this kind or to come to terms with it. Resignation (whether accompanied by astrology or not) is always the disconsolate consolation of unbelief. There is, of course, a Christian patience and submission, as there is also a Christian waiting upon God. But it shows itself to be genuine by the fact that it is always accompanied by the haste and restlessness of the prayer which runs to God and beseeches Him, by the haste which rests on the knowledge that God takes our distress to heart, and expects that we for our part will take His mercy to heart and really live by it, so that in our mutual turning to one another He may be our God and therefore a Helper in our distress, allowing Himself to be moved by our entreaties : εἰ ὑπομένομεν, καὶ συμβασιλεύσομεν (2 Tim. 2¹²). This does not mean that God puts the reins of world government in the hands of believers or that believers may feel or act as sharers of His throne. In spite of all its untiring insistence and its likeness to the passionate prayer of the importunate widow, the prayer of faith has also the characteristic of the prayer in Gethsemene, in which the will of God is resolutely and finally set above the will of men. It is only prayer of this kind which has the promise that it will be heard. " And this is the confidence that we have in him, that, if we ask anything according to his will, he heareth us : and if we know that he hear us, whatsoever we ask, we know that we have the petitions that we desired of him " (1 Jn. 5¹⁴⁻¹⁵). But the " reigning with him " does mean that while God alone exercises the government of the world believers are not simply to be servants under Him. They may stand beside Him as His friends. Thus it is said of Moses that " the Lord spoke unto him face to face, as a man speaketh unto his friend " (Exod. 33¹¹). Similarly Jesus says to His disciples : " Ye are my friends, if ye do whatsoever I command you. Henceforth I call you not servants ; for the servant knoweth not what his lord doeth : but I have called you friends ; for all things that I have heard of my father I have made known unto you " (Jn. 15¹⁴⁻¹⁵). It is in this way that God reveals Himself and acts in the history of salvation. He does not alter when He reveals Himself as the One who listens to prayer. He remains the One He was and is, the Creator and Lord of all creation. But as such He has now made clear this other aspect of His being, that He wills not only to hear but to hearken, that He does actually hearken, that His own can meet Him in what is finally not a passive but a supremely active attitude, that He has, indeed, expressly commanded that they should do so—not, of course, in the work of a creaturely freedom, in competition with His sole sovereignty and activity, but in the freedom of friends, a freedom which He has specially given them. God's glory is not diminished by the fact that He gives this new activity to His creatures on the basis of His new work, being manifested as the One who is so free, so much the Master and Worker of all things, that He can limit Himself and let Himself be conditioned by faith in Him. What else is revealed when God hears and answers prayer but that He is the Creator and Lord of all things ? And how can this fact be more gloriously revealed, or be revealed at all, except by His hearing and answering prayer ? This activity of His creatures over against Him, surrounded as it is by God's eternal activity, is certainly something new and special. Yet it only reveals what is old and general, the meaning, the significance, the power and the truth of the divine activity which embraces all things and all men. Again it is quite inconceivable that this new and special characteristic should be the distinctive mark of the order of grace, that God's hearing prayer and granting this activity to the creature should belong to His dealings with the sinful world, and that it should be sinful men whom God should raise to such an unheard of dignity and function as they are awakened to faith and enabled to be vigilant in faith. But its inconceivability is no reason why we should deny that prayer is heard or even forget it or treat it as something which is dispensable or inessential to faith. For what is inconceivable is God's grace. But faith cannot try to live by anything but by God's inconceivable grace in its fulness and totality. It can will only to be obedient to grace, fully obedient, however inconceivable this may seem to be to it. It is therefore essential for faith to be faith in the God who listens to prayer—no less essential than for it to be faith in the God who elects men freely and has given us an eternal hope. Therefore the hearing of believing prayer is not to be reduced to the general truth that we are to live before God in humility as His servants and in gratitude as His children. We should recognise that in the realisation of this general truth we participate in the special.

" No tear before Thee is so small, Thou dost not wipe away " (P. Gerhardt) ; and even more forcibly, as the Gospel says : " If ye have faith as a grain of mustard seed, ye shall say unto this mountain, Remove hence to yonder place ; and it shall remove ; and nothing shall be impossible unto you " (Mt. 17²⁰).

The meaning and secret of the creation and preservation of the world is revealed in the history of salvation. But the meaning and secret of the history of salvation itself is Jesus Christ. Here too, then, we must speak finally and supremely about Him—not only as the Last, but as both the First and the Last—if we are to speak correctly about the confirmation and manifestation of God's immutable vitality. The special form in which God is immutably alive in the history of reconciliation and revelation is not first and originally the fact of Israel and the Church. It is this too. But we have always called it the special act of God. We must now explain rather more precisely how far it is this, and how far as such it also belongs specially to Israel and the Church. It belongs specially to them because properly and essentially it belongs specially to the incarnate Word of God, Jesus Christ. Even the general truth of God's being and action as Lord and Creator of the world is both hidden and disclosed to us in the history of salvation, in the life of Israel, and the Church. It is only there that it can be found by us. For it is the will of God that it should be only at the place where the work of God's free grace is real and active. But the history of salvation is first and last, at its centre and in its origin, the history of Jesus Christ. For these reasons we can seek and find the general truth about God only in Jesus Christ and not apart from Him, according to the will of God that it should have the seat of its truth and activity in Him and in Him alone. What is revealed under the name of Jesus Christ is the confirmation and manifestation of the immutable vitality of God in particular—and because in particular in general too—the confirmation and manifestation of His free love. Necessarily, therefore, it will bear this name for all time and indeed for all eternity. The fact and way that God is the immutably living One is primarily and definitely revealed in the person and work which bears this name. The real act of God, the basis and presupposition of creation, reconciliation and redemption, is what has occurred and still occurs in accordance with God's will under the name of Jesus Christ. It is not, then, a movement only within the reality which is distinguished from God. Here if anywhere in this work, which embraces all others, we have to do with God Himself. If this is so, God's reality for its part cannot in any circumstances be understood in separation from what has occurred and occurs in this work. It belongs always to the essence and conception of God's constant vitality that He is the One who was able, who had the ability and capacity, to will and execute that which occurred and occurs here ; that He is the constantly living God in this willing and executing since it is not merely something which He has willed and for which He has the ability and capacity, but something which He has actualised by Himself. In the investigation and knowledge of the constant will and being of God we cannot go behind Jesus Christ. In all circumstances we must understand God as the One who has done and does that which took place and still takes place in Jesus Christ. He is immutably this God, and not another.

Again, this event has in common with the work of creation and that of reconciliation the fact that it is an act of God's free love. God is indeed God, and glorious in this event, in His power and capacity for it, in His will and resolve to bring it about, and in the actuality of the event itself. We must remember however that, while this event as a happening in and on the created world makes, magnifies and enhances the glory of God outwardly, inwardly it neither increases nor diminishes His glory, His divine being. For this is neither capable nor in need of increase or decrease. God did not and does not owe this happening to the world or to us any more than He did creation or the history of salvation. God was and is bound to cause this event to take place and to be only in so far as He has bound Himself. The fact that He was able and willing to do this and actually did it is the decisive and final demonstration of what His being is—His free love. It was not the case, nor is it, that His being necessitated Him to do it. In that case, where would there be freedom in His love ? He would be the One He is even if He did not give Himself to be known as such. If He is not the One He is without this self-disclosure, this claims our gratitude and worship, and calls us to faith and obedience, but it does not permit us to understand this bond with which He has bound Himself as anything other than the fact of His nature for the sake of which we are bound to Him. He did not need to bind Himself to us as He has in fact done in this event. But He has actually bound Himself in this way. What we see in Jesus Christ is that creation, too, and reconciliation and redemption are a real act, but that they are the real act of God's free love. We learn this in faith and obedience to Him, to His person and work. We recognise it in the grace of His revelation and reality.

God's work in Jesus Christ, as the centre and content, the presupposition and ground, of creation and reconciliation makes clear to us that in Jesus Christ God Himself has become a creature. That is to say, He has become one with the creature, with man. He has not simply entered into fellowship as He did in creation, causing the creature to become and be as His creature, or as He does in reconciliation, befriending His fallen creature, or as He does in redemption, granting life in His perfect kingdom to His creature. Among all the events in which God in His free love has granted His fellowship to what He has created, this event is distinguished by the fact that in it, in Jesus Christ, He becomes one with the creature. Where this creature, the man Jesus Christ is, God Himself is present : not only as the Creator and Lord ; not only in His reconciling grace to the creature ; not only as its King and Helper and Master ; not only, then, in the witness of the creature ; but, in addition to all these ways, in direct attestation of Himself in and with the existence of this creature.

Jesus does not simply speak about God—of course He does this too—but God Himself speaks through Him in such a way that He Himself is the speaker in Him. Jesus does not simply act in obedience to God—of course He does this too—but in His act God acts, He Himself doing fully and conclusively what is to be done by the creature for God's sake. Jesus does not simply live and suffer and die under the protection and promise of God—of course He does this too—but He does it in the full glory, first hidden and then revealed, of God Himself, in full possession of all the divine perfections, because He does it as God's own Son. It is in this way that He lives and suffers and dies. That is why He does it as the One who provides and brings salvation for all who believe in Him. But it is also why He moves to His own resurrection and ascension. It is why He does it, first hidden and then revealed, as the occupier of the throne of God from eternity to eternity.

It is because God was in this way one with the creature in Jesus Christ, that there was and is fellowship between God and the creature.

We can say already that the reason why God created the world and set up in it the office of reconciliation, is because He was able, willing and ready to be one with the creature in Jesus Christ and because He did in fact do this. Because He is the One who did and still does this, He is constant in all His works and constant also in Himself. Note that this " constancy " of His involves the point that it is grace that He did and still does this. He did not and does not have to do it. He did it and He does it in free love. The God in whose essential nature it lies to do this, not of necessity but in free love, is the constant God. But this " constancy " also involves the fact that He has actually done this in free love. Therefore God is constant, He does not alter, when He becomes and is one with the creature in Jesus Christ. For this happening is simply God Himself, His free life, in which He is inexhaustible, untiring, incapable of being diverted from His purpose. God does not contradict Himself in this act, but confirms and reveals Himself as the One He is, and as the Creator and Reconciler of His creation. He does this as the One He is because the incarnation is as such the confirmation of the triunity of God. Without abrogation of the divine unity, there is revealed in it the distinction of the Father and the Son, and also their fellowship in the Holy Spirit. He does it as the Creator because the incarnation is as such the confirmation of the distinctive reality of creation; for in the fact that God becomes one with creation there is revealed that God and creation as such are two distinct realities, and that the creature has its own reality over against God. He does it finally as Reconciler and Redeemer, because the incarnation as such confirms and explains the fact that God has befriended and continually befriends fallen creation, and will lead it on to a full redemption. It reveals the place and manner in which God pledges Himself to be true to His creation, in which He has actually bound Himself to it, so that He would be untrue to Himself if He were not to befriend it further and in other circumstances. To this extent it is the constancy of God which is revealed and which is recognisable in Jesus Christ.

All the older theology rightly stressed the fact that the incarnation of the Logos, the God-manhood of Jesus Christ, could not mean any alteration in the divine being, any declension of God from Himself, any transformation of His divine nature into another or admixture with another. For it consisted in the assumption of human nature, which was not abrogated or destroyed as such, into unity with the divine Word. *Nam Deus manifestatus in carne mansit quod erat et assumpsit, quod non habebat, non mutatione divinae naturae suae in humanam, nec transfusione proprietatum humanitatis in deitatem aut proprietatum deitatis in humanitatem, sed copulatione humanae naturae nostrae cum divina sua in unitatem personae* (Polanus, *Synt. Theol. chr.*, 1609, *col.* 979). This is true. But what we have to do at this point is to say much more strongly and positively that the incarnation not only does not mean any curtailment or compromising of the immutable divine nature, but that it means the revelation of it in its perfection, a perfection which we recognise in God the Creator,

Reconciler and Redeemer only because He is the God revealed, present and active in the God-manhood of Jesus Christ.

We read in Phil. 2st· that Jesus Christ emptied Himself (ἑαυτὸν ἐκένωσεν), taking the form of a servant, going about in the likeness of man and being found in appearance (ἐν σχήματι) as a man ; and that as such He humbled Himself (ἐταπείνωσεν ἑαυτόν), becoming obedient to death, even the death of the cross. All the expressions selected by Paul in this statement make it quite clear that like the older theology he did not believe that in all this Jesus Christ surrendered, lost, or even curtailed His deity. For He did it all ἐν μορφῇ θεοῦ ὑπάρχων, being in the form of God. The self-emptying does not refer to His divine being. It refers in a negative sense to the fact that He did not consider or treat His equality with God as His one exclusive possibility. He did not treat it as a robber does his booty. It was not an inalienable necessity for Him to be only like God and only distinct from the creature. Positively His self-emptying refers to the fact that, without detracting from His being in the form of God, He was able and willing to assume the form of a servant and go about in the likeness of man, so that the creature could know Him only as a creature, and He alone could know Himself as God. In other words, He was ready to accept a position in which He could not be known in the world as God, but His divine glory was concealed from the world. This was His self-emptying. His humbling of Himself—the meaning and goal of His self-emptying—consisted in the fact that (in the form of a servant which He had assumed and in the likeness of man) He did what man does not do because he is a sinner in revolt against the destiny imposed on him by his nature. That is to say, He was obedient unto death, and more than that, in His obedience He took upon Himself, even to the death of the cross, the curse and punishment of the rebellion which He had not Himself committed. This self-emptying and self-humbling has nothing to do with a surrender or loss of His deity. The only thing involved is the self-offering of God to the being and fate of men, a self-offering in which He makes them so much His own that His deity becomes completely invisible to all other eyes but His own. What distinguishes Him from the creature disappears from everyone's sight but His own with His assumption of the human form of a servant, with its natural end in death, and above all with His death as that of a criminal on the cross. *Paulisper interea delitescebat eius divinitas, hoc est vim suam non exserebat: sa divinité se tenoit pour un peu de temps comme cachée, c'est-à-dire qu'elle ne démonstroit point sa vérité* (Calvin, *Cat. Genev.*, 1542, edited by W. Niesel, *Qu.* 68.) No one here knows the Son but the Father. This does not mean, however, that the Son ceases to be the Son and therefore true God along with the Father. It is not at all the case that it belongs to the essence of God to be incapable of this self-offering and self-concealment, that to be God and assert Himself He must " snatch after " His position, hardening Himself to be only like Himself, only in His own form, One only with Himself. His freedom is seen in the fact that He is able to do something different. He can so empty Himself that, without detracting from His form as God, He can take the form of a servant, concealing His form of life as God, and going about in the likeness of man. He does not, however, do despite to Himself when He humbles Himself in this form of a servant, not shrinking from a descent into the lowest depths even of creaturely life. It is He Himself who empties and humbles Himself. There is no reason why in so doing He should do despite to Himself. It all takes place in His freedom and therefore not in self-contradiction or with any alteration or diminution of His divine being. But if we follow Phil. 2 we cannot stop here. After depicting Jesus Christ's self-offering the passage continues : " Wherefore God also hath highly exalted him, and given him a name which is above every name : that at the name of Jesus every knee should bow, of things in heaven, and things in earth, and things under earth ; and that every tongue should confess that Jesus Christ is Lord, to the glory of the Father." Note that the exaltation of Jesus Christ by the power of God, and therefore the revelation of the divine form hidden under the form of a servant, is not introduced with a Nevertheless or an And so but with a Therefore. The name *Kyrios* does not belong to Him in spite of the fact that the self-offering and concealment of God took place in Jesus Christ, but just because it took place. Because He emptied and humbled Himself this name is His as His resurrection reveals. And as the One who bears it He glorifies God in all creation, or in its acknowledgment creation must glorify God. " Come unto me, all ye that labour and are heavy laden, and I will give you rest. . . . For I am meek and lowly in heart " (Mt. 11²⁸ᶠ·). This means that so far from being contrary to the nature of God, it is of His essence to possess the freedom to be capable of this self-offering and self-concealment, and beyond this to make use of this freedom, and therefore really to effect this self-offering and to give Himself up to this self-concealment. The meaning and the goal of His self-emptying is His self-humiliation. In this above all He is concealed as God. Yet it is here above all that He is really and truly God. Thus it is above all on account of this that He must and will also be revealed in His deity by the power of God. It is not the case, then, that His self-emptying and self-humiliation compromises His deity. The case is rather that they reveal His true divinity. It is not the case that God has in a sense to be excused or justified for the condescension which has taken place in Jesus Christ. The older theology did not go far enough when it defended the *mansit quod erat* against all conceptions of an alteration brought about by the incarnation in or on God. The truth is that it is by the incarnation that God has revealed His truly immutable being as free love in the perfection in which, on the basis of the incarnation, we recognise it again and find it confirmed in His acts as Creator, Reconciler and Redeemer. God is " immutably " the One whose reality is seen in His condescension in Jesus Christ, in His self-offering and self-concealment, in His self-emptying and self-humiliation. He is not a God who is what He is in a majesty behind this condescension, behind the cross on Golgotha. On the contrary, the cross on Golgotha is itself the divine majesty, and all the " exaltation " necessary on account of His deity (i.e., the revelation of what He is) can reveal only, and all the worship in heaven and on earth which is the necessary response to it can confirm only, that God on high is the One who was able and willing and in fact did condescend so completely to us in His Son. This free love is the one true God Himself. All divine exaltation is exalted and divine because it is the exaltation and divinity of this free love. Everything that claims to be exaltation and divinity is to be tested by whether it is identical or not with the free love disclosed in its reality in the ταπεινοφροσύνη of Jesus Christ. The spirits may be tested, and with them all doctrine and exhortation, and all the forms of the Church and its message, by their conformity to this standard. All that claims to be exalted and divine must in all circumstances consist in an acknowledgment and confirmation of the self-offering and self-concealment of God that has taken place in Jesus Christ, and in an act of praise, adoration and gratitude towards the humility He manifested on the cross on Calvary. For it is in this that God has revealed Himself, and it is only as it is acknowledged that God is glorified by His creation. All statements about God and His exaltation which omit or deviate from this deny and violate His constancy, even though they may be made in the name of Jesus Christ. We must not forget that the only reason why the name of Jesus is " the name above every name," the name of God's glory itself, is that it is the name of Him who emptied and humbled Himself, the name of the God who did not count it beneath Him to make this condescension, but in it manifested His divine glory and caused it to triumph. (This is also the practical significance of Phil. 2⁵ᶠ·. It serves, cf. verses 1-4, directly to emphasise the apostolic exhortation to humility, in which each member of the community is to subordinate himself to the other, not seeking his own but the things of others. In the community we are to be intent on the reality " in Jesus Christ." And this is the divine condescension, the self-emptying and self-humbling. In it Christ is Christ and God is God. In it alone can Christians be Christians. Any " mind " which is not directed to it, however exalted or penetrating it may be, passes by Christ and therefore passes by God, and is therefore an unchristian " mind ".)

We have already stated that the constancy of the being of God revealed in Jesus Christ is the constancy of His freedom. But we must now underline and explain this. God has limited Himself to be this God and no other, to be the love which is active and dwells with men at this point and in this way, in Jesus Christ. God has bound Himself in His own Son to be eternally true to His creation. But He has done this Himself, and the fact that He has acted in this and not in any other way has its basis in and from Himself. He was not under any obligation to befriend creation by giving it no less than Himself in His Son, by Himself assuming and adopting its form. He was not under any obligation either to it or to Himself to be one with it in this specific form, thus constituting and instituting Himself the pledge of His faithfulness.

There are two important insights in this connexion and they belong and cohere together.

The first is that what did and does happen to and for creation in Jesus Christ must be understood as God's free decision. As He has in fact effected this, we cannot and should not form any conception of God in abstraction from what He has effected, His reality in Jesus Christ. By the very nature of the case we are dealing with a movement and a decision that takes place in the nature of God Himself. For grace is grace, and we are concerned with a real condescension, when God befriends us. In other words, God is not compelled to become man by any superior inward or outward necessity. He has decided to act in this way because it was His free good-pleasure to do so. In the light of the decision taken in the fulness of His free love, and therefore included in it, it is also to be understood as the free decision of God that He willed to become and be the Creator of the world and the Reconciler and Redeemer of man.

The second insight is complementary, that what has taken place and takes place in Jesus Christ must be understood as a necessary decree of God. If we are to have a right understanding of the grace of God's decision and therefore of its divine freedom, we must in all circumstances face the fact that God has made this free decision of His a decree, and has executed it as such, and that we are therefore bound to it and cannot ignore it or live without it. By the very nature of the case we cannot try to seek or find Him except where and how He has given Himself to be sought and found. For God is God, the One who has condescended to us and befriended us. His freedom is the basis of our necessity. And again it is in the light of the great decree which compellingly reveals the fulness of

His free love that we are also to understand concretely the compulsion of God's government as Creator, Reconciler and Redeemer.

To sum up, because we have to do with the immutability of the freedom of God, what we have to recognise and acknowledge in Jesus Christ is unalterably the grace of God, but it is also unalterably His will and command and ordinance.

The older theology, especially in the Reformed Church, used the concept of the divine decree to describe this free divine decision which becomes a compelling ordinance for us. Under this term was included whatever Scripture refers to as the will, counsel, design, good-pleasure or hand of God. The *decretum* was treated first among all God's works, the *opera externa*. It was understood as the *opus internum Dei* (J. Wolleb, *Chr. Theol. comp.*, 1626, I, *cap.* 3), *quatenus in ipsa Dei essentia permanet*. It was not, therefore, separate from the being of God, i.e., from God Himself—for *quicquid in Deo est, Deus est*—although it was an *opus ad extra, quatenus ad creaturas seu rem extra Deum refertur*. Wolleb defined it as follows: *Decretum Dei est interna voluntatis divinae actio, qua de iis, quae in tempore fieri debebant, ab aeterno liberrime et certissime statuit*. The divine will which lies at the basis of this decree and is active in it is called the *voluntas Dei beneplaciti* inasmuch as its content is completely a matter of the free, divine decision and disposal. It is *voluntas antecedens* in that it completely precedes the existence and form of the created world. It is *voluntas absoluta* in that it is completely independent of everything that happens in time. Finally it is *voluntas occulta* in that no man or angel by himself can know its content. *Proprie*, it is explained, the *voluntas beneplaciti* is the one and only will of God and everything that takes place in consequence of it does not stand over against it as a second reality, but is simply a revelation of it to us (*voluntas signi* or *revelata*), its product (*voluntas consequens*) or its form as conditioned by God's dealings with creation (*voluntas conditionalis*). It is only *improprie* that these are separated from it, because in God there cannot really be any separate will. It is then explained that although in the creaturely sphere there may be an occurrence *contra*, there cannot be any occurrence *praeter voluntatem Dei*, i.e., there may be resistance to the *voluntas signi* but not to the *voluntas beneplaciti* ; for even evil takes place under the will of God, under a *voluntas permittens Dei*, although it does not on that account have to be referred back to God as its author. This necessity by which everything that happens must do so in accordance with the divine will and decree is not a *necessitas coactionis*. It is a *necessitas immutabilitatis*, the necessity in virtue of which everything in its final result must correspond in all circumstances to the one unalterable divine will. This necessity does not mean, then, that the freedom and contingency of the creature are taken away. On the contrary, while the divine decree is in itself unique and simple, without a " before " and " after," such distinctions have to be made *rerum decretarum respectu, ut quo ordine eveniunt, eo ut evenirent, Deus decrevisse dicatur*.

We must first acknowledge the service which this teaching rendered by at least indicating the problem and insight which concern us. In the relation between God and creation we certainly have to do with the one immutable God, with the *essentia Dei*. But the relationship is not simply a fixed one. It is determined and ordered by a decree, a decision of God's will. Therefore in the one immutable essence of God we have to do with something special in God, an *interna voluntatis divina actio*. But in the concreteness which it has by its relation with the created world, this *actio* cannot be expressly placed in the essence of God and therefore identified with God Himself, without involving a notable contradiction of the order of God's absolutely simple and immovable essence. This was underlined by the equally express acknowledgment of the freedom and contingency of the created world which were not removed by the divine decree although it had reference to this world. It was also emphasised by the remarkable way in which all along the reality of evil was not denied, and yet it was so subordinated to the divine decree as to preserve intact both the immutability of God's will and its righteousness and freedom from responsibility for evil. According to this chapter of Reformed orthodox theology there is, then, something special in God, a movement, change and decision, in virtue of which He both can be and is the One He is in relation to His creation. We certainly cannot say, according to what is at any rate the embryonic teaching of this chapter (in contrast with that on the *essentia Dei*), that death is God and God is dead. The doctrine of a living God does at least begin to emerge ; it does at least become possible. What is difficult to see is how the older dogmaticians could speak, as they did, about the essence of God as if they had never heard of this *actio interna* which is now identified with God's essence.

Closer examination forces us to admit that here too the knowledge of the living God and of His immutability unfortunately does not have more than an initial effect. For the distinction between the *voluntas beneplaciti* and the *voluntas signi*, and the explanation that in the latter we are dealing only *improprie* with the will of God Himself, compromises again the conception of a special act which takes place in the essence of God, and the doctrine of the simple and immovable essence of God re-emerges. For according to this distinction everything that might be called action in the divine decree belongs to the *voluntas signi* which only improperly can be reckoned the true will of God. In the light of this distinction it appears that it is only provisionally true, only in relation to us, perhaps only from our standpoint, that God is alive and active in the senses enumerated by Wolleb in a hexameter :

Praecipit et prohibet, permittit, consulit, implet.

Again, God's relationship with a free creature as such, His dealings with a creature which in its own way is equally real, can be regarded only as provisional. The real will of God remains somewhere in the background. It is something unmoved and immovable. It has no connexion with or relation to anything else except that of the highest necessity ruling over everything else. About it we can know nothing except that it is the one thing necessary and as such inscrutable. In face of it the Word of God has the significance of an exposition in which we are told this or that about God, but not about God Himself and this one unique decree of His will. Since it is obscure how far the *voluntas beneplaciti* is God's free grace, it must also be obscure how far the *voluntas signi* is binding on us.

This is the first shadow which hangs over the orthodox doctrine of the divine decree. The second is that not only in its less good elements, but also in what are undoubtedly its good elements, in marked contradiction to the Bible passages quoted in support, it is so obviously an abstract general doctrine of the essence and relation of God to the created world, in other words, a general doctrine of providence. Wolleb expressly identifies the divine decree with the *aeterna providentia Dei*. This is not in itself untrue. The divine decree is in fact identical with eternal providence too. But the older theology identified it with this and this alone. As a consequence, all the contents of the decree, the creation, preservation and government of the world on the one hand, reconciliation and redemption on the other, and above all the incarnation of the Son of God and the existence of Jesus Christ—all form a single series as mere *opera externa* with a common denominator, as specific instances of the *voluntas signi* which has somewhere behind it the unmoved inscrutable *voluntas beneplaciti*, as mere instances of the divine providence. Compare with this the biblical passages by which they tried to establish the divine decree. Is. 46⁹⁻¹³ : " I am God, and there is none else ; I am God, and there is none like me, declaring the end from the beginning, and from ancient times the things that are not yet done, saying, My counsel shall stand, and I will do all my pleasure : calling a ravenous bird from the east, the man that executeth my counsel from a far country : yea, I have spoken it, I will also bring it to pass ; I have purposed it, I will also do it. Hearken unto me, ye stouthearted, that are far from righteousness : I bring near my righteousness ; it shall not be far off, and my salvation shall not tarry : and I will place salvation in Zion for Israel my glory." Ps. 2⁷⁻⁸ : " I will declare the decree : the Lord hath said unto me, Thou art my Son ; this day have I begotten thee. Ask of me, and I shall give thee the heathen for thine inheritance, and the uttermost parts of the earth for thy possession." Eph. 1⁹⁻¹¹ : " Having made known unto us the mystery of his will, according to his good-pleasure which he hath purposed in himself : that in the dispensation of the fulness of times, he might gather together in one all things in Christ, both which are in heaven, and which are on earth ; even in him : in whom also we have obtained an inheritance, being predestinated according to the purpose of him who worketh all things after the counsel of his own will." Ac. 2²³ : " Him, being delivered by the determinate counsel and foreknowledge of God, ye have crucified and slain." Ac. 4²⁷⁻⁸ : " For of a truth against thy holy child Jesus, whom thou hast anointed, both Herod, and Pontius Pilate, with the Gentiles, and the people of Israel, were gathered together, for to do whatsoever thy hand and thy counsel determined before to be done." It is astonishing that it was possible to quote all these passages and not notice that, while they do of course speak very clearly about the government of general eternal providence, it is evident that they all refer concretely to a supremely particular event. In defining what is to be understood as the divine βουλή, εὐδοκία, πρόθεσις, χείρ, etc., it is impossible to abstract from the content of this event in the interests of a general conception of the relation of God to the world. On the contrary, we must deduce from its particularity what is always involved in the general relation between God and the world as determined and ordered by the divine will. When the Old and New Testaments speak of what the older theology called the divine decree, directly or indirectly they always speak about Jesus Christ, as is obvious in all the passages adduced and in all the others that might be quoted here in this connexion. They all deal with what the older Reformed theology after Coccejus (again in a very late chapter) called the *foedus gratiae* and tried to expound, with many finely drawn distinctions, from the point of view of the eternal testament of the Father, the compact between the Father and the Son, the *fideiussio* (pledge) undertaken by the Son, and finally, based on this, God's covenant of grace with the elect. But it is difficult to see how a statement which really did look to Holy Scripture could fail to take into account, in its evaluation of the very essence of God, the divine truth which underlies and is operative in God's action in His special covenant with Israel and the Church. It is difficult to see especially how it could fail to take this truth into decisive account as the content of the divine decree which essentially precedes all its other contents and is not therefore parallel but superior to them. It is difficult to see how, if we seek to be true to Scripture, we can avoid discovering, in the meaning and basis of the *foedus gratiae*, and therefore in Jesus Christ Himself, the decree and decision of God, His will, His hand and His good-pleasure, the one reality of the divine decision, which includes everything else that God also wills and therefore everything else that is the content of His decree, but in such a way that this is conditioned by and subordinate and adjusted to it. In the older Reformed theology the doctrine of the decree was generally placed directly after the doctrine of the Trinity. But when this was its starting-point how could it possibly continue in the form of a general doctrine of providence ?—as if the doctrine of the Trinity had no practical significance, and all haste must be made (as if nothing had happened) to take up the thread again at the point where it had been left—unsatisfactorily enough !—in the doctrine *De essentia Dei*. If at this point Jesus Christ had been spoken of as the decree of God, the doctrine of the divine decree would not have been left an unsubstantially philosophical outline. It would at once have acquired a Christian content and could have formed a solid basis for the doctrine of the *opera Dei*. The doctrine could then have controlled and conditioned all that followed. Above all, the false distinction between a proper and an improper will of God could never have been made, nor could the idea of a non-living God have re-emerged. There would surely have been hesitation to resolve the *actio divina* which took and takes place in Jesus Christ into a *voluntas signi* which only improperly can be described as the will of God. If this decree and its content had been maintained, the *voluntas beneplaciti* and the real content of the decree would have been found in the concrete reality of Jesus Christ. In this decree the constant God would certainly have been acknowledged and honoured, but the constancy of His freedom would have been recognised and extolled : the freedom which God does in fact possess, and of which He does in fact make use is the freedom of His love. There would then have been a recognition of the fact and manner that God is unalterably gracious and therefore that His will and commandment and ordinance lay upon us an unalterable obligation. The *voluntas signi* would then have been understood as the true and proper revelation of the *voluntas beneplaciti*. There would thus have been found what could not be found by the method actually used—a knowledge of the *decretum Dei* which is *in se unicum et simplicissimum*, but is also *in se* and *quoad nos* the *decretum* of the living God.

Against the perfection in which God is constantly the One He is we have now to set the perfection in which He is able to do what He wills, the perfection of His omnipotence. This will show us how necessary it was to mark off and safeguard the right understanding of God's constancy from the conception which directly or indirectly means that death is God and that consequently God is dead.

God loves as the One who is free. In our first sub-section we have taken this to mean that as the One He is omnipresent. We now add the further meaning that as the constant One He is omnipotent. The earliest creeds obviously thought it sufficient to ascribe only this one attribute to God. *Credo in Deum patrem omnipotentem*, παντοκράτορα. Clearly they saw in this attribute that which embraced all the others ; what might be called a compendium of them. But this attribute describes very especially the positive character of the divine freedom, that which distinguishes it from the freedom that might be ascribed to a being unmoved and immovable in itself. An " immutable " being of this kind could only be conceived of as powerless. God, on the other hand, is not powerless but powerful, indeed all-powerful, with power over everything that He actually wills or could will. God is able, able to do everything ; everything, that is, which as His possibility is real possibility. God has possibilities—all the possibilities which, as the confirmation and manifestation of His being, are true possibilities. As this omnipotent God, He is constant. As this omnipotent God, He is distinct from the changeable : which means, on the one hand, that which is not capable of everything that it wills, that which cannot do everything that is a real possibility, that which does not have all true possibilities ; and on the other hand that which is capable of what it does not will, that which can do what is not really possible, that for which untrue and impossible possibilities are not impossible. As this omnipotent God, He is also distinct from the unchangeable, whose unchangeableness inevitably means utter powerlessness, complete incapacity, a lack of every possibility, and therefore death. God omnipotent distinguishes Himself from all these positions (which are occupied by the creature or his false gods) as God, and as the true, the living God. In His omnipotence He stands over the reality which He has created as its Lord, and revealing Himself He is exalted in its midst. In His omnipotence He is the source of all created life and its preservation. It has its life in and by His. At the same time He is in His omnipotence sovereign over its death, which has no place in Him and as negation can be only under His feet. In His omnipotence He is from eternity and to eternity (in virtue of His existence) the refutation of all real or possible illusions and errors in relation to gods that are no gods, whether creatures regard themselves as gods of this kind or think they should acknowledge and worship such gods in reflections of their own non-divine existence. As and because He is omnipotent, He is the one, unique and simple God, and as such omnipresent. This clearly raises His grace and holiness, mercy and righteousness, patience and wisdom above the perfections which, under these or similar names, could be ascribed to the creature or any of its fictitious creations. They possess the strength and truth to be perfections of the true God, and each of them individually the true God Himself, because they are all of them omnipotent, omnipotent grace, omnipotent holiness, etc. For they are all in themselves the omnipotence of God.

The essential content of the usual definitions of the omnipotence of God in the older theology has already been expressed in what has just been said. *Potentia Dei essentialis Dei proprietas, qua potest et efficit omnia in omnibus et singulis.* This is how Polanus puts it and his comment is as follows. While it is not to be separated from God's will, it is to be described as *omnipotentia: natura sua et per se,* because it is identical with the infinite being of God ; *respectu obiectorum,* because its sphere is infinite ; *respectu effectuum* because this is also true of its results ; *respectu actionis,* because there is no limit to its activity (*Synt. theol. chr.,* 1609, col. 1191). *Potentia Dei quae est principium exsequens operationum divinarum, nihil aliud est quam ipsa essentia divina extra se productiva, per quam concipitur ut potens facere ea omnia quae vult et velle potest* (F. Turrettini, *Inst. Theol. el.,* 1679, I, L. 3, qu. 21, I). *Potentia Dei est, qua Deus independenter per essentiae suae aeternae actuositatem facere potest omnia in universum: non ea tantum quae vult, sed et ea quae ullo modo possibilia sunt adeoque omnia illa, quae contradictionem non involvunt* (Quenstedt, *Theol. did. pol.,* 1685, I, c. 8, sect 1, th. 26). We recognise at once in these formulations the principal problem which we have now to tackle. What is the meaning of the resurgent concept of the infinite as a condition of the omnipotence and therefore of the existence and essence of God ? What are the things that God can do, that can be ascribed to Him as the real and possible object of His ability ? How far is God's capacity unlimited and how far is it limited by the fact that it is His capacity and therefore the standard of what is possible, to the exclusion of what is impossible for Him and is therefore completely impossible ? In a word, what is the meaning of power as God's power and therefore as omnipotence, but at the same time as real power in distinction from total or partial impotence and also in distinction from the power which is power only in appearance, because it is able to do and actually does do the impossible ?

It is best to begin here too with the decisive statement that we are not dealing with any kind of power, or power in itself, or even omnipotence in itself and in general. On the contrary, we have to do with the power of God, and in this way and to this extent with omnipotence, with real power. Here, too, the forgetfulness which would lead us to define the subject by the predicate instead of the predicate by the subject would lead to disastrous consequences. It is just at this point that it would become especially clear how wrong a method this is at every point. More clearly even than the definition of God by the abstract concepts of the infinite, the simple, the immovable, etc., to define Him in terms of power in itself has as its consequence, not merely a neutralisation of the concept of God, but its perversion into its opposite. Power in itself is not merely neutral. Power in itself is evil. It is nothing less than freedom from restraint and suppression ; revolt and domination. If power by itself were the omnipotence of God it would mean that God was evil, that He was the spirit of revolution and tyranny *par excellence*.

This leads, of course, to a conclusion which has already presented itself on more than one occasion. The infinite, simple or immovable in itself, provided (contradictorily enough !) potency and dynamic are also attributed to it, provided it is now suddenly to be understood as powerful impotence, is not really so harmless and neutral as appears at first sight. The final thing has not been said about it when it is declared that it is not God. If it is really that which is powerful, indeed the all-powerful in itself, we must say of it, not merely that it has nothing to do with God, but also that it has a great deal to do with the devil, or at least with what the devil would like to be and to have.

But Holy Scripture and the revelation to which it bears witness do not lead us on this dangerous path. In it, it is God who is revealed as full of power and therefore as omnipotent. It is not power or even omnipotence which is revealed there as divine in itself. If we are to continue our previous course, and understand God's omnipotence too in accordance with Scripture and therefore by the standard of God's self-revelation, we must in all circumstances understand it in this way, refusing to reverse subject and predicate.

Already in the creed the *omnipotentem* is not to be separated from the *Deum patrem* nor is the latter to be explained by the former. The omnipotence of which the creed speaks is the omnipotence of God the Father, the omnipotence of the God and Father who reveals Himself to be God and Father in accordance with the remaining content of the creed, and is therefore of one essence with the Son and the Holy Spirit. It is not a matter of our already knowing by ourselves what omnipotence is and then learning from God's self-revelation that He is this and acknowledging the One defined as omnipotent in this way as our Father. What we by ourselves can think we know as power and omnipotence can be only that evil power in itself. It is blasphemy to ascribe power of this kind to God; and to require men to call a God of this kind " Father " is a piece of sentimentality which reveals with remarkable clarity the vicious and fundamentally cruel irony behind all sentimentality. On the other hand, the revelation of God the Father is itself the revelation of the divine omnipotence. This is the source from which we have to learn basically what power and omnipotence is, in opposition to every preconception. " The Almighty " *in abstracto* has probably more to do with that revolutionary and tyrannical spirit than with God. The constitution of the Swiss Confederacy is right when it begins with the words : " In the name of God, the Almighty."

In the saying of God to Abraham in Gen. 17[1f.] : " I am the Almighty God " (El Shaddai), we must not overlook the " I." It is interpreted later in the words : " Walk before me, and be thou perfect. And I will make my covenant between me and thee, and will multiply thee exceedingly." The same " I " said earlier to Abraham (Gen. 12[1f.]) : " Get thee out of thy country, and from thy kindred, and from thy father's house, unto a land that I will shew thee : and I will make of thee a great nation, and I will bless thee, and make thy name great ; and thou shalt be a blessing ; " and (Gen. 15[1]) " Fear not, Abram : I am thy shield, and thy exceeding great reward " ; and (Gen. 15[7]) " I am the Lord that brought thee out of Ur of the Chaldees, to give thee this land to inherit it." This One, this " I " who has announced all these purposes and already partially fulfilled them, now calls Himself the Almighty God (according to the composition of Genesis it is the final and supreme title, immediately before the establishment of circumcision as the visible sign of the covenant and the decisive promise of the birth of Isaac). It is not a numen of overpowering majesty, powerful in itself, and therefore forcing on Abraham the knowledge of a kind of power in itself that confronts him. It is the One who attests His essence in this command and promise. It is the One who now defines His essence as almighty, and therefore His command and promise as an almighty command and promise. Before Him Abraham falls on his face. It is in Him, in this God, that Abraham has faith, and it is the fact that He has faith in this God that is reckoned to him for righteousness by this God (Gen. 15[6]). We hear John the Baptist say of this same Abraham (Mt. 3[9]) that God—obviously this God again—could raise up children to him from the stones of the wilderness. " Our God is in the heavens : he hath done whatsoever he hath pleased " (Ps. 115[3]). This One is the God to whom nothing is impossible according to the saying of Abraham to Sarah (Gen. 18[14]), and of Jeremiah (Jer. 32[17]), which is taken up again in what the angel says to Mary (Lk. 1[37]). Again, the reference is obviously to this God—the topic is that of the saving entrance into the kingdom of God which is so difficult for the rich of this world—when, according to Mt. 19[26], Jesus says : " With man this is impossible, but with God all things are possible." " I know that thou canst do every thing " (Job 42[2]). It is noteworthy that the predicate " almighty " is nowhere so frequent in the Old Testament as in the book of Job, and that in the New Testament it occurs only in a series of passages in Revelation (with the exception of 2 Cor. 6[18]). For it is in these two writings that the figure of God is particularly concrete as that of the Lord—in the one case confronting us in the life history of one elect person, in the other in the history of the Church as it hastens to share the victory of Jesus Christ. The context and connexion in which this attribute is ascribed to God is shown by the doxology in Eph. 3[20f.] : " Unto him that is able to do exceeding abundantly above all that we ask or think, according to the power that worketh in us, unto him be glory in the church by Christ Jesus throughout all ages, world without end." This is true also of Phil. 3[21], where it is expressly said of Jesus Christ that he will " change our vile body, that it may be fashioned like unto his glorious body, according to the working whereby he is able even to subdue all things unto himself." In a word, whatever it may mean that God is almighty, and can therefore do all things, and possesses all possibilities, it is at least certain that we depart from Scripture in any statement which either openly or secretly has any other subject than God the Father, the Maker and Lord of the covenant with Abraham, the Father of Jesus Christ, and with Him His Son and His Holy Spirit, or in which we fail to understand the predicates "mighty" and "almighty" as wholly filled out and defined by this subject.

The first statement leads us on at once to a second. To let this subject give content and definition to the concept of power means concretely that the power of God is never to be understood as simply a physical possibility, a *potentia*. It must be understood at the same time as a moral and legal possibility, a *potestas*. God's might never at any place precedes right, but is always and everywhere associated with it. Like all true might, it is in itself and from the beginning legitimate power, the power of the holiness, righteousness, and wisdom which is grounded in itself, in the love and freedom of the divine person. It is the power which is the origin of legality and is always exercised in the fulness of this legality. It is the power which never lacks or can lack the dignity of the Godhead, of the Creator, Reconciler and Redeemer. What God is able to do *de facto*, He is also able to do *de jure*, and He can do nothing *de facto* that He cannot also do *de jure*. This can all be stated equally well in reverse. God's moral and legal potentiality is also His physical. His *potestas* is complete *potentia*. His holiness, righteousness and wisdom is almightiness. What He can do *de jure* He can also do *de facto*. And there is nothing He can do *de jure* that He would not also do *de facto*. In this context our interest is in the first statement that God's *potentia* is in all circumstances *potestas*. It cannot be otherwise, if as we stated first, this power is God's power, and not merely any kind of power.

Potestas, ἐξουσία Dei est jus ejus ac dominium universale, independens et absolutissimum in omnes creaturas statuendi de ipsis plane ex sententia. Jus enim ei competit. . . . Cujus juris fundamentum in sola est deitatis ὑπεροχῇ (Petrus van Mastricht, *Theor. pract. Theol.*, 1698, II, 20, [51]). If God can act as the potter does (Jer. 18[6] ; Rom. 9[20f.]), His power is the complete power of the One to whom the clay belongs. He is free to do with His own what He will (Mt. 20[15]). " All souls are mine " (Ezek. 18[4]). " We are the Lord's " (Rom. 14[8]). " Is not he thy father that hath bought thee ? hath he not made thee, and established thee ? . . . for the Lord's portion is his people ; Jacob is the lot of his inheritance " (Deut. 32[6, 9]). The overruling of His power is, then, the control of the One who may and must claim it because it has its basis in His right which is right itself, and because by His control of it His right, right itself, is established. *Imo quicquid potestatis quivis obtinent, non aliunde obtinent, quam ab hoc potestatis fonte:* Rom. 13[1] ; Col. 1[16] ; Jas. 4[12] (P. v. Mastricht, *loc. cit.*, 20, 8f.).

A third and necessary clarification is that the confession of God's omnipotence involves a statement about God which, although like every such statement it refers to what, according to His self-revelation, God has done, does and will do in His actual work, is not actually exhausted in content by an affirmation and description of this work.

It is not the case that this work as such completely coincides with the omnipotence and therefore with the essence of God, because it takes place by His will and in virtue of His perfect power. In that case God's omnipotence would be simply his omnicausality and the latter the divine omnipotence. Of course it is God, and God alone, who is active in His work, and He has revealed Himself within it. His omnipotence, then, is naturally the power manifest in His activity, the power in the activity of the One who has fulfilled and does and will fulfil this work, and who reveals Himself as the One He is within this work. We have neither to fear nor to hope nor in any sense to expect that He will be utterly different, and not the Shepherd of Israel and Lord of the Church, in other work not known to us or in His divine essence. Nevertheless we must reject the idea that God's omnipotence and therefore His essence resolves itself in a sense into what God actually does, into His activity, and that it is to be identified with it. It is not the case that God is God and His omnipotence omnipotence only as He actually does what He does. Creation, reconciliation and redemption are the work, really the work of His omnipotence. He is omnipotent in this work. Loyally binding Himself to this work He does not cease to be omnipotent in Himself as well as in this work. He has not lost His omnipotence in this work. It has not changed into His omnicausality in this work, like a piece of capital invested in this undertaking, and therefore no longer at the free disposal of its owner. The love with which He turns to us in this work, and in which He has made Himself our God, has not made Him in the least degree poorer or smaller. It has its power and its reality as love for us too in the fact that it continues to be free love, that God has bound and still binds Himself to us as the One who is able thus to bind Himself and whose self-binding is the grace and mercy and patience which helps us, because primarily He is not bound, because He is the Lord, because stooping down to us He does not cease to be the Lord, but actually stoops to us from on high where He is always Lord. He is wholly our God, but He is so in the fact that He is not our God only. This means that when we recognise and worship God's omnipotence in His work we must ascribe it to Him as the omnipotence behind this work. It is, then, to be loved and praised by us in this work, yet as His omnipotence in this work. Only as we do this shall we acknowledge and revere His omnipotence rightly, as divine omnipotence, and show it the awe and the trust which are free from and unaffected by the suspicion that God's total activity is perhaps only a name for reality in general, which (including its religious aspects) may perhaps then be understood as not the work of God but something else. If we are to gain a right understanding of the omnipotence of God which confirms and manifests itself in the divine activity in its totality, in creation, reconciliation and redemption, it all depends upon a perception of the height from which the divine omnipotence comes, plunging as it were in the execution and fulfilment of its works. We have to realise that it is not the omni-causality of God simply and in itself. In that case God would be bound to the reality which is distinct from Himself, and more or less resolved into it. We have to see that His omnipotence becomes His omnicausality as God takes up and binds this other reality to Himself in love, but without ceasing to be God and omnipotent in Himself, in the height from which He can also be omnipotent for this other reality, for us, and for us in His omnicausality. It is important to per-ceive the thrust of grace and mercy and patience in which God makes Himself our omnipotent God and applies His omnipotence bene-ficially to us as His omnicausality, although He does not need to do this or lose anything by doing it. If we do not see this, how can we acknow-ledge and worship it as divine omnipotence, and show it the awe and trust it deserves and claims as divine omnipotence. Absolutely every-things depends on whether we know God as the One who is omnipotent in Himself, and therefore recognise His omnipotence, of course in His omnicausality in creation, reconciliation and redemption on the basis of His self-revelation, but really as His omnipotence. Absolutely every-things depends on whether we distinguish His omnipotence from His omnicausality : not to the glory of an unknown omnipotent being who is beyond and behind His work ; but to the glory of the omnipotent God who is present to us in His work and is known to us by His self-revelation ; to the glory of His divinity, of the freedom of His love, without which His love would not be divine love or recognisable as such.

A simple and to that extent dangerous identification of God's omnipotence with His omnicausality in the very way that must be avoided is to be found in the definition given by Quenstedt. In it the *potentia Dei* is described directly as the *principium exsequens operationum divinarum*. It is expressly said to be the *essentia Dei extra se productiva*. If this is all there is to say, is not the con-clusion irresistible that no *potentia* can be described to God *intra se*, as distinct from His *operationes ad extra*, and therefore that *impotentia* must be ascribed to Him in Himself ? Does God begin to be omnipotent only with the existence of a reality distinct from Himself, an *extra* in which His omnipotence can be omni-causality ? Does it first exist as His relationship to this *extra* ? But how is this in any sense possible if there is no corresponding being in God Himself ? And how can God's relation *ad extra*, His omnicausality, be distinguished from all this out-ward activity ? In Polanus we find the actual statement (*loc. cit., col.* 1191) that God's omnipotence is His *principium agendi in aliud*. Along with this Polanus draws a distinction which throws a good deal of light on the identifica-tion of God's omnipotence and His omnicausality. Polanus wants to distin-guish between the *potentia essentialis Dei* and the *potentia personalis*. In virtue of the latter God the Father eternally begets the Son, the Son is eternally be-gotten of the Father, the Father and Son eternally cause the Holy Spirit to pro-ceed from them (*spirare*), and the Spirit can eternally proceed from the Father and the Son (*spirari*). According to Polanus this power within the Trinity has nothing to do with God's omnipotence. This explains everything—or more cor-rectly nothing. It is understandable that in his attempt to differentiate this inter-trinitarian power Polanus can find no place for a power which is proper to

God, but only for a *principium agendi in aliud*. But this being the case, it is hard to see what is the purpose of the whole doctrine of the Trinity, with all its elaborate and polemical discussion of the supposedly decisive mystery of the divine essence, if in the exposition of this essence the insights gained can be left on one side (for no apparent reason), and (again for no apparent reason) liberty allowed to speak of a double *potentia* in God, the one being significant " only " inside the Trinity, the other being " only " a *principium agendi in aliud*. Here again we can see clearly how orthodoxy prepared the way for the later abandonment of the basic Christian truths grounded in the doctrine of the Trinity. It did not intend to do this. It had an honest concern for the doctrine. But it failed to apply the doctrine. It presented God's attributes as the description of a supreme world principle which at a later date could easily be stripped of its theological character and interpreted as the (supposed) philosophical truth in which it was thought a complete substitute could be found for belief in God. The most excellent preparation for both the abandonment of the old and the construction of the new view can be seen in these statements of Polanus, which hardly fifty years after Calvin's death he could casually toss off as supremely self-evident. It is essential at this point to say what Polanus would not say. God is the omnipotent God as He is the trinitarian God; in His life as this God; in His power to be the Father, Son and Holy Spirit; in the power by which He is the One by and in the Other, all being equal in origin, necessity and glory; in the power in which He is in Himself the One whose life consists in the begetting and being begotten, the causing to proceed and proceeding, in which God has and is in Himself the reality and therefore the possibility of this divine life. It is as this God that He is omnipotent, and not first or only in His omnicausality, *agendo in aliud*. He is omnipotent on high, and in Himself, before and beyond every *aliud* and every *agere in aliud*.

The full-scale theological and systematic identification of God's omnipotence with His omnicausality first becomes a theologumenon in the developed Neo-Protestantism of Schleiermacher and his school. The perception that God is the Subject over His works is now lost and God is finally denied as such. The summary at the head of §54 of Schleiermacher's *Christian Faith* declares : " In the conception of the divine omnipotence two ideas are contained : first, that the entire system of nature, comprehending all times and spaces, is founded upon divine causality, which, as eternal and omnipresent, is in contrast to all finite causality ; and second, that the divine causality, as affirmed in our feeling of absolute dependence, is completely presented in the totality of finite being, and hence everything really happens and occurs for which there is a causality in God." This summary itself makes clear that Schleiermacher is not concerned with God as the Subject of omnipotence, but with the concept of divine omnipotence as such, and with this, as the first half of the statement shows, only as it denotes the causal basis of the natural system, i.e. the totality of finite causes and effects : " Each exists through all and all exists completely through the divine omnipotence, so that all undividedly exists through One." But according to the second half of the statement this existence is of such a nature that the totality of finite being is the complete and exhaustive presentation of the divine causality. Thus there is no divine causality or omnipotence which does not have its corresponding development or occurrence in the totality of finite being. The sense of dependence, the only basis on which we and others can state that God is omnipotent, is itself related to the universal system. For it is in it alone that we experience the divine causality. " We lack any point of contact by which we could make claims on the divine causality such as extend beyond the system of nature which this feeling of dependence embraces." But our pious self-consciousness does not guide us to the idea of a possible outside the totality of the actual. If it were to do that, it would express a self-limitation of the divine omnipotence, thus destroying the whole presupposition and finally itself. At this point Schleiermacher quoted a saying of Basil (*Hom.* I *in Hexaem.*), that the Creator possesses not only the power to create this one world, but creative power εἰς τὸ ἀπειροπλάσιον (for infinitely many worlds). His comment is that we must explain such statements " by the paltriness of the contemporary knowledge of the universe which we have now surpassed to reach the ἀπειρο-πλάσιον ". The question of the possibility of divine power beyond the totality of the actual did not exist for Schleiermacher—as it is not raised in the saying of Basil—quite apart from the possibility of the ἀπειροπλάσιον which has happily come to our knowledge in the intervening period. Because will and power, will and action, and power and action are not to be separated in God, " the entire omnipotence, undivided and unabbreviated, is the omnipotence that does and effects all ", and beyond this, i.e., the divine omnicausality, there is no more to be said about omnipotence. The mistake which appeared in orthodoxy has now become more serious and final. Orthodoxy thought it sufficient to define omnipotence as basically God's *potentia agendi in aliud*, but agreed that God could do more than He actually wills and does (Polanus, *loc. cit., col.* 1192). Here, however, the divine power is simply dissolved and disappears into His actual willing and action. We can now appreciate the full consequences of the nominalists' doctrine of the attributes, what it means when the identity of the divine attributes is understood as a real *simplicitas*, but not as a real *multiplicitas*. God is His own prisoner because the identity of His attributes is understood only as something single (in Schleiermacher as the source of the utter sense of dependence, itself without utterance or act). But He is also the prisoner of that which is supposed to be based on His causality, the prisoner of the world from which the theologians will not permit Him to stand apart. R. A. Lipsius made a very detailed and explicit statement of the same kind. God's omnipotence is " to be defined as His self-directed omnicausality which is to be equated with the timeless and non-spatial causality behind every real event in the world—in relation to the world of nature with its natural order, the world of morality with its moral order and the world of redemption with its order of redemption, so that it never does anything of its own over and above the totality of its orderly work " (*Lehrb. d. ev. prot. Dogm.*, 2nd ed., 1879, p. 239). We can see that as distinct from Schleiermacher Lipsius is concerned to make clear the inner differentiation of the divine omnicausality and therefore of the divine omnipotence. But in so doing, he has only more zealously affirmed the complete congruence of the divine omnipotence with the divine omnicausality. " To want to ascribe to it all kinds of other activities outside the totality of God's orderly working (in the orders of nature, morality and redemption) would be simply absurd " (p. 241). Thus in nature the natural order is the revelation of God's omnipotence as the totality of the divine activity, directed to nature and ordered in it, and expressed in the laws of nature. In the moral world this revelation, or the divine omnipotence itself, consists in the moral order, and the same is true of the order of redemption, which holds sway in the world of redemption. " The religious content of the doctrine of the divine omnipotence is the actual expression of the pious consciousness that as in nature and morality, so also in the life of redemption man is completely dependent on the divine causality, so that he can never at any point withdraw from the divine ordinances, but, if he bows humbly before the divine will, can always be sure of God's nearness to help him, a confidence that is vindicated in the experiences of the life of redemption as a real consciousness of the power of God bringing about every good wish and action in us " (p. 243). " This divine power, which reveals itself in the consciousness of the believer, is for faith identical with the power behind all things in which the world of nature and of morality also have their being and existence " (p. 244). It would be impossible to put more clearly than this the very thing which we must not say, that in the last resort the omnipotence of God means simply the power of God experienced in the religious consciousness as identical with the power of God in nature and morality. And it would be impossible to ignore or forget more openly the very thing which must not be ignored or forgotten, that as the living Lord, God is mighty in Himself, before and beyond all activity in us or any worlds, and all the orders which obtain in these worlds. R. Seeberg, too, does not appear to have had any inkling of the gravity of this kind of speech or forgetfulness (*Chr. Dogm.*, Vol. I, 1924, pp. 355 f., 405 f.). As he saw it, God's omnipotence does not consist in the fact that He can do all things, but in the fact that He does all things, that " in pure activity He wills all that is and occurs, and that accordingly the range of His working is infinite and the execution of His work unlimited ". He would rather see this expressly called His omnicausality. And at the end of the Schleiermacher era H. Stephan simply shrugs his shoulders in face of the question of the relation and distinction between God's omnipotence and His omnicausality, expressing surprise at " a piety that was not accustomed to experience God in actuality and preferred to conceive Him in the airy forms of the intellect, the piety of the monk or of the man whose home is abstract thought " (*Glaubenslehre*, 2nd ed., 1928, p. 108).

The mischief of this view, which first appears in orthodoxy and reaches its full development in the school of Schleiermacher, consists directly in its abandonment of the distinction between what God can do and what He does do. This destroys our understanding of God's freedom in His action. It makes it impossible for us to glorify His work as His (in distinction from every other happening), to glorify it as an action which is done and applied to us in free love, graciously, mercifully and patiently. The mischief of it also consists indirectly in the fact that it leads inevitably to the fatal identification of the power of God with the general power at work in the world. The triumphant reference to real experience of God says either nothing at all or something very godless. For what is this real experience ? or Schleiermacher's " total system of nature, embracing all spaces and times " ? or the threefold world order of Lipsius ? All this is not simply given in unity with the omnipotence of God, so that it has only to be experienced or enjoyed to make us at once participate in an encounter with the omnipotence of God. God's omnipotence is the omnipotence of His free love, which is not as such identical with any system or order of His works and from which we must not abstract if there is to be serious discussion of the system and order of His works. In His works we are concerned with His activity and therefore with Himself. But apart from the revelation of the particular and proper omnipotence of God, which is not exhausted by His omnicausality, the omnipotence of the Father, the Son and the Holy Spirit, all that we can and will enjoy and experience in so-called reality, in what is supposed to be the divine order of the world (including the so-called order of salvation), is not God's omnicausality, but merely a vast flood of unrealities, of revelations of the power of impotence, of demonic forces, and therefore of impossibilities of every kind. God and God alone has real power, all the real power. This is the statement of the Christian knowledge of God. The alternative that all the real power that we encounter (what we think real) is God's power is the statement of a blind deification of nature or history or fate, and finally of man himself. The identification of God's omnipotence with His actual omnicausality drives us to this deification, which is more or less concealed in it. That is why it is to be rejected. Certainly all true reality is based on God's omnipotence as the only true possibility. But what this true reality is cannot in any way be known *a priori*. It is God's revelation which decides what true reality is, and therefore what may and must be the occasion and object for our glorification of the divine omnipotence. If we do not know this distinction and therefore the omnipotence proper to God, we have no protection against the temptation which constantly threatens to bestow our praise of God's omnipotence, and the awe and trust which we owe it, on one or other of the powers of falsehood and apostasy which are to be understood only as impossibilities, as powers of impotence ; or on the epitome of all such impossibilities, the power of the devil.

Our fourth step is to maintain that the omnipotence of God, which is peculiarly His own, which is not to be confounded with any power in itself, and which does not exhaust itself in His omnicausality, is a very specific capacity, i.e., a power which is not empty but has real content, not neutral but wholly and utterly concrete. God has the power, as Father, Son and Holy Spirit, to be Himself and to live of and by Himself. This is His omnipotence. Everything else which He has the power to do, He has the power to do in virtue of this power. And further, everything else which He has the power to do is simply a manifestation, revelation and application of this power. For if God is not only omnipotent, but effects everything as such, i.e., if in His omnipotence He is active outwards, in relation to another, all His activity consists simply in a recapitulation of His own being. It means that He is also *Himself* outwards in relation to another, though He does not have any need of this and it is not in any way obligatory for Him. How can He be active, or active in a better or higher way, than by being Himself again, and this time fully, in His outward as in His inward relationship ? The goodness and power and truth of all God's acts consist in the fact that in them He is Himself, He recapitulates Himself, He is always true to Himself and proves this to be the case. It is in this, too, that His words and dealings are incomparable —the words and dealings of God. Knowing God's omnipotence, we also know His power to do this, and therefore the power of His constant vitality. In this power God is the criterion of all genuine possibilities. And in the actualisation of all genuine possibilities, God is the criterion of all genuine actualities. That and that alone is real in which God recapitulates and confirms Himself. The reason why He created the world and man was to be the scene and instrument and servant of His self-manifestation. And the reason why His grace withstands falsehood and rebellion in the world is to enable Him to continue and ever and again to be in the world and in man. This opposition itself consists in the fact that He is fully Himself in the world and in man. And all the future glory of His work in the realm of redemption consists in the fact that in them He will be " all in all ", as 1 Cor. 15^{28} says, and therefore again and in a new way Himself. That which has nothing to do with God's reality, that which withstands it, that which tries to be like God as an ostensible and supposed reality by affirming its being, as if it were God instead of serving God's being : a reality of this kind is an unreal and demonic reality, and any capacity for it is an unreal and impossible possibility—impossible because it is a possibility excluded by the divine possibility, which is the standard of everything possible.

It can be said that God can do " everything " only if the " can " is understood to mean that He Himself in His capacity to be Himself is the standard of what is possible, and if the " everything " is understood as the sum of what is possible for Him and therefore genuinely possible, and not simply the sum of what is " possible " in general. God cannot do everything without distinction. He can do only what is possible for Him and therefore genuinely possible. This does not imply any limitation of His omnipotence. Rather, it defines His omnipotence as His and therefore true omnipotence. It is omnipotence, the true omnipotence over all and in all, in the very fact that He cannot do " everything," that the possibility of the impossible, the power of impotence, is alien to Him and excluded from His essence and His activity. God's power is the power both to do the sum of what is possible for Him and therefore genuinely possible and also not to do what is impossible for Him and therefore completely impossible. It is the power to set up a superior opposition to what opposes Him, the power of exclusion, of treading under His feet the possibility of the impossible. To this extent and only to this extent does the latter possibility exist in His sphere. To possess the power to do everything without distinction would be a limitation, or rather the removal of His power, and not its extension. Possessing that power, He would not be God. He would be continually disturbed and threatened in His genuine possibilities by His own possibility of the impossible. But this means that He would Himself be a creature, a fallen creature. It is against this misunderstanding that we have to safeguard the assertion of God's omnipotence by making clear that God's omnipotence consists positively in His power to be Himself and therefore to be true to Himself.

Augustine gave a correct answer to the question whether God could alter Himself and, if not, whether this was not a limitation of His omnipotence, when he said : *Tanquam laudabile est omnipotentem non posse mutari quam laudabile quod omnipotens non potest mori. . . . Hoc quia non potest, non deficienter non potest, sed potenter* (*C. serm. Arian.* 14). All the older theology gave similar correct answers to such questions as whether and how far God Almighty cannot tell a lie, deny Himself, sin, or be deceived or die. These questions will not be dismissed as mere conundrums when it is realised to what extent we are inclined to toy with the general idea of capacity and actually to deal with God as if He could be anything at all, a sinner, a liar, a dead God. The correct answer given by the older theologians is that all this would be impotence, not power. *Deus omnipotens est et cum sit omnipotens, mori non potest, falli non potest, mentiri non potest et, quod ait apostolus, se ipsum negare non potest* (2 *Tim.* 2¹³). *Quam multa non potest et tamen omnipotens est. Et ideo omnipotens est, quia ista non potest: nam, si mori posset, non esset omnipotens ; si mentiri, si falli, si fallere, si inique agere, non esset omnipotens ; quia si hoc in eo esset, non fuisset dignus, qui esset omnipotens* (Augustine, *De symb. ad. cat.* 1, 2). Or systematically more fully : God is not able to do certain things *non ob defectum . . . sed abundantiam et perfectionem potentiae, quae in eo consistit, quod potest* θεοπρεπῆ, *Deo, summo infinito et perfectissimo ente digna, non ea, quae ab eius natura et entitate degenerant et ad nihilum vergunt . . . Non potest ergo, sed potentissime non potest, quae naturae eius repugnant . . . non potest, quae impotentiam, debilitatem, defectionem a semetipso et perfectionibus suis arguunt* (H. Heidegger, *Corp. Theol.*, 1700, III, 107, quoted in Heppe ², p. 84, E.T. p. 101). Or with special reference to God's will and action : *Omnipotentia Dei non est a sapientia, voluntate et iustitia eius separanda; non enim potest illa Deus facere, quae sapientiae, voluntati et iustitiae eius repugnant . . . Itaque potentia Dei licet infinita sit, nunquam tamen agit nisi prout a sapientia et voluntate Dei modificata sit* (Polanus, *Synt. theol. chr.*, 1609, *col.* 1196). Or more shortly : *Deo nihil impossibile nisi quod non vult* (Tertullian, *De carne Christi* 3). *Quod autem voluit et potuit et ostendit* (*Adv. Prax.* 10). Everything is right and clear so long as the conditions and limits of what is possible for God are in some way sought and found in God Himself. In this connexion it is worth noting that if we examine the contexts we shall find that at least the first of the two passages quoted from Augustine and the two passages in Tertullian refer to the possibilities or impossibilities of the trinitarian God as such.

But we have already met Quenstedt's statement that the object of the divine omnipotence is *omnia illa, quae contradictionem non involvunt*. This introduces a general concept of what is possible which is independent of the concept of God, and must be stoutly resisted. It was Thomas Aquinas (*S. theol.* I, qu. 25, *art.* 3) who at this point lured even Protestant theology to some extent on to a false track. Thomas thought that the argument moved in a circle if no more was said than that God is omnipotent in the fact that He can do everything in His power. As he saw it, God is omnipotent *quia potest omnia possibilia absolute*. Whatever can be the object of the divine omnipotence must be absolutely (*absolute*) possible, i.e., it must come under the concept of being. Whatever comes under the concept of its opposite, non-being, is as such absolutely impossible, and therefore cannot form the object of the divine omnipotence : *non propter defectum divinae potentiae, sed quia non potest habere rationem factibilis neque possibilis. Quaecumque igitur contradictionem implicant, sub divina omnipotentia non continentur, quia non possunt habere possibilium rationem. Unde convenientius dicitur, quod non possunt fieri, quam quod Deus non potest ea facere.* On this basis it is said to be impossible for the Almighty to do not only things which contradict Himself, which is the sense of the patristic citations, but also generally, i.e., in the sphere of His creation, things which have an inherent contradiction, *quae rei definitioni repugnant*, for example, to undo what has been done, or to make man into an animal, or to make a triangle whose three angles are not equal to two right angles, or to make a circle whose radii are unequal. *Talia impossibilia Deus non potest . . . Haec tamen non posse non est impotentiae sed potentiae*, because *ille maxime potens est, qui constantem et immutabilem potestatem habet*, and because *omnino potentis est, in optimo perseverare* (Polanus, *loc. cit., col.* 1193). In this direction the statement could even be hazarded : *Prius enim est, res ex se non implicare contradictionem, quam Deum ad ipsas actu referri ut omnipotentem* (A. Heidanus, *Corp. Theol. chr.*, 1686, p. 88). Now, of course, there is no more question of asserting the opposite here than there is in the case of the possibilities or impossibilities which compromise God Himself. We do not argue that the possibilities of God are of such a kind that, for example, He can make two and two five. But the *prius* must certainly be rejected. We cannot accept the idea of an absolutely possible or impossible by which even God's omnipotence is to be measured. On the contrary, we have to recognise that God's omnipotence is the substance of what is possible. Necessarily, then, we dispute the reasons offered by Thomas and his followers for rejecting the statement that even what is to be described as absurd in creation is the object of God's omnipotence. As against this reasoning it is hard to see how the legitimate concern which underlies it, a recognition of relative unity and continuity in God's works, and therefore of relative unity and consistency in our human knowledge, is not equally or even better safeguarded in the following argument of H. Heidegger : *Potentiae divinae obiectum est δυνατόν, possibile, non in se, quasi extra Deum quicquam sit, quod possibilitatis suae causam in se, extra potentiam et voluntatem Dei habeat—sed in potentia et voluntate Dei, quae sola omnis possibilitatis fundamentum et radix est. Omnes enim res extra Deum essentiam et realitatem suam inde habent, quod Deus uti eas ad gloriam suam facere intelligit, ita esse vult et producit . . . Sic ergo id demum possibile est, quod Deus ad gloriam suam velle, iubere, vocare, facere potest—impossibile, quod ad gloriam suam iubere, vocare, facere non potest. Neque enim in Deo agnoscimus potentiam eiusmodi absolutam, quae a rerum possibilium essentia earum respectum ad finem, glorificationem Dei, a quo ad quem et propter quem est quicquid est vel esse potest, separet* (ib., III, 106 f., quoted in Heppe [2], pp. 83 f., E.T., pp. 100 f.). Similarly P. van Mastricht, *loc. cit.*, 20, 12 : *Res est possibilis, quia Deus eam potest. Prout vice versa : Deus hoc aut illud non potest, non quia illud est impossibile ; sed impossibile est, quia Deus illud non potest.* We have, indeed, to keep an inflexible grip on the truth that God is omnipotent in the fact that 'He and He alone and finally (because He is who He is) controls and decides what is possible and impossible for Himself and therefore at all. Whatever confirms Him is possible for Himself and therefore generally, and in the created world. Whatever contradicts His own being is impossible for Him and therefore generally and in the world. It cannot be ; it is only in unreality. But again it is He and He alone who controls and decides what manifests Him and is therefore possible, and what contradicts Him and is therefore impossible. God's omnipotence consists in the fact that in this sense His power and His will are *sola omnis possibilitatis fundamentum et radix*. They are not subordinate and responsible to any higher and independent idea of what is possible and impossible, in regard to what is possible and impossible for Him either as concerns Himself or as concerns His works. The very thing which Thomas was trying to avoid as circular is unavoidable if we are to describe the matter as it confronts us. We are forced to say that God is omnipotent in the fact that He can do everything that is in His power. But His power is not any kind of power defined by any kind of idea of what is possible. On the contrary, God is power, the one, unique, and only power. And as such He is also the substance of everything that is possible. This does not mean that there are not also creaturely powers and corresponding ideas of what is creaturely possible. But what we know as creaturely power is real only in virtue of its basis in the power of God. It is real only in as far as it honours its basis, conforming to God's power and not withstanding it. This is true also of the conceptions of what is creaturely possible. Up to and including the statement that two and two make four, these do not have their value and truth and validity in themselves or in a permanent metaphysical or logical or mathematical system which is " absolute " in itself, i.e., independently of God's freedom and will and decision. They have their value and truth and validity by the freedom and will and decision of God as the Creator of all creaturely powers. As such God is also the basis and origin and limit of all that is creaturely possible. The system or the various systems within which the ideas of what is creaturely possible have their place as we can know it, and within which this or that can be labelled as impossible either by definition or in itself, are to be understood only as relative systems, related to creaturely reality and power as a whole, and devised in what is itself the creaturely power and reality of human reason. If we ascribe value and truth and validity to them, if we count on their constancy, or on the constancy of the decisive axiomatic elements in them, and therefore on the legitimacy and necessity of our definitions, and therefore on predicates which are impossible by definition, if we count on the law of contradiction as that which sets limits to what is possible, this is all done in confidence in the unity and continuity of the creaturely reality and power to which there also belongs our own reason, which as such reflects this creaturely reality and power. But as such this confidence can only be relative. It is based on the reliability which we believe we ought to ascribe to the object of our thought, to its relation to us, our relation to it and so finally to ourselves. The limit of this confidence and of the reliability which is its basis is fixed by the fact that the reliability we ascribe to ourselves is only a creaturely reliability, and that again the confidence in which we turn to it can only be a creaturely confidence. But the system—and within it that which we have to hold as the limit of what is possible—can be regarded as permanent " absolutely " (in itself) only if we find the creaturely as such absolutely worthy of trust and have therefore absolute confidence in ourselves ; only if we reckon the created as such to be creative, thus denying the distinction between God and the world. But if this does not arise, we must maintain the relative character of the system and the limits to what is possible posited in the system. This does not mean the collapse but the true and proper establishment of that reliability and confidence. It is not, of course, the creature as such which is reliable, but God, the Creator of the creature. We shall give our trust to Him and not to the creature. We shall always seek and find the limit of what is possible in Him, not in what is created. But we have really to *give* our trust to Him. We have really to *seek and find* in Him the limit of what is possible. As there is nothing outside God that is real in itself, so there is nothing outside Him which is possible in itself. As there is nothing real outside God which has not been created and is not based on Him as the One who is real in Himself, so there is nothing possible outside God, except the possible which corresponds to the reality created by and based on God. And as there is nothing unreal except what is not based on Him as the One who is real in Himself because it has not been created by Him, so there is nothing impossible or absurd except what cannot have any possibility of being in itself because it has not been created by or based in Him. The limit of the possible is not, therefore, self-contradiction, but contradiction of God. It is not the impossible by definition, but that which has no basis in God and therefore no basis at all because it was not created by God. As we have seen, statements about God are absurd in which God contradicts Himself and is not therefore God ; in which in fact God as God is denied. Similarly, statements about what is real and powerful in creation are absurd in which real existence or the possibility of existence is ascribed to what has not been created by God, is not therefore real and cannot be possible—statements therefore in which God is denied as the standard of everything real, and therefore as the basis and limit of everything possible and therefore as the Creator of the creature. In view of the absolute reliability of the Creator and on that basis, there does exist also a relative reliability of the creature, and with the absolute confidence in God given in faith there is a relative confidence in the constancy of what is created, of its relation to us and of our relation to it, and finally even in ourselves and the limit of the possible as we, being what we are, necessarily see it in this world, being what it is. It is only by faith that there is this confidence, based not on creation but on the Creator. But by faith there is this confidence. It does not originate from creation but it refers to creation. Thus it cannot try to impose any limits on God, but it does recognise the limits God has imposed on His creation. It does not rebel against God by thinking that as the Creator He could have done what He clearly did not choose to do. But in what He has clearly chosen, it honours both the relative capacity of God, the capacity manifested by Him as the Creator of the real world willed by Him, and also His absolute capacity *in* this creation. We not only have no cause, but, bound by faith in God, we have neither the permission nor the freedom to ascribe to God, in respect of the world He has created, other possibilities than those which He actually chose and actualised in the creation and preservation of the world. We are not summoned by God's Word to honour Him by ascribing to Him a capacity which He did not choose to use as Creator, which He thus rejected as His capacity in relation to His creation, and which He thus disqualified as a genuine possibility. We are not summoned by God's Word to honour Him by calling in question the grace of

His creation, the patience with which He upholds it, or the wisdom in which He governs it, allowing instead an imaginary God to rule in an imaginary world. For example, we are not summoned by God's Word to assert that through God's omnipotence two and two could also be five. We will not be restrained from doing this out of respect for the law of contradiction, or owing to the absolute value and truth and validity of the relative systems within which the statement that two and two make five is impossible. It is well known that respect for the law of contradiction is not able in fact to protect us from this kind of absurdity and all kinds of much more serious absurdities. What can protect us is the fear of God, and the knowledge of the grace and patience and wisdom in which He has called the world into existence and causes it to consist in its nature and existence for His own sake and by Himself. It is this knowledge alone in the realm of creaturely reality and reason which can definitely and finally protect us from holding the impossible to be possible. God's omnipotence is not without limits either in itself or in relation to the world, but it is determined and therefore limited by the fact that it is His omnipotence—and it is this alone which can effectively hinder us from reckoning with the possibility of the impossible. Those who recognise and respect these limits will abide by them. But they are shown us by God's Word. It is there that we are told who and what God is and therefore what is possible and impossible for Him. Every meaningful statement about God's omnipotence must be able to base itself on God's Word. If it cannot do this, it is directed against God and is a denial of His omnipotence, even if, as far as its content goes, it seeks to say the most tremendous and wonderful things about the infinity of His power. If it is not based on God's Word, it denies His omnipotence just as definitely as a statement which denies or limits the capacity which according to His Word is His will and is therefore a real capacity. We have to consider whether it is possible by this standard, in obedience to God's Word, to state and justify a real *contradictio in adjecto* in reference to the omnipotence of God, and even to praise God's omnipotence by describing it as the power to bring about a *contradictio in adjecto* ; or whether if we do this we do not transgress the limits of what is humanly possible and therefore pass over from glorifying God to wantonly blaspheming Him. We have also to consider, on the other hand, whether, if we abandon this standard, and pay no attention to the question of obedience to God's Word, but try to seek the limit of the possible in an absolutised system of relationships alongside or in place of God's Word, we can avoid the headlong plunge into a *contradictio in adjecto* which rests on the discovery of an imaginary God and an imaginary world, the fundamental dissolution of all systems of relationships and therefore complete scepticism and anarchy in the realm of creation, the irruption of a Third Reich of madness. In these circumstances can we really safeguard the justifiable desire for relative certainty in regard to the constancy of the being of the world and man ? Nothing in the realm of creation can be treated as absolute, nor can the creature be proclaimed as reliable, nor confidence be commanded, except this arises from the same spirit of presumption on the part of the creature as does the assertion of its own so-called value and truth and validity and therefore its opposition to the real and genuine value and truth and validity of its existence. The law of contradiction, as the limit of the possible imposed by the creature itself, is so far from being tenable in all circumstances that sooner or later it will inevitably be directed against itself and without the slightest doubt will render impossible all certainty and every certain advance in the realm of creation. The limit of what is possible, if it is to hold good and therefore if there is to be any certainty or security in the created realm, must be guaranteed by God's Word as the order of the divine grace, patience and wisdom which is set up and maintained by God because freely chosen by Him, and is therefore to be accepted and respected by us and not therefore doubted through any discoveries of our imagination. In the last resort we must reject the Thomist limitation of the omnipotence of God to the possible in itself and as such because if we introduce a possible in itself and as such which has in a sense the role of an independent and equal partner and corrective side by side with God, we bring into the realm of creation the very element of disquiet, uncertainty and insecurity which the thesis of Thomas was designed to exclude. The real and effective limit of the possible is the one which God has imposed on Himself and therefore on the world and on us. If, as Leibnitz believed (quoted in D. F. Strauss, *Glaubenslehre*, Vol. I, p. 599), there existed a *nature des créatures raisonnables, avant que Dieu décerne de les créer*, and if the fact that two and two make four is not based completely on God's will, and therefore on His omnipotence, and in virtue of it on His work of creation, what real basis could it have ? If it is based merely on itself, it has no true basis. Since we are not summoned either by God's work or by His Word to any other arithmetic, we must regard that which we have, and alone can have on the presupposition of our world and ourselves, as safeguarded and guaranteed by God's work and Word, so that it is only wantonly and irrationally that we can aspire to the statement that two and two are five.

Our fifth step is to maintain that as His own power, and therefore as concrete power, determined in relation both to Himself and to the world, God's power is power over everything. This means the power of all powers, the power in and over them all. It does not mean the sum or the substance of all powers—this is excluded by what we have said already. Created powers, and above all the powers of opposition and therefore of powerlessness, are always distinct from God's power. He permits them to exist as powers apart from and beside His power. He gives them a place, and this applies not only to the powers created through His work but also to the powers of opposition and powerlessness, to the possibility of the impossible, of that which has been excluded by His own act. Yet this does not mean that He abandons even part of His lordship over them, that He is even partially powerless over against them, or that they have even partially an independent position and function in relation to Him. On the contrary, it is by His power that He creates or at any rate tolerates other powers. In this His power is always power in and over them, and He is always first and last the only one who is full of power. He is not at any point limited or determined by them, but at every point He limits and determines them. He is the " King of kings " as their true Creator and Preserver or as their righteous Judge. Thus none of them can escape Him, but all must serve Him and will definitely serve Him in one way or another. God in Himself is power of this kind over all things to the extent He is able as Father, Son and Holy Spirit to be Himself and to live of and by Himself. This ability of His is His omnipotence, true power, the power of lordship, not blind power, but the power of eternal wisdom. It is also not a power that cannot endure another beside it. On the contrary, it is the power of the eternal love in which before all worlds God is not only full of power in Himself but as Father and Son always has power in another. It is not finally an imperfect power, nor on the other hand an unlimited. It is the perfect and for that reason the perfectly definite power of His divinity. As real power this is power over all things, the divine omnipotence.

We shall insert at this point what we have to say concerning the distinction customarily made in the older theology between *potentia absoluta* and *potentia ordinata*.

According to Thomas Aquinas (*S. theol.* I, qu. 25, art. 5, ad I) *potentia absoluta* is the power of God to do that which He can choose and do, but does not have to, and does not actually choose and do. *Potentia ordinata*, on the other hand, is the power which God does actually use and exercise in a definite *ordinatio*. Interpreted in this way, the distinction is simply a description of the freedom of the divine omnipotence. It was in connexion with the question : *Utrum Deus possit facere quae non fecit*? that Thomas came to maintain this position. The question is certainly to be answered in the affirmative. God would not have power, nor would His power be in His hands, nor would it be the power of a Lord, real power over everything, if it amounted only to His omnicausality (the position we have already rejected), to what He actually chooses and does ; if His actual choice and action were not a real decision and did not take place in freedom ; if the capacity which He actually uses did not contrast with the different capacity which He does not use. And this being the case, the grace of creation, reconciliation and redemption would not then be grace, but God would be under obligation to the created powers over which He is Lord. He would not be their real Lord if as their Lord He had lost or never had the power to be Lord without them, apart from the lordship exercised over them, in Himself, in an infinity of very different inward or even outward possibilities. We therefore endorse the distinction between *potentia absoluta* and *potentia ordinata* in so far as it reminds us that God's omnipotence is His own power and therefore free power.

But a quite different meaning has been given to these terms, and in view of this they should be adopted with caution, with a basic loyalty to this first interpretation. For one thing, the *potentia absoluta* has been made into a *potentia extraordinaria* and the *potentia ordinata* into a *potentia ordinaria*. Thomas had understood by the *potentia ordinata* the omnipotence which, in accordance with God's will, had in fact been used and exercised and in this sense regulated. This was now turned into the omnipotence used and exercised according to a regular scheme, in the framework of definite laws. Over against it was set a *potentia extraordinaria*, the divine omnipotence which breaks through this regular system as a miraculous power and in that way demonstrates its freedom. There is, however, no reason to introduce into the concept of God this distinction between a regular and a miraculous omnipotence, and to do so leads to dangerous consequences. God is obviously omnipotent in the case of a miracle, and no doubt He is so in a special, even an extraordinary way, if measured against the natural and historical context in which the miracle takes place. This is the human point of view—and the divine one too, since apart from God it does not happen. But in the case of a miracle God is not different from what He is otherwise. The power in which God is Lord over all created powers is in itself one and the same power, whether God uses and manifests it for us in the usual or in an unusual way. It is certainly not the function of biblical miracles to present to men a special divine omnipotence, a higher one, exercised and used in a series of exceptions. On the contrary, their function is to remind men by signs, by visible illustrations of His Word, that God is omnipotent (as He calls us into His kingdom by His Word), and therefore that the omnipotence of God and God Himself are not to be identified with the created powers in themselves and as such, or with their sum or substance, as we are constantly inclined to think in view of the usual course of events. We are to remember that we are not subject to them or bound to them, but that they are His subjects and servants, and therefore that God is Lord over the usual course of events which we constantly misinterpret. It is to point us to this that God's revelation is accompanied by miracles. The fact that they break into the regular course of events, and therefore break through our picture of a *potentia divina ordinaria*, our picture of the law of the divine exercise of omnipotence, is of course true, but it is the least important and not the decisive element in the essence of biblical miracles. For this element, according to the Bible itself, possesses only temporary existence and relative significance. According to the testimony of the Bible, it is not a matter of setting up a second *ordo extra ordinem*, or the establishing of a special world of miracle in and alongside the remaining world of nature and history. We are not told that the feeding of 5000 became or ought to have become a regular institution of the Christian Church, or that Lazarus, once raised from the dead, did not die later, or above all that the Virgin Birth and ascension of Jesus Christ became universally possible for mankind, or even for Christ's own people, or even for one of them. Biblical miracles involve " supernaturalism " in principle only because they are signs of the divine reality, and therefore, of course, of our own future reality. There is no question of the emergence of the picture of a divine *potentia extraordinaria* alongside a *potentia ordinaria*. On the contrary, these two are mutually inclusive. By the occurrence of the miracle the special picture of a *potentia ordinaria*, a " usual " course of events, is, so to speak, resolved into its elements and built up afresh. It can no longer be a picture of the lordship of powers which perhaps are not even subservient to God and may even wish to rule us as gods. In the light of the divine miracle, we can no longer ascribe to these powers an independence and value and truth and validity of their own. In the miracle it is made clear to us that all the kingdoms of this world will be those of God and His Christ, and in fact are this already. Thus there are no autonomous rules or laws of a so-called " regular " course of events. There are no rules or laws distinct from the ordinances of God's own good and free will which are established by Him and bound to Him, and which we have to recognise only as we recognise Him, and therefore in no sense as ordinances with a position or validity outside or even above Him. There is far more reason to call the *potentia ordinaria* the miraculous power which reveals His omnipotence. For in it it is not the interruption but the reality of the divine order which is manifested as the order in all and over all, and God Himself is revealed as the God who orders all things. We should, therefore, believe in Him, in the One whose ordinary power is just the same as the power revealed in His miracles, even at those points where He performs no miracle and where we are constantly inclined to see other powers ruling in His stead. And there is far more reason to describe as the *potentia extraordinaria* the omnipotence which is hidden in the usual course of events, constantly mistaken by us for the other powers, and not yet finally and exclusively revealed as His omnipotence. For in it the divine ordering is not yet complete. In appearance, at least, it is an *ordo extra ordinem*. And in it the freedom in which God is Lord over all—and which is revealed in His miraculous power as such—can be believed in particular cases, but is not yet visible in general as the only principle of all order. Since, then, this matter is correctly understood only when there is this inversion, and in view of the fundamental misuse of the term " order " which is involved, it is best to drop completely the distinction between *potentia ordinaria* and *extraordinaria*. Miracle is not the proof of a special divine omnipotence. It is a special proof of the one divine omnipotence. It is certainly something fundamentally new in the realm of creation. But it is not for that reason something either different or alien, any more than the God who reveals Himself in His Word is different from the Creator. It is certainly a revelation of the divine life and is, therefore, to be respected and not identified *simpliciter* with anything else, but it is no less a revelation of the one constant life of God. Miracle reveals the richness and comprehensiveness of the divine ordering of things, but not that God sets aside or destroys His own order. If it belongs to this divine order that He should give and allow us a usual picture of His omnipotence, the not yet complete picture which is broken by miracles for the sake of a right understanding and with a view to the future revelation of His perfection, then this irruption of miracle does not take place outside this order, setting it aside and destroying it, but it belongs to the order as a legitimate element and member in the right functioning of the order. There is thus no reason to ascribe to God—in respect of this irruption, the interruption of the regular—a special omnipotence exercised and used in an extraordinary way. On the contrary, we have every reason to recognise and respèct it in this actual interruption (but not only in it) as the omnipotence which God ordinarily uses and exercises.

The distinction between God's normal and His miraculous omnipotence is also suspect because it can lead and has led to obviously dangerous consequences. The *potentia divina absoluta* was understood by the Nominalists of the later Middle Ages in such a way as to retransfer the *potentia extraordinaria* into the essence of God. In virtue of His *potentia ordinata* God was indeed able actually to do everything in the way He chose. But in virtue of His *potentia absoluta* He could actually have done everything, and still can, very differently. Originally and properly, then, He had a power in the use of which He was and is perfectly free to create and maintain a world ruled either by His wisdom and righteousness or equally by their opposites. More or less accidentally, on the basis of a completely inscrutable decision, God chose and did and therefore was able to do what now presents itself to us as His will and action and power. But after as well as before there stands behind this work, and the choice and action and power revealed in it, a quite different capacity in God and therefore a quite different possibility of manifesting and revealing Himself in a quite different work as a quite different being, a "wholly Other." It cannot be denied that Luther sometimes spoke of his *Deus absconditus* as if he understood by this concept a *potentia absoluta* or even more a *potentia inordinata*. The power to work miracles alongside and behind the power active in the sphere of order and regularity has now become an arbitrary power beside or behind a power of order which corresponds only accidentally to God's real work. Understood in this sense, the whole distinction has become completely intolerable. Now that God has in fact chosen and acted as He has, now that He has revealed His capacity, it is both true and important to maintain with Thomas that this capacity is most certainly to be understood as free, but it is completely invalid to ascribe to Him a capacity different from that which He has in fact revealed in His work, and one which contradicts it. God neither was nor is bound to the one possible way. He chose it, and it must always be understood as His free choice that He remains faithful to this particular way, that He wills and does and therefore can, as we actually see Him according to His revelation. But since God has actually chosen and still chooses this possibility, since in virtue of His will He actually applies His capacity to this possibility, we must recognise His capacity, His *potentia absoluta*, only in the capacity chosen by Him, in His *potentia ordinata*. We no longer need reckon with the possibility that He could have acted differently. We must come to terms with the fact that in His freedom He was able to act in this and not in another way, that His capacity directed to the creation and government of the world and His whole action in this world is His true and proper capacity, and that every other conceivable capacity is a capacity which He Himself has excluded and rejected. His real capacity is not one which contradicts and therefore compromises the capacity in which He actually manifests Himself. It is not a capacity which goes on existing somewhere on high or in the background, as if He had not chosen and as if we did not see Him in His Word choosing daily, as if He did not take this choice quite seriously, and might in certain circumstances go back on this and choose quite differently. If this were the case, we could not rely on His Word, or could do so only partially.

We should have the prospect of seeking and finding Him at least partially in other places than in His work and Word. We certainly must reckon with other capacities of His in addition to that known to us ; for God is free. We must reckon with a capacity that is richer and greater, embracing other regions and dimensions than those we know. We have not, however, to reckon with the fact that His other capacity in the infinity of its (undeniable) possibilities is essentially different at any place or time from the power known to us and demonstrated in His work. It is not a capacity without order, or in its *ordinatio* distinct from the capacity we know, or contradictory to it. As Luther clearly saw, and ultimately this was the issue of his controversy with medieval theology, it is obvious that if what the Nominalists understood by *potentia absoluta* was correct, there could be no assurance of salvation and therefore no stability and confidence in life and death. At bottom there could never be more than a restless seeking and asking for God's true capacity, and on high or in the depths it could actually be quite different from and even contradictory to the capacity with which we might assure ourselves on the basis of His work. What is not so obvious, however, is how far Luther really thought he could overcome this difficulty by his advice that we should worry as little as possible about the *Deus absconditus* and cling wholly to what he called God's *opus proprium*, to the *Deus revelatus*, and therefore to the God revealed in Jesus Christ. For how can we do this genuinely and seriously if all the time, as in Luther's teaching about the Law, there is not denied but asserted a very different existence of God as the *Deus absconditus*, a very real *potentia inordinata* in the background ? Is the correct reference to the *Deus revelatus* adequate if it is not quite certain that this *Deus revelatus* as such is also the *Deus absconditus*, and that in all His possibilities, all His capacity in the regions and dimensions inaccessible to us, the *Deus absconditus* is none other than the *Deus revelatus* ? In opposition to the thesis of the Nominalists, even in its Lutheran form, it is necessary to maintain that in the choice and action and capacity which He exercised in His freedom God has finally and definitively revealed His *potentia absoluta* as *potentia ordinata*. We are no longer free but forbidden to reckon on an essentially different omnipotence from that which God has manifested in His actual choice and action, as if God could exercise a different choice and action and capacity from what He has done. We can count on a greater omnipotence, but not on a different one. We can reckon with the freedom with which God willed to choose and did choose the possibility of His work revealed to us in His Word. But we cannot for this reason reckon on possibilities which are materially different. God is the power over all things. But here too we can and must accept the fact that it was and is His business to decide what " everything " is and also what " nothing " is, so that the latter exists in the sphere of His power only in its " nothingness ".

Let us summarise the points so far made. God is omnipotent in the fact that as such all real power is His power, all actual capacity His capacity, every genuine possibility His possibility. His being, essence and life are constantly the being, essence and life of real power, actual capacity and genuine possibility as such. God not only has these things, but is these things. Everything outside Him, on the other hand, is not these things but only has them, and has them only by Him and from Him, so that without Him it could not have them, but would be powerless. But again, His power is not real and actual and genuine and divine because it is power. On the contrary, it is all these because it is His power, because He has it and is it. Again,

His power is not exhausted in the fact that He allows what is outside Himself to have power. For this can and does come about only as He Himself has and is power in superabundance over against everything that may have power by Him and from Him. But again, His power is not neutral. It is conditioned by His deity. It is His own power, the power of His right, the power Himself to be true and true to Himself. As this it is, again, the measure and limit of all power even outside Himself. But again, this power is free power over all, the power over all powers.

Properly speaking, however, these are only the distinguishing and delimiting, not the positive characteristics of the divine omnipotence. We must now push on to these in an attempt to understand the power of God expressly and in detail as the power of the divine knowledge and will. It is in this way alone that the God confronts us whom Holy Scripture attests as the omnipotent God. According to Scripture, His freedom, and therefore the divinity of His love, is the freedom of His personality. This freedom is the sovereignty, the superiority, the penetrating and comprehensive capacity of His knowledge, decision and resolve. If for a moment we chose to employ the concept apart from its proper trinitarian use, we might say that God's freedom is the freedom in which He is spirit—spirit in distinction from nature, from extended, multiple, finite and visible being. At more than one point already we have seen that these opposites to spirit are not excluded from the essence of God; that God is also extended, multiple, finite and visible; that He also has and is " nature," since He is not dead but the living God. How can we ascribe power to Him if we try to deny that He is nature? But God has and is the nature which as such is spirit, spiritual nature, personal nature, the nature which has not first to be the object of the knowledge and will of another, which is not nature only in this antithesis but also beyond this antithesis, which is as much the subject as object of a knowing and a willing. It is the freedom of God that the antithesis between nature and spirit is overcome in Him, that He has fully mastered it, although the antithesis itself is there. For how could He be God if He were only nature, or only spirit? In a positive definition of the divine omnipotence the decisively important thing is that without detriment to His " nature," indeed in the glory in which He is nature, in the mystery of the essence of His nature as His own, God is also spirit. Unlike created nature He is not only the theme but also the subject of a knowing and willing. He is, in fact, the knowing and willing itself. Thus as the presupposition and creative ground of all nature He is also the presupposition and creative ground of all knowing and willing, the personal Creator of all personal being, the spiritual Creator of all spirit. As such He is omnipotent in His knowing and willing, and His omnipotence is the omnipotence of His knowing and willing.

It is to be noted how all our previous critical statements on the idea of omnipotence acquire form and colour from this point. Indeed they stand or fall by it.

God's being, essence and life are constantly the being, essence and life of His real power, actual capacity and genuine possibility, because they are themselves God's knowing and willing. There is nothing higher than this knowing and willing. It is not the object of any other knowing or willing in the sense that its reality, actuality and genuineness can be compromised by it. That is real power, the power of God. It is not merely a possession and instrument in the hand of one which might equally well be in the hand of another. Yet it is not an uncontrolled capacity, power in itself. It is power which is its own master, which wills and knows itself. It is only in this respect that it is distinguished from power in itself ; that it is really His power, God's power ; the power which He Himself has and is ; *potestas* and not merely *potentia* ; the power known and willed by Him and itself the power of His knowing and willing.

This is also the basis of the fact that His power is greater than His work, in which He permits other things outside Himself also to have power. Because God's power is the power of His personality, the power of His knowing and willing, we can say that it also belongs to God's will not to will many things. That is why God's omnipotence cannot be resolved into His omnicausality. It is also His power not to do what He knows to be impracticable and therefore will not do.

That God's omnipotence is the omnipotence of His knowing and willing is also the basis of the fact that it is not power for anything and everything, but His power with a definite direction and content. It is both His power to will and His power not to will. It is, therefore, His power to know both what has been willed by Him and what has not been willed by Him. What God's omnipotent will wills or does not will is characterised by the fact that He wills or does not will it as light or darkness, as the object of His omnipotent capacity and His equally omnipotent in-capacity. And what God's omnipotent knowledge knows as that which in omnipotent positivity He wills and therefore has done, does or will do, is thereby distinguished from what in equally omnipotent negativity He does not will and therefore never has done, does or will do. " Everything " is the object of His omnipotence, but, because His omnipotence is the omnipotence of His knowledge and His will, it is its object in a definite, distinct, concrete way. He is the master of His omnipotence and not its slave. He is the judge of what is wise and foolish, possible and impossible. He is, therefore, always holy and righteous in His actions. Because it is not willed by Him, and only the object of His will and knowledge in this sense, sin is always sin, folly folly, and the devil the devil, with no prospect even in eternity of ever becoming the object of His omnipotence in any other sense. And the reason is that His omnipotence is that of His personal judgment and decision, which is negative towards sin, folly and the devil, and can only continue to be so for all eternity, since God does not cease to be God.

Finally we have here the basis and explanation of the fact and way that God is the free power over and in all powers. He stands above them in freedom, and is their Lord in the strict and proper sense only if they have no other power but that which He wills to give them and knows as that which He has given. And they for their part have power only in such a way that they are limited and determined by His will and His knowledge of His will. Surrounded by His knowledge and His will, governed by His Spirit as by His omnipotence, they can have their creaturely independence and even the freedom of self-determination. But they can also be subordinated to the all-predestinating omnipotence of God as the concrete power which differentiates and judges. In different ways therefore, in obedience or in opposition, willingly or unwillingly, they can serve Him who Himself alone is and therefore originally has power.

But this also throws light, perhaps, on the reason why the concept of omnipotence occupies a kind of key position for the understanding of all the perfections of the divine freedom and therefore indirectly of all the divine perfections whatsoever—a view which was obviously that of the earliest Christian creeds. It is only retrospectively in the light of the fact that His divine power is the power of His person, His knowledge and will, His judgment and decision, that we can properly explain what is meant by the constancy of His life. It is constant, and constant life, because it is not capacity in itself, which might vary widely according to its application, and apart from its application might just as well be incapacity as capacity. It is the capacity of a person. It is a capacity which is spiritual and manifests itself in knowledge and will. It is the capacity of judgment and decision. That it is constant and living is based on the constancy of this person and His life, on the continuity of His judgment and decision. Defined in this way, God's omnipotence is also the root of the relationship between His unity and His omnipresence. In virtue of the unity of His constant knowledge and will and in the continuity of His judgment and decision God is unique and simple. In this personal activity of His, which is also His judging and deciding, He is omnipresent in that He creates and maintains objects for Himself, and is already an object to Himself and wills and knows as such. Above all, this is the basis of all the perfections of His love. We have already established the fact that they are all perfections of His omnipotence. Otherwise they would not be divine attributes. But obviously they really are what they are; God really is the One who is gracious and holy, righteous and merciful, patient and wise; these are not merely ideas added to Him or titles attached to Him, only if He can be and really is all this as the One who knows and wills omnipotently, and not merely in our conception of Him or in His relation to us. His power and essence must, therefore, be those of One who knows and wills to be gracious and holy, merciful and righteous, patient and wise, these being the real determinations of His knowledge and will and therefore of His power. It is of this that we speak when we speak of God's omnipotence and supremely magnify His freedom by acknowledging and confessing Him as Lord over all. In so doing, we do not magnify something neutrally divine which in itself might be the predicate of another subject than eternal love. On the contrary, we magnify the love which God alone is. And so when we now turn, as we must, to the knowledge of God's spirituality, of His knowing and willing, we do so with the strictest reference to the whole of our knowledge of the divine reality.

To understand that it is true that God knows and wills, and therefore that in His omnipotence He is the personal God, we should start from the simple and sure place where all Christian knowledge of God has its origin, but where the truth that God knows and wills is the simplest of simple truths, the surest of all, and therefore the most wonderful.

All Christian knowledge of God has its source in the revelation of God. And it is there that God meets us as the One who knows—Himself, and us whom He meets, and all things. He does, of course, speak in His revelation. He speaks about Himself. But He speaks to us. And in speaking about Himself to us He speaks about us. And in speaking about Himself and us He speaks about all things. For all things exist between Him and us. All things are in different ways both His and ours. Even if we do not understand here and now how God speaks about all things and what He says about them when He reveals Himself, yet in His self-revelation, in His speaking about Himself and us, we cannot fail to hear Him also speaking about all things as the

One who knows them all. The disclosed secret of His divinity and our humanity is also the not yet disclosed secret of all that is, which is no secret for Him. The disclosure of the secret of His divinity and our humanity takes place in the form of this speaking and by our hearing of it. Already this form of the disclosure, this speaking and hearing, discloses also the fact that God is not simply a new light reaching our eyes or a new object laying its claim on our imagination. As certainly as He speaks and lets Himself be heard, He is One who knows, a spirit, a person. Revealing Himself through speech and hearing, God discloses Himself as One who knows and permits us to know ourselves as those who are known by Him. Uncovering a vast waste of falsehood God's revelation dissipates the fundamental falsehood that this waste is infinite and that there exists only falsehood. We may have gone utterly astray and there may not be a single person who has not. But God is not in error. God knows. He says this to us with His revelation. Giving us the lie, it scatters the illusion that we can tell lies successfully and deceive God. We might deceive the whole world, and above all each might deceive himself—but God cannot be deceived. He knows, and so we gain no success with our lies. He says this to us in His revelation. And what happens at that simple and sure place, in God's self-revelation, is that God gives us fellowship with Himself in spite of all our errors and lies ; fellowship with His own knowledge. If God speaks to us and lets Himself be heard by us, this means that we too may now know—know Him and ourselves whom He knows. Sharing His knowledge with us, He becomes and is our God ; He becomes and is gracious, merciful and patient, but also holy, righteous and wise in the fulness of His lordship. Giving us a share in His knowledge He loves us, He draws us to Himself, He upholds us to prevent us from falling again, He makes Himself ours and us His. It is from this shared knowledge, the *conscientia* awakened by His revelation from the sleep of death that we believe and confess Him. We cannot believe and confess Him except as the One who knows, the One who knows primarily and originally and properly, the One whom we can only follow as sharers of His knowledge, but whom on account of His revelation we may and must follow. The confession that God knows is simply the response to and confirmation of the event in which God stooped down and gave Himself to us, the event of His love which allows and commands us to know Him, without which we could neither know nor confess Him, but on account of which we cannot but know Him. Once awakened by His revelation, our conscience can never again forget or deny that God knows. We demonstrate only that we know nothing about God, and prove ourselves without any conscience, if we try to maintain that we do not know this. And confessing that we do know this, and that it is true, we confess the simplest and yet also the most profound and comprehensive thing that we have to confess of God. For in a sense this is the most obvious thing that can be said about God. Children and savages can at once understand and accept the fact that " God knows." Yet this statement declares a truth about God, ourselves and all things, than which the most fundamental reflection and understanding will not easily discover a statement more moving, terrifying or soul-rewarding. What greater thing is there to be known than that God knows and that we are known of Him ? It requires nothing more or less than the divine revelation for the words " God knows " really to be inscribed on our hearts. No one can really have the knowledge that God knows or really live with this knowledge, unless he has come from this one, sure place. And if we have come from this place, we do not need deeper reflection, more extensive experience, or successful dialectic really to live with this knowledge and therefore with God, and to have a real share in the whole power and riches of His essence.

But this is also true of God's will. The place of divine revelation is also and in itself the place of divine reconciliation. God reveals Himself in this definite act, reconciling the world to Himself. He does not do it then merely as One who looks at us and is the object at which we look. He does not do it merely as One who knows and has only knowledge to share with us. He does not do it merely as a passive knower and a passive object of knowledge, in relation to which we on our side can continue neutral. What He establishes with the revelation of His knowledge is fellowship between Himself and us. This knowledge itself, then, is a complete act of will, an utterly definite willing. Note that it is not a mere striving, a kind of natural life force, a mechanically or organically necessary movement. This does not arise in God's relation to us. We ourselves are not God. We do not belong to His life. In His relation to us, therefore, He is not fulfilling a kind of function necessary to Himself. We have sinned and are not worthy that He should turn to us. We deserve that He should turn away from us, and not to us. We do not deserve that He should raise us up to share His knowledge. If He does this, it is an act of His own free self-determination, His decision and disposing, and therefore of His resolve and His will. God's meeting with us here enables us to understand Him, retrospectively in His action as our Creator, and prospectively in His action as our Redeemer, only as the One who wills, freely determining and deciding about us in Himself. If we begin at this point, it breaks through and sets aside every conception of God as the slave of His own immutable life. On the contrary, He stands before us as the free person who controls His own immutable life and who in His knowledge of Himself and of everything else He knows is bound to the objects of His knowledge only in so far as He binds Himself, so that every possible object is bound first and foremost to His will. If we start from this place, it becomes clear that it is not a question of ascribing only necessity to the being and essence of God and excluding contingency. There is in God both supreme necessity and supreme contingency. This supreme contingency in the essence of God which is not limited by any necessity, the inscrutable concrete element in His essence, inscrutable because it never ceases or is exhausted—is His will. He not only is and lives and has power and knows. But in all this He wills, and in doing this He finally reveals and confirms the fact that He is a person, a spirit. Because He wills, He is not only God, but there is a Word of God and a work of God, and He is to be sought and found in His Word and work and not elsewhere. Everything that God is and does must be understood as His free will. Otherwise we may have understood all kinds of ideas or powers, fate or nature or history, but we have not understood God. We must, therefore, test all our conceptions of God's government and action, and of our existence and behaviour towards Him, by the fact that to say " God " is to say " God's will." His will cannot for a moment retire into the background in favour of a power or law or truth or order distinct from it. All other powers and orders can certainly bear witness to it, but cannot take its place or supplant it. If we come from that one sure and simple place, we cannot forget or deny that God wills. For as God takes us up into the fellowship of His knowledge, He takes us up also into the fellowship of His will. God's love for us does not simply mean that He knows us ; it means also that He chooses us. This does not imply that in God's reconciling the world to Himself our will becomes God's will or God's will our will. Equally in that event our knowledge does not become God's knowledge or His knowledge ours. In both cases it is not a matter of identity but of fellowship when in response to what God does we are awakened in faith to make this response by God's action itself and to become those whom God has willed, His children. God's reconciling the world to Himself means the confronting of our will by His, its subordination to Him, fear and joy before Him, the prayer : " Thy will be done," and therefore a fundamentally new direction for our created and sinful wills, the establishment of divine sovereignty over them. This new direction of our wills means that, whatever their subjective position, we cannot forget or deny that God does will. For we cannot believe Him or confess Him except as the One who wills. How can we conceal the fact that He wills from ourselves who are those willed by Him ? Again, we inevitably conceal ourselves from ourselves if we try to have another conception of God, or set up another God. And again, the very simple thing we profess when we grant that God wills is also the very highest thing. It is clear to every child, and yet it is a continuing miracle for the deepest knowledge of God. It is the acknowledgment of the eternally new thing which God has done, surpassing all thought and understanding. It is a recognition that can be brought about only by the grace of His Holy Spirit. And yet it is also the acknowledgment of the very simple fact that God is God in the fact that He wills what He wills in the way and for the end which He wills.

The further understanding of the statements that God knows and that God wills, and of the fact that in them we have the positive characteristic of the divine omnipotence, depends wholly on whether or not we keep to the firm ground of the divine revelation where we meet God as the One who knows, and of the divine reconciliation where we meet God as the One who wills. In substance the biblical witness to God's knowledge and will never loses its connexion with God in His revelation and with His action in the covenant with Israel and the Church. It is only by speaking in this way that it speaks truly about God's knowledge and will as distinct from a completely different kind of knowledge and will. We dare not move away from this connexion. It is only if we retain it that we shall avoid those questions, some of them superfluous and some of them false, which inevitably frustrate Christian teaching and even falsify it if it is not clear whether we are in fact speaking about the omnipotence of God and of His knowledge and will or about another knowledge and will and its omnipotence, a supposedly supreme knowledge and will as such, which is ultimately the conception of our own knowledge and will. In the statements of orthodox theology this was far from clear, as is inevitable if the relation between what has to be said and the original source of all Christian knowledge of God and therefore the divine revelation and reconciliation, is not strictly preserved.

1. If we enter our theme with this presupposition, if on this basis we cannot but understand the divine knowledge and will as the knowledge and will of the divine omnipotence and therefore as itself omnipotent, we must affirm first that with the two statements " God knows " and " God wills " we are describing the one total essence of God. God's knowledge is God Himself, and again God's will is God Himself.

Thus God's knowledge does not come about in virtue of a special capacity or in a special act that might well come to an end and be discontinued. It does not first require the existence and essence of its objects and it does not come about by the indirect method of the forming of specific concepts of the objects. On the contrary, by the very fact that He is God, God knows before there are any objects and without any means. His being is itself also His knowledge. When we have to do with Him, we have to do directly and inescapably with the One who knows Himself, us and all things. Having fellowship with God involves being known by Him, knowing this and therefore knowing oneself.

The old symbolic way of representing God, a triangle indicating the Trinity, and an eye in the middle of it fixed on the observer, is apposite in a way both terrifying and comforting. " He does not have an eye ; He is eye. His essence is His knowledge " (H. Martensen, *Chr. Dogm.*, 1856, p. 87). He is *totus spiritus et totus sensuabilitas et totus ἔννοια et totus ratio* (Irenaeus, *Adv. o.h.* II, 13, 3). *In illius naturae simplicitate mirabili non est aliud sapere, aliud esse, sed quod est sapere, hoc est et esse* (Augustine, *De trin.* XV, 13, 22). *Necesse est dicere, quod intelligere Dei est eius substantia* (Thomas Aquinas, *S. theol.* I, qu. 14, art. 4c). *Novit Deus omnia per se ipsum, per suam essentiam* (Polanus, *Synt. Theol. chr.*, 1609, col. 1001).

Fundamentally the same thing is to be said about God's will. God is His own will, and He wills His own being. Thus will and being are equally real in God, but they are not opposed to one another in the sense that the will can or must precede or follow the being or the being the will. Rather, it is as He wills that He is God, and as He is God that he wills. Thus we can have no dealings with God without having direct and inescapable dealings with the One who wills Himself and us and in different ways all things. To have fellowship with God means always to be drawn into the decision made by His being as God (which is itself His will), and therefore to be placed face to face with a real decision of the will.

This is the logical consequence of the insight into the unity of the divine knowledge and will, provided this insight is based on the real divine action in reconciliation and not on an idea of our own construction. The conclusion is inescapable that the Reconciler Himself is the reconciliation, and the reconciliation the Reconciler. The result of this insight is, then, that we may and must revere God's being wholly under the form of His will, and in His will His being. This means that we cannot think of God at all without being summoned in the same instant to faith, obedience, gratitude, humility and joy. *Voluntas Dei . . . Deus ipse est* (Augustine, *Conf.* VII, 4). We do not think of God if confrontation with His will does not in some way challenge us, bringing us face to face with a decision. The consequence of this insight cannot be that God's concrete will is swallowed up and disappears in the idea of His being, or that the thought of God fails basically and necessarily to have the character of a call to personal decision. We are at the least threatened by this false result if with B. Bartmann (*Lehrb. d. Dogm.*[7] Vol. I, 1928, p. 145) we think of the divine will as self-grounded and hovering in eternal regularity over all changeable materials and states, and if we argue that what the Bible says about the stirrings and movements of the divine will does not " quite do justice " to the absolute essence of God on account of its anthropomorphism. If this is the case, we on our side do not " quite do justice " to the will of God in the decisions of faith, obedience, gratitude, etc., required by these stirrings and movements. Beyond these decisions there is a higher and more real attitude to the will of God which consists simply in a neutral contemplation or even a mere endurance of the divine essence self-grounded and hovering in eternal regularity. But this is very different from what the Bible at any rate describes as the true human attitude to the will of God. And it would mean that the Bible gives us strange advice when it so plainly directs us to make these definite decisions. No. Against this position we must hold firm to the fact that the divine reconciliation in which we are confronted with God's real will is one great " anthropomorphism," but that we may not cease to see in it, and in it alone, the absolute essence of God. We have to seek this essence, then, in the highly concrete " stirrings and movements " of the divine will and not anywhere else. We have not to look for it in a divine being self-grounded and hovering in eternal regularity. We have to revere the divine being very seriously, and without looking for what are called better possibilities, by the concrete decisions of faith and obedience which correspond to the concrete will of God. Polanus' statement is correct (*loc. cit.*, p. 1025) : *Voluntas Dei reipsa est unica, quia est ipsamet essentia Dei*. But when he continues *nostrae tamen infirmitatis causa est multiplex*, this is only a half truth, and dangerous in the same way as the opinion already quoted. It suggests that the *multiplicitas* in which the will of God confronts us does not belong to the real essence of God, but is only an appearance assumed by God to help our human weakness. If, however, we are to take seriously the will of God which confronts us in the divine reconciliation as itself the true and real will of God, we must see in it and there-fore in its multiplicity the simple essence of God Himself.

2. If God's knowledge is God Himself, and again if God's will is God Himself, we cannot avoid the further statement that God's knowledge is His will and God's will His knowledge. But this further equation must be made with caution. It cannot mean that God can be deprived of the particular characteristic of either knowledge or will ; that if possible His knowledge and will are to be understood only as figurative ; that they are to be expunged from the divine essence as anthropomorphisms in favour of a higher third thing which as such is neither real knowledge nor real will. But again, the equation cannot mean that God's will is to be reduced to His knowledge if the thinker's taste is intellectualistic, or His knowledge to His will if it is voluntar-istic ; that a so-called primacy is to be ascribed to the one, while the other is thought of as merely a figurative description of the essence of God. On the contrary, we have to take quite seriously both that God knows and that God wills. We have to treat His knowledge seriously as knowledge and His will as will, and God Himself in the unity and also in the particular characteristics of both as spirit, as a divine person. He would not be a person if properly and finally in Himself He were something other than knowledge and will, or were only the one or the other. He is a person as He is both, and both with their particular characteristics. He is the divine person in the fact that He is one in both, completely the knower and completely the willer : not conditioned and limited in His knowledge by His will nor in His will by His knowledge ; but conditioned and limited in both—for He Himself is both—only by Himself ; in both of them freely and completely Himself. That God's knowledge is His will and His will His knowledge means, then, that His knowledge is as extensive as His will and His will as His knowledge. Everything that God knows He also wills, and everything that He wills He also knows. In every way God's knowledge is also His will and His will is a will that knows. And knowing and willing He is one and the same person. But He is so as the One who both knows and wills in a way which is true and divine. He knows and wills, therefore, as is proper to Himself in accordance with His holiness, righteousness and wisdom. He knows Himself as the original and proper being which is the creative ground of everything else. And He wills Himself as the incomparably good which is the source and standard of everything else that is good. He knows what is real outside Him as that which has been raised to reality by Himself, and as this He also wills it. He knows the possible as that which has its possibility in and by Him, whether as that which He will raise to reality in its own time, or as that which will always be a possibility from Him and by Him, but only a possibility. And He also wills this possibility as such,

whether it is to be realised in the future or not at all. He knows also the impossible, that which from Him and by Him is not possible. He knows it as that which He has rejected, excluded and denied : sin as sin ; death as death ; the devil as the devil. And He also wills it to be this, to be what it is in virtue of His rejection of it, in the way which belongs to it as the impossible. Even His non-willing is really a powerful willing, which fixes limits and therefore directs and governs. We can never escape the knowledge and will of God, either in the heights or the depths, in heaven or in hell, as believers or unbelievers. Either way He will always know of us. And either way He will always will us.

This is the logical consequence to be drawn from the insight into the unity of the divine knowledge and will, provided this insight derives only from the perception of the unity of the divine revelation and reconciliation and is therefore the correct insight into this unity. If this is the case, we know that we are never forgotten by God and also that we can never forget Him. We know that we can never be forgotten by Him because He never wills anything without also knowing about us. And we can never forget Him because knowing us He also wills us, in some way, in His love and grace and holiness. Dangerous conclusions can be drawn from a false understanding of the unity of God's knowledge and will. If we fail to keep in mind the reality of them both, and therefore of the real divine presence, we may be dealing with the kind of God who is really only a Beyond without consciousness or purpose, of which we can be quite certain that it forgets us, while we on our side forget it just as easily. Or we may remember His knowledge of us, and therefore that we are in some sense before Him and kept by Him, but not that His knowledge of us is His complete will by which a claim is laid upon us and we are called to decisions. Or, on the other hand, we may remember only His will and try to satisfy Him without perceiving that God knows us—our impurity in His holiness but also in His mercy our weakness. It can be seen that there is here a whole series of closely related practical mistakes directly connected with the theoretical. For this reason it is hard to be too strict or too cautious in our understanding and teaching of the unity of the divine knowledge and will.

3. Moving on from this point, and taking up again expressly the thread of the doctrine of the omnipotence of God, we reach the statement that the divine knowledge and will, being divine, is free, i.e., superior in relation to all the objects distinct from itself.

In this connexion we must speak first of that aspect of God's knowledge which is traditionally called His omniscience. To put the simplest point first, God's knowledge, as omnipotent knowledge, is complete in its range, the one unique and all-embracing knowledge. We will not call it in this respect an infinite knowledge. It is, of course, infinite in its power. But although the realm of the knowable is infinite for us, for God, who knows everything, it is a finite realm, exhausted and therefore limited by His knowledge. We have seen already that God knows all things, each in its own peculiar way, but still all things. That which is not knowable and known by Him does not exist, either as actuality or possibility, as being or non-being, good or bad, in bliss or perdition, life or death. Whatever is in any sense is known by God in exactly the sense proper to it. The limit of being is not the concept of mere possibility or even of non-being. For both possibility and non-being exist in their own way. It is the knowledge of God—and with it His will—which defines the limits of being. For this reason God's knowledge, as it embraces all things—all that is—is a knowledge which is finite, not limited from without, but by itself. There is no limit set to it. But it sets itself a limit, declaring that which is not its object as *ipso facto* null and void.

Omnis infinitas quodam ineffabili modo Deo finita est, quia scientiae ejus incomprehensibilis non est (Augustine, *De civ. Dei* XII, 19). This insight has a practical, i.e., a disciplinary significance. If it is true, the infinitude of human striving after knowledge must be regarded as only relative. If our knowledge does not reach any end—because it does not have the power of the divine knowledge—this does not mean that it is infinite. Since God's knowledge is in itself and fixes the limit of the existent and therefore of the knowable, it is also the objective limit of our knowledge. " Thought is free." But if, at any stage of its relatively infinite movement, it wishes to be absolutely infinite and cross the boundary of the knowable and therefore of being, it can no longer be thought, and how then can it be free ? For the sake of the freedom of thought we have every reason to allow our thinking to be accompanied always by a recollection of the knowledge of God which embraces all being and is for that reason finite. At each stage in our thinking we must submit to the question whether in the true sense we do not perhaps cease to think if we forget God and therefore the limit of true being.

Within the limit of being imposed by God Himself, God knows everything. Again, this includes even non-being, even the merely possible and the impossible, even evil, death and hell, all things in their own way—but still all things. Non-being also exists in its own way, not as something infinite, but as something finite, conditioned by the fact that God knows it. There is, therefore, nothing hidden from God. Anything hidden from God would constitute a realm of being or non-being independent of Him, and therefore the realm of a second god.. If all second gods are rejected and excluded by God Himself, and if no second god exists, there does not exist any being or non-being independent of Him, any object which is not an object of His knowledge, and therefore anything hidden from Him. Anything hidden from God would not be something but nothing. It would not simply be without being like sin or death. It would be *nihil pure negativum*, which cannot even be hidden from God, because it does not exist in any sense. And so, since nothing that exists can be hidden from God, and since God knows everything, there is no self-concealment from God. There is, of course, a desire for self-concealment which is the direct consequence of sin and the unwilling, compulsory, impotent admission of it. There is the flight to the denial of the undeniable God, dictated by anxiety, which is all that remains, when the desire to trespass has run its full course. There is the ostrich's strategy which confirms and seals the headlong fall into the realm of the non-existent and impossible before God, the overpowering by death and hell. But this policy can have no success. There can be no real secession to a realm hidden from God, the realm of a being or non-being independent of Him, the kingdom of another god. For there is no such kingdom. Even the non-being to which we turn, and into which we can fall, actually is before God even though He turns away from it. In the form of His turning away from it, it is no less the object of the divine knowledge than that which is before Him. Our escape fails because, being an escape from God, it has no goal. Every goal that can be reached lies within the realm of the one God and therefore within the realm of His knowledge. At every one of these goals we again stand before God. We are seen and known by Him. We are no more inaccessible to Him than He is to Himself. We may fall into sin and hell, but whether for salvation or perdition we cannot fall out of the realm of God's knowledge and so out of the realm of His grace and judgment. This is the comfort and the warning contained in the truth of the divine omniscience in this simplest sense of the term.

" The Lord is the God who knoweth all things " (1 Sam. 2³). " God is greater than our heart, and knoweth all things " (1 Jn. 3²). " Neither is there any creature that is not manifest in his sight : but all things are naked and opened unto the eyes of him with whom we have to do " (Heb. 4¹³). " I know Ephraim, and Israel is not hid from me " (Hos. 5³). " Thou hast set our iniquities before thee, our secret sins in the light of thy countenance " (Ps. 90⁸). " Behold, I will send for many fishers, saith the Lord, and they shall fish them ; and after will I send for many hunters, and they shall hunt them from every mountain, and from every hill, and out of the holes of the rocks. For mine eyes are upon all their ways : they are not hid from my face, neither is their iniquity hid from mine eyes " (Jer. 16¹⁶⁻¹⁷). " O Lord, thou hast searched me, and known me. Thou knowest my downsitting and mine uprising, thou understandest my thought afar off. Thou compassest my path and my lying down, and art acquainted with all my ways. For there is not a word in my tongue, but, lo, O Lord, thou knowest it altogether. Thou hast beset me behind and before, and laid thine hand upon me. Such knowledge is too wonderful for me ; it is high, I cannot attain unto it. Whither shall I go from thy spirit ? or whither shall I flee from thy presence ? . . ." (Ps. 139¹f·). All these passages read like commentaries on the dark and menacing text, Gen. 3⁸f·, where Adam after the fall thinks he can hide himself and his wife from God under the trees in the garden, and yet God knows it and calls : " Where art thou ? " and Adam has to give an account and cannot. Nevertheless we should not overlook the comfort with which this very text speaks of the fact that God does not allow even fallen man to fall out of His knowledge and His thoughts. Therefore we must listen to the other biblical commentaries on this text. " Thou tellest my wanderings : put thou my tears into thy bottle : are they not in thy book ? " (Ps. 56⁸). " Are not two sparrows sold for a farthing ? and one of them shall not fall on the ground without your Father. But the very hairs of your head are all numbered. Fear ye not therefore, ye are of more value than many sparrows " (Mt. 10²⁹⁻³¹). " The Lord knoweth them that are his " (2 Tim. 2¹⁹). He " knoweth the way of the righteous " (Ps. 1⁶), and " seeing in secret " He is the rewarder of their alms, their prayers and their fasts (Mt. 6⁴·⁶·¹⁸). " They break in pieces thy people, O

Lord, and afflict thine heritage. They slay the widow and the stranger, and murder the fatherless. Yet they say, The Lord shall not see, neither shall the God of Jacob regard it. Understand, ye brutish among the people : and ye fools, when will ye be wise ? He that planted the ear, shall he not hear ? he that formed the eye, shall he not see ? " (Ps. 94⁵ᶠ·). Over all God's knowledge of the heights and the depths of the reality that is distinct from Himself there stands, basically and decisively, the comforting and warning knowledge of Himself, the Father's knowledge of the Son, and the Son's of the Father (Mt. 11²⁷), the Spirit's knowledge of the deep things of God (1 Cor. 2¹⁰). " For I know the thoughts that I think toward you, saith the Lord, thoughts of peace, and not of evil, to give you an expected end. Then shall ye call upon me, and ye shall go and pray unto me, and I will hearken unto you. And ye shall seek me, and find me, when ye shall search for me with all your heart. And I will be found of you, saith the Lord " (Jer. 29¹¹ᶠ·). As certainly as God knows Himself and His thoughts in this way, Jacob-Israel cannot escape the divine judgment, but equally, it may and must not say : " My way is hid from the Lord and my judgment is passed over from my God " (Is. 40²⁷). " Behold he that keepeth Israel shall neither slumber nor sleep " (Ps. 121⁴). God knows Himself, and therefore He knows about us and all things.

In view of these biblical passages it is natural to add to what we have said the express statement that God's knowledge is a complete knowledge not only in the sense of a comprehensive but also in that of a penetrating knowledge. It is not merely an outer knowledge of its objects ; it is also an inner knowledge. It is not partial ; it is total. It not only knows them individually ; it knows them in their inter-connexion. It knows the individual in the whole and the whole in each constituent individual. Only in this way can we say unreservedly what must be said about God—that nothing is hidden from Him. For His knowledge is exempt in every way from uncertainty, obscurity and error. Everything is open before Him not only in its existence but in all its limitations, possibilities and relationships. It is a knowledge which is absolutely clear, plain, definite, and intensive in its exhaustiveness. Everything which is in any way knowable is known by Him. " God is light, and in him is no darkness at all " (1 Jn. 15). " If I say, Surely the darkness shall cover me ; even the night shall be light about me. Yea, the darkness hideth not from thee, but the night shineth as the day " (Ps. 139 ¹¹⁻¹²).

Over against this simplest definition of the divine knowledge, we shall set the simplest definition of God's will. Rightly understood it is as right and necessary to speak of God's " omnivolence "—His willing all things—as of His omnipotence. For God's will also, being omnipotent will, is in its sphere a complete and exhaustive will, embracing and controlling not only being which has no will but all other wills, although without detracting from their character as wills. There is no being not subject to the will of God. There is also no other will outside or beyond God. There is no will which conditions or hinders God's will. Again, we shall not describe God's will as infinite in regard to the sphere of its objects. It is infinite in power. But if we at any rate seem to be able to will infinitely, God's will is different from ours in that it fixes a sphere which it does not overstep. It keeps to it, and therefore it is a will which is finite in its compass. If we say that God wills everything, we must interpret this as meaning everything that can be willed by God, and everything in the way in which it can be willed by Him. When we say of God's will that everything is subject to it, it is " everything " in this sense. This is really everything. For whatever cannot be willed in some way by Him, and is not sooner or later willed by Him in some way and under some determination, simply is not. Only what in some sense can be and is willed by Him is. It is by God's affirming and accepting will that the actual is, and also the possible which has not yet received actuality from God's will or may never receive it. But it is by God's refusing and rejecting will that the impossible and non-existent before Him is, since it is only by God's rejecting will, His aversion, that it can have its particular form of actuality and possibility. Outside the sphere of God's will there can be only the pure, negative nothing to which we have already referred. There is no outside this sphere. The sphere of His will is as such the sphere of spheres. In this sense it may and must be said that God wills everything in some way, and that defined in this sense His will is a finite will.

This also has practical significance for conduct. We deceive ourselves if we think we can will infinitely much. The extent of what can be willed is in fact fixed by the will of God and fixed in such a way that only that can be willed which is either affirmed and accepted by God's will or denied and rejected by it, i.e., the possible or the impossible, the good or the bad. All volition is dependent on and limited to this finite sphere, to the decision marked out by the pattern given by God Himself. For God Himself does not will except in this way, i.e., in this sphere. He therefore prescribes the law and limit of all volition. Within this sphere our willing may be in harmony with the will of God or in opposition to it. But it can possess no other sphere. We can choose differently from God, but we cannot make any other kind of choice than that delineated by His will. We cannot make a third, neutral choice, and will something outside that which God has either accepted or rejected. This first possibility out of the apparently infinite other possibilities of choice simply does not exist, not even as a possibility. We cannot will at all if we are not willing to decide within the sphere fixed by the will of God.

Within this sphere, which is itself the only sphere of being, God wills everything. God's willing something can therefore mean that He loves, affirms and confirms it, that He creates, upholds and promotes it out of the fulness of His life. His willing it can also mean that in virtue of the same love He hates, disavows, rejects and opposes it as that which withstands and lacks and denies what is loved, affirmed and confirmed by Him and created, upheld and promoted by Him. He still wills it in the sense that He takes it seriously in this way and takes up this position over against it. He wills it in so far as He gives it this space, position and function. He does not do so as its author, recognising it as His creature, approving and confirming and vindicating it. On the contrary, He wills it as He denies it His authorship, as He refuses it any standing before Him or right or blessing or promise, as He places it under His prohibition and curse and treats it as that from which He wishes to redeem and liberate His creation. In this way, then, in His turning away from it, He wills what He disavows. It cannot exist without Him. It, too, is by Him, and is under His control and government. There is nothing that is withdrawn from His will, just as there is nothing hidden from His knowledge. There is no sphere of being or non-being which is not in some way wholly subject to His will. For such a sphere would inevitably be that of another god. Anything withdrawn from His will can be only pure nothing. Whatever exists belongs either (as it is affirmed by Him) to being or (as it is disavowed by Him) to non-being. In either case it is subject to His will. Thus nothing that exists is withdrawn from His will. His will is therefore done in all and by all. There is no escape from what is done by His will. Again, of course, there is the desire to escape. But there is no goal where this desire can be realised. We can adopt an independent attitude to the divine Yes and No. We can hate what God loves and love what He hates. We can accept what He rejects and reject what He accepts. This is our sinful will. But it does not lead us to a sphere where we have withdrawn from the will of God or hidden and secured ourselves against its realisation and fulfilment in us and by us. If we will to sin, we enter the sphere of the divine prohibition and curse, disavowal and rejection; the realm of death. We can certainly attain this goal. But even if we do, we do not leave the sphere of the divine will or escape from God. Here, too, we cannot actually govern ourselves. In fact we are under no other government than that of the will of God. By our decision, our decision against God, we merely fulfil God's decision. Besides willing and deciding for God or against Him there is no third possibility of choice or decision. There is no neutrality in which we can slip between the divine Yes and the divine No (which circumscribe the area of being), thus saving ourselves in this neutrality from the will of God in a middle position between faith and belief. There is no such place outside that area. The Yes and No of the divine will are absolutely and definitely the true circumscription of the area of being. There is nothing beyond. If we want to be neutral, we definitely want to be disobedient. For to struggle against adopting the position of agreement with the divine Yes and No, to look instead for a third possibility beyond the antithesis set up by the divine decision, to make a refusal to will the object of our will is a piece of folly in which we have already hated what God loves and loved what He hates and therefore sinned. If there is no neutrality towards God, we are already against God if we will to remain neutral. It is, therefore, impossible—really impossible—to fall out of or escape from the lordship of the divine will. His will is done in heaven and on earth both when we are obedient and when we are disobedient. This is no less true when our disobedience takes the form—as it usually does—of trying to avoid the decision marked out for us in the divine pattern. But God's will is God Himself, and God is gracious and holy, merciful and righteous. Therefore, again, to say that God is the One to whose will all things are subject is a word which is full of warning and yet at the same time full of comfort.

This is why in Scripture the prayer : " Thy will be done," stands so close to : " Search me, O God, and know my heart : try me and know my thoughts : and see if there be any wicked way in me, and lead me in the way everlasting " (Ps. 139²³⁻²⁴). The two together form the substance of all prayer. In such prayer what do we pray for ? Clearly that God will make us obedient and set us at His right hand, but no less clearly that even in our disobedience, when we must stand on His left hand, nothing except His will may be done to us. We pray that in some way God will deal with us in His gracious and holy knowledge and will. In contrast with this prayer, it is impossible to try to dispute with God, as if it is not His will that is done to us, or as if His will (although it is His) is not really gracious and holy. At what point and from what position can we dispute with God ? " Shall the thing formed say to him that formed it, Why hast thou made me thus ? Hath not the potter power over the clay, of the same lump to make one vessel unto honour, and another unto dishonour ? What if God, willing to shew his wrath, and to make his power known, endured with much longsuffering the vessels of wrath fitted to destruction : and that he might make known the riches of his glory on the vessels of mercy, which he had afore prepared unto glory ? " (Rom. 9²⁰ᶠ·). Within the sphere described here there is obviously no escape. We are obviously either lost and remain lost, or we pray the prayer which means either way that we leave the realm of neutrality and acknowledge God to be in the right instead of disputing with Him. When we do this we go over from disobedience to obedience, and therefore from God's left hand to His right, and we are therefore saved and not lost. According to Scripture the will of God is neither to be extolled nor feared as our fate. It is to be adored and done as the will of our Lord which is always justified and right. " For I know that the Lord is great, and that our Lord is above all gods. Whatsoever the Lord pleased, that did he in heaven, and in earth, in the seas, and all deep places " (Ps. 135⁵⁻⁶). " But he is in one mind, and who can turn him ? and what his soul desireth, even that he doeth. For he performeth the thing that is appointed for me : and many such things are with him. Therefore am I troubled at his presence : when I consider, I am afraid of him " (Job 23¹³⁻¹⁵). " Let all the earth fear the Lord : let all the inhabitants of the world stand in awe of him. For he spake, and it was done ; he commanded, and it stood fast. The Lord bringeth the counsel of the heathen to nought : he maketh the devices of the people of none effect. The counsel of the Lord standeth for ever, the thoughts of his heart to all generations. Blessed is the nation whose God is the Lord ; and the people whom he hath chosen for his own inheritance " (Ps. 33⁸⁻¹²). We are not speaking of God's will at all if we do not grant it this range and worship it in it.

4. We now take a further step and say of the divine knowledge first that it possesses the character of foreknowledge, *praescientia*, in relation to all its objects, with the exception of God Himself in His knowledge of Himself. This concept deepens that of omniscience in so far as it characterises the divine knowledge explicitly as a knowledge which is superior to all its objects that are distinct from God. This is the meaning of the " fore," the *prae*, which has, therefore, much more than a purely temporal connotation. God's knowledge does not consist only in His knowing all things before they are and have been, in His actually knowing them when they are still future. It does, of course, consist in this. But the decisive thing is that God and

therefore His knowledge of all things is what it is in eternal superiority to all things and eternal independence of all things : a knowledge of them which is complete in every respect ; which not only eternally corresponds to them and follows them as human knowledge corresponds to and follows its objects, but is eternally their presupposition. It is not that God knows everything because it is, but that it is because He knows it. For primarily, in the basis and origin of its being, everything does not exist in itself but in God, in His knowledge of its possibility and its actuality. Thus the " fore " in the divine foreknowledge denotes the absolute priority and superiority of God Himself to every possible existence distinct from His own, His dignity as the Creator of being and as the Lord and master even of non-being. In Him both being and non-being would be what they are even if they had no existence outside Him, even if He had not created being and given no place to non-being. Everything that exists outside Him does so because it exists first and eternally in Him, in His knowledge. It is for this reason that His knowledge is not actually tied to the distinction between past, present and future being. For this reason, too, all things in all ages are foreknown by God from all eternity, or, to put it in temporal terms, always—no less and no differently in their future than in their present and past.

Quid improvisum tibi qui nosti omnia et nulla natura est, nisi quia nosti eam (Augustine, *Conf.* VII, 4, 6). *Nos ista quae fecisti videmus, quia sunt, tu autem quia vides ea, sunt* (*ib.* XIII, 38). *Iste mundus nobis notus esse non posset, nisi esset; Deo autem nisi notus esset, esse non posset* (*De civ. Dei* XI, 10, 3). *Universas creaturas . . . non quia sunt, ideo novit Deus, sed ideo sunt quia novit* (*De. trin.* XV, 13). *Non enim more nostro ille vel quod futurum est, prospicit, vel quod praesens est, aspicit, vel quod praeteritum est, respicit . . . Ille quippe non ex hoc in illud cogitatione mutata, sed omnino incommutabiliter videt ita ut . . . omnia stabili ac sempiterna praescientia comprehendat nec aliter oculis, aliter mente . . . nec aliter nunc, aliter autem et aliter postea, quoniam non sicut nostra, ita eius quoque scientia trium temporum . . . varietate mutatur* (*De civ. Dei* XI, 21). But: *Unico simplicissimo semperque eodem et praesentissimo actu omnia intelligit et veluti unico aspectu et intuitu omnia lustrat et emetitur . . . Est enim unica et simplicissima in Deo idea, quae est idea ipsius, adeoque ipsa Dei essentia, in qua Deus omnia videt et contemplatur* (F. Burmann, *Syn. Theol.*, 1678, I, p. 113). *Omnia cognoscit per genesin et non per analysin, ideo omnia sunt prius in ipsius mente, quam in semetipsis, neque scientiam suam mutuatur aut emendicat a rebus* (A. Heidanus, *Corp. Theol. chr.*, 1686, I, p. 113).

Thomas Aquinas went a step farther at this point when he described the divine *scientia* directly as the *causa rerum*. For God's knowledge, he holds, is related to created things in the same way as the knowledge of an artist is related to his work. But as the *forma intellectus* the artist's knowledge is the *principium operationis* from which his work proceeds when it actually becomes the corresponding *actio*. To this extent it might be said : *Deus per suum intellectum causat res* (*S. theol.*, I, qu. 14, *art.* 8c.). This is true in the context in which Thomas meant and said it, i.e., in regard to God's knowledge of what has actually been created or is to be created by Him. But it could not be applied to what is only possible for the simple reason that this is an object of the divine foreknowledge only as the possible and not the actual, so that it cannot have its cause in it. What is not an effect cannot have a cause. The most that can be said of what is only possible is that the divine foreknowledge (and will) is the presupposition of its possibility. And of course Thomas' statement is even less applicable to what is the object of God's knowledge as the impossible, as that which has been disavowed and rejected by God. Sin, death and the devil do exist within the sphere of the divine creation, of *res creatae*, as principles of disobedience, evil and rebellion. But they do not belong to these *res*. They are not themselves created by God. Their being is simply the non-being which disturbs and denies God's creation. As this they are certainly just as much objects of the divine foreknowledge (and will) as the being created by God. But they are objects in a different way, in the way peculiar to non-being, as the limit of the being known by God, but not as an effect which has something corresponding to it as such, a cause, in the divine knowledge. Thus God in His foreknowledge is the Lord and source of being, and He is also the Lord but not the source of non-being. He is not the *actor*, but the *judex peccati*. Finally it is worth while noting at this point that among the *res creatae* are also the created wills of angels and men. If we say of them that they, too, have their cause in the divine foreknowledge and are its effect, this cannot mean that they are not real as wills (as created wills), that they do not have freedom of choice and therefore contingency (even if a created freedom and contingency). For the contingency of being is no more set aside by the fact that God is its originator than is its necessity. Both are established by this. God knows about everything in His creation in its own way. He knows about nature as nature, spirit as spirit, the necessary as necessary, and the contingent as contingent. This correspondence between God's will and created things does not have its origin and norm in created things themselves—in this we must agree with Augustine—but in God their Creator and therefore in His foreknowledge. The created corresponds to the divine foreknowledge, and it is only for this reason that the divine foreknowledge corresponds to the created. Thus everything created certainly has its origin in the foreknowledge of God. But if this is the case, it is so in such a way that as the effect of this cause it is this specific thing, determined in a particular way. It is, therefore, granted its own contingency. The created will does not lose its character as a will, and therefore its freedom (a created freedom, but freedom nevertheless) because it is an effect of this cause. On the contrary, it is given it.

In respect of God's will, what corresponds to the divine foreknowledge is freedom. The freedom of God's will means that it precedes and is superior to all its objects—with the exception of God Himself, to the extent that God also and first of all wills Himself. God is not dependent on anything that is not Himself ; on anything outside Himself. He is not limited by anything outside Himself, and is not subject to any necessity distinct from Himself. On the contrary, everything that exists is dependent on His will. It is conditioned by Him and happens necessarily in accordance with His will. And His will is pure will, determined exclusively by Himself, to act or not to act, or to act in a particular way. In this self-determination it has no law over it. It does not have an external law in which one of its objects is necessarily in its existence or nature a motive either as a goal or a means to other goals. Nor does it have an internal law, because it is itself God, and therefore the standard of everything divinely necessary and the substance of everything holy and just and good, so that there can be nothing divine which must first be its motive or norm, or which it needs as a motive or rule, in order to be the divine will. There is only one thing which the divine will cannot will, and that is the absurd. It cannot will to cease to be the divine will, to be God Himself. This, however, is not a limitation. It is the condition of its freedom. It would not be a more free, but a less free will, if it chose to surrender its divinity. In the constancy of its divinity it is always a free will and needs no stimulus to determine itself and nothing higher to condition itself as holy and righteous and good. As God's will it is itself the stimulus, the higher thing, the reason which leaves no further place for questioning because it is itself the substance of every true and justifiable reason. Thus the freedom of God's will, too, denotes the absolute superiority of God in relation to every possible or real power distinct from His power ; His dignity as the Creator of being and also the Lord and master of non-being. The place of each of these—in all their difference—is the place that He chooses to give them, controlling or permitting, and really controlling even in His permission. Thus each owes its (distinctive and absolutely different) being wholly to the will of God and not to itself or to any other necessity distinct from the divine will. If we ask why creation or each of us or everything has to be as it is, the only answer is that it must be so by God's free will. If we ask further why being is limited by non-being or why creation has to be obstructed and contradicted by sin and death and the devil, again the only answer we can give is that by the same free will of God by which it was created creation has to have this limitation by what is not created, by non-being, and even non-being must also have this definite place and therefore its peculiar being. If we ask the further question why there must be reconciliation, why the decision in which God shows Himself as Lord and Victor in His creation by saying Yes at this place and No at that, here accepting and there rejecting ; and if we ask further why for this reconciliation and this decision there has to take place what does take place, why God Himself must become man, Himself enduring this limiting of His creation by sin and death and the devil in all its fearful totality, and in this way conquer—the only answer we can finally give is that this is how God has known it from eternity, and this is also how He has willed it from eternity, in His divine freedom. And if we ask further why we must believe the Word of God spoken in this event, and obey it, again and above all the only answer we can give is that this is God's free will, and therefore His holy and righteous and good will, and as such His omnipotent will. This is all absolutely above us, and we are absolutely accountable to it all, because it is all in some way God Himself, and God is free to be God in this way both in Himself and therefore also for us.

" The spirit bloweth where it listeth " (Jn. 3[8]). " He worketh all things after the counsel of his own will " (Eph. 1[11]). " He hath mercy on whom he will have mercy, and whom he will he hardeneth," and who is to challenge Him on the

point ? (Rom. 9¹⁸ᶠ·). " O the depth of the riches both of the wisdom and knowledge of God ! how unsearchable are his judgments, and his ways past finding
out ! For who hath known the mind of the Lord ? or who hath been his counsellor ? Or who hath first given to him, and it shall be recompensed unto him
again ? For of him, and through him, and to him, are all things " (Rom. 11³³⁻³⁶).
Libertas non necessitas Deo competit (Tertullian, *Adv. Hermog.* 16). *Non decet
eum, qui super omnia sit Deus, cum sit liber et suae potestatis, necessitati servisse
dicere* (Irenaeus, *Adv. o. h.* II, 5, 4). *Voluntas Dei est liberrima, ita ut Deus omnia
quaecunque vult, libere et absque impedimento velit et faciat: utque nihil agat aut
fieri permittat, nisi libere volens, nihilque coactus.* God's will has *nullam sui
causam efficientem et promoventem.* And *nullus etiam finis divinam voluntatem
alliciendo causalitatem erga illam exercet.* But the same is also true of all the
means to these ends. And *praeter voluntatem Dei nihil fit etiam quod fit contra Dei
voluntatem.* But in everything it is true that God's will is unalterable and :
*Voluntas Dei semper iusta est et summa iustitiae regula, ita ut quicquid Deus vult,
eo ipso quod vult, iustum habendum sit* (Polanus, *Synt. Theol. chr.*, 1609, *col.* 1025 f.).

The right understanding of the freedom of God's will excludes all those
views which seek to represent the relation between God and the reality distinct
from Himself as a relation of mutual limitation and necessity. In the first instance
this includes all pantheistic and panentheistic systems, according to which the
existence of this other reality belongs in some way to the essence and existence of
God Himself. The reason why God gives them real being and why from eternity
they are objects of His knowledge is not that God would not be God without their
actual or even possible existence, but because He wills to know them and to
permit them to be actuality. As real objects of His will, and therefore already
as real objects of His knowledge, they are distinct from Him. He is not conditioned by them. They are conditioned by Him. They have not proceeded
from His essence. On the contrary, He has called them and created them out
of nothing. He was not obliged to do this. He did not do it to satisfy some
need in His own being and life. The eternity and necessity of the divine will
do not involve the eternity and necessity of its objects. With whatever necessity God acts in Himself, He is always free in relation to these. As God He wills
the world, but He does not will a second God. In relation to the world He is
always the one and only God. He eternally wills what is temporal, but He wills
it as what is temporal and not as a second eternity. It is the same freedom of
His will, and this alone, which prevents Him from not continuing to will what
He has already willed, or from willing it in another form, or willing something completely different. It is in His freedom that He still wills, and wills
to be as it is, what He has already willed. He is not bound by the essence or
the existence of what has been willed by Him. It is also in His freedom that
He still does not will what He did not will when He willed what He did. Thus
the necessity of the world is always based, like its origin, on the freedom of
God, and not on any necessity of its own, nor on a necessity which was bestowed
on it by God in creation and which has now become independent. The decision
in which He wills it, and wills it in a particular form, alone is and posits necessity
in heaven and earth. But it also limits necessity, as happens in His revelation,
not in order to set it aside, but in order to confirm it as necessity, yet that which
is established solely by His will.

The right understanding of the freedom of God's will also excludes all non-
deterministic and deterministic standpoints—the two really belong together.
According to these the creature constitutes a factor which in some way conditions
and limits the will of God. It does so either by its relative contingency on the
basis of its *liberum arbitrium* or by its relative necessity in the continuity and
limitation of its existence as it obeys the law of its being. Pelagianism and
fatalism are alike heathen atavisms in a Christian doctrine of God. They both
ascribe to the will of the creature an autonomy in relation to God's will which

it cannot possess either in its relative freedom or its relative subjection. Whether he believes himself capable of absorbing the Godhead into his own personal will or whether he sees his own personal will as a mere link in a chain of fate which rules over space and time and which, as indicated perhaps in the stars, has decided about the possibilities and limits of willing and non-willing, the created individual is guilty of exaggeration and error. For if the creaturely individual has a personal will, and if there are " great, eternal, brazen laws " within the framework of which he will make use of his will, neither his will nor these laws form a stronghold against God in which the creature can live his own life in rivalry with God, whether forsaken by Him or secured against Him in his freedom or subjection. The truth is that both the freedom and the necessity which belong to the creature exist only by the will of God, which, because it wills and posits both, does not cease to be wholly free in relation to its objects and their limitations, as it is wholly necessary in itself.

Finally, a right understanding of the freedom of God's will makes all dualistic ways of thought impossible. This position is taken up when the limitation of being, and therefore of what is willed by God, is replaced by the limitation of God and His will, as if there stood at this limit a second divine will, the will of an evil power, a counter-god, who is inevitably a kind of adversary. But what exists as non-being, *contra Dei voluntatem*, does not on this account exist and occur *praeter voluntatem Dei*. We deceive ourselves if we think that we should take sin, death, and the devil seriously in the sense of ascribing to them a divine or semi-divine potentiality or the rôle of a real antagonist to the living God. It is when we see them as powers which are in their own peculiar way subordinate and subject to the will of God that we really take them seriously as powers of temptation, evil and eternal destruction. It is only then that we know conclusively that we ourselves do not have the power to combat and conquer them. We cannot do this because it is not our business. They are powers combated and conquered by God, and our business is to acknowledge and accept the decision about them made by God's will and to deal with them accordingly. They are not really taken seriously when a mythology of evil and wickedness gives the appearance that God is dead or has abdicated. In Christian faith in God, in the light of the resurrection of Jesus Christ, we have no other choice than to understand the limitation of being (no less than being itself) in this sense, as the concern of the will of God.

5. We turn, finally, to what I might call the essential nature of the divine knowledge and will, its character as real knowing and willing.

It might seem that the character of the divine knowledge as real knowledge, knowledge properly so called, is compromised by its identity (1) with God's essence, and (2) with His will, (3) by its designation as omnipotence and (4) as foreknowledge. We have thought of God and described Him as the One who, in the one unique act of His divine being, knows (and wills) in Himself and by Himself both Himself and all things, quite independently of their existence. But does this mean that we have really recognised Him as the One who knows? Have we really understood God's omnipotence as the omnipotence of His divine knowledge? Is God just as much the One who genuinely and really knows as He is the Almighty, and is He the One who knows even in this perfection of omnipotence? Is He more than generally the One before whom and by whom all things are? Is He concretely the One before whom and by whom all things are as they are known by Him ? And first, is He more than just the One who exists in and by Himself ? Is He concretely the One who knows Himself, and who in this knowing is who He is ? Nothing less is at stake here than that the spirituality and personality of the omnipotent God, and therefore the love in which He is the free God, should be taken with absolute seriousness and not merely understood as figurative or mere *nomina*. Our ability to understand the divine knowledge as real knowledge also depends on it. The same is true of our ability to understand the divine will as real will without affecting the fact that it embraces everything as a single act and is completely free in itself. Because the will is also involved the question will have to be put in a twofold form. But first we must ask to what extent the divine knowledge is real knowledge—divine and in that very way true and genuine knowledge.

The question is raised at once at our starting-point by the fact that God's knowledge is the knowledge of divine omnipotence, and is therefore omnipotent knowledge. But if this is the case, how can it be knowing, i.e., consciousness and conscious representation of itself and other objects ? If God knows Himself and all things in one unique act, to what extent does He really know ? To what extent does His knowing amount to more than His being, which is self-grounded and the ground of all other being ? To what extent is there real knowing here ? In our attempt to answer this question we cannot, of course, disturb the fact that God's being is His knowing and His knowing His being and as such omnipotent knowing. But we must obviously take account of all the critical conclusions reached in our general analysis of the conception of divine omnipotence : that God's omnipotence is not power in itself and as such but His power, and therefore real power as distinct from powerless power, and legitimate power as distinct from arbitrary power ; that it is not simply coincident with God's all-reality but greater than this ; that it does not exhaust and lose itself in God's omnicausality *ad extra*, but is always God's own power even in His omnicausality ; and that it consists decisively in the fact that God has the power to be Himself, and that only then and in this way He is the power over all things. It is with this differentiation, of which God Himself is always the criterion and limit as Himself the meaning and possessor of His power and the Lord of its use, that the omnipotence of God is what it is, real power, the divine perfection, God Himself, the being which is self-grounded and the ground of everything else. It is with this differentiation that His being itself is what it is, although without prejudice to its unity. As stated much earlier, it is not being in an ascribed simplicity and pure actuality which is God, but God who is being. We do not believe in and pray to being, but to God who is being. Who and what God is, is not something to be learned from a knowledge of being. Our conception of being is to be drawn from our knowledge of God.

But if we know God, it is only with this differentiation that we can also know the being which is self-grounded and the ground of everything else, and therefore true omnipotence. Power, yes—but God as power, God who is and possesses power, His own power before and over all activity, His power, He Himself, and therefore His power to be Lord over everything. This differentiation, this critical determination, cannot possibly be subtracted from the concept of divine omnipotence. The whole picture is distorted if we put this differentiation in the background or neglect it when we think or speak about omnipotence or use it to explain other concepts in the doctrine of God or other theological concepts. We may boldly assert that even in the depths of His being God is not omnipotent in any other way than with this differentiation. It is this that prevents God's knowledge from disappearing in His omnipotence. It is this that prevents God from being confused with the idea of an unconscious being which is self-grounded and the ground of everything else. It is this that reveals God's knowledge to us as the knowledge of the One who is Himself a knower, who is self-grounded and therefore the ground of all things in the sense that He knows Himself and all things, and knows them genuinely and properly, with the knowledge which we must recognise and revere as the origin and prototype of all creaturely knowledge. It is from the revelation of God, in which He speaks to us and causes us to hear Him and in which by our call to faith from the sleep of death He awakens our conscience to be real con-science, that the statement that " God knows " is told us and laid on our lips. But, in this divine revelation God's omnipotence confronts us only with this differentiation. We do not learn from it either by words or by an overpowering experience that the world and we ourselves are subject to a higher power. That is how the false religions of the heathen arise. What is said to us in revelation is : " I am the Lord thy God." He is certainly the Lord, and therefore the substance of all power, but He is not any kind of Lord. He is the Lord who in His speech and action makes Himself our Lord and declares Himself to be such : " I am the Lord and as such thy God." When God reveals Himself, His omnipotent speech and action are not self-exhausting but point back beyond themselves to the One who speaks and acts. In all its omnipotence His speech and action only serve the fact that, as the One who addressed us as " I " and declares Himself our God, He wills Himself to be for us and among us. The ultimate power involved in this speech and action is incomparable and unlimited. We are subject to it as the supreme power. Yet it can no longer be understood in abstraction. God cannot, as it were, disappear in it and behind it. For He is its subject, conditioning, possessing and using it. He is Himself this supreme power. There is, then, a differentiation between God and power. And it is only with this differentiation that there is the recognition that God is power and to that extent power is God. This differentiation remains. If the simple statement that " God knows " is our plain answer to God's revelation it is not exposed to the appearance of being only figuratively meant. It certainly describes God's omnipotent knowledge and therefore His omniscience and foreknowledge. Yet it also refers to the real divine omnipotence, which is what it is only in this differentiation. And it is in this differentiation that it is knowledge. For in virtue of this differentiation God is not the prisoner of His own power. He is not conditioned by possessing it. But He Himself conditions it. He is not bound to use it. He controls it. He is its Lord. He is it and has it as His own power. He therefore is it and has it in His own way, distinguishing it from all demonic power and impotence, causing it to be real power, and using it in accordance with His own decision. This differentiation characterises the act of divine being and therefore the act of His omnipresence and omnipotence as a spiritual and personal act. Hence He cannot be conceived as a thing, mechanical or calculable. By the standard of the true and the good, which He Himself is, He differentiates between Himself and what He Himself is and does. And in this differentiation, which He Himself makes, He is both in one—Himself and what He is. This means in the first instance that He knows Himself and what He is. He knows also what He is and does *ad extra*. He is not unconscious in all His being and action. He has awareness. He establishes and grasps His own being, and with it all being, in an act of knowing. This is, of course, an act of His being, but is not to be reduced to an act of a being without knowledge, a neutral and impersonal presence and power. On the contrary, it characterises His presence and power as an act of His differentiating awareness. It is for this reason that there is the inner differentiation without which we could not have given a true description of His omniscience and foreknowledge. This is also the source of the distinction between God and the possibility and reality distinct from Himself which is His creation. It is also the source of the distinctions between the real, the possible, and the impossible, between being and non-being among the objects of His knowledge. It also gives us the unavoidable concept of a definite and finite realm of the real and possible objects of His knowledge, and its differentiation from what as *nihil pure negativum* does not exist in any sense. If God is omnipotent, all these distinctions are originally and properly grounded in God Himself, and not in the objects that are distinct from God, or in a being of God which limits and imprisons Him as God. This can mean only that all these distinctions are made in God's Spirit, that the decision about all these distinctions is made by His knowledge, and that He Himself considers what He is and what He is not, what is real or possible or impossible, what is being or non-being, what is to be affirmed and what is to be denied, and finally what in no sense exists at all. It means not only that He is over all things, but that as the One who is over all things He knows all things, and that as the One who knows He has power over Himself and over all things.

At this point the older theology was at great pains to clarify the conception of the divine knowledge. To this end it tried to make certain distinctions which were all designed to show that God's knowledge is the knowledge of God and therefore omnipotent knowledge, but that it is still real knowledge. Since this conclusion is indispensable to our own position, it is worth while listening to what it had to say.

1. A distinction was drawn between God's *scientia necessaria* and His *scientia libera*. The first stood for God's knowledge of Himself, which is necessary because even in accordance with His free will—indeed just because of it—God cannot *not* be, and therefore cannot *not* be the object of His own will. But His knowledge of the world created by Him, its nature and its changes, is a free knowledge, because, again in accordance with His free will, the world might not be, or might be in a very different form, and therefore might not be the object of His knowledge, or might be so in a very different way.

2. A distinction was drawn between a divine *scientia speculativa* and a divine *scientia practica*. The first stood for God's knowledge as it is applied as pure contemplation or consideration to the inner truth of God Himself and of all things. This leaves out of account all questions of possibility or actualisation. God does not need these, nor does He owe them to all other things. Therefore they cannot either of them be the presupposition of His knowledge. On the contrary, His knowledge, as *scientia speculativa*, is the presupposition of them. As distinct from this *scientia practica* is God's knowledge of things in their eternal possibility and actualisation on the basis of His will. It can be identified with God's wisdom in so far as this is active in the decisions of His will with regard to creation, reconciliation and redemption.

3. There was a further distinction between a divine *scientia simplicis intelligentiae* and a *scientia visionis*. The first is God's knowledge of what, according to His will, is only possible but never actual. In His external action He could certainly will it in accordance with the freedom of His will. But in this same freedom He does not will it. He excludes it as impossible in practice. But as a purely theoretical possibility, it is still an object of His will. In contrast with this, in the *scientia visionis* He knows things which not only could, but, according to His will, do actually exist in the past, present and future, and are therefore demonstrated to be possible in practice.

4. A final distinction was made between a *scientia approbationis* and a *scientia reprobationis* on God's part. The former is a knowledge which affirms Himself and His creation in their genuine being, in their goodness. The latter is the knowledge which denies and rejects non-being or evil as the limit of being and good ; the powerful " not-knowing " of God attested in the saying : " I never knew you : depart from me, ye that work iniquity " (Mt. 7^{23}, 25^{12}).

In these distinctions we cannot fail to be impressed by the trouble taken to set out clearly both the divine nature of God's knowledge and its distinctive character. Without these distinctions it would be impossible to bring out the essence of the divine omnipotence which decides and differentiates both in itself and over all things, and therefore its spiritual character and peculiar characteristics as omniscient knowledge. In so far as both terms in the various pairs of concepts used by the older theology denote the one knowledge of God, the terms refer clearly to its divine nature ; and in so far as they designate distinction in this unity, they refer to its particular nature, its character as knowledge. To this extent the distinctions are worthy of consideration and are more or less unavoidable, as our own discussion has shown.

The legitimate desire that we have described is, however, crossed by a second, which appears actually to play the dominant role in what is presented in Roman

Catholic theology. This is an interest in the distinctive nature of the objects of the divine knowledge as such. We must recognise, of course, that this too is a legitimate interest. If there is genuine, real knowledge on the part of God, it involves conclusively the existence of its genuine and real objects. The reality of the world of possible or real objects distinct from Himself depends on His nature as Spirit and on the character of His knowledge as real knowledge. If these distinctions were not fundamentally valid, and if there were no genuine and real knowledge on God's part, all things would exist only in God and not in themselves. Because God knows not only Himself, but also these other possible or real things, in His *scientia libera* or *practica* or *visionis* He becomes as He wills it the Creator, Ruler and Upholder of these possibilities and realities. In addition to the existence that they have in Him, He gives them an existence outside Him and in themselves. He therefore gives them a reality distinct from His own, yet without detracting from the fact that He is reality, and therefore their reality. It is, then, quite legitimate in itself to have this interest in these distinctions, and by them to establish the special nature of the objects of the divine knowledge. But this interest can and necessarily will become dangerous if it means ascribing to the creature, as the object of the divine knowledge, not merely a distinctiveness but an autonomy which on its side limits the divine knowledge. This is just what happened in relation to the possibility and reality of the creaturely will as one of the objects of the divine knowledge.

It is easy to see how the problem arose. If the divine knowledge embraces itself and all things does it not inevitably constitute for man's free will a danger which is unavoidable and which takes away man's responsibility ? If in this knowledge everything (including what is future) is eternally what it is in the manner in which it is, is not this knowledge inevitably the basic cause of man's sin ? Augustine had already given the correct answer to this question : *religiosus animus utrumque eligit, utrumque confitetur et fide pietatis utrumque confirmat*, God's infallible knowledge of our actions including their character as acts of will. The former does not involve the unreality of the latter. On the contrary, *ipsae nostrae voluntates in causarum ordine sunt, qui certus est Deo eiusque praescientia continetur*. The One who knows all things and the cause of all things also knows our wills as the cause of our actions (*De civ. Dei*, V, 9, 2 f.). He knows our wills as such : *illo praesciente est aliquid in nostra voluntate*. Therefore we do not need to diminish either God's knowledge or our own willing as such : *sed utrumque amplectimur, utrumque fideliter et veraciter confitemur: illud* (the divine knowledge) *ut bene credamus, hoc* (our willing) *ut bene vivamus. Male autem vivitur, si de Deo non bene creditur*. It is because of the divine knowledge of us that we are and become free, and as we have faith in this knowledge (and in it alone) we shall make the right use of our freedom, just as we shall also understand the admonitions and commands that come to us as objects of this divine knowledge. If man sins, this is not because God knew, as He certainly did from eternity, that man would sin. For the object of the divine foreknowledge was not a *fatum* or *fortuna*, but the man who sinned of his own will (*ib.*, 10, 2). Our earlier qualification of the Thomist doctrine that the divine knowledge is the *causa rerum* is relevant in this connexion. We agree with Polanus : *Non omnium, quae Deus praescit, ipse est autor, sed tantum eorum, quae ipse facere decrevit sive per se, sive per alios*. And therefore *praescientia Dei non est causa eorum, quae Deus decrevit non facere, sed solummodo permittere, ut peccati*. As God's necessary and infallible knowledge does not at all remove the contingency of the things created by Him, this knowledge is not the source of any *coactiva necessitas peccandi*, since it does not destroy the nature of man and therefore does not destroy his will (*Synt. Theol. chr.*, 1609, *col.* 1014). All this is important and correct.

But it is not legitimate to do more than establish the distinctiveness of man's free will as the object of the divine knowledge—the necessary safeguard against a fatalism that removes the will as a will. In part at least, however, the post-Tridentine theology of Roman Catholicism has gone a good deal further than this, with a theory which can only be described as an illegitimate interest in an autonomy of the human will in its relation to the divine knowledge and to God generally. Augustine ascribed no such autonomy to it. But following the precedent of Petrus Fonseca and others, the Spanish Jesuit theologian Louis Molina (1535–1600) took this step in his doctrine of the divine *scientia media*. The name signifies that the object of this knowledge is to be found between the objects of all those pairs of concepts described above and especially between the objects of the *scientia necessaria* and the *scientia libera*. Its object is the *futuribile*, the conditionally future, i.e., what will occur on the presupposition that certain circumstances and conditions are given, on the basis of free decisions on the part of the creature. According to this theory God knows what the free creature will do in its freedom under these circumstances and conditions, and in accordance with this knowledge He saves or condemns it. The indispensable but not finally decisive circumstances and conditions are given by prevenient grace. But it lies in the will of the creature to make use of them or not and therefore to make the grace operative or not. Justification depends on the union of creaturely will with prevenient grace. The two work together like two men pulling a boat. The result of this co-operation (or the negative result of the non-co-operation) of will and grace is the conditionally future as the object of God's " middle " knowledge. It cannot, therefore, be the object of His necessary knowledge, since it cannot be essentially necessary for God to know this conditionally future as it is for Him to know Himself. Nor can it be the object of God's free knowledge, because God's will is not unconditioned in regard to this conditionally future, but is conditioned *ex consensu hominis praeviso*. For His decree, His predestination, does not precede but follows His knowledge of this *consensus*. In this respect the divine knowledge is " free " rather from its own freedom : *est scientia conditionatorum independens ab omni decreto absoluto et efficaci eoque anterior* (J. Pohle, *Lehrb. der Dogm.*, Vol. I, 1902, p. 187).

As may be seen, this is not primarily an express contribution to the doctrine of God's knowledge. The very title of Molina's book (1588) tells us that his subject is a *Concordia liberi arbitrii cum gratiae donis*. It is, therefore, an essay on the doctrine of grace. The doctrine of the *scientia media* is not advanced for its own sake, but from a specific interest in the object of the divine knowledge, human free will. It was the express intention of the Jesuits, who are the representatives of this theory of the doctrine of grace, to aid a new semi-Pelagianism to gain its necessary place and right in the new situation in opposition to the Augustinian–Thomist teaching of the Dominicans, which they accused of being dangerously near to Luther and Calvin. It is, therefore, no accident that the Jesuits even reported appearances of the Virgin Mary to confirm this teaching during the great controversy which followed its discovery. The Virgin Mary of the Roman Catholic tradition would certainly have to intervene at this point (cf. *C.D.* I, 2, pp. 138-146). By this discovery the Jesuits did in fact show a very sensitive feeling for what it has become unavoidable and indispensable for Counter-Reformation Catholicism to assert. It is worth noting, however, that Molinism has not completely carried the day even in Roman Catholic theology. To this day it is opposed by those schools which look to Aquinas, and the controversy has not in any sense been decided by the teaching office of the Church in the Molinist sense, but has been left without a definite decision. A decision in favour of the Thomistic position neither was nor is to be expected. For since the anathematising of Reformation teaching it is impossible that there should not be at least the Jesuit tendency in the Roman Catholic system. Yet we have to recognise that the continued existence of the Thomistic counter-theory means that the door to the Reformation doctrine has not been altogether slammed. It remains an inch open.

We will now develop the question within the framework of the particularly relevant and interesting Thomistic view (cf. for what follows : from the Thomistic standpoint, F. Diekamp, *Kath. Dogm.*[6] Vol. I, 1930, pp. 199-215 ; from a middle position, B. Bartmann, *Lehrb. d. Dogm.*[7] Vol. I, 1928, pp. 139 f. ; representing a more or less explicit Molinism, J. Pohle, *Lehrb. d. Dogm.* Vol. I, 1902, pp. 181-203). The Thomists, too, naturally recognise the problem of the relation between the divine omniscience and foreknowledge on the one hand and the conditionally future free actions of the creature on the other. Both sides constantly quote as a biblical example of this problem the passage 1 Sam. 23[11f.]. David at Keilah, fleeing from Saul, asks God : Will Saul come down hither ? God replies that he will. David asks further : Will the men of Keilah deliver me and my men into the hand of Saul ? And God replies : They will deliver you. Then David leaves Keilah, and when this is reported to Saul he does not go either, and David is not delivered to him there. In this case, then, God knew a *conditionale futurum* which did not actually take place but which was known to Him as such. Saul and the people of Keilah would have acted in this way if David had remained in Keilah. Reference is also made to Mt. 11[21] : " Woe unto thee, Chorazin ! woe unto thee, Bethsaida ! For if the mighty works which were done in you, had been done in Tyre and Sidon, they would have repented long ago in sackcloth and ashes." These mighty acts were not actually done in Tyre and Sidon, and therefore they were not converted. Their conversion is thus a mere *futuribile*, but it is no less an object of the divine knowledge than an event that had really taken place. The Thomists, too, hold that this divine knowledge does not remove the freedom of the human actions in question. " God foresees eternally every free activity which takes place in time, not only in regard to its actuality, but also in regard to its nature, i.e., He foresees it as free activity " (Diekamp, *loc. cit.*, p. 201). God's foreknowledge does not compel the creature to act in this or that way. But it is necessarily this action in God's knowledge and as known by Him. What is the nature of God's knowledge of it ? Is He simply One who knows about something which will occur, or not occur, or occur in a particular way, independently of His will ? Is the infallibility with which it occurs, or does not occur, or occurs in a particular way, only based on the infallibility of the divine knowledge to the extent that it was infallibly known beforehand by God in its occurring, or not occurring, or occurring in this or that form ? Is God simply the One who knows it infallibly because in His eternity He is the observer who sees time and all that is in time in all its dimensions ? The Thomists do not take this view. As they see it, God knows it within the eternal decrees of His will, by which the actual free actions of the creatures are " actively caused." No *virtus ad actionem* or *motio ad agendum* exists without God. God's determination and decision has infallibly as its result the free action of the creature. *Semper hoc homo eligit quod Deus operatur in eius voluntate* (Thomas Aquinas, *S. c. gent.* III, 92). In the decrees and decisions which determine this *operari*, and therefore in His will, God knows the content of the free actions of the creatures infallibly. This is no less true of what is conditionally future. If certain conditions and the free actions connected with them do not occur, this does not alter the fact that these free actions are objects of the divine decree, decision and will, and therefore objects of His knowledge. According to the Molinist view God's influence on the free actions of the creature is limited to His giving the created will a general bias to the good, and His seeking to move it in this direction by " moral " means, commands, counsels, warnings and threatenings. Thus He is the active cause of these free actions only *ab extrinseco*. God knows (1) what a certain man *can* do with his free will in every conceivable circumstance. He knows (2) what he *would* do in all possible relationships should they become actual. He knows (3) what he *will* do in his freedom when He has given him the necessary external conditions in accordance with His will. Thus according to Jesuit teaching God knows what man would do in all possible relationships even before He has resolved on this action, i.e., His own co-operation in it. Thus the divine co-operating will is guided by this knowledge, by the *scientia media*. It is the knowledge of the eternal objective truth of the free creaturely will to which God stretches out His hand to help in accordance with His will (as guided in this way). It is the reflection in the being of God of the eternal objective truth of the free actions of the creature, to which the divine will reacts. The Thomists decisively reject this *scientia media*. On their view the biblical passages which speak of a divine knowledge of the conditionally future free actions of the creature are not to be taken to mean that there is a knowledge which precedes the divine will and decision and is independent of it. At the most only Origen can be adduced from tradition in favour of this hypothesis. It is incomprehensible, they hold, that anything future or even conditionally future can exist if it is not decreed by God in the freedom of His will, and therefore is not an object of His *scientia libera*. It is impossible to understand how there can be an infallible divine knowledge of the decisions of the will of the creature if there is actually ascribed to this will a freedom independent of the divine will. The fact that a certain act follows under certain conditions, the certainty of even its conditional occurrence in the future, can have its basis only in a corresponding divine decree and therefore in a divine knowledge that precedes it not merely as a spectator but as an active influence. If certain knowledge exists about the future free actions of the creatures, it comes from their causes. But can created causes—including the created free will—be of such a nature that by a knowledge of them the consequence, and in the case of free will the content, of the action decided can be infallibly foreseen? If not, there is no alternative but to base the divine foreknowledge of free acts on the cause which is grounded in the uncreated divine cause, in the self-operative decree of God's will. According to the Thomistic criticism the doctrine of the *scientia media* is also to be rejected on theological grounds. It ascribes to the human will the capacity to make a decision to which it is not determined by a self-operative divine movement. It therefore detracts at a decisive point from the being of God as the Creator, the *primum movens*, from God's unconditioned overlordship, from the independence of divine providence, and from the divine omnipotence. It means the setting aside, at the most important point, of the necessity of prayer. If it is true, it limits the divine activity to the offering of grace to men and the producing of the circumstances necessary for human decision. According to Molina, " man's decision to make good use of grace is not caused by God, through the inner working of grace. On the contrary, the human will determines itself here by its own power alone. Thus the most important and decisive thing, that the offered grace should not be received in vain or remain inoperative but come into operation, depends purely on the human will. It can certainly ask God to bestow the grace on it in particularly favourable circumstances, but it cannot ask God for what is most important and decisive, because it does not receive this from God but must provide it for itself." And not without a certain passion Augustine is quoted (*De dono persev.* 2, 3) : *Ista irrisoria petitio est, cum id ab eo petitur, quod scitur non ipsum dare, sed ipso non dante esse in hominis potestate; sicut irrisoria est etiam illa actio gratiarum, si ex hoc gratiae aguntur Deo, quod non donavit ipse nec fecit* (Diekamp, *loc. cit.*, p. 211). But what about that objection which forms the centre of the whole problem, and which in their opposition to the Thomists the Molinists never fail to raise ? What about the accusation that the freedom of the creaturely will, its character as self-determination, and therefore the responsibility of the rational creature, is taken away if we understand it as the object of God's free knowledge, itself determined by the divine will ? How can a will that is moved by the divine will be a free will ? And if we assume that God's will moves the human will in all circumstances, do we not inevitably interpret and understand God as the author of sin too ? To this the Thomists reply : The idea that a created will determines its activity without God having determined to move it effectively is itself a *contradictio in adjecto*. It is not a created will if it is free in this absolute sense. Again, the freedom of the human will is not taken away by God deciding and moving it. On the contrary, it is in virtue of this that it attains to its free action as a creature. *Deus est prima causa, movens et naturales causas et voluntarias. Et sicut naturalibus causis movendo eas non aufert, quin actus earum sint naturales, ita movendo causas voluntarias non aufert, quin actiones earum sint voluntariae, sed potius hoc in eis facit; operatur enim in unoquoque secundum eius proprietatem* (Thomas Aquinas, *S. theol.* I, qu. 83, art 1, ad 3). The movement of the created will by God is infallible : *immutabiliter propter efficaciam virtutis moventis, quae deficere non potest.* But it is not compulsory. It does not involve coercion. Freedom is preserved for the human will in accordance with its nature as such. Indeed, it is confirmed in the fact that it is moved by God. This is also true of its decision to act *in malam partem*. It is undeniable that there is a foreknowledge of sin too in the counsels of God, that there is a divine movement even of the sinful human will. But this does not make God the author of sin any more than it excuses man. God does not will that sin should occur. He also does not will that it should not occur. He wills to permit its occurrence. That is, He will not make its occurrence a physical impossibility. He wills the movement in the creature in which sin occurs. But in this He wills the good and the good only. For the evil, when sin occurs, is not the movement in the creature itself. It is the defect, the wickedness, the lie, the ugliness, which occurs in it. If the movement in the creature is to be referred completely to God's authorship, to His positive will, and if it is thus contained in the divine foreknowledge, this is also to be said of the defect, but only in so far as it occurs by the divine permission. As a defect, it does not rest on God's authorship. Nor is it not based on a capacity in the creature and therefore on its freedom, though it occurs in the use or rather the misuse of this freedom. It can be understood only as a defect, as actual treachery on the part of the creature, as revolt. But this means that it cannot be understood. From the point of view of both God and man it is the absolutely incomprehensible. As such it comes under the responsibility of the creature, and in virtue of the divine permission under the decree of God's will, and therefore under the divine foreknowledge. God in His free will is not under obligation to the creature to protect it by not permitting sin. Rather it is His good will to permit it, and therefore to let the free creature be guilty towards Himself. God foreknows infallibly that this will occur. It thus occurs infallibly, but as the (permitted) incurrence of guilt by the free creature, so that the inevitability is not an excuse for man's sin, or an invitation to him to will it.

So much for the opposition to the Molinist doctrine stirred up in Catholic theology itself. The half irenic, half polemical paragraph with which J. Pohle concludes and crowns his defence of Molinism is not uninteresting in another respect (*loc. cit.*, p. 203). " Thomism is an imposing and strictly consistent view which gives impressive and lively expression to the omnipotence of God, His ability to initiate movement and cause all things, His supreme control and sovereignty. Yet the relentless out-working of its basic ideas in all spheres leads at specific points to a hardness and roughness which seriously disturb the harmonious integration of the architectonic plan, producing a most unpleasant effect like sharp and hard points and angles. Psychologically it produces gloom, inclines to moral earnestness and gives rise to a conception of God that impels to fear. It is most congenial to characters of strong faith, while it can easily drive weak natures to despair. Therefore it is suitable only for lectures from the rostrum and cannot be utilised in rousing and inspiring preaching for ordinary Christian people. On the other hand, in Molinism we see softer and milder features, a high conception of God's loving providence, His merciful will to save, His grace that seeks men, His power to comply with feeble wills, coupled with His infinite leniency. Psychologically it inclines more to unswerving trust in God, strengthens the mind in its own power of co-operation, spurs men on to great personal activity in the salvation of their souls and produces peace and gladness of heart. It is, therefore, the natural language of the preacher and the unconscious form of instruction of the catechist as he addresses a group of Christian children. It is not unnatural that one of the most lovable of the saints, Francis de Sales, was a Molinist. Both systems, irreconcilable in their fundamental principles, extending far in their practical results, and yet based alike on the common teaching of the Church, will retain their power to enlist support, making disciples in every age, and in their respective spheres continuing their work of encouragement and edification, so long as blind passion and pernicious partisanship do not maliciously disturb the cordial relationships of their representatives."

Turning from these disputes within Catholicism, it is a shock to have to state that 17th century Protestant theology did not react to the appearance of the Molinist theory with a wholly unanimous rejection. As we have seen, even within Roman Catholicism the attacking Jesuits still find at this point the opposition of two " uncompromising " principles, in spite of the fact that both are based on the common teaching of the Church. And even to-day a Thomist like Diekamp is not prepared to yield an inch on the matter. Yet even on a point like this we do not find that whole-hearted opposition to the Jesuit teaching that one would expect from a theology which derived from the Reformation (the very theology which the Jesuits were attacking when they diverged from the Dominicans, who for their part did not hesitate to oppose the Jesuits for fear of the compromising proximity of this theology). Surely Protestant theologians ought to have resisted the Jesuits with even greater determination than the Thomists. Yet it was not only the heterodox Socinian and Arminian factions but a whole powerful wing of orthodox theology in both confessions which adopted the Jesuit teaching with a few unimportant corrections and reservations, just as an interesting scientific discovery of an objective kind has to be accepted even though sometimes the discoverer happens to be a Jesuit. It seems as if no objection could be found to the intentions and implications and even the very substance of the doctrine. On the contrary, the Protestants would appear to have been glad that with its help they could say and prove something which they themselves had basically wanted to say and prove for a long time. For all their hatred of the Jesuits, they seem to have been secretly waiting to give a place of honour in Protestantism to the particular concern of the Jesuits.

It must certainly be noted first that only one wing of the older Protestant theology was involved, and in the case of the Reformed theologians this formed a numerically much weaker wing. There were not lacking Protestants who did not share this concern at all, and therefore did not have to agree with the Jesuits on this matter, but could and necessarily did radically oppose their doctrine. Whether Polanus belonged to this group it is hard to say. At the time when he composed his *Syntagma* he appears to have had no knowledge of the new discovery, although this was chronologically possible. But we can certainly count among them Gisbert Voetius, the alert Utrecht theologian, who did not hesitate to describe the doctrine of the *scientia media* as the *asylum omnium pelagianizantium*, and to state with grim humour what the occasion was beginning to reveal in the Protestant sphere : *Inventum illud Jesuitarum*—this *profana novitas et evanida speculatio, toti antiquitati, omnibus theologorum scholis incognita—novitate sua vix notum in Batavia, nedum examinatum, commodissimum Remonstrantibus nostris visum fuit muniendis insulsis et infruitis illis . . . contra gratiam Dei et praedestinationem teretismatis.* Nor did he fail to ask concerning the much vaunted consensus of Roman Catholic theology in view of such a fundamental difference within it (*Disput. theol.*, I, 1648, pp. 254 f.). The new doctrine was also definitely rejected by J. Coccejus (*S. Theol.*, 1662, *ed.* 1669, p. 147) and his pupils (e.g., F. Burmann, *Syn. Theol.*, 1678, I, pp. 118 f.) on the one side, and by the Cartesian A. Heidanus (*Corp. Theol.*, 1676, *ed.* 1686, I, pp. 122 f.) on the other. At the end of the century Petrus van Mastricht also opposed it (*Theor. Pract. Theol.*, 1698, II, 13, 20 f.), and it was basically and comprehensively resisted by the last great "orthodox" teacher of the Genevan church, F. Turrettini (*Instit. Theol. el.*, I, 1679, L. 3, *qu.* 13). The direction taken by his polemic becomes clear in the following sentences : *Scientia media tollit dominium Dei in actus liberos, quia ea stante actus voluntatis supponuntur esse antecedenter ad decretum, ideoque futuritionem non habent a Deo, sed a se; imo Deus hoc pacto videtur potius pendere a creatura, dum nihil potest decernere vel disponere, nisi posita humanae voluntatis determinatione, quam Deus in tali connectione rerum viderit* (13). *At nulla causa secunda cum Deo concurrere potest ad causandam rerum futuritionem, quia futuritio facta est ab aeterno, at causae omnes tantum sunt in tempore. Unde patet rerum futuritionem non aliunde pendere quam a Dei decreto, atque adeo non aliunde quam ex decreto praesciri posse* (23). With regard to Reformed orthodoxy it can certainly be said that the majority of its representatives recognised the danger of the Jesuit teaching and therefore wisely and staunchly refrained from any attempt to enrich their knowledge from this source. Among the arguments which these writers produced against a *scientia media* this is one which constantly recurs. Far from erecting an effecting barrier against fatalism, with its presupposition of a final freedom and partial aseity of creaturely decision this conception introduces into theology a *fatum plus quam Stoicum* (to use the phrase of van Mastricht), a necessity independent of the will of God and superior to it, an *ens aliquod independens a summo ente. Hoc est fundamentum fundamentorum, cui tota causae moles incumbit; hoc est postulatum illud, quod et nos adversariis concedere et ipso nobis probare non possunt. Hoc est centrum illud, ex quo ducuntur deformes et absurdae illae hypotheses, quibus tum philosophiam tum sacram quoque theologiam misere conspurcant doctores isti Hypothetici ;* as if God's will could be distinguished from blind force by ascribing to it an object independent of it, while all the time it was itself declared to be limited by another (and an unknown) blind force (Voetius, *loc. cit.*, p. 336). If the vehemence with which these men uttered their polemic shows that they had to reckon with opposition very near home, it is all the more remarkable to relate that this opposition did not come only from the Arminian camp, but that, with L. Crocius and H. Alsted, two outstanding representatives of what we may call Reformed orthodoxy in the narrowest sense, Gomarus and Walaeus, wholeheartedly accepted the doctrine of the *scientia media* with one or two modifications.

F. Gomarus, the famous opponent of Arminius, the doughty representative of Supralapsarianism at the Synod of Dort, stated explicitly in a disputation *De divina hominum praedestinatione* (*Opera*, 1644, Vol. III, p. 34) that there is a *praescientia conditionata: qua Deus ex infinito scientiae suae lumine quaedam futura non absolute sed certa conditione posita, novit. Praescientia haec indefinita a decreto definiente minime dependet, sed illud necessario* (*tanquam obiectum suum adiunctum*) *naturae ordine antecedit.* By this divine decree, which does not determine certain objects of the divine foreknowledge, Gomarus meant, of course, only the decree of predestination as such, which as he saw it is simply a special qualification of God's general decision and will directed to the creation, preservation and government of the world. Within this general divine plan for the world all things and events, including the free decisions of man, have their definite place and meaning. If they are thus objects of the divine foreknowledge, they are so not because of the decree of predestination but because of God's general foreordination, the *ordo naturae*, the *series rerum*. The decree of predestination, being determined by the will of God, is included in this and is in a sense only an executive determination. The divine foreknowledge is not therefore dependent on or determined by it. On the contrary, it is itself dependent on the foreknowledge and determined by it, while the foreknowledge on its side has its natural limits in God's plan for the world. It is clear, then, that Gomarus had not the slightest intention of approximating to the semi-Pelagianism of the Jesuits. On the contrary, he wanted to strengthen his rejection of it and the doctrine of the *servum arbitrium* by basing the divine sovereignty over everything on a plan for the world which precedes the whole executive will of God and even the divine foreknowledge. This plan itself is put into effect without qualifications, but as a system of conditions within which there are also free actions. We cannot call this a happy exaggeration of the Protestant position. It is dangerous playing with fire. For it is difficult to see how this conception can, in fact, be distinguished from fatalism, since in it the divine knowledge and will threaten finally to disappear behind a divine world plan, and the divine omnipotence behind the divine omnicausality. Surely this involves an imminent (and perhaps secretly effected) transformation of the idea of the divine government of the world into that of a self-constitutive and self-operative world order in which even the decree of predestination may well disappear. But if this is the case, the door can no longer be kept closed against the unfailing partner of all fatalism, the most primitive Pelagianism. It was obviously a piece of over-cleverness for this representative of the Reformed position to think that he could make capital out of its most radical and dangerous opponent in this way. He did it at the price of being compelled actually to speak of the will of God as if it were fate. At this price elements of truth can certainly be found in the Jesuit doctrine. But what profit and loss does this involve ? And what weapons remain to combat the fundamental error that lies behind this doctrine ? Why do we really want to find elements of truth here ? The question cannot be evaded : Was there not in fact a very deep and solid community of interest between the hyper-Calvinism of a Gomarus and the ultimate intentions of Molinism in spite of the fact that historically they were as different as day and night ?

Following in the footsteps of Gomarus, A. Walaeus, one of the editors of the famous Leiden *Synopsis*, acknowledged (in his *Loci comm.*, 1640, pp. 160 f.) that it was impossible to oppose the Jesuit teaching in principle, though like Gomarus he did not mention it by name. It has the value, he held, *ut immutabilitas omnium Dei decretorum possit servari et aliquo modo explicari possit, quomodo Deus per decretum suum non sit autor aut causa mali*. But the matter now seems to have been dangerously coarsened. For we read of *scientia hypothetica in Deo ante omne decretum*, and we are told expressly of an alteration of the divine *propositum* by *causae liberae*. The following syllogism is employed : *Omnis veritas est obiectum divinae praescientiae. At in conditionalibus, ex quibuscumque causis pendeant, est aliqua veritas. Ergo conditionalia illa sunt obiecta divinae praescientiae*. The *decretum hypotheticum* as such is described as " necessary." In other words, at least a part of the *veritas*, a part too of the *immutabilitas*, of the divine decrees is withdrawn from God and is ascribed to certain objects of His knowledge and will as such, to what are called " free causes " in His creation. What use was it for Walaeus subsequently to protest, with biblical citations, against the misuse that the Jesuits had made of this doctrine, as if the doctrine had not been invented for the sake of this " misuse " ? Ascribe to the freedom of the creature the truth and immutability on the basis of which it forms a factor independent of God's will, and it is too late to profess in the doctrine of grace that it is not a matter of him that wills or runs, but of God who has mercy. This can be said only if, with the Molinists, we take it to mean that it is not a matter only of him that wills or runs, but also of God who has mercy by creating the necessary conditions. And it is obviously only a matter of technical interest when Walaeus explains that the special distinction of a *scientia media* is " not necessary," since what is meant can be explained partly as *scientia necessaria* and partly as *scientia libera* : as *scientia necessaria* in the factuality in which God necessarily foresees every future possibility in its conditionality ; and as *scientia libera* in so far as the general laws according to which every future possibility becomes actuality (for example, the law that only believers in Christ will be saved) are known to God as such—the only qualification being that in the case of *exempla singularia* God's free knowledge is a knowledge conditioned by the objects and to that extent hypothetical. This technical correction of the teaching of the Molinists only shows the more clearly the reorientation which was about to take place or had already taken place. Indeed, the uncorrected Molinist doctrine has the advantage in so far as it sought to preserve at least for the *scientia necessaria* and the *scientia libera* as such the character of an unconditional divine knowledge, while in this weak Reformed imitation the whole conception of God's omniscience and foreknowledge was in danger of slipping into a knowledge of the necessity and contingency of the world which might finally be interpreted as the world's knowledge of itself or, concretely, man's knowledge of himself.

But matters were even worse in the older Lutheran theology. For in the tradition, not of Luther himself in the *De servo arbitrio*, but of the later Melanchthon, there was a direct and positive interest in the very thing which the *scientia media* signified for the doctrine of grace. It was J. Gerhard (*Loci theol.*, 1610 f., L. II, 244) who first took the *scientia media* into his theology. But he did not relate it to this matter or discuss it in any detail. Indeed, it is obvious that he had charitably misunderstood the concept. He distinguishes the *scientia necessaria* and the *scientia libera* as the knowledge which precedes and the knowledge which follows God's will, and then asserts that *scientia media praecedit quidem actum voluntatis (Dei), sed ex hypothesi illius aliquid futurum videt*. The conditioning of God's knowledge of future possibility is simply its conditioning by the divine will. It is remarkable that though Gerhard quoted the text of the Jesuit Becanus, who speaks explicitly of its being conditioned by the freedom of the creature, he did not gather that this was the meaning and only possible sense of the concept formally taken over by him, and that the sense in which he adopted it did not go beyond the conception of the *scientia libera*, so that in his own outline the *scientia media* was entirely superfluous. It is no wonder that he had no further use for it and that later—in his *Disputationes Isagogicae*—he did not return to it. But the later Lutheran theologians found what was here to be found : *Sine hac scientia (media) non poterit commode explicari electio ex praevisa fide, qua Deus ex praevisione fidei perseveraturos nos ad aeternam elegit vitam* (A. Calov, *Syst. loc. theol.*, 1655 f., II, p. 524). To be sure, Quenstedt (*Theol. did. pol.*, 1685, I, *c.* 8, sect. 2, *qu.* 7), like Walaeus, declared on logical grounds that the distinction of a special *scientia media* was " not necessary ". Yet it is obvious that in substance the dangerous intentions which are at the root of the new concept gain in him complete and triumphant recognition. He achieved a masterpiece of polemic by appearing to combat the doctrine of the Jesuits from the standpoint that it could clearly be used to establish and advance an extremely Calvinistic determinism. We have seen in the instance of Gomarus that it could in fact be employed for this purpose. Even in the case of a few of its bolder Jesuit representatives like Suarez, it pressed in this deterministic direction, from which Gomarus approached it. Yet originally and properly it had been introduced into the doctrine of God for the sake of establishing man's *liberum arbitrium*, and this was something which Quenstedt was evidently not willing or able to see for the simple reason that this was an aim not at all alien to his own mind. He rejected the *scientia media* as a special distinction, but he explained in the same breath : *Mediam et conditionatam scientiam . . . non repugnamus, dummodo appellationis ratio non sit principium Jesuiticum, Praedeterminatisticum, Calvinisticum*, and with this reservation he found in it something " sound " which must be protected against the Calvinists' denial of the *decreta conditionalia*, and especially their denial of the *electio ex praevisa fide*. The only actual correction he finally adduced was that it is

better to speak of a *scientia conditionatorum* than of a *scientia conditionata.
Conditio enim . . . non est in Deo, sed in obiectis extra Deum.* Thus the very
kernel of Jesuit doctrine here invaded Protestant theology under the standard
of specifically Lutheran orthodoxy and its traditional conflict with Rome and
Geneva. Later still, Lutheran theologians like J. W. Baier (*Comp. Theol. pos.,*
1686, I, *c.* 1, § 15), D. Hollaz (*Ex. theol. acroam.,* 1707, I, 1, *qu.* 41), and J. F.
Buddeus (*Instit. Theol. dogm.,* 1724, II, 1, § 22) gave up Quenstedt's opposition
to the Jesuit terminology. Actual opposition on the Lutheran side was from
the very outset isolated and ineffective, so that the *scientia media* became a
solid constituent of Lutheran doctrine. God's will and decision in election for
the salvation of individual men is not absolute. It is conditioned by human
faith and human perseverance. To establish this proposition of the Lutheran
doctrine of grace the theory of the *scientia media* was far too well adapted not
to be grasped. The decree of the divine will which precedes the divine knowledge
of free causes in creation, and therefore also of man's freedom (to believe or
not, to persevere in faith or not), is after all only hypothetical and not irresistibly
efficacious. Man's freedom is not governed by the divine knowledge, nor foreordained in it. It forms a factor over against it which God knows, but cannot,
or will not, or at any rate does not control.

The period which followed in the history of Protestant theology was that of
the developing Enlightenment. Its characteristic was not that it solved many
of the problems which had agitated the 17th century, but with a wry gesture
of weariness abandoned them altogether as scholastic subtleties. There is not,
therefore, a great deal more to say about the further history of the *scientia
media* in Protestant theology. We cannot really argue that the acceptance of
it by a part of orthodoxy formed the door through which the new Pelagianism
made its invasion. Certainly Pelagianism was now to enjoy a long period of
dominance in the Protestant Church and its theology. But for the most part
it was to do this in a form which gave an almost Augustinian look to Molinism
and its hedge of careful reservations, as to Roman Catholic semi-Pelagianism in
general. The most that we can say is that the acceptance of the *scientia media*
is a symptom of the fact that the door was actually wide open for Pelagianism, and for a powerful humanistic reaction to the Reformation knowledge of
God and of life, to enter the Protestant Church in the twofold form of Pietism
and Rationalism. This reaction found so much nourishment in a certain supposedly orthodox way of understanding Luther and Calvin that it was not able
at the time to achieve any consistent insight into the nature of this Jesuit discovery. It was simply classified with the scholastic sophistries once orthodoxy
had made it substantially its own as a proclamation in the doctrine of God of
the independence of the free creature. It was not really abandoned because it
was forgotten in the particular form in which it had once agitated their fathers
(and still agitates Roman Catholic theology to-day). And even when it was not
forgotten, it was not abandoned just because it was rejected with horror on
account of its scholastic form or Jesuit origin and without any closer examination.
It has happened more than once in the history of Protestantism that an element
which had a scholastic form in the Middle Ages has won a place in Protestant
doctrine. And more than once this element which seems so alien in its original
form has had to be eliminated for the survival or revival of the Reformation
Church.

But what is the point at which the resistance ought to have been offered ?
In our reply we can and must refer to the position which even in Catholicism
itself the Thomists took up and defended against the Molinists. Much would
have been gained if Protestant theology on its side had at least held to the
Thomistic position without qualification, not allowing itself to be driven back
behind the line of Augustinian teaching which was defended even in Catholicism,
and therefore forced to fight on the Jesuits' own ground. As things are, it has

19

to be admitted that the Thomists have always been more Evangelical in this matter than the wing of our orthodoxy which completely accepted the position of the Jesuits, and obviously much more Evangelical than the popular Protestant Pelagianism which followed. Our first task, then, is simply to assert for our part the decisive themes of the Thomistic doctrine. We must not fail to admit that at certain points their polemic against the Molinists is more profound and effective than that brought by the Protestant opposition. As they saw it, God does not know free human actions merely as their spectator, or even partially as their spectator. He is absolutely the One who has willed and effected their occurrence. His knowledge is no mere contemplation. It is this, but it is also a foundation and actualisation. God's knowledge, will and action cannot be divided. What God knows He also wills, and what He wills He also does. Consequently God knows free creaturely actions too with eternal, objective truth. For eternal objective truth cannot be ascribed to the actions in themselves any more than it can to other things. God knows them in the same way as everything else. Like all other created things they are the objects of His knowledge both as what they are and in the way in which they are. They have an objectivity and truth which is relative rather than absolute, dependent not independent, temporal rather than eternal; and this they owe to God as the Creator and Lord of all being and all occurrence. The Thomists are right when they establish against the Molinists the fact that the doctrine of creaturely freedom as a limitation of God's omnicausality and omnipotence, and therefore a denial of His sovereignty, involves an attack on His deity and makes prayer, if not impossible, at least superfluous. Obviously this criticism is true also against the *praescientia conditionata* of Gomarus and the *praescientia conditionatorum* of Quenstedt, and one could wish that the Protestant opponents of the *scientia media* as well had shown more energy than they did in making use of this conclusive and truly theological argument. However highly one may value their courageous opposition, it cannot be denied that all of them from Voetius to Turrettini handled the matter too much as a problem of logic and metaphysics, and so far as I see did not, for example, appreciate at all its significance for the question of prayer. But the Thomists made a further true and important contribution in their answer to the question of the responsibility of the free acts of the creatures as actually governed by the knowledge and will of God. There can, they said, be no question of the abolition of this responsibility even in these circumstances —indeed especially in these circumstances. For the creaturely will based on and governed by God's knowledge and will is a real will and therefore free and responsible in itself. And although the occurrence of sin as such has its ground in God's permission and therefore in God's knowledge and will, this is in such a way that sin does not take place on account of creation and therefore of a capacity in the creature, but purely by the rebellion and guilt of the creature. Sin belongs to the sphere which God knows as the sphere of nonbeing and wills as the sphere of what He has not willed. In this sphere the sinner has neither excuse nor possibility of restitution. Yet for all that he is still in the hands of the merciful and righteous God. As we recall what the Thomists said in this respect, we cannot suppress a second wish that in the Protestant polemic against the *scientia media* as well more attention had been given to this question and also to the justifiable aspects of the concern represented by the Jesuit theory. All this must be penitently acknowledged on our side, with a confessional penitence in which we admit that at this point the Protestant doctrine of grace was better defended in Roman Catholic theology than by our own orthodox—to say nothing of the others or of those who came later.

The question must now be raised whether it is really an accident that the conflict about the *scientia media* has never been decided and does not seem likely to be decided in Roman Catholic theology. Why is it possible for Roman Catholic theology to fluctuate so easily and obviously indefinitely between thesis

and antithesis, affirmation and denial, on this matter ?   Why can Roman Catholics
speak of " two irreconcilable principles " and yet say that they are both based
on the " common teaching of the Church " and prophesy that they will both
" retain their power to enlist support, making disciples in every age, and in
their respective spheres continuing their work of encouragement and edification,"
so that the last word can and must be a mild warning against " malicious disturbance " by " blind passion and pernicious partisanship " ?   What is it that
may not and must not be disturbed, and obviously never will be disturbed even
by a dispassionate and impartial decision ?   When the last word is really a
recommendation to this kind of inexplicable but highly desirable peace, it is
usually justifiable to ask the question whether those involved in the conflict
have not in the last resort a common basis of error.   On this basis they can and
must certainly dispute, but no genuine decision is to be expected.   Therefore
on this basis they cannot dispute with final seriousness or with the prospect of
truth triumphing, so that in the last resort they can be counselled only to mutual
forbearance.

Of course, we on the Protestant side have to be very cautious when we raise
this question of the conflict between the Thomists and the Molinists and try
to make it a matter for reproach.   The reason for this is that in our own camp
we too have a conflict which at the moment we cannot see being overcome.   To
this day it has had the character of a conflict between two " irreconcilable principles".   Yet we do not want to regard it as something which divides the Church
and in our treatment of it we have to advise and observe a certain mutual tolerance and respect without attempting to efface or suppress the conflict.   I am
referring to the antagonism between Lutheran and Reformed theology which
emerges at certain points in Christology and the doctrine of the Lord's Supper,
and is also not without significance, and sometimes of great practical effect, in
a whole series of other questions.   In view of this beam in our own eye we must
be careful not to launch too easily into the criticism that this inner and as yet
unresolved conflict in Roman Catholicism proves that it is in the grip of an error
that embraces both parties.   " Whatsoever ye would that men should do to
you. . . ."   On the other hand, it must be said that we neither may nor can
treat the antagonism in our own camp in any sense as one in whose existence
we can acquiesce or in face of which tolerance must be the last word.   We must
certainly regard this controversy in Protestantism as an opposition of two
schools in the one Church.   But for that reason we must hold firm to the expectation that when both sides have listened and learned sufficiently, the meaning and purpose of the whole conflict will prove to be, not a common error
embraced by both sides, but an ultimate error on the one side and therefore the
untenability of its opposition to the other.   The conflict will thus end with a
decision, with the victory of truth, and the side convicted of error will have no
justification for continued life, because it will have no inward force.   In the same
way, we have both the right and the duty to maintain in regard to the conflict
in Roman Catholicism that if Roman Catholic theology does not cease seeking
the truth, it cannot acquiesce in the juxtaposition of an affirmation and its
denial, or claim a lasting character for the armistice so finely proclaimed.   If it
still seeks truth, the expectation must not be given up on the Thomist side
that one day (when at last all the arguments and counter-arguments have been
heard and compared and applied) it will be clear that the Molinists have been
wrong, that their counter-position is untenable, and that Jesuitism has no vital
force in Catholic theology, and therefore no justification for continued life.   As
they wait and prepare for this conclusion the Thomists must state their opposition to Molinism in such a way that it is attacked and removed at its root.   But
if, with these considerations, we try to put ourselves really on a level with Roman
Catholic theology, and pass the same judgment on the form of their inner controversy as on our own, in so doing we must at once admit that we are demanding

from the tendency in Roman Catholic theology which we feel we would ourselves naturally espouse if we were Roman Catholics something which it cannot possibly accomplish as long as it is and remains a tendency of Roman Catholic theology.

For what would it mean if the Thomists were to take their rejection of the *scientia media* to such a length that the Jesuit theory were not merely attacked but actually excluded, and the conflict reached a decision, and one in which there was a clear affirmation of the sovereignty of the divine knowledge in relation to all objects distinct from it ? It would mean nothing less than that the distinction and relationship between God and the creature (including that of the divine knowledge and all its non-divine objects) would be so stated theologically that this distinction and relationship would exclude in principle the affirmation of an autonomy of the creature in the sense of a capacity to impose conditions on God. The relation between the divine and the non-divine spheres could not then in any sense be viewed or conceived in such a way that their juxtaposition may even momentarily appear to be the neutral relationship of an A with a B, or that theoretically at least it may sometimes be viewed and conceived equally well in the direction B–A as in that A–B. In the comparison of the two spheres their utter incomparability would have to have and always to retain and recapture absolutely a present and actual significance. There could never emerge the picture of a system in which the creature has its place in the same way as God. God and the creature could never be thought of together under any other concept than in the name of Jesus Christ. Though God could compete and co-operate with the creature—if He did not do this He would not be its Creator—there could not be even the remotest possibility of the creature competing and co-operating with God. Logically the second possibility cannot be excluded if the first is said of any other A in relation to any other B. Whoever competes and co-operates also experiences competition and co-operation. What conditions is also conditioned. But this natural logical conclusion is necessarily ruled out in this case. For the distinction between God and the creature and the relation between them must always be understood in principle in such a way that the inversion is not possible under any circumstances. The reason is this. God is God and the creature is creature. In this unique and incomparable relationship—because it is this—there can only be God's competition and co-operation with the creature, but not the reverse. An inversion would compromise and abrogate the very presupposition of the relationship : the character of God as God, and of the creature as creature, and of the distinction and relationship between them. In that case the relationship under consideration would not be that between God and the creature, but a very different one. The Jesuits have achieved this inversion with their assumption of a freedom in the creature which conditions the divine omniscience and foreknowledge. They have given the creature an autonomy which enables him to constitute a riddle for the divine knowledge. The solution of this riddle is his own concern and not God's, and God can read it only as this solution is given by the creature. The Thomists are right to regard and reject the adoption of this view as blasphemous. The creature which conditions God is no longer God's creature, and the God who is conditioned by the creature is no longer God. (While it is an open question whether this leads to dualism or pantheism, there is no doubt that if we start from this point we will constantly lose sight of both the reality of God and the reality of the creature.) We must be glad that in Catholicism itself a resistance so strong and wise was offered—stronger and wiser than anything achieved by our Protestant orthodoxy. Yet the question remains whether this opposition springs from such an appreciation of the total distinction and relationship between God and the creature that it could really be carried through successfully, not merely offering an impressive resistance to the view adopted by the Jesuits, but basically excluding it. There is no reason to doubt the determination of the Thomists to resist, or the carefulness and consistency of their resistance. The only question is whether it springs from a source which is adequate not only for resistance but also for the achievement of victory. The answer is in the negative. The Thomists will not join in this inversion in the interests of the creature. As the whole affair makes clear, they are effectively hindered and actually prevented from doing this by their medieval master, by Augustine and perhaps also by the Bible. Yet it is not really possible to say that they were or are prevented by a fundamental necessity. For the Thomist conception of the relation of God and the creature also offers the picture of a system, of the relationship of two quantities which in the last resort are comparable and can be grouped together under one concept. God's infinite superiority and the infinite subordination of the creature are beautifully set out and secured in this system. Yet in this remarkable relationship the two quantities are embraced in the common concept of being. This is filled out by God in a divine manner and by the creature in a creaturely one, but at the same time it is described as the substance of both and therefore as a substance common to both. In this fundamental standpoint, which has priority over all the others, Thomist and Molinist are unfortunately one. On their own ground they strive for the unconditional primacy of the being of God. But how can they really and conclusively contend for it on this ground? On this ground is it not possible and even perhaps necessary, not to attack this primacy (the Molinists themselves did not wish to do this), but to interpret it in such a way that the distinctness of creaturely being will become its autonomy in relation to God, thus limiting the perfection of the divine knowledge by opposing to it, in the form of creaturely freedom, that final riddle which only the creature itself can solve? Is this remnant of creaturely independence not so modest that you can say in its defence that the primacy and sovereignty of God cannot be seriously threatened by it? Do we not have to speak of a remnant of this kind if we are to keep to the position that the creature participates with God in being, and that its being, however utterly dependent, is real being? On this common ground is it not possible and even necessary to raise this question? And, raised on this ground, has it been satisfactorily taken into consideration and answered by the Thomists? On this ground can the concern of the Jesuits be refused both ultimate legitimacy and also—if the Thomists have not quite done it justice—practical vindication? If God and the creature are both really within a system of being superior to both, the occasional inversion of the concept A–B into that of B–A is not to be rejected absolutely or *a limine*. The same is true of the idea of a competition and co-operation on the part of the creature in relation to God. It is difficult to see how far this conception is to be ruled out by the distinction between the infinitude of the one and the finitude of the other. On the contrary, where there is this distinction and therefore this relationship, this inversion is necessary, in its own place, for a complete estimation of what is involved, and it must be admitted that in its own way the finite is just as much the limit of the infinite as is the infinite in its way of the finite. And where it is a matter of this distinction and this relationship, it necessarily seems legitimate and even desirable that overemphasis on the one side should be met by reaction in favour of the other. Theology will thus be healthy if it oscillates as equally as possible between the two sides, and when its health is threatened the easiest cure will be to make a special effort in the direction that has at the time been neglected. Therefore it cannot possibly be the task of a wise teaching office in the Church to come to a decision. On the contrary, it must prevent one, since a decision would only serve error. Instead it must take care that there is preserved at bottom a *complexio oppositorum*, a desirable oscillation between the two extremes. In other words this ground means that there can be no question of a victory either for Molinism or for Thomism. This is ruled out by the wisdom of the principle that lies at the basis of all Catholic theology. And the teaching office of the Church has shown itself, and will no doubt

continue to show itself, the true defender of this principle by an attitude of inde-
cision, and indeed of opposition to decision.

But this particular controversy belongs to post-Reformation Catholicism.
The Church had been severely shaken. And doctrinally the shaking had come
from the Thomistic side. For the sake of equilibrium, and its own existence,
the Church needed a reaction to the opposite side. It was the Jesuits who
achieved this reaction—adopting in some respects the tradition of the later
Scotists whose position had been directly attacked by the Reformation. The
Jesuits were the special representatives of the opposition which had become
so necessary in the history of the Church. In this situation there was automatically a prejudice against any movement to the other side. For however
well-meant and justified it might be generally in the framework of the whole,
it could lend support to Protestantism. It is of a piece with this that even
the father of the Dominican school, Aquinas himself, to whom the older Protestants often used to appeal, was not exactly discredited, but was for many
years forced into the background with a certain distaste, until in the 19th century
it became necessary for quite different reasons, in the fight against modern
philosophy, seriously and definitely to reach back to him again, as Leo XIII
did in the encyclical *Aeterni patris* (1879). This is really the first time that a
balance was again reached officially between the two conflicting tendencies in
the Catholic Church. But that is as far as it went. As a balanced philosophy
and theology Thomism was then actually declared to be the standard Catholic
method for all Catholic schools, expressly including the Jesuits. Thus the Thomist
opponents of the Jesuits were certainly strengthened. They could hold their
position with a perfectly good conscience. But the Jesuits for their part were
now recognised as Thomists. Their teaching was accepted as a legitimate interpretation of Thomas, a possible nuance and tendency on a common basis. We
cannot pursue the question of the historical correctness of this decision (in
favour of non-decision). What is certain is that by it both tendencies, and
therefore the Thomist too, were robbed of the possibility of representing their
individual position in such a way as to exclude the opposing one. In fact the
position of the Jesuits has necessarily had the advantage, both before and after,
because in the fight against Protestantism it could and can give the sharpest
expression to the general aim of Catholic theology. It has always been impossible to be a representative of the Thomist hypothesis without continually revealing willy nilly that the door is very slightly open to Protestantism. The
Thomists are obviously hindered by this fact from trying to establish and carry
through their theory too radically.

And now we must go a step farther. Let us assume, as we must assume,
that J. Pohle is right. On Roman Catholic grounds the final word is neutrality,
the *complexio oppositorum* (and therefore, in terms of ecclesiastical policy, toleration, a concordat between the two tendencies). This concordat has to be observed
because in the system of being equal justice has to be done to both God and
the creature in their different ways. Let us assume that this is the ground of
Roman Catholicism itself and as such. How else can we interpret this basic view
itself as such except as a confirmation and application of the very freedom which
in the *scientia media* controversy the Jesuits always wished to ascribe and preserve
to the creature ? For what else is the establishing of such a system embracing
God and the creature, the attempt to see and correlate them on the one level, but
the kind of act in which the creature arrogates to itself the ability to control itself
and therefore God, to apprehend itself in such a way that *eo ipso* God is also
apprehended and comprehended with it ? What else can it be if it is not the
act of a will that holds itself to be free, a would-be *liberum arbitrium* ? But this
act is the ground, the basic view of the whole Roman Catholic system in all
its details. This act is the basic act of its doctrines of grace, of the sacraments,
of the Church, of Scripture and tradition, of the Roman primacy and the infalli-

bility of the Pope, and above all of its Marian doctrine. On this ground there is room for movement. The sovereignty of God can later be had in great honour —so great indeed that a dissipated Protestantism has good reason to be deeply ashamed before it. On this ground Thomism is always possible and even desirable as a corrective. But on this ground the Jesuits will always have the advantage because quite apart from the historical necessity of their function they have a better understanding of the inmost nature of the basis than the Thomists, even perhaps than St. Thomas himself. For their position and their theory is congenial and adapted to the nature of this basis at the deepest level. They are what we might call its true children. If it had been otherwise, it would have been enough for the Reformers to choose to emerge and work as a strengthening Augustinian tendency in the Catholic system, and conversely they would necessarily have been greeted and accepted by the representatives of the Augustinian system as the bearers of a legitimate corrective. Or at least all those in the Catholic Church who were Augustinian in outlook would necessarily have heard the call to reformation and recognised the legitimate continuation of the *una sancta* in the Protestant Church. None of these things happened. The Reformers were not able to see any place for their insight on the platform of the Roman Church, and this place was explicitly refused and denied them. Dominicans and Jesuits combined as their most conscious and implacable opponents. This all confirms the fact that the common ground of Roman Catholicism as such, the *complexio oppositorum*, itself involves an affirmation of the Molinist tendency which cannot afterwards be set aside by any qualifying denial. The Jesuits can and must be " Thomistic," at least since 1870, because the Thomists for their part were and are utterly " Jesuit," and can outline and present their counter-theory only in the framework of the Molinist theory which obtained long before Molina. The experimental demand we made on them is, therefore, quite impossible of achievement. They cannot radicalise their theory in such a way that Molinism is completely rejected. For if they do, they will no longer stand on Roman Catholic ground as such. They can do it only if they become Protestant, and Reformed at that. The door that is open an inch would then be wide open.

For an effective denial of Molinism is possible only when we cease to think in a God-creature system, in the framework of the *analogia entis*. It is possible only when theology dares to be theology and not ontology, and the question of a freedom of the creature which creates conditions for God can no longer arise. But this can happen only when theology is orientated on God's revelation and therefore Christology. It has to be determined to think and teach about the relation between God and the creature only in the way prescribed by the fact of the assumption of the flesh by the divine Word in the person of Jesus Christ and the consequent assumption of sinful man to be the child of God. Where this is the case, there is no question of speaking of a being that embraces both parties, or creation's grasping at itself and therefore at God. There can be no dream of a freedom that belongs to the creature in face of God. It will necessarily be seen that the decision about the existence and nature of the relation between God and the creature lies exclusively with God, as does the validity and continuity of this decision. God competes and co-operates with the creature in Jesus Christ. But in Him there cannot be any competition and co-operation of the creature with God. For a theology orientated on God there can be no question of the inversion made by the Jesuits. Everything depends, of course, on whether or not there is this orientation. Only if it begins with the knowledge of Jesus Christ can theology so think and speak that the divine and the creaturely spheres are automatically distinguished and related in a way that makes wholly impossible the replacement of the order A–B by the order B–A. It must be wholly and from the very first, and not merely occasionally or subsequently, a theology of revelation and grace, a christological theology, if it is to speak at this point conclusively and effectively. If it is not this, or not this absolutely, then the protest against the inversion will come too late and can never be effective. It will be forced to admit that within the *complexio oppositorum* the counter-theory is always possible. Indeed, if it is to speak in wider terms it will somehow have to fit the counter-theory in with its own position. If it does not do this, but maintains its protest, it will necessarily cut the respectable but rather narrow-minded figure which emerges from the theology of Diekamp as compared with that of Pohle. Yet with all its narrowmindedness it still cannot reach a decision, and all its goodwill will not enable it to utter a really conclusive word. This is the tragedy of the efforts of the Thomists in the Catholic camp. They want to say what is true, but they cannot do so finally and definitely because they are the victims of the same erroneous presupposition as their opponents. We cannot refuse the Thomists our sincere sympathy. But we must also admit that we do not know how to advise them because we are fully aware that the only advice that we can give them is not practicable for them as Romanist, and even, we may say, as Thomistic theologians. For the school of Thomas has done far more than its opponents to consolidate the basis it has in common with the Jesuits, the great error of the *analogia entis* as the basic pattern of Catholic thinking and teaching. The most secure basis for this pattern is the work of Thomas Aquinas himself, so that every step a Thomist takes, even if it seems to take him far from the Jesuit counter-thesis, really serves implicitly to justify this counter-theory in advance. Those who practise theology as ontology have not merely to admit the doctrine of the freedom of the creature. Willy-nilly they must themselves espouse it even if it means omitting some of the radical conclusions of their protest. They affirm this doctrine when they undertake to practise theology as ontology. And it is not only Catholic theology in general which stands or falls with this undertaking, but Thomism in particular.

Once we have grasped this point, we are in a position to understand how the doctrine of the *scientia media* was able to invade Protestant theology. It is quite simply that from about 1600 theology was again beginning to be understood and pursued more and more obviously as ontology on the Protestant side as well. We have constantly come up against this phenomenon in the doctrine of God. The theology of the Reformers had made a great initial step towards a thinking dominated by the view of the person and work of Christ. But instead of being followed up more energetically, their lead was ignored. Revelation, grace and justification were understood as the predicates of a *summum ens*, and the creaturely *ens* could be thought of as belonging to the same sphere as this *ens*. With this view as a basis it was inevitable that the problem raised by the Jesuits should be recognised as legitimate and their solution greeted as a helpful one. It must be admitted that the wing of Protestant orthodoxy which yielded here had, unfortunately, consistency on its side. And on the Protestant side there was no compensating basic principle, and no teaching office of the Church to safeguard its authority and enforce its observance, and thus to prevent the headlong fall into all kinds of popular Pelagianism. The danger of Jesuitism, the humanising and secularising of the Church, was for this reason much more acute, and there was much more unrestrained and gross and flagrant sin in this direction, than in Roman Catholicism itself. It is only too easy to understand how in modern Protestantism there constantly arises a homesickness or a longing for the peace and security of the Roman Catholic *complexio oppositorum*. But it is here that we have the greatest delusion. A return to Rome and to Thomas means a return to a place where all kinds of inner and outer precautions and correctives against certain dangerous consequences of Jesuitism may have developed and operated, but where these consequences themselves are always a possibility and a threat. For the root has not been attacked. Indeed, the error which in the last resort these consequences necessarily reveal is native to this place and hallowed in it. It is, in fact, the principle underlying this so-called peace and its security. There is no doubt that 17th century Protestant theology did adopt to a considerable extent the basis of Catholic thought about God and the creature, in spite of all its anti-Roman polemics. That is why it was radically exposed to the Jesuit doctrine. It did in fact accept it to a considerable extent. It actually lapsed into certain conclusions against which there appears to be both external and internal protection in Roman Catholicism. But Protestant theology has always a decided advantage over Roman Catholic owing to what might seem to be its disadvantage, its lack of a compensating principle and a teaching office to watch over it. It derives from sources where there is at least a disposition not merely to heal the evil, but to set it aside; not to meet error merely by a dialectical balancing of its false conclusions, but by cutting it away. Recollection of its original sources means that in contrast with Roman Catholic theology Protestant theology has a door open to freedom. It is not bound either in principle or by an office of the Church to what happened to it from the beginning of the 17th century. It can recover from the apostasy which began at that time. It is free; free in relation to its own tradition and history. And more than that, it is sooner or later thrown back on its original source by virtue of the Scripture principle set up at that time and never completely abandoned or rendered inoperative. Its freedom is the freedom to glorify the grace of God in the way prescribed for it in the witness of Holy Scripture in relation to the person and work of Jesus Christ. Its freedom is therefore the true and genuine freedom not only to combat the error in regard to the independence of the creature over against God, but to exclude it. By nature it is not merely an anti-Jesuit but a non-Jesuit theology. It has to be untrue to itself to be able either then or later to turn in this direction. It has only to be true to itself to put itself in a position which excludes the Jesuit theory. For in its true position there cannot exist in any form the dialectic or the *sic et non* within which alone the Jesuit theory can and must flourish. Roman Catholic theology is of a different nature. It is dialectic at heart, and so it cannot exclude Jesuitism. Even in its most sincere attempts to combat it, it can only uphold it. ·

Thus our own opposition to the doctrine of the *scientia media* must have as its starting-point the simple recognition that the relation between God and the creature is grace, a free act of the divine mercy. This is true generally, and it is therefore true of the relation between His omnipotent knowledge and the free creaturely actions. There are, then, genuine and proper objects of the divine knowledge. For this grace is reality. There are objects distinct from God Himself and to that extent at least independent. They actually include in its own way the free creaturely will and all its choice and decision. But it is from God alone that this is what it is. And it can never be anything different. It cannot therefore be anything, or in any way, which would enable it to lay down conditions for God or to be a riddle for Him. God does not destroy it by knowing it omnipotently, i.e., by knowing it as God, as its Creator and Lord. But God is not under any obligation to it. He is not conditioned by it, nor is it a mystery to Him, because He permits it to be what it is by Him and before Him. That God chooses to know it, and knows it, and competes and co-operates with it, is grace, the sovereign decision of God. In its relation to God it exists simply in virtue of the fact that God establishes and maintains this relationship, and therefore simply by the grace of God. This alone is the way in which the creature exists in its oneness with God in the person and work of Jesus Christ. With this in view we must avoid any kind of speculation with regard to God and the creature. It is here that we must learn what the Creator and the creature are in their relationship. We have to understand our own free will by faith in God's grace revealed to us in Jesus Christ, and therefore to understand its freedom as freedom by grace, under grace, and for grace. If we do this, there can be no room for the thought, or even a possibility of the thought, that our will on its side is not completely and omnipotently perceived and therefore foreordained by God in all the possibilities of its choice. Nor can there be any room for the idea of a possibility given us with this freedom to assert ourselves in relation to God. And of course there is no place either for the notion that the freedom of our wills is destroyed by this foreordination, or that our choice is not responsible choice, or that our evil choice is thereby excused. We are foreordained and perceived by God in our genuine human self-determination. That it is under divine foreordination does not alter the fact that it is genuine human self-determination. On the other hand, that it is genuine human self-determination does not alter the fact that it is completely under God's foreordination and does not in any way include a foreordination of God by men. What source is there to give strength and meaning to an inversion of this kind ? How can our self-determination be a foreordaining of God when we exist in God's sight only by grace, and we cannot be gracious to God in return but only thankful ? And how can the impossibility of this inversion, the one-sidedness, the fact that God conditions us but we do not have to condition Him, lead to the despair, defiance and recklessness which presume to say that justice is done to God's claim on the creature and the creature's own dignity only if we can lay down conditions for God and propound Him a riddle ? Is it not rather a defence of human freedom and responsibility, which tries to secure this possibility for man, that inevitably leads to the despair and defiance and recklessness which it is ostensibly seeking to avoid ? If we are really to avoid it, we must give up this kind of defence. To be thankful of our own free will it is necessary that we should have unconditionally acknowledged the divine foreordination of our free will. It is in this acknowledgment that gratitude to God consists. Our only intention is not to be really and fully thankful if we do not acknowledge the divine foreordination ; if we try to exclude our self-determination from it by keeping back some remnant and securing it against it ; if we make it, as it were, a condition of our obedience that we must be assured that we can lay down conditions for God by our obedience or its opposite. Thus the only source of the assertion of the freedom of our will over against God is a suspension of the right use of this freedom. Its proper use consists in our being thankful to God, not only for this or that but for ourselves, and therefore for God's fore-ordination which governs our self-determination. If we want to play off our self-determination against His foreordination and assert it, this simply means a despair that is self-chosen, a defiance that is superfluous, and a recklessness that is out of place. The doctrine of the autonomy of the free creature over against God is simply the theological form of human enmity against God's grace, the theological actualisation of a repetition of the fall. Where grace is not extolled, there can only be sin. There is no third possibility. But the doctrine of the *scientia media* is not an extolling of grace. It will not deny it, but it hedges it round with so many reservations and limitations that it is only too clear that there is in it no love for grace as grace. And because there is no love, there is hatred of it. This doctrine is a unique expression of the fear of God's omnipotent knowledge. It is the theological form of a desire for a God who certainly appears to know everything, but does not will everything which He knows, and so does not really know everything. It is the desire for a God who is not wholly God and so is not God at all. It should not be forgotten that Jesuitism is the Roman Catholic form of modern Humanism. It is deeply involved in an undertaking which from the very start savours of a denial of God, and in which, as we can clearly see to-day, humanity itself is very largely set aside. When this has once been recognised objectively and historically, there is adequate protection against it. It is therefore our task to declare plainly, with an emphasis and in a sense that are never possible in Roman Catholic theology, that we can have no use at all for the *scientia media*. The fact that the divine knowledge of the free decisions of the creature is real knowledge of a real object is a clear statement which can only be obscured through the Jesuit elucidation that it is a limited knowledge in relation to this object.

As a parallel to the foregoing discussion, we have now to speak of the genuineness and reality of the divine will, of its character as a true will. Will this compromise the fact that it is an all-embracing and free will, the living act in which He affirms and posits Himself and everything that is? Is the One who is conceived of in this living act to be thought of as One who wills, and not merely as One who works omnipotently, positing and maintaining Himself, and through Himself all that is, without a decision or a goal, and therefore arbitrarily and without a will? Everything that we have said so far has prepared us for the fact that this cannot possibly be the case. But in this respect, too, we have now to make explicit the recognition of the spirituality and personality of this One who acts in omnipotence and omnipresence. God's will is in all things as His eternal living act, and it is wholly and utterly free in itself. In this it is true and genuine and proper will.

The question is posed at this point too by God's omnipotence, and the answer is given by a right understanding of God's omnipotence. How can an omnipotent will really be a will, a purpose, the setting of a goal, a resolve? For everything which can be the object of this willing and will already exists in the realm of its power, indeed of its omnipotence. Therefore it does not first have to be willed by it, indeed it cannot first be willed by it; just as it is far too much the master of itself to have first to will itself or to be able to do so.

It is obvious, however, that if we try to raise this as a serious objection we are again confusing God's omnipotence with blind power in itself, with lifeless force. We are again overlooking the fact that God's omnipotence does not merge into His omnicausality. We are speaking of God as One who is the prisoner of His own power, and therefore not at all of the divine omnipotence. The divine omnipotence is God Himself as the One who is and has power. It is His power, the power at His disposal and used by Him, because it belongs to Him. It is His before and beyond all the use He makes of it in His omnicausality. It is His power to be God and therefore Lord over everything else. We cannot go back behind this differentiation if our thinking and speaking remain bound to this object, the divine omnipotence, and if we are not to begin speculating in empty space about omnipotent being as such. It is precisely when we know the deepest depths of the divine being that we do not go back behind this differentiation but have to respect the divine being in this differentiation. Just as this differentiation rejects and hinders the absorption of the concept of the divine knowledge by that of the divine omnipotence, it rejects and hinders the absorption of the divine will. Everything depends, of course, on whether our thinking and speaking remain bound to this object because they are continually directed to the place where this has dealt with us as divine omnipotence in such a way that it can no longer be alien to us, that we are forced to

recognise it as what it is, that we may not and cannot any more mis-
understand it.   The divine omnipotence itself is a real hindrance which
necessarily makes the confusions we have mentioned impossible.
Without this it is hard to see why we should remain bound to that
object, or how the differentiation can be not only illuminating but
compulsory.   Without it, it is hard to see how the absorption of the
concept of the divine will by that of His omnipotence can come up
against a real barrier in our thinking and speaking.   Our thinking
and speaking do not really have of themselves the power to keep
true to this object, or even in the first instance to grasp it.   But the
place where this object itself lays hold of our thinking and speaking
and compels them to be true to it is our reconciliation with God as
accomplished by God Himself.   This is our starting-point if we are
to think and speak correctly about the divine omnipotence.   But in
it we have also attained to the proposition that " God wills."   For
in it God's will meets us as omnipotent will, as a free and irresistibly
and finally compelling power confronting our own will, as a decisive
determination not of this or that but of ourselves, as our own determination to obedience to it.   What other source can we have for our
knowledge of what divine omnipotence is than the one at which we
ourselves cannot in any sense be spectators or observers of it, but
where it concerns us and engages us and deals with us as it alone can ?
But at this point it confronts us definitely as will, not as blind force,
or with the dead weight of a falling stone, or as the sum of all causality
or activity.   It meets us as a decision that stands out conspicuously
from every other activity or causality, interrupting, surpassing and
controlling the course of all normal occurrences.   It meets us as an
occurrence that does not take place by the ordinary, but by a special
necessity, specially decided and therefore weighed and willed.   It
does not meet us only as an event, but as an action.   How can we
fully appreciate the undeserved nature, the grace of reconciliation
without also appreciating the freedom of this omnipotent event ?
If our thinking and speaking are directed to this place, the whole
weight of the omnipotence of the event forbids them to capitulate
to their own dialectic and therefore seek the deep things of God at
a point beyond the differentiation which tells us that God is omnipotent and not that this or that omnipotence is God.   If our mind
is directed to this place we will recognise as the final depth of the
being of God only the fact that He, God, is omnipotent.   " I am the
Lord thy God."   God takes us up into fellowship with Himself with
this " I " and this " thy."   He binds Himself to us and us to Himself
without any deserts on our part, quite contrary to our deserts, out of
sheer mercy.   That He does this settles the question that it is not contrary to His omnipotence but in harmony with it for it to be purpose,
the setting of a goal, a resolve and therefore will.   God is not compelled to do what He does.   Nor is He forced to any of the apparent

consequences of His action. On the contrary, He does what He does because He wills it. And when He does it again, again it is because He wills it. And every consequence of His action is again necessary only because it rests on His will and only to the extent that it does so. He is under no obligation to us to lift us up to fellowship with Himself because we are His creatures and He our Creator. On the contrary, even as He does this it is plain that He is not under any obligation to us to do it. Indeed we cannot even deny that He is under no obligation to do the first thing of all for us, to give us existence at all, to be our Creator and let us be His creatures. This, too, is completely the act of His will. His act of reconciliation prevents any counter-question about a necessity other than that which rests on His will. It completely cuts away the counter-question about our own existence and about the existence of God. It means that we see here the omnipotent will of God simply deciding our own existence as well as His. The inescapable conclusion to be drawn from this is that it is pure sophistry to object that, if God is pure omnipotence, in the last resort He can be only power and not omnipotent will. It points no less conclusively and cogently to the necessity of the differentiation of which we have spoken and therefore to the recognition of the will of God. There is no place where we can relativise or remove this differentiation and therefore suppress the recognition of God's will. Only the unreconciled man can try to take up a position of this kind, giving rein to the dialectic of his human thinking and speaking, trying to devise and produce a " supreme being " in the form of active omnipotence without a will, conceiving himself without the will of God directed towards him and therefore questioning the reality of that will. But what has this unreconciled man, his thinking and speaking, his " supreme being," to do with God ? And therefore what has his chattering to do with our theme, the divine omnipotence ? It is in the reconciliation accomplished by God that the decision is made what this is—and the decision is that it is the omnipotence of the divine will. If, then, our statement that " God wills " is simply our response to the omnipotent divine act of reconciliation it is definitely protected against the suspicion that it can be meant and understood only figuratively. For thought and spoken as this response, it makes the distinction that God is omnipotent in such a way that He uses the power that He is and has as He Himself pleases and disposes. The statement characterises the act of the divine omnipotence as a spiritual, personal act. Where there is a will and not merely an event running its necessary course, there is also one who wills and the so-called event is his decision and action. In this case, of course, it is an all-embracing and free action, since the One who acts is God Himself. And it is an action which is not distinct from the divine nature itself. But it must still be said that that which is all-embracing and completely free in God, the divine nature itself, is active will or willed action. To try to rob Him of this character is no less to deny His deity than to try to dispute His character as omnipotence, and indeed it is *ipso facto* to rob Him of His character of omnipotence as well. For if God does not really will and act, how can He really be omnipotent? Or how can His being be an all-embracing and utterly free being?

God wills in a genuine and proper sense because He is what He is and therefore omnipotent in this differentiation. That this is the case is confirmed when we consider the other distinctions without which we cannot correctly describe the all-embracing and free nature of His will. There is, for example, the distinction between His willing of Himself and His willing of the possibility and reality of His creation as distinct from Himself. There is the distinction between the real and the possible and the impossible, between being and non-being in the realm of His creation, among the objects of His will. There is the distinction of this whole realm from that which has no being of any kind, which is absolutely nothing before Him and therefore in every sense. We have seen that these distinctions do not rest in the nature of things. We referred them in the first instance to the omnipotent knowledge of God, which is not only the standard of all that is true, but its source and therefore the source of these distinctions. And in these necessary distinctions we also found a confirmation of the character of the divine omnipotence as knowledge. But these distinctions are equally based on the will of God. This is inevitable, since we have to understand His knowledge as an omnipotent, creative, productive knowledge, the eternal knowledge of the divine decrees. What God knows He wills, and what He wills He knows. And so all these distinctions are also distinctions of His will. He is not conditioned in any of these spheres, but He Himself conditions. And He does not do this uniformly or everywhere in one and the same sense. He lays down different conditions for Himself and the world, for the possible and the actual and the impossible, for being and non-being, for good and evil, for nature and history, for His creation and everything that exists and occurs in it, whether affirmed or denied by Him, and the nothingness which is nothingness only by His will. If His conditioning were uniform, how could it be recognised as His or in the last resort distinguished from a conditionality imposed on Him? But the distinct forms of His conditioning confirm the fact that what occurs does not occur by an inner compulsion, but is a totality of willed action and grounded in the active will of God.

At this point, too, the older theology worked with a series of distinctions which are justified in so far as they show that God's will is both omnipotent and at the same time true and genuine will. We have already met with these (p. 519 f.) at the point where we found it necessary to understand God's constant being as the being of the living God, the unity of His being and His decree. We quote them again—with the necessary reservations and criticisms—in the somewhat altered form in which they were presented when interest was particularly focused on the characteristics of the divine will in its relation to the divine omnipotence.

In this connexion a distinction was drawn (1) between God's *voluntas naturalis* or *necessaria: qua vult, quod non potest non velle*, and God's *voluntas libera: qua vult quod posset non velle*. It is natural or necessary for God to will Himself and in Himself the basis and standard of everything else. But He wills freely the possibility and reality of everything else. This distinction may be allowed to stand as an instructive one, provided we add that the will of God is free even in His necessity to will Himself, and necessary even in His freedom to will everything else, so that the *non posse non velle* is determined by His will and the *posse non velle* is rejected by His will. The distinction concerns the ontological side of the problem. It differentiates between God as the sovereign Subject of all His works and God in the effecting of all these works of His. This differentiation is necessary if God's omnipotence is to be understood as the omnipotence of His will.

It was also helpful that (2) a distinction was drawn between God's *voluntas occulta* or *beneplaciti* and His *voluntas revelata* or *signi*. This distinction concerned the noetic problem—the problem of our knowledge. It referred to the fact that God's omnipotence as omnipotent will is not only active, and can be known not only as active, but also as will, purpose, determination and decision, so that it can be distinguished from a mere being or occurrence which is not the achievement of a will. This is true because the reconciliation in which God's will confronts us does not only occur but is revealed. For as God's own act it is also His self-manifestation. Now if this is so it is necessary to acknowledge that the will of God as the will of the sovereign Subject of all His works is first of all hidden and therefore unknown to us because in the first instance we can view and apprehend only His works. It is the will of His own good-pleasure, His own will in His works, which as such and in itself cannot be the object of any other knowledge but its own. If this hidden nature is not true of it, it is not a true and genuine will. For there is will only where there is the mystery of freedom in which a subject decides on its act in a way that is known only to itself in the first instance, before the decision is actually carried out. Now while the mystery of creaturely freedom of will in our actions is no mystery to God, the divine freedom of will is always an absolute and quite impenetrable mystery for all knowledge which is distinct from God's knowledge, and therefore for all creaturely knowledge when it is face to face with the works of God. But this hidden will of God is revealed to us by Himself. For God Himself, being love, is not only hidden in Himself but also revealed. The decision of His will is executed not only in His works, but also within His works in what is called in the distinction the *signa voluntatis divinae*, the instruction, comfort and admonition which God causes to come to lost man by the work of reconciliation, in order to give him the indispensable explanation and exposition of all His works. What man cannot know by himself, what he has not deserved to be able to know, what he has no claim on God to know, God did and does really permit him to know. He reveals to him His own will, and with it the origin and meaning and goal of all His works, and revealing this He reveals the first and last thing man has to know with regard to his own existence. The *voluntas occulta* or *beneplaciti* is known to us in its execution as God's free grace, being in itself also *voluntas revelata* or *signi*. It is in this way that it becomes for us a genuine and inescapable encouragement and also demand. It is in this way that we are subjected to God's will—for our salvation and our sanctification. We have, of course, presented the distinction in a way which makes it both instructive and meaningful. This can be said only partially of the way in which it was presented in the older theology. There the hidden will of God was understood as God's immovable and inscrutable inner being, and as such it was regarded as the will of God properly so called, and contrasted with the revealed will of God, which was looked on as figurative, an arrangement and appearance for the benefit of the creature. We have already rejected this interpretation of the distinction at the earlier point where we argued that the real inner being of God is falsely represented as the immutability of a lifeless God, and that this representation does not take into account the perfection and scope of the Word of God as the divine self-revelation. We would add the further criticism that the knowledge of the reality and genuineness of the divine will are not advanced but hindered and finally made quite impossible by this interpretation of the distinction. For how can God will in His inner life if this inner life is in fact immovable ? But if He cannot will, what truth or binding force remains for our knowledge of His revealed will as such ? Do not the truth and binding force of our confrontation by the will of God, and the reality of our subjection to it, depend absolutely on the fact that in them we are dealing unreservedly with God Himself in His inmost life and not with a mere divine arrangement or appearance ? We cannot recognise a will if we do not recognise One who wills. In that case we have to accept the belief that there is no one who really and genuinely wills, but only a being unmoved in itself which for our benefit has assumed the form, but only the form, of a will. We therefore correct the theologoumenon of our fathers by finding in both the *voluntas occulta* or *beneplaciti* on the one hand and the *voluntas revelata* or *signi* on the other the one will of God, the one God who wills, the will of the divine love. This is in itself both God's hidden and His revealed will, so that God can both possess it for Himself from eternity to eternity and also in time reveal it to a knowledge distinct from His own. This revelation is the divine arrangement for our benefit. But in this arrangement we have to do with nothing less than with God Himself. We have to do with God's own will in a real and binding way. This is so because God's will does not first require this particular revelation in order to be revealed. It is revealed in itself, and it reveals itself in this self-revelation and therefore genuinely and properly as God's will.

We will take collectively (3) the distinctions of God's *voluntas absoluta* and *conditionalis*, His *voluntas antecedens* and *consequens*, His *voluntas efficiens* and *permittens*, and finally—this is a distinction we shall have to reject—His *voluntas efficax* and *inefficax*. The difference between all these distinctions and those cited above is that they seek to make intelligible the reality and genuineness of God's omnipotent will in its relation to the objects distinct from itself and therefore in relation to a real or possible divine creation. At this point, too, we must add the interpretation " intelligible from God's being itself, from the nature of His will." All these distinctions speak of a movement, a multiplicity of acts in God's own life. They speak of a real divine " inner " and " outer," a real " before " and " after," a real " thus " and " otherwise." We cannot, therefore, accept the reservations made by the older theology and still made by Roman Catholic theology to-day. According to these the distinctiveness of the divine will, in virtue of which it can be directed to objects distinct from itself, has no real basis in God, and therefore its particular character as creative will is not a characteristic of the divine being and will as such. We may recall what we said against a false, because abstract, conception of the divine immutability, and about the relation of the *simplicitas* and *multiplicitas* of God in our basic investigation of the problem of the divine attributes. God's immutability is not immovability, and His simplicity is not poverty. On the contrary, God is one in the fulness of His deity and constant in its living vigour. He does not therefore acquire fulness and life from His relation to creation. He has it in Himself before all creation and every relation to it, in a way incomparably higher, richer and stronger than all the fulness and life which is in creation or which He displays in His relation to it. We have, therefore, no reason to say (rather uneasily) of these distinctions that they are only " virtual." On the contrary, we can take them more seriously, i.e., more concretely than the older theology ever did.

If we distinguish between God's *voluntas absoluta* and His *voluntas conditionalis*, we have on the one hand the will of God in its omnipotence and therefore in its perfect freedom, a freedom to determine and decide, and to do so in different ways under differing circumstances and in relation to these circumstances. We have, therefore, the will of God as the omnipotent God Himself coinciding with God's aseity. And on the other hand we have the same will of God to the extent that in His freedom God is love and therefore a definite and decided will, not at all arbitrary, but directed to what His freedom has chosen from eternity, and will choose in eternity, because it is the divine freedom. We have God's will to the extent that it has decided, and does and will decide, not apart from definite conditions, for His eternal decision is also a decision in time and is therefore to be described genuinely and compulsorily in these temporal forms, but in such a way that the conditions themselves are created and posited by His decision, so that they are in force in fulfilment of His will, not in their own strength, but in that of their divine creation and positing. Thus, whether we speak of the *voluntas absoluta* or the *voluntas conditionalis*, we speak of the will of God which is His eternal being itself, not of mere conditions of His relationship to the world and to time. For that which is operative in the relationship of God to the world and to time, in the act of His creation, is simply God Himself, His innermost will, which decides in freedom and love. His *voluntas absoluta* is to be recognised in His *voluntas conditionalis*, and His *voluntas conditionalis* in His *voluntas absoluta*. We have, then, no reason to fear at this point the conception of a hidden God who in His final and innermost sovereignty is not free, and in His freedom is not love. Equally, there is no escape from the revealed God, as though He were not free to give to us and command us according to His will which is the will of the one God.

When a distinction is drawn between God's *voluntas antecedens* and His *voluntas consequens*, it is clear that we are dealing with a special aspect of the *voluntas conditionalis*, namely, with its aetiology. Strictly speaking, from creation onwards the whole of the divine volition *ad extra* comes under the concept of the *voluntas consequens* to the extent that this presupposes creation and applies to its preservation and government, or at least to objects within it. But it does not cease to be also the *voluntas antecedens* to the extent that it is bound to creation and its sphere only as it continually binds itself to it and the presupposition is firmly posited only as it rests on a continual divine positing. In virtue of its freedom God's will is always *voluntas antecedens*, or beginning, just as it is always *voluntas consequens*, or end, in virtue of its love. Eternity does not cease when time begins, but time begins and continues in the lap of eternity. For this reason God's will cannot be only *voluntas antecedens*. It works under the presupposition created and posited by God Himself. It is, therefore, *voluntas consequens* as much as *antecedens*. And this *antecedere* and *consequi* is not a mere appearance in which God conceals Himself for our benefit and in order that we may be able to know Him. On the contrary, as it is true that we have always God's will behind us and before us, it is equally true that we have to do here with God Himself and not with a mere appearance. The before and after correspond to a before and after peculiar to the divine will itself in its eternity, to the extent that His majesty does not prevent His condescension and His condescension cannot in the least injure His majesty. God in Himself wills a first and therefore a second. And conversely He wills a first for the sake of a second. Again, He wills a second and therefore a first, and, again conversely, a second for the sake of the first. To say that God moves in certain directions is not a mere figure of speech, nor is it a reality only in His relation to what He has created. It is an eternal reality in Himself. It is the actuality and genuineness and distinctiveness of His will, of His eternal decision and determination, which when it confronts us confronts us in a way which is unreservedly true and compelling. The importance of the fact that we have our refuge beneath the " everlasting arms " of God according to Deut. 33²⁷, or under God's " wings " according to Psalms 36⁷, 57¹ and 61⁴, can be forcibly brought home to us in the distinction between the *voluntas antecedens* and *consequens*. On the other hand, it is obviously a mistake to try to use this distinction to introduce at this point the idea of an autonomy of the creature over against God, an autonomy which is certainly preceded by God's will, but which also conditions it and is therefore followed by it. To be sure, the creature is not forgotten along these ways of God in the course of His willing and achieving. On the contrary, it is remembered in the best and most worthy manner. But it is only along God's ways that the creature can ever have its place and its function. And it is only because there is a divine before and after, following the divine reality and based on the grace of the divine creation and preservation, that a before and after can have in the creaturely sphere also the relative reality proper to it.

Further, if a distinction is drawn between God's *voluntas efficiens* and His *voluntas permittens*, this is obviously done in the first instance in relation to the problem of theodicy. In a certain sense evil, sin, wickedness, the devil, death and non-being also exist. If this whole realm exists it does so in its own way by the will of God and not without it. Otherwise it would form a realm independent of God and therefore itself divine. If existence is conceded to it, and if we cannot grant a dualism between God and another principle or lord of the world really based on himself—and it is impossible for us to do this in the context of the Christian knowledge of God—we have no alternative but to seek the basis even of this realm in the will of God. But how does God will this realm when according to His own Word it is disavowed and condemned by Him ; when it is the anti-god which He Himself characterises as the enemy which has already been conquered, the guilt which has already been uncovered and forgiven, the fetter which has already fallen off, the misery of His creature which has already been set aside ; when He obviously wants us to recognise and acknowledge and treat it as that which is impossible in His sight ? How can we say that it is not absolutely non-existent, but non-existent only in this fulfilment and order of His will, and yet also existent in this order and to that extent willed by Him ? In what way is it willed ? The distinction between *efficere* and *permittere* provides the answer to this question. *Efficere* means *creare, causare, producere*. What God creates, causes and produces is what He affirms, the positive and final goal in His intention. But this is the good creature, the creature that honours Him in willing obedience and is for that reason blessed. It clearly cannot and may not be said that He creates, causes and produces the realm of opposition to this obedience and blessedness and therefore to Himself, or that it is the object of His will in this sense. On the other hand, we may not and cannot say that it is not the object of His will at all ; that it escapes His lordship and control. It may not and cannot be said, therefore, that God's will confines itself to *efficere*. There is a divine volition which is no less real and powerful, no less righteous and good and no less omnipotent than His affirmative will, but of a very different character. This is the volition of God in virtue of which He not only gives the creature its existence and being, the independence and freedom which belongs to it, and therefore its true creaturely existence, but in virtue of which, because He wills its free obedience and therefore its blessedness, He refrains from making absolutely impossible the misuse of its independence and freedom, and therefore the incapacitating and destruction of its creaturely existence. It is the volition in virtue of which He does not absolutely prevent the emergence of this realm of opposition, or utterly exclude the limitation of being by non-being. His will, His real and powerful will, consists also in this refraining, non-preventing, and non-excluding. The one will which is *efficiens* is also *permittens*. God wills to create, cause, and produce in such a way that He also " permits." And in this negative form, not as creative but as controlling will, He takes up into His fore-ordination and therefore His will, and has indeed done so from all eternity, the revolt of creation against Him and against itself, its self-merited distress, and therefore the sphere of evil and wickedness. God's good will, the omnipotent goodness of His will, is of such a nature that He does not will to create, cause and produce without this permission. But it is also of such a nature that He does not will to permit without this being as such a negating, judging, condemning and overcoming. And again it is of such a nature that He does not will to negate without the necessary subordination of the negation to His positive will, and its service of it. Hence all this does not exist outside His freedom, or in such a way that His freedom ceases in the least to be the freedom of His love. *Nec dubitandum est, Deum facere bene etiam sinendo fieri quaecunque fiunt male. Non enim hoc nisi iusto iudicio sinit; et profecto bonum est omne, quod iustum est* (Augustine, *Enchir.* 96). There must not be at any point a diminution either of the character of evil as evil, of the unconditioned goodness of the divine creative will, of the omnipotence of the divine will as that of the Lord over the evil which He has not created, or of the goodness of this will of the Lord which is identical with His will as Creator. Nor must there be a diminution of the unity of the divine will as the willing of what is good even as it works through the evil that is rejected and nevertheless permitted by it. If the *voluntas permittens* certainly stands for what is only a provisional and subordinate and in itself revocable volition on the part of God, it is not for that reason merely figurative, or in its own way to be taken less seriously than His positive will. It is just as much to be feared as the other is to be loved, and just as much to be avoided as the other is to be sought. God wills to be glorified equally in both ways, so that it is quite another matter if they happen so differently, and we can fear Him only when we have loved Him even more, and avoid His *voluntas permittens* only by subordinating ourselves even more to His *voluntas efficiens*. In its own context, corresponding to the nature of the subject, the *voluntas permittens* is no less *voluntas divina* than the *voluntas efficiens*. If we did not know that even in the midst of sin and death we were utterly in God's hands and at His disposal, how could we hope to become obedient and blessed ? If God's freedom ended at the very point where we need God most, and if we found ourselves suddenly outside His foreordination and dependent on our own freedom, how could His love find us, or we participate in it ? We may, of course, raise the basic charge against God : Why is not His will for creation wholly and utterly a *voluntas efficiens*, and a good will only in this form ? Why does this refraining, this not preventing and not excluding exist only in the utterly terrifying power which is proper to it as the divine will, and seems so fatefully to conceal the goodness of His will ? To this our only answer is that God's supreme and truest good for creation, and therefore the good determined for and promised to creation, is revealed in its full splendour only when its obedience and blessedness are not simply its nature, the self-evident fulfilment of its existence, its inevitable course, but when they are salvation from the edge of an abyss, when in its obedience and blessedness creation is constantly reminded of its creation out of nothing and its preservation from nothingness by the menacing proximity of the kingdom of darkness, when its obedience and blessedness are therefore grace and salvation. It is the very essence of our reconciliation as grace to depend on the existence of a divine *voluntas permittens*, and in virtue of this on the reality of disgrace, damnation and hell. If God is greater in the very fact that He is the God who forgives sins and saves from death, we have no right to complain but must praise Him that His will also includes a permitting of sin and death. God is not less but greater—He does not come under suspicion, but shows Himself to be holy and righteous, in the fact that He not only *efficit*, but also *permittit*. For in this way His will appears as the will of the gracious God who in His grace is the glorious God. But if this is so, we have also no reason to look on this distinction merely as one in the divine relation to the world. On the contrary, it too describes the will of God as it is in itself. Certainly in God there is absolutely no inclination to evil or evil purpose. To the very depths of His being, we can expect only that He will will His own glory and therefore our willing obedience and blessedness. But even in God Himself there is no simple or as it were physical or mechanical exclusion. On the contrary, in God Himself there is a mighty not-willing of evil. There is light as the denial of darkness, holiness, righteousness and wisdom as the rejection of their opposites. To this extent and in this way there is a mighty permission of them to go their own way. It is, of course, only permission, a restricted toleration, the forbearance of God which aims at a goal and has therefore an end. Yet God does not simply practise this patience. He is patient in Himself, that is, He is the One who can permit as well as cause, because His will as the divine will is one which permits as well as causes. His judgment, too, will have an end, but He will not on that account be any the less the God of righteousness from eternity to eternity. God is not God if He is not a will which causes. But He is equally not God if He is not a will which also permits and forbears. The will which does not will to cause is not a perfect will, but neither is the will which is only causation and does not put limits to its own action. It is not a free will which wills only to act and not also to refrain from action. And it is not a divine will but a demonic, satanic will which so wants its own way—even if this way is the divine holiness and righteousness—that it can only assert and enforce and not also make concessions. Without detriment to its holiness and righteousness, rather in confirmation of its holiness and righteousness, in its very omnipotence, the divine will wills also to make concessions. God's causation and forbearance are equally God's eternal being—each in its own way, the one unlimited, the other limited, the one in authority, the other in subordination, the one positively, the other negatively, the one independently, the other dependently, the one the *voluntas major* or *pura*, the other the *voluntas minor* or *indulgentiae* (Tertullian, *De exh. cast.* 3). If we are willing to be taught about God's will by His reconciling action in Jesus Christ, we cannot see any other way of saying this. And the more truly we understand both the *efficere* as *efficere* and the *permittere* as *permittere*, the more securely we will avoid the errors which certainly threaten on both sides.

The last of the usual distinctions drawn in this connexion is false and misleading. God's will is in all circumstances a *voluntas efficax*. There is no such thing as a *voluntas Dei inefficax*. God's will in relation to His creation is conditioned, yet not by the creature but by His own will as Creator, by the conditions to which He has Himself subjected and continually subjects His creature. It is not conditioned from outside itself, by another. In no sense is it a powerless will, an empty wish, mere volition. On the contrary, whatever God wills also comes about. God wills whatever He wills in the different orders indicated by the other distinctions to which we have referred. Thus different things happen in the different spheres of the objects of His will. But in whatever happens, it is always His will that is active, and never finally and properly another will independent of His, effectively resisting it and capable of opposition to it. Always and everywhere His will is operative, and it is only conditioned and limited by itself, and in this sovereignty it is the determination and delimitation of all things and all occurrence. This is true without in any way destroying the contingence of creaturely being and occurrence. The contingence of the divine will sovereignly precedes it, but it is not destroyed or even disturbed by it. This happens in the sovereignty of the Creator which is operative in the freedom of His creature without robbing it of freedom. It is true, therefore, without the free will of man having to be understood as unfree in itself. This will is free in itself, but in its freedom it is always at the disposal of the ever-active will of God. It is also true without the character of evil as evil either having to be re-interpreted or put to the charge of God ; for if God permits it and therefore effectively wills His creature to assume this character, this is His good and righteous will and serves to increase His glory. His will in this activity does not make the evil good or make it His own as evil. For in this activity it is a wholly negating will, permitting in power but only permitting and not affirming. Yet at no point or level is the will of God one to which we can presume to ascribe inactivity and therefore non-omnipotence.

A long tract lies behind us. We have posed and examined the equation that God's omnipotence is that of His knowing and willing, and therefore God's knowing and willing are those of His omnipotence. By the very nature of the case we have been particularly concerned with the second form of the equation. It is at this point that the problems and therefore the errors constantly arise. It has always to be asserted and accepted that in this distinctiveness God's knowing and willing are an omnipotent, an unconditionally superior, comprehensive and permeating knowing and willing. To this extent our whole consideration of the divine knowing and willing is simply an exposition of the statement that God is omnipotent. To this extent, when viewed in the wider context, it belongs to the doctrine of the perfections of the divine freedom. But if this form of the equation : " that God's knowing and willing are those of His omnipotence," has had to have the material predominance in this connexion, we could not work this out without constantly coming up against the stumbling-block to which we have finally had to give more expanded treatment. We have had to weigh and respect the divine knowing and willing as such, its special character as knowing and willing in distinction from pure power and causality. This distinction has necessarily determined our analysis of the concept of omnipotence in general. In the light of it we are brought face to face with the problem of the divine knowing and willing as a whole. Thus our exposition of the statement that God knows and God wills was not exhausted when we had filled out its predicates with the concept of omnipotence. We did do this and took all the necessary precautions to protect ourselves from the concept of a divine knowing and willing which are even partially impotent. Yet although this was very important and necessary, we must be clear that in the last analysis the taking of these precautions was not the real nerve and point of our consideration of the divine knowing and willing, and that its decisive motif and results could not consist in this, that is, in the application and confirmation of the fact that God's knowing and willing are omnipotent. On the contrary, the aim of this consideration lay in the first form of the equation, in the knowledge that God's omnipotence is that of His knowing and willing, the power of His person and His Spirit. It lay, therefore, in the very elements which held up the discussion, and especially in their final phase (5), where we were expressly and specifically concerned with an understanding of the distinctiveness of the divine knowing and willing. Our understanding of the divine omnipotence is complete when it confronts us free from every taint of a merely neutral capacity and efficacy, of a blind and dumb causality and force. It is complete when we can know it and honour and fear and love it only in its pure spirituality, which as God's spirituality is omnipotent, mighty and effective, but omnipotent in a divine way as God's knowing and willing and Spirit. The divine profundity of true omnipotence consists in the fact that it is itself the omnipotent person of God. It is in this alone, and therefore never at any time impersonally, without consciousness and will, that it is omnipotence, and mighty and effective. In this it is wholly omnipotence, but solely and exclusively in this.

False systematisations of the relation of God to the creature inevitably impair a knowledge of God's omnipotence. They are based on a failure to see clearly that in this relationship we are dealing with the omnipotence of the divine knowing and willing, of the divine person and the divine Spirit, and therefore with *His* power and activity and not another. When this is clear, there can be no place for the idea that the independence of the creature is impaired by God's omnipotence, an idea which can then be removed only by impairing the knowledge of God's omnipotence. Since God is Spirit, He is not *per se* omnipotent in a way which threatens and destroys the independence of His creature. As Spirit, He is omnipotent in the freedom of His creatures. His omnipotent and irresistibly commanding power and activity are those of His knowing and willing. He controls and moves by the fact that He knows His creatures and wills them in their own movements. And this means that He honours this independence and robs us of any pretext for safeguarding them before Him by ascribing the controlling and moving only partially to Him, and therefore making certain deductions from His omnipotence for the benefit of the power of His creatures. These deductions are not only impossible in relation to God's omnipotence. They are also unnecessary. They rest on a profound misunderstanding of God's omnipotence and therefore of God Himself. They can be contemplated only when there is no clear knowledge of God's spirituality and personality and therefore of the profundity of His omnipotence. If we understand that God's omnipotence is the omnipotence of His knowing and willing, and if this is a genuine understanding because it has its source in the divine revelation and reconciliation, and therefore if the knowing and willing of His omnipotence is known as that of His love, the problem of competition, from which all the errors necessarily and constantly derive, withers away of itself. In face of the omnipotence of the divine love the creature has never to think of struggling and bickering for an ability of its own power to compete. It will never see its own power threatened or destroyed by the power of God's love. It will never jealously oppose its own power to this power, but rather place it at its disposal, in the knowledge that it already belongs to the divine love even before it has decided to put its power at its disposal, and that it can decide to do so only because the divine power has itself disposed concerning its power.

This is the deepest concern in the whole consideration of God's knowing and willing. It is by their distinctiveness, by the knowledge of the true spirituality and personality of God, that formally if not materially—and the formal side is also indispensable—it is decided that we can know God genuinely and properly as love, as the One who loves. We could not take or say this seriously if we could speak of God's knowing and willing only figuratively and metaphorically and not with ultimate truth. If God does not know and will, He does not love either. A mere blind force can possess power and efficacy, but it cannot love. What might be called its love would be a decorative epithet arbitrarily ascribed to it, but not having any basis or truth. There is love only where there is knowing and willing. But the divine knowing and willing meets us at the point where it does meet us, in the divine revelation and reconciliation, wholly and altogether as love. As God's love meets us there, we are met also by God's knowing and willing. And because it meets us there as omnipotence, we must now say as the final thing about God's omnipotence that we must recognise the omnipotence of the divine knowing and willing, the only real divine omnipotence, as the omnipotence of love. It is in this way that God knows and wills, in His love. This is what we mean by knowing and willing in its divine origin and truth. This is the eternal knowing and the eternal will which determines all other knowing and willing by the grace of creation. It is love. And it seeks its own only in fellowship with another. It establishes and lifts up the other as a beloved object, as belonging to itself. In this act it is true knowing and willing, but at the same time omnipotent, free in itself, and irresistible in relation to the other. Again, its omnipotence, and therefore God's omnipotence in general, is simply and exclusively the omnipotence of this action. And again, with the statement that God's omnipotence is the omnipotence of His knowing and willing we have confirmed the one essence of God in its twofold nature, that His freedom is the freedom of His love.

It only remains for us to name and reveal the final and decisive ground on which we have made this statement. As we have been reminded again, our knowledge of God's omnipotent knowing and willing has been deduced generally from the knowledge of the divine revelation and reconciliation. It is as God says something to us there that we recognise that He knows, and as He does something there that we recognise that He wills. It is as He speaks and acts there in omnipotence that we recognise the omnipotence of His knowing and willing. But this basis and its strength are surely exposed to the menace of that suspicion of arbitrariness which attaches to every conceptual construction. We therefore repeat it in conclusion in the concrete and irrefutable form in which it is given us in Holy Scripture itself. It is this alone which can and will make it an ultimately reliable and solid basis even in the abstract form in which we accepted it in the first instance. If we consult the biblical witness to God's omnipotence, it emerges at once that the differentiation and relationship between the concepts of God and power, upon which we have constantly insisted, are necessary because power is from the very first described as residing in a single hand and revealed as the power of this one hand. This one hand is the hand of the One whom the Bible calls God, and according to the Bible real power is not to be separated from this hand and its sway. What this hand brings about is brought about with real power. There is no real power which is not the power of this hand and which does not in some way reveal itself as the power of this hand.

" O Lord God, thou hast begun to shew thy servant thy greatness, and thy mighty hand : for what God is there in heaven or in earth, that can do according to thy works, and according to thy might ? " (Deut. 3^{24}). It cannot be maintained, of course, that the idea of natural and neutral divine powers, of every kind of dynamic *Mana*, is absolutely alien to biblical ways of thinking and speaking. Yet it is very noticeable that this view common to all nature-religion is as it were filtered in the biblical sphere and stripped of its importance. In the Bible apparently different, distinct and neutral powers are drawn into the conception of the one God. So then, although the existence of a variety of powers and activities is not denied but assumed, He alone remains as the One who first and last controls their destiny. In fact, then, nothing remains of a neutral divine energy and activity, a nameless dynamic, which man as such must respect and fear and honour. In the Bible the mysticism of an *exousia* as such, the mystery of a natural force or an historical sequence, is from the very first attacked at the root. It is not worth considering. It can only be rejected. Israel can be impressed by this kind of divine power only when it falls back and away to the idols of Canaan, Egypt or Babylon. When it is obedient, it counts on God's power and God's power alone, and therefore not on any divine powers. For all powers are His powers. He is the " Lord of hosts." We have only to think of the teaching on angels in Colossians and Ephesians to remember that this same concentration and mobilisation in respect of the idea of power is the characteristic tendency of New Testament thinking as well. " All power is given unto me in heaven and in earth " (Mt. 28^{18}). In the light of the testimony of the Bible we certainly cannot omit the differentiation and relationship between God and power which we have attempted to make.

We certainly have to speak of a "hand" which emerges at this point as the source and centre of all power ; for from the beginning the owner of it appears as a person, an I, who disposes of His own power and therefore of all power in accordance with His insight and will. His action is a conscious and planned activity ; His operation is history.

Who and what is God in the Old Testament ? He is definitely the One who leads Israel out of Egypt, and saves it at the Red Sea from the power of Pharaoh, and leads it forward into the wilderness to Sinai and through the wilderness to the land of Canaan. This history and the recollection of this history as the primal history of the covenant between God and man are for all time the revelation of the God of the Old Testament, and therefore the revelation of His being as power. But His being as power is the being of His personal knowing, planning and willing. It is a unique action in which He knows Israel for the sake of its elected fathers, and therefore calls Moses and sets him face to face with Pharaoh, strikes Egypt with all the plagues, lets the waves of the sea pile up so that the people may pass through, lets them close again over Pharaoh and his host, and finally confirms and seals His election and will by publicly concluding His covenant : I am thy God, and thou art my people. " The enemy said, I will pursue, I will overtake, I will divide the spoil ; my lust shall be satisfied upon them ; I will draw my sword, my hand shall destroy them. Thou didst blow with thy wind, the sea covered them : they sank as lead in the mighty waters. Who is like unto thee, O Lord, among the gods ? who is like thee, glorious in holiness, fearful in praises, doing wonders ? Thou stretchedst out thy right hand, the earth swallowed them. Thou in thy mercy hast led·forth the people which thou hast redeemed : thou hast guided them in thy strength unto thy holy habitation. The people shall hear, and be afraid : sorrow shall take hold on the inhabitants of Palestina. Then the dukes of Edom shall be amazed ; the mighty men of Moab, trembling shall take hold upon them ; all the inhabitants of Canaan shall melt away. Fear and dread shall fall upon them ; by the greatness of thine arm they shall be as still as a stone ; till thy people pass over, O Lord, till the people pass over, which thou hast purchased. Thou shalt bring them in, and plant them in the mountain of thine inheritance, in the place, O Lord, which thou hast made for thee to dwell in, in the Sanctuary, O Lord, which thy hands have established. The Lord shall reign for ever and ever (Ex. 15⁹⁻¹⁸). Here we have the two together. A sovereign power is put forth which everything obeys and nothing can withstand. But it is in the hand of the One and exercised in accordance with His purpose. It all leads, then, to the goal which He has appointed, His self-revelation as God, King and Lord of those for whose benefit it all takes place. That is why the song begins : " The Lord is my strength and song, and He is become my salvation ; he is my God, and I will prepare him an habitation : my father's God, and I will exalt him. The Lord is a man of war ; the Lord is his name " (vv. 2-3). What begins with this event in which there is such a mighty display of power (cf. Ps. 78, 105, 106) is not, then, a natural history but the history of a strictly personal relationship and action on the part of this mighty God. What is revealed is not a divine power but this mighty God and His person as the possessor of all power. It is He who is recognised and praised. It is He who continues to deal with this people. The knowledge that Yahweh knows and wills does not merely derive from this event, and it is certainly not an interpretation of this event. But the event itself is the revelation of this knowledge. As Yahweh's self-revelation it is the revelation of His knowing and willing, and only as such is it the revelation of His being as power.

That God's activity is an action, His operation a history and He Himself a person, includes rather than excludes the fact that the power with which He wills is omnipotent or unlimited power over everything. That is the reason why the witness of the Bible to God achieves, from the very first, the distinctive concentration and mobilisation to which we have referred. It is obviously compelled at this point by its object. It knows and says emphatically that God is the Creator and Lord of heaven and earth. It bears witness to the fact that He is revealed as such. It testifies to the voice of the thunder, the sea and the earthquake as the proclamation of His power. But not for a moment does it lose sight of Himself, His knowing and willing, His person revealed in that historical event, as the Subject even of His power in the universe. We cannot hold, therefore, that there is first a divine power generally in nature, and then in the whole of the course of history, which can be identified in an undefined and rather uncertain way with the power of God, but that this is a matter more of supposition and inkling than of knowledge, perhaps the recognition, in common with heathen religions, of the substance of a neutral supreme power and activity before which, as an obscure but true revelation of divine omnipotence, we can stand reverently for a moment (and at a pinch a little longer) before going on to God's special, concrete, historical capacity and activity and therefore to the true and clear knowledge of God. The contexts in which the Bible bears witness to God's power as the power over everything make it quite impossible for us to entertain this idea of a forecourt to the real shrine of the true knowledge of the omnipotent God. The Bible is not interested in God's power over everything, the power that creates, upholds and moves the world, as a reality to be considered for itself. On the contrary, it is interested in it because it forms the ground and place, the space and framework, in which He is active in power as the Lord of this history. It is not the general which comes first, but the particular. The general does not exist without this particular and cannot therefore be prior to the particular. It cannot, then, be recognised and understood as the general prior to it, as if it were itself a particular. Thus we cannot move from the general to this particular, but only in the opposite direction—from this particular to the general. It is from this particular that we come to this general.

Tenendum est axioma, perverse eos vagari, qui de potentia Dei imaginantur extra verbum, si quid visum est; quia sic consideranda est eius immensitas, ut spei et fiduciae nobis sit materia. Iam vero non temere solum et inutiliter, sed etiam periculose disputatur, quid sit Deo possibile, nisi simul occurrat, quid ipse velit . . . Notandum tamen est, potentiam Dei vera fide effectualem, ut ita loquar, apprehendi. Potens enim est atque agnosci vult Deus, ut ipso opere veracem se demonstret (Calvin, *Comm. on Luke* 1³⁷, C.R. 45, pp. 32 and 33).

So powerful is the Lord of this history that His power is the power—and makes itself known as the power—that preserves the stars, moves the sea, and directs the lightning. The power that is in the universe is revealed as His power and therefore as the power of His knowing and willing, as the power of His choosing and calling, as the power of the One who has mercy on Israel and who leads it out to make covenant with it, as the power of the Word by which He comforts and judges Israel. It is as this power that it evokes our wonder and veneration. As such it is no longer obscure but perfectly clear, having a final clarity as His power. As such it is distinct from all anonymous and neutral powers. As such it is the same holy and gracious, righteous and merciful power which is the power of that particular history and yet as such real, eternal power.

It can be stated with confidence that everything that the Old Testament says about God's power in general, and therefore abstractly about His lordship over nature and history, is simply a reflection of what He has done in His power in particular in His covenant with Israel. " The portion of Jacob . . . is the former of all things ; and Israel is the rod of his inheritance : the Lord of hosts is his name " (Jer. 10¹⁶). " Ah, Lord ! behold, thou hast made the heaven and the earth by thy great power and stretched out arm, and there is nothing too hard for thee " (Jer. 32¹⁷). But of whom is this said ? The passage continues : " Thou shewest lovingkindness unto thousands, and recompensest the iniquity of the fathers into the bosom of their children after them : the Great, the Mighty God, the Lord of hosts, is his name. Great in counsel, and mighty in work : for thine eyes are open upon all the ways of the sons of men : to give every one according to his ways, and according to the fruit of his doings : which hast set signs and wonders in the land of Egypt, even unto this day, and in Israel, and among other men ; and hast made thee a name, as at this day ; and hast brought forth thy people Israel out of the land of Egypt with signs, and with wonders, and with a strong hand, and with a stretched out arm, and with great terror ; and hast given them this land, which thou didst swear to their fathers to give them, a land flowing with milk and honey " (Jer. 32¹⁸⁻²²). It is, then, only of the God of the covenant and salvation history that the first and general statements are made. Or take Is. 40²¹⁻²⁶ : " Have ye not known ? have ye not heard ? hath it not been told you from the beginning ? have ye not understood from the foundations of the earth ? It is he that sitteth upon the circle of the earth, and the inhabitants thereof are as grasshoppers ; that stretcheth out the heavens as a curtain, and spreadeth them out as a tent to dwell in : that bringeth the princes to nothing ; he maketh the judges of the earth as vanity. Yea, they shall not be planted ; yea, they shall not be sown : yea, their stock shall not take root in the earth : and he shall also blow upon them, and they shall wither, and the whirlwind shall take them away as stubble. To whom then will ye liken me, or shall I be equal ? saith the Holy One. Lift up your eyes on high, and behold who hath created these things, that bringeth out their host by number : he calleth them all by names by the greatness of his might, for that he is strong in power ; not one faileth." The passage continues : " Why sayest thou, O Jacob, and speakest, O Israel, My way is hid from the Lord, and my judgment is passed over from my God ? " (v. 27). It is clear that the power at work in the universe is here traced back to the power, plan and will of the One who will not forget Israel and as whose special possession Israel is continually claimed. Thus it is clear that His power in general is not recognised apart from the knowledge of the power shown in this way, and that without it it cannot be the object of this song of praise. The song of praise illustrates the confession of the power of God which protects Israel and not *vice versa*. Psalm 29 is often quoted in this connexion, but we cannot understand this Psalm if we fail to see that " God's glory in the storm " is only the theme and not the text of the Psalm, and that " the voice of the Lord " of which it speaks is the voice of One who, according to verse 11, gives His people power and blesses it with salvation. This inner order and teleology of the testimony of the Bible to God's omnipotence is best verified by the fact that it never slips into the eulogising of an arbitrary power. This would inevitably happen if its object had secretly been the power active and manifest in the universe in itself and as such. This kind of eulogy does of course follow in relation to astounding elements in the universe, as at the end of the book of Job. But even there the astonishment is not an end in itself. On the contrary, in what astonishes us, the final thing, the real mystery revealed is the righteousness and holiness of God, and not a mere *tremendum*. The Bible bears testimony to these in their unfathomable greatness and divine pre-eminence. But it does bear witness to them, to God's will, and not to a mysterious arbitrary power which is for that reason divine.

God's righteous and holy will is the upholding and fulfilling of His covenant with Israel, revealed as a grace and mercy which punishes and saves. This divine will is the often unseen but always active criterion of the testimony to His omnipotence. We must mention finally the simple fact which plainly distinguishes the biblical history of creation from the cosmogonic myths of the rest of antiquity. This fact is that according to Scripture God created heaven and earth simply by His Word. "And God said." No one who hears or reads the account controlled by this statement can fail to think at once of that speaking of God by the mouth of Moses and the prophets which established and upheld the existence of Israel in covenant with this God. The God whose speech confronts us in His promise and His command also said : " Let there be light : and there was light." He said this for the sake of His promise and His command ; indeed He spoke it as His command and His promise. And it is by these words that heaven and earth exist and all that therein is. This speaking of His is His creating and upholding, ruling and moving. It is the omnicausality of His omnipotence. Thus, on the first page of the Bible, all power is mobilised and concentrated in the person and Spirit of God. And this is the person and Spirit later attested as the Lord of the special history contained in the Bible. Thus from this very beginning there is no possibility of any power in the universe which as such is not first of all the power of this Lord. There is no attestation or eulogising or knowledge of such a power which is not the attestation or eulogising or knowledge of God, applying at once to the power of this Lord, the power of the One who speaks and therefore knows and wills, the power of the true God. If this condition is observed the attestation and eulogising and knowledge of His omnipotence will not be indefinite or confused or obscure. This is certainly not true of what the Bible has to say in this respect. It is true only when for some reason there is dissatisfaction with the biblical mobilisation and concentration in relation to the concept of the divine omnipotence.

But this concentration and mobilisation does not refer only to the fact that all power is described as the character and predicate of the one personal God. It is not that this personal God, and in Him the One who wields and has all real power, moves as it were anonymously and restlessly through the successive ages of biblical history, and then through the following ages right up to our own time. Nor is it that this concentration and mobilisation is purely conceptual, whereas in fact what is seen as the one personal God and His power is really, as it were, diffused through all ages and equally present in them all, having its location similarly in all ages, which means having no definite and distinct location. Under these circumstances, to say that God is not a generally existent and moving something, but the personal Lord of history, is simply an assumption or assertion which can later be abandoned. We have reached only the idea of a world-power which knows and wills but not the knowledge of the Lord of the world who possesses and exercises all power in His knowing and willing. This knowledge depends on the fact that God has a definite location in history distinct from other places, a concrete temporal centre from which God knows and wills and from which he exercises His power in all ages. It is the existence of this place which marks out and characterises the testimony of the Bible to the omnipotence of the personal God as testimony to the true and living God. Of course, the Bible's testimony is aware of God's personal omnipotence permeating all ages and over-ruling them. But just because it is aware of this as personal omnipotence, it ascribes a concrete temporal centre to it, and it always points and refers back to this centre, to a definite place, from which God exercises His power in all other places too, in the strength of the knowing and willing which proceeds from this place. It is from this centre that He sees and conditions, elects and calls, exercises grace and judgment. It is from this centre that He loves the world. For He Himself is in this centre. This centre is His omnipotent Word by which He created and governs and upholds the world, withstands its rebellion and restores it to Himself, not only calling it back from all sides, but omnipotently bringing it back to peace with Himself. As witness to the personal omnipotence of God which holds sway in this centre and therefore in all ages, the biblical witness stands out clearly from the claim and also the weakness of every general doctrine of a general existence and willing of the omnipotent God. It is smaller, and for that reason greater, than this type of doctrine. It is testimony to the Messiah, to the One who is born in His own time as the fulfilment of all time, the crucified and risen Son of God and Son of Man, Jesus Christ. For this reason it has both an Old and a New Testament form as the wide and varied witness of expectation and the short and univocally definitive witness of recollection. Everything that is to be said about the omnipotent God is said with this twofold testimony. This is He who was and is and will be omnipotent. He is the Lord of the exodus from Egypt, and He is the Lord who in days to come will consummate His Church. He is also the Lord of everything that takes place between that beginning and this end. He is the Lord also of the universal space in which the Church lives. We do not have here an omnipotent knowing and willing without place or name. It is the omnipotent knowing and willing that bears His name, the knowing and willing of the person designated by that name, a knowing and willing which flows out from the place occupied by this person into all other places. It is, therefore, a true and objective knowing and willing, a personal Logos, which, since it is the Logos of God, is also omnipotent.

Paul is not ashamed of the Gospel of Jesus Christ, and the Word of the cross is no foolishness to him, because he knows it for what it is. It is the δύναμις θεοῦ, and therefore the power to save all those who believe in Him (Rom. 1[16]; 1 Cor. 1[18]). But it is this wholly in virtue of its content, because it is the Gospel of Jesus Christ. He, the crucified One, is the power of God (1 Cor. 1[24]). Note that He not only has this power but that in His existence He Himself is it. He certainly has it as well. Like Moses He is an ἀνὴρ προφήτης δυνατὸς ἐν ἔργῳ καὶ λόγῳ ἐναντίον τοῦ θεοῦ καὶ παντὸς τοῦ λαοῦ (Lk. 24[19]; cf. Ac. 7[22]). According to the creaturely-historical side of His existence, He is a miraculous product of this power, of the " overshadowing " of Mary by " the power of the Most High " (Lk. 1[35]). He is promised and expected as the One produced and active by the miraculous power of God, the One " who bears the government on his shoulder " (Is. 9⁶). It is in this way that He comes. For this reason He causes astonishment, teaching the people ὡς ἐξουσίαν ἔχων and not as the scribes (Mk. 1²², Mt. 7²⁸ᶠ·). " Never spake man like this man " (Jn. 7⁴⁶). " With authority and power commandeth he the unclean spirits and they come out " (Lk. 4³⁶). It can even be said of Him generally that " a virtue came out of him and healed them all " (Lk. 6¹⁹). He is a man whom even ·the winds and the sea obey (Mt. 8²⁷). If His acts are called τέρατα as regards their strange relation to all other occurrence, and σημεῖα as regards their meaning and purposes for those on and before whom they took place, they are called δυνάμεις, acts of power, in relation to their own inner being. According to John's Gospel He does that which He can do only because God is with Him (3², 5¹⁹· ³⁰, 9¹⁶· ³³), only because He is provided by God with this δύνασθαι, and therefore equipped to produce unique results. But the epitome and sum of all the power He enjoys as given and active in Him by God is the fact that God in His power raised Him from the dead (1 Cor. 6¹⁴ ; 2 Cor. 13⁴). And in this decisive proof of power it is also quite clear that the Christ of the New Testament not only has this power of His as something that comes to Him from outside, flowing in Him, and received and therefore exercised by Him. He has it only to the extent that as the Son He can do and does nothing without the Father. But to that extent what He can do and does is also His own power belonging to Him as the Son of the Father. The passages that speak of His resurrection by " God " can be understood only when we compare with them those expressly ascribing it to " God the Father " (Gal. 1¹) or to the " glory of the Father " (Rom. 6⁴). We can see how little this power is a power alien to Himself when we consider Acts 2²⁴. Here it certainly says again that God raised Him by loosing the pains of death. There is, however, the remarkable addition καθότι οὐκ ἦν δυνατὸν κρατεῖσθαι αὐτὸν ὑπ' αὐτοῦ. He is the One for whom it was impossible that the resurrection from the dead should not take place. This was only His declaration as the Son of God, and therefore as the possessor of the power of His Father, which He gained by this event, according to Rom. 1⁴. He did not have to become this. He is from the very beginning the possessor of " the power of an endless life " (Heb. 7¹⁶). He is from the very beginning the One whose countenance " is as the sun shineth in its strength " (Rev. 1¹⁶), who upholds " all things by the word of his power " (Heb. 1³). He is worthy to receive what He receives with His resurrection from the dead as the visible proof of His worth : power, riches, wisdom, strength, glory and praise (Rev. 5¹²) ; the power in which according to Mt. 24³⁰ He will return to fulfil all things as they are already fulfilled in Himself. For this reason the acts of power which precede and herald the resurrection do not have their meaning and purpose in themselves, or in the help and deliverance accomplished by them, or in their miraculous character. They have their meaning and purpose in their character as " signs." It makes no odds, therefore, whether they are understood as signs of the kingdom of God which is still to come and therefore hidden, or as signs of the mystery of the being of the One who performs them. For He Himself is the kingdom of God which is destined to come but still hidden, and the being of this kingdom is simply His own being. Therefore to believe in Him means " to taste the powers of the world to come " (Heb. 6⁵), as is obviously done by those who do not fail to notice the meaning and purpose of those signs, but learn from them what they have to indicate beyond their character as acts of mercy and miracles. It is all summed up in the words of 1 Cor. 1²⁴. Jesus Christ is not merely the bearer and executive of a power of God which is given Him but which is not originally and properly His. On the contrary, Jesus Christ has the power of God because and as He Himself is it. And alongside this decisive equation we must notice two others in 1 Cor. 1²⁴.

The first is this. Jesus Christ is the power of God and He is also the wisdom of God. The meaning is undoubtedly that He is the power of God and as such the wisdom of God, the wisdom of God which is the power of God. This same truth is implicit in 1 Cor. 1[18], where we read that the word of the cross is foolishness to those that are perishing, but the power of God to those that are saved. By implication the power of God is equated with the wisdom hidden to those that are lost. Similarly the people in Mark 6[2] were astonished both by the wisdom given to Jesus and the acts of power wrought by His hands. Similarly the power which over-shadowed Mary in Lk. 1[35] was none other than the power of the Spirit of God. Again, even in Is. 11[2] the Messiah is promised as the One on whom will rest the Spirit of the Lord, that is, " the spirit of wisdom and understanding, the spirit of council and might, the spirit of the knowledge and the fear of the Lord." Again, according to 1 Kings 3[9] it is the " understanding heart to judge thy people and to discern between good and evil " which forms the Messianic distinction of King Solomon. The Logos which was with God and was God Himself, and which in His revelation is known as Jesus, is the One by whom are all things, and without whom nothing is that is (Jn. 1[1f.]). Thus Jesus Christ, the power of God, is a power that knows and wills. To put it the other way round, what finally decides that the power which is active here is a power which knows and wills is the fact that it is identical with Him and is His own power. For as His power it is necessarily the power of the wisdom of God.

The second thing to be learned from 1 Cor. 1[24] is that it is Jesus Christ the Crucified who is Himself the power of God. This is true in just the same sense as that the power of God is the power of His wisdom. It is in Him as the Crucified that all this is revealed and can be learned. The first lesson this teaches us is that we must really keep before our eyes God's reconciliation along with His revelation, that we must really understand His reconciliation itself as His revelation, if we are to know that God knows and wills, and that He does so omnipotently and therefore in reality and truth. It is the Son crucified for us, and therefore offered up to the world in God's love, whom the Father has raised from the dead, and therefore revealed as the divine power that is itself the divine wisdom. But the consequence of this is that it is actually to those who are called, both Jews and Greeks, that He is what He is, God's power and wisdom, the One who knows and wills omnipotently, the Logos by whom all things have come into being. The statements " God knows " and " God wills " can really be understood only as the answer given by those who have been called to this knowledge, called out of darkness to God's marvellous light. For according to 1 Cor. 1[18] and Rom. 1[16] we have to be saved and therefore to have faith if we are to recognise this δύναμις θεοῦ at the very point at which alone in all ages it can be recognised, and therefore to gain the key to the secret of the being of God, ourselves and all things. We cannot gain this key ourselves. We can only receive it. No one will really recognise God at the point at which He can be recognised if he is not saved and does not have faith. This means that a man cannot recognise God if in the real power of the reconciling action of God he has not been sanctified by God's grace, justified by His mercy, made a partaker of His wisdom by His patience and born anew by His Word. We are told quite expressly by 1 Cor. 1[24] that the crucified One is God's power and God's wisdom. Obviously, then, He can be known as such only by God Himself, by the power of His calling. This cannot be accomplished by the knowledge of an omnipotent knowing and willing even under what is claimed to be the name of Jesus Christ. This would only be a profane and finally an imaginary knowledge. The genuine name of Jesus Christ is the name of the One who has been crucified. It is, therefore, the knowledge of Jesus Christ the Crucified which is the knowledge of the omnipotent knowing and willing of God. It is in Jesus Christ the Crucified that that is loosed which is to be loosed here, and that is bound which is to be bound here. Therefore it is the knowledge of Him and this alone which is the real and incontrovertible knowledge of the omnipotent God.

3. THE ETERNITY AND GLORY OF GOD

There lies before us a consideration of God's freedom in a third and final grouping of its perfections. Its divinity consists and confirms itself in the fact that in Himself and in all His works God is eternal and therefore glorious.

God's eternity, like His unity and constancy, is a quality of His freedom. It is the sovereignty and majesty of His love in so far as this has and is itself pure duration. The being is eternal in whose duration beginning, succession and end are not three but one, not separate as a first, a second and a third occasion, but one simultaneous occasion as beginning, middle and end. Eternity is the simultaneity of beginning, middle and end, and to that extent it is pure duration. Eternity is God in the sense in which in Himself and in all things God is simultaneous, i.e., beginning and middle as well as end, without separation, distance or contradiction. Eternity is not, therefore, time, although time is certainly God's creation or, more correctly, a form of His creation. Time is distinguished from eternity by the fact that in it beginning, middle and end are distinct and even opposed as past, present and future. Eternity is just the duration which is lacking to time, as can be seen clearly at the middle point of time, in the temporal present and in its relationship to the past and the future. Eternity has and is the duration which is lacking to time. It has and is simultaneity.

Eternity is not, then, an infinite extension of time both backwards and forwards. Time can have nothing to do with God. The infinity of its extension cannot help it. For even and especially in this extension there is the separation and distance and contradiction which mark it as time and distinguish it from eternity as the creature from the Creator. It is quite correct, as in the older theology, to understand the idea of eternity and therefore God Himself first of all in this clear antithesis. In the sense mentioned, it is in fact non-temporality. *Aeternitas ipsa Dei substantia est, quae nihil habet mutabile; ibi nihil est praeteritum, quasi iam non sit; nihil est futurum, quasi nondum sit. Non est ibi nisi " est "*—and so no *fuit* and no *erit*, no "no more" and no "not yet." (Augustine, *Enarr. in Ps.* 101[2, 10]). *Fuit, quia nunquam defuit; erit, quia nunquam deerit; est, quia semper est (in Joann. tract.* 99). *Non ergo fuisti heri et eris cras, sed heri et hodie et cras es—imo nec heri nec hodie nec cras es; sed simpliciter es extra omne tempus. Nam nihil aliud est heri et hodie et cras quam " in tempore." Tu autem, licet nihil sit sine te, non es tamen in loco et tempore, sed omnia sunt in te. Nihil enim te continet, sed tu contines omnia* (Anselm of Canterbury, *Prosl.* 19). *Aeternitas Dei est essentialis proprietas Dei, per quam Deus nullo tempore finiri et nec principium secundum tempus nec finem exsistendi habere ullum, sed omni tempore antiquior et omni fine posterior et absolute citra successionem semper totus simul esse significatur* (Polanus, *Synt. Theol. chr.*, 1609, col. 928). From the witness of the biblical passages (especially in Deutero-Isaiah and Revelation), the older theology recalled the definitions in which God is spoken of as " the first and the last," as Alpha and Omega. " Before me there was no God formed, neither shall there be after me " (Is. 43[10]). " Before the mountains were brought forth, or ever thou hadst formed the earth and the world, even from everlasting to everlasting thou art God " (Ps. 90²). The final duplication, " from everlasting to everlasting," which is so common in both Old and New Testaments, may be regarded as particularly significant. It can be taken to mean from duration to duration, that is, in pure duration. This is how God exists in distinction from us who exist from one time to another, but never in pure duration. In the light of this we can understand the continuation of the passage which runs : " Thou turnest man to destruction ; and sayest, Return, ye children of men. For a thousand years in thy sight are but as yesterday when it is past, and as a watch in the night " (Ps. 90³⁻⁴ ; cf. 2 Pet. 3⁸). And Ps. 102²⁵⁻²⁷ : " Of old hast thou laid the foundation of the earth ; and the heavens are the work of thy hands. They shall perish, but thou shalt endure ; yea, all of them shall wax old like a garment ; as a vesture shalt thou change them and they shall be changed : but thou art the same, and thy years shall have no end."

In this duration God is free. It is the principle of the divine constancy, of the unchangeableness and therefore the reliability of the divine being, which we previously recognised as the determination of His freedom. Because and as God has and is this duration, eternity, He can and will be true to Himself, and we can and may put our trust in Him. God is really free to be constant, and so we may put our trust in the fact that He is. The reason why He is free to be constant is that time has no power over Him. As the One who endures He has all power over time. He is God in His eternity. But this duration is exclusively His being. " Everything has its time." Only God is eternal ; only His love in all its inner and outer, positive and negative forms—except that in the act of His love God exalts something else to share in His eternity, so that there is now and for this reason an eternal life of which even we may live in hope and an eternal fire which even we have to fear. Yet even in God's fellowship with His creature, this eternity still belongs exclusively to God. In its fellowship with God the creature is permitted to taste it in one way or another, but it does not on that account itself become God and therefore eternal. Viewed from this side eternity is thus the principle of the divine unity, uniqueness and simplicity. When we refer back to God's constancy and unity, we find that when we speak of God's eternity we have to do with a final word concerning the divine freedom. Time—which is in a sense the special creation of the " eternal " God—is the formal principle of His free activity outwards. Eternity is the principle of His freedom inwards. As the eternal One God is the One who is unique and one with Himself. He is also present to Himself and therefore omnipresent. Again, as the eternal One God is constant, and He is also the One who omnipotently knows and wills.

Whenever Holy Scripture speaks of God as eternal, it stresses His freedom. It takes Him emphatically out of the realm of man and men, away from all history and all nature. It sets Him at the beginning and end of all being and on high above it and unfathomably beneath it. But it does this in order to understand Him as the One who is utterly present to man and has

20

complete power over him in His own person. Eternity is the source of the deity of God in so far as this consists in His freedom, independence and lordship. At the very place at which later theology fell under the influence of Greek philosophy and made the concept of being predominant, the Bible speaks of the eternal God. According to the Bible it is not being as such, but that which endures, duration itself, which is the divine. It is this which also characterises and distinguishes the holiness and righteousness and wisdom of God, and also His grace and mercy and patience, or in a word, His love as divine. Eternity is before and after, above and below being. Being does not include eternity, but eternity includes being. The genuineness of being is examined and weighed and measured and tested by eternity. It is being or non-being according to its relation to eternity. God Himself is eternal, and for that reason and in that way He is.

This means that it is a poor and short-sighted view to understand God's eternity only from the standpoint that it is the negation of time. That it is duration without separation between beginning, succession and end is true only against the background of the decisive and positive characteristic that as true duration, the duration of God Himself is *the* beginning, succession and end. That it does not possess beginning, succession and end is true only to the extent that it is not " possessed," qualified, dominated, and separated by them as by a general principle of being foreign to itself. In so far as it is itself the sovereign God it does also possess beginning, succession and end. These are grounded and made possible and limited in it as true duration. It decides and conditions all beginning, succession and end. It controls them. It is itself that which begins in all beginnings, continues in all successions and ends in all endings. Without it nothing is or begins or follows or ends. In it and from it, in and from eternity everything is which is, including all beginning, succession and end. To that extent it is and has itself beginning, succession and end.

It is to be noted again that, in distinction from the concept of eternity which later dominated the Church, the Bible is interested predominantly, if not exclusively, in this primary and positive quality of eternity, and scarcely or not at all in the secondary quality which is its character as non-temporality. It is not to be explained as naive, Semitic realism, but by a conception that is incomparably more profound and goes to the heart of the matter, if in the Bible an abstract qualification of eternity as non-temporality emerges explicitly only on the very circumference of its consideration. By the terms *'olam* and αἰών the Bible understands a space of time fixed by God, and eternity is generally ascribed to God under the categories of beginning, succession and end. The biblical writers do not hesitate to speak of God's years and days, or to describe these as eternal. In God actual years and days are enumerated before numbers existed and when He did not need them. Years and days could not exist if this were not the case, if, without being bound to them, God were not their beginning, succession and end, and did not possess them in Himself. This positive quality of eternity is finely expressed in the definition of Boethius which is classic for the whole Middle Ages : *Aeternitas est interminabilis vitae tota simul et perfecta possessio* (*De consol. phil.* V, 6). This goes farther and deeper than the statements of Augustine and Anselm, which are far too occupied with the confrontation between eternity and time. It is surprising that although later this statement of Boethius was constantly quoted as authoritative it was never properly exploited. (We can see this clearly in its defence by Thomas Aquinas, which is obviously only partially convinced and certainly only partially convincing (*S. theol.* I, *qu.* 10, *art.* 1). " Total, simultaneous and complete possession of unlimited life " is eternity in fact only in so far as it is the eternity of God prior to and after, above and under all being, and not the eternity of being itself. But if it is this, it is not sufficient to contrast it as the *nunc stans* with the *nunc fluens* of time, as Boethius did in the *De trin.* 4. The interpretation of *aeternitas* by the *possessio vitae* and the *possessio vitae* by the *nunc* is correct. As the divine possession of life, God's eternity is undoubtedly the " now," the total simultaneous and complete present of His life. But the totality, simultaneity and perfection in which He possesses His life are not related to the dividedness, non-simultaneity and imperfection in which we possess ours as *stare* is to *fluere*, nor is this true of the relation of eternity to time. If an unmoving, persistent present is distinguished from our fluid and fleeting present, which can be understood only as a mathematical point, this distinction rightly describes the problem of our concept of time, but it does not rightly describe the concept of eternity in so far as this is to be understood as the *possessio vitae*. If there is a *nunc* of the total simultaneous and perfect possession of life, then this *nunc*, this " now," certainly cannot be touched by the problem of our " now," or by the instability bound up with its *fluere*. It must undoubtedly be a *nunc stans*. But the concept of the divine *nunc* must not exclude the times prior to and after the " now," the past and the future, nor may it exclude the *fluere*. On the contrary, it must include it no less than the *stare*. Eternity is the *nunc* which is undoubtedly not subject to the distinctions between past, present and future. But again, it is not subject to the abolition of these distinctions. The usual way of treating the concept of eternity in theological tradition leads to the dangerous position that there appears to be no eternity if there is no time and if eternity cannot be non-temporality ; and that there appears to be no knowledge of eternity except through time, in the form of a negation of the concept of time : *in cognitionem aeternitatis oportet nos venire per tempus* (Thomas Aquinas, *ib.*, *art.* 1 *c.*). But we know eternity primarily and properly, not by the negation of the concept of time, but by the knowledge of God as the *possessor interminabilis vitae*. It is He who is the *nunc*, the pure present. He would be this even if there were no such thing as time. He is this before and beyond all time and equally before and beyond all non-temporality. He is this *nunc* as the possessor of life completely, simultaneously and perfectly, and therefore to the inclusion and not the exclusion of the various times, beginning, succession and end. His *stare* is also a *fluere*, but without the instability that belongs to all creaturely *fluere*, the *fluere* of empirical time. Again, His *fluere* is also a *stare*, but without the immutability that belongs to all creaturely *stare*, the *stare* which is proper to the various times as they become a problem in our reflection on them. The theological concept of eternity must be set free from the Babylonian captivity of an abstract opposite to the concept of time.

God's eternity is itself beginning, succession and end. To this extent it also has them, not conditioned by them but itself conditioning as beginning, succession and end. It has them actively, not passively, not from another being or from time, but from itself and therefore in itself. God is both the prototype and foreordination of all being, and therefore also the prototype and foreordination of time. God has time because and as He has eternity. Thus He does not first have it on the basis of creation, which is also, of course, the creation of time. He does have time for us, the time of revelation, the time of Jesus Christ, and therefore the time of His patience, our life-time, time for repentance and faith. But it is really He Himself who has time for us. He Himself is time for us. For His revelation as Jesus Christ is really God Himself.

There is no place here for the reservation or secret complaint or accusation that basically and in Himself God is pure eternity and therefore has no time, or that he has time for us only apparently and figuratively. Those who do not have time are those who do not have eternity either. In fact it is an illegitimate anthropomorphism to think of God as if He did not eternally have time; as if he did not have time, and therefore time for us, in virtue of His eternity.

Nothing less than the assurance of faith and the possibility of trust in the enduring God depends on the fact that time is not excluded from His duration but included in it, so that we in our time may recognise and honour His time, the time given us by Him. This is just what we may and ought to do. We have seen again and again that God is alive. His unity does not exclude but includes multiplicity and His constancy movement. And God does not first create multiplicity and movement, but He is one and simple, He is constant, in such a way that all multiplicity and movement have their prototype and pre-existence in Himself. Time, too, pre-exists in this way in Him, in His eternity, as His creation, i.e., with space, the form of His creation. The form of creation is the being of God for a reality distinct from Himself. But the form of God's being for us and our world is space and time. The prototypes in God's being in Himself which correspond to this form are His omnipresence in regard to space, and His eternity in regard to time (cf. pp. 464 f.). If God in Himself is the living God, this prototype, too, is in Himself identical with His eternity. The fact that He is the enduring God, duration itself, does not prevent God from being origin, movement, and goal in and for Himself. What distinguishes eternity from time is the fact that there is in Him no opposition or competition or conflict, but peace between origin, movement and goal, between present, past and future, between " not yet," " now " and " no more," between rest and movement, potentiality and actuality, whither and whence, here and there, this and that. In Him all these things are *simul*, held together by the omnipotence of His knowing and willing, a totality without gap or rift, free from the threat of death under which time, our time, stands. It is not the case, then, that in eternity all these distinctions do not exist.

If this were so, if this and therefore abstract non-temporality were the truth about eternity, it would be far too akin to time; indeed it would be only an image of time in the mirror of our reflection, as was actually held by L. Feuerbach. But it is eternity in that it carries and prefigures all this in itself. It is in this way and this way alone that it is God's eternity, and God Himself. Thomas Aquinas was therefore right to admit *quod verba diversorum temporum attribuuntur Deo, inquantum eius aeternitas omnia tempora includit*. This is true irrespective of the fact *quod ipse non varietur per praesens praeteritum et futurum*

(*S. theol.* I, *qu.* 10, *art.* 2, *ad.* 4).   And if in his view eternity and time are to be distinguished by the fact that *aeternitas est tota simul, in tempore autem est prius et posterius* (*ib., art.* 4, *s.c.*), we must also agree with him when he says : *Deus videt omnia in sua aeternitate, quae, cum sit simplex, toti tempore adest et ipsum concludit* (*S. theol.* I, *qu.* 57, *art.* 3 *c.*).   *Cuilibet tempori vel instanti temporis praesentialiter adest aeternitas* (*S. c. gent.* I, 66).   *Nunc aeternitatis invariatum adest omnibus partibus temporis* (*In* I *Sent. d.* 37, *qu.* 2, *art.* 1, *ad.* 4). This *adesse, includere* or *concludere* clearly denotes a positive relation to time which is the special possession of eternity.   That it is this must be brought into greater prominence than in the older theology, without cancelling or blurring the distinction between the two, or imposing upon eternity the limitations of time. Eternity does not lack absolutely what we know as present, as before and after, and therefore as time.   Rather this has its ultimate and real being in the *simul* of eternity. Eternity simply lacks the fleeting nature of the present, the separation between before and after.   Eternity is certainly the negation of created time in so far as it has no part in the problematical and questionable nature of our possession of time, our present and our beginning, continuation and ending. But eternity is not the negation of time *simpliciter*.   On the contrary, time is absolutely presupposed in it.   Eternity is the negation of time only because and to the extent that it is first and foremost God's time and therefore real time, in the same way as God's omnipresence is not simply the negation of our space, but first and foremost is positively God's space and therefore real space.

It is on this positive meaning of the concept of eternity, which the older theologians denoted by the term *sempiternitas*, that the main stress, and not merely a secondary stress, must significantly fall. For, rightly understood, the statement that God is eternal tells us what God is, not what He is not. It is only from this point that the negation which is certainly necessary, the knowledge of what God is not, has force behind it. The force behind this negation is the perfection of the Creator of time over against His creation. But in the perfection of the Creator even time is not simply nothing. It is perfect in contrast to His creation.   It is real duration, real beginning, continuation and ending. If all this exists in an imperfect and intrinsically unintelligible way, yet with relative reality in the form of created time, as the form of our existence and our world, the reason for this is that it has its basis (in its relativity and also in its reality) in the decree of the will of God in creation and providence. The presupposition of this basis in God Himself is His eternity. As the eternal One who as such has and Himself is absolutely real time, He gives us the relatively but in this way genuinely real time proper to us.   As the eternal One He is present personally at every point of our time. As the eternal One it is He who surrounds our time and rules it with all that it contains. How can He be and do all this if as the eternal One He does not Himself have His own time, superior to ours, undisturbed by the fleetingness and separations of our time, simultaneous with all our times, but in this way and for this reason absolutely real time ?

It is because God is the eternal One that Psalm 31[15] is to be taken literally : " My times are in thy hands." God's hands, the workings of His omnipotence, are not themselves timeless but supremely temporal, so that our time can be really in them, and can be not merely apparent but real time. As the tree on the river's bank is always beside it, yet does not flow with it ; as the Pole Star is at the zenith of the vault of heaven, yet does not move round with it ; and as the ocean surrounds the land on all sides and yet is not land itself—so the eternal God co-exists with the time created by Him. The second of these illustrations is used by J. Gerhard : *Ut circa polum immobilem coelestis machina perpetuo circumgyratur motu, ita ut nec poli immobilitas per motum machinae coelestis turbetur, nec motus machinae per poli immobilitatem sistatur: sic aeternitas coexistit partibus temporis sibi invicem succedentibus, ut nec fixa aeternitatis immobilitas et immobilitas per continuam temporum fluentium successionem turbetur, nec temporum successio per fixam aeternitatis immobilitatem aboleatur* (*Loci theol.*, 1609 f., II, 143). But all these illustrations are imperfect and must be at once abandoned. For God is the Creator and Lord of our time, and therefore eternity is the *tota simul et perfecta possessio vitae*, and co-exists with time and all it contains with a superiority which the tree cannot have over the river or the Pole Star over the vault of heaven or the ocean over the continent. Consequently the statement that God co-exists with our time cannot be reversed, as is possible with the elements in the illustrations. Roman Catholic theology betrays at this point its ineradicable interest in an equilibrium between the being of God and the being of the creatures by hazarding this reversal and, on the ground that *aeternitas* means *sempiternitas*, ascribing to temporal and created things, not indeed eternal creation, but a co-existence with God's eternity which is not simply one of intention but is physically real (cf. especially F. Diekamp, *Kath. Dogm.*[6] Vol. I, 1930, pp. 169 f.). In the first instance too little is ascribed to time (i.e., God's time), and then all at once too much is ascribed to it (i.e., created time). It is true that God knows and wills temporal things eternally, that He can know and will them, and really does know and will them, in their temporal existence because He is eternal, and that He co-exists with them as the One who is eternal. But this does not permit us to reverse the matter and say that they for their part eternally co-exist with Him and His eternity. They exist in time and only in time, in the time given and proper to them and not in God's time, enclosed and ruled, then, by God's time, but in their own created form of time, in the time that is granted them by the grace of creation. On the basis and presupposition of this divine permission and in virtue of it they are objects of the eternal knowing and willing of God in this order and co-exist with Him—but not in any other order, not as if in virtue of the time granted them they for their part had a right or a claim to share in God's time and therefore in eternity, not as if the statement about God could be transformed into a statement about them. *Quod licet Jovi non licet bovi !* From the fact that God's eternity in its eternal Now embraces and contains all parts of time and all things in itself simultaneously and at one moment, we cannot deduce the general truth that things are present to God either in physical reality or even in intention in a *nunc aeternitatis* and therefore from eternity. God knows them and wills them. In this way they are certainly present to Him from eternity, enclosed in the Now of eternity even before their existence and without it. But they have their existence and also their co-existence with God only in the positive act of the divine creation, which can only be understood in its character as an act of divine grace if we refrain from finding a partner for God's eternity in the co-existence of the result of this act, in the co-existence of the creature. We glorify God by seeking the basis of our temporal existence in His eternity. But we do not glorify Him if we try to use His eternity in its character as the basis of our temporal existence as a pretext for giving our temporal existence the character of something analogous to His eternity, as is obviously the case if we allow ourselves to make this reversal. The part-truth of the concept of eternity in Augustine and Anselm is of particular relevance in this connexion, as is also the recognition of the freedom of God in relation to our time and all it contains. For they make this reversal quite impossible.

A correct understanding of the positive side of the concept of eternity, free from all false conclusions, is gained only when we are clear that we are speaking about the eternity of the triune God. We are speaking about the God who is eternally the Father, who without origin or begetting is Himself the origin and begetter, and therefore undividedly the beginning, succession and end, all at once in His own essence. We are speaking about the God who is also eternally the Son, who is begotten of the Father and yet of the same essence with Him, who as begotten of the Father is also undividedly beginning, succession and end, all at once in His own essence. We are speaking about the God who is also eternally the Spirit, who proceeds from the Father and the Son but is of the same essence as both, who as the Spirit of the Father and the Son is also undividedly beginning, succession and end, all at once in His own essence. It is this " all," this God, who is the eternal God, really the eternal God. For this " all " is pure duration, free from all the fleetingness and the separations of what we call time, the *nunc aeternitatis* which cannot come into being or pass away, which is conditioned by no distinctions, which is not disturbed and interrupted but established and confirmed in its unity by its trinity, by the inner movement of the begetting of the Father, the being begotten of the Son and the procession of the Spirit from both. Yet in it there is order and succession. The unity is in movement. There is a before and an after. God is once and again and a third time, without dissolving the once-for-allness, without destroying the persons or their special relations to one another, without anything arbitrary in this relationship or the possibility of its reversal. If in this triune being and essence of God there is nothing of what we call time, this does not justify us in saying that time is simply excluded in God, or that His essence is simply a negation of time. On the contrary, the fact that God has and is Himself time, and the extent to which this is so, is necessarily made clear to us in His essence as the triune God. This is His time, the absolutely real time, the form of the divine being in its triunity, the beginning and ending which do not mean the limitation of Him who begins and ends, a juxtaposition which does not mean any exclusion, a movement which does not signify the passing away of anything, a succession which in itself is also beginning and end.

Hoc principium ordinis non excluditur aeternitate, nec opponitur aeternitati (Polanus, *Synt. Theol. chr.*, 1609, *col.* 929). But it is not enough to distinguish this *principium ordinis* (which is not to be denied to the essence of God in view of His being as Father, Son and Holy Spirit) from the *principium temporis* as it belongs to creatures. On the contrary, this *principium ordinis* is clearly identical with a *principium temporis* in God Himself. It is certainly to be distinguished from the idea of created time, which along with time itself belongs

to creation and not to God, and as such can only be distinguished from eternity.
Yet it is a *principium temporis*, indeed *the principium temporis*, in so far as the
ordering here is also time. It is the absolutely unique time of God distinct from
all other times, but for that reason true time, the duration which makes possible
and actual all other duration, duration in the space of creation. A co-existence
of the creature can be ascribed to God's eternity understood in this way only as
the co-existence of the creature taken up into fellowship with God by the grace
of the Son and the Holy Spirit, and not as an attribute of the creature as such.
Thus God's essence cannot in any sense be burdened by an eternal partnership
with the creature.

Again, a correct understanding of the concept of eternity is reached
only if we start from the other side, from the real fellowship between
God and the creature, and therefore between eternity and time.
This means starting from the incarnation of the divine Word in Jesus
Christ. The fact that the Word became flesh undoubtedly means
that, without ceasing to be eternity, in its very power as eternity,
eternity became time. Yes, it became time. What happens in Jesus
Christ is not simply that God gives us time, our created time, as the
form of our own existence and world, as is the case in creation and
in the whole ruling of the world by God as its Lord. In Jesus Christ
it comes about that God takes time to Himself, that He Himself,
the eternal One, becomes temporal, that He is present for us in the
form of our own existence and our own world, not simply embracing
our time and ruling it, but submitting Himself to it, and permitting
created time to become and be the form of His eternity.

The fulfilment of (and within) the positive relation of God to the world established by the creation is the fact that God as the Creator and Lord of the world
Himself becomes a creature, man, in His Word and His Son. Note that He
not only creates and preserves man. He is not only beside him and with him.
He not only deals with him as his Lord, Judge and Redeemer. He certainly
does all these things in Jesus Christ. But beyond all this He Himself becomes
man, and in that way reconciles man with Himself. This does not mean that
He who is utterly above us ceases to be who He is in His superiority. But while
He is still this, He humbles Himself and lifts us up by becoming one of us, like
us in all things. In this fulfilling and surpassing of creation in Jesus Christ
God actually takes time to Himself and makes it His own. He raises time to a
form of His own eternal being. For our being, as created human being, has
this form, and He could not assume our being, could not become and be like
us and reconcile us to Himself, without taking time also and concealing and
revealing His eternal being in it. His own time, eternity, is not so precious to
Him, it is obviously not so conditioned in itself, nor is it the case that God has
and is eternity in such a way, that He must set it over against our time and
keep it far away with the distance of the Creator from the creature. And on
the other hand our created time is not of such little value, and in its creatureliness
it does not have such independence or autonomy over against the eternal Creator,
nor do we have it for ourselves in such a way, that God is prevented from causing
it to be His own garment and even His own body. No contraction or diminution of
deity takes place, but the true and fullest power of deity is displayed, in the
fact that it has such power over itself and its creature that it can become one
with it without detriment to itself. This is just what takes place in Jesus Christ.
His name is the refutation of the idea of a God who is only timeless. His name

describes a divine presence which is not only eternal but also temporal. God Himself is present, not only eternally as He is to all time, but temporally in His eternity in the act of the epiphany of the Messiah Jesus, and again in every act of faith in the Messiah Jesus. That this presence of God is genuinely temporal is shown by the fact that Jesus Christ's epiphany has a " before " and an " after." It could and had to be the object of expectation in a " not yet " and of recollection in a " no more." Again, it could and had to be the object of recollection (of the Exodus from Egypt) even in the " not yet," and of expectation (of the final appearance of Jesus Christ) even in the " no more." Faith in the One who is present always was and is faith in the One who has come and comes again. Thus in the fulfilment and surpassing of His positive relation to the world established by creation God has subjected Himself to time, and made it His own, and subjected it to Himself in such a way that to know and have Him as the eternal One we must cling utterly to His temporality, to His presence, to the fact that He has come and will come again in Jesus Christ.

If this is so, from this standpoint too we cannot understand God's eternity as pure timelessness. Since it became time, and God Himself, without ceasing to be the eternal God, took time and made it His own, we have to confess that He was able to do this. He was not only able to have and give time as the Creator, but in Jesus Christ He was able Himself to be temporal. If we say that God's eternity excluded this possibility, we are not speaking of the eternity which He has revealed to us, and therefore not of God's real eternity, the true eternity. We are speaking of a poor, sham eternity. True eternity includes this possibility, the potentiality of time. True eternity has the power to take time to itself, this time, the time of the Word and Son of God. It has the power itself to be temporal in Him. We cannot deny it this power. It has exercised it in Jesus Christ. In Jesus Christ it has been revealed as its power. But this being the case we cannot understand eternity only as the negation of time. It is obvious that we are dealing with the power of the Creator and Lord of the world. It is pure power. To use it does not burden God with the being of the creature, and to apply it does not lay Him under obligation to the creature. He always maintains His superiority in it. When He subjects Himself to time He does freely what He does not have to do. He masters time. He re-creates it and heals its wounds, the fleetingness of the present, and the separation of past and the future from one another and from the present. He does not do this in an alien and distant way, but as present Himself. Real created time acquires in Jesus Christ and in every act of faith in Him the character and stamp of eternity, and life in it acquires the special characteristics of eternal life. The God who does this and therefore can do it is obviously in Himself both timeless and temporal. He is timeless in that the defects of our time, its fleetingness and its separations, are alien to Him and disappear, and in Him all beginning, continuation and ending form a unique Now, steadfast yet moving, moving yet steadfast. He is temporal in that our time with its defects is not so alien to Him that He cannot take it to Himself in His grace, mercy and patience, Himself rectifying and healing it and lifting it up to the time of eternal life. This power exercised in Jesus Christ consists in His triune being. But this means that it consists in His grace and mercy and patience. For, benefiting us in God's revelation and reconciliation, these have their inner divine basis in God's triune being. If we try to cling to the idea of a divine eternity that is purely timeless, we must be careful that we are not compelled to deny both God's revelation and reconciliation in Jesus Christ, and also the triune being of God revealed and active in them. If we cannot deny these, we cannot deny that although God's eternity is not itself time it is as such the absolute basis of time, and therefore absolute readiness for it.

The reversal in which an eternal co-existence with God is ascribed to created time and temporal things is made quite impossible for us from the christological standpoint. In the light of the incarnation in which eternity itself became time, and this readiness of eternity for time was conclusively manifest, we cannot and will not speak of more than a readiness of eternity for time. God neither was nor is bound to take time to Himself. The readiness which belongs to His essence, and without which eternity would not be true eternity, does not compel Him to actualise it. He does not need our time. Nor as Creator does He need to give us time. Nor as Reconciler does He need Himself to become temporal. He has time, that is, true and absolute time, in His eternity, for this itself is a readiness for time. He gives us time by creating and preserving time. He takes time to Himself for us by Himself becoming temporal. Thus we can glorify only the grace of God, the grace of creation and the grace of reconciliation, when we declare that God Himself is not only timeless, but that in this readiness for time, in the timeless ordering and succession of His triune being, He is also temporal. The fact that we have time in virtue of this grace, or further that in faith in Jesus Christ we are allowed to be God's contemporaries, to live in God's eternity, in the new time of the Son and Word of God, even in the midst of our time, does not justify us in setting up a corresponding predicate for the creature and his time as such, or in saying that we co-exist eternally with God as He in His eternity certainly co-exists with us. The comfort and power of this latter statement stand or fall by whether we leave and accept it unreversed.

For the same reason as in the case of the Roman Catholic inversion we must question and reject A. Ritschl's peculiar conception of eternity (*Unterricht* [3], 1886, § 14 : *Justification and Reconciliation*, E.T., 1900, pp. 296 ff.). Ritschl tried to see God's eternity in " the unchanging continuity and identity of the divine will in relation to its goal," in the fact that " in all the changes in things which denote the alteration in His working He is Himself the same, as He also maintains the final goal and plan in which He creates and governs the world." His will, continuous and identical in itself, is directed towards the kingdom of God as the goal of His whole creation. In relation to this purpose and goal of creation, the time which precedes is cancelled, i.e., it is of no " value " as that which has not attained it. " The realisation of each subordinate means by the divine will is reflected in its self-feeling or blessedness as the realisation of the whole." The final purpose of God thus consists concretely in the creating and preserving of the Church as the community of the kingdom of God. Therefore God's eternity is the continuity which overcomes the limits of time, the continuity of His will directed towards this community. It is to be noted that in this thought there is a genuine concern to produce a positive conception of eternity. We must object, however, that at this point the Creator and the creature, God's will and His purpose in the world, are brought too close to one another. In this mutual relationship God and the Church are not in fact bound to one another. It is certainly true that God's continuous and identical will is directed to the establishment of the Church and preservation of the Church. Yet God is eternal quite apart from this goal adopted by His will, and therefore quite apart from the direction of His will to it. Its direction gives us confidence and draws its strength from the fact that it is this will already in itself. The fact that God has bound Himself and undertaken to establish and preserve His Church in Christ is again not a reversible sentence. It must not be misused to make the Church itself, as the object of God's eternal election, the *telos* of His will, and therefore a moment in His eternity. God co-exists with the Church too, but that does not mean that it co-exists with Him. As God's omnipotence is more than His omnicausality, and is not exhausted but merely operative in it, God's eternity is more than the unity of all times with the goal and purpose of His will, and is not exhausted by this unity. It is rather the presupposition of this unity, without which it cannot be believed and known as accomplished and maintained by God.

Defined and delimited in this way against misuse, the temporality of eternity may be described in detail as the pre-temporality, supra-temporality and post-temporality of eternity. With these terms we return to the direct proximity of the biblical outlook. After what has been said it will be at once apparent that it is not a matter of naïvety that in the Bible the idea of eternity is continually brought into a positive relationship to time, irrespective of the fact that this concept distinguishes God from the world and therefore also from time. For even as it points to this distinction it also indicates the relationship between the two, describing God as the One who is and rules before time, in time and again after time, the One who is not conditioned by time, but conditions it absolutely in His freedom. He does this in a threefold respect. He precedes its beginning, He accompanies its duration, and He exists after its end. This is the concrete form of eternity as readiness for time. It is God's power, indeed God Himself, who has the power to exist before, above and after time, before its beginning, above its duration and after its end.

In hac aeternitate tanquam in fonte amplissimo vel potius vastissimo quodam oceano innatat gutta illa fluxa (Polanus, *Synt. theol. chr.*, 1609, *col.* 930). Once again the illustration is inadequate, but every improvement on it is inadequate too. We might be inclined to compare time with an island instead of a drop in the ocean of eternity, as a better indication of the distinctiveness and demarcation of the two realms. But then we would have to admit that Polan's illustration brings out the relation between the two better—God's complete lordship over time. But where God's reality is a matter of faith, there is no question of seeing anything, and so there can be no adequate illustration. What is certain is that God and eternity must be understood as the element which surrounds time on all sides and therefore includes its dimensions. It is the element which is able to comprehend time, to create it and control it. Yet this does not mean that it was necessary for it to create time and therefore to give it reality. It does not mean that God would be any less eternal if time did not exist outside Himself. The case is exactly the same as in God's omnipresence, omnipotence and unity. In relation to all spaces God is the original and proper space, the Omnipresent ; in relation to all powers He is the original and proper power, the Omnipotent ; and in relation to all unities He is the original and proper

One, unique and simple. And He is all these things even if apart from Him there was no space or power or unity. It is in this way that eternity has and is a positive relationship to time, that it is itself temporal, and would be so even if no time existed apart from it.

In virtue of this readiness of His for time, God also creates, preserves and rules it. Because His eternity is this readiness for time, it is no mere figure of speech to say that God is before, above and after all things. On the contrary, it is unreservedly serious and divine truth. In virtue of this character as readiness for time, He, His eternity itself, is able to be before it, above it and after it. And since God did choose to create time and did create it He is all this : " He who was, and is, and is to come." And again He is it, not figuratively or metaphorically, but in a divine, unsurpassable reality which is not to be relativised. We have good reason to give clear emphasis to this truth and therefore to the concepts of the pre-temporality, supra-temporality and post-temporality of the eternal God. For a great deal depends on this truth and on the legitimacy of these concepts. It is only if they are true and legitimate that the whole content of the Christian message—creation as the basis of man's existence, established by God, reconciliation as the renewal of his existence accomplished by God, redemption as the revelation of his existence to be consummated by God (and therefore as the revelation of the meaning of His creation)—can be understood as God's Word of truth and not as the myth of a pious or impious self-consciousness, the comfortless content of some human monologue which lays no real claim upon us, the substance of a well-meant pastoral fiction, mere wishful thinking or a terrifying dream. The Christian message cannot be distinguished from a myth or dream of this kind unless God's eternity has temporality in the sense described, and God is really pre-temporal, supra-temporal and post-temporal. If God's eternity is not understood in this way the Christian message cannot be proclaimed in any credible way or received by faith. For the content of this message depends on the fact that God was and is and is to be, that our existence stands under the sign of a divine past, present and future, that in its differentiation this sign does not point away into space, to a God who, in fact, is neither past, present nor future. Without God's complete temporality the content of the Christian message has no shape. Its proclamation is only an inarticulate mumbling. Therefore everything depends on whether God's temporality is the simple truth which cannot be attacked from any quarter because it has its basis in God Himself, which is not then a mere appearance, a bubble constructed by human feeling or thought. And it is as well to consider this whole matter from the other side too. In the temporality of all its statements the Christian message is the truth which binds and comforts men. In the One who, according to this message, was and is and is to come we have to do with the true God Himself.

The message calls us to faith in virtue of its own weight. It attests itself as God's Word and therefore destroys, so to speak, from within the suspicion that we have to do only with the imaginative drama of a myth. But because this is the case, it is quite impossible to deny to God's eternity the possession of preparedness for time and therefore temporality. It is for this reason that this is true, and the concepts of pre-temporality, supra-temporality and post-temporality are legitimate because they simply spell out and analyse what the Christian message guarantees to be the Word of God and therefore the truth. This message can neither be proclaimed nor believed as the truth without the proclaiming and believing of these statements about God. They are not simply inferences from the Gospel. As certainly as the Gospel tells us the truth about God, they are elements in the Gospel itself and as such. The Gospel itself and as such cannot be spoken and take shape without these statements being made and this understanding of the divine eternity forcing itself upon us—not indirectly, as a scholastic parergon, but directly, because the Gospel must either remain unproclaimed or be spoken in the form of these statements. We shall go through them quickly to remind ourselves of the two aspects—that the truth of God's Word depends on their truth, and that they themselves are based on and preserved by the truth of God's Word.

God is pre-temporal. This means that His existence precedes ours and that of all things. It does not do this only in its own way in correspondence with its essence and dignity. It does it physically as well, so that there can now be no question whatever of the possibility of an inversion. It may sound trivial to say that God was before we were, and before all the presuppositions and conditions of our existence. Yet in its unqualified, literal sense it is profound and decisive. God was in the beginning which precedes all other beginnings. He was in the beginning in which we and all things did not yet exist. He was in the beginning which does not look back on any other beginning presupposed by this beginning itself. God was in Himself. He was no less Himself, no less perfect, not subject to any lack, superabounding from the very first even without us and the world. This is God's eternity as pre-temporality. Always and everywhere and in every way God exists as the eternal One in the sense of this pre-temporality.

God's freedom and therefore His love, His grace and mercy and patience, can be measured only if we start from this point, or rather they can be known and understood in their immeasurability only from this point. It is because God is pre-temporal that He does not owe us anything ; either our existence, or that He should establish and maintain fellowship with us, or that He should lead us to a goal in this fellowship, to a hereafter which has a place in His own hereafter. He need not have done this. For He could have done without it, because He is who He is before it and without it. For the very same reason, of course, He need not do without it, but can have it as a reality in His sight without owing it to us or to Himself. And as the One who was before it, He did in fact choose not to be without us. His eternal grace and mercy and patience are displayed in the fact that He knew us, and knew about us and all things; that He willed to create us and elect us and give us eternal bliss. The knowledge of this actual knowing and willing on God's part depends on whether it is understood as His knowing and willing which preceded all time and established and upholds time itself. We cannot understand Him without this pre-existence in His divinity, in His holiness and righteousness and wisdom, and also in His omnipotence. We are not from eternity, and neither is our world. There was a time when we and the world did not exist. This was the " pre-time," the eternity of God. And in this time, before time, everything, including time itself, was decided and determined, everything that is in time. In this time God wrote His decrees and books, in which everything is marked down that is to be and occur, including every name and the great and the small events of every bearer of every name. In this time God decided to call into being the world and man by His Word, in the wisdom and power of His eternal Word. In this time He determined to send this eternal Word into this created world to this created man. Therefore, to reconcile the world with Himself He determined to permit the world itself, man, flesh, to be. In this time God exercised the providence and foreordination by which all the being and self-determination of created things is enclosed. In this time He decided on the Church as the fellowship of those who are to be wakened to faith in His Word by His Holy Spirit and to be preserved in this faith. And with this He determined the goal of all His willing, the salvation of all who believe and their blessedness in His own eternal hereafter. All this—we must say it in view of its centre in Jesus Christ— was determined beforehand by and in God Himself. For this pre-time is the pure time of the Father and the Son in the fellowship of the Holy Spirit. And in this pure divine time there took place the appointment of the eternal Son for the temporal world, there occurred the readiness of the Son to do the will of the eternal Father, and there ruled the peace of the eternal Spirit—the very thing later revealed at the heart of created time in Jesus Christ. In this pure divine time there took place that free display of the divine grace and mercy and patience, that free resolve to which time owes its existence, its content and its goal. The name in which this is manifested and known to us is Jesus Christ. To say that everything is predestined, that everything comes from God's free, eternal love which penetrates and rules time from eternity, is just the same as to say simply that everything is determined in Jesus Christ. For Jesus Christ is before all time, and therefore eternally the Son and the Word of God, God Himself in His turning to the world, the sum and substance of God in so far as God chose to create and give time, to take time to Himself, and finally to fix for time its end and goal in His eternal hereafter. In this turning to the world, and with it to a time distinct from His eternity, this God, Yahweh Sabaoth, is identical with Jesus Christ. If we understand eternity as pre-time— and we must understand it in this way too—we have to recognise that eternity itself bears the name of Jesus Christ. Jn. 8[58] is relevant in this connexion: " Verily, verily, I say unto you, before Abraham was, I am." So, too, is Eph. 1[4f.] : " He hath chosen us in him before the foundation of the world, that we should be holy and without blame before Him in love : having predestinated us unto the adoption of children by Jesus Christ to himself, according to the good pleasure of his will, to the praise of the glory of his grace." So, too, is 1 Pet. 1[18f.] ; " Ye were redeemed . . . with the precious blood of Christ, as of a lamb without blemish and without spot : who verily was foreordained before the foundation of the world, but was manifest in these last times for you, who by him do believe in God." Note how in all these and similar passages the eternal presence of God over and in time is established by reference to a pre-time in which time, and with it the existence of man and its renewal, is foreseen and determined.

What is to be said about time and its relation to eternity derives from the fact that eternity is also before time.

God is supra-temporal. This concept is not adequate to express what has to be expressed here. For completeness we should have to coin a new English word like " co-temporal " or " in-temporal." We retain " supra-temporal " because, like " pre-temporal " and " post-temporal," this expresses the fact that eternity is the element which embraces time on all sides. However, after all that we have said, this " supra-temporal " must not have the flavour of " timeless." Here too, and especially, we have to do with the positive relationship of eternity to time. This consists, as we now are going to contend, in the fact that eternity faithfully accompanies time on high, so to speak, just as on a journey we are accompanied from one horizon to another by the vault of heaven which begins and ends beyond every horizon. Or to be more precise it consists in the fact that eternity does not will to be without time, but causes itself to be accompanied by time. God is as we are. God endures in His pure and perpetual duration as we have our confused and fleeting duration. It is not that God merely was and will be. This is also true, and everything depends on whether eternity is understood as the divine *perfectum* and *futurum*, and our past and future as surrounded by God's eternity. But everything also depends on whether God's " before " and " after " are not separated from one another, and our time is not thought of as a self-enclosed middle separated from the beginning and end. It is certainly separated from its own beginning and end. It would not be time if it did not possess extension or existed without this separation. But it is not separated from its beginning and end in God's eternity. God's eternity accompanies it ; and it, too, may accompany God's eternity by which it is created and in which it also has its goal. God's eternity goes with it ; and it, too, goes, it has its own confused and fleeting and yet constant and real movement, because eternity goes over it, and above its movement the unalterable hours of eternity strike, which the strokes of our clocks can only echo and answer in a childlike or even childish way. God's eternity is in time. Time itself is in eternity. Its whole extension from beginning to end, each single part of it, every epoch, every lifetime, every new and closing year, every passing hour : they are all in eternity like a child in the arms of its mother. Time does not limit eternity. It is not its *constituens*. It does not exist in independent reality over against it. It is its creation. But as such it is preserved and kept in it. As such it is under the law and confidence of its presence. This, the divine life which bears time, is God's eternity as supra-temporality. Always and everywhere and in every way God is who He is in the sense of this supra-temporality too.

According to Lk. 2¹⁴ the message of the angels which proclaims the birth of Jesus Christ is : " Glory to God in the highest and on earth peace, good will toward men." This is the most accurate description of God's supra-temporality. For these words declare that, since God is in the highest over the earth, and all glory belongs and is due to the One who is there, there is peace on earth, there is not to be any lack of security on earth, that is, among the men to whom this God who dwells in the highest has turned His good will. God's love and there-fore His freedom, His holiness, righteousness and wisdom, are to be measured in all their immeasurability by His supra-temporality. It is as God is supra-temporal that He realises His love, giving us that which He is under no obliga-tion to give us—our existence, fellowship with Him, and in this fellowship a living hope. It is as He is supra-temporal that He wills not to be alone, not to be apart from us, that He exercises and interprets His freedom in our favour, that He causes His holiness, righteousness and wisdom to be not merely barriers, but at the same time and as such doors to us, that He wills to be not only God, but God among and for the men of His good will, and that He creates for the glory proper to Him in the highest a complement on earth in the peace which is guaranteed to us to magnify His glory and to be thankful to Him. It is in this way that God knows and wills us and all things. Everything now depends on our right understanding of God's supra-temporality, of the accompaniment of our time by His eternity, of the height in which He has His glory, to which our peace may correspond. God's love would not be divine, gracious, merciful and patient if it were not the love which dwells in this way on high, but which really comes to us from high heaven—eternal grace, eternal mercy and eternal patience, eternal in the positive sense, just described, of supra-temporality. We are not God. We only have time. But it is the Lord of time who is God. Eternity is over time. Time itself is with and in eternity. We have time as it is en-closed by eternity. We may and must seek to know God as present not only in that which is before all time, but in all time and in each single part of time. Mysticism is wrong, of course, when it chooses to forget the divine " before " in its supposed apprehension of God in the present. And any conception of the relation of time and eternity is in error which tries to find eternity only in an immediate perpendicular connexion with each moment of time, and does not see that the basis of time is also in the divine " before " and " after." The God who was not " before " and will not be " after " is not " now." A doctrine of God which consists and results in the hypostatising of our " now " between the times, what we think we know as our present, or perhaps of our temporal consciousness, or in speculation on the connexion of all times with God, is more the doctrine of an idol than the doctrine of God. Only supra-time, which is also pre-time and post-time, is divine. This is unequivocally withdrawn from our oversight and control, and from the utterly foolish confusion of the real and eternal present of eternity with the present which belongs to our time and is only given us in its fleetingness. When, however, these errors are set aside, the truth remains that we really do have to seek God in the perpendicular relationship as well, in each present of our time, although we have also to seek Him in the past and future which surround each present of our time. It is His love, the comple-ment of the glory which is His possession and His due in the highest, that He is actually to be sought and found even here in time. Eternity did not cease when time began, to begin again when time ceases. Eternity is in the midst, just as God Himself is in the midst with us. It is not a divine preserve. On the con-trary, by giving us time, God also gives us eternity in a real sense. Our decisions in time occur with a responsibility to eternity which is not partial but total, and we may and must understand and accept the confidence with which we can undertake them as a complete confidence which we gain from eternity. Having loved us from eternity, and granted us from eternity our existence, fellowship with Himself, life in hope and eternal life itself, God also loves us here and now, in the temporality ordained for us from eternity, wholeheartedly and unreservedly, so that any doubt or lack of assurance is a burden which we impose on ourselves, while from His side there is only one message even to our life in its temporality, and that is : " Be not over-anxious." In all its inaccessible distance the divine " before " does not separate us from God's love. It does so as little as the divine " after " in its equally inaccessible distance. It cannot do this because it is the distance of that high heaven of which the complement on earth is peace among the men of the divine good will. If mysticism, and the existentialism which secretly draws its life from mysticism, is satisfied merely to uphold this truth, to the extent that it does this there is no need to oppose it. Equally the well-known statement of L. von Ranke, that the meaning of each epoch is immediate to God, is not without theological truth. It can be understood as a statement whose subject is not history in itself but God as the Lord of history. It can mean that God gives its meaning directly to each epoch because He is in fact directly eternal over each epoch. The statement can mean that we are bidden, as we look at any epoch, not to fail to see that the God who has given it its meaning is gracious, merciful and patient, but also holy, righteous and wise. Understood in this way the statement is a guarantee against all such views of world history as optimistically or pessimistically anticipate the final judgment, arbitrarily exalting an epoch here and equally arbitrarily debasing an epoch there. To be consistent we must add that the meaning of all world history as such is also immediate to God, determined by the decision of His judgment and His goodness, by the dominion of His wrath and His mercy. All time is really in His hands. It is from this standpoint, and only from this standpoint, that we have to consider our own and every epoch. This means, to be concrete, that because the concrete work of God's hands in time is the Church which has its root in Israel, every epoch, every period of history and every life-time has its significance from Israel and the Church and with a view to Israel and the Church. In its innermost content, its final riddles and revelations, its true possessions and privations, its real height of achievement and its catastrophes, and no less in the times which are neither white nor black, which seem empty and are really most decisive, the history of the world is not really " world-history," but the history of Israel and the Church. Of course, it is only when we see and understand time and its significance in this concentrated way that the assertion of God's supra-temporality and the security of time in His eternity is credible and effective, and von Ranke's statement is more than a speculation in which the decisive word " God," being undefined, can be filled in arbitrarily and will finally have only the character of a symbol for the Unknown, so that its connexion with the idea of a " meaning " is quite illegitimate. The angels' message in Lk. 2¹⁴, from which we began, does not proclaim a general truth. It proclaims the fulfilment of the promise to Israel and the basis and meaning of the Church—the birth of Jesus Christ. It is in this that time is secured in eternity. It is in this that time has its meaning immediately to God. Our statements cannot be separated from it. They are statements of faith, confessing the One who is the fulfilment of time and of all times. We must speak of the supra-temporality of God the Father, Son and Holy Spirit if under the title of eternity we are not to speak secretly of a time-less God and therefore of a godless time, again taking refuge in a desperate hypostatising of the " now " of our time which cannot be hypostatised. In the last resort the older theology was quite right to return again and again to the passage in Ps. 2⁶ᶠ·, in which God says to the King set " on Zion my holy mountain " : " Thou art my Son, this day have I begotten thee." The " to-day " of the setting up of the King is the temporal present, which is contemporary with the *nunc aeternitatis*, and itself in the full sense eternal time. In his exposition of this passage (C.R. 31, 46 f.) Calvin rightly perceived that this *hodie* cannot mean eternity in itself, so that the begetting cannot be the eternal begetting of the Son by the Father. But this makes it all the more certain that what is meant is the appearing of the Messiah King in time. And in this appearing, as Calvin says, eternity is revealed, or, as we should now say more specifically, the supra-temporality of God as His presence in time : *Quod autem Deus se illum genuisse pronuntiat, referri debet ad hominum sensum vel notitiam . . . Itaque adverbium Hodie tempus illius demonstrationis notat, quia postquam innotuit creatum divinitus fuisse regem, prodiit tanquam nuper ex Deo genitus.* In this appearing, time and all times have their direct meaning in relation to God. In it they are not only reality created by God, but reality upheld and ruled by Him. From it there is in all times and for all times that peace on earth among men of good will. " That was the true light, which lighteth every man that cometh into the world. He was in the world, and the world was made by him, and the world knew him not. He came unto his own, and his own received him not. But as many as received him, to them gave he power to become the sons of God, even to them that believe on his name " (Jn. 1ᵒᶠ·). This occurrence is the concrete form to which we must hold fast in relation to God's supra-temporality. It is the space within which it can be recognised and understood by us. God's eternity is so to speak the companion of time, or rather it is itself accompanied by time in such a way that in this occurrence time acquires its hidden centre, and therefore both backwards and forwards its significance, its content, its source and its goal, but also continually its significant present. Because, in this occurrence, eternity assumes the form of a temporal present, all time, without ceasing to be time, is no more empty time, or without eternity. It has become new. This means that in and with this present, eternity creates in time real past and real future, distinguishes between them, and is itself the bridge and way from the one to the other. Jesus Christ is this way. For it is Jesus Christ who in His person decides what has happened and is therefore past, and what will be and is therefore future, Himself distinguishing between the two. It is He who draws the distinction between disobedience and obedience, sin and righteousness, guilt and freedom from guilt, fate and freedom, death and life, alien lordship and the kingdom of God, damnation and blessedness. These are not timeless, objective spheres. They appear to be so to moralistic and physico–metaphysical thinking, like two worlds joined in a parallel way through all times, or two full scales balancing each other in time and even in eternity. Yet this is not the Christian but a heathen view of these two spheres. Considered from a Christian standpoint, and therefore in fact from the distinction and decision made in Jesus Christ, they do belong to the one created time. But in this unity of time the first of these spheres is basically the sphere of what is past, and the second is no less basically the sphere of what is to come. The first is the old aeon which is passing, and the second the new aeon which is coming. Between them there is not contemporaneity, but its opposite ; not equilibrium, but the tipping of the scales to the detriment of the first and the advantage of the second. There is not between them endless repetition of event and existence, but the overcoming and dissolution of the first by the second with a view to its final removal. In His death on the cross Jesus Christ slew and buried the old man of the first sphere. He destroyed in Himself the disobedience of Adam. He bore in His person the sin of Israel, thus bringing it under the divine forgiveness. He paid the debt of the human race. He fulfilled and ended the fate that pressed on it. He suffered death, and in so doing robbed it of its power. He endured the alien lordship of the world powers opposed to God, and thereby broke it. Permitting Himself to be affected by the condemnation to which the world is subject, He changed it into the condemnation to which the world was once subject but is so no longer. And in His resurrection Jesus Christ brought to light and life in Himself the new man of the second sphere. He fulfilled as man the obedience which makes man the object of the divine good will. He carried out the sentence of the divine righteousness in accordance with which man does not belong to himself or anyone else but to God alone. He was perfectly innocent. He not only brought man back into the ambiguous freedom of the creature, for which sin and therefore bondage to fate are not impossible, but He led men upwards and forwards to the freedom in which man will no longer be a sinner or the slave of any fate. He made him the heir of eternal life. In Himself He brought the kingdom of God near for all who believe in Him. In Himself He has already saved them and made them blessed. The person and work of Jesus Christ are quite misunderstood, they are necessarily understood very differently from the way in which they are attested, if we have Word of Jesus Christ, and conceive of His appearing, His words and deeds, His suffering, death, and resurrection, only as a particularly energetic emphasising of the existence and antithesis of two objective spheres. In the sense of the Old and New Testament witness, Jesus Christ is taken seriously only when we see that as He comes between the two spheres He makes the one really past and the other no less really future, constituting time itself the way from this past to this future. Again, the existence and antithesis of the two spheres are rightly understood only when He is seen in this relationship to them. Jesus Christ and Jesus Christ alone is the One who has made the antithesis of these spheres the antithesis between past and future, thus making time itself something new by giving it its centre in Himself. For He has not merely explained and interpreted it as the way from this past to this future, from the old to the new aeon, but has really made it this way, in the power of the Creator of time and of all things. This and this alone is, therefore, the Christian conception of time which is the real conception of time, the conception of human existence moving in Jesus Christ out of the first and into the second sphere. The fact that we have time and live in time means, from a Christian point of view and therefore in reality, that we live in this turning. It always involves the relapse into a heathen point of view if we understand the past and the future, and ourselves between them, as anything else but our living in this turning. It really is a turning. The consequence is that the contemporaneity of our being in both spheres is always to be understood as non-contemporaneity, as the overcoming and dissolution of the past by the future, not as an equilibrium or see-saw between the right and validity of the two realms. Luther's *simul iustus et peccator* cannot and should not, in Luther's sense, be taken to mean that the totality with which we are righteous and sinners involves an equal and equally serious determination of our existence. It is not a justification and demand to see ourselves as righteous and sinners in the same sense. It is not just as legitimate for us to sin as to practise our righteousness. Our righteousness is not a condition of our life only with the same truth and power as our sin is on the other side. The two things which are " at the same time " are our past and our future. Our sin has been, and our righteousness comes. God affirms our righteousness as He negates our sin. We are at the same time righteous and sinners only under this determination, with this preponderance, and with this decision. This *simul iustus et peccator* has nothing whatever to do with a Hercules always at the crossroads. The same is true of all the other determinations in which we can speak of a contemporaneity of the old and the new aeon. This contemporaneity never means in any sense that we belong to both spheres in the same way. St. Paul, in 2 Cor. 6⁸ᶠ·, says of himself that he approved himself as the minister of God in " honour and dishonour, evil report and good report, as a deceiver and yet true, as unknown and yet well-known, as dying and behold we live, as chastened and not killed, as sorrowful, yet always rejoicing, as poor, yet making many rich, as having nothing and yet possessing all things." This description of the apostle's life and also the inward analysis more fully made in the inter-related chapters Romans 7 and 8, are quite misunderstood if it is not perceived that if here one reality is continually opposed by another, the one in its particular reality is infinitely less and fleeting and passing because it is repressed and ejected by the whole power of God, while the other in its particular reality is infinitely superior as one which comes breaking in triumphantly with the whole power of God. It is in this relationship alone that the two spheres are contemporary, and not with the vibrating balance of scales or in an endless dialectic. We stand between the two, between yesterday and to-morrow, that which lies behind and that which lies before us, what is above and what is below. But these are not like two partners with the same rights and powers and competence. We are certainly placed between them. But first of all and above all Jesus Christ stands between them. It is in this way and in Him that we are in this position. But in Him the equilibrium between them has been upset and ended. He is the way from the one to the other and the way is irreversible. He is the turning. If we try to hold any other view of the relationship between the two and to make them equal, we will have to forget and abandon Him—whatever our pretext may be, even if it is on grounds of the greatest verisimilitude. And it is a matter of this turning if we live in time. We are not concerned about the turning from an empty or an arbitrarily and imaginatively filled past to a no less empty or no less imaginatively filled future. On the contrary, both are fixed and filled. For not we and our present, but Jesus Christ and His present are the turning from the one to the other. The past is that from which we are set free by Him, and the future that for which we are set free by Him.

The first consequence of this is that there is no sense in looking back with tears and complaints, or even doleful yearning, to " what once was mine " and is so no more, to the past. If it is a matter of looking back, it must be with Ps. 103² : " Forget not all his benefits." But benefits which lie behind us have always been as such the future, the benefits of the new age to which we could even then move : " who forgiveth all thine iniquities and healeth all thy diseases, who redeemeth thy life from destruction, who crowneth thee with loving kindness and tender mercies." This future was already the benefit of yesterday. By its very nature it cannot be a thing of yesterday. It cannot be taken from us. It cannot, then, be the object of a sorrowful looking backwards. From what is really past, from what can disappear and be taken from us, we have to be set free and we are set free. To be able to look back to its disappearance, and no longer to have to keep it as a thing present, is a new reason for thankfulness and not for sorrow. We can say of it: " I forget those things that are behind " (Phil. 3¹³), and Paul calls this forgetting the one thing which he can and will do in the present as one who does not think that he has already attained the future. *Quod vixi tege.* What God in Jesus Christ has cast behind Him, we cannot and are not to set before ourselves again. The middle point set up and secured in Jesus Christ divides us from it. This middle point we cannot and are not to forget, but as we remember it we are to forget what lies behind us. We did not make it good then, and no repentance will ever enable us to make it good. We would not do better than we did even if we could do it all over again from the beginning. There must be no yearning to be able " to do it over again." This yearning passes by Jesus Christ. For in Him our past is judged, but also ended as what is past. It should be completely given over to Him. Anything else is sentimentality, a waste of time, and a secret deception.

A further consequence is that there is just as little sense in worrying as we look into the future. This is not because we are unable to survey the future and determine it. That would be true enough if we regarded the future merely as empty time in front of us. But it is not true absolutely because it is to some extent possible to survey and determine this future. And it is not so true that it can effectively repel the desire to make use of this possibility and the anxiety attached to it. But the future is not this empty time. It is the coming new age with all its benefits for which we are set free in Jesus Christ. As men set free in this positive way we can look and move to the future—this is the meaning of the evangelical admonition not to worry. *Quod vivam rege.* Even that which still lies before us apparently as actualities and possibilities of the old aeon, even that which may await us at any point as future sin and adversity and approaching death, awaits us in truth as that which has already been, as that which lies behind us, as that which when it comes is something passing and past ; just as all the benefits of the past could not as such disappear but were our future then as they are now. We therefore await what belongs to the old age as that which has already been and is past, so that we cannot in any circumstances be afraid of it. Seen from the centre of time, from Jesus Christ, and therefore in reality, there is no such thing as a future that is dark and therefore no fear of the future. To be afraid would again be sentimentality, a waste of time, and a secret deception. Already in created time, what is to come is not a kingdom of darkness but the kingdom of God, life not death, God's acquittal and not our sin—if only we keep to the Christian, to the real understanding of time, to the fact that time has acquired its middle point in Jesus Christ, and has therefore been made new.

Therefore to have time and to live in time means to live in this turning. In this turning we live—not in eternity, but in the real time healed by God, the time whose meaning is immediate to God. Living in this turning we recognise and experience God's supra-temporality and therefore here and now already His eternity. In this form of supra-temporality eternity is near and not distant. This form is the revelation of eternity. In this revelation of itself eternity is the foundation of a real consciousness of time on our part. This is a consciousness of the present, the past and the future, of beginning and goal, of succession and order. It is a consciousness of the content of time. It is a consciousness in which it is possible to live. But this life has to be the life of faith for which the revelation of eternity has not occurred in vain, or Jesus Christ has been born and died or raised again in vain. Everything depends on whether time has a different centre from the constantly disappearing and never coming " now " of the pagan concept of time. But time really has this centre, and being related to eternity in this centre, it is accompanied and surrounded and secured by eternity. True time-consciousness depends on a consciousness of this middle point. It stands or falls by the gift and decision of faith. And faith is faith in Jesus Christ or it is not faith at all.

God is post-temporal. This statement completes the conception of eternity as that which embraces time. Just as God is before and over time, so He is after time, after all time and each time. We move to Him as we come from Him and may accompany Him. We move towards Him. He is, when time will be no more. For then creation itself, the world as a reality distinct from God, will be no more in its present condition, in everything which now constitutes its existence and being. And the same will also be true of man in his present existence and essence. For everything will have reached its goal and end. Man here and now reconciled to God will be redeemed. Eternity is also this " then," just as it is the " once " before all time and the " now " over all time. Eternity is also the goal and the end beyond which and over which another goal and end cannot exist. All roads necessarily lead to it. It is the sum of that to which anyone or anything can move. Any roads leading away from it can lead only to utter nothingness, and therefore cannot be roads at all. Since movement away from it is movement into utter nothingness, there can be no such movement. The meaning and necessity of all ways and movement are fulfilled and exhausted in it. It is the perfection which remains, so that over and beyond it there is no new horizon. This perfection is God Himself in His post-temporality. It is God in His Şabbath rest after the completion of all His works, the execution of all His will *ad extra*, the attainment of the goal of all His purposes in so far as these are distinct from His free necessity to be Himself. God is the Last as He was the First. He is, therefore, the absolute, unsurpassable future of all time and of all that is in time. There is no life in time that can develop and reach its end at any other point than with Him, i.e., at the goal which He has ordained and appointed for it. There is no history in time that can end except with Him, i.e., under the judgment which He holds over it, and the results which He gives it. There is no part of time that with all its specific contexts must not be revealed as a part of the completed divine plan. God will exist after all things and everything. He will look back on everything outside Himself as what has been in its totality. As He looks back, He will in reality decide what it has been and how far it has really been, just as He had already decided when it did not yet exist. This He did and does in His love and therefore in accordance with His grace and mercy and patience. But He does it also in His freedom and therefore in accordance with His holiness and righteousness and wisdom. He will judge, and against His judgment there is no appeal. It is final. Corresponding to this judgment, all that has been will be before Him what it must be, accepted or rejected, acquitted or condemned, destined for eternal life or eternal death. Everything that has been, everything that was in all completed time, will be what He will be to each, and what is proper to it because it is His good will for it. And as in this sense He is what is proper to everything that has been, He will be, as 1 Cor. 15^{28} says, "all in all," and all that has been will have been to Him as it was from Him and by Him, and will have fulfilled its purpose as being in its own place and way, and to that extent will have been vindicated in some sense according to the plan and order of God. This vindication, involving both the eternal life and the eternal death of what has been, will be the revelation of the kingdom of God. For the kingdom of God consists in the fact that in some sense He is all in all. It is only in its revelation that the kingdom of God is post-temporal and therefore lies in the future. Already pre-temporally God was, and supra-temporally He is, all in all without reservation or reduction. But if we believe this and recognise it in faith, we believe in its future revelation. God's revelation stands before us as the goal and end of time. We wait for it even as we look back on its occurrence in the middle of time and grasp it as the kingdom of God that has drawn near, in the way in which it is possible to grasp this in time, in the way in which it wills to grasp us, and has grasped us in time. After time, in post-temporal eternity, we shall not believe in it. We shall see it. It will be without the concealment which surrounds it in time and as long as time continues. Without deprivation or the danger of deprivation, and without the veil of hope, we shall then have that for which we must now pray, and which we do really receive in its fulness, but in the veil of hope, so that we must continually pray for it again. Post-temporal eternity is free from this fluctuation. It is the same revelation which we have had, but it is now without a veil, whereas in time we may believe in it under the veil of hope and therefore with the fluctuation of praying and receiving and praying again. God is also post-temporal eternity, the eternity to which we move. To this extent He is the God of all hope, the imminent peace which is prepared and promised to His people, into which it has not yet entered but will enter. God has and is also that which so far we do not have and are not. He therefore embraces time and us too from a position in front of us. Thus in having Him we have really everything—including what so far we do not have. His *is* the kingdom. He *is* the Last. He *is* the One who is all in all. It is only then, at the goal and end of time, that He will be revealed as this and no longer veiled at all. But He is this already in Himself. He was it from the beginning. So then, even the alternation in which we recognise Him in time as the eternal One can and necessarily will be blessedness. The fact that He is veiled in time cannot be a cause for complaint. If we must live in hope, this means only that we may live in hope. Always and everywhere and in every way God is also the eternal One in the sense of His post-temporality.

It is perhaps relevant to say at this juncture that there can be no basic rivalry with regard to the three forms of eternity. The conceptions of God's pre-temporality, supra-temporality, and post-temporality have all to be emphasised in their different ways. But they are not to be played off the one against the other, as if God could be better known and were to be taken more seriously under one of these forms and less so or not at all under another. When in Rom. 11³⁶ Paul adopted into his message about God the words ἐξ αὐτοῦ καὶ δι' αὐτοῦ καὶ εἰς αὐτὸν τὰ πάντα (and there may perhaps be a verbal connexion with certain ideas found in the mystery religions), coming as it does at the end of Rom. 9-11 this surely points to the fact that in equal divinity, or as we should say, in the same love and freedom, God is the One and all, the beginning, the middle and the end, the One who was, and is, and is to come, at perfect peace within Himself. So then, if we are to love Him and know Him, we must give Him equal attention and seriousness in all three dimensions as the source and content of all time and all that is in time. We must emphasise this because, when our thinking is by nature systematic, it is so easy to be guilty of some kind of preference, selection or favouritism in this matter, and therefore of the corresponding omissions. But this cannot really be our procedure in relation to God's eternity. It may, perhaps, be possible in this way to achieve a certain clarity and concentration of our Christian knowledge, but it is even more clear that in doing this we are inevitably entangled in ideologies or even mythologies which partially and in the long run totally endanger the truth and are almost unavoidably followed by reactions in the neglected direction which for their part, it is to be feared, involve further over-emphasis, and the consequent concealment and truncation of the truth and therefore the loss of its character as truth.

For example, we cannot but be aware that the theology of the Reformers showed an interest not free from dangerous one-sidedness in the ἐξ αὐτοῦ, in eternity as pre-temporality, and therefore in the doctrine of election and divine providence. It was the source of the power and strength of this theology that it taught man so emphatically to see himself with a reference back to the God who was before Him and who from all eternity, without co-operation or merit on man's part, and before there were any means for man's salvation, had already decided on his whole salvation. This being the case, human life can consist only in a confidence and clear performance of the eternal divine decree and the eternal divine will. No one would or should deny this. But in this theology time itself in its duration, and human life in time with its responsibilities, problems and possibilities, came to have the position of a kind of appendix, though one that was expressed with force. We can only say that in view of the truth of God's supra-temporality time must not in any circumstances be reduced to a mere appendix. For God's presence in time, the δι' αὐτοῦ, is just as seriously God's eternity as His pre-temporality and all that is to be said about our life from this standpoint. There is the even more serious objection that God's post-temporality, the εἰς αὐτόν and therefore eschatology, hope, the determination of human life by the coming kingdom of God, were treated far too summarily in Reformation theology, or at least they were not honoured as they should have been. It was only the appendix of an appendix that we have been placed on a way and may proceed along it to reach a goal, because there is a divine plan which is not merely determined but is also to be fulfilled, and we can expect its revealed completion, so that our life is necessarily a life of expectation. This whole side of eternity is certainly mentioned by the Reformers, but it is subsidiary, because they have thought about it much more from the point of view of God's pre-temporality. Over wide tracts of their doctrine there is therefore a gloom, and even a hopelessness, which cannot be based on or justified by Scripture. This can be avoided only if we refrain from the definite one-sidedness with which the Reformers handled the problem of time in their doctrine of God, and if we give more honour to God's supra-temporality and above all His post-temporality than they did.

Far more dangerous, of course, was the one-sidedness with which the 18th and 19th centuries tried to achieve a partial reaction against the one-sidedness of the 16th century by determining to give the preference to what we have called God's supra-temporality. Too much attention was now paid to man in time, his needs and problems, but above all his positive possibilities. The actual relationship of God to time in its duration, His presence and government in the world and the soul and in the religious experience of the individual, now became central to an understanding of His eternity. What of God's pre-temporality? With everything belonging to it, this now came under the suspicion of idle speculation without objective basis or at any rate practical significance. Even where this judgment was not passed, it was regarded only as an introduction to the main and really serious statement about the centre, the eternity present to us in time, and as such it must be rushed through as hastily and even unceremoniously as possible. And what about God's post-temporality? The Reformers and orthodoxy after them had never had their heart in this, and even less so the age which followed. Therefore eschatology, the εἰς αὐτόν, remained the appendix which it had been. Everything was now to be δι' αὐτοῦ and only δι' αὐτοῦ. "To be eternal in a single moment," as Schleiermacher said at the close of his second Address—for a whole age attempts seemed to be made to compress into this all that they had to say about the eternal God, and significantly it was not said about Him at all but about religious man. Even the Gnostic doctrine of the eternity of the creation and constitution of the world, and their co-existence with the eternal God, now became the view of wide theological circles. In a really distressing way—infinitely more distressing than in the 16th century—the conception of eternity had lost in depth and perspective, so that finally the point was reached where the assertion of it was hardly if at all to be distinguished from the denial of its contents. In the last resort—here if anywhere we can see the results of one-sidedness in this matter—it became little more than an exclamation mark which had no positive content, so that it could be placed not only behind the word " God " but behind any word at all denoting a supreme value, even in the very last analysis, as we have seen under National Socialism, behind the word " Germany." Preferences and prejudices of this kind in the sphere of Christian truth are usually the beginning of its total secularisation.

At the end of the 19th century and the beginning of the 20th there has finally been a reaction to the third side that had hitherto been neglected, and unfortunately we have to say again that it has been a one-sided reaction. Eschatology, and therefore the post-temporality of God, was re-discovered after it had for centuries claimed the interest only of certain sects and certain isolated individuals among the theologians of the Church, as, for example, J. A. Bengel. One focus in this movement of discovery was the message of the kingdom of God expounded by the older and the younger Blumhardt ; the other focus was the application of scientific exegesis, especially of the New Testament, to the attainment of a previously unknown exactness in both secular and religious history, which—whether a strictly optimistic concept of time was retained or not—made it quite impossible to overlook or deny the fact that Jesus and the apostles themselves had had a very different conception of time determined by a direct looking for the coming of the new age.

It is worth noting that the opponent against whom the post-temporality of God was effectively maintained by the two Blumhardts and their most influential theological spokesman, F. Zündel, was not the cultural optimism of Liberal Protestantism. On the contrary, it was the more recent, positively Church-centred Christianity, and especially its pietistic qualities, which they accused of a complete and utter lack of the characteristic of hope which is so distinctive in the message of the New Testament and New Testament faith, of diluting to a purely individual hope of a future life for the soul the confidence and unsettlement of the expectation of the kingdom of God which will rectify the whole world and all life even to its deepest recesses. They therefore called the world of piety with its apparently very definite faith in Christ to a conversion, to faith in the living Christ who is to come again and make all things new. They gave a central position to the prayer : " Thy kingdom come," and : " Even so, come, Lord Jesus," and therefore to post-temporal eternity, although this involved them in conflict with the most earnest representatives of the anthropocentric Christianity of the post-Reformation period. The younger Blumhardt, H. Kutter and especially L. Ragaz, gave this " fight for the kingdom of God " a particularly surprising turn when they linked it with the eschatology and hope of the Socialist Labour movement. They expressly approved this movement and contrasted it with the Church, theology and Christendom, as the representative realisation for our time of the faith that Jesus did not find in Israel. Yet this application was not so remarkable as seems at first sight. It had already been prepared by the elder Blumhardt, in whose proclamation of hope the emphasis, strictly speaking, was less on the return of Christ and the coming of the kingdom than on the new outpouring of the Holy Spirit which was to precede this true end and new beginning and the return of the mighty works and the miracles which, in apostolic times, had proclaimed the imminent kingdom of God in time. It was hard to see any basic reason why this should not be seen in a secular movement like Socialism. If this application to a temporal hope clarified the problems involved in the new discovery, further clarification came when H. Lhotzky and, above all, Johannes Müller (also under the inspiration of the two Blumhardts, found it quite possible to transpose back into general teaching the whole dynamic of the hope proclaimed in Bad Boll. The accent now was on the present and not on the future, and, in good Neo-Protestant fashion, on the present as experienced in individual personal existence. Inevitably, then, the final result was only a

Pietism of a supposedly higher order, that is, of an expressly secular character. Again, there could be no place for looking to a real hereafter beyond all time, to a real coming of Christ, and therefore for the reality of a confidence and assault invading the world of men from beyond. There was so little place for it that Müller found at last, inevitably, an inglorious end in the slough of the " German Christian " movement of 1933.

Under the impression made by the first world war and its compromising both of those who held the Socialist expectation and also of those who again taught an uneschatological inwardness of " personal life," many of us tried to make a fresh start at what we saw to be the original point of departure of the elder Blumhardt. We did not wish to return either to the older secularised piety or with Johannes Müller and others to its modern form. We believed that what we found in the teaching of Schleiermacher was the theological kernel of a Christianity-of-the-present compatible neither with the Bible nor the real world. We were convinced that we must oppose this. We also felt compelled to put behind us the view of the younger Blumhardt, Kutter and Ragaz, which combined the Christian expectation of the kingdom of God and the Socialist expectation for the future. It was far too easy for them to understand this, not as a combination, but as an identification, and in fact this is just how they did understand it. We felt compelled to press beyond all temporal expectations whether individual, cultural or political; even beyond what necessarily seemed to us to be the foreground view of the elder Blumhardt—to the view of a pure and absolute futurity of God and Jesus Christ as the limit and fulfilment of all time. It was due to the inner and outer circumstances of these years that the divine No of judgment, now understood as a No directed both to the present position and to all possible and attempted religious and cultural developments, had to be expressed more loudly, and certainly more clearly heard, than the gracious Yes that we believed we genuinely heard, and genuinely wished to express, from the end, the real end, of all things. In the critical form in which it was presented, this could not unjustly be connected with the spiritual shaking experienced by European man through the world war. It was violently welcomed by some as an expression of the spirit of this time, and no less forcibly rejected by others, less receptive to this spirit, as a " post-war phenomenon." Beyond this the impression was not a bad one, and could have been corrected with time. The real danger was material. Because we were more consistent and proceeded in a more clear-cut way than our predecessors we were well on the way to just as systematic a reduction of God's eternity to the denominator of post-temporality, the eternally future, as the Reformers had that of pre-temporality and the Neo-Protestants of supra-temporality. In the attempt to free ourselves both from these early forms of one-sidedness, especially from that of pietistic and Liberal Neo-Protestantism, and also from the unsatisfactory corrections with which our predecessors had tried to overcome them, we took the surest possible way to make ourselves guilty of a new one-sidedness and therefore to evoke a relatively justifiable but, in view of the total truth, equally misleading reaction, involving all kinds of protests and opposition to even the justifiable aspects of our own concern. Expounding Rom. 8[24], I even dared to say at that time : " Hope that is visible is not hope. Direct communication from God is not communication from God. A Christianity that is not wholly and utterly and irreducibly eschatology has absolutely nothing to do with Christ. A spirit that is not at every moment in time new life from the dead is in any case not the Holy Spirit. ' For that which is seen is temporal ' (2 Cor. 4[18]). What is not hope is a log, a block, a chain, heavy and angular, like the word ' reality.' It imprisons rather than sets free. It is not grace, but judgment and destruction. It is fate, not divine fulfilment. It is not God, but a reflection of man unredeemed. It is this even if it is an ever so stately edifice of social progress or an ever so respectable bubble of Christian redeemedness. Redemption is that which cannot be seen, the inaccessible, the impossible, which confronts us as hope. Can we wish to be anything other and better than men of hope, or anything additional ? " Well roared, lion ! There is nothing absolutely false in these bold words. I still think that I was right ten times over against those who then passed judgment on them and resisted them. Those who can still hear what was said then by both the religious and worldlings, and especially by religious worldlings, and especially the most up-to-date among them, cannot but admit that it was necessary to speak in this way. The sentences I then uttered were not hazardous (in the sense of precarious) on account of their content. They were hazardous because to be legitimate exposition of the Bible they needed others no less sharp and direct to compensate and therefore genuinely to substantiate their total claim. But these were lacking. If we claim to have too perfect an understanding of the Gospel, we at once lose our understanding. In our exposition we cannot claim to be wholly right over against others, or we are at once in the wrong. At that time we had not sufficiently considered the pre-temporality of the Reformers or the supra-temporality of God which Neo-Protestants of all shades had put in such a distorted way at the centre. Hence we had not seen the biblical conception of eternity in its fulness. The result was that we could not speak about the post-temporality of God in such a way as to make it clear that we actually meant to speak of God and not of a general idea of limit and crisis. That we had only an uncertain grip of the matter became apparent, strangely enough, in those passages of the exposition in which I had to speak positively about the divine future and hope as such. It emerged in the fact that although I was confident to treat the far-sidedness of the coming kingdom of God with absolute seriousness, I had no such confidence in relation to its coming as such. So when I came to expound a passage like Rom. 13$^{11f.}$ (" Now it is high time to awake out of sleep : for now is our salvation nearer than when we believed. The night is far spent, the day is at hand "), in spite of every precaution I interpreted it as if it referred only to the moment which confronts all moments in time as the eternal " transcendental meaning " of all moments in time. The tension between the " then " when we believed and the " now " of " disturbing recollection," a new awareness of Christ's *parousia*, was only a continual tension, having no connexion with the tension of two points in time and the time of Church history. The " last " hour, the time of eternity, was not an hour which followed time. Rather at every moment in time we stood before the frontier of all time, the frontier of " qualified time." We had to awaken to a recollection of this situation and a consciousness of its special nature instead of either waiting for a kind of finale or " consoling ourselves with the utterly frivolous ' piety ' of convinced ' Culture-Protestants ' that this finale would never happen.' We were to recognise that moment as " eternal," and therefore as a metaphysico-ethical qualification of our moments in time, because, in accordance with its nature, it never has " come " and never will " come." It is clear that I did say there things which can and have to be said at the periphery if Rom. 13$^{11f.}$ is to be correctly understood. But it is also clear that with all this art and eloquence I missed the distinctive feature of the passage, the teleology which it ascribes to time as it moves towards a real end. Above all, it is clear and astonishing that in my exposition the one thing which continues to hold the field as something tangible is the one-sided supra-temporal understanding of God which I had set out to combat. It was at this point that the objection could be made, as it was in fact made by both friends and critics, that while I had radically disturbed the optimism of the Neo-Protestant conception of time in itself it had really been confirmed by the extreme form it had been given by me. It was at this point that P. Tillich with his Kairos-philosophy, and later R. Bultmann with his reduction of New Testament anthropology to the terms of an existentialist philosophy, believed that they could welcome me as one of themselves. It was at this point that there could be rejoicing that the naivety seemed to have been overcome with which the two

Blumhardts and their nearest disciples transposed the Christian hope into expectations in time, yet also regret that the sublimity which this hope in its relation to time had introduced into temporal Christian life and thinking was again being threatened and was in danger of being reduced to an impulse to look radically but with no concrete hope or movement to what is absolutely beyond time. It was no light task gradually to put right these not undeserved misunderstandings, including my own misunderstandings on which much that I said at that time rested, and to guide theology out of the suspicion under which it had fallen of being only " the theology of crisis." It could not actually be the " theology of crisis " for more than a moment. And that it could be it only for a moment showed that the basic, eschatological application on which it rested was too strong and arbitrary and independent like all reactions. It was necessary and right in face of the Immanentism of the preceding period to think with new seriousness about God's futurity. But it was neither right nor necessary to do this in such a way that this one matter was put at the head of all Christian teaching, just as the previous epoch had wanted to make what they claimed to be the knowledge of God's presence the chief point in Christian doctrine. Such interesting concentrations in theology must be completely avoided if we are not to come in some way under the domination of compelling ideas, which we can enjoy ourselves and with which we can for a while give pleasure to others, yet of which sooner or later we will inevitably tire, because what is merely interesting always becomes tedious in the course of time. The doctrine of the living God will not tolerate any such concentrations. There is therefore a fundamental reason why among both older and younger representatives of this recent eschatological movement in theology so many compelling ideas have in fact circulated, and, after they have been operative for a time, lost their interest and had to be discarded for the sake of freshness and vitality.

All this becomes, if possible, even more obvious if attention is paid to the origin of this movement as seen in the history of New Testament exegesis. It was in the second half of the 19th century that the thesis was propounded and defended that the whole of primitive Christianity was chiefly concerned with the end of all things. F. Overbeck was the first to adopt this position, in opposition to the tradition of the Tübingen school from which he himself had sprung, and also in opposition to what was then the modern school of Ritschl, especially A. von Harnack. The view was then taken up by the emerging religious historical movement, and especially by Johannes Weiss (*Die Predigt Jesu vom Reiche Gottes*, 1892). Finally Albert Schweitzer (*Von Reimarus zu Wrede*, 1906), with special reference to what he claimed were the unfulfilled words of Jesus about the immediate proximity of His return, built it up into the theory that the whole momentum of the New Testament message and the New Testament faith lay in the hope of Jesus' return and the setting up of the kingdom of God on earth—a hope that had not been fulfilled and was therefore erroneous. Certain of his disciples (as had happened also in the case of Overbeck) took this to mean that in their decisive historical form these had to be abandoned. Schweitzer himself was influenced by it to the extent that he gave his positive teaching the form of an ethic of the philosophy of culture in which the Gospel lives on only in the form of the doctrine (identical with all kinds of Eastern wisdom) that the fashion of this world passes away and our portion can only be active sympathy with its irremediable misery. Here, too, secularisation follows hot foot on systematisation and the tedious on the all too interesting. The disciples of Albert Schweitzer might well be reminded that it is the same in exegesis as in dogmatics. There can be no vitality and freshness in theology where there is only one insight, no matter how true and important it may be in itself. It was certainly high time for New Testament historical research to penetrate to a recognition of the extent to which its message and faith are determined and permeated by the expectation of the return of Christ and the end of all things. And this expectation is in fact misunderstood if there is failure to see that it does not reckon with long periods of time, but is on the contrary the expectation of something near. The problem of exposition posed by this is obvious. But to solve it by the categorical assertion that this expectation of something at hand " was not fulfilled " is too obvious to be convincing. And in any case it is not wise in the field of New Testament exegesis, as in any other, to regard this one insight, problem and solution as a kind of " open sesame " to unlock all doors to all secrets. We cannot try to confine ourselves for decade after decade to the one theme, repeating with pathetic monotony that primitive Christianity lived in the expectation of Christ's imminent return, that this did not happen, that all its other statements are therefore radically affected and that all that remains is the mysticism of reverence for life and nothing more. If we are to avoid the punishment of sterility we must never stop at a single insight, however sure we may be of our facts. To be sure, the eschatological interpretation of the New Testament and Christianity in general had to be given its place after centuries of neglect of this side of the truth. But this does not justify the misfortune, or a continued acceptance of the misfortune, that a system is again created and God's post-temporality is made a principle or even a fetish in exactly the same way as had happened with God's supra-temporality in the preceding period and to some extent with God's pre-temporality in the age of the Reformation. As in the movement which proceeded from the two Blumhardts, so in the purely historical exegesis of the New Testament there was the temptation and danger of turning back from pure eschatology to a wholly non-eschatological and Liberal way of thinking (and sometimes trivially so). This danger was a warning signal. It was a summons to see that even the post-temporality of God, what the New Testament calls the expectation of the return and the end, is bracketed with other things and stands in a larger context. It is indeed the whole truth about God. But merely as such it is not something which can be seized and handled by us as an instrument or weapon. On the contrary, it seizes and handles us. It shows itself at once to be so powerful in its particularity that we cannot tie it, as it were, to this particularity, but have to recognise its inner movement and are compelled to follow this movement.

Therefore it was most fortunate that in part at least a new consciousness of the theology of Luther and Calvin was successfully linked, before it was too late, with the awakening to eschatology which proceeded from Blumhardt and the exegesis of the New Testament. Without detriment, then, to the necessary recognition of God's post-temporality, His pre-temporality was again perceived, though it had been neglected in the 18th and 19th centuries no less than His post-temporality. Everything depends on there being no new rivalry between these conceptions. In the truth of God there is certainly dynamic particularity, but for that reason there is no rivalry, and therefore we have no right to ride hobby horses in its exposition and proclamation. The establishing and preserving of sound teaching in the Church is wholly dependent on two important factors : the post-temporality of God must not become the content of a mere appendix, or the pre-temporality the content of a mere introduction ; and a dislike of the truth of God's supra-temporality (which is historically understandable through the misuse of this truth in the past) must not be allowed to dictate what is said. Even in this latter respect we must maintain or regain an open mind, so that we know and say what really is to be known and said, even if it seems to involve a dangerous proximity to certain propositions dear to the 18th and 19th centuries. The errors of those centuries are not overcome by suppressing the element of truth which lay at the basis of the errors. They can be overcome only by seeing and establishing this truth in the context from which it should not be separated. In this context it has been necessary recently to speak much more clearly and positively, for example, about the relationship between Church and state, than was for a long time possible in the unavoidable opposition to the one-sidednesses and omissions of Neo-Protestantism. In this context the life of man in time and his various responsibilities must be brought into the light of God's true supra-temporality in a manner quite different from that previously practised. There can be no question of our being ashamed of it, and therefore of our taking those responsibilities lightly or anxiously seeking to escape them. What right have we to do that ? Is it not true that in this second, middle step we reach the true, christological basis of the concept of eternity ? Have we not had to see God's supra-temporality as the particular form of the revelation of His eternity ? If we have not to forget Him who was and will be as well as Him who is, and if we correctly understand man in time only when we see his time and himself in time surrounded by eternity before and behind, we have also not to forget, and perhaps we must learn again, the fact that the One who was and will be is also the One who is, who is Himself above and in time, and from whom we are not separated so long as time endures, as if He were only at the beginning or at the end. It is He whose presence is our comfort in the time left us between, and to whom in this time we must be loyal both in big things and small. God in His supra-temporality is to be distinguished from a mere sum or principle of time by the fact that He is also pre-temporal and post-temporal. He is not, therefore, bound to our time as such a principle would be, but time is in His hands and at His disposal. This is also the reason why time itself is not empty and yet has not to be filled arbitrarily by us, but from beginning to end is filled and therefore meaningful through the real and therefore the comforting and commanding presence of God. If, then, ethics becomes a new problem for us in the future, this does not mean that any of the insights that we have previously gained are to be forgotten, or that the doctrines of the Trinity and of predestination on the one hand and of eschatology on the other, with all the corrections and warnings which they provide, are again to become matters of indifference and even to be completely abandoned. On the contrary, it is because of this background, because time has a beginning and an end, and the omnipresent God is also the One who was before time and will be after time, that ethics must be a problem for us. Indeed, it is only on this basis that this can and will happen. For ethics depends on its proclamation of the command of the supra-temporal God, and the only supra-temporal God is the One who is also pre-temporal and post-temporal, bound to no time, and therefore the Lord of all times.

Pre-temporality, supra-temporality and post-temporality are equally God's eternity and therefore the living God Himself.

Non enim aliud anni Dei et aliud ipse Deus, sed anni Dei aeternitas Dei est (Augustine, *Enarr. in Ps.* 101². ¹⁰).

This is the last thing which we have to emphasise in connexion with the concept of eternity. Like every divine perfection it is the living God Himself. It is not only a quality which He possesses. It is not only a space in which He dwells. It is not only a form of being in which He shares, so that it could belong, if need be, to other realities as well, or exist apart from Him in itself. We cannot for one moment think of eternity without thinking of God, nor can we think of it otherwise than by thinking of God, by knowing Him and believing in Him and obeying Him—for there is no knowledge of God without this— by loving Him in return when He has first loved us. Eternity is the living God Himself. This radically distinguishes the Christian knowledge of eternity from all religious and philosophical reflection on time and what might exist before and after time. It distinguishes it from all speculations about different aeons, all the mythologies of past, present and future worlds, their essence and their relations to one another. The Christian knowledge of eternity has to do directly and exclusively with God Himself, with Him as the beginning before all time, the turning point in time, and the end and goal after all time. This makes it a complete mystery, yet also completely simple. In the last resort when we think of eternity we do not have to think in terms of either the point or the line, the surface or space. We have simply to think of God Himself, recognising and adoring and loving the Father, the Son and the Holy Spirit. It is only in this way that we know eternity. For eternity is His essence. He, the living God, is eternity. And it is as well at this point, in relation to the threefold form of eternity, to emphasise the fact that He is the living God.

The above-mentioned over-emphases and omissions in relation to this three-fold form are perhaps connected with the fact that it was thought possible to advance and maintain the idea of a pre-temporal, supra-temporal or post-temporal as such. Involuntarily, then, thinkers became the slaves of a systematisation and finally a secularisation, forgetting that under all these conceptions they were really dealing with the living God, and with the person of God, which cannot be tied to concepts of this kind or exhausted by them. The unity of tl e three forms of eternity is guaranteed if here too the knowledge of God is the knowledge of the personal God. In this case the demand that they must be known in their context and not played off against one another, the necessary theological programme of our day, a comprehensive consideration of God's true eternity, will be both possible and practicable. It will be possible to understand eternity in each of the three forms in its particularity, but in a mutually inter-related particularity, so that the foolish idea of a constantly threatening rivalry will be avoided. There is just as little place for this rivalry here as between the three persons of the Trinity, whose distinction is really in the last resort the basis of these three forms. In this connexion, too, there is in God both dis-tinction and peace. If it is utterly necessary to know Him in His distinction, this certainly does not mean that we can expect to find real contradictions. For here, too, the whole distinction takes place in the one, complete unity of God and therefore without contradiction.

Once we are clear that eternity is the living God Himself, it is impossible to look on eternity as a uniform grey sea before, above and after time, or to smooth out the distinctions between before, now and after, divesting them of the special characteristics which they possess as before, now and after. Again, it is impossible to involve this before, now and after in the problems which mark off time from eternity. Eternity is really beginning, really middle, and really end because it is really the living God. There really is in it, then, direction, and a direction which is irreversible. There really is in it an origin and goal and a way from the one to the other. Therefore there is no uniformity in it. Its forms are not to be exchanged or confused.

Its symmetry is strict, but is not to be reduced to a geometrical formula. Both the ball and the point with which it has so often been compared are very poor illustrations of eternity. For the irreversible direction without which eternity would not be God's eternity does not apply to either of them.

God *lives* eternally. It is for this reason that He has the distinctions mentioned. It is for this reason that they are not to be evaporated or assimilated to one another. It is for this reason that no one can be preferred to the detriment of another or neglected to the other's advantage. It is for this reason that God is equally truly and really pre-temporal, supra-temporal and post-temporal. But since He is God, He is all this in divine perfection. Thus " before " in Him does not imply " not yet " ; " after " in Him does not imply " no more " ; and above all His present does not imply any fleetingness. In each of the distinctions of perfection He has a share in the others. His beginning includes not only His goal and end, but also the whole way to it. In His present there occurs both the beginning and the end. At God's end, His beginning is operative in all its power, and His present is still present. At this point, as in the doctrine of the Trinity itself, we can and must speak of a *perichoresis*, a mutual indwelling and interworking of the three forms of eternity. *God* lives eternally. It is for this reason that there are no separations or distances or privations. It is for this reason that that which is distinct must be seen in its genuine relationship. In the future course of dogmatics we shall often have occasion to think of both the distinction and the unity in God's eternity. Perfect theological expression is that in which they are both constantly before our eyes as equally real and both expressed constantly with equal reality and seriousness. It is in this way at any rate, in this distinction and unity, that God is eternal, and therefore the Creator and Lord of time, the free and sovereign God.

The point we have reached makes it both possible and necessary to take our last step and say that God has and is glory. For God is glorious in the fact that He is eternal, as He is omnipresent in the fact that He is One and omnipotent in the fact that He is constant. It would be a poor conception of eternity which barred us from a view of God's glory or did not require us to contemplate it, just as God's freedom in general would be poorly understood if by our understanding of it we were not compelled to recognise the love which is mighty in it. God endures ; He is before, above and after time, and therefore its Creator and Lord, and therefore the free and sovereign God. We have established this to be the meaning of His eternity. But we must now interpret and expound this meaning and say that God endures in glory. It is not His being as such, mere abstract being, which is eternal. God has no such being. His being is eternal in glory. For the specific nature of God's eternity, the distinction and unity in which He is eternal, is also and as such the specific nature of God as the God of glory. Thus a consideration of His freedom has led us again and for the last time to a consideration of His love. For while the glory of God describes especially His freedom, majesty and pre-eminence, and therefore definitely belongs to the second series of divine perfections dealt with in this section, yet this final and supreme predicate of the divine freedom can be understood as such only if the divine freedom itself and as such is seen to be God's freedom to love.

Adopting at once the biblical usage, we can say that God's glory is His dignity and right not only to maintain, but to prove and declare, to denote and almost as it were to make Himself conspicuous and everywhere apparent as the One He is. He does this negatively by distinguishing Himself from what He is not, and positively by naming Himself, pointing to Himself, manifesting Himself in various ways. It is further His dignity and right to create recognition for Himself, in some sense to impose or intrude Himself in such a way that not only is He not overlooked, but He is not mistaken for another or again forgotten. He cannot possibly be avoided, nor can the reality which is distinct from Him exist at all without Him. Looking back on what has been said, we may say that God's glory is His competence to make use of His omnipotence as the One who is omnipresent, and to exercise lordship in virtue of His ever-present knowledge and will. But we must add at once, God's glory is not only His right but His power to do all this. It is the power of His divine being to be in control and to act as God. And again, as it is this right and power, it is also the actual accomplishment of all this. To sum up, God's glory is God Himself in the truth and capacity and act in which He makes Himself known as God. This truth and capacity and act are the triumph, the very core, of His freedom. And at its core it is freedom to love. For at the core of His being, and therefore in His glory, God is the One who seeks and finds fellowship, creating and maintaining and controlling it. He is in Himself, and therefore to everything outside Himself, relationship, the basis and prototype of all relationship. In the fact that He is glorious He loves.

The New Testament term δόξα must be our starting-point. Like many other words, when the Greek tongue was impressed into the service of the proclamation of the Gospel of Jesus Christ, it underwent a decisive and particularly striking change of meaning. In secular Greek δόξα denotes the opinion which anyone has, and the opinion others have of him, the standing or reputation which he enjoys. In the New Testament the first of these meanings has entirely disappeared, and the second is replaced by the objective conception of the honour which a man has in himself and which is therefore his due, the dignity which is his and is therefore accepted by others, the magnificence which he displays because he has a right to it, the splendour which emanates from him because he is resplendent. It is in this sense that the New Testament speaks of God's glory or of the glory of Jesus Christ or even of the glory that belongs to us. It refers to the legitimate, effective, and actual self-demonstration, self-expression and self-declaration of a being whose self-revelation is subject to no doubt, criticism or reservation. This being is glorious. It achieves recognition for itself in such a way that it need not and cannot be questioned. The recognition is such that it consists simply in the declaration of the one who makes it that he has done so because he could do nothing else. " Thine " or " His " *is* the glory, runs the prayer of the New Testament Church. For since the δόξα of which it speaks is no mere opinion or assertion or hypothesis, it cannot be the object of mere opinions or wishes or titles. It can be the object only of a statement of fact. Philologically the basis is to be found in the fact that the New Testament continually rests on the Old. In the Old Testament *kabod* denotes that which constitutes the importance and value of a being, giving it prestige and honour because it belongs to it (as for example wealth). *Kabod* is the inner, essential, objective strength which a man has and which expresses itself in the force of his appearance and activity, in the impression that he makes on others. *Kabod* is light, both as source and radiance. In this sense *kabod* is ascribed to Yahweh, and Yahweh's being and presence and activity are described in terms of various natural forms of light, the lightning or the sun or fire, and are recognised in these natural phenomena. The glory or honour of God is the worth which God Himself creates for Himself (in contrast to what He is not) simply by revealing Himself, just as light needs only itself and has only to be light in the midst of darkness to be bright and to spread brightness in contrast to all the darkness of heaven and earth. It is in this way that God is glorious. It is in this way that glory belongs to Him, and in a literal and true sense to Him alone. Only God is light in this sense. All other light and also all other glory (especially all the glory of men) can only copy Him. It can only be the glory which is not the possession of those that have it, but is granted them and can be taken away from them again. Belonging to God and therefore to God alone, glory is the substance of His presence in Israel. Glory is God Himself in His activity as the King of Israel, its Leader, Ruler and Saviour, not chosen by Israel but Himself choosing Israel, the One who therefore dwells on Sinai, in the cloud that goes before the people, in the tabernacle and the ark, in the temple and in the promised land. According to Is. 6³, the whole land is full of the glory of the Lord. This is not contradicted by the fact that, according to Ps. 72¹⁹, it is still something that is to come. For the revelation of God's glory (Is. 40⁵) is always future, as its truth and power and activity are already present. This Old Testament use of the term teaches us how utterly foolish it is to suggest even a distant connexion between the glory of God and a kind of divine vanity or self-seeking, and therefore to contrast it with God's grace and mercy, His condescension and His friendliness to men, although it was customary to do so for a time especially in explaining the difference between Reformed and Lutheran Christianity. It is in the revelation of His glory as such that God reveals to Israel His grace and mercy, His condescension and friendliness to men. It is itself His love that He incontestably asserts Himself as God, not merely preserving and maintaining Himself, but forcefully creating this recognition of Himself. Thus the New Testament is simply repeating the fulfilled testimony of the Old when in its decisive strand it describes the glory of God as the glory of Jesus Christ. There are, of course, two subsidiary strands which we must not neglect. In the New Testament, too, there is a " glory of the Father " (Rom. 6⁴), a " glory to God in the highest " (Lk. 2¹⁴), a " glory of God " which is apparently general and abstract (Jn. 11⁴⁰). There is also the glory which certain men are to share and in a certain sense already do share [the apostle as the holder of his office (2 Cor. 3¹⁸) and all Christians as receivers of the ἀπαρχή, the ἀρραβὼν τοῦ πνεύματος], in order that it may one day be unveiled and revealed in them as embracing the whole man, including his bodily nature (Rom. 8¹⁸). But these two strands are held together by the decisive central strand in which the δόξα is the δόξα of the Lord Jesus Christ, a glory which is based on the δόξα of God the Father—He is glorified by the Father and He glorifies the Father (Jn. 13³¹)—and which itself forms the basis of the future yet present δόξα of the men in question. Jesus Christ appears now with both a retrospective and a prospective reference, to Israel on the one hand and the Church on the other. On the one hand He is the reflection of the divine glory. In Him the divine self-manifestation is accomplished. God's love becomes an event and a person, God's fellowship, powerful and a fact. On the other hand He is the prototype of all participation by creation in the glory of God. For it is in Himself, and in Himself first, that the divine self-manifestation has its distinctive future yet present form. His δόξα is His revelation as the One who is alive from the dead. It is therefore the future of His own life and the future of His second appearing which brings all time to an end. If it certainly belongs to Him already before His resurrection and ascension, it does so in a hidden way. Yet as is shown by the record of the transfiguration in Mark and its parallels it can be seen and known before His end and therefore definitely before the end of the world. In all its futurity it can also be the object of a backward look : " We beheld his glory " (Jn. 1¹⁴). God glorifies Himself on high. He does so in such a way that He glorifies His Son on earth. He in turn is glorified on earth among men who gain a part in His own glorifying, so that they themselves are called to glorify God. The totality as it is brought together at its middle point in Jesus Christ represents and is the glory of God according to the New Testament. The *kabod* has this middle point, this concrete form and name. This is the new element in the New Testament. But what is here described both was and is also the *kabod* according to the testimony of the Old Testament. We cannot fail to see that according to the testimony of the Bible the conception of the glory of God belongs to the context of the doctrine of the love of God. It is a matter of the *free* love of God. This is what we have to bear in mind in view of the great objectivity of the concept. But it is a matter of God's *love*. We shall not fail to notice this if we do not lose sight of the clear soteriological relationship of the concept in both Old and New Testaments, its relationship to Israel and the Church, its concentration in the person of Jesus Christ.

It is now perhaps legitimate and even requisite to ask in what sense the glory of God is to be understood as the truth and power and act of His self-demonstration and therefore of His love. What is the more precise meaning of the honour and the glory of God, of the *gloria Dei*, of God as the source and radiance of light ? The most obvious answer, which is also correct and important in itself, is as follows. It is the self-revealing sum of all divine perfections. It is the fulness of God's deity, the emerging, self-expressing and self-manifesting reality of all that God is. It is God's being in so far as this is in itself a being which declares itself.

Many of the older theologians understood the *gloria Dei* in this way : *quae nihil aliud est, quam Dei essentia et essentiales eius proprietates* (J. Gerhard, *Loci theol.*, 1610 f., II, 300). Or Polanus : *Gloria Dei est essentialis eius maiestas, per quam intelligitur eum revera esse eundem essentia sua esse revera id, quod esse dicitur: simplicissimum, perfectissimum, infinitum, aeternum, immensum, immutabilem, viventem, immortalem, beatum, sapientem, intelligentem, omniscium, prudentem, volentem, bonum, gratiosum, amantem boni, misericordem, iustum, veracem, sanctum, castum, potentem imo omnipotentem, et talem se in omnibus operibus suis declarare. Breviter, essentialis gloria Dei sunt virtutes in ipso Deo existentes et in operibus eius relucentes* (*Synt. Theol. chr.*, 1609, *col.* 1213). It is indeed the glory of God that He gives Himself to be known as all this, that He not merely is all this and maintains Himself as all this, but that He demonstrates Himself as all this, not holding back or concealing anything of it as He does not lack anything of it, but proving Himself to be God in it all : the One who is it all in His own divine way, in His free love, the Father, the Son and the Holy Spirit. The glory of God consists in the fact that He declares Himself as all this and in all this. It would not be divine glory if any one of His perfections were lacking from His self-declaration, or if any one of the attributes declared fell short in perfection or if any one of them were not a divine perfection because less or other than Himself. From this point of view God's *gloria* is identical with His all-sufficiency, *omni-sufficientia*. God is He who declares Himself as the One who in virtue of His being and in the fulness of His perfection is sufficient for Himself, and—because it is His creation—for everything else. He is sufficient as He is known to Himself and therefore able to be known and actually known to everything else. In Him nothing is lacking and therefore nothing can be lacking at the place where He gives Himself to be known. In the words of P. Gerhardt : " Thou fillest up what life doth lack." God does this decisively in the fact that He is glorious, that He declares Himself in this perfection. He declares Himself in such a way that by His declaration He overcomes from the very outset all questions, counter-questions, hesitations, reservations and doubts concerning Him. These are only subjective and not objective. They do not have any corresponding reality. To remove them it is necessary only to repeat what has already been done on God's side—to open our eyes to the light with which they have for long been surrounded. This repetition, this opening of the eyes, is itself the work of His glory, for it is His glory that makes it necessary. It is in itself the truth and power and act by which blind eyes come to see. Thus it is really God's *maiestas, per quam intelligitur Deus revera esse eundem essentia sua esse revera id quod esse dicitur*. Our lack of ability to know Him is filled up by His glory, and our ability to know Him is healed and restored by it. In face of the named centre of the divine *kabod* in the New Testament, this is the first thing we have to say at this point. But it inevitably leads us to see God Himself as the One who has no need of amplification or confirmation in His inner life, in His existence or His essence as God ; the One who is not conditioned or controlled by any higher authority. This, then, His freedom, is the energy behind His self-declaration. This is what makes it, too, a sovereign, irresistible event, so that from the very first our knowledge can only follow, and even as that which follows can only come about as His own work. And if this divine self-sufficiency is understood in the light of the sovereign and irresistible activity of the divine revelation, we can also see that the filling up of what is lacking in us is not limited to the lack of our ability to know. Rather, since God's self-declaration is the self-declaration of the God who is sufficient in Himself, the supplying of our lack of ability to know God carries with it a supplying of every lack in our life. All the problems and worries of our life, all the riddles of the world and the riddles of our existence, are put into that secondary place to which we have referred, and being put there are thereby clarified and resolved by Him. This comes about in whatever way He chooses, according to His order and standard, but they are really clarified and resolved, i.e., they are elucidated and illuminated in such a way that there can no longer be any independent reality corresponding to them. He who has God has really everything. He may not have it in the way he would choose himself. But this only means that he has it the more certainly in the way that God wills that he should have it, and therefore in such a way that he can be satisfied and content. Let him only be content with God. Let him simply recognise that God is God who is and has all things, who is completely self-sufficient and who declares Himself to us as such, and who therefore loves us and permits us to have fellowship with Himself. This fellowship is the root of true Christian contentment. In this fellowship it cannot become or be anything else. It is true, and therefore

Christian, as the response to God's love, to the self-declaration of the One who is self-sufficient, and therefore definitely sufficient for everyone to whom He declares Himself and with whom He has fellowship. Man most certainly does not have of himself a glory which will give him contentment. Is. 40⁶ᶠ· tells us what is to be said about the glory of man. Man is not sufficient, and therefore there is no regard in which he can have self-sufficiency. For, of course, he is only man and not God. Indeed, he is in opposition to God. But *gloria hominis est Deus*, as Polanus says (*loc. cit., col.* 1225), finely expounding how in the fact that God is glorious in the fulness of His divine being, and that He has attested His glory to us, He has from the very first covered and removed all the shame of our position, all terror at the death and dissolution of our body, and also all our fear of Jesus Christ's return. In all these things, and under threat of all these things, we are effectively and finally comforted if we look to God's glory. To be comforted by God's glory is genuine, Christian contentment. It do s not involve any presumptuous claims that it is what we have a right to receive through God's glory, that is ours by right. It is God's glory that it can be received in this way, that God does not keep to Himself the fulness and therefore the sufficiency of His divine being, that He does not simply maintain and protect it as His own preserve, but that, on the contrary, He declares it and makes it known and therefore shares it, that He is self-sufficient in the fact that He is our Shepherd, as the Twenty-Third Psalm says. Where this is perceived and heard, the only possible answer is : " I shall lack nothing." Any lack can consist only in the fact that our eyes are closed to the glory of God and that we therefore resist His rule over us as our Shepherd. This blindness and opposition are not under any circumstances to be explained in terms of the divine glory. For this is always and in every way light and not darkness. From the point of view of God's glory and His Shepherd-rule, the sin in which this blindness and opposition consist can only be regarded as quite incomprehensible. God's glory is God's love. It is the justification and sanctification of us sinners out of pure, irresistible grace. What place is there then for our sin, our blindness and opposition ? From what source do we draw it ? How do we come to be obtuse and rebellious ? Since the Lord is my Shepherd, I shall lack nothing, and this means that I do not have to be obtuse and rebellious. We can and must say that it is just there that we see most clearly the frightfulness of sin—in its complete impossibility, in its character as that which is utterly excluded. It is, of course, explicable that it is recorded of the earthly shepherds (Lk. 2⁹) that when the glory of the Lord shone round about them, they were sore afraid. But more attention should be paid to the answer of the angel : " Fear not, behold I bring you good tidings of great joy." It is, of course, true, as Rom. 3²³ says, that all men are in the position that they all inevitably come short of the glory of God, and the reason is because they have all sinned, and face to face with the glory of God must confess that they have come short because they are closed to it, and that they are closed to it because they have closed themselves to it and resisted it. But the other side is even truer, and the first truth can be rightly understood only as we look back at this other side. And the other side is that in Jesus Christ sinful, blind and disobedient man has as such been so encircled by the light of God's glory that he can and must see it and he will lack nothing in Jesus Christ. In face of the " Fear not," and the *gloria hominis est Deus* which has its origin in that glory, there is no way back. This is the truth and importance of our first answer to the question of the nature of the divine glory. The older theologians were right. God's glory is also the fulness, the totality, the sufficiency, the sum of the perfection of God in the irresistibility of its declaration and manifestation.

But it is worth while to put the question rather more precisely and in that way perhaps to penetrate to a more definite answer. How far does it belong to God in the fulness of His divine being to be glorious in the sense described, to have and to be the source and radiance of light, the possibility and actuality of that outshining, the self-declaration to which we have referred ? It is obvious that in biblical usage this is what is specifically meant when we speak of His glory, and not simply of His being, of the sum of all His perfections, or rather when we speak of His being as that to which glory in particular belongs, which is itself glory. From the beginning we have had to see the glory of God as the truth and power and act of His self-declaration, corresponding to the fact that in the New Testament the term is found in significant proximity to the terms " power " and " kingdom." It is true enough that He who declares Himself in His glory is God in that fulness and sufficiency. We can also say that the divine glory as such is contained in this fact. But it is necessary and rewarding to ask specifically to what extent His glory is this outshining, this self-declaration.

1. If we start from our first answer, we must say that His glory consists in the fact that His being is His fulness and self-sufficiency, and distinct from every other being, because it is *God's* being. God is the being which is absolutely pre-eminent among all other beings and excels them absolutely. For this reason and in this way He is the source of light. In His positive and definite differentiation He is in relation to everything else what light is to darkness.

2. This statement does not exhaust the matter. A being can exist in such contrast to all other things, so marked off from them, that it can have no significance for them. There can be no relationship between it and their existence. In fact, it does not exist for them at all. There can be so great a distance between light and darkness that the light can do nothing to alter the darkness. In the universe, for example, there may be immense sources of light which have never been seen by any human eye and never will be so seen. Now this might well be the case between God and His creatures. But a God of whom this was true would not be the God whose is the kingdom, the power and the glory. As the living God is the source of light, and light in Himself, He also has and is the radiance of light. Standing in contrast to all other beings and marked off from them, He is the radiance of light that reaches all other beings and permeates them. He is not separated from them by any distance, but changes such distance into proximity. God's omnipotence is the positive meaning of His freedom. Thus His light is omnipotent light, and so omnipresent light. His glory means, then, that His self-declaration does not go out into empty space. On the contrary, He seeks and at once finds those to whom He declares Himself. As light He penetrates the darkness, even the farthest darkness. He shines round about it and through it. He illumines it in some way, so that nothing is hidden from Him, but everything is revealed and open.

3. We cannot stop even at this point. This reaching and permeating of other things by God does not take place in such a way
that when God declares Himself He is always at one point and we
are at another. What reaches us from Him and permeates us is not
merely an effect to be distinguished from Him, a creaturely or a half-
divine, half-creaturely force. Certainly to reach us God does also
make use of creaturely powers both of a higher and a lower rank.
But what reaches us through them is His own power and kingdom
and glory, and therefore Himself. No angel of God is this, no divine
sign or sacrament, no divinely instituted service of creatures, unless
it includes God's own presence, unless God Himself reaches us and is
present with us in it, unless by it we are in some way placed before the
face of God. God's face is more than the radiance of light. And
God's glory is the glory of His face, indeed His face itself, God in person,
God who bears a name and calls us by name. God is glorious in the
fact that He does this, that He reaches us in this way, that He Himself
comes to us to be known by us.

4. There still remains something to be added. God's glory is revealed when God is not present in vain, when the distinction and
worth of His person are not merely immanent but are recognised and
acknowledged as such, when to that extent they reach over to us.
Where there is light and light shines, there is an illuminating and
an illumination. This means that another object is illuminated which
is not light in itself and which could not be light without being illuminated. Where there is radiance there is also reflection of the radiance. And the final thing which we must say in this connexion
about God's glory is that it is God Himself in the truth and power
and act of His self-glorification on and in and through that which is
dark in itself because it is distinct from Himself and is not divine
but opposed to the divine. God's glory is the answer evoked by
Him of the worship offered Him by His creatures. This is not of
their own ability and inclination, their creaturely capacity and good
will, least of all the wisdom and desire of man who is flesh. It derives
from the presence of the Creator which is granted to the creature.
This is not an idle or unfruitful presence. It is not the presence of a
cold confrontation. It is not a presence which leaves blind eyes blind
or deaf ears deaf. It is a presence which opens them. It is a presence
which also looses at once tongues that were bound. God's glory is
the indwelling joy of His divine being which as such shines out from
Him, which overflows in its richness, which in its super-abundance
is not satisfied with itself but communicates itself. All God's works
must be understood also and decisively from this point of view. All
together and without exception they take part in the movement of God's
self-glorification and the communication of His joy. They are the
coming into being of light outside Him on the basis of the light
inside Him, which is Himself. They are expressions of the infinite

exultation in the depth of His divine being. It is from this point of view that all His creatures are to be viewed both first and last. God wills them and loves them because, far from having their existence of themselves and their meaning in themselves, they have their being and existence in the movement of the divine self-glorification, in the transition to them of His immanent joyfulness. It is their destiny to offer a true if inadequate response in the temporal sphere to the jubilation with which the Godhead is filled from eternity to eternity. This is the destiny which man received and lost, only to receive it again, inconceivably and infinitely increased by the personal participation of God in man's being accomplished in Jesus Christ. The reaction of God even against sin, the meaning even of His holiness, even of His judgment, the meaning which is not extinguished but fulfilled even in damnation and hell, is that God is glorious, and that His glory does not allow itself to be diminished, to be disturbed in its gladness and the expression of that gladness, to be checked in the overflowing of its fulness. And this is what is expected from all creation because this is the source from which they come. It is in this light that they are to be seen and heard. This is their secret that will one day come out and be revealed. And it is to this that we are always required and will always find it worth our while to attend and look. It is for this revelation that we should always wait. The creature has no voice of its own. It does not point to its own picture. It echoes and reflects the glory of the Lord. It does this in its heights and its depths, its happiness and its misery. The angels do it (and unfortunately we have almost completely forgotten that we are surrounded by the angels as crown witnesses to the divine glory). But even the smallest creatures do it too. They do it along with us or without us. They do it also against us to shame us and instruct us. They do it because they cannot help doing it. They would not and could not exist unless first and last and properly they did this and only this. And when man accepts again his destiny in Jesus Christ in the promise and faith of the future revelation of his participation in God's glory as it is already given Him here and now, he is only like a late-comer slipping shamefacedly into creation's choir in heaven and earth, which has never ceased its praise, but merely suffered and sighed, as it still does, that in inconceivable folly and ingratitude its living centre man does not hear its voice, its response, its echoing of the divine glory, or rather hears it in a completely perverted way, and refuses to co-operate in the jubilation which surrounds him. This is the sin of man which is judged and forgiven in Jesus Christ, which God Himself has made good and cast behind man's back. It is this which in Jesus Christ has once for all become his past. In the eternal glory before us it will not exist at all even as the past. In the eternity before us the groaning of creation will cease, and man too will live in his determination to be the reflection and echo of God and therefore the witness to the divine glory that reaches over to him, rejoicing with the God who Himself has eternal joy and Himself is eternal joy.

I owe this fourfold development to the inspiration of Petrus van Mastricht (*Theor. pract. Theol.*, 1698, II, *cap.* 22). So far as I can see, he alone among the Reformed orthodox attempted a detailed examination and presentation of the concept of the *gloria Dei* in a way which does justice to all the biblical statements and references. His definition of the *gloria Dei* is that it is the *infinitae eminentiae fulgor agnoscendus et manifestandus*. The glory of God consists in the fact that God is great *non mole sed perfectionis majestate* ; that He is always magnificent and wonderful ; that He is supreme among His works ; that as such He is active and above all gods ; that He is worthy to be praised and calls us to give this praise. But van Mastricht was not satisfied with this affirmation, and rightly so. He found a basis for it, and developed it, in an exposition of the definition. 1. God's glory has its basis in the *eminentia* of His being and His perfection. 2. It is the *fulgor* which belongs to this *eminentia* as such, which goes out from it, which strikes and enlightens our spiritual eyes, and which, according to biblical testimony to revelation, never wholly lacks the symbolical accompaniment of physical light. 3. It is the *agnitio istius eminentiae a qua facies Dei dicitur*. And 4 it is *agnitae per fulgorem eminentiae celebratio seu manifestatio, quae magis proprie glorificatio quam gloria appellatur*. And here van Mastricht enumerates : the glorification which God prepares for Himself by His being within the Godhead ; the glorification of the Son by the Father and of the Father by the Son ; the glorification of God as it may and should be offered by angels and men ; His glorification in His Word, in the Gospel, in Jesus Christ Himself ; His glorification in the works of the creation, preservation and overruling of the world, and especially in the miracles of the history of revelation ; His glorification in His grace granted to the Church and in the secrets of its ways and constitution. And van Mastricht concludes by referring to the honour which is to be offered God by the intelligent creation in an intelligent, conscious and purposeful way, and therefore to the worship of angels, the praise of Israel and the thanksgiving (*eucharistia*) of the Church, to which also belong its *supplicationes*, its praying and beseeching, *quibus omnibus Dei omnipotentia, omniscientia, inexhausta bonitas agnoscitur et extollitur*.

But at this point a question arises which has not yet been answered even by this development of the concept. The question is whether we cannot in some sense give a name and a more precise designation even to the form in which the divine transition takes place in which we have always to see the heart of the concept of the divine glory. To what extent is God's light in His self-declaration really light and therefore enlightening ? To what extent, when God is present to Himself and others, does He really convince and persuade ? In what way does He move Himself to glorify Himself, and move others, that which is outside Himself, to join in His self-glorification ? Or we might simply ask : What is the thing revealed in the divine revelation and what is the nature and form of its revealing ? Here again we have to begin by considering the revelation in which God is revealed to Himself, going on from this point to understand how in fact He is revealed to us. Or do we go too far when we ask this question ? Is it a forbidden and foolish question ? Should we be satisfied simply to state that

God is actually glorious and therefore convincing and persuasive, enlightening and revealed ? Must we refuse to answer the question how He is this, in what shape and form—because the question itself is refused us ? Can we only point to the fact and its content, because we ourselves are pointed to this, and can and must be satisfied with it ? Or can we perhaps say positively of the method of God's glory, of His self-glorification, only that it has the whole omnipotence of God behind it, that it persuades and convinces by ruling, mastering and subduing with the utterly superior force which as such creates the fact that light gives light, that there is a being enlightened by it, that there is a thing enlightened which as such, receiving light, itself becomes light ? Well, in many other matters we can be satisfied with a negative reply, or a positive reply of this kind. But this is not possible in a connected consideration of the concept of God's glory. It would be always most unsettling if all that could be given were the negative answer which dismisses the question ; if in dealing with the knowledge of God's glory we had to be satisfied with the existence of a *brutum factum*, and therefore of a blind spot in our knowledge ; if we had to count and declare ourselves convinced and persuaded when face to face with this dark spot. The question would inevitably arise whether this was worthy of the knowledge or revelation of the God who is the truth. Is this a knowledge or revelation which in the last resort is a mere object—without shape or form ? When the Bible uses the term " glory " to describe the revelation and knowledge of God, does it not mean something other and more than the assertion of a brute fact ? And the very same question arises in relation to the positive answer given above. We have seen that when we speak of God's glory we do emphatically mean God's " power." Yet the idea of " glory " contains something which is not covered by that of " power." For the idea of " kingdom " which precedes the other two concepts in the doxology of the Lord's Prayer seems to say something of wider range than can be described by " power " alone. Light, too, has power and is power, but it is not this that makes it light. Has not and is not God more than is covered by the idea of power when He has and is light and is glorious ?

The concept which lies ready to our hand here, and which may serve legitimately to describe the element in the idea of glory that we still lack, is that of beauty. If we can and must say that God is beautiful, to say this is to say how He enlightens and convinces and persuades us. It is to describe not merely the naked fact of His revelation or its power, but the shape and form in which it is a fact and is power. It is to say that God has this superior force, this power of attraction, which speaks for itself, which wins and conquers, in the fact that He is beautiful, divinely beautiful, beautiful in His own way, in a way that is His alone, beautiful as the unattainable primal beauty, yet really beautiful. He does not have it, therefore, merely as a fact or a power. Or rather, He has it as a fact and a power in such a way that He acts as the One who gives pleasure, creates desire and rewards with enjoyment. And He does it because He is pleasant, desirable, full of enjoyment, because He is the One who is pleasant, desirable, full of enjoyment, because first and last He alone is that which is pleasant, desirable and full of enjoyment. God loves us as the One who is worthy of love as God. This is what we mean when we say that God is beautiful.

When we say this we reach back to the pre-Reformation tradition of the Church. We think of the famous passage in Augustine's *Confessions* (X, 27) where he addresses what we may call a hymn to God. *Sero te amavi, pulchritudo tam antiqua et tam nova! sero te amavi! Et ecce intus eras et ego foris et ibi te quaerebam; et in ista formosa quae fecisti deformis irruebam. Mecum eras et tecum non eram. Ea me tenebant longe a te, quae si in te non essent, non essent. Vocasti et clamasti et rupisti surditatem meam. Coruscasti, splenduisti et fugasti caecitatem meam. Fragrasti et duxi spiritum et anhelo tibi. Gustavi et esurio et sitio. Tetigisti me et exarsi in pacem tuam.* Pseudo-Dionysius (*De div. nom.* IV, 7) expanded this in detail. He said that the beautiful in its identification with the good is the ultimate cause which produces and moves all things, that which is in and for itself, identical in form with itself, the ever beautiful, the beauty which, as the source, possesses all beauty already in a more eminent degree, by which all the harmony of the universe, all friendships and all fellowships have their existence, and by which everything is ultimately and finally united. This is a hardly veiled Platonism, and there is good reason why traces of the application of this idea are, generally speaking, very rare even in the ancient Church. Reformation and Protestant orthodoxy, so far as I can see, completely ignored it. Paul Gerhardt dared to sing: " I think me, Thou art here so fair." And the popular hymn " Fair Lord Jesus " found its way from the Middle Ages even into the Protestant Church or at least into the exercise of its piety. But this was always an alien element, not accepted with a very good conscience, and always looked on and treated with a certain mistrust. Theology at any rate hardly knew what to make of the idea and would have nothing to do with it. Even Schleiermacher, in whom we might have expected something of this kind, did not achieve anything very striking in this direction. It is no less surprising that Roman Catholic theology did not return expressly and seriously to this conception until the 19th century with J. M. Scheeben (*Handb. d. kath. Dogm.*, Vol. I, 1874, pp. 589 f.; cf. J. Pohle, *Lehrb. d. Dogm.*, Vol. I, 1902, pp. 131 f.; F. Diekamp., *Kath. Dogm.*[6], 1930, Vol. I, pp. 174 f.). It may well be asked if it is a good thing to follow its example. Owing to its connexion with the ideas of pleasure, desire and enjoyment (quite apart from its historical connexion with Greek thought), the concept of the beautiful seems to be a particularly secular one, not at all adapted for introduction into the language of theology, and indeed extremely dangerous. If we say now that God is beautiful, and make this statement the final explanation of the assertion that God is glorious, do we not jeopardise or even deny the majesty and holiness and righteousness of God's love? Do we not bring God in a sinister because in a sense intimate way into the sphere of man's oversight and control, into proximity to the ideal of all human striving? Do we not bring the contemplation of God into suspicious proximity to that contemplation of the world which in the last resort is the self-contemplation of an urge for life which does not recognise its limits? Certainly we have every reason to be cautious here. But the question is even more pressing whether we can hesitate indefinitely, whether we can avoid this step. Has our whole consideration of the matter not brought us inevitably to the place where what would otherwise remain a gap in our knowledge can be filled only in this way? Finally and above all, does biblical truth itself and as such permit us to stop at this point because of the danger, and not to say that God is beautiful ?

Attention must first be paid to the context. We have spoken of the divine glory as the sum of the divine perfections and as the divine self-sufficiency that is a self-sufficiency which overflows and declares itself. We have spoken of the superiority and irresistibility of the divine self-declaration. There can be no question of withdrawing or relativising this, as if it were insufficient and not wholly true in itself. There can be no question of giving it full reality by bringing it under the denominator of the beautiful, as if this conception were the key to the being of all things, or even this being itself. In our discussion of the leading concepts of the Christian knowledge of God, we have seen that no single one of them is this key, and that if any one of them is claimed as such it inevitably becomes an idol. There can be no question, then, of finally allowing an aestheticism to speak which if it tried to have and keep the last word would inevitably be as false and unchristian as any dynamism or vitalism or logism or intellectualism or moralism which might try to slip into the doctrine of God in this role and with this dignity.

For all that, it is as well to realise that the aestheticism which threatens here is no worse than the other " isms " or any " ism." They are all dangerous. Indeed, as we have more or less clearly encountered them all, we have seen that in their place they are all mortally dangerous. But we have also seen that there is a herb that is a match for them. There is no reason to take up a particularly tragic attitude to the danger that threatens from the side of aesthetics —which is what Protestantism has done according to our historical review. Nor is there any reason to shrink back at this point with particular uneasiness or prudery, suppressing or dismissing out of sheer terror a problem that is set us by the subject itself and its biblical attestation.

Attention should also be given to the fact that we cannot include the concept of beauty with the main concepts of the doctrine of God, with the divine perfections which are the divine essence itself. In view of what the biblical testimony says about God it would be an unjustified risk to try to bring the knowledge of God under the denominator of the idea of the beautiful even in the same way as we have done in our consideration of these leading concepts. It is not a leading concept. Not even in passing can we make it a primary motif in our understanding of the whole being of God as we necessarily did in the case of these other concepts.

To do this is an act of philosophical wilfulness of which Pseudo-Dionysius is guilty in the passage quoted and elsewhere, and which even lurks behind the passage in Augustine's *Confessions*. The Bible neither requires nor permits us, because God is beautiful, to expound the beauty of God as the ultimate cause producing and moving all things, in the way in which we can and must do this in regard to God's grace or holiness or eternity, or His omnipotent knowledge and will.

Our subject is still the glory of God. We speak of God's beauty only in explanation of His glory. It is, therefore, a subordinate and auxiliary idea which enables us to achieve a specific clarification and emphasis. With the help of it we are able to dissipate even the suggestion that God's glory is a mere fact, or a fact which is effective merely through God's power, a formless and shapeless fact. It is not this. It is effective because and as it is beautiful. This explanation as such is not merely legitimate. It is essential.

It is certainly true that the idea of the beautiful as such and *in abstracto* does not play any outstanding or at least autonomous part in the Bible.

The only serious appeal is to Ps. 104[1f.], where magnificence and sublimity and especially light are mentioned as God's garment and apparel. Ps. 45[2] could also be mentioned, where the Messiah-king is addressed as " fairer than the children of men ; grace is poured into thy lips : therefore God hath blessed thee for ever." In addition it is worth asking whether an important contribution could not and would not be made by a new and more penetrating exposition of the Song of Songs—which if it was once interpreted much too directly has more recently not been understood at all. Even then, the fact still remains that the idea of beauty does not have any 'independent significance in the Bible. Yet this does not mean that it is unimportant for the Bible or alien to it.

We must now point to the purely philological fact that the significance of the word " glory " and its Hebrew, Greek, Latin and even German equivalents, at least includes and expresses what we call beauty. At each point where the idea of glory appears we can apply the test and we shall see that in no case can it be interpreted as something neutral or something which excludes the ideas of the pleasant, desirable and enjoyable and therefore that of the beautiful. We have already said that God's glory is His overflowing self-communicating joy. By its very nature it is that which gives joy. This is not contradicted by the fact that it can unleash fear and terror. It works by contraries on the man who cannot have it, just as bright light can only blind eyes unaccustomed to it. But the cause in this case is subjective. The objective meaning of God's glory is His active grace and mercy and patience, His love. In itself and as such it is worthy of love. In and with this quality it speaks and conquers, persuades and convinces. It does not merely assume this quality. It is proper to it. And where it is really recognised, it is recognised in this quality, with its peculiar power and characteristic of giving pleasure, awaking desire, and creating enjoyment.

Medieval theology knew and used the concept of a *frui* or *fruitio Dei*. It understood by it the activity of a desire possible and proper only to man among created beings. Whether fulfilled or not it was directed towards that which stands in relation to all other desirable things as the end to the means, so that its proper object as the *finis ultimus hominis* can only be God Himself. Too much of what cannot be overlooked in the Bible would have to be struck out if the legitimacy of this concept of beauty were denied out of an excessively Puritan concern about sin. It is true that the imagination of the heart of man is wicked from his youth (Gen. 8²¹), that there is sinful and deadly desire, and that this is the desire natural to man. But this does not alter the fact that the God who stoops down to the man whose heart is like this in judgment and mercy, slaying and making alive, is Himself supremely and most strictly an object of desire, joy, pleasure, yearning and enjoyment. This is a fact, and the radically evangelical character of the Biblical message has to be denied if this is rejected. " My soul doth magnify the Lord, and my spirit hath rejoiced in God my Saviour " (Lk. 1⁴⁶ᶠ·). " Rejoice in the Lord alway " (Phil. 4⁴). The good and faithful servant will enter into the joy of his lord (Mt. 25²¹). Paul desires to be absent from the body and present with the Lord (2 Cor. 5⁸). According to Ps. 1², 112¹ and Rom. 7²² there is a necessary and legitimate delight in the Law of God, while according to Ps. 119⁴ (and *passim*) there is a desire, a gladness and a pleasure in its commands and precepts. It is not true that the lines of Joachim Neander which run : " Hast thou not seen, How thy heart's wishes have been Granted in what He ordaineth," are a *pudendum* in our hymn books, as some of the over-zealous maintain. We are bidden expressly in Ps. 37⁴ : " Delight thyself in the Lord, and he shall give thee the desires of thine heart." And Prov. 23²⁶ says : " My son, give me thine heart and let thine eyes have pleasure in my ways " ; and Ps. 5¹¹ : " Let all those that put their trust in thee rejoice : let them ever shout for joy " ; and Ps. 145¹⁶, " Thou openest thine hand and satisfieth the desire of every living thing." " In thy presence is fulness of joy ; at thy right hand there are pleasures for evermore " (Ps. 16¹¹). " Thou hast multiplied the nation and increased their joy : they joy before thee according to the joy of harvest, and as men rejoice when they divide the spoil " (Is. 9³). We are invited to taste and see how good the Lord is (Ps. 34⁸). All this has nothing whatever to do with an optimistic glossing over of the need and the condition of mankind. On the other hand, the latter cannot alter but is confuted and overcome by the fact that God must be the object of joy. " Thou hast turned for me my mourning into dancing : thou hast put off my sackcloth, and girded me with gladness " (Ps. 30¹¹). " Yea, in the way of thy judgments, O Lord, have we waited for thee ; the desire of our soul is to thy name, and to the remembrance of thee. With my soul have I desired thee in the night, yea, with my spirit within me will I seek thee early : for when thy judgments are in the earth, the inhabitants of the world will learn righteousness " (Is. 26⁸⁻⁹). According to Ecclus. 1¹¹ the fear of the Lord is also gladness. It is the meek who according to Is. 29¹⁹ " shall increase their joy in the Lord, and the poor among men shall rejoice in the Holy One of Israel." For this reason it is always " good to draw near to God " (Ps. 73²⁸). We must " serve the Lord with gladness " and " come before his face with singing " (Ps. 100²). If this is so—and it could be illustrated directly or indirectly from hundreds of other passages—if the God attested in Holy Scripture is the God who Himself radiates joy, and would not be understandable in His Godhead or be what He is without it, there is no reason to avoid the medieval concept (merely on account of the misuse to which it was put by mystics). We can only ask to what extent we are to say of God that He can be the object of this *frui*, of this pleasure, desire and enjoyment, fulfilled or not yet fulfilled.

Are we saying something excessive or strange when we say that God also radiates this joy because He is beautiful ? We say " also " deliberately, not forgetting that we are speaking only of the form and manner of His glory, of the specifically persuasive and convincing element in His revelation. The substance and content of His glory is God Himself in the fulness of His perfection. He is also its power. He is glorious in His self-declaration because He is gracious and merciful and patient, holy and righteous and wise, because He is love, and because He is all this in the freedom of His unity and omnipresence, His constancy, omnipotence and eternity. It is in this way that He also radiates this joy and it is possible, necessary and permissible to have joy in Him and before Him. But the question remains : Why also joy, why specifically joy, according to the witness of Holy Scripture ? Why not simply awe, gratitude, wonder, submission and obedience ? Joy, desire, pleasure, the yearning for God and the enjoyment of having Him in the fellowship with Him which He Himself gives us, is all along something which is obviously special and distinctive in all this. The special element to be noted and considered is that the glory of God is not only great and sublime or holy and gracious, the overflowing of the sovereignty in which God is love. In all this it is a glory that awakens joy, and is itself joyful. It is not merely a glory which is solemn and good and true, and which, in its perfection and sublimity, might be gloomy or at least joyless. Joy in and before God—in its particular nature, distinct from what we mean by awe, gratitude and the rest—has an objective basis. It is something in God, the God of all the perfections, which justifies us in having joy, desire and pleasure towards Him, which indeed obliges, summons and attracts us to do this. That which attracts us to joy in Him, and our consequent attraction, is the inalienable form of His glory and the indispensable form of the knowledge of His glory. But this being the case, how can we dispense with the idea of the beautiful, and therefore with the statement that God is also beautiful ? It is again to be noted that we use the cautious expression that God is " also " beautiful, beautiful in His love and freedom, beautiful in His essence as God and in all His works, beautiful, that is, in the form in which He is all this. We shall not presume to try to interpret God's glory from the point of view of His beauty, as if it were the essence of His glory. But we cannot overlook the fact that God is glorious in such a way that He radiates joy, so that He is all He is with and not without beauty. Otherwise His glory might well be joyless. And if a different view of His glory is taken and taught, then even with the best will in the world, and even with the greatest seriousness and zeal, the proclamation of His glory will always have in a slight or dangerous degree something joyless, without sparkle or humour, not to say tedious and there finally neither persuasive nor convincing. We are dealing here solely with the question of the form of revelation. But this must not on any account be neglected. Where it is neglected, and the legitimate answer to the question is not perceived or understood, the element in God's glory which radiates joy is not appreciated and His glory itself is not really perceived. But where this element is not appreciated—and this is why the question of the form is so important—what becomes of the evangelical element in the evangel ?

If, then, we must pursue our enquiry, what is actually the beautiful element in God which makes Him an object of joy as the One He is, and therefore in His glory, in the fulness and self-sufficiency of His being, in the power of His self-declaration ?

In answering this as all other questions in the doctrine of God we must be careful not to start from any preconceived ideas, especially in this case a pre-conceived idea of the beautiful. Augustine was quite right when he said of the beautiful : *Non ideo pulchra sunt, quia delectant, sed ideo delectant, quia pulchra sunt* (*De vera rel.* 32, 59). What is beautiful produces pleasure. *Pulchra sunt, quae visa placent* (Thomas Aquinas, *S. th.* I, qu. 5, art. 4, ad. 1). Yet it is not beautiful because it arouses pleasure. Because it is beautiful it arouses pleasure. In our context Augustine's statement is to be expanded into : *Non ideo Deus Deus, quia pulcher est, sed ideo pulcher, quia Deus est.* God is not beautiful in the sense that He shares in an idea of beauty superior to Him, so that to know it is to know Him as God. On the contrary, it is as He is God that He is also beautiful, so that He is the basis and standard of everything that is beautiful and of all ideas of the beautiful.

We have to ask about God Himself, about the content and sub-stance of His revelation, and therefore also of His revealed divine being. This as such is beautiful. We have to learn from it what beauty is. Our creaturely conceptions of the beautiful, formed from what has been created, may rediscover or fail to rediscover themselves in the divine being. If they do rediscover themselves in it, it will be with an absolutely unique application, to the extent that now, subse-quently as it were, they have also to describe His being.

Strictly speaking, to give even a generally adequate answer to our question we should again have to work through the whole doctrine of God which we have now completed. We should have to refer back to the whole doctrine of the Word of God. We should also have to survey all the sections of dogmatics which we have yet to consider, and indeed all theology as such.

At this point we may refer to the fact that if its task is correctly seen and grasped, theology as a whole, in its parts and in their interconnexion, in its con-tent and method, is, apart from anything else, a peculiarly beautiful science. Indeed, we can confidently say that it is the most beautiful of all the sciences. To find the sciences distasteful is the mark of the Philistine. It is an extreme form of Philistinism to find, or to be able to find, theology distasteful. The theologian who has no joy in his work is not a theologian at all. Sulky faces, morose thoughts and boring ways of speaking are intolerable in this science. May God deliver us from what the Catholic Church reckons one of the seven sins of the monk—*taedium* —in respect of the great spiritual truths with which theology has to do. But we must know, of course, that it is only God who can keep us from it.

The beauty of theology is an insight to which there is occasional allusion in Anselm of Canterbury. The *ratio* which *fides quaerens intellectum* has to seek is not only *utilitas*. It is also *pulchritudo*. When it is found, and as it is sought, it is *speciosa super intellectum hominum* (*Cur Deus homo* I, 1), a *delectabile quiddam* (*Monol.* 6). In the *Cur Deus homo* there is a great attempt to offer proofs, but the fact should not be overlooked that Anselm makes this *delectari* (*loc. cit.*) explicitly the first of his tasks and polemics and apologetics only the second. The fact that he seeks truth in sincere despair and with fervent prayer (cf. the introductions to *Prosl.* and *Cur Deus homo*) includes rather than excludes the joy which he finds in this and desires to spread. A theological proof is in itself a *delectatio.* There is, however, a reason why even in Anselm there are only allusions to this thought in all its truth. No more than allusion is possible because, however much we may try to illustrate it in detail, this insight depends too much on the presence of the necessary feeling to allow of theoretical development. But again, and above all, reflection and discussion of the aesthetics of theology can hardly be counted a legitimate and certainly not a necessary task of theology. Yet it must not be forgotten that there is actually something here which must be perceived rather than discussed and that the theologian has good cause for repentance if he has not perceived it.

It belongs to the nature of the subject that the real proof of our statement that God is beautiful can be provided neither by few nor by many words about this beauty, but only by this beauty itself. God's being itself speaks for His beauty in His revelation. All that we can do here is to indicate by several examples the fact that this is so, or rather in view of certain decisive features of the Christian knowledge of God to put the question whether what is known in it, quite apart from anything else, is not simply beautiful. And what is known itself gives us a positive answer. That it does this is the one thing which can be said here with unambiguous certainty. But it is the only thing which can give this answer. It is part of the border-line character of this whole subject that whatever we say can be only with this qualification.

We mention first that aspect of God with which we have just been dealing—God's being as it unfolds itself in all His attributes, but is one in itself in them all. All these attributes are perfections because they are God's attributes. And both together and individually they are nothing other or less than God Himself. They are the perfections of His being, and this perfect being itself. The perfection of the divine being consists in the fact that God is all that He is as God, and therefore originally, and therefore in truth, completeness and reality, and therefore uniquely and unsurpassably. Both in Himself and in His works God is what He is in this perfection. In every relationship to His creation He is this perfect being. He speaks and acts with this perfection. The inexhaustible, unfathomable, inaccessible source and meaning of all these relationships is, again, this perfect divine nature. But is it not the case that, in addition to all this, with a delight that is certainly subsequent, but cannot subsequently be suppressed, we have to maintain that the form or way or manner in which God is perfect is also itself perfect, the perfect form? The form of the perfect being of God is, as we have seen all along, the wonderful, constantly mysterious and no less constantly evident unity of identity and non-identity, simplicity and multiplicity, inward and outward, God Himself and the fulness of that which He is as God. It has not been either possible or legitimate to overlook either the one side or the other in our discussion, to reduce the one to the other, or to deny the one for the sake of the other. We have always had to remember that we have to do with God Himself, and not with an object which we can clearly survey and control. We have also had to remember, however, that God Himself in the fulness of His revelation of His being has entered the sphere of our survey and control. In embarrassment at our inability to know or say anything about God, we have always had to flee to God Himself, and we have always returned as those who are permitted to know and say something about Him. And again, what we have been allowed to know and say of Him has always been at one and the same time one thing and many things, both a simple statement and a new exposition of limitless wealth, in which, however, we have never been able so to lose ourselves that the simplicity in which God is who He is has not always reappeared. Thus the freedom of God and the love of God have become comprehensible to us in all their incomprehensibility as the basic determinations of His being. We have seen their identity and their non-identity, the movement and the peace in which they together constitute the life of God, so that neither of them is lost in any single moment of His being and life. Thus both are His self-determination. Both are God Himself. And in both He is and remains one and the same. This unity of movement and peace has accompanied us through our consideration of the whole series of divine perfections. Again and again we have inevitably had to notice how each of them as God's perfection is this or that in real differentiation from all the others, and yet how they are not only inter-related but, bursting through every system and relativising from the very first the surveys we try to make, each is one with every other and with the sum of them all. Yet this is not so in such a way that we have not been permitted and bidden in full consciousness of the relativity but also of the necessity of our undertaking to take a definite way from one to the other, and also to take definite ways in detail. We have not made any presumptuous claim that these are the only right ways or that our ways are God's ways. Yet we have done it without the fear that we cannot be accompanied by the absolute on these relative ways, that we are necessarily forsaken by God. It is here that we have the form in which God's perfect being makes itself known in its revelation. And clearly, if God is not deceiving us, but is truly the One He is, this form is really His own. If this is so, then, assuming that this form has been visible to us and has made an impression on us, we cannot avoid the question whether this form of God's perfect being is not itself perfect ; whether this, the perfect being of God, is not itself and as such beautiful. We must be very clear what we are doing. There can be no question of distinguishing between the content and the form of the divine being and therefore of seeking the beauty of God abstractly in the form of His being for us and in Himself. The beauty of God is not to be found in the unity of identity and non-identity, or movement and peace, as such.

Here, too, our final recourse must be to God Himself. He is the perfect content of the divine being, which also makes His form perfect. Or, the perfection of His form is simply the radiating outwards of the perfection of His content and therefore of God Himself. But this content does actually make this form perfect, clearly because the form is necessary to the content, because it belongs to it. And in this form the perfect content, God Himself, shines out. The glory, the self-declaration of God, is based entirely on the fact that He Himself has His life in it both inwards and outwards. And so the question cannot be whether there might not be other examples of this unity and distinction, distinction and unity. That, of course, may be so. The question is : Where is this form the garment in which God wraps Himself ? Where is it so perfect and incomparably beautiful because and as it is the form of this content ? Where is it the form of the being of Him whose perfections are those of the Lord, the Creator, Reconciler and Redeemer ? Where does it radiate this perfection ? Where does it do so more than anything imperfect ? Where, then, will it not show itself on a closer inspection to be highly imperfect ? Only the form of the divine being has divine beauty. But as the form of the divine being it has and is itself divine beauty. And where it is recognised as the form of the divine being it will necessarily be felt as beauty. Inevitably when the perfect divine being declares itself, it also radiates joy in the dignity and power of its divinity, and thus releases the pleasure, desire and enjoyment of which we have spoken, and is in this way, by means of this form, persuasive and convincing. And this persuasive and convincing form must necessarily be called the beauty of God.

We take as our second example the triunity of God. God's perfect being is the one being of the Father, the Son and the Holy Spirit. It is only as this that it has the perfection of which we have spoken. But as this it does have it. Yet it is not just being in itself. God's freedom is not an abstract freedom or sovereignty, nor is God's love an abstract seeking and finding of fellowship. Similarly, all the perfections of the divine freedom and love are not truths, realities and powers which exist in themselves, and God's being is not self-enclosed and pure divine being. What makes it divine and real being is the fact that it is the being of the Father, the Son and the Holy Spirit, and it is in the fact that they exist in this triune God in His one but differentiated being that God's freedom and love and all His perfections are divine in this concretion. In just the same way, the form of His being, which is our present concern, is not form in itself but the concrete form of the triune being of God, the being which is God the Father, the Son and the Holy Spirit. It is in such a way that everything that may be said about His being, existence and nature must always, strictly speaking, be understood and described as the being, existence and nature of the Father, the Son and the Holy

Spirit. Even the particular form of the divine being has its necessity and significance in the triunity of God. Here first and in final truth we have to do with a unity of identity and non-identity. Here God lives His divine life, which may be brought neither under the denominator of simplicity nor under that of multiplicity, but includes within itself both simplicity and multiplicity. There are here three in God who stand in definite irreversible and non-interchangeable relationships to one another and are definitely a plurality of divine modes of being in these relationships. Here God in Himself is really distinguished from Himself: God, and God again and differently, and the same a third time. Here there is no mere point, nor is the circle or the triangle the final form. Here there is divine space and divine time, and with them extension, and in this extension, succession and order. But here there is no disparity or dissolution or contradiction. Here there is always one divine being in all three modes of being, as that which is common to them all. Here the three modes of being are always together—so intimate and powerful are the relationships between them. We can never have one without the others. Here one is both by the others and in the others, in a *perichoresis* which nothing can restrict or arrest, so that one mode is neither active nor knowable externally without the others. Note that the divine being draws from this not only its inner perfection, its great truth and power, and therefore also that of its works, as the truth and power of the Father, the Son and the Holy Spirit. But from it, too, it draws the outer perfection of its form, its thorough-going distinctiveness, as the unity of identity and non-identity, movement and peace, simplicity and multiplicity. This is inevitable if God is triune. It does not follow from His triunity that His being is three-fold in the sense that His perfection consists of three parts and is to be seen and understood by us as it were in three divisions. His being is whole and undivided, and therefore all His perfections are equally the being of all three modes of the divine being. But it certainly follows from God's triunity that the one whole divine being, as the Father, the Son and the Holy Spirit whose being it is, must be at the same time identical with itself and non-identical, simple and multiple, a life both in movement and at peace. In this relationship, and therefore in its form, what is repeated and revealed in the whole divine being as such, and in each divine perfection in particular, is the relationship and form of being of the Father and the Son in the unity of the Spirit, to the extent that these three are distinct in God but no less one in God, without pre-eminence or subordination but not without succession and order, yet without any jeopardising or annulment of the real life of the Godhead. We can now state more explicitly the decisive truth that it is the content of the divine being which creates the particular form of the divine being. This form is particular to this content. It is not based on a general necessity but on the necessity of the triune being and life of God. As the triunity—and by this we mean in the strictest and most proper sense, God Himself—is the basis of the power and dignity of the divine being, and therefore also of His self-declaration, His glory, so this triune being and life (in the strict and proper sense, God Himself) is the basis of what makes this power and dignity enlightening, persuasive and convincing. For this is the particular function of this form. It is radiant, and what it radiates is joy. It attracts and therefore it conquers. It is, therefore, beautiful. But it is this, as we must affirm, because it reflects the triune being of God. It does not do this materially, so that a triad is to be found in it. It does it formally, which is the only question· that can now concern us. It does this to the extent that in it there is repeated and revealed the unity and distinction of the divine being particular to it as the being of the triune God. To this extent the triunity of God is the secret of His beauty. If we deny this, we at once have a God without radiance and without joy (and without humour !); a God without beauty. Losing the dignity and power of real divinity, He also loses His beauty. But if we keep to this, fulfilling the whole Christian knowledge of God and all Christian theology with a knowledge of this basic presupposition that the one God is Father, Son and Holy Spirit, we cannot escape the fact either in general or in detail that apart from anything else God is also beautiful.

Our third example is the incarnation. We are now assuming that we have here the centre and goal of all God's works, and therefore the hidden beginning of them all. We are also assuming that the prominent place occupied by this divine work has something corresponding to it in the essence of God, that the Son forms the centre of the Trinity, and that the essence of the divine being has, so to speak, its *locus*, and is revealed, in His work, in the name and person of Jesus Christ. But this work of the Son as such reveals the beauty of God in a special way and in some sense to a supreme degree.

This is not to qualify what we have already said about the beauty of the being of God as such and of the Trinity in particular. But how do we know God's being and the Trinity except by revelation and therefore from the existence of the Son of God in His union with humanity ? We must even say that the Son or Logos of God already displays the beauty of God in a special way in His eternal existence and therefore within the Trinity, as the perfect image of the Father. *Aliqua imago dicitur esse pulchra, si perfecte repraesentat rem* (Thomas Aquinas, *S. theol.* I, qu. 39, *art.* 8 *c.*) The *species* or *pulchritudo* of God is, therefore, present *ubi iam est tanta congruentia et prima aequalitas et prima similitudo nulla in re dissidens et nullo modo inaequalis et nulla ex parte dissimilis, sed ad identidem respondens ei cuius imago est.* But this is the Son of God. He is the *Verbum perfectum, cui non desit aliquid et ars quaedam omnipotentis et sapientis Dei . . . ipsa unum de uno, cum quo unum* (Augustine, *De trin.* VI, 10). We find ourselves directed to the same point when we recall that according to Scripture we have in Jesus Christ the revelation of the glory of God *par excellence*, His supreme self-declaration (according to Heb. 1³ He is the ἀπαύγασμα τῆς δόξης καὶ χαρακτὴρ τῆς ὑποστάσεως αὐτοῦ; according to 2 Cor. 4⁶ His face is the instrument

to enlighten us " in the knowledge of the glory of God "). But it is the work o
the Son and therefore His incarnation which causes us to speak in this way of
His eternal being.

We should not know anything about that which attracts us as the
beauty of God's being and of the triunity of His being, nor should we
have any conception or idea of the unity in God of identity and non-
identity, simplicity and multiplicity, movement and peace, nor should
we have found delight in the vision of His inner life, if this life had
not been presented to us in the distinction in which it arouses joy,
in the self-representation of God which consists in the fact that He
becomes flesh in His eternal Word, that He becomes One with us
men in Jesus Christ, that He adopts us into unity with Himself, by
Himself, very God, becoming and being very man in Jesus Christ.
He has done this without encroaching in the least on His divinity or
losing it. On the contrary, His divinity overflows in its glory in the fact
that the true God became true man in Jesus Christ. This is the miracle
of all the miracles of His divinity. Nowhere could God's love or His
freedom be greater than in this work. It is here that each must be
recognised and acknowledged in its divinity. If it is impossible to
over-emphasise the inner unity, the supreme exercise and confirmation of
this unity, in which God acts in Jesus Christ, it is equally impossible
to over-emphasise the depth with which He here differentiates Himself from Himself. For He makes Himself free and accessible, He
gives Himself, to one who is utterly different from what He is. He
grants to this other perfect fellowship with Himself. He in a sense ex-
tends His own existence to co-existence with this other. He becomes
very man and yet remains very God. Indeed He lives as very God under
these conditions. Note, He *becomes* man. He not only creates and
upholds and governs him. This is the work of creation which is presupposed in the other greater work, and for all its inconceivability
it merely precedes that other and is surpassed by it in a way for which
there is no parallel. For the fact that God becomes and is Himself
man in Jesus Christ is more than creation, preservation and government. It is the condescension of God Himself. This means that
God makes His own the being of this other, man. He causes His
divine being to be man's being and man's being to be divine being.
What a differentiation in the unity of God emerges at this point !
God is so much One, and simple, and at peace with Himself, that He
is capable of this condescension. This estrangement, this union with
a stranger, is not strange to Him. It.is not just natural to Him.
But the fact that He becomes man is the confirmation and exemplification of His unity, the work of the unity of the Father with the Son
and of the Son with the Father, and therefore the work of the one
divine being. Note further that He becomes *man* : not the semblance
of a man but a real man. And a real man does not mean man in the
glory of his original determination in which even as a creature he is

addressed as at least the crown of creation. The man with whom
God has become one has lost this glory. This glory is to be granted
him again through this union. It is the *terminus ad quem* but not
the *terminus a quo* of the incarnation of the divine Word. The man
with whom God becomes one is the child of Adam with the weight of
the curse upon him, the offspring of the stock of Abraham and David
which fell into one act of unfaithfulness after another and was overtaken by one judgment after another. What is chosen is no noble
vessel which redounds to God's glory, but one which has all the marks
of corruption. The one who adopts it is certainly the eternally holy
God. But the one who is adopted is lost man. And God not only
endures and bears with him, although his life stands forfeit in His
sight. He not only loves him at a distance. He not only guides and
instructs him, gives him promises and commands, lets him have a
share of the crumbs of His goodness. He not only makes an agreement
with him, as can be made between very dissimilar parties. Rather
He bestows on him nothing other and nothing less than Himself. He
so enters into fellowship with him, and into so complete a fellowship,
that He Himself, God, takes his place, to suffer for him in it what
man had to suffer, to make good for him the evil he had done, so that
he in turn, man, may take God's place, that he, the sinner, may be
clothed with God's holiness and righteousness and therefore be truly
holy and righteous. This change and interchange of position and of
predicates is the perfect fellowship between God and man as it has been
realised in the incarnation, in the person of Jesus Christ, in the death
of the Son of God on the cross and in His resurrection from the dead.
God allowed this humiliation to come upon Himself and this exaltation to be the lot of the other, man. It is in this way that He exercises
and confirms His unity with Himself, His divinity. This is how His
self-declaration is realised, and He reveals His glory. It is with this
depth that He differentiates Himself from Himself. Again, this does
not mean surrender or loss of His divinity. God could not be more
glorious as God than in this inconceivable humiliation of Himself to
man and the no less inconceivable exaltation of man to Himself.
He is glorious in this very differentiation, this renunciation of Himself. And this, His supreme work towards what is outside Him, is
the reflection and image of His inner, eternal, divine being. In this
reflection and image we see Him as He is in Himself. He is One, and
yet not imprisoned or bound to be merely one. He is identical with
Himself, and yet free to be another as well ; simple and yet manifold ;
at peace with Himself, yet also alive. The One who is and does what
we see God to be and do in Jesus Christ can, of course, be all this at
the same time. He is it without tension, dialectic, paradox, or contradiction. If the opposite seems true to us, it is our mistaken thinking,
not God, which is to blame. He is it in the real unity of the divine
being which has this form, this beautiful form that arouses joy—as

we may now say again with a new fulness of meaning. For the beautiful in God's being, that which stirs up joy, is the fact that so inexhaustibly and necessarily (although the necessity is not one of outward compulsion, but the inward movement of His own being) He is One and yet another, but One again even as this other, without confusion or alteration, yet also without separation or division. What is reflected in this determination of the relationship between the divine and the human nature in Jesus Christ is the form, the beautiful form of the divine being. In this way, in this rest and movement, God is the triune, and He has and is the divine being in the unity and fulness of all its determinations. Because He is this in this way, He is not only the source of all truth and all goodness, but also the source of all beauty. And because we know that He is this in this way in Jesus Christ, we must therefore recognise the beauty of God in Jesus Christ.

This should throw some light on a remarkable contradiction. The Old Testament—and this is increasingly true of the Book of Isaiah as it mounts to its climax—is full of the notes of joy, exultation and jubilation which the prophets and the people with them strike all the more loudly, and apparently more and more so, as the times are sombre. Yet the object of all this joy, the beauty which justifies and evokes it, not only appears to be lacking, but is also never referred to as such. There is only one context in which earthly, human glory plays an independent and legitimate part. This is the story and the form of king Solomon, and it is significant that the Song of Songs appears to be connected with his person both in material and literary form. Solomon's glory is bound up inseparably with his wisdom. On closer inspection, however, it can be seen that in Solomon's glory as such we are not really dealing with beauty but rather with its preconditions: riches, brilliance, magnificence, inexhaustible possessions and the lavish development of material means for it. There is such a thing as a cold magnificence, and, if we are not wholly deceived, Solomon's glory appears to have possessed more of the nature of this cold magnificence than true beauty. The artistic skill exercised at this high point in Jerusalem may well have had more to do with skill than with art in the true sense. The shadow of the second commandment. must also have hung heavily over this high point. It passed just as it had come. At very best (and the texts do not actually say this) there was attained only a very fleeting joy even in the cold magnificence of this glory. It went by like a dream, and even during the king's lifetime and in spite of his wisdom it sank at once into sin and shame, to live on only as the dream of a beauty which had never really existed but for which there had been a longing and a brilliant preparation. In spite of Solomon beauty continued to be, for Israel, a promise like Solomon's other predicates of power and wisdom. And if this same Israel did produce so many strong notes of joy, and appeared to know in its own way something about beauty—for otherwise there could not have been rejoicing—it is clear that this joy had to do with the divine beauty, or with a human beauty which had still to come, which was still awaited in spite of Solomon or indeed in the very form of Solomon. In this respect, too, Israel had to be and have less than the other nations. Beside Athens Jerusalem had to appear rather barbarous even in its recollection of Solomon. For it had a greater hope. As opposed to Athens it awaited the divinely human beauty of its God in the form of its Messiah. It could, therefore, desire and prepare for human beauty, but it could not manifest or perceive or enjoy it. God Himself had promised and was resolved to give it His own image, and with it beauty in personal form. That is why it could not make images. That is why Jerusalem could not become an Athens. That is why there was no flowering of a humanity portraying and enjoying itself. That is also why, according to Mt. 6[29], even Solomon in all his glory was not arrayed like one of the lilies of the field. His glory could be beautiful only in so far as it was a prophecy of the glory of Jesus Christ.

The beauty of Jesus Christ is not just any beauty. It is the beauty of God. Or, more concretely, it is the beauty of what God is and does in Him. We must not fail at this point to see the substance or model of the unity of God's majesty and condescendence; His utter sublimity and holiness, and the complete mercy and patience in which this high and holy One not only turns towards man but stoops down to him; the unity of faithfulness to Himself and faithfulness to the creature with which He acts. Nor must we fail to see the love in which God is free here or the freedom in which He loves. If we do not see this, if we do not believe it, if it has not happened to us, how can we see the form of this event, the likeness of the essence of God in Jesus Christ, and how can we see that this likeness is beautiful? In this respect, too, God cannot be known except by God.

Is. 53[2-3] teaches us how we can go astray even in this respect, even in face of Jesus Christ, and how much we need instruction on this point : " For he shall grow up before him as a tender plant, and as a root out of a dry ground : he hath no form nor comeliness ; and when we shall see him, there is no beauty that we should desire him. He is despised and rejected of men ; a man of sorrows, and acquainted with grief : and we hid as it were our faces from him ; he was despised, and we esteemed him not." Jesus Christ does present this aspect of Himself, and He always presents this aspect first. It is not self-evident that even—and precisely—under this aspect He has form and comeliness, that the beauty of God shines especially under this aspect, that the crucified is revealed and known as the risen Christ. We cannot know this of ourselves. It can only be given us. If the beauty of Christ is sought in a glorious Christ who is not the crucified, the search will always be in vain. But who does not do this ? And who finds it at this point ? Who of himself does not find the opposite here ? Who sees and believes that the One who has been abased is the One who is exalted, that this very man is very God ? The glory and beauty of God shines out in this unity and differentiation. In this it persuades, convinces and conquers. This unity and differentiation is God's καλόν which itself has the power of a καλεῖν. It is the beauty which Solomon did not have, but which with all his equipment he could only prophesy. It is the beauty of which we must also say that even Athens with all its beautiful humanity did not have and could not even prophesy it, because unlike Jerusalem it thought it had it. Beautiful humanity is the reflection of the essence of God in His kindness towards men as it appeared in Jesus Christ (Tit. 3[4]). In this self-declaration, however, God's beauty embraces death as well as life, fear as well as joy, what we might call the ugly as well as what we might call the beautiful. It reveals itself and wills to be known on the road from the one to the other, in the turning from the self-humiliation of God for the benefit of man to the exaltation of man by God and to God. This turning is the mystery of the name of Jesus Christ and of the glory revealed in this name. Who knows it except the man to whom it gives the power to know it ? And how can it be known except in the face of Him who Himself gives us power to know it ? There is no other face of this kind. No other face is the self-declaration of the divine loving-kindness towards men. No other speaks at the same time of the human suffering of the true God and the divine glory of the true man. This is the function of the face of Jesus Christ alone.

And this is the *crux* of every attempt to portray this face, the secret of the sorry story of the representation of Christ. It could not and cannot be anything but a sorry story. No human art should try to represent—in their unity—the suffering God and triumphant man, the beauty of God which is the beauty of Jesus Christ. If at this point we have one urgent request to all Christian artists, however well-intentioned, gifted or even possessed of genius, it is that they should give up this unholy undertaking—for the sake of God's beauty. This picture, the one true picture, both in object and representation, cannot be copied, for the express reason that it speaks for itself, even in its beauty.

We now return to the main line of our discussion. While the statement that God is also beautiful must not be neglected, since it is instructive in its own place, it cannot claim to have any independent significance. What we wanted to know was how God in His glory, in His self-declaration, makes Himself clear to man. The statement about God's beauty answers this question in an appropriate parenthesis.

In a similar parenthesis, here at the end of this first part of the doctrine of God, we might address a question to all those who hold that in order to answer the question raised above a " natural " knowledge of God is indispensable, demanded and permitted. Can they not see that in a much better way, in one that is much more appropriate to Himself, God Himself has provided and continues to provide in His revelation, in the very being of His Godhead, that He should be attractive to the natural man and worthy of His love, " to the Jew first and also to the Greek," and that He has done this simply by giving them joy, and given them joy by being beautiful ? The enterprise of natural theology is surely a questionable one for the further reason that it is so profoundly tedious and so utterly unmusical. With a seriousness more animal than human, and certainly more human than divine, it misses the fact that according to Proverbs 8[31] it has pleased the wisdom of God to take pleasure in the circle of the earth and to have its delight in the children of men, and thus to reply in this happy way to the vexed question how God can be clear to us as God, how Jews and Greeks can come to know the Gospel as Gospel. Is it possible to hear the answer given by God and the Gospel themselves, that pleasure and desire are evoked and enjoyment created by the eternal beauty, and still to seek another mode of enlightenment apart from the revelation and Gospel of God ? And if we do, can we really have understood God's answer or even our own question ? Is not the undertaking of natural theology ruled out and rendered impossible by the fact that it seems to be a strangely sullen and even barbarous undertaking in face of the shape and form of God's being, in face of the living form of the divine triunity, in face of the self-declaration of God in His Word, in face of the radiance that grace, not nature, has in everything ? But this is to be said only in passing. Our decision for or against natural theology is made for other reasons. At the very most we have here only a later illustration of the decision against it.

The whole question of the manner of God's glory is important, and we are not at a loss for an answer, but we can now leave it and return to the statement that God's glory is the truth and power and act of His self-declaration and therefore of His love. God stands in need of nothing else. He has full satisfaction in Himself. Nothing else can even remotely satisfy Him. Yet He satisfies Himself by showing and manifesting and communicating Himself as the One who He is. He is completely Himself and complete in Himself. But He comes forth and has an outer as well as an inner side. He is not only immanent in Himself but He moves over to others. He is what He is in irresistible truth and power and act even for that which is not God, which is something else, which exists only through Him. He can and will not only exist but co-exist. This is the δόξα τοῦ θεοῦ, the *gloria Dei*, and all God's works from the greatest down to the least, each in its own way, are works of this divine glory, witnesses of the overflowing perfection of His Godhead. But the beginning, centre and goal of these works of the divine glory is God's Son Jesus Christ. He is their beginning because prior to all God's action *ad extra*, the self-declaration of God as His glory has its true and original place in the eternal co-existence of the Father and the Son by the Holy Spirit ; because the Son in His relation to the Father is the eternal archetype and prototype of God's glory in His externalisation, the archetype and prototype of God's co-existence with another. He is their centre because in Him, in the union of God and man which has taken place in Him, and the reconciliation of the world with God accomplished by Him, there has taken place that which the glory of all His other works can attest only in a preliminary or subsequent way, in preparation or development. He is their goal because God's glory as His externalisation can reach its end (which as such cannot be an end) only as He is external in His Son and His lordship and the fulfilment of His office and His task, only as all things are to Him in His Son as they are also from Him.

It belongs to the essence of the glory of God not to be *gloria* alone but to become *glorificatio*.

We have certainly to maintain with Polanus (*Synt. Theol. chr.*, 1609, *col.* 1214 f.) : *Gloria Dei aeterna est, semper eadem fuit ab aeterno et semper eadem manet in aeternum, eique nec accedere quicquam nec decedere potest, Deusque perpetuo gloriam suam habuisset licet nulla res fuisset condita. Haec gloria Dei a nemine dari nec minui augerive potest sed eadem in ipso fuit et manet semper.* Indeed God does not need the creature as the other for whom and by whom to be glorious, because before all creation He is the other in Himself as the Father and the Son and therefore glorious in and for and by Himself. But when Polanus continues : *Glorificatio vero fit in tempore a creaturis et est extra Deum et fundamentum suum habet in cognitione gloriae Dei,* we certainly do not deny this, but we must add that the *cognitio gloriae Dei* which the creature has *extra Deum* has its own *fundamentum* in the *gloria Dei* itself, and that it could not really be *cognitio* without this, without the actual communication of it to the creaturely other. Therefore properly and decisively we can understand even the *glorificatio Dei* which takes place in time by the creatures, only as the work of the divine glory.

God's glory is not exhausted by what God is in Himself, nor by the fact that from eternity and to eternity He is not only inward but also outward. God's glory is also the answer awakened and

evoked by God Himself of the worship offered Him by His creation
to the extent that in its utter creatureliness this is the echo of God's
voice. But it is only in the light of this beginning, centre and end of
all God's works, of Jesus Christ, that we can be bold to say that there
does exist this echo to be given by creation, and to be given only
as the echo of God's voice ; that there does exist this divine-creaturely
worship, a *glorificatio* which itself springs from the *gloria Dei* and has
a share in it. Otherwise we cannot possibly interpret our own voice
or the voice of any creature as an echo of this kind, thus claiming
for it the divine glory itself. We cannot possibly escape confessing
the unlikeness, indeed the opposition to God, at least of our own voice,
and our inability to glorify God. Are we not forced to admit that
since our ears are just as creaturely and sinfully impotent as our
tongues we cannot even perceive this echo in the chorus of all other
creaturely voices surrounding us and therefore their participation in
the divine glory ? But as we look to Jesus Christ we not only profess
our faith in the revelation of the divine being in its glory. We also
confess that there is a sinner reconciled by Him and in Him, and
therefore a loosing of tongues that were dumb, and therefore a reply
awakened to His glory and evoked by God Himself, and as awakened
and evoked by Him having a share in His glory. It is not only that
we magnify Him in this answer but that He magnifies Himself through
us. Looking to Jesus Christ, in faith in Him, in the unity of all the
children of God with this their elder Brother, in the life of the Church,
looking away from ourselves and all other created beings, looking to
the creature which is God's own Son, in whom God willed to accept
and has accepted creation, speaking of this centre of God's glory
because it has made itself the centre of creation too and our own
centre—we not only may but must say also that even in His glorification through creation God wills to be and actually is God and
glorious, that it is not too small a thing for God's self-glorification
to take place also in the form of His glorification through creation.
But we must keep strictly to Jesus Christ. It is indeed only of Him
that we can speak when we dare to say such extravagant things about
ourselves and the rest of creation. We can say them only as we look
to our acceptance by Him and in Him, to the undeserved and inconceivable grace of the incarnation of the Son of God. We can do so
only in the sense and form of a thanksgiving for the atonement that
has taken place for us in Him. We can do so only by way of supplement, just as we can ourselves understand in our fellowship with
God, and a reconciled world generally, only as a supplement to the
existence of Jesus Christ. But the children of God, and God's Church
and a world reconciled to God do really exist as a supplement to the
existence of Jesus Christ. Therefore we can now say (supplementarily)
that God's glory is not only pleased to accept at a distance its glorification through the creatures, but that it makes this glorification its

own in all its creatureliness. There is, therefore, a genuine creaturely *glorificatio*. It does not cease to be creaturely. It does not escape its own inner problems. It takes place this side of redemption and has to wait for it. But all the same it has already a part in the genuine divine *gloria*, and the divine *gloria* is not ashamed to dwell in it and to shine through it. Because God is glorious and is glorious also in the world, in His only begotten Son, in the pronouncement of His eternal Word, this world is no longer without His glory and God is no longer glorious for it in vain. But this is concretely real wherever God's glory and therefore the glory of His Son and Word is known, and the creature has to recognise that it is created and reconciled and will one day be redeemed by Him, and therefore to recognise Him as its Lord and Saviour, and therefore its own existence before His face, in co-existence, in confrontation with Him. This creature is itself a new creature, not taken out of darkness by its own powers and efforts but by the light which has fallen upon it from God, and of which it has become the witness and been made the reflection. This creature is free for God's glory, not because it was able or willed to be so on its own account, but because it has been made free for it by God's glory itself. This creature is grateful. It knows God, and itself becomes a new creature, by being thankful. To believe in Jesus Christ means to become thankful. This is to be understood as radically as it must be in this context. It is not merely a change of temper or sentiment or conduct and action. It is the change of the being of man before God brought about by the fact that God has altered His attitude to man. It is the change from the impossible and dangerous position of ingratitude to that of gratitude as a new and better position before God which alone is possible and full of hope. Gratitude is to be understood not only as a quality and an activity but as the very being and essence of this creature. It is not merely grateful. It is itself gratitude. It can see itself only as gratitude because in fact it can only exist as this, as pure gratitude towards God. What the creature does in its new creatureliness, which in Jesus Christ has become gratitude to God, is to glorify God. This is certainly a creaturely work. But seeing it takes place in Jesus Christ, in the life of His Church, it cannot take place outside the glory of God Himself or without it. It is the Creator and Lord of this new creature, the new man who lives in it, Jesus Christ Himself, who rules and sustains and motivates this creaturely work, giving it its start and course and goal.

It is as well to realise at this point that the glory of God is not only the glory of the Father and the Son but the glory of the whole divine Trinity, and therefore the glory of the Holy Spirit as well. But the Holy Spirit is not only the unity of the Father and the Son in the eternal life of the Godhead. He is also, in God's activity in the world, the divine reality by which the creature has its heart opened to God and is made able and willing to receive Him. He is, then, the unity between the creature and God, the bond between eternity and time. If God is glorified through the creature, this is only because by the Holy Spirit the creature is baptised, and born again and called and gathered and enlightened and sanctified and kept close to Jesus Christ in true and genuine faith. There is no glorification of God by the creature that does not come about through this work of the Holy Spirit by which the Church is founded and maintained, or that is not itself, even in its creatureliness, this work of the Holy Spirit. It is the Holy Spirit who begets the new man in Jesus Christ whose existence is thanksgiving. It is in virtue of His glory, which is the glory of the one God, that what this new man does is the glorification of God, and therefore the creature may serve this glorification. It is in this way that it has its part in His glory and therefore in the glory of God.

This, then, is how we must describe what the creature can do. It serves God's self-glorification in the same way as an echoing wall can serve only to repeat and broadcast the voice which the echo "answers." But it does really serve it. This is what may be done by the man who is thankful, who is called and appointed in Jesus Christ by the Holy Spirit to thanksgiving, who is created anew and as such directed and upheld. He is permitted to serve the divine self-glorification, and in this way and to this extent what he does can have a share in God's own glory to which his action is directed.

It is to be noted that δόξα in the New Testament means not only the honour which God Himself has or prepares for Himself, but also that which the creature gives Him, as well as finally the honour which He for His part gives to the creature. So, then, δοξάζειν means both to honour, praise, extol and glorify as a creaturely action and also to transfigure as a divine. And δοξάζεσθαι means both the glorification of God by the creature and of the creature by God. The coincidence of what appear to be opposite meanings in the same concept is absolutely necessary in view of the subject. If God prepares honour for Himself this necessarily means that the creature may pay Him honour, and as it does so it acquires and takes a share in the glory of God. We must also point out that there is the same relationship in regard to the terms specially used to denote the δοξάζειν of the creature, i.e., thanksgiving (εὐχαριστία) and service (δουλεία, λατρεία, λειτουργία). Χάρις calls for εὐχαριστία. But εὐχαριστία is itself the substance of the creature's participation in the divine χάρις. And if God requires and makes possible that He should be served by the creature, this service itself means that the creature is taken up into the sphere of divine lordship. We have always to remember that God's glory really consists in His self-giving, and that this has its centre and meaning in God's Son, Jesus Christ, and that the name of Jesus Christ stands for the event in which man, and in man the whole of creation, is awakened and called and enabled to participate in the being of God. If we do this, we will be kept from what seems to be the threatened danger of a deification of the creature and therefore of pantheism. We will also be kept from saying too little, or failing to say what must be said here, out of fear of this danger. And what must be said is that the self-declaration of God is true and real, which means that God Himself is God, in such a way that He wills to have the creature as a creature with Him, that He does not will to be God without it, without claiming it, but also without being personally present to it.

Let us conclude, therefore, by considering what it means that the creature is permitted to thank and serve the glory of God, honouring and praising God. In the first instance, everything depends on whether we understand this as real permission. All the ability, necessity and obligation of which we must also speak are included in this permission, but their power and truth are in the permission.

Everything that has to be said about our relationship to the divine glory will be on a false note if our ability, necessity and obligation are made decisive and central. In the abstract, it is a complete untruth to say that we have the power to thank and serve the glory of God. It does not belong to the essence of the creature to have or to be the power or ability to glorify God. This ability is God's. It does not belong to the creature at all, nor is God bound to give it to the creature by its creation. Whoever is able to glorify God is able to do more than the creature can of itself. Therefore when we establish and expound the praise of God given by the creature, it is wrong to refer it to the creature's own ability. Again, it is quite untrue in the abstract to say that the creature is under an obligation to serve the glory of God. For this would mean a summons to will what we cannot actually do, to arrogate to ourselves what we do not have or own. It is a dangerous presumption if the creature ascribes to itself the honour of being under obligation to will the glory of God from its own resources. There is no divine command for such presumption. It is also untrue to say, in the abstract, that the creature must serve the glory of God. This service is not a natural necessity. It does not take place merely with the existence and essence of the creature or the presence and course of creaturely things as such. But just as the glory of God itself is the superabundance, the overflowing of the perfection of the divine being, so the glorification of God through the creature is in its own way equally an overflowing, an act of freedom and not of force or of a self-evident course of events. We do not deny that there is also an ability, obligation and necessity in this thanksgiving and service on the part of the creature. But none of these is primary, decisive, or comprehensive. None of them can stand alone as the basis and explanation of this thanksgiving and service.

But there is something which stands alone and includes this ability, obligation and necessity. This is the fact that the creature is permitted to praise God. It is the permission which flows from the mercy of God to the creature in the fact that God befriends the creature, that He not only creates and claims and governs it, but that in all this He loves it, that He seeks it out in order that He may be God with it and not without it, and that in so doing He draws it to Himself, in order that it for its part can henceforth be a creature only with Him and not without Him. God gives Himself to the creature. This is His glory revealed in Jesus Christ, and this is therefore the sum of the whole doctrine of God. And the creature to whom God gives Himself may praise Him. What can ability and obligation and necessity mean when everything depends on the gift of the divine love and therefore everything consists in this permission ? Certainly, there is here an ability, an obligation, a necessity of supreme power and truth. But the power and the truth of the ability, obligation and necessity under consideration are wholly those of the permission which precedes them. They are those of the liberation of the creature brought about by the divine gift—its liberation from powerlessness and presumption and the limitations of its existence as a mere creature. It is from this liberation that the praise of God springs. This is the occasion of it and the source of it. This liberation is the standard by which the genuineness and purity of the praise are to be judged. It is from this that the praise of God receives its forms, the words and acts in which this praise is offered. It is from this liberation that it gains its inexhaustible strength. If God did not give Himself to us and therefore liberate us, how could we say that we may praise Him ? And if we had not the permission, where would be the ability, obligation, desire or necessity ? But the gift of the divine love is not wanting. We only need to see the glory of God at the point where it is revealed and where at the same time it has its eternal centre in Jesus Christ, and we shall see it at once as the divine gift, and therefore as our permission, and therefore as our liberation through which we can and should and will and must praise God together.

The most important thing about this permission to serve the glory of God has not yet been said. That God gives Himself to us certainly means that He is not bound or obliged to give us a share in His glory. And that we are permitted to praise Him in virtue of His gift means that we have no claim to praise Him and to have a share in His glory. This gift and this permission mean from the very outset that what the creature does as a result of and in this liberation does not have in itself the character of a glorification of God, a turning to Him, a participation in His being. On the contrary, it has this character in the divine liberating as such, and therefore in the fact that even as a creaturely action it is accepted by God, that it is the object of His good-pleasure, of His grace and mercy and patience, and that for this reason it is righteous and holy praise of God, and therefore directed to God's glory and participant in it. The creature's liberation from its powerlessness, presumption and limitations as a creature does not consist in the fact that as a creature it is free in itself, or that it ceases to exist as a creature. It consists in the fact that God co-exists with it in such a way that in its peculiar form as a creature, and as it were in addition to this form, it acquires the new form in which it may praise God and therefore can and should and will and must praise Him. That the creature may do this is not only grace in the sense that it is wholly and utterly a gift given him. It is grace also in the sense that it is wholly and utterly as grace that it is true for him and in him. It is, therefore, always God's self-glorification which is accomplished even in His glorification by the creature. So completely does His glorification by the creature participate in His self-glorification.

But presupposing this divine gift and this creaturely permission in view of Jesus Christ as the basis and explanation of the creature's gratitude and service to the divine glory, what does it mean that God may be honoured and glorified in this way by the creature ? The divine glory consists in God's self-glorification. This is the over-flowing of the divine existence into co-existence with the creature, the superabundance of the divine being which establishes fellowship between Him and our created being. This being so, the fact that God is honoured by us, the glorification of the divine glory by our thanksgiving and service, must consist essentially in the fact that our existence is fulfilled in the co-existence with God which has be-come its determination by reason of God's co-existence with it, that it is fulfilled, therefore, in the fellowship of our being with God's being, created by the superabundance of the divine being. Our existence cannot itself be divine existence. It can, however, be creaturely testimony to God's existence. This is what it may be, and therefore can and should and must be. This is what remains for it on the basis of God's self-glorification. This is its portion. It is granted, we recall, only by grace, and therefore in its truth always by grace alone. But it is really granted in this way. The creature which has been awakened and called to glorify God becomes as such the confirmation of the divine existence. If we remember that the being of this new creature is in Jesus Christ, we can also say with confidence that it becomes an image, *the* image of God. It is asserted in the biblical account of creation that man's destiny is to be the image of God. And this meaning and purpose of all creation must indeed be realised and revealed in man, and it has already been realised and revealed once for all in Jesus Christ. The whole point of creation is that God should have a reflection in which He reflects Himself and in which the image of God as the Creator is revealed, so that through it God is attested, confirmed and proclaimed. For this reflection is the centre and epitome of creation concretely represented in the existence of man. God wills to find again in another the reflection and image which He finds in Himself from eternity to eternity in His Son. It was in order that there should be this reflection that the Son of God became flesh. And the children of God born subsequently are those in whose exist-ence this reflection appears. In their existence they do not themselves become gods, but creaturely reflections of the divine glory and there-fore of the divine being. In virtue of the superabundance of this being in His Son Jesus Christ there is both the possibility and the actuality of the existence of these children of God (in co-existence with God), and therefore of these reflections of the divine glory.

" Be ye therefore followers of God (μιμηταὶ τοῦ θεοῦ) as children dear (to him) ; and walk in love, as also Christ hath loved you, and hath given himself for you

22

an offering and a sacrifice to God for a sweetsmelling savour " (Eph. 5¹⁻²). This is
our task and programme as we are permitted to praise and thank and serve
God. It can be formulated only in this way. Its only basis and explanation
is the divine gift and human permission actualised in Jesus Christ.

Glorifying and honouring God can only mean " following " (or
imitating) Him. The meaning and purpose of this glorifying cannot
be fulfilled by any form of existence, speech or action that is arbitrary
or follows any other pattern. The glory of God in its glorification
by the creature must assume the form of correspondence, or it does
not take place at all. No other image or copy, however perfect, has
any significance in this respect. As it is only possible to praise God
by God Himself, on the basis of being awakened and called by Him,
so too we can do this only along with God, i.e., as we confirm and
justify Him, as we conform to Him and attest Him as God. To give
honour to God means that in our existence, words and actions we
are made conformable to God's existence ; that we accept our life as
determined by God's co-existence, and therefore reject any arbitrary
self-determination. Self-determination comes about when God is
honoured by the creature in harmony with God's predetermination
instead of in opposition to it. It happens when we accommodate
ourselves, not to the dominion of any power (history or fate, for instance), but to that of the One to whom alone there belongs right and
finally might.

To give honour to God means " to be willing and ready from the heart to
live henceforth unto Him " (*Heidelberg Catechism, Qu.* 1). To live henceforth
unto Him means no longer to live our own lives to ourselves, but to live them
to the end that the being of God in all its perfections can find in them a sign
and likeness. To be willing and ready means not to loathe but to love this
purpose, not to oppose but to be open to its realisation : and this " from the
heart." It is only by a heart's willingness and readiness to live unto Him that
God can be honoured, thanked and served. It is to this and this only that we
are pointed by that divine self-giving and creaturely permission, by the liberation which is the beginning of all glorifying of God by the creature.

In this sense, then, the glorifying of God consists simply in the
life-obedience of the creature which knows God. It has no alternative
but to thank and praise God. And in this thanks and praise it has
nothing else to offer God—nothing more and nothing less than itself.
This self-offering can have no other meaning—no higher and no lower—
than that its existence becomes a reflection of the perfection of the
divine being. To know God is the only possibility of this self-offering
and its only necessity. In the conformity with God into which it
enters, with this self-offering, in accordance with God's call and its
own knowledge of Him, it may honour God and therefore acquire
and have a share in God's own honour. In this sense the way and
theatre of the glorification of God is neither more nor less than the
total existence of the creature who knows God and offers Him his

life-obedience. Nothing can be omitted from the gift, the task, and the new gift here revealed and actual as the purpose of its existence. There can be no frontier in its being beyond which it no longer may and therefore no longer can or should or must glorify God ; beyond which it has no share in the glory of God.

But it is only when we turn our thoughts to the angels of God or the company of men made perfect in post-temporal eternity that we can say all that has to be said about the glorifying of God through the creature. The Church does not forget the total thanksgiving and service which it will one day offer God in all its members and the lives of all its members and which is already given God on high by His angels. The Church finds comfort in this future, post-temporal, but already supra-temporally eternal worship. It yearns to have a part in its perfection. It conforms itself to its perfection. But it lives in time and therefore in the distinction between this perfection and what it can itself display here and now. It cannot display the totality of life-obedience in which it may thank and serve God. It can certainly believe but cannot see that it is itself the place where the honour of God is all in all. On the contrary, in distinction from the angels of God and the company of men made perfect, it finds in itself, both as a whole and in all its members, certain limits, not in the divine self-giving but in its own knowledge, its own freedom and the form in which it may respond. It does not see the totality in which God is here and now glorified in its existence. It can certainly find this glorifying in its Head, Jesus Christ, but not in itself as His body. Finding it in Him, it necessarily misses it in itself. But missing it in itself, it continually finds it again in Him. Yet these limits, this difference between it and Him, remain. This does not mean that it is excluded from the glory of God, or even from its full reality. But it does mean that the form in which it shares in it here is another and special form—a temporal and therefore a provisional form in contrast to the perfect form for which we may here and now wait, and to which the Church may move.

The Church's prayer here and now is as follows : " O mighty and majestic God, whom the angels and all the blessed in heaven praise, grant us men in our poverty the grace to worship Thee in righteousness on earth and to serve Thee according to Thy good-pleasure. May we stand in Thy holy house in true reverence and a heavenly mind, and in faith adore Thy glory. Lift up our thoughts and desires unto Thyself. Sanctify our worship, bless our service and may the praise of our lips be pleasing unto Thee. Hearken to our prayers before the throne of Thy mercy, and bestow upon us in Thy grace all things necessary for our blessedness, through Jesus Christ, our Lord " (*Berne Liturgy*, 1888). Here, as we can see, we men in our poverty on earth are distinguished in our worship from the angels and the blessed in heaven with their praise. In both cases it is a matter of worship and service according to God's good-pleasure. The difference is that our part here consists in adoring God's glory in faith (and not with sight). When this happens here and now (as distinct from there one day) it does so in a special " holy house." This holy place exists, yet here and now it exists, not as the totality, but as a special corner of our existence ; although this does not mean that in other places we are consigned to what is unholy and therefore excluded from the glory of God. We wait for this to become visible in the totality of our existence. But because we are still waiting for this, it is necessary that our thoughts and desires, which in the first instance are directed to something else that is visible, should be " lifted up," raised up to God. Because of our waiting, we on earth need this special uplifting (which God alone can accomplish). We need the special " worship " (which only God can sanctify). We need the special " service " (which only God can bless). We need, too, the special " praise of our lips " (whose success depends completely on God's gracious acceptance of it). We need our prayers (which are dependent on God's hearkening). We need, in short, a holy place on earth in which we can stand " in true reverence and a heavenly mind," if God permits us to do so. This prayer, its concrete content and its fulfilment through Him to whom it is directed, is the temporal and provisional form of our participation in the glorification of God and therefore in God's glory itself.

We are not here and now excluded from the glory of God. But the form in which we are surrounded by it, and in which we participate in it, is the form of the Church, proclamation, faith, confession, theology, prayer. The temporal form of God's glorification through the creature is the form of this special sphere. It is only in this way that the life-obedience which is the meaning of all glorification of God can take shape here and now. We are careful not to say that it may not and cannot and does not actually take place in any other way. But that which takes shape and is visible is this special sphere. We are careful not to say that this sphere in its particularity involves and attests only a particular aspect of the whole. It most certainly involves and attests and indeed virtually is the whole. But what takes shape and is therefore visible is this particular sphere. It is as we are gathered to the Church, as the Word is proclaimed to us, as we believe and profess our faith, as theology does its work, as all this being and action is a single prayer and yet also in particular presents itself before God as prayer, that we really glorify God and therefore share in His self-glorification : no less really in this form than in the future form which here and now we still await and to which the Church moves. We do it in the simple sense of life-obedience. And we do not do so only partially but totally. Here, however, the whole as such is hidden from us. This is the limit of this form. We can share in the totality of the glorification of God by the creature only within this limit and therefore only within this special sphere. Because this part as such is virtually the whole, the part may stand for the whole. We may not, then, seek the whole beyond this part. We may not be sad but glad to be in the Church, to hear the proclamation of the Word, to respond in faith to this proclamation of God, to confess this faith, seriously to present this profession in theology. We may be glad to pray. The whole energy of the awakening and calling of the creature to its destiny to give glory to God works itself out here and now wholly and utterly in the fact that the Church may be. It is not as if much else too, indeed everything, may not be done to the glory of God. It is not as if these other things, when they occur, occur less to the glory of God. But in order that all other things, and indeed everything, may occur to the glory of God, the Church may be ; and preaching, believing, professing, teaching and praying. The Word of God may come to those who have not yet heard it, and again and again among those who have already heard it. In all this the fundamental law of our existence is confirmed which signifies both the limit and the promise. This is that we must just as certainly miss the glory of God in ourselves as we may find it in Jesus Christ, and that we may find it just as certainly in Jesus Christ as we must miss it in ourselves. For the confirmation of this fundamental law, for the sake of this limit and promise, the Church may be in all the significance and range of its activity, and the being of the Church is both the indispensable blessing and at the same time the most urgent task in human existence and history. We do not confine God's glory when we call the Church its provisional sphere. This does not mean that only the Church is its sphere. Rather, we shall be both comforted and shamed by the fact that there is no sphere in heaven or on earth which even here and now is not secretly full of the glory of God. It is in the Church that this is known and more and more of this secret reality is seen in faith. But it cannot be seen and known outside the Church. Nowhere else can either the truth or the secret nature of this content be known, or the certainty of its future revelation. It is only the faith of the Church which can see what can already be seen here. Remembering that this knowledge and perception is not only the Church's grace but also its judgment, and that all its missed opportunities and errors cannot be more severely punished than by the fact that in God's grace it has this particular perception and knowledge, not trying to avoid either the unsettlement which this chastisement involves or the peace which is given us by the fact that this chastisement is also grace, we can sum up in the confession *Credo ecclesiam* everything that is to be said about God's glory, and doctrinally about His being. He is the God who is glorious in His community, and for that reason and in that way in all the world.

We do not detract from this *Credo ecclesiam*, but confirm it, if—looking out confidently from the narrower to the wider sphere—we close with some sentences from Polanus (*Synt. Theol. chr.*, 1609, *col.* 1125) : *Deus vult gloriam suam praedicari, idque necessario: inprimis a ministris verbi Dei. Si nolunt ministri verbi Dei, si nolunt episcopi, laici id facient, ut ministros verbi Dei, ut episcopos confundant. Si nolunt viri, feminae id facient. Si nolunt divites et potentes in hoc mundo, pauperes et egentes id praestabunt. Si nolunt adulti, ex ore infantium et lactentium perficiet sibi Deus laudem. Imo si homines id nolint facere, potest sibi Deus filios ex lapidibus excitare, imo ipsas potest creaturas inanimatas gloriae suae praecones constituere. Ac profecto caeli enarrant gloriam Dei, ut dicitur Psal.* 19 *v.* 1.

INDEXES

I. SCRIPTURE REFERENCES

GENESIS

CHAP.					PAGE
1 f.	.	.	.	.	104, 117, 507
1¹ᶠ.	.	.	.	.	. 117
1³ᶠ.	.	.	.	.	366, 604
1²⁶	.	.	.	.	. 496
1²⁷ᶠ.	.	.	.	.	. 118
2⁵ᶠ.	.	.	.	.	. 118
2¹⁷	.	.	.	.	. 392
2¹⁷ᶠ.	.	.	.	.	. 118
2¹⁹ᶠ.	.	.	.	.	. 187
2²⁴	.	.	.	.	. 118
3¹	.	.	.	.	. 140
3⁵	.	.	.	.	. 433
3⁸	.	.	.	.	. 403
3⁸ᶠ.	.	.	.	.	507, 554
4¹ᶠ.	.	.	.	.	412 f.
6 f.	.	.	.	.	. 413
6⁵	.	.	.	.	103, 393
6⁶ᶠ.	.	.	.	.	. 496
6⁸	.	.	.	.	103, 413
7¹	.	.	.	.	. 413
8²¹	.103, 117, 393, 431, 496, 654
8²¹ᶠ.	.	.	.	.	. 118
9	.	.	.	.	. 496
9⁸ᶠ.	.	.	.	.	. 117
9¹¹ᶠ.	.	.	.	.	. 413
9¹²ᶠ.	.	.	.	.	124, 413
9¹⁶	.	.	.	.	. 413
12¹ᶠ.	.	.	.	.	. 525
15¹	.	.	.	.	. 525
15⁶	.	.	.	.	. 385
15⁶ᶠ.	.	.	.	.	. 525
17¹ᶠ.	.	.	.	.	. 525
18¹⁴	.	.	.	.	. 525
18¹⁷ᶠ.	.	.	.	.	496 f.
18²⁰ᶠ.	.	.	.	.	. 507
19²⁶	.	.	.	159, 161, 393
28¹⁶ᶠ.	.	.	.	.	. 479
32¹⁰	.	.	.	.	. 459
32²²ᶠ.	.	.	.	.	. 507

EXODUS

3¹ᶠ.	.	.	.	.	60 f.
3²	.	.	.	.	. 366

CHAP.					PAGE
3⁵	.	.	.	.	. 479
3¹⁴	.	.	.	302, 492, 495
4¹⁰ᶠ.	.	.	.	.	. 221
8¹⁰	.	.	.	.	. 302
15²ᶠ.	.	.	.	.	. 601
15⁹ᶠ.	.	.	.	.	. 601
15¹¹	.	.	.	.	302, 361
20	.	.	.	.	. 451
20²	.	.	.	.	. 302
20⁵	.	.	.	.	. 452
20⁶	.	.	.	.	. 372
24¹⁶	.	.	.	.	. 479
25⁸	.	.	.	.	. 479
29⁴⁵	.	.	.	.	479, 482
32⁹ᶠ.	.	.	.	.	. 497
32¹¹ᶠ.	.	.	.	.	. 389
33¹¹	.	.	.	.	. 511
33¹¹ᶠ.	.	.	.	.	18 f.
33¹⁹	.	.	.	61, 353, 371 f.
34⁶	.	.	.	.	. 407
34⁹	.	.	.	.	. 355
34¹⁴	.	.	.	.	. 452

LEVITICUS

11⁴⁴	.	.	.	.	. 364
17 f.	.	.	.	.	364 f.
26¹¹ᶠ.	.	.	.	.	. 482

NUMBERS

11	.	.	.	.	. 497
14¹⁹	.	.	.	.	. 355
22²⁸	.	.	.	.	. 221
23¹⁹	.	.	.	.	492, 496

DEUTERONOMY

3²⁴	.	.	.	.	. 600
4³²ᶠ.	.	.	.	.	. 451
4³⁵	.	.	.	.	. 302
5¹ᶠ.	.	.	.	.	. 451
5²⁸ᶠ.	.	.	.	.	. 28
6⁴	.	.	.	.	. 451
7⁸	.	.	.	.	. 279
7⁹	.	.	.	.	. 459
9²³ᶠ.	.	.	.	.	. 389

Deuteronomy (*continued*).

CHAP.					PAGE
$12^{1f.}$	.	.	.	.	479
18^{18}	.	.	.	.	221
27^{26}	.	.	.	.	392
$32^{4f.}$	.	.	.	.	459
32^{6}	.	.	.	.	526
32^{9}	.	.	.	.	526
33^{16}	.	.	.	.	353
33^{27}	.	.	.	.	594

Judges

$2^{11f.}$	.	.	.	.	415

1 Samuel

2^{2}	.	.	.	.	361
2^{3}	.	.	.	.	554
$23^{11f.}$	.	.	.	.	568

1 Kings

$3^{4f.}$	.	.	.	.	433
3^{9}	.	.	.	.	607
$3^{16f.}$	.	.	.	433 f.
$5^{9f.}$	.	.	.	.	433
8	.	.	.	.	389
$8^{23f.}$	.	.	.	.	540
8^{27}	.	.	.	.	534
$8^{27f.}$	.	.	.	469, 474
$8^{31f.}$	.	.	.	.	391
$10^{1f.}$	.	.	.	.	433
22^{19}	.	.	.	.	474

2 Kings

19^{15}	.	.	.	.	302
$19^{16f.}$	.	.	.	.	452

1 Chronicles

17^{20}	.	.	.	.	302

Nehemiah

9^{17}	.	.	.	.	407

Job

$9^{2f.}$	.	.	.	.	388
$9^{19f.}$	.	.	.	.	388
$9^{29f.}$	.	.	.	.	388
$11^{7f.}$	.	.	.	.	469
$13^{18f.}$	.	.	.	.	388
$14^{1f.}$	.	.	.	.	388
15^{8}	.	.	.	.	50
$16^{19f.}$	.	.	.	.	388
$19^{25f.}$	.	.	.	.	388
$23^{13f.}$	.	.	.	.	558
27^{6}	.	.	.	.	385

CHAP.					PAGE
28	.	.	.	.	429 ff.
29^{14}	.	.	.	.	385
36^{26}	.	.	.	.	184
38 f.	.	.	.	115 f., 603
40 f.	.	.	.	.	115
42^{2}	.	.	.	.	525
42^{3-6}	.	.	.	.	115
42^{7}	.	.	.	.	388

Psalms

1^{2}	.	.	.	.	654
1^{6}	.	.	.	.	554
2^{4}	.	.	.	.	479
$2^{6f.}$	.	.	.	.	625
$2^{7f.}$	.	.	.	.	521
4^{1}	.	.	.	.	385
4^{9}	.	.	.	.	10
$5^{4f.}$	.	.	.	.	392
5^{8}	.	.	.	381, 385
5^{11}	.	.	.	.	654
7	.	.	.	.	387
7^{8}	.	.	.	.	387
7^{17}	.	.	.	.	381
8	.	.	.	108, 113
$8^{1f.}$	.	.	.	.	113
8^{2}	.	.	.	.	108
8^{9}	.	.	.	.	113
11^{4}	.	.	.	302, 474
$14^{2f.}$	.	.	.	104, 393
14^{7}	.	.	.	.	104
16^{11}	.	.	.	.	654
17^{15}	.	.	.	.	385
$18^{20f.}$	.	.	.	.	498
18^{25}	.	.	.	.	496
19	.	.	.	101, 108
$19^{1f.}$	.	.	.	108, 677
19^{3}	.	.	.	.	112
$19^{8f.}$	.	.	.	.	108
22^{31}	.	.	.	.	385
23	.	.	.	.	645
23^{4}	.	.	.	.	75
$24^{1f.}$	.	.	.	.	107 f.
26^{8}	.	.	.	.	480
$29^{1f.}$	.	.	.	.	108
29^{11}	.	.	.	108, 603
30^{5}	.	.	.	415, 421
30^{11}	.	.	.	.	654
31^{1}	.	.	.	381, 385
31^{5}	.	.	.	.	459
31^{15}	.	.	.	.	613
32^{5}	.	.	.	.	380
33^{4}	.	.	.	.	459
$33^{5f.}$	.	.	.	.	108
$33^{8f.}$	.	.	.	.	558

Psalms (*continued*).

CHAP.	PAGE
33¹³ᶠ.	302
33¹⁴	474
34⁸	654
34¹⁶	392
35²⁸	385
36⁵ᶠ.	107 f.
36⁶	432
36⁷	594
36⁹	108, 111, 263
37⁴	654
45²	653
46⁴ᶠ.	480
48¹¹ᶠ.	381
50²	482
50⁶	385
50⁷ᶠ.	283
50¹⁰ᶠ.	107
50¹⁵	511
51¹	378
51⁴ᶠ.	104
51¹³ᶠ.	104
51¹⁴	378
51¹⁵	221
56⁸	554
57¹	594
61⁴	594
65⁷ᶠ.	107
66¹ᶠ.	108
66⁴	107
67⁵	107
68¹⁶	479
68¹⁷ᶠ.	477
71¹⁵	385
72¹⁹	642
73²³ᶠ.	277
73²⁵	33
73²⁸	14, 654
74²	480
74¹³ᶠ.	108
77¹³	361
78	601
78³⁷ᶠ.	373
82¹	107
84¹ᶠ.	480
84⁷	482
84¹ᶠ.	480
85¹⁰ᶠ.	385
86⁸	302
86¹⁵	407
89³	353
89⁷	302
89¹⁴	207
90¹	108

CHAP.	PAGE
90²ᶠ.	609
90⁸	554
90¹³ᶠ.	108
91⁴	207
93¹ᶠ.	108
93²	474
93⁴ᶠ.	108
94⁵ᶠ.	555
94⁹	230
95⁴ᶠ.	107
96	107
96¹³	383
97	107
97⁶	385
98²	385
98³	207
99	107
99²	482
100¹	107
100²	654
101²	608, 638
101¹⁰	608, 638
102	686, 720
102¹⁹	302
102²⁵ᶠ.	492, 609
102²⁶ᶠ.	498
103	353
103²	628
103⁸	407
103⁸ᶠ.	356
103¹¹	353
103¹²	372
103¹⁹	302, 474
103²²	479
104	108, 114
104¹ᶠ.	653
104²⁴	114
104²⁷ᶠ.	114
104³³ᶠ.	114
104³⁵	108
105	601
106	611
106⁴	354
108⁵	353
109²⁶	354
111³	385
111⁹ᶠ.	430
112¹	737
112³	385
115¹	207
115³	525
117	108
117²	207
118¹⁹	385

Psalms (*continued*).

CHAP.					PAGE
119	.	.	.	.	. 381
119⁴	.	.	.	.	. 654
119¹⁶	.	.	.	.	. 381
119⁸⁸	.	.	.	.	. 354
119¹⁵⁶	.	.	.	.	. 381
121⁴	.	.	.	.	. 555
127¹ᶠ.	.	.	.	.	6
132¹³	.	.	.	.	. 480
135¹ᶠ.	.	.	.	.	479 f.
135⁵ᶠ.	.	.	.	.	. 558
135²¹	.	.	.	.	. 408
139¹	.	.	.	.	. 228
139¹ᶠ.	.	.	.	.	. 554
139²	.	.	.	.	. 258
139⁵ᶠ.	.	.	.	469, 476, 478
139⁶	.	.	.	.	. 184
139¹¹ᶠ.	.	.	.	.	. 555
139¹⁹ᶠ.	.	.	.	.	. 108
139²³ᶠ.	.	.	.	.	. 558
143	.	.	.	.	. 388
143¹	.	.	.	.	. 385
143²	.	.	.	.	. 387
143⁸	.	.	.	.	. 354
143¹¹	.	.	.	.	. 385
145⁸	.	.	.	.	. 407
145⁹	.	.	.	.	. 371
145¹⁵	.	.	.	.	. 471
145¹⁶	.	.	.	.	. 654
145¹⁸	.	.	.	.	. 511
147	.	.	.	.	. 107
148	.	.	.	.	. 108
148¹ᶠ.	.	.	.	.	. 108
148¹⁴	.	.	.	.	. 108
150⁶	.	.	.	.	. 107

Proverbs

1⁷	.	.	.	.	192, 428
1²⁰ᶠ.	.	.	.	.	. 428
3	.	.	.	.	. 428
3¹²	.	.	.	.	. 361
3¹⁴ᶠ.	.	.	.	.	. 428
3¹⁸ᶠ.	.	.	.	.	. 428
3¹⁹ᶠ.	.	.	.	.	. 428
3²⁶	.	.	.	.	. 428
8	.	.	.	.	429 ff.
8¹ᶠ.	.	.	.	.	. 429
8¹⁷	.	.	.	.	279, 429
8²²ᶠ.	.	.	.	.	. 429
8³¹	.	.	.	.	. 666
8³⁵	.	.	.	.	. 429
9¹⁰ᶠ.	.	.	.	.	429 f.
9¹⁶	.	.	.	.	. 429
9¹⁸	.	.	.	.	. 429

CHAP.					PAGE
10²	.	.	.	.	. 385
11⁵	.	.	.	.	. 385
11¹⁸	.	.	.	.	. 385
13⁶	.	.	.	.	. 385
14³⁴	.	.	.	.	. 385
15²⁹	.	.	.	.	. 511
23²⁶	.	.	.	.	. 654

Ecclesiastes

12¹³ᶠ.	.	.	.	.	. 430

Song of Songs

1 f.	.	.	.	.	653, 664

Isaiah

1²¹ᶠ.	.	.	.	.	. 496
1²⁴ᶠ.	.	.	.	.	. 383
, 2³	.	.	.	.	. 482
6¹	.	.	.	.	302, 474
6¹ᶠ.	.	.	.	.	. 366
6³	.	.	.	.	125, 642
6⁵ᶠ.	.	.	.	.	. 221
7⁹	.	.	.	.	. 390
7¹⁵ᶠ.	.	.	.	.	. 433
9³	.	.	.	.	. 654
9⁶	.	.	.	.	. 606
9⁷	.	.	.	.	. 385
10¹⁷ᶠ.	.	.	.	.	. 366
11²	.	.	.	.	. 607
11³ᶠ.	.	.	.	.	. 386
18⁴	.	.	.	.	. 505
26⁸ᶠ.	.	.	.	.	. 654
28¹⁶	.	.	.	.	. 390
29¹⁴	.	.	.	.	. 435
29¹⁹	.	.	.	.	. 654
29²³	.	.	.	.	. 361
30¹⁸ᶠ.	.	.	.	.	. 381
32¹⁷	.	.	.	.	. 385
33⁵	.	.	.	.	. 479
40	.	.	.	.	431 f.
40⁵	.	.	.	.	. 462
40⁶ᶠ.	.	.	.	.	. 645
40¹²ᶠ.	.	.	.	.	. 431
40¹³ᶠ.	.	.	.	.	. 50
40¹⁸	.	.	.	.	. 431
40²¹ᶠ.	.	.	.	.	431, 603
40²⁷	.	.	.	.	. 555
40²⁷ᶠ.	.	.	.	.	431 f.
40²⁸	.	.	.	.	. 504
41¹⁴	.	.	.	.	. 361
42⁸	.	.	.	.	. 16
43³	.	.	.	.	. 361
43¹⁰	.	.	.	.	361, 608
43¹⁴	.	.	.	.	. 361

ISAIAH (continued).

CHAP.					PAGE
43²²ᶠ·	.	.	.	.	. 389
44¹ᶠ·	.	.	.	.	. 389
44⁶	.	.	.	.	. 302
44⁶ᶠ·	.	.	.	.	. 452
45⁸	.	.	.	.	. 385
46⁹ᶠ·	.	.	.	.	520 f.
47⁴	.	.	.	.	. 361
48⁹	.	.	.	.	. 410
48¹¹	.	.	.	.	. 16
48¹⁷	.	.	.	.	. 361
49⁷	.	.	.	.	. 361
49¹⁵	.	.	.	.	. 230
50⁴	.	.	.	.	. 221
51⁶	.	.	.	.	. 385
53²ᶠ·	.	.	.	.	665 f.
54⁵	.	.	.	.	. 361
54⁷ᶠ·	.	.	.	.	. 373
54⁸	.	.	.	353, 415, 421
54¹⁰	.	.	.	.	. 505
55¹⁰ᶠ·	.	.	.	.	. 417
56¹	.	.	.	.	. 385
57¹⁵	.	.	.	.	. 477
57¹⁹	.	.	.	.	. 221
59⁹ᶠ·	.	.	.	.	. 389
59¹⁵ᶠ·	.	.	.	.	. 389
61¹⁰	.	.	.	.	. 385
63⁹	.	.	.	.	. 279
64⁶	.	.	.	.	. 389
65¹ᶠ·	.	.	.	.	. 415
66¹	.	.	.	.	. 474

JEREMIAH

1⁶ᶠ·	.	.	.	.	. 221
2¹³	.	.	.	.	. 263
7³ᶠ·	.	.	.	.	. 480
7¹⁴ᶠ·	.	.	.	.	. 480
9²³ᶠ·	.	.	.	.	. 436
10¹ᶠ·	.	.	.	.	. 432
10¹²	.	.	.	.	. 428
10¹⁴	.	.	.	.	. 263
10¹⁶	.	.	.	.	. 603
16¹⁶ᶠ·	.	.	.	.	. 554
17¹³	.	.	.	.	. 263
18¹ᶠ·	.	.	.	.	. 497
18⁶	.	.	.	.	. 526
23⁶	.	.	.	.	. 385
23¹⁸	.	.	.	.	. 50
23²³ᶠ·	.	.	.	.	. 469
25²⁹	.	.	.	.	. 367
26²ᶠ·	.	.	.	.	. 498
26¹³	.	.	.	.	. 498
26¹⁹	.	.	.	.	. 498
29¹¹ᶠ·	.	.	.	.	. 555

CHAP.					PAGE
31³	.	.	.	.	279, 504
31³⁵ᶠ·	.	.	.	.	. 118
32¹⁷	.	.	.	.	. 525
32¹⁷ᶠ·	.	.	.	.	. 603
33¹⁶	.	.	.	.	. 385
36³	.	.	.	.	. 498
42¹⁰	.	.	.	.	. 498

LAMENTATIONS

3²³	.	.	.	.	. 371

EZEKIEL

1	.	.	.	.	124 f.
3²⁷	.	.	.	.	. 221
10⁸ᶠ·	.	.	.	.	124 f.
11²²	.	.	.	.	. 124
18⁴	.	.	.	.	. 526
18²¹ᶠ·	.	.	.	.	. 414
23	.	.	.	.	. 452

DANIEL

9⁴	.	.	.	.	. 354
9⁴ᶠ·	.	.	.	.	. 389
10¹⁵ᶠ·	.	.	.	.	. 221

HOSEA

1 f.	.	.	.	.	. 452
2¹⁹	.	.	.	.	. 385
5³	.	.	.	.	. 554
10¹²	.	.	.	.	. 385
11⁴	.	.	.	.	. 453

JOEL

2¹¹	.	.	.	.	. 390
2¹³	.	.	.	381, 407, 498

AMOS

5¹⁸ᶠ·	.	.	.	.	. 390
5²⁴	.	.	.	.	. 386
7¹ᶠ·	.	.	.	.	. 497
7⁷ᶠ·	.	.	.	.	. 497
9¹ᶠ·	.	.	.	.	477 f.

JONAH

1 f.	.	.	.	.	413 f.
2³ᶠ·	.	.	.	.	. 414
3 f.	.	.	.	.	. 414
4²	.	.	.	407, 414, 498
4⁵ᶠ·	.	.	.	.	. 414

MICAH

7⁷ᶠ·	.	.	.	.	. 388

HABAKKUK

CHAP.   PAGE
2^4 390

ZEPHANIAH

1^{14} 390

MALACHI

3^6 492
$3^{6f.}$ 496

MATTHEW

3^2 384
3^9 525
4^9 444
4^{17} 384
5^3 389
5^6 389
$5^{17f.}$ 384
5^{34} 474
5^{45} 508
6^4 554
6^6 554
6^9 474
6^{10} 558, 633
6^{13} . . . 26, 642, 650
6^{18} 554
6^{29} 665
$7^{7f.}$ 511
7^{11} 230
7^{12} 579
7^{23} 567
$7^{28f.}$ 606
8^{27} 606
9^{36} 390
10^8 355
$10^{19f.}$ 221
$10^{29f.}$ 554
$11^{16f.}$ 436
11^{21} 568
11^{27} . . . 50, 202, 555
11^{28} 390
$11^{28f.}$ 517
12^{42} 434
13^{12} 382
15^{24} 278
16^{17} 50
17^{20} 511
18^{20} . . . . 488 f.
18^{33} 381
19^{17} 454
19^{26} 525
20^{15} 526
21^{16} 113

CHAP.   PAGE
$21^{18f.}$ 392
22^{13} 392
$23^{8f.}$ 456
24^{30} 606
24^{35} 415
$24^{41f.}$ 392
$25^{11f.}$ 392
25^{12} 567
25^{18} 336
25^{21} 11, 654
25^{30} 392
26^{39} 558
27^4 363
$28^{1f.}$ 363
28^{18} . . . . 488 f., 600

MARK

1^{11} 367
1^{15} 384
1^{22} 606
1^{24} 363
6^2 607
$9^{2f.}$ 643
15^{34} 253, 422

LUKE

1^{35} 605, 607
1^{37} 525, 602
$1^{46f.}$ 654
1^{50} 372
1^{78} 371
$1^{78f.}$ 372
$2^{9f.}$ 645
2^{14} . . . 623, 625, 642
2^{40} 439
2^{52} 439
4^{36} 606
$5^{4f.}$ 363
5^8 . . . . 362, 366
$5^{31f.}$ 278
6^{19} 606
6^{36} 371, 381
10^{18} 177
$10^{41f.}$ 454
15 278
15^7 454
15^{10} 454
$18^{1f.}$ 507
$18^{6f.}$ 511
19^{10} 278
24^{19} 605
24^{34} 460

John

CHAP.	PAGE
1$^{1f.}$	481, 607
1^{3}	317, 432 f.
1$^{4f.}$	42
1^{9}	42
1$^{9f.}$	459, 626
1^{10}	317
1^{14}	20, 151, 162, 207, 481, 643
1$^{14f.}$	208
1^{18}	50, 208
3^{2}	606
3^{8}	561
3^{16}	275, 278, 397
3^{33}	460
4$^{20f.}$	481
4^{24}	208, 268
5^{19}	606
5^{26}	263
5^{30}	606
5^{37}	50
6^{46}	50
6^{63}	263
6^{69}	42
7^{46}	606
8^{12}	42
8^{19}	50
8^{32}	208
8^{46}	397
8^{58}	622
9^{5}	42
9^{16}	606
9^{33}	606
9^{41}	278
10^{1}	172, 177
10^{9}	172, 177
10$^{14f.}$	50
10^{16}	454
10^{17}	279
10$^{30f.}$	456
11^{40}	625
12^{46}	42
13^{31}	643
14^{6}	29, 42, 172, 177, 208, 263, 320
14$^{9f.}$	42
14^{10}	483
14^{21}	279
14^{23}	279
15^{1}	202
15$^{14f.}$	511
16$^{8f.}$	363
16^{27}	279
17^{3}	42
17^{11}	364, 456

CHAP.	PAGE
17^{17}	208
17^{19}	367
17$^{23f.}$	279

Acts

2$^{3f.}$	221
2^{23}	521
2^{24}	606
3^{14}	363
3^{15}	263
4$^{27f.}$	521
4^{32}	455
6^{7}	29
7^{22}	605
7^{49}	474
9^{2}	29
13^{18}	420
14^{3}	354
14^{15}	263
14$^{15f.}$	122
17	107, 121 f.
17$^{16f.}$	121
17$^{22f.}$	104, 107, 122
17$^{24f.}$	481
17^{25}	283
17$^{27f.}$	469
17^{28}	475, 484 f.
17^{30}	383, 420
17$^{30f.}$	383
17^{32}	435
17$^{32f.}$	104, 123
20^{32}	354
22^{4}	29
24^{14}	29

Romans

1	120 f., 123
1 f.	104, 107, 109, 123
1^{4}	606
1^{5}	37, 354, 385
1$^{15f.}$	119
1^{16}	119 f., 605, 607, 666
1$^{16f.}$	382
1^{17}	119, 390
1^{18}	362, 396
1$^{18f.}$	104, 119 f., 382
1$^{19f.}$	101, 104
1^{20}	120, 184
1$^{20f.}$	120
1$^{22f.}$	118
1^{23}	496
1^{32}	121
2 f.	120
2$^{1f.}$	119 f.

ROMANS (*continued*).

CHAP.	PAGE
$2^{3f.}$	120
2^4	414
$2^{8f.}$	120
$2^{9f.}$	119 f.
2^{12}	119 f.
$2^{12f.}$	101, 104
3^3	390
$3^{3f.}$	459
3^4	208
$3^{5f.}$	399
3^9	119 f.
3^{20}	119 f., 393, 398
3^{21}	119
$3^{21f.}$	104
3^{23}	119, 645
$3^{24f.}$	382
3^{25}	239, 420
$3^{25f.}$	418
3^{26}	383
3^{28}	383
$3^{29f.}$	453
3^{31}	384
4^5	279, 383
4^{17}	279
$4^{24f.}$	404
5^1	161
$5^{4f.}$	277
5^6	398
5^8	278, 398
5^9	398
5^{10}	398
$5^{12f.}$	456
5^{15}	355
5^{17}	355
5^{20}	153, 355
$6^{1f.}$	361
6^4	606, 642
6^{10}	398
6^{15}	361
$6^{16f.}$	398
6^{17}	37
6^{18}	361
6^{23}	392
7 f.	120, 627
7^7	381
$7^{12f.}$	381
7^{16}	381
7^{22}	654
$7^{24f.}$	157
8^1	398, 403
8^3	396, 398
8^9	483
8^{10}	263
$8^{17f.}$	422
8^{18}	642
8^{19}	649
8^{24}	633
8^{28}	422
$8^{29f.}$	148
8^{31}	399
$8^{31f.}$	156
8^{32}	276, 396
8^{34}	154, 390
8^{37}	406
$8^{38f.}$	277
9	372
9 f.	631
9^{11}	505
9^{16}	372
9^{18}	372
$9^{18f.}$	562
$9^{20f.}$	526, 558
$9^{21f.}$	498
$9^{22f.}$	414
10^3	384
$10^{6f.}$	470
10^{12}	454
10^{16}	37
$11^{5f.}$	355
11^{29}	390, 498
11^{32}	131, 372
$11^{33f.}$	50, 558
$11^{35f.}$	302
11^{36}	631
12^1	381
$12^{4f.}$	454
13^1	526
$13^{11f.}$	635
14^8	526
14^{10}	381
$15^{5f.}$	455
15^9	375
16^{26}	37, 385
16^{27}	438

I CORINTHIANS

CHAP.	PAGE
1 f.	120, 146 f., 435 f., 439
1^9	459
1^{18}	56, 605, 607
$1^{18f.}$	435
1^{21}	56
1^{23}	122
$1^{23f.}$	56
1^{24}	605 f.
$1^{26f.}$	56
1^{30}	56, 390, 432, 435

I CORINTHIANS (*continued*)

CHAP.	PAGE
2	. 104
2^1f.	436 ff.
2^2	56, 109
2^8	. 324
2^9	. 10
2^9f.	. 50
2^10	364, 555
3^16f.	. 483
6^14	. 606
6^19	. 483
7^14	. 110
8^1f.	. 42 f.
8^4f.	. 454
8^6	. 455
10^17	. 454
12^11f.	454 f.
13^8f.	. 52
13^9	. 187
13^12	42, 56
14^33	. 353
15^10	. 354
15^12f.	. 82
15^21f.	. 456
15^28	532, 630
15^51	. 11

2 CORINTHIANS

CHAP.	PAGE
1^3	. 371
1^18f.	. 460
1^19f.	. 75
3^9	. 381
3^18	. 642
4^1	. 381
4^2	. 42
4^5f.	. 42
4^6	56, 661 f.
4^18	. 634
5^1	. 483
5^7	. 53
5^8	. 654
5^10	. 381
5^14	. 456
5^16f.	. 56
5^17	. 506
5^19	157, 398
5^21	367, 397 f., 404
6^7	. 208
6^8f.	. 627
6^16	. 483
6^18	. 525
8^9	. 397
10^5	. 37
12^2	. 474

CHAP.	PAGE
12^9	. 483
12^18	. 455
13^4	. 606
13^14	. 251

GALATIANS

CHAP.	PAGE
1^1	. 606
2	24, 404
2^20	. 397
3^1	. 496
3^3	. 496
3^13	. 398
3^20	. 454
3^28	. 455
4^4	. 397
4^5	. 398
4^8f.	. 42
4^16	. 208
5^7	. 496
5^14	. 454
6^7f.	. 405

EPHESIANS

CHAP.	PAGE
1^4	. 279
1^4f.	505, 622
1^5f.	. 355
1^6	. 279
1^7f.	. 438
1^9-11	. 521
1^11	. 560
1^13	. 208
1^17	. 438
2^4	. 371
2^4f.	. 373
2^5	. 355
2^7f.	. 355
2^14f.	. 454
2^18	. 455
2^21	. 483
3^8f.	. 438
3^11	. 505
3^17	. 483
3^18	. 469
3^19	. 42
3^20f.	. 525
4^4f.	. 455
4^10	488 f.
4^15	. 208
5^1f.	673 f.
5^15	. 439
5^31f.	. 118

PHILIPPIANS

CHAP.	PAGE
1^8	371
1^{21}	263
1^{27}	455
2^1	371
$2^{1f.}$	517
2^2	455
$2^{5f.}$	516 f.
$2^{6f.}$	397
$2^{7f.}$	398
2^8	398
2^9	367
$2^{9f.}$	516
2^{11}	221
2^{12}	37
$2^{12f.}$	381
2^{27}	371
$3^{9f.}$	14
$3^{12f.}$	25
3^{13}	170, 628
3^{21}	525
4^4	654
4^7	42

COLOSSIANS

1^5	208
1^9	439, 486
1^{12}	154
1^{15}	54, 184, 317
1^{16}	526
1^{18}	54, 488
1^{19}	483, 486
1^{22}	398
$1^{25f.}$	438
1^{28}	439
$2^{2f.}$	40
2^3	252, 432
2^9	483, 486
3^1	159
$3^{1f.}$	475
3^2	159
3^3	149, 459
3^4	263
3^{12}	371
3^{16}	483
4^5	439

2 THESSALONIANS

$1^{6f.}$	392
1^8	37
3^3	460

1 TIMOTHY

CHAP.	PAGE
1^{11}	283
1^{16}	415
1^{17}	184, 438, 496
2^4	508
2^5	454
6^{15}	283, 302
6^{16}	50, 479

2 TIMOTHY

1^9	355, 505
1^{14}	483
2^{12}	511
2^{13}	459, 533
2^{19}	554

TITUS

$2^{11f.}$	361
2^{14}	397 f.
3^4	665
3^5	372

HEBREWS

$1^{2f.}$	420
1^3	416, 606, 661
$2^{5f.}$	113
$2^{8f.}$	113
2^{17}	460
4^{13}	477 f., 554
$4^{14f.}$	157
4^{15}	398
6^5	606
$6^{13f.}$	492
7^{16}	606
7^{25}	390
$9^{23f.}$	481
9^{24}	482
$10^{11f.}$	457
$10^{26f.}$	361 f.
11^1	57, 159
11^8	37
11^{13}	59
11^{27}	42
12^6	361
$12^{28f.}$	367
13^8	262
13^{15}	221

JAMES

$1^{2f.}$	248
1^5	439
1^{12}	248
1^{17}	283, 492
1^{18}	208

JAMES (*continued*).

CHAP.					PAGE
2¹	.	.	.	.	314
3¹³ᶠ.	.	.	.	.	439
3¹⁷	.	.	.	.	439
4⁵	.	.	.	.	483
4¹²	.	.	.	.	526
5¹⁶ᶠ.	.	.	.	.	511

1 PETER

1¹ᶠ.	.	.	.	.	37
1³	.	.	.	373, 406, 510
1⁵ᶠ	.	.	.	.	528
1¹⁴	.	.	.	.	37
1¹⁵ᶠ.	.	.	.	.	364
1¹⁷	.	.	.	.	381
1¹⁸ᶠ.	.	.	.	.	622
1²⁰	.	.	.	.	505
1²²	.	.	.	.	385
2⁴ᶠ.	.	.	.	.	483
2⁹	.	.	.	.	42
2¹⁰	.	.	.	.	372
2²⁴	.	.	.	.	398
3¹⁸	.	.	.	.	398
3²⁰	.	.	.	.	413
4¹⁷	.	.	.	.	367

2 PETER

1¹	.	.	.	.	384
2²	.	.	.	.	29
3⁸	.	.	.	.	609
3⁹	.	.	.	.	415

1 JOHN

1²	.	.	.	.	263
1⁵	.	.	.	.	555
1⁹	.	.	.	.	389, 459

CHAP.					PAGE
2¹	.	.	.	.	157, 390
2³	.	.	.	.	28
2²⁰	.	.	.	.	364
3¹⁹ᶠ.	.	.	.	.	157
3²⁰	.	.	.	.	554
4	.	.	.	.	275, 286
4⁸ᶠ.	.	.	.	.	275
4¹²	.	.	.	.	50
4¹⁵ᶠ.	.	.	.	.	275
4¹⁸	.	.	.	.	34
5⁶	.	.	.	.	208
5¹⁴ᶠ.	.	.	.	.	511
5²⁰	.	.	.	.	263, 460

REVELATION

1⁵	.	.	.	.	460
1⁸	.	.	.	.	302, 620
1¹⁶	.	.	.	.	606
1¹⁷	.	.	.	.	302
1¹⁸	.	.	.	.	263
3⁷	.	.	.	.	363, 460
3¹⁴	.	.	.	.	54, 460
3¹⁹	.	.	.	.	361
4¹ᶠ.	.	.	.	.	124 f.
5¹²	.	.	.	.	606
11¹⁵	.	.	.	.	117
15 f.	.	.	.	.	396
15¹	.	.	.	.	396
17¹⁴	.	.	.	.	302
19¹⁰	.	.	.	.	444
19¹¹	.	.	.	.	460
19¹⁶	.	.	.	.	302
21¹ᶠ.	.	.	.	.	114
21²ᶠ.	.	.	.	.	482
21⁶	.	.	.	.	302
22¹³	.	.	.	.	302
22²⁰	.	.	.	.	633

II. NAMES

«Aeterni Patris», Encycl., 582.
Alsted, H., 574.
Anselm of Canterbury, 4, 92 f., 185, 191, 195, 302, 305, 323, 379 f., 391, 444, 446 f., 608, 610, 614, 656 f.
Apostolicum, Symb., 14, 525, 677.
Aristotle, 84, 127, 265, 305, 382.
Arminius, 574.
Arnobius, 190 f.
Asmussen, Hans, 175.
Athanasius, 185, 202, 222.
Athenagoras, 185.
Attalus, 185
Augustine, 10 f., 127, 154, 185, 187, 191, 193 f., 197 f., 202, 222, 228, 263, 283, 285, 323, 328 f., 380, 446, 470 f., 493, 516, 533 f., 549 ff., 559, 568 ff., 595, 608, 610, 614, 638, 651 f., 656, 661.
Pseudo-Augustine, 197.
Aurelius, 185.

Baier, J. W., 302, 577.
Barlaam, 332.
Barmen, Synod of (*Theological Declaration*), (1934), 172, 175 f.
Bartmann, Bernhard, 305, 341, 353, 550, 570 f.
Basil of Caesarea, 193, 200, 530.
Bavinck, Hermann, 186.
Becanus, Martin, 576.
Belgica, Confessio, 127, 185.
Bengel, J. A., 633.
Bernard of Clairvaux, 331, 363, 380.
Berne Liturgy (1888), 675 f.
Biedermann, Alois E., 195, 282, 289, 292 ff., 337 f., 466.
Biel, Gabriel, 327.
Blumhardt, Christoph, 633 f.
Blumhardt, J. Christoph, 633 f.
Boethius, 610 f.
Böhl, Eduard, 282, 341.
Braun, J., 222.
Buddeus, J. Franz, 577.
Bullinger, H., 195.
Bultmann, R., 635.
Burmann, Franz, 559, 574.

Cajetan, Jacob, 238.
Calov, A., 576.
Calvin, John, 13, 27 f., 124, 127, 154, 180, 185, 323, 328, 444 f., 494, 516, 529, 569, 577, 602, 625, 637.
Chalcedonense, Conc., 664.
Chemnitz, Martin, 194.
Clemens, Alexandrinus, 190, 195, 199, 200.
Coccejus, J., 521, 573.
Constantine, 127.
Constantinople, Synod of (1351), 373.
Constitution of the Swiss Confederacy, 590.
Cremer, Hermann, 260 f., 282, 299, 341, 372, 383, 426.
Crocius, Louis, 574.
Cyril of Alexandria, 202.
Cyril of Jerusalem, 192, 195.

Dahlem, Synod of (1934), 175.
Dibelius, Martin, 275.
Diekamp, Franz, 305, 310, 341, 570 ff., 614, 651.
Pseudo-Dionysius, The Areopagite, 193, 347, 651 f.
Dorner, Isaak August, 330, 493.
Dort, Synod of, 574.
Dostöevski, Fedor Michailovitch, 88.
Duns Scotus, 237.

Eckhart, Meister, 327.
Ephraem, 200
Eugenius III, 331.
Eunomius, 327.
Eusebius of Caesarea, 185.

Fehr, J., 81 ff.
Feuerbach, L., 292 f., 449, 467, 613.
Feuling, Daniel, 81 ff.
First Epistle of Clement, 185.
Francis de Sales, 573.
Frank, Franz Hermann Reinhold, 330, 341, 344.

Gallicana Confessio, 127, 185.

Gerhard, J., 180 f., 185, 191, 195, 464 f., 484, 487 f., 576, 614, 643.

Gerhardt, Paul, 512, 651.

Gilbert de la Porrée, 331 f.

Goethe, J. W., 466, 563.

Gomarus, Franziscus, 574 f.

Gregorius Eliberitanus, 200.

Gregorius Palamas, 331 f.

Gregory of Nyssa, 202, 222, 333.

Häring, Theodor, 341, 344.

v. Harnack, Adolf, 636.

Hegel, Georg W. F., 73, 270, 282, 288, 294, 449.

Heidanus, A., 426, 559, 574.

Heidegger, J. H., 426, 534 f.

Heidelberg Catechism, 13, 396, 400 f., 404, 489, 674.

Hermes Trismegistos, 471.

Hilary of Poitiers, 191, 193, 470,

Hitler, Adolf, 173, 444.

Hollaz, David, 577.

Hurter, Hugo, 341.

Irenaeus of Lyons, 190, 198, 328, 333, 443, 549, 562.

Jerome 305.

Jerusalem, Missionary Conference (1928), 97.

Jesus Sirach, 654.

John Chrysostom, 187, 193, 202.

John of Damascus, 328.

John XXII, 327.

Justin Martyr, 185, 191, 195, 200.

Kaftan, Julius, 339.

Kant, Immanuel, 183, 270, 310 f., 464.

Kirn, Otto, 341.

Kutter, Hermann, 663 f.

Kuyper, A., 173.

Lateran Council IV (1215), 185.

Leibniz, G. W., 538.

Leiden, *Syn. pur. Theol.*, 283, 575.

Leo XIII, 582.

Lhotzki, H., 633.

Libellus in modum Symboli (5th c.), 444.

Lipsius, R. Adelbert, 341, 530.

Lotze, Hermann, 291, 292 f.

Lüdemann, Hermann, 277, 289.

Luther, Martin, 18, 35 f., 42, 57, 210, 339, 363 f., 372, 378 ff., 390 f., 412, 494, 541, 569, 577, 627, 637.

Marcion, 296.

Marius Victorinus, 222.

Martensen, Hans Lassen, 341, 549.

v. Mastricht, Petrus, 328 f., 332, 359, 451, 458, 526, 535, 574, 649.

Melanchthon, P., 259 f., 576.

Minucius Felix, 190, 192, 195, 203.

Missale Romanum, 507.

Mohammed, 448 f., 455.

Molina, Louis, 569 ff.

Müller, J., 633 f.

Neander, Joachim, 654.

Nicephorus Gregoras, 332

Nitzsch, Carl Immanuel, 328.

Nitzsch, F., 339, 382.

Novatian, 192, 444.

Oetinger, F. Christoph, 268.

Origen, 200, 443, 571.

Otto, R., 359, 365.

Overbeck, Franz, 636.

Petrus Fonseca, 569.

Petrus Lombardus, 484 f.

Phidias, 269.

Philo, 317, 427.

Plato, 183, 185 f., 265, 474.

Plotinus, 185 f.

Pohle, Joseph, 569 ff., 582 ff., 651.

Polanus, Amandus, 190, 194, 237, 261, 263, 265 ff., 278, 283, 328 f., 333 f., 353, 359, 370 f., 378, 385, 398, 410, 471, 488, 492 f., 515, 523, 528 f., 534, 549 f., 562, 568, 573, 608, 615, 619, 643 ff., 667, 677.

Poljak, A., 482.

Quenstedt, 186 f., 237 ff., 263, 278, 328 f., 353, 359, 370, 377 f., 410, 523, 528, 576.

Ragaz, Leonhard, 633.

v. Ranke, Leopold, 625.

Reims, Synod of, 331.

Rilke, Rainer Maria, 282.

Ritschl, A., 173 f., 228, 270, 279 f., 291 f., 364 f., 382, 391, 619, 636.

Rothe, Richard, 173, 291 f.

Scheeben, Matthias Josef, 341, 651.
Scheffler, J. (Angelus Silesius), 281 f.
Schell, Hermann, 305 f.
Schelling, F. W. Josef, 73.
Schiller, F., 444.
Schleiermacher, F. Daniel Ernst, 73, 173 f., 185, 193, 270, 327, 338 f., 347, 370, 377 f, 432 f., 449, 466, 495, 506, 529 f., 632 f., 651.
Schütz, J. J., 411.
Schweitzer, Albert, 636.
Schweizer, A., 338 f., 347.
Scotica, Confessio, 185, 445, 457.
Seeberg, Reinhold, 277, 327, 338 f., 531.
Siebeck, Hermann, 291 ff.
Simonides, 185.
Söhngen, Gottlieb, 81 f.
Soliloquia animae ad Deum, 197.
de Spinoza, Benedictus, 288.
Stegmann, Josua, 459.
Stephan, Horst, 339, 341, 531.
Stirner, Max, 449.
Stöcker, Adolf, 173.
Strauss, D. F., 289, 292 ff., 330, 538.
Suarez, 576.

Tertullian, 443, 534, 562, 596.
Thomas Aquinas, 127, 185, 187, 190, 200, 237, 239, 263, 277, 310 f., 328, 411, 444, 534, 539 f., 549, 559 f., 569 ff., 611 ff., 656, 661.
Thomasius, G., 277, 330.
Tillich, Paul, 635.
Toletanum, Conc., 323.
Troeltsch, Ernst, 73, 341.
Turrettini, Franz, 523, 574, 578.

Vaticanum Conc., 79 f., 83 f., 127, 164 f.
Vischer, W., 118, 412.
Voetius, Gisbert, 573 f., 578.

Walaeus, Anton, 575 f.
Wegscheider, Julius A. L., 328, 340.
Weiss, J., 636.
Westminster Confession, 187.
Wichelhaus, J., 269, 338, 341, 364, 466.
William of Occam, 327.
Wolleb, J., 269, 328, 333, 447, 465, 519 f.
Wyder, H., 97.

Zündel, F., 633.

III. SUBJECTS

Aesthetics, 652.

Angels, 266, 316, 560, 648, 675.

Anthropology, 144, 149, 154 ff., 162, 292.

Anthropomorphism, 222 f., 264, 286, 369 f.

Anthropopathism, 550.

Apologetics, 8, 93 ff.

Aseity of God, 269 ff., 302 ff., 333, 339, 349, 532, 538.

Being, 268 f., 555 f., 561.
  non-being, 552 f., 555, 560, 609.
  cf. Nothingness.

Being of God, 51, 74 f., 80 f., 257 ff., 267, 272 f., 279 ff., 331, 333 f., 351, 475 f., 542, 547, 549, 659 f.
  content, 660.
  form, 657 ff.
  cf. Essence of God.

Biblicism, 195.

Calling, 390, 565, 607.

Catholicism, Roman, 586 f., 614.
  analogia entis, 81 ff., 232, 243, 310 f., 580 f.
  God, concept of, 305 ff., 329, 559 f., 568 ff., 651.
  grace, concept of, 356.
  knowability of God, 79 ff.
  knowledge of God, 237 ff.
  mariology, 569.
  Molinism, 569 ff.
  natural theology, 99.
  omnipotence, 537, 539 .
  scientia media, 569 ff.
  Thomism, 569 ff.

Christ, *v.* Jesus Christ.

Christian Life, 148.
  Christian contentment, 645.
  simul justus et peccator, 627.
  suffering, 371, 373 f., 395, 406, 420 f.
  cf. Faith, Holy Spirit, New Birth, Obedience.

Christology, 148 ff., 162, 171, 251, 320, 582, 618, 638.
  adoptio, 485.

Christology (*continued*)—
  ubiquity, 487.
  unio, 485.
  cf. Jesus Christ.

Church, 15 f., 20, 160 ff., 193, 209, 318, 361, 404 f., 618 f., 622, 625, 643, 668, 675.
  Body of Christ, 160 f., 404, 485, 675.
  as human achievement, 140 ff.
  mission, 97, 109.
  pastoral care, 91 ff., 145 f.
  Spirit, Holy, 160.
  and state, 386 f.
  visibility, 483.
  Word of God, 5 f., 176 f., 181, 258.
  and world, 144 ff., 198, 318, 320.

Comfort, *v.* Faith.

Confession, 284, 676.

Confessional Church, German, 172 ff.

Churches, Protestant, 579.
  Christology, 487 f.

Conscience, 546 f., 565.

Constancy, of God, 491 ff., 545, 608 f.
  immutability?, 492 ff.
  mutability, 495 ff.

Creation, 57, 76 f., 189, 228 ff., 272, 274, 302 f., 317, 319, 461 ff., 476 ff., 499, 514, 536, 560 f., 585, 593, 602, 629, 662, 668.
  heaven, 266, 474 f.
  out of nothing, 76, 562.
  praise, 647 f., 677.
  preservation, 419, 428.
  reconciliation, 117, 502 ff., 616.
  revelation, 112 ff., 201.
  " new creation," 506.

Creature, 53 ff., 266, 278, 284, 323, 368 f., 401, 410 ff., 481, 500 ff., 514, 537, 562, 578, 589, 594, 608, 616, 667.

Death, 274, 323, 373, 386, 404, 419 ff., 494, 501, 552 ff., 560, 563, 626, 630.

Decree, Divine, 519 ff., 622.

Deism, 269.

693

Determinism, 562 f.
Devil, 524, 544, 552, 560, 563, 594 f.
Doctrine of God, 32, 233, 267 ff., 348 f., 352 f., 447.
Doctrine of the Trinity, 261, 288, 326 f., 329, 528 f.
  Modalism, 326.
Dogmatics, 257 f., 316 f., 336.
  cf. Doctrine of God, Doctrine of the Trinity.
  Anthropology, Christology, Ecclesiology, Eschatology.
Dualism, 501, 562.

Ecclesiology, 144 f., 148 f., 155 ff.
Election, 116, 362, 374, 390, 443, 450 f., 500, 508 f., 541, 622, 663.
Enlightenment, 288 ff., 570.
Eschatology, 116, 631 ff.
  heathen, 393.
Essence of God, 74 f., 206 f., 261, 266, 269, 272 f., 279 ff., 322, 325 f., 329, 332 ff.
Eternity of God, 464 ff., 559, 593, 608 ff., 622.
  infinitude, 464 ff., 608.
  non-temporality, 610 f.
  post-temporality, 619, 629 ff.
  pre-temporality, 619 f., 621 ff., 630 ff.
  sempiternitas, 613.
  supra-temporality, 619 f., 623 ff., 630 ff.
  temporality, 610 ff.
Ethics, 638.

Faith, 12 f., 21, 53, 57, 155, 158 f., 246 ff., 252 f., 325, 362, 384, 387, 404, 406, 418 ff., 435 ff., 453, 460 f., 505, 574, 606, 629, 675 f.
  analogia fidei, 82, 320.
  comfort, 249 f., 253 f., 262, 373 f., 385, 554.
  decision, 387, 550, 557, 624, 629.
  knowledge, 12 ff., 33 f., 183, 191 f., 244, 246 ff., 275.
  object, 13 ff.
  promise, 307, 378.
  sanctification, 15 f.
  trust, 374, 392 f., 536, 612.
  v. Knowledge of God.
Father (God), 47 ff., 229 f., *v.* Trinity.

Freedom of God, 301 ff., 337 f., 342 f., 348, 351 f., 357, 440 ff., 518, 531, 542, 560 f., 592 f., 608 ff., 658.

Glory of God, 324 ff., 461, 513, 640 ff.
  all-sufficiency, 644 f.
  doxa, kabod, 641 f., 670.
  fruitio Dei, 653 f.
  glorificatio, 668 ff.
  light, 649 f.
  power, 650.
  self-declaration, 645 f.
God—
  absoluteness, 308.
  aseity, *q.v.*
  attributes, *v.* perfections.
  beauty, 650 f.
  being, *q.v.*
  blessedness, 283.
  condescension, 55, 62, 200, 354, 358, 517 f., 662.
  constancy, *q.v.*
  Creator, 76 f., 79 f., 172, 228 ff., 284, 301 f., 304, 462 ff., 505 ff., 535 f., 547, 596 f., 613.
  decision, 565.
  deity, 263, 274 f., 297 ff., 331, 528, 561, 564, 587, 643, 660.
  essence, *q.v.*
  eternity, *q.v.*
  existence, 304 ff., 321, 463, 559, 562.
  co-existence, 614 ff., 619.
  face, 647.
  faithfulness, 303, 314, 318, 384 f., 393, 400 ff., 407, 419, 459 f., 657 f.
  freedom, *q.v.*
  glory, *q.v.*
  grace, *q.v.*
  hiddenness, *q.v.*
  holiness, *q.v.*
  joy, 647 f., 653 f., 661.
  knowability, *q.v.*
  life, *q.v.*
  lordship, 45 ff., 75 f., 230, 301, 324 ff. 461, 565.
  love, *q.v.*
  mercy, *q.v.*
  name, 59, 273, 647.
  " nature," 543.
  objectivity, 13 ff., 206 f.
  omnicausality, *q.v.*
  omnipotence, *q.v.*

God (*continued*)—
  omnipresence, q.v.
  perfections, q.v.
  personality, q.v.
  Reconciler, 77, 301, 304, 618.
  Redeemer, 78, 301, 304, 547.
  repentance, 496 ff.
  riches, 307, 331, 368, 375, 406, 461, 473, 657, 660.
  simplicity, q.v.
  " Spirit," 267, 543, 551, 597 f.
  triunity, q.v.
  truth, 67 ff., 197 ff., 207, 228 ff., 334, 343, 362 f.
  uniqueness, q.v.
  unity, q.v.
  will, q.v.
  wisdom, q.v.
  works, 51, 115, 259 ff., 273, 301, 318, 429, 499, 506 ff., 513, 527, 531, 547, 591, 647 f., 668.
    individuation, 316.
  wrath, 274, 362 ff., 373, 382, 394 ff., 402, 410, 421 f.
Grace, 20 ff., 69 ff., 129 f., 138 f., 152 f., 169, 172, 188 f., 192, 197 f., 203, 205 f., 213 f., 220, 224, 235, 243, 245, 251, 281, 287, 341, 353 ff., 369, 371, 375 f., 382, 407 f., 411, 509, 515, 539, 554, 585, 617 f., 622, 677.
Gratitude, 76 ff., 183, 192, 198, 216 ff., 374, 381, 421, 514, 586, 628, 669.

Heaven, v. Creation.
Hell, 274, 373, 553.
Heresy, 319.
Hiddenness of God, 39 ff., 55 ff., 182 ff., 235, 243, 335, 516.
  incomprehensibility, 186 ff.
  ineffability, 186 ff.
  inexpressibility, 186 ff.
History of Salvation, 506 ff.
Holiness of God, 358 ff.
Hope, 78, 624, 631, 634.
Humility, 50, 204, 213 f., 342, 344, 375, 517 f.
  v. Knowledge of God.

Images, Commandment against, 431, 665.
  representation of Christ, 666 ?.
Immanence, 212, 264, 303, 313 ff., 427, 446.

Immanence (*continued*)—
  differentiation, 315 ff.
  Jesus Christ, 317 ff.
Incarnation, v. Revelation/incarnation.
Indeterminism, 633.
Islam, 448.
Israel, 14, 19, 23, 54, 60 f., 100 f., 108 f. 116, 262, 304, 360 f., 363 f., 373, 384, 386 ff., 394 ff., 417 ff., 451, 479, 485, 554, 600 f., 603, 625, 642 f., 664.

Jesus Christ, 54 f., 74 f., 116 f., 148 ff., 189 f., 199, 250 ff., 286, 304, 315 ff., 367, 373, 384, 394, 419, 432, 455 f., 483 f., 512 ff., 521, 605 f., 622, 625 f., 661 f., 664, 667.
  ascension, 540.
  assumptio carnis, 151, 252 f., 316 ff., 662.
  and the Church, 154, 160 f., 163 f., 319 f., 373, 405.
  cross, 56, 151, 154, 279, 394 ff., 422, 516 f., 607, 626 f., 665.
  divine-humanity, 19, 150 f., 317, 355, 400, 485 f., 514 ff., 665, 667.
  divinity, 318, 486, 514, 606 f.
  humanity, 53 f., 150 f., 373, 397, 662.
  imago Dei, 665.
  King, 116, 514, 605 ff.
  name, 153, 249, 373 f., 517, 615.
  Priest, 152 ff., 253, 374, 390, 397 ff., 418, 622, 626, 643, 666.
  resurrection, 56 f., 78, 107, 116, 120 f., 154, 253, 272, 316, 394, 404, 482, 563, 627, 665.
  return, 78, 645.
  self-emptying, 397 f., 516, 663.
  sinlessness, 397 f.
  ubiquity, 487 ff.
  Virgin Birth, 540.
  v. Immanence, Triunity cf. Revelation/incarnation.

Judaism, 119 ff., 395 f., 481 f.
Judgment of God, 153, 167, 171, 192, 253, 356, 360 ff., 380 ff., 386, 391 ff., 403 ff., 419 f., 554, 595, 677.

Kingdom of God, 277, 318, 606, 630, 635 f., 650.

Knowability of God, 5 ff., 63 ff., 150, 196 f.

Knowledge (God's), 9, 15, 44, 57, 67 ff., 150 f., 237, 543 f.
  omniscience, 553 f.
  particularity, 563.
  praescientia, 558 f.
  scientia approbationis, 567.
    ,,   *libera*, 567.
    ,,   *media*, 569 ff.
    ,,   *necessaria*, 567.
    ,,   *practica*, 567.
    ,,   *reprobationis*, 567.
    ,,   *simplicis intelligentiae*, 567.
    ,,   *speculativa*, 567.
    ,,   *visionis*, 567.

Knowledge of God, 3 ff.
  awe, 220 ff.
  beneficia Christi, 259 f.
  certainty, 7 ff., 37 ff., 197 ff., 344, 382.
  Church, 5 f.
  concepts, 224, 229 f., 264, 333 ff., 360, 651.
    analogia attributionis, 238.
    analogy, 225 f.
    disparity, 224 f.
    parity, 224 f.
  Deus absconditus, 210, 362 f., 541 ff., 593.
  Deus revelatus, 542.
  direct?, 9 ff.
  faith, 12 f., 52 f., 191 f., 244, 246 ff.
  fear, godly, 33 ff.
  goal, 204, 214, 233.
  grace, 22 ff., 69 ff., 192, 203, 206 f., 213 f., 230 f., 241, 251 ff., 341 f., 358 f., 591 f.
  human achievement, 216.
  humility, *q.v.*
  indirect ?, 9 ff.
  Jesus Christ, 250 ff., 317 ff.
  joyfulness, 219.
  limit, 52 ff., 179 ff., 233 ff.
  love, 32 ff.
  natural ?, 85 f., 299, 453.
  necessity, 216.
  obedience, 26 f., 35 f., 201 ff., 214, 342.
  object, 6 ff., 194, 205 ff.
  prayer, 22 ff., 223.
  proof of God ?, 342 ff.
  reality, 210 ff.
  revelation, 3 ff., 224 ff., 245, 261 f., 299, 320, 350, 545.

Knowledge of God (*continued*)—
  sacrifice, 217 f.
  sacrificium intellectus ?, 9, 423.
  Spirit, Holy, 48 f.
  subject, 3 ff., 43 f., 181, 252.
  success, 214, 223, 227.
  veracity, 208 ff.
  via triplex, 346 ff.
  Word of God, 3 ff., 43, 423 f.

Law, 120 f., 167, 362 ff., 379, 381 f.
  command, 262, 364, 518.
  and Gospel, 166 f., 236, 349, 362 f., 391 f., 518.
  "Holiness Code," 364 f.

Life, eternal, 78, 422, 509, 630.

Life of God, 263 ff., 272, 275, 337, 350, 492, 495 ff., 638.

Lordship, *v.* God.

Love, 230, 275, 281 f., 407, 598 f.
  fear, 33 ff.
  for God, 32 ff.

Love of God, 206 f., 230, 274 ff., 321, 337 ff., 342 ff., 349, 350 f., 440 f., 461 ff., 499, 514, 528, 545, 592 f., 598 f., 624 f., 641, 658.
  end in itself, 279 f.
  fellowship, 274 ff., 344, 362, 369, 546 ff.
  lack of nothing, 280.
  miracle, 278.
  self-communication, 276.

Man, 110 ff., 128 ff., 145 ff.
  Christian, 146 ff.
  comfort, 169, 171.
  death, 386 f., 393, 404, 421, 494.
  existence, 131 ff., 159, 325, 409 ff., 421, 424, 465 f., 559, 589, 621, 629.
  flesh, 151.
  imago Dei, 188.
  incapacity for revelation, 129 ff., 182, 211 f.
  knowledge, 71, 130, 189 f., 205, 290, 535.
  personality, 355 ff.
  vitality, 165.
  will, 556, 560.
    free, 563, 585 f., 596.
  wisdom, 430 ff., 553.
  woman, 118.
  v. Scripture.

Mercy of God, 74 f., 354 f., 369 ff.,
  377 ff., 410, 617 f.
  sympathy, 370 f.
Metaphysics, 73, 269 f.
Miracle, 130, 197 ff., 220 f., 278, 509,
  539, 548, 662.
Monism, 500 f.
Monotheism, 448 f.
  Jewish ?, 453.
Mysticism, 10 f., 57, 192 f., 197, 200,
  281 f., 309, 332, 409, 472, 600,
  624.
  Hesychasts, 332.
Mythology, 117, 620 f., 639.

Neo-Protestantism, 287 ff., 296, 632 f.
  concept of God, 291 ff., 529 f.
  Liberalism, 232.
  revelation, 291 ff., 529 f.
Nominalism, 327 f., 335, 345, 541 ff.
  semi-nominalism, 327 ff.
Nothingness, 556, 566, 590.

Obedience, 33 ff., 201 f., 213, 342, 385,
  393, 398, 419, 514, 516, 557 f.,
  594 f., 626, 674.
  disobedience, 594 f.
Omnicausality of God, 527 ff.
  v. Knowledge of God.
Omnipotence of God, 522 ff.
  definite, 527 ff.
  divinity of, 523 ff.
  legality (potestas), 526.
  potentia, 526.
    absoluta, 539.
    extraordinaria, 539.
    ordinaria, 539.
    ordinata, 539.
  cf. Will of God, Knowledge (God's).
Omnipresence of God, 461 ff., 612.
  general, 468 ff.
  in Jesus Christ, 483 ff.
  spatiality, 468 ff.
  special, 477 ff.
  the throne of God, 474 f., 487.
Optimism, 501 f.
Orthodoxy, Older Protestant, 190 f.,
  237 ff., 261, 266, 287 ff., 328 ff.,
  337 ff., 345, 377 f., 391, 398,
  426, 447, 457 f., 464 ff., 492 f.,
  519 f., 673 f., 649, 651.

Paganism, 84, 117 ff., 299, 319, 393,
  448 f., 472, 494, 565, 618, 626.

Panentheism, 312, 315, 562.
Pantheism, 269, 312, 315, 450, 562.
Patience, 171 f., 230, 352, 407 ff., 600,
  618.
Pelagianism, 562.
Penitence, 154, 384 f., 391, 399, 414 f.
  417 f.
Perfections of God, 322 ff., 657 ff.
  perfections of the divine freedom,
    440 ff.
  perfections of the divine love, 351 ff.
  division and classification, 335 f.
  historico-intuitive grouping, 339 f.
  psychological grouping, 337 f.
  religious-genetic grouping, 338 f.
Pessimism, 501 f.
Pietism, 633 f.
Possibility, 533 ff., 542, 551 ff., 556.
Power, 286, 523 f., 531 f., 535 f., 538 ff.
  542 ff., 548, 599 f., 602.
Powers, 326, 538 ff., 544, 563, 600.
Prayer, 22, 25 f., 308, 390 ff., 510 f.
  548, 558, 675 ff.
  adoration, 675 ff.
  hearing of prayer, 510 ff.
  v. Knowledge of God.
Proclamation of the Church, 19 f., 154,
  162, 167 f., 170 ff., 193, 220 f.
  232, 257.
  commission, 211.
  joy, 655.
  love, 171.
  promise, 220, 231.
  task, 170.
Providence, 302, 427, 520.

Realism, 268, 331.
Reality, 568.
Reconciliation, 77, 151, 264, 274, 366,
  397 ff., 503 ff., 514, 547 ff., 550,
  561, 588, 591, 599, 607, 616,
  620, 663, 668.
Redemption, 78, 209, 509, 514, 532,
  620, 629.
Reformation, 127, 288, 457, 583 f.,
  631 f., 651.
Regeneration, 57, 144, 149, 158, 315,
  373, 406, 669.
Religion, 444.
Revelation, 51 ff., 197 ff., 210, 259,
  264, 280, 343, 346, 362, 504,
  545 f., 565, 592, 598, 630,
  658.
  aeons, old and new, 626 f.

Revelation (*continued*)—
 as divine act, 263 ff.
 covenant, 44 f., 59, 103, 362 ff., 384,
  390, 412 ff., 479, 521, 600.
 God as Subject, 3 ff., 39 ff., 209 f.,
  260 ff.
 history, 61, 262 ff., 601, 604, 617.
 incarnation, 151, 253, 265, 274, 317,
  418, 446, 515 ff.
 mystery, 40 ff., 56 f., 151, 210 f.,
  283 f., 348 f., 357 f., 423 ff., 546,
  591, 603 f.
 necessity, 206, 402, 518.
 offence, 55 f., 146.
 order, 317 f., 348 f., 352, 375 f., 540,
  603.
 reality, 210 ff.
 revelations, 173 ff.
 signs, 17, 51 f., 198, 395 ff., 398,
  412 f., 419 f., 539.
 unity in O.T. and N.T., 364 ff.,
  381 f.
 veiling and unveiling, 37 ff., 54 ff.,
  193 f., 210 f.
 veracity, 209 ff., 223 f., 341.
Revolution, 468.
Right, 386 f., 526.
Righteousness of God, 375 ff.
 decision, 390 ff.
 faithfulness, 385 ff.
 iustitia distributiva, 381.
 judgment, 393 ff.
Romanticism, 290.

Sabbath, 117, 630.
Sacraments, 50, 52 ff., 315, 647.
Sacrifice, 217 f., 219.
Salvation, History of, 506 ff.
Sanctification, 15, 110, 360 f., 364.
Scripture, Holy, 98 ff.
 anthropogony, 116 ff.
 apostolate, 24 f., 54, 99 ff., 125, 151,
  223, 299, 316, 364, 642.
 authority, 98.
 cosmogony, 116 ff. ·
 language, 264 f., 286.
 man as object, 100 ff.
 natural theology ?, 98 ff.
 prophecy, 19, 24 f., 99 ff., 125, 151,
  223, 289.
 source of revelation, unique, 109
 unity, 364, 392, 605.
 v. Witness.
Signs, *v*. Revelation.

Simplicity, 234, 324 ff., 332 f., 406,
 445 ff., 592, 609, 657, 660.
Sin, 213, 279, 323, 355 ff., 361, 364,
 371 ff., 388, 392 f., 395 ff., 504 ff.,
 544, 552 f., 557, 560, 563, 586,
 594 f., 626 f., 645.
 fall, 188, 503 f.
Singleness of God, *v*. Uniqueness.
Space, 465 ff., 468 ff., 474, 612.
 cf. Omnipresence of spatiality.
Spirit, Holy, 48 f., 100, 141 ff., 249,
 261, 267, 361, 607, 669.
 blasphemy, 201.
 deity, 615.
 divine Sonship, 158, 485, 548, 668 f.,
  673.
 work, 170, 509.
 v. Knowledge of God, cf. Church,
 Regeneration, Triunity.
Spirit-Nature, 265 ff.
Spiritualism, 265 ff.

Temptation, 170, 247 ff., 307.
Theodicy, 395 f., 405 f., 419 f., 503 f.,
 594 ff.
Theology, 168 f., 194 f., 245, 320, 336,
 555 f., 640.
 certainty, 203 f., 210.
 Church history, 126 ff., 315 f.
 language, 195, 223 ff., 286.
 natural theology, 86 ff., 129 ff., 200,
  666.
  analogia entis, 81 ff., 193, 240 ff.
  anthropology, 143 ff., 292, 303.
  Christian, 97 ff., 137 ff., 303.
  direct knowledge of God ?, 10 ff.,
   85 ff.
  ontology, 583.
  point of contact, 88 f., 131 f.
  "provisional understanding," 230 f.
  respectability, 141, 164.
  scriptural basis ?, 97 ff.
  vitality, 165.
 Protestant, 584 f.
 theologia viatorum, 209.
Time, 61, 409 ff., 417 ff., 465 ff., 592 ff.
 expectation, 616 f.
 fulfilment, 625 ff.
 future, 626 ff.
 past, 626 ff.
 present, 611, 617 f., 624 f.
 recollection, 695.
Tragedy, 374.
Transcendence, 264, 302 ff., 313.

Trinity, Doctrine of the, 261, 288, 326 f., 329, 528 f.
Modalism, 326.
Triunity, 47 ff., 67 f., 79 f., 156, 252 f., 267 f., 297, 305 f., 317 f., 323, 326, 349, 357 f., 368, 372, 463, 468, 475 f., 487, 531, 538 f., 615 f., 622, 625 f., 640, 659 ff., 667.
Truth, *v.* God/truth.

Unbelief, *v.* Faith.
Uniqueness of God, 297, 442 ff., 609.
Unity of God, 79 f., 319, 325, 345 ff., 358 f., 363, 369, 375 ff., 406.

Will of God, 210, 212, 277, 356, 379, 423 f., 518 f., 535, 543 ff., 555 ff., 587 ff.
genuineness, 587 ff.
voluntas absoluta, 519, 592.
   ,,   *antecedens*, 519, 592.
   ,,   *beneplaciti*, 519 f., 591 f.
   ,,   *conditionalis*, 519, 592.

Will of God, *(continued)*—
voluntas consequens, 519, 592.
   ,,   *efficax*, 592, 596.
   ,,   *efficiens*, 592, 594.
   ,,   *inefficax*, 592, 596.
   ,,   *occulta*, 519, 591 f.
   ,,   *permittens*, 592, 599.
   ,,   *revelata*, 519, 591 f.
   ,,   *signi*, 519, 591 f.
Wisdom of God, 422 ff.
Witness, 54, 100 f., 199, 283, 405.
Holy Scripture, 99 ff.
man in the cosmos, 99 ff.
self-witness of God, 44 ff., 100 ff., 150 f., 456.
Word of God, 3 ff., 39 ff., 259, 315, 403 f., 416 f., 423, 478, 537, 604, 622.
and the cosmos, 110 f.
World, 124, 211, 261, 280, 304 f., 315 ff. 427, 446, 499 ff., 532, 536 f., 562, 593, 622, 629.
world history, 395, 399, 405, 625.
Worship, 293, 670 ff.